# MODERN

# LOCOMOTIVE CONSTRUCTION

BY

J. G. A. MEYER

Associate Editor of the "American Machinist;" Member American Society Mechanical Engineers; formerly Chief Draftsman at the Grant Locomotive Works

## Fully Illustrated

NEW YORK

JOHN WILEY AND SONS

53 East Tenth Street

1892

©2010 Periscope Film LLC
All Rights Reserved
ISBN #978-1-935700-20-3
www.PeriscopeFilm.com

The principles upon which the methods of construction are based are generally given, so as to enable any one who designs with the necessary regard to theory to make modifications to suit his own ideas. In writing the original articles I have aimed to make each one as complete as possible. This necessarily required a few repetitions, which were allowed to remain in this book, as it was thought such a course would make the book more convenient for reference.

My thanks are due to Mr. P. Arnot, Supt. of the Grant Locomotive Works, when these works were located at Paterson, N. J.; to Mr. John Headden, formerly Supt. of the Roger Locomotive Works; Mr. D. Shirrell, draftsman at the Richmond Locomotive Works; and other friends, for valuable suggestions and assistance in the preparation of this work. I am also indebted to Mr. Theo. N. Ely, General Supt. of Motive Power, Pennsylvania R. R.; the Grant Locomotive Works; the Cooke Locomotive Works, of Paterson, N. J.; the Rogers Locomotive Works, of Paterson, N. J.; the Rhode Island Locomotive Works, Providence, R. I.; the Baldwin Works, Philadelphia, Pa.; the Richmond Locomotive and Machine Works, Richmond, Va.; and Mr. A. J. Pitkins, Supt. of the Schenectady Locomotive Works, Schenectady, N. Y., for kindly furnishing me with drawings and data.

PATERSON, N. J., September, 1892.

# CONTENTS.

### CHAPTER I.
INTRODUCTORY REMARKS.—CLASSIFICATION OF LOCOMOTIVES.—TRAIN RESISTANCE.—TRACTIVE POWER.—WEIGHT OF ENGINES..................................................... 1

### CHAPTER II.
CONSTRUCTION OF CYLINDERS.—STEAM PIPES.—SLIDE VALVES........................... 20

### CHAPTER III.
VALVE GEAR.—CONSTRUCTION OF LINKS ............................................. 74

### CHAPTER IV.
PISTONS.—CROSSHEADS.—SLIDES.—STUFFING BOXES..................................... 138

### CHAPTER V.
FRAMES AND PEDESTALS.—AXLE BOXES................................................. 182

### CHAPTER VI.
DRIVING AXLES.—DRIVING WHEELS.—COUNTERBALANCE................................... 214

### CHAPTER VII.
MAIN-RODS.—SIDE-RODS.—CRANK-PINS ................................................ 267

### CHAPTER VIII.
THROTTLE PIPES.—THROTTLE VALVE GEAR.—SAFETY VALVES.—WHISTLE.—PUMPS.—CHECK VALVES ........................................................................... 343

### CHAPTER IX.
SPRING GEAR AND SPRINGS........................................................... 400

### CHAPTER X.
BOILERS.—GRATE SURFACE.—HEATING SURFACE.—RIVETED JOINTS.—EXTENSION FRONTS ... 417

## CHAPTER XI.
ASH-PANS.—SMOKE-STACKS.—EXHAUST-PIPES ............................................. 491

## CHAPTER XII.
SAND-BOXES.—BELLS.—PILOTS.—ENGINE-BRACES ........................................ 510

## CHAPTER XIII.
ENGINE TRUCKS ............................................................................. 535

## CHAPTER XIV.
OIL-CUPS.—VALVES.—COCKS.—INJECTOR ................................................. 552

## CHAPTER XV.
TENDERS.—TENDER-TRUCKS ................................................................ 563

## CHAPTER XVI.
USEFUL RULES, FORMULAS, AND DATA ..................................................... 595

## CHAPTER XVII.
COMPOUND LOCOMOTIVES .................................................................. 617

# MODERN LOCOMOTIVE CONSTRUCTION.

## CHAPTER I.

INTRODUCTORY REMARKS.—CLASSIFICATION OF LOCOMOTIVES.—TRAIN RESISTANCE.—TRACTIVE POWER.—WEIGHT OF ENGINES.

1. In late years a change in the management and treatment of the locomotive has taken place on most of our principal railroads. This change necessarily caused, also, a change in the construction of the locomotive, besides other improvements that have been added from time to time.

2. It is the writer's intention to give in these chapters a general description of the principal parts of the modern locomotive, illustrated by good and correct drawings, and indicate the improvements that have been added.

Since all the illustrations represent separate parts of the modern locomotive, and since some of them will be arranged in a tabular form (an arrangement the writer has not seen in any book, and consequently believes it to be new), we trust that these illustrations will be appreciated by the professional designer, and by the young designer in particular.

3. In order to make the reading of these papers profitable to the mechanic, we will, in connection with the illustrations, give rules relating to the proportioning of the parts in as plain and simple language as we can command, so that any one engaged in the building and running of the locomotive may easily understand these rules. We also hope that the description of the locomotive, which is almost inseparable from a subject presented in a manner as we propose to do, will prove interesting to the ordinary reader.

Should any of our professional friends pronounce the rules given as something superfluous, because they may be found in the many excellent books already published, or should any of our friends find fault with the practical method of treating this subject, we would kindly remind them that these chapters are intended for a large class of readers—for the mechanic and engineer in particular—and not for a favored few.

4. When a comparison is made between the locomotives built recently and the locomotives in use about ten or twelve years ago, a change in their construction and appearance will be noticed. This change is due to the desire of railroad managers to reduce the cost of transportation of passengers and freight, and to a great extent this desire has been realized.

5. In former times it has been the custom to place an engine in the hands of one engineer, and whenever the engine was attached to a train this same engineer had his hand on the throttle lever. When the trip was completed, the engine was carefully housed and cleaned, and, so to speak, was put to rest. In fact, we once heard an engineer say (and we have reason to believe that he was in earnest) that engines needed rest as well as engineers, because he noticed that his engine never worked as well when nearing the end of a trip as it did when starting. If this engineer is still among the living, he must either have changed his opinion or stepped off the footboard to stay off. The trips also were comparatively short, and generally the trains comparatively light. Indeed, when we carefully consider the management of the locomotive and the treatment it received in former times, we might almost conclude that the locomotive was looked upon as a delicate piece of machinery that needed extraordinary care to keep it in good working order.

But now, mark the change of treatment of the engine that has taken place on some of our best railroads. Notice, for instance, on these roads the modern freight locomotive as it starts off with as heavy a train as it can possibly haul on a trip of great length, the engineers relieving each other at designated stations, instead of one engineer having charge of the engine during the whole trip, as in former times; notice also the scanty accommodations, if any, for cleaning or housing the engine when the trip is completed; the short time the engine is allowed to stand still after it has been examined and found to be in good working order; the heavy train it must haul on the homeward journey, run by any engineer that is competent to run an engine; and when the starting point has been reached, no time is lost in coupling it to another train, and thus it is kept running almost continually in all kinds of weather. Compare this treatment to the former and the change must become apparent.

6. The passenger engines are sometimes subjected to the same severe treatment, but generally an engine is placed in the charge of only two engineers, one of these running the engine during one trip, and the other having charge of it during the next trip, and so relieving each other alternately.

7. Allowing different engineers to run the same engine has this advantage, namely: that only competent engineers can hold their positions, because after a competent engineer has once shown what the engine can do, the other engineers must make the engine perform a like amount of work in the same time, or give good reasons for not doing so. Here then we perceive that no incompetency is admissible.

8. The passenger trains are also heavier now than in former times, and the trips longer. Generally speaking, all engines are now required to do more work than formerly. Engines placed in such severe service must naturally be strong, powerful and durable, well put together, bolt holes reamed, bolts turned and fitted, and driven in tightly. In the modern locomotive the boiler is larger than in former practice, the frames and cylinders are heavier, and generally all working parts are made stronger.

9. In the appearance and outside finish of the engine we also notice a decided change. For instance, the landscape paintings and pictures of birds and horses on the side of the tender, have of late disappeared, and the tanks are plainly painted with good paint, and well varnished.

This is, in the writer's opinion, as it should be, because pictures on the side of the tank seem to him to be out of place. A tender is made for the purpose of carrying water and fuel, and is ill adapted for a picture-gallery. The brass finish on the engine and fancy ornaments, such as eagles, etc., are also things of the past, because these require too much time and expense to keep clean and in good condition.

From these remarks the reader must not conclude that in former times the engines had a better and more pleasing appearance. This is not the case, because years of experience have exposed faulty constructions in former locomotives, which have been corrected and otherwise improved in the modern engine, and since correct construction and distribution of metal must always improve the appearance of a machine, we conclude that our American locomotives as now built (although by no means perfect) possess elegance in form, compactness in the arrangement of the different pieces of mechanism, and gracefulness in movement.

## CLASSIFICATION OF LOCOMOTIVES.

10. We may divide the different kinds of locomotives into two distinct classes; in one class we may place the ordinary passenger and freight locomotive, and in the other the switching engine and other locomotives designed for some special service.

At present we will consider only the first class, namely, the passenger and freight locomotives. These engines are again divided into four different classes, namely: 1st, the eight-wheeled engine; 2d, the Mogul engine; 3d, the ten-wheeled engine; 4th, the consolidation engine.

An eight-wheeled engine, sometimes called the American locomotive, because this design was first brought out in this country and used here more than elsewhere, is an engine that has four driving wheels and four truck wheels, as shown in Fig. 1. On some roads the eight-wheeled engine is used for both passenger and freight service, but generally it is recognized as the passenger engine. A Mogul engine is an engine that has six driving wheels and two truck wheels, as shown in Fig. 2. These engines are used principally for freight service; occasionally they are used for passenger service, but generally they are recognized as freight engines.

A ten-wheeled engine is one that has six driving wheels and four truck wheels, as shown in Fig. 3. Ten-wheeled engines are used for fast freight service, for hauling heavy passenger trains, or for a mixed traffic.

A consolidation engine is an engine that has eight driving wheels and two truck wheels, as shown in Fig. 4. These engines are used for heavy freight service on roads having steep grades.

Now, notice the eight-wheeled engine and the Mogul engine; each one has eight wheels. In the passenger engine four wheels of the whole number are driving wheels, and in the Mogul engine six wheels of the whole number are driving wheels.

Again, notice the ten-wheeled engine and the consolidation engine; each one has

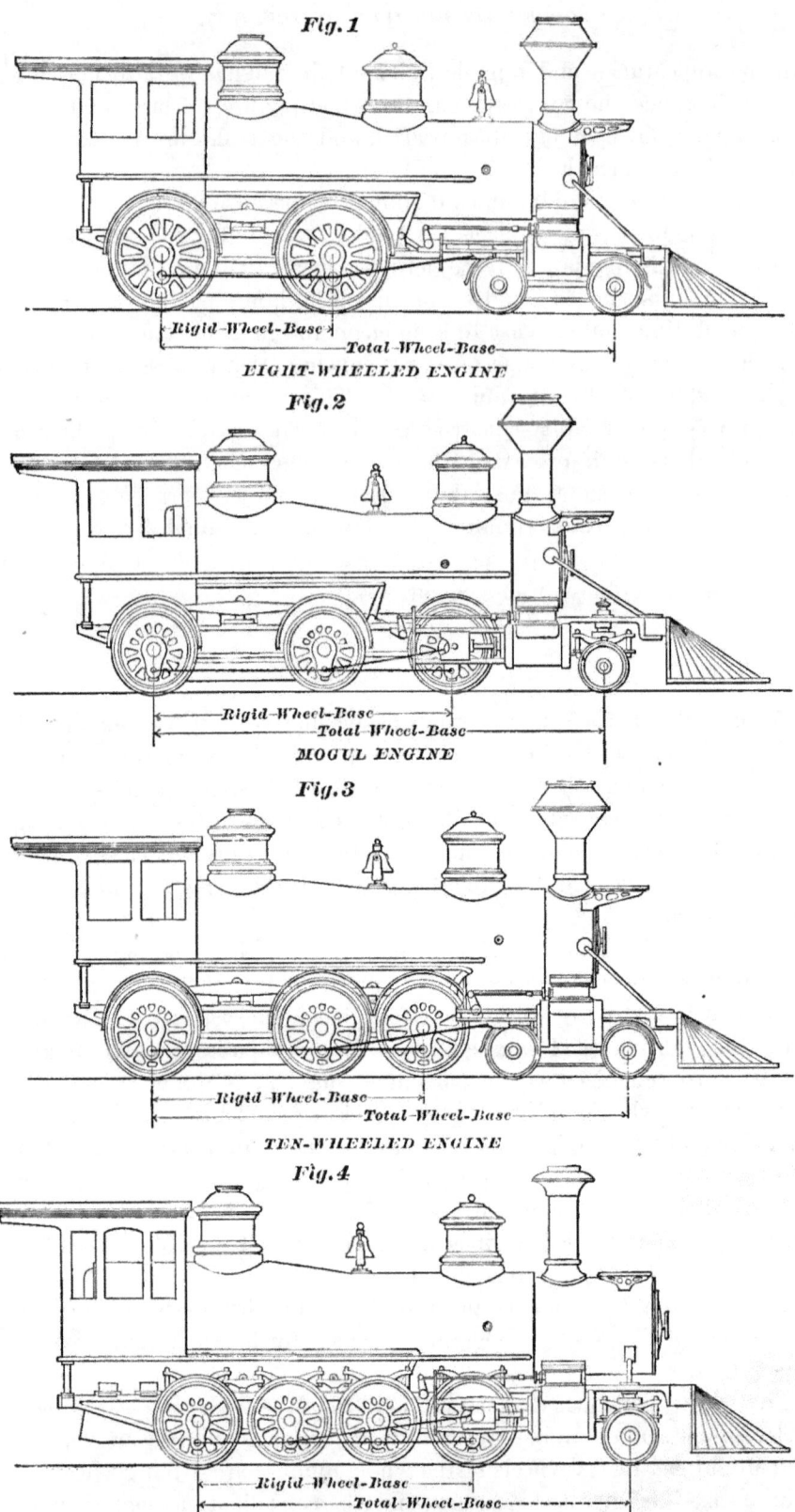

Fig. 1 — EIGHT-WHEELED ENGINE

Fig. 2 — MOGUL ENGINE

Fig. 3 — TEN-WHEELED ENGINE

Fig. 4 — CONSOLIDATION ENGINE

ten wheels. In the ten-wheeled engine six wheels of the whole number are driving wheels, and in the consolidation eight wheels of the whole number are driving wheels.

## WHEEL BASE.

11. The rigid wheel base of any engine is the distance from the center of rear to the center of the front driving wheel, plainly shown in figures. The total wheel base of any engine is the whole distance from the center of the rear driving wheel to the center of the front truck wheel, also plainly shown in figures.

## DATA REQUIRED.

12. Before we can decide what type of a locomotive to adopt, and before we can determine the dimensions of this engine, we must know the following particulars: 1st, the total weight of the train—that is, the combined weight of the load and cars; 2d, the speed of train; 3d, the grades and curves of the road on which the engine is to run; 4th, gauge of track—that is, the exact distance between the rails; 5th, the weight on the drivers that the rails of the road can bear; 6th, kind of fuel to be used; 7th, kind and height of couplings of cars; 8th, limitations, if any, in width, height, length, etc., by tunnels, overhead bridges, turn-tables, etc.

For the sake of simplicity, let us first find the type and the dimensions of a locomotive capable of hauling a train of given weight on a straight and level track, leaving the speed and all other particulars out of the question.

## TRAIN RESISTANCE.

13. The principal resistance which a locomotive must overcome in slowly hauling a train over a straight and level road, is rolling and axle friction. Hence the resistance to motion of a train, or the train resistance, is simply rolling and axle friction combined. But it must be remembered that when a train is to run fast, or against strong winds, other forces must be overcome.

By rolling friction is meant the resistance to motion that takes place where the circumference of the car wheel comes in contact with the rail. Axle friction is the resistance to motion that takes place between the axle journal and its bearing.

14. An ordinary train, composed of cars whose wheels are, say, from 28 inches to 32 inches in diameter, and having journals, say, from 3 inches to $3\frac{1}{4}$ inches in diameter, will require a force of $7\frac{1}{2}$ pounds for every ton of 2,000 pounds to move it. Thus, for instance, if the total weight of the cars and the load is 1,000 tons, we have 1,000 × $7\frac{1}{2}$ = 7,500 pounds; this means that a train of 1,000 tons requires a force of 7,500 pounds to move it, or, in other words, it requires a force of 7,500 pounds to overcome the combined rolling and axle friction.

On some roads it may require only 6 pounds for every ton, and on other roads it may require 9 pounds to move a ton weight. This difference is caused by the degree of smoothness and irregularities of the rails, the different proportions of the wheels and journals, the kind of springs under the cars, the kind and quantity of oil used, and other minor conditions. We believe that 7½ pounds per ton will be suitable for the average railroads, and this figure we shall hereafter adopt in all our calculations in which speed and the grade is not taken into account.

15. The amount of the combined rolling and axle friction of a train, which a locomotive must overcome, can be found by several practical methods. For instance: Assume that one end of a rope is attached to a car, and the other end, $c$, of rope passed over pulley, $b$, as shown in Fig. 5. The bearings of this pulley are supposed to be firmly fastened to the track, and the height and position of the pulley being such that portion $a\,b$ of the rope will be parallel to the rail; then a weight fastened to the end, $c$, of the rope, and sufficiently heavy to move the car, and no more, will be the force in pounds necessary to move it, or, in other words, this weight will be the force necessary to overcome the combined rolling and axle friction. Hence, if the weight of this car is 20 tons, we may expect to find that a weight from 120 to 180 pounds will move it, this difference of weight being caused by the conditions of the rail, etc., as before explained. Now, the mean between 120 and 180 is 150 pounds to move 20 tons, which is equivalent to 7½ pounds per ton.

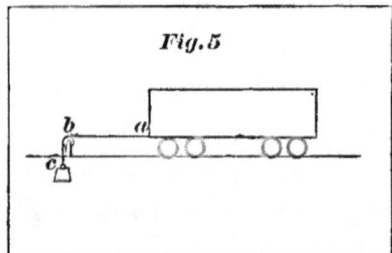

Again, we may try another method. Instead of placing a coupling-bar between the tender and cars, let us couple these by an instrument capable of measuring a force. Such an instrument is called a dynamometer. There are different kinds of dynamometers, the simplest being a spring balance, sufficiently strong to withstand the pull, and yet elastic enough to indicate correctly the force in pounds exerted by the engine in pulling the train. Although the spring balance is not always the best instrument to use for this purpose, and is adapted only for moderate forces, we draw attention to it because its action is familiar to the reader, and probably best understood. Now suppose a correct spring balance is placed between the tender and a train whose weight is 1,000 tons, then, as soon as the engine commences to pull and move the train, our spring balance will show a force from 6,000 to 9,000 pounds. The mean between 6,000 and 9,000 pounds is 7,500 pounds, which is again equivalent to 7½ pounds per ton.

We may also determine by observation the force necessary to move the train. It has been found that railroad cars, with wheels and axles as before described, will begin to roll down a grade when it is as steep as from 16 to 24 feet per mile. Of course, this difference is caused by the condition of the track and other considerations before mentioned.

Let the length of the line $a\,c$, Fig. 6, represent a mile, and the length $b\,c$ the rise of the grade, namely, 16 feet. In that branch of science called mechanics it has been proved that the force necessary to overcome friction is as much smaller than the weight* of the cars as the length of the line $b\,c$ is shorter than the length of the line $a\,c$.

---

* Instead of the word "weight," we should have said "pressure," because the weight and pressure are equal only on a level track, and not on a grade; but in this particular case, the difference being so small, we have, for the sake of simplicity, used the word "weight." How to find this difference will be explained hereafter.

Now, the line $a\,c$ represents one mile, or 5,280 feet, and the line $b\,c$ 16 feet; dividing 5,280 feet by 16 feet, we have $\frac{5280}{16} = 330$, that is, the line $a\,c$ is 330 times longer than the line $b\,c$, hence the weight of the cars will be 330 times greater than the force necessary to overcome friction. Now, there are 2,000 pounds in a ton, hence $\frac{2000}{330} = 6.06$. This means that it requires 6 pounds per ton to move the train. If we assume the grade to be 24 feet in a mile when the cars begin to roll down the grade, then the line $b\,c$, Fig. 6, will be 24 feet long, and $\frac{5280}{24} = 220$, that is, the line $a\,c$ is 220 times longer than the line $b\,c$, therefore $\frac{2000}{220} = 9$ pounds per ton to move the train, or to overcome rolling and axle friction; the mean between 6 and 9 pounds is 7½ pounds, as before.

From this we may establish a rule for finding the force necessary to overcome the train resistance, the speed not being taken into consideration.

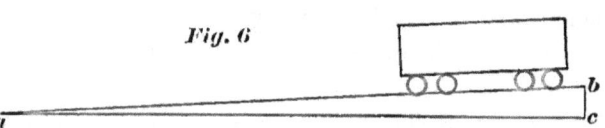

Fig. 6

RULE 1.—Multiply the weight of the train in tons (of 2,000 pounds) by 7½; the answer will be the force in pounds necessary to overcome the train resistance. If to this we add the resistance of the tender and its load, also the force necessary to move the engine itself, we then know the force an engine must exert to haul the total load.

For all practical purposes we may assume that 7½ pounds per ton is not only sufficient to move the train, but also includes the force necessary to move the engine and overcome the friction of its machinery, hence no separate calculation for this is necessary.

The resistance of the tender is found by Rule 1—that is, multiply the weight in tons of the tender and its load by 7½, and the answer will be the force in pounds required to overcome this resistance. Or, still simpler, add the weight of the tender and its load to the weight of the train and multiply the sum by 7½. Thus,

EXAMPLE 1.—The weight of a train is 1,200 tons, and the weight of the tender 20 tons; find the force in pounds necessary to haul this train; $1,200 + 20 = 1,220$ tons, $1,220 \times 7\frac{1}{2} = 9,150$ pounds, hence the engine must be capable of exerting a total pulling force of 9,150 pounds.

## ADHESION.

16. The effort to haul a train which a locomotive can exert is limited by the adhesion between the driving wheels and the rails. This adhesion is simply friction between the driving wheels and rails acting so as to prevent slipping. If, for instance, the train resistance exceeds the adhesion, the driving wheels will slip, or, in other words, turn round without advancing.

The adhesion depends upon the weight placed on the drivers. When the rails are dry and in comparatively good condition, we may assume that the adhesive force is equal to $\frac{1}{5}$ of the weight on the drivers. Thus, for instance, if the weight on the drivers is 40,000 pounds, the adhesive force will be 8,000 pounds. This adhesive force enables an engine to pull a train, and must not be less than the train resistance.

When the rails are wet, muddy, or greasy, this adhesive force will be considerably less, and snowy or frosty weather will also reduce the adhesion.

In the following calculations we shall consider the track to be in good condition, and therefore shall assume the adhesion to be equal to $\frac{1}{5}$ of the weight on the drivers. If the condition of the track is not known, the writer believes that the adoption of $\frac{1}{6}$ of the weight on the drivers for the adhesion will not lead to disappointment as often as when $\frac{1}{5}$ is adopted.

### WEIGHT ON DRIVERS.—NUMBER OF DRIVING WHEELS.

17. From the foregoing remarks we have learned that when the weight of the train and tender is known we can find the train resistance; also, that the adhesion must at least be equal to the train resistance, and since the adhesion is equal to $\frac{1}{5}$ of the weight on the driving wheels, we multiply the train resistance or the adhesion by 5, the product will be the total weight on all the drivers.

EXAMPLE 2.—In Example 1 we found the train resistance to be 9,150 pounds; what must be the total weight on the driving wheels? $9,150 \times 5 = 45,750$ pounds, hence the total weight in all the drivers will be 45,750 pounds.

On some roads heavy rails are used, on other roads lighter rails are adopted. The heavy rails can, of course, bear a greater weight on the drivers than the lighter rails, therefore, before we can find the number of drivers under an engine, we must know the weight that the rails can bear.

18. When an engine is running on light rails—about 30 pounds per yard—we may place 4,000 pounds on each driver; and when an engine is running on heavy rails we may place 15,000 pounds on each driver. In late years the tendency has been to crowd all the weight on the drivers that can possibly be placed on them, so that now on some roads more than 15,000 pounds are placed on a driver. But there must be a limit to this weight, because when too much weight is placed on the drivers, either the tires, the rails, or both, will be injured. The exact amount of weight that can be placed on the drivers has not yet been satisfactorily established, but we believe that the foregoing figures, namely, 4,000 to 15,000 pounds on each driver, according to size of rail, may be safely adopted.

From these remarks it must be evident that before we can decide which of these two figures we can use, or what amount of weight between these two limits we may adopt, we must know the material of which the rails are made, and the weight of rail per yard, that is, their form and size. Of course, we are now alluding only to rails for ordinary passenger and freight engines on roads of 3 feet gauge, or other roads up to 4' 8½" gauge, and we do not include the rails for mining engines, plantation engines, or wooden rails.

Another important fact that we must not overlook is the weight the bridges can bear, because the rails may be suitable for a heavy load, and the bridges may not be so.

19. If, then, we know the weight that can be safely placed on each driver, we can find the number of drivers to be placed under an engine by:

RULE 2.—Divide the weight that must be placed on all the drivers by the weight that can be safely placed on one driver, and the quotient will be the number of driving wheels required.

EXAMPLE 3.—The greatest weight on each driver that the rails of a given road can bear is 10,000 pounds, and the weight necessary on all the drivers to haul the train is 40,000; how many driving wheels must be placed under the engine? According to the rule we have $\frac{40000}{10000} = 4$, hence the number of drivers will be four. If the necessary weight on all the drivers had been 60,000 pounds, we then would have to place six drivers under the engine so as not to exceed 10,000 pounds on each.

### DIAMETERS OF DRIVING WHEELS.

20. The diameter of the driving wheels under an engine will, to a great extent, depend upon the speed of the locomotive. Driving wheels of large diameter are necessary for fast speeds; and, on the other hand, driving wheels for heavy freight engines must necessarily be comparatively small in diameter. There are several causes which

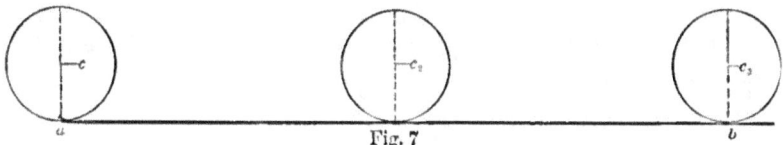

Fig. 7

will place a limit to the diameter of a driving wheel in either direction. We will name two: The diameter must not be too large, because, if it is, the engines will stand too high. The diameter must not be too small, because, if it is, difficulty will be experienced in getting steam out of the cylinder on account of the high piston speed which may be necessary for the required speed of train. Between these two limits no exact rule for finding the diameter of a driving wheel can be given. The following tables will greatly aid us in determining the diameters of these wheels. These tables show the diameters of driving wheels for the different classes of engines, such as are generally adopted by builders and master mechanics, and giving good satisfaction.

In these tables we see that, for an eight-wheeled engine with cylinders 10″ in diameter and 20″ stroke, we may use driving wheels 45″ diameter, or larger, up to 51″ diameter; or, if it is an eight-wheeled engine with 17″ × 24″ cylinders, we may adopt driving wheels 60″ diameter, or larger, up to 66″. Of course, these limits of driving wheels for the different classes of engines are not absolute. We may change, and, indeed, may be compelled to change, these diameters to suit some particular service.

But it must be remembered that when the number of revolutions of the driving wheel per mile are given, then the diameter of the driver is not a matter of choice, but must be found accurately by calculation, which is an easy matter. Thus, for instance, the number of revolutions of the driving wheel per mile is 336; what must be the diameter of the wheel? One mile is equal to 5,280 feet; then dividing 5,280 by the number of revolutions, namely, 336, we have $\frac{5280}{336} = 15.71$. This quotient is the number of feet in the circumference of the wheel. Now, if we refer to a table of circumferences, we find that the diameter of a circle, whose circumference is 15.71 feet, is equal to 5 feet. If such a table is not at hand, then divide the 15.71 feet by

3.1416, because the circumference is always 3.1416 times greater than the diameter, and the quotient in this case will be 5 feet, which is the diameter of the wheel.

TABLES SHOWING THE DIAMETERS OF DRIVING WHEELS AS GENERALLY ADOPTED FOR DIFFERENT CLASSES AND SIZES OF LOCOMOTIVES.

ALL DIMENSIONS IN INCHES.

| TABLE 1. EIGHT-WHEELED ENGINES. || TABLE 2. MOGUL ENGINES. || TABLE 3. TEN-WHEELED ENGINES. || TABLE 4. CONSOLIDATION ENGINES. ||
| Cylinders. Diameter. Stroke. | Driving Wheels. Diameter. | Cylinders. Diameter. Stroke. | Driving Wheels. Diameter. | Cylinders. Diameter. Stroke. | Driving Wheels. Diameter. | Cylinders. Diameter. Stroke. | Driving Wheels. Diameter. |
| Column 1. | Column 2. | Column 1. | Column 2. | Column 1. | Column 2. | Column 1. | Column 2. |
|---|---|---|---|---|---|---|---|
| | | | | | | ......... | For Narrow Gauge. 3' 0" to 3' 6" |
| 10 × 20 | 45 to 51 | 11 × 16 | 35 to 40 | ......... | ......... | | |
| 11 × 22 | 45 to 51 | 12 × 18 | 36 to 41 | 12 × 18 | 39 to 43 | 14 × 16 | 36 to 38 |
| 12 × 22 | 48 to 54 | 13 × 18 | 37 to 42 | 13 × 18 | 41 to 45 | 15 × 18 | 36 to 38 |
| 13 × 22 | 49 to 57 | 14 × 20 | 39 to 43 | 14 × 20 | 43 to 47 | | |
| 14 × 24 | 55 to 61 | 15 × 22 | 42 to 47 | 15 × 22 | 45 to 50 | ......... | ......... |
| 15 × 24 | 55 to 66 | 16 × 24 | 45 to 51 | 16 × 24 | 48 to 54 | For 4' 8½" Gauge. | |
| 16 × 24 | 58 to 66 | 17 × 24 | 49 to 54 | 17 × 24 | 51 to 56 | 20 × 24 | 48 to 50 |
| 17 × 24 | 60 to 66 | 18 × 24 | 51 to 56 | 18 × 24 | 51 to 56 | 22 × 24 | 50 to 52 |
| 18 × 24 | 61 to 66 | 19 × 24 | 54 to 60 | 19 × 24 | 54 to 60 | | |

The reason why 5,280 is divided by the number of revolutions per mile is simple, and yet it is not so generally understood among mechanics as we might expect, therefore the following explanation is offered:

Let the line $a\,b$, Fig. 7, represent one mile—that is, 5,280 feet—and $c$ the center of the wheel when it stands at the end, $a$, of the line $a\,b$, as shown in the figure. Carefully rolling this wheel without slipping along the line $a\,b$ until it has completed one revolution, or made one complete turn, the number of feet that it has traveled along the line $a\,b$ is equal to the number of feet in its circumference. Now, if this wheel is 5 feet in diameter, its circumference will be 15.71 feet, nearly, and the distance from the center $c$ to the center $c_2$, which is equal to the distance that it has traveled along the line $a\,b$, will be 15.71 feet. Again, if we continue rolling this wheel along the line $a\,b$ until it has made another complete turn, then its center will be at $c_3$, and the distance that the wheel has traveled from the point $a$ along the line $a\,b$ will be equal to the distance between the first center $c$ and $c_3$—that is, 31.42 feet—which is obtained by multiplying $15.71 \times 2$; and so on for every revolution it will travel 15.71 feet further; and therefore, if we divide the length of the line $a\,b$, or one mile, by the circumference of a wheel, which is, in this case, 15.71 feet, we will know the number of revolutions that it must make to travel from $a$ to $b$. And conversely, if we know the number of revolutions per mile, we divide the number of feet in a mile, or, as in our example, the length of the line $a\,b$ by the number of revolutions, and the quotient will be the circumference of the wheel, and dividing this circumference by 3.1416, will give its diameter.

## TRACTIVE POWER.—DIAMETER OF CYLINDERS.

21. We now come to the consideration of the size of cylinders necessary to turn the driving wheels. Neglecting the friction of the machinery, we may say that the cylinders with a given steam pressure must be large enough to almost slip the wheels, that is, to turn the wheels without advancing on the rails, when the engine is attached to the heaviest train that it was designed to haul. Or, in other words, if a certain amount of weight is placed on the drivers to haul a given train, we must design our cylinders so that a sufficient power can be obtained to turn the wheels, and not more and not less, when the engine is attached to this train. This power which is necessary to turn the driving wheels under the above conditions is called the "tractive power" of a locomotive. If the cylinders are too small in proportion to the weight placed on the drivers, then the engine cannot haul the train that it was intended it should do with the correct weight on the drivers. If, on the other hand, the cylinders are too large in proportion to the weight placed on the drivers, then the engine cannot employ all its tractive power. In these cases, there will be either a waste of material or steam. Here, then, we see that in a correctly designed engine there is a fixed relation or proportion between its tractive power and the weight placed upon the drivers. The tractive power is not only dependent upon the diameter of the cylinders, but also upon the diameters of the drivers, the length of stroke, and the mean effective steam pressure per square inch of piston.

22. In Fig. 8 we have represented a pair of cylinders and *one* of the front pair of driving wheels of an eight-wheeled engine, such as shown in Fig. 1. One of the cylinders in Fig. 8 is connected to the driving wheel; the other cylinder is connected to a crank fastened to the same axle, and not connected to a driving wheel, because we have assumed that there is only one driving wheel on the axle. Let us also assume that the cylinders in Fig. 8, with frames, valve gear, and all necessary mechanism, are firmly fastened to blocks or a foundation, so that this figure represents a complete stationary engine. The driving wheel is not to touch the track, but the whole engine is set high enough so that a rope can be fastened to the lower part of the driving wheel, in such a manner that when the other end of the rope is attached to a train this rope will be parallel to the track, as shown. When this engine is set in motion in a direction as shown by the arrow, it will haul the train towards the engine. Now, the power that this engine exerts in doing this is precisely the same as the tractive power of a locomotive designed to do the same amount of work. Should the total weight of this train be 1,000 tons, then, according to what has been said before, it will take 7,500 pounds to move it, and therefore the stress or the pull on the rope will be 7,500 pounds.

If, instead of fastening this rope to the train, we pass it over a pulley, *a*, and attach a weight, *w*, to it weighing 7,500 pounds, as shown by the dotted lines in Fig. 8, then the stress or the pull on the rope will not be changed, but will still remain as before, namely, 7,500 pounds, and therefore we conclude that the power necessary to move the train is exactly the same as the power necessary to hoist a given weight.

For the sake of clearness and simplicity, when calculating the tractive power of a locomotive, we shall hereafter always assume that the train resistance is represented by a weight, *w*, fastened by the means of a rope to *one* driving wheel, as shown in

Fig. 8, and that the cylinders must be made large enough so as to be capable of lifting this weight.

But the reader may say that a locomotive has more work to do than the stationary engine here represented, because the locomotive must move its own weight, which the stationary engine does not have to do. This is true, but it must be remembered that we are allowing 7½ pounds for every ton of the weight of train that is to be moved, and, as we have stated before, this may be considered—and we do consider it so—as not only sufficient to move the train, but also sufficient to move the weight of the locomotive and overcome the friction of its mechanism. Yet we must again call the attention of the reader to the fact, that any particular or given speed is not yet taken into consideration; we are simply proportioning an engine capable of moving a train very slowly.

23. The foregoing being thoroughly understood, the solution of the following example will not be difficult:

EXAMPLE 4.—Find the diameters of the cylinders for an eight-wheeled locomotive, whose total weight on drivers is 20,000 pounds, the diameter of the driving wheels, 45 inches; the stroke, 20 inches; and the mean effective steam pressure 90 pounds per

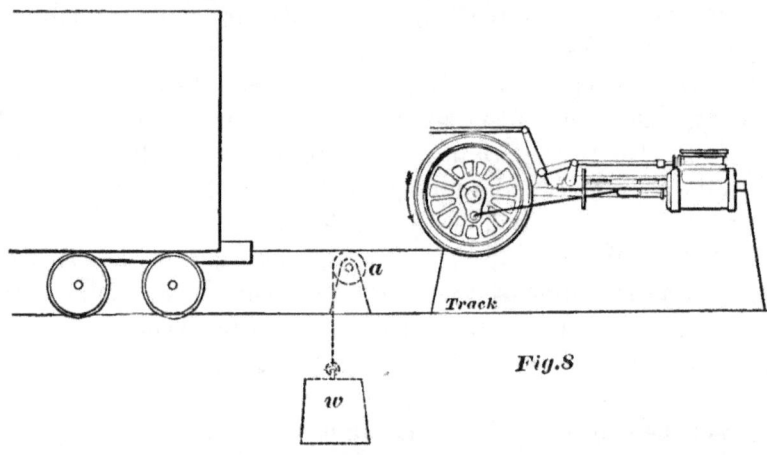

Fig. 8

square inch of piston area. (The writer believes that for the mean effective steam pressure 90 pounds per square inch is a good average, and this will always be adopted unless otherwise stated.)

From what has been said before, we know that the total adhesive force will be $\frac{1}{5}$ of the weight placed on the drivers; hence the total adhesive force will be $\frac{1}{5}$ of 20,000, which is equal to 4,000 pounds. We have also seen that the adhesion is equal to the train resistance; hence the weight $w$, in Fig. 8, which represents the train resistance, must weigh 4,000 pounds. Now, all we have to do is to find the diameters of the two cylinders, as shown in Fig. 8, capable of lifting this weight of 4,000 pounds; and so for all locomotives when the total weight on the drivers is known, no matter how many driving wheels are to be placed under an engine, we always assume that the train resistance is represented by the weight $w$; that all this weight, or train resistance, is applied to only one driving wheel; and that the two cylinders must be made large enough, so that their combined effort will be sufficient for lifting this one weight $w$, which we assume to be $\frac{1}{5}$ of the total weight placed on all the drivers.

In our example, as we have already seen, this weight $w$ is equal to 4,000 pounds, and the diameters of the driving wheels 45 inches each. When the wheel has made one revolution, the weight $w$ will then have been raised through a distance equal to the circumference of the wheel, and this circumference is 141.37 inches, or 11.781 feet.

In raising this weight, a certain amount of energy must be expended; and, to know exactly how much has been expended, we must compare it to some standard or unit of energy.

The amount of work required to raise or lift one pound one foot high is equal to a unit of energy or foot-pound; hence, if two pounds are lifted one foot high, two units of energy have been expended, or, if five pounds are lifted one foot high, five units of energy have been expended; and, if the five pounds are raised five feet high, then 25 units of energy have been expended, because, to raise the five pounds through the first foot, five units of energy will be required; to raise them through the second foot another five units will be required; the same for the third, and so on up to the fifth, making a total of 25 units of energy, or foot-pounds.

In our example a weight of 4,000 pounds must be raised 11.781 feet high. To raise this weight through the first foot, 4,000 units of energy or foot-pounds will be required; and the same amount of energy will be required to raise it through the second foot, and again the same through the third foot, and so on until the height of 11.781 feet has been reached; therefore, the total number of units of energy, or foot-pounds, that must be expended to raise this weight through a distance of 11.781 feet is $4,000 \times 11.781 = 47,124$ foot-pounds. In a similar way, for all engines, we multiply the weight, $w$, in pounds, which represents the adhesion, by the circumference of the wheel in feet, and the product will be the number of foot-pounds or units of energy that must be expended during the time the wheel makes one revolution.

But the energy necessary to raise this weight is derived from the steam pressure in the cylinder, and since the mean effective steam pressure per square inch of piston is already given—namely, 90 pounds—it only remains to make the cylinder of such a diameter that we can obtain 47,124 units of energy for every turn of the wheel with a weight attached, as shown in Fig. 8.

But now notice the fact that during the time the wheel makes one turn, raising the weight 11.781 feet high, the piston travels through a distance equal to twice the length of the stroke; the stroke being 20 inches, the piston travels through a distance of 40 inches, or 3.33 feet. During the time that the piston travels through a distance of 3.33 feet, 47,124 units of energy or foot-pounds must be expended, and therefore, dividing 47,124 by 3.33 feet, we have $\frac{47124}{3.33} = 14,151$ pounds. This last answer simply means that to raise the 4,000 pounds weight through a distance of 11.781 feet, the weight being attached to the wheel, as shown, will require as many units of energy as to raise a weight of 14,151 pounds 3.33 feet high, the weight being attached directly to the end of the piston rod, as shown in Fig. 9.

Now, it will be readily understood that the mean effective steam pressure on each square inch of piston will lift a portion of this weight of 14,151 pounds, and the amount that the pressure per square inch of piston will lift is 90 pounds; hence, dividing 14,151 pounds by 90 pounds, we have $\frac{14151}{90} = 157.2$ square inches. This means that the total piston area must be 157.2 square inches. But we have two cylinders; therefore $\frac{157.2}{2} = 78.6$ square inches in the area of one piston; and a piston having an area of 78.6 square inches, must be 10 inches diameter. Hence a locomotive having four driving wheels, with 20,000 pounds placed upon them, the driving wheels being 45 inches in diameter, and a mean effective steam pressure of 90 pounds per square inch, will require cylinders 10 inches in diameter and 20 inches stroke.

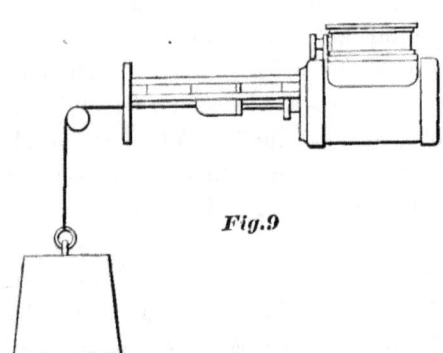

Fig. 9

Here we have calculated the diameters of the cylinders suitable for a given weight placed on the drivers. We may reverse the order of this calculation, and find the necessary weight that must be placed on the drivers, when the dimensions of cylinders and diameters of driving wheels are given.

EXAMPLE 5.—The diameter of each cylinder is 10 inches; stroke, 20 inches; diameter of driving wheels, 45 inches; mean effective steam pressure, 90 pounds per square inch of piston. What is the tractive power of such an engine? And how much weight must be placed on the drivers?

The area of a piston 10 inches in diameter is 78.54 square inches. Multiplying the area of the piston by the steam pressure per square inch, we have 78.54 × 90 = 7068.6 pounds total steam pressure on one piston; but there are two pistons, hence 7068.6 × 2 = 14137.2 pounds, which is the total steam pressure on both pistons. The stroke is 20 inches, and during the time that the wheel makes one turn, the piston has traveled through twice the length of the stroke; hence 20 × 2 = 40 inches, or 3.33 feet. Multiplying the total steam pressure on the pistons by 3.33 feet, we have 14137.2 × 3.33 = 47076.876 foot-pounds, or units of energy the cylinders can exert during one revolution of the wheel. The driving wheels are 45 inches in diameter; hence the circumference of each wheel will be 141.37 inches, or 11.78 feet.

Dividing the units of energy the cylinders are capable of exerting by the circumference of the wheel, we have $\frac{47076.876}{11.78} = 3{,}996$ * pounds. The tractive power of the engine is, therefore, capable of lifting a weight of 3,996 pounds attached to the driving wheel, as shown in Fig. 8; or, in other words, the tractive power of this engine is capable of overcoming a train resistance of 3,996 pounds. In a similar manner, the tractive power of any engine may be found, namely, by multiplying together twice the area in square inches of one piston, the mean effective steam pressure per square inch, and

---

* This answer would have been 4,000, instead of 3,996, if the decimal fraction in the 3.33 feet (obtained by multiplying the stroke by 2) had been exact.

twice the length of the stroke in feet; then dividing this product by the circumference in feet of the wheel, the quotient will be the tractive power of the engine.

This rule can be greatly simplified, as we shall presently show. The tractive power and the adhesion are represented by the same number of pounds; therefore multiplying the tractive power by 5, we have $3,996 \times 5 = 19,980$ pounds, which is the weight that must be placed on the drivers of this particular engine. Our answer, then, to Example 5 is: Tractive power, 3,996 pounds; weight on drivers, 19,980 pounds.

## WEIGHT OF ENGINES.

24. In Example 4 it has been shown how to find the diameters of the cylinders when the weight on the drivers and the diameters of the same are known; and in Example 5 it has been shown how to find the weight on the drivers when the dimensions of the cylinders and diameters of driving wheels are known. From the reasoning connected with these examples, we conclude that the tractive power should not be more or less than the adhesion—a fact which we have stated before. We may also reasonably conclude that, when the dimensions of the cylinders and the diameters of the driving wheels of any engine are given, and if we assume that, in all cases, the mean effective steam pressure per square inch of piston is 90 pounds, we may at once arrange, for future use and reference, a table for each class of engine, showing the tractive power of each, the necessary weight on the drivers, and the number of tons of 2,000 pounds that each engine can haul on a straight and level track. Indeed, we may extend these tables so that the weight on the truck, and consequently the total weight of each engine, will at once be seen.

With these objects in view, the following tables have been prepared. In these tables, columns 1 and 2 are exactly the same as those given in tables 1, 2, 3 and 4. In column 3 of all the following tables the adhesion is given and, since the adhesion and tractive power are expressed by the same number of pounds, these figures are obtained by finding the tractive power of each engine, and for this purpose the small diameters of driving wheels given in column 2 are always used. The weight on drivers is shown in column 4, which is obtained by multiplying the adhesion by 5 for all classes of engines. Column 5 gives the weights on the trucks; the calculations for these weights are based upon observations. Thus, it has been noticed that the weight on the truck for an eight-wheeled engine is about one-half of that placed on the drivers; hence, multiplying the weight placed on drivers by the decimal .5, the weight on the truck will be known.

For Mogul engines, we multiply the total weight on drivers by the decimal .2, and the product will be the weight on the truck.

For ten-wheeled engines, the total weight on the drivers multiplied by the decimal .32 will be equal to the weight on the truck.

And lastly, for consolidation engines, the total weight on drivers multiplied by the decimal .16 will determine the weight on the truck.

For instance, to find the weight on the truck for an eight-wheeled engine with cylinders $17'' \times 24''$, we multiply the total weight on drivers for this engine, given in column 4, by .5; hence, we have $52,020 \times .5 = 26,010$ pounds, which is the weight on truck.

For a 17″ × 24″ Mogul engine, we have 63,697 × .2 = 12,739 pounds = weight on truck.

For an 18″ × 24″ ten-wheeled engine, we have 68,611 × .32 = 21,955 pounds = weight on truck.

And for a 20″ × 24″ consolidation engine, we have 90,000 × .16 = 14,400 pounds = weight on truck.

In column 6, the total weight of each engine is given, which is obtained by adding the weight on the drivers to the weight on the truck. Dividing the adhesion given in column 3 by 7½, will give us the number of tons of 2,000 pounds that the engine is capable of hauling on a straight and level track; these figures are given in column 7.

The weight of engines given in these tables will be found to agree generally very closely with the actual weights of locomotives recently built, although it must not be expected that these weights will agree in every case with the actual weights, because different builders do not build their engines alike.

The given weights on the trucks for Mogul or consolidation engines may differ considerably from the actual weights, yet this should not be a matter of surprise, because the weight on a truck for either of these engines can be changed without changing the total weight of engine, and, indeed, often the pieces of mechanism connecting the truck to the engines are so arranged that a heavy or light weight can be thrown on the truck while the engine is standing on the track.

Yet the figures in these tables, indicating the weights on the trucks, can be safely taken as guides in constructing and proportioning an engine.

The actual weight on trucks for eight-wheeled or ten-wheeled engines will not differ much from those given in the tables, because these weights depend greatly on the difference between the total and rigid wheel bases, and these are not often changed by the different builders. The ratio of the rigid and total wheel bases is generally the same in all eight-wheeled engines, and the same may be said of ten-wheeled engines.

It has already been stated that the rule (as before given) for finding the tractive power of an engine can be greatly simplified. To explain this, we will again state the former rule, but, instead of writing it in the ordinary language, we will employ a number of simple arithmetical signs. This will enable us to bring the whole mode of operation under the eye, and follow it without taxing our memory; hence this rule will read as the following:

### Rule A.

$$\frac{\text{Area of piston in sq. in.} \times \text{mean effective steam pressure per sq. in.} \times \text{stroke in ft.} \times 2 \times 2}{\text{Circumference of driving wheel in feet}} = \text{tractive power.}$$

For the sake of distinction we have called this Rule A. Now, remembering that the area of a piston is found by multiplying the square of its diameter by .7854, and also that the circumference of a wheel is found by multiplying its diameter by 3.1416, we can put in the place of "*area of piston in square inches,*" in Rule A, the method of finding this area, namely, square of diameter in inches × .7854; and, in the place of "*circumference of wheel in feet,*" we may put diameter of wheel in feet × 3.1416; consequently, the wording of the Rule A will be changed, and read like Rule B:

## Rule B.

$$\frac{\text{Sq. of diam. of piston in in.} \times .7854 \times \text{mean effective steam pressure per sq. in.} \times \text{stroke in ft.} \times 2 \times 2}{\text{Diameter of driving wheel in feet} \times 3.1416} = \text{tractive power.}$$

If, now, we multiply the decimal .7854 by 2, and again by 2 (figures which are found above the line in Rule B), we have a product of 3.1416. Below the line, in Rule B, we find the same figure—that is, 3.1416; hence we may cancel all these figures, or, in other words, we may throw out of the Rule B the decimal .7854 and the figures 2 × 2, all found above the line, and the figure 3.1416, which is found below the line. Doing so, the wording of the Rule B will be changed to that of

## Rule 3.

$$\frac{\text{Square of diameter of one piston} \times \text{mean effective steam pressure per square inch} \times \text{stroke in feet}}{\text{Diameter of driving wheel in feet}} = \text{tractive power.}$$

In ordinary language, Rule 3 would read: multiply together the square of the diameter in inches of one piston, the mean effective steam pressure per square inch and the length in feet of one stroke. The product thus obtained, divided by the diameter in feet of one wheel, will be the tractive power.

EXAMPLE 6.—What is the tractive power of a locomotive whose cylinders are 17 inches in diameter and 24 inches stroke? The mean effective steam pressure is 90 pounds per square inch, and the driving wheels 60 inches in diameter.

$$\frac{17 \times 17 \times 90 \times 2}{5} = 10404 = \text{tractive power.}$$

If the tractive power had been calculated according to Rule A, the result would have been the same. But Rule 3 is evidently the simplest, and a great amount of time and labor will be saved by using it.

All the figures expressing the adhesion in pounds, as shown in column 3 in all the following tables, have been found according to Rule 3:

### TABLE 5.

#### EIGHT-WHEELED LOCOMOTIVES.

| Cylinders. Diameter. Stroke. | Diameter of Driving Wheels. | Adhesion. | Weight on Drivers. | Weight on Truck. | Total Weight. | Hauling Capacity on Level Track in Tons of 2,000 Pounds, including Tender. |
|---|---|---|---|---|---|---|
| Column 1. | Column 2. | Column 3. | Column 4. | Column 5. | Column 6. | Column 7. |
| Inches. | Inches. | Lbs. | Lbs. | Lbs. | Lbs. | |
| 10 × 20 | 45 to 51 | 4000 | 20000 | 10000 | 30000 | 533 |
| 11 × 22 | 45 to 51 | 5324 | 26620 | 13310 | 39930 | 709 |
| 12 × 22 | 48 to 54 | 5940 | 29700 | 14850 | 44550 | 792 |
| 13 × 22 | 49 to 57 | 6828 | 34140 | 17070 | 51210 | 910 |
| 14 × 24 | 55 to 61 | 7697 | 38485 | 19242 | 57727 | 1026 |
| 15 × 24 | 55 to 66 | 8836 | 44180 | 22090 | 66270 | 1178 |
| 16 × 24 | 58 to 66 | 9533 | 47665 | 23832 | 71497 | 1271 |
| 17 × 24 | 60 to 66 | 10404 | 52020 | 26010 | 78030 | 1387 |
| 18 × 24 | 61 to 66 | 11472 | 57360 | 28680 | 86040 | 1529 |

Figures in columns 1 and 2 are the same as those in Table 1.
Figures in column 3 are obtained according to Rule 3.

Figures in column 4 are obtained by multiplying the figures in column 3 by 5.

Figures in column 5 are obtained by multiplying the figures in column 4 by .5.

Figures in column 6 are obtained by adding the figures in column 4 to those in column 5, and are the weight of engines in working order with water and fuel.

Figures in column 7 are obtained by dividing the figures in column 3 by 7½.

## TABLE 6.

### MOGUL ENGINES.

| Cylinders. Diameter. Stroke. | Diameter of Driving Wheels. | Adhesion. | Weight on Drivers. | Weight on Trucks. | Total Weight. | Hauling Capacity on Level Track in Tons of 2,000 Pounds, including Tender. |
|---|---|---|---|---|---|---|
| Column 1. | Column 2. | Column 3. | Column 4. | Column 5. | Column 6. | Column 7. |
| Inches. | Inches. | Lbs. | Lbs. | Lbs. | Lbs. | |
| 11 × 16 | 35 to 40 | 4978.2 | 24891 | 4978 | 29869 | 663 |
| 12 × 18 | 36 to 41 | 6480 | 32400 | 6480 | 38880 | 864 |
| 13 × 18 | 37 to 42 | 7399.4 | 36997 | 7399 | 44396 | 986 |
| 14 × 20 | 39 to 43 | 9046 | 45230 | 9046 | 54276 | 1206 |
| 15 × 22 | 42 to 47 | 10607 | 53035 | 10607 | 63642 | 1414 |
| 16 × 24 | 45 to 51 | 12288 | 61440 | 12288 | 73728 | 1638 |
| 17 × 24 | 49 to 54 | 12739.5 | 63697 | 12739 | 76436 | 1698 |
| 18 × 24 | 51 to 56 | 13722.3 | 68611 | 13722 | 82333 | 1829 |
| 19 × 24 | 54 to 60 | 14440 | 72200 | 14440 | 86640 | 1925 |

Figures in columns 1 and 2 are the same as those in Table 2.

Figures in column 3 are obtained according to Rule 3.

Figures in column 4 are obtained by multiplying the figures in column 3 by 5.

Figures in column 5 are obtained by multiplying the figures in column 4 by .2.

Figures in column 6 are obtained by adding the figures in column 4 to those in column 5, and are the weight of engines in working order with water and fuel.

Figures in column 7 are obtained by dividing the figures in column 3 by 7½.

## TABLE 7.

### TEN-WHEELED ENGINES.

| Cylinders. Diameter. Stroke. | Diameter of Driving Wheels. | Adhesion. | Weight on Drivers. | Weight on Truck. | Total Weight, with Water and Fuel. | Hauling Capacity on Level Track in Tons of 2,000 Pounds, including Tender. |
|---|---|---|---|---|---|---|
| Column 1. | Column 2. | Column 3. | Column 4. | Column 5. | Column 6. | Column 7. |
| Inches. | Inches. | Lbs. | Lbs. | Lbs. | Lbs. | |
| 12 × 18 | 39 to 43 | 5981.5 | 29907 | 9570 | 39477 | 797 |
| 13 × 18 | 41 to 45 | 6677.5 | 33387 | 10683 | 44070 | 890 |
| 14 × 20 | 43 to 47 | 8204.6 | 41023 | 13127 | 54150 | 1093 |
| 15 × 22 | 45 to 50 | 9900 | 49500 | 15840 | 65340 | 1320 |
| 16 × 24 | 48 to 54 | 11520 | 57600 | 18432 | 76032 | 1536 |
| 17 × 24 | 51 to 56 | 12240 | 61200 | 19584 | 80784 | 1632 |
| 18 × 24 | 51 to 56 | 13722.3 | 68611 | 21955 | 90566 | 1829 |
| 19 × 24 | 54 to 60 | 14440 | 72200 | 23104 | 95304 | 1925 |

Figures in columns 1 and 2 are the same as those in Table 3.

Figures in column 3 are obtained according to Rule 3.

Figures in column 4 are obtained by multiplying the figures in column 3 by 5.

Figures in column 5 are obtained by multiplying the figures in column 4 by .32.

Figures in column 6 are obtained by adding the figures in column 4 to those in column 5, and are the weight of engines in working order with water and fuel.

Figures in column 7 are obtained by dividing the figures in column 3 by 7½.

## TABLE 8.

### CONSOLIDATED ENGINES.

| Cylinders. Diameter. Stroke. | Diameter of Driving Wheels. | Adhesion. | Weight on Drivers. | Weight on Truck. | Total Weight, with Water and Fuel. | Hauling Capacity on Level Track in Tons of 2,000 Pounds, including Tender. |
|---|---|---|---|---|---|---|
| Column 1. | Column 2. | Column 3. | Column 4. | Column 5. | Column 6. | Column 7. |
| Inches. | Inches. | Lbs. | Lbs. | Lbs. | Lbs. | |
| 14 × 16 | 36 to 38 | 7840 | 39200 | 6272 | 45472 | 1045 |
| 15 × 18 | 36 to 38 | 10125 | 50625 | 8100 | 58725 | 1350 |
| 20 × 24 | 48 to 50 | 18000 | 90000 | 14400 | 104400 | 2400 |
| 22 × 24 | 50 to 52 | 20908.8 | 104544 | 16727 | 121271 | 2787 |

Figures in columns 1 and 2 are the same as those in Table 4.

Figures in column 3 are obtained according to Rule 3.

Figures in column 4 are obtained by multiplying the figures in column 3 by 5.

Figures in column 5 are obtained by multiplying the figures in column 4 by .16.

Figures in column 6 are obtained by adding the figures in column 4 to those in column 5, and are the weight of engines in working order with water and fuel.

Figures in column 7 are obtained by dividing the figures in column 3 by $7\frac{1}{2}$.

# CHAPTER II.

## CONSTRUCTION OF CYLINDERS.—STEAM PIPES.—SLIDE-VALVES.

25. The general practice in the United States is to place the cylinders outside the frames $A$, $A$, as shown in Figs. 10 and 11; but on further examination of these two figures, we find that there is a considerable difference in the construction of the cylinders, so that we may divide these into two classes. In one class we may place the cylinder with half the saddle cast in one piece; and in the other class we may place the cylinder with the saddle cast separate. The following explanation will help the reader to gain a clearer understanding of the difference of these constructions.

Fig. 10 shows an end view of a cylinder with half the saddle cast to it. In this case the cylinder casting is extended over the frame $A$ to the center of the boiler, and here meets a similar extension from the opposite cylinder (not shown in this figure), the two being bolted together by the bolts $b$, $b$, $b$. These extensions of the cylinders, or those parts of the castings which extend from frame to frame, constitute the cylinder saddle; hence this type of cylinder is known by the term "cylinder and half-saddle cast in one."

26. Fig. 11 shows a locomotive cylinder belonging to the second class, in which the saddles are cast separate, the cylinder being bolted to the saddle by the bolts $C$, $C$; the manner of fastening these to the frames is similar to that of the former cylinders.

Cylinders with half-saddle cast in one are generally used, because only one pattern is needed for both cylinders in a locomotive; whereas, the saddle being cast separately, we need a greater number of patterns.

27. In this chapter we will consider only the cylinders with half-saddle cast in one because they are the most popular ones. The arrangement of the steam-ways, steam passages, exhaust passages, as well as all other details of these cylinders, are shown in Figs. 12, 13, and 14.

Fig. 12 shows a section lengthways of the cylinder, the section being taken through the line $a$, $b$, drawn in Fig. 14.

Fig. 13, right-hand side, shows a section of the cylinder and saddle taken through a line $c$, $d$, drawn in Fig. 14.

Fig. 13, left-hand side, shows an outside end view of the cylinder and half-saddle.

Fig. 14 shows a plan of the cylinders and saddle; the right-hand side of this figure shows a section of half the saddle, the section being taken through the line $e$, $f$, drawn in Fig. 13. Similar letters in these three views indicate the same pieces or parts of the cylinder and saddle.

In Fig. 12 the cylinder heads, piston, and piston-rods are shown, but these have been omitted in all the other figures.

*A, A* are sections of the frames to which the cylinders are firmly bolted.
*B* represents the cylinder.
*C* represents the back cylinder head.
*D* represents the front cylinder head.
*E* represents the piston.
*F* represents the piston-rod.
*G* represents the piston-rod gland.
*H* represents steam-chest seat, that is, the surface on which the steam-chest rests

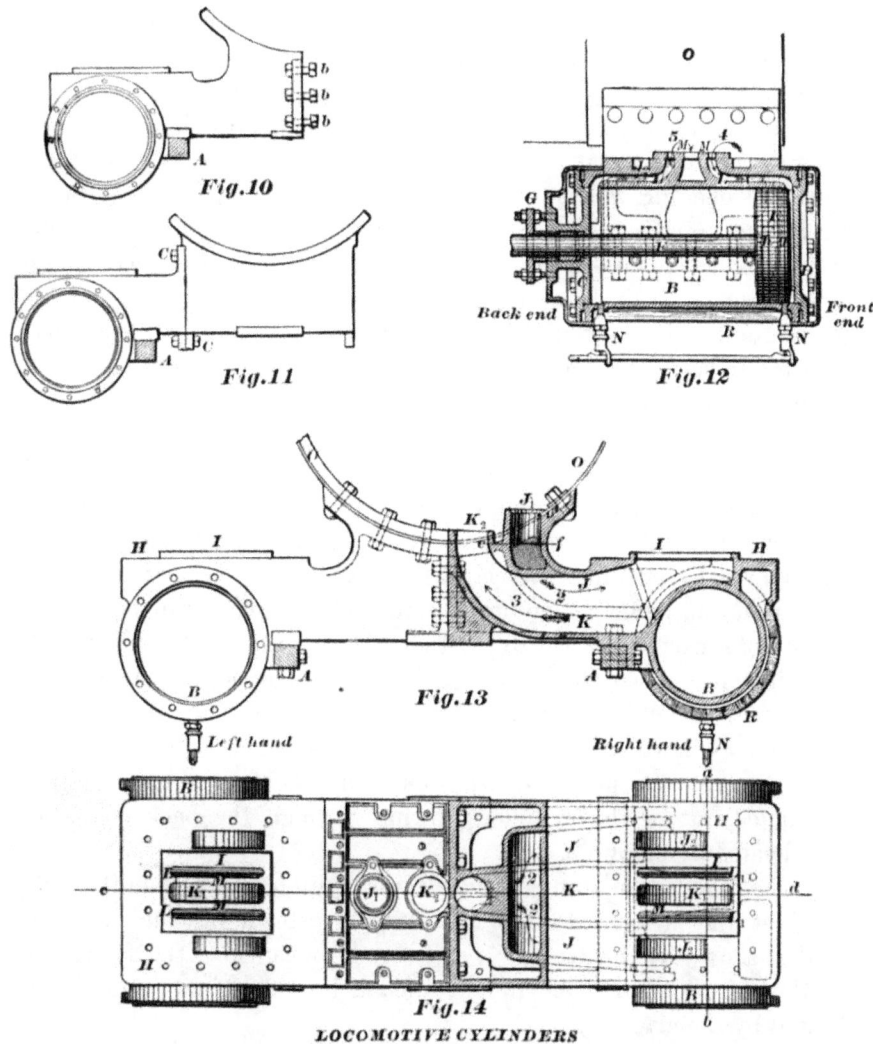

LOCOMOTIVE CYLINDERS

*I* represents the valve seat, that is, the surface on which the slide-valve moves backward and forward.

*J* represents the steam passage. This steam passage terminates at one end (that is, the end in the saddle), with a round hole, as shown at $J_1$. Before this passage reaches the other end, it is divided into two branches, each one terminating in the steam-chest seat with the openings marked $J_2$, $J_2$, and both of these openings lie inside the steam-chest (the steam-chest is not shown in these illustrations).

28. By dividing this steam passage into two branches three advantages are gained. First, the steam will be delivered at each end of the steam-chest, so that the steam can freely enter the steam ports. Second, a right and left-hand cylinder pattern will be avoided, and only one pattern needed for both cylinders. Third, if the cylinders are accurately planed and fitted to gauges, they will be interchangeable; that is, we can use such a cylinder for either side of the engine.

29. The duty of the steam passage is to conduct the steam into the steam-chest; the steam enters the opening $J_1$, and is delivered into the steam-chest through the openings $J_2$, $J_2$. This is the only duty the steam passages have to perform, and consequently the steam in these passages will always flow in one direction, as shown by arrows 2.

30. $K$ represents the exhaust passage. This terminates with one opening in the valve seat, and this opening, marked $K_1$, is called the exhaust port; the other end terminates with a round opening $K_2$, a little above the saddle. Some designers make the form of this opening a semicircle; others, again, will make it a square or oblong; and which of these forms is to be adopted will depend greatly upon the judgment and fancy of the designer. The duty of the exhaust passage is to conduct the steam out of the cylinder after it has performed its work. In this passage the steam will always flow in a direction as indicated by arrow 3.

31. On each side of the exhaust passage, Fig. 12, is a channel or passage marked $L L$; these passages are called the steam-ways. For the sake of distinction we shall call the steam way nearest the front cylinder head, the "front steam-way," and the other one, the "back steam-way." These steam-ways terminate with the openings $L_1$, $L_1$ in the valve seat, and these openings are called the steam ports. The steam-ways have a double duty to perform, namely, they must conduct the steam into the cylinder, and after the steam has performed its work, they must conduct the steam out of the cylinder. For instance, when the piston stands in the position as shown in Fig. 12, the steam will be conducted through the front steam-way into the cylinder space between the front cylinder head and piston, and the steam will flow through this steam-way in a direction as shown by arrows 4. On the other side of the piston the steam is conducted out of the cylinder, flowing through the back steam-way in a direction as indicated by arrows 5.

But now, when the piston stands near the back cylinder head, then the back steam-way will conduct the steam into the cylinder, the steam flowing in an opposite direction, to that shown by the arrows 5, and, in the meantime, the front steam-way will conduct the steam out of the cylinder, causing it to flow in an opposite direction to that indicated by the arrows 4.

Here, then, the reader will perceive what was meant by saying the steam-ways have a double duty to perform. We draw particular attention to this fact, as we shall allude to it again.

The metal or small bars marked $M$, between the steam ports and the exhaust port, are called bridges.

32. $N$, $N$ represent the cylinder cocks. $O$ represents the boiler, or to be more precise, the smoke-box of the boiler, to which the cylinders are firmly bolted as shown.

## PISTON AND ENGINE CLEARANCE.

33. Piston clearance is the distance $P$ between the piston and cylinder head at the end of a stroke. In locomotive cylinders it varies from $\frac{1}{4}$ to $\frac{1}{2}$ inch; it is generally equal to $\frac{3}{8}$ of an inch. The term "piston clearance" must not be confounded with the term "engine clearance," or simply clearance, which is the space between the piston and head plus the volume of the steam-way, or we may say, that the engine clearance is the whole minimum space between the piston and the valve face at the completion or beginning of a stroke.

## COUNTERBORE.

34. The cylinder is counter-bored at each end, generally $\frac{1}{4}$ of an inch larger in diameter than the bore of the cylinder. The depth of the counterbore should be such, that when the piston stands at the end of a stroke, as shown in Fig. 12, the packing ring, $g$, will not project more than $\frac{1}{4}$ of an inch beyond the edge of the counterbore, or when the piston stands at the opposite end of the stroke, the packing ring, $h$, will not project more than $\frac{1}{4}$ of an inch beyond the edge of the corresponding counterbore. In any case care must be taken to regulate the depth of the counterbore so as not to allow the whole width of any of the packing rings to pass over it. It will be readily understood that should any of the packing rings travel beyond the edge of the counterbore, they will at once adjust themselves to the larger diameter, and thus prevent the piston from returning without doing considerable damage.

35. For the cylinders such cast-iron should be selected as will wear well and equally; it must be hard and homogeneous, yet not so hard as to prevent the tools from cutting during the process of boring, planing, drilling, and turning.

36. The joints between cylinder and cylinder heads are made metal to metal, and ground; the part to be ground is allowed to project a little beyond the face of the flange, as shown in Figs. 12 and 14.

The bolts securing the cylinder heads to the cylinder are usually placed from $4\frac{1}{2}$ to $5\frac{1}{2}$ inches from center to center, and these distances will determine the number of bolts to be used. Their diameter should be such that the stress brought upon them by the steam pressure alone will not exceed 5,000 pounds per square inch.

## CYLINDER PROPORTIONS AND DETAILS.

37. To find the diameter of a cylinder-head bolt we must first know the initial steam pressure in the cylinder, that is, the steam pressure at the beginning or near the beginning of the stroke. We believe that 120 pounds per square inch for the initial steam pressure will agree very closely with ordinary practice, but the tendency is to work with higher steam pressure than this. Assuming that 120 pounds per square inch for the initial pressure is correct, the diameters of the bolts for the cylinder head can easily be found.

For example, let it be required to find the diameter of the cylinder-head bolts, the cylinder being 16 inches in diameter, and the bolts to be placed about 5 inches from center to center.

The area of a circle 16 inches in diameter is 201 square inches; multiplying this area by the initial steam pressure per square inch, we have 201 × 120 = 24,120 pounds; this is the force which the combined strength of all the bolts in one cylinder head must be capable of resisting, independent of the stress that is already placed on these bolts by the use of the screw wrench. Placing these bolts about 5 inches from center to center, we find that twelve bolts are needed. Dividing the 24,120 pounds by 12, we have $\frac{24120}{12} = 2,010$ pounds. This means that each bolt must be capable of resisting a pulling force of 2,010 pounds.

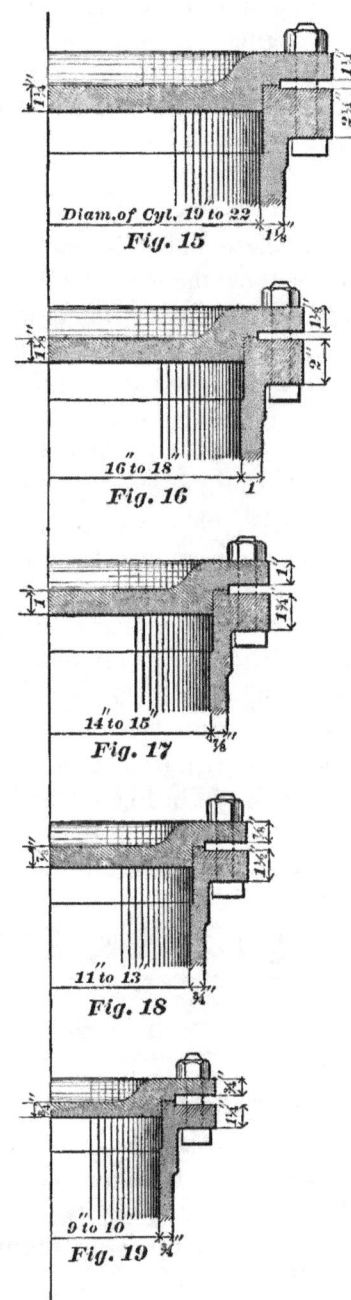

The area of the cross-section of a bolt must be such that each square inch will be subjected to a stress of not more than 5,000 pounds. But now the pulling force on the bolt is less than 5,000 pounds, hence the area will also be proportionately less than one square inch. Therefore, to find the area of cross-section of the bolt we divide 2,010 by 5,000, and $\frac{2010}{5000} = .4$; this means that the area of the cross-section of the bolt must be $\frac{4}{10}$ of a square inch, and consequently will be very nearly $\frac{3}{4}$ of an inch diameter. Adding to this diameter, twice the depth of thread, we find that the bolts for a 16-inch cylinder head should be $\frac{7}{8}$ of an inch in diameter.

38. Some master mechanics object to bolts in the cylinder head, and demand studs in place of them. Their objection to bolts is, that in case a bolt should break, the whole cylinder lagging (marked R, R in Figs. 12 and 13) must be taken off in order to place a new bolt in position. On the other hand, should a stud break, that part left in the cylinder flange can be drilled out, without disturbing the cylinder lagging, and hence the preference for studs.

39. The cylinder lagging consists of strips of ordinary pine fitted around the cylinder, the thickness of these strips filling the whole space between the body of the cylinder and the outside of the flanges. The writer believes that a few thicknesses of asbestos paper placed around the cylinder, and then the remaining space filled with wood, as shown in Figs. 12 and 13, is the best practice.

40. Figs. 15, 16, 17, 18, and 19 show the thicknesses of metal in locomotive cylinder heads, cylinders, and their flanges. These dimensions have been obtained by actual measurements of the metal in cylinders belonging to acknowledged first-class modern locomotives, and suitable for an initial pressure of 120 pounds per square inch. In these figures it

will be noticed that the cylinder flanges are considerably thicker than those of the cylinder head; this is certainly a good practice, because in case a fracture should take place through some obstruction between cylinder head and piston, the break will occur in the cylinder head, and not in the cylinder flange; and thus, on account of the comparative cheapness with which a cylinder head can be replaced, costly repairs and vexing delays will be avoided, such as are sure to follow when the cylinder flange is injured.

41. In order to insure a good cylinder casting, the thickness of the bridges should be about the same as that of the cylinder barrel, and the thickness of metal around the exhaust passages, the steam passages, and sides of the saddle may be made about $\frac{1}{16}$ of an inch less for the smaller cylinders, and about $\frac{1}{8}$ of an inch less for the larger cylinders.

42. It sometimes occurs in connection with railroads, that ferry-boats must be used in which the cylinders are very large in diameter. To determine the thickness of metal in these cylinders, the following facts must be taken into consideration: first, the thickness of metal must be such, that when the cylinder is subjected to the maximum steam pressure, fracture cannot take place; second, a sufficient amount of metal must be allowed for reboring; third, the cylinder must be sufficiently stiff to prevent jarring during the process of boring and planing; and lastly, cylinders must be sufficiently strong to maintain their circular form. Rules for finding the thickness of metal in cylinders that will satisfy all the foregoing demands have been given by a number of eminent writers.

The following rule has been copied from J. D. VanBuren's book on "formulas for the strength of the iron parts of steam machinery." In the writer's opinion this is the best rule, and will always give the proper thickness for all marine or stationary steam-engine cylinders. For locomotive cylinders the thickness found according to this rule will be rather light when compared with the thicknesses given in Figs. 15, 16, 17, 18, and 19.

RULE 4.—To find the thickness of metal in cylinders: Multiply the diameter of the cylinder in inches by the steam pressure per square inch, also multiply this product by the constant decimal fraction .0001; add to this last product the square root of the diameter of the cylinder in inches multiplied by the constant decimal fraction .15; the result will be the thickness of metal in the barrel of the cylinder. Or we may write this rule thus:

$$(\text{Diam. of cyl. in inches} \times \text{steam pressure per sq. inch} \times .0001) + .15 \sqrt{\text{diam. of cyl. in inches}} = \text{thickness of cyl. wall.}$$

EXAMPLE 7.—What must be the thickness of metal in the barrel of cylinder, 49 inches in diameter, for 60 pounds' steam pressure per square inch?

$$(49 \times 60 \times .0001) + .15 \sqrt{49} = 1.34 \text{ inch} = \text{thickness of metal.}$$

Now let us find, according to rule, the thickness of metal in a locomotive cylinder 16 inches diameter. Assuming that the greatest steam pressure these cylinders have to resist is 120 pounds per square inch, we have

$$(16 \times 120 \times .0001) + .15 \sqrt{16} = .7920 \text{ of an inch,}$$

that is, the thickness of metal in the barrel of cylinder should be fully $\frac{3}{4}$ of an inch. Comparing this thickness with that given in Fig. 16, we find that the thickness found according to this rule is light; in locomotive cylinders it should have been one inch, as shown. By a little reflection we can discover the reason why the thickness of metal in locomotive cylinders should be more than in cylinders for marine or stationary engines. In locomotive cylinders more metal must be allowed for reboring than in cylinders for the other classes of engines, because in a locomotive the piston speed is generally very high, and besides this, in locomotive engines ashes accumulate around the exhaust nozzle in the smoke-box, and should then the engine be in motion with steam shut off (which occasionally occurs), ashes are sometimes drawn in the cylinder through the exhaust passage, and the consequence of such an evil, and the necessity of reboring, can easily be conjectured. Hence, the thickness of metal in a cylinder found according to this rule should be increased from $\frac{1}{8}$ to $\frac{1}{4}$ of an inch for locomotives.

### STEAM PORTS AND EXHAUST PORT.

43. Figs. 20 and 21 show the steam ports and the exhaust port. The form of these, also the length, breadth, and area of the same, are now to be considered and determined.

In Fig. 21 it will be noticed that the ends of the steam ports have the form of a semi-circumference of a circle, and the straight lines surrounding the exhaust port are joined by arcs, whose radii are equal to those of the semi-circumferences of the ends of the steam ports. Ports formed in this manner are superior to ports with square ends, because the sliding surface of the valve, and the valve seat having square-

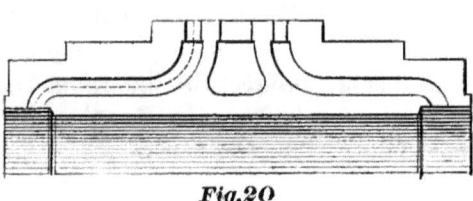

*Fig. 20*

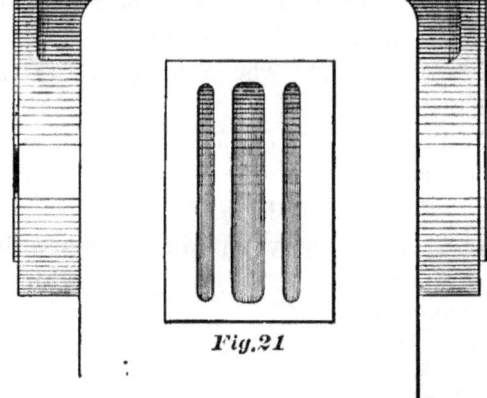

*Fig. 21*

ended ports, are liable to wear into grooves and ridges, particularly at the angles. Again, making the ends of the ports semicircular, as shown, adds strength to the bridges. This form of ports will also enable us to true up the whole port with a milling tool, and facilitate the application of a template which is to guide the milling tool, thus providing for making the ports in all cylinders of one class exactly alike in regard to length, breadth, and distance between them; such accuracy is a matter of great importance in locomotive engineering.

The length of a steam port is, within certain limits, a matter of choice. The length is often made equal to the diameter of the cylinder, sometimes a little less, but should never be less than $\frac{3}{4}$ of the diameter of the cylinder. When the length of a steam port has been established, then its breadth must be such that the port will have the proper area. Here, then, we see that before both the length and the breadth of a port can be decided upon, the area of the port must be known. We have already pointed out in Art. 31 that the steam-way has a double duty to perform, namely, to admit steam into the cylinder, and to conduct it out of the same. To conduct the steam out of the cylinder requires a steam-way of greater cross-section than that which simply admits the steam; and since the port area really represents the cross-section of a steam-way, we conclude that the port area for conducting the steam out of the cylinder must be greater than would be required for admitting the steam. The reason of this is that, when the steam is admitted into the cylinder, the pressure of the steam is very nearly constant, because the pressure is sustained by the flow of steam from the boiler, and, consequently, the velocity of the steam will be nearly constant. But, on the other hand, when the steam is allowed to escape, the pressure of the steam is generally less than it was when it entered the cylinder, and therefore the velocity of the steam will be slower. Again, as the steam continues to escape the pressure in the cylinder becomes gradually lower, and consequently the velocity also decreases. Now, the steam must be discharged as quickly, or nearly so, as it was admitted; but, since the velocity of the steam is slower when it flows into the air than when it flowed into the cylinder, the area of the steam port for the release of steam must be larger than the area that would be required for the admission of steam. We therefore conclude that if the area of a steam port is large enough for the release of steam, it will always be large enough for the admission of steam.

We find in the valuable work of D. K. Clark on "Railway Machinery," that for a piston speed of 600 feet per minute, a good exhaust will be obtained when the area of the steam port is $\frac{1}{10}$ the area of the piston, the steam being in an ordinary state as to dryness. Assuming that for a slower piston speed the area of the steam port must be proportionately less, and for a faster piston speed proportionately larger, we have all the data necessary to find the area of the steam port suitable for any given diameter of cylinder and piston speed. Now, since for a piston speed of 600 feet per minute the port area must be $\frac{1}{10}$ of the area of the piston, and for other speeds the port area must be in proportion, we may put our data in the following form:

600 is to the given piston speed in feet as $\frac{1}{10}$ of the piston area in inches is to the port area; or thus:

600 : the given piston speed in feet :: $\frac{1}{10}$ of the piston area in inches : the port area.

But writing our data in this form, we recognize a statement of the simple rule of proportion; in order, then, to find the required port area, we must follow the rule of proportion, consequently we have

### Rule 5.

$$\frac{\text{Given piston speed in feet per minute} \times .1}{600} = \text{port area in fractional parts of piston area.}$$

In ordinary language this rule would read: The given piston speed in feet per minute multiplied by $\frac{1}{10}$, and this product divided by 600, will be equal to the port area in fractional parts of the piston area.

Then, multiplying the area in square inches of the piston by the port area found by Rule 5, we obtain the number of square inches that the steam port area must contain.

EXAMPLE 8.—Find the steam port area suitable for a cylinder 17 inches in diameter, and a piston speed of 650 feet per minute.

According to Rule 5, we have—

$$\frac{650 \times .1}{600} = .108$$

that is, the port area must be equal to $\frac{108}{1000}$ part of the piston area. The area of a piston 17 inches in diameter is 226.98 square inches, hence 226.98 × .108 = 24.51384. This means that the steam port area must be equal to 24½ square inches for this particular piston speed. Of course, for a slower piston speed, this port area should be less. For instance, if the piston speed is to be 500 feet per minute, and the diameter of the cylinder 17 inches, as before, we have—

$$\frac{500 \times .1}{600} = .083;$$

and the piston area 226.98 × .083 = 18.8 square inches for port area.

With the aid of Rule 5 we may arrange the following table, showing the ratio of port area to piston area. This table will be found useful and convenient, because with it the area of the steam port can be found with less time and labor.

TABLE 9.

PROPORTIONAL STEAM PORT AREA.

| Speed of Piston in Feet Per Minute. | Port Area in Fractional Parts of Piston Area. |
|---|---|
| 200 | .033 |
| 250 | .041 |
| 300 | .050 |
| 350 | .058 |
| 400 | .066 |
| 450 | .075 |
| 500 | .083 |
| 550 | .091 |
| 600 | .1 |
| 650 | .108 |
| 700 | .116 |

RULE 6.—To find, with the aid of Table 9, the area of a steam port suitable for a given diameter of cylinder and a given piston speed: Multiply the area in square inches of the piston by the decimal fraction found in Table 9 on the same line that the given piston speed is indicated, the product will be the steam port area in square inches.

EXAMPLE 9.—Find the area of a steam port suitable for a cylinder 14 inches in diameter, and a piston speed of 450 feet per minute.

The area of a piston 14 inches in diameter is 153.9 square inches; referring to the piston speed of 450 feet in the Table 9, we find on the same line the decimal fraction .075, hence 153.9 × .075 = 11.5425; that is, the steam port area should be equal to 11½ square inches.

We have already stated that the length of the steam port should be equal, or very nearly so, to the diameter of the cylinder, and not less than ¾ of the same. If, then, the length has been decided upon, we simply divide the area of the steam port by the length, and the quotient will be the necessary width of port. Or, if we are compelled to adopt a certain width for the steam port, we divide the area of the port by the width, and the quotient will be the length of the port. In these calculations, for the sake of simplicity, we consider the ports to have square ends, as the area that is lost in making the ends circular is so small that it may be neglected.

44. The length of the exhaust port is always made equal to that of the steam port. For finding the breadth of the exhaust port, a graphic process has been here adopted, and such as, the writer believes, will be easy to follow and understand. Fig. 22 shows a section of a slide-valve, exhaust and steam ports. The valve is shown to stand in two positions on the valve seat. When in the position marked $A$ the valve stands in a central position, that is, midway of its extreme travel, and when in position $B$ it

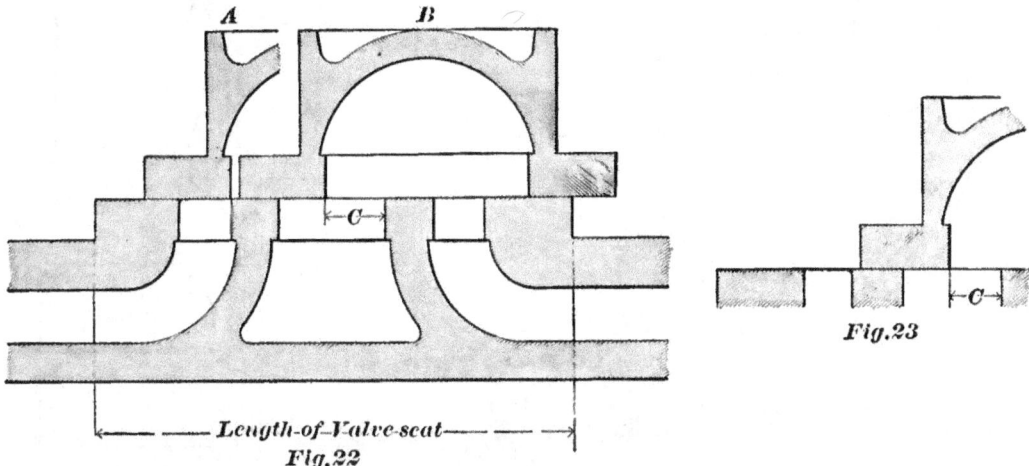

Fig. 22

Fig. 23

stands at one end of its extreme travel. In this latter position we notice that the opening of the exhaust port is considerably contracted, and should, then, the opening $C$ be much smaller than the width of the steam port, the free escape of the exhaust steam would be interfered with.

We consider it to be good practice to make the exhaust port wide enough so that when the valve stands in an extreme position, as at $B$, the opening $C$ will then be equal to the width of the steam port. Therefore, to find the width of the exhaust port, first indicate on paper the width of the steam port and the thickness of the bridge (see Fig. 23). On these draw a portion of the slide valve in an extreme position, as shown, and then make the exhaust port wide enough so that the opening $C$ will be equal to the width of the steam port. Generally, when this rule is followed, the width of the exhaust port will be equal to about twice that of the steam port for locomotive engines; hence it is often said, that the width of the exhaust port should be equal to twice that of the steam port for all engines. This statement should be received with caution, as it might lead to error. Following the graphic method here explained, satisfactory results will always be obtained.

45. The valve seat for locomotive cylinders is generally raised one inch above the surrounding surface, so as to allow for wear.

The length of the valve seat (see Fig. 22) should be such that the valve may considerably overshoot it at each end of the travel when in full gear; this will promote uniformity in wear, but care must be taken not to make the valve seat too short, because then the steam would pass underneath the valve into the steam port.

### STEAM PIPES.—STEAM AND EXHAUST PASSAGES.

46. Figs. 24 and 25 show the steam pipes and the manner of connecting these to the cylinders. The steam pipe has only one duty to perform, namely, conducting the

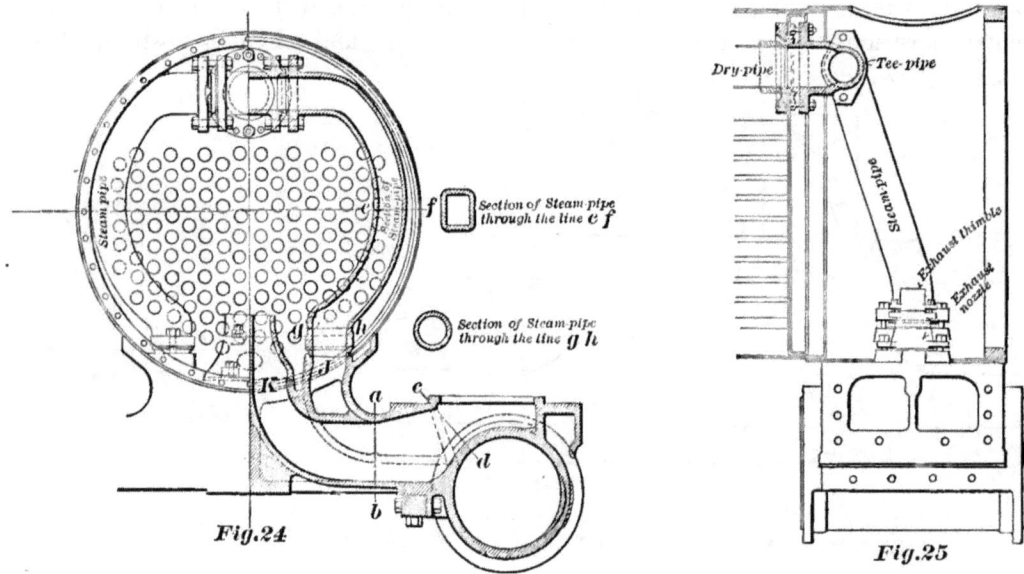

steam to the cylinder, and therefore its cross-sectional area is made less than the area of a steam port through which the steam is both admitted and exhausted.

It has been found that for a piston speed of 600 feet per minute good results will be obtained when the cross-section area of the steam pipe is equal to .08 (that is, $\frac{8}{100}$) of the area of the piston; for slower piston speeds proportionally less, and for higher piston speeds proportionally greater. Consequently, to find the cross-sectional area of a steam pipe, we again apply the rule of proportion, thus:

600 : given piston speed : : 0.08 : steam-pipe area in fractional parts of piston area.

From the foregoing remarks, we can establish—

RULE 7.—Multiply the given piston speed in feet per minute by the decimal .08, and divide the product by 600; the quotient will be the cross-sectional area of the steam pipe in fractional parts of the piston area. Or, writing this rule in the form of a formula, we have—

$$\frac{\text{Given piston speed per minute} \times .08}{600} = \text{steam-pipe area in fractional parts of piston area.}$$

Then, multiplying this proportional area by the piston area in square inches, we obtain the number of square inches in the steam-pipe area.

EXAMPLE 10.—Find the cross-sectional steam-pipe area suitable for a cylinder 17 inches in diameter, and a piston speed of 500 feet per minute.

According to Rule 7, we have—

$$\frac{500 \times .08}{600} = .0666$$

This means that the steam pipe area must be equivalent to $\frac{666}{10000}$ of the piston area. The area of a piston 17 inches in diameter is 226.98 square inches; therefore, $226.98 \times .0666 = 15.116868$. That is, the cross-sectional steam-pipe area should be $15\frac{1}{8}$ square inches.

With the aid of Rule 7, the following table has been arranged, showing the ratio between the steam-pipe area and the piston area for different speeds.

Using this table when the steam-pipe area is to be found, time and labor will be saved. To find the cross-sectional area of the steam pipe with the aid of this table, we have—

RULE 8.—Multiply the area of the piston in square inches by the decimal fraction found in Table 10, on the same line that the given piston speed is indicated; the product will be the number of square inches in the cross-sectional area of the steam pipe.

TABLE 10.

PROPORTIONAL STEAM-PIPE AREA.

| Speed of Piston in Feet Per Minute. | Steam-pipe Area in Fractional Parts of Piston Area. |
|---|---|
| 200 | .026 |
| 250 | .033 |
| 300 | .04 |
| 350 | .046 |
| 400 | .053 |
| 450 | .06 |
| 500 | .066 |
| 550 | .073 |
| 600 | .08 |
| 650 | .086 |
| 700 | .093 |

EXAMPLE 11.—Find the steam-pipe area suitable for a cylinder 16 inches in diameter, and a piston speed of 450 feet per minute.

Referring to Table 10, we find on the same line with the given piston speed of 450 feet the decimal .06. The area of a piston 16 inches in diameter is 201 square inches; therefore, $201 \times .06 = 12.06$. That is, the steam-pipe area should contain 12 square inches.

47. In Fig. 24, the area of the opening $J$ of the steam passage should be the same as that of the steam pipe, because the steam passage is a continuation of the steam pipe. Consequently, when we know the area of the steam pipe, we also know the area of the opening $J$, and when we know the area of this opening, its diameter is easily found by referring to a table of areas of circles, or by one of the simple rules of mensuration. From these remarks, we may correctly infer that, for instance, a cylinder 17

inches in diameter and a piston speed of 600 feet per minute will require a larger area in the opening $J$ than the same cylinder would require for a piston speed of 500 feet per minute; and, since the piston speed is not the same in all locomotives, we would naturally expect to find a number of core boxes of different size for each cylinder, so that the size of a steam passage could be changed in a cylinder pattern to suit some particular piston speed. To carry out such a system would require too great a variety of patterns; and to avoid this, master mechanics and manufacturers generally group the cylinders, according to their diameter, into different classes, and adopt for each class some particular diameter for the opening $J$.

In the following table, in column 2 are given the diameters of the openings $J$ for the different classes of cylinders, such as are generally adopted; of course, some makers will vary slightly from these figures. In column 3 the diameters of the exhaust opening (marked $K$, Fig. 24) are given. If these exhaust openings are made square, or of some other form, their area should contain about the same number of square inches as the circular openings corresponding to the diameters given in column 3, Table 11.

TABLE 11.

SIZE OF STEAM AND EXHAUST OPENINGS.

| Column 1. | Column 2. | Column 3. |
|---|---|---|
| Diameter of Cylinders. | Diameter of Steam Opening $J$, in Inches. | Diameter of Exhaust Opening $K$, in Inches. |
| 10 | 3 | $3\frac{1}{4}$ |
| 11 | 3 | $3\frac{1}{2}$ |
| 12 | $3\frac{1}{4}$ | 4 |
| 13 | $3\frac{1}{4}$ | 4 |
| 14 | $4\frac{1}{4}$ | 5 |
| 15 | $4\frac{1}{4}$ | 5 |
| 16 | $4\frac{1}{4}$ | 5 |
| 17 | $4\frac{3}{4}$ | 5 |
| 18 | $4\frac{3}{4}$ | 5 |
| 19 | $4\frac{3}{4}$ | 5 |
| 20 | 5 | 5 |
| 22 | 5 | 5 |

When an engine is to be designed for a very fast speed, we would advise to determine the area of the opening $J$ according to Rule 7, and not follow the diameters given in the last table. The area of any cross section of the steam passage should contain the same number of square inches as the opening $J$.

In regard to the exhaust passage, good results will be obtained when the area of any cross section in the neighborhood of the line $a\,b$, Fig. 24, is made larger than the exhaust opening $K$; in fact, we have always obtained good results by making it as large as possible. With large exhaust passages the flow of exhaust steam will not be so irregular as when smaller passages are used. In the writer's opinion, large exhaust passages will improve the draft of an engine, and to some extent lessen the back pressure in the cylinder. No rules have been established to determine the area of the exhaust opening $K$. The diameter for these openings, given in Table 11, have been obtained by actual measurements.

48. Often it will be found that, in designing a locomotive cylinder, the space allotted for the steam passages and exhaust passage in the neighborhood of the line $c\ d$, Fig. 24, is very small; therefore, great care and good judgment must be used to obtain the proper cross-sectional area in either passage. The result of carelessness right here will be that either one or the other passage is too small, and the engine will fail to do the work that it was intended it should do.

## STEAM PIPES.

49. Steam pipes, Figs. 24 and 25, for locomotives are made of cast-iron; their thickness of metal for smaller engines is about $\frac{1}{2}$ of an inch, and for larger engines about $\frac{5}{8}$ of an inch.

On account of some practical difficulties that must be overcome, ordinary flat joints cannot be used between the **T** pipe and the steam pipe, neither between the steam pipe and cylinder saddle.

The first difficulty that presents itself is the expansion and contraction due to the great change of temperature to which the steam pipes in locomotives are exposed, and therefore we must adopt a joint which possesses a small amount of flexibility.

The second difficulty that presents itself is of a practical nature, namely, the impossibility to construct a boiler and fit the cylinder saddle to the outside of the smoke-box with absolute accuracy, yet a steam pipe of proper length is expected to fit at once in its place, without any more labor than would be required if everything else had been perfectly accurate; hence, the joint must possess a small amount of adjustability.

Adopting a ball joint, the foregoing difficulties can be overcome. These ball joints are made (as shown in Fig. 24) by interposing a brass ring between the **T** pipe and steam pipe, and another one between the steam pipe and cylinder saddle. Each brass ring has a spherical and a flat surface. Now, it must be readily perceived that with such rings interposed the steam pipe can be slightly moved up or down or sideways, and still maintain a steam-tight joint. This kind of ball joint will also be sufficiently flexible to allow for the contraction and expansion of the steam pipe.

## PISTON SPEED.

50. To determine the piston speed in feet per minute according to the following rule, we must know the speed of train in miles per hour, the diameter of the driving wheels in feet, and the length of stroke in feet:

RULE 9.—To find the piston speed in feet per minute in a locomotive, multiply the number of feet in a mile by the speed of train in miles per hour, divide the product by the circumference in feet of the driving wheel multiplied by 60, and multiply the quotient by twice the length of the stroke in feet; the product will be the piston speed in feet per minute. Or, writing this rule in the shape of a formula, we have—

$$\frac{\{\text{Number of feet in a mile}\} \times \{\text{Speed of train in miles per hour}\}}{\{\text{Circumference of driving wheel in feet}\} \times 60} \times \text{twice the stroke in feet} = \{\text{piston speed in feet per minute.}\}$$

EXAMPLE 12.—Find the piston speed in feet per minute in a locomotive whose driving wheels are 5 feet in diameter; stroke, 2 feet; and speed of train, 35 miles per hour.

According to Rule 9, we have—

$$\frac{5280 \times 35}{15.7 \times 60} \times 4 = 784.68$$

That is, the piston speed will be $784\frac{68}{100}$ feet per minute. In order to assist the reader to understand the foregoing rule, the following explanation is offered:

First, we multiply the number of feet in a mile by the speed of train in miles per hour; this product will give the number of feet the locomotive travels in one hour, and, since there are 5,280 feet in a mile, and the speed of train in our example is 35 miles per hour, we have $5,280 \times 35 = 184,800$ feet that the locomotive travels during one hour. To find the number of feet that the locomotive travels during one minute, we divide the number of feet per hour by 60, because there are 60 minutes in one hour; hence, in our example, $\frac{184800}{60} = 3,080$ feet; that is, during one minute the locomotive travels through a distance of 3,080 feet. To find the number of revolutions of the wheel per minute (which is necessary in this case), we divide the distance traveled per minute by the circumference of the driving wheel. In our example, the diameter of the driving wheel is 5 feet; the circumference of such a wheel is 15.7 feet; therefore, $\frac{3080}{15.7} = 196.17$ number of revolutions per minute. During every revolution of the wheel the piston travels through twice the length of the stroke; therefore, multiplying the number of revolutions per minute by twice the length of the stroke, the piston speed per minute will be obtained. In our example, the stroke is 2 feet; therefore, $196.17 \times 4 = 784\frac{68}{100}$ feet. That is, the piston speed is $784\frac{68}{100}$ feet per minute.

## SLIDE-VALVES, AND MOVEMENT OF SLIDE-VALVES.

51. Slide-valves are sometimes made of brass, but generally of cast-iron. Cast-iron slide-valves are more durable than brass valves, but the latter do not wear the valve's seat as quickly as the cast-iron valves.

The ordinary form of slide-valve, such as is generally used in locomotives, is shown in Figs. 26 and 27. Fig. 26 represents a cross-section of the valve; one-half of

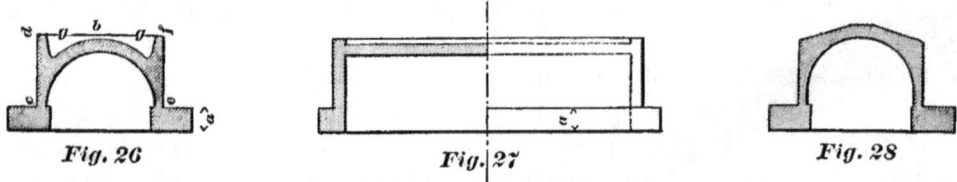

*Fig. 26*  *Fig. 27*  *Fig. 28*

Fig. 27 shows a section lengthwise of the valve, and the other half an outside view of the same. The thickness of metal at $a$ is generally made 1 in., and at $b$ about $\frac{1}{2}$ in. The sides $c\,d$, $e\,f$ are extended upwards until they become flush with the top, $b$, of the valve; in some cases these sides are extended a little beyond the top of the valve. This has been done for the following practical reasons: In the first place, a large surface is obtained against which the valve yoke can bear. Secondly, this form of valve can be laid on its back, and thus speedily and conveniently secured to the planer, when the valve face is to be planed; this is a matter of no small importance in a large locomotive establishment where a number of valves have to be planed daily. The recesses $g\ g$, shown in Fig. 26, are simply for the purpose of making the valve as light as possible. Some master mechanics object to these recesses, because they believe that they will hold the oil (which is usually admitted through the top of the steam chest), and prevent the oil from falling upon the valve seat, and thus not find its way into the cylinder. For this reason a valve has been adopted having a form as shown in Fig. 28. This form of valve, although used on some roads, has not been favorably received on other roads, because it takes up too much room in height, and besides it is an inconvenient casting to fasten to the planer when the face is to be planed or replaned. The writer would recommend the adoption of a valve having a form as shown in Fig. 26, and believes that the fear of the recesses $g\ g$ preventing the oil from flowing into the cylinder is groundless, and that the constant flow of steam into the chest will not allow the oil to lay still on any part of the valve.

52. The duty of the slide-valve is to control the flow of steam into and out of the cylinder, that is, the valve (as its name implies) slides backward and forward on the

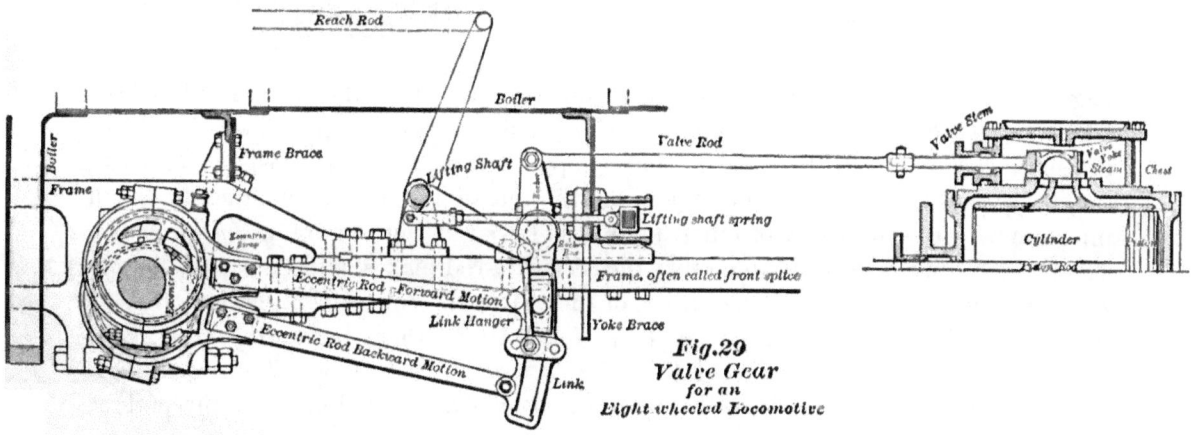

Fig. 29
Valve Gear
for an
Eight wheeled Locomotive

valve seat, thus opening and closing the steam ports at proper times. Whether it will perform this duty or not, depends upon the form and motion of the valve.

Fig. 29 shows a complete locomotive valve gear; the names of the different pieces of the mechanism are plainly marked on the drawing, so that here any further definitions of these pieces will be unnecessary.

53. To construct a slide-valve and assign to it the proper motion, such as shown in Fig. 29, may seem to be a difficult subject for solution; and so it would be, if, right in the beginning, we do not—wheresoever we can—throw out of consideration all such pieces of mechanism as have a complicating influence upon the motion of the valve. Hence it is of the utmost importance first to reduce this subject to its simplest form. It will be noticed that the operation of the valve is controlled by two eccentrics: one eccentric is used for the forward motion and the other for the backward motion of the engine. Here we may simplify our subject by leaving out of consideration the back-

ward eccentric, because when the valve is made to accomplish the desired results with one eccentric its form will not have to be changed when the other eccentric is added. But leaving the backward eccentric out of the question, we may also leave the link out of consideration, because the link only serves to connect the two eccentric-rods so as to enable the engineer to put wholly or partly into gear one or the other eccentric. The lifting-shaft is simply used for moving the link up or down as the case may be; and since the link has been thrown out of consideration, we may treat the lifting-shaft likewise. The rocker is simply used for the purpose of connecting the eccentric-rod to the valve-rod, and although it affects the position of the eccentrics, and in some cases the travel of the slide-valve, it will not affect the laws relating to the construction of the valve, and therefore we also throw this out of consideration.

54. Reducing our subject as described, and connecting the eccentric-rod directly to valve stem, we obtain a simple arrangement, Fig. 30, such as is often used in stationary

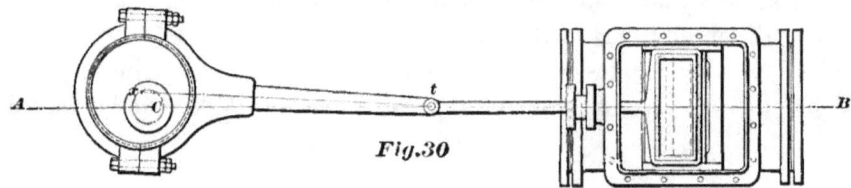

Fig. 30

engines; of course, in this arrangement we must assume that the driving axle of the locomotive is represented by the crank shaft $C$, and the eccentric placed on the end of the shaft as shown. In this arrangement, simple as it is, a feature exists which has a somewhat complicating influence upon the motion of the valve, and therefore will interfere with the simplicity of our study of the laws relating to the form of the valve. The feature alluded to is the angle that the eccentric-rod makes with the center line, $A B$. This angle varies during the travel of the valve, and consequently the motion of the valve will be slower during one half of the travel than during the other half. Thus, for instance: Let the line $A B$ in Fig. 31 represent the line $A B$ shown in Fig. 30. The circle $s_1 t_1 u_1$, Fig. 31, will represent, in an exaggerated manner, the path of

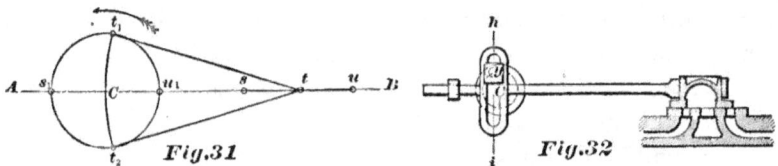

Fig. 31    Fig. 32

the center $x$ of the eccentric shown in Fig. 30, and lastly, the distance from the center $x$ to the center $t$ of the eccentric-rod pin in Fig. 30 is represented by the line $t_1 t$ in Fig. 31. Now, referring only to Fig. 31, when the valve stands in an extreme position of its travel, the center of the eccentric-rod pin will be at $u$, the center of the eccentric will be at $u_1$, and the center line of the eccentric-rod will lie in the line $A B$. Again, when the valve stands in the other extreme position of its travel, the center of the eccentric-rod pin will be at $s$, the center of the eccentric will be at $s_1$, and the center line of the eccentric-rod will lie in the line $A B$. When the slide-valve stands central that is, midway between the extreme ends of its travel, the center of the eccentric-rod pin will be at $t$, exactly midway between the points $s$ and $u$.

From the point $t$ as a center, and with a radius equal to the distance $C\,t$, describe an arc; this arc will intersect the circumference $s_1\,t_1\,u_1$ in the points $t_1$ and $t_2$. Join the points $t$ and $t_1$ by a straight line, also draw a straight line from the point $t$ to the point $t_2$; then the straight line $t\,t_1$ or $t\,t_2$ will represent the center of the eccentric-rod when the valve stands in a midway position of its travel; the point $t$ will be the center of the eccentric-rod pin and the point $t_1$, or the point $t_2$ will be the center of the eccentric. Assume that the shaft is turning in the direction indicated by the arrow. When the eccentric-rod pin has traveled from $u$ to $t$, equal to half the travel, the slide-valve has also completed one-half of its travel, and the center of the eccentric has traveled through the arc $u_1\,t_1$. Again, during the time that the eccentric-rod pin travels from $t$ to $s$, equal to half the travel, the center of the eccentric will travel through the arc $t_1\,s_1$. But now notice the difference of length of the two arcs $t_1\,s_1$ and $t_1\,u_1$; this plainly shows that the eccentric-rod pin will travel slower from $u$ to $t$ than from $t$ to $s$, and consequently the travel of the valve will be affected likewise. Or, we may say, that the angle formed by the lines $t\,t_1$, and $A\,B$ destroys the symmetry of the valve motion. Now, in the study of the laws relating to the motion of the valve and the duties it has to perform, such a motion will complicate matters, and will prevent us from tracing the action of the valve so readily as when both halves of the travel are described in equal times, and therefore the reader will perceive the necessity of changing the valve gear to one which will give the valve a perfectly symmetrical motion.

In the first place, it will be easily seen that the longer we make the eccentric-rod —leaving the travel of the valve the same—the smaller will be the angle between the line $t\,t_1$ (which represents the center of eccentric-rod), and the line $A\,B$, and consequently the times in which the halves of the travel of the valve are described will be nearer equal, and when we assume the eccentric-rod to be of an infinite length the angle will vanish and each half of the travel of the valve will be described in equal times, and the motion will be symmetrical; in fact, the valve will have precisely the same motion as that obtained with a valve gear, as shown in Fig. 32, to which we shall now call attention.

55. In this figure, in place of using an eccentric-rod, the valve-stem is lengthened, and to its end a slotted cross-head is forged. The eccentric has also been dispensed with, and in its place a pin $y$ fastened into the end of the crank-shaft has been adopted. The distance between the center $C$ of the crank-shaft and the center of the pin $y$ must always be equal to the distance between the center $C$ and the center $x$ of the eccentric shown in Fig. 30. This distance from $C$ to $x$ is called the eccentricity of the eccentric, and is equal to one-half of the throw, or in other words the throw of an eccentric is equal to twice its eccentricity. In this particular case, as shown in Fig. 30, the throw is equal to the travel of the valve; by the travel of the valve is meant the distance between the extreme points of its motion. In all direct acting valve motions, that is when no rocker or link is used, the throw of the eccentric will be equal to the travel of the valve. In locomotives, the travel of the valve is not always equal to the throw of the eccentric, the difference being due to the influence of the link, and often to the unequal length of the rocker-arms.

Now, turning our attention to Fig. 32, we notice that by substituting for the eccentric a pin $y$ in the end of the crank-shaft, we really adopt a crank, and this we can do without affecting the correctness of the reasoning relating to the movement of the valve, because the action of the eccentric is precisely the same as that of a crank whose length is equal to half the throw; the only reason why eccentrics are adopted is that they are more convenient to use; in fact, cranks in many cases cannot be used, the peculiar construction of the machine preventing their adoption; in no case is an eccentric adopted because a different motion to that due to a crank is desired.

We have drawn particular attention to this fact, because some mechanics (a good many of them) have a misty notion of the action of an eccentric.

As the shaft revolves (see Fig. 32) the pin in the end of the shaft will move in the slot of valve-stem's cross-head, and thus always allowing the center line of the valve-stem to coincide with the line $A B$.

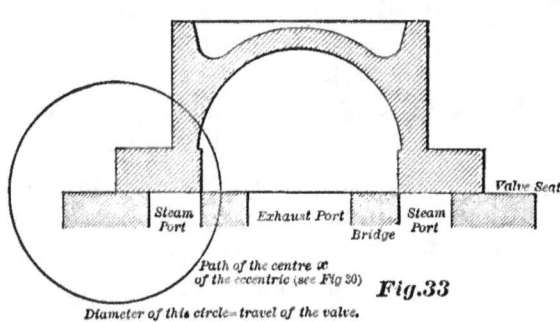

Fig. 33

It must also be plain that as the shaft revolves the center of the pin will describe a circle, and it is the circumference of this circle that will enter into the solutions of the following problems. Once more, the reader will readily perceive that the length of the valve-stem will in no wise affect the motion of the valve, hence we may leave this also out of consideration, and place the circumference of the circle which represents the path of the pin $y$ on the end of the slide-valve, as shown in Fig. 33. Here, then, we notice that our original subject, that of finding the proper motion and form of a valve, a subject in which all the different pieces of mechanism as shown in Fig. 29 had entered, has been reduced and simplified to that having only the pieces of mechanism as shown in Fig. 33.

### THREE CONDITIONS A SLIDE-VALVE MUST FULFILL.

56. The entrance of steam into the cylinder is regulated by the two outside edges, $a\,b$ and $c\,d$, of the slide-valve, Fig. 34; the exit of the steam is regulated by the two inner edges, $e\,f$ and $g\,h$, of the slide-valve; and the correct admission and exhaust of the steam depends upon these edges, the motion of the valve—that is, the travel of the valve—and the position of the eccentric.

All slide-valves must be capable of fulfilling the three following conditions, and if a slide-valve cannot do this, the engine will not work satisfactorily:

*First Condition.*—Steam must be admitted into the cylinder at one of its ends only at one time. To satisfy this condition, the length of the valve from $a$ to $c$ must at least cover both steam ports, when the valve stands in a central position, as shown in Fig. 34. This length of the valve cannot be less, because if it is made less, steam will enter both ends of the cylinder at one time, and consequently bad results will follow.

*Second Condition.*—The valve must allow the steam to escape from one end of the cylinder, at least as soon as it is admitted into the other end of the cylinder. To fulfill this second condition, the length of the exhaust cavity in the valve, or, in other words, the distance between the two inner edges, $e\,f$ and $g\,h$, Fig. 34, must be equal to the sum of the widths of the two bridges added to the width of the exhaust port. The length of the exhaust cavity in a valve whose outside edges just cover the steam ports, must not be made less than shown in Fig. 34, because if it is made less, steam will be admitted into one end of the cylinder, some time before the steam in the other end of the cylinder is released, and consequently a considerable amount of back pressure will be the result. When the outer edges of a valve overlap the steam ports, such as shown in Fig. 36, then its exhaust cavity can be made less, within certain limits, and still satisfy the second condition.

*Third Condition.*—The valve must cover the steam ports so as not to allow the steam to escape from the steam chest into the exhaust port. To fulfill the third con-

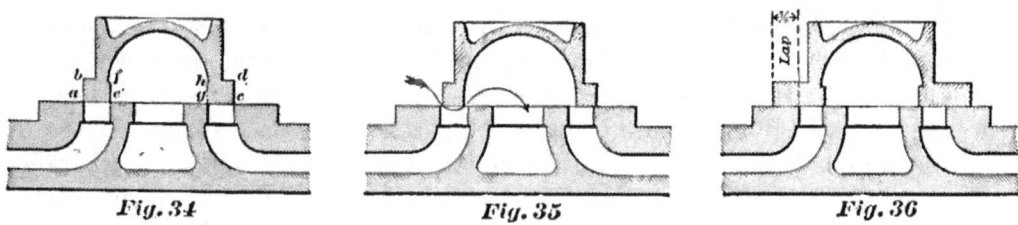

Fig. 34    Fig. 35    Fig. 36

dition, the length of the exhaust cavity, that is, the distance between the edges $e$ and $g$, Fig. 34, must not be made greater than the sum of the width of the two bridges added to the width of the exhaust port, in a valve whose outside edges just cover the steam ports. If the length of the exhaust cavity in such a valve is made greater, then the distance between the edges $a$ and $e$, or the distance between the edges $g$ and $c$ will be less than the width of steam ports, and consequently the steam will be permitted to pass from the steam chest directly into the exhaust port, as indicated in Fig. 35, or, as the practical man would say, the steam will blow through, and therefore an unpardonable waste of steam will be the result.

If the outside edges of the valve overlap the steam ports, as shown in Fig. 36, then the exhaust cavity can be made within certain limits a little longer, without interfering with the third condition.

57. For the sake of distinction we may divide slide-valves into two classes. In one class we may place all slide-valves whose outside edges just cover the steam ports, such as shown in Fig. 34. These valves will admit steam into the cylinder during the whole stroke of the piston, or, as the practical man would say, "the valve follows full stroke."

In the other class we may place all slide-valves whose outer edges overlap the steam ports, such as shown in Fig. 36. These valves will not admit steam into the cylinder during the whole stroke of the piston, but will close the steam ports, and thus cut off the flow of the steam into the cylinder, before the piston has reached the end of a stroke. The position of the piston at the moment that steam is cut off is called the point of cut-off, and this point depends upon the amount of lap.

58. When a valve of this kind is placed in a central position, that is, midway of its travel, as shown in Fig. 36, then the amount of overlap at each end is called "outside

lap," or simply lap. Thus, if as in Fig. 36, the valve overlaps each port ⅞ of an inch, then the valve is said to have ⅞ of an inch lap. Under no circumstances should one of the outside edges of the valve be placed flush with an outside edge of the steam port, and then the total amount of overlap at the other end of the valve be called lap, because that would be wrong according to the universal acceptation of the term "lap."

### TRAVEL OF THE VALVE.

59. Since it is always taken for granted that the steam ports are made just large enough—and no more—to give a free exhaust, we must give the valves that have no lap, as shown in Fig. 34, such a travel that the outside edges of these valves will wholly open the steam ports. We cannot make this travel any less, because if it is less the steam port will not be fully open to the action of the exhaust. On the other hand, theoretically, the travel of a valve that has lap need not be such that the steam port will be fully opened to the admission of steam; all that is really needed for this purpose is an opening of $\frac{8}{10}$ of the width of the steam port, and if this does not interfere with the free action of the exhaust, that is, if it does not prevent the full opening of the steam port for the escape of steam, satisfactory results will follow. In practice, such niceness in the travel of the valve is seldom aimed at. In fact, it is customary to assign such a travel to a valve that the outside edges of the valve will not only fully open the steam ports, but travel a little beyond them. Adopting such a practice, we gain the following advantages: When a valve that has no lap travels a little further than necessary to fully open the steam port, we have the assurance that a slight inaccuracy in workmanship, which cannot always be prevented, will not interfere with the full opening of the steam port. Again, it is always desirable that when the valve is to cut off steam, it will do so as quickly as possible, hence, when valves that have lap and their travel is greater than absolutely necessary, the motion of these valves will be quicker than the motion of valves with shorter travel; therefore, when the former are employed, the cut-off will be sharper and more decisive.

EXAMPLE 13.—To find the travel of a valve that has no lap, the width of the steam port being given, let the steam port be 1¼ inch wide. The travel of a valve without lap must at least be equal to twice the width of the steam port. The truth of this must be perceived when we examine Fig. 34, and remember the remarks just made. Consequently the travel of the valve in our example will be $1¼ \times 2 = 2½''$. From the foregoing we may establish the following:

RULE 10.—To find the travel of a valve without lap, the steam port to be fully opened and no more. Multiply the width of steam port in inches by 2, the product will be the travel of the valve.

Now, if the travel of the valve is to be such that the valve shall move ¼ of an inch beyond the steam port, then we must add this amount to the width of steam port, and make the travel equal to twice this sum. Thus:

EXAMPLE 14.—Width of steam port 1¼ inch, the valve to travel ¼ of an inch beyond the steam port, find the travel. $1¼ + ¼ = 1½$, and $1½ \times 2 = 3$ inches = travel of the valve. From the foregoing we have the following:

RULE 11.—To find the travel of the valve without lap, the travel to extend a given amount beyond the steam port. Add the given amount which the valve must travel beyond the steam port to the width of the steam port, multiply the sum by 2; the product will be the travel of the valve.

60. When this valve is used in an engine with no rocker interposed, then the eccentricity of the eccentric, or, in other words, the distance between the center, $C$, of the crank shaft and the center, $x$, of the eccentric, Fig. 30, will be $1\frac{1}{2}$ inch, and the throw of the eccentric will be equal to the travel of the valve, namely, 3 inches.

To find the travel of a valve that has lap, the lap and width of the steam port being given:

EXAMPLE 15.—The width of the steam port is $1\frac{1}{4}$ inch, the lap is $\frac{7}{8}$ of an inch, find the travel.

If the valve is to open the steam port fully, and no more, for the admission of steam, then the travel cannot be less than twice the sum of the width of the steam port and lap. Hence in our example we have $1\frac{1}{4} + \frac{7}{8} = 2\frac{1}{8}$, and $2\frac{1}{8} \times 2 = 4\frac{1}{4}$ inches = travel of the valve. If the valve is to move $\frac{1}{4}$ of an inch beyond the steam port, then we have $1\frac{1}{4} + \frac{1}{4} + \frac{7}{8} = 2\frac{3}{8}$, and $2\frac{3}{8} \times 2 = 4\frac{3}{4}$ inches = travel of the valve. When no rocker is interposed, the throw of the eccentric is equal to the travel, that is, $4\frac{3}{4}$ inches. From the foregoing we can establish the follow rules:

RULE 12.—To find the travel of the valve with lap, the travel not to extend beyond the steam port. Add the width of the steam port to the lap, multiply the sum by 2; the product will be the travel of the valve.

RULE 13.—To find the travel of a valve with lap, the travel to extend beyond the steam port. Add the width of the steam port, the lap, and the amount of travel beyond the steam port, multiply this sum by 2; the product will be the travel of the valve.

### POSITION OF ECCENTRIC WHEN NO ROCKER IS USED.

61. Assume that a valve without lap is to be used in an engine similar to that shown in Fig. 37, that is, an engine in which the axis of the cylinder will pass through the center of the crank-shaft; also let it be required that at the precise moment at

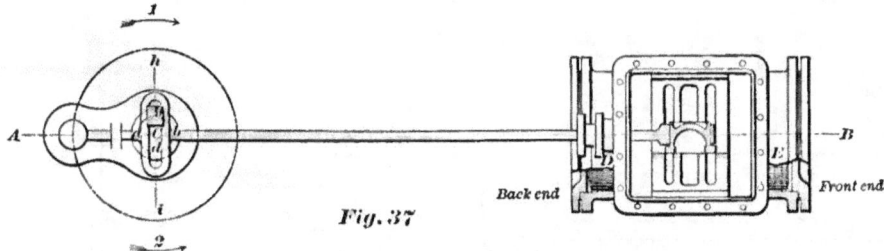

Fig. 37

which the piston reaches the end of a stroke, the valve shall open the steam port. In Fig. 37, it will be noticed, that instead of showing the back of the slide-valve as it should be, we have assumed the valve and seat to be turned around the valve stem, so as to see a section of the valve and seat; this will make the illustration more intelligible for our purpose. Now, assume that the piston stands at $D$, the back end of the stroke, then the crank will be in the position as shown, and according to our proposition, the valve must at that instant open the back steam port, consequently the valve must stand in the position as indicated in the figure. Again, assume that the piston stands at $E$, the front end of the stroke, then the valve must stand in a position so that the least movement will open the front steam port, consequently the valve will occupy the same position as before. In fact, when the piston stands at either end of the stroke, the valve, having no lap, must stand in a central position, that is, midway of its travel. To find the suitable position of the eccentric when this valve stands central, we proceed as follows:

From the center $C$ describe a circle $a\ b\ d$ (Fig 37), whose diameter is equal to the travel of the valve; the circumference of this circle will represent the path of the center of the eccentric, or, what amounts to the same thing, the path of the center of the pin $y$; consequently the exact location of the center of this pin must be found somewhere in the circumference $a\ b\ d$. Now, the diameter $a\ b$ is equal to the travel of the valve, hence we may assume that the point $a$ will represent one end, and the point $b$ the other end of the travel, and $C$ the center of the travel.

Therefore to find the location of the pin $y$, draw through the center $C$ a line $i\ h$ perpendicular to the line $A\ B$; the line $i\ h$ will intersect the circumference $a\ b\ d$ in the points $y$ and $d$. If the crank-pin is to turn in the direction of the arrow marked 1, then the point $y$ will be the center of the pin or the center of the eccentric; if the crank is to turn in an opposite direction, as indicated by arrow 2, then the point $d$ will be the location of the pin $y$.

From the foregoing we learn that the center of the eccentric, or the pin $y$, will always travel ahead of the crank in either direction, providing no rocker is used. Secondly, we learn that for a valve without lap the center of the eccentric will be found in a line drawn perpendicular to a line passing through the center of crank-pin and the center of crank-shaft, providing the valve has no lead.

The straight line drawn through the center of crank-shaft and center of crank-pin will, in the future, be called "*the center line of crank.*"

62. By "lead" is meant the width of the opening of the steam port at the commencement of the stroke of the piston. Thus, in Fig. 38, when the piston stands at the

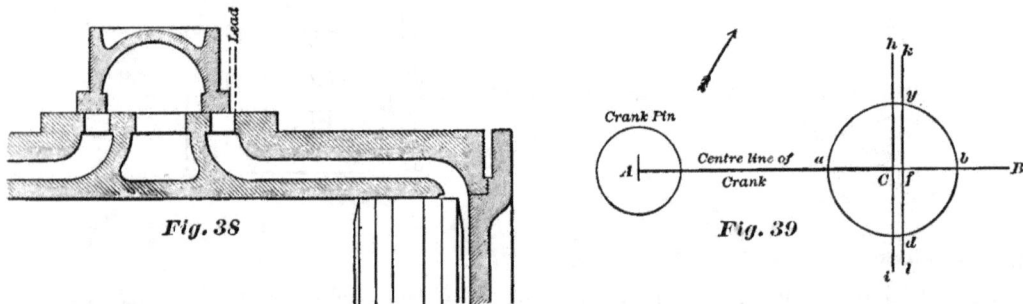

Fig. 38   Fig. 39

beginning of the stroke, and the valve has then opened the steam port $\frac{1}{16}$ of an inch, that $\frac{1}{16}$ of an inch of opening is called "lead," and the valve is said to have $\frac{1}{16}$ of an inch lead. Again, if the valve has opened the steam port $\frac{1}{8}$ of an inch, instead of $\frac{1}{16}$ of an inch, the valve is said to have $\frac{1}{8}$ of an inch lead. In our previous example the valve had no lead, therefore the question arises, where shall we place the eccentric when the valve has lead?

EXAMPLE 16.—Let $AB$, in Fig. 39, represent the center line of crank; the direction in which the crank is to move is indicated by the arrow. The lead is to be $\frac{1}{16}$ of an inch, the travel of the valve 5 inches; find the position of the eccentric. From the center $C$ draw a circle $a\ b\ d$, whose diameter is equal to the travel of the valve, namely, 5 inches; on the line $AB$ lay off a point $f$, $\frac{1}{16}$ of an inch from the center $C$; through the point $f$ draw a line $k\ l$ perpendicular to the line $AB$, this line $k\ l$ will intersect the circumference $a\ b\ d$ in the points $y$ and $d$; the point $y$ will be the center of the eccentric. If the crank had been designed to move in the opposite direction, then the point $d$ would have been the center of the eccentric. If no lead had been required, then the center of the eccentric would have been found in the line $i\ h$ drawn through the center $C$.

From this we learn that when the valve is to have lead the center of the eccentric must be moved forward of the line $i\ h$, and the amount that the center of the eccentric must be moved forward (or away from the crank-pin) is equal to the lead.

63. The line $i\ h$ is an important one, because the position of the eccentric is always laid off from this line. In this particular case, Fig. 39, the line $i\ h$ has been drawn perpendicular to the center line of crank. But from this we must not conclude that in every case the line $i\ h$ must be drawn perpendicular to the center line of crank. The line $i\ h$ in every case is drawn perpendicular to the center line of motion of the valve gear, irrespective of the position of the crank. In Fig. 39 the center line of motion of the valve gear coincides with the center line of crank, and it is for this reason that the line $i\ h$ has been drawn perpendicular to the latter. This will be made plainer as we proceed. By "the center line of motion of the valve gear" is meant a line drawn through the center of the shaft parallel to the direction in which the valve moves when no rocker or other mechanism between the shaft and valve is used. The definition of the center line of the motion of the valve gear in cases where rockers are used will be given later.

### TO FIND THE POSITION OF THE ECCENTRIC CORRESPONDING TO ANY ONE OF THE DIFFERENT POSITIONS OF THE VALVE.

64. We have stated in Art. 55, that for the construction of a slide-valve and for the purpose of following the movements of the same, all that will be required is a section of the valve, the valve seat, and the circumference of a circle to represent the path of the center of eccentric, and such we shall now employ in the solution of the following problems.

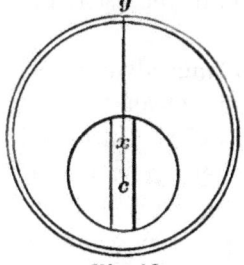

Fig. 40

By the center of eccentric we mean the center $x$, Fig. 40, and not the center $c$ of the hole. The center line of an eccentric is a straight line

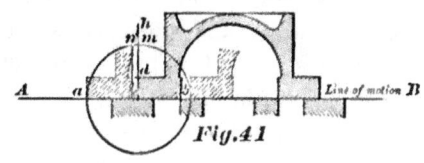

Fig. 41

drawn through the centers $x$ and $c$, and produced to the circumference of the eccentric Fig. 41 shows the valve seat with the steam ports and exhaust port, also the valve standing in the center of its travel. This position of the valve is an important one, because to this we generally refer when any other position of the valve is to be considered. From the point $c$ (the intersection of the lines $A B$ and $d c$) as a center and a radius equal to half the throw of the eccentric, a circle has been drawn; the circumference of this circle will represent the path of the center $x$ of the eccentric. Now, it must be remembered that in studying the laws relating to the construction and movement of the slide-valve, the length of the eccentric rod is always considered to be an infinite length, or, in other words, that the eccentric acts precisely in the same manner as a pin working in a slotted cross-head forged to the valve stem, such as we have described in Arts. 54 and 61. Keeping this in mind, the following explanation will be easily understood:

Since the circumference $a\ b\ m$, Fig. 41, represents the path of the center of the eccentric, it must be readily perceived that the center $c$ of this circle also represents the center of the shaft, and since the line $A B$ is drawn through the center of the shaft, we may call it the center line of motion of the valve gear, because in this particular case the line $A B$ is parallel to the direction of motion of the valve. The diameter $a b$ of the circle $a\ b\ m$ coincides with the line of motion $A B$, consequently when the center of the eccentric is at $b$ the valve will be at the forward end of its travel, as shown in dotted lines, and at the same time indicating how far the valve will travel beyond the edge of the steam port. When the center of the eccentric is at $a$, the valve will then stand at the opposite end of its travel, also shown by dotted lines. Now, when the valve stands in its central position, the center of the eccentric must also stand in the center of its path from $a$ to $b$, and consequently will be at $m$. To find the point $m$ we draw a straight line $c\ h$ through the center $c$ of the circle, and perpendicular to the line of motion $A B$, the point of intersection of the line $c\ h$ and the circumference will be the point $m$. So also in a similar manner we may find the position of the center of the eccentric for any other position of the valve. For instance, if the edge $c$ of the valve stands at $g$, we draw through the point $g$ a line perpendicular to the line $A B$; the point of intersection $n$ of this line and the circumference $a\ b\ m$ will be the center of the eccentric, when the valve stands at $g$.

In order to save time and labor, and to make the solutions of the problems as simple as possible, it is always best to place the valve, as we have done, in the center of its travel, and then adopt $c$, the point of contact of the outer edge of the valve and the valve seat as the center of the circle whose circumference is to represent the path of the center of eccentric.

By adopting the foregoing suggestion we also gain the following advantages; namely, we can see at once how far the valve will travel beyond the steam port in either direction; and we can also see how much the exhaust port will be contracted when the valve is at end of its travel. Hence it must be distinctly remembered that to trace the motion of any slide-valve, the valve should be placed in a central position, and the center of circle whose circumference represents the path of the center of the eccentric should be the point in which one of the outer edges of the valve touches the valve seat.

## LINEAR ADVANCE OF THE VALVE AND ANGULAR ADVANCE OF THE ECCENTRIC.

65. In connection with the setting of the eccentric two terms are used, namely, "linear advance of the valve" and "angular advance of the eccentric." Between these two there exists such a close relation that if we change one we must also change the other, and if there is no linear advance of the valve there will be no angular advance of the eccentric, therefore it is of great importance to understand the meaning of these terms.

In Fig. 42 we have shown the valve in two positions. The dotted lines represent the valve standing in the center of its travel, and is marked $D$. The section of the valve in full lines, marked $E$, represents its position at the commencement of the

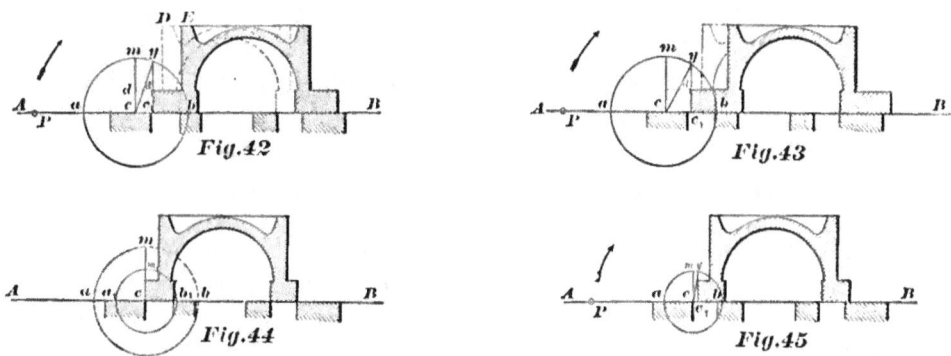

stroke of the piston (it will be noticed here that the valve has lead), the distance from $c$ to $c_1$ is called linear advance of the valve, and is equal to the lap and lead, plainly shown in the figure; in short, linear advance of the valve means the distance the valve has traveled beyond its middle position when the piston has reached the end of the stroke. When the valve stands in the middle position $D$, the center of the eccentric will be at $m$, and a line drawn from $c$ to $m$ will represent the center line of the eccentric. Again, when the valve stands at $E$, the center of the eccentric will be at $y$, and a line drawn from $c$ to $y$ will again represent the center line of the eccentric. The angle formed by the lines $c\,m$ and $c\,y$ is called the angular advance of the eccentric; or, in other words, by angular advance is meant the angle that is formed by the position of the center line of the eccentric when the piston is at the commencement of the stroke, and the position of the center line of the eccentric when the valve is in the center of its travel, the length of the eccentric rod being assumed to be infinite.

66. If the lap is increased without changing the travel and lead, as shown in Fig. 43, the linear advance will be greater, and consequently the angular advance $m\,c\,y$ will also be increased, which is plainly indicated in the figure. Here also notice that the center $c$ has been moved away from the outside edge of the steam port, because when the valve is placed central, its outside edge $c_1$ will be at $c$, which, according to what has been stated before, should be adopted for the center of the circle, whose circumference $a\,m\,b$ represents the path of the center of the eccentric. By so doing, we see at a glance how far in either direction the valve will travel.

In this figure we notice that the valve does not travel as far beyond the inner edge of the steam port as in Fig. 42.

If the lap is made less than shown in Fig. 42, without changing the travel and the lead of the valve, the linear advance will be less, and consequently the angular advance will be smaller. In this particular case the center $c$ would have to be moved closer to the edge of the steam port, because the lap is smaller. When the valve has no lap and lead, as shown in Fig. 44, there will be no linear advance, and consequently no angular advance. In this case the center $c$ will be on the outer edge of the steam port. If the travel of the valve is the same as that in Fig. 43, and indicated by the diameter of the dotted circle $a\ m\ b$ in Fig. 44, we notice that in the latter figure the travel is too great; our circle shows that the valve will travel beyond the bridge, and thus open the exhaust port to the steam in the steam chest; therefore, the travel must be reduced, as shown by the circumference $a_1\ m_1\ b$ in a full line. Lastly, if lead be given to a valve that has no lap, as shown in Fig. 45, then we have again linear advance, and consequently there will be a corresponding amount of angular advance. In this case the center $c$ will remain on the outside edge of the steam port.

### TO FIND THE RELATIVE POSITION OF THE ECCENTRIC TO THAT OF THE CRANK.

67. In Art. 61 it was shown how to set an eccentric for a valve without lap and lead. In that particular example the center line of the eccentric was placed perpendicular to the center line of crank. These relative positions are only true for engines in which all the connections are direct, such as shown in Fig. 30 (see Art. 63). When other connections are used, such as rockers, etc., it may happen that for some engines the eccentric would have to be set at right angles to the crank, or, as the practical man would say, "the eccentric set square with the crank," and yet for other engines this would be wrong.

Here we will consider only the relative position of eccentric to that of the crank in simple engines such as represented by Fig. 30.

The position of the valve in Fig. 45 indicates that the piston stands at the commencement of its stroke, because the small opening of steam port there shown is supposed to be lead and no more. Now, assume that the point $c$ is not only the center of the circle whose circumference represents the path of the center of eccentric, but is also the center of the crank-shaft, consequently the center line of crank must pass through $c$, and since all the connections between crank-shaft and cylinder are direct, the center line of crank must coincide with the line $A\ B$. Again, the valve has opened the left-hand steam port, therefore the center $P$ of the crank-pin must also be on the left-hand side of $c$, and in the line $A\ B$. Lastly, the point $y$ is the center of the eccentric, and since the eccentric must travel ahead of the crank (Art. 61) in this class of engines, we conclude that the crank is designed to turn in the direction as indicated by the arrow. In a similar manner, and for similar reasons, it can be proved that when the small openings of the steam ports, as shown in Figs. 42 and 43, represent lead, then the crank-pin $P$ must occupy the position shown in these figures.

Notice now the fact that in all the Figs. 42, 43, and 45, the center line $c\ m$ is perpendicular to the center line of crank $P\ c$, and the angular advance is laid off from the line $c\ m$ towards the right (away from the crank-pin). Also notice another important fact; the distance between the lines $c\ m$ and $c_1\ y$ in all these figures is equal to the linear advance; therefore in order to find the point $y$ we must lay off the linear advance on a line perpendicular to the line $c\,m$, and not on the arc $m\,y$.

These facts are principles which are applicable to every-day practice. For instance:

EXAMPLE 17.—Travel of the valve is 5 inches, lap 1 inch, lead $\tfrac{1}{16}$ of an inch, and the direction in which the crank is to move is indicated by the arrow, Fig. 46. Find the relative position of the eccentric to that of the crank.

Draw the straight line $A\,B$ as in Fig. 46, let the point $P$ on the line $A\,B$ represent the center of the crank-pin, and the point $c$ on the same line represent the center of the shaft. From $c$ as a center, and with a radius equal to $2\tfrac{1}{2}$ inches (which is half the

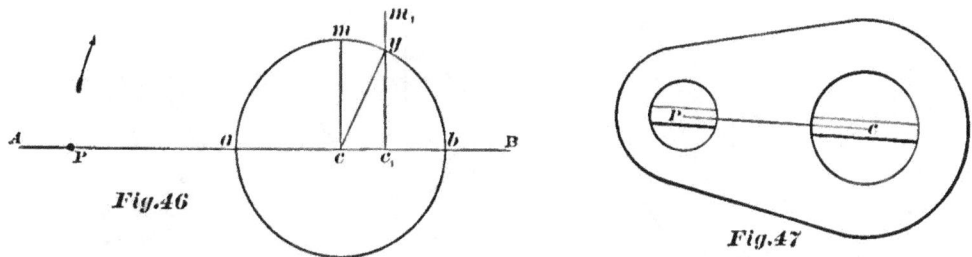

Fig.46

Fig.47

throw of the eccentric), draw a circle $a\,b\,m$, the circumference of this circle will represent the path of the center of the eccentric. From $c$ lay off towards the right a point $c_1$ $1\tfrac{1}{16}$ inch from $c$ (this $1\tfrac{1}{16}$ inch is the sum of the lap and lead), through $c_1$ draw a line $c_1\,m_1$ perpendicular to $A\,B$, this line $c_1\,m_1$ will intersect the circumference $a\,b\,m$ in the point $y$, and this point will be the center of the eccentric when the crank occupies the position as shown. Through the point $c$ draw a line perpendicular to $A\,B$, also a line through the points $c$ and $y$, then the angle $m\,c\,y$ will be the angular advance, and the distance from $c$ to $c_1$ the linear advance.

These principles are also applicable to shop practice.

EXAMPLE 18.—Fig. 40 represents an eccentric; Fig. 47, a crank; Fig. 48, the end of a crank-shaft. It is required to fasten to the crank-shaft the crank and eccentric in their correct relative positions before the shaft is placed in its bearings. The lap of the valve is $\tfrac{7}{8}$ of an inch, and the lead $\tfrac{1}{16}$ of an inch.

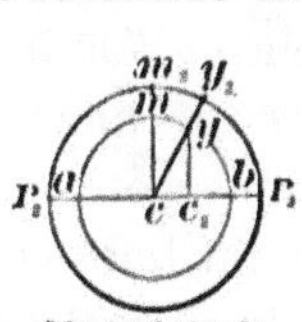

We must first find the half-throw of the eccentric. In this case, see Fig. 40, the diameter of the shaft being greater than the throw of the eccentric, we must force a strip of wood in the hole of the eccentric, and on this strip find the center $c$ of the hole, and the center $x$ of the eccentric; the distance between $c$ and $x$ is equal to half the throw. Through $c$ and $x$ draw a straight line $c\,g$; this line will be recognized as the center line of the eccentric.

End of shaft
Fig.48

Fig. 47.—On the face of the crank draw through the centers $c$ and $P$ a straight line, which will be the center line of crank.

Fig. 48.—Through the center $c$ of the shaft draw any straight line, as $P_2\,P_3$. From the center $c$, and with a radius equal to half the throw of the eccentric, draw on the end of the shaft a circle $a\,b\,m$. On the line $P_2\,P_3$ lay off a point $c_2$ $1\tfrac{5}{16}$ of an inch from the center $c$; through the point $c_2$ draw a straight line perpendicular to $P_2\,P_3$, intersecting the circumference $a\,b\,m$ in the point $y$; through the points $c$ and $y$ draw the straight line $c\,y_2$.

Fig. 49.—Place the crank on the shaft so that its center line $P\,c$ will coincide with $P_2\,c$ on the shaft, and then fasten the crank.

Place the eccentric on the shaft so that its center line $g\,c$ will coincide with $c\,y_2$ on the shaft, and fasten the eccentric.

The crank and eccentric will then have the correct position on the shaft, and must not be changed for a valve having $\tfrac{7}{8}$ of an inch lap and $\tfrac{1}{16}$ of an inch lead. We here

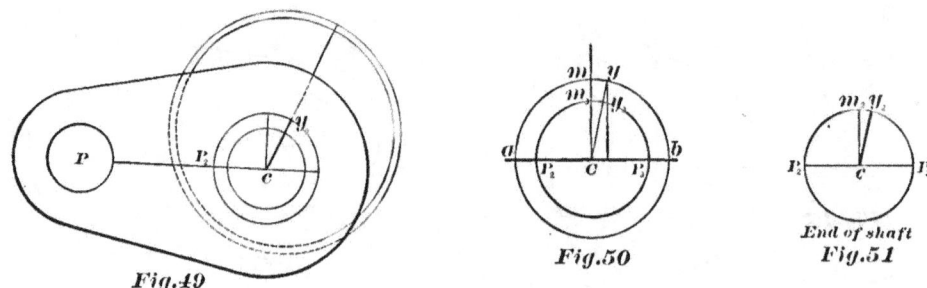

Fig. 49  Fig. 50  Fig. 51

again call the attention of the reader to the fact that these relative positions of crank and eccentric are only correct for engines in which all the connections are direct, and in which no rocker is used.

When it is necessary to place the crank and the eccentric some distance from the end of the shaft, it will be an easy matter to draw on the outside of the shaft lines through the points $P_2$ and $y_2$ parallel to the axis of the shaft, and then set the crank and eccentric to these lines.

Should it so happen that the throw of the eccentric is larger than the diameter of the shaft (but which seldom occurs), draw on paper or on a board any straight line $a\,b$, as in Fig. 50, and from a point $C$ on this line as a center, and with a radius equal to half the throw of the eccentric, draw the circle $a\,b\,m$. Find the point $y$ in the circumference $a\,b\,m$ in the same manner as the point $y$ in Fig. 46 has been found, and then draw the lines $m\,C$ and $y\,C$. From the center $C$, and with a radius equal to half the diameter of the shaft, draw the circle $P_2\,P_3$, whose circumference will intersect the straight lines $m\,C$ and $y\,C$ in the points $m_3$ and $y_3$. Through the center $c$ of the shaft, see Fig. 51, draw a straight line $P_2\,P_3$, and also the line $m_2\,c$ perpendicular to $P_2\,P_3$; make the arc $m_2\,y_2$ equal to $m_3\,y_3$ in Fig. 50; draw on the end of the shaft the line $y_2\,c$; set the eccentric to the line $y_2\,c$, and the crank to the line $c\,P_2$.

## THE EFFECT OF LAP.

68. When only one slide-valve is used for the whole distribution of steam in one cylinder, as in locomotives, and the valve has no lap, we may justly name the form of such a valve a primitive one, because valves without lap, or with only a trifling amount, about $\tfrac{1}{16}$ of an inch, were used in locomotives years ago, when the great necessity for an early and liberal exhaustion was not so well understood as at present, the chief aim then being to secure a timely and free admission of steam. Such valves, as

we have stated before, will admit steam during the whole length of the stroke, or, in other words, follow full stroke, and release the steam in one end of the cylinder at the same moment, or nearly so, that the steam is admitted into the other end; this is certainly no profitable way of using steam, for the following reason:

The process of exhausting steam requires *time*, and therefore the release of steam should begin in one end of the cylinder some time before steam is admitted into the other end, or, we may say, the steam which is pushing the piston ahead should be released before the end of the stroke has been reached. This cannot be accomplished with a valve having no lap, and consequently, when such a valve is used, there will not be sufficient time for the exhaustion of steam, thus causing considerable back pressure in the cylinder. In order then to secure an early exhaust, lap was introduced; first, $\frac{3}{8}$ of an inch lap was adopted, then $\frac{1}{2}$ of an inch. But it soon became apparent that working the steam expansively (a result of lap, besides gaining an early exhaust) additional economy in fuel was obtained, hence the lap was again increased until it became $\frac{7}{8}$ of an inch, and in some cases 1 inch, and even more than this. At the present time the lap of a valve in ordinary locomotives with $17'' \times 24''$, or $18'' \times 24''$ cylinders is $\frac{7}{8}$ to 1 inch, and in a few cases slightly exceeding this. From these remarks we may justly conclude that in these days the purpose of giving lap to the valve is to cause it to cut off steam at certain parts of the stroke of the piston, so that during the remaining portion of the stroke the piston is moved by the expansion of the steam. When steam is used in this manner, it is said to be used expansively.

Now, since the aim of giving lap to a valve, is to cause it to cut off steam at designated parts of the stroke of the piston, it will be necessary first to study the existing relation between the motion of the crank-pin and the motion of the piston.

## RELATION BETWEEN MOTION OF CRANK-PIN AND MOTION OF PISTON.

69. In order to illustrate this subject plainly, we have adopted in Fig. 52 a shorter length for the connecting rod than is used in locomotives.

The circumference of the circle $A\ B\ M\ D$, drawn from the center of the axle, and with a radius equal to the distance between the center of axle and that of the crank-pin, represents the path of the latter. We will assume that the motion of the crank-pin is uniform, that is, that it will pass through equal spaces in equal times. The direction in which the crank-pin moves is indicated by the arrow marked 1, and the direction in which the piston moves is indicated by arrow 2.

In order to trace the motion of the piston it is not necessary to show the piston in our illustration, because the connection between the cross-head pin $P$ and the piston is rigid; hence, if we know the motion of the former, we also know the motion of the latter.

The line $A\ C$ represents the line of motion of the center of cross-head pin $P$, consequently no matter what position the crank may occupy, the center $P$ will always be found in the line $A\ C$. The semi-circumference $A\ B\ D$ will be the path of the center of the crank-pin $P$ during one stroke of the piston; the point $A$ will be the position of the crank at the beginning of the stroke; and $B$, the position of the same at the end of the stroke. The semi-circumference $A\ B\ D$ is divided into 12 equal parts, although any other number would serve our purpose as well. The distance between the centers $D$ and $P$ represents the length of the connecting-rod.

From the point $A$ as a center, and with a radius equal to $DP$ (the length of the connecting-rod), an arc has been drawn, cutting the line $AC$ in the point $a$; this point is the position of the center $P$ of the cross-head pin, when the center of the crank is at $A$. Again, from the point 1 on the semi-circumference as a center and with the radius $DP$, another arc has been drawn cutting the line $AC$ in the point $1p$, and this point indicates the position of the cross-head pin when the crank-pin is at the point 1. In a similar manner the points $2p$, $3p$, $4p$, etc., have been obtained, and these points indicate the various positions of cross-head pin when the crank-pin is in the corresponding positions, as 2, 3, 4, etc.

Now notice the fact that the spaces from $A$ to 1 and from 1 to 2, etc., in the semi-circumference $ABD$ are all equal, and the crank-pin moves through each of these spaces in equal times, that is, if it requires one second to move from $A$ to 1, it will also require one second to move from 1 to 2. The corresponding spaces from $a$ to $1p$ and from $1p$ to $2p$, etc., on the line $AC$ are not equal, and yet the cross-head pin must move through these spaces in equal times; if it requires one second to move from $a$ to $1p$, it will also require one second to move from $1p$ to $2p$. But this last space is greater than the first. Here, then, we see that the cross-head pin, and therefore the piston, has a variable motion, that is, the piston will, at the commencement of its stroke, move comparatively slow, and increase in speed as it approaches the center of the stroke, and when the piston is moving away from the center of stroke, its speed is constantly decreasing. This variable motion of the piston is mostly caused by changing a rectilinear motion into a uniform rotary motion, and partly by the angle formed by the center line $DP$ of the connecting-rod and the line $AC$, an angle which is constantly changing during the stroke. Also notice that the distance from $a$ to $1p$ nearest one end of the stroke is smaller than the distance from $b$ to $11p$ nearest the other end of the stroke, and if we compare the next space $1p$ to $2p$ with the space $11p$ to $10p$, we again find that the former is smaller than the latter, and by further comparison we find that all the spaces from $a$ to $6p$ are smaller than the corresponding spaces from $b$ to $6p$, and consequently when the crank-pin is at point 6, which is the center of the path of the crank-pin during one stroke, the cross-head pin $P$ will be at $6p$, and not in the center of its stroke. Thus we see that the motion of the piston is not symmetrical, and this is wholly due to the varying angularity of the connecting-rod during the stroke. If we make the connecting-rod longer, but leave the stroke the same, the difference between the spaces $b$ to $11p$ and $a$ to $1p$ will be less, and the same can be said of the other spaces. Again, if we consider the length of the connecting-rod to be infinite, then the difference between the spaces nearest the ends of the stroke will vanish, and the same result is true for the other spaces. Hence, when the length of the connecting-rod is assumed to be infinite, the motion of the piston will be symmetrical, but still remain variable; in fact, the piston will have the same motion as that shown in Fig. 53. In this figure we have dispensed with the connecting-rod, and in its place extended the piston rod, and attached to its end a slotted cross-head in which the crank-pin is to work. Although such mechanism is never used in a locomotive, yet with its aid we can establish a simple method for finding the position of the piston when that of the crank is known. In this figure, as in Fig. 52, the circumference $A\ B\ D\ M$ will represent the path of the center of the crank-pin, and from the nature of this mechanism it must be evident that at whatever point in the circumference $A\ B\ D\ M$ the crank-pin

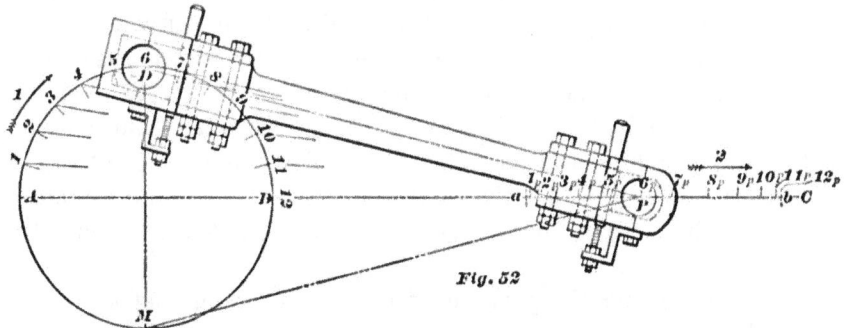

Fig. 52

center may be located, the center line $i\ h$ of the slotted cross-head will always stand perpendicular to the line $A\ C$, and also pass through the center of crank-pin.

In Fig. 53, when the crank-pin is at $A$, the piston will be at the commencement of its stroke. During the time the crank-pin travels from $A$ to point 8 the piston will travel through a portion of its stroke equal to the length $A\ E$, which is the distance between the dotted line $i\ h$ and the full line $i\ h$. If now we assume the points 1, 2, 3, etc., in the semi-circumference $A\ B\ D$ to be the various positions of the crank-pin during one stroke, and then draw through these points lines perpendicular to the line $A\ C$, cutting the latter in the points $1p$, $2p$, $3p$, etc., we obtain corresponding points for the

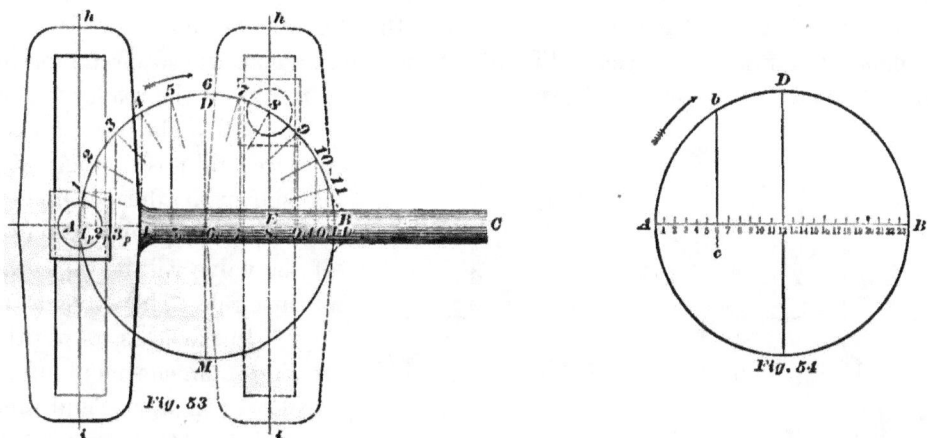

Fig. 53

Fig. 54

position of the piston in the cylinder. Thus, for instance, when the crank-pin is at point 1, the piston will then have moved from the commencement of its stroke through a distance equal to $A\ 1p$, and when the crank-pin is at point 2, the piston will then have traveled from $A$ to $2p$, and so on.

70. From the foregoing, we can establish a simple method, as shown in Fig. 54, for finding the position of the piston when that of the crank is known. The diameter $A\ B$ represents the stroke of the piston, and the semi-circumference $A\ B\ D$ represents the path of the center of the crank-pin during one stroke. For convenience, we may

divide the diameter into an equal number of parts, each division indicating one inch of the stroke. In this particular case (Fig. 54), we have assumed the stroke to be 24 inches; hence the diameter has been divided into 24 equal parts. Let the arrow indicate the direction in which the crank is to turn, and $A$ the beginning of the stroke; then, to find the distance through which the piston must travel from the commencement of its stroke during the time that the crank travels from $A$ to $b$, we simply draw through the point $b$ a straight line $b\,c$ perpendicular to $A\,B$; the distance between the line $b\,c$ and the point $A$ will be that portion of the stroke through which the piston has traveled, when crank-pin has reached the point $b$. In our figure we notice that the line $b\,c$ intersects $A\,B$ in the point 6; hence the piston has traveled six inches from the commencement of the stroke.

If this method of finding the position of the piston when that of the crank is known is thoroughly understood, then the solutions of the following problems relating to lap of the slide valve will be comparatively easy.

### PROBLEMS RELATING TO LAP OF THE SLIDE-VALVE.

71. To find the point of cut-off when the lap and travel of the valve are given, the valve to have no lead.

The principles upon which the following problems relating to the construction of the slide-valve are based, have been taken from the excellent "Practical Treatise on the Movement of Slide-Valves by Eccentrics," by Prof. C W. MacCord.

EXAMPLE 19.—Lap of valve is one inch; travel, 5 inches; no lead; stroke of piston, 24 inches. At what part of the stroke will the steam be cut off?

We must first find the center $c$, Fig. 55, of the circle $a\,b\,m$, whose circumference represents the path of the center of eccentric, and this is found, as the reader will re-

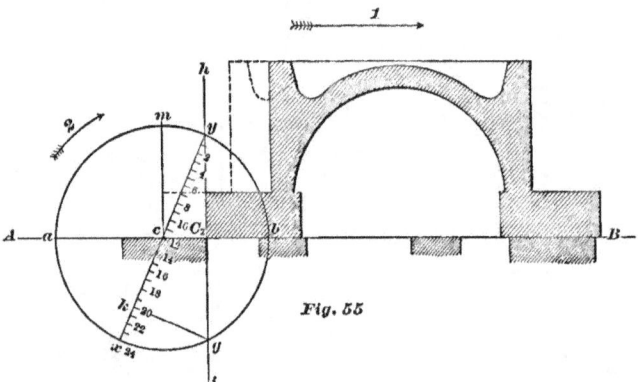

Fig. 55

member, by placing the valve in a central position (Art. 64), as shown in dotted lines in this figure. Then the edge $c$ of the valve will be the center of the circle. The valve drawn in full lines shows its position at the commencement of the stroke of piston; and since the valve is to have no lead, the edge $C_2$ will coincide with the outer edge of the steam port. Through the edge $C_2$ draw the line $i\,h$ perpendicular to the line $A\,B$; the line $i\,h$ will intersect the circumference $a\,b\,m$ in the point $y$, and this point will be the center of eccentric when the piston is at the beginning of its stroke. Now, assume that the circumference $a\,b\,m$ also represents, on a small scale, the path of the center of the crank-pin; then the diameter $y\,x$ of this circle will represent the length of the stroke of the piston; the position of this diameter is found by drawing a straight line through the point $y$ (the center of the eccentric when the piston is at one end of its stroke) and the center $c$. Also assume that the point $y$ represents the center of the crank-pin when the piston is at the beginning of its stroke. To make the construction as plain as possible, divide the diameter $y\,x$ into 24 equal parts, each representing one inch of the stroke of piston, and for convenience number the divisions as shown. The arrow marked 1 shows the direction in which the valve must travel, and arrow 2 indicates the direction in which the center $y$ must travel. Now it must be evident, because the points $y$ and $C_2$ will always be in the same line, that during the time the center $y$ of the eccentric travels through the arc $y\,g$, the valve not only opens the steam port, but, as the circumference $a\,b\,m$ indicates, travels a little beyond the port, and then closes the same, or, in short, during the time the center of eccentric travels from $y$ to $g$, the port has been fully opened and closed; and the moment that the center of eccentric reaches the point $g$, the admission of steam into the cylinder is stopped. We have assumed that the point $y$ also represents the position of the center of crank-pin at the beginning of the stroke; and, since the crank and eccentric are fastened to the same shaft, it follows that during the time the center of eccentric travels from $y$ to $g$ the crank-pin will move through the same arc, and when the steam is cut off the crank-pin will be at the point $g$. Therefore, through the point $g$ draw a straight line $g\,k$ perpendicular to the line $y\,x$; the line $g\,k$ will intersect the line $y\,x$ in the point $k$, and this point coincides with the point mark 20; hence steam will be cut off when the piston has traveled 20 inches from the beginning of its stroke.

The manner of finding the point $k$ is precisely similar to that of finding the point $c$ in Fig. 54. The angle $m\,y\,c$ will be the angular advance of the eccentric.

## LEAD WILL AFFECT THE POINT OF CUT-OFF.

72. In Fig. 55 the valve had no lead; if, now, in that figure, we change the angular advance $m\,y\,c$ of the eccentric so that the valve will have lead, as shown in Fig. 56, then the point of cut-off will also be changed. How to find the point of cut-off when the valve has lead is shown in Fig. 56.

EXAMPLE 20.—The lap of valve is 1 inch, its travel 5 inches; lead ¼ of an inch (this large amount of lead has been chosen for the sake of clearness in the figure); stroke of piston, 24 inches; at what part of the stroke will the steam be cut off?

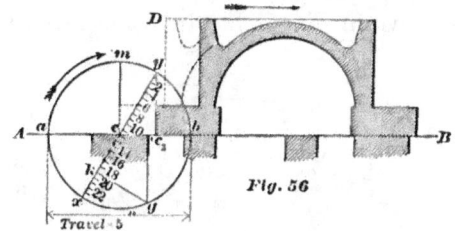

Fig. 56

On the line $A\,B$, Fig. 56, lay off the exhaust and steam ports; also on this line find the center $c$ of the circle $a\,b\,m$ in a manner similar to that followed in the last construction, namely, by placing the valve in a central position, as shown by the dotted lines and marked $D$, and then adopting the edge $c$ of the valve as the center of the circle $a\,b\,m$; or, to use fewer words, we may say from the outside of the edge $s$ of the steam port, lay off on the line $A\,B$ a point $c$ whose distance from the edge $s$ will be equal to the lap, that is, 1 inch. From $c$ as a center, and with a radius of 2½ inches (equal ½ of the travel), describe the circle $a\,b\,m$, whose circumference will represent the path of the center of eccentric. The lead of the valve in a locomotive is generally $\frac{1}{32}$

and sometimes as much as $\frac{1}{16}$ of an inch, when the valve is in full gear, in this example we have adopted a lead of $\frac{1}{4}$ of an inch for full gear, hence, draw the section of the valve, as shown in full lines, in a position that it will occupy when the piston is at the beginning of its stroke, and consequently the distance between the edge $c_2$ of the valve and the edge $s$ of the steam port will, in this case, be $\frac{1}{4}$ of an inch. Through $c_2$ draw a straight line perpendicular to $A B$, intersecting the circumference $a b m$ in the point $y$; this point will be the center of the eccentric when the piston is at the beginning of its stroke, and since it is assumed that the circumference $a b m$ also represents the path of the center of the crank-pin, the point $y$ will also be the position of the center of the crank-pin when the piston is at the commencement of its stroke. Through the points $y$ and $c$ draw a straight line $y x$, to represent the stroke of the piston, and divide it into 24 equal parts. Through the point $s$ draw a straight line perpendicular to $A B$, intersecting the circumference $a b m$ in the point $g$, and through $g$ draw a straight line perpendicular to $y x$, and intersecting the latter in the point $k$; this point will be the point of cut-off. If now the distance between the point $k$ and point 19 is $\frac{1}{8}$ of the space from 19 to 20, we conclude that the piston has traveled $19\frac{1}{8}$ inches from the beginning of its stroke when the admission of steam into the cylinder is suppressed.

Here we see that when a valve has no lead, as in Fig. 55, the admission of steam into the cylinder will cease when the piston has traveled 20 inches; and when the angular advance of the eccentric is changed, as in Fig. 56, so that the valve has $\frac{1}{4}$ of an inch lead, the point of cut-off will be at $19\frac{1}{8}$ inches from the beginning of the stroke, a difference of $\frac{7}{8}$ of an inch between the point of cut-off in Fig. 55 and that in Fig. 56. But the lead in locomotive valves in full gear is only about $\frac{1}{32}$ of an inch, which will affect the point of cut-off so very little that we need not notice its effect upon the period of admission, and, therefore, lead will not be taken into consideration in the following examples.

### THE TRAVEL OF THE VALVE WILL AFFECT THE POINT OF CUT-OFF.

73. Fig. 57 represents the same valve and ports as shown in Fig. 55, but the travel of the valve in Fig. 57 has been increased to $5\frac{3}{4}$ inches. The point of cut-off $k$ has been

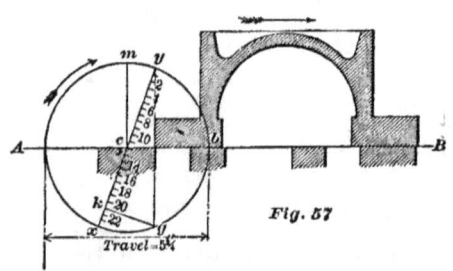

Fig. 57

obtained by the same method as that employed in Figs. 55 and 56, and we find that this point $k$ coincides with point 21. Now notice the change caused by an increase of travel; when the travel of the valve is 5 inches, as shown in Fig. 55, the admission of steam into the cylinder will cease when the piston has traveled 20 inches from the commencement of its stroke, and when the travel of the same valve is increased $\frac{3}{4}$ of an inch, as shown in Fig. 57, the admission of the steam will not be suppressed until the piston has traveled 21 inches. Here we notice a difference of 1 inch between the two points of cut-off. But it must be remembered that when the travel of a valve for a new engine is to be found or established, the point of cut-off does not enter the question; we simply assign such a travel to the valve that steam ports will be fully opened, or give it a slightly greater travel when the valve is in full gear; and how to find this travel has been explained in Art. 59. The point of cut-off is regulated by the lap and position of the eccentric.

74. In order to find the point of cut-off it is not necessary to make a drawing of the valve, as has been done in Fig. 55. The only reason for doing so was to present the method of finding the point of cut-off to the beginner in as plain a manner as possible. In order to show how such problems can be solved without the section of a valve, and consequently with less labor, another example, similar to Example 19, is introduced.

EXAMPLE 21.—Lap of valve is $1\frac{3}{8}$ inches; travel, $5\frac{1}{2}$ inches; stroke of piston, 24 inches; width of steam port, $1\frac{1}{4}$ inches; find the point of cut-off.

Fig. 58. Draw any straight line, as $A B$; anywhere on this line mark off $1\frac{1}{4}$ inches, equal to the width of the steam port. From the edge $s$ of the steam port lay off on the line $A B$ a point $c$, the distance between the points $s$ and $c$ being $1\frac{3}{8}$ inches, that is,

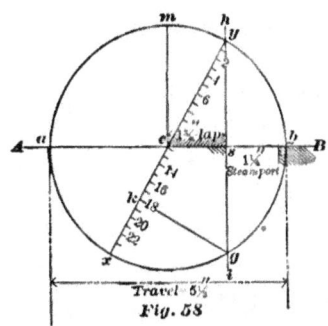
Fig. 58

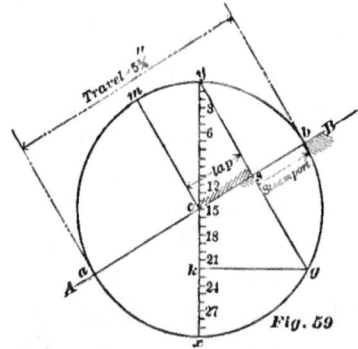
Fig. 59

equal to the amount of lap. From $c$ as a center, and with a radius equal to half the travel, namely, $2\frac{3}{4}$ inches, draw a circle $a\,b\,m$; the circumference of this circle will represent the path of the center of the eccentric, and also that of the crank-pin. Through $s$ draw a straight line $i\,h$ perpendicular to $A B$; this line $i\,h$ will intersect the circumference $a\,b\,m$ in the points $y$ and $y$. Through the points $y$ and $c$ draw a straight line $y\,x$; the diameter $y\,x$ will represent the stroke of the piston. Divide $y\,x$ into 24 equal parts; through the point $y$ draw a straight line $y\,k$ perpendicular to $y\,x$, and intersecting $y\,x$ in the point $k$, this point is the point of cut-off. Since $k$ coincides with the point 18, it follows that the piston had traveled 18 inches from the beginning of its stroke when the flow of the steam into the cylinder ceased.

75. Now we may reverse the order of this construction and thus find the amount of lap required to cut off steam at a given portion of the stroke.

EXAMPLE 22.—Travel of valve is $5\frac{3}{4}$ inches; stroke of piston, 30 inches; steam to be cut off when the piston has traveled 22 inches from the beginning of the stroke; find the lap.

Fig. 59. Draw a circle $a\,b\,m$ whose diameter is equal to the travel of the valve, viz., $5\frac{3}{4}$ inches. Through the center $c$ draw the diameter $y\,x$. In this figure we have drawn the line $y\,x$ vertically, which was done for the sake of convenience; any other position for this line will answer the purpose equally well. The circumference $a\,b\,m$

represents the path of the center of the eccentric, also that of the crank-pin; the diameter $y\,x$ will represent the stroke of the piston, and therefore is divided into 30 equal parts. The steam is to be cut off when the piston has traveled 22 inches from the beginning of the stroke, therefore through the point 22 draw a straight line $g\,k$ perpendicular to $y\,x$, the line $g\,k$ intersecting the circumference $a\,b\,m$ in the point $g$. Join the points $y$ and $g$ by a straight line. Find the center $s$ of the line $y\,g$, then, through $s$ and perpendicular to the line $y\,g$, draw the line $A\,B$; if the latter line is drawn accurately it will always pass through the center $c$. The distance between the points $s$ and $c$ will be the amount of lap required, and in this example it is $1\frac{7}{16}$ inches.

Examples like the foregoing are often given in a somewhat different form. For instance, let the travel of the valve be $5\frac{3}{4}$ inches, stroke 30 inches, steam to be cut off at $\frac{3}{4}$ stroke; find the lap.

Here we draw the circle $a\,b\,m$ and the diameter $y\,x$ as before; but instead of dividing the diameter $x\,y$ into 30 equal parts to correspond to number of inches in the stroke, we divide it into four equal parts; the point of cut-off $k$ will then be at $\frac{3}{4}$ of the diameter from its extremity $y$. Through the point $k$ draw $k\,g$ perpendicular to $y\,x$, and proceed as before, and thus obtain the lap required.

It may also be stated that this construction will give the amount of opening of the steam port; thus, in Fig. 59 the distance from $s$ to $b$ shows the amount of opening of the steam port. If, for instance, $s\,b$ is equal to the width of the steam port, the latter will be opened fully; if $s\,b$ is greater than the width of the steam port, the edge of the valve will travel beyond the inner edge of the steam port; and if $s\,b$ is less than the width of the steam port, the latter will not be opened fully. This is obvious from what has been said in relation to Figs. 33, 41, 42, 43, and 44.

76. It sometimes occurs in designing a new locomotive, and often in designing stationary or marine engines, that only the width of steam port and point of cut-off is known, and the lap and travel of the valve is not known. In such cases both of these can be at once determined by the following method.

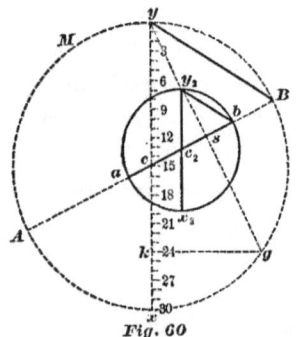
Fig. 60

EXAMPLE 23.—The width of the steam port is 2 inches; the stroke of piston, 30 inches; steam to be cut off when the piston has traveled 24 inches from the beginning of its stroke; find the lap and travel of the valve.

Fig. 60. Draw any circle, as $A\,B\,M$, whose diameter is larger than what the travel of the valve is expected to be. Through the center $c$ draw the diameter $y\,x$, and, since the stroke of the piston is 30 inches, divide $y\,x$ into 30 equal parts. Steam is to be cut off when the piston has traveled 24 inches; therefore through point 24 draw a straight line $g\,k$ perpendicular to the diameter $y\,x$, intersecting the circumference $A\,B\,M$ in the point $g$. Join the points $y$ and $g$ by a straight line; through the center $s$ of the line $y\,g$ draw a line $A\,B$ perpendicular to $y\,g$. So far, this construction is precisely similar to that shown in Fig. 59, and in order to distinguish this part of the construction from that which is to follow, we have used dotted lines; for the remainder full lines will be used. It will also be noticed by comparing Fig. 60 with Fig. 59 that, if the diameter $A\,B$ had been the correct travel of valve, then $c\,s$ would have been the correct amount of lap. But we commenced this construction with a travel that we knew to be too great; hence, to find the correct travel and lap, we must proceed as follows: Join the points $B$ and $y$. From $s$ towards $B$, lay off on the line $AB$ a point $b$; the distance between the points $s$ and $b$ must be equal to the width of the steam port plus the amount that the valve is to travel beyond the steam port, which, in this example, is assumed to be $\frac{1}{8}$ of an inch. Therefore the distance from $s$ to $b$ must be $2\frac{3}{8}$ inches. Through $b$ draw a straight line $b\, y_2$ parallel to $B\, y$, intersecting the line $y\, g$ in the point $y_2$. Through the point $y_2$ draw a straight line $y_2\, x_2$ parallel to the line $y\, x$, and intersecting the line $AB$ in the point $c_2$. From $c_2$ as a center, and with a radius equal to $c_2\, b$, or $c_2\, y_2$, describe a circle $a\, b\, y_2$. Then $a\, b$ will be the travel of the valve, which, in this case, is $7\frac{5}{8}$ inches, and the distance from $c_2$ to $s$ will be the lap, which, in this example, is $1\frac{11}{16}$ inches.

## PRACTICAL CONSTRUCTION OF THE SLIDE-VALVE.

77. It should be obvious, and therefore almost needless to remark here, that the foregoing graphical methods employed in the solutions of the problems relating to the slide-valve are applicable to every-day practice. The writer believes that these methods are the simplest and best to adopt for ordinary use, and without these it would be difficult to construct a valve capable of performing the duty assigned to it. Of course, when a graphical method is employed, great accuracy in drawing the lines is necessary.

We will give a practical example, in which one of the objects aimed at is to show the application of one of the foregoing methods to ordinary practice.

EXAMPLE 24.—The width of the steam ports is $1\frac{1}{4}$ inches; length of the same, 14 inches; thickness of bridges, $1\frac{1}{8}$ inches; width of exhaust port, $2\frac{1}{2}$ inches; travel of valve, $4\frac{3}{4}$ inches; stroke of piston, 24 inches; steam to be cut off when the piston has traveled $20\frac{3}{4}$ inches from the beginning of its stroke; the edges of the exhaust cavity are to cover the steam ports, and not more, when the valve stands in a central position; construct the valve.

Fig. 61. Draw a straight line $AB$ to represent the valve seat; through any point in $AB$ draw another line $DC$ perpendicular to $AB$; the line $DC$ is to represent the center of exhaust port and the center of valve. Draw the exhaust port, bridges, and steam ports as shown.

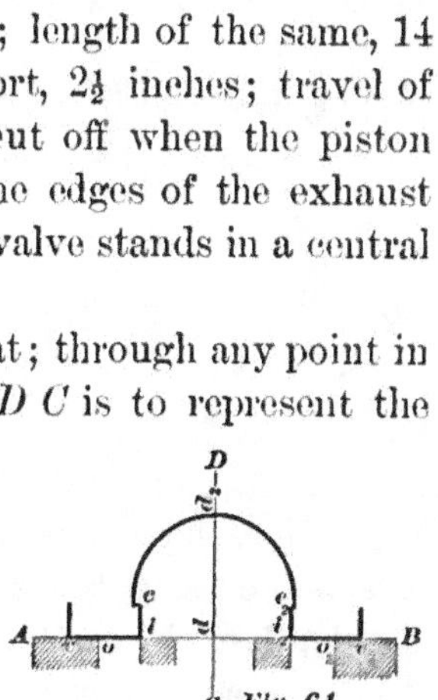

The question now arises: How long shall we make the valve? Or, in other words, what shall be the distance between the outside edges of the valve $c$ and $c_2$? If the valve had to admit steam during the whole stroke of the piston, or, as the practical man would say, "follow full stroke," then the distance between the edges $c$ and $c_2$ would be equal to the sum of twice the width of one steam port plus twice the width of one bridge plus the width of the exhaust port, hence we would have $2\frac{1}{2} + 2\frac{1}{4} + 2\frac{1}{2} = 7\frac{1}{4}$ inches for the length of the valve. But according to the conditions given in the example, the valve must cut off steam when the piston has traveled $20\frac{3}{4}$ inches, therefore the valve must have lap, and the amount of lap that is necessary for this purpose must be determined by the method shown in Fig. 59, and given in connection with Example 22. Following this method, we find that the required lap is $\frac{7}{8}$ of an inch, therefore the total length of the valve will be $7\frac{1}{4} + (\frac{7}{8} \times 2) = 9$ inches: or we may say that the distance between the edges $c$ and $c_2$ must be equal to twice the width of one steam port plus twice the width of one bridge plus the width of the exhaust port plus twice the lap, consequently we have $2\frac{1}{2}+2\frac{1}{4}+2\frac{1}{2}+1\frac{3}{4} = 9$ inches for the length of the valve. Through the points $c$ and $c_2$ (each point being placed $4\frac{1}{2}$ inches from the center line $C\,D$), draw lines perpendicular to $A\,B$; these lines will represent the outside surfaces containing the edges $c$ and $c_2$. These surfaces must be square with the surface $A\,B$, because, if they are not so, but are such as shown in Fig. 64, the distance between the edges $c$ and $c_2$ will decrease as the valve wears, and when this occurs the valve will not cut off the steam at the proper time. Now, in regard to the cavity of the valve. One of the conditions given in our example is, that the edges of the cavity must cover the steam ports, and no more, when the valve stands in a central position, therefore the inner edges $i$ and $i_2$ of the valve must be $4\frac{3}{4}$ inches apart, which is equal to twice the width of one bridge plus the width of the exhaust port; consequently, when the valve stands midway of its travel, the inner edges of the valve (being $4\frac{3}{4}$ inches apart) and the inner edges of the steam ports coincide. Through the points $i$ and $i_2$ (each being placed $2\frac{3}{8}$ inches from the center line $C\,D$), draw the straight lines $i\,e$ and $i_2\,e_2$ perpendicular to $A\,B$. These lines will represent the sides of the cavity containing the inner edges $i$ and $i_2$ of the valve, and these sides must be square with the surface $A\,B$; if these are otherwise, for instance such as shown in Fig. 64, the distance between the edges $i$ and $i_2$ will change as the valve wears, and then the valve will not perform its duty correctly. The depth $d\,d_2$ of the cavity is generally made from $1\frac{1}{4}$ to $1\frac{1}{2}$ times the width of the exhaust port. The writer believes that making the depth of the cavity $1\frac{1}{2}$ times the

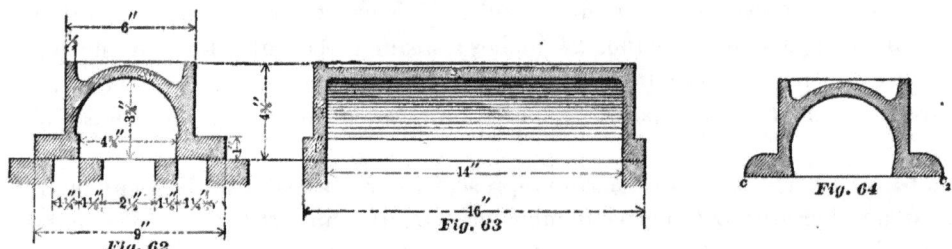

Fig. 62  Fig. 63  Fig. 64

width of the exhaust port is the best practice. In our example the width of the exhaust port is $2\frac{1}{2}$ inches, and $2\frac{1}{2} \times 1\frac{1}{2} = 3\frac{3}{4}$ inches, which will be the distance from $d$ to $d_2$, that is, the depth of the cavity. The curved surface of the cavity is generally a cylindrical surface, and when it is so, as in our example, this surface must be represented in Fig. 61 by an arc of a circle. The sides $i\,e$ and $i_2\,e_2$ must be planed, and to do this conveniently, these sides must extend a little beyond the curved surface, towards the center $C\,D$. Consequently, through the point $d_2$ draw an arc whose center is in the line $C\,D$, and whose radius is such that will allow the sides to project about $\frac{1}{16}$ of an inch. Here we have lines which completely represent the cavity of the valve and the valve face. If we now add to these lines the proper thickness of metal, as shown in Fig. 62, this section of the valve will be complete.

Fig. 63 shows a section of the valve taken at right angles to that shown in Fig. 62. Since the ports are 14 inches long, the cavity of the valve must be 14 inches wide, as shown. The amount that the valve overlaps the ends of the steam ports must be sufficient to prevent leakage. For a valve of the size here shown, 1 inch overlap is allowed, and the thickness of metal around the cavity is generally $\frac{1}{2}$ of an inch. For smaller valves the overlap at each end of the steam port is from $\frac{3}{4}$ to $\frac{7}{8}$ of an inch, and the thickness of metal around the cavity is $\frac{3}{8}$ of an inch.

The valve here shown is suitable for a locomotive cylinder 16 inches in diameter, and a piston speed of 525 feet per minute, and the dimensions here given agree with those of the valves that are at present in use.

### INSIDE LAP, CLEARANCE AND INSIDE LEAD.

78. Now, a few words in regard to some other terms used in connection with the slide-valve.

INSIDE LAP.—The amount that the inside edges $i$ and $i_2$ of the valve, Fig. 65, overlap the inside edges $s$ and $s_2$ of the steam ports, when the valve stands midway of its

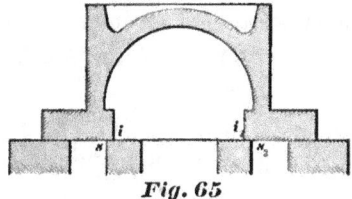
*Fig. 65*

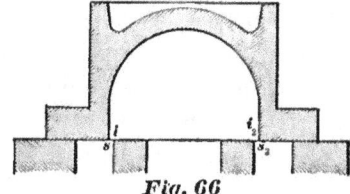
*Fig. 66*

travel, is called inside lap; thus, the distance from $s$ to $i$, or from $s_2$ to $i_2$, represents the inside lap. Its purpose is to delay the release of steam.

The amount of inside lap is comparatively small, rarely exceeding $\frac{1}{8}$ of an inch, and in many locomotives the valves have no inside lap. Rules for determining the inside lap cannot be given, because engineers do not agree on this subject. The writer believes that for slow-running locomotives, particularly if these have to run over steep grades, a little inside lap will be beneficial. For ordinary passenger locomotives running on comparatively level roads, no inside lap should be used.

79. INSIDE CLEARANCE.—When the valve stands midway of its travel, as shown in Fig. 66, and its inside edges $i$ and $i_2$ do not cover the steam ports, then the amount by which each edge of the valve comes short of the inner edges of the steam ports is called inside clearance; thus, the distance from $i$ to $s$, or from $i_2$ to $s_2$, represents inside clearance. The purpose of inside clearance is to hasten the release, and is sometimes adopted in very fast-running locomotives. It seldom exceeds $\frac{1}{64}$ of an inch. Good judgment and great experience are required for determining the amount of clearance, and in deciding for what classes of locomotives it should be used. In ordinary passenger locomotives the valves have no inside clearance.

80. The width of opening of the steam port for the release of steam at the beginning of the stroke is called inside lead; thus, when the piston is at the beginning of its stroke, and the valve occupying the position as shown in Fig. 67, then the distance between the inner edges $i_2$ of the valve and the inner edge $s_2$ of the steam port is called inside lead. The simple terms "lead" and "lap" are used among engineers to desig-

nate outside lead and lap; hence, the necessity of using the terms "inside lead" and "inside lap" when such is meant.

## THE EVENTS OF THE DISTRIBUTION OF STEAM.

81. In the distribution of steam during one revolution of the crank, four distinct events occur, namely:

1st. The admission of steam.
2d. The cutting off, or, in other words, the suppression of steam.
3d. The release of steam.
4th. The compression of steam.

Fig. 67. The outside edges $c_2$ and $c_3$ of the valve, and the outside edges $o$ and $o_2$ of the steam ports, will regulate the admission and suppression of steam; the inner edges $i$ and $i_2$ of the valve and the inner edges $s$ and $s_2$ of the steam ports control the release and compression of steam. The parts of the stroke of the piston during which these events will happen can be found by the following methods:

EXAMPLE 25.—Travel of valve, 5 inches; lap, 1 inch; lead, ¼ of an inch; stroke of piston, 24 inches; no inside lap or clearance. Find at what part of the stroke the admission, suppression, release, and compression will take place.

In Figs. 67, 68, and 69 the valve occupies different positions, but the sections of the valve in these figures are exactly alike, because they represent one and the same

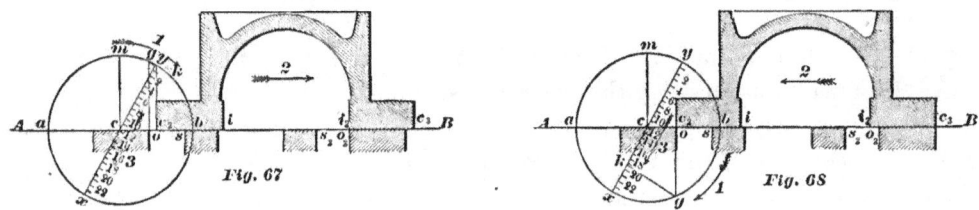

Fig. 67.   Fig. 68.

valve. In Fig. 67 the distance between the edge $c_2$ of the valve and the edge $o$ of the steam port is ¼ of an inch, which is the amount of lead given in our example; hence, this position of the valve indicates that the piston is at the beginning of its stroke, and the angle $m\,c\,y$ is the angular advance of the eccentric. In Fig. 68 the edge $c_2$ of the valve and the edge $o$ of the steam port coincide, and, since the valve is moving in the direction indicated by arrow 2, the suppression commences, or, in other words, the valve is cutting off steam when it is in the position as here shown. In Fig. 69 the inside edge $i$ of the valve coincides with the inner edge $s$ of the steam port, and, since the valve is moving in the direction indicated by arrow 2, the release must commence when the valve arrives in the position here shown.

In Figs. 67, 68, and 69 the distances from the outside edge $o$ of the steam port to the center $c$ of the circle $a\,b\,m$ are equal; that is, the points $c$ and $o$ are one inch apart, which is the amount of lap. The diameters of the circles $a\,b\,m$ are all five inches, which is the travel of the valve given in the example, and the circumference of each circle represents the path of the eccentric, and also the path of the center of the crank-pin. The point $y$ in these figures represents the position of the center of eccentric when the piston is at the beginning of its stroke. The distance between the point $y$

and $m$ is the same in all figures, and consequently the angles formed by the lines $y\,x$ and $m\,c$ are equal and represent the angular advance of the eccentric.

When the valve occupies the position as represented in Fig. 67, the center line of crank will coincide with the line $A\,B$; and since the piston will then be at the beginning of its stroke, it follows that the line $A\,B$ will indicate the direction in which the piston must move. In order to compare the relative position of the piston with that of the valve with as little labor as possible, we shall assume that the direction in which the piston moves is represented by the line $y\,x$, instead of the line $A\,B$; hence the point $y$ will not only show the position of the center of the eccentric, but it will also indicate the position of the center of the crank-pin when the piston is at the commencement of its stroke. If these remarks are thoroughly understood, there will be no difficulty in comprehending that which is to follow.

Now let us trace the motions of the valve and piston and thus determine at what part of the stroke the events (previously named) will take place. When the crank-pin is moving in the direction as indicated by the arrow marked 1, Fig. 67, the center of eccentric will move through part of the circumference, $a\,b\,m$, and the valve will travel in the direction indicated by the arrow 2, thus opening the steam port wider and wider until the end $b$ of the travel is reached; then the valve will commence to return, and as it moves toward the center $c$, the steam port gradually closes, until the valve reaches the position as shown in Fig. 68; then the steam port will be closed and steam cut off. To find the position of the piston when the valve is cutting off steam, we draw through the edge $c_2$ of the valve, Fig. 68, a straight line $c_2\,g$, perpendicular to $A\,B$, intersecting the circumference $a\,b\,m$ in the point $g$; through this point draw a line perpendicular to $y\,x$ intersecting the latter in the point $k$, and this point $k$ being 19¼ inches from $y$ indicates that the piston has traveled 19¼ inches from the beginning of its stroke before the steam is cut off, and that steam has been admitted into the cylinder during the time the piston traveled from $y$ to $k$. As the piston continues to move towards the end $x$ of the stroke, the valve will move in the direction of the arrow 2, Fig. 68, and the steam port will remain closed so that no steam can enter the cylinder or escape from it; hence the steam that is now confined in the cylinder must push the piston ahead by its expansive force, but the moment that the valve reaches the position as shown in Fig. 69 the release of steam will commence. To find the corresponding position of piston we draw through the edge $c_2$ of the valve, Fig. 69, a line $c_2\,g$, perpendicular to $A\,B$, intersecting the circumference $a\,b\,m$ in the point $g$. Through this point draw a line

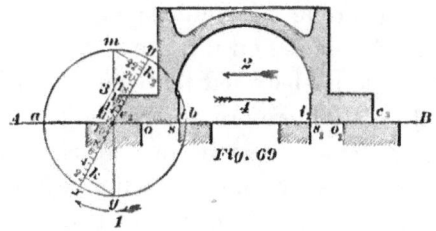

Fig. 69

$g\,k$ perpendicular to $y\,x$, intersecting the latter in the point $k$, and this point $k$ being 22⅜ inches from the beginning of the stroke indicates that the piston has traveled through this distance when the release of steam commences. Now notice, the steam is cut off when the piston has traveled 19¼ inches, and the release of steam commences when the piston has traveled 22⅜ inches; consequently the steam is worked expansively during the time the piston moves 3¼ inches of its stroke. The steam port will remain open to the action of the exhaust during the time the piston completes its stroke and moves through a portion of its return stroke. In the meantime the valve will move to the end $a$ of the travel and return as indicated by arrow 4, and the moment that the valve again reaches the position shown in Fig. 69, the release of steam will be stopped. To find the corresponding position of the piston, draw through the edge $c_2$ of the valve, Fig. 69, a straight line $c_2\, m$ perpendicular to $A\, B$, intersecting the circumference $a\, b\, m$ in point $m$. Through this point draw a straight line $m\, k_2$ perpendicular to $y\, x$, and intersecting the latter in the point $k_2$. Since the distance between the points $x$ and $k_2$ is $22\tfrac{3}{8}$ inches, it follows that the piston has moved through $22\tfrac{3}{8}$ inches of its return stroke, by the time that the release of steam will cease. As the valve continues its travel in the direction of arrow 4, Fig. 69, the steam port will remain closed until the edge $c_2$ of the valve coincides with the outer edge $o$ of the steam port, and during this time, the steam which remained in the cylinder is compressed, but as soon as the edge $c_2$ of the valve passes beyond the steam port edge $o$, the admission of steam into the cylinder will commence. To find the corresponding position of the piston, draw through the outer edge $o$ of the steam port, Fig. 67, a straight line $o\, g$ perpendicular to $A\, B$, and intersecting the circumference $a\, b\, m$ in the point $g$; through this point draw a line $g\, k$ perpendicular to $y\, x$, intersecting the latter in the point $k$, and since the distance between the points $x$ and $k$ is $23\tfrac{7}{8}$ inches, we conclude that the piston has moved through $23\tfrac{7}{8}$ inches of its return stroke before the admission of steam will begin. Here we see that steam will be admitted into the cylinder before the return stroke of the piston is completed, and that is the object of lead, as has been stated before. Notice once more: the compression of steam will commence when the piston has traveled $22\tfrac{3}{8}$ inches of its return stroke, and will cease when the piston has traveled $23\tfrac{7}{8}$ inches of its return stroke; hence the steam is compressed during the time that the piston travels through $1\tfrac{1}{2}$ inches.

In each one of these figures the point $g$ represents the relative position of the center of eccentric to that of the valve. The point $g$ will always be found in the circumference $a\, b\, m$, and in a straight line $c_2\, g$ drawn perpendicular to $A\, B$, the former passing through the outer edge $c_2$ of the valve.

The reason why the point $g$ should in all cases be found in the straight line $c_2\, g$ drawn through the outside edge $c_2$ of the valve is this: the center $c$ of the circle $a\, b\, m$ has been placed on the line $A\, B$ in such a position (as shown in these figures), so that the distance between the center $c$ and the outside edge $o$ of the steam port is equal to the lap, therefore the center $g$ of the eccentric and the outer edge $c_2$ of the valve will always lie in the same straight line drawn perpendicular to $A\, B$. If the distance between center $c$ and the outer edge $o$ of the steam port is greater or less than the lap, then the center of the eccentric and outside edge of the valve will not lie in the same straight line drawn perpendicular to the line $A\, B$. Here, then, we can conceive the necessity of placing the center $c$ of the circle $a\, b\, m$ in the position as shown in these figures. The correctness of these remarks must be evident to the reader if the explanations in the previous article have been understood. Again, since we have assumed that the point $g$ not only represents the center of the eccentric, but also the center of the crank-pin, it follows that, in order to determine how far the piston has moved from the beginning $y$ of its stroke when the crank-pin is at $g$, we must draw a straight line through the point $g$ perpendicular to $y\, x$, as has been done in these figures. See Art. 69.

From these constructions we can obtain our answer to Example 25, namely:

Steam will be cut off, or, in other words, suppression will commence when the piston has traveled 19¼ inches from the beginning of its stroke, and steam will be admitted into the cylinder during the time that the piston travels through this distance. The steam will be released when the piston has traveled 22⅜ inches from the beginning of its stroke, consequently the steam will be worked expansively during the time the piston travels through 3¼ inches. The release of steam will continue until the compression commences, which will occur when the piston has traveled 22⅜ inches of its return stroke. The compression will cease, and the admission of steam commence when the piston has traveled 23⅞ inches of its return stroke.

The same answer to our example could have been obtained with less labor by a construction as shown in Fig. 70, which is nothing else but a combination of the three preceding figures; the methods of finding the different points in Fig. 70 have not been changed, and therefore an explanation in connection with this figure is unnecessary.

## POWER REQUIRED TO WORK PLAIN SLIDE-VALVE, ROLLER VALVES AND BALANCED SLIDE-VALVES.

82. The great aim of engineers in constructing a slide-valve for a locomotive is to produce a valve that will require as little power as possible to work it. Consequently,

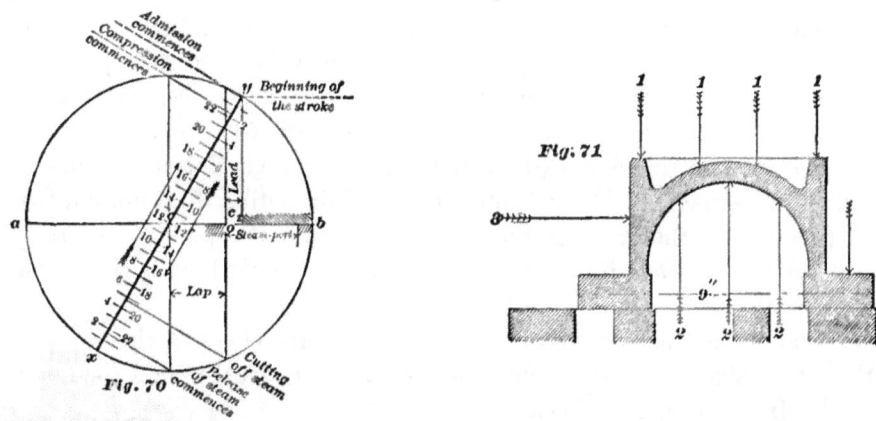

when a plain slide-valve is to be used, such as we have shown in some of the foregoing articles, the valve face is made as small as it can be made, without interfering with the duties which the valve has to perform.

Again, it is of very great importance to have the mechanism inside of a steam-chest as simple as possible; therefore, on account of the great simplicity of the plain slide-valve, it is more extensively used than any other kind. Yet it has its drawbacks, besides requiring a considerable amount of force to move it forward and backward on its seat; for instance, it is liable to cut the valve seat, wear the link, rocker, pins, and eccentrics comparatively fast, and when the valve is large, it is difficult to reverse the engine.

Let us for a moment consider the amount of force that will be required to move an ordinary plain slide-valve. The resistance which must be overcome in moving any slide-valve is simply the friction between the valve and its seat. This friction depends upon the pressure of the valve against the seat,* and this pressure is equal to the total steam pressure upon the back of the valve, minus the reaction of the steam pressure in the steam and exhaust ports.

This state of affairs we have endeavored to illustrate in Fig. 71, in which the arrows marked 1 indicate the pressure of the steam on the back of the valve, and the arrows marked 2 indicate the reaction of the steam pressure in the ports.

To present in a plain manner the subject of finding the amount of this friction, let us take the following example: The valve is 9 inches long (see Fig. 71) and 16 inches wide; the steam pressure in steam-chest is 120 pounds, it is required to find the amount of force necessary to move the valve.

The total pressure on the back of the valve is found by multiplying the area of the valve face by the steam pressure, hence we have $9 \times 16 = 144$ inches, which is the area of the valve face, and $144 \times 120 = 17,280$ pounds, which is the total pressure on the back of the valve, but it is not the pressure of the valve against its seat.

To obtain the latter, we must deduct from the total pressure on the back of the valve the reacting pressure in the ports. The reaction of the steam pressure in the ports can only be obtained approximately, because there are no data from which we can make the calculation. It will readily be seen that the reaction of the steam pressure in the ports, when the valve is in full gear, is affected by, and depends upon, the size of the exhaust nozzle, the speed of engine, the lap of valve, and some other details.

This pressure is also variable during the travel of the valve. For our purpose here, we will take the average. From observation the writer is led to believe that in ordinary locomotives the reacting pressure is equal to one-third of the pressure on the back of the valve. Grant that this is true, then the total pressure acting in the direction of the arrows 2 will be equal to $\frac{17280}{3} = 5,760$ pounds. Subtracting this quotient from the total steam pressure on the back of the valve, we obtain the pressure of the valve against its seat, hence we have $17,280 - 5,760 = 11,520$ pounds, which is the pressure of the valve against the seat.

In order that the reader may obtain a better idea of the effect of this pressure, we may say that this valve has to be moved forward and backward with a load of 11,520 pounds (nearly six tons) upon its back.

The friction between two cast-iron surfaces which are straight, smooth, and lubricated generally ranges from $\frac{1}{10}$ to $\frac{1}{14}$ of the pressure. In this case we will adopt the former proportion. Therefore, the friction between the valve and seat is found by dividing the pressure on the valve seat by 10, hence $\frac{11520}{10} = 1,152$ pounds.

This 1,152 pounds is the friction, or, we may say, the resistance which must be overcome in moving the valve, therefore a force of 1,152 pounds is required to move the valve on its seat in a direction as indicated by arrow 3, and the same amount of force is also required to move the valve in an opposite direction. To work such a valve as quickly as must be done in a locomotive will need a great amount of power; also, whatever power is used for this purpose is a loss, because the engine will have that amount less with which to perform useful work, that is, to haul the train.

It must also be plain to the reader that a valve working under such a pressure is

---

* The weight of the valve being comparatively small, it is left out of the question.

very liable to cut the valve seat, and the only way that this evil may be prevented to some extent is to use the best of metal in the cylinders, and keep the valve well oiled. We have shown that this valve requires a considerable amount of force to move it on its seat, and since this force is transmitted through the eccentrics, links, rockers, and pins, it follows that these will also wear very quickly. Again, to pull the reverse lever from one notch to another, on a locomotive having cylinders about 16 inches in diameter, is often laborious work for an engineer, and still more so in modern engines, because these generally have larger cylinders, and consequently larger valves.

From the foregoing remarks we infer that although the plain slide-valve is extremely simple, and can and must be made to distribute the steam correctly, the steam pressure on the back of this valve impairs its usefulness; and consequently there is a desire existing among engineers to procure a valve in which the evil effects of pressure on the back of the same will be removed.

### ROLLER VALVES.—BALANCED VALVES.

83. There are in use two distinct kinds of valves which require less power to work than the plain slide-valve. One kind comprises the roller valves, and to the other kind belong the balanced valves, or, as sometimes called, the equilibrium slide-valve.

Although less power is required to work the roller valve than is needed for the plain slide-valve—and therefore when a roller valve is used the wear of the valve gear will be reduced—this valve has never been, and is not now very extensively used, and, in the writer's opinion, this should not be a matter of surprise, because in the construction of these valves, no attempt has been made to remove the steam pressure on the back of the valve, which so impaired the usefulness of the plain slide-valve. But since the roller valve is sometimes adopted, the writer believes that a description of it will be interesting to the reader.

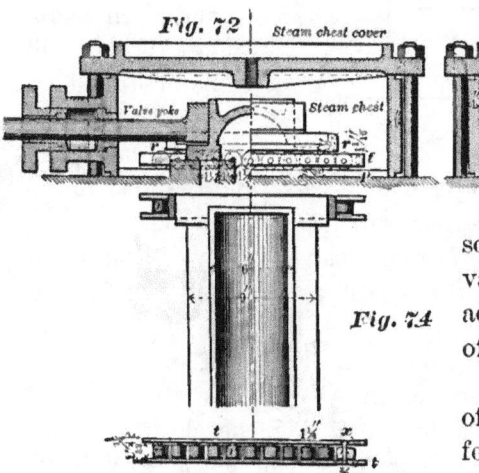

Figs. 72, 73, and 74 represent different views of this valve, and, as will be seen, the only difference between the roller valve and the plain slide-valve, is that the former is constructed in such a manner as to make room for the rollers $r\ r\ r$, which are interposed between the steam-chest seat and the valve. These rollers are prevented from touching each other by the small axles $x\ x\ x$, and around these the rollers turn. These axles, with the rollers placed upon them, are riveted to the bars $t\ t$, so that when this arrangement is completed, as shown in Fig. 74, a small carriage is obtained on which the valve is to work. To prevent wear of the steam-chest seat and valve as much as possible, steel plates $p\ p$, Figs. 72 and 73, are laid on the steam-chest seat, but not fastened to it. Two other plates *u u* are attached to the valve, and between these plates the carriages are made to roll. The most important dimensions are given in the figures, and the general arrangement is also plainly shown, so that a further description is unnecessary.

84. A balanced slide-valve is represented in Figs. 75, 76, and 77. This valve is extensively used in modern locomotives, and seems to be growing in favor. In the construction of these valves the correct principle has been followed, namely, the removal of the steam pressure on the back of the valve. This is accomplished by cutting grooves around the back of the valve, and care must be taken to cut these grooves perfectly true; in these, strips *s s s* of cast-iron are accurately fitted, so that the latter may move up and down in the grooves without any perceptible play. The strips are held up by spiral springs *t t t*, as shown. Some mechanics make these springs of hard brass wire, while others prefer to use steel wire.

The diameter of the wire ranges from $\frac{1}{16}$ to $\frac{1}{8}$ of an inch. The number of springs generally employed is shown in the figures. When the balanced valve is to be used the under side of the steam-chest cover must be accurately planed and scraped, because, against this surface, the strips must press and make a steam-tight joint when the valve is in the steam-chest, as shown in Fig. 78. This arrangement will prevent the steam from coming into contact with the greater portion of the back of the valve,

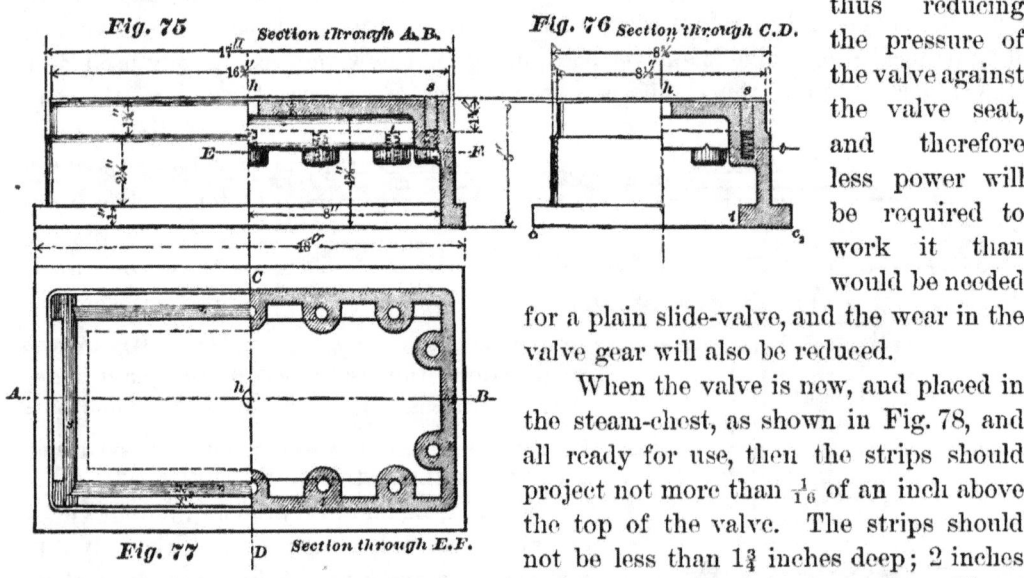

thus reducing the pressure of the valve against the valve seat, and therefore less power will be required to work it than would be needed for a plain slide-valve, and the wear in the valve gear will also be reduced.

When the valve is new, and placed in the steam-chest, as shown in Fig. 78, and all ready for use, then the strips should project not more than $\frac{1}{16}$ of an inch above the top of the valve. The strips should not be less than $1\frac{3}{4}$ inches deep; 2 inches is better; in fact, these should be made as deep as they can be made without choking the exhaust cavity of the valve; and $\frac{1}{2}$ inch is about the proper width of the strips. The manner of joining them at the corners is plainly shown in the plan of the valve, Fig. 77. For the sake of distinctness the strips have been shaded in this figure.

85. Some master mechanics object to the spiral springs, because the pockets in which these springs are placed will in time fill up with tallow, and thus prevent the springs from working freely. Therefore, in place of spiral springs for holding the strips, elliptic springs made of flat steel are used, as shown in Figs. 79 and 80, and, of

course, when these springs are to be used, the grooves must be cut deep enough to receive them, and the pockets, as shown in Figs. 75 and 76, left out.

Yet these elliptic springs are not free from objections. Some master mechanics disapprove of them because they are too strong when new, and consequently are liable to cut the steam-chest cover.

On the other hand, if these elliptic springs are made weaker, so that they will work satisfactorily in the beginning, they will not remain so long, and become too weak to

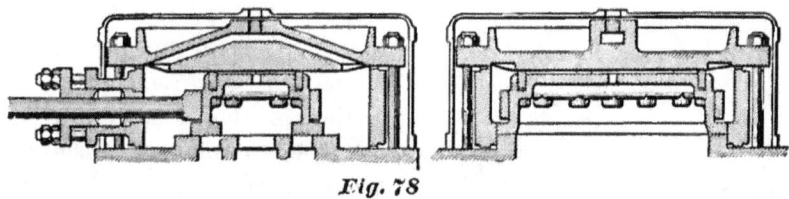
Fig. 78

hold up the strips. The result of this disagreement, among master mechanics, is that there are about as many valves wth spiral springs in use as there are with elliptical springs.

All balanced valves of this kind should have a hole $h$, about $\frac{3}{4}$ of an inch in diameter, through the top of the valve; without this hole the valve will lift off its seat. When a locomotive is running and then steam shut off, a partial vacuum will be formed in the steam-chest, causing the valve to chatter, and thus ruin its mechanism. To prevent the forming of a vacuum in the steam-chest, and consequently its evil effects, a vacuum valve must be attached to the steam-chest to admit air into the latter when steam is shut off during the time the engine is in motion. Without this vacuum valve

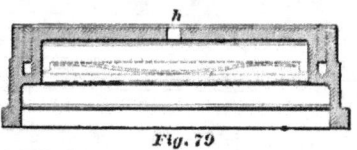
Fig. 79

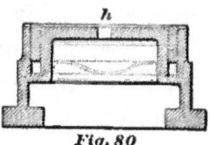
Fig. 80

no balanced slide-valve must be expected to work successfully. Indeed, it is good practice to attach a vacuum valve to all steam-chests in which a plain slide-valve is working, as this will often be the means of preventing the ashes from being drawn into the cylinder and the steam-chest.

When these balanced valves are properly made by *mechanics*, not cheap labor, good results can certainly be looked for. We find it recorded in the annual report of the "American Railway Master Mechanics' Association," for the year 1884, that a passenger locomotive with 16″ × 22″ cylinders, driving wheels 5½ feet in diameter, fitted with Morse balanced valves, ran 166,000 miles without any need of facing the valve seat.

Another good result obtained by using the balanced valves, is that the reverse lever can easily be handled, something to be appreciated by the engineer having charge of the engine. The balanced valve, which of late seems to be the favorite, is shown in the figures, and is called the "Richardson" balanced slide-valve. But by this remark the writer does not wish to be understood that this is the only good balanced valve; he simply wishes to state facts as they appear to him.

## ALLEN VALVE.

86. The Allen valve is shown in Fig. 80A. Its general design is the same as that of an ordinary D valve with the exception that it has a supplementary steam passage $PP$ cast into it.

In this valve, as in the ordinary D valve, the outside lap, or simply lap, is equal to $ag$, that is to say, it is equal to the distance by which it overlaps the outer edge $g$ of

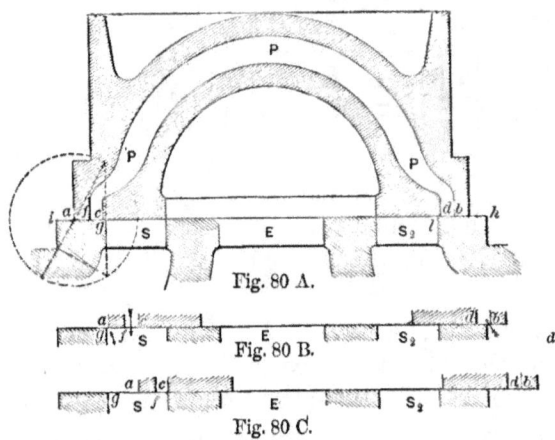

Fig. 80 A.

Fig. 80 B.

Fig. 80 C.

the steam port, and this lap is in nowise affected by the supplementary steam passage; in fact, all the definitions of lap, lead, linear advance of valve, angular advance of eccentric, etc., remarks and rules given in connection with the plain slide-valve, are not changed when the Allen valve is used.

Fig. 80c shows the valve at the end of its travel. It will here be noticed that the thickness $af$ of the metal outside of the supplementary port covers a portion of the steam port $S$, and therefore a somewhat wider steam port may be required than for an ordinary slide-valve.

To find the proper width of steam port for an Allen valve under these conditions, we should proceed as follows: First, find the width of steam port required for a free exhaust for an ordinary slide-valve, as explained in Art. 43. Now referring to Art. 59, we find that for the admission of steam we require only $\frac{8}{10}$ of this width of port; consequently, if the thickness of the wall $af$ is greater than $\frac{2}{10}$ of the width of the port, we must make the latter correspondingly wider. To illustrate:

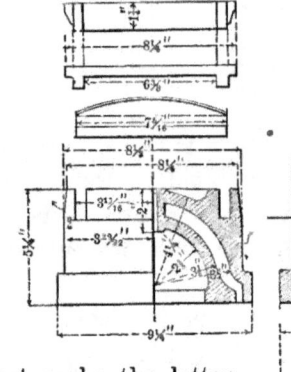

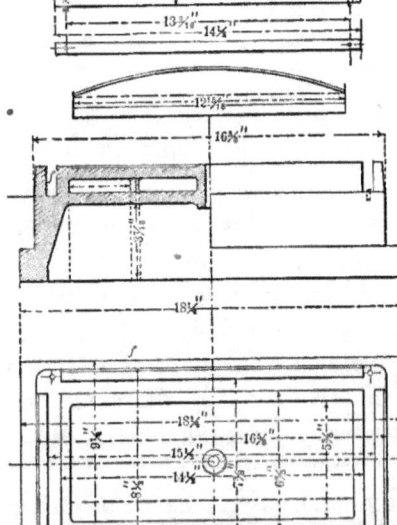

Fig. 80 D.

If we find by computation, as explained in Art. 43, that the width of the steam port for a free exhaust should be $1\frac{1}{4} = 1.25$ inches, then for the admission of steam we shall require an opening of $1.25 \times .8 = 1$ inch. If, now, the thickness of the wall $af$ is $\frac{3}{8}$ inch, then we shall require for the Allen valve a steam port $1 + \frac{3}{8} = 1\frac{3}{8}$ inches wide. This shows us that in this particular case the width of steam port for an Allen valve should be $\frac{1}{8}$ inch greater than for a plain valve,

When the correct width of steam port has been found as above, and the inner edge $e$ of the supplementary port is to be in line with the inner edge of the steam port when the valve is at the end of its travel, as shown in Fig. 80c, then the travel of the valve will be equal to twice the sum of the width of the steam port plus the amount that the edge $e$ overlaps the outer edge of port. It will be noticed that this rule differs slightly from that given in Art. 59 for finding the travel of an ordinary slide-valve. The correctness of this travel should be checked by drawing the valve seat with the valve at the end of its travel, as shown in Fig. 80c. If in this position the steam port is fully or very nearly uncovered so as to give a free exhaust, the travel as previously found is correct. Generally, when the steam ports are correctly proportioned, the travel of an Allen valve will be less than that of an ordinary valve.

The arrangement of the valve and seat should be such that when the outer edge $a$ (Fig. 80b) of the valve admits steam into the cylinder, then the edge $b$ of the supplementary port should also admit steam into the same end of cylinder; the flow of steam under these conditions is indicated by the arrows. To attain this object, it is necessary to assign to the valve seat a correct length, which is done by making a drawing of the seat and the valve in its central position, as shown in Fig. 80a, and then making $b\,h$ equal to $a\,g$, the lap.

The following advantage is claimed for this valve: In high speed locomotives with the link well hooked up, say, so as to cut off at 6 inches of the stroke, the greatest width of steam port opening with an ordinary valve is about $\frac{3}{8}$ of an inch only; with this contraction great difficulty is often experienced to keep up a full steam pressure from the beginning of the stroke of piston to the point of cut-off; in fact, diagrams taken under these conditions always show a marked fall of steam pressure during this period.

If, now, an Allen valve is used with supplementary ports $\frac{3}{8}$ inch wide, then, instead of having a steam port opening of $\frac{3}{8}$ inch in width, as will be the case when the ordinary valve is used, we shall have a port opening of double that amount, which gives a freer admission of steam, and consequently the engine, with its links hooked up, will be capable of making better time, and in some cases do the work with less fuel. But the fact that this valve is not universally adopted seems to indicate a want of confidence in its advantages; indeed, we have heard mechanics of ability express the opinion that the two currents of steam flowing into the same steam port will interfere with each other's flow, thereby losing the advantage gained by an increased port opening.

Fig. 80d shows different views and details of a balanced Allen valve. It is used in an $18 \times 24$ inch passenger engine.

TO FIND THE POINT OF CUT-OFF WHEN LENGTH OF CONNECTING-ROD IS GIVEN.

87. During one revolution of the crank the piston makes two strokes; one stroke we will call the forward stroke, and the other, the return stroke. When the length of the connecting-rod is assumed to be infinite, and the valve constructed according to the foregoing methods, having the same amount of lap at each end, then the valve will cut off equal portions of steam in the forward and return strokes.

When a connecting-rod of definite length is introduced, instead of a rod whose length is assumed to be infinite, but leaving everything else unchanged, then the portions of steam cut off in the forward stroke will not be equal to that cut off in the return stroke. To illustrate this, let us take the following example:

EXAMPLE 26.—The length of the connecting-rod is 4 feet (this short length has been adopted for the sake of clearness); stroke of piston is 24 inches; lap of valve, 1¼ inches; no lead, and travel of the valve 5¼ inches; find at what part of the forward stroke, and also at what part of the return stroke, steam will be cut off.

In order not to complicate matters, we will assume the length of the *eccentric-rod* to be infinite. This problem will be divided into two parts. 1st. It will be shown at what part of the forward, and also at what part of the return stroke, steam will be cut off when the length of the connecting-rod is assumed to be infinite.

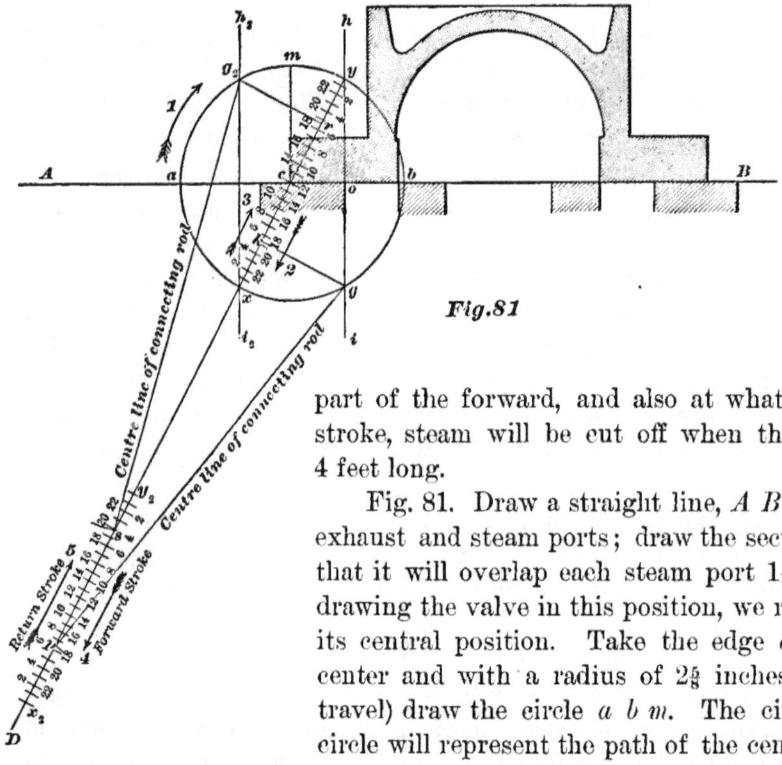

2d. It will be shown at what part of the forward, and also at what part of the return stroke, steam will be cut off when the connecting-rod is 4 feet long.

Fig. 81. Draw a straight line, $AB$; on this lay off the exhaust and steam ports; draw the section of the valve so that it will overlap each steam port 1¼ inches, as shown; drawing the valve in this position, we represent it to be in its central position. Take the edge $c$ of the valve as a center and with a radius of 2⅝ inches (equal to half the travel) draw the circle $a\ b\ m$. The circumference of this circle will represent the path of the center of the eccentric, and also that of the crank-pin (see Example 19).

The direction in which the crank-pin is to move is indicated by the arrow marked 1. Since there is to be no lead, draw through the outside edge $o$ of the steam port a straight line $i\ h$ perpendicular to $A\ B$, intersecting the circumference $a\ b\ m$ in the point $y$ and $g$. The point $y$ will be the center of the eccentric, and also the center of the crank-pin when the piston is at the beginning of its forward stroke, and the point $g$ will represent the center of the eccentric and that of the crank-pin at the moment that steam is cut off in the forward stroke. Through the points $y$ and $c$ draw the diameter $y\ x$, which will represent the stroke of the piston; divide $y\ x$ into 24 equal parts; each part will then represent one inch of the piston's stroke. The direction in which the piston moves during the forward stroke is indicated by the arrow 2, and consequently, in the return stroke the piston must move in the direction as indicated by the arrow 3. Since $y$ is the beginning of the forward stroke, we commence at $y$ in marking the inches 2, 4, 6, etc., on the right-hand side of $x\,y$; and because $x$ is the beginning of the return stroke, we commence at $x$ in marking the inches 2, 4, 6, etc., on the left-hand side of $x\,y$.

Through the point $g$ draw a straight line perpendicular to $y\,x$, intersecting the latter in the point $k$, which is found to be located $18\frac{5}{8}$ inches from the point $y$, therefore the piston will travel $18\frac{5}{8}$ inches from the beginning of its forward stroke before steam is cut off. So far, the construction is similar to that shown in Fig. 55, and explained in Example 19. We have assumed that the diameter $y\,x$ represents the stroke of the piston, the point $y$ the beginning of the forward stroke, and the point $x$ the beginning of the return stroke. But in these constructions, the center of the crank-pin and the center of eccentric are always assumed to be represented by the same point, therefore the point $x$ will also represent the position of the center of eccentric, when the piston is at the beginning of the return stroke. Since the amount of lap is the same at either end of the valve, the center of eccentric must travel from the beginning $x$ of the return stroke through an arc equal to the arc $y\,g$ in order to reach the position at which the steam will be cut off in this stroke; therefore the arc $x\,g_2$ must be made equal to the arc $y\,g$. The best way to accomplish this is to draw a line $i_2\,h_2$ through $x$, and perpendicular to $A\,B$, intersecting the circumference $a\,b\,m$ in the point $g_2$, then the arc $x\,g_2$ will be equal to the arc $y\,g$, and the point $g_2$ will be the position of the center of eccentric at which steam will be cut off in the return stroke.

Through the point $g_2$ draw a straight line $g_2\,r$ perpendicular to $y\,x$, cutting the latter in the point $r$. The distance from $x$ to $r$ will represent the portion of the stroke during which steam will be admitted into the cylinder, and since, according to our construction, the point $r$ is situated $18\frac{5}{8}$ inches from $x$, it follows that the piston will reach the point of cut-off when it has traveled $18\frac{5}{8}$ inches from the beginning of the return stroke. Here, then, we see that when the length of the connecting-rod is assumed to be infinite, steam will be admitted into the cylinder during equal portions of the two strokes, or, in other words, the distance from the beginning of the forward stroke to the point of cut-off will be equal to that in the return stroke. Now let us consider at what part of the stroke steam will be cut off when the connecting-rod is 4 feet long.

If the valve is drawn full size in the construction, then the diameter $y\,x$ will be $5\frac{1}{4}$ inches long; but we have assumed that this diameter also represents the length of the stroke of piston, which is 2 feet; therefore, when we lay off the length of the connecting-rod, we must adopt the diameter $y\,x$ as a scale 2 feet long, consequently one-half of this diameter (which is equal to the radius of the circle $a\,b\,m$) will represent one foot, and the length of the connecting-rod, which is 4 feet long, will be equal to four times the radius of the circle $a\,b\,m$. Prolong the line $y\,x$ to any length, say, to $D$, then the path of the cross-head pin will lie in the line $y\,D$, or, in other words, the center of cross-head pin will always be found somewhere in the line $y\,D$. From the point $y$ as a center, and with a radius equal to the length of the connecting-rod (equal to four times the radius of the circle $a\,b\,m$), describe an arc cutting the line $y\,D$ in the point $y_2$; this point will represent the position of the center of the cross-head pin when the piston is at the beginning of its forward stroke. From the point $x$ as a center, and with a radius equal to the length of the connecting-rod, describe an arc cutting the line $y\,D$ in the point $x_2$, and this point will represent the center of the cross-head pin when the piston is at the end of the forward stroke or the beginning of the return stroke.

The distance between the points $y_2$ and $x_2$ will represent the length of stroke, and will be equal to the diameter $y\,x$. Divide the distance between $y_2$ and $x_2$ into twenty-four equal parts and number them as shown. The arrow marked 4 indicates the direction in which the piston moves during the forward stroke, and arrow 5 indicates the direction of the motion of the piston during the return stroke. From the point $g$ in the circumference $a\,b\,m$ as a center, and with a radius equal to the length of the connecting-rod, describe an arc cutting the line $y\,D$ in the point $p$; this point $p$ will be the center of the cross-head pin, when steam is cut off in the forward stroke of the piston, and, as will be seen in the figure, the point $p$ is situated midway between the divisions marked 17 and 18, and therefore indicates that steam will be cut off when the piston has traveled $17\frac{1}{2}$ inches from the beginning of the forward stroke $y_2$.

From the point $g_2$ (in the circumference $a\,b\,m$) as a center, and with a radius equal to the length of the connecting-rod, describe an arc cutting the line $y\,D$ in the point $s$; this point $s$ will be the position of the center of the cross-head pin when steam is cut off in the return stroke, and, as will be seen in the figure, it is situated $19\frac{3}{4}$ inches from the beginning of the return stroke $x_2$, and therefore indicates that steam will be cut off in the return stroke when the piston has traveled $19\frac{3}{4}$ inches from $x_2$. Here, then, we see that when the connecting-rod is 4 feet long, steam will be cut off in the forward stroke when the piston has traveled $17\frac{1}{2}$ inches, and in the return stroke steam will be cut off when the piston has traveled $19\frac{3}{4}$ inches, making a difference of $2\frac{1}{4}$ inches between the two points of cut-off. This difference is caused by the angularity of the connecting-rod, or, in other words, by the angle formed between the center line of the connecting-rod and the line $y\,D$. This angle can be reduced by making the connecting-rod longer, but not changing the length of the stroke; with this change the difference in position between the points of cut-off in the forward and return strokes will be decreased. But in all engines in which the valve receives its motion direct from the eccentric, with an equal amount of lap and lead at each end of the valve, there will always be a difference in the position of the points of cut-off, even if the connecting-rod is comparatively long.

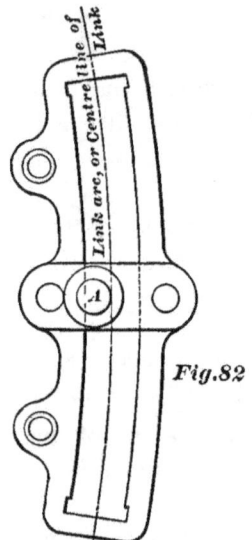

Fig. 82

Should it be desirable to make the valve in these engines to cut off equal portions of steam in the return and forward strokes, then the only way that this can be accomplished is by giving the valve more lap or lead at one end than at the other. When a link is interposed between the valve and the eccentric as shown in the locomotive valve gear, Fig. 29, then the valve can be made to cut off equal portions of steam in the forward and return strokes, without making a difference in the lap or lead of the valve. Indeed, in locomotives the amount of lap at each end of the valve is always equal, and the lead for full stroke at each end of the valve is also equal.

88. When the valve, or the valve gear, is constructed so as to make the valve cut off equal portions of steam in the forward and return strokes, the cut-off is said to be

equalized. To equalize the cut-off in a locomotive, the saddle-pin $A$ is moved out of the center of the link, as shown in Fig. 82, that is, the center of the saddle-pin is moved a certain distance towards the center from which the link has been drawn; and besides this, the lifting-shaft arms must be made of the proper length, and the lifting shaft placed in the correct position. To determine how much the saddle-pin must be moved out of center, and what length the lifting-shaft arms should be made, and where to place the lifting shaft so that the cut-off will be equalized, we shall show later.

In a locomotive it is of great importance to equalize the cut-off, as this will cause the engine to work smoother and better than with a cut-off not equalized. Again, an equalized cut-off will produce an exhaust at regular and equal intervals, an attainment which is in itself of the greatest importance, because when an engine is running the sound of the exhaust indicates to the engineer the working conditions of such parts of mechanism as are out of sight; hence the engineer, besides keeping a strict look-out for the parts of mechanism which are in sight, and performing other duties imposed upon him, constantly listens to the exhaust, and as long as this beats at regular and equal intervals he knows that the valve and valve gear are in good working order, or, so to speak, are in a healthy condition; but as soon as the exhaust commences to beat at irregular or unequal intervals, the engineer accepts this fact as a warning that something is seriously wrong, and that an immediate examination of his engine is absolutely necessary.

89. In the foregoing construction we have assumed that the eccentric-rod is of an infinite length. Such an assumption will in no wise interfere with the positions of the points $y$ and $x$, which indicate the position of the center of eccentric when the piston is at the beginning of the forward and return strokes, and if these points are located with absolute exactness, according to foregoing instructions, the positions of these points will be absolutely correct. But these remarks do not apply to the points $g$ and $g_2$, which indicate the positions of the center of eccentric at the moment that the steam is cut off in the forward and return strokes.

To find the correct positions of the points $g$ and $g_2$, we should take into consideration the length of the eccentric-rod, which, on account of its angularity during the travel of the valve, will somewhat affect the positions of the points $g$ and $g_2$, and consequently the points of cut-off will also be affected. Yet the change in the positions of the points $g$ and $g_2$ which will occur when the length of the eccentric-rod is taken into consideration, will be so slight, that for ordinary engines it will hardly be appreciable, and therefore may be neglected. But, in equalizing the cut-off in locomotives, the length of the eccentric-rod is taken into account, as will be seen later.

# CHAPTER III.

## VALVE GEAR.—CONSTRUCTION OF LINKS.

### ROCKERS.

90. Figs. 83 and 84 represent a rocker such as is used in American locomotives. The general practice in locomotive construction is to make the rockers of wrought-iron, although occasionally we find them made of cast-iron. The arms and the shaft are forged in one piece. The holes in the end of the arms should be tapered, the taper being equal to $\frac{1}{8}$ of an inch in 12 inches; that is, in a hole 12 inches deep its diameter at one end should be $\frac{1}{8}$ of an inch larger than the diameter at the other end. Some makers adopt a greater taper, sometimes as great as $\frac{3}{4}$ of an inch in 12 inches. The pins are made to fit these holes very accurately, so that they must be driven home with a hammer. The pins are made of wrought-iron, and are case-hardened.

The reason for making the holes in the rocker-arms tapered, is that the pins can be driven out with greater ease, and without injuring or upsetting their ends. On the other hand, if these holes have no taper, and the pins are fitted into the rockers as firmly as is required in a locomotive, then the pins will need so much hammering in driving them into or out of the holes as to produce injurious result.

The design of the locomotive generally limits the length of the rocker-shaft between the arms, but when there is room enough the length of the rocker-shaft should be at least 12 inches for large locomotives, and not less than 9 inches for smaller engines. The diameter of the shaft must be such that it will have sufficient strength to resist the severest stress to which the rocker may be subjected without springing or twisting the shaft to any appreciable extent.

The greatest stress to which a rocker can be subjected will occur when an engine is to be started after it has been allowed to stand still for some time, for the following reasons:

1st. When an engine is to be started after standing still for some time, the valve seat will be dry, and it will not be lubricated until the engine has made a few turns, consequently a greater force will be required to move the valve when the engine is commencing to move than after it has been in motion for some time.

2d. Besides the force necessary to overcome the friction, an additional force will be required to overcome the adhesion caused by the oil that remained between the valve and its seat when the engine was stopped.

3d. In starting an engine the valve may occupy a position as shown in Fig. 84, that is, the valve covering both steam ports. When this happens the friction between the valve and its seat will not be diminished by any reaction of steam pressure in the exhaust or steam ports; therefore the friction between the valve and its seat will be proportional to the total steam pressure upon the back of the valve. Here, then, we see that, in starting an engine, considerably more power will be required to work the valve than will be necessary to work the same valve after the engine has been in motion for some time. Again, we must not neglect the force required to overcome the friction between the packing in the stuffing-box and the valve-stem, which at times may be considerable, caused by carelessly tightening the stuffing-box gland. Thus we can understand what forces a rocker has to overcome; and it must be made strong enough to do it. But to calculate the exact amount of force necessary to move a slide-valve under the foregoing conditions is impossible; we can only adopt an empirical rule, the correctness of which is based upon close observation in actual practice. The writer believes that, by making a rocker strong enough to overcome $\frac{1}{3}$ of the total steam pressure on the back of the valve, good results will be obtained. Thus, for instance:

EXAMPLE 27.—The length of the slide-valve is 9 inches, its breadth 16 inches, and the steam pressure in the steam-chest is 120 pounds per square inch; what will be the greatest force that the rocker must be capable of overcoming?

The total steam pressure upon the back of the valve is obtained by multiplying the area of the valve face by the steam pressure per square inch; hence we have $9'' \times 16'' \times 120 = 17,280$ pounds, which is the total pressure upon the back of the valve, and $\frac{1}{3}$ of this pressure will be the force that the rocker must be capable of overcoming without twisting or springing the shaft; therefore $\frac{17280}{3} = 5,760$ pounds will

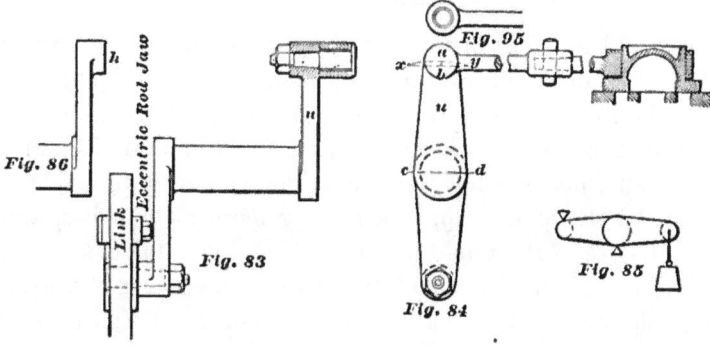

be the greatest stress to which the rocker can be subjected, or, in other words, the greatest force that it must overcome. Now, when we know this force we can easily determine by computation the suitable diameter of the rocker-shaft.

91. We find in books relating to the strength of material, that in the instance of a shaft which is firmly fixed at one end, having a lever attached to its other end with a force applied to the end of the lever, its diameter, which will be sufficiently large to resist twisting, is determined by multiplying the length of the lever in inches by the force in pounds applied to the end of the lever, then dividing this product by a constant quantity which has been previously obtained by actual experiment, and extracting the cube root of the quotient; the result will be the diameter of the shaft in inches.

This rule is used for determining the diameter of a rocker-shaft, and when we apply it we must assume the upper rocker-shaft arm *u*, Figs. 83 and 84, to be the lever attached to the shaft, its length being the distance between the center of shaft and the center of pin; the constant quantity (before alluded to) may be taken at 1,200. Hence, to find the diameter of a rocker-shaft made of wrought-iron, we have the following:

Rule 14.—Multiply the length of the upper rocker-arm in inches by $\frac{1}{3}$ of the total steam pressure upon the back of the valve; divide this product by 1,200, and the cube root of the quotient will be the diameter of the shaft in inches; or putting this rule in the shape of a formula, we have

$$\text{Diameter of shaft} = \sqrt[3]{\frac{\text{Length of rocker-arm in inches} \times \frac{1}{3} \text{ steam pressure on back of valve.}}{1200}}$$

If the rocker-shaft is to be made of cast-iron, then the same rule is applicable, with this exception, instead of using the constant quantity 1,200, we must use the constant 1,000.

Example 28.—Find the diameter of a wrought-iron rocker-shaft which has to move a slide-valve 9 inches long and 16 inches wide; the steam pressure in the steam-chest is 120 pounds per square inch, and the length of the upper rocker-arm 10 inches.

We have seen in Example 27 that $\frac{1}{3}$ of the total steam pressure on the back of the valve 9 inches long and 16 inches wide is 5,760 pounds. This 5,760 pounds is the force applied to the end of the upper rocker-arm; therefore, according to Rule 14, we have,

$$\frac{10'' \times 5760 \text{ pounds}}{1200} = 48,$$

and the cube root of 48 is 3.63, consequently the shaft must be $3\frac{5}{8}$ (nearly) inches in diameter. To find the cube root in an easy manner of any quantity, we simply refer to a table of cube roots, which will be found in any good engineer's pocket-book.

92. The length of the upper rocker-arm *u*, Figs. 83 and 84, is limited in either direction; that is, it must not be made too long or too short. For a slide-valve having 5 inches travel, the length of the upper arm is generally 10 inches, and for valves with less travel, the length of the upper arm can be, and should be, somewhat reduced. The reason for this is: If the length of the upper rocker-arm for a valve having 5 inches travel is made much longer than 10 inches, then the shaft will be subjected to a greater twisting stress, and consequently the diameter of the shaft must be increased, which is not always desirable. The reason why the diameter of the shaft should be made larger when the upper rocker-arm is made longer can easily be seen by examining Rule 14.

Again, this arm should not be made much shorter than 10 inches for a valve with 5 inches travel, on account of the custom that is followed by the majority of locomotive-builders and master-mechanics of keying the valve-rod to the valve-stem, as shown in Fig. 84, thus making a rigid connection. Now notice, in Fig. 84, that the path of the valve-rod pin is an arc, as *x y*, and to this arc the end of the valve-rod must accommodate itself; and since the valve-stem must travel in a straight line, and since there is not a flexible joint between the valve rod and stem, it follows that the valve-rod must be sprung out of a straight line during the travel of the valve, and the amount that the latter is sprung out of a straight line is equal to the line $a\,b$, Fig. 84. Now, if the upper rocker-arm is made much shorter than 10 inches, leaving the travel of the valve the same as before, then the line $a\,b$ will be longer, and consequently the amount that the valve-rod must be sprung out of a straight line during the travel of the valve will also be greater than before, producing injurious results.

The width of the rocker-arms on the line $c\,d$, passing through the center of the shaft, as shown in Fig. 84, is not made the same by the different locomotive-builders or master-mechanics, yet the following arbitrary rule will give a width agreeing very closely with the present practice:

RULE 15.—To the diameter of the rocker-shaft add one-half of the same diameter, and from this sum subtract $\frac{1}{8}$ of an inch. Or, in the shape of a formula we have:

Diameter of shaft $+ \frac{1}{2}$ of diameter of shaft $- \frac{1}{8}$ of an inch $=$ width $c\,d$ of rocker-arm.

EXAMPLE 29.—Diameter of the rocker-shaft is $3\frac{5}{8}$ inches; what must be the width of the rocker-arm at $c\,d$?

$$3\tfrac{5}{8}'' + 1\tfrac{13}{16}'' - \tfrac{1}{8}'' = 5\tfrac{5}{16}'', \text{ say } 5\tfrac{3}{8}''.$$

When the width $c\,d$ of the rocker-arm is known, its thickness can be easily ascertained in the following manner: Assume that the arm is a lever firmly fixed at one end and loaded at the other end, as shown in Fig. 85. Then, according to rules found in books relating to the strength of material, we find that the load which a beam or lever, firmly fixed at one end and loaded at the other, can support with safety is determined by multiplying the square of the width $c\,d$ by the thickness, and by a constant quantity, previously found by experiment (this quantity is generally called the "coefficient"), and dividing this product by the length of the beam or lever. In applying this rule to the rocker we shall adopt 1,200 for the constant quantity or coefficient, and the dimensions of the rocker will be taken in inches; therefore we have,

$$\frac{\text{Square of the width } c\,d \times \text{thickness} \times 1200}{\text{Length in inches.}} = \text{load.}$$

Now, if we know the load, the width at $c\,d$, and the length of the rocker-arm, but not its thickness, we can establish a rule from the foregoing formula which will enable us to find the thickness of the rocker-arm.

RULE 16.—Multiply the load in pounds by the length of the rocker-arm in inches, and divide this product by the square of the width in inches into 1,200; the quotient will be the thickness of the arm. Or, in the shape of a formula we have,

$$\frac{\text{Load} \times \text{length in inches}}{\text{Square of the width } c\,d \text{ in inches} \times 1200} = \text{thickness in inches.}$$

EXAMPLE 30.—What must be the thickness of the upper rocker-arm, its width $c\,d$ being $5\frac{1}{2}$ inches; length, 10 inches; and the valve which the rocker has to move is $9'' \times 16''$; the steam pressure in the steam-chest is 120 pounds?

The total load which a rocker has to support is equal to the greatest stress to which it can be subjected, and, as we have seen before, the latter is equal to $\frac{1}{8}$ of the total steam pressure upon the back of the valve.

Now, according to Example 27, we know that ⅓ of the total steam pressure upon the back of the valve 9″ × 16″ and with a pressure of 120 pounds per square inch is equal to 5,760 pounds, which must now be considered as the load; consequently we have, according to Rule 16,

$$\text{Thickness} = \frac{5760 \times 10''}{(\text{square of } 5\tfrac{1}{2}) \times 1200} = 1.58 \text{ or } 1\tfrac{9}{16}'' \text{ inch nearly,}$$

which is the thickness of the rocker-arm without the hub.

93. In a great many locomotives we find the hub $h$ on the upper rocker-arm placed upon the outside of the latter, as shown in Fig. 86. This should be avoided as much as possible, because when the hub is so placed the arm will not only have to resist a transverse stress, but also an increased twisting stress, and therefore the arm and shaft must be made correspondingly strong. If the hub is placed upon the inside of the rocker-arm, as shown in Fig. 83, then the twisting stress will be reduced, but yet not altogether removed. To allow for this extra twisting stress which still remains, we have adopted in the foregoing rules a coefficient of 1,200. If the rocker-arm had no twisting stress to resist,

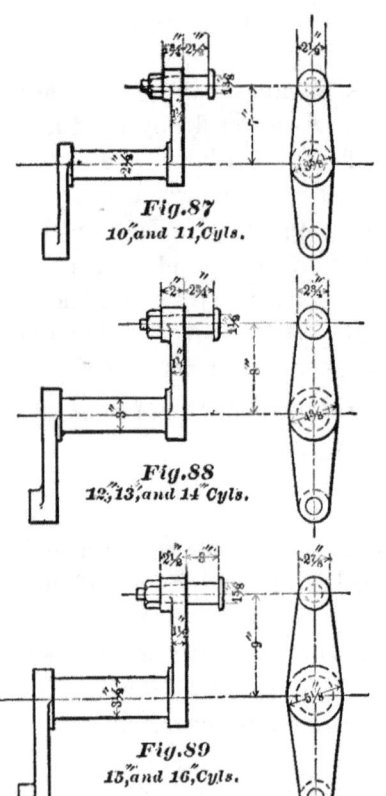
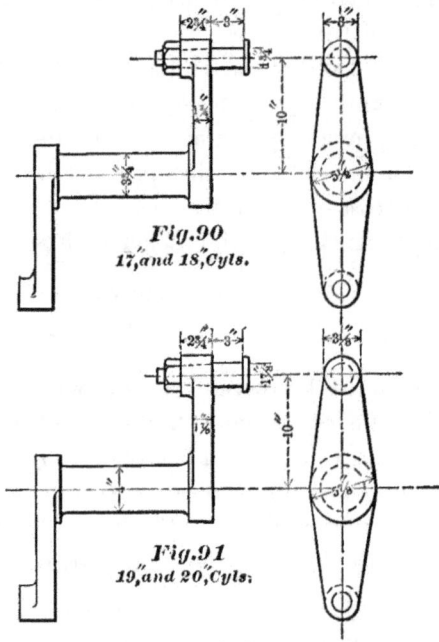

but simply a transverse stress, then the coefficient of 1,200 could have been increased to 1,800; the result of this would have been a thinner rocker-arm.

On the lower rocker-arm we are generally compelled to place the hub on the outside of the arm, because room is required to clear the eccentric-rod jaw and pin, as shown in Fig. 83. Figs. 87, 88, 89, 90, and 91 show the wrought-iron rockers for the different sizes of locomotives. The diameters of the shafts and dimensions of rocker-arms have been obtained according to the foregoing rules, and are suitable for cylinders whose ports are proportioned for a piston speed of 600 feet per minute, the valves having the ordinary amount of lap, with a steam pressure 120 pounds per square inch in the steam-chest. Comparing the dimensions given in these illustrations with the dimensions of rockers in actual use in modern locomotives, it will be seen that the former agree very closely with the latter. Of course, the length of arms given in the illustrations may have to be changed to suit some particular design of engine, and when the change is very great, then the dimensions of arms and shaft should be determined according to the foregoing rules.

Again, to be very exact, we should have given a differently proportioned rocker for each size of cylinder, but this would cause a complication of patterns, which managers of private establishments and master-mechanics on railroads seek to avoid; hence one size of rocker is generally used for two or three different sizes of cylinders—that is, cylinders varying in diameter.

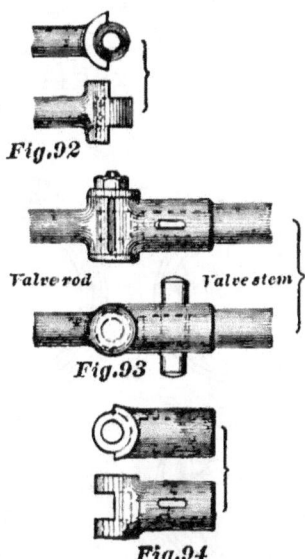

Now, as simple as a rocker may appear to an ordinary observer, it requires care to proportion it. If the rocker is made too weak, it may still be strong enough to move the valve, yet it will spring sufficiently to derange the whole valve motion. Indeed, we have met with locomotives which, on leaving the round-house, had such an irregular exhaust that the engineers stopped the engines and examined the valve motions, but found that the cause of all the trouble was the springing of the rocker-shaft—a trouble which would disappear after the valve face and seat became lubricated by running the engines a short distance.

94. When the valve-rod is comparatively very short, a knuckle-joint must be introduced between valve rod and stem, as illustrated in Figs. 92, 93, and 94, and which needs no further explanation.

In a few cases the valve-rod end which connects to the rocker-pin is provided with brasses and a key, so as to take up the wear. But the almost universal practice in the construction of American locomotives is to drive a bush into the eye of the valve-rod, as shown in Fig. 95 (page 75). This bush is made of wrought-iron, generally $\frac{3}{16}$ of an inch thick for large locomotives and $\frac{1}{8}$ of an inch for smaller engines. The bush is bored and turned, and then case-hardened, and finally forced into the eye of the valve-rod by an hydraulic press. Valve-rods with case-hardened bushes will need but very little repair, as the wear is comparatively slow, and when the wear of the bush becomes too great, it can be easily removed and replaced by a new one with very little expense.

### ECCENTRICS AND STRAPS.

95. In the following illustration we have represented various eccentrics and their straps, with all the important dimensions marked upon them. These have been selected from a number of designs adopted by some of our best locomotive builders. Figs.

143 and 144 represent two views of an eccentric, Figs. 145 and 146 represent two views of its strap, and Fig. 147 a section of the same. Such eccentrics and straps are used on some of our large locomotives, that is, consolidation engines having cylinders 20″ in diameter and 24″ stroke. Figs. 152 and 153 represent an eccentric, and Figs. 154, 155, 156 represent the strap for the same. Eccentrics and straps of this size are used on our smallest locomotives, namely, eight-wheeled passenger engines, with cylinders 10″ in diameter and 18″ stroke. When we say "smallest locomotives" we do not include locomotives for mining purposes, or very light narrow-gauge locomotives.

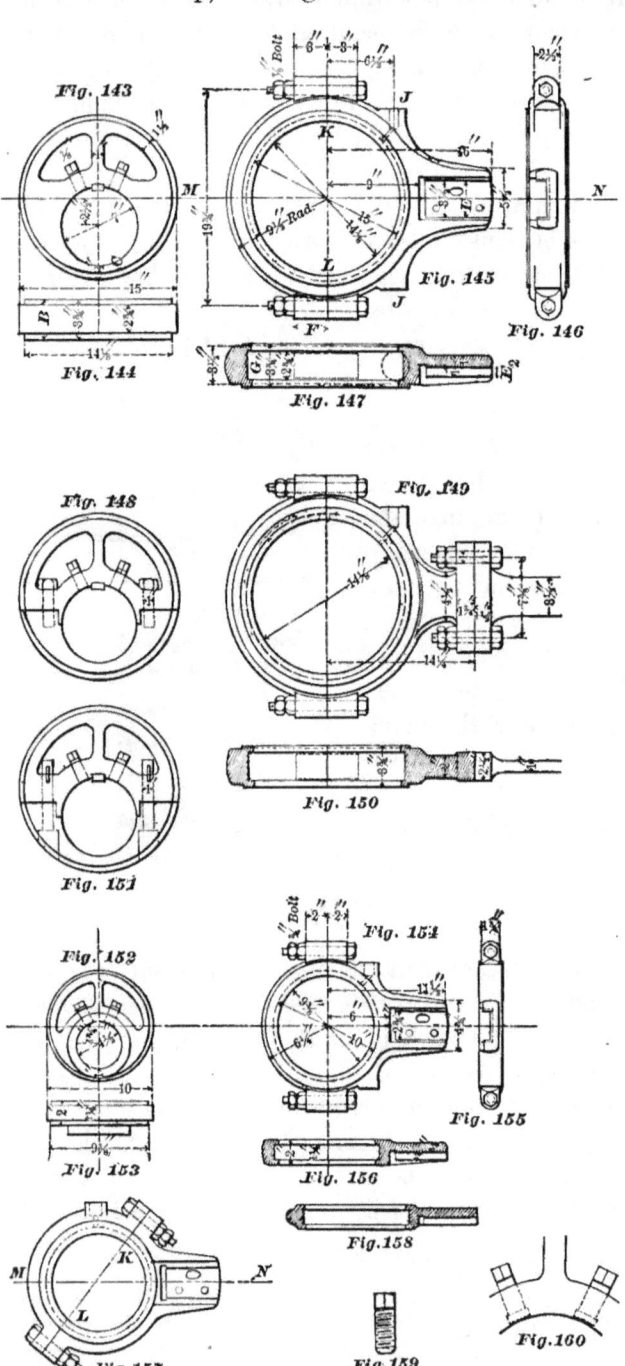

The duty of an eccentric and its strap is to move the slide-valve forward and backward; and when, a few years ago, pumps were used in locomotive engines, then occasionally an eccentric was employed to work the pump. The action of an eccentric, as we have stated in Art. 55, is precisely the same as that of a crank. No peculiar movement must be expected by the use of an eccentric; the slide-valve will perform its functions as correctly when it receives its movement from a crank as when it receives its movement from an eccentric; the only reason why an eccentric is adopted is, that the use of the crank is impracticable. In American locomotives the eccentrics and straps are generally made of cast-iron; indeed, we may say they are always made of cast-iron, as we seldom find a locomotive whose eccentrics and straps are made of brass or of wrought-iron. To prevent the strap from slipping sideways off the eccentric, a recess marked $G$,

Fig. 147, is turned in the strap, which fits a corresponding projection turned on the eccentric.

Some builders make the joint $K L$, Fig. 145, perpendicular to the center line $M N$ of the eccentric-rod; others make this joint not at right angles to the center line $M N$, as shown in Fig. 157. The advantage claimed for the latter is that the stress will be less on the nuts of the bolts which hold the two parts of the strap together. The advantage claimed for the former design is that no right- and left-hand pattern for the strap will be required. The oil-cup is screwed in one of the hubs $J$, Fig. 145; the reason why two hubs are cast on the strap is, as before, to avoid a right- and left-hand pattern.

The eccentric-rod fits into the recess marked $E E_2$, Figs. 145 and 147, and is secured to the strap by three bolts. It will be noticed in Fig. 145 that the hole for one bolt is oblong; this will allow the rod to be moved outward or inward in the recess, as may be required, and then fastened. After the correct position of the rod in the recess has been found, then the other two holes are drilled, reamed, and the bolts driven in tight, so that the distance from the center of the strap to the extreme end of the rod cannot be changed. Some master-mechanics object to this arrangement, and prefer to let the eccentric-rod butt against the eccentric-strap, as shown in Fig. 149. In this case, the distance between the center of the strap and the extreme end of the rod can be changed by placing some thin copper strips between the strap and the rod.

The eccentric is generally cast in one piece, but sometimes, for the sake of convenience in repairing, it is made in two parts, as shown in Figs. 148 and 151. For holding the two parts of the eccentric firmly together, some master-mechanics use studs and nuts, as shown in Fig. 148; others use studs with split keys or cotters, as shown in Fig. 151. The writer believes that the latter method is the best, since for the want of room in the design shown in Fig. 148 it is often extremely difficult to gain access with a wrench to the nuts.

During the time of setting the valve gear the eccentrics are held in position by the set-screws, but afterwards, in the majority of locomotives, they are keyed to the axle. Of course, in a small number of locomotives, as may be inferred from the foregoing remark, the eccentrics are not keyed to the axle, and are held in position by the set screws only. The set-screws are made of steel, cupped as shown in Fig. 159, and then hardened. The key-way in the eccentric is cut before the latter is placed on the axle, but the key-way in the axle is cut after the correct position of the eccentric has been found. To cut this key-way—which must be done by hand—is very troublesome; hence some master-mechanics cut no key-ways in the axle, but use two keys, as shown in Fig. 160. In this case each key has teeth cut lengthways on one of its sides, as shown, so that when the keys are driven home the teeth will grip the axle.

The set-screws in this case are used as an extra security against the slipping of the keys out of position.

The form of the section of the strap can be made as shown in Figs. 150 and 156, or as represented in Fig. 158. By adopting the form shown in the latter figure, the strap can be made lighter, and still have the same strength as that shown in Fig. 156, but the outside diameter of the strap in Fig. 158 will necessarily be somewhat larger than that in Fig. 156.

96. The diameter of the eccentric, and also that of the strap, should be made as

small as possible, since by so doing not only material will be saved, but also the work expended in friction will be reduced; and lastly, less space will be required for the eccentric to work in. This last fact is of great importance, because in a great number of locomotives the space required for the revolving of the eccentrics limits the length of the fire-box; and since the available space for the fire-box is often barely sufficient, it follows that space should not be wasted by making the eccentrics larger than necessary. Thus, for instance, in eight-wheeled passenger engines the main driving-axle on

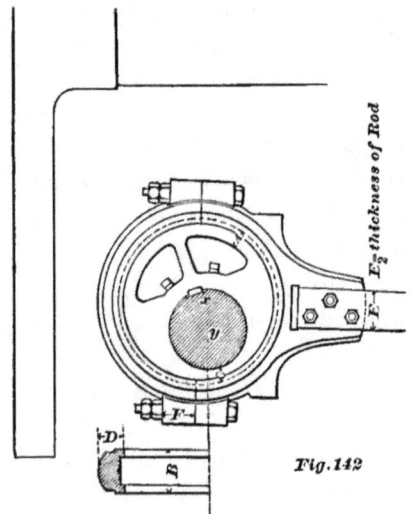

Fig. 142

which the eccentrics are fastened is placed comparatively close to the front end of the fire-box, as shown in Fig. 142, and this distance between the main axle and the fire-box is determined by the space required for the working of the eccentrics. Now, whatever amount the radius of the eccentric is made too large, that same amount must be taken from the length of the fire-box, thus, to some extent, reducing the steaming capacity of the engine.

Here, then, we see the necessity of making the diameter of the eccentric and that of its strap as small as possible. The distance between the center of the main axle and that of the fire-box is generally 14 to $14\frac{1}{2}$ inches in large locomotives, and from 10 to $10\frac{1}{2}$ inches in the smaller locomotives. But here, then, the question arises, How can the correct diameter of the eccentric be determined? In order to find the diameter of an eccentric, we must know its eccentricity; that is, the distance between the center $y$ of the axle and the center $x$ of the eccentric, Fig. 142. We must also know the diameter of the axle on which the eccentric is fastened, and the thickness of the metal at $C$. When these items are known, we add together the distance between the centers $x$ and $y$, half the diameter of the axle, and the thickness of the metal at $C$, and multiply this sum by 2. Thus, for instance, in Fig. 143 (Art. 95) we see that the distance between the center of axle and the center of eccentric—that is, the eccentricity—is $2\frac{1}{2}$ inches, half the diameter of the axle is $3\frac{1}{2}$ inches, and the thickness of metal at $C$ is $1\frac{1}{2}$ inches. Adding these dimensions together, we have $2\frac{1}{2} + 3\frac{1}{2} + 1\frac{1}{2} = 7\frac{1}{2}$, and $7\frac{1}{2} \times 2 = 15$ inches, which is the diameter of the eccentric. From this we see that there are three items whose dimensions determine the diameter of the eccentric, namely, its eccentricity, the thickness of metal at $C$, and the diam-

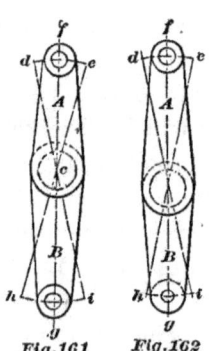

Fig. 161   Fig. 162

eter of the axle. Here, then, another question arises: How can we find the dimensions of these three items? The diameter of the axle is determined by rules to be explained hereafter; hence there remain only the two former items, whose dimensions will claim our consideration.

97. In Art. 55 we have stated that the throw of an eccentric is equal to twice its eccentricity, hence the throw of the eccentric shown in Fig. 143 will be 5 inches; we have also stated that the throw is equal to the travel of the valve for engines in which

no rocker is interposed. We will now add to this statement that, when a rocker is used whose arms are of equal lengths, then the throw of an eccentric will still be equal to the travel of the valve; on the other hand, if a rocker is used whose arms are not of equal lengths, then the throw will not be equal to the travel of the valve. Consequently, when the travel of the valve is given for an engine that has no rocker, or when the travel of a valve is given for an engine in which a rocker is employed whose arms are of equal length, in either case we must make the eccentricity of the eccentric equal to one-half of the travel of the valve; we cannot make it less or more; hence, in these two cases the shortest distance between the centers $x$ and $y$, Fig. 142, will be equal to half the travel of the valve.

When a rocker is used whose arms are not of equal lengths, then the eccentricity of the eccentric will be either more or less than half the travel of the valve.

Thus for instance:

EXAMPLE 31.—Fig. 161. If the upper arm $A$ of the rocker is 10 inches, and the lower arm $B$ is 12 inches long, and the travel of the valve 5 inches, what will be the eccentricity of the eccentric?

Let the line $fg$ represent the position of the center of the rocker when the valve stands midway of its travel; from the center $c$, and with a radius of 10 inches, describe the arc $d\,e$; on this arc lay off a point $d$ $2\frac{1}{2}$ inches (one-half of the travel) from the center line $fg$, not measured on the arc, but on a straight line perpendicular to $fg$; in a similar manner lay off the point $e$ $2\frac{1}{2}$ inches from $fg$; then the point $d$ will represent the position of the center of the rocker-pin when the valve stands at one end of its travel, and the point $e$ will represent the position of the center of the rocker-pin when the valve stands at the other end of its travel. From the point $c$ as a center, and with a radius of 12 inches, describe the arc $h\,i$; through the point $d$ and the center $c$ draw a straight line intersecting the arc $h\,i$ in the point $i$; also through the point $e$ and the center $c$ draw another straight line intersecting the arc $h\,i$ in the point $h$. The distance between the points $h$ and $i$ will be equal to the throw of the eccentric, and half of this distance will be the eccentricity of the eccentric. If this drawing is accurately made it will be found that the throw is 6 inches, hence, in this case, 3 inches will be the distance between the centers $x$ and $y$ in Fig. 142, and is $\frac{1}{2}$ inch more than half the travel of the valve.

EXAMPLE 32.—But now suppose the upper arm $A$ of the rocker is 12 inches long, and the length of the lower arm $B$, 10 inches, and the travel of the valve 5 inches as before, then what will be the eccentricity of the eccentric?

Fig. 162. From the center $c$, and with a radius of 12 inches, describe arc $d\,e$; on this arc lay off as before points $d$ and $e$, each point being placed $2\frac{1}{2}$ inches from the center line $fg$; then the distance between these two points will be equal to the travel of the valve. From $c$ as a center, and with a radius of 10 inches, describe the arc $h\,i$; through the point $d$ and the center $c$ draw a straight line intersecting the arc $h\,i$ in the point $i$, also through the point $e$ and the center $c$ draw a straight line intersecting the arc $h\,i$ in the point $h$; the distance between the points $h$ and $i$ will be equal to the throw of the eccentric, and half of this distance will be the eccentricity of the eccentric. If this drawing is correctly made, it will be found that the distance between the points $d$ and $i$—that is, the throw of the eccentric—is 4.16 inches, consequently the eccentricity of the eccentric will be 2.08 inches, say 2 inches, ½ of an inch less than the travel of the valve.

The throw of an eccentric in the last two examples can also be found by the "simple rule of three," or, as it is sometimes called, "the simple rule of proportion." Thus, take Example 31; instead of finding the throw graphically as shown, we may find it thus:

$$10'' : 12'' :: 5'' : \text{throw}$$
$$\frac{5}{10)\overline{60}}$$
$$6 \text{ inches} = \text{the throw.}$$

Or, if we take Example 32, we have,

$$12'' : 10'' :: 5'' : \text{throw}$$
$$\frac{5}{12)\overline{50}}$$
$$4.166 \text{ inches} = \text{throw.}$$

### PROPORTIONS OF ECCENTRICS.

98. Table 12 gives the proportional dimensions of the important parts of the eccentric and strap. For instance, this table indicates that to find the thickness at $C$, Fig. 142, we multiply a given unit by 1, and thus obtain the dimension at $C$ in inches. By "unit" is meant a certain number regarded as one, so that when this unit is multiplied by the numbers as indicated, the important dimensions in inches of an eccentric and strap will have been obtained. This unit is found in the following manner: We may assume that the friction which the eccentric has to overcome is proportional to the total steam pressure on the back of the valve, which is equal (Art. 82) to the area of the valve face multiplied by steam pressure per square inch, consequently, for finding the unit we have the following empirical rule:

Multiply the square root of the total pressure on the back of the valve by the decimal .01, the product will be the unit required; or, putting this rule in the shape of a formula, we have,

$$.01 \sqrt{\text{total pressure on the back of the valve.}}$$

Here the decimal .01 is arbitrary, and should only be used in locomotive practice, in which it always remains the same, no matter whether the locomotive is large or small. Again, notice that the total pressure on the back of the valve depends upon the size of the valve face and the steam pressure per square inch; and since the sizes of the valve faces vary in the different locomotives, it follows that this unit in Table 12 will also vary for the different classes of engines.

EXAMPLE 33.—Take, for example, a consolidation engine with cylinders 20 inches in diameter; the average size of the valve face for these engines is 10 inches long and 20 inches wide, hence the area of the valve face is $10'' \times 20'' = 200$ square inches. Assume that the steam pressure in the steam-chest is 120 pounds per square inch, we have 120 × 200 = 24,000 pounds, which is the total pressure on the back of the valve. The square root of 24,000 is 154 (here the fraction has been neglected), and 154 × .01 = 1.54, which is the unit required. If now we multiply this unit 1.54 by the numbers given in Table 12, we shall obtain the following dimensions of an eccentric and strap suitable to work a slide-valve with a total pressure of 24,000 pounds upon its back. Thus (see Fig. 142):

TABLE 12.

$A = \text{Unit} \times 1$
$B = \text{Unit} \times 2.25$
$C = \text{Unit} \times 1$
$D = \text{Unit} \times 1.75$
$E = \text{Unit} \times 2.3$
$E_2 = \text{Unit} \times .7$
$F = \text{Unit} \times 2$

The dimensions at A will be 1.54 × 1 = 1.54 inches.
" " " B " " 1.54 × 2.25 = 3.46 "
" " " C " " 1.54 × 1 = 1.54 "
" " " D " " 1.54 × 1.75 = 2.69 "
" " " E " " 1.54 × 2.3 = 3.54 "
" " " $E_2$ " " 1.54 × .7 = 1.07 "
" " " F " " 1.54 × 2 = 3.08 "

EXAMPLE 34.—Now take a small eight-wheeled passenger engine, with cylinders 10 inches in diameter. The average size of the valve face for this class of engines is 6 inches long and 11½ inches wide. Again, assume that the steam pressure per square inch in the steam-chest is 120 pounds. In this case we have 6″ × 11.5″ × 120 = 8280 pounds pressure on the back of the valve, and $.01 \sqrt{8280}$ (that is, the square root of 8280 × .01) = .91, which is the unit required. Consequently, the dimensions of an eccentric and strap suitable to work a valve with 8,280 pounds pressure upon its back will be (see Fig. 142):

The dimensions at A = .91 × 1 = .91 inches.
" " " B = .91 × 2.25 = 2.04 "
" " " C = .91 × 1 = .91 "
" " " D = .91 × 1.75 = 1.59 "
" " " E = .91 × 2.3 = 2.09 "
" " " $E_2$ = .91 × .7 = .63 "
" " " F = .91 × 2 = 1.82 "

If we now compare the dimensions found in Example 33 with the dimensions obtained by measurements of eccentrics in use as shown in Figs. 143 and 145, we find these to agree very closely. The greatest difference between any two dimensions is that of the breadth of the strap at B. In our illustration the breadth is ¼ of an inch greater than that obtained by the rule, but it must be remembered that the eccentric and strap shown in Figs. 143 and 145, although frequently used in modern locomotives, is very heavy in comparison with those employed in a great many other locomotives. We also find that the dimensions found in Example 34 agree closely with those shown in Figs. 152 and 154. Here the greatest difference between any two dimensions is that of the width of the recess $E$ for the eccentric-rod. The writer believes that if the width of the recess is made according to the rule given, namely, $2\frac{3}{8}$ inches instead of $2\frac{3}{4}$ inches, good results will follow.

Lastly, to those who are acquainted with locomotive work, it may appear that depth of the lug at $F$ is very great when compared with the lugs on ordinary eccentric straps, but in the writer's opinion this is a great improvement, because when the holes in these lugs are reamed, the bolts turned and fitted, so that they must be driven into position, this increased depth of lug will to a great extent prevent the strap from springing out of its true circular form.

LINK MOTION.

99. In Art. 61 we have seen that, when a direct connection is made between the eccentric and valve (that is, when no rocker is employed), as shown in Fig. 163, the

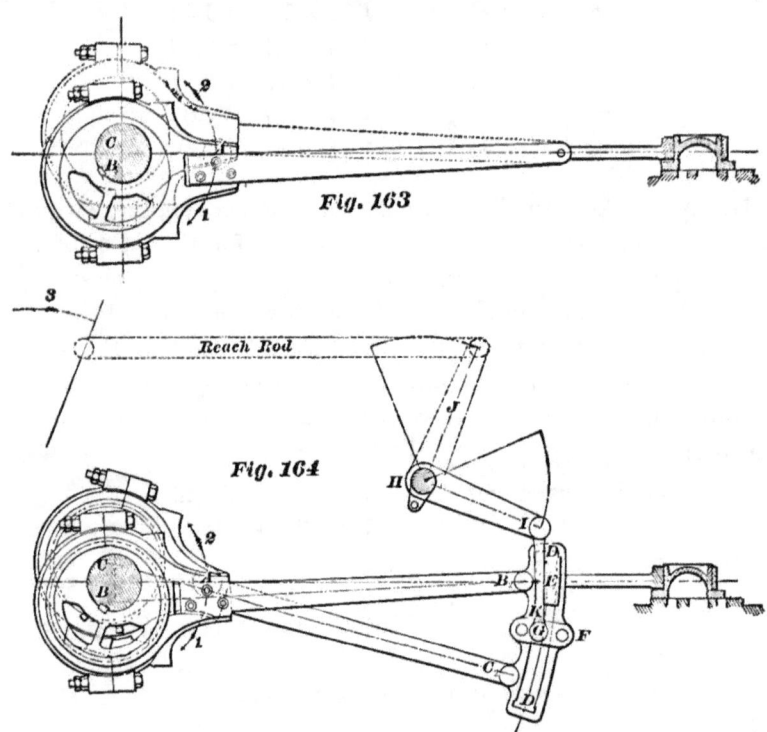

eccentric will always travel ahead of the crank. Consequently, if, as in Fig. 163, the crank-pin occupies the position $A$ as shown, and is to rotate in the direction as indicated by the arrow marked 1, then the position occupied by the eccentric will be as shown in full lines and with its center at $B$. If, on the other hand, the crank-pin occupies the position $A$, as before, but is to rotate in the direction indicated by the arrow 2, then the position occupied by the eccentric must be as shown in dotted lines and with its center at C. Now if the engine is to rotate at one time in a given direction, and at another time in an opposite direction, or, in other words, if the motion of the engine is at any time to be reversed, then we must have some device by which one eccentric can be moved from its position B to C, or we must have two eccentrics fixed on the axle for each slide-valve. The latter method, namely, the use of two eccentrics for each slide-valve, has been adopted in locomotive engines. At present, and for the sake of simplicity, we will continue the investigation of the link and its motion as used in a valve gear in which no rocker is employed.

Referring now to Fig. 163, it will be readily perceived that when the engine is to turn in the direction as indicated by arrow 1, then the eccentric drawn in full lines, and whose center is at B, and that alone, must move the slide-valve; and when the engine is to rotate in the opposite direction, as indicated by the arrow 2, then the eccentric drawn in dotted lines (and not the other one) must move the slide-valve.

From the foregoing we conclude that in order to reverse the engine we must disengage one eccentric and engage the other, and for this purpose the link, as shown in Figs. 164 and 165, is employed. In Fig. 164 we see that one end of each eccentric-rod is attached to the link. In this link a slot or opening D D is cut lengthwise in which a block E, called the link-block, can freely but accurately move from one end to the other end of the link. The piece F is

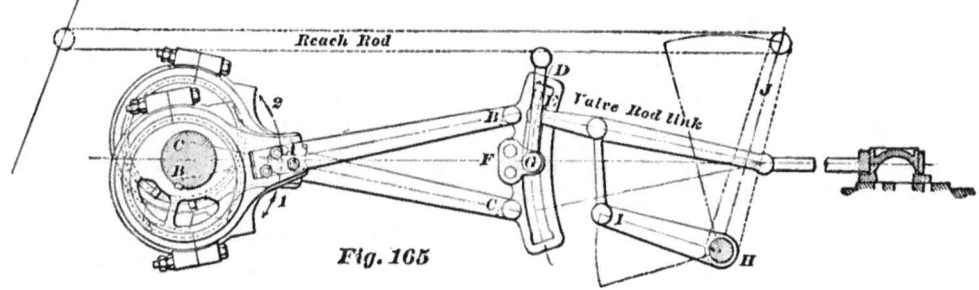

Fig. 165

called the saddle and is bolted to the link. To the saddle the pin G is forged, and is called the link saddle-pin. The shaft H is called the lifting-shaft, or the reversing shaft; and the arms I, J are called the lifting-shaft arms. A pin is fastened to the end of the lifting-shaft arm I. This pin and the link saddle-pin G work freely in a piece K, called the link hanger; this link hanger is simply a connection between the link and the lifting shaft. To the lifting-shaft arm J, one end of the reach rod is attached, as shown. The other end of the reach rod connects with the reversing lever, which is placed in the cab of the locomotive. The reversing lever is here represented by its center line only; more of this hereafter. It will readily be seen that, by moving the reverse lever in the direction as indicated by the arrow 3, the link can be raised to any position desired, and thus the motion of the engine reversed.

100. There are two methods of applying the link. First, it may be applied as shown in Fig. 164. In this case, if we move the reverse lever, we also move the link and not the block, and thus set the link to any desired position. Of course, in moving the link, the end of the eccentric-rods, which are attached to it, are carried with it.

Links which are moved by the reversing lever, so as to reverse the motion of the engine, are called "shifting links."

The second method of applying the link is illustrated in Fig. 165. Here the reversing lever moves the valve-rod link to which the link-block is attached, but does not move the link; or, in short, we may say that, in order to reverse the motion of the engine, the link-block is shifted in the link. In this case the link is called a "stationary link."

By the term "stationary" is simply meant that the link is suspended from a stationary or fixed point; the link itself is not stationary, because, when the engine is running, either one or the other eccentric, or both, will act upon the link, and thus keep it continually on the move.

101. It will readily be seen by referring to Fig. 164 that when a shifting link is used, and the engine is to rotate in the direction indicated by arrow 1, then the link must occupy the position as here shown; that is, it must have been moved downwards, and for full gear the eccentric-rod pin $B_2$ and the center of the link-block $E$ will lie in a horizontal line. If the engine is to rotate in an opposite direction, then the link for full gear must be lifted up until the center of eccentric-rod pin $C_2$ and the center of the link-block will be in the same horizontal line.

Now, referring to Fig. 165, we see that when the stationary link is used, and the engine is to rotate in the direction as indicated by arrow 1, the link-block, not the link, must be moved upwards until its center and the center of the eccentric-rod pin $B_2$ lie in a horizontal line, as here shown, and when the engine is to move in an opposite direction, then the link-block must be moved downwards until its center and the center of the eccentric-rod pin $C_2$ are again in a horizontal line for full gear.

102. It may also be of interest to the reader to note some of the differences in the construction of the shifting and that of the stationary links. In the former the curvature of the link is towards the axle; that is, the center from which the link has been drawn is located towards the axle. On the other hand, the center from which the stationary link is drawn is located towards the slide-valve. Again, notice that in the shifting link the eccentric-rods are coupled to the concave side of the link, and in the stationary link the eccentric-rods are coupled to the convex side of the link. It can also be shown that when the latter link is used the lead of the slide-valve will be constant at whatever point of the stroke steam may be cut off, but when a shifting link is used the lead of the slide-valve will not be constant; that is, the earlier that the steam is cut off the greater will be the lead. This we shall presently explain. We must also note the fact that when a shifting link is employed in a manner as here shown, the angular advance of the eccentric is found according to the rule given in Arts. 65, 67, but when the stationary link is used the angular advance of the eccentrics will be less. In American locomotives the shifting link is mostly used, and the stationary link is seldom found; therefore, hereafter we will generally confine our attention to the investigation of the shifting link.

103. From the foregoing the reader may be led to believe that the whole purpose of the link is to take one eccentric out of gear and place the other into gear; and, indeed, the writer believes that when the link was first discovered no one expected to use it for any other purpose. But soon afterwards engineers became aware of the fact that

the link could be used for cutting off steam in the cylinder at different parts of the stroke, and that on account of its simplicity it was particularly well adapted in locomotive engines for this purpose. Hence we may say that the purpose of the link is twofold: first, because with it the motion of the engine can readily be reversed; second, the point of cutting off steam in the cylinder can easily be changed. Thus, for instance, if the link is placed in the position as shown in Fig. 164 it will in nowise affect the point of cutting off steam in the cylinder; that is, if the eccentrics are set to cut off steam at $\frac{7}{8}$ of the stroke, and the valve has the proper amount of lap, the link will not change this point of cutting off. Again, when the link is raised up so that the center of the eccentric-rod pin $C_2$ will be in line with the center of the link-block, then the motion of the engine will be simply reversed, and, as before, the point of cut-off will not be interfered with. If now, on the other hand, the link is raised a short distance only, so that the center of the link-block will be located, say, about midway between the end of the link and the link saddle $F$, then the travel of the valve will be shortened and the point of cutting off steam in the cylinder will be changed.

### DEFINITIONS.

104. Since the cylinders are placed in front of the locomotive, it follows that when the engine is traveling ahead, the crank must turn in the direction as indicated by the arrow 1, Fig. 164; but we have seen that when the crank rotates in this direction the eccentric $B$ must work the valve; therefore the eccentric $B$ is called the forward eccentric, and the rod connected with it is called the forward eccentric-rod. The eccentric $C$ is the backward eccentric, and the rod connected with it is called the backward eccentric-rod. Again, when the link occupies the position shown in Fig. 164, or when it occupies the other extreme position, that is, when the link is moved up, then the link is said to be in full gear. When the link-block stands midway between either one of its extreme positions and the center of the saddle-pin, the link is said to be in half gear; and lastly, when the center of the link-block is in line with the center of the saddle-pin, the link is said to be in mid gear.

The backward stroke of the piston is that described from the front end of the cylinder towards the crank, and the forward stroke is that described from the back end of the cylinder towards the front.

For the sake of brevity, and according to custom, we shall hereafter call the distance from the center of the eccentric to the center of the eccentric-rod pin, the length of the eccentric-rod; or, in other words, we shall consider the eccentric and rod to be one piece, and therefore the distance from the center $B$ to $B_2$, or from $C$ to $C_2$, Figs. 164 and 165, will be the length of the eccentric-rod.

By the term radius of link is meant the radius of the arc $D\,D$, drawn through the center of the opening of the link.

### LEAD AND ANGULAR ADVANCE IN CONNECTION WITH LINKS.

105. In Art. 102 we have stated that when a stationary link is employed the lead remains constant at whatever point of the stroke the steam may be cut off. The truth

of this will be evident by referring to Fig. 166. Here, as the position of the slide-valve indicates, the piston stands at the beginning of the forward stroke, and consequently the center of the crank-pin will be at $u$ on the center line of motion $L\,M$. In order to enable us to trace the action of the mechanism of the valve gear as clearly as possible, we have represented the latter by its center lines. All lines drawn in full represent the position of the different parts of the valve gear when the piston is at the beginning of the forward stroke, and consequently correspond with the position $u$ of the crank as shown. All the dotted lines represent the position of the mechanism when the piston is at the

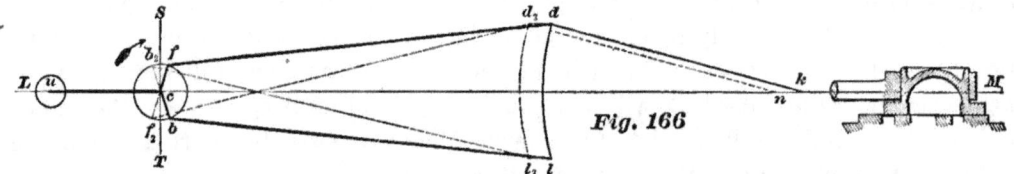

Fig. 166

beginning of the backward stroke, and consequently will correspond with a position of the crank opposite to that of $u$. The line $d\,k$ represents the center of the valve-rod link, and the distance from $d$ to $k$ represents the length of the valve-rod link from center to center of pins. The arc $d\,l$ represents the link arc, that is, an arc drawn through the center of opening in the link. And here again, for the sake of simplicity, we have assumed that the center of eccentric-rod pins are located in the same arc $d\,l$. In this case such an assumption will not affect the correctness of our reasoning. The distance between the points $d$ and $l$ on the arc $d\,l$ represents the distance between the eccentric-rod pins. The circumference of the circle $f\,b$ represents the path of the center of eccentric. The point $f$ in this circumference represents the position of the forward eccentric, and the point $b$ in the same circumference represents the center of the backward eccentric. Both centers $f$ and $b$ are shown in the correct relative positions to that of the crank, when the piston is at the beginning of the forward stroke. When in this position the points $f$ and $b$ will lie in a line parallel to the line $S\,T$, which is drawn perpendicular to $L\,M$. The point $f_2$ represents the position of the forward eccentric, and $b_2$ represents the position of the backward eccentric when the piston is at the beginning of the backward stroke. These points $f_2$ and $b_2$ will also lie in a straight line parallel to the line $S\,T$. And since the points $f$ and $b$ lie in the same circumference, and also in a line perpendicular to $L\,M$, it follows that the points $f$ and $b$ are equally distant from the center line of motion $L\,M$. The same remarks apply to the points $f_2$ and $b_2$. The full lines $f\,d$ and $b\,l$ represent the center lines of the eccentric-rods when the piston is at the beginning of the forward stroke, and the dotted lines $b_2\,l_2$ and $f_2\,d_2$ represent the center lines of the eccentric rods when the piston is at the beginning of the backward stroke. The link is suspended in such a manner that when the piston is at the beginning of the backward or forward stroke, the center line of motion $L\,M$ will pass midway between the ends of the link, or, in other words, the line $L\,M$ will pass midway between the points $d$ and $l$. In stationary links the radius of the link arc $d\,l$ is equal to the length $d\,k$ of the valve-rod link. Now, since the centers $f$ and $b$ of the eccentrics lie in a straight line perpendicular to $L\,M$, and since the lines $f\,d$ and $b\,l$ are equal in length, and also, since the lines $f\,d$ and $b\,l$ when produced towards $L$ would form equal angles with the line

$L\,M$, it follows that the point $k$ from which the arc $d\,l$ is drawn will also lie in the line $L\,M$. Consequently, when the link-block is lowered, or, that is to say, when the center $d$ of the valve-rod link is moved towards $l$, the point $k$ will remain stationary, and therefore the lead will not be changed, no matter what position the link-block may occupy in the arc $d\,l$. But when the link-block is at $d$, the valve motion is assumed to be in full-gear; on the other hand, when the link-block occupies a position on the arc $d\,l$ anywhere between the points $d$ and $l$, the valve motion is not in full-gear; hence the travel of the valve is changed, and consequently the point of cut-off is also changed without changing the lead of the valve.

106. When a shifting link is employed and no rocker used, then the linear advance of the valve and the angular advance of the eccentric, measured as explained in Art. 67, will be equal to each other, and consequently the angular advance of each eccentric must be found as shown in Arts. 65 and 67.

In Art. 102 we have stated that when a stationary link is used the angular advance of the eccentric will be less than that which is necessary when a shifting link is employed. In the first place, then, let us consider why this should be so; and secondly, let us establish a method for finding this angular advance of the eccentrics, with stationary link.

We have already seen that when the piston stands at the beginning of the forward stroke, one end of the valve-rod link will be at $k$, Fig. 166, and when the piston is at the beginning of the backward stroke, the same end of the valve-rod link will be at $n$. The distance between the points $k$ and $n$ on the line $L\,M$ must be equal to twice the linear advance of the valve. Again, since the two lines $d\,k$ and $d_2\,n$ are parallel, it follows that the line $d_2\,d$, which is drawn parallel to $L\,M$, must be equal to the distance between the points $n$ and $k$, or in other words, the distance between the point $d$ and $d_2$ must be equal to twice the linear advance of the valve. Now notice that when the piston stands at the beginning of the forward stroke the eccentric-rods $f\,d$ and $b\,l$ do not cross each other; on the other hand, when the piston stands at the opposite end of the stroke the eccentric-rods do cross each other, as shown by the dotted lines $b_2\,l_2$ and $f_2\,d_2$. Consequently the angle formed by the line $f\,d$ (when it is produced towards $L$) and the line $L\,M$ will be less than the angle formed by the lines $f_2\,d_2$, and $L\,M$, and therefore, on account of the inequality of these angles the distance between the straight line that may be drawn through the points $f_2\,b_2$ and the straight line drawn through the points $f$ and $b$ will be less than the distance between the points $d_2$ and $d$. But the angle formed between the line $S\,T$ and a straight line joining the points $f$ and $c$ is equal to the angular advance of the eccentric. Or again, the angle formed between the line $f\,c$ and the line $b_2\,c$ is equal to twice the angular advance of the eccentric. But we have just seen that the distance between the points $b_2$ and $f$ is less than that between the points $d_2$ and $d$, and consequently the angular advance of the eccentric will be less than the linear advance of the valve; and lastly, since in a valve gear in which the shifting link is used, as shown in Fig. 164, the angular advance of the eccentrics is equal to the linear advance of the valve, it follows that when a stationary link is used the angular advance of the eccentrics will be less than that which is necessary when a shifting link is employed.

## METHOD FOR FINDING THE ANGULAR ADVANCE.

107. In order to show clearly how to find the angular advance of the eccentric in a case as shown in Fig. 166, we will take the following example:

EXAMPLE 35.—Lap of valve is 1 inch, lead $\frac{1}{16}$ of an inch, travel of valve 5 inches, length of eccentric-rods 3 feet, and the distance between the eccentric-rod pins in the link is 12 inches, throw of the eccentrics is 5 inches. Find the angular advance of the eccentrics suitable for a stationary link.

Let $c$ on the line $L\,M$, Fig. 167, be the center of the driving axle. From $c$ as a center and with a radius equal to $2\frac{1}{2}$ inches (that is, half the throw of the eccentric) describe the circle $f\,b$. The circumference of this circle will represent the path of the

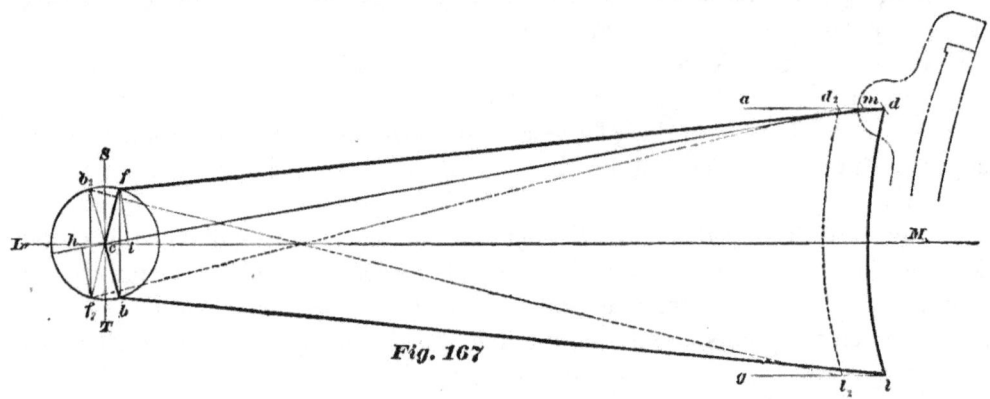

Fig. 167

centers of the eccentrics. Draw two lines $a$ and $g$ parallel to the horizontal line of motion $L\,M$ and each line equally distant from $L\,M$. The total distance between the lines $a$ and $g$ must be equal to that between the centers of the eccentric-rod pins in the link, namely 12 inches. From the center $c$ and with a radius of 3 feet (which is equal to the length of the eccentric-rods) draw a short arc intersecting the line $a$ in the point $m$. Through the point $m$ and the center $c$ draw a straight line $m\,c$, and prolong it to the circumference $f_2\,b_2$, on this line, from the center $c$, and with a distance of $1\frac{1}{16}$ inches (which is equal to the linear advance of the valve), lay off the point $h$; and also with the same distance ($1\frac{1}{16}$ inches) lay off from the center $c$ on the line $c\,m$ the point $i$. Through the points $i$ and $h$ draw lines perpendicular to the line $c\,m$, intersecting the circumference of the circle in the points $f$ and $f_2$. The point $f$ will be the center of the forward eccentric when the piston is at the beginning of the forward stroke, and the point $f_2$ will be the center of the same eccentric when the piston is at the beginning of the backward stroke. From the points $f$ and $f_2$ as centers, and with a radius equal to the length of the eccentric-rod, describe small arcs intersecting the line $a$ in the points $d$ and $d_2$. Through the points $d$ and $f$ draw a straight line, then this line $d\,f$ will be the center line of the forward eccentric-rod when the piston is at the beginning of the forward stroke. Through $d_2$ and $f_2$ draw a straight line, then this straight line $d_2\,f_2$ will be the center of the same eccentric-rod when the piston is at the beginning of the backward stroke.

The distance between the points $d$ and $d_2$ will be equal to twice the linear advance of the valve very nearly. We say "nearly," because this method of finding the angular advance is empirical, and can be accepted only as an approximate method. Yet in ordinary cases the difference between the line $d\,d_2$ and the linear advance is inappreciable, and even in extreme cases, such as represented in the figure in which the eccentric-rods are comparatively very short, the result is very nearly correct. Yet in every case the distance between the points $d_2$ and $d$ found by the foregoing method should be compared with the linear advance of the valve, and when it is found that the distance between the points $d$ and $d_2$ is greater than twice the linear advance, the former must be corrected by changing the positions of the points $f$ and $f_2$. The difference is generally so small that the correction necessary for the positions of the points $f$ and $f_2$ can very readily be seen. In this example the linear advance of the valve is $1\frac{1}{16}$ inches, and according to the construction in Fig. 167 the angular advance of the eccentric is $\frac{11}{16}$ of an inch measured on a line drawn through the point $f$ perpendicular to the line $S\,T$. The point $b$ represents the center of the backward eccentric when the piston is at the beginning of the forward stroke, and the point $b_2$ represents the center of the same eccentric when the piston stands at the beginning of the backward stroke. The position of the point $b$ is found by drawing through the point $f$ a straight line $f\,b$, parallel to the line $S\,T$. The point $b$ in which the line $f\,b$ intersects the circumference of the circle is the center of the backward eccentric. In a similar manner we find $b_2$ by drawing a line through $f_2$ parallel to $S\,T$.

### LEAD WITH SHIFTING LINKS.

108. In Art. 105 we have seen that the lead of the valve remains constant when a stationary link is employed.

But now let us examine the state of affairs when a shifting link is used; by so doing we will find that the lead of the valve increases when the link is moved from full-gear towards mid-gear.

Fig. 168 represents a valve gear with a shifting link, and here again, for the sake of simplicity, its mechanism is represented by center lines. Also, in order to enable

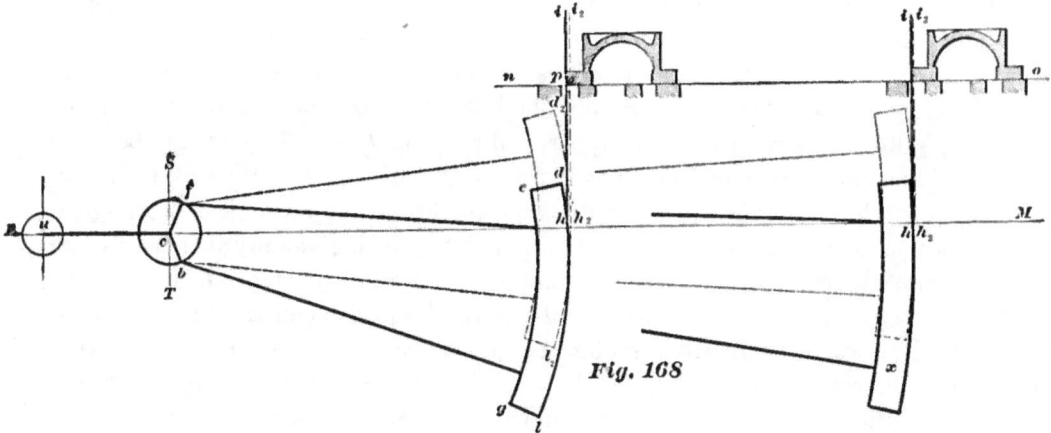

Fig. 168

us to trace quickly and clearly the effect of the position of the link on the lead of the slide-valve, we have shown the latter and its seat above the line $L\,M$ and parallel to it. The distance between the valve seat and the line $L\,M$ is immaterial; it can be placed at any convenient height, without affecting the correctness of our reasoning; but the distance between the line $S\,T$ and the end of the valve seat is important, and should be placed in a position as will be presently explained.

In Fig. 168 the point $c$ represents the center of the driving axle; the circumference $f\,b$ represents the path of the centers of the eccentrics—$f$ the center of the forward eccentric and $b$ the center of the backward eccentric. The arc $d\,l$ represents the link arc, that is, an arc drawn through the center of the link opening; and the arc $e\,g$ represents the arc in which the centers of the eccentric-rod pins are located. In this figure the link motion is shown to be in full-gear. The center of the crank-pin is at $u$, and consequently the piston will be at the beginning of its forward stroke.

When the link motion is in full-gear, or in mid-gear, or in any intermediate position, the point of intersection $h$ of the line $L\,M$ with the arc $d\,l$ will always represent the position of the center of the valve-rod pin; and since the distance between the valve-rod pin and the slide-valve is constant, it follows that if we know the position of the former we also know the position of the latter. If, therefore, through the point $h$, a straight line $h\,i$ be drawn perpendicular to $L\,M$, and the valve seat placed in a position in which the distance between the line $h\,i$ and the outer edge $p$ of the port will represent the lead when the link motion is in full-gear, then we can easily determine the amount of lead when the link is set to cut off at any other portion of the stroke. Thus for instance: Let the arc $d\,l$ represent the position of the link arc when the link motion is in full-gear and the piston at the beginning of the forward stroke, and also assume that the valve has $\frac{1}{16}$ of an inch lead when the link motion is in this position. Draw a straight line $n\,o$ any convenient distance above and parallel to $L\,M$. Through $h$, the point of intersection of the line $L\,M$ with the arc $d\,l$, draw a straight line $h\,i$ perpendicular to $L\,M$; the point of intersection of the line $h\,i$ with the line $n\,o$ will represent the edge of the valve as shown.

From the line $h\,i$ and on the line $n\,o$ lay off a point $p$ $\frac{1}{16}$ of an inch from $h\,i$, then this point $p$ will represent the outer edge of the steam port, and the distance between the point $p$ and the line $h\,i$ is the lead when the link motion is in full-gear. Let us now assume that the link has been moved into mid-gear as shown by the dotted lines, but without disturbing the position of the crank and that of the eccentric centers $f$ and $b$. Through $h_2$, the point of intersection of the line $L\,M$ with the new position of the link arc $d_2\,l_2$, draw a straight line $h_2\,i_2$ perpendicular to $L\,M$; the distance between this line and the outer edge $p$ of the port will represent the lead when the link is in mid-gear, and, as will be seen, this lead is greater than the lead when the link is in full-gear.

109. In a similar manner it can be shown that the lead gradually increases when the link is moved from full-gear towards mid-gear. Again, by simply increasing the length of the eccentric-rods the difference between the lead when the link is in full-gear and the lead when the link is in mid-gear is decreased. Thus, for instance, making the length of the eccentric-rods equal to twice the length as before, but not changing the position of the crank and the centers $f$ and $b$ of the eccentrics, the link will occupy the position as shown at $x$; then by drawing the valve seat in the correct place, following the same method of construction as before, it will be seen that the difference in the lead (or in other words the distance between the line $h\,i$ and $h_2\,i_2$) when in full-gear and the lead when the link is set in mid-gear is less than when shorter eccentric-rods are used. From this we learn that the magnitude of the variable character of the lead

depends upon the length of the eccentric-rods, and that in practice, where it is generally desirable to keep the lead as nearly constant as possible, we must make the eccentric-rods as long as the design of the engine will admit. In locomotives when in full-gear the lead is generally $\frac{1}{16}$ of an inch, sometimes a little less, and this lead is increased to $\frac{1}{4}$ or $\frac{3}{8}$ of an inch, and sometimes even more, by moving the link into mid-gear.

In order to avoid hereafter any misunderstanding, we again call attention to the fact that the foregoing remarks refer to link motions in which rockers are not employed.

#### CONNECTION OF ECCENTRIC-RODS TO THE LINK.

110. It is always desirable that locomotive slide-valves should have some lead, no matter in what position the link is placed, and it certainly would be injurious if the slide-valve lapped over the steam port at the beginning of a stroke of the piston. Now

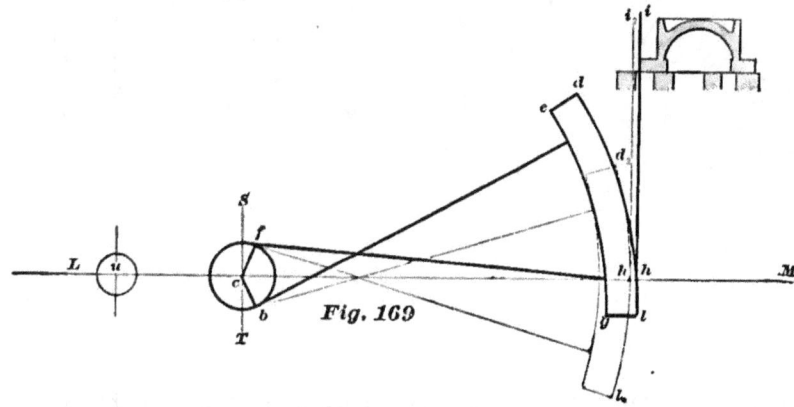

to avoid having lap at the beginning of a stroke, the eccentric-rods must be correctly connected to the link. Notice, for instance, the manner in which the eccentric-rods are connected to the link in Fig. 168. There, it will be seen, the eccentric-rods do not cross each other when the piston is at the beginning of the forward stroke. But now let us examine Fig. 169, which represents precisely the same valve gear as that shown in Fig. 168, but with this difference—the eccentric-rods are crossed when the piston is at the beginning of the forward stroke. Note the result. If it is the intention to use the link simply for the purpose of reversing the motion of the engine, then this manner of connecting the eccentric-rods to the link would work very well; but as soon as the link is used for the purpose of changing the point of cut-off, then this arrangement of eccentric-rods will have an injurious effect, particularly so in locomotive engines, as we can readily see by inspecting Fig. 169. In this figure the full lines represent the mechanism in full-gear, and the dotted lines represent the same in mid-gear. Drawing a line $h\ i$ perpendicular to the line $L\ M$, and placing the valve seat in its proper position as explained in connection with Fig. 168, the distance between the line $h\ i$ and the outer edge of the steam port, Fig. 169, will be the amount of lead when the link is placed in full-gear. On the other hand, when the link is placed in mid-gear, as shown by the dotted lines, and drawing a line $h_2\ i_2$ through the point $h_2$ perpendicular to the line $L\ M$, we find that instead of having lead—as we should have—the slide-valve laps over the steam port when the piston is at beginning of the stroke, which is a bad feature, and must be avoided in locomotive construction.

PRACTICAL APPLICATION OF THE PRINCIPLES RELATING TO THE VALVE MOTION.

111. In our previous articles we have endeavored to explain the mode of procedure in laying out on paper a simple valve gear, so that its mechanism can be correctly proportioned, drawn, and made in the shop.

After the different parts of the valve gear are finished, they must then be correctly set in the engine. Although the methods employed in the shop for finding the position of the eccentric and other mechanism of the valve gear may appear to be different from those employed for finding the positions of the same pieces on paper, the principles on which these methods are based do not differ.

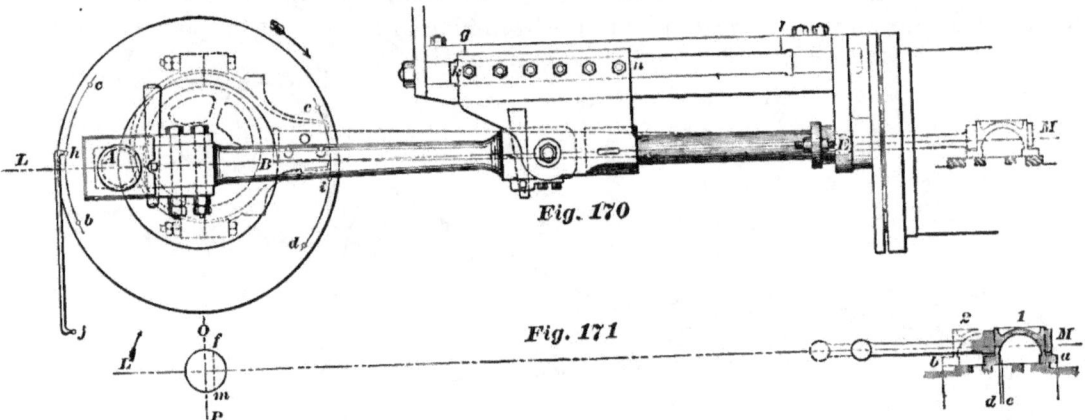

Fig. 170

Fig. 171

In setting a simple valve gear such as is illustrated in Fig. 170, the great aim is to obtain equal leads of the slide-valve; to obtain these we must first determine the correct length of the eccentric-rod; second, we must find the locations of the dead centers of the crank; and lastly, the correct positions of the eccentric on the shaft.

In order to show clearly the practical method employed in setting the valve gear in an engine of this kind, we will take the following example:

EXAMPLE 36.—The distance, as shown in Fig. 170, between the center of the crank-shaft and the line drawn midway between the steam ports of the cylinder is 8 feet 4 inches, the length of the valve-rod from center of valve to center of valve-rod pin is 20 inches, lap $\frac{5}{8}$ of an inch, lead $\frac{1}{16}$ of an inch, and travel of the valve 5 inches. In this example it must be understood that the cylinder, shaft, and the other parts of the engine have been correctly set in line, and that all we have to do is to set the valve gear.

LENGTH OF ECCENTRIC-ROD.

Our first duty is to find the length of the eccentric-rod; on paper this can be easily accomplished. Here we have only to draw the valve and rod in the center of its travel, and measure the distance from the center $E$ of the valve-rod pin in mid position to the center of the shaft, which is equal to $100 - 20 = 80$ inches, and this distance of 80 inches is the length of the eccentric-rod.

Now if the workmanship of all the other parts of the engine is positively perfect, so that all the dimensions of the mechanism are absolutely correct, all that we need to do is to make the eccentric-rod from the center of the eccentric-strap to the center of the valve-rod pin 80 inches long. But such perfect workmanship is seldom procured, and therefore the eccentric-rods are generally made in two pieces, namely, the eccentric-strap and the rod proper, and constructed so that the distance between the center of strap and the center of pin $E$ can be adjusted to suit the other parts of the machinery, and thus enabling all to work harmoniously and correctly.

To obtain in an engine by measurement the distance from the center of shaft to the center $E$ is often a difficult matter if not impracticable, and therefore the following practical method for finding the correct length of the eccentric-rod is employed.

Fasten the eccentric on the shaft in a position which will allow it to be connected to the valve-rod. In fastening the eccentric in this position, no attention need or should be paid to the position of the crank. Place and connect in position the eccentric-rod, which we will assume to be somewhat short. Turn the crank-shaft in a direction in which the shaft is designed to run, and when the valve arrives in the position marked 1, drawn in full lines (Fig. 171), representing it to be at one extreme end of its travel, draw along the edge $a$ of the valve a line on the valve seat; again turn the shaft in the same direction as before, and when the valve arrives in the position marked 2, shown in dotted lines, representing it to be at the other extreme end of its travel, draw along the edge $b$ of the valve a line on the valve seat. Also on this surface draw a short line $d$ midway between the lines $a$ and $b$ and parallel to the same. The distance from the line $d$ to the line $e$ drawn midway between the steam ports indicates that the length of the eccentric-rod is just that much too short and must be increased by an amount equal to this distance. If this measures $\frac{1}{4}$ of an inch the length of rod must be increased by $\frac{1}{4}$ of an inch. Again, if the point $d$ had fallen on the other side of the center line $e$, then the distance between $d$ and $e$ would have indicated that the eccentric-rod is just that much too long, and must be shortened by an amount equal to this distance.

In Art. 61 we find that when a valve has no lap the center of the eccentric is placed in a line perpendicular to the center line of motion, and in Art. 67 we find that when a valve has lap the angular advance of the eccentric must be laid off from this same line. Therefore in Fig. 171 the angular advance of the eccentric must be laid off from the line $O P$ drawn perpendicular to the center line of motion $L M$. Consequently, on paper, the position of the eccentric is easily found, for we have only to draw a circle whose diameter is equal to the travel of the valve, namely, 5 inches; and draw a straight line $f m$ parallel to $O P$ and $\frac{11}{16}$ of an inch (which is equal to the lap and lead) away from it. The point $f$ in which the line $f m$ intersects the circle is the center of the eccentric when the crank is at $L$, the crank-shaft rotating in the direction as indicated by the arrow. But in setting the valve gear in an engine, lines like $L M$ and $O P$, from and on which measurements can be taken, would be a difficult matter to locate, and therefore we must seek another method, but not new principles, for laying off the angular advance of the eccentric. To do so we must find the dead centers of the crank.

### TO FIND THE DEAD CENTERS OF A CRANK.

The dead centers $A$ and $B$ of the crank-pin, in Fig. 170, are represented by the points in which the center line of motion $L M$ intersects the circumference of the circle representing the path of the center of the crank-pin. But, as stated before, we cannot locate in the engine the line $LM$; we must, therefore, in this case also adopt a practical method by which these dead centers can be readily and correctly found. For the sake of simplicity in our illustration we have represented a crank-disk instead of a locomotive wheel. This will not affect the correctness of our reasoning, for what is true in one instance will also be true in the other.

On the crank-disk describe arcs $b\,c$ and $e\,d$; if the periphery of the disk is turned, then the arcs $b\,c$ and $e\,d$ can be described with the aid of a gauge; if the periphery is not turned, then these arcs should be described with the aid of a scriber or sharp-pointed instrument held against the face of the disk while the shaft is revolving in its bearings; but whichever way the arcs are described these must be true. Next turn the shaft in the direction of the arrow, until the crosshead is within a short distance from the end of the stroke, say $\frac{1}{2}$ of an inch; while in this position mark on the slides a line $g$ even with the end $k$ of the crosshead. Also, while the shaft and the crosshead is in this position, place a center-punch mark $j$ on the frame or any other fixed surface. From this point $j$ as a center, and with a tram of any convenient length, $j\,h$, as a radius, describe a short arc intersecting the arc $b\,c$ in the point $c$ (this point $c$ will at this instant coincide with the end $h$ of the tram, and not as shown in the figure). Now turn the shaft in the same direction as before, causing the crosshead to complete its full stroke and part of the return stroke, and when during this motion the edge $k$ of the crosshead touches the line $g$ on the slide, stop turning the shaft, and while in this position describe from the point $j$ as a center, and with the same tram as before, a short arc intersecting the arc $b\,c$ in the point $b$. Find the point $h$ on the arc $b\,c$, midway between the points $b$ and $c$. Now turning the shaft into a position in which the ends of tram will touch the points $h$ and $j$, the crank will then be on one of its dead centers, as shown.

In a similar manner we can find the point $i$, but for this purpose we must draw another line, $l$, on the slide; this time $l$ must be drawn even with the edge $n$ of the crosshead when it is about one-half of an inch from the beginning of the backward stroke. Then from the point $j$, and with the same tram, and in the same manner as before, the points $d$ and $e$ are found, and the point $i$, midway between these points on the arc $d\,e$, is established. Turning the shaft into a position in which the points of the tram will touch the points $j$ and $i$, the crank will then be on the other dead center.

### PRACTICAL METHOD OF FINDING THE ANGULAR ADVANCE OF THE ECCENTRIC.

When now the crank is placed on a dead center, the valve must then be in a position in which the steam-port opening is equal to the lead. Therefore place the crank on a dead center, say on $A$, and move the eccentric (which is now assumed to be connected to the valve-rod $E$) into a position so that the valve will have $\frac{1}{16}$ of an inch lead, thereby giving the eccentric the correct angular advance. Fasten the eccentric in this position. If no inaccuracies exist in the valve gear, then by turning the crank-shaft we will find the same amount of lead when the crank is at $B$. If the valve has not the same lead at each end of the stroke, then inaccuracies do exist, which must be found and rectified. In setting the valve extreme accuracy is necessary; without this failure will be the result.

112. A direct-acting valve gear, as shown in Fig. 170, is not used on locomotives.

This kind of valve has been shown here to enable us to point out some fundamental principles which must be remembered in laying out any kind of valve gear. We will repeat here the most important ones in an order in which they will present themselves in laying out a valve gear for any locomotive:

1. The position of the eccentrics must be laid off from a line drawn perpendicular to the center line of motion of the valve gear, and not to the center line of crank. If the center line of motion coincides with the center line of crank, then the line drawn perpendicular to the former will also be perpendicular to the latter; but this is merely a case of coincidence, and does not prove that the line from which the positions of the eccentrics are laid must be drawn perpendicular to the center line of crank. (See Art. 63, page 43.)

2. When no rocker is used the linear advance will be equal to the angular advance of the eccentric, the latter being measured on a line drawn from the center of the eccentric perpendicular to the line from which it is laid off. (See Art. 67, page 46.)

3. When no rocker is employed the eccentric will travel ahead of the crank. (See Art. 67, page 46.)

4. The use of a shifting link does not change the angular advance of the eccentric. The use of a stationary link will change the angular advance of the eccentric. (See Art. 102, page 88.)

5. When no rockers and links are employed the throw of the eccentric will be equal to the travel of the valve. (See Art. 55, page 37.) When rockers with arms of unequal lengths are used the throw of the eccentric will not be equal to travel of the valve. When the rocker-arms are of equal length the throw will be equal to the travel of the valve. (See Art. 97, page 82.)

6. The lead varies with a shifting link; the lead is constant with a stationary link. (See Art. 102, page 88.)

7. The eccentric-rods must be connected correctly to a shifting link, otherwise there will be no lead when the link is moved towards mid-gear. (See Art. 108, page 93.)

## CLASSIFICATION OF LINKS.

113. When links are classified with reference to the manner of their suspension, we have, according to Art. 100, the shifting link and the stationary link.

When these same links are classified with reference to their form, we have the following two classes, namely, the box link as shown in Fig. 172, and the open link as shown in Figs. 173 and 175. In American locomotives the former is seldom employed, the open link being the favorite; and therefore we will consider the latter only.

The open link can again be divided into two classes, namely, the solid link, as shown in Fig. 173, and the built-up link, generally called the skeleton link, shown in Fig. 175. The term "skeleton link" we shall hereafter adopt for this class of links.

## DEFINITIONS.

In all links the link arc is an arc, as $a\,b\,c$, drawn through the center of the opening, as shown in Fig. 173.

Length of link is the length of the opening measured on a straight line joining the ends $a$ and $c$ of the arc $a\,b\,c$.

# MODERN LOCOMOTIVE CONSTRUCTION.

Radius of link is the radius with which the link arc $a\,b\,c$ has been described, as stated in Art. 104.

Eccentric-rod pin arc is an arc, as $e\,d$, drawn through the centers of the eccentric-rod pin-holes $F\,F$; this arc is described from the same center as that used in describing the link arc $a\,b\,c$.

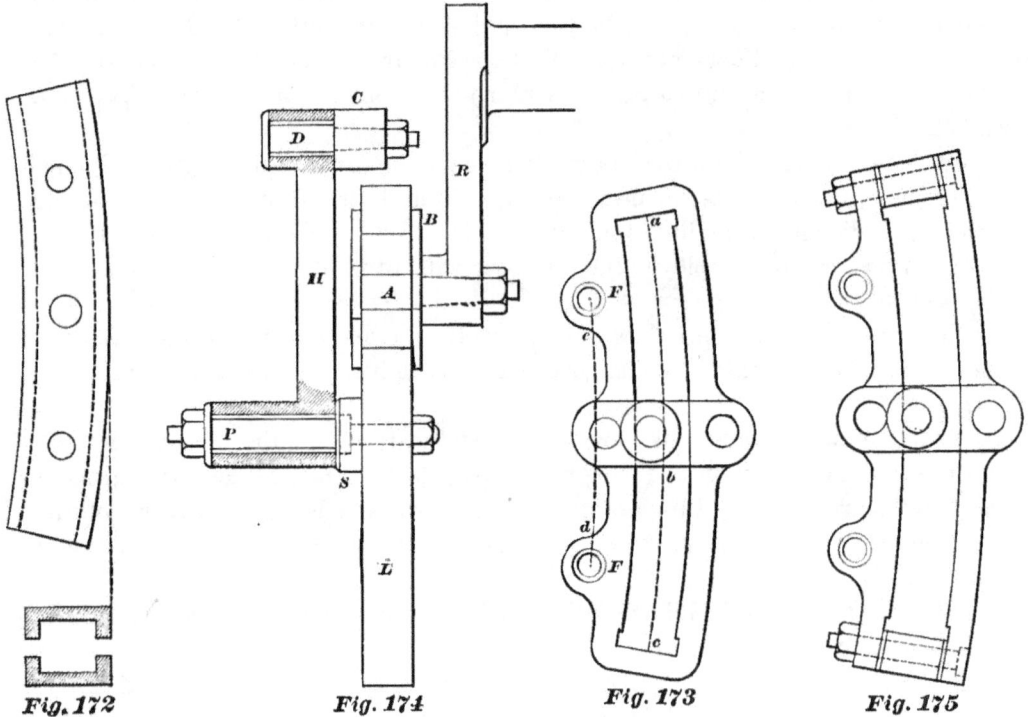

Fig. 172    Fig. 174    Fig. 173    Fig. 175

The manner of suspending the link and attaching the same to the rocker is plainly shown in Fig. 174. $R$ is the lower rocker-arm; $A$, the link-block pin; $B$, the link-block; $L$, the link; $S$, the link-saddle; $P$, the link-saddle pin; $H$, the link hanger; $C$, the end of the lifting shaft arm; and $D$, the lifting shaft pin.

### LINK-BLOCK PIN.

114. The link-block pin $A$ (Fig. 174) is made of wrought-iron case hardened, and is fastened to the lower rocker-arm. Its end, which fits into the lower rocker-arm, should be tapered and accurately fitted into the latter. The taper should be the same as that of the valve-rod pin, as given in Art. 90.

The diameter of the link-block pin at $A$ is generally made equal to that of the valve-rod pin. Hence, the diameters of these pins will be:

For 10 and 11 cylinders............................ $1\frac{3}{8}$ diam.
" 12, 13, and 14 " ............................ $1\frac{1}{2}$ "
" 15 and 16 " ............................ $1\frac{5}{8}$ "
" 17 " 18 " ............................ $1\frac{3}{4}$ "
" 19 " 20 " ............................ $1\frac{7}{8}$ "

Comparing these figures with the diameters of the pins in actual practice, it will be found that the diameters of the pins given for the smaller cylinders agree very closely with those in use, and the diameters given for 17, 18, 19, and 20 cylinders are rather large. But it must be remembered that the diameters here given have been calculated for cylinders having steam ports suitable for piston speed of 600 to 800 feet per minute, which will be required for fast passenger service, and with a steam pressure of 120 pounds in the cylinder. For freight engines in which the steam ports are often smaller than those adopted for fast passenger service, and consequently have smaller slide-valves, the diameter of these pins may be somewhat reduced, because they will have less work to do.

## LINK-BLOCKS.

115. The link-block is made of wrought-iron and is case hardened; it works freely and accurately on the pin $A$ (Fig. 174). For skeleton links the link-block is generally made in one piece; but when the solid link is used the link-block consists of two or three pieces. Fig. 176 represents a side view; Fig. 177 an end view; and Fig. 178 a

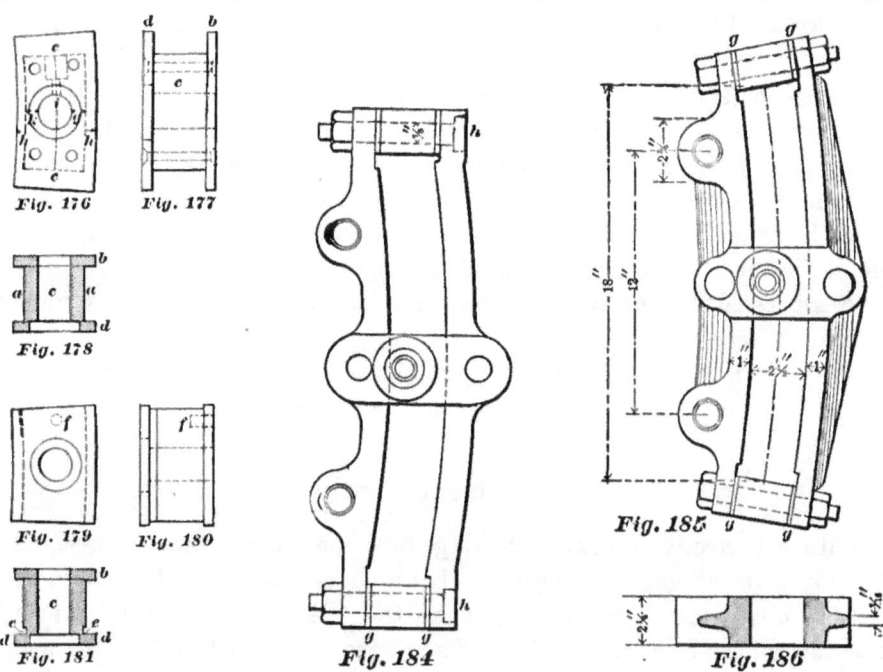

section of a link-block which is made in three pieces, namely, the plates $b$ and $d$, and the block $c$; after the block $c$ has been placed in the opening of the link, the plates $b$ and $d$ and the block $c$ are riveted together with four $\frac{3}{8}''$ rivets when link-block is large, and with four $\frac{1}{4}''$ rivets when the link-block is small; the position of the rivets is shown in Fig. 176.

The advantage claimed for a link-block made in this manner is, that the curved surfaces $a\ a$ of the block $c$ and the edges of the plates $b$ and $d$ can be finished in a slotting machine, which in some shops is more convenient to do than turning the curved surfaces of the block. Some master-mechanics prefer to make the link-block in two pieces, as shown in Figs. 179, 180, and 181. Link-blocks made in this manner consist of the plate $b$ and the block $c$ with the projections or flanges $d\ d$ forged on to it. Close to the flanges $d\ d$ small grooves $e\ e$, about $\frac{1}{16}$ of an inch deep and $\frac{3}{32}$ of an inch wide, are turned into the curved surfaces; with these grooves the surfaces can be finished completely with an emery wheel, without using special tools for finishing the corners after the link-block has been case hardened. Sometimes the plate $b$ is riveted to the block, as shown in Fig. 176, and at other times the plate $b$ (Fig. 181) is not fastened to the block $c$ in any manner. In this case the plate $b$, when the link-block is in position, must be next to rocker-arm, and is prevented from turning around by a pin $f$, $\frac{3}{8}$ of an inch diameter, as shown in Figs. 179, 180; the block and plate being held together by the link-block pin. All link-blocks, no matter whether they are made in one piece or several pieces, are counterbored, as shown in the figures to receive the head of the link-block pin.

The length of the block $c$ is generally from one and one-quarter to one and one-half times the throw of the eccentric. This distance is measured on a straight line joining the ends $c\ c$ of an arc drawn through the center of the block, as shown in Fig. 176.

The thickness at $g$ or $k$, Fig. 176, between the pin and the link is generally $\frac{7}{16}$ of an inch.

In a number of engines the plates $b$ and $d$ extend beyond the ends of the block $c$, as shown in Fig. 177; this is done to gain larger wearing surfaces. But since the extension of these plates will occasionally cause trouble in oiling the link-block, the plates are sometimes cut flush with the ends of the block, as shown in Fig. 179.

The depth of the flanges at $h\ h$, Fig. 176, is generally $\frac{7}{16}$ of an inch, and we have seen them $\frac{5}{8}$ of an inch deep; but in the latter case the distance between the link arc and the eccentric-rod pin arc was greater than desirable. The plates $b$ and $d$ are generally made $\frac{3}{8}$ of an inch thick.

The oil hole at $i$, half way through the metal, is $\frac{1}{4}$ of an inch in diameter, and then increased to 1 or $1\frac{1}{4}$ inches in diameter, to hold the waste and oil.

## PROPORTIONS OF LINKS.

116. With a correctly designed shifting link motion, we obtain an equal lead when the link is in full-gear, and very nearly an equal lead when the link is in half-gear; we also obtain an equal cut-off when the link is in half-gear, and as little slip of the link on the block as possible. The slip is greater when the link is in full-gear than when it is in mid-gear, and generally the slip in forward gear will exceed the slip in the backward gear. But since there will be always more or less slip, and since this will cause wear and create "lost motion," the link must be made of such metal as will enable it to run as long a time as possible without wearing to any appreciable extent, thereby preserving the delicacy of its action.

We therefore find the majority of the locomotive links made of wrought-iron, case hardened, which gives a smooth and excellent service to resist wear.

During late years cast-iron links and links cast of steel have been adopted and used. These will wear faster than wrought-iron links case hardened. But the lost motion caused by wear is not undesirable, therefore cast-iron or cast-steel is mostly used for the skeleton links. In these links very thin copper strips are inserted at $g\ g\ g\ g$, Figs. 184, 185, so that, when the lost motion affects the correct action of the link to an extent which is hurtful to the engine, a strip or liner is taken out, and the delicate action of the link restored. Again, if the wear of these links becomes excessive, they can be easily replaced by new links, as the cost of these is comparatively small. Figs. 185 and 186 represent the form of a skeleton link made of cast-iron, and used on a number of mogul engines having cylinders 18 inches in diameter. The same form is also adopted when the link is to be cast of steel. We have met with a few locomotives having cast-iron links of a form similar to that of a solid wrought-iron link, such as is shown in Fig. 182.

But skeleton links are not always made of cast-iron or cast of steel; often we find skeleton links made of wrought-iron case hardened, as shown in Fig. 175, and these are preferred on many railroads.

In skeleton links a difficulty is experienced in putting back the end bolts after some of the liners have been taken out, because these bolt holes—which incline towards each other—will then not be in line; therefore, in order to avoid this difficulty, some master-mechanics make the form of the links as shown in Fig. 184, in which the bolts $h\ h$ are parallel to each other.

117. The eccentric-rod pins will, in a comparatively short time, wear the holes of the link oblong; and therefore, in order to preserve the link as long as possible, the holes $e$ and $f$, Fig. 182, are bushed; the bushing is made of wrought-iron about $\frac{3}{16}$ or $\frac{1}{8}$ of an inch thick, case hardened, and then forced into the link, usually with a hydraulic pressure of four tons. This bushing is used in wrought-iron, and also in cast links. When the wear of the pin and bushing becomes so great as to affect the action of the link, the pin and bushing can be easily and cheaply replaced by new ones. Sometimes we find links in which the bushing has been fitted loosely in the holes; in these cases the bushing is slightly longer than the width of the link, and held fast in the eccentric-rod jaw by tightening the nut of the eccentric-rod pin, allowing the bushing to move freely in the link. Loose bushing is better adapted for cast links than for wrought-iron case-hardened links, because the former can be more readily and in less time rebored, or replaced by a new link if necessary, and with less expense than the latter.

118. The eccentric-rod pins are also case hardened. The cross-sectional area of one of these pins should not be less than half the area of the rocker-pins given in Art. 114; locomotive builders generally make the area of an eccentric-rod pin a little larger than half the area of rocker-pin, so as to obtain a larger bearing surface. The diameter of the eccentric-rod pins for engines having cylinders 19 or 20 inches in diameter is usually $1\frac{1}{4}$ inches; for engines having cylinders 16, 17, or 18 inches in diameter, $1\frac{1}{8}$; and for smaller engines, 1 inch.

119. For locomotives having cylinders 10 inches in diameter and upwards, the distance between the centers of the eccentric-rod pins $e$ and $f$, Fig. 182, generally varies from 9 to 10 inches; and for locomotives having cylinders 16 inches in diameter and upwards, the distance between these eccentric-rod pin centers generally varies from 11 to 12 inches; sometimes, but rarely, this distance is 13 inches. The distances between the eccentric-rod pin centers should not be made less than those here given, because if we do so the slip of the link on the block will be increased. Neither can these distances be made much longer, because generally the room under the locomotive will not admit longer links.

120. In locomotives having cylinders 10 inches in diameter and upwards, the throw of the eccentric is from 3½ to 4 inches; and in locomotives having cylinders 16 inches in diameter and upwards, the throw of the eccentric is from 4½ to 5½ inches, oftener 5 inches. Now, comparing the throw of the eccentrics with the distances between the eccentric-rod pin centers, we find that this distance varies from 2¼ to 2½ times the throw of the eccentric. Hence, in designing a locomotive link we may make the distance between the eccentric-rod pin centers equal to 2¼ or 2½ times the throw of the eccentric. Although this is an empirical rule, it is a good rule to adopt, provided it does not make the link too long.

121. The distance between the eccentric-rod pin arc and the link arc must not be greater than necessary; it should be such as will allow $\frac{1}{16}$ of an inch clearance between the flanges of the link-block and the ends of the eccentric-rods. By increasing this distance we also increase the slip, which must be avoided. In ordinary locomotive practice this distance varies from 2¼ to 3 inches, and occasionally reaches 3⅛ inches.

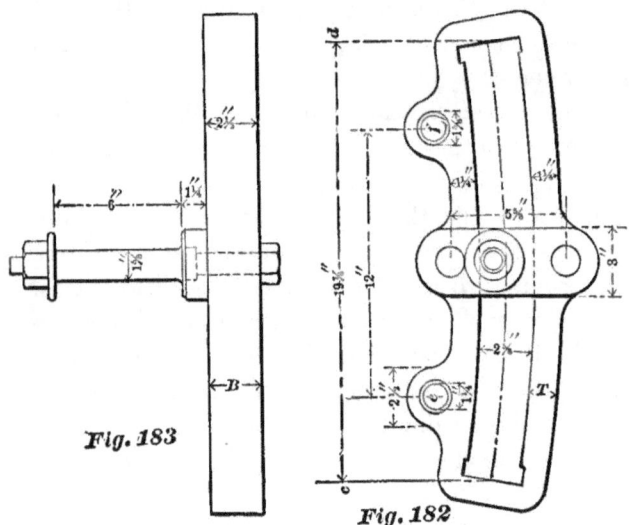

Fig. 183

Fig. 182

122. The length of the link, that is, the distance from $c$ to $d$, Fig. 182, should be sufficiently great to allow the center of the link-block to be placed in line with the center of either one of the eccentric-rod pins, leaving a clearance sufficient for the slip, so that when running in this gear the link-block will be prevented from coming in contact with the end of the link opening. In fact, ¼ of an inch for the least amount clearance between the link-block and end of link opening is preferable.

Consequently, to determine the length of a link, we must know the distance between eccentric-rod pins, the length of the link-block, the maximum slip, and the desired amount of clearances. The sum of these items will be the length of the link.

EXAMPLE 37.—The distance between the eccentric-rod pins is 12 inches; the length of the link-block is 6 inches; the maximum slip is 1⅛ inches; and the desired clearance at either end must not be less than ¼ of an inch.

$$12'' + 6'' + 1\tfrac{1}{8}'' + \tfrac{1}{4}'' + \tfrac{1}{4}'' = 19\tfrac{5}{8}'' = \text{length of link.}$$

The length of links in the different locomotives having cylinders 16 inches in diameter and upwards varies from 18 inches to 19⅞ inches, rarely exceeding the latter dimension.

123. The radius of links in nearly all locomotives is equal to the distance between the center of the main driving axle and the center of link-block pin (sometimes called the lower rocker-arm pin) when the latter stands in the center of its travel.

It has been found that, with this radius, the variation of the lead is sensibly equal for the front and back strokes of the piston. Sometimes, when greater accuracy in the equalization of the lead is required, this radius of the link is made a little shorter.

124. In order to obtain the breadth $B$, Fig. 183, and the thickness $T$, Fig. 182, of a wrought-iron link, we should know the pressure of the valve against its seat; but since the existing data is not sufficient to determine this pressure accurately, we will assume that the friction of the valve on its seat—and which the link has to overcome in moving the valve—is proportional to the total steam pressure on the back of the valve.*

Consequently, for the purpose of obtaining these dimensions of the link we will adopt the same rule as that used for finding the principal dimensions of an eccentric, given in Art. 98.

Therefore, for finding the breadth $B$ and thickness $T$ of a wrought-iron link we use the same units found in Art. 98, and multiply the unit by the numbers given in the following table:

TABLE 13.

Breadth $B$ of wrought-iron link = unit × 1.62
Thickness $T$ " " " = unit × .81

EXAMPLE 38.—Find the breadth $B$ and the thickness $T$ of a wrought-iron link suitable for a consolidation engine having cylinders 20 inches in diameter; the length of valve is 10 inches; breadth of the same 20 inches; and pressure of the steam in the steam-chest 120 pounds per square inch.

We find in Art. 98 that the unit for this size of slide-valve is 1.54, hence:

$$1.54 \times 1.62 = 2.49'' = \text{breadth of link.}$$
$$1.54 \times .81 = 1.24'' = \text{thickness } T.$$

EXAMPLE 39.—Find the breadth $B$ and the thickness $T$ of a wrought-iron link suitable for an eight-wheeled passenger locomotive having cylinders 10 inches in diameter; slide-valve being 6 inches long and $11\frac{1}{2}$ inches wide; steam pressure in steam-chest 120 pounds per square inch.

We find in Art. 98 that the unit for this size of slide-valve is .91, hence:

$$.91 \times 1.62 = 1.47'' = \text{breadth of link.}$$
$$.91 \times .81 = .73'' = \text{thickness } T.$$

Now, comparing the dimensions obtained in Example 38 with the dimensions of the link in Figs. 182 and 183, which is a drawing of a link used in a consolidation engine with cylinder 20 inches in diameter, lately built and now in active service, we find that these dimensions agree very closely. It will also be found that the dimensions of other wrought-iron links obtained by this rule, suitable for locomotives having cylinders 13 inches in diameter, and others having cylinders of larger diameter, up to 20 inches, will agree very closely with the dimensions of the links in locomotives of the foregoing sizes at present in active service.

* It should be understood that the total steam pressure on the back of the valve is greater than the pressure of the valve against its seat (see Art. 82).

106 MODERN LOCOMOTIVE CONSTRUCTION.

But the dimensions of links for smaller locomotives obtained by our rule are less than the dimensions of links made according to the present practice of locomotive builders.

Take, for instance, Example 39. In this we find that the breadth of the link suitable for locomotives having cylinders 10 inches in diameter is 1.47 inches, say 1½ inches, whereas the breadth of links in locomotives of this size, and at present in active service, is 1¾ and sometimes 2 inches. But when it is necessary to build a very light locomotive, the writer believes that links proportioned by this rule will give good satisfaction, although they will wear somewhat faster than those having a greater width.

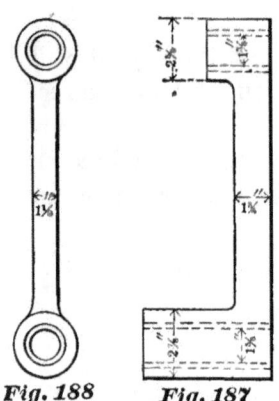

Fig. 188   Fig. 187

125. The tendency in modern locomotive construction is to make the saddle-pin longer than formerly. This, in the writer's opinion, is a great improvement. The saddle-pin for locomotives having cylinders 17 up to 20 inches in diameter is now generally 6 inches long, as shown in Fig. 183. For smaller locomotives the length of saddle-pin is decreased; a saddle-pin 4 inches long will work very satisfactorily in locomotives with cylinders 10 inches in diameter. These saddle-pins should not be made shorter, unless compelled to do so by the narrow gauge of the road.

The diameter of the saddle-pin is usually about one-eighth of an inch less than the diameter of the link-block pin.

Figs. 187 and 188 represent a link hanger. The dimensions given are suitable for locomotives having cylinders 19 inches and others having cylinders 20 inches in diameter. Usually the holes are bushed with wrought-iron ferrules case hardened.

### LIFTING SHAFT.

126. Fig. 189 represents an end view and Fig. 190 a plan of the "lifting shaft," or sometimes called the "reverse shaft." Two arms $B$ $B$—one for each link—are forged to the shaft $D$; the holes for the lifting-shaft pins $A$ $A$ in the end of these arms are tapered; the taper should be the same as that of the valve-rod pin (see Art. 90).

The case-hardened lifting-shaft pins $A$ $A$ are made to fit these holes very accurately. On these pins the link hangers vibrate. The arm $E$ is generally forged to the shaft $D$; occasionally it is keyed to the shaft. The hole at $C$ for the reach-rod pin is bushed with a wrought-iron ferrule, case hardened, usually from $\frac{1}{8}$ to $\frac{3}{16}$ of an inch thick. The reach-rod pin, which connects the reach-rod to the arm $E$, is straight and case hardened. The other end of the reach-rod is connected to the reversing lever at $C$, as shown in Fig. 192. The line $L$ $B$ (Fig. 192) represents the center line of the reverse lever when it stands in full-gear forward, and the line $A$ $B$ represents the center line of the reverse lever when it stands in full-gear backward; and when the reverse lever stands in center of the arc as shown, the link motion is said to be in mid-gear. Now when the reverse lever (which is connected by the reach-rod to the lifting shaft) is moved from $A$ to $L$ the motion of the engine will be reversed; or if the reverse lever is moved to any intermediate position, the travel of the valve will be reduced, and steam in the cylinder will be cut off sooner.

The diameter of the lifting shaft (Figs. 189 and 190) and the size of its arms must be sufficiently large to prevent the shaft and arms from springing. The dimensions given in the figures are those of lifting shafts generally used in locomotives which have cylinders 20 inches in diameter. For smaller locomotives, which have cylinders 10 inches in diameter, the lifting-shaft arms $B\ B$ measured close to the shaft are usually 2½ inches wide and ⅝ of an inch thick; the arm $E$ is 2¼ inches wide and ¾ of an inch thick; and the shaft 2 inches in diameter. These dimensions are gradually enlarged as the diameter of the cylinder is increased.

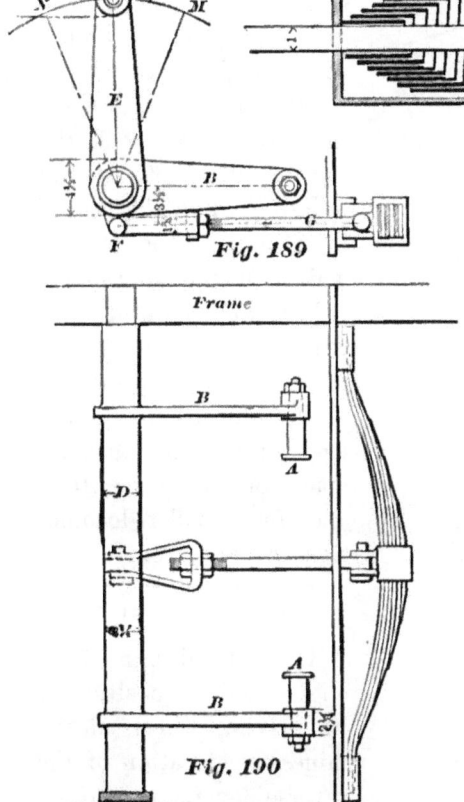

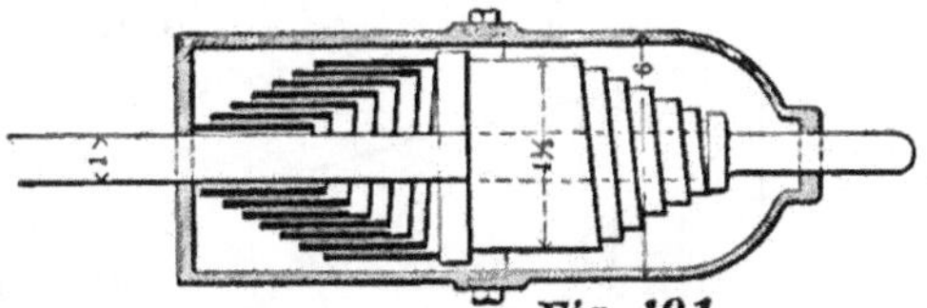

Fig. 191

Fig. 189

Fig. 190

The location of the lifting shaft and the length of its arms $B\ B$ will influence the equalization of the cut-off; therefore it is very important to assign the correct position to the lifting shaft and make the arms $B\ B$ of the proper length. How to find the position of the lifting shaft and the correct length of the arms $B\ B$ will be explained later. The length of the arm $E$ is generally limited by the design of the locomotive; that is, the length of this arm must be such as will prevent the reach-rod from coming in contact with other parts of the engine.

The center lines of the arms $B\ B$, and that of the arm $E$, do not often stand at right angles to each other as shown; they should have the following relative positions: The center line $A\ F$ of the arm $E$ should stand perpendicular to the reach-rod when the link motion is in mid-gear; and the center lines of the arms $B\ B$ should then stand in the center of their total vibration. This will allow the end of the arm $E$ to pass through equal arcs on each side of the line $A\ F$ during the time the links are moved from full-gear forward to full-gear backward. The short arm $F$ is usually forged to the shaft $D$; occasionally it is bolted to the shaft. To this arm $F$ a spring counter-balance is attached which acts against the weight of links, hangers, etc., relieving the engineer of considerable hard work in reversing the engine, and enabling him to move the reverse lever as easily in one direction as in the other. Sometimes, for the purpose of counterbalancing the weight of the links, hangers, etc., volute springs are used, as shown in Fig. 191, but the writer believes that a half elliptic spring, as shown in Figs. 189 and 190, will give better satisfaction.

127. Volute springs, as shown in Fig. 191, are made of steel 3 inches wide, $\tfrac{3}{16}$ of an inch thick, the springs are 6 to $6\tfrac{1}{2}$ inches long for large locomotives. For small locomotives these springs are made of steel 3 inches wide, $\tfrac{1}{8}$ of an inch thick, and the same length as that of the larger ones. The cast-iron casing around these springs is generally bolted to the yoke brace.

Elliptic springs are usually made nearly as long as the space between the frames will allow. For large engines, $4'\ 8\tfrac{1}{2}''$ gauge, the length of these springs is usually 40 inches before compression, and having 5 or 6 leaves of steel $2\tfrac{1}{2}$ inches wide and $\tfrac{5}{16}$ thick.

When these half elliptic springs are used, the rod $G$ (Fig. 189) should be attached to the arm $F$ in a manner as shown, which will allow the spring to be tightened or loosened without disconnecting the rod $G$ from the spring.

Reach-rods for large locomotives are usually made of $2\tfrac{3}{4}'' \times \tfrac{3}{4}''$ iron; and for smaller locomotives $2'' \times \tfrac{5}{8}''$ iron.

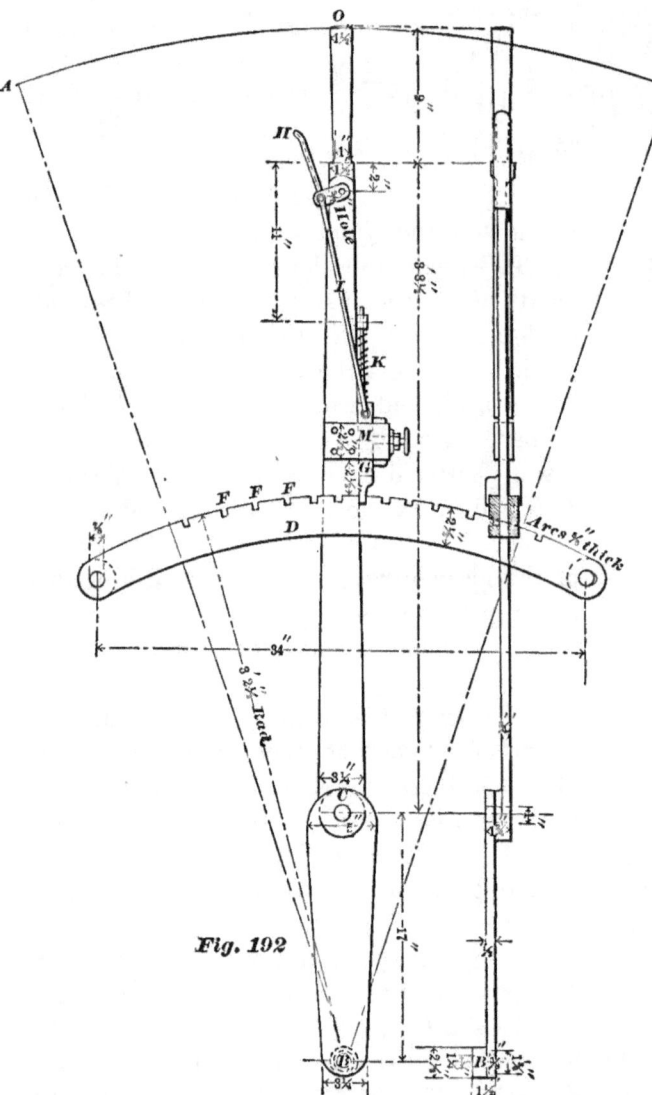

Fig. 192

### REVERSE LEVER.

128. The design of an engine and the position of its driving wheels determines the location of the reverse lever. Generally, in engines having a footplate the lower end of the lever can be attached to the same; in consolidation engines or hard-coal burners we are generally compelled to attach the lever to the frame. In all cases the reverse lever is located on the right-hand side of the engine. The reverse lever is usually made of wrought-iron; but when the part of the lever below the arc $D$, Fig. 193, is very crooked—which often occurs—then in order to save labor in forging, the lower part is sometimes made of cast-iron and bolted to the upper part, which is made of wrought-iron. The form of the lower end of the reverse lever is determined also by

the design of the engine. In consolidation engines it often happens that the reverse lever has to move between one of the rear driving wheels and the boiler, and therefore its lower part has to be made comparatively thin and very wide, as shown in Fig. 192. In engines which have the reverse lever attached to the foot-board, the lower end of the lever is shaped as shown in Fig. 193, and its thickness is the same throughout; usually ¾ of an inch for large engines, and ⅝ of an inch for smaller ones.

The total length of the reverse lever and the location of the reach-rod pin in the same must be such as will allow the top of the reverse-lever handle $O$, Fig. 192, to move through a distance of about 4 feet in large engines; and through a distance of about 3 feet 6 inches in smaller engines during the time that the link is moved from full-gear forward to full-gear backward. Now, since the distance through which the link is moved is equal to the distance between the centers of eccentric-rod pins, and since these are placed from 11 to 12 inches apart in large engines, and from 9 to 10 inches in small engines (Art. 119), we may say that the distance through which the reverse-lever handle moves should be about four times the distance through which the link moves.

The diameter of the reverse-lever pin $B$, Fig. 192, is usually 1 inch for small locomotives and 1¼ inches for large ones. These pins are case hardened.

The hole $C$ for the reach-rod pin in the reverse lever is sometimes bushed with a case-hardened bushing.

129. The arcs $D$ are usually made of steel, fastened to the boiler, or to the foot-plate and running board. In a number of engines two arcs are employed, one on each side of the lever, as shown in Fig. 192. In other locomotives one arc only is used, which passes through an opening in the reverse lever as shown in Fig. 194. When a single arc is used it is made comparatively wide, as will be seen by comparing Fig. 192 with Fig. 194. Whether to use two arcs or the single arc is a matter of choice and judgment. The arcs should be placed as high as the design of engine will permit; by so doing more notches, $F F$ (Fig. 192), can be cut in the arcs, with sufficient metal for strength between them, than can be cut in arcs placed lower down. The notches $F F$ receive the latch $G$. This latch is connected to the latch-handle $H$ by the links $I$, so that, when the latch-handle is pressed towards the handle of the reverse lever, the latch $G$ will be lifted out of the notch, and when the pressure on the latch-handle ceases, the spring $K$ presses the latch into the notch. With this arrangement the lever can be placed and held in any desired position. The writer believes that it will give better satisfaction by placing the latch $G$ (which slides in the clamp $M$) in front of the reverse lever, as shown in Fig. 192, and not in the rear of the reverse lever, as shown in Fig. 193. By adopting the former method the reverse lever will press against the latch; but by placing the latch in the rear of the lever, the tendency will be to pull the reverse lever away from the latch, which will in a short time cause the lever to rattle and interfere with the correct action of the link motion.

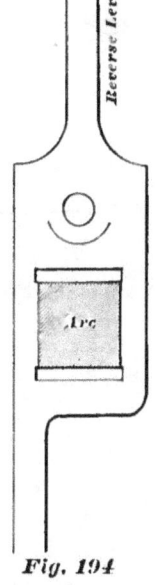

Fig. 194

130. Master-mechanics differ in opinion in regard to the number and the position

of the notches in the arcs. First: A number of master-mechanics prefer the notches arranged in a manner which will hold the reverse lever in positions that cause the steam to be cut off in the cylinder at some full number of inches of the stroke. Consequently, we find arcs with notches cut in such positions as will cause the steam to be cut off at 6, 9, 12, 15, 18, and 21 inches of the stroke; or at 6, 8, 10, 12, 15, 18, and 21 inches of the stroke. Besides these notches one notch is cut in the arcs to hold the link in mid-gear. With this arrangement of notches a difficulty arises, namely, it is often found that when a particular notch—say the 6-inch notch—holds the reverse lever, the cylinders do not receive a sufficient amount of steam to haul the train, and when the reverse lever is moved to the next notch—the 9-inch notch—the cylinders receive too much steam, and therefore the steam has to be throttled, causing the locomotive to work under disadvantages. To overcome this difficulty, May's Reverse Lever Latch has been invented, by which a finer gradation is obtained without changing the notches. This latch is shown in Figs. 195 and 196, and, as will be seen, is a very simple device. The only difference between this and the ordinary latch is, that the former is a double latch instead of a single one; consequently, it can easily be applied to the reverse levers at present in use without any change in the levers or arcs. Now, since a finer gradation is not a matter of convenience, but it is a saving of fuel, the advantages of May's latch, or some equally good device, will easily be perceived.

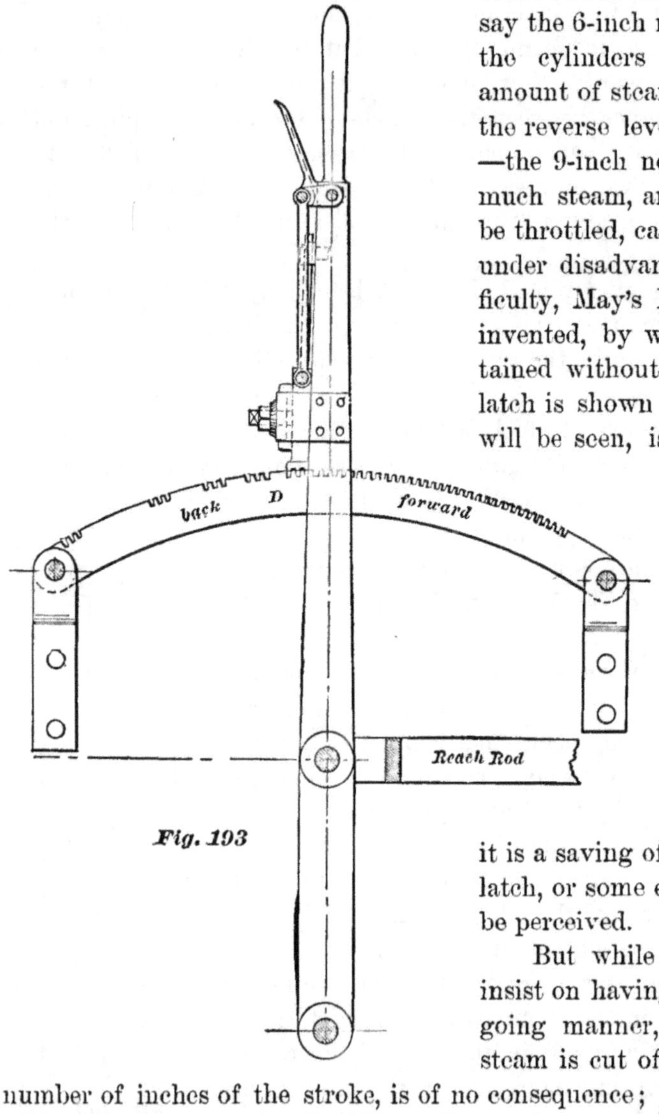

But while some master-mechanics will insist on having the notches cut in the foregoing manner, others believe that whether steam is cut off at full inches, or a fractional number of inches of the stroke, is of no consequence; hence these master-mechanics will cut as many notches in the arc as there is room for, and as close together as the strength of metal will allow. Fig. 193 shows an arc with notches cut in this manner. The distance between the centers of these notches is half an inch; sometimes the notches are cut closer than this. With notches cut in this manner a very fine gradation of cut-off is obtained, and fuel saved.

*Fig. 193*

## VALVE GEARS WITH ROCKERS.

**131.** Heretofore we have shown, theoretically and practically, how to set the eccentrics in simple valve gears in which rockers are not employed, and in which the connections between the eccentric and valve are direct, and also in which the center line of motion of the valve gear coincided with that of the piston.

Let us now continue the subject of setting the eccentrics, in the following order: First, how to find the position of an eccentric in a valve gear in which a rocker with arms of equal length is used, and in which the center line of motion of the valve gear coincides with the center line of motion of the piston. Second, how to find the position of the eccentric in a valve gear in which a rocker whose arms are not of equal length is used, and in which the center line of motion of the valve gear coincides with that of the piston. Third, to find the position of an eccentric in a valve gear in which a rocker is used, and in which the center line of motion of the valve gear does not coincide with that of the piston.

### TO FIND THE POSITION OF AN ECCENTRIC IN A VALVE GEAR HAVING A ROCKER WHOSE ARMS ARE OF EQUAL LENGTH, AND THE CENTER LINE OF MOTION OF THE VALVE GEAR COINCIDING WITH THAT OF THE PISTON.

In order to make this subject as plain as possible, let us take the following example:

EXAMPLE 39a.—Lap of valve, $\frac{15}{16}$ of an inch; lead, $\frac{1}{16}$ of an inch; travel of valve, 5 inches; length of each rocker-arm, 10 inches; find the position of the eccentric.

In Art. 67 we have explained how to find the position of an eccentric in a simple valve gear in which no rocker is employed, and in Art. 61 we have pointed to the fact that in simple valve gears of this kind the eccentric must travel ahead of the crank.

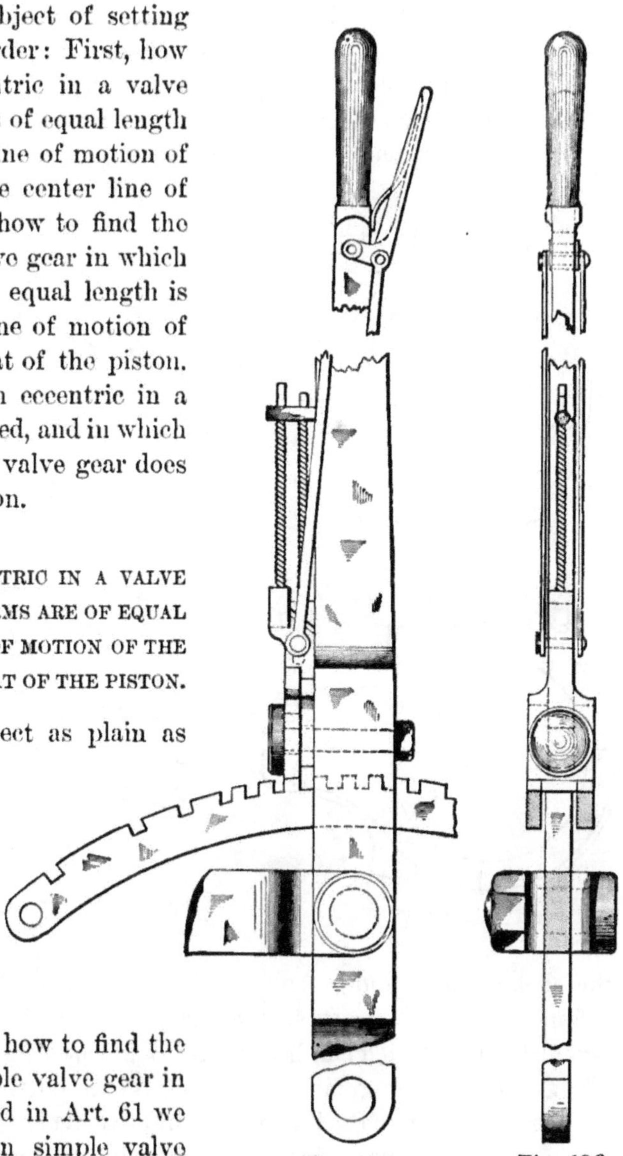

*Fig. 195*     *Fig. 196*

It is now to be shown that, when a rocker is interposed between the eccentric and valve without making any other changes in a simple valve gear, the eccentric must follow the crank, instead of traveling ahead of the same; and it is also to be shown

112                    MODERN LOCOMOTIVE CONSTRUCTION.

that, when the rocker whose arms are equal in length is used, the angular advance of the eccentric will be laid off in a different direction from that in a simple valve gear; but the amount of angular advance will remain the same in both cases.

In order to point out clearly the reason why this should be so, we have illustrated in Fig. 197 two connections between the valve and eccentric. 1st. The upper connection, marked "Case 1," is that in which no rocker is employed. 2d. The lower connection, marked "Case 2," is that in which a rocker is interposed.

In Case 1 the center $C$ of the crank-shaft is in line with the valve; in Case 2 the center $C_2$ of the crank-shaft is situated below the valve so as to admit a rocker.

In Art. 61 we have seen that the angular advance of the eccentric is laid off from a line drawn perpendicular to the center line of crank. This method is also applicable

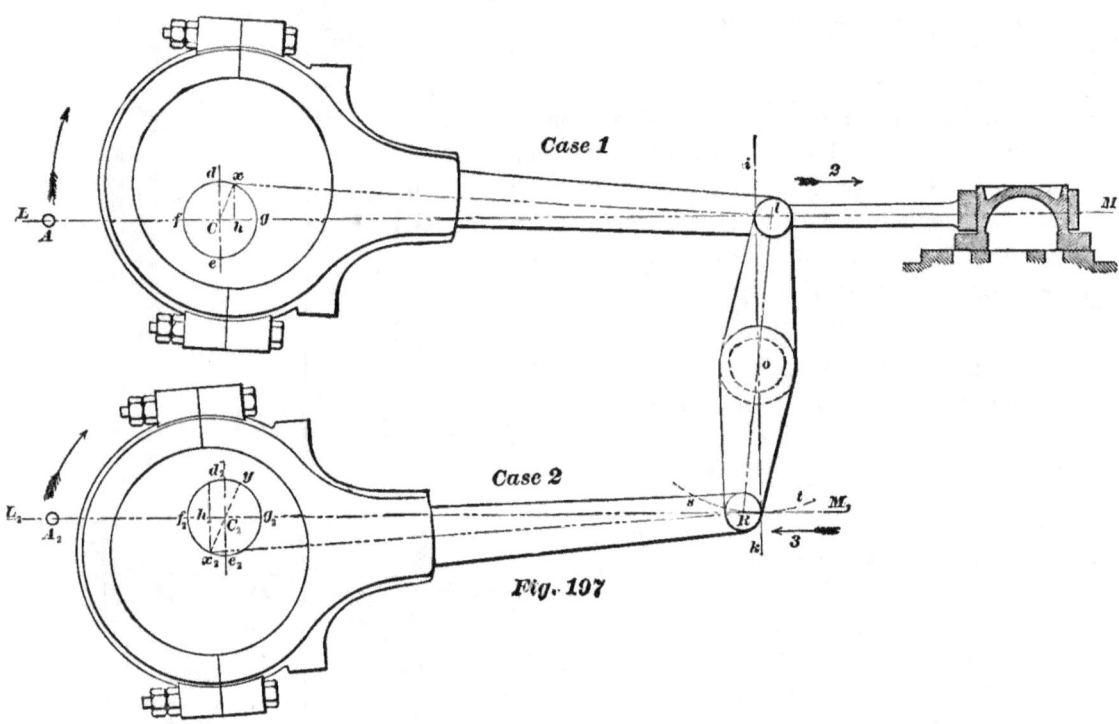

Fig. 197

to the example now under consideration; but since this will not give correct results in laying out all valve gears, such as are to be considered hereafter, it will be best first to establish a rule which can be applied to all cases. It is this:

RULE 17.—The angular advance of the eccentric must be laid off from a line drawn perpendicular to the line of motion of the valve gear (see Art. 63). Hence, before we can comply with this condition so as to find the position of the eccentric in Case 1, or in Case 2, Fig. 197, we must draw the center line of motion of the valve gear. To do this in Case 1, we draw a line $L M$ through the center $C$ of the shaft in a direction in which the valve moves. This line $L M$ will be the center line of motion of the valve in Case 1, and agrees with the definition given in Art. 63. In Case 2 we draw a line $L_2 M_2$ through the center $C_2$ of the shaft, and tangent to the arc $s\,t$, described by the center $R$ of the lower rocker-arm pin.* This line $L_2 M_2$ will be the center line of motion of the valve gear in Case 2.

Now let us apply the method given in Art. 61 for finding the position of the eccentric in Case 1, Fig. 197. From the center $C$ of the shaft, and with a radius of $2\frac{1}{2}$ inches (equal to half the throw of the eccentric in our example), describe a circle $f d g$; the circumference of this circle will represent the path of the center of the eccentric. Through the center $C$ of the shaft draw a line $d e$ perpendicular to $L M$. Let $A$ represent the position of the center of the crank-pin when the crank is on the dead center, or, in other words, when the piston is at the beginning of the stroke.

Now, since the conditions in our example demand that the center line of the valve gear shall coincide with that of the piston, it follows that the center $A$ of the crank-pin must lie in the line $L M$—and when in this position the valve must have opened the steam port $\frac{1}{16}$ of an inch, which is equal to the given amount of lead—and occupy the position as shown in the figure. To find the position of the eccentric which will correspond with that of the valve, and enable the shaft to revolve in the direction indicated by the arrow, we continue our construction as follows: From the center $C$ on the line $L M$, away from the crank-pin $A$, lay off a point $h$; the distance between $C$ and $h$ must be equal to the sum of the lap and lead, namely 1 inch. Through the point $h$ draw a straight line $h x$ parallel to the line $d e$, cutting the circumference $f d g$ in the point $x$; this point $x$ will be the required center of the eccentric, and will travel ahead of the crank; the valve will open the steam port more and more during the time the shaft revolves through a certain distance, and then close the port, as it should do. In Art. 61 we have drawn the line $d e$ perpendicular to the center line of crank. In this example we have drawn the line $d e$ perpendicular to the center line of motion; but since the center line of crank and the line of motion coincide, the result is the same.

The position of the eccentric when a rocker is used, as shown in Case 2, Fig. 197, is found in the following manner: For the sake of convenience and easy comparison, let us draw the center line of motion $L_2 M_2$ of the valve gear parallel to $L M$ in Case 1; also let us place the center $C_2$ of the shaft in a line drawn through $C$ perpendicular to the line $L M$, and low enough to admit a rocker with arms each 10 inches long. Let $o$ represent the fixed center of the rocker-shaft, and let the line $i k$, drawn through $o$ perpendicular to $L_2 M_2$, represent the center line of the rocker-arms when these stand midway of their travel, corresponding to the position of the slide-valve when the latter stands in a central position, not indicated in these illustrations. Now, it must be evident that when the valve stands in the position as shown in the figure it has moved 1 inch (the sum of the lap and lead) out of its central position, and consequently the center of the upper rocker-arm pin must have moved out of its central position the same amount in a horizontal direction (not measured on the arc described by the center of the pin), and therefore the center of the pin will be at $l$ when the valve stands in the position as shown. Through the centers $l$ and $o$ draw a straight line $l R$, cutting the arc $s t$, described by the lower rocker-pin, in the point $R$. This

---

* Drawing this center line of motion tangent to the arc described by the lower rocker-arm pin is not absolutely correct, but is near enough, and generally considered so, for all practical purposes in locomotive construction, or in engines having eccentric-rods of the ordinary length; that is, engines not having very short eccentric-rods.

point $R$ will be the position of the center of the lower rocker-pin when the upper pin is at $l$; and, as will be seen, these pins will then be located in the opposite sides along the line $i\,k$; but the distance between the center $R$ and the line $i\,k$ will be the same as that between the center $l$ and the line $i\,k$, namely, 1 inch, because the rocker-arms are of equal lengths. Also notice that as the pin $l$ travels in the direction of the arrow 2, as it should do, the pin $R$ will travel in an opposite direction, indicated by the arrow 3. When the valve stands in the position as shown, the crank-pin $A_2$ in Case 2 will be on the same side of the shaft as $A$ in Case 1, and will lie in the line $L_2\,M_2$, because, according to the condition in our example, the center line of motion of the valve gear coincides with that of the piston. Therefore the following construction will give us the position of the eccentric to correspond with that of the crank. Through the center $C_2$ of the shaft draw a line $d_2\,e_2$ perpendicular to $L_2\,M_2$; and from the center $C_2$, and with a radius of $2\frac{1}{2}$ inches, describe a circle $f_2\,d_2\,g_2$; the circumference of this circle will represent the path of the center of the eccentric. From the center $C_2$ on the line $L_2\,M_2$, and towards the crank-pin $A_2$, lay off a point $h_2$; the distance between the center $C_2$ and the point $h_2$ must be equal to 1 inch, because the horizontal distance between the point $R$ and the line $i\,k$ is 1 inch. Through the point $h_2$ draw a line $h_2\,x_2$ parallel to the line $d_2\,e_2$, and cutting the circumference $f_2\,d_2\,g_2$ at the point $x_2$; this point $x_2$ will be the required position of the eccentric in Case 2 when the crank-pin is at $A_2$ and the shaft rotating in the direction indicated by the arrow. If in Case 2 we had found the position of the eccentric in precisely the same manner as that employed in Case 1, and had placed the eccentric at $y$ and thus caused the eccentric to travel ahead of the crank as in Case 1, a movement in the wrong direction would have been communicated to the rocker-pin $R$, which would make the valve close the steam port at this particular time instead of opening the same, as it should do. Also notice that $y$ is one end of the diameter of the circle $f_2\,d_2\,g_2$, and $x_2$ is the other end of the same diameter.

132. From this we learn that in a valve gear in which a rocker with arms of equal lengths is introduced the eccentric must be placed in a position directly opposite to that of an eccentric in a valve gear in which no rocker is used; also, when the amount of lap and lead in Case 1 is the same as that in Case 2, then the angular advance in both cases will be equal, although laid off in opposite directions.

When two eccentrics and a link are to be used, as in locomotives, then, in order to find the position of the second eccentric, prolong the line $h_2\,x_2$ so as to cut the circumference $f_2\,d_2\,g_2$; this point of intersection will be the center of the second eccentric. (See Art. 99.)

POSITION OF ECCENTRICS WHEN A ROCKER WITH ARMS OF UNEQUAL LENGTHS IS USED.

133. In Fig. 197 we have shown the position which the eccentrics must occupy when the lengths of the rocker-arms are equal.

If, however, the lower rocker-arm is made either longer or shorter than the upper arm, then the position of the eccentrics on the shaft must be changed from that position they would occupy when the arms of the rocker are of equal lengths.

EXAMPLE 40.—The length of the lower rocker-arm is $11\frac{1}{4}$ inches; the length of the upper arm, 9 inches; throw of eccentric, 5 inches; lap, $\tfrac{15}{16}$ of an inch; lead, $\tfrac{1}{16}$ of an inch; the center line of motion of the valve gear coincides with that of the piston; it is required to find the position of the eccentrics.

Fig. 198. Draw the center line $i\,k$; this line will represent the center line of the rocker-arms when these stand midway of their travel. On the line $i\,k$ locate any point $o$ to represent the center of the rocker-shaft. From the center $o$, and with a radius equal to 9 inches, describe an arc $u\,v$ to represent the path of the center $l$ of the upper rocker-pin; also from the center $o$, and with a radius equal to $11\tfrac{1}{4}$ inches, describe an arc $s\,t$ to represent the path of the center of the lower rocker-pin. On the arc $u\,v$ lay

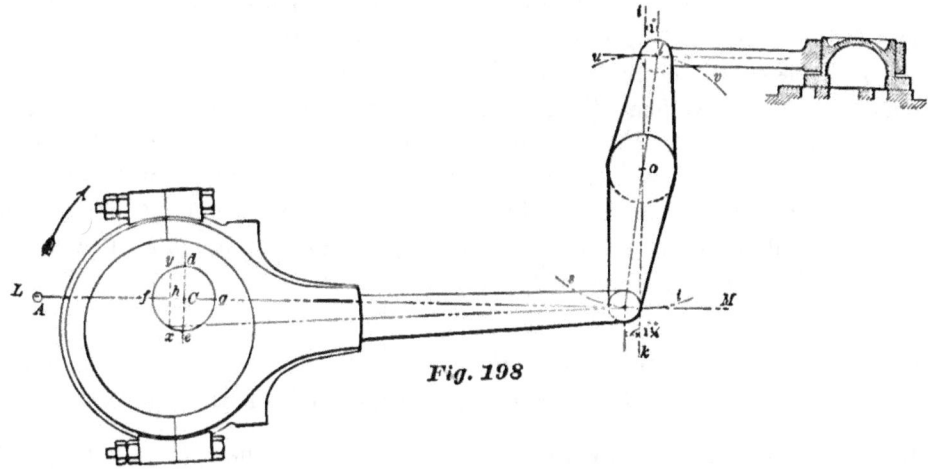

Fig. 198

off a point $l$; the distance between the line $i\,k$ and the point $l$ must be equal to the sum of the lap and lead, namely 1 inch, measured on a line perpendicular to $i\,k$, and not on the arc $u\,v$. Through the point $l$ and the center $o$ draw a straight line $l\,R$, cutting the arc $s\,t$ in the point $R$. Draw $L\,M$, the center line of motion of the valve gear, perpendicular to the line $i\,k$ and tangent to the arc $s\,t$. On the line $L\,M$ lay off the center $C$ of the shaft. When the valve stands in the position as shown in the figure, the crank-pin will be at $A$, or, in other words, the shaft $C$ will be between the crank-pin and the rocker. Through the center $C$ draw a straight line $d\,e$ perpendicular to $L\,M$; also from the center $C$, and with a radius equal to half the throw, namely $2\tfrac{1}{2}$ inches, describe a circle; the circumference of this circle will represent the path of the center of eccentrics. From the center $C$ and on the line $L\,M$ lay off a point $h$; the distance between these points must be $1\tfrac{1}{4}$ inches; through the point $h$ draw a line parallel to the line $d\,e$, and cutting the circumference $f\,d\,g$ in the points $x$ and $y$. The point $x$ will be the center of the eccentric when the crank-pin $A$ has to move in the direction of the arrow; and the point $y$ would be the center of the eccentric if the crank-pin $A$ had to move in a direction opposite to that of the arrow. If two eccentrics and a link are to be employed, then one eccentric is placed at $x$ and the other at $y$.

Since the valve has $\tfrac{15}{16}$ of an inch lap and $\tfrac{1}{16}$ of an inch lead, the linear advance of the valve must be 1 inch; that is, when the valve is in the position as shown, it has traveled 1 inch away from its central position; and since the valve is connected to the upper rocker-arm, the distance between the center $l$ and the line $i\,k$ was made equal to

1 inch. According to Art. 97, the distance between the line *i k* and the center *R* of the lower rocker-pin must be greater than 1 inch, because the lower rocker-arm is longer than the upper one. In our present example the distance between the line *i k* and the center *R* is $1\frac{1}{4}$ inches. But the eccentric-rod is connected to the lower rocker-arm, and therefore the distance between the center *C* and the point *h* must be $1\frac{1}{4}$ inches, as we have made it. Hence, lengthening the lower rocker-arm necessitated an increase in the angular advance. If the lengths of the rocker-arm had been equal, the distance between *C* and *h* would have been 1 inch, or, in other words, the centers *x* and *y* of the eccentrics would have been placed 1 inch away from the line *d e*, instead of $1\frac{1}{4}$ inches as shown in Fig. 198. In the same manner it can be shown that, when the length of the lower rocker-arm is less than the length of the upper arm, then the angular advance of the eccentric will be less than the linear advance of the valve.

From this example we learn that, when the lower rocker-arm is longer than the upper one, the angular advance will be greater than the linear advance; and when the lower rocker-arm is shorter than the upper one, the angular advance is less than the linear advance—in short, the angular advance of the eccentric is equal to the distance between the central position of the lower rocker-pin and that in which it will stand when the piston is at the beginning of the stroke.*

## POSITION OF THE ECCENTRIC WHEN A ROCKER IS USED AND THE CENTER LINE OF MOTION OF THE VALVE GEAR DOES NOT COINCIDE WITH THAT OF THE PISTON.

**134. EXAMPLE 41.**—The length of each rocker-arm is 10 inches; lap, $\frac{5}{16}$ of an inch; lead, $\frac{1}{16}$ of an inch; throw of the eccentric, 5 inches; center line of motion of the valve gear does not coincide with that of the piston; to find the position of the eccentric.

Fig. 199. In this figure the axis of the cylinder is assumed to be in a line with the center *C* of the shaft; that is, if the axis of the cylinder is prolonged towards the shaft, it will pass through the center *C*. Hence the line *N P* will be the center line of motion of the piston. Again, when the crank is on a dead center, the crank-pin must lie in this line *N P*; and when the valve has opened the steam port $\frac{1}{16}$ of an inch, that is to say, when the valve has $\frac{1}{16}$ inch lead, as shown in the figure, the center of the crank-pin must be at *A*. Let *o* represent the center of the rocker-shaft. From the center *o*, and with a radius equal to the length of the lower rocker-arm, namely 10 inches, describe the arc *s t*; also from the center *o*, and with the same radius as before, describe the arc *u v*. Through the center *C* draw the line *L M* tangent to the arc *s t*. Then *L M* will be the center line of motion of the valve gear; and, as will be seen, the center line of motion *L M* does not coincide with the center line of motion *N P*.

Cases of this kind, in which one end of the center line of motion of the valve gear is depressed, are not of rare occurrence in locomotive construction; we frequently have to do this in order to give sufficient clearance between the lifting-shaft arms or the link and the boiler when the valve gear is placed in full-gear back. But when this

---

* It should be remembered that increasing the length of the lower rocker-arm, and leaving the throw of the eccentric the same, the travel of the valve will be decreased. Also by decreasing the length of the lower rocker arm without changing the throw of the eccentric, the travel of the valve will be increased. Therefore care and thought must be given to the subject when the lower rocker-arm is made longer or shorter than the upper rocker-arm

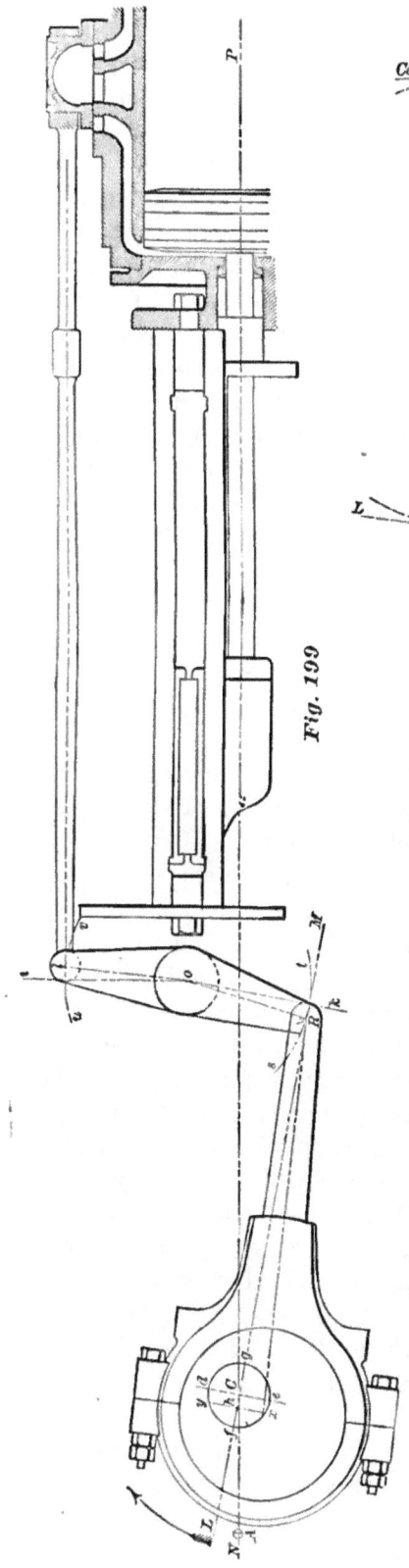

Fig. 199

Fig. 200

expedient is resorted to, we must also make a change in the relative positions of the rocker-arms on the shaft, as shown in Fig. 200. In this figure it will be noticed that the center lines of the rocker-arms do not lie in one straight line, as shown in all our previous figures, but that these arms incline towards each other. By giving the rocker-arms these positions on the shaft we will preserve the identity and symmetry of their motion. The relative positions of the rocker-arms are found in the following manner: Through the center $o$, Fig. 199, draw a line $o\,k$ perpendicular to $L\,M$; this line will represent the center line of the lower rocker-arm when it stands midway of its travel. Also through the center $o$ draw the line $o\,i$ perpendicular to the center line of the valve-rod; the line $o\,i$ will represent the center line of the upper rocker-arm when it stands midway of its travel. The lines $o\,i$ and $o\,k$ show the required amount of inclination of the rocker-arms towards each other.

To draw the rocker in a position corresponding to that of the valve at the beginning of the stroke, lay off from the line $i\,o$ on the arc $u\,v$, towards the valve, a point $l$; the distance between this point $l$ and the line $i\,o$ must be equal to the linear advance, namely 1 inch. Through the point $l$ and the center $o$ draw a straight line $l\,o$; this line will be the center line of the upper rocker-arm when in a position corresponding to that of the slide-valve. From the line $o\,k$ on the arc $s\,t$, and towards the center $C$ of the shaft, lay off a point $R$; the distance between the point $R$ and the line $o\,k$ must also be equal to the linear advance (1 inch), because the length of the upper rocker-arm is equal to that of the lower one. The line $o\,R$ represents the center line of the lower rocker-arm when in a position corresponding to that of the valve. From the center $C$, and with a radius equal to $2\frac{1}{2}$ inches, describe the circle $f\,d\,g$; the circumference of this circle will represent the path of the center of eccentric. Through the center $C$ of the shaft draw a line $d\ e$ perpendicular to the line $L\ M$; from the same center $C$ lay off on the line $L\ M$, towards the crank-pin $A$ a point $h$; the distance between the points $C$ and $h$ must be equal to the linear advance (1 inch). Through the point $h$ draw a line $x\ y$ parallel to the line $d\ e$, cutting the circumference $f\ d\ g$ at the points $x$ and $y$. The point $x$ will be the center of the eccentric when the crank-pin $A$ is to travel in the direction of the arrow; and the point $y$ will be the center of the eccentric when the crank-pin $A$ is to travel in the direction opposite to that of the arrow. If a link is to be used so that the motion of the crank-shaft can be reversed, then the point $x$ will be the center of one eccentric, and the point $y$ the center of the other eccentric.

Now notice in this case the angular advance of the eccentric is laid off from the line $d\ e$, which is not perpendicular to the center line $A\ C$ of the crank. From this we learn that the angular advance must be laid off from a line drawn perpendicular to the center of motion of the valve gear, as stated in Rule 17, and this rule holds true in all cases. On the other hand, the expressions, "the eccentric is set at right angles to the crank," and "the angular advance is laid off from a line drawn perpendicular to the crank," are true only in cases in which the center line of motion $L\ M$ of the valve gear coincides with the center line $A\ C$ of the crank.

## LAYING OUT A LOCOMOTIVE VALVE GEAR.

135. In Fig. 199 we have shown a valve gear without a link. Now, adding a link will not change the position of the eccentrics, neither will it make any difference in the positions of the rocker-arms; the off-set in the arms and the position of the rocker are not interfered with—in fact, no change whatever will be required excepting a change in the length of the eccentric-rods. Hence all the remarks relating to the valve gear shown in Fig. 199 are true also for a valve gear in which a link is used.

136. In regard to the position of the center $o$ of the rock-shaft in any valve gear, it may be said that it is usually located in the most convenient position, which in the meantime will give as long eccentric-rods as possible. Hence we find the rocker placed either in front of the yoke-brace or in the rear of it, as shown in Fig. 29. In either case care must be taken to place the rocker far enough away from the yoke-brace to give sufficient clearance between the latter and the link when hooked up; again, it often happens that, when we attempt in ten-wheeled engines to place the rocker in front of the yoke-brace, the link will strike the engine truck frame, and under these circumstances we are compelled to place the rocker as shown in Fig. 29. The vertical distance from top of frame to the center of rock-shaft is usually determined by the location of the valve-rod, and when the boiler is set comparatively low, we may have to lengthen the upper rocker-arms so as to lower the position of the rocker for the purpose of obtaining sufficient clearance between the bottom of the boiler shell and the top of link and hanger when the latter are placed in full backward gear. The preceding remarks indicate that for determining the position of rocker-box computations are not required, but good judgment guided by experience must be exercised.

137. The correct working of the valve not only depends on the correct position of the eccentrics, but it will also depend, when a link is used, on the position of the

saddle-pin on the link, the length of the lifting-shaft arms from which the links are suspended, and the position of the lifting shaft.

The position of the driving axle in the pedestal will also affect to a small extent the equality of the cut-off, and since this axle is free to move up and down in the pedestal, the question which presents itself is: Where shall we place the driving axle for the purpose of laying out the valve gear? The axle should be drawn in a position corresponding to that which it will have when the engine is in first-class working order; and this position can be taken from Figs. 271 to 279, in which the positions of axles in the pedestals for different sizes of engines in working order are clearly indicated. After the axle and rocker-box have been located, we are then ready for laying out the valve gear, and in order to show plainly the manner of doing so, we shall take the following example and work out the solution in the same way as many draftsmen will do; the only difference being that the draftsman will work out the whole solution in one diagram, whereas we shall use three to enable us to point out the construction more clearly.

EXAMPLE 42.—It is required to lay out a valve gear such as is shown in Fig. 29. This gear is to be used on an eight-wheeled passenger engine with a piston stroke of 24 inches. The length of each rocker-arm is 10 inches; throw of eccentrics, 5 inches, which will make the eccentricity equal to $2\frac{1}{2}$ inches; lap, $\frac{7}{8}$ inch; lead, $\frac{1}{16}$ inch; length of link, 18 inches; distance between centers of eccentric-rod pins in link, 12 inches; length of link-hanger, 13 inches; horizontal distance from the center of axle to the center of rock-shaft, 55 inches; length of connecting-rod, 84 inches; axis of cylinder, $1\frac{1}{2}$ inches above the center of driving axle when the engine is in good working order. We will also assume that after the driving axle has been correctly drawn in the pedestal, and the rocker properly located, it is found that the vertical distance from the center of axle to a horizontal line drawn through the center of rock-shaft is 6 inches. It is required to find, in the order here given, the off-set in the rocker-arms; the position of crank-pin for full and half stroke of piston; the radius of links; the position of eccentrics; the length of eccentric-rods; the position of eccentrics for half strokes of piston; the position of the saddle-pin on the links; the position of lifting shaft and the length of the lifting-shaft arms from which the links are suspended. Indeed, it may be said that to determine each one of these particulars is a problem by itself, so that the matter of laying out a valve gear consists of the solutions of a number of simple problems.

### TO FIND THE OFF-SET IN THE ROCKER-ARMS.

138. Let the point $A$ in Fig. 200A be the center of the driving axle; through this center draw a vertical line, and make the distance from $A$ to $i$ equal to 6 inches; through the point $i$ draw a horizontal line $i\,o$, and make the distance from $i$ to $o$ equal to 55 inches, as given in the example; the point $o$ will be the center of the rock-shaft. From $o$, and with a radius of 10 inches, describe two arcs, $U\,V$ and $S\,T$; through the center $A$ draw a line $L\,M$ tangent to the arc $S\,T$; this line will be the center line of motion of the valve gear. (See Art. 131.) Through the center $O$ draw a line $O\,R$ perpendicular to $L\,M$; the line $O\,R$ will be the center line of the lower arm of the rocker when the valve stands in the center of its travel. Again, through $O$ draw the

vertical line $O I$; we say vertical, because the valve is supposed to move in a horizontal direction; if the valve-rod moves in any other direction, then $O I$ should be drawn perpendicular to that direction. The line $O I$ represents the center line of the upper

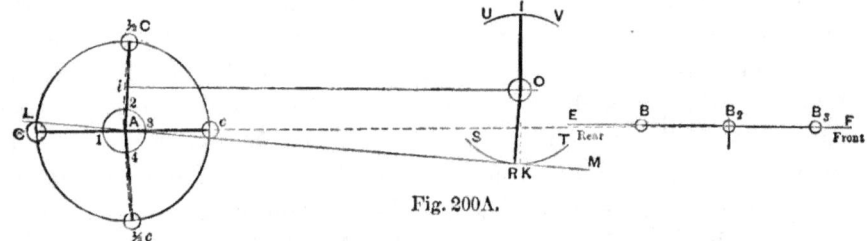

Fig. 200A.

arm of rocker when the valve stands in the center of its travel. Prolong $I O$ to $K$, then $K R$ will be the off-set in the rocker-arms.

### TO FIND THE POSITION OF CRANK-PIN FOR FULL AND HALF STROKES OF PISTON.

139. According to the conditions given in the example, the axis of the cylinder is to be $1\frac{1}{2}$ inches above the center $A$ of the axle; hence, on the line $A i$ lay off a point at a distance of $1\frac{1}{2}$ inches above $A$, and through this point draw the horizontal line $E F$, which will be the axis of the cylinder. From $A$ as a center, and with a radius equal to the length of the connecting-rod, namely, 84 inches, describe a short arc cutting $E F$ in the point $B_2$; this point will be the center of the crosshead pin when midway of its travel. Towards the rear of $B_2$ lay off the point $B$ at 12 inches from $B_2$; also lay off the point $B_3$ towards the front of $B_2$ at a distance of 12 inches from the latter; the points $B$ and $B_3$ will be the position of the center of the crosshead pin when the piston is at the extremities of a stroke. It should be remarked here that the foregoing way of finding the points $B$ and $B_3$ is correct only when the axis $E F$ of the cylinder and the center $A$ lie in one and the same straight line; but when these do not lie exactly in the same straight line, as is the case in the example before us, then the construction is not correct, but it is sufficiently close for all practical purposes, in cases in which the axis of cylinder is only $1\frac{1}{2}$ inches above the center $A$ of axle. In extreme cases, say when the line $E F$ is from 3 to 4 inches above the center $A$, it is best to find the points $B$ and $B_3$ accurately, which is done in the following manner: From $A$ as a center, and with a radius equal to the length of the connecting-rod minus the length of the crank, describe a short arc cutting $E F$ in the point $B$; again, from $A$ as a center, and with a radius equal to the length of the connecting-rod plus the length of the crank, describe a short arc cutting $E F$ in the point $B_3$; the distance from $B$ to $B_3$ will be the length of stroke of piston, which is a little less than twice the length of crank; of course the length of crank is the distance from the center of axle to the center of crank-pin. With a radius of 12 inches describe from $A$ the circle $C$, $\frac{1}{2}C$, $c$, $\frac{1}{2}c$; its circumference will represent the path of the center of the crank-pin. Through $A$ and $B$ draw a straight line, and prolong it to $C$ on the circumference of the circle; this point $C$ will be the center of the crank-pin when the crosshead pin is at the end $B$ of the stroke. Through $A$ and $B_3$ draw a straight line cutting the path of the crank-pin at $c$; this point will be the position of the crank-pin when the crosshead pin is at the end $B_3$

of the stroke. For laying out the valve gear, it is customary to find the points $C$ and $c$ in a somewhat simpler way—namely: through $A$ and $B_2$ draw a straight line cutting the path of the crank-pin in the points $C$ and $c$, which will be the centers of the crank-pin corresponding to the extremities of the piston stroke. This way of finding the centers is not quite as accurate as the first method given, but the error is so small that it may be safely neglected. In laying out the valve gear, we have to find another two important positions of the crank-pin, namely, those corresponding to the positions of the piston when it is in the center of each stroke, or, in other words, when the crosshead pin is at $B_2$. These positions are found in the following manner: From $B_2$ as a center, and with a radius equal to $A B_2$ (that is, the length of the connecting-rod), describe an arc cutting the path of the center of crank-pin in the points $\tfrac{1}{2}C$ and $\tfrac{1}{2}c$, which will be the required points. Join the points $A$ and $\tfrac{1}{2}C$, also $A$ and $\tfrac{1}{2}c$, by straight lines; these lines will be the center lines of the crank corresponding to $\tfrac{1}{2}$ stroke of the piston; and the lines $A\,C$ and $A\,c$ will be the center lines of the crank when the engine is on its dead centers. From $A$ as a center, and with a radius equal to $\tfrac{1}{2}$ of the throw of the eccentric, $2\tfrac{1}{2}$ inches, describe a circle cutting the center lines of the crank in the points 1, 2, 3, and 4.

### TO FIND THE RADIUS OF THE LINK.

**140.** According to construction, the point $R$ in Fig. 200A is the center of the lower rocker-arm pin or link-block pin when the valve stands midway of its travel; hence, according to Art. 123 the radius of the link is equal to the distance $A R$. If this radius is made either longer or shorter than $A R$, the tendency will be to produce an unequal lead when the link is placed in mid-gear.

### TO FIND THE POSITIONS OF THE ECCENTRICS FOR FULL STROKES OF PISTON.

**141.** This construction is shown in Fig. 200B, which, for the sake of clearness, is drawn to a larger scale than Fig. 200A, but in both figures the lines and points which have the same letters affixed represent the same parts of the valve gear.

On the line $L\,M$ lay off from $A$ a distance $A\,p$ equal to the sum of the lap

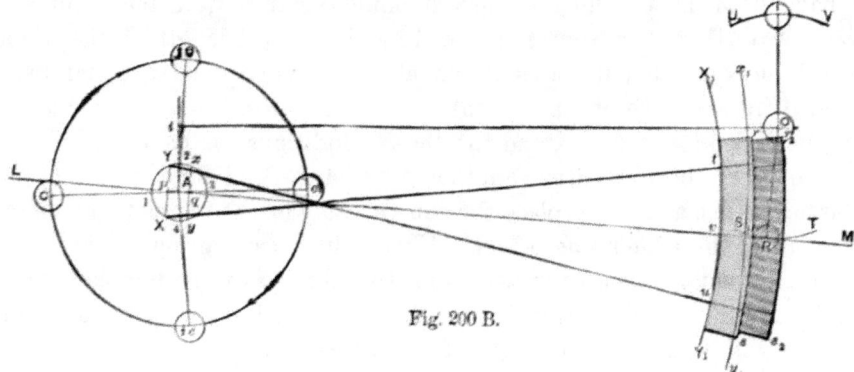

Fig. 200 B.

and lead, $\tfrac{15}{16}$ inch, and through the point $p$ draw a line $X\,Y$ perpendicular to $L\,M$ cutting the circle 1, 2, 3, 4, in the points $X$ and $Y$; the point $X$, according to Art. 131, will be the center of the forward eccentric; and $Y$ will be the center of the backward eccentric when the crank-pin is at $C$. In this case we have made $A p$ equal to the lap and lead, because the lengths of the rocker-arms are equal. (See Art. 131.) If the lower rocker-arm had been longer or shorter than the upper one, then the distance $A p$ would have been made respectively greater or less than the sum of the lap and lead. (See Art. 132.) On the line $L M$ lay off from $A$ a distance $A q$ equal to $A p$, and through the point $q$ draw a line $x y$ parallel to $X Y$, cutting the circumference 1, 2, 3, 4, in the points $x$ and $y$. The point $x$ will be the center of the forward eccentric and $y$ that of the backward eccentric when the crank-pin is at $c$. Here, then, we have found the position of eccentrics when the engine is on its dead centers.

### TO FIND THE CORRECT LENGTH OF ECCENTRIC-RODS.

142. For this purpose we shall need a template. Let Fig. 200C represent the link. Cut out a template represented by the shaded portion of this figure. The edge $r s$ of the template must coincide with the link arc; and the arc $t u$ of the template

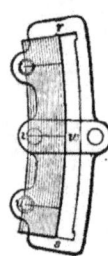

Fig. 200 C.

must pass through the centers of the eccentric-rod pins. Through the centers of the eccentric-rod pins $t$ and $u$ draw straight lines on the template, and also through a point midway between these centers draw on the template a line $v w$ towards the center from which the link has been drawn; the lines through $t$ and $u$ may be drawn parallel to $v w$, or they may also point to the center from which the link has been drawn; either way will answer the purpose, so long as the points $t$, $v$, and $u$ on the concave edge of the template are correctly located as explained.

From the points $X$ and $x$ as centers (Fig. 200B), and with a radius equal to $A R$ minus the width of $v w$, draw two arcs $X_1$ and $x_1$ above the line $L M$; and with the same radius draw from the centers $Y$ and $y$ two arcs $Y_1$ and $y_1$, below $L M$. Now place the template with its center line $v w$ on $L M$, and with its points $t$ and $u$ on the arcs $X_1$ and $Y_1$ respectively, and along the edge $r s$ draw an arc on the paper. Again, place the template with its center line $v w$ on $L M$, and with its points $t$ and $u$ on the arcs $x_1$ and $y_1$ respectively, and along the edge $r s$ draw another arc $r_2 s_2$. If now these two arcs which have been drawn along $r s$ are at equal distance from the point $R$, then the line drawn from $X$ to $t$ or from $Y$ to $u$ will be the correct length of the eccentric-rod; but the chances are that the arcs drawn along $r s$ will not be at equal distances from $R$, because in one position the eccentric-rods will cross each other, and in the other position they will not do so, and for these conditions we have not made any allowance. We must therefore draw another set of arcs $X_1$ $Y_1$ and $x_1$ and $y_1$, with a somewhat larger radius, and again place the concave side of the template on these arcs and draw arcs along the edge $r s$ as before. With a little care and good judgment in drawing $X_1$, $Y_1$, $x_1$, and $y_1$, the arcs drawn along the edge $r s$ of the template will now be at equal distances from the point $R$, and therefore the lines joining the points $X$ and $t$ or $Y$ and $u$ will be the correct length of eccentric-rods.

143. The heavy lines $X t$ and $Y u$ represent the position of the center lines of the eccentric-rods when the crank-pin is at $C$; it is seen that these rods cross each other; but when the crank-pin is at $c$ the eccentric-rods will not cross each other; they are then said to be "open." If we connect the rods so that they will not cross each other

MODERN LOCOMOTIVE CONSTRUCTION. 123

when the crank-pin is at $C$, we shall have no lead when the link is placed in mid-gear, and this is not admissible in locomotive practice, although it may be advantageously employed in hoisting engines, because when there is no lead with the link in mid-gear the engine can be stopped simply by raising the link without touching the throttle-valve.

#### TO FIND THE POSITION OF ECCENTRICS FOR HALF STROKES OF PISTON.

144. To show this construction we shall refer to Fig. 200D, to which nearly all the lines shown in the former figure have been transferred. We have seen that the center lines of the crank corresponding to full and half stroke of piston cut the path of the center of eccentrics in the points 1, 2, 3, and 4. Now when the crank-pin is at $C$

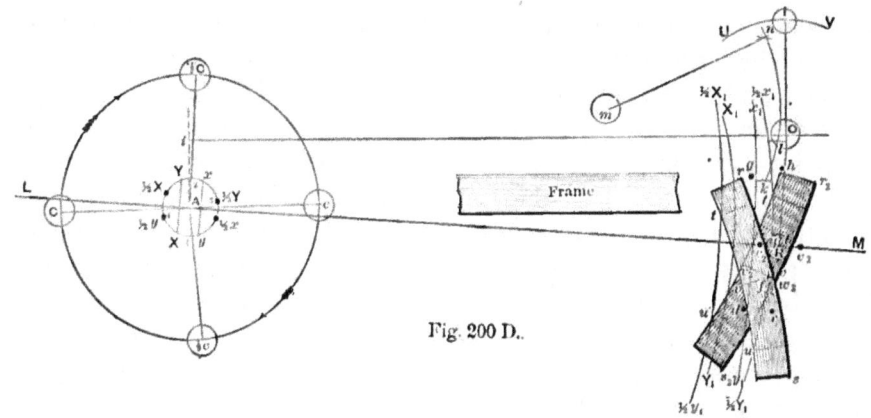

Fig. 200 D.

the forward eccentric will be at $X$, and the length of the arc from the point 1 to $X$ is fixed; it cannot be changed in whatever position the crank may be; hence, when the crank-pin is at $\tfrac{1}{2}C$ the arc from the point 2 to $\tfrac{1}{2}X$ must be equal to that from 1 to $X$. Therefore, making the arc $\tfrac{1}{2}X$-2 equal to $X$-1, we obtain the point $\tfrac{1}{2}X$, which is the center of the forward eccentric when the piston is in the center of the forward stroke. For similar reasons we make the arc $\tfrac{1}{2}x$-4 equal to $X$-1; the point $\tfrac{1}{2}x$ will be the center of the forward eccentric when the piston is in the center of its return stroke. Of course, care must be taken to lay these points off on the path of the center of eccentrics, that is, on the circumference $X\,Y\,x\,y$, and these points should be laid off to follow the crank. We know that the point $Y$ is the center of the backward eccentric when the crank is at $C$, and the length of the arc from 1 to $Y$ remains fixed for all positions of the crank; therefore make the arc $\tfrac{1}{2}Y$-2 equal to $Y$-1, also make the arc $\tfrac{1}{2}y$-4 equal to the same arc; of course, the points $\tfrac{1}{2}Y$ and $\tfrac{1}{2}y$ must be ahead of the crank. Now the point $\tfrac{1}{2}Y$ will be the position of the backward eccentric when the piston is in the middle of its forward stroke, and the point $\tfrac{1}{2}y$ will be the position of the backward eccentric when the piston is in the middle of its return stroke.

#### TO FIND THE CENTER OF THE SADDLE-PIN.

145. From the centers $\tfrac{1}{2}X$ and $\tfrac{1}{2}x$, and with a radius equal to $X\,t$ or $Y\,u$ (Fig. 200B), describe in Fig. 200D above the line $L\,M$ the arcs $\tfrac{1}{2}X_1$ and $\tfrac{1}{2}x_1$; from the centers $\tfrac{1}{2}Y$ and

$\tfrac{1}{2}y$, and with the same radius, describe below the line $L\,M$ the arcs $\tfrac{1}{2}Y_1$ and $\tfrac{1}{2}y_1$. It will be remembered that the point $R$ is the center of the link-block pin when the valve stands midway of its travel; from this point $R$ as a center, and with a radius equal to the lap of valve $\tfrac{7}{8}$ of an inch, describe the lap circle, cutting the line $L\,M$ in the points $a$ and $b$. Now place the template with its point $t$ on the arc $\tfrac{1}{2}X_1$, and with the point $u$ on the arc $\tfrac{1}{2}Y_1$, and its outer edge $r\,s$ touching the point $a$; in this position draw on the paper along the outer edge of the template an arc $r\,s$, and also mark off the points $v$ and $w$; lift off the template, and through the points $v$ and $w$ draw a straight line $v\,w$; this line represents the position of the center line of the link when steam is being cut off at $\tfrac{1}{2}$ of the forward stroke. Again, lay the template in a position as indicated by the darker shading; the point $t$ must lie on the arc $\tfrac{1}{2}x_1$; the point $u$, on the arc $\tfrac{1}{2}y_1$; and its outer edge $r_2\,s_2$ must touch the point $b$. In this position draw on the paper an arc $r_2\,s_2$ along the outer edge of the template, and also mark off the points $v_2\,w_2$; then lift off the template and join the points $v_2\,w_2$ by a straight line; this line will be the center line of link when steam is cut off at $\tfrac{1}{2}$ of the return stroke. On the line $v\,w$ lay off a point $f$, and on the line $v_2\,w_2$ lay off a point $f_2$, to comply with the following conditions: The distance from the point $f$ to the arc $r\,s$ must be equal to the distance from the point $f_2$ to the arc $r_2\,s_2$, and these points $f, f_2$ must also lie in a line parallel to $L\,M$; the position of these points are found by trial—usually two or three trials will locate them correctly. The distance from the arc $r\,s$ to the point $f$, or the distance from the arc $r_2\,s_2$ to the point $f_2$ (these distances being equal), will be the amount that the saddle-pin has to be set inwards from the link arc. Mark off correctly this point $f$ on the template.

### TO LOCATE THE LIFTING SHAFT.

146. On the line $L\,M$ lay off from $R$ a point $c_2$; the distance from $R$ to $c_2$ must be equal to the sum of the lap and lead $\tfrac{15}{16}$ inches. Also from $R$ lay off on $L\,M$ a point $c_3$; the distance from $R$ to $c_3$ must again be equal to the sum of the lap and lead. Let it now be remembered that the arcs $X_1, Y_1, x_1$ and $y_1$ in Fig. 200D represent the same arcs as those which have the same letters affixed in Fig. 200B. Now place the template as low as possible, with its point $t$ on the arc $X_1$, the point $u$ on the arc $Y_1$, and the outer edge $r\,s$ touching the point $c_2$. In this position prick off through the point $f$ on the template the point $d$ on the paper. Now move the template to as low a position as possible, so that its outer edge $r\,s$ will touch the point $c_3$ with the point $t$ on the arc $x_1$, and the point $u$ on the arc $y_1$, and in this position prick off through $f$ on the template a point $e$ on the paper. From the points $d$ and $e$ as centers, and with a radius equal to the length of the link-hanger, 13 inches, describe two arcs intersecting each other in the point $k$. Now move the template as high as possible, and let its outer edge $r\,s$ touch the point $c_2$, and let the point $t$ be on the arc $X_1$, and the point $u$ on the arc $Y_1$, then through the point $f$ on the template prick off on the paper a point $g$. Again, move the template to as high a position as possible, and let its outer edge $r\,s$ touch the point $c_3$, and let the point $t$ be on the arc $x_1$, and $u$ on the arc $y_1$; through $f$ on the template prick off on the paper a point $h$. From the points $g$ and $h$ as centers, and with a radius equal to the length of the link-hanger, describe two arcs intersecting each other

in the point $n$. Lastly, from the points $f$ and $f_2$ previously located on the paper, describe with a radius of 13 inches two arcs intersecting each other in the point $l$. Now find by trial a point $m$ from which an arc passing through the points $k\ l\ n$ can be described; this point $m$ will be the center of the lifting shaft, and the radius $m\ n$ will be the length of the lifting-shaft arms from which the links are to be suspended.

This completes the whole construction. It will be noticed that in this valve motion the valve will have equal lead at full stroke, and cut off steam at the center of the forward and return stroke. Under these conditions steam will be cut off at equal portions of the forward and return strokes, or very nearly so, for all intermediate positions of the link.

147. In designing an engine the foregoing construction is essential; it gives us the required data for several details which can be made and completely finished before they are sent into the erecting shop. But there are other details which have to be adjusted to the imperfect workmanship which cannot always be avoided; for instance, the length of eccentric-rods will have to be adjusted under the engine, also the eccentrics will have to be set on the axle, and there are other points which cannot be exactly transferred from the paper to the engine; it will therefore be advantageous to examine now the mode of procedure in setting the valves on the engine in the shop.

**PRACTICAL EXAMPLE OF SETTING THE VALVE GEAR OF A LOCOMOTIVE IN THE ERECTING SHOP.**

EXAMPLE 43.—Throw of the eccentric is 5 inches; lap, $\frac{15}{16}$ of an inch; lead, $\frac{1}{16}$ of an inch; clearance between piston and each cylinder head is $\frac{3}{8}$ of an inch; type of locomotive is one in which the eccentrics are placed on the main axle, that is, the axle to which the main rod is connected: it is required to set or adjust the valve gear. In this example the position of the saddle-pin on the saddle is assumed to be correct, so that in setting the valve gear no loose saddle is to be used.

To the young mechanic it may appear that setting the valve gear of a locomotive is a very mysterious and difficult operation. Yet, if he understands the theory of the valve motion, which we have endeavored to explain and to make plain in the foregoing articles, and proceeds in setting the valve gear in a systematic manner, this operation will lose all its mystery, and will not be such a difficult problem as it first appeared to be. True, in attempting to set the valve gear we are confronted with that which may seem to be a very mixed-up problem, because the correct position of the eccentrics on the axle and the exact length of the eccentric-rods must be determined; and since these two items are intimately connected, we may often be in doubt as to which of the two has been correctly found. But by dividing this problem into a number of simpler ones, its solution will be comparatively easy. In connection with the setting of the valve gear a few preliminary preparations are necessary; this whole subject will be treated in the following order:

1st. Blocking up the main axle boxes in the pedestals of the frames.

2d. To find the exact position of the crank-pin when the piston is at the beginning of a stroke.

3d. To test the amount of clearance between the piston and cylinder heads.

4th. To connect the eccentric-rods correctly to the link.

5th. To find the correct length of the eccentric-rods.
6th. To find the correct position of the eccentrics on the axle.
7th. To lay off the notches in the reverse arcs or quadrants.

In this example it is assumed that the quadrants are properly fastened in their position, and that they have no notches. Also that the reverse lever and lifting shaft are in correct positions; and that the reach-rod connects the reverse lever and lifting shaft; and lastly, that the links are suspended from the lifting-shaft arms, and that the former are properly attached to the lower rocker-arms; and also, that the connections between the upper rocker-arms and the valves are complete.

### BLOCKING UP THE MAIN AXLE BOXES IN THE PEDESTALS OF THE FRAMES.

148. The locomotive should rest securely on blocks, so that the main driving wheels can be lifted off the track and held in a position which will allow the main driving wheels to be easily turned around in their boxes. In lifting the main driving wheels off the track, they should be raised to a position in the pedestal which corresponds to the position of their boxes in the frame when the engine is hauling a train.

The general practice is to give $1\frac{1}{2}$ inches clearance between the axle box and pedestal cap, and about 3 inches clearance between the top of axle box and frame. In smaller engines whose axle boxes have less clearance in the pedestals, the proportion between the upper and lower clearances should be about the same as that just given; namely, the clearance on top of the axle box should be about twice as great as that below the box. (See Figs. 271 to 279.) If then $1\frac{1}{2}$ inches is to be the clearance at the bottom, blocks each $1\frac{1}{2}$ inches thick are inserted between the main axle boxes and the pedestal caps, which will hold the main driving wheels off the track and in the correct position during the time the valve motion is to be adjusted. No attention need be paid to the other boxes and wheels, since in this class of engines it is not necessary to put on the side rods for the purpose of setting the valve gear; in fact, the side rods would be in the way, and would give unnecessary labor in revolving the main driving wheels.

### TO FIND THE EXACT POSITION OF THE CRANK WHEN THE PISTON IS AT THE BEGINNING OF A STROKE; OR, IN OTHER WORDS, TO LOCATE THE DEAD CENTERS OF THE CRANK.

149. Fig. 201. The following remarks refer only to the setting of the valve gear on the right-hand side of the engine; the manner of setting the valve gear on the left-hand side of the engine is precisely the same as that adopted for the right-hand side. First set or adjust one side, and then the other side. On the face of the tire describe with the aid of a gauge two arcs $d\ e$ and $f\ g$ in about the same relative positions to that of the crank, as shown in the figure; care should be taken to describe these arcs as true as if they had been described in the lathe. Attach the main rod to the crank-pin and crosshead; but at present do not fasten the piston-rod to the crosshead. Now turn the driving wheel in the direction of the arrow until the crosshead is within a short distance from the end of the stroke, say $\frac{1}{2}$ an inch; while in this position mark on the slides a line $i$ even with the end $j$ of the crosshead. Also, while the wheel and crosshead are in this position, place a center punch mark $c$ on the side

of the fire-box or any other convenient fixed piece of mechanism. From this point $c$ as a center, and with a tram of any convenient length as a radius, describe on the face of the tire a short arc, cutting the arc $d\ e$ (previously marked on the tire) at the point $d$ (this point $d$ will at this instant coincide with the end $h$ of the tram, and not as shown in the figure). Now turn the wheel in the same direction as before, causing the crosshead to complete its full stroke and a very small portion of its return stroke; and when during this motion the edge $j$ of the crosshead touches the line $i$ on the slides, stop turning the shaft, and while in this position describe from the center punch mark $c$ as a center, and with the same tram as before, a short arc on the face of the tire, cutting the arc $d\ e$ at the point $e$. Midway between the points $d$ and $e$ on the arc $d\ e$ lay off a point $h$. Turn the wheel in a position in which the tram will touch the points $c$ and $h$; the crank-pin will then be at $B$, and the piston will be at the beginning of its forward stroke; or, in other words, the crank will then be on one of its dead centers. While the crank stands at $B$ draw on the slides a line $k$ even with the end $j$ of the crosshead; this line $k$ will indicate the end of the stroke—that is, the end $j$ of the crosshead will not travel beyond the line $k$ with the connecting-rod attached. In order to locate the other dead center $A$ we again turn the wheel in

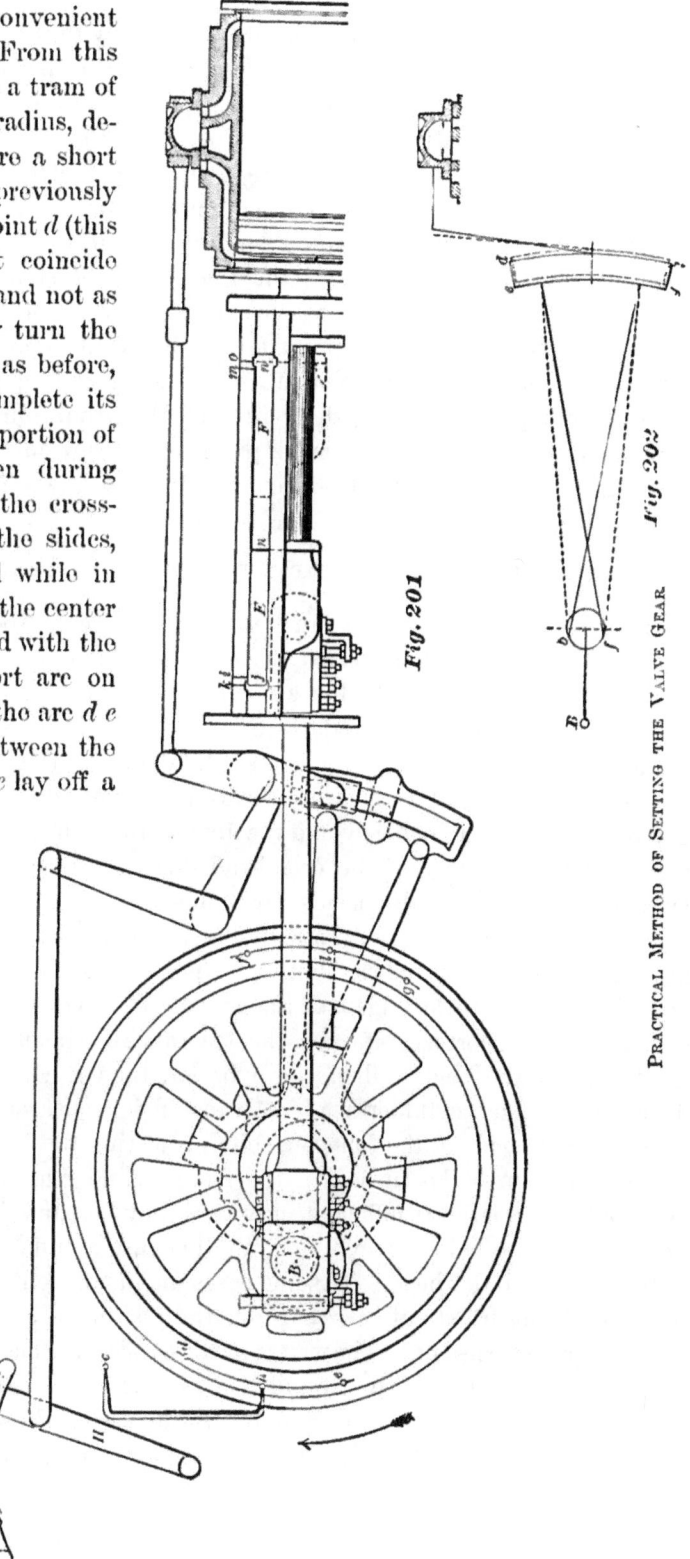

Fig. 201

Fig. 202

Practical Method of Setting the Valve Gear

the direction of the arrow until the crosshead is within a short distance of the front end of the stroke, say $\frac{1}{2}$ an inch, and while in this position mark on the slides a line $m$ even with the end $n$ of the crosshead; also, before the wheel and crosshead are moved out of this position, describe on the face of the tire from the point $c$ as a center, and with the same tram as used before, a short arc, cutting the arc $fg$ at the point $g$. Next turn the wheel in the same direction as before, causing the crosshead to complete its forward stroke and a small portion of its backward stroke, and when the edge $n$ of the crosshead again touches the line $m$ on the slides, stop turning the wheel. From the center $c$, and with the same tram, describe on the face of the tire a short arc, cutting the arc $fg$ at the point $f$. Mark off the point $l$ on the arc $fg$ midway between the points $f$ and $g$. Now, turning the wheel in a position in which the tram will touch the points $c$ and $l$, the center of the crank-pin will be at $A$, which is the other dead center. While the crank-pin is at $A$ draw on the slides a line $o$ even with the end $n$ of the crosshead; this line $o$ will indicate the other end of the stroke.

### TO TEST THE AMOUNT OF CLEARANCE BETWEEN THE PISTON AND CYLINDER HEADS.

150. For this purpose we must take off the main rod, fasten the piston to the piston-rod, key the piston-rod to the crosshead, and bolt the cylinder heads to the cylinder. Our example calls for $\frac{3}{8}$ of an inch clearance between piston and cylinder head at each end of the cylinder. Consequently the crosshead with piston-rod and piston must be pulled out as far as can be done; if then the edge $j$ of the crosshead overlaps the line $k$, $\frac{3}{8}$ of an inch, the clearance is correct; if the edge $j$ of the crosshead only reaches $\frac{1}{4}$ of an inch beyond the line $k$, then the clearance is $\frac{1}{8}$ of an inch too small; or if the edge $j$ of the crosshead does not reach the line $k$, then there is no clearance, and the cylinder heads are liable to be broken if we attempt to turn the crank over the dead centers. In a similar manner we find the amount of clearance at the front end of the cylinder; that is, we push the crosshead towards the front as far as it will go, then, if the edge $n$ of the crosshead moves $\frac{3}{8}$ of an inch beyond the line $o$, the clearance is correct; if less, the clearance is insufficient. If the clearance is insufficient at the back end of the cylinder, then a corresponding amount must be turned off the back cylinder head. An insufficient clearance at the front end may be caused by the heads of the follower bolts projecting too far beyond the piston; in that case a groove must be turned in the front cylinder heads, to clear the heads of the follower bolts; or the insufficient clearance may be caused by the front cylinder head projecting too far into the cylinder; in this case a sufficient amount must be turned off the front cylinder head. In some cases an insufficient clearance may be caused by the piston being fitted out of square on the piston-rod; in that case the faces of the piston must be turned off. The writer in his experience has seldom found the clearance to be too great, but has often found it to be too small, generally owing to the roughness of the faces of the piston and inside surface of the cylinder heads, as these are seldom turned unless it is absolutely necessary to do so for the correct amount of clearance.

## TO CONNECT THE ECCENTRIC-RODS CORRECTLY TO THE LINK.

**151.** In locomotives it is necessary to preserve the lead, no matter in what position the link may be placed. In Art. 108 we have shown that the eccentric-rods can be connected to the link in a manner which will increase the lead as the link is moved from full-gear to mid-gear. In Art. 110 it is also shown that the eccentric-rods can be connected to the link in a manner which will give lap instead of lead when the link is in mid-gear. Now, since we must have lead in whatever position the link may be placed, it follows that the eccentric-rods must be connected to the link in a manner which will accomplish the desired result. In Fig. 201 the piston is at the beginning of its forward stroke, and the eccentric-rods are shown to cross each other, and, consequently, when the axle has made one-half of a revolution, and the piston is at the beginning of the backward stroke, the eccentric-rods will not cross each other, as shown in Fig. 29 (Art. 52). This manner of connecting the eccentric-rods to the link is correct, because it will give lead, no matter in what position the link is placed, although in mid-gear the lead will be greater than in full-gear. (See Art. 108.) The reason why the manner of connecting the eccentric-rods to the link should affect the lead is clearly shown in Fig. 202. In this figure the different parts of the valve gear are represented by center lines; the arc $d\,l$ represents an arc drawn through the center of the link opening, and the arc $e\,g$ represents the arc in which the centers of eccentric-rod pins are located. The full lines show the correct manner of connecting the eccentric-rods to the link, and the dotted lines represent the incorrect manner of doing this. Here it will be seen that by connecting the eccentric-rods, as shown by the full lines, we have lead when the link is placed in mid-gear; and by changing the connections, as shown in dotted lines, we push the lower rocker-arm pin away from the axle, which causes the upper rocker-arm pin to pull the valve towards the axle, and thus close the port and destroy the lead when the link is in mid-gear. In connecting the eccentric-rods to the link, as shown in Fig. 201, we must not forget that a rocker is employed. If a rocker had not been interposed, then the eccentric-rods would not cross each other when the piston is at the beginning of the forward stroke, but would be open, as shown in Fig. 168 (Art. 108).

## TO FIND THE CORRECT LENGTH OF THE ECCENTRIC-RODS.

**152.** Fig. 203, to which we now shall refer, is supposed to represent the same valve gear as that shown in Fig. 201. But for the sake of clearness we have left out all details not necessary for a clear conception of the subject. For instance, instead of showing the driving wheel with arms and crank, as has been done in Fig. 201, we have simply shown the tire of the same driving wheel with the arcs $d\,h\,e$ and $f\,l\,g$ marked upon its face. Of course, these arcs represent the same arcs as shown on the face of tire in Fig. 201. In Fig. 203 the center line of crank is represented by the straight line $B\,C$ or $A\,C$; $B$ being the center of crank-pin when it is on the rear dead center, and $A$ the center of crank-pin when on the front dead center; $C$ is the center of the driving axle. The circumference $x\,y$ represents the path of the centers of eccentrics. The distance between the rocker and the slide-valve has been shortened and the slide-valve

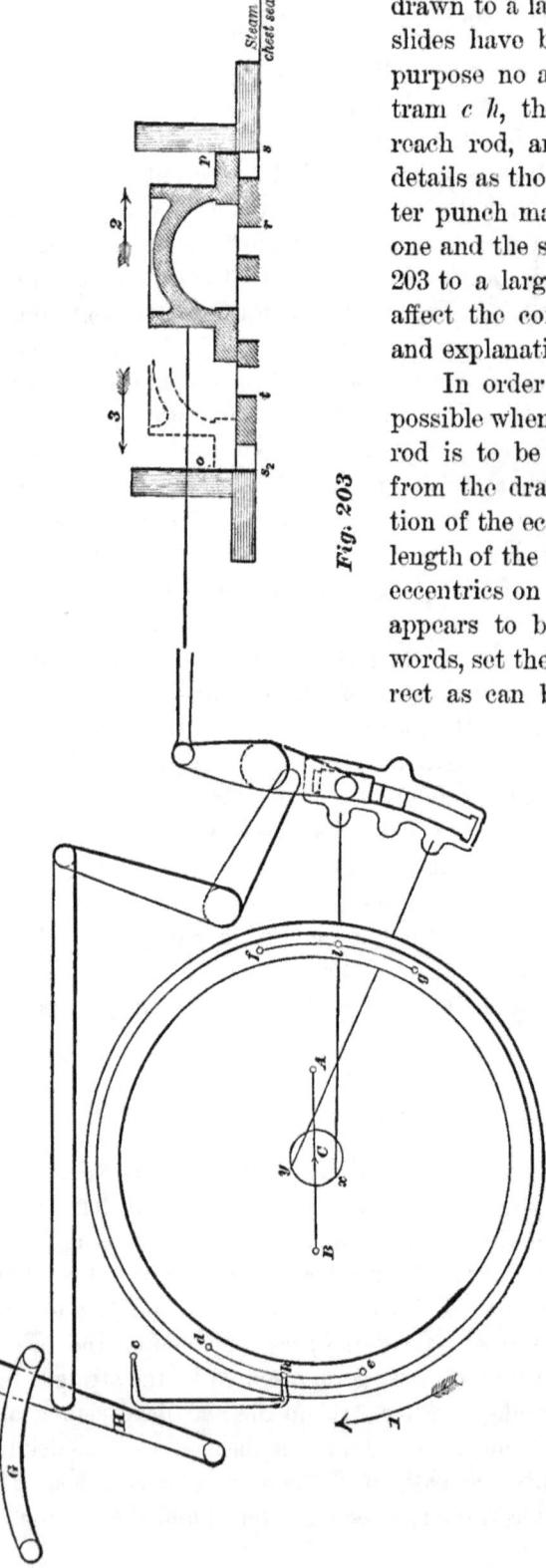

Fig. 203

drawn to a larger scale than the other details. The slides have been left out, because for the present purpose no attention need be paid to them. The tram *c h*, the reverse lever *H*, the quadrant *G*, reach rod, and lifting shaft represent the same details as those shown in Fig. 201. Also, the center punch marks *c* in Figs. 201 and 203 represent one and the same point. Drawing a part of Fig. 203 to a larger scale than the other part will not affect the correctness of the following reasoning and explanation:

In order to save as much time and labor as possible when the correct length of each eccentric-rod is to be determined, it will be best to obtain from the drawing-room the correct relative position of the eccentrics to that of the crank, also the length of the eccentric-rods; and then first set the eccentrics on the driving axle in a position which appears to be sufficiently accurate, or, in other words, set the eccentrics on the axle as nearly correct as can be done without spending too much time, or making special measurements. Also adjust the length of the eccentric-rods to the length obtained from the drawing-room, and bolt the rods to the eccentric-strap, and connect the rods to the link as previously explained. Now, the eccentric-rods being properly connected to the link, our next step will be to find the correct elevation or location of the link, and the position of the reverse lever *H* when the valve motion is in full-gear forward, and also in full-gear backward. The general practice is to sufficiently raise or lower the link which will not allow the link-block to approach the ends of the slot in the link closer than ½ or ⅜ of an inch during any one stroke. Hence, we may say the least clearance between the link-block and the link is from ⅜ to ½ an inch.

Let us assume that this clearance is to be $\frac{1}{8}$ an inch. Hence, turn the driving wheel in the direction of the arrow 1 (Fig. 203), and in the meantime move the reverse lever $H$ into the forward gear, and when the lever is in a position which will cause the least clearance between the top of the link-block and the end of the slot in the link, during one revolution of the wheel, to be equal to $\frac{1}{8}$ an inch, stop turning the wheel and clamp the lever $H$ to the quadrants $G$. This location of the link will be that to which it must be lowered when the valve motion is in full-gear forward; and since the elevation or location of the link is regulated by the reverse lever $H$, it follows that the position of the lever $H$ as found is for full-gear forward. Therefore on the quadrants $G$ mark this position of the reverse lever $H$, so that at any time afterwards it can again be readily placed in the same position. Next turn the wheel in a direction opposite to that of the arrow, and in the meantime move the reverse lever $H$ towards the rear end of the quadrants $G$, and when the link is sufficiently raised so as to cause the least clearance between the bottom end of the link-block and end of the slot in the link to be equal to $\frac{1}{8}$ an inch during one revolution of the wheel, stop turning the same, clamp the lever $H$ to the quadrants $G$, and mark its position on the quadrants for future use. Now, to determine the length of the eccentric-rods, we simply lengthen or shorten the rods so that the distance between the forward end $s$ of the extreme travel of the slide-valve and the outer edge $r$ of the front steam port will be equal to that between the rear end $s_2$ of the extreme travel of the valve and the outer edge $t$ of the rear steam port. In adjusting the length of the eccentric-rods, we may commence with the forward or backward eccentric-rods; let us commence with the former. Place the reverse lever $H$—and thus the whole valve motion—into the full forward gear, and clamp the lever $H$ to the quadrants $G$. Place a small ordinary square against the edge $p$ of the slide-valve; then turn the driving wheel in the direction of the arrow 1, causing the slide-valve to move in the direction of the arrow marked 2, and pushing the small square before it. When the valve has reached its extreme end $s$ of travel, the valve will commence to move in an opposite direction, as indicated by the arrow 3, and the square will be left standing, indicating the distance between the outer edge $r$ of the front steam port and the extreme end $s$ of the travel of the valve. While the square is in this position draw on the steam-chest seat a line touching the edge $s$ of the square. Next place the square against the edge $o$ of the valve, and continue turning the driving wheel in the same direction as before, causing the valve to travel in the direction of the arrow 3, and pushing the square towards the rear end $s_2$ of the travel. When the valve has pushed the square towards the rear as far as it can do, draw on the steam-chest seat a line touching the edge $s_2$ of the square; this line $s_2$ indicates the rear end of the extreme travel of the valve, and the distance $s_2 t$ shows the amount of travel of the valve beyond the outer edge $t$ of the rear steam port. If the distance $s_2 t$ is equal to the distance $r s$, the length of forward eccentric-rod is for the present considered to be correct. If $r s$ is greater than $s_2 t$, the eccentric-rod is too short and must be lengthened; if $r s$ is less than $s_2 t$, the eccentric-rod must be made shorter. Now place the reverse lever $H$ into full-gear backward, and clamp it to the quadrants $G$. Turn the wheel in a direction opposite to that of the arrow 1, and with the aid of the small square find the extreme travel of the slide-valve in a manner precisely the same as that just explained. And if in this case the distances $s_2 t$ and $r s$ are equal, the length of the

132                MODERN LOCOMOTIVE CONSTRUCTION.

backward eccentric-rod is for the present considered to be correct. If these distances $s_2\,t$ and $r\,s$ are not equal, the backward eccentric-rod must be lengthened or shortened as the case may require. If the backward eccentric-rod has to be lengthened or shortened, the valve motion should again be set into full-gear forward and examined, so as to determine that the adjustment of the length of the backward eccentric has not affected the action of the forward eccentric-rod. It is possible that the length of the forward eccentric-rod may want a little readjustment.

### TO FIND THE CORRECT POSITION OF THE ECCENTRICS ON THE AXLE.

153. Place the reverse lever $H$ into full-gear forward; turn the driving wheel in the direction of the arrow 1, Fig. 203, till the tram will touch the center punch marks $c$ and $h$, and then stop turning the wheel. When the wheel is in this position, the crank-pin will be on the rear dead center $B$. Move the forward eccentric around the driving axle until the required lead is obtained—that is, until the valve has opened the rear steam port $\frac{1}{16}$ of an inch. Again, turn the driving wheel in the same direction as before, till the tram will touch the center punch marks $c$ and $l$; then stop turning the wheel. While the wheel is in this position, the crank-pin will be on the front dead center $A$. And if now the workmanship of the valve gear is absolutely perfect, the lead, when the crank is in this position, will also be $\frac{1}{16}$ of an inch. But to obtain such workmanship is very difficult, if not impossible, and therefore it must not be surprising to find the lead at the front end of the cylinder to be somewhat incorrect. Assume the lead at the front end is $\frac{1}{8}$ of an inch, and at the back end $\frac{1}{16}$ of an inch. Now, since, according to our example, $\frac{1}{16}$ of an inch is the required lead, and since the lead at both ends of the cylinder must be equal, it follows that the lead at the front end must be reduced, without changing the lead at the back end of the cylinder. To do this we must shorten the forward eccentric-rod $\frac{1}{32}$ of an inch, and move the center $x$ of the eccentric towards the center line $B\,C$ of the crank, until the valve has just opened the front steam port $\frac{1}{16}$ of an inch. Turn the driving wheel once or twice around its axis and examine the lead; if the lead is equal to $\frac{1}{16}$ of an inch at each end of the cylinder, consider, for the present, the setting of the forward gear to be correct. Next move the reverse lever $H$ into full backward gear, and find the correct position of the backward eccentric $y$ in a similar manner to that adopted for finding the position of the forward eccentric $x$. In finding the position of the backward eccentric $y$ or setting the backward motion of the valve gear, the driving wheel should always be turned in a direction opposite to that indicated by arrow 1. Now put the valve motion in full-gear forward, and see that the adjustment of the backward gear has not deranged the valve motion when in the forward gear. Perhaps a little readjustment will be necessary; if so, the valve motion will generally indicate where the readjustment is to be made. When the valve motion is in the forward gear, the driving wheel should always be turned in the direction of the arrow 1—never in the opposite direction. Should the wheel be turned a little further than was intended, we must either turn the wheel completely around its axis, or turn it back considerably beyond the stopping point, and then turn slowly and carefully in the direction of the arrow 1, until it arrives at the stopping point. By so doing, any slack motion which may exist will not interfere with the correct

setting of the valve motion. If now it is found that the lead is $\frac{1}{16}$ of an inch at each end of the cylinder when the valve motion is in full backward gear, and also in full forward gear, the setting of the valve gear is correct and complete. Since we have assumed that the position of the saddle-pin on the saddle is correct, and that the location of the lifting shaft and reverse lever is also correct, according to drawing received from the drawing-room, the slide-valve will cut off equal portions of steam at each end of the cylinder.

### TO LAY OFF THE NOTCHES IN THE QUADRANTS.

154. In Fig. 204 we have represented the same mechanism as that shown in Fig. 201, but for the sake of clearness some of the details have been left out.

In Fig. 204, the line $k$ on the rear end of the slides represents the extreme end of the travel of the crosshead end $j$, and the line $o$ on the front end of the slides represents the extreme end of the travel of the crosshead end $n$. It is now to be shown how the notches on the quadrants $G$ can be located, so that when the reverse lever latch $L$ is placed in one of these notches steam will be cut off when the crosshead is in a corresponding given position between the lines $k$ and $o$ marked on the slides.

For this purpose we must attach the connecting-rod to the crank-pin and crosshead, so that when the wheel is in motion the crosshead will also be in motion.

In Art. 130 we have seen that there are two ways of arranging the notches in the quadrants $G$, namely:

1st. The notches may be cut as close together as the strength of material will allow.

2d. The notches may be cut so as to hold the reverse lever in positions which will cause the steam to be cut off

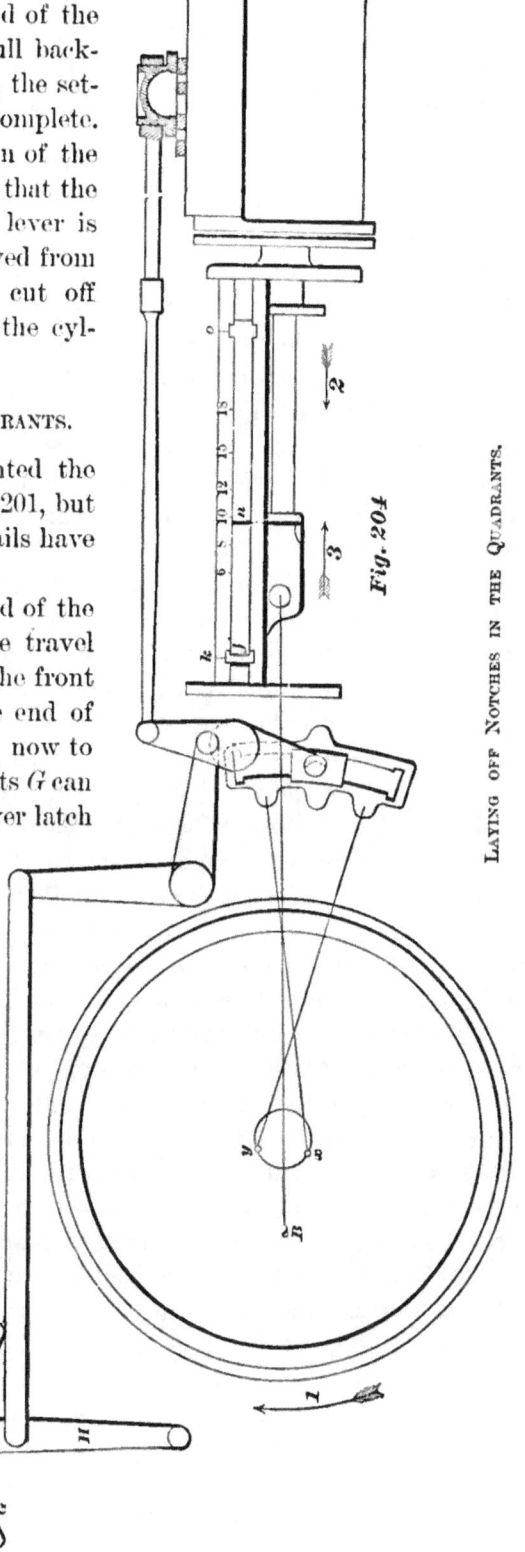

in the cylinder at some full number of inches in the stroke. We will first consider how to locate the notches in the quadrants when steam is to be cut off at a number of full inches in the stroke.

Assume that the stroke, in Fig. 204, is 24 inches, and that steam is to be cut off when the piston has traveled 6, 8, 10, 12, and 15 inches from the beginning of the stroke; it is required to find the positions of the notches in the quadrants $G$, and also, as is always customary, find the center notch which will hold the valve motion in mid-gear.

In Art. 152 we have shown how to locate the notches for full-gear forward, and also for full-gear backward; it now remains to be shown how to locate the intermediate notches. First, let us find the location of the center notch, or, in other words, the notch which will hold the valve motion in mid-gear. To do this move the reverse lever $H$ (Fig. 204) towards the middle of the quadrants $G$, and in the meantime turn the driving wheel in the direction of arrow 1—that is, in the direction of the forward motion of the wheel; also watch the movement of the slide-valve. When finally the reverse lever $H$ arrives in a position in the central portion of the quadrants which gives the shortest travel to the slide-valve, the reverse lever is then in the desired position, and will hold the whole valve motion in mid-gear, and the latch of the reverse lever will indicate the position of the center notch; therefore on the arcs $G$ scribe off the end of the latch $L$, and to these marks the center notch must be cut. To locate the other notches lay off on the slides a number of fine and distinct lines, as represented in the figure by the lines marked 6, 8, etc.; in scribing these lines on the slides care should be taken not to disfigure them. The first line, marked 6 in our figure, must be 6 inches from the line $k$; the second line, marked 8, must be 8 inches from the line $k$; and the third 10 inches from $k$; and so on for all the given points of cut-off. Now turn the driving wheel in the direction of the arrow 1, causing the crosshead to move away from $k$; as soon as the edge $j$ of the crosshead touches the line marked 6, stop the motion of the wheel, and then slowly move the reverse lever $H$ from the center notch towards the forward end of the quadrants $G$ until the slide-valve has just closed the rear steam port; then on the arcs mark off the end of the latch, and thus locate the notch which will hold the valve motion in a position that will cut off steam at 6 inches from the beginning of the stroke. Again, turn the driving wheel in the direction of the arrow 1, and when the edge $j$ of the crosshead touches the line marked 8 on the slide, stop the motion of the wheel, and then move the reverse lever towards the forward end of the quadrants until the slide-valve has just closed the rear steam port; then again, on the quadrants, mark off the end of the latch $L$ and thus locate the 8-inch notch. In a similar manner the locations of all the other notches in the forward gear are obtained. In this example we have assumed that the valve motion has been correctly designed in the drawing-room, and also correctly put up in the erecting shop, and consequently we do expect that, when the driving wheel moves in the direction of arrow 1, and the crosshead in the direction of the arrow 2, and the reverse-lever latch is in the notch marked 6, the valve will close the front steam port when the crosshead edge $n$ has moved 6 inches away from the line $o$, which was previously marked on the slide; or when the latch is in the notch marked 8, the valve will close the front steam port when the crosshead edge $n$ has moved 8 inches from the line $o$.

To lay off the notches for the backward motion a similar method is pursued, and the same lines indicating the points of cut-off previously described on the slides, and used for the forward motion of the valve gear, can also now be used for the backward motion. Hence, to lay off the notches for the backward motion, again place the reverse lever $H$ in the center notch, and place the wheel in a position in which the edge $j$ of the crosshead will touch, or nearly so, the line $k$ on the slides. Then turn the driving wheel in a direction opposite to that of arrow 1, and when the edge $j$ of the crosshead touches the line marked 6 on the slide, stop the motion of the wheel, and move the reverse lever $H$ towards the back end of the quadrants, until the slide-valve closes the rear steam port; then mark off on the quadrants the end of the latch, thus obtaining the location of the 6-inch notch for the backward motion. In a similar manner the position of all the notches in the backward gear are obtained; and since we have assumed that the valve gear has been correctly designed, it is expected that when the reverse lever latch is in the 6, 8, or 10 inch, etc., notches steam will also be cut off at 6, 8, or 10 inches when the crosshead travels in the opposite direction, namely, in the direction of arrow 2. Of course, a perfect, equal cut-off is hardly to be expected; that is, when the crosshead moves in the direction of arrow 3, and steam is cut off at 6 inches, it is not to be expected that steam will also be cut off at 6 inches when the crosshead moves in the direction of arrow 2; but we do expect that, as long as the reverse-lever latch remains in one notch, the points of cut-off will not vary more than $\frac{1}{4}$ of an inch. If the difference is greater than $\frac{1}{4}$ of an inch, an inaccuracy exists in the fitting up of the valve gear, or it is due to a faulty construction; in either case it should be rectified.

The notches must be correctly located for both cylinders, so that when steam is cut off at 6, 10 inches, etc., in one cylinder the steam must be cut off at the same points in the other cylinder, or, in other words, both cylinders must receive the same amount of steam. Hence, after the notches have been correctly located for one cylinder, we must test their accuracy for the other cylinder; and if then one cylinder receives more steam than the other, we generally find that the cause for this inaccuracy is in the position of the lifting-shaft arms, which are out of line—that is, one of the arms may hold the link too high or too low, and consequently this arm must be sprung into the proper position, which is often accomplished while the shaft is cold, without taking it out of the engine.

When steam is to be cut off equally without regard to any particular points of cut-off or full number of inches in the stroke, the notches are spaced off evenly between the two outside ones and as close together as the strength of the material will allow, and therefore generally have $\frac{1}{2}$ an inch pitch—that is, $\frac{1}{2}$ an inch from center to center of notch. (See Art. 130.) In this case also the same care must be taken to arrange the valve motion in a manner which will supply both cylinders with the same amount of steam.

It should be remembered that the foregoing instructions in setting the valve gear are intended for new work only. When the valve gear for an old engine is to be readjusted, the wear of the different parts must be taken into consideration, which sometimes makes the readjustment a difficult process, requiring experience and a knowledge of the principles connected with the design of the valve motion.

## REMARKS RELATING TO THE VALVE MOTION IN WHICH THE ECCENTRICS ARE NOT ON THE MAIN DRIVING AXLE.

**155.** Sometimes it happens that in designing small locomotives the eccentrics cannot be placed on the main axle, consequently we occasionally meet with a valve gear as shown in Fig. 205. In this valve gear the eccentrics are placed on the axle in front of the main axle. Placing the eccentrics on the front axle instead of the main axle will not change the previous rules we have given for designing the valve motion; but it should be noticed that, in order to preserve the lead, no matter in what position the link may be placed, as explained in Art. 151, the eccentric-rods are

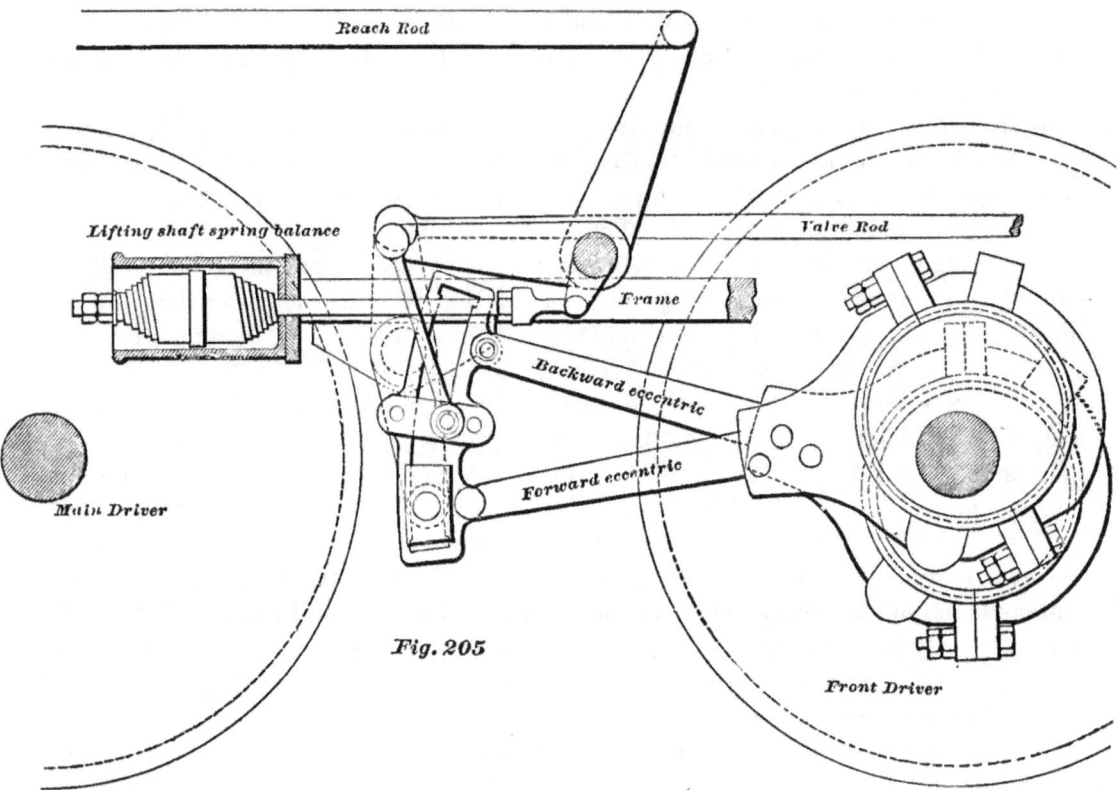

Fig. 205

connected to the link in a manner which will put the lower end of the link in action when the engine is going ahead, or, in other words, the link must be raised when the engine is to run forward, and lowered when the engine is to run backward. Of course the eccentric-rods could be connected to the link so that it would be in the lower position when going ahead, and in the upper position when running backward—that is, the link could be made to occupy a similar position to that in the link motions previously illustrated, and for that matter would also work all right while in full-gear, but the lead will be destroyed when the link is placed in any of the intermediate positions for the same reasons as explained in Art. 151; and since we must have lead in whatever position the link is placed, we must suspend the link as shown in Fig. 205

It will also be found that in locating the lifting shaft according to the rules previously given, it will have to be placed in front of the link, instead of being placed in the rear of it as has been found necessary in all the foregoing link motions. But by placing the lifting shaft, in the case now under consideration, in front of the link, we will gain an additional advantage, namely, in connecting the lifting-shaft arm to the reverse lever, the latter will be made to point ahead when the engine is going forward—an important fact which should not be neglected or forgotten, because if the valve motion should happen to be arranged in a manner which would cause the reverse lever to point back while the engine is going ahead, the engineer may be thrown into confusion when, in an emergency, the engine has to be quickly reversed, and thus lead to accidents.

# CHAPTER IV.

### PISTONS.—CROSSHEADS.—SLIDES.—STUFFING BOXES.

#### PISTONS.

156. Locomotive pistons consist of two principal parts, namely, the piston head and the packing. Locomotive pistons may also be divided into three classes, according to the construction of the head; the first class embracing all those in which the piston head is made up of more than one piece, such as shown in Figs. 206 and

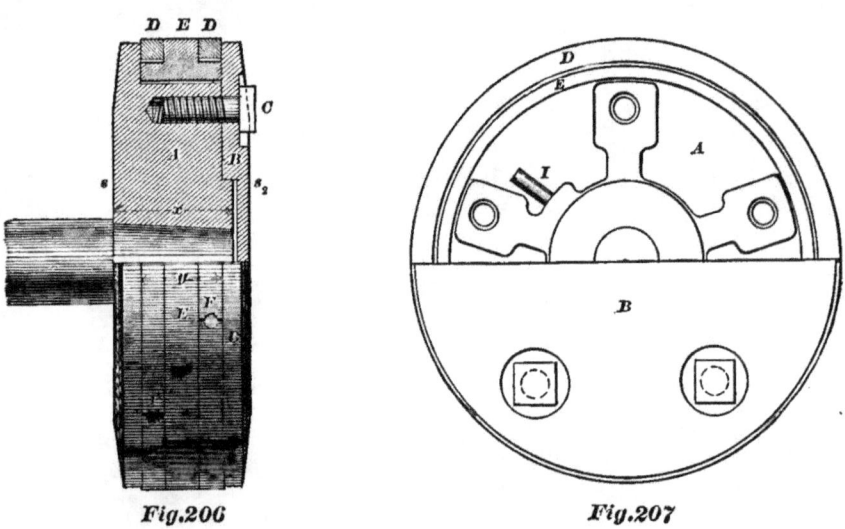

Fig. 206    Fig. 207

207; this class of pistons we may call the "built-up piston." The second class will embrace the pistons in which the head is cast hollow, such as shown in Fig. 208; this class of piston we may call the hollow piston. To the third class belong the solid piston, such as is shown in Fig. 209.

#### THE BUILT-UP PISTON.

157. Figs. 206 and 207. In this figure the piston head is made up of the following pieces: The spider, which is marked $A$; the follower plate, or simply the follower, marked $B$; and the follower bolts $C$, which unite the follower to the spider.

In American locomotives the spider $A$ is made of cast-iron. It should be made, in fact the whole piston should be made, as light as possible, and consequently its metal must be judiciously distributed, so as to obtain the required strength with the least amount of metal. By so doing, less counterbalance will be required, besides gaining other advantages. The spider is generally keyed to the piston-rod by the key $I$; sometimes the piston is secured to the rod by means of a nut, as shown in Fig. 208. In very large pistons, such as are used in stationary or marine engines, the depth of the spider (corresponding to the depth $x$ in Fig. 206) is computed for strength; the width of the packing (corresponding to the width $y$ in Fig. 206)—that is, the distance from the face of the flange of the spider to the face of the follower—is generally made equal to $\frac{1}{9}$ to $\frac{1}{6}$ of the diameter of the piston; the latter proportion being adopted for pistons of comparatively small diameter (as large as a locomotive piston 22 inches in diameter) and the former proportion for pistons of very large diameter. Consequently, in stationary engines, and also in marine engines, we often find pistons whose depth

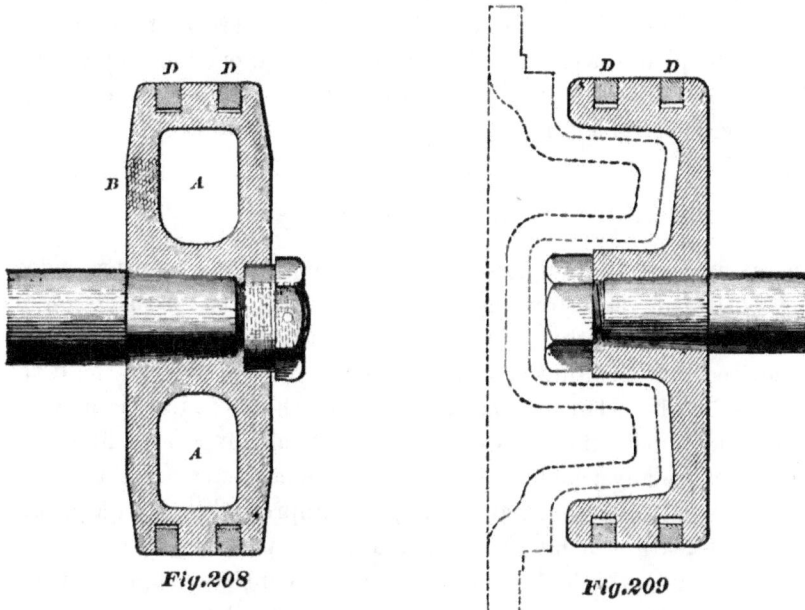

at the center is greater than that at the circumference, so that when one face of these pistons is flat the other face will be part of a spherical surface. In locomotive pistons the depth $x$ of the spider is determined by the key which holds it to the piston-rod. The dimensions of these keys, depth of spider, and size of piston-rods are given in Figs. 220 to 232. Now, practically, in locomotive pistons of small diameter the necessary depth $x$ of spider does not give us an excessive depth for the packing, and in those of larger diameter the depth $x$ will give a depth of packing agreeing with the proportions given for stationary and marine engines. Therefore the faces $s$ and $s_2$ of locomotive pistons are generally flat, sometimes slightly tapered towards the circumference, as shown in the figures.

The follower plates (Figs. 206 and 207) are made of cast-iron, and usually cover the whole open end of the spider when follower bolts are used, as shown in the figure.

### FOLLOWER BOLTS.

158. In any mechanism having such a high rate of reciprocating motion as a locomotive piston, bolts, unless carefully fitted, are liable to become loose and work

out. To prevent the follower bolts from becoming loose, they are extended into the spider through a distance which is at least equal to three times the diameter of the bolt, and great care is taken to make a good fit of the thread. Sometimes, on account of the rust, trouble is experienced when the follower bolts are to be taken out of the spider. To obviate this difficulty a few locomotive builders insert brass plugs into the spider. (See Fig. 210.) These plugs are tightly screwed into the spider and then riveted over at the ends. In these brass plugs holes are drilled and tapped to receive the follower bolts, preventing any rust from causing a difficulty in removing the bolts when it becomes necessary to do so.

The construction of the hollow piston, shown in Fig. 208, needs no explanation, with the exception to state that a number of core holes $B$ are cast in one side of the piston, and when the piston is cleaned the core holes are tapped and plugged up.

The solid piston shown in Fig. 209 is used when extreme lightness is required. This form of piston is suitable for cast-iron, wrought-iron, or steel.

### PISTON PACKING.

159. A great amount of thought, labor, and expense has been expended in constructing and perfecting a piston packing which shall give satisfaction under all circumstances, and consequently many different kinds of piston packing are in use. But we have noticed that the kind of piston packing which has given the best satisfaction so far is one in which two distinguishing features are found, namely, durability and simplicity; and indeed these two features we should expect to find in any good piston packing, because any packing that will not remain steam tight for a considerable length of time is troublesome, annoying, and unprofitable; and a packing which does not possess the feature of simplicity is dangerous, particularly so in fast-running engines. The packing in the hollow piston, Fig. 208, consists simply of two cast-iron rings $D\ D$, which are sprung into the grooves turned into the periphery of the piston. Each ring is cut in one place; the favorite form of the cut is shown in Figs. 214 and 215. This piston, on account of its great simplicity, is a favorite one on many roads. It is more suitable for cylinders of large diameter than smaller ones, because in the latter there is danger of breaking the rings in attempting to spring them into the grooves. Similar packing rings are used for the solid piston shown in Fig. 209.

In Figs. 206 and 207 we have represented another piston packing which, on account of its simplicity and durability, has in late years gained great favor among engineers, and is certainly an excellent piston packing for locomotives. It consists simply of two cast-iron rings $D\ D$, and one cast-iron T-ring marked $E$. We call this ring a "T-ring" because its cross-section resembles a T. The rings $D\ D$ are cut open in one place, and consequently are called single-cut rings. Two ways of cutting these rings are generally adopted. Some master-mechanics will have the rings $D\ D$ cut as shown in Fig. 213. Here a hole $F\ F$ is first drilled and made oblong in the direction of $F\ F$, then through the center of the hole the ring is cut open square across. Care should be taken to cut out a sufficient amount of metal, so that when the packing ring is placed in the cylinder the two ends will not touch each other, but will leave an opening sufficiently great to allow for the expansion of the ring when it becomes hot. The same remark applies to the hole $F\ F$; this should be made long enough, as shown, to allow a sufficient clearance around the pin which is inserted in this hole and driven into the T-ring, otherwise the expansion will force the ends of the packing ring against the pin and prevent the ring from acting as it should do. The object of this pin is to prevent the ring $D$ from moving around the

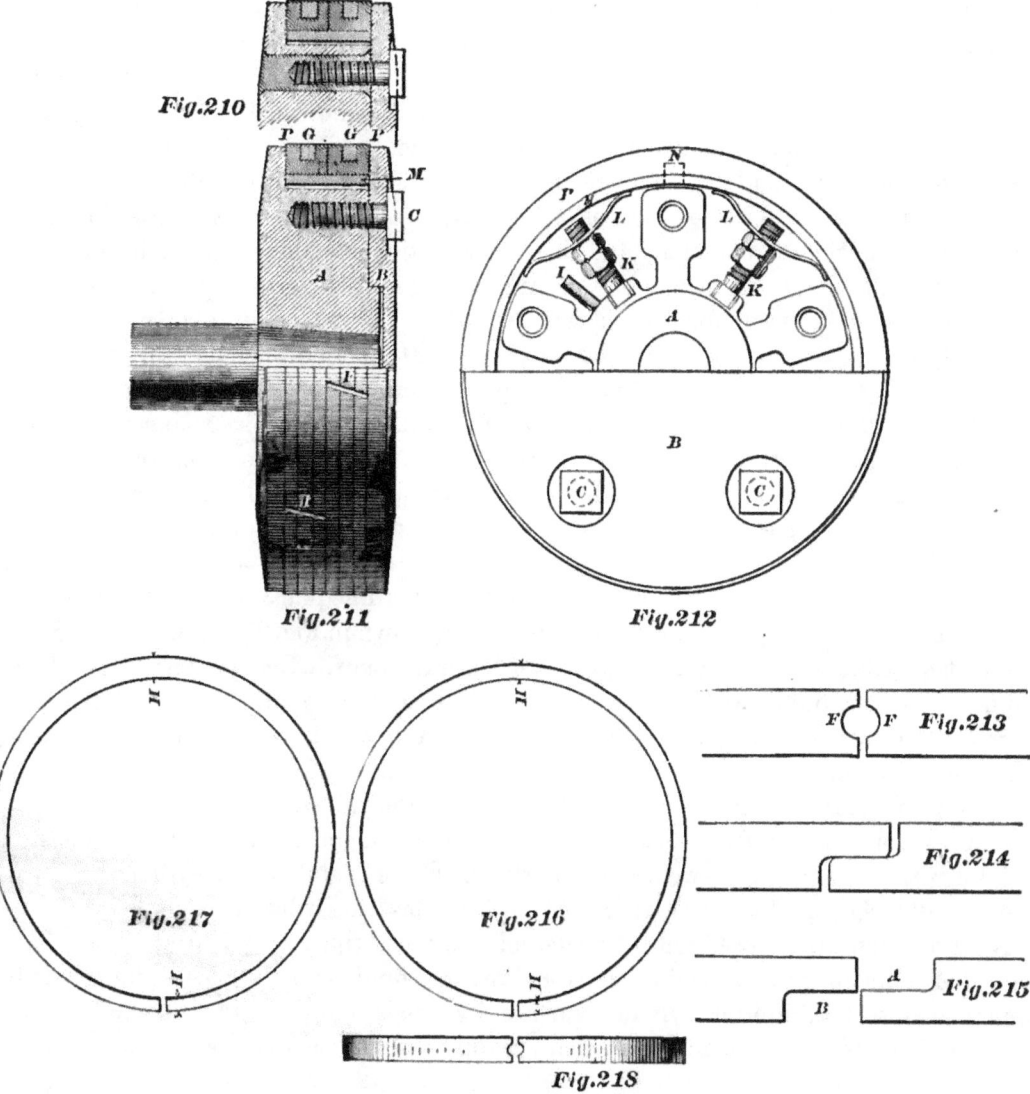

T-ring. When the rings $D\ D$ are cut in the manner just described, they are turned about $\frac{3}{16}$ to $\frac{5}{16}$ of an inch larger in diameter than the bore of the cylinder, so as to give the rings an inherent elasticity. The other way of cutting these rings is shown in Fig. 214. Here half the width of the ring is cut out through a distance of about $\frac{7}{8}$ of an inch, which enables the ends of the ring to overlap each other about $\frac{3}{4}$ of an inch. The writer believes that when a ring is to be cut in this manner the best method to pursue will be as follows: First turn the ring large enough in diameter to allow for

142                    MODERN LOCOMOTIVE CONSTRUCTION.

the metal to be cut out. Then cut the openings A and B, Fig. 215, through half the width of the ring, and each about ⅞ of an inch long. When these are cut press the ends together, so that the ends will overlap each other about ¾ of an inch; through these reduced ends drive a small temporary pin, and then again turn the ring to fit the bore of the cylinder; after that take out this pin, as it has served its purpose. Other pins are driven in the T-ring, which fit loosely in holes drilled in the packing rings, to prevent the latter from turning around the T-ring.

As to the proportions of the cross-section of the rings D D (see Fig. 206), a difference of opinion exists. Some master-mechanics make the width of the ring greater than the depth, others will insist on having the width smaller than the depth, but more frequently we find the cross-section to be a square. The writer believes that packing rings whose cross-section is ½ inch square will give good satisfaction for cylinders 9 inches in diameter; and this cross-section should be gradually increased for cylinders of larger diameter, in a manner which will bring the cross-section of the ring to ¾ inch square for locomotive cylinders 22 inches in diameter. In the majority of locomotives the depth H of rings D D remains the same throughout, as shown in Fig. 216. They are made to press against the interior surface of the cylinder by their inherent elasticity, and when this elasticity is exhausted through constant wear, it can be partially restored by a few judicious light blows of the hammer in the inside of the ring. Since these rings will wear most at the opening, and in time wear the cylinders oval instead of cylindrical, it has been assumed that they have not a uniform pressure all around against the cylinder surface, and this is true. Hence, on account of this unequal pressure, some master-mechanics make these packing rings of the form as shown in Fig. 217, in which the depth H at the opening of the ring is less than the depth H opposite the opening. The object aimed at is, of course, to obtain as nearly as possible an equal pressure of the ring against the interior surface of the cylinder. But from the writer's experience, and upon careful inquiry, he is led to believe that rings of uniform depth throughout, as shown in Fig. 216, will give as good satisfaction as the ring shown in Fig. 217.

Cast-iron is generally considered to be as good a metal as can be used for piston packing rings, as it wears well, particularly when the metal in the cylinder is hard, as it should be; furthermore, rings of the kind just described need but very little inspection, and can be used for a considerable length of time.

160. Sometimes the packing rings are cut into four or more pieces, and made to press against the interior cylinder surface by the aid of springs; the advantage claimed for this arrangement is an equal pressure against the cylinder surface.

### DUNBAR PACKING.

A notable packing of this kind is the Dunbar packing shown in Fig. 219A. The packing consists of two kinds of rings: one has an L-shaped cross-section and the other a square section. Each ring is cut into a number of sections—in this case six in number—and when put together the joints are staggered. These sections are pressed out by a number of springs made of round steel wire extending around the T-ring; the latter is of the same form as is usually used for the ordinary class of pistons. But cutting the rings into so many pieces, and then introducing springs, interferes with the simplicity of construction, and therefore packings of this kind have not been as frequently used in late years as formerly.

T-RING.—POSITION OF PACKING RINGS.

161. Fig. 206. The outer surface of the T-ring is turned to fit easily the bore of the cylinder, so that when the T-ring becomes hot its expansion will not

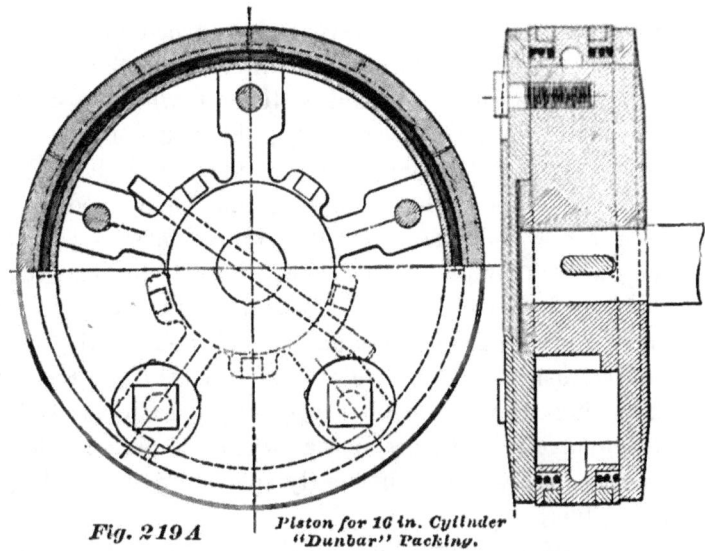

Fig. 219A  Piston for 16 in. Cylinder "Dunbar" Packing.

interfere with its free motion in the cylinder. The width of this ring must be turned to such dimensions that it can be held firmly in position by the follower plate, when the latter is screwed to the spider. The recesses turned at each corner of the ring will form the grooves for the packing rings when the piston is put together. Of course, the T-ring is not cut open. The advantage obtained by the use of this ring is that the packing rings can be readily placed in or taken out of the piston, without forcing the ends of the packing rings apart to place them into the grooves, as must be done when the solid piston is used. The packing rings must fit in the grooves very accurately, not too loose, yet free enough to allow the rings to adjust themselves to the interior surface of the cylinder. When both the packing rings are placed in position, their openings or cuts should not be in a straight line, but should be staggered, having a distance of 5 or 6 inches between them, as indicated by distance between the openings $F F$ in Fig. 206. It is always best to allow the openings of the rings to lie in the lower part of the cylinder; but in no case should they be placed over a steam way. The reason for this is that, since the rings are turned a little larger in diameter than the bore of the cylinder, they must be compressed in placing them into the cylinder; and now, should the hold or grip upon them be lost through some accident or mishap while in the act of placing them in position, the ends of the rings may fly into the steam way, and generally in such cases they must be ruined by cutting them into several pieces, in order to take the rings out.

BRASS PISTON PACKING.

162. Another very good packing for locomotive pistons is shown in Figs. 211 and 212. In former years this packing was the favorite, and even in late years some master-mechanics show a reluctance in giving it up, and consequently it is at present frequently met with. This packing consists of two brass packing rings $P P$, one inside cast-iron ring $M$, the packing bolts $K$ with nuts, and the packing springs $L$. The

packing rings $P\ P$ have grooves $G\ G$ turned in them, and these grooves are filled with Babbitt metal. This metal will prevent the scratching of the interior of the cylinder surface, such as would be the case when brass alone is used. The rings $P\ P$ are turned all over very accurately; the width of each of these rings is equal to half the space between the flange of the spider and the follower plate, so that the rings will fill this space without binding, and have freedom to adjust themselves to the bore of the cylinder as the piston moves forward and backward. Consequently—as will be seen by the illustrations, Figs. 220 to 232—the width of each packing ring for large pistons will be $1\frac{1}{2}$ inches, and for the smaller pistons $1\frac{1}{16}$ inches. The depth of these rings is generally equal to $\frac{2}{3}$ of their width. Each ring $P\ P$ is cut open in one place, usually at an angle as shown at $F\ F$, Fig. 211. The diameter of these packing rings should be sufficiently large to allow only for the amount of metal that is to be cut out of them, so that when the ring is placed in the cylinder the ends of the opening will be sufficiently apart to prevent the expansion from forcing the ends together.

The cast-iron ring $M$ is turned to fit the inside of the brass rings $P\ P$, is cut in one place square across, and its width must be exactly equal to the sum of the widths of the brass rings, so as to give it freedom to adjust itself to the inside of the brass rings. The thickness of the ring $M$ is usually about $\frac{3}{8}$ of an inch for large pistons, and about $\frac{5}{16}$ for smaller ones. The purpose of the ring $M$ is to furnish a bearing for the springs $L\ L$, and to distribute their pressure equally on the packing rings; also to form a steam-tight joint with the interior of the brass rings $P\ P$. Dowel pins $N$, Fig. 212, are driven into the ring $M$ and allowed to project into holes drilled into the brass rings $P\ P$, preventing the latter from moving around the ring $M$.

The brass rings $P\ P$ have but very little inherent elasticity, and consequently the packing springs $L\ L$ are needed for the purpose of pressing the packing rings against the interior cylinder surface. In large locomotive pistons the springs $L\ L$ are usually about 5 inches long, $2\frac{1}{2}$ inches wide, and $\frac{1}{4}$ of an inch thick in the center; the thickness is reduced towards the ends. For smaller pistons these springs are about 4 inches long, 2 inches wide, and $\frac{1}{8}$ of an inch thick.

The packing bolts $K\ K$ are generally $\frac{5}{8}$ of an inch in diameter; their heads, which are of the T form, are set into grooves cast into the hubs of the spider, which will prevent the bolts from turning when the nuts are screwed against the springs to press out and adjust the packing rings as may be required.

### PISTON-RODS.

163. Locomotive piston-rods, and, in fact, piston-rods for nearly all kinds of steam engines, are subjected alternately to a tensile and compressive stress. By tensile stress is meant that force which tends to produce fracture by pulling or tearing the piston-rod apart; and by compressive stress is meant that force which tends to produce fracture by crushing the rod. In calculating the strength of any piston-rod the tensile and also the compressive stress to which it is subjected must be considered; thus, for instance: We first find the diameter which will give the piston-rod sufficient

strength to resist the tensile stress; then we find the diameter which will give the piston-rod sufficient strength to resist the compressive stress. If we find that the diameter must be 3½ inches to resist tensile stress, and only 3 inches to resist compressive stress, then the diameter of the rod must be made equal to 3½ inches, otherwise there is danger of producing fracture by tearing; if, on the other hand, we find that the diameter of the piston-rod must be 3 inches to resist compressive stress, and only 2¼ inches to resist tensile stress, then the diameter of the piston-rod must be 3 inches, otherwise there is danger of buckling or producing fracture by crushing it. From these remarks we may conclude that in some cases the diameter of the piston-rod is determined and limited by the tensile stress, and in other cases by the compressive stress. Generally speaking, long rods—that is, rods which are long in comparison with their diameters—cannot resist as much compressive stress as tensile stress, consequently their diameters are determined by the former; short rods, on the other hand, cannot usually resist as much tensile stress as compressive stress, hence the diameters of short rods are determined by the tensile stress. Locomotive rods are comparatively short when compared with their diameters, and their ends are weakened by key ways or threads; therefore the diameters are determined by the tensile stress alone, and consequently in the following, compression will be left out of consideration.

In speaking of the diameter of a piston-rod, we mean the diameter of that part of the rod which reaches from the piston to the crosshead.

164. When built-up pistons are used, the piston is keyed to the rod in the majority of cases; occasionally we find the two united by a nut. The ends of the rod which fit in the piston and crosshead are made smaller in diameter than that of the rod, so as to form shoulders. The object of these shoulders is twofold: first, they will allow the rods to be re-turned when that becomes necessary through constant wear; and secondly, it is considered to be good practice to have a shoulder against which the piston can be driven. The ends are tapered ⅛ of an inch in 4 inches—that is, in 4 inches the diameter decreases ⅛ of an inch. The end of the rod which fits in the piston must be made as short as the design will permit, so as to reduce the depth of the piston as much as possible. The crosshead end must be made a little longer than the piston end, because in the former the distance between the key and the shoulder of the piston-rod must be increased to obtain sufficient metal in the crosshead hub from the key to the end of the hub. The taper of the keys is ¼ of an inch in 12 inches.

165. Figs. 220 to 232 inclusive form an illustrated table of the pistons and rods from which all the principal dimensions can at once be obtained. In making this table the writer obtained the dimensions of rods and pistons used in modern locomotives and doing good work, but, as was to be expected, there was found to be no uniformity of proportions; but yet these proportions seemed to indicate that the tensile stress should not be greater than 10,000 pounds per square inch on the weakest part of the piston-rod. With this data and these proportions as a basis the writer formed this table, in which the dimensions have been obtained by calculation, so that when these dimensions are adopted and the pressure in the cylinder is 120 pounds, the tensile stress per square inch on the weakest part of the piston-rod and key will not exceed 10,000 pounds.

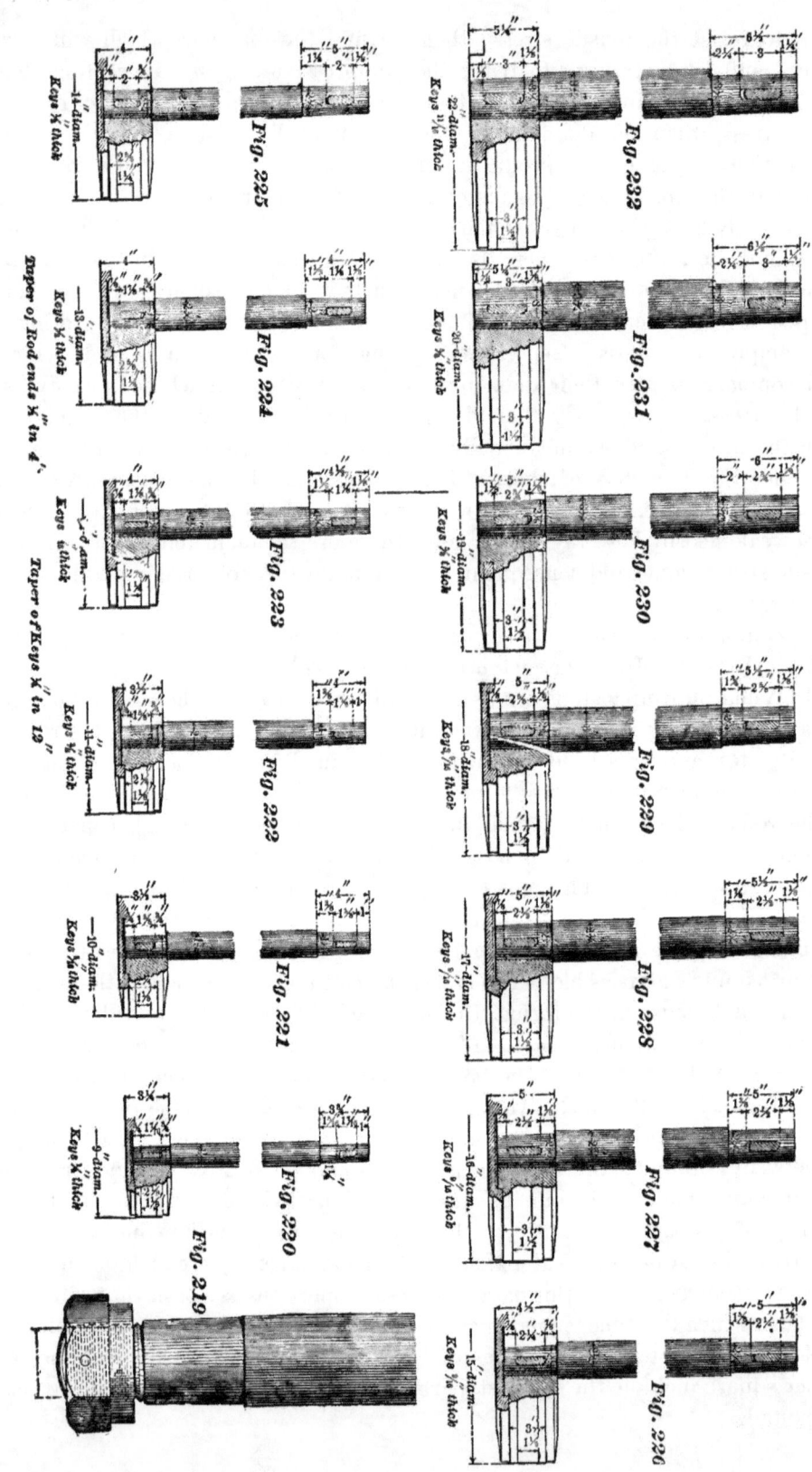

Mostly all the dimensions given in these figures agree, and the others very nearly agree, with the sizes of pistons and rods used in first-class locomotives. The writer believes this table to be reliable.

Locomotive piston-rods are made of iron, steel, and cold rolled iron. When cold rolled iron is used the piston-rods are not turned, the iron being rolled to the required size.

In order to reduce the number of patterns as much as possible, it is customary to retain the same diameter for steel and iron piston-rods for a given diameter of cylinder; that is to say, when a steel rod is to be used in place of an iron rod, the diameter of the former is made the same as that of the latter.

Consequently, our remarks in regard to strength of locomotive piston-rods apply to iron as well as steel rods. But the reader must not be led to understand that there is no difference between the strength of steel and iron rods, and that in designing piston-rods for other engines the difference between the strength of steel and iron can be neglected. We simply wish to be understood that in locomotive practice only, the difference between the strength of steel and iron rods is left out of the calculation, so that the rod made of the weakest material will still be strong enough to do the work, and thus enable us to establish an interchangeability of wider range of the mechanism whose dimensions depend upon the diameter of the piston-rod, and also reduce the number of patterns.

It is the general practice to allow on the piston-rod a tensile stress of 5,000 pounds per square inch, and not to exceed this. But it should also be remembered that new locomotive piston-rods are usually made $\frac{1}{8}$ of an inch larger in diameter than is necessary for the strength of the rod, so that in case the rod needs to be turned down on account of wear, it will still be strong enough to do the work. Consequently, after having found the correct diameter which the strength of the rod demands, we must increase this diameter by $\frac{1}{8}$ of an inch, which will be the allowance for wear. Hence, when it is desirable to determine by calculation the diameter of a piston-rod suitable for a size of cylinder and a steam pressure not given in the table, the following rule may be employed:

RULE 18.—Multiply the area in square inches of the piston by the maximum steam pressure per square inch in the cylinder; the product will be the total pressure on the piston, and therefore the total tensile stress on the piston-rod.

Divide this product by 5,000; the quotient will be the area in square inches of the cross-section of the piston-rod; the corresponding diameter of this area, and an addition of $\frac{1}{8}$ of an inch to this diameter, will be required diameter of the piston-rod. Putting this rule in the shape of a formula, we have:

$$\frac{\text{Area of the piston in square inches} \times \text{pressure per square inch}}{5,000} = \text{area of the piston-rod, without allowance for wear;}$$

then,

diam. of area found + $\frac{1}{8}$ of an inch = required diameter of piston-rod.

EXAMPLE 44.—What should be the diameter of a piston-rod for a locomotive cylinder 18 inches in diameter; steam pressure in cylinder, 120 pounds per square inch?

$$\frac{254.47 \times 120}{5000} = 6.1 = \text{area of piston-rod, without allowance for wear.}$$

Diameter of an area of 6.1 square inches = $2\frac{13}{16}$ inches, nearly.

$2\frac{13}{16} + \frac{1}{8} = 2\frac{15}{16}$ inches = required diameter of piston-rod.

In Fig. 229 we find this diameter to be 3 inches. There are in this table several diameters which will slightly exceed the diameters found by this rule. The reason of this is that in making this table the writer has followed the general practice of locomotive builders, namely, avoiding $\frac{1}{16}$ of an inch in the diameters of the piston-rods; also making the increase of the diameters of rods for the different sizes of cylinders as gradual as possible. The piston-rod in Fig. 232 is about $\frac{1}{8}$ of an inch less in diameter than would be obtained by calculation.

We have given this small diameter because such was used in the few engines of this size that we have met. The figures obtained by the rule will give sufficient strength to the piston-rods; the figures in table agree closer with practice. It will

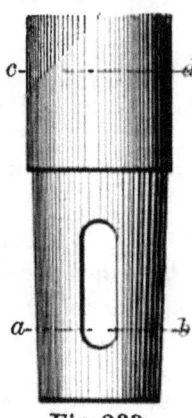

Fig. 233

be well to remark here that the area of the weakest part of the piston-rod is practically equal to one-half the area of the cross-section of the rod; and this remark applies equally well to the piston-rods which are keyed to the piston, and those which are united to it by a nut. Thus, for instance: Let Fig. 233 represent one end of the piston-rod; then the section through $a\,b$ will obviously be the weakest part of the rod to resist tensile stress; and it will generally be found that the area of this section is equal to one-half the area of the section through $c\,d$. Or, again, when the piston-rod is united to the piston by a nut (such a rod is represented in Fig. 219), then the area of a section through the bottom of the thread, which is the weakest part, will be equal to about one-half the area of the rod. Consequently it follows that, by allowing 5,000 pounds per square inch of section at $c\,d$, Fig. 233, the tensile stress cannot exceed 10,000 pounds per square inch at $a\,b$, which is correct, and agrees with practice.

In calculating the strength of the key, we may assume, and do so without fear of error, that the tensile stress is equal to the shearing stress. The key is subjected to a double shear; that is, shearing must take place at two places before fracture can occur. Hence, the area of one cross-section of the key must be equal to one-half the area at $a\,b$ in Fig. 233.

TABLE 14.

| Diameter of Piston. | Diameter of Piston-rod. | Large Diameter of Tapered End. |
|---|---|---|
| 9 inches. | $1\frac{1}{2}$ inches. | $1\frac{1}{4}$ inches. |
| 10 " | $1\frac{3}{4}$ " | $1\frac{1}{2}$ " |
| 11 " | 2 " | $1\frac{5}{8}$ " |
| 12 " | $2\frac{1}{8}$ " | $1\frac{3}{4}$ " |
| 13 " | $2\frac{1}{4}$ " | 2 " |
| 14 " | $2\frac{3}{8}$ " | $2\frac{1}{8}$ " |
| 15 " | $2\frac{1}{2}$ " | $2\frac{1}{4}$ " |
| 16 " | $2\frac{5}{8}$ " | $2\frac{3}{8}$ " |
| 17 " | $2\frac{3}{4}$ " | $2\frac{1}{2}$ " |
| 18 " | 3 " | $2\frac{3}{4}$ " |
| 19 " | $3\frac{1}{8}$ " | $2\frac{7}{8}$ " |
| 20 " | $3\frac{1}{4}$ " | 3 " |
| 22 " | $3\frac{3}{8}$ " | $3\frac{1}{4}$ " |

The dimensions in the foregoing table agree with those given in the illustrations. The principal dimensions of pistons are given in Figs. 220 to 232.

### CROSSHEADS.

166. The function of a crosshead is to form a connection between the piston-rod and the connecting-rod, making the piston-rod move in its true course, in a straight line, while the connecting-rod moves through various oblique positions. Consequently we may say the crosshead consists essentially of a socket, to which the piston is keyed; a journal, on which one end of the connecting-rod works; and lastly, sliding surfaces, which are compelled to remain in contact with the guides, and thus guiding

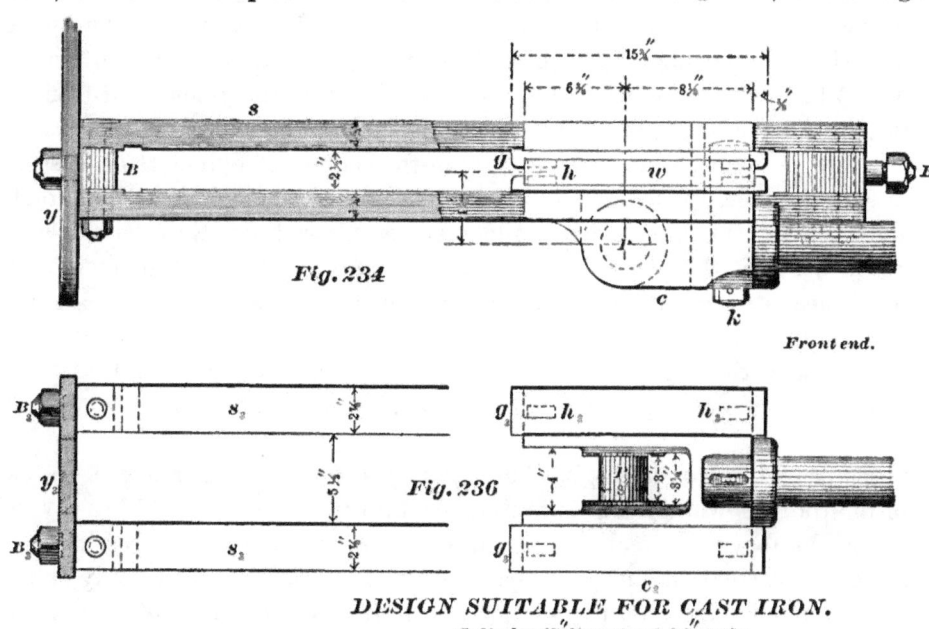

Fig. 234

Front end.

Fig. 236

DESIGN SUITABLE FOR CAST IRON.
Cylinder 17″ diameter & 24″ stroke.

the end of the piston-rod in its true course, preventing the thrust of the connecting-rod from bending or injuring the former.

It will hardly seem necessary to give names to such familiar mechanism as here represented; but since the different pieces are not named alike by all mechanics, the writer deems it advisable to name the pieces, so as to avoid misunderstanding hereafter. Similar letters in the different views represent the same piece.

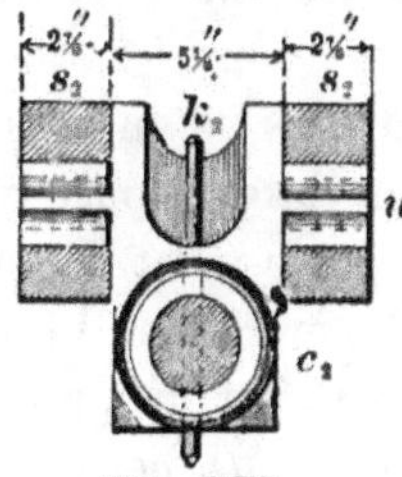

Figs. 234, 235, and 236. $S$ represents the guides, frequently called slides (some mechanics call these the slide-bars or guide-bars; we shall simply name these the guides or slides); $B$, the guide-blocks; $c$, the crosshead; $w$, the crosshead wings, or simply the wings (in some books these are called slides or slide-blocks); $g$, the gibs; $P$, the crosshead pin; $k$, the crosshead key; and $y$, the guide-yoke.

Fig. 235

In locomotive construction three styles of crossheads are used, and these we may classify as follows:

First, crossheads which require four guides; second, crossheads which require two guides; third, crossheads which require one guide.

167. Fig. 234 represents a side view, Fig. 235 an end view, and Fig. 236 a plan of a crosshead and guides. This crosshead, as will be seen, requires four guides. This style of crosshead is generally used (not always) in eight-wheeled locomotives such as shown in Fig. 1, and ten-wheeled locomotives as shown in Fig. 3. When a crosshead is to be designed for one of these engines, we must keep in mind the following conditions. In the eight-wheeled and ten-wheeled locomotives the rear truck wheels are situated directly behind the cylinder saddle and between the guides and the frames, and these wheels must have a sufficient space for the lateral play when the engine is running over a curve. Now this space is limited by the position of the cylinders. Thus, for instance, the centers of the cylinders are always placed as close to the frames as possible, which, of course, will limit the space between the guides and frames and often give an insufficient space for the lateral play of the rear truck wheels. But, since it is always of great importance to keep the centers of cylinders as close to the frames as can be done, we should not attempt to spread the cylinders so as to obtain sufficient space for the wheels until all other resources fail. Now let us consider the distance between the center of the cylinders and the top of the track, and see if by some means sufficient room can be obtained for the wheels to pass underneath the guides and thus gain for them a sufficient space for their lateral play. In the first place, the centers of cylinders are usually placed from 1 to 2 inches above the centers of driving wheels when the engine is in the ordinary good running condition.

The center of the crosshead pin $P$ must, of course, remain in line with the center of the piston-rod, or—what amounts to the same thing—the center line of the cylinder; hence the height above the track to the center of the cylinder or the crosshead pin $P$ will also to a great extent limit the space we wish to obtain. Now, only one more resource remains by which we may obtain the desired space, and that is, raising the guides above the center of the crosshead pin $P$. If this fails to give us sufficient space, then we must either spread the centers of the cylinders, or adopt a crosshead such as is shown in Fig. 241, or do both. Usually it is found that a crosshead with the guides raised above the center of pin $P$, as shown in Fig. 234, will answer the purpose and still allow the center of the cylinders to remain as close to the frames as they can possibly be placed. This arrangement will enable the truck wheels to pass underneath the guides as far as will be necessary. Here the flanges have not entered into our consideration, and indeed it is not necessary that they should, as there will always be, in this class of engines, sufficient space between the frames and guides for the lateral play of the flanges. Sometimes in narrow-gauge engines the side of the frames must be cut in order to clear the truck wheel. It must also be remarked that the engine and truck springs, particularly the latter, will cause the cylinders and guides to move up and down, and since the wheels have not this movement, a sufficient clearance between the under side of the guides and top of truck wheels must be allowed, to prevent the guides from striking the top of truck wheels when the springs impart a vertical movement to the guides.

This style of crosshead, Fig. 234, is usually made of cast-iron, sometimes of malleable iron. The crosshead pin $P$ and the crosshead are cast in one piece. The pin $P$ is generally finished off by hand, sometimes with special machinery.

In order to take up quickly and readily any wear between the guides and the wings of the crosshead, the brass gibs $g$ are introduced. The lips at the ends of these gibs prevent them from moving endways, and the lugs $h$ cast to the gibs and fitting in the slots cut in the wings of the crosshead will prevent the gibs from slipping out sideways. When the wear is to be taken up, thin copper liners are inserted between the gibs and the wing.

168. Some master-mechanics prefer crossheads with brass gibs, because, the brass being softer than the iron, they believe that there is not so great a liability to cut the guides as when cast-iron bears directly against them, which will be the case when crossheads without the gibs are used. Cutting the guides is always a serious matter,

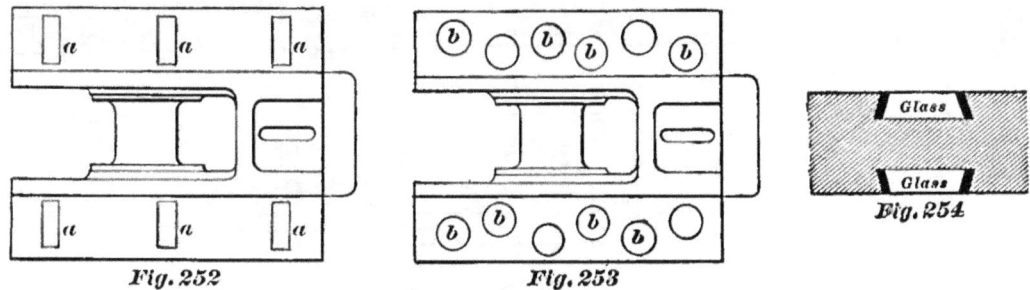

and if cutting does occur, it is always preferable that the gibs should be cut or ruined, rather than the guides, as the former are cheaper to replace, and can be replaced in less time (another important matter in railroading) than ruined guides. Yet experience also teaches that when guides are properly case hardened, and crossheads without gibs are used, so that cast-iron bears directly against the guides, cutting of the guides is prevented by running a new engine at first slowly and carefully, allowing the cast-iron wings to wear down to smooth, hard surfaces; after that there is little danger of cutting the guides, providing they are kept oiled. Consequently we meet with many locomotives in which the crossheads have no brass gibs and give perfect satisfaction.

Crossheads without gibs have the wings babbitted, as shown at $a\ a\ a$ in Fig. 252. Three or more rectangular recesses, about $\frac{1}{2}$ or $\frac{3}{8}$ of an inch deep, $\frac{3}{4}$ of an inch wide, and as long as the width of the wing will allow, are cast in the wing, and then filled with Babbitt metal. Sometimes as many recesses, $\frac{1}{2}$ or $\frac{3}{8}$ of an inch deep, $1\frac{1}{2}$ inches in diameter, as there is room for, arranged in a manner as shown at $b\ b\ b$ in Fig. 253, are bored in the wing, and then filled with Babbitt metal. A few years ago these recesses were sometimes filled with glass disks. When these were used, the bottom diameter of the recess was larger than the upper diameter, and also the lower diameter of the glass disk larger than the upper one. This disk was then placed in the recess, and Babbitt metal poured around it, as shown in Fig. 254, and thus held firmly in the recess.

169. Objections are sometimes raised against crossheads with the pins $P$ cast in one piece, as it is difficult to true up these pins when necessary, and therefore crossheads similar to that as represented in Figs. 237, 238, 239, and 240 are sometimes preferred.

This crosshead consists of several pieces. Fig. 240, $H$ is a wrought-iron hub with fork end. This hub is keyed to the piston-rod. The wings $w_3 \, w_3$, with flanges $l_3 \, l_3$, are made of cast-iron. The bushing $F$ is made of wrought-iron case hardened, the grain of the iron running around the bushing, and not in the direction of its length; the fork end of the hub $H$ is bored out large enough to receive the bushing. The bolt $o_3$ is made of wrought-iron not case hardened; the outer plate $a_3$ is made of brass and

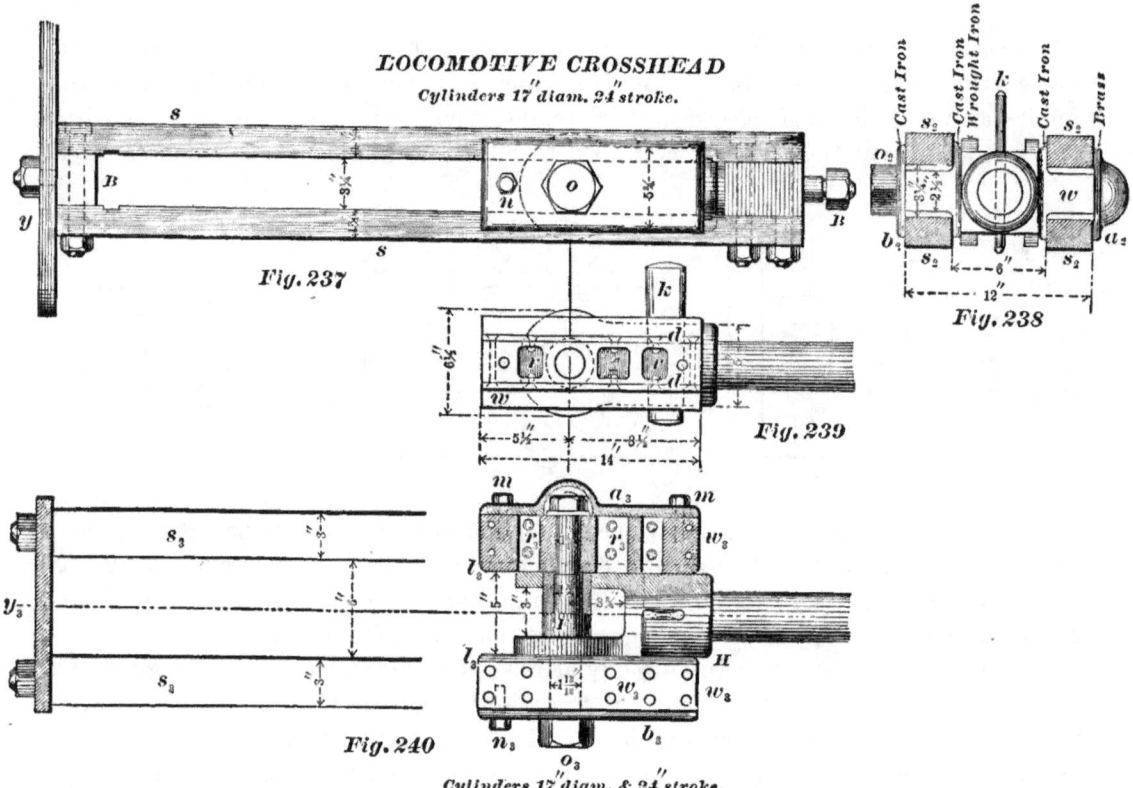

Fig. 237
Fig. 238
Fig. 239
Fig. 240

LOCOMOTIVE CROSSHEAD
Cylinders 17″ diam. 24″ stroke.

Cylinders 17″ diam. & 24″ stroke.

the inner plate $b_3$ of cast-iron. The purpose of the holes $r_3 \, r_3$ in the wing is to reduce the weight of the latter. Thin brass plates $d \, d$ (Fig. 239) are riveted to the bearing surfaces of the wing, as shown. In putting this crosshead together, the bolt $o_3$ (Fig. 240) is passed through the cast-iron plate $b_3$, and through the wings, with the hub $H$ and bushing $F$ between them. In screwing these together, the wings $w_3 \, w_3$ bear hard against the ends of the bushing $F$, and thus prevent the closing up of the fork on the hub $H$. The brass plate $a_3$ is then fastened to the outer wing by two ⅝ screw bolts, covering up the nut of the bolt $o_3$ and giving a nice and clean outer appearance to the crosshead. The ⅝ screw bolt $n_3$ prevents the cast-iron plate from turning on the bolt $o_3$. The bushing $F$ forms the crosshead pin, and when it becomes worn, can easily be removed and replaced. This design makes a very good crosshead, but on account of its expense is not often used.

When crossheads of this kind or those without gibs are used, thin copper strips are inserted between the guide-blocks $B \, B$ and the guides $s \, s$ at the time the engine is being built. Then when it becomes necessary to take up the wear between the guides and the crosshead, these copper slips are one by one removed, thereby bringing the guides together.

170. The pressure of locomotive crossheads against the guides caused by the thrust of the connecting-rod should not exceed 50 pounds per square inch; and how to find this thrust we will presently explain. From this remark we conclude that the sliding surfaces of the wings of crossheads shown in Figs. 234 and 237 must contain a certain number of square inches, and consequently if the width of the guides is increased the length of the wings is made less, and when the length of the wings is shortened the guides are also shortened, which is always desirable. When four guides are employed, as shown in Figs. 234 and 237, we naturally obtain a wide sliding surface, and consequently the crossheads and guides shown in these figures are comparatively short; the guides, being placed well up above the rails, are kept comparatively free from dust; the crosshead is light; in fact, the whole arrangement is well adapted for eight-wheeled passenger engines, or engines having a four-wheeled truck in front.

The vertical distance between the guides, as shown in Figs. 234 and 237, should be only sufficient to admit a wing of a minimum depth. In these figures it will also be noticed that the crosshead pin $P$ is, horizontally, somewhat out of the center of the wings or sliding surfaces of the crosshead. The reason for this is that designers will always endeavor to make the crosshead, and consequently the guides, as short as possible. Now, because the required strength of the crosshead will fix the distance between the center of the pin $P$ and the front end of hub, this distance is limited, but by moving the wings a little ahead of the pin $P$, which can often be done, the distance from the front of the hub to the rear end of the wing is somewhat decreased, and therefore the guides can also be made a little shorter. But in the writer's opinion such practice should be avoided as much as possible, and the pin $P$ should be kept central with the wings or sliding surfaces of all crossheads; by so doing the latter will wear more evenly.

171. The type of crosshead of which a side elevation is shown in Fig. 241, an end elevation in Fig. 242, and a plan in Fig. 243, is occasionally used for eight-wheeled passenger engines, but the writer believes that this crosshead is better adapted for a mogul engine, such as is shown in Fig. 2, and a consolidation engine, such as is shown in Fig. 4, and for these engines it is very often used. This design of crosshead is suitable for cast-iron, of which these crossheads are made, and the dimensions here given are suitable for a cylinder 20 inches in diameter. The crosshead pin $P$ is either made of steel or wrought-iron case hardened. The head of the pin is always placed towards the driving wheels; by so doing—as will be obvious—the cylinders can be brought closer together and still leave room enough for the crosshead to pass the crank-pin of the front driving wheels. The side of the crosshead in which the head of the pin $P$ is inserted we shall hereafter call the inner side of the crosshead, and the opposite one the outer side. In the majority of crossheads of this type brass gibs $g_2 g_2$ (Fig. 242) are used. In order to take these out quickly when necessary, or to put in liners when the wear demands it, the outer flanges $f_2 f_2$ are bolted to the crosshead; the inner flanges are cast to it. These flanges and the lips cast on the ends of the gibs will prevent the latter from slipping out of place. In designing a crosshead one great object aimed at is to make it as light as possible, and still leave it strong enough

154  MODERN LOCOMOTIVE CONSTRUCTION.

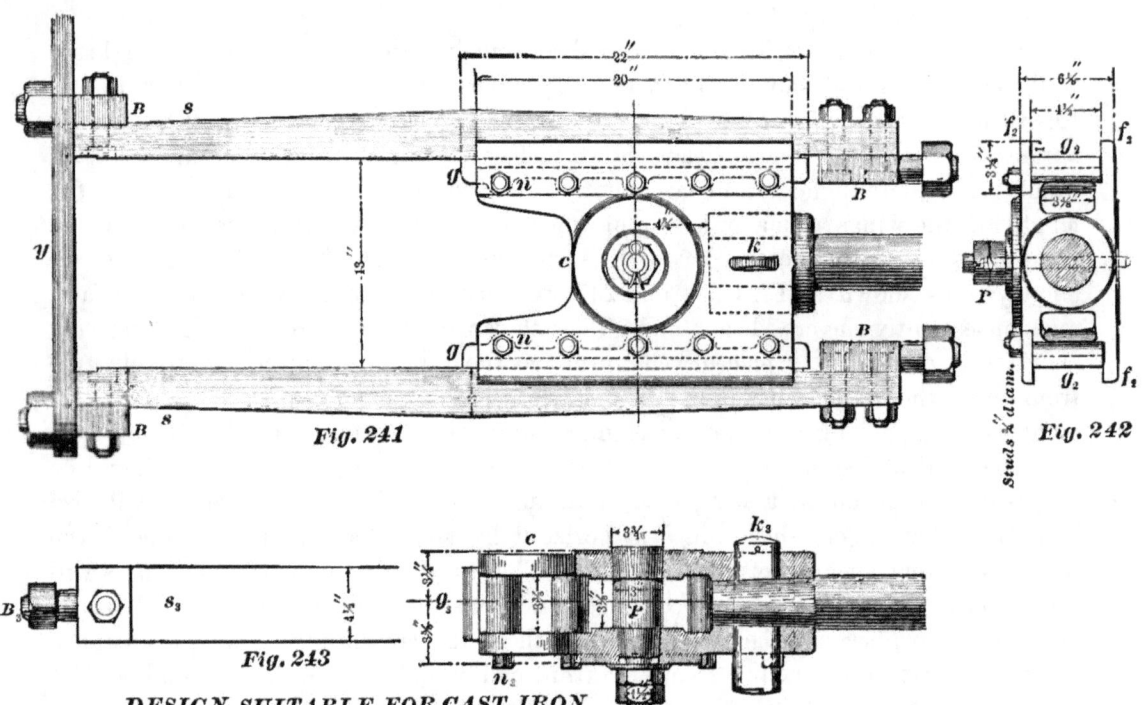

DESIGN SUITABLE FOR CAST IRON

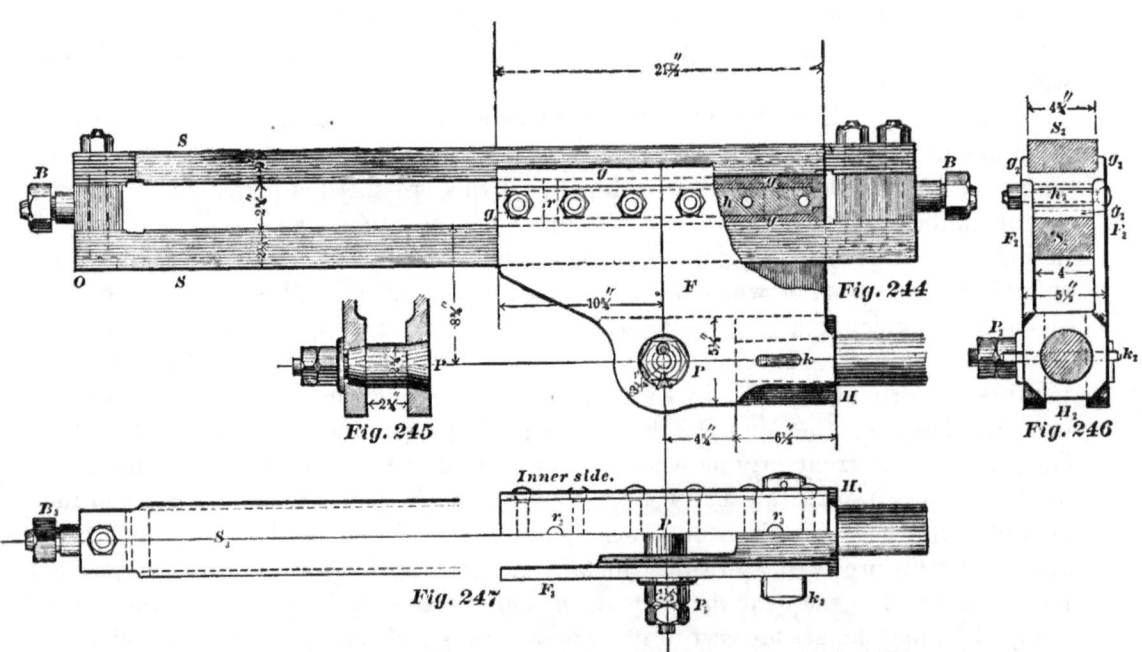

DESIGN SUITABLE FOR WROUGHT IRON OR CAST STEEL.
Cylinder 20 inches diameter. 24 inches stroke.

to meet any emergency; consequently the distance between the guides must be as short as possible. This distance is determined by the oblique positions of the connecting-rod. The method employed for finding the distance between the guides will be explained hereafter. Some master-mechanics raise an objection to this type of crosshead, because when it is used in engines which have driving wheels of comparatively small diameter, as is the case in freight engines, the guides are brought too close to the rails and consequently exposed to the dust, which will wear the guides and crosshead too fast. To avoid this difficulty, crossheads are used of which Fig. 244 is a side elevation, Fig. 246 an end elevation, Fig. 247 a plan, and Fig. 245 a view of the crosshead pin $P$. This design of crosshead is adapted for wrought-iron or cast steel, and is made of either one or the other material. The dimensions here given are suitable for cylinders 20 inches in diameter with a maximum steam pressure of 120 pounds per square inch. Some types of wrought-iron crossheads are very expensive to make, and if wrought-iron is insisted upon, then this design recommends itself, as the expense connected with making a crosshead of this type is comparatively small. Referring to Figs. 244 and 246 it will be seen that this crosshead consists simply of a hub $H H_2$, to which the piston-rod is keyed. To this hub are forged two deep flanges $F F_2$. These flanges extend upwards and terminate a little below the upper guides $S S_2$. Between these flanges a cast-iron block $h h_2$ is bolted by a number of bolts $\frac{3}{4}$ of an inch in diameter; these bolts extend through the flanges and the cast-iron block. To the upper and lower faces of the block $h h_2$ the brass gibs $g g_2 g_2$ are fitted. The gibs are held in position sideways by the flanges $F_2 F_2$, and endways by the lips cast to the gibs; for additional safety two pins $r r$ one inch in diameter are driven through the gibs $g g$ and the block $h$. The flanges of the upper gib $g_2$ slide along the sides of the upper guide, and the flanges $F_2 F_2$ slide along the sides of the lower guides, thus forming good deep sliding surfaces which will guide the end of the piston-rod in a straight line laterally, although not with such steadiness as the crosshead shown in Fig. 241 will do; and in this respect the crosshead represented in Fig. 244 is somewhat inferior to the one shown in Fig. 241. The gibs in the crosshead shown in Fig. 244 are not so readily removed as in those shown previously, because in the case before us, in order to take out the gibs the upper guide must be taken off, besides taking out all the bolts which hold the block $h$, and this is not always an easy matter. The distance from the center of the crosshead pin $P$ to the lower surface of the bottom guide must be as short as possible; it should be only sufficient to allow the connecting-rod when in an oblique position to clear the edge $o$ of the lower guide.

172. Fig. 248 is a side elevation, Fig. 250 an end elevation, and Fig. 251 a plan of another crosshead and guide; and Fig. 249 shows the crosshead pin $P$.

This crosshead is made of cast-iron, and, as will be seen, requires only one guide. This design of crosshead should only be used for small locomotives; the dimensions here given are suitable for a cylinder 15 inches in diameter, and indeed this crosshead is seldom used on engines having cylinders larger than 15 inches in diameter. This crosshead, with the exception of the plate $F F_2$ which is bolted on, is cast in one piece; this arrangement allows the brass gibs to be readily placed in position, and quickly removed when necessary. The distance between the guide and the pin $P$ must be such as will allow the end $O$ of the guide to clear the connecting-rod

156   MODERN LOCOMOTIVE CONSTRUCTION.

when in an oblique position. The writer believes this crosshead to be inferior to all the others shown, because in his opinion it will not guide the end of the piston-rod laterally as steadily as the others. Yet it is a very cheap crosshead, and seems to work well in small engines.

TO FIND THE THRUST OF THE CONNECTING-ROD.

173. When the connecting-rod stands in an oblique position, for instance such as will occur when the crank is at half stroke, the connecting-rod will force the crosshead

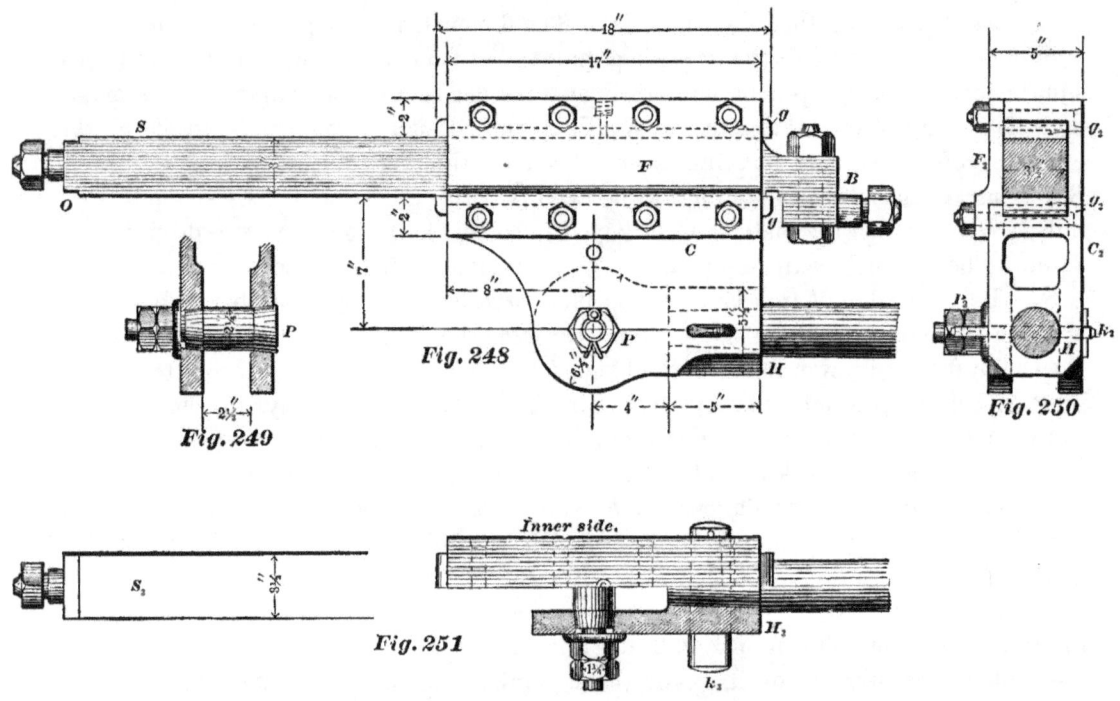

DESIGN SUITABLE FOR CAST IRON.
Cylinder 15 inches diameter. 20 inches stroke.

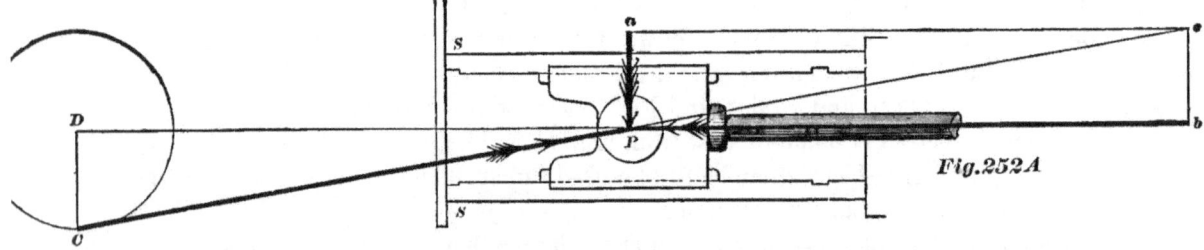

against the guides; and this force which presses the crosshead against the guides is called the thrust of the connecting-rod. The amount of this thrust, or the magnitude of this force, can be found by two methods: The graphic method, and by calculation.

We will first explain how this thrust can be found by the graphic method.

Fig. 252A. Let $D$ be the center of the driving axle, $C$ the center of the crank-pin, $P$ the center of the crosshead pin, $S S$ the guides, $D b$ the center line of motion, and the circumference $R C$ the path of the center of crank-pin. We shall assume that steam follows the full stroke of piston. It is required to find the thrust of the connecting-rod, or the pressure of the crosshead against the guides.

The total steam pressure on the piston is transmitted through the piston-rod to the crosshead pin $P$, and from thence it is transmitted through the connecting-rod to the crank-pin $C$. The directions in which this steam pressure acts is in the direction of the center line of the piston-rod, and in the direction of the center line of the connecting-rod.

At the beginning of a stroke, the center line of the piston-rod and the center line of the connecting-rod will lie in one and the same straight line, and therefore we assume that in this position there will be no thrust, or, in other words, the steam pressure will not cause any pressure between the crosshead and the guides.

When the crank stands perpendicular to the center line of motion $D b$, we may assume that for the purpose of finding the thrust the angle formed by the line $D b$ and the center line $C P$ of the connecting-rod will be the greatest, and therefore we conclude that in this position the thrust of the connecting-rod will also be the greatest. It is now our object to find the intensity of the thrust, or the magnitude of this force, when the crank $D C$ stands at right angles to the center line of motion $D b$.

Draw the center line of motion $D b$; on this line take any point, as $D$, to represent the center of the driving axle; through the point $D$ draw a line $D C$ perpendicular to the line $D b$, and make $D C$ equal to the length of the crank. From $C$ as a center, and with a radius equal to the length of the connecting-rod, draw a short arc cutting the line $D b$ at the point $P$; this point will be the center of the crosshead pin, and the line $C P$ will represent the center line of the connecting-rod. Prolong the line $C P$ to $e$, making $P e$ equal to $C P$. Through the point $P$ draw a line $P a$ perpendicular to the line $D b$; through the point $e$ draw a line $e b$ parallel to $P a$, and again through the point $e$ draw a line $e a$ parallel to $P b$; then $P a e b$ will be a parallelogram, which is called the parallelogram of forces.

Now in mechanics, which is that branch of science which treats of the effects of forces upon matter, it is shown that forces can be completely represented by straight lines, or, in other words, the magnitude of a force and the direction in which it acts can be represented by a straight line. It is also further shown that in a parallelogram of forces, such as we have just completed, the magnitudes of the forces are proportional to the lengths of the sides of the parallelogram of forces; that is to say, if the length of the side $P a$ in our parallelogram is equal to $\frac{1}{2}$ the length of the side $P b$, then the force represented by the side $P a$ will be one half of the force represented by the side $P b$; or again, if the length of the line $P a$ is equal to $\frac{1}{4}$ of the length of $P b$, then the force represented by the line $P a$ will be one quarter of the force represented by the line or side $P b$.

Here, then, it may be said that we have a point $P$ which is held in equilibrium by three forces. The magnitude of these forces and the direction in which they act are completely represented by the length and the direction of the three straight lines $C P$, $P b$, and $P a$. The line $P b$ represents the total steam pressure on the piston, which is

158                    MODERN LOCOMOTIVE CONSTRUCTION.

acting in the direction of the center line of the piston-rod; the line $CP$ represents a force acting in the direction of the center line of the connecting-rod; and the line $Pa$ represents a force acting in a direction perpendicular to the guides, and is the thrust of the connecting-rod, or, in other words, the line $Pa$ represents the magnitude of the force which presses the crosshead against the guides, and which, according to our problem, was to be found.

**174.** In order to find the force or thrust $Pa$ it is not necessary to draw the crosshead, guides, piston-rod, and as many lines as we have done in this figure (this was simply done to make the principles plain), but we can, without adding any new principles or changing the foregoing ones, obtain the same forces by constructing the triangle, Fig. 253A, which may be drawn full size, half size, or to any convenient scale thus:

Draw any straight line $Pb$ (Fig. 253A); on this line take any point, as $b$, and through this point draw a line $be$ perpendicular to the line $Pb$; on the line $be$ lay

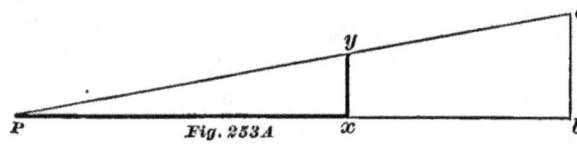

off a point $e$; the distance between the points $b$ and $e$ must be equal to the length of the crank. From the point $e$ as a center, and with a radius equal to the length of the connecting-rod, describe a short arc cutting the line $Pb$ in point $P$; join the points $P$ and $e$ by a straight line, and complete the triangle $Pbe$. Now, if the dimensions of engine and steam pressure in Fig. 253A remain the same as those in Fig. 252A, the triangle shown in Fig. 253A will be equal to any of the triangles as $Pbe$, $Pae$, and $PDC$ in Fig. 252A, and consequently the sides of the triangle in Fig. 253A will represent the same forces as the sides $Pa$, $ae$, and the diagonal $Pe$ of the parallelogram $Pabe$ in Fig. 252A.

### PRACTICAL APPLICATIONS OF THE FOREGOING PRINCIPLES.

**175. EXAMPLE 45.**—Diameter of the piston is 16 inches, the stroke is 24 inches, length of connecting-rod 84 inches, and the steam pressure is 120 pounds per square inch; steam follows full stroke: find the thrust of the connecting-rod or the pressure of the crosshead against the guides.

Draw the line $Pb$ (Fig. 253A); at any point $b$ on this line erect the perpendicular $be$; make the length of $eb$ equal to 12 inches (which is the length of the crank or half the given stroke). From $e$ as a center, and with a radius equal to 84 inches (the given length of connecting-rod), describe a short arc cutting the line $Pb$ at the point $P$; join $P$ and $e$ by a straight line, and the triangle will be completed.

The total steam pressure on the piston is found by multiplying its area in square inches by the steam pressure per square inch, and this total pressure will be equal to 24,120 pounds (the fraction has been omitted); hence the length of the line $Pb$ will represent 24,120 pounds.

Now assume that we have a narrow strip of paper whose length is exactly equal to the length of the line $Pb$, and that this paper is divided lengthwise into 24,120 equal parts, then each division will represent one pound; laying this piece of paper (or scale, as we may call it) on the line $eb$, we find that this line will contain 3,481 (nearly) of the number of divisions on the paper; hence we conclude that the thrust, or the pressure of the crosshead against the guides, is 3,481 pounds.

But to divide the line $P\ b$ into 24,120 equal parts would require too much time and labor, hence the following method is used:

Let us adopt $\frac{1}{2}$ of an inch to represent 1,000 pounds; then since 24,120 pounds is represented by line $P\ b$, we lay off from the point $P$ on the line $P\ b$ twenty-four $\frac{1}{2}$ inches, which will then represent 24,000 pounds, because each $\frac{1}{2}$ inch represents 1,000 pounds. In order to represent the remaining 120 pounds, which are very nearly equal to $\frac{1}{8}$ of 1,000 pounds, we must add $\frac{1}{8}$ of $\frac{1}{2}$ inch (which is equal to $\frac{1}{16}$ of an inch) to the twenty-four $\frac{1}{2}$ inches; or, in short, from the point $P$ on the line $P\ b$ lay off a point $x$; the distance between the points $P$ and $x$ must be equal to $12\frac{1}{16}$ inches. Through the point $x$ draw a line $x\ y$ perpendicular to the line $P\ b$ and cutting the line $P\ e$ in the point $y$; then the line $x\ y$ will represent the thrust of the connecting-rod, and since the length of this line is very nearly equal to $1\frac{3}{4}$ inches, which we obtain by measurement, and since each $\frac{1}{2}$ inch represents 1,000 pounds, we know that the pressure of the crosshead against the guide is not quite but very nearly equal to 3,500 pounds; and this answer is in most cases near enough for practical purposes.

But should it be necessary to find the amount of this thrust accurately, then the simplest way to determine it is by calculation; and if the foregoing graphic method is understood, then there should not be any difficulty in understanding the following calculations, which are based on the principles already introduced in connection with the graphic method, thus:

176. We have already seen that the magnitudes of the three forces which hold the point $P$ in Fig. 252A in equilibrium are represented by the three sides of the triangle shown in Fig. 253A. Now we know the length of the line $P\ e$, which, according to our example, is 84 inches; we also know the length of the line $b\ e$, which is 12 inches, but the length of the line $P\ b$ we do not know, yet we do know that the length of this latter line must represent 24,120 pounds. If we now find by calculation (instead of construction as before) the length of the line $P\ b$, then, since we know the lengths of the other lines or sides of the triangle we shall have no difficulty in computing the number of pounds that each of the sides of this triangle represents, because the magnitudes of the forces are proportional to the length of the lines.

The triangle $P\ e\ b$ is by construction a right-angled triangle, and consequently to find the length of the side $P\ b$ we subtract the square of the side $b\ e$ from the square of the side $P\ e$; the square root of the remainder will be the length of the side $P\ b$.

The length of $P\ e$ is 84 inches, the length of $b\ e$ is 12 inches. The square of 84 is equal to $84 \times 84 = 7,056$, and the square of 12 is equal to $12 \times 12 = 144$, and $7,056 - 144 = 6,912$. The square root of 6,912 is equal to 83.13+ inches, which is the length of the side $P\ b$. But the side $P\ b$ and consequently the 83.13 inches represent 24,120 pounds; therefore the number of pounds of the force represented by the side $b\ e$, which bears the same proportion to 24,120 pounds as the length of $b\ e$ bears to $P\ b$, is found by the simple rule of proportion, thus:

83.13 inches : 12 inches :: 24,120 : the answer;

hence,

$$\frac{24{,}120 \times 12}{83.13} = 3{,}481 \text{ pounds}.$$

Therefore the magnitude of the force represented by the side $b\,c$ is equal to 3,481 pounds, which is the pressure of the crosshead against the guides. Now putting the whole foregoing calculations in the shape of a formula, we have the following:

FORMULA AND RULE FOR FINDING THE THRUST OF THE CONNECTING-ROD BY CALCULATION.

$$\text{Total pressure of steam on piston} \times \frac{\text{Length of crank in inches}}{\sqrt{(\text{length of connecting-rod in inches})^2 - (\text{length of crank in inches})^2}} = \text{thrust of connecting-rod.}$$

Or, in ordinary language, we have the following:

RULE 19.—Multiply the total steam pressure in pounds on the piston by the length of the crank in inches, and call this product $a$; then from the square of the length of the connecting-rod in inches subtract the square of the length of the crank in inches, and find the square root of the remainder; divide the product $a$ by the last answer, the quotient will be the thrust of the connecting-rod in pounds.

177. The foregoing rule will give the thrust of the connecting-rod correctly in stationary and marine engines, or in all engines in which the center $D$ of the crank-shaft (Fig. 252A) cannot move out of the center line of motion $D\,b$; but such conditions do not exist in locomotives, hence the foregoing rule must be somewhat modified, so that it will apply to them.

Fig. 254A. Let $D\,b$ represent the center line of motion; $D$, the center of driving

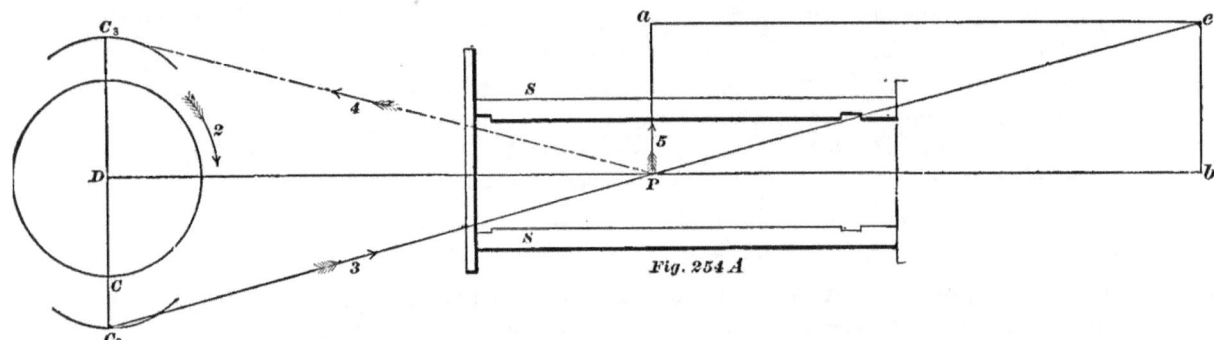

Fig. 254 A

axle; $C$, the center of crank-pin; the circumference $R\,C$, the path of the center of crank-pin; and $P$, the center of the crosshead-pin.

In locomotives the driving-axle box can move up and down in the pedestals, and consequently the center $D$, and with it the path $R\,C$ of the center of crank-pin, will move out of the center line of motion $D\,b$.

In order to obtain the greatest thrust of a connecting-rod in a locomotive, we find the extreme lower and upper position $C_2$ and $C_3$ of the crank-pin when the center line $D\,C_2$ of the crank stands perpendicular to the center line of motion $D\,b$. Now let $C_2$ represent the center of crank-pin in its extreme lower position; then in order to construct the parallelogram of forces we proceed in a manner similar to that adopted before, namely:

From the point $C_2$ as a center, and with the length of the connecting-rod as a radius, describe a short arc cutting the center line of motion $D\,b$ at the point $P$, which will be the position of the center of crosshead-pin when the crank stands at right angles to the center line of motion and the crank-pin in its extreme lowest position. From $C_2$ and through $P$ draw a straight line, and produce it towards $e$; make the line $P\,e$ equal in length to that of $C_2\,P$, or, in other words, to the length of the connecting-rod. Through the point $e$ draw a straight line $e\,a$ parallel to $P\,b$, and through the points $P$ and $e$ draw the lines $P\,a$ and $b\,e$ perpendicular to $P\,b$, thus completing the parallelogram of forces $P\,a\,b\,e$.

Now, if in Fig. 254A the length of the connecting-rod, crank, and the total steam pressure is the same as those in Fig. 252A, the line $b\,e$ in Fig. 254A must be considerably longer than $b\,e$ in Fig. 252A, and therefore the thrust represented by the line $b\,e$ in the former figure must be greater than the thrust in the latter figure. Consequently the formula for determining the thrust of a locomotive connecting-rod will be as follows:

RULE 20, IN SYMBOLS.—TO FIND THE THRUST OF A LOCOMOTIVE CONNECTING-ROD.

Let $P$ represent the total pressure of the steam in pounds on the piston; $L$, the length in inches of a line drawn perpendicular to the center line of motion $D\,b$ and measured from the line $D\,b$ to the extreme lowest position of the center $C$ of the crank-pin; $K$, the length of the connecting-rod in inches; $T$, the thrust of the connecting-rod, or the pressure of the crosshead against the guides in pounds. Then

$$P \times \frac{L}{\sqrt{K^2 - L^2}} = T.$$

If the line $D\,C_3$ should be greater than $D\,C_2$, then the thrust will be the greatest when the crank-pin is in its extreme upper position, and in the calculation the length of $D\,C_3$ should be taken in place of $D\,C_2$.

APPROXIMATE RULE FOR FINDING THE THRUST OF A CONNECTING-ROD.

178. When the length of the connecting-rod is very great in comparison with that of the crank, then the difference between the lines $P\,e$ and $P\,b$ is very slight, and for many practical purposes this difference may be neglected. In such cases we assume that the length of the line $P\,e$ will represent the total pressure on the piston, and consequently the rule for finding the thrust becomes very simple.

APPROXIMATE RULE 21.—Divide the length of the crank in inches by the length of the connecting-rod, and multiply the quotient by the total steam pressure on the piston; the product will be the thrust of the connecting-rod against the guides, in pounds.

Applying this rule to Example 45, we have the following result:

It will be remembered that the total steam pressure on the piston was found to be equal to 24,120 pounds, the length of the connecting-rod is 84 inches, and the length of the crank, 12 inches. Hence

$$\tfrac{12}{84} \times 24{,}120 = 3{,}445.71+ \text{ pounds} = \text{thrust of the connecting-rod}.$$

The thrust of the connecting-rod found by Rule 19 was 3,481 pounds. The difference between the two answers is so slight that it may be neglected, and in cases of this kind the simplest rule can be used.

179. In Fig. 255 we have shown the method of finding the thrust of the connecting-rod for any other position of the crank. Let $D\,P$ represent the center line of motion; $D$, the center of driving axle; $C$, the center of crank-pin; $D\,C$, the position of the center line of crank; and the circumference $R\,C$, the path of the center $C$. Now, in order to find the thrust of the connecting-rod when the crank-pin is in this position,

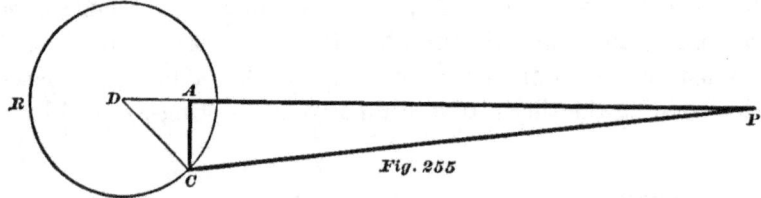

Fig. 255

we draw through the center $C$ a line $A\,C$, perpendicular to the center line of motion $D\,P$. And from $C$ as a center, and with a radius equal to the length of the connecting-rod, describe a short arc cutting the line $D\,P$ at the point $P$; join $C$ and $P$ by a straight line, thus completing the triangle $A\,C\,P$, shown in heavy lines for distinction. The line $A\,P$ will again represent the total steam pressure on the piston, and the line $A\,C$ the thrust, or the pressure of the crosshead against the guide. To find the magnitude of the force represented by the line $A\,C$, we have the following approximate rule:

RULE 22.—Divide the length of the line $A\,C$ in inches (that is, the perpendicular distance from the center of the crank-pin to the center line of motion) by the length of the connecting-rod in inches, and multiply the quotient by the total pressure of steam on the piston; the product will be the thrust in pounds.

Thus: EXAMPLE 46.—If the total pressure is 24,120 pounds, the length of the connecting-rod is 84 inches, and the length of the line $A\,C$ is equal to 8 inches (by measurement), what will be the thrust of the connecting-rod?

$\frac{8}{84} \times 24{,}120 = 2{,}287$ pounds = pressure of the crosshead against the guides, or thrust of the connecting-rod.

Should it be desirable to obtain this thrust more accurately, then apply Rule 19, and instead of using the length of the crank as stated in that rule, use the length of the line $A\,C$ in Fig. 255; the length of the line $A\,C$ is always found by measurement. Remember that in all these examples the steam follows full stroke.

180. In passenger locomotives, or other locomotives in which the crank generally turns in the same direction, the upper crosshead gibs will wear faster than the lower gibs. This is explained in the following manner:

Let the arrow 2 in Fig. 254A represent the direction in which the crank turns when the locomotive is running in a forward direction; then when the crank-pin is at $C_2$ the reaction of the connecting-rod will be in the direction of the arrow 3, causing the crosshead to be forced against the upper guide, as indicated by arrow 5; when the crank-pin is at $C_3$ the reaction of the connecting-rod will be in the direction of arrow 4, and again force the crosshead against the guides, as indicated by arrow 5 as before.

In fact, throughout the stroke when the engine is going ahead, the crosshead will press against the upper guide; but it should be remembered that, when the center line of crank stands perpendicular to the center line of motion, then the pressure of the crosshead against the guides will be the greatest; or, we should say, that in the neighborhood of the center of the guides the pressure will be the greatest, and will gradually decrease as the crosshead approaches the ends of the guides. In switching engines which are run as often backward as forward, the upper and lower gibs of the crosshead will wear very nearly alike, because in running forward the pressure of the crosshead is against the upper guides, and in running backward the pressure is against the lower guides.

## PROPORTIONS OF CROSSHEAD.

181. The sliding surfaces of a crosshead should not be too large, as this will make the crosshead too heavy; neither should they be too small, because with small sliding surface the pressure per square inch on these surfaces will be increased to an extent which will heat the guides and cause abrasion or cutting. Now it will be apparent that before we can determine the dimensions of the sliding surfaces, we must know the pressure which can be allowed per square inch on these surfaces for the best practical results. Knowing this pressure, and also the total pressure of the crosshead against the guides, which must be provided for, the calculations for obtaining the dimension of the sliding surfaces or the length and breadth of the gibs will be an easy matter.

According to the dimensions of crossheads in different classes of locomotives made by various builders and master-mechanics, and under the assumption that the maximum steam pressure in the cylinders is 120 pounds per square inch, the writer finds that 50 pounds per square inch of sliding surface is a good average; in a few cases the pressure per square inch was somewhat less than 50 pounds, and in a number of crossheads 75 pounds per square inch was reached. In the writer's opinion 50 pounds pressure per square inch will give very good results, and may be adopted for determining the dimensions of the sliding surface or the gibs of a crosshead which is to be designed.

In the following we shall adopt 50 pounds per square inch as the standard. The total pressure of the crosshead against the guides is obtained by Rule 20 or 21. Our next step will be to determine the area of the sliding surface or gibs.

RULE 23.—Divide the total pressure of the crosshead against the guides by 50; the quotient will be the area in square inches of the gibs or sliding surface.

EXAMPLE 47.—The cylinders in a locomotive are 17 inches in diameter; stroke, 24 inches; steam pressure, 120 pounds per square inch; length of connecting-rod, 7 feet: it is required to find the area in square inches of the crosshead gibs.

The area of a piston 17 inches in diameter is 226.98 square inches; the total pressure on the piston will be equal to $226.98 \times 120 = 27237.6$ pounds. According to Rule 21, the total pressure of the crosshead against the slides will be equal to $27237.6 \times \frac{1}{7} = 3891$ pounds. And lastly, according to Rule 23, we have $\frac{3891}{50} = 77.8$ square inches for the area of the gibs, or sliding surface of the crosshead. The dimensions of crosshead given in Fig. 240 are those of a crosshead in actual use for a 17 × 24 engine, and has given good satisfaction. In this crosshead we find the area of the sliding surface to be equal to $(3'' + 3'') \times 14'' = 84$ square inches. According to our rule, it should have 77.8 square inches. Here, then, is a difference of 6.2 square inches, which is due to the fact that we have made no allowance for the play of the driving box in the pedestal; this play should have been added to the length of crank; but when we remember that this size of sliding surface is sometimes used in locomotives having cylinders 18 inches in diameter, we may conclude that the area found according to our rule will give satisfactory results.

Assuming that in all locomotives the maximum steam pressure in the cylinder is 120 pounds per square inch, and the ratio of the length of crank to length of the connecting-rod is as 1 to 7, and that the pressure per square inch of the crosshead sliding surface should be about 50 pounds, we may find the area of the sliding surface by the following simple rule:

RULE 24.—Multiply the area of the piston by the decimal .34; the product will be the area in square inches of the sliding surface or of gibs.

This rule will give results approximately correct, for all ordinary locomotive practice in which the maximum pressure does not exceed 120 pounds.

EXAMPLE 48.—What must be the area of the sliding surface of a crosshead for a locomotive having cylinders 20 inches in diameter?

The area of a 20-inch piston is 314.16 square inches; hence $314.16 \times .34 = 106.81+$ square inches, which is the area of the sliding surface of the crosshead. Comparing this area with that of the crosshead shown in Fig. 244, we find the area obtained by calculation to be slightly in excess of that in the illustration.

## TO FIND THE LENGTH AND BREADTH OF THE GIB.

182. Examining the illustrations of the crossheads, we find that the length of each gib is very nearly equal to five times its breadth; in some it is more, in others a little less; let us adopt the ratio of 1 to 5 as the correct proportion of the breadth to the length of these surfaces. Now, when we know the area of the gib and the ratio of its length to breadth, the dimensions of the latter are easily obtained by the following rule:

RULE 25.—Divide the area of the surface by 5, and extract the square root of the product; the answer will be the breadth in inches; this breadth multiplied by 5 will give the length.

EXAMPLE 49.—The area of a gib or sliding surface is 45 square inches: it is required to find the length and breadth of the gib.

$45 \div 5 = 9$, and the square root of 9 or $\sqrt{9} = 3$ inches.

Three inches is the breadth, and $3 \times 5 = 15$ inches is the length of the gib.

EXAMPLE 50.—What should be the length and breadth of a gib for a crosshead with two guides in a locomotive having cylinders 18 inches in diameter?

The area of a piston 18 inches in diameter is 254.47 square inches.

The area of the gib or sliding surface, according to Rule 24, must be $254.47 \times .34 = 86.5198$ square inches. Then by Rule 25 we have $86.5198 \div 5 = 17.3039$

and $\sqrt{17.3039} = 4.15$ inches for the breadth of the gib; and $4.15 \times 5 = 20.75$ inches for the length.

EXAMPLE 51.—What should be the length and breadth of a gib for a crosshead with four guides in a locomotive having cylinders 18 inches in diameter?

In the solution of this problem it should be remembered that when a crosshead has four guides, as shown in Figs. 234 and 237, the area of the sliding surface is the sum of the areas of two gibs, as $F$ and $G$ in Fig. 257; hence, notice the following solution:

The total area of the sliding surface will be 254.47 square inches $\times .34 = 86.5198$ square inches, as in Example 50; but, as already stated, this sliding surface is made up of two gibs, hence the area of each gib must be $86.5198 \div 2 = 43.2599$ square inches, then $43.2599 \div 5 = 8.6519$, and $\sqrt{8.6519} = 2.94$ inches for the width of gib, say 3 inches; and $3 \times 5 = 15$ inches for the length of the gib.

Gibs are generally made from $\frac{1}{2}$ inch to $\frac{5}{8}$ inch thick.

### WIDTH OF CROSSHEADS AND DIAMETER OF HUBS.

183. In locomotive cast-iron crossheads into which the piston rods are fitted with tapered ends, and sometimes not resting against a shoulder, as shown in Fig. 255A, the area of the hub around the key, as shown in Fig. 256, should be sufficiently large, so

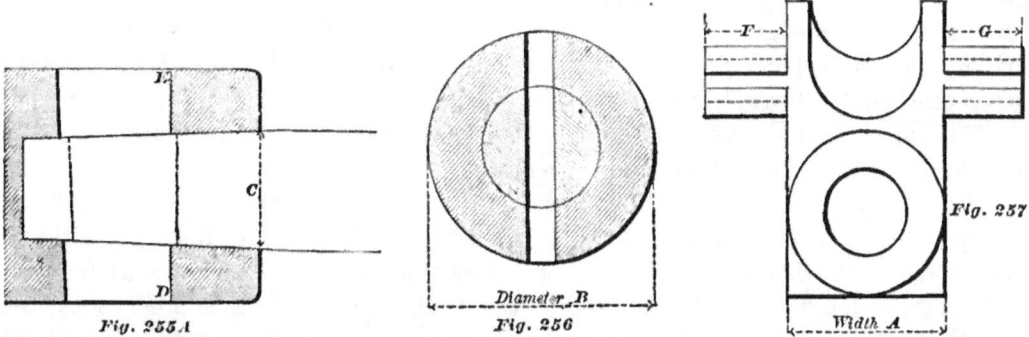

Fig. 255A.   Fig. 256.   Fig. 257.

that the tensile stress or pull will not exceed 3,000 pounds per square inch of section. This section is, of course, assumed to be taken through $D E$, Fig. 255A, where the area of the hub will be smallest. Hence, to find the diameter $B$ of the hub, Fig. 256, or the width $A$, Fig. 257, we may use the following approximate rule:

RULE 26.—For cast-iron crossheads, multiply the large diameter of the tapered end of piston-rod, as given in Table 14, by 2; the product will be the outside diameter of the hub.

When the piston-rod has no shoulder fitting against the end of the hub, as shown in Fig. 255A, then make the outside diameter of the hub equal to twice the diameter of the tapered end measured at $C$—that is, the diameter of the hole in the face of the hub.

For wrought-iron crossheads multiply the large diameter of the tapered end, or the diameter at $C$, by 1.8; the product will be the outside diameter $B$ of the hub, Fig. 256, or the width $A$, Fig. 257.

EXAMPLE 52.—Find the diameter or the width of a locomotive cast-iron crosshead suitable for four guides, cylinders 17 inches in diameter.

According to Table 14, the large diameter of the tapered end of a piston-rod for a cylinder 17 inches in diameter is $2\frac{5}{8}$ inches; hence $2\frac{5}{8} \times 2 = 5\frac{1}{4}$ inches for the outside diameter of hub.

EXAMPLE 53.—What must be the diameter of the hub of a wrought-iron crosshead suitable for two guides, cylinders 20 inches in diameter? According to Table 14, the large diameter of the tapered end of the piston-rod is 3 inches; hence $3 \times 1.8 = 5.4$ inches, which is the diameter of hub.

The width of the latter class of crossheads will frequently have to be determined by the width of guides, or the length of the crosshead pin.

## DIMENSIONS OF GUIDES.

184. The guides should be made as short as possible. In practice half an inch for clearance at each end of the crosshead is generally considered to be the least amount that should be allowed. Consequently, if in Fig. 234 the stroke is 24 inches, the length of the sliding surfaces (which in this case is equal to the length of the gibs) is equal to $15\frac{3}{4}$ inches, and the clearance at each end is equal to half an inch, then the shortest distance between the guide-blocks is equal to $24'' + 15\frac{3}{4}'' + \frac{1}{2}'' + \frac{1}{2}'' = 40\frac{3}{4}$ inches. If to this distance is added the necessary amount for bolting the guide to the guide-blocks, then the shortest length of guides will have been obtained.

Sometimes the general design of a locomotive, generally the position of the driving wheels, will compel us to make the length of the guides greater than that determined by the foregoing figures.

The breadth of the guide is equal to the breadth of gib or sliding surfaces of the crosshead, according to rules already given.

In order to determine the thickness of a guide we must consider it to be a beam firmly fastened at the ends and loaded in the middle. The rule for finding the thickness of a beam when all its other dimensions and load are known is as follows: Multiply the length of beam in feet by the load, and divide this product by the breadth in inches multiplied by a constant number. The square root of the quotient will be the thickness in inches. The constant number alluded to is determined by experiment, and is not the same for different kinds of material. From these remarks we would infer, and correctly too, that a different constant should be used for steel than is used for iron beams. But in locomotive practice, for the sake of interchangeability, it is customary to use the same constant for wrought-iron and steel guides, and this practice we shall follow in these articles. The constant number used in calculating the strength of guides is 1,200.

In these calculations we shall, for the sake of simplicity, call the distance between the guide-blocks the "length of the guides." Hence, for finding the thickness of a wrought-iron or steel guide we have the following rule:

RULE 27.—Multiply the length of the guide in feet by the load in pounds; divide this product by the breadth in inches into the constant number 1,200; extract the square root of the quotient, then the answer, increased by an amount deemed necessary for re-planing and wear, will be the thickness of the guide in inches.

EXAMPLE 54.—Find the thickness of the guides (two guides being used for one crosshead) for a locomotive having cylinders 20 inches in diameter, 24 inches stroke, length of guides 4 feet, breadth of guides 4¾ inches, length of connecting-rod 7 feet, steam pressure in cylinders 120 pounds per square inch.

In the first place we must find the load which these guides will have to support. The load is equal to the greatest pressure of the crosshead against the guide, and consequently can be found by Rule 21. Now, we have for the total steam pressure on the piston, 314.16 square inches × 120 pounds = 37699.2 pounds, and according to Rule 21, we have 37699.2 × ⅐ = 5385.6 pounds of pressure of crosshead against the guides, which is now considered to be the load that one guide will have to support.

Now, to find the thickness we have, according to Rule 27,

$$\frac{5385.6 \times 4}{4.75 \times 1200} = 3.77;$$ and the square root of 3.77, or $\sqrt{3.77} = 1.9$, say 2 inches; adding to this ¼ of an inch for truing up, when that becomes necessary through wear, we have 2¼ inches for the thickness of guide.

EXAMPLE 55.—Find the thickness of the guides (four guides being used for one crosshead) for a locomotive having cylinders 17 inches in diameter, 24 inches stroke, length of guides 3 feet 4½ inches (= 3.375 feet), breadth of guide 3 inches, length of connecting-rod 7 feet, and steam pressure in cylinder 120 pounds per square inch.

Area of piston = 226.98; hence 226.98 square inches × 120 = 27237.6 pounds total steam pressure on the piston, and 27237.6 × ⅐ = 3891.08 pounds, which is the load two guides bearing against the gibs $F$ and $G$, Fig. 257, will have to support; consequently one guide will have to support

$$\frac{3891.08}{2} = 1945.54 \text{ pounds,}$$

and

$$\frac{1945.54 \times 3.375}{3 \times 1200} = 1.82;$$

the square root of 1.82, or $\sqrt{1.82} = 1.34$, say 1⅜ inches; add to this ¼ of an inch for truing up, we have 1⅝ inches for the thickness of guides.

185. Sometimes the thickness of the guides is greater at the center of their length than at the ends, as shown in Fig. 241; this is done to reduce the weight of the guides; or, in other words, this form of guide will give the maximum strength with the minimum amount of metal. Tapering the guides adds considerably to the expense of labor; and since the extra weight of guides with parallel faces, or of straight guides, is not objectionable, the writer believes that the latter, such as are shown in Fig. 260, and whose thickness or depth throughout is equal to the thickness at the center of tapered guides having the same work to do, are more desirable to use, and will give as good, if not better, results; again, observing that the majority of locomotives have straight guides, we are led to believe that many master-mechanics and locomotive builders share our opinion.

186. In determining the depth of a guide for a crosshead requiring one guide only, as shown in Fig. 248, good judgment must be used, because in this case we must not only make the guide sufficiently strong to resist the thrust of the connecting-rod, but

we must also make it deep enough to guide the end of the piston-rod in a straight line laterally. It should also be remembered that, since guides of this kind will wear on the upper and lower surfaces, we must allow double the amount for re-planing that has been allowed in the other classes of guides; that is to say, when only one guide is used for a crosshead, then we should allow for re-planing $\frac{1}{4}$ of an inch on the upper sliding surface, and $\frac{1}{4}$ of an inch for the lower sliding surface. Taking these things into consideration, we may employ for determining the depth or thickness of a guide such as shown in Fig. 248 the following rule:

RULE 28.—Find the depth of the guide by Rule 27; add the necessary amount for re-planing, and increase this sum by 25 to 35 per cent. to obtain sufficient depth of guide to keep the piston-rod in a straight line laterally.

When the crank is turning in the direction of arrow 1, Fig. 260—that is, when the engine is running ahead—the weight of the crosshead has a tendency to reduce the thrust of the connecting-rod against the upper guide; but when the engine is running in the direction of arrow 2—that is, running backward—the thrust of the connecting-rod against the lower guide will be increased by the weight of the crosshead. But in locomotives the thickness of the upper guide is always equal to that of the lower one. For extreme accuracy in determining the thickness of either guide, the weight of the crosshead should be taken into account; and furthermore a part of the weight of the guide should also enter into our calculation. For the sake of simplicity, we omitted referring to these items in Rule 27, but they were taken into consideration when the constant number 1,200 was determined upon. Hence these rules should only be used for determining the thickness or depth of locomotive guides, or those for engines of similar design.

### CAST IR-ON GUIDES.

187. Sometimes locomotive guides are made of cast-iron. In Figs. 258 and 259 we have shown the form and given the dimensions of cast-iron guides working satisfactorily in ten-wheeled engines having 19 × 24 inch cylinders.

### GUIDE BOLTS.

188. The guides are held in position at one end by the guide-yoke $y$, Fig. 260, and at the other end they are fastened to the cylinder head. The guide-yoke is made strong enough to prevent the end of the guide moving in a vertical direction, but has not sufficient strength to resist a force acting against it in a horizontal direction, consequently it cannot resist the horizontal force due to the friction between the guides and crosshead. Therefore, for holding the guides in position only one bolt is used at the yoke end, and two bolts are used at the cylinder end. The bolt at the yoke end and one of the bolts at the cylinder end, we may say, are for the purpose of resisting the thrust of the connecting-rod, and the second bolt at the cylinder end is for the purpose of resisting the force acting in a horizontal direction or the pull due to friction between the guides and crosshead. These bolts are generally $\frac{3}{4}$ of an inch in diameter for small locomotives; $\frac{7}{8}$ and sometimes 1 inch in diameter for larger locomotives; and occasionally we meet with bolts $1\frac{1}{16}$ inches in diameter for locomo-

tives having cylinders 20 inches in diameter. It is always best to use tapered bolts for this purpose, because these must have a good fit, and if they are made straight, it would require too much labor or the bolt may be ruined in driving it out, when that becomes necessary to take out the thin strips of copper placed between the guide-blocks and guides to take up the wear. It should also be noticed that in locomotives having cylinders of the same diameters but different design of crosshead, the diameters of the guide bolts in the designs such as shown in Figs. 234 and 237 are about the same as those used in the design shown in Fig. 260; yet, when we compare the manner of fastening the guides at the yoke end in these designs, it would seem that in the

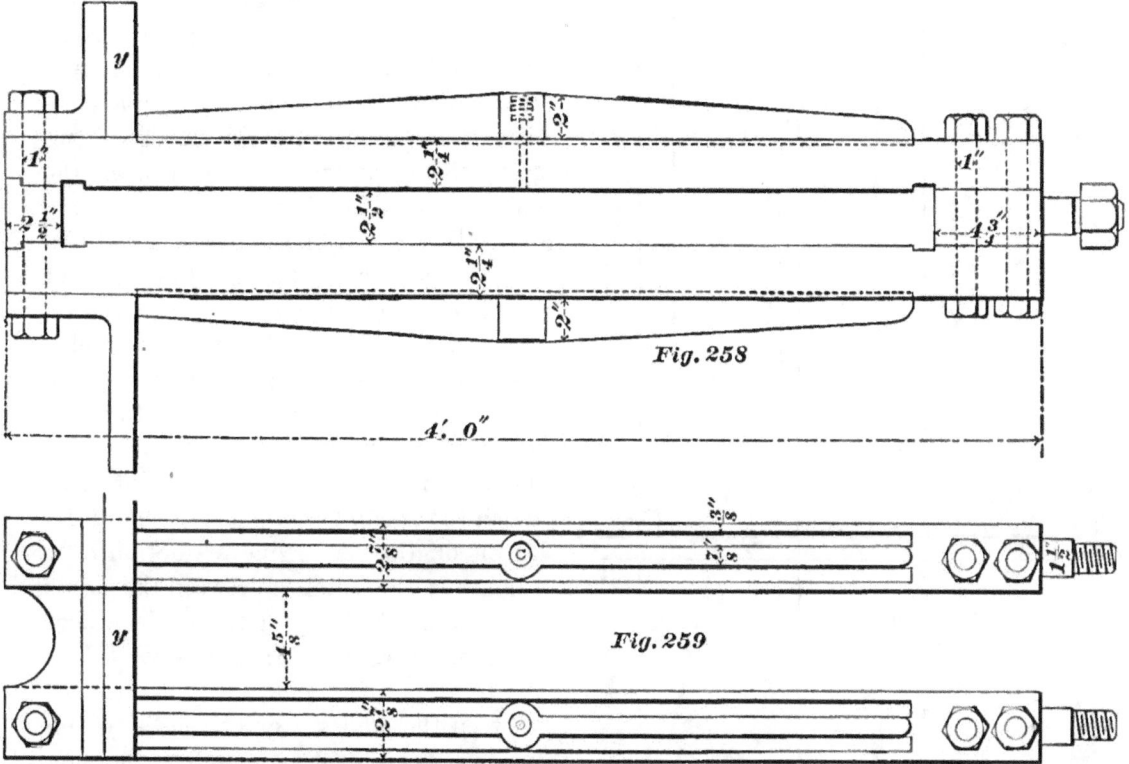

Fig. 258

Fig. 259

design Fig. 260 guide bolts of smaller diameter can be used than in the designs shown in Figs. 234, 237; because in the latter two designs some of the thrust of the connecting-rod acts directly against the bolts; whereas in the former design the same amount of thrust seems to act directly against the guide-blocks $B$ $B$. But a closer examination of the design in Fig. 260 will make it apparent that, should the guides spring, which may occur, and often does occur, then the thrust will act with a long leverage against the bolt which has but a very short leverage—the edge $t$ of the guide-block being the fulcrum—and thus greatly increase the stress in the bolt at the yoke end. For these reasons, then, we may assume that the amount of stress in the guide bolts in design Fig. 260 is the same as the amount of stress in the guide bolts in designs Figs. 234 and 237 when the thrust of the connecting-rod in one case is equal to that in the other case.

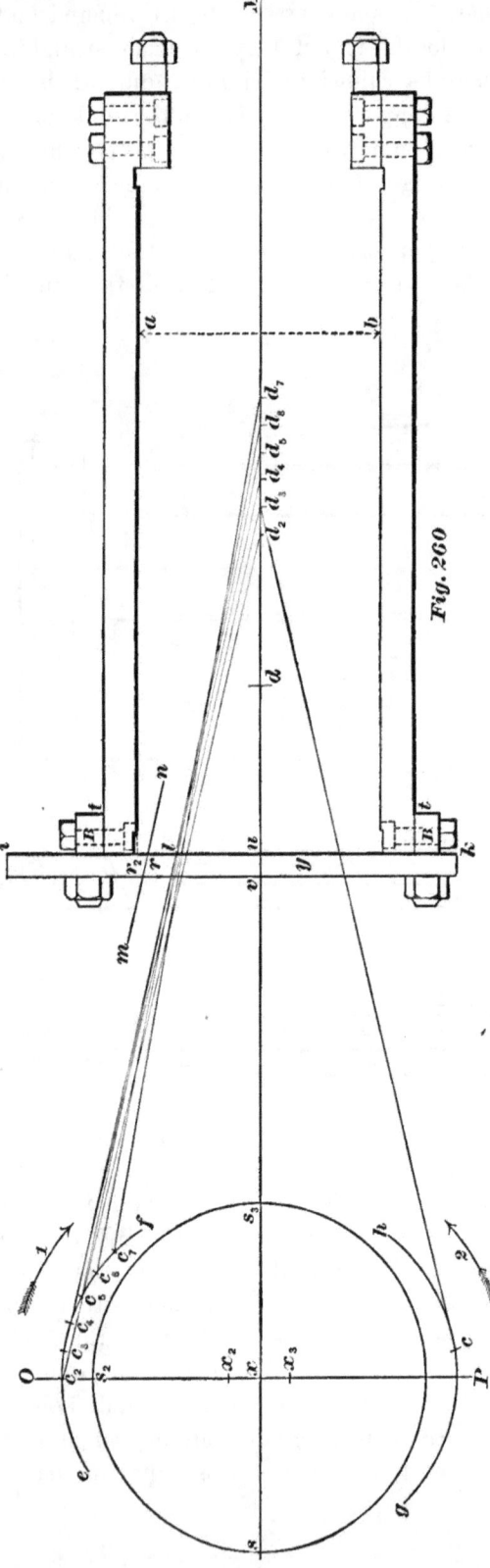

Fig. 260

## DISTANCE BETWEEN THE GUIDES.

**189.** The distance from $a$ to $b$ between the guides in Fig. 260 (this distance also determines the depth of the crosshead) must be sufficient to clear the connecting-rod in any oblique position which it may occupy during the revolution of the crank. Our first step, then, will be to find the position of the guide-yoke $y$ when the length of the connecting-rod, stroke, and length of crosshead are given; and secondly, we must find that oblique position of the connecting-rod which will require the greatest distance between the guides. Let $L\,M$ (Fig. 260) represent the center line of motion of the crosshead pin, and the point $x$ on this line the center of the axle. From the point $x$ as a center, and with a radius equal to half the stroke, describe a circle $s\,s_2\,s_3$; the circumference of this circle will represent the path of the center of the crank-pin when the center of the axle is at $x$. From the point $s$, at which the circumference cuts the line $L\,M$, lay off on the center line of motion $L\,M$ a point $d$; the distance between the points $s$ and $d$ must be equal to the length of the connecting-rod. From the point $d$ towards $s$ lay off a point $u$; the distance between the points $d$ and $u$, measured on the line $L\,M$, must be equal to the sum of the clearance at the rear end, and the horizontal distance between the center of crosshead pin and the rear end of the sliding surfaces of the crosshead, or the rear end of the gib when one is used; also, on the line $L\,M$ lay off from the point $u$ towards $s$ a point $v$; the distance between the points $u$ and $v$ must be equal to the thickness of the guide-yoke. Through the points $u$ and $v$ draw straight lines perpendicular to the center line of motion; these lines will represent the inner and outer faces of the guide-yoke, and thus establish its position. This position of the guide-yoke is the closest to the cylinder head which it can occupy; sometimes the guide-yoke may have to be moved towards the center of axle in order to clear the driving wheel or to suit other parts of the design. Secondly, to find the oblique position of the connecting-rod which will require the greatest distance between the guides. Through the point $x$ draw a straight line $O\,P$ perpendicular to $L\,M$; on this line $O\,P$ lay off above the center $x$ a point $x_2$; the distance between the points $x$ and $x_2$ must be equal to the distance through which the driving box can move before it strikes the frame; hence the point $x_2$ will be the center of the axle when the driving box occupies its highest position in the pedestal of the frame. Again, on the line $O\,P$ lay off below the center $x$ a point $x_3$; the distance between the points $x$ and $x_3$ must be equal to the distance through which the driving box can move before it strikes the pedestal cap; hence the point $x_3$ will be the center of the axle when the driving box occupies its lowest position in the pedestal. From the point $x_2$ as a center, and with the radius equal to half the stroke, describe an arc $e\,f$; also, from the point $x_3$ as a center, and with the same radius, describe an arc $g\,h$. When the driving box is in its extreme highest position the arc $e\,f$ will be a part of the path of the center of crank-pin; and when the driving box is in its extreme lowest position the arc $g\,h$ will be a part of the path of the center of crank-pin. From the point $c_2$ at which the line $O\,P$ cuts the arc $e\,f$ lay off on this arc a number of points $c_3$, $c_4$, $c_5$, $c_6$, $c_7$; the distance between these points should be about 2 inches or a little less. From these points as centers, and with a radius equal to the length of the connecting-rod, describe a number of short arcs cutting the center line of motion $L\,M$ at the points $d_3$, $d_4$, $d_5$, $d_6$, $d_7$. Join by straight lines the points $c_3$ and $d_3$, $c_4$ and $d_4$, $c_5$ and $d_5$, etc.; then the line $c_3\,d_3$ will represent the center line of the connecting-rod when the crank-pin is at $c_3$, and the lines $c_4\,d_4$, $c_5\,d_5$, etc., will represent the center line of connecting-rod when the crank-pin is at $c_4$, $c_5$, etc. Now select that center line of the connecting-rod which cuts the inner face $i\,k$ of the guide-yoke at a point furthest from the line $L\,M$. In our illustration the line $c_5\,d_5$ cuts the line $i\,k$ at the point $l$, and there is no other line representing the center line of connecting-rod which will cut the line $i\,k$ at a point above the point $l$; hence the line $c_5\,d_5$ will represent the center line of the connecting-rod in such an oblique position as will require the greatest distance between the upper guide and the line $L\,M$, and consequently the upper guide must be placed high enough to clear the connecting-rod in this position. Above the center line $c_5\,d_5$ draw a line $m\,n$ to represent the upper edge of the connecting-rod; the space between the line $c_5\,d_5$ and the line $m\,n$ must be equal to that between the center line of connecting-rod and its outer edge at a corresponding distance from either end of the rod to the guide-yoke; if the edges of the rod are parallel to each other, then of course the line $m\,n$ will also be parallel to $c_5\,d_5$; if the rod is tapered, then the line $m\,n$ must have the same inclination to $c_5\,d_5$ as the edges of the rod have to its center line.

The line $m\,n$ cuts the line $i\,k$ at the point $r$, and theoretically the distance between the points $u$ and $r$ would be the required distance between the center line of motion $L\,M$ and the lower face of the upper guide. But, since small inaccuracies in workmanship are very difficult to avoid, we must allow some extra space for these inaccuracies; and besides this the ends of the slot in the yoke, shown in Fig. 261, are usually semicircular, and the face of the guide is placed even with the ends of the slot, or, in other words, tangent to the curved part, and therefore some allowance in the distance between the guides must be made to enable the edges of the rod to clear the curved surface in the slot of the yoke. Therefore, above the point $r$ lay off on the line $i\,k$ a point $r_2$; the distance between the points $r$ and $r_2$ must be equal to a clearance considered to be sufficient to allow for the inaccuracy of workmanship and the semicircular form of the end of the slot. In the case before us let the distance between the points $r$ and $r_2$ be equal to $\frac{1}{2}$ an inch. Through the point $r_2$ draw a horizontal line $r_2\,a$; this will be the lower surface of the upper guide, and thus the position of the upper guide is established. Frequently the distance between the centers $x$ and $x_2$ is greater than the distance between the centers $x$ and $x_3$; hence it may appear that the distance between the center line $L\,M$ and the upper guide should be greater than that between the line $L\,M$ and the lower guide; but in such cases, after the position of the upper guide has been determined, we simply place the lower one at a distance from $L\,M$ equal to that from $L\,M$ to the upper guide.

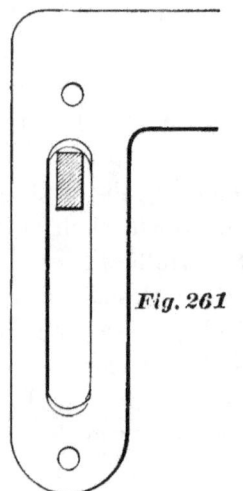

Fig. 261

If, on the other hand, the distance between $x$ and $x_3$ is greater than from $x$ to $x_2$, then we must find, by a construction similar to the foregoing, the distance from $L\,M$ to the lower guide, and place the upper one at the same distance so found above $L\,M$, because it is always desirable to have the guides equidistant from the crosshead pin.

The construction in Fig. 260 shows plainly that the distance between the guides depends upon the position of the guide-yoke. Again, drawing the connecting-rod in a position so that its center line will be tangent to the path of the crank-pin, as shown by the line $c_3\,d_3$ (Fig. 260), and then making the distance between guides to clear only this oblique position of connecting-rod, as is often done, may result in bringing the guides too close together, and lead to considerable trouble, annoyance, and waste of labor in having to chip the ends of the guides, and increase the length of slot in guide-yoke.

### PROPORTIONS OF CROSSHEAD PINS.

190. In establishing rules for determining the dimensions of a locomotive crosshead pin it will be best to base these rules on the dimensions of pins used in locomotives in actual and successful service. A great difference in the sizes of these pins exists; but in the writer's opinion the sizes given in Table 15 are a good average, and will be used in establishing the following rules. The greater number of the smaller pins whose dimensions are here given are made of cast-iron, and the greater number of the large pins are made of wrought-iron.

TABLE 15.

AVERAGE DIMENSIONS OF CROSSHEAD PINS AS AT PRESENT USED IN LOCOMOTIVES.

| Diameter of Cylinder. | Stroke. | Diameter of Crosshead Pins. | Length of Crosshead Pins. |
|---|---|---|---|
| 12″ | 20″ | 2″ | 2″ |
| 13″ | 22″ | 2½″ | 3″ |
| 14″ | 22″ | 2¾″ | 3″ |
| 15″ | 22″ | 2¾″ | 3″ |
| 15″ | 24″ | 3″ | 3″ |
| 16″ | 22″ | 3″ | 3″ |
| 16″ | 24″ | 3⅛″ | 3⅛″ |
| 17″ | 22″ | 3⅛″ | 3⅛″ |
| 17″ | 24″ | 3¼″ | 3¼″ |
| 18″ | 22″ | 3¼″ | 3¼″ |
| 18″ | 24″ | 3⅜″ | 3⅜″ |
| 19″ | 22″ | 3⅜″ | 3⅜″ |
| 19″ | 24″ | 3½″ | 3½″ |
| 20″ | 24″ | 3⅝″ | 3⅝″ |
| 21″ | 24″ | 3¾″ | 3¾″ |

Crosshead pins are subjected to a shearing stress, and therefore it would seem that by making the diameter of a pin sufficiently large to give it the necessary strength to resist shearing, and then assigning to it some given length, would be all that is required. But in examining the dimensions given in the table we find the diameters of these pins to be larger than is necessary for their adequate strength. Another notable feature is that the length of the pins is, in all cases excepting three, equal to the diameter. Here, then, we conclude, and rightly too, that there must be other considerations besides that of strength which the designers have kept in view in determining the dimensions of these pins.

Let us first turn our attention to the length of these pins. We find that their lengths compared with their diameters are less than the lengths of pins ordinarily used in stationary or marine engines. The reason for making the length of a locomotive

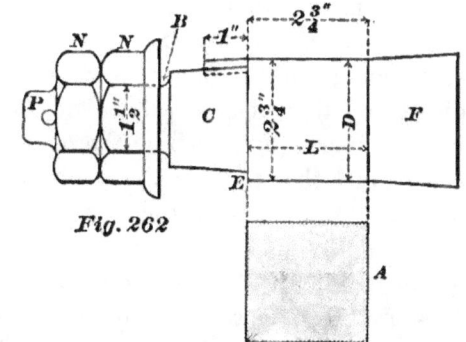

Fig. 262

crosshead pin comparatively so short is that considerable lateral play is allowed between the hubs of the driving wheels and their boxes; and consequently, when the locomotive is running over a curve the mechanism between cylinders and wheels will become out of alignment, which will create an extra stress on the crosshead pin. Now, in order to reduce this extra stress as much as possible, the pin should be made as short as good practice will allow, and thus reduce the leverage of the pin. Another reason for making these pins so short is that in many locomotives the space for the crosshead, and consequently its pin, is limited.

From these considerations, and also from the dimensions given in the table, it will be seen that the length of a locomotive crosshead pin should be equal to its diameter.

By the expression "length of crosshead pin" is meant the length marked $L$ in Fig. 262—that is, the length of that part of the pin which is covered by the connecting-rod brass; and by "diameter of pin" is meant the diameter marked *D*—that is, the diameter of the same part of the pin.

Our next step will be to establish a rule for finding the diameter of the pin. Here a consideration of the greatest importance presents itself, namely, we must not only make the pin large enough to give it the required strength to do the work, but it must also have a large working surface, so as to avoid heating. Right here it may be remarked that when locomotive crosshead pins are correctly proportioned so that they will not heat, they will also have adequate strength for the work, and for this reason we will leave the consideration of strength out of the question. But it must be distinctly understood that these remarks apply only to locomotive crosshead pins, or pins which are as short in comparison with their diameters.

The pressure on the piston is transmitted to the crosshead pin, and experience has shown that when the pressure on the crosshead pin exceeds a certain amount the oil will be forced out of the bearing, and consequently heating or abrasion will follow, and the only means at hand to avoid such results is to make the working surfaces sufficiently large to reduce the pressure per square inch. The area of the working surface is estimated by the projected area as shown at *A* in Fig. 262. This area is always equal to that of a rectangle whose length and breadth is equal to the length and diameter of the pin.

Since the pressure per square inch on the pin is estimated by the pressure per square inch on its projected area, we must proportion this area in a manner which will not allow the pressure to exceed a given limit. Here, then, the question arises, what is this limit? To answer this question let us find the projected area of each pin given in Table 15, which is obtained by multiplying the length by the diameter; the product will be the area required. Let us assume that the greatest pressure per square inch on the piston is 120 pounds; then the total pressure on the piston, and therefore on the projected area of the pin, will be equal to the product obtained in multiplying the area of the piston by 120.

Now, dividing this product by the projected area of the pin we will obtain a quotient which will be the pressure per square inch. By so doing we find that the pressure per square inch of the projected area varies from about 2,200 to 3,200 pounds; and since these pins in Table 15 have given satisfaction, and since their dimensions are suitable for cast-iron pins, and are also often used for wrought-iron pins, we may adopt either 2,200 or 3,200, or any other figure between these two, as a limit or standard of pressure per square inch of projected area. Let us adopt 2,880 pounds per square inch as a standard. We are now in a position to establish a rule for finding the dimensions of any locomotive crosshead pin.

RULE 29.—Divide the total pressure on the piston in pounds by 2,880 and extract the square root of the quotient; the result will be the diameter and the length of the pin in inches. Or, putting this rule in the form of a formula, we have,

$$\sqrt{\frac{\text{Area of piston in sq. inches} \times \text{pressure per inch of piston}}{2880}} = \text{diameter and length of crosshead pin in inches.}$$

EXAMPLE 56.—Find the diameter of a locomotive crosshead pin suitable for a cylinder 18 inches in diameter, and a steam pressure of 120 pounds per square inch of piston.

$$\text{Area of 18-inch piston} = 254.47;$$

hence,

$$\frac{254.47 \times 120}{2880} = 10.60;$$

and the square root of 10.60 is $3\frac{1}{4}$ (nearly); therefore the diameter of the pin will be $3\frac{1}{4}$ inches, and the length will also be $3\frac{1}{4}$ inches.

In a similar manner we can obtain the dimensions of the crosshead pins for all locomotives when the diameter of cylinder and steam pressure is given. But if we assume that in all locomotives the maximum steam pressure per square inch of piston is 120 pounds, then the foregoing rule can be made simpler, and we obtain the following:

RULE 30.—Divide the area of the piston in square inches by 24, and extract the square root of the quotient; the answer will be the diameter and length of the crosshead pin.

Or, putting this rule in the shape of a formula, we have,

$$\sqrt{\frac{\text{Area of piston in square inches}}{24}} = \text{diameter and length of crosshead pin in inches.}$$

By this last rule the dimensions of the crosshead pins in Table 16 have been obtained. As will be seen, the dimensions of pins in Table 16 agree very closely with those in Table 15, and may therefore be adopted as the standard sizes of cast-iron pins for locomotives in which the steam pressure in the cylinders does not exceed 120 pounds per square inch. A number of locomotive builders make the diameters of wrought-iron pins somewhat less than that of cast-iron ones, but leave the length of the former the same as that of the latter. But, on the other hand, quite a number of builders make the diameters of cast-iron and wrought-iron pins alike, and thereby obtain a greater uniformity in the patterns for the connecting-rod brasses.

TABLE 16.

DIMENSIONS OF CROSSHEAD PINS SUITABLE FOR LOCOMOTIVES IN WHICH THE STEAM PRESSURE PER SQUARE INCH DOES NOT EXCEED 120 POUNDS.

| Diameter of Cylinders. | Diameter of Crosshead Pins. | Length of Crosshead Pins. |
| --- | --- | --- |
| 9″ | $1\frac{5}{8}″$ | $1\frac{5}{8}″$ |
| 10″ | $1\frac{7}{8}″$ | $1\frac{7}{8}″$ |
| 11″ | 2″ | 2″ |
| 12″ | $2\frac{1}{4}″$ | $2\frac{1}{4}″$ |
| 13″ | $2\frac{3}{8}″$ | $2\frac{3}{8}″$ |
| 14″ | $2\frac{1}{2}″$ | $2\frac{1}{2}″$ |
| 15″ | $2\frac{3}{4}″$ | $2\frac{3}{4}″$ |
| 16″ | $2\frac{7}{8}″$ | $2\frac{7}{8}″$ |
| 17″ | 3″ | 3″ |
| 18″ | $3\frac{1}{4}″$ | $3\frac{1}{4}″$ |
| 19″ | $3\frac{1}{4}″$ | $3\frac{1}{4}″$ |
| 20″ | $3\frac{3}{8}″$ | $3\frac{3}{8}″$ |
| 21″ | $3\frac{5}{8}″$ | $3\frac{5}{8}″$ |
| 22″ | $3\frac{3}{4}″$ | $3\frac{3}{4}″$ |

## REMARKS RELATING TO THE FORM OF CROSSHEAD PINS.

191. Cast-iron pins are cast to the crosshead; wrought-iron or steel pins are put in separately, and fit into tapered holes in the crosshead. The taper of these holes should not be too great, as an excessive taper will throw too much stress on the nuts and is liable to tear the pin at $B$, Fig. 262. A good taper, and one which is often used, is $1\frac{1}{4}$ inches in 12 inches—that is, the diameter of one end of the 12 inches will be $1\frac{1}{4}$

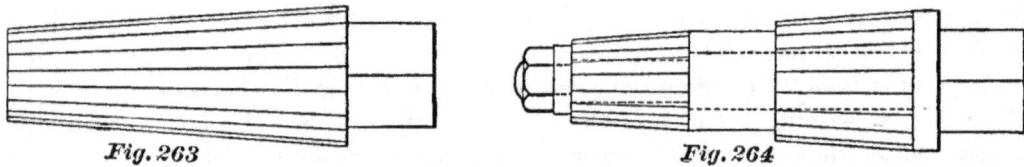

Fig. 263.  Fig. 264.

inches less than at the other end. Many master-mechanics use one taper reamer only, as shown in Fig. 263, for reaming both holes which fit the pin at $C$ and $F$. Some master-mechanics object to this plan, because in their opinion it does not leave a shoulder sufficiently large at $E$, and therefore the diameter of the pin at $C$ is reduced, although the taper per inch is left the same as before. For pins of this kind a step reamer similar to that shown in Fig. 264 will have to be used.

The crosshead pin is held in position by two nuts $NN$, and to obtain further security a split pin $P$ is inserted in the end of crosshead pin.

All crosshead pins should be prevented from turning by a dowel pin or a small feather, as shown at $C$.

Crosshead pins made of wrought-iron should be case hardened.

## STUFFING BOXES AND GLANDS.

192. The purpose of the stuffing box and gland is simply to hold some kind of packing close against the piston-rods, valve-rods, or spindles of valves, etc., thus forming a steam-tight passage for the rods or spindles. The packing may be divided into two distinct classes, namely, metallic packing and hemp packing. In the latter we include all packing made of fibrous material.

Most of the metallic packing at present in use is manufactured by firms who make the manufacture of it a special business, and these firms furnish the dimensions of the stuffing boxes to hold this packing; hence the only kind of stuffing boxes to be considered here will be those which are to hold hemp packing.

Fig. 265 represents a stuffing box with gland similar to those cast to locomotive cylinder heads. Fig. 266 represents a stuffing box with gland similar to those cast to locomotive steam chests. Fig. 267 represents a stuffing box with screw-cap, as is generally used for small valves, cocks, etc.

In order to find the principal dimensions of the stuffing box, glands, and studs, the following rules may be used; and the dimensions thus obtained will agree with good practice:

RULE 31.—To find the thickness $t$ of the stuffing box shown in Figs. 265 and 266,

Add ¼ of an inch to ¼ the diameter of the rod; the sum will be the thickness of the stuffing box at $t$.

EXAMPLE 57.—Find the thickness at $t$ for a piston-rod stuffing box, the piston-rod being 2½ inches in diameter.

hence,
$$\tfrac{1}{4} \text{ diam.} + \tfrac{1}{4} \text{ of an inch} = \text{thickness};$$
$$\tfrac{5}{8}'' + \tfrac{1}{4}'' = \tfrac{7}{8}'', \text{ thickness at } t.$$

EXAMPLE 58.—What should be the thickness at $t$ for a valve-rod stuffing box, the valve-rod being 1½ inches in diameter?

hence,
$$\tfrac{1}{4} \text{ of } 1\tfrac{1}{2} \text{ inches} = \tfrac{3}{8};$$
$$\tfrac{3}{8}'' + \tfrac{1}{4}'' = \tfrac{5}{8}'', \text{ thickness at } t.$$

In practice the thickness at $t$, Fig. 266, is about ½ inch for small valve-rods, and ¾ of an inch for the large valve-rods. The thickness at $t$ for piston-rod stuffing

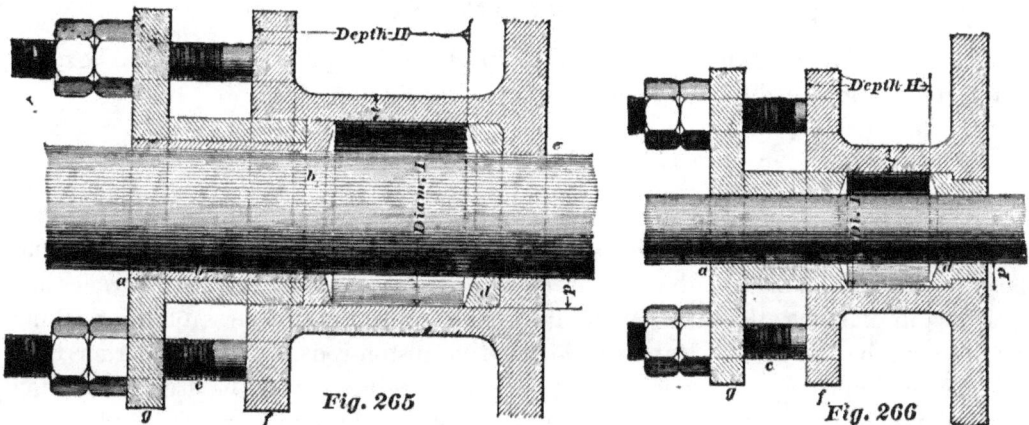

Fig. 265    Fig. 266

boxes, Fig. 265, ranges generally from ¾ inch for small piston-rods and 1 to 1⅛ inches for the larger ones.

The thickness of the stuffing-box flange $f$ should be sufficient to obtain a good depth of thread for the studs; hence, to find thickness $f$ of the stuffing-box flange, we have the following rule:

RULE 32.—To ¼ of the diameter of the rod add ⅜ of an inch, and increase this sum 25 per cent. This sum will be the thickness of the stuffing-box flange. Putting this rule in the shape of a formula, we have,

$$\tfrac{1}{4} \text{ diameter of rod} + \tfrac{3}{8} \text{ inch} + \frac{\tfrac{1}{4} \text{ diameter of rod} + \tfrac{3}{8} \text{ inch}}{4} = \text{thickness of the stuffing-box flange.}$$

EXAMPLE 59.—Find the thickness of a valve-rod stuffing-box flange, the rod being 1½ inches in diameter.

hence,
$$\tfrac{1}{4} \text{ of } 1\tfrac{1}{2} \text{ inches} = \tfrac{3}{8} \text{ inch};$$
$$\tfrac{3}{8}'' + \tfrac{3}{8}'' + \frac{\tfrac{3}{8}'' + \tfrac{3}{8}''}{4} = \tfrac{15}{16} \text{ inch thickness of flange.}$$

The flange of the piston-rod stuffing box, Fig. 265, generally forms part of the cylinder head casing, and therefore it is often made from 14 inches to 16 inches in diameter. The guide-blocks are also fastened to this flange, and consequently its thickness cannot be exactly determined by the foregoing rule; the thickness of the flange near the body of the box will always be more than that obtained by this rule.

In large engines the thickness of this flange will often be from $1\frac{3}{4}$ to 2 inches, and this thickness extends from the stuffing box to beyond the guides; and from the guides to the edges of the flange, its thickness is reduced to about $\frac{1}{2}$ inch.

193. For determining the packing thickness $p$ we may employ the following rule:

RULE 33.—To $\frac{1}{4}$ of the diameter of the rod add $\frac{1}{4}$ of an inch; the sum will be the thickness $p$ of the packing. Putting this rule in the shape of a formula, we have,

$$\tfrac{1}{4} \text{ diameter of rod} + \tfrac{1}{4} \text{ inch} = \text{thickness } p \text{ of packing.}$$

EXAMPLE 60.—Find the thickness of the packing in a stuffing box for a valve-rod, the rod being 1 inch in diameter.

$$\tfrac{1}{4}'' + \tfrac{1}{4}'' = \tfrac{1}{2} \text{ inch for the thickness of the packing.}$$

EXAMPLE 61.—Find the thickness of the packing in a piston-rod stuffing box, the piston-rod being $3\frac{1}{4}$ inches in diameter.

$$\frac{3\frac{1}{4}''}{4} + \tfrac{1}{4}'' = 1\tfrac{1}{16} \text{ inches for the thickness of packing.}$$

In good locomotive practice we find the average thickness of packing for rods of small diameter $\frac{1}{2}$ inch, and for large piston-rods $1\frac{1}{8}$ inches. Here we see that the dimensions obtained by the rule agree with practice. If the rods are larger than $3\frac{1}{2}$ inches in diameter, this rule cannot be used, because the thickness of the packing so found will be too great. But, since locomotive piston-rods are seldom larger than $3\frac{1}{2}$ inches in diameter, we may conclude that the foregoing rule can be used for finding the thickness of the packing in all stuffing boxes used in locomotives.

As soon as we know the thickness of the packing, the diameter $I$ of the stuffing box is readily obtained, for we have only to add twice the thickness of the packing to the diameter of the rod; the sum will be the diameter $I$.

194. Generally speaking, the greater the depth $H$ of the box the longer the engine will run without renewing the packing. In locomotives the depth $H$ of the piston-rod stuffing boxes is often limited, therefore the general practice is to make this depth equal to $1\frac{1}{4}$ to $1\frac{1}{2}$ times the diameter $I$ of the stuffing box; this proportion of diameter to the depth of the box is also adopted for the valve-rod stuffing boxes.

195. Stuffing-box glands for the valve-rod are sometimes made of brass, and many are made of cast-iron; piston-rod glands are nearly always made of cast-iron.

In order to reduce the number of patterns as much as possible, and also to reduce the number of tools and templets necessary for boring and turning the glands, the dimensions of a brass gland and a cast-iron gland are alike; hence the following rules apply to glands made of either metal:

For valve-rods of small diameter the glands are often made entirely of brass, as shown in Fig. 266. When the larger glands are made of cast-iron, they are lined with a brass bushing (Fig. 265) in the same way as all large glands are lined where the cost of labor in making the bushing is less than the cost of making the gland entirely of brass. In the smaller cast-iron glands the bushing is generally $\frac{1}{8}$ inch thick, and in larger glands $\frac{3}{16}$ inch thick. The end $b_2$ of the bushing is enlarged; sometimes this enlarged part will cover the whole end of the gland as shown, and this the writer believes to be the best practice; at other times the diameter of this end is only a very little larger than the diameter of the bushing, the cast-iron part being counterbored to receive the enlarged end. The bushing is forced into the cast-iron; its object is to prevent the collection of rust on the inside of the gland when the engine stands still for any considerable length of time, and thus prevent scratching or injuring the rod.

196. For finding the thickness $g$ of the flange on gland, Fig. 265, we may use the following rule:

RULE 34.—To $\frac{1}{4}$ of the diameter of the rod add $\frac{3}{8}$ of an inch; the sum will be the thickness $g$ of the flange.

EXAMPLE 62.—Find the thickness of the flange on a piston-rod gland, the rod being 3 inches in diameter.

$$\tfrac{3}{4}'' + \tfrac{3}{8}'' = 1\tfrac{1}{8} \text{ inches for the thickness of the flange.}$$

The flanges on the piston-rod gland are generally made oblong in form, as shown in Fig. 268; sometimes oil chambers are cast in these flanges, as shown in Fig. 269; the thickness of the latter flanges is somewhat greater than the thickness obtained by

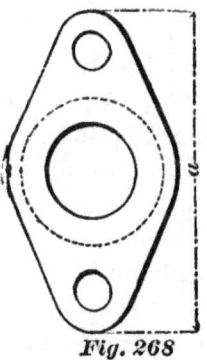

Fig. 268

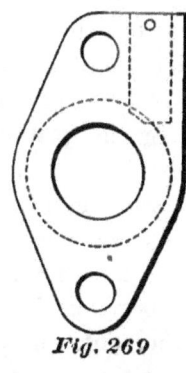

Fig. 269

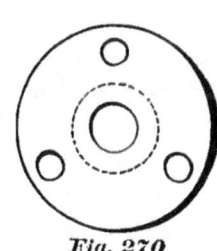

Fig. 270

the rule. The flanges on the valve-rod glands are generally circular in form, as shown in Fig. 270. The length (Fig. 268) of the piston-rod gland, and the diameter of the valve-rod gland (Fig. 270) must be made sufficiently great to allow the edges of the flanges to project a little beyond the nuts of the studs.

The length of the gland measured from the flange to the end is generally made equal to $\frac{3}{4}$ or $\frac{4}{5}$ of the depth $H$ of the stuffing box.

197. A brass ring $d$, as shown in Fig. 265, is placed inside of the stuffing box. The hole in this ring is just large enough to allow the piston-rod to pass through easily, whereas the hole $e$ through the cylinder head, or, in other words, the hole $e$ through that portion of the cast-iron which forms one end of the stuffing box, is generally made $\frac{1}{8}$ inch larger in diameter than that of the piston-rod. This arrangement prevents iron and iron from touching each other, and consequently what

little rust may form and collect in the hole *e* through the cylinder head cannot scratch or injure the rod. Sometimes we find the brass ring *d* extending through the cylinder head; in cases of this kind the form of the ring *d* will be similar to that of the ring *d* shown in Fig. 266. Allowing the ring *d* to pass through the cylinder head in this manner is, in the writer's opinion, bad practice, because this ring is liable to break, and sometimes it does break; then if pieces of it fall into the cylinder, more or less damage to the cylinder head or piston may be the result; the writer has known accidents of this kind to happen, incurring a great expense for repairing the damage. Although brass rings *d* similar in form to that shown in Fig. 266 should not be used in any kind of stuffing boxes, the use of this form of ring cannot be avoided in a valve-rod stuffing box for the following reason:

The valve-stem is forged to the valve yoke, and therefore it must be entered into the stuffing box from the inside of the steam chest; this cannot be done without canting the valve-stem, because the form of the steam chest will not allow it to enter the hole squarely, and consequently this hole must be considerably larger in diameter than that of the valve-stem; when the stem is in position the hole is reduced by the brass ring *d*, hence this shape. From the fact that a large hole is required for entering the valve-stem into the stuffing box, it will be readily perceived that the valve-stem cannot be taken out of the steam chest or placed into the same without first removing the ring *d*, and therefore this ring must not be fitted very tightly in the stuffing box.

The face of the ring *d* and the end of the gland which touches the packing are generally turned slightly concave, so as to help to force the packing against the rod.

198. To keep the packing in place, and to compress it sufficiently to prevent leakage, the gland must be forced against the packing, and for this purpose the studs *c c* (Figs. 265 and 266) are used. In the piston-rod stuffing box two studs are generally employed; the limited space for the gland prevents the use of a greater number of studs. In the valve-rod stuffing box two or three studs are used, the number of studs depending on the fancy and judgment of the designer.

In the piston-rod stuffing box the studs should be placed sufficiently far apart to allow the hub of the crosshead to pass between the nuts on these studs. In the valve-rod stuffing box the distance from the center of the studs to the center of the box should be sufficiently great to allow the tap to pass the outside of the box when the holes for these studs are being tapped.

For finding the diameter of these studs when two are used in each box we have the following rule:

RULE 35.—To ¼ of the diameter of the rod add ¼ inch; the sum will be the diameter of the stud. Putting this rule in the shape of a formula, we have,

$$\tfrac{1}{4} \text{ diameter of rod} + \tfrac{1}{4} \text{ inch} = \text{diameter of stud}.$$

EXAMPLE 63.—Find the diameter of the studs for a piston-rod stuffing box, the rod being 3 inches in diameter.

$$\tfrac{3}{4}'' + \tfrac{1}{4}'' = 1 \text{ inch for the diameter of the stud}.$$

The same rule may be used in finding the diameter of the studs for the valve-rod stuffing box when three studs are used for each box; although, theoretically, when more than two studs are employed, the diameter of each stud can be made somewhat less than that found by the rule.

The general practice is to make all studs for small piston-rod stuffing boxes ¾ inch in diameter; for piston-rod stuffing boxes on cylinders 12 inches in diameter and up to 17 inches in diameter ⅞" studs are used; for cylinders 18 to 20 inches in diameter 1" studs are used; and for larger cylinders 1⅛" studs. For the valve-rod stuffing boxes the diameter of the studs varies from ⅝ to ¾ inch, according to the size of the rod.

Two nuts are always used for each stud; often both nuts are placed outside of the gland, as shown in the illustrations, but sometimes the nuts are placed so that one will be outside, and the other nut inside of the flange $g$.

These nuts are case hardened to prevent their corners from becoming worn; and for the sake of convenience (so that one wrench can be used) the nuts for the piston-rod gland and those for the valve-rod gland are made the same size, even when larger studs are used for the former than for the latter.

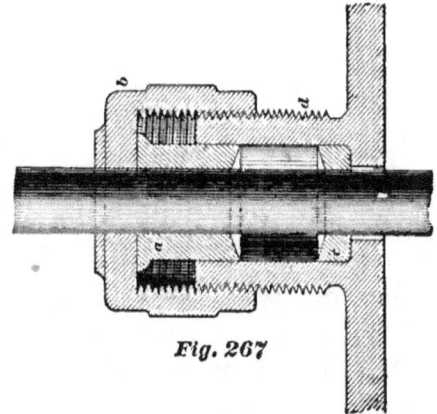

Fig. 267

When only two studs are employed great care must be taken to have the center of the studs and the center of the rod in one straight line, otherwise trouble will be experienced in screwing up the gland; in fact, when the two studs cannot be placed exactly in line with the center of the rod it is better to use three studs.

Another manner of compressing the packing is shown in Fig. 267. Instead of having a gland, we have here a brass sleeve $a$ fitting the rod and the inside of the stuffing box. This sleeve is pressed against the packing by means of the nut $b$, which is tapped to fit the thread cut on the outside of the stuffing box $d$. It will be noticed that the sleeve $a$ has a small flange on top; the purpose of this flange is simply to prevent the sleeve from being pressed too far into the box, and to provide some means of pulling it out of the box.

# CHAPTER V.

## FRAMES.—AXLE BOXES.

### FRAME PEDESTALS.

199. The figures numbered 271 up to 279 represent the proportions of frame pedestals for passenger locomotives of different sizes.

The function of the pedestal is to hold the axle box—often called the driving box—at a given distance from the cylinder, but in the meantime allowing the axle box to move in a vertical direction. The pedestals are made of wrought-iron, and each one, as shown in Figs. 271 and 280, consists of a portion of the upper frame brace $B$, the pedestal legs $A$ $A_2$, and the mechanism used for preventing an increase of the opening at the bottom of the jaw. The three parts, namely, the portion $B$ of the frame brace and the two pedestal legs $A$ $A_2$, form what is called the pedestal jaw. The pedestal legs in large locomotives are often connected at the bottom by the bolt $D$ passing through a frame thimble $T$ inserted in the opening of the jaw, as shown in Fig. 271; in smaller engines the legs are connected by a pedestal cap $C$ as shown in Figs. 277, 278, 279, and also in 280. The frame thimbles $T$ are made of cast-iron, the caps $C$ are made of wrought-iron. The reason for not using the bolts $D$ and frame thimbles in smaller locomotives is that the bolt $D$ will interfere with the wedge bolt $E$, as will be presently explained.

The pedestals are united in each frame by the upper frame brace $B_2$ and the lower frame brace $L$; these braces are forged to the pedestal jaws.

There are two distinct forms of pedestal jaws used; one is represented in Fig. 271 and the other in Fig. 280. The difference between these two forms consists in the shape of one of the pedestal legs, thus: The jaw represented in Fig. 271 has one straight and one tapered leg—that is to say, the inside of one of the pedestal legs, as $A_2$ (called the straight leg), is planed square with the top of frame, the inside of the other one, $A$, is planed so as to form an angle with the top of frame, making the opening at the bottom of the jaw greater than at the top. In the pedestal represented in Fig. 280 both legs are tapered. The form of pedestal shown in Fig. 280 has been used very extensively in former years; but lately the use of the form shown in Fig. 271 has increased. Some master-mechanics prefer to use for all locomotives the pedestal caps as shown in Figs. 277, 278, and 279 in place of the cast-iron frame thimbles $T$ and the bolts $D$; but the writer believes that the use of the thimble and bolt will add to the stiffness of the pedestal, because by the use of the bolt $D$ the lower frame brace $L$ will be brought nearer in line with the

MODERN LOCOMOTIVE CONSTRUCTION.

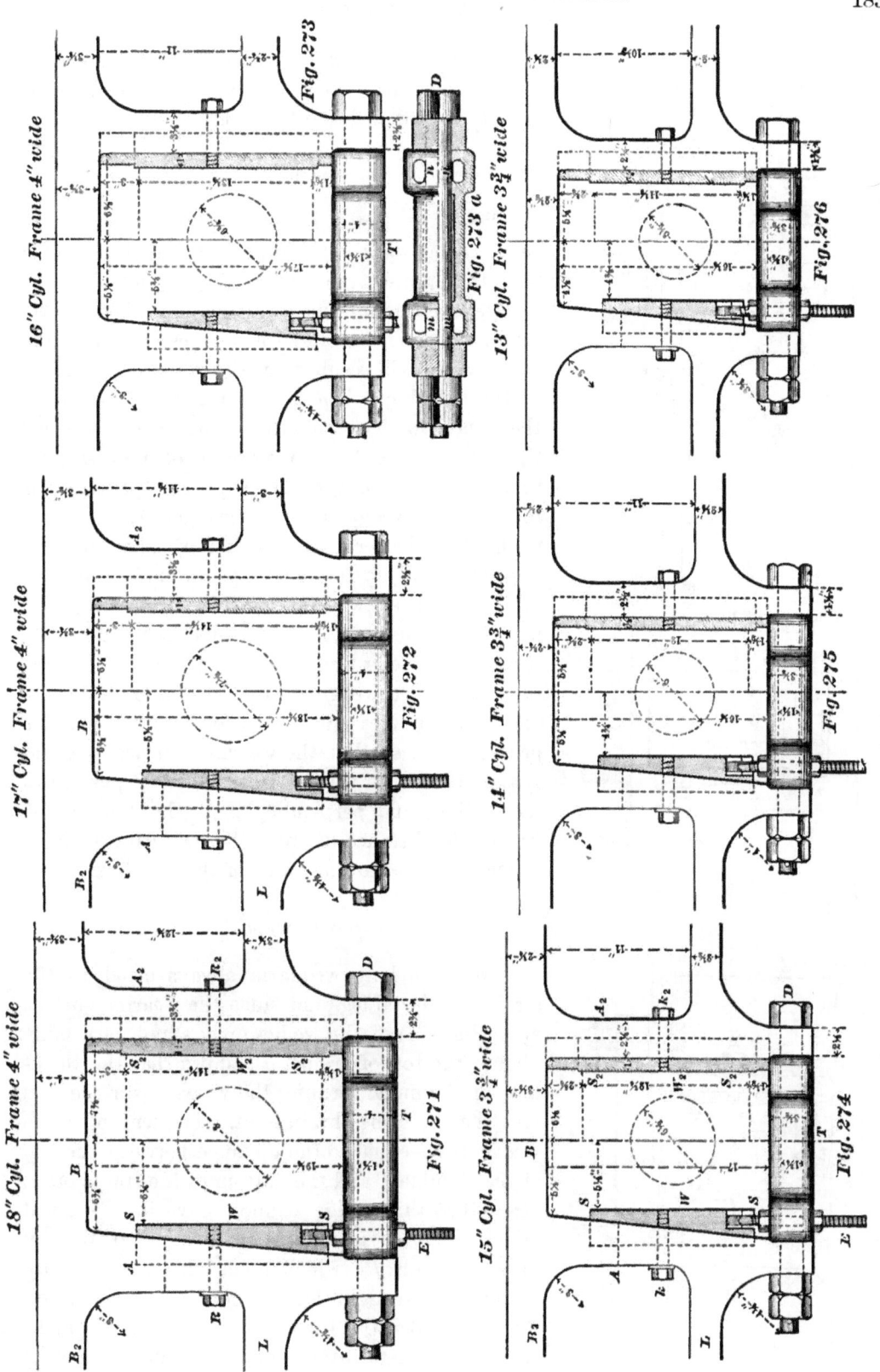

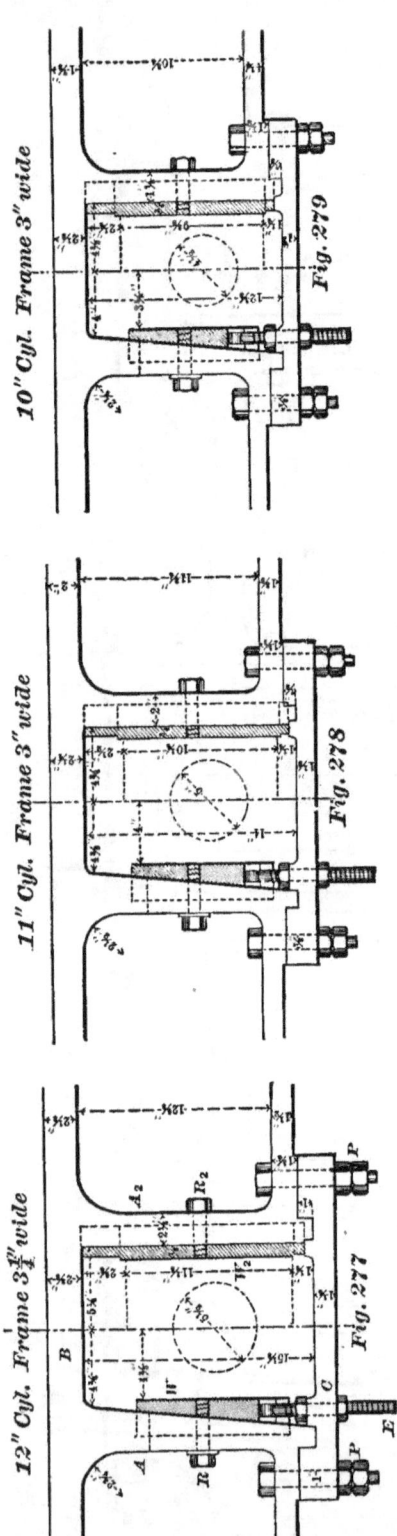

center of driving axle; by so doing a better distribution of metal in the frame is secured and the stiffness of the pedestal legs increased.

## WEDGES.

200. The function of the wedges—shown in section, and marked $W \; W_2$ in Fig 271—is twofold: first, they protect the pedestal legs from wear; secondly, with these wedges the play is taken up between the axle box and the wedges caused by the wear, which will result from the vertical movement of the axle box. The wedge marked $W$ is called the "short wedge," and that marked $W_2$ is called the "long wedge." It may here be necessary to remark that the long wedge $W_2$ in this pedestal has in nowise a wedge shape, consequently "a shoe" would be a better name for it; we shall for the sake of simplicity follow the usual custom and retain the term "wedge," as this term will cover both wedges used in the pedestal shown in Fig. 280, in which the long wedge $W_2$ must necessarily have the shape of a wedge similar to that of the short one. The wedges must be accurately fitted in the pedestal jaw, so that the wearing surfaces $s \; s$ and $s_2 \; s_2$ of these two wedges will be exactly parallel to each other, and perpendicular to the top of the frame; the distance between these wearing surfaces should be equal to the width of the axle box.

### LONG WEDGE.

201. The long wedge is always fitted to the straight pedestal leg, and since the wearing surface $s_2 \; s_2$ (Fig. 271) of the wedge must stand perpendicular to the top of frame, it follows that the thickness of the metal forming the wearing surface $s_2 \; s_2$ must be the same throughout. The length of the wedge $W_2$ is equal to the distance between the top of the thimble $T$ and the bottom of the frame brace $B$, so that this wedge cannot move in a vertical direction, and it is further secured in position by the screw bolt $R_2$, which holds the wedge firmly against the straight leg. In order to prevent on the long wedge the formation of ridges, the thickness of the metal at the ends is reduced, causing

MODERN LOCOMOTIVE CONSTRUCTION. 185

the wearing surfaces on three sides of the wedge to project beyond the metal at the ends, and these projecting surfaces are accurately planed. The long wedge is shown in detail in Figs. 281 and 282.

### SHORT WEDGE.

202. A reduction of the metal at the ends of the short wedge $W$ (Fig. 271) is not necessary, because the length of the wedge is always made equal to, or a little less than, the length of the axle box, and consequently ridges cannot be formed on it, as the axle box in its vertical movement will move beyond the ends of the

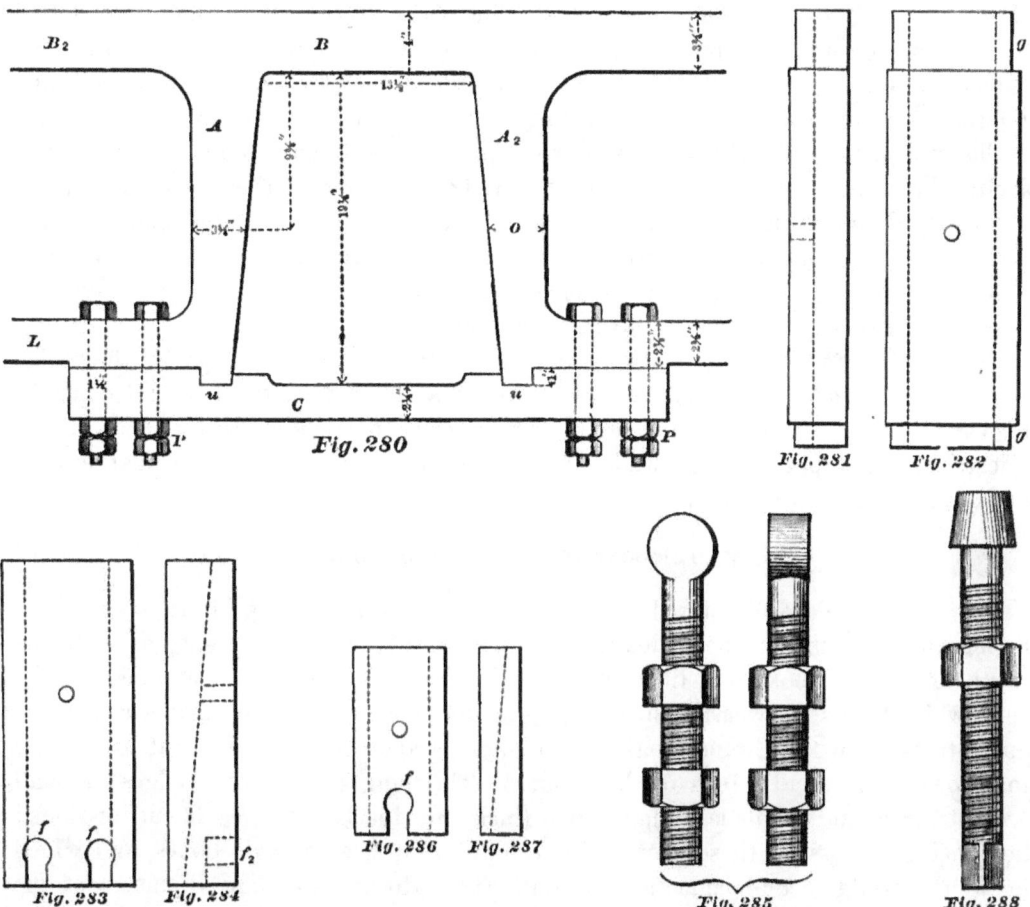

wedge. Since the wearing surface $s\ s$ must be perpendicular to the top of frame, and since this wedge has to fit the tapered pedestal leg, it follows that the part of it against which the side of the axle box slides must have a wedge form, as shown. The play between the wedges and the axle box is taken up by moving the short wedge upwards by means of the wedges bolt $E$. By so doing the short wedge will slide against the inner surface of the tapered pedestal leg $A$, and thereby reduce the distance between the wedges. When the short wedge has been adjusted to the correct position, it is held there by the wedge bolt $E$, and also by the screw bolt $R$, which holds it firmly against the pedestal leg. For the bolt $R$ a slot is cut in the leg, so

186               *MODERN LOCOMOTIVE CONSTRUCTION.*

that the bolt can be moved up or down with the wedge to any desired position. The short wedge is shown in detail in Figs. 283 and 284.

### WEDGE BOLTS.

203. When a cast-iron thimble is used, as shown in Fig. 271, two wedge bolts $E$ are employed for each short wedge. These bolts pass through slots $m$ $n$, Fig. 273$a$, cast into the thimble near the end, one on each side of the bolt $D$. The reason for casting slots near both ends of the thimble, as shown, is to make the thimble reversible. The heads of the wedge bolts are cylindrical in form, as represented in Fig. 285. These heads fit into recesses $f f$ cast in the short wedge, as shown in Fig. 283. In small locomotives the frames are not sufficiently wide to admit two wedge bolts and therefore only one can be used, and this bolt must be placed in the center of the wedge, as indicated by the recess $f$ in the wedge shown in Fig. 286. But placing the wedge bolt in the center of the wedge will prevent the use of a pedestal bolt $D$, which must also pass through the center of the pedestal legs, and therefore these two bolts will interfere with each other. It is for this reason that in small locomotives wrought-iron pedestal caps $C$, as shown in Fig. 277, are employed in place of the cast-iron thimble $T$ and pedestal bolts $D$.

In the writer's opinion it is always best not to tap the pedestal caps for the wedge bolts $E$, but to allow this bolt to pass through a slot cut in the pedestal cap. In this case the wedge bolt will have the same form of head as shown in Fig. 285. If the pedestal cap is tapped for the wedge bolt, then the head of this bolt must have a conical form, as shown in Fig. 288.

### PROPORTIONS OF WEDGES AND BOLTS.

204. We have already stated that the length of the long wedge must be equal to the length of opening in the pedestal; and the length of the short wedge equal to the length of the axle box, or a little shorter. In the long wedge the thickness of the metal which forms the wearing surface $s_2$ $s_2$ should not be less than that given in the illustrations; and the thinnest part of the short wedges should be about $\frac{1}{2}$ inch for small locomotives, and $\frac{5}{8}$ inch for large ones. The flanges of all the wedges in small locomotives should not be less than $\frac{5}{8}$ inch thick, and for larger ones $1\frac{1}{4}$ inches thick; the exact thickness of these flanges for the different sizes of axle boxes, and which the writer would recommend, are given in Figs. 316 to 340. The diameter of the wedge bolts $E$ is usually $\frac{3}{4}$ inch for the small locomotives, and $\frac{7}{8}$ inch for larger ones. The bolts which hold the wedges to the pedestal legs are generally made $\frac{3}{4}$ inch in diameter.

205. All the principal dimensions of the pedestals for passenger locomotives are given in our illustration, and these dimensions agree with modern locomotive practice. In connection with this subject it may here be remarked that in late years the mechanisms of the larger locomotives have been made heavier and their weights increased. It will therefore be found by comparison that the dimensions of the larger pedestals will exceed the dimensions of pedestals made a few years ago, and the dimensions given for the smaller pedestals will agree very closely with the

dimensions of the average pedestals now in use. The dotted circle, with the diameter given in each pedestal, represents the driving axle journal suitable for each one of these pedestals. It will be noticed that the diameter of the journal given in Fig. 271 is considerably larger than the average diameter of journals used in passenger locomotives built some years ago; but in modern engines of this class journals as large as shown in this figure are now used, and the writer believes it is only a matter of time when this size of axle will be generally adopted for fast passenger engines having cylinders 18 inches in diameter.

### ENGINE FRAMES.

206. Fig. 289 represents the main frame for an eight-wheeled passenger engine, such as is shown in Fig. 1, and suitable for a locomotive having cylinders 18 inches in diameter. Fig. 290 represents the front splice of the same frame; the front splice is fastened to the main frame, as shown in Fig. 289, in which that portion marked $S$ represents one end of the front splice.

Fig. 291 represents the main frame for a locomotive of the same class as the foregoing, but having cylinders 10 inches in diameter.

The back ends of these main frames, Figs. 289 and 291, are suitable for a footboard, and, since nearly all locomotives which carry footboards burn soft coal or wood, it may be said that these frames are for soft coal and wood burning locomotives. For this class of locomotives the horizontal distance

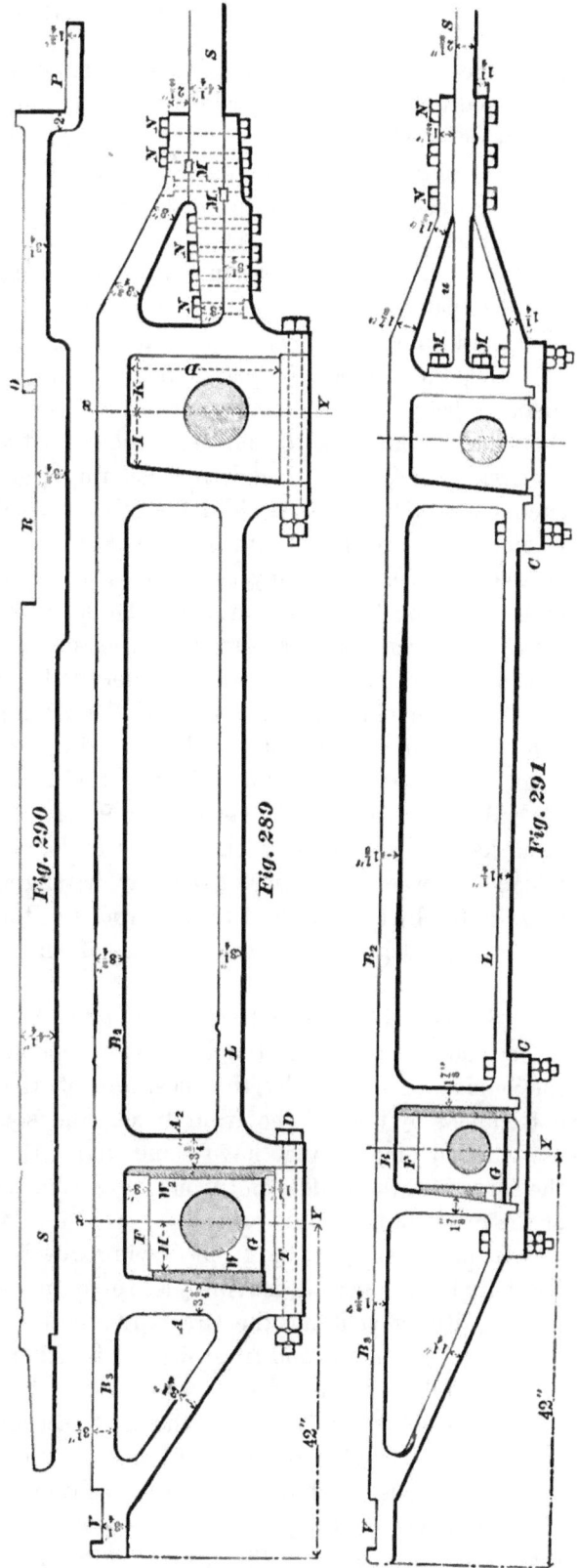

from the center of the rear axle to the back end of frame is usually 42 inches. For hard coal burning locomotives this distance may have to be changed, and made either longer or shorter to suit the design of boiler.

In designing a locomotive frame the first step is to locate the centers of the driving wheels and the position of the cylinders. It may be said that the relative position of the driving wheels and the cylinder depend upon the proper distribution of the weight on the drivers, and also on the length of the boiler. Again, in all eight-wheeled passenger engines, such as shown in Fig. 1, ten-wheeled engines, shown in Fig. 2, and mogul engines, shown in Fig. 3, which are designed for burning soft coal or wood, the fire-box is placed between the two rear axles, and consequently the distance between these axles must be sufficiently great to admit the fire-box between them; there must also be sufficient room for the working of the eccentrics, space for the axle boxes, room enough for cleaning the water space around the furnace, and such space as may be required for other special mechanism which the design of the locomotive may call for. But in the meantime it must be remembered that the distance between the centers of any two wheels which are connected by a side rod must not exceed 8' 9" or 9' 0" at the utmost; the latter distance is seldom used. If the distance between the centers of the driving wheels exceed these distances, the length of the side rods will become too great, and consequently dangerous; because, on account of the great number of revolutions per minute of the driving wheels, the change of motion of the side rods from an upward to a downward or from a downward to an upward motion becomes so sudden that the weight of the rods will be an element of danger, causing the side rods which are longer than 8' 9" or 9' 0" to be shaken to pieces. From these remarks we learn that in the classes of locomotives before mentioned the greatest distance between the center of the rear driving wheel and the center of the one next to it is limited by the length of the side rod, and the shortest distance between the centers of the same drivers in the same classes of engines is limited by the length of the fire-box.

In ten-wheeled locomotives the distance between the center of the middle driving wheel and the center of the front one depends greatly upon the general design of the engines; but usually the position of the front drivers in these engines is determined by that of the front truck, and sometimes by the valve motion. In all ten-wheeled engines that have come under the writer's notice, the distance between the centers of the middle and front drivers has been less than that between the centers of the rear and middle drivers.

In mogul engines, the front driving wheels are generally placed as far forward as the cylinder will permit, leaving just room enough for removing the cylinder head and casing without striking the tire. In these engines, too, the distance between the centers of the middle and front drivers is generally less than that between the centers of the middle and rear drivers.

In consolidation we have the first, second, third, and fourth pair of driving wheels; the pair of driving wheels next to the cylinder is called the first pair. The same conditions which determine the position of the front drivers in a mogul engine will also determine the position of the first pair of drivers in the consolidation engine; that is, in these engines the front drivers are placed as far forward as the cylinders will permit, so that the cylinder head and casing can readily be taken off. The distance between the centers of the first and second pair of drivers must be sufficiently great to admit the rocker between the tires of these wheels. The distances between the centers of the second and third pair, and between the third and the fourth pair, are generally arranged so as to leave 1 inch or 1½ inches clearance between the flanges of the tires.

207. In small locomotives the total wheel base generally depends on the proper distribution of the weight of the engine on all the wheels. For instance, moving the front truck nearer to or further from the center of gravity of the locomotive, we throw more or less weight on the truck. In larger engines we may often, if it is desirable, be able to move the front truck nearer to the center of gravity of the locomotive; but if we attempt to move the truck away from the center of gravity of the engine, we may meet with obstacles, namely, the sharp curves of the track over which the engine has to run, and for which the wheel base must be kept as short as possible. The turn-tables of the road may also limit the length of the wheel base. Therefore it will be seen that the arrangement of the wheels, and the determination of the total wheel base of large locomotives, is brought within very narrow limits. And it may be said that, in cases of this kind, the ingenuity of the designer is often taxed to the utmost to obtain satisfactory results; and even then he may have to be satisfied with results not as desirable as they should be.

208. The relative positions of the wheels under hard-coal burners are sometimes the same as those under soft-coal burners; at other times conditions will arise which will compel a change in the arrangement of the wheels under the hard-coal burners.

## DEPTH OF PEDESTAL.

209. The depth of the pedestal—that is, the distance $D$, Fig. 289, from the top of the cast-iron thimble to the under side of the upper frame brace $B$—should be sufficient to allow the driving box to move a given amount in a vertical direction, thus: In Fig. 289 the line marked $F$ represents the top, and the line marked $G$, the bottom of driving box. The depth of the space between the top of the box and the frame brace $B$, plus the depth of the space between the bottom of the box and the thimble, represents the total vertical movement of the driving box. When a locomotive is in good working order, with the usual amount of fuel and water, the driving box should occupy in the pedestal a position in which the upper clearance—that is, the space between the top of box and frame brace—is greater than the lower clearance, or the space between the bottom of the box and thimble. Thus: In Fig. 289 we see that the upper clearance is 3 inches, and lower clearance is 1½ inches. The total amount of clearance and the difference between the top and bottom clearance is arbitrary and is not always alike in the same class of locomotives. The average amount of clearance at the top and bottom of the boxes for the different sizes of locomotives, as generally adopted by locomotive builders and master-mechanics, is given in Figs. 271 to 279, in which the dotted lines immediately over and under the axle represent the top and bottom of the driving boxes; the dimension given from the top of the box to frame brace $B$ represents the amount of

the upper clearance, and the dimension given from the bottom of the box to the thimble or pedestal cap represents the amount of the lower clearance.

### WIDTH OF PEDESTAL OPENING.

210. The width of the opening of the pedestal, or the distance from leg to leg, Fig. 289, should be such as will not admit the short wedge further into the pedestal after the driving box and long wedge are in position than is necessary for it to clear the wedge-bolt nut on the top of the thimble, leaving as great a distance as possible between the top of the short wedge and the frame brace $B$, through which the short wedge can be moved to take up the play. The distance $H$ given in Fig. 289, from the center line $x Y$ to the face of the short wedge, represents one-half the width of the driving box; and so also the dimensions from the vertical center lines to the face of the short wedges in Figs. 271 to 279 represent one-half the width of the axle boxes.

### TAPER OF PEDESTAL LEGS, AND POSITION OF STRAIGHT LEG.

211. When pedestals are used like those shown in Figs. 289 and 291, the straight leg should always be placed towards the cylinder; by so doing the distance from the cylinders to the center of the driving wheels cannot be readily changed, and therefore the distance from center to center of the brasses in the main rod need not be so often adjusted. The amount of taper for the inner surface of the tapered legs is generally $1\frac{1}{8}$ inches in 12 inches; and this taper is used for all pedestals of the form shown in Figs. 289, 291, and 280.

### POSITION OF CENTER LINES.

212. In connection with this subject it may be advantageous to the reader to call his attention to the fact that when pedestals such as shown in Figs. 289 and 291 are used, the vertical center line drawn through the center of the axle does not pass through the center of the opening of pedestal at the top; that is to say, the distance $K$ (Fig. 289) from the center line $x Y$ to the straight leg will be greater than the distance $I$ from the center line $x Y$ to the top of the tapered leg; at the bottom of the pedestal the conditions are reversed. When pedestals such as shown in Fig. 280 are used, the vertical center line drawn through the center of the axle will pass through the center of the opening of pedestal, both at the top and bottom.

It is well to note these facts, because in designing a frame the position of these center lines have a very important bearing in determining the position and dimensions of other parts of the locomotive. Hence in designing a frame having pedestals as shown in Figs. 289 and 291, the distance from the straight pedestal leg to the vertical center line $x Y$ must be equal to the thickness of the long wedge added to one-half the width of the driving box, whereas for the pedestals shown in Fig. 280, the vertical center line must be drawn through the center of the opening of the pedestal. In all pedestals the horizontal center line drawn through the center of the axle must be in a position which will give about the same relative clearance on top and bottom of driving box as given in Figs. 271 to 279; or, in other words, in designing a locomotive frame the driving boxes must be drawn in the same positions as they would occupy when the engine is in first-class working order and running on the road; and the boxes must be considered to be stationary during the time the locomotive is being designed.

## WIDTH OF FRAME.

213. For small locomotives the width of frame should not be less than 3 inches, so as to provide on top of frame a surface sufficiently wide to which the rocker box, lifting-shaft bearings, and other mechanism can be bolted without interfering with the necessary strength of the frame. In large locomotives the space between the driving wheels and the fire-box will limit the width of the frame, and is seldom, if ever, wider than 4 inches. We may therefore conclude that the width of locomotive frames ranges from 3 to 4 inches; the suitable width of frame, such as is usually adopted for any one of the different sizes of passenger locomotives, will be found in Figs. 271 to 279.

## DIMENSIONS OF FRAME BRACES.

214. To the upper frame brace $B_2$ in Fig. 292 (also see Figs. 271 and 274) are bolted and attached some of the principal parts of the locomotive. The forces acting upon the braces are of a complex character, and therefore to find the exact dimensions of the braces, which will give them the required strength—no more and no less—to resist the forces acting upon them, would be a very difficult matter.

Consequently, rules which are to be of any practical value for finding the dimensions of a locomotive frame, can only be empirical or arbitrary rules.

The following rules are founded upon the observation of the writer, and he believes that the results obtained by them will agree with the best practice.

We have already established the width of the frames for the various sizes and classes of locomotives; our next step will be to find the cross-sectional area of the upper frame brace $B_2$.

One of the principal forces to which locomotive frames are subjected is the pulling force, or the horizontal force, which acts parallel to the frame braces $B_2$ and $L$. This pulling force is not equal to the total steam pressure on the piston, but for the sake of simplicity in establishing the following rules, and for convenience in finding the dimensions of other locomotive frames, we may assume it to be so, without falling into any serious errors. Therefore we will again assume, as before, that the maximum steam pressure in the cylinder is 120 pounds per square inch. Comparing the total steam pressure on the piston with the cross-sectional area of the frame brace $B_2$ in the frames lately made, we find that when the cylinders are 11 inches and up to 18 inches in diameter, then 1 square inch for every 2,000 pounds of the total steam pressure on the piston is allowed in the cross-sectional area of the frame brace $B_2$; for cylinders 19 and 20 inches in diameter, 1 square inch for every 2,200 pounds; for cylinders 21 and 22 inches in diameter, 1 square inch for every 2,400 pounds; and for cylinders 10

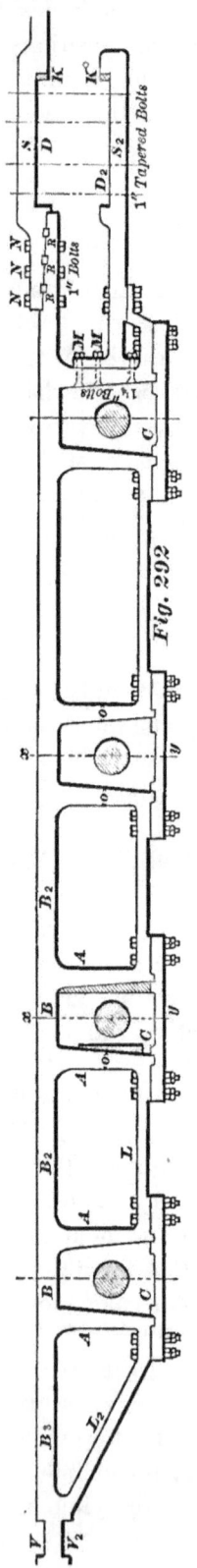

Fig. 292

inches and less in diameter, 1 square inch for every 1,700 pounds of the total steam pressure on the piston is allowed.

According to these figures, it will be seen that the cross-sectional area of the smaller braces is greater than that of the larger braces, when these are compared with their respective piston pressures. This is as it should be, because the ratio between the depth and width of the smaller braces, or, we may say, the distribution of the metal in the smaller braces, is not as good for obtaining the necessary strength to resist the forces which act in a vertical direction as the distribution of the metal in or the ratio between the depth and breadth for the larger braces, and therefore the larger frame braces can resist all the forces acting upon them with comparatively less metal than the smaller ones. It may be asked: Why cannot we make the form of cross-section in smaller frames similar to that of the larger ones? To this we answer that the widths of the frames are determined by certain conditions, as explained in Art. 213, and cannot be changed; therefore if we attempt to make the depths of the smaller frame braces $B_2$ equal or nearly equal to the breadth of the frame, as is often the case in larger frames, we waste material and obtain frames too heavy for the smaller locomotives.

Hence, for finding the area of those portions of the upper frame braces which are marked $B_2$ in Figs. 292, 271, and 274, we have the following rules:

RULE 33a.—For locomotives having cylinders 21 or 22 inches in diameter, divide the total maximum steam pressure in pounds on the piston by 2,400; the quotient will be the number of square inches in the cross-sectional area of the part of the frame brace marked $B_2$.

For locomotives having cylinders 19 or 20 inches in diameter, divide the total maximum steam pressure on the piston by 2,200.

For locomotives having cylinders 18 inches or less in diameter down to 11 inches in diameter (the latter included), divide the total maximum steam pressure on the piston by 2,000; and for cylinders 10 inches and less in diameter, divide by 1,700; the product in each case will be the required area in square inches of the frame brace $B_2$.

EXAMPLE 64.—What should be the cross-sectional area of the upper frame brace in a locomotive having cylinders 17 inches in diameter? Maximum steam pressure on the piston is 120 pounds per square inch.

The area of a piston 17 inches in diameter is equal to 226.98 square inches; hence,

$$\frac{226.98 \times 120}{2000} = 13.618 \text{ square inches in the sectional area of the upper frame brace.}$$

**215.** When the area of the upper frame brace $B_2$ is known and the width of the frames established, as in Figs. 271 to 279, the depth of the upper frame brace can be readily obtained, thus:

RULE 34a.—Divide the area of the frame brace $B_2$ by the suitable width of frame given in Figs. 271 to 279.

EXAMPLE 65.—What should be the depth of the upper frame brace for a locomotive having cylinders 18 inches in diameter? Maximum steam pressure on the piston is 120 pounds per square inch.

The area of a piston 18 inches in diameter is 254.47 square inches; hence, according to Rule 33a, the area of the upper frame brace must be

$$\frac{254.47 \times 120}{2000} = 15.26+ \text{ square inches.}$$

In Fig. 271 we see that the suitable width of the frame for a locomotive with cylinders 18 inches in diameter should be 4 inches.

According to Rule 34a, the depth of the brace will be

$$\frac{15.26}{4} = 3.81 \text{ inches.}$$

Comparing this answer with the dimension given in Fig. 271, we find the two to agree very nearly. By the same rules the depths $B_2$ of all the upper frame braces in Figs. 272 to 279 have been obtained; and in order to avoid in these dimensions fractions of $\frac{1}{16}$ inch, the depths of the upper frame braces given in some of these figures are very nearly $\frac{1}{8}$ of an inch deeper than obtained by computation.

The part of the upper frame brace marked $B$, which forms the top of the pedestal jaw, is generally made $\frac{1}{4}$ inch deeper—sometimes more—than the depth of that part of the upper brace marked $B_2$; by so doing, the stiffness of the pedestal jaw is increased, and will to some extent prevent injury to it when the bolt $D$ or the pedestal cap $C$ is removed.

The portion of the upper frame brace marked $B_3$, between the rear pedestal and the rear end of frame, in Figs. 289, 291, 292, is not subjected to such severe vertical stress as some of the other portions of the brace, and therefore the depth of that part marked $B_3$ is generally made $\frac{1}{4}$ inch less than the depth found by Rule 34a.

**216.** The thickness, marked $o$, of the pedestal legs in Figs. 292, 295, and 280 is not always made alike by the different locomotive builders. Our practice has been to make the thickness $o$ for straight pedestal legs equal to the depth of the frame brace $B_2$, as found by Rule 34a, and for the tapered pedestal legs, the thickness $o$ in the center of the length of the leg was also made the same depth. These dimensions of the pedestal legs have always given good satisfaction, and we believe can be safely adopted.

**217.** It will be noticed that when the cast-iron thimble $T$ and the bolt $D$ at the bottom of the pedestal, Fig. 295, are used, we are compelled to place the lower frame brace $L$ nearer in line with the center of the driving axles than when pedestal caps are adopted, as shown in Fig. 292; and therefore the lower frame brace $L$ in Fig. 295 will be subjected to a greater pulling force than that in Fig. 292. Hence, for finding the depth of the lower frame brace $L$, we have the following rules:

Rule 35a.—When cast-iron thimbles at the bottom of the pedestal are used, as shown in Fig. 295, multiply the depth of the upper frame brace $B_2$, as found by Rule 34a, by the decimal .86; the product will be the depth of the lower frame brace $L$.

Rule 36.—When pedestal caps are used, as shown in Fig. 292, multiply the depth of the upper frame brace $B_2$, as found by Rule 34a, by the decimal .69; the product will be the depth of the lower frame brace $L$.

Example 66.—What should be the depth of the lower frame brace for a locomotive having cylinders 18 inches in diameter, when cast-iron thimbles are to be used at the bottom of the pedestal, and the maximum steam pressure is to be 120 pounds per square inch of piston?

We find in Fig. 271 that the depth of the upper frame brace $B_2$, suitable for this size cylinder and steam pressure, is 3¾ inches; hence we have, according to Rule 35a:

$$3.75 \times .86 = 3.22 \text{ inches for the depth of the lower frame brace } L.$$

Example 67.—What should be the depth of the lower frame brace for a locomotive having cylinders 11 inches in diameter, when pedestal caps are to be used at the bottom of the pedestal, and the maximum steam pressure is to be 120 pounds per square inch of piston?

In Fig. 278 we find that the suitable depth of the upper frame brace for this size cylinder and steam pressure is 2 inches; hence we have, according to Rule 36:

$$2 \times .69 = 1.38 \text{ inch for the depth of the lower frame brace } L.$$

Since the bottom surface of this brace is not planed along the entire length, that part of the same brace to which the pedestal cap is bolted is usually made ⅛ to ¼ inch deeper than the depth found by the rule. This extra depth of the lower frame brace will restore some of the strength lost by the holes drilled for the pedestal cap bolts.

### THICKNESS OF THE PEDESTAL CAP.

218. The thickness $C$ of central portion of the pedestal cap, Fig. 280, is usually made ¼ inch less than the depth of the lower frame brace $L$.

The projections $u$, Fig. 280, of the pedestal jaw generally extend into the cap ⅞ of an inch for the smaller engines, and 1 inch for the larger engines; and since the bottom of the projections $u$ are generally in line with the top of the central portion $C$ of the cap, it follows that the ends of the pedestal cap must be made that much thicker.

The projections $u$ are slightly tapered, so that they can be easily entered into the recesses in the cap, and when the cap is screwed fast into position they will firmly hold the ends of the pedestal jaw.

### NUMBER OF BOLTS IN PEDESTAL CAPS.

219. It is the general practice to secure the pedestal caps in small engines with two bolts, and in larger engines with four bolts. We believe that it is good practice to use two bolts for each pedestal cap in locomotives having cylinders 14 inches and less in diameter. In larger locomotives four bolts should be used for

each pedestal cap. The diameters of these bolts are given in Figs. 277, 278, 279, and 280.

Fig. 292 represents a frame for a consolidation engine, having cylinders 20 inches in diameter, with all the pedestal legs tapered. Formerly nearly all frames had pedestals of this kind, but lately a great number, if not the majority, of frames have pedestals in which one leg is straight, as shown in Fig. 294. It will be noticed that all these pedestals have caps. Fig. 295 represents a frame for the same class and size of engine in which cast-iron thimbles are used at the bottom of the pedestal jaw. We have frequently seen frames with this kind of pedestal in Mogul, ten-wheeled, and eight-wheeled engines, but have not seen them used in frames for consolidation engines. This frame has been designed for this book, and we believe it to possess advantages of its own for consolidation engines.

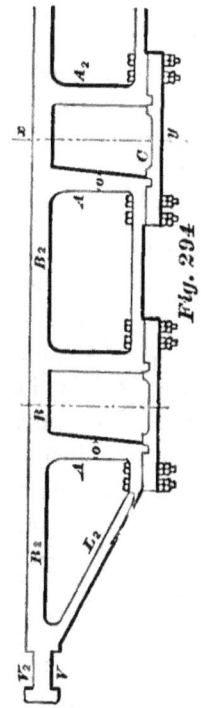

## BUILT-UP FRAMES.

220. Fig. 297 represents a frame which may be called the built-up frame, because, instead of it being forged in one piece, the same as all the frames previously shown, the lower brace $L$ is fitted between the pedestals and bolted to the same. This class of frames is looked upon with favor by a number of master-mechanics, and is used to a comparatively small extent. In our opinion the built-up frame is not as good as either one of the solid frames shown in Figs. 292 and 295; it lacks that simplicity

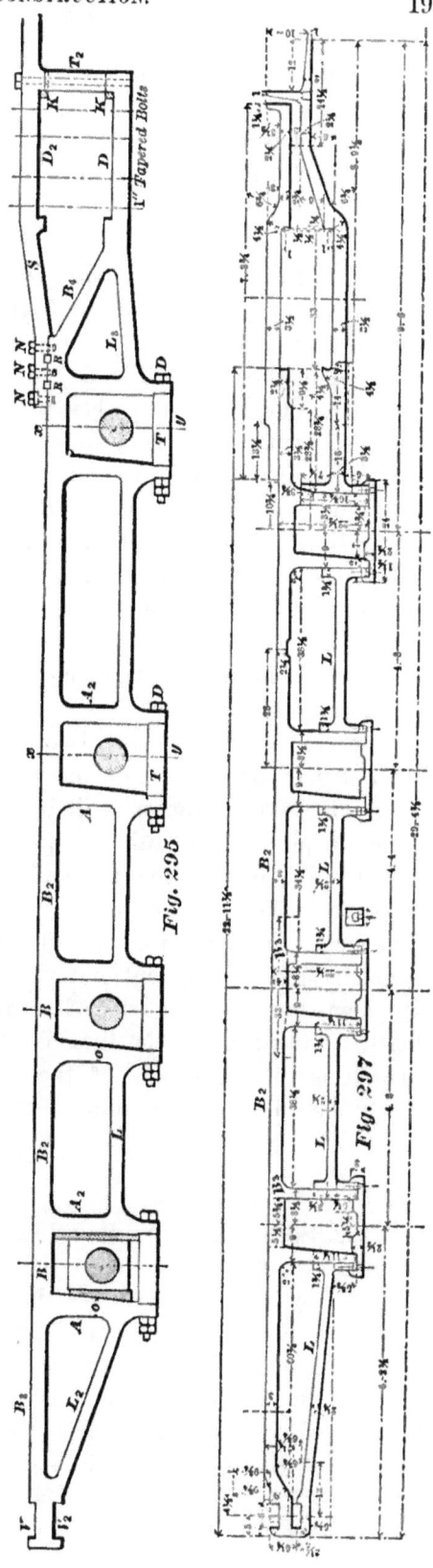

which is so desirable and essential in a locomotive. The frame represented in Fig. 297 is one of the frames used in a number of consolidation engines having cylinders 20 inches in diameter. We consider this frame to be too light for engines with cylinders of this size.

### LIGHT FRAMES.

221. It has been found that when the depth $B_2$ of the upper frame brace is the same throughout, as shown in Figs. 292 and 295, and when the brace is rather light for the forces which it has to resist, fracture will take place somewhere in the neighborhood marked $B_3$ in Fig. 297, near the pedestal, and seldom midway between the pedestals. Consequently, when it is necessary to make the frames as light as possible to comply with given conditions of a railroad, or when a load must be hauled with a locomotive of minimum weight, as on elevated railroads, the weight of the frames can be reduced by making the depth $B_2$ less at the center of that portion of the upper frame brace which connects any two pedestals without weakening the frame. When the depth of the brace midway between the pedestals is to be reduced, then make the cross-sectional area and the depth $B_3$ near the pedestal equal to that found according to Rules 33a and 34a; and for the center of the upper frame brace, reduce the depth so found in about the same proportion as shown in Fig. 297.

For ordinary locomotives in which a little extra weight is not objectionable, in fact where this extra weight is often desirable, it is always best to leave the depth of the upper frame brace the same throughout, and plane the under side of the brace. By so doing an advantage will be gained which at first sight may appear trivial, but which in private locomotive shops is appreciated. We allude to the bolts which are required for bolting the mechanism to the upper frame braces. These bolts are generally made before they are actually needed in the erecting shop, and according to dimensions obtained from the drawing room. If now the upper frame braces are equal in depth throughout and planed to correct dimensions, not only will confusion, and sometimes the necessity of throwing bolts away, or often altering the lengths of bolts, be avoided, but the time lost by the workmen waiting for bolts, and the delay in getting the engine out of the erecting shop, will be prevented, which otherwise would have amounted to quite an item of loss to the proprietors.

### SLAB FRAMES.

222. Sometimes it is desirable, and particularly so in narrow-gauge locomotives, to obtain more room between the frames for the fire-box of the boiler than can be obtained by leaving the frames the full width throughout. In cases of this kind the the width of the upper frame brace $B_2$ along the side of the fire-box is reduced, as shown in Fig. 299, and the depth of the brace $B_2$ increased, as shown in Fig. 298. In designing locomotives of this kind, precautions are taken to bring the bottom of fire-box within one inch from the top of the lower frame brace $L$, and never allow the bottom of the fire-box to extend below this brace; by so doing the lower frame brace is allowed to remain the full width of the frame, and room is also provided for the spring gear.

When the upper frame brace is to be made in the form of a slab, as shown, its cross-sectional area for any given diameter of cylinder should be equal to that of the brace suitable for the same diameter of cylinder, and found according to Rule 33a. The width of the slab is arbitrary, and is generally made as small as is practicable in the designer's judgment. The least thickness of slab that we have seen was 1¼ inches, used on a locomotive having cylinders 15 inches in diameter; the depth of the same brace was 7½ inches.

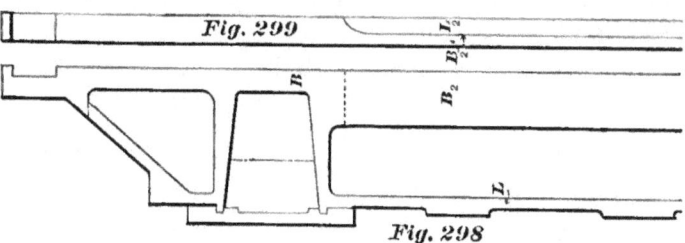

Fig. 299

Fig. 298

From the foregoing we can establish the following rule for finding the depth of the frame brace $B_2$ when it is to be of the slab form:

RULE 37.—First find the cross-sectional area of the frame brace according to Rule 33a, then divide this area by the given width of the slab; the quotient will be the depth of the upper frame brace or slab.

EXAMPLE 68.—What should be the depth of the frame brace $B_2$ whose width is 1¼ inches for a locomotive having cylinders 14 inches in diameter? The maximum steam pressure in the cylinder is to be 120 pounds per square inch.

The area of a piston 14 inches in diameter is 153.94 square inches. Hence, according to Rule 33a, the area of the upper frame brace will be

$$\frac{153.94 \times 120}{2000} = 9.23 + \text{ square inches.}$$

According to Rule 37, the depth of this brace will be

$$\frac{9.23}{1.25} = 7.38, \text{ say } 7\tfrac{3}{8} \text{ inches.}$$

## FRONT SPLICES FOR PASSENGER LOCOMOTIVES.

223. The general design of the front splice, sometimes called the front end of the frame, depends upon the class of locomotives in which it is to be used. Fig. 290 represents the front splice for an eight-wheeled passenger locomotive. The manner of fastening the front splice to the main frame depends on the kind of pedestals adopted. The manner of fastening the splice to the frame, or, we may call it, the connection between the two, when pedestals with cast-iron thimbles and bolts are used, is shown in Fig. 289. In this connection the keys $M\,M$ are usually placed in a position which will necessitate the drilling out a small portion of the keys so as to allow the bolts $N\,N$ to pass through the frame; this will prevent the keys $M\,M$ from working out of position.

In Fig. 291 is seen the manner of fastening the splice to frame when pedestals with wrought-iron caps are used. In this connection the bolts $M\,M$ which fasten the T-end of the splice to the pedestal leg are liable to give trouble or break; to prevent this, great care must be taken in determining the diameters of these bolts, and to make them as large in diameter as possible without impairing the strength of the pedestal leg. To determine the diameter of these bolts, we have the following rule, which is based upon observation:

RULE 38.—Multiply the width of the frame in inches by the decimal .32; the product will be the diameter of the bolt in inches for fastening the T-end of splice to pedestal leg.

EXAMPLE 69.—What should be the diameter of the bolts for fastening the T-end of splice to pedestal leg? The width of frame is 4 inches.

$$4 \times .32 = 1.28, \text{ say } 1\tfrac{1}{4} \text{ inches.}$$

These bolts have usually conical heads, and countersunk into the pedestal leg.

In the connection of splice to frame, it is also of great importance to have a sufficient number of bolts $N\,N$ to hold the end of the frame to splice. The diameter of these bolts should be equal to about $\tfrac{1}{4}$ of the width of the frame, and the shearing stress should not exceed 3,000 pounds per square inch. Assuming as before, for the sake of simplicity, that the total pulling force is equal to the total steam pressure on the piston, we can use, for determining the number of bolts through frame and splice, the following rule:

RULE 39.—Divide the total steam pressure on the piston in pounds by 6,000; the quotient will be the total cross-sectional area of all the bolts; divide this quotient or total cross-sectional area by the cross-sectional area of one bolt; the quotient will be the number of bolts required through the end of frame and splice.

NOTE.—The reason for dividing the total steam pressure on piston by 6,000 instead of 3,000 is, that some of these bolts, frequently all, are subjected to a double shear; that is to say, they must be sheared off in two places before the frames can be pulled apart.

EXAMPLE 70.—What should be the number of bolts marked $N\,N$ in Fig. 289, passing through the end of frame and splice, for a locomotive having cylinders 18 inches in diameter, maximum steam pressure in cylinder 120 pounds per square inch? The diameter of each bolt to be equal to $\tfrac{1}{4}$ the width of the frame.

In Fig. 271 we see that the suitable width of frame for a locomotive having cylinders 18 inches in diameter is 4 inches; hence the diameter of each bolt must be 1 inch. The cross-sectional area of a bolt 1 inch in diameter is .7854 of a square inch.

The area of a piston 18 inches in diameter is 254.47 square inches; hence, according to Rule 39, we have, $\dfrac{254.47 \times 120}{6000} = 5.089$ square inches = total cross-sectional area of all the bolts; and $\dfrac{5.089}{.7854} = 6.4+$ say $7 =$ the number of bolts required.

If the connection of frame and splice is similar to that shown in Fig. 289, and the number of bolts found according to Rule 39, and also assuming that the total pulling force is equal to total steam pressure on the piston, the shearing stress per square inch of cross-sectional area of the bolts will appear to be greater than 3,000 pounds, because four of the bolts $N\,N$ are subjected to a shear in one place only; but the keys $M\,M$ will reduce the shearing stress to less than 3,000 pounds per square inch on the bolts, so that the foregoing rule can be safely applied in designs of this kind.

EXAMPLE 71.—What should be the number of bolts $N\,N$, Fig. 291, passing through the end of the frame and splice for a locomotive having cylinders 14 inches in diameter, the diameter of each bolt is to be equal to ¼ of the width of the frame? The maximum steam pressure in cylinder is 120 pounds per square inch.

In Fig. 275 we see that the suitable width of frame for a cylinder 14 inches in diameter is $3\frac{3}{4}$ inches, consequently the diameter of each bolt $N\ N$ must be $\frac{3\frac{3}{4}}{4} = \frac{15}{16}$ inch. The area of a piston 14 inches in diameter is 153.94 square inches; hence, according to Rule 39, we have,

$$\frac{153.94 \times 120}{6000} = 3.0788 \text{ square inches for the total cross-sectional area of all the bolts.}$$

The area of a bolt $\frac{15}{16}$ inch in diameter is equal to .69 of a square inch, and

$$\frac{3.0788}{.69} = 4.4+ \text{ say 5 bolts.}$$

224. The recess marked $R$, Fig. 290, near the front end of the frame splice, is for the purpose of receiving the cylinder saddle, which generally butts against the rear end of the recess. The cylinder saddle is bolted to the front splice, as shown in Fig. 12, page 21, by bolts running in a horizontal direction through the flange of saddle and splice, and also by the vertical bolts $B$. In order to provide further security and prevent the cylinder from moving in a longitudinal direction—that is, the direction in which acts the greatest force which the cylinders have to resist—a key $D$ is driven between the front face of the cylinder saddle and end of recess. Occasionally we find master-mechanics using two keys in each frame, one at the front face of saddle and another one at the rear face. We prefer to use only one key at the front; and believe this to be the best practice, because two frames (sometimes four) are usually slotted at one time, and consequently the distances in the frames between the pedestals and recesses will be exactly alike; the facing strips on the cylinder saddles are planed in line and square with the axis of cylinders, and therefore by placing the cylinder saddle directly against the rear ends of the recesses, the cylinders are brought in the true position with less labor than when two keys are used in each frame.

225. In passenger engines, the lifting-shaft bearing and rocker-box, besides other mechanism, are bolted to the front splice, consequently it is subjected to the action of vertical forces of considerable magnitude, and it has also to resist the pulling force due to the pressure on one piston; therefore in this class of locomotives it is generally made somewhat deeper than the upper frame brace $B_2$ in Fig. 289, but uniformity in the proportion of these depths does not exist. As a result of observation on this point, we believe that the following rule will give a depth for the front splice which will agree with good modern practice.

Rule 40.—Multiply the depth of the upper frame brace $B_2$, Fig. 289, by 1.15; the product will be the depth of the front splice.

According to this rule the depth of the front splice is 15 per cent. deeper than that of the upper frame brace.

Note.—When the maximum steam pressure on the piston is 120 pounds per square inch, then take the depth of the upper frame brace $B_2$ from a pedestal, suitable for the given diameter of cylinder, shown in the group Figs. 271 to 279.

When the maximum pressure is more or less than 120 pounds per square inch of piston, then find the depth of the upper frame brace $B_2$ by Rules 33a and 34a.

EXAMPLE 71a.—What should be the depth of the front splice for a locomotive having cylinders 18 inches in diameter? Maximum steam pressure on pistons is 120 pounds per square inch.

In Fig. 271 we see that the depth of the upper frame brace $B_2$ for an 18-inch cylinder is $3\frac{3}{4}$ inches; hence, according to Rule 40, we have,

$$3.75 \times 1.15 = 4.3125 \text{ inches,}$$

which is the depth of the front splice. The depth of the front splice at the recess should be equal to the depth of that portion of the upper frame brace which is marked $B_2$ (see Fig. 289), and the depth of the splice from the cylinders to the bumpers should be equal to the depth $B_3$.

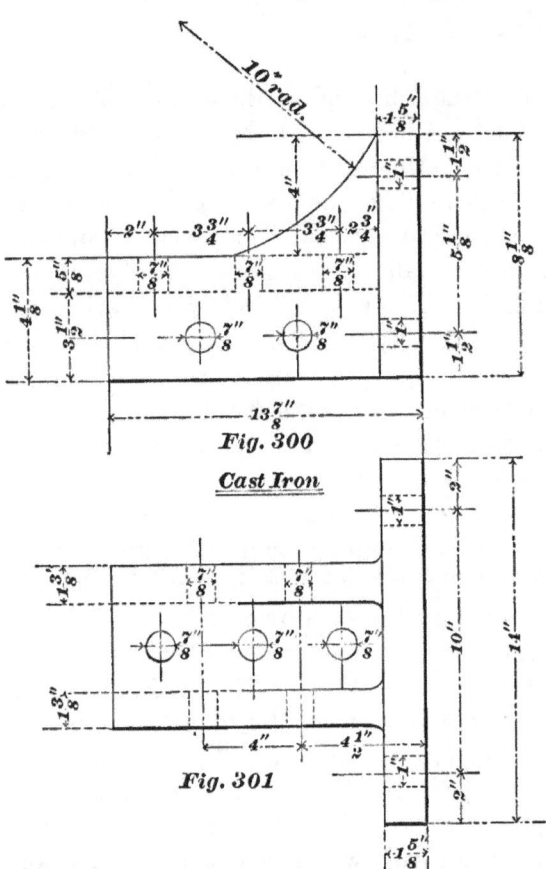

Fig. 300
Cast Iron

Fig. 301

226. The front end $P$ of the splice is often turned down, forming an offset, as shown in Fig. 290. To this offset is bolted the bumper, usually made of wood. In some locomotives the offset at $P$ is in an upward direction, so as to bring the bumper to a suitable height above the rails for convenience in coupling to the cars.

In cases of accidents or collision, the front end $P$ of the splice is very liable to be broken off or otherwise injured, and to repair the damage the whole splice will have to be taken off. To obviate this difficulty and thus save considerable time and labor, many master-mechanics now make the splice perfectly straight at the front end, and in place of the offset $P$ use a casting, of which an elevation and plan are shown in Figs. 300 and 301. This casting here shown is suitable for locomotives having cylinders 17 inches in diameter; for smaller engines the dimensions may be somewhat decreased, and for larger ones they should be increased.

227. Figs. 293 and 296 represent the front splices for consolidation engines, and a similar form of splice is also often used for Mogul engines. These splices pass over the top of cylinder saddle, and are fastened by bolts $D\,D$, Figs. 292 and 295, passing through the front splice, cylinder saddle, and front end of main frame; they are also fastened to the main frame by the bolts $N\,N$, and further secured in position by the keys $R\,R$, and also by the keys $K\,K$ between the cylinder saddle and end of recess in the splice.

## DEPTH OF FRAME SPLICES FOR MOGUL AND CONSOLIDATION ENGINES.

228. When the form of the splice is like that shown in Fig. 295, the depth of that part of the splice marked $S$ between the main frame and saddle, and also that portion of the splice which lies on top of cylinder saddle, should be equal to that of the upper frame brace marked $B_2$. The depth of the splice in front of the cylinder saddle can be made equal to that of the upper frame brace which is marked $B_3$.

## FRONT SPLICE AND MAIN FRAME FORGED IN ONE PIECE.

229. Sometimes the front splice and main frame are forged in one piece, as shown in Fig. 302. This we consider to be very bad practice, because, should the front end

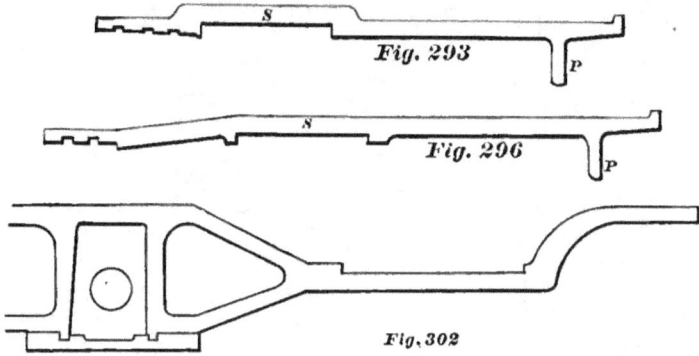

be injured, the whole frame will have to be taken down to repair the damage, which will involve a great amount of unnecessary labor and expense.

## FRAME BOLTS.

230. The bolts which are used for bolting the different parts of the engine to the frames are, by the majority of locomotive builders, made straight, accurately turned to fit reamed holes, and driven home. Other builders make these bolts tapered, generally $\frac{1}{8}$ inch to the foot—that is, in the length of one foot the diameter is increased $\frac{1}{8}$ inch—and turn them to such dimensions as will allow the bolts to enter the reamed holes to within $\frac{1}{4}$ of an inch from the head of the bolt; through this distance of $\frac{1}{4}$ inch the bolts are driven home. We are inclined to believe that the use of tapered bolts is the best practice, as when these bolts become slack, then by turning a small amount off the under side of head, the bolts can again be driven tightly into the holes. We also believe that tapered bolts will hold the parts more firmly together than straight bolts. Bolts which are very long, as those marked $D\ D$ in Figs. 292 and 295, should always be tapered, which we believe to be the best practice.

## SPRING SADDLES.

231. Fig. 303 represents the pedestal $P$, with driving axle box $B$, wedges $W\ W_2$, and spring saddle $S$ in position. A portion of the spring $I$ and also the spring strap $H$ are shown. Fig. 304 represents a vertical section through the centers of the same

mechanism. Spring saddles of the form here shown are made of cast-iron, and are suitable for locomotives having cylinders larger than 12 inches in diameter. The base *E E* of these saddles is made as wide as the space between the wedges will permit, leaving a sufficient amount of metal around the recesses in top of the driving box in which the base of the saddle is placed. Part of the metal at *F*, in the base *E E* of the

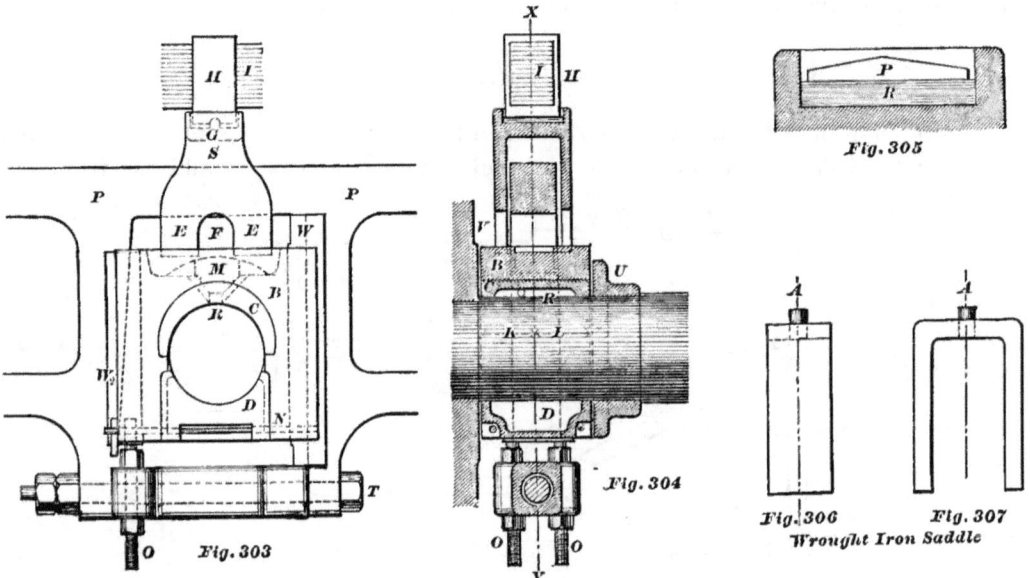

saddle, is cut out, thereby giving access for oiling the axle journal. A saddle with this kind of base will have a firmer support than, and is not so liable to upset, as a saddle with a narrow base, similar in form to that shown in Fig. 306.

The width of the spring saddle is made to allow at least ¼ inch clearance at each side of the frame, as shown in Fig. 304. A recess is cast in the top of the saddle to receive the spring strap *H*. At the center, in the bottom of the recess, a fulcrum *G* is cast to fit into a groove cut in the bottom of the spring strap *H*, the whole arrangement being such as will allow the spring *I* to rock through a short distance.

232. Some locomotive builders do not cast the fulcrum *G* in the recess, but make the bottom of it perfectly flat, as shown in Fig. 305. In this recess a piece of rubber *R* is placed, with a wrought-iron plate *P* on top. This plate is about ¼ inch thicker in the center than at the ends, so that when the spring strap (in this case without a groove cut in it) is placed on top of the plate, the spring can rock the required amount. In this kind of spring saddle the recess should always be deep enough to allow the spring strap to enter it at least ¼ inch, to prevent the spring from moving out of position.

233. Sometimes the spring saddles are made of wrought-iron, their form being similar to that of the cast-iron ones, with the exception of the recess, which is left off. The tops are straight, and a pin *A*, as shown in Fig. 306, screwed into the top. This pin is made to fit loosely in a hole in the bottom of the spring strap, and prevents the spring from moving out of position. The bottom of the strap is made convex, to allow the spring to rock.

Occasionally, when wrought-iron spring saddles are used, a roller is inserted between the saddle and strap, lying in suitable grooves cut into both. The roller has also collars at each end, to prevent the spring from slipping sideways.

For locomotives having cylinders 12 inches in diameter and less, the straps are made of wrought-iron, of a form as shown in Figs. 306 and 307, which need no further explanation.

### DRIVING AXLE BOXES.

234. The play or clearance between the axle box and hub of driving wheel $V$, Fig. 304, is generally $\frac{1}{16}$ inch, and the clearance between the axle box and collar $U$ is equal to the same amount, giving the driving axle a total amount of $\frac{1}{8}$ inch play or movement in the direction of its length.

Occasionally we find driving axle boxes in which the distance $K$ (Fig. 304), that is, the distance from the center line $X Y$ to the outside face of box, is less than the distance $L$ from the center line $X Y$ to the inner face of box, the difference generally

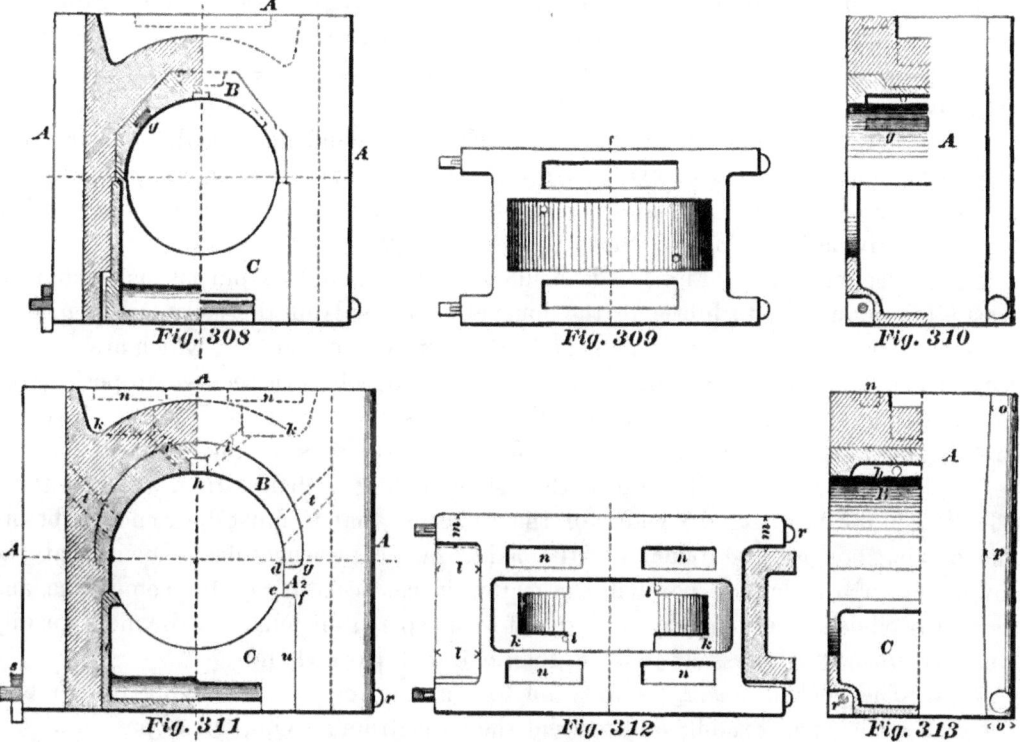

being $\frac{1}{8}$ to $\frac{3}{16}$ inch. The object of this difference is for the purpose of turning the axle box around to take up the wear between it and the face of wheel, when that becomes excessive.

235. Driving axle boxes, or which, for the sake of brevity, are often called driving boxes, consist essentially of three parts, namely, the casting marked $A A$ in Fig. 308, an oil cellar $C$, and the brass $B$. The driving boxes may be divided into two classes, the form of the brass $B$ being the distinguishing feature.

Figs. 308, 309, 310 represent different views of one class of driving boxes, in which the octagonal form of brasses are used, and Figs. 311, 312, 313 represent the other class of driving boxes, in which the cylindrical form of brasses are used.

Occasionally we find the casting $A\ A$ made of brass; in such cases a separate brass bearing is not used; but boxes of this kind are seldom adopted, and therefore we will confine our attention to that class of boxes which are called cast-iron driving boxes.

In proportioning these boxes great care must be taken to have the depth $g\ f$ of the lug $A_2$, Fig. 311, sufficiently great so that it cannot be broken off by pressing the brass into the box, or the strength of the lug $A_2$ impaired, causing it to break off when the engine is running. In large driving boxes the depth $g\ f$ should be at least $1\frac{1}{4}$ inches.

In a great number of locomotives the inner faces of the flanges $m\ m$, Fig. 312, are planed parallel to each other, and in a small number of engines the inner surfaces of these flanges are planed to a form, as shown in Fig. 313; that is, when planed the flanges are about $\frac{1}{16}$ inch thicker in the center $p$ than at the ends $o\ o$. The object of this form of driving-box flange is to prevent the same from binding against the pedestal wedge, and at the same time give the box a greater freedom to adjust itself to the journal when one end of the axle stands higher than the other end, caused by running over an uneven track.

The width $l\ l$ of the flanges, Fig. 312, should be sufficient to allow their lower ends, when the box is in the lowest position in the pedestal, to cover the pedestal legs. By this arrangement the lateral stress on the flanges of the wedges will be less than when the driving-box flanges do not reach the pedestal legs.

236. The oil cellar $C$, Fig. 311, is made of cast-iron, and its purpose is to hold the waste, tallow, and oil to lubricate the journal. The ends of the cellar are planed to fit accurately in the box; and it is held in the box by two bolts $r\ r$, which are roughly turned and fit in the holes somewhat loosely; these bolts are secured in position by means of the split keys $s$. In many driving boxes the end surfaces $u\ u$ of the cellar are parallel to each other; in others we find these surfaces inclined towards the center, making the width at the top of the cellar about $\frac{1}{8}$ inch less than at the bottom. The reason for tapering the width of the cellar is, that it must be removed before the driving box can be taken off the axle; but experience has shown that the lower ends of the driving box will close after it has been in use for some time, and clasp the oil cellar very tightly, and therefore a tapered oil cellar can be more readily removed when it is necessary to do so than one with parallel ends.

237. The pockets $n\ n$, Figs. 311 and 312, in the top of the driving box, receive the ends of the spring saddle and prevent the latter from moving out of position.

The recesses $k\ k$ are for the purpose of leading all the oil which may be poured on the top of the box into the oil holes $i\ i$.

### DRIVING-BOX BRASSES.

238. There are some objections to the use of octagonal brasses; for instance, they require a considerable amount of labor to fit them in the box as accurately as they should be; and again, since the ends of these brasses are not firmly secured in the box, they are liable to close, press against the axle journal, and consequently become

hot in a very short time, and for these reasons the octagonal form of brass is not extensively used.

The cylindrical form of brass shown in Fig. 311 gives better satisfaction, and is the form adopted in a large majority of locomotives. Its outer surface is accurately turned, the casting $A\ A$ is slotted, and the brass pressed in with a pressure of about five to seven tons. The edge $d$ of all driving-box brasses generally extends $\frac{1}{2}$ to $\frac{3}{4}$ inch below the center of the axle; and the edge $g$ generally extends $\frac{1}{8}$ inch below the edge $d$; the object of this form is to hold the ends securely in position, so as to prevent them from closing, and thereby avoid hot journals. Even when these brasses are accurately fitted and pressed in the box very tightly, they will in time become loose, and will have to be replaced. In order to make these brasses remain tight in the box for a greater period of time, some master-mechanics will drive two brass pins $t\ t$, about $\frac{3}{4}$ inch in diameter, through each side of the box and brass. These pins are, for obvious reasons, driven at an angle with the sides of the box, as shown in Fig. 311. Another advantage gained by these pins is that, when collars on the driving axle are not used, as is sometimes the case, the brasses, when they have become loose, cannot slip out of the box.

In the top of the brass is cast an oil groove $h$, about $\frac{3}{4}$ inch square. This groove extends to within 1 inch from the ends of the brass. The oil is led into this groove by two oil holes $i\ i$, each about $\frac{3}{4}$ inch in diameter.

Babbitt metal is used in many driving-box brasses. Grooves, about $\frac{3}{4}$ to 1 inch in width, and extending sometimes the whole length of the brass, and at other times to about $\frac{3}{4}$ inch from the end of the same, are cast into and near the top of the brass, as indicated by $g\ g$ in Figs. 308 and 310.

We believe that the Babbitt metal in driving-box brasses is worse than useless, because the waste in the oil cellars will accomplish the same purpose for which Babbitt metal is intended, namely, to prevent the dust from spreading around the axle journal. Besides, in our experience, we have found that, since the pressure of the brass against the journal is very great and acting constantly, and since the Babbitt metal will collect and hold the dust, the axle journal will wear comparatively very rapidly, and for these reasons the brass is better without it.

## PROPORTIONS OF DRIVING AXLE BOXES.

239. In designing a locomotive driving box we must not lose sight of the fact that all the weight which is placed upon it must be supported by the upper part of the axle journal. Indeed, herein lies a great difference between a locomotive driving box and an ordinary pillow block similar to those used in many stationary engines. In the former the pressure is against the upper part of the box, and consequently the oil which is fed through the oil holes in the top of the box will be aided to flow away from the elements of contact. In the ordinary pillow block the pressure is against its lower part, and if the pressure is not sufficiently intense to force out the lubricant from between the surfaces, the oil will be aided to some extent to flow towards the element of contact.

It must also be remembered that the vertical pressure on a locomotive axle journal is almost constant, which will in nowise assist in the lubrication of the journal. In pillow blocks of stationary engines, although the pressure is generally towards the bottom of the block, it will shift a little from one side of the pillow block to the other as the piston changes the direction of its motion, and thereby assist in the lubrication of the journal.

These considerations lead us to conclude that locomotive axle journals are more liable to become hot than the main journals of stationary engines. To prevent as much as possible hot axle journals, we must proportion them in a manner which will allow upon them a comparatively low pressure per square inch. The pressure on any journal is estimated by the pressure per square inch of its projected area. By the projected area is meant the area of a rectangle whose length and breadth are respectively equal to the length and diameter of the journal.

240. The pressure on an axle due to the weight of the engine is not the only pressure which the axle journal has to resist; it has also to resist a pressure due to the load which the engine has to haul. The latter pressure is not a constant quantity, but the ratio between the pressure due to the weight of the engine and that due to the maximum load is about the same in all engines; and therefore, for the sake of simplicity, we may leave the pressure due to load out of the question, and proportion the journal according to the pressure due to the weight of the engine.

Close observation and experience in modern locomotive construction lead us to believe that a pressure of about 160 and not over 175 pounds per square inch of projected area, due to the weight of the engine, agrees with the best modern practice and may be adopted; the former figure, namely, 160 pounds per square inch, should be preferred; it will give the best results.

241. From the foregoing it will be seen that, in order to design the driving box, we must first determine the total weight which the driving axle journals will have to support.

The weight on the driving axle journals for new locomotives can generally be estimated only approximately, because the design is not sufficiently advanced to obtain the exact weights of the different parts of the engine and running gear; yet experience will enable us to estimate this weight close enough for all practical purposes. In Art. 24, tables will be found which give the weights on drivers in the various classes of locomotives. Table 5 contains the weights on drivers in eight-wheeled passenger engines, to which we shall refer here. Now, in order to determine the weight which the driving axle journals in eight-wheeled passenger engines will have to support, we must subtract the sum of the weights of the wheel centers, tires, axles, side rod, etc., in fact, the weight of all pieces which are supported directly by the track, from the total weight on drivers given in Table 5; one-fourth of the remainder will be the weight on each journal.

If the design of the engine is not sufficiently advanced to obtain the accurate weights of the driving wheels, axles, side rods, etc., we can generally estimate the sum of these weights by assuming them to be from $\frac{1}{5}$ to $\frac{1}{4}$ of the total weight on the drivers. Thus, let it be required to find the weight on the driving axle journals for an eight-wheeled passenger engine having cylinders 16 inches in diameter. In Table 5 we find the total weight on the drivers for a locomotive of this size to be 47,665 pounds. One-

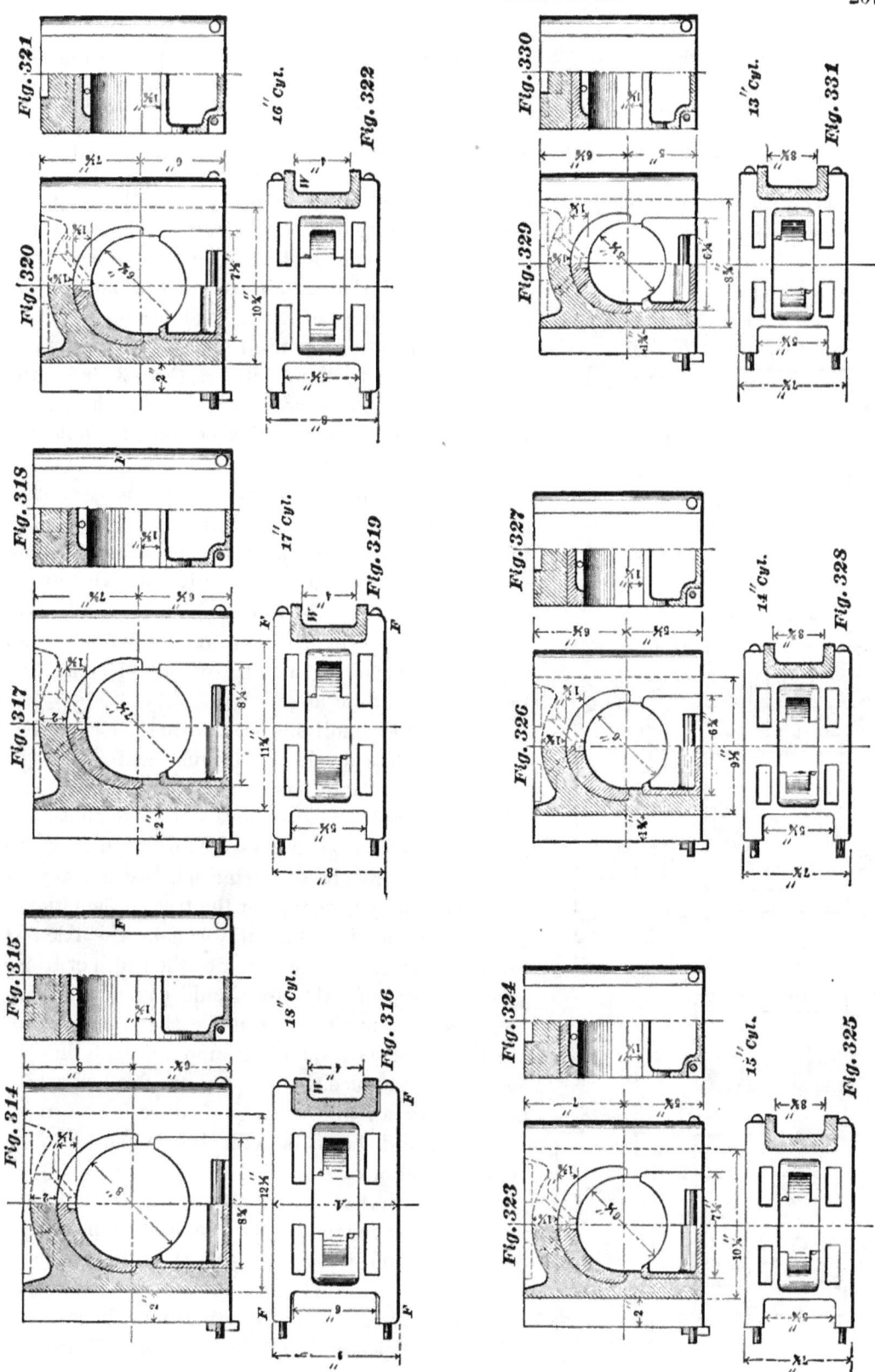

fourth of this weight will be the estimated sum of the weights of the parts supported directly by the track. Hence, $47665 - \dfrac{47665}{4} = 35749$ pounds, which is the total weight supported by all the driving axle journals; and $\dfrac{35749}{4} = 8937$ pounds supported by each driving axle journal; or, we may say that the pressure on the projected area of the journal is 8,937 pounds; and since the pressure per square inch is to be about 160 pounds and not exceed 175 pounds, we must proportion the diameter and length of the journal accordingly. By the term "length of journal" we mean that length which is equal to the width $A$ (Fig. 316) of the driving box, and neglecting the short length of journal required for the play between the axle box and hub of driving wheel.

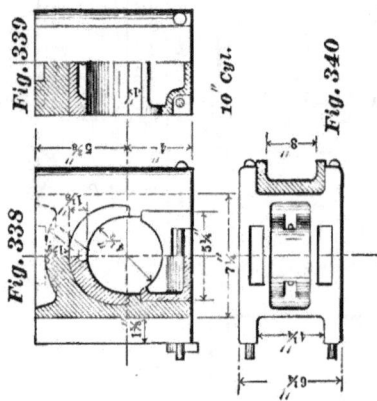

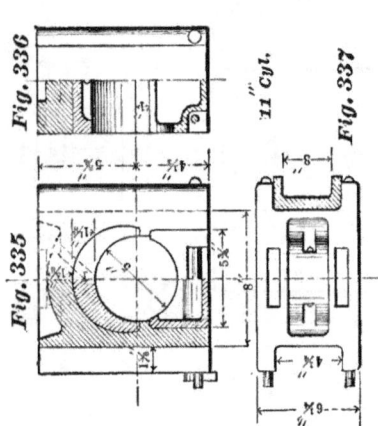

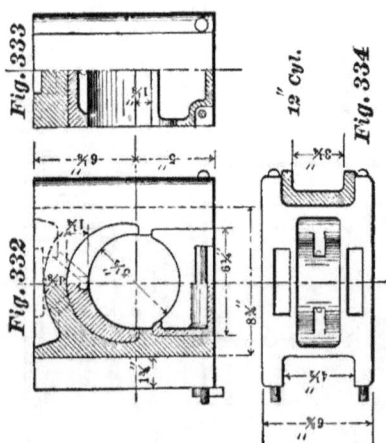

242. When the driving axle is made large enough to prevent heating, and, to fulfill conditions peculiar to the locomotive, also properly fitted into the hub of the wheel, we have generally an axle strong enough to resist all the forces which may act upon it, and therefore in determining the diameter and length of journal we may throw out of consideration the strength of an axle.

One of the conditions peculiar to the locomotive, and to which a driving axle must conform, is the width $A$ of the axle box (Fig. 316), which is short when compared with the lengths of pillow blocks in stationary or marine engines. This width $A$ of the axle box is limited by the distance between the cylinders and also by the gauge of the track; the latter is established, and therefore if we make the axle box too wide, then, since the center of the width of frame and the center of axle box should coincide, or very nearly so, we must either move the frames closer together to a corresponding amount, and thus be compelled to reduce the width of the fire-box, which is decidedly an objectionable feature, or we must increase the distance between the cylinders, which is also objectionable.

The width $A$ of the axle box should be only sufficient to allow for the proper thickness of the flanges on the box and wedges to give these the requisite strength.

Figs. 314 to 340 represent driving boxes suitable for the pedestals shown in Figs. 271 to 279, and are designed for eight-wheeled passenger locomotives of various sizes, including those having cylinders 10 inches in diameter, and up to 18 inches in diameter. The given dimensions of these boxes agree with the average modern locomotive practice. From these illustrations we can readily obtain the width of the boxes, and all the main dimensions. The part shown in section at the right-hand side of all the plans of the boxes, such as Figs. 316, 319, 322, etc., and marked $W$ in some of them, represent a section of the long wedge; the distance between the flanges of the wedges is the thickness of the frame, and this thickness subtracted from the distance between the flanges of the boxes and divided by two will give the thickness of each flange on the wedge.

243. Having established the width of the driving boxes, the diameter of the journal is easily obtained by the following rule:

RULE 41.—Divide the weight on the journal by 160; the product will be the number of square inches in the projected area; divide this quotient by the width $A$ (Figs. 316 to 340) of the driving box in inches; the quotient will be the diameter of the journal in inches.

EXAMPLE 72.—What should be the diameter of a driving axle journal for an eight-wheeled passenger engine having cylinders 16 inches in diameter?

We have already seen in Art. 241 that the total pressure on the projected area of one driving axle journal for this class and size of engine is 8,937 pounds. In Fig. 322 we find that the width of box should be 8 inches. Hence to find the diameter we have, according to Rule 41, $\frac{8937}{160} = 55.8$, which is the number of square inches in the projected area, and $\frac{55.8}{8} = 6.97$ inches = diameter of the journal. If we make the diameter of this axle equal to that given in Fig. 320, namely, $6\frac{3}{4}$ inches, the pressure per square inch on the projected area will be 165.5 pounds, providing our estimated weight of wheels, tires, axles, etc., is exactly correct.

EXAMPLE 73.—Find the diameter of a driving axle suitable for an eight-wheeled passenger engine whose cylinders are 12 inches in diameter.

In Table 5 we find the total weight on the drivers to be 29,700 pounds. Allowing $\frac{1}{5}$ of the total weight on the drivers for the mechanism whose weight is not supported by the journals, we have, $29700 - \frac{29700}{5} = 23760$ pounds pressure on all the four journals and $\frac{23760}{4} = 5940$ pounds pressure on the projected area of each journal. Again, $\frac{5940}{160} = 37.12$ square inches in each projected area. In Fig. 334 we find that for a passenger locomotive with cylinders 12 inches in diameter, the width of the driving box should be $6\frac{3}{4}$ inches, and consequently the diameter of the journal should be $\frac{37.12}{6.75} = 5.49$ inches. These dimensions agree with those given in the illustrations.

From the foregoing it will be seen that in determining the dimensions of a locomotive driving axle journal, we have followed the law of simple proportionality of friction to pressure. In relation to this law, Prof. W. J. M. Rankine says: The law of simple proportionality of friction to pressure is only true for dry surfaces, when the pressure is not sufficiently intense to indent or grind the surfaces; and for greased surfaces, when the pressure is not sufficiently intense to force out the unguent from between the surfaces where it is held by capillary attraction. If the proper limit of intensity of pressure be exceeded, the friction increases more rapidly than in the simple ratio of the pressure. That limit diminishes as the velocity of rubbing increases, according to some law not yet exactly determined. The following are some of its values, deduced from experience:

RAILWAY CARRIAGE AXLES.

|  | Limit of pressure per square inch. |
|---|---|
| Velocity of rubbing surface, 1 foot per second | 392 |
| " " " 2½ feet " " | 224 |
| " " " 5 " " " | 140 |

The limit of the pressure on journals given by Professor Rankine is exceeded on the journals proportioned by the foregoing rules, and such as are used in modern locomotives, yet these journals are giving good results, and seem to be suitable for the purpose intended. But if the average speed of the present locomotive is to be increased, so that the velocity of the circumference of the journal exceeds 9 feet per second, the lengths of these journals may also have to be increased, so as to reduce the pressure per square inch to considerably less than 160 pounds, even if we are compelled to increase the distance between the cylinders.

244. The driving boxes shown in Figs. 314 to 340 were proportioned to suit one particular class of locomotives, namely, eight-wheeled passenger engines. From our remarks in Art. 243 it will be seen that the size of a box for a passenger engine depends upon the weight on the drivers; and since the cylinders are proportioned in accordance with the weight on the drivers, we may assume and say, as our illustrations indicate, that the size of a box depends upon the diameter of the cylinder used. In Mogul, ten-wheeled, and consolidation engines the diameter of cylinder is also proportioned in accordance with the weight on drivers; but under any one of these engines there are more driving wheels than under an eight-wheeled passenger engine, and consequently the size of the axle box suitable for an eight-wheeled passenger engine, with cylinders of given diameter, may or may not be suitable for a Mogul, ten-wheeled, or consolidation engine having cylinders whose dimensions are equal to those of the cylinders in the passenger engine. It therefore remains for us to consider the conditions which influence the size of the journal in these engines, thereby enabling us to determine its dimensions and select the proper size of driving box, from the number shown in Figs. 314 to 340. In Mogul, ten-wheeled, and consolidation engines, as well as in passenger engines, the weight on the journals must be distributed in such a manner as to prevent heating; and the rules given for finding the dimensions of the driving axle journal for a passenger engine may also, with a slight change, namely, less pressure per square inch on the projected area of the journal, be used for computing the dimensions of driving axle journals in the other classes of engines.

From the foregoing we perceive that in all locomotives the driving axle journals are proportioned to the pressure due to the weight on the driving wheels, and when this is correctly done, sufficient allowance will then have been made for the pressure due to the load which the engine has to haul; we therefore leave the load to be hauled out of consideration in the calculations. In determining the sizes of journals for Mogul, ten-wheeled, and consolidation engines, we must not lose sight of the fact that, in these classes of engines, particularly in Mogul and consolidation locomotives, the driving wheels are smaller in diameter than those in eight-wheeled passenger engines, and consequently the axles are brought closer to the track and exposed more to the dust, thereby raising conditions favorable for cutting the journals. Again, it often happens that, on the road, the counterbalance weights are in the way of oiling the journals, and therefore, if the time is limited, it may happen that the oiling of some of the journals will be neglected. These classes of locomotives are also more or less looked upon as freight engines, and do not always receive the same care as bestowed upon passenger engines. For these reasons it is always advisable to make the journals for freight engines comparatively large in diameter. We therefore recommend that their driving axle journals shall be so proportioned as not to allow more than 160 pounds per square inch on the projected area of the journal; in fact, 160 pounds should be the limit, instead of 175 pounds, as given for passenger engines, and when the design or other given conditions will allow, the pressure per square inch should be even less than 160 pounds.

The dimensions of driving axle journals in the following tables are recommended. The pressure per square inch on the projected area of these journals will be less than 160 pounds, when the weight of the engines correspond to the weights given in Tables 5, 6, 7, and 8:

TABLE 17.

DIMENSIONS OF DRIVING AXLE JOURNALS FOR MOGUL ENGINES.

| Diameter of Cylinders. | Diameter of Journals. | Length of Journals. |
|---|---|---|
| 11 inches. | 5 inches. | 6¼ inches. |
| 12 " | 5½ " | 6¾ " |
| 13 " | 5½ " | 7¾ " |
| 14 " | 6 " | 7¾ " |
| 15 " | 6½ " | 7¾ " |
| 16 " | 6¾ " | 8 " |
| 17 " | 6¾ " | 8 " |
| 18 " | 7½ " | 8 " |
| 19 " | 8 " | 9 " |

TABLE 18.

DIMENSIONS OF DRIVING AXLE JOURNALS FOR TEN-WHEELED LOCOMOTIVES.

| Diameter of Cylinders. | Diameter of Journals. | Length of Journals. |
|---|---|---|
| 12 inches. | 5 inches. | 6¼ inches. |
| 13 " | 5½ " | 6¾ " |
| 14 " | 6 " | 7¾ " |
| 15 " | 6 " | 7¾ " |
| 16 " | 6½ " | 7¾ " |
| 17 " | 6¾ " | 8 " |
| 18 " | 7½ " | 8 " |
| 19 " | 8 " | 9 " |

## TABLE 19.

DIMENSIONS OF DRIVING AXLE JOURNALS FOR CONSOLIDATION LOCOMOTIVES.

| Diameter of Cylinders. | Diameter of Journals. | Length of Journals. |
|---|---|---|
| 14 inches. | 5 inches. | 6¼ inches. |
| 15 " | 5½ " | 7½ " |
| 20 " | 7½ " | 8 " |
| 24 " | 8 " | 9 " |

245. Although there are many locomotives with cylinders of the same diameters as given in these tables running with smaller journals, yet the dimensions given in the tables agree with the average sizes of journals in modern locomotives.

For the sake of comparison, we append Table 20, in which are given the dimensions of a few driving axle journals in modern locomotives doing excellent service:

## TABLE 20.

| Class of Locomotive. | Dimensions of Cylinders. | Diameter of Driving Axle Journal. | Diameter of Main Driving Axle Journal. | Length of Journals. |
|---|---|---|---|---|
| Eight-wheeled Passenger...... | 17″ × 24″ | 7¾ inches. | 7¾ inches. | 8 inches. |
| " " " ...... | 18″ × 24″ | 8 " | 8 " | 8½ " |
| " " " ...... | 18″ × 24″ | 8 " | 8 " | 12½ " |
| Moguls...................... | 18″ × 24″ | 7½ " | 7½ " | 8 " |
| Ten-wheeled .............. | 18″ × 24″ | 7½ " | 7¾ " | 8 " |
| " " .............. | 19″ × 24″ | 7½ " | 7¾ " | 8 " |
| Consolidation .............. | 20″ × 24″ | 7½ " | 7¾ " | 8 " |

In Table 20 it will be seen that in some of the locomotives the journals of the main driving axle—that is, the axle to which the connecting-rods are attached—are made ¼ inch larger in diameter than the other driving axle journals. Although this is good practice, there are master-mechanics who object to such an arrangement, because it compels them to keep, for each class of engine, two sizes of driving boxes on hand ready to replace worn-out ones, thereby increasing the stock which must be kept to facilitate quick repairs.

The dimensions of the driving axle journals given in Tables 17, 18, and 19 also establish the sizes of driving boxes; and consequently we have only to select, from the number of boxes shown in Figs. 314 to 340, that box which will fit the journal to be used.

When the right driving box has been selected, we then select the corresponding pedestal from the number of pedestals shown in Figs. 271 to 279. It should be remembered that the dimensions of the upper braces $B_2$, and the lower braces $L$, uniting the pedestals, must be computed to suit the diameters of the cylinders; and therefore in frames for freight engines the braces uniting the pedestals will be heavier than those shown in the illustrations. To make this plain, we will take an example. Let it be required to find the principal dimensions of a frame for a consolidation engine with cylinders 20 inches in diameter. In Table 19 we see that the driving axle journal must be 7½ inches diameter and 8 inches long, hence the box to be used is that one which is represented in Fig. 317; and the pedestal to be used for this box is represented in Fig. 272. But now, the dimensions for the upper and lower frame braces must be determined according to Rules 33a, 35a, and 36, to suit a cylinder 20 inches in diameter, and consequently these braces will be heavier than shown in Fig. 272, but the dimensions of the pedestal itself will remain as they are given. There are also a few cases in which the choice of the axle box will either compel us to change the width of frame suitable for a given diameter of cylinder as established in the illustration of pedestals, or we must increase the width of the axle box to suit the given width of frame.

# CHAPTER VI.

### DRIVING AXLES.—DRIVING WHEELS.—COUNTERBALANCE.

#### DRIVING AXLES.

246. The driving axles are made of iron or steel; the writer prefers good hammered-iron axles.

Some of the different forms of driving axles, such as are generally adopted under all classes of locomotives, are shown in Figs. 341, 342, and 343.

Fig. 341 represents a main driving axle suitable for eight-wheeled passenger locomotives, with cylinders 16 inches in diameter; a Mogul engine with cylinders 16 inches in diameter; or a ten-wheeled locomotive with cylinders 17 inches in diameter. Those parts of the axles marked $A\ A$ are generally called the wheel fits, and are usually turned to $\frac{1}{8}$ inch less in diameter than the journals of the axles marked $B\ B$; in fact, in this style of axles the difference between the diameter of the wheel fit and that of the journal should never be greater than $\frac{1}{8}$ inch, as this will give a shoulder sufficient for all practical purposes; on the other hand, if the difference between these diameters is greater than $\frac{1}{8}$ inch, the axle will be unnecessarily weakened, and will be liable to break off at the hub of the wheel. Sharp corners at $ff$ are another cause which will lead to the breaking of the axles near the hub, and therefore sharp corners should not be tolerated; the junction between the wheel fit and the journal should always be a curve. Although this manner of forming the wheel fit $A$, that is, turning it to a smaller diameter than that of the journal, is quite a common practice, we believe it to be inferior to that shown in Fig. 344. In this design the diameter of the wheel fit is equal to that of the journal, and consequently the strength of the axle is in nowise impaired. The shoulder against which the hub of the wheel is pressed is formed in turning by leaving on the axle a small collar $H$, about $\frac{3}{16}$ inch larger in diameter than the journal, the thickness of this collar being about $\frac{1}{8}$ inch at the top. Here, also, sharp corners at $i\ i$ must be avoided, and the junction between the collar and axle nicely rounded out. The hub of the wheel is counterbored to receive the collar, as shown in the illustration. This design of an axle has an advantage over those shown in Figs. 341, 342, and 343, namely, in axles with wheel fits like that shown in Fig. 344; the journal can be trued up when necessary and still leave the shoulder $H$ unimpaired.

247. Sometimes we find the main axles turned to equal diameters from hub to hub of wheels, and frequently we find them formed as shown in Fig. 341. In

the latter axle the central part C is left smooth forged; the parts B B are made sufficiently long to receive the axle box and eccentrics.

Fig. 342 represents the rear driving axle of an eight-wheeled passenger engine with cylinders 16 inches in diameter. The same size and form of axle is also used

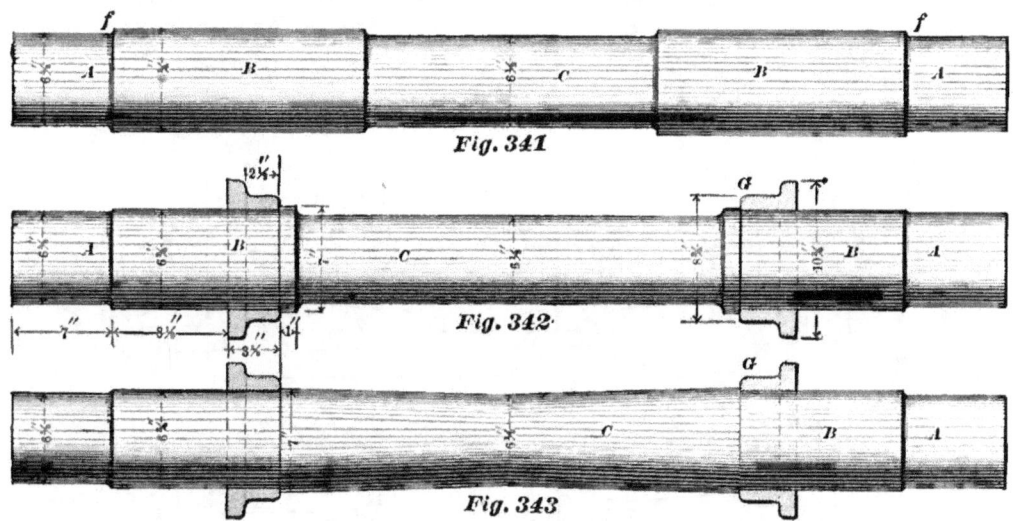

under other engines under which a main axle like that in Fig. 341 is used. In these driving axles the central part C and the projections which form the shoulders are left smooth forged; the amount of projection is equal to amount of metal allowed for turning the journals B. The cast-iron collars G G are either shrunk on the axle, or held in position by two set screws. Occasionally we find the driving axle made as shown in Fig. 343. The only difference between the axle shown

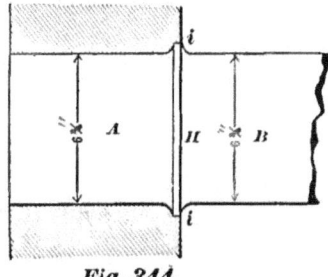

in Fig. 342 and that in Fig. 343 will be found in the form of the central part C C; in the latter the diameter is gradually reduced from the collar to the center; and in the former it is of equal diameter throughout.

### DRIVING WHEELS.

248. Fig. 345 represents the front view, Figs. 346, 347, sections of a driving wheel, and Figs. 348, 349 represent sections of its arms. This wheel was designed for and is successfully used under eight-wheeled fast passenger engines with cylinders 18 inches in diameter.

A driving wheel consists of two parts, namely, the driving wheel center marked C, and the tire marked T. In this country the driving wheel centers are made, almost universally, of cast-iron. Sometimes the spokes are cast solid, but usually they and the rim are cast hollow. The crank N and the counterbalance O O form part of the wheel center.

The most common practice in fastening the tires on the wheel center is to shrink them on the center. To do this, the wheel centers are turned square across (not

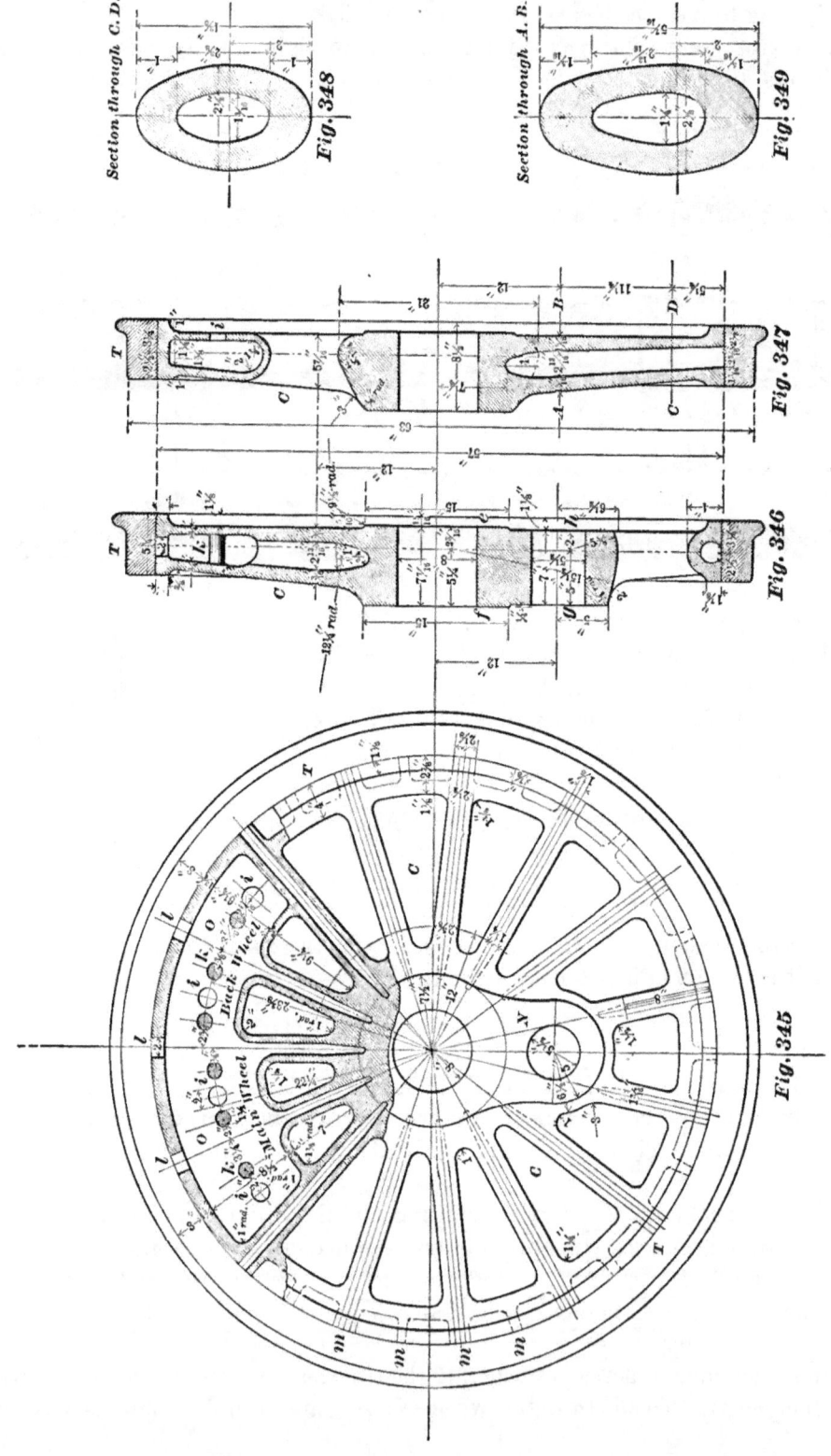

Fig. 345. Fig. 346. Fig. 347. Fig. 348. Fig. 349.

tapered), and the tire bored out somewhat smaller in diameter than that of the wheel center. The tire is then heated, generally on account of cleanliness, by means of a number of gas flames arranged for the purpose. When the tire, by these means, has been sufficiently expanded, it is then slipped on the wheel center and allowed to cool, thereby contracting and binding it firmly around the cast-iron center.

TABLE 21.

STANDARD SIZES OF WHEEL CENTERS.

| Diameter of Wheel Centers. | Inside Diameters of Tires. |
|---|---|
| 38 inches. | 38 inches, less 0.040 |
| 44 " | 44 " " 0.047 |
| 50 " | 50 " " 0.053 |
| 56 " | 56 " " 0.060 |
| 62 " | 62 " " 0.066 |
| 66 " | 66 " " 0.070 |

A uniformity in the diameters of wheel centers has not yet been thoroughly established. In 1886 the American Railway Master Mechanics' Association recommended and adopted the above diameters as standards.

In this table we see that, for the given diameters of wheel centers, the shrinkage allowance in the bore of the tires is 0.040, 0.047, 0.053, 0.060, 0.066, and 0.070 of an inch respectively, and these are claimed to be the average of the wide range of shrinkage allowance used in actual practice.

249. Figs. 350, 351, and 352 represent the different views of a driving wheel designed for a ten-wheeled engine having cylinders 19 inches in diameter; Fig. 353 represents the sections of the spokes.

In this wheel the spokes are solid and the rim is cast hollow, with the exception of that part which forms the counterbalance $O\ O\ O$, extending from $u$ (Fig. 250) to an equal distance on the other side of the center line; this part of the rim is cast solid.

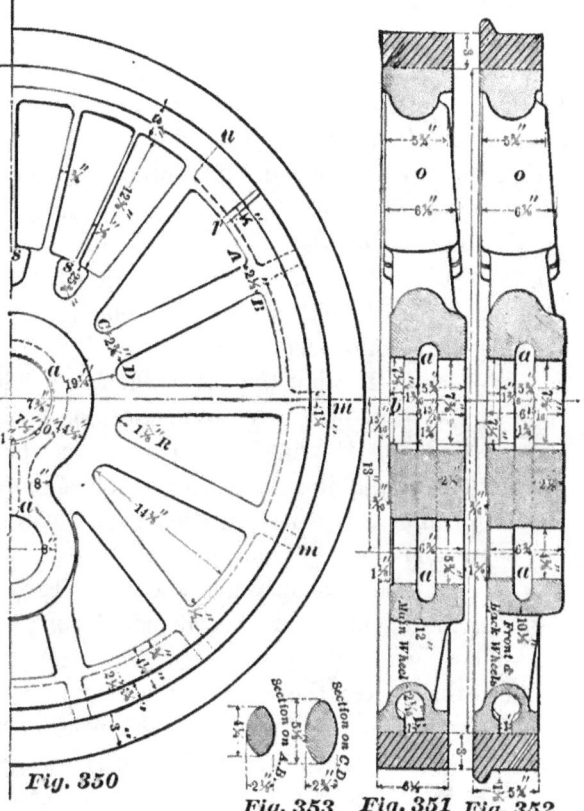

Fig. 350  Fig. 353  Fig. 351  Fig. 352

In order to avoid a shrinkage stress, the counterbalance is parted at $s\ s$; these openings extend to the rim, but not through it; the latter is parted or cored through at $r$ and in a corresponding place on the other side of the center line. The openings $r$ are generally slotted and cast-iron liners driven in.

In this wheel the whole crank is cored out, the cored part extending to the axle, and leaving all around it an opening $1\frac{3}{4}$ inches wide. There is an objection to this opening: it will interfere with the guidance of the axle when it is to be pressed into the hub of the wheel. It seems to us that a few ribs cast into the core opening around the axle will be an improvement, by which considerable annoyance may sometimes be avoided.

It will be noticed that the hub of the wheel is counterbored at $b$; the reason for doing so is to allow the full diameter of the axle to extend into the wheel, bringing the shoulder of the wheel fit inside of the hub, instead of against the hub, as explained in Art. 247. The object of this design is to prevent the breaking of the axle, which occasionally occurs when the shoulder of the wheel fit is pressed against the outside of the hub.

The ribs $m\ m$, shown in Figs. 345 and 350, are for the purpose of stiffening the hollow rims.

In some wheels the ribs are placed at the end of each spoke, as shown in Fig. 350; in other wheels they are placed at the end of each spoke and midway between them, as shown in Fig. 345.

250. Figs. 354 to 357 inclusive show different views of a driving wheel designed for an eight-wheeled passenger engine having cylinders 19 inches in diameter. In this wheel the spokes and rim are cast solid. One peculiarity of this wheel, not often found in others, is that the rim of the wheel center has a shoulder against which the tire is pressed. The object of this shoulder is to prevent the tire from slipping inwards when the flange is working against the rail. At first sight, it may appear that a shoulder of this kind is unnecessary, but when locomotives are fitted up with driver brakes, and these applied, the tire will in some instances become sufficiently hot to expand and thereby loosen it, and hence the importance of the shoulder will be apparent.

We also notice that for these wheels the wheel fit is tapered; its large diameter is the same as that of the journal, and consequently there are no shoulders, such as shown in Figs. 341 and 342. This is another method sometimes adopted for the prevention of breaking the axles near or at the hub of the wheel.

The rim of this wheel is cored through in two places $r\ r$, and at the center $r_2$ of the counterbalance. In our opinion, the positions of the openings $r\ r\ r_2$ are better located than the two openings shown in Fig. 350; because in Fig. 354 the distances between the openings are nearly equal, and the openings $r\ r$ through the rim are placed between such spokes where the strength of the hub is reinforced by ribs cast between the spokes, the result being that in this wheel the openings through the rim will not widen as easily nor as much as the openings in the wheel shown in Fig. 350, when the axle is forced into the hub of the wheel.

251. Figs. 358 to 362 inclusive represent a driving wheel designed for an eight-wheeled passenger engine having cylinders 18 inches in diameter. This wheel has solid spokes. The rim is cast hollow, but differs from those previously shown, in the fact that in this wheel the cored part in the rim does not extend to the periphery; it

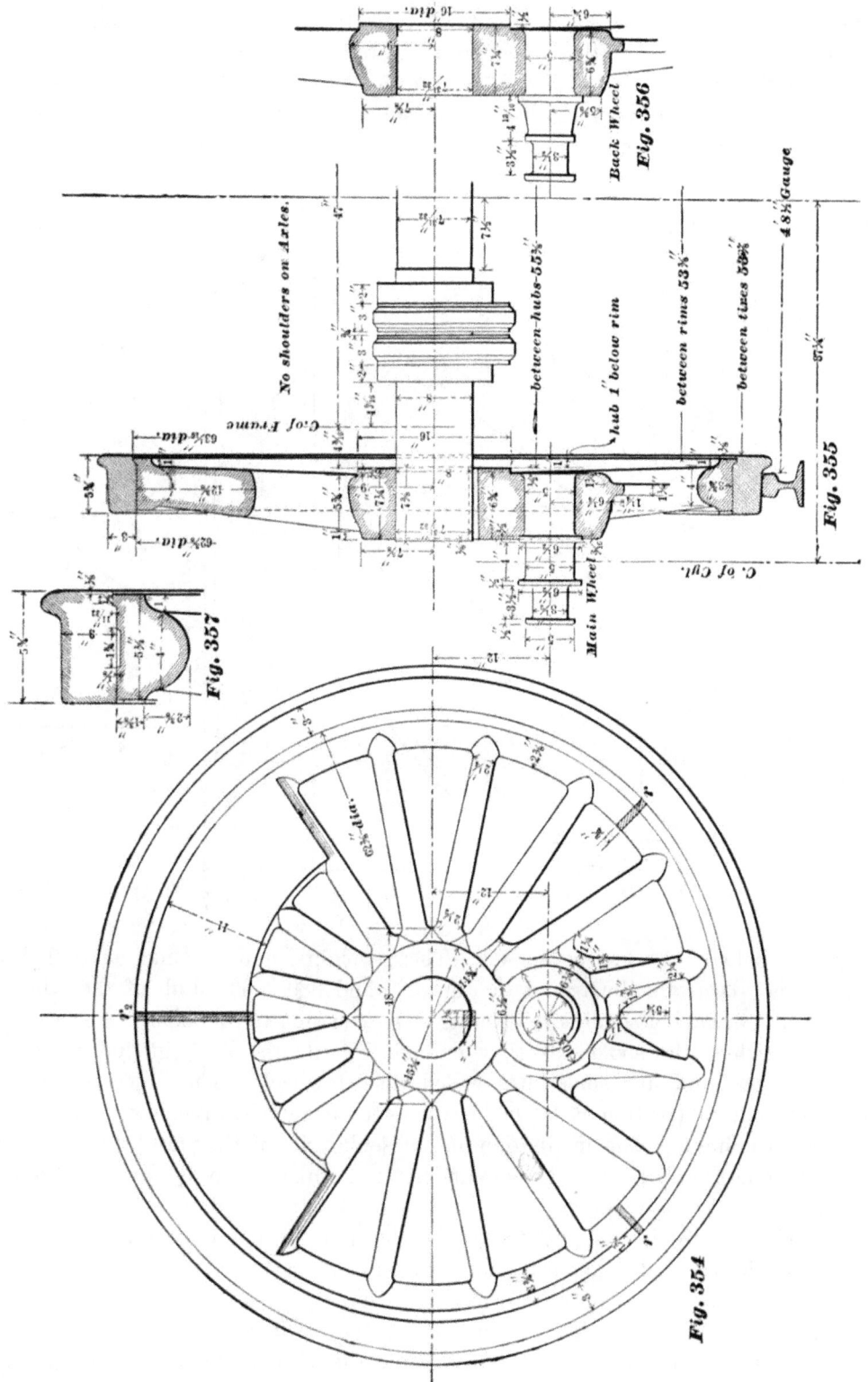

is closed, as shown in Fig. 362, and indicated by the dotted lines in Fig. 358. The only openings in the rim of this wheel are the core holes *w w*; ribs in the rim, similar to those marked *m m* in Figs. 345 and 350, are not used. The rim from *u* to *u* is cast solid, but the extra metal thus obtained is not sufficient for counterbalancing, and therefore two or four separate pairs of counterbalance weights, as the case may

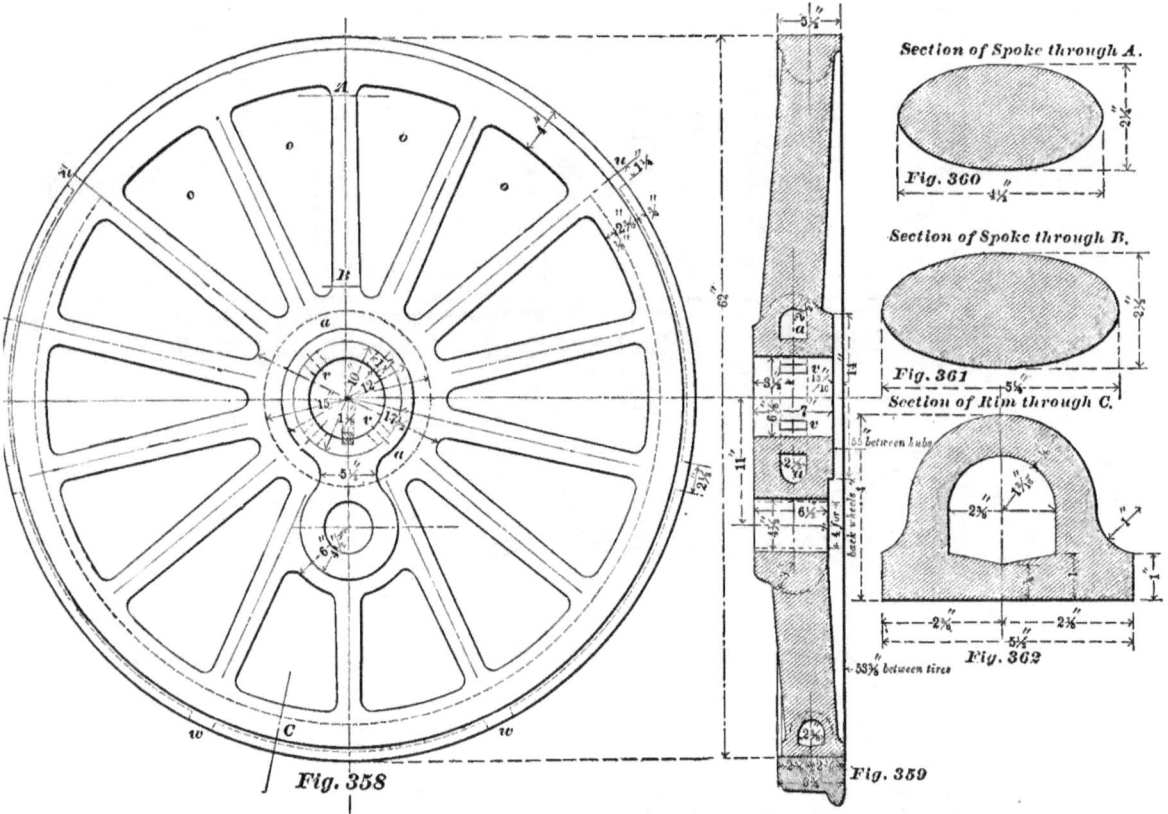

require, are bolted between the spokes. These weights, and the manner of bolting them to the wheel, are illustrated in Figs. 388 and 389. The hub of the wheel is cored out at *a a*, having small core openings *v v* extending to the axle.

In this wheel the spokes, as they extend towards the hub, incline outwards; wheels of this kind are sometimes called dished wheels. The object of placing the spokes in this position is to make room for a comparatively wide axle box; but there is a limit to the inclination of the spokes, for if they are brought out too far, it will be necessary to spread the cylinders also, which is always an objectionable feature.

252. The wheels are usually forced on the axle with a hydraulic press. The pressure should be equal to about 9 tons per inch of diameter, so that an axle 6 inches in diameter will be forced into the wheel with a pressure of $6 \times 9 = 54$ tons; or an axle 7 inches in diameter, with a pressure of $7 \times 9 = 63$ tons.

To add further security, keys are driven into the wheel and axle. These keys are generally made $\frac{7}{8}$ inch square for axles less than 6 inches in diameter; 1 inch square for axles varying from 6 to 7 inches in diameter; and 1¼ inches square for axles 7 inches and over in diameter.

The illustrations represent driving wheels such as are used on some of our prominent railroads; they have been taken directly from working drawings kindly given to the writer by locomotive builders for the purpose of illustrating these pages. The designs of these wheels also indicate the study and care bestowed upon this subject by master-mechanics, so as to obtain a strong and safe wheel, thereby greatly promoting the safety of the passengers.

253. Figs. 363 and 364 represent the two views of a driving wheel designed for a consolidation engine having cylinders 20 inches in diameter. Fig. 365 represents a section through the rim, and Figs. 366, 367 represent sections of one of the arms. These are cast solid, the rim hollow, its form being similar to that of the rim shown in Fig. 358. The counterbalance weight is cast solid throughout, without any openings to prevent shrinkage stress.

Figs. 368 and 369 represent two views of another driving wheel designed for a consolidation engine with cylinders 20 inches in diameter. The construction of this wheel is somewhat different from that shown in Fig. 363; it has hollow spokes and a hollow rim, the hollow part of the rim extending to the periphery of the wheel and strengthened by the ribs $m\ m$; the counterbalance has—for the purpose of avoiding shrinkage stress—openings $r\ r$ cast into it, and extending to the rim.

In Fig. 368 we see that the inner face of the wheel center projects beyond the inner face of the tire.

This style of wheel is adopted for locomotives designed for roads having tracks of 5 feet gauge, which in the near future are to be reduced to a gauge of 4 feet 8½ inches. Now, locomotives designed for a 5 feet gauge, and having the tires placed on the wheel centers, as shown in Fig. 368, can readily be changed to suit a gauge of 4 feet 8½ inches, as all that need be done is to heat the tires and move them inwards on the wheel centers, and then turn off the outer face of the latter to suit the tires.

## COUNTERBALANCE.

254. In traveling in a railroad car it may sometimes be noticed that the motion of the train is not uniform, but is accompanied by jerks occurring at regular intervals. This kind of irregular motion is often due to the locomotive, which is imperfectly counterbalanced. Consequently, we may say—in a general way—that in a locomotive, all parts whose weights have a bad influence on the smooth forward and backward motion of the engine, and tend to produce jerks in its motion, must be counterbalanced; and therefore not only the weight of the crank and its pin, and other parts attached to the crank-pin which have a rotary motion, must be counterbalanced, but also those parts which are attached to the crank-pin and have a reciprocating motion. Hence in locomotives the weights of the cranks, pins, connecting- and side-rods, piston-rods, crossheads, and pistons must be counterbalanced.[*]

In order to explain as clearly as possible the method of counterbalancing these

---

[*] A difference of opinion exists in regard to the amount of weight to be counterbalanced, as will be seen farther on.

# MODERN LOCOMOTIVE CONSTRUCTION.

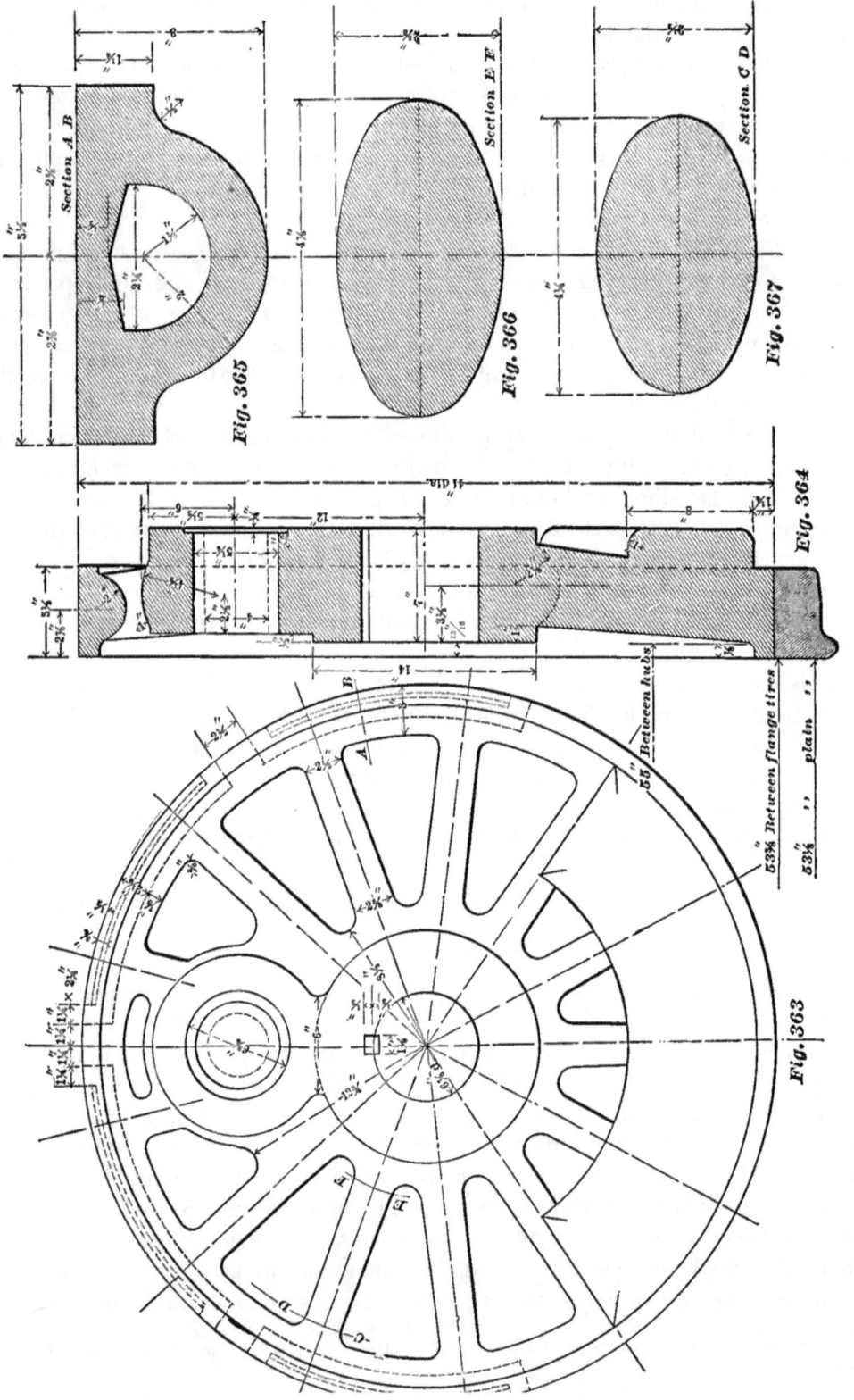

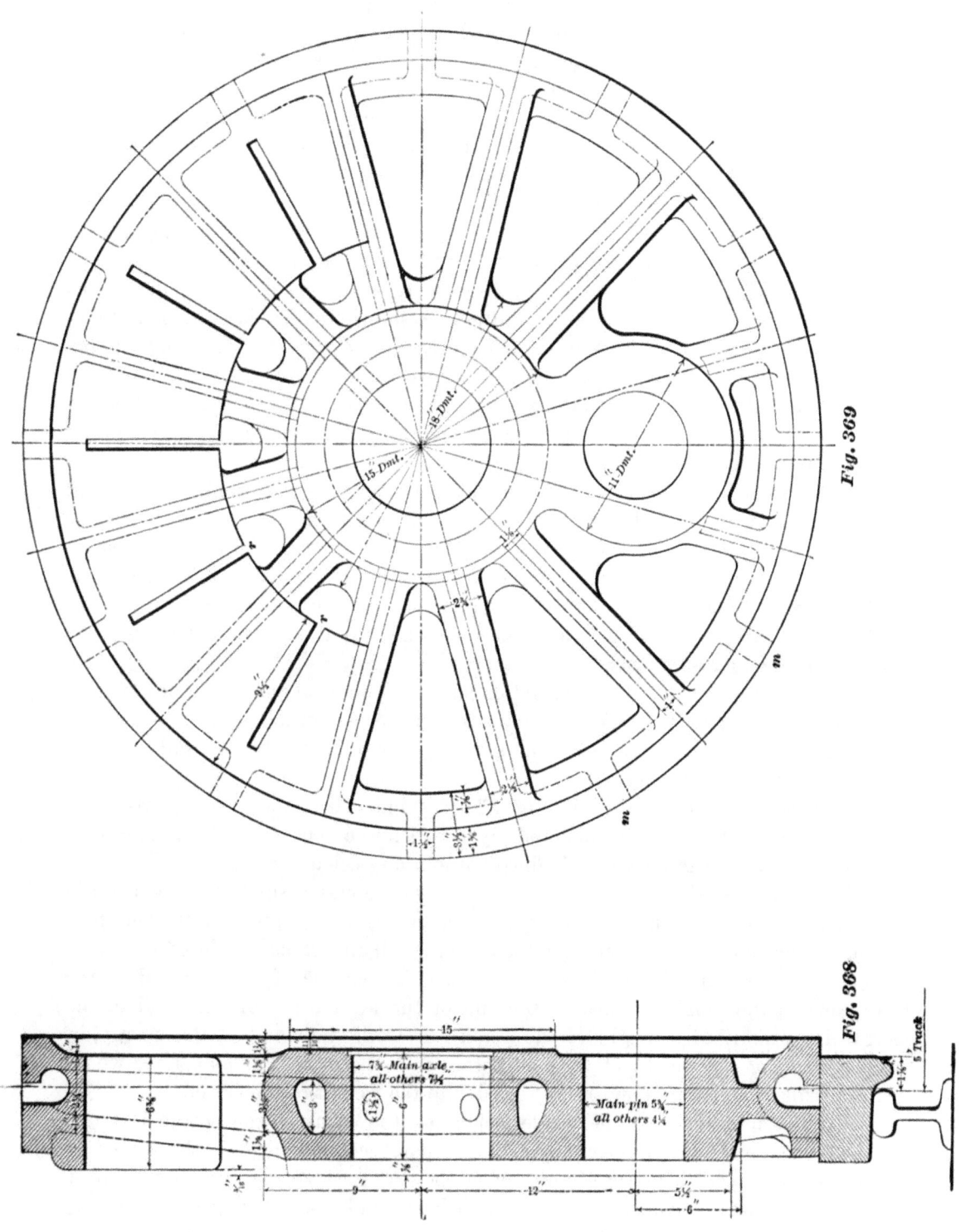

Fig. 369

Fig. 368

parts of the engine, and reduce this subject to simple problems, we will first consider the principles upon which the method is based, and the application of these principles to the method used for finding the counterbalance for objects of simple outline.

In the first place, then, we will determine the amount of counterbalance required for a crank such as is shown in Fig. 370. This crank is supposed to be of equal thickness throughout, and its form is perfectly symmetrical—that is to say, the diameter of the hole for the axle is equal to that of the hole for the crank-pin, the ends of the crank are exactly alike, and the depth $c\,d$ or $e\,f$ the same throughout.

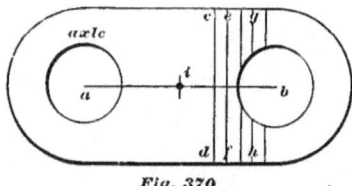

Fig. 370

Assume now that the crank stands in a horizontal position, as shown in our illustration, and that it is divided by vertical planes represented by the lines $c\,d$, $e\,f$, etc., into any number of parts; then the weight of each part with a leverage corresponding to the distance between it and the center $a$ of the axle will act with a certain amount of energy, tending to turn the axle around its center, bringing the center line $a\,b$ of the crank in a vertical position below the axle.

Now, in order to enable us to compare readily the amount of this energy with that of a force applied to some other point at a given distance from the center $a$, we assume that the weights of the different parts $c\,d$, $e\,f$, etc., of the crank are concentrated on the line $a\,b$ at a single point $i$, so that the same amount of energy be developed as is developed by distributing the weight of the parts along the center line $a\,b$; this point $i$ will coincide with the center of gravity of the crank. Hence our first step will be to determine this center of gravity.

The center of gravity of every solid or body is a point about which all the parts of the solid acted upon by the force of gravity balance each other, so that, if the solid be suspended from that point (center of gravity), the solid will be in equilibrium in any position it may be placed.

Since the crank represented in Fig. 370 is symmetrical, its center of gravity $i$ must lie in the center line $a\,b$, and midway between the centers $a$ and $b$. Hence in this case the center of gravity $i$ is obtained without any calculation.

After the center of gravity has been determined, we may assume that the distance between the center $a$ of the axle and the center of gravity $i$ represents the length of an arm of a lever whose fulcrum is at the center $a$. If the whole weight of the crank is applied to the extremity $i$ of the lever arm $a\,i$, then the effect produced or the energy due to the weight applied to the end of the lever arm will be equal to the energy of the distributed weight of the crank. It is the influence of this energy, in counterbalancing the weight of the crank, that is to be destroyed by a force whose energy is equal and acting opposite to that due to the weight of the crank.

By the assumption that the whole weight of the crank is concentrated at one point—the center of gravity—or applied to a point coinciding with the center of gravity, we obtain an easy way of comparing the energy developed by the weight of the crank and that developed by the counterbalance, and also an easy way for determining the number of pounds of metal required in the latter.

In determining the counterbalance we must also find its center of gravity, and, as in the case of the crank, assume its weight to be concentrated at its center of gravity.

These conditions will reduce the whole method of counterbalancing to a simple problem, in which the given conditions are such as represented in Fig. 371. In this figure the point $a$ represents the center of the axle; the line $k\,b$, passing through the center $a$, represents a lever whose fulcrum is at $a$; the line $a\,b$ is the arm of the force $C$, its length is equal to the distance between the center of the axle and the center of gravity of the crank. The line $a\,k$ is the arm of the force $R$, its length is equal to the distance between the center of the axle and the center of gravity of the counterbalance. The weight of the crank is represented by $C$ which is attached to the point $b$; the weight of the counterbalance is represented by $R$, which is attached to the point $k$.

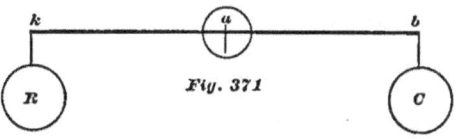

Fig. 371

Now, since in all levers of this kind which are in equilibrium the product obtained by multiplying the length of the arm $a\,b$ by the weight $C$, which is suspended from this arm, must be equal to the product obtained by multiplying the length of the arm $a\,k$ by the weight $R$ suspended from it, we can find the number of pounds of metal required in the counterbalance by the following rule:

RULE 42.—Multiply the distance between the center of the axle and the center of gravity of the crank in inches by the weight of the crank in pounds, and divide this product by the distance between the center of the axle and the center of gravity of the counterbalance in inches; the quotient will be the weight of the counterbalance in pounds.

EXAMPLE 74.—The length of the crank (Fig. 370) from the center $a$ to the center $b$ is 12 inches; the weight of the crank is 300 pounds. It is required to find the weight of the counterbalance, which is placed so that the distance between its center of gravity and the center of the axle is 9 inches.

Since the form of this crank is symmetrical, and since its length is 12 inches, the distance between its center of gravity and the center of axle is 6 inches; hence we have,

$$\frac{6 \times 300}{9} = 200 \text{ pounds};$$

which is the weight necessary for counterbalancing the weight of the crank only.

255. In order to express concisely that which is to follow, it will be necessary to give a more general definition of the term "arm of the force," or simply "arm," and also a definition of the term "moment of a force" which we shall introduce.

Fig. 371. Let $k\,b$ represent a lever, $a$ its fulcrum, $R$ and $C$ weights attached to the ends $k$ and $b$ of the lever.

By the term "arm of the force" is meant the perpendicular distance from the fulcrum to the line of direction of a force applied to the arm. For instance: The weight $C$ when applied to the end $b$ of the lever will act in a vertical line $b\,C$, and therefore, according to our definition, the line $a\,b$, which is perpendicular to the line $b\,C$, will be the arm of the force $C$. The line $a\,k$ is the arm of the weight $R$, because $a\,k$ is the perpendicular distance from the fulcrum $a$ to the line $k\,R$ in which the weight $R$

acts. In fact, we may say that the arm of the force is the shortest line that can be drawn from the fulcrum to the line of direction of the force.

By the term "line of direction of a force" is meant a line indicating the direction in which the force acts; the length of this line is not limited by the distance between the arm and the weight attached to it. Thus, in Fig. 372, let the lever on one side of the fulcrum be bent as indicated by the line *d a*. In this case the line of direction in which the force, due to the weight *R*, acts is not limited by the end of the lever *d* and the weight *R*, but the line of direction is represented by the line *d e* extending below the fulcrum, so that the line *a k* can be drawn from the fulcrum *a* perpendicular to the line of direction *d e*. In this case the line *a k* is the arm of the weight *R*.

Since the weight *R* acts with a leverage *a k*, we say that *a k* is *R*'s arm, and for a similar reason we say that *a b* is *C*'s arm.

## MOMENT OF A FORCE.

256. The moment of a force with respect to a point is the product obtained by multiplying the force by the perpendicular distance from the point to the line of direction of the force. When the forces are applied to a lever, then the product of each force multiplied by its arm is the moment of that force. Thus:

In the lever *k b*, Fig. 371, the force due to the weight *R* tends to turn the lever around the point or fulcrum *a*, and the same thing may be said of the force due to *C*, that is, it tends to turn the lever around the same fulcrum *a*, but in an opposite direction. The weight *R* acts with a leverage *a k*, hence the product of the weight *R* multiplied by its arm *a k* is the moment of the force due to the weight *R*. In like manner, the product obtained by multiplying the weight *C* by its arm *a b* is the moment of the force *C*.

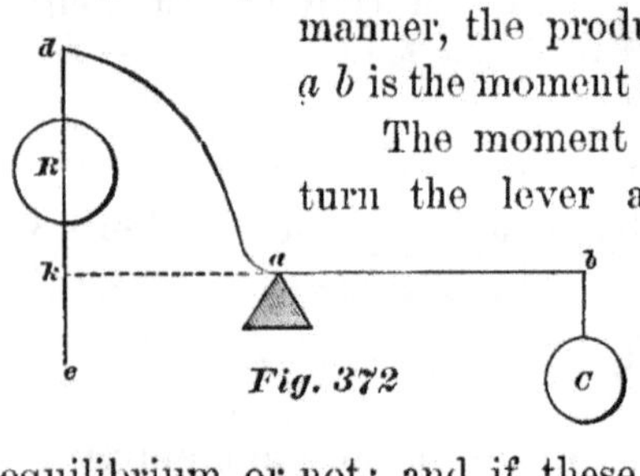

The moment of a force is used as a measure of its tendency to turn the lever around a point, or the fulcrum *a*. By establishing this measure we obtain an easy method for comparing the effect of the two forces applied to a lever; that is to say, we can readily determine whether the forces applied to a lever will hold it in equilibrium or not; and if these forces do not hold the lever in equilibrium, we are enabled to calculate quickly the amount by which one of the forces must be increased or decreased, and this is exactly what we have to do in counterbalancing some of the weights in a locomotive.

Fig. 372

When a lever is in equilibrium, the moments of the forces are equal to each other.

To make the foregoing principles clear let us take the following example:

EXAMPLE 75.—Suppose that in Fig. 371 the length of the arm *a k* is two feet, and the weight *R* attached to it is 150 pounds, the length of the lever arm *a b* is four feet, and the weight *C* is 75 pounds. Will the lever *k b* under these conditions be in equilibrium? The moment of the force due to *R* is equal to the product of the weight *R* into its arm *a k*; hence we have: 150 pounds × 2 feet = 300 foot pounds = moment of *R*.

The moment of the force $C$ is equal to the product of the weight $C$ into its arm $a\,b$, hence we have: 75 pounds × 4 feet = 300 foot pounds = moment of $C$.

Here, then, we see that the moments of the weights $R$ and $C$ are equal, and consequently the lever must be in equilibrium. Let us take another example.

EXAMPLE 76.—The length of the arm $a\,k$ in Fig. 371 is two feet, the weight $R$ attached to it is 300 pounds; the length of the arm $a\,b$ is four feet, and the weight $C$ attached to it is 75 pounds. Will the lever under these conditions be in equilibrium? If not, what change must be made in the weight $R$?

The moment of the weight $R$ is equal to 300 pounds × 2 feet = 600 foot pounds.

The moment of the weight $C$ is equal to 75 pounds × 4 feet = 300 foot pounds.

Here we see that the moment of $R$ is 600, and the moment of $C$ is 300, and since the moments are not equal, the lever cannot be in equilibrium. This also indicates, that because the moment of $R$ is greater than the moment of $C$, the weight of $R$ is too great, and consequently it will turn the lever around the point or fulcrum $a$ and pull the end $k$ downwards.

In order to produce equilibrium, we would have to change one of the arms, or change one of the weights; but according to the conditions given in our example, we can make only one change, and that is in the weight $R$. Hence, our next step will be to determine by calculation the amount of reduction in the weight $R$.

We have seen that in order to produce equilibrium the moments of the two forces must be equal. We know that the moment of the weight $C$ is 300, and we also know that the length of $R$'s arm is 2 feet; now, since the product of 2 feet into the weight $R$, that is, the moment of $R$, must be equal to 300 to produce equilibrium, we simply divide the moment of $C$ by the length of $R$'s arm and obtain $\dfrac{300}{2}$ = 150 pounds for the weight of $R$. Here we see that $R$ must be reduced to one-half of its original weight.

In calculating the moments we must always use the same unit of length for both lever arms, and also the same unit of weight for the forces applied to the lever. That is to say, when we multiply the arm $a\,k$ in feet by the weight of $R$ in pounds, we must also multiply the arm $a\,b$ in feet (not inches) by the weight of $C$ in pounds. If we multiply the arm $a\,k$ in inches (which we are at perfect liberty to do) by the weight $R$ in pounds, then we must also multiply the lever arm $a\,b$ in inches (not feet) by the weight $C$ in pounds. Or, if we adopt ounces as the unit of measurement for the weight $R$, we must also adopt ounces for the unit of measurement for the weight $C$. To make this plain, let us consider the conditions given in Example 76, namely, that the arm $a\,k$ is equal to 2 feet, the arm $a\,b$ equal to 4 feet, the weight $R$ equal to 300 pounds, and the weight $C$ equal to 75 pounds. Taking feet as the unit of measurement for the length of the arms, we have, for the moments of $R$ and $C$:

$$300 \times 2 = 600 \text{ foot pounds} = \text{moment of } R; \text{ and}$$
$$75 \times 4 = 300 \text{ foot pounds} = \text{moment of } C.$$

Here we see that the moment of $R$ is equal to twice that of $C$.

Taking inches as the unit of measurement for the length of the arms, we have for the moments of $R$ and $C$:

$$300 \times 24 = 7200 \text{ inch pounds} = \text{moment of } R; \text{ and}$$
$$75 \times 48 = 3600 \text{ inch pounds} = \text{moment of } C.$$

Here, again, the moment of $R$ is equal to twice that of $C$. Hence we see that, for the purpose of comparing the effects of the forces applied to the lever, it makes no difference whether we adopt feet or inches for the unit of measurement, so long as we keep the same unit for both arms.

If these principles are understood, considerable of the difficulty in determining the counterbalance for an engine will disappear.

## AMOUNT OF COUNTERBALANCE.

257. In Art. 254 it was seen that in determining the counterbalance for the crank, we simply assumed the line drawn from the center of gravity of the crank to the center of gravity of the counterbalance to represent a lever with the fulcrum at the center of the axle, and then calculated the weight attached to one end of the lever that would counterbalance the total weight of the crank attached to the opposite end of the lever.

As we proceed, it will be seen that, for the sake of convenience in calculating the total amount of counterbalance required in a locomotive, it is desirable to adopt, in place of the whole weight of the crank applied to its center of gravity, a smaller weight applied to the center of the crank-pin, which will have the same effect as the whole weight of the crank applied to its center of gravity. This smaller weight is determined in the following manner:

EXAMPLE 77.—Fig. 373. Let $a$ represent the center of the axle, and let the horizontal line $k\,d$ drawn through $a$ represent a lever with its fulcrum at $a$; also let $a\,d$ represent the length of the crank—that is, the distance between the center $a$ of the axle and the center $d$ of the crank-pin; $b$ the center of gravity of the crank; $C$ the whole weight of the crank applied to $b$; and $R$ the weight of the counterbalance applied to the point $k$ coinciding with the center of gravity of the counterbalance. Let the total weight of the crank be 300 pounds, the length of the crank 12 inches, and the distance from the center of axle $a$ to the center of gravity $k$ of the counterbalance 9 inches, and the distance from the center of axle to the center of gravity of the crank 6 inches; it is required to determine by calculation the weight $W$ applied to the center $d$ of the crank-pin; the weight $W$ is to have the same effect or tendency to turn the crank around the center $a$ of the axle as that of the whole weight of the crank (300 pounds) applied to the center of gravity $b$.

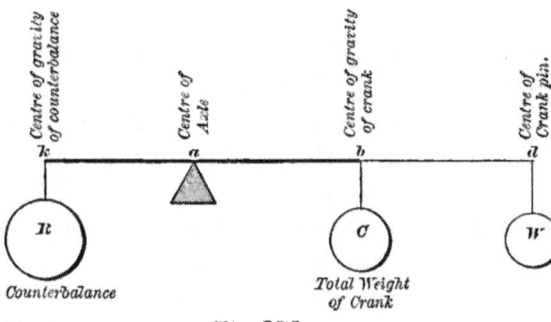

Fig. 373

We have seen in Example 74 (Art. 254) that to counterbalance the weight of this crank under the given conditions, we require 200 pounds, and this counterbalance cannot be changed as long as the weight of the crank, its center of gravity, and the center of gravity of the counterbalance remain as they are given.

But we have already seen that the moment of a force is a measure of its tendency to produce rotation. The moment of the counterbalance $R$ in our example is equal to $200 \times 9 = 1800$ inch pounds; and if the lever $k\,b$ is to remain in equilibrium, the moment of weight $C$ must also be equal to 1,800 inch pounds, which we find to be the case in this example, for the distance from the center $a$ of the axle to the center of gravity of the crank is 6 inches, and the weight of the crank is 300 pounds, hence the moment of $C$ is $300 \times 6 = 1800$ inch pounds.

If we now replace the weight $C$ of the crank applied to its center of gravity by another weight $W$ applied to the center of the crank-pin $d$, and at the same time preserve an equilibrium, it will easily be perceived that the moment of $W$ must be equal to the moment of $R$. Again, since the moment of $C$, as we have shown, is equal to the moment of $R$, we may say that the moment of $W$ must be equal to the moment of $C$. Therefore, when to the center $d$ of the crank-pin a weight $W$ is to be attached, which shall have the same tendency to turn the crank around the center $a$ of the axle, we have, for determining the amount of the weight $W$, the following rule:

RULE 43.—Multiply the distance from the center of gravity of the crank to the center of the axle in inches by the total weight of the crank in pounds; divide this product by the length of the crank in inches; the quotient will be the number of pounds in the weight $W$.

Therefore, the required weight $W$ in our example will be

$$\frac{6 \text{ inches} \times 300 \text{ pounds}}{12 \text{ inches}} = 150 \text{ pounds}$$

Generally in locomotives the center of gravity of the crank is not in the center of its length; but Rule 43 will apply to all cases in which the center of gravity is in the center of the length or otherwise. How the center of gravity in bodies of different forms can be obtained will soon be explained.

The advantage of determining the weight $W$ applied to the center of crank-pin in place of the whole weight $C$ of the crank applied to its center of gravity, is, that the counterbalance for the crank and other parts attached to the crank-pin, which must also be counterbalanced, can be found with less labor.

## POSITION OF THE CENTER OF GRAVITY OF THE COUNTERBALANCE.

258. So far we have assumed that the center of gravity of the crank and that of the counterbalance lie in one straight line passing through the center of axle. We have also stated that the length of the arm of the counterbalance is equal to the distance between the center of the axle and the center of gravity of the counterbalance. It is now to be explained how the position of the center of gravity of the counterbalance can be determined.

Let the full lines in Figs. 374 and 375 represent two views of a counterbalance; it is required to find the distance between its center of gravity and center of the axle; the arc $f\,b\,g$ is described from the center of the axle, and its radius is 11 inches. The middle point $b$ of the arc $f\,b\,g$, the center of gravity of the weight, and the center of axle are to lie in one straight line.

From the conditions given, we know that the distance from the point $b$ to the center of axle is 11 inches; it therefore remains to find only the distance between $b$ and the center of gravity of the weight.

Fig. 375 shows that the thickness of the weight is the same throughout; we have, therefore, two methods for finding the position of its center of gravity: first, a geometrical method; and second, a practical method.

## GEOMETRICAL METHOD.

For the purpose of finding the distance between the center of gravity and the point $b$ when the thickness of the weight is uniform, we have only to find the center of gravity of the surface or plane $e\,a\,d\,g\,b\,f$, Fig. 374.

Fig. 374. Join the points $e$ and $d$ by a straight line, and bisect this line by the perpendicular line $a\,b$, cutting the arc $f\,g$ in the point $b$. The line $a\,b$ will divide

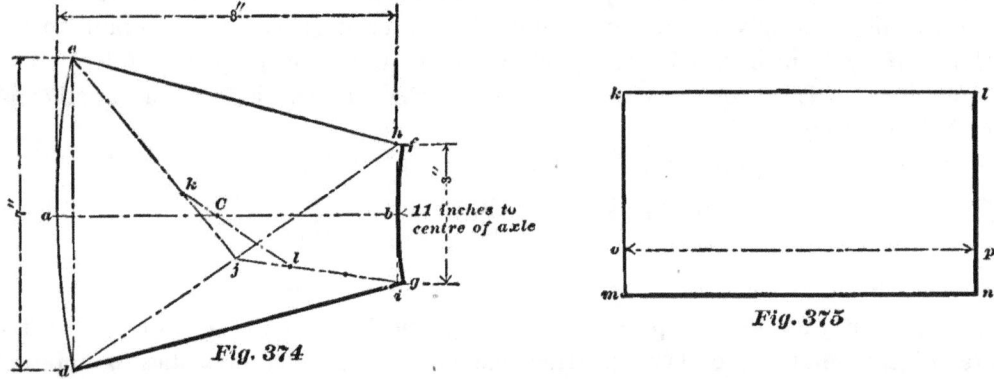

Fig. 374.

Fig. 375.

the plane $e\,a\,d\,g\,b\,f$ into two equal parts, and is therefore a center line; it also contains the center of gravity of the plane, because it passes through the centers of all lines drawn parallel to the line $e\,d$. Through the point $b$ draw a line $h\,i$ perpendicular to $a\,b$, cutting the line $e\,f$ in the point $h$, and the line $d\,g$ in the point $i$. For the sake of simplicity we will now consider the plane to be bounded at the ends by the straight lines $e\,d$ and $h\,i$ in place of the arcs $e\,a\,d$ and $f\,b\,g$. Join the points $d$ and $h$ by a straight line $d\,h$, bisect this line—that is, find the point $j$ midway between the points $d$ and $h$; join the points $j$ and $e$, also the points $j$ and $i$, by the straight lines $e\,j$ and $j\,i$. Divide the line $e\,j$ into three equal parts, and thus obtain the point $k$, which is the first point of division from the line $d\,h$. Also divide the line $j\,i$ into three equal parts, thereby obtaining the point $l$, which is the first point of division from the line $d\,h$. Join the points $k$ and $l$ by a straight line $k\,l$ cutting the line $a\,b$ in the point $C$; this point $C$ will be the center of gravity of the plane $e\,d\,h\,i$—that is, the center of gravity of the plane bounded by the straight lines $e\,d$, $h\,i$, $e\,h$, and $d\,i$; but it will not be the exact center of gravity of the plane bounded at the ends by the arcs $e\,a\,d$ and $f\,l\,g$; for all practical purposes we may consider the point $C$ to be the center of gravity of the plane bounded by the arcs, as in this case the error will not amount to more than $\frac{1}{8}$ inch—that is to say, the distance between the point $a$ in the arc $e\,a\,g$ and the center of gravity $C$ found by the foregoing construction, will only be $\frac{1}{8}$ inch greater than the distance between $a$ and the true center of gravity of the plane bounded by the arc $e\,a\,d$ and $f\,b\,g$.

To prove that the point $C$ is the correct center of gravity of the plane $e\,d\,h\,i$, it may be stated that the line $d\,h$ divides the plane into two triangles, $d\,e\,h$ and $d\,h\,i$; the point $k$ is the center of gravity of the triangle $d\,e\,h$, and the point $l$ is the center of gravity of the triangle $d\,h\,i$. We may now consider the two triangles to form a system of bodies; under these conditions the point about which the two triangles will balance each other must lie in a line joining the centers of gravity $k$ and $l$; but the two triangles make up the plane $d\,e\,h\,i$, and we have seen that the center of gravity of this plane must lie in the center line $a\,b$, therefore its center of gravity $C$ must be the point in which the lines $a\,b$ and $k\,l$ intersect.

To show that the method of finding the centers of gravity $k$ and $l$ of the triangles is correct, we have the following demonstration, taken from "Theoretical Mechanics," by J. Weisbach.

In a triangle $d\,e\,h$, Fig. 376, every line drawn from an angle to the center of the opposite side will contain the center of gravity of the triangle. Thus the line $e\,m$ drawn from the angle $e$ to the center $m$ of the opposite side $d\,h$ will contain the center of gravity, because the line $e\,m$ bisects all lines such as $o\,p$, $r\,s$, which are drawn parallel to the side $d\,h$. The line $d\,n$ drawn from the angle $d$ to the center $n$ of the opposite side $e\,h$ will also contain the center of gravity of the triangle, because the line $d\,n$ will bisect every line drawn parallel to the side $e\,h$, and therefore the point of intersection $k$ of the two lines $e\,m$ and $d\,n$ must be the center of gravity of the whole triangle.

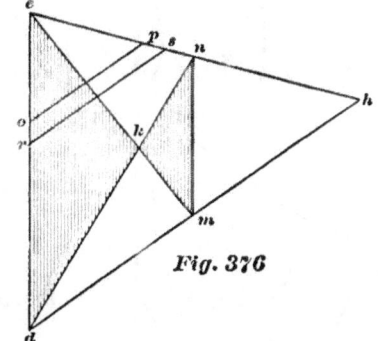

Fig. 376

Join the points $n$ and $m$ by a straight line; this line $m\,n$ must be parallel to the side $e\,d$, because the line $m\,n$ is drawn from the center of the side $e\,h$ to the center of the side $d\,h$. Again, the length of the line $n\,m$ must be equal to one-half of the length of the side $d\,e$, because the line $n\,m$ is drawn from the center $n$ of the side $e\,h$ parallel to $e\,d$. Since $n\,m$ is parallel to $d\,e$, it follows that the triangles $m\,n\,k$ and $d\,e\,k$ are similar; and because $m\,n$ is equal to one-half of $e\,h$, the line $m\,k$ is equal to one-half of the line $e\,k$, and consequently the line $k\,m$ must be equal to one-third of the whole line $e\,m$. Hence the center of gravity $k$ of the triangle $d\,e\,h$ is at a distance equal to $\frac{1}{3}\,e\,m$ from the middle point $m$ of the side $d\,h$, and at a distance equal to $\frac{2}{3}\,e\,m$ from the angle $e$.

### PRACTICAL METHOD.

259. Before the practical method for determining the center of gravity is explained, let us first obtain an insight into an important property of gravity. Let the outline in Fig. 377 represent the shape of an iron plate of equal thickness through-

out, and let A, B, C, and D represent holes drilled anywhere near the edges of this plate. Assume now that from a pin driven into a wall the plate is suspended by the hole A, the diameter of the pin being a little less than that of the hole, so that the plate can freely turn on the pin. We now find that after the plate has made a few oscillations, it will come to rest in only one position; even if we withdraw it from this position, the plate, as soon as it is free to move, will again come to rest in the same place. Let us carefully mark this position; to do so, we suspend a chalked line $h\,i$, and plummet from the pin; then, when the plate is at rest, we carefully snap the string against the plate and thus obtain on the plate a chalked mark which represents a vertical line drawn through the center of the hole A. We now remove the plummet and suspend the plate by the hole B, then replacing the plummet we draw on the plate in the same manner as before another vertical chalked line through the center of the hole B. In a similar manner we suspend the plate, in succession, from the holes C and D, and from the center of these holes draw vertical chalked lines, thereby obtaining four chalked lines, which are represented in the figure by broken lines drawn through the centers of the holes A, B, C, and D. We now find this remarkable

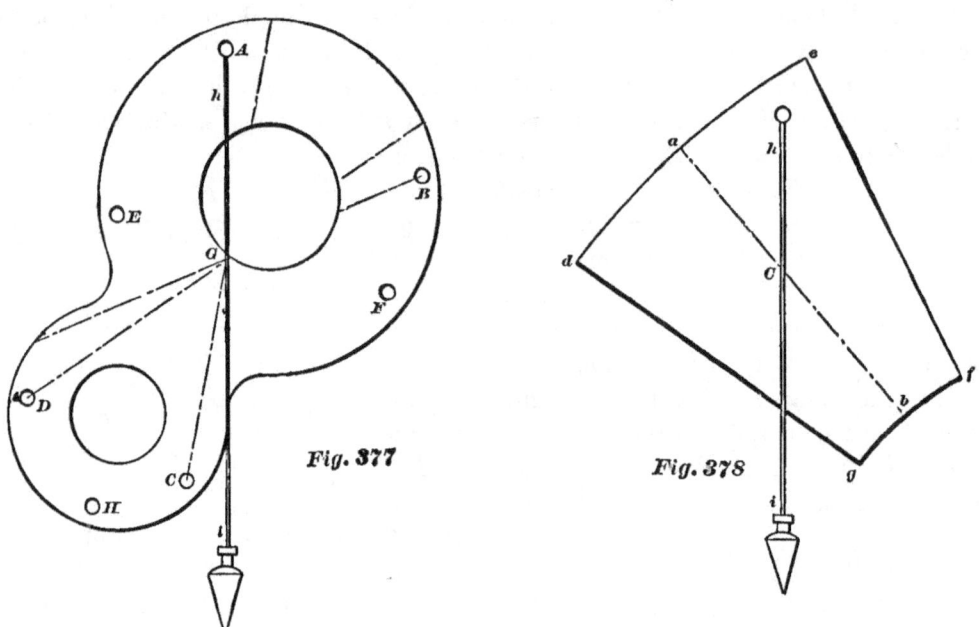

Fig. 377  Fig. 378

condition, namely, all these lines will intersect in one and the same point G. If additional holes, E, F, and H, are drilled anywhere in the plate—near its edge—and the plate suspended from these holes in succession, and chalked lines drawn in a manner as described, we will find that these additional lines through the centers of the holes E, F, and H will also pass through the same point G. This point is the center of gravity of the plate. Hence we may say that a vertical line drawn through the point from which the plate is suspended will pass through or contain the center of gravity of the plate. The lines which pass through the center of gravity of a body are called "lines of gravity."

In precisely the same manner we can find the position of the center of gravity of the weight shown in Fig. 374, thus: Cut a templet to the form of the surface shown in Fig. 374. When the templet is to be cut to full size, it will be best to make it of wood; its thickness must be the same throughout; indeed, this condition is very important; the real thickness makes no difference; it may either be $\frac{1}{8}$ or $\frac{1}{4}$ of an inch, or 1 inch, but it must be uniform. When the templet is to be cut to a scale, it may be made of stiff paper; in this case care must be taken to keep it perfectly flat.

On this templet draw the center line $a\,b$; this line will contain the center of gravity. Anywhere in and near one of the corners of the templet, punch a small smooth hole, and from a pin suspend the templet by the hole, as shown in Fig. 378. In doing so care must be taken to allow the templet perfect freedom to turn on the pin. From the same pin suspend a plummet line, and when the templet is at rest mark off the point $C$ in which the plummet line intersects the center line $a\,b$; this point $C$ will be the center of gravity of the surface shown in the figure, and will give the distance between the center of gravity of the weight and the point $b$, which is equal to $4\frac{1}{2}$ inches. Therefore the distance between the center of axle and the center of gravity of this counterbalance, which was to be found, is equal to $11 + 4\frac{1}{2} = 15\frac{1}{2}$ inches. Or, we may say, the arm of the counterbalance is $15\frac{1}{2}$ inches long.

260. In order to become familiar with the principles given in the previous articles, we will apply them to a simple case.

EXAMPLE 78.—Let $a$ in Fig. 379 represent the center of the axle, $b$ the center of the crank-pin; the distance between these two centers is 12 inches; $i\,j\,k\,l$ represents

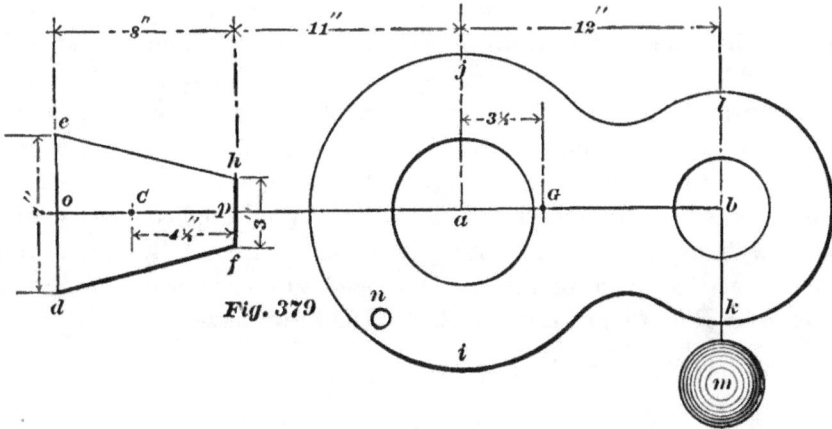

Fig. 379

the cast-iron crank, which is of uniform thickness. The weight of the crank is 250 pounds. In addition to this weight of the crank, another weight $m$ of 100 pounds is applied to the center $b$ of the crank-pin. One view of the counterbalance is shown by the outline $e\,d\,f\,h$, and all the dimensions of the counterbalance except its thickness are given. The edge $f\,h$ of the counterbalance is to be placed 11 inches from the center $a$ of the axle; the center line $o\,p$, and the center line $a\,b$ of the crank, are to lie in one straight line $o\,b$. It is required to find the weight of this counterbalance, which will hold in equilibrium the sum of the weight of the crank and the additional weight of 100 pounds applied to the center $b$ of the crank-pin. It is also required to find the thickness of the counterbalance. Our first step will be to find the center of gravity of the crank and also that of the counterbalance.

In order to avoid hereafter a misunderstanding, we deem the following remarks necessary. In these calculations, and in fact for all calculations employed for determining the counterbalance in locomotive wheels, we only need to know the positions of the centers of gravity—that is to say, we need only to know the distances of the centers of gravity of the crank and the counterbalance from the center of the axle. Hence, for the sake of brevity, we shall speak of the center of gravity as if it was located in the surface of the crank or counterbalance, whereas in reality it lies in the center of the thickness. Thus, in saying that $G$ is the center of gravity of the crank, it must be understood that the point $G$ simply indicates the distance of the center of gravity from the center of the axle, or the position it occupies between the center $a$ and $b$.

To find the center of gravity of the crank, cut out a templet to the shape of the crank, and on this templet draw the center line $a\,b$. Anywhere near the edge of the templet punch a small smooth hole $n$, and then suspend the templet by the hole $n$ from a pin, as shown in Fig. 377, allowing it to have freedom to oscillate. From the same pin suspend a plummet line and mark off the point $G$ in which the plummet line intersects the center line $a\,b$; this point $G$ will be the center of gravity of the crank. Suppose, now, that by this method we have found the distance between the center of gravity $G$ and the center $a$ of the axle to be $3\tfrac{1}{2}$ inches.

To find the center of gravity of the counterbalance $e\,d\,f\,h$, we proceed in a manner as shown in Fig. 378, and explained in Art. 259. Also assume that by this method we have found the distance between the center of gravity $C$ and the edge $f\,h$ to be $4\tfrac{1}{2}$ inches.

Since the distance between the edge $f\,h$ and the center $a$ of the axle has been given, namely, 11 inches, it follows that the total distance between the center $a$ and the center of gravity $C$ must be equal to $11'' + 4\tfrac{1}{2}'' = 15\tfrac{1}{2}$ inches.

Our next step will be to find the weight, which, when applied to the center $b$ of the crank-pin, will have the same effect in producing rotation of the crank around the center $a$ as that of the weight of the crank applied to its center of gravity $G$. This weight is found by Rule 43, given in Art. 257. Hence we have,

$$\frac{250 \text{ pounds} \times 3\tfrac{1}{2} \text{ inches}}{12 \text{ inches}} = 72.91 \text{ pounds.}$$

This weight of 72.91 pounds applied to the center $b$ will have the same tendency to produce rotation as the weight of the crank (250 pounds) applied to the center of gravity $G$, and therefore the 72.91 pounds applied at $b$ will require the same counterbalance as 250 pounds applied at $G$.

But to the center $b$ of the crank-pin is to be applied an additional weight of 100 pounds, represented by $m$. Consequently, the total weight applied to the crank-pin, and which must be counterbalanced, is 172.91 pounds.

We may now reduce our problem to a very simple one. Thus: Fig. 380. Let the line $c\,b$ represent a straight lever, and $a$ its fulcrum; the distance between the fulcrum $a$ and the end $b$ of the lever arm is equal to the distance between the center of axle and the center of crank-pin, namely, 12 inches; and the distance between the fulcrum $a$ and the end $c$ of the other lever arm is equal to the distance between the center of the axle and the center of gravity of the counterbalance, namely, 15½ inches. Now we know that the weight applied to the end $b$ is equal to 172.91 pounds, consequently all we have to do is to find the amount of weight, which, when applied to the end $c$, will hold the lever in equilibrium.

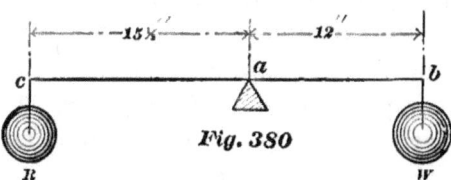

Fig. 380

To find this weight, or, we may say, to find the weight of the counterbalance for any given weight on the crank-pin, we have the following rule:

RULE 44.—Multiply the distance in inches between the center of the axle and the center of the crank-pin by the total weight in pounds applied to the crank-pin, and divide this product by the distance in inches between the center of the axle and the center of gravity of the counterbalance; the quotient will be the weight in pounds of the counterbalance.

According to this rule, we have,

$$\frac{172.91 \text{ pounds} \times 12 \text{ inches}}{15\frac{1}{2} \text{ pounds}} = 133.86 \text{ pounds},$$

which is the weight of the counterbalance.

In order to find the thickness of this weight or counterbalance, we must first find the number of cubic inches contained in it. One cubic inch of cast-iron is generally reckoned to weigh .26 of a pound; hence the following rule:

RULE 45.—Divide the number of pounds in the counterbalance by .26; the quotient will be the number of cubic inches in the counterbalance.

The number of pounds in our counterbalance is 133.86; consequently, according to Rule 45,

$$\frac{133.86}{.26} = 514.84 \text{ cubic inches in the counterbalance.}$$

To determine the thickness of the counterbalance, we have the following rule:

RULE 46.—Divide the number of cubic inches contained in the counterbalance by the area in square inches of its face; the quotient will be the thickness of the counterbalance in inches.

The area of the face $e\ d\ f\ h$ (Fig. 379) is found by multiplying one-half the sum of the parallel sides $e\ d$ and $f\ h$ by its length $o\ p$; the product will be the number of square inches in the surface $e\ d\ f\ h$. Thus:

$$\frac{7'' + 3''}{2} \times 8'' = 40 \text{ inches.}$$

Now, according to Rule 46, the thickness of the counterbalance will be,

$$\frac{514.84 \text{ cubic inches}}{40 \text{ square inches}} = 12.87 \text{ inches, say } 12\frac{7}{8} \text{ inches.}$$

261. Generally in locomotives there is not sufficient room for a counterbalance $12\frac{7}{8}$ inches in thickness, consequently we must employ two weights, each similar in form

to that shown in Fig. 379, so that the thickness can be reduced and still have sufficient weight for counterbalancing.

EXAMPLE 79.—Let $i\,j\,k\,l$, Fig. 381, represent the same cast-iron crank of 250 pounds, and $m$ the same additional weight of 100 pounds applied to the center of the crank-pin, as given in Example 78. The sum of the weights of this crank and weight $m$ are now to be counterbalanced by two weights whose dimensions, except their thicknesses, are given, and these dimensions of each weight are the same as those of

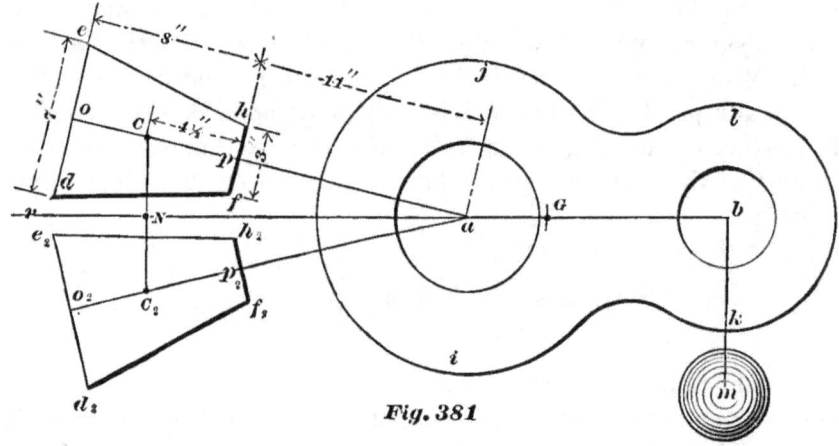

Fig. 381

the weight given in Example 78. The space between the two weights is equal to the thickness of the spoke of the wheel; the weight of the spoke, as in the previous example, is, for the sake of simplicity, left out of consideration. The edge $f\,h$ of the upper weight is to be placed 11 inches from the center $a$ of the axle, and the same distance is to be maintained between the edge $f_2\,h_2$ of the lower weight and the center $a$. In fact, the only difference between this example and the former one is that two weights for counterbalancing, instead of one, are to be used. It is required to find the number of pounds in these weights and their thickness.

Since the size and weight of the crank, and also the additional weight $m$, are the same as before, it follows that the total weight as considered to be applied to the crank-pin will be 172.91 pounds, and this weight must be counterbalanced. Again, since the size of each counterbalance weight, except the thickness, is equal to the size of the weight shown in Fig. 379, it follows that the center of gravity $C$ of the upper weight must be in the same relative position as before—that is, the distance between the center of gravity $C$ and the edge $f\,h$ must be equal to $4\frac{1}{2}$ inches. The same remarks apply to the center of gravity $C_2$ of the lower weight. Consequently the distance between the centers $C$ and $a$ will be equal to $15\frac{1}{2}$ inches, and the distance between the center $C_2$ and $a$ will also be equal to $15\frac{1}{2}$ inches, both distances remaining the same as in the previous example.

We may now consider the weight $e\,d\,f\,h$, and the weight $e_2\,d_2\,f_2\,h_2$ to be segments of one counterbalance. Now, considering these two weights to form one counterbalance $e\,d_2\,f_2\,h$, it must be apparent that neither the center $C$ nor the center $C_2$ can be the center of gravity of the whole counterbalance $e\,d_2\,f_2\,h$; we must therefore find a new center of gravity $N$, or we may say a common center of gravity of the two segments $e\,d\,f\,h$ and $e_2\,d_2\,f_2\,h_2$. To find this new center of gravity, we simply join the centers

$C$ and $C_2$ by a straight line; the point $N$ in which this line cuts the center line $r\,b$ will be the center of gravity required. Now assume that, by this construction, we find the distance between the center of gravity $N$ and the center $a$ of the axle to be equal to 15 inches; we have then all the data necessary for determining the weight and thickness of the counterbalance.

In fact, we may now reduce our problem to that of the simple straight lever, as shown in Fig. 380, in which the line $c\,b$ represents the lever, $a$ the fulcrum, $a\,b$ a lever arm 12 inches long, and $c\,a$ the other lever arm 15 inches long. To the end $b$ is applied a weight $W$ of 172.91 pounds. It is now required to find the weight $R$, which, when applied to the end $c$, will hold the lever in equilibrium. It will be noticed that the only difference between this problem and the previous one represented by this figure consists in the length of the lever arm $c\,a$, which in the previous problem was $15\tfrac{1}{4}$ inches long instead of 15 inches, as we must now consider it to be.

Remembering that the new center of gravity $N$ is the common center of gravity of the two segments, and is the only center of gravity that can now enter in our calculation, we can find the sum of the weights of the segments by Rule 44. Hence we have

$$\frac{172.91 \text{ pounds} \times 12 \text{ inches}}{15 \text{ pounds}} = 138.32 \text{ pounds},$$

which is the sum of the weights of the two segments. Consequently the weight of one segment will be

$$\frac{138.32}{2} = 69.16 \text{ pounds}.$$

It will be noticed that in this example the sum of the weights of the two segments is somewhat greater than the weight of the counterbalance used in Fig. 379, and yet in both examples the weights applied to the crank-pin, which were to be counterbalanced, are equal. This is as it should be, because in Fig. 381 the distance between the center of gravity $N$ and the center $a$ of the axle is less than that between $C$ and $a$ in Fig. 379.

We have found that the weight of one segment of the counterbalance in Fig. 381 is equal to 69.16 pounds. In order to find the thickness of one of these segments, we must first find by Rule 45 the number of cubic inches contained in each segment.

Hence we have,
$$\frac{69.16}{.26} = 266 \text{ cubic inches}.$$

Now, since we know the area of the face $c\,d\,f\,h$ of one segment is equal to 40 square inches, the thickness of the segment will be, according to Rule 46, equal to

$$\frac{266 \text{ cubic inches}}{40 \text{ square inches area}} = 6.65 \text{ inches}.$$

262. In Art. 261 we explained the manner of finding the common center of gravity of two segments of a counterbalance. When more than two segments are to be used—a frequent occurrence—the common center of gravity may be found by the following methods:

238  MODERN LOCOMOTIVE CONSTRUCTION.

EXAMPLE 79a.—Let $A$, $B$, $D$ in Fig. 382 represent three segments of a counterbalance; all these segments are equal in form and weight; it is required to find the common center of gravity of these segments.

RULE 47.—Draw the three segments in their correct position—that is, leaving the correct spaces for the spokes between them—and draw the center lines $e f$, $e_2 f_2$, $e_3 f_3$; these center lines will, when produced, pass through the center of axle. Find the center of gravity of one of the segments, say of the segment $B$, by the method shown in Fig. 374, or by the method shown in Fig. 378, and thus obtain the center of gravity $C_2$. From the center $a$ of the axle draw an arc passing through the center $C_2$, cutting the line $e f$ in the point $C$, and the line $e_3 f_3$ in the point $C_3$. Then $C$ will be the center of gravity of the segment $A$; and $C_3$ the center of gravity of the segment $D$. The centers $C$, $C_2$, $C_3$ must lie in an arc described from the center of the axle, because the segments are all placed at equal distances from the center of axle, and are alike in form and weight. Through the points $C$ and $C_3$ draw a straight line cutting the center line $e_2 f_2$ in the point $i$. Divide the distance between the center of gravity $C_2$ and the point

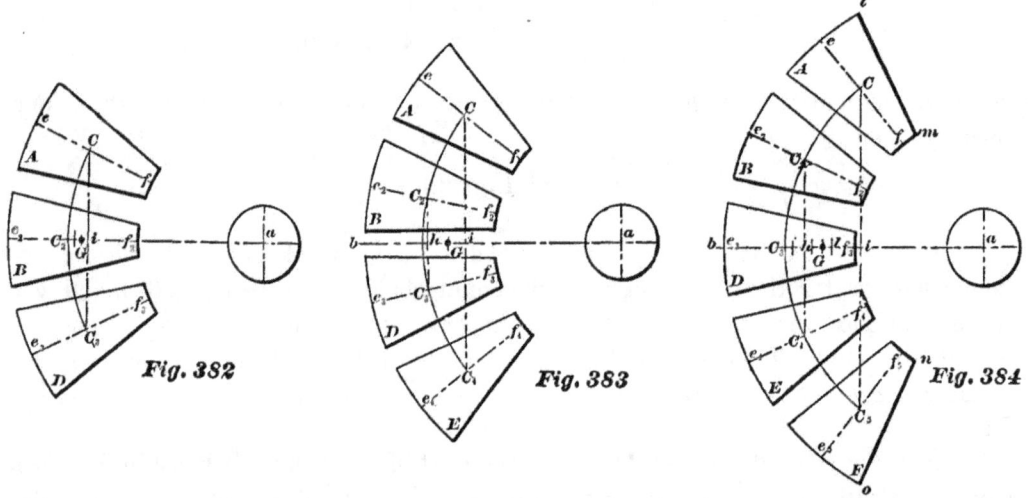

Fig. 382  Fig. 383  Fig. 384

$i$ into three equal parts; the point of division $G$, which is nearest to the point $i$, will be the common center of gravity of the three segments. Here we see that the distance between $G$ and $i$ is equal to one-third of $C_2 i$.

EXAMPLE 79b.—Let $A$, $B$, $D$, $E$ in Fig. 383 represent four segments of a counterbalance; all these segments are equal in form and weight; it is required to find the common center of gravity of these segments.

RULE 48.—Draw the segments in their correct position, leaving the exact amount of space for the spokes between them. Two of these segments must lie above the line $b a$, and two of the segments below it. The line $b a$ must pass through the center of the space for the wheel spoke, and when produced pass through the center $a$ of the axle and also through the center of the crank-pin. Draw the center lines $e f$, $e_2 f_2$, $e_3 f_3$, and $e_4 f_4$. Find the center of gravity of one of the weights, say $C$ of the segment $A$, according to the method shown in Fig. 374 or Fig. 378. From the center $a$ of the axle describe an arc passing through the center of gravity $C$ and cutting the line $e_2 f_2$ in the point $C_2$, $e_3 f_3$ in the point $C_3$, and $e_4 f_4$ in the point $C_4$. The point $C_2$ will be the center of gravity of the segment $B$, $C_3$ the center of gravity of $D$, and $C_4$ that of the segment $E$. Through the centers $C$ and $C_4$ draw a straight line, cutting the line $a\ b$ in the point $i$; also through the centers $C_2$ and $C_3$ draw a straight line, cutting $a\ b$ in the point $h$; the point $G$ midway between $i$ and $h$ will be the common center of gravity of the four segments.

EXAMPLE 79c.—Let $A$, $B$, $D$, $E$, $F$ in Fig. 384 represent five segments of a counterbalance, all of them equal in form and weight; it is required to find the common center of gravity of these segments.

RULE 49.—Through the center $a$ of the axle draw the horizontal line $a\ b$; on this line draw the segment $D$, making its center line $e_3 f_3$ coincide with $a\ b$. Draw the segments $A$ and $B$ above, and the segments $E$ and $F$ below, the segment $D$—all in the correct position, with the correct spaces for the spokes between them. Find the center of gravity $C_3$ of the segment $D$, according to the method shown in Fig. 374 or Fig. 378. From the center $a$ of the axle describe an arc passing through $C_3$ and cutting the center lines $e\ f$, $e_2 f_2$, $e_4 f_4$, $e_5 f_5$ of the segments $A$, $B$, $E$, $F$ in the points $C$, $C_2$, $C_4$, $C_5$; these points will be the centers of gravity of their respective segments. Join the points $C$ and $C_5$ by a straight line, cutting $a\ b$ in the point $i$. Also join the points $C_2\ C_4$ by a straight line, cutting $a\ b$ in the point $h$. On the line $a\ b$ lay off a point $l$ midway between $i$ and $h$; and then divide the distance between $l$ and $C_3$ into five equal parts. The point of division marked $G$ nearest to the point $l$ will be the common center of gravity of the five segments.

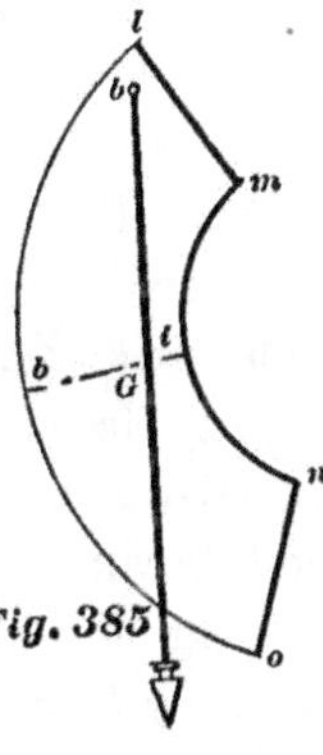

The common center of gravity $G$ of the five segments may also be found approximately, but often near enough for practical purposes, in the following manner:

Cut a templet conforming with the outline $l\ m\ f_3\ n\ o$ of all the five segments shown in Fig. 384.

This templet is represented on a smaller scale in Fig. 385. Anywhere in this templet punch a small smooth hole $b$ and suspend it by this hole from a pin, allowing it freedom to oscillate. From this pin suspend a plummet-line; the point $G$ in which the plummet-line crosses the center line $i\ b$, previously drawn on the templet, is the center of gravity of the five segments.

Fig. 385.

263. A knowledge of the principles upon which the foregoing methods are based may not only prevent mistakes in the applications of the methods, but will also enable us to find the common center of gravity of a number of segments under varied conditions.

In Fig. 386 we may consider the horizontal line $G$ to $d$ to represent a lever, whose fulcrum is at $a$—that is, the center of the axle. This lever is held in equilibrium by the weight $W$ applied at $d$, and the counterweights $A$ and $B$ applied at the end of the other lever arm. The segments $A$ and $B$ are equal in form and weight, and are placed at equal distances from the center $a$ of the axle, consequently their centers of gravity, $C$ and $C_2$, must also be at equal distances from the center $a$. Again, since the distance between the center of gravity $C$ and the line $b\ d$ is equal to that between the center $C_2$ and the line $b\ d$, it follows that the straight line $C\ C_2$ joining the centers of gravity of the two segments must be perpendicular to $b\,d$. From statements made in previous articles, we may assume that the whole weight of the segment $A$ is concentrated at the point $C$, and if this point $C$ is left free to move, the force of gravity will cause it to move in the straight line $C\,C_2$. Also the whole weight of the segment $B$ may be considered to be concentrated at its center of gravity $C_2$, and if this point is left free

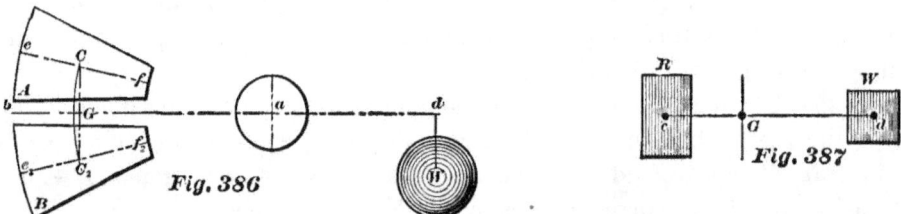

Fig. 386    Fig. 387

to move, the force of gravity will cause it to move in the same line $C\,C_2$ prolonged. Therefore we may say that the line $C\,C_2$ is the line of direction in which the forces due to the weights of the two segments act; and according to the remarks in Art. 255, the line $G\,a$, which is the perpendicular distance from the fulcrum $a$ to the line of direction $C\,C_2$, is the length of the arm, and we may consider the segments $A$ and $B$ to be directly applied to the point $G$; or, in other words, we may assume that the sum of the weights of the two segments is concentrated at the point $G$, producing precisely the same effect in holding the lever in equilibrium as the combined effect of the weight of $A$ acting at $C$, and the weight of $B$ acting at $C_2$.

264. But we may consider this problem in another light. Treating the two segments $A$ and $B$ as two distinct bodies, similar to those shown in Fig. 387, each one equal to any given weight—that is to say, they may be, or may not be, equal in weight, placed in any given position, either one above the other, or side by side, or otherwise, the common center of gravity of these bodies or weights can be found in the following manner:

Fig. 387. Let $R$ represent one body weighing 10 pounds, and $W$ another body weighing 5 pounds; it is required to find the common center of gravity of these two bodies.

RULE 50.—First find the center of gravity $c$ of the weight $R$, and also the center of gravity $d$ of the weight $W$; join the points $c$ and $d$ by a straight line; this line will contain the common center of gravity $G$ of the two weights $R$ and $W$. Now, in order to find the exact location of the point $G$ on the line $c\,d$, we have the following proportion:

The sum of the weights $R$ and $W$ : the line $c\,d$ :: weight of $R$ : $G\,d$;

or,

The sum of the weights $R$ and $W$ : the line $c\,d$ :: weight of $W$ : $G\,c$.

Now, supposing we find that by measurement the line $c\,d$ is 12 inches long, then we have,

$$(10 + 5) : 12 :: 10 : G\,d.$$

Working out this proportion, we have,

$$\frac{12 \times 10}{15} = 8 = G\,d,$$

which shows that the common center of gravity $G$ is located at 8 inches from $d$. Again,

$$(10 + 5) : 12 :: 5 : G\,c.$$

Working out this proportion, we have,

$$\frac{12 \times 5}{15} = 4 = G\,c,$$

which indicates that the common center of gravity $G$ is located at 4 inches from $c$.

Now notice the product of the weight $R$ multiplied by its arm $G\,c$ is equal to the product of the weight $W$ multiplied by its arm $G\,d$. This is as it should be, otherwise the solution is not correct, because $G$ is the point about which the weights $R$ and $W$ must balance each other, and consequently the moment of the force $R$ must be equal to the moment of the force $W$. (See Art. 256.)

In Fig. 386 the weights of the two segments $A$ and $B$ are equal, and consequently, according to the foregoing rule, the common center of gravity $G$ must lie midway between $C$ and $C_2$ in a straight line joining these two points.

The usefulness of Rule 50 will become apparent as we proceed.

265. Let us now examine the method for finding the common center of gravity of three segments as shown in Fig. 382.

In the first place, let us assume that the center segment $B$ has been removed; in this way our problem becomes similar to that shown in Fig. 386, and we find that the point $i$ (Fig. 382) in which the vertical line $C\,C_3$ cuts the horizontal line $a\,c_2$ is the common center of gravity of the two segments $A$ and $D$. We now may assume that simply a weight equal to the sum of the weights of the segments $A$ and $D$ is applied at the point $i$, and throw the idea of segments $A$ and $D$ out of mind. Replacing the segment $B$ in its proper position, and remembering that in determining the effect of this weight we assume the whole of the weight of the segment is concentrated at its center of gravity $C_2$, we have then two weights applied to the line $a\,c_2$, namely, one at $C_2$ and the other at $i$; the weight at $i$ is twice as great as that applied at $C_2$. Now to find the effect of these two weights we must find their common center of gravity $G$ by Rule 50. For the sake of simplicity we will say the weight of the segment $B$ is equal to 1; and consequently the weight applied at $i$ will be equal to 2; hence we have,

The sum of the weights at $i$ and $C_2 = 3$ : line $C_2\,i$ :: weight at $C_2$ : $G\,i$.

Working out this proportion, and assuming that by measurement the line $C_2\,i$ is equal to $1\frac{1}{2}$ inches, we have,

$$\frac{1\frac{1}{2} \times 1}{3} = \frac{1}{2} \text{ inch} = G\,i;$$

that is, the common center of gravity $G$ is located $\frac{1}{2}$ inch from the point $i$ towards $C_2$. Now $\frac{1}{2}$ inch is equal to $\frac{1}{3}$ of $1\frac{1}{2}$ inches—that is to say, $G\,i = \frac{1}{3}$ of $C_2\,i$, which agrees with the previous construction.

266. Now let us take Fig. 383. Here we have four segments which make up the counterbalance. The point $i$ in which the line $C\,C_4$ cuts the line $a\,b$ is the common center of gravity of the two segments $A$ and $E$; and the point $h$ in which the line $C_2\,C_3$ cuts the line $a\,b$ is the common center of gravity of the two segments $B$ and $D$.

We may now assume that we have simply a weight applied at $h$, and another one at $i$; and, since the weights of the segments are equal, the weight applied at $h$ is equal to that applied at $i$. In order to determine the effect of these two weights at $h$ and $i$, we must find their common center of gravity $G$; and since these weights are equal, we find, by Rule 50, that the common center of gravity $G$ is located midway between $h$ and $i$, which agrees with the construction.

267. Lastly, Fig. 384. Here we find the counterbalance composed of five segments. The point $i$ in which the line $C\,C_5$ cuts the line $a\,b$ is the common center of gravity of the two segments $A$ and $F$. The point $h$ in which the line $C_2\,C_4$ cuts the line $a\,b$ is the common center of gravity of the two segments $B$ and $E$. According to the construction in Fig. 383, the point $l$ in Fig. 384, midway between $h$ and $i$, is the common center of gravity of the weights applied at $h$ and $i$—that is, of the four segments $A$, $B$, $E$, and $F$. We may now assume that there are two weights applied to the line $a\,b$, one at $l$ and another at $C_3$. The weight at $l$ is four times as heavy as that at $C_3$. We may now determine the location of the common center of gravity $G$ of the two weights, namely, the weight at $C_3$, and that applied at $l$ by Rule 50; hence we have,

The sum of the weights at $l$ and $C_3 = 5$ : line $C_3\,l$ : : weight at $C_3$ : $G\,l$.

Working out this proportion, and assuming that by measurement we find the line $C_3\,l$ to be equal to $3\tfrac{3}{4}$ inches, we have,

$$\frac{3\tfrac{3}{4} \times 1}{5} = \tfrac{3}{4} \text{ inch} = G\,l;$$

that is, the common center of gravity is located at $\tfrac{3}{4}$ inch from $l$ towards $C_3$. But $\tfrac{3}{4}$ inch is $\tfrac{1}{5}$ of $3\tfrac{3}{4}$, which agrees with the construction.

In all counterbalances which are composed of segments, we always consider the sum of the weights of the segments to be concentrated at their common center of gravity, and the distance from this point to the center of the axle—that is, from $G$ to $a$—to be the lever arm.

268. Figs. 388 and 389 represent the form of one of the cast-iron segments of a counterbalance designed to be bolted between the spokes. As will be seen, this

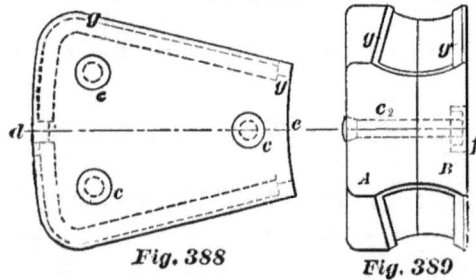

Fig. 388  Fig. 389

segment is made in two pieces, $A$ and $B$. The piece $A$ is placed in the outer face of the driving wheel, and $B$ in the inner face of the wheel. They are held together and clamped to the wheel by the three bolts $c\,c\,c_2$. In large wheels these bolts are $\tfrac{7}{8}$ of an inch diameter; in small wheels, $\tfrac{3}{4}$ inch diameter. Since the space through which the counterbalance has to move is nearly always limited, the bolt heads are generally made conical and countersunk into the outer piece $A$; in the inner piece $B$ pockets $f$ are cast to receive the nuts. The strips $g\,g$ are simply chipping strips, so that the weights can be snugly fitted between the spokes and rim.

The thickness of the outer piece $A$ depends upon the available space through which—in connection with the axle—it can revolve. In some cases, the thickness of this piece depends upon the amount of weight required. The inner piece $B$ is usually kept even with the spokes. The length $d\,e$ also depends upon the amount of weight required, and varies from about one-half to three-quarters of the distance between the rim and hub of the wheel. These segments should never fill the whole space from rim to hub, because, if these spaces are closed by the segments, it will, when the wheels are in certain position, be very difficult to oil the axle journals.

In calculating the weight of the counterbalance it is always best to establish first the length $d\,e$ of the segment, and then find its thickness.

EXAMPLE 80.—It is required to find the dimensions of the segments of a counterbalance for an eight-wheeled locomotive—that is, an engine having four driving wheels and a four-wheeled truck, such as is shown in Fig. 1. Cylinders, 18 inches in diameter; stroke, 24 inches; weight of crosshead, 154 pounds; piston and rod, complete, 306 pounds; main-rod, 280 pounds; side-rod, 240 pounds; crank-pin, 60 pounds. The form of wheel is shown in Fig. 390.

Not only the revolving parts, but also the reciprocating parts of a locomotive will have a disturbing influence on the smooth running of the engine. To obtain a steady motion, the weight of all the parts which produce a disturbing influence must be counterbalanced. Engineers agree that the sum of the weights of all the revolving parts must be counterbalanced; but as to the proportion of the weight of the reciprocating parts which ought to be counterbalanced, they are not unanimous. A few believe that only two-thirds of the weight of the reciprocating parts should be counterbalanced. Our practice has been to counterbalance the sum of the weights of all the reciprocating parts, and we believe it is safe to say that this is the practice of the majority of engineers, and will give the best results; we will follow this practice in the example under consideration.

In determining the dimensions of the counterbalance, we need to confine our attention to only one side of the engine, and consequently in our calculation we have to deal with only two driving wheels through which the counterbalance must be distributed. Each wheel should have enough weight to counterbalance one-half of the weight of the reciprocating parts, in addition to the total weight of the parts which revolve with the wheel. Hence our first step will be to separate the weights of the revolving and the reciprocating parts.

The parts, and their weights, which revolve with the main driving wheel, are:

  Crank-pin .................................... 60 lbs.
  Weight of crank referred to pin .......................180 "
  One-half side-rod.........................................120 "
  One-half main-rod ......................................140 "
  Total weight of the revolving parts ....................500 lbs.

The parts, and their weights, which revolve with the rear driving wheel, are:

  Crank-pin .................................... 60 lbs.
  Weight of crank referred to pin .......................180 "
  One-half of side-rod....................................120 "
  Total weight of revolving parts........................360 lbs.

By the term weight of the crank referred to the crank-pin is meant that weight which, when applied to the crank-pin, will have the same effect in tending to turn the axle as the whole of the weight of the crank applied to the center of gravity of the crank, as explained in Art. 257. To find the weight of the crank referred to the crank-pin, we must first find the center of gravity of the crank by the method shown in Fig. 377, and then compute the weight by Rule 43. Of course, in this case, the thickness of the crank is supposed to be uniform. When the thickness is not uniform, another method is often adopted, which will be explained in Art. 270.

Reciprocating parts, and their weights, are:

$$\begin{aligned}
&\text{Crosshead, pin, etc.} && 154 \text{ lbs.} \\
&\text{Piston and rod} && 306 \text{ "} \\
&\text{One-half of main-rod} && \underline{140 \text{ "}} \\
&\text{Total weight of reciprocating parts} && 600 \text{ lbs.}
\end{aligned}$$

One-half of this weight must be counterbalanced in the main wheel, the other half in the rear wheel. Consequently, the total weight to be counterbalanced in the main driving wheel will be

$$500 + 300 = 800 \text{ pounds;}$$

and the weight to be counterbalanced in the rear driving wheel will be

$$360 + 300 = 660 \text{ pounds.}$$

We will first determine the dimensions of the segments composing the counterbalance in the main driving wheel. In this wheel we have to counterbalance 800 pounds applied to the crank-pin, and since the distance between the center of crank-pin and center of axle is 12 inches, the moment of the force produced by the 800 pounds is

$$800 \times 12 = 9600.$$

Our next step will be to establish the number of segments in the counterbalance, and also the length $d\,e$ of each. No regular rules for determining the number of segments, and their lengths, can be given. An experienced engineer will readily see that four segments, $A$, $B$, $D$, and $E$ (Fig. 390), will be necessary. A smaller number of segments would make their thickness too great for the available space through which they have to move. Hence we will decide that four segments are to be used, and that the length $d\,e$ of each one is to be 12 inches.

We now find the center of gravity $C$ of one of the segments in the manner shown in Fig. 374 or 378, and then find the common center of gravity $G$ of the four segments by the method shown in Fig. 383 and explained in Art. 266. Measuring the distance between the common center of gravity $G$ and the center $a$ of the axle, Fig. 390, we find it to be $18\frac{3}{4}$ inches. Now, since the moment of force due to the weight of the four segments, that is, the product obtained by multiplying the total weight of the four segments by the $18\frac{3}{4}$ inches, must be equal to the moment of the force due to the weight applied to the crank-pin, namely 9,600 (previously determined), we can find the total weight of the four segments by Rule 44. Hence we have

$$\frac{800 \times 12}{18.75} = \frac{9600}{18.75} = 512 \text{ pounds.}$$

Since the weight of a cubic inch of cast-iron is .26 of a pound, the total number of cubic inches in the four segments will be, according to Rule 45,

$$\frac{512}{.26} = 1969 \text{ cubic inches.}$$

Assuming that in Fig. 390 the area of $f\,g\,h\,i$ of one segment is 80 square inches, then the area of the four segments will be

$$80 \times 4 = 320 \text{ square inches.}$$

And lastly the thickness of the counterbalance, or, which amounts to the same thing, the thickness of each segment, will be, according to Rule 46,

$$\frac{1969}{320} = 6.15+ \text{ inches.}$$

The dimensions of the segments for the rear driving wheel are found in a manner

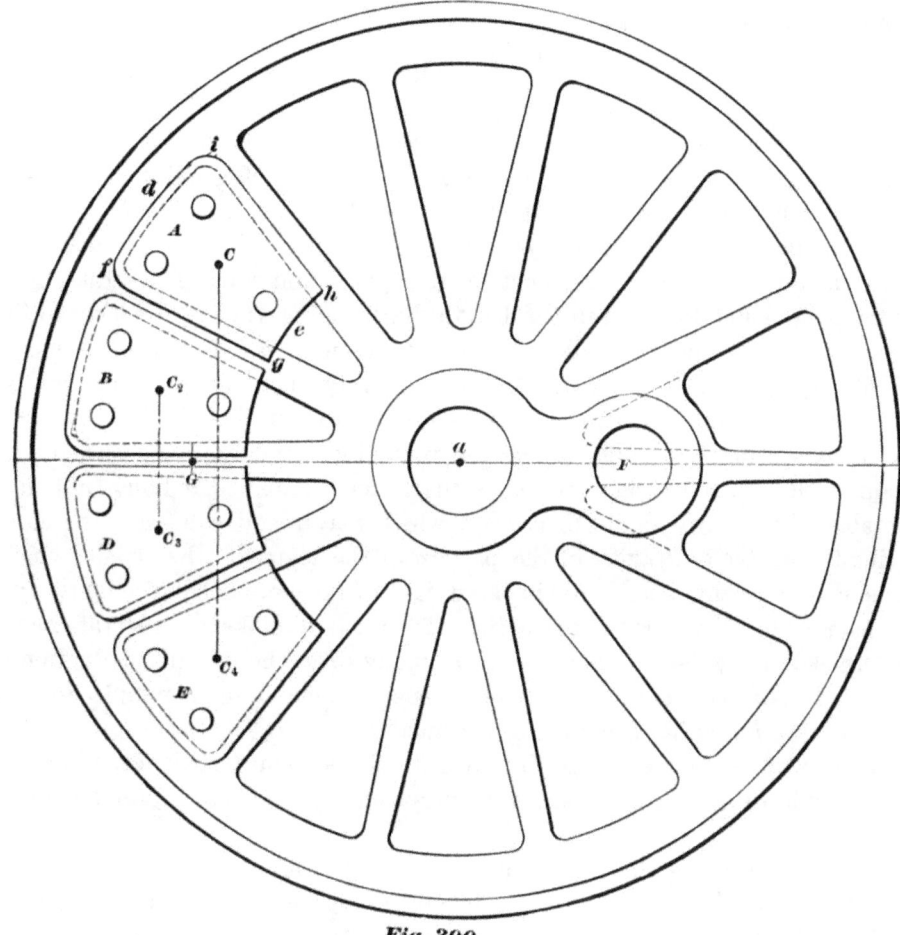

**Fig. 390**

precisely similar to the foregoing—that is, we first establish the length $d\,e$ of the segments, and then find the thickness. We will make the calculations without explanatory remarks.

Let us decide that the length $d\ e$ of each one of the four segments in the rear driving wheel is to be 12 inches—that is, equal to the length of segments in the main driving wheel.

Under these conditions the common center of gravity $G$ will be $18\frac{3}{4}$ inches from the center $a$ of the axle, the same as in the main driving wheel. Now, remembering that the total weight applied to the crank-pin in this wheel, and which must be counterbalanced, is 660 pounds, we have,

$$\frac{660 \times 12}{18.75} = 422.4 \text{ pounds,}$$

which is the total number of pounds in the four segments. Again,

$$\frac{422.4}{.26} = 1624 \text{ cubic inches}$$

in the four segments, and lastly,

$$\frac{1624}{320} = 5 \text{ inches,}$$

which is the thickness of each segment in the rear driving wheel.

269. It must be remarked here, that when the center of gravity $C$ of one of the segments is to be found by the method shown in Fig. 378, the templet must be cut somewhat smaller than the face $f\ g\ h\ i$ of the segment (Fig. 390), to allow for the amount of metal cut out of the segment for the spokes and rim. The reduction in the size of templet should be made in the length $d\ e$, bringing the arc $f\ i$ closer to the arc $g\ h$; the reduction should be made at the end $f\ i$, none at $g\ h$, because the end $g\ h$ is not to fit any part of the wheel, and consequently there is no metal cut out at this end. A small reduction should also be made in the width, bringing the two sides $f\ g$ and $h\ i$ closer together. The amount of reduction is generally governed by good judgment rather than by calculation, as the latter method is tedious and involves considerable labor. Any slight inaccuracy which may result can easily be corrected by finding the center of gravity of the pattern of the segment when made, which will enable us to correct any small error in the weight of the counterbalance by readjusting the common center of gravity $G$ of all the segments, and make such slight changes in the pattern as may be deemed necessary. In many cases the required reduction of the templet will be so small that for practical purposes we may cut the templet to conform to the surface $f\ g\ h\ i$ without making any reduction.

It must also be noticed that the weight of the counterbalance, found in the manner as we have done, will be slightly—very slightly—too heavy, for the following reason:

If the wheel center is made without the crank-pin hub, and if the workmanship is absolutely perfect, the wheel center itself will be perfectly balanced. In putting in the crank-pin hub, a portion $F$ of the spokes must be cut out, and for this amount of metal thus cut out no allowance has been made, and consequently the counterbalance is not only sufficient for the weight of the crank, but also for the amount $F$ cut out of the spokes, and therefore the counterbalance is slightly too heavy, but by an amount barely appreciable.

270. Again, engineers and draftsmen often find it difficult to determine the exact location of the center of gravity of the crank, and therefore, instead of finding the weight of the crank referred to the crank-pin, content themselves by finding the weight of the crank-pin hub—that is, the weight of the metal around the crank-pin as indicated by the shaded portion in Fig. 391—and then adding this weight to the revolving parts to be counterbalanced, in place of the weight of the crank referred to the crank-pin; by this method the necessity of finding the center of gravity of the crank is avoided.

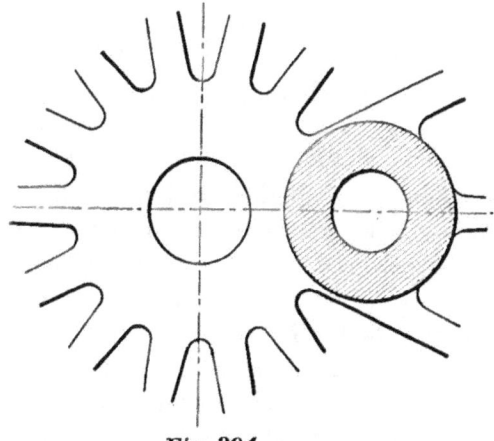

Fig. 391

This method of adding the weight of the crank-pin hub to the revolving parts, which must be counterbalanced, saves considerable labor in all cases, and is usually adopted when the crank is not of uniform thickness.

271. Frequently, in fact in the majority of locomotives, the counterbalance and the wheel center are cast in one piece, as shown in Fig. 392. To determine the dimensions of a counterbalance of this kind, we should follow the rules given in Art. 268. That is to say, we should consider the solid counterbalance to be made up of a number of segments bolted between the spokes, as shown in Fig. 390, and then determine the thickness by a method precisely similar to that given in Art. 268.

The correctness of the result of the calculation depends upon the correct position of the common center of gravity $G$ (Fig. 390) of the segments, and this center, of course, depends upon the correct position of the center of gravity $C$ of each segment; therefore we conclude that when the centers of gravity $C_1$ $C_2$, etc., of the segments are placed in incorrect positions, the results of our calculations will be erroneous.

If in these segments metal had not to be cut out of the sides $i\,h$ and $f\,g$ to fit the spokes, and also out of the end $f\,i$ to fit the rim, we could find very accurately and easily the centers of gravity $C_1$ $C_2$ of these segments of uniform thickness by the method shown in Fig. 378. But it is not such an easy matter to find the center of gravity of segments of irregular shapes, as shown in Fig. 390, or Fig. 389; in fact, to find correctly the center of gravity of one of these segments involves a great amount of labor, unless we have the pattern of which the center of gravity may be found by balancing it on a knife edge.

Now, when a solid counterbalance, as shown in Fig. 392, is considered to be made up of segments, we cannot lose sight of the fact that the sides of the segments and their outer ends must be formed to fit the spokes, and consequently we have to do with segments of irregular shape. To reduce the labor of finding the common center of gravity of these segments, or, in other words, to reduce the labor of finding the center of gravity $G$ of the counterbalance shown in Fig. 392, we may generally adopt the following method; the results obtained by this method, although not absolutely correct, will be sufficiently accurate for practical purposes:

Instead of considering the counterbalance (Fig. 392) to be made up of segments, as we should do, we treat it as it appears to be, namely, as one solid weight. Now, assume that the dimensions of this weight are such as will give a sufficient amount of metal, and not more, to counterbalance all the weights applied to the center of crank-pin; then, by inserting, so to speak, this counterbalance into the wheel center, we must cut portions out of several spokes, and also cut a part out of the rim; by so doing we leave unbalanced portions of other spokes and a part of the rim on the crank-pin side, all of which are precisely similar in amount and form to those cut out. It must be evident that by leaving portions of the wheel itself unbalanced we create new disturbing forces, which will be just as injurious as a similar amount of unbalanced weight applied to the crank-pin. Therefore the thickness of our present counterbalance must be increased, so that not only the weights applied to the crank-pin are counterbalanced, but also have sufficient weight to counterbalance those portions of the wheel opposite those which had to be cut out to make room for the counterbalance. In the following example it will be seen how a close approximation to the exact thickness can be determined.

EXAMPLE 81.—The distance from the center of axle to the center of crank-pin is 12 inches; the total weight applied to the crank, which must be counterbalanced, is

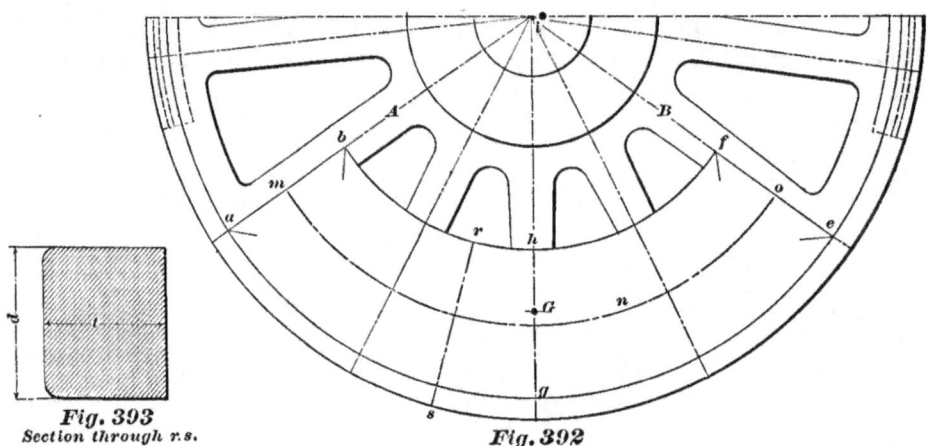

Fig. 393
Section through r.s.

Fig. 392

500 pounds; the depth of the counterbalance from $h$ to $g$ is to be 8 inches, and is to terminate in the centers $a\,b, f\,e$ of the spokes $A$ and $B$ (Fig. 392). It is required to find the thickness of the counterbalance; this thickness is indicated by $t$, in Fig. 393. This figure represents a cross-section of the counterbalance through the line marked $r\,s$, in Fig. 392.

In the first place, make a drawing of the wheel, as shown in Fig. 392, then cut a templet conforming to the outline $a\,b\,h\,f\,e\,g$ of the counterbalance, and find its center of gravity $G$ in the manner shown in Fig. 385. Mark off this center of gravity $G$ on the drawing, and measure its distance from the center $i$ of the axle. Assume that we find the distance between $G$ and the center $i$ to be 16 inches, we will then have all the data necessary for determining the thickness by calculation. The moment of the force due to the weight applied to the crank-pin is equal to

$$500 \times 12 = 6000.$$

The moment of the force due to the weight of the counterbalance must also be equal to 6,000; hence, by dividing 6,000 by the distance of the center of gravity $G$ from the center $i$, we have,

$$\frac{6000}{16} = 375 \text{ pounds,}$$

which is the weight necessary to counterbalance the weight applied to the crank-pin. But this counterbalance cuts portions out of five spokes and also a portion out of the rim. Suppose now that by calculation we find the total amount thus cut out of the wheel center to be equal to 80 pounds. Adding this weight to 375 pounds previously found, we have,

$$375 + 80 = 455 \text{ pounds}$$

for the total weight of the counterbalance.

We now find the thickness of the counterbalance in a manner precisely similar to that given in Art. 268, thus: Dividing the total weight of 455 pounds by the weight of a cubic inch of cast-iron, we have,

$$\frac{455}{.26} = 1750 \text{ cubic inches}$$

required in the counterbalance.

And lastly, dividing the number of cubic inches by the area of the face $a\,b\,h\,f\,e\,g$ of the counterbalance, we have,

$$\frac{1750}{256} = 6.83 \text{ inches,}$$

which is the thickness of the counterbalance.

272. The simplest way of finding the area of the surface $a\,b\,h\,f\,e\,g$ of the counterbalance will be to describe an arc $m\,n\,o$ midway between the arcs $a\,g\,e$ and $b\,h\,f$ (not drawn through the center of gravity $G$), then find by measurement the length of the arc $m\,n\,o$, and multiply this length by the depth $a\,b$; the product will be the number of square inches in the face of the counterbalance.

273. Now it must not be understood that we claim to obtain, by the foregoing method, an absolutely correct thickness for the counterbalance; the thickness thus found, although close enough for practical purposes, is only approximate, for the following reason: In the first place, we should have considered the counterbalance to consist of a number of segments fitted around the spokes and part of the rim, and then found the common center of gravity of these segments. Instead of this, we found the center of gravity of the whole counterbalance without making the proper allowances for the amount of metal which must be cut out of the counterbalance for the spokes and rim.

Consequently the center of gravity $G$, as we have determined it, will be somewhat —a very small amount—too far away from the center $i$ of the axle. Secondly, simply adding the weight of those portions of the spokes and rim which are cut out for the purpose of making room for the counterbalance to the weight required for counterbalancing the weights applied to the crank-pin, is not quite correct. The exact procedure would be to find the common center of gravity of the portions cut out of the wheel center, so as to obtain the correct distance between this center of gravity and the center of axle, and then find the amount of weight which, when applied to the center of gravity $G$ of the counterbalance, will have the same effect as the weight of the portions of the spokes and rim, cut out of the wheel center, applied to their own center of gravity, and then add this weight, so found, to the weight required for counterbalancing the weights applied to the crank-pin. But such a course requires a great amount of labor, and may, on account of its complicacy, and the errors which may creep into it, give no better results than those obtained by the simpler method.

274. In ten-wheeled, Mogul, and consolidation engines, the weight of the reciprocating parts which are to be counterbalanced is often equally distributed throughout the driving wheels, thereby making the counterbalances in all wheels, excepting the main wheel, equal in size. The counterbalance in the main wheel will, of course, be a little larger than the others, because it has to counterbalance a heavier crank-pin than those in the other wheels, and has also to counterbalance the weight of one-half of the connecting-rod, which the counterbalances in the other wheels have not to do. In some instances this arrangement will require in the main wheel a counterbalance whose thickness is too great to pass through the available space; consequently, in such cases, the total weights of the revolving and reciprocating parts are assumed to be equally distributed throughout all the wheels, and calculations of the counterbalance made accordingly, making the counterbalances in all the wheels (main wheel included) equal in size and weight.

275. Even with this arrangement, considerable difficulty is often experienced in the endeavor to obtain sufficient weight in the counterbalance for narrow-gauge locomotives having driving wheels of comparatively small diameter, say 3 feet. In fact, in many of these small wheels it is impossible to obtain sufficient weight with cast-iron, and therefore these counterbalances are frequently cast hollow and filled with lead—for instance, such as is shown in Fig. 394. This figure represents

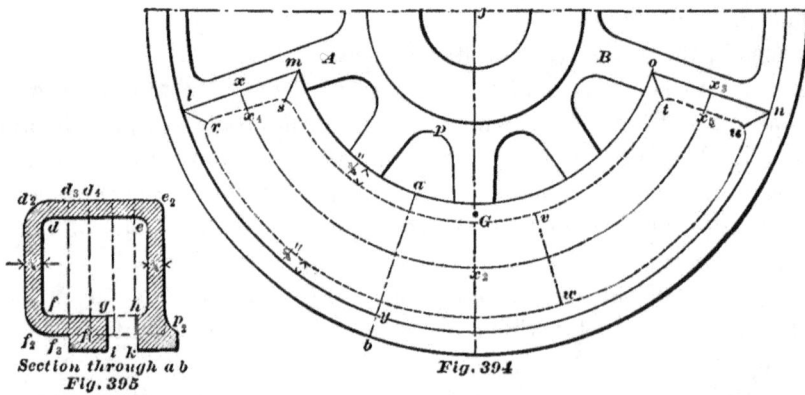

Section through $ab$
Fig. 395

Fig. 394

a wheel center 33 inches diameter, and is designed for a narrow-gauge (3 feet, or 3 feet 6 inches gauge) locomotive. Fig. 395 represents a section of the counterbalance through the line $ab$ (Fig. 394), and, as will be seen, it is cast hollow, so that it may be filled with lead. We use lead because it is considerably heavier than cast-iron, and consequently we can obtain a counterbalance which will need less room than a cast-iron counterbalance of the same weight. We are compelled to use a counterbalance of small dimensions, and yet a heavy one, because, on account of the small diameter of the wheel, the length of the arc $x\ x_2\ x_3$ (which is the length of the counterbalance) and also the depth $a\ y$ are limited. The available space through which the counterbalance has to move will also limit the thickness $d_2\ e_2$ in Fig. 395. Another fact we must not lose sight of, is that, occasionally, in small wheels, the distance between the center of gravity $G$ of the counterbalance and the center of the axle will be less than the length of the crank; consequently in cases of this kind the weight of the counterbalance will be greater than that applied to the crank-pin; such conditions do not occur in large wheels. Small wheels leave us but very little choice in the length $x\ x_2\ x_3$ of the counterbalance, which frequently must be extended around the wheel as far as we can possibly go with advantage. The choice of the width $a\ y$ is also limited; all we can do is to make it as wide as we can, leaving only sufficient room between the counterbalance and the hub, that is, between $a$ and $p$, for oiling the axle journals when the counterbalance stands above the center $j$.

276. The thickness of this class of counterbalances can be determined by the following method, which saves labor and promotes simplicity, but will give only approximate results, though close enough for practical purposes.

EXAMPLE 82.—The length of the crank is 9 inches; total weight applied to the crank-pin, which is to be counterbalanced, is 300 pounds; it is required to find the thickness of the counterbalance.

Make a drawing of the wheel center as shown in Fig. 394. Lay in the counterbalance, and let it extend from the center $l\ m$ of the arm $A$ to the center $o\ n$ of the arm $B$. This length of the counterbalance is arbitrary; an experienced designer will know that, under the conditions, it must be made as long as possible; and anything beyond the lines $l\ m$ and $o\ n$ will add little, if any, appreciable effect to the counterbalance. Let us also decide to make the width $a\ y$ equal to 6 inches; this will leave about as little room between $a$ and $p$ as we can get along with in oiling the axle journal. Let us now consider that our counterbalance is simply a cast-iron box whose cross-section is rectangular, as represented by the lines $d_2 f_2$, $f_2 p_2$, $p_2 e_2$, and $d_2 e_2$, in Fig. 395; also let us consider that the cross-section of the lead is represented by the rectangle $d\ e f g\ h$. Now the depth $d_2 f_2$ of the box is established, the thickness of the sides of this box is also established, which is to be $\frac{3}{4}$ of an inch. We may, therefore, find at once the weight of sides $d_2 f_2$ and $e_2 p_2$ in the following manner: Midway between the arcs $m\ a\ o$ and $l\ y\ n$ draw, from the center $j$, the arc $x\ x_2\ x_3$; multiply the length of this arc by the depth $a\ y$, by the thickness of the side, and by the weight of a cubic inch of cast-iron; the product will be the weight required; thus:

Assume that by measurement we find the length of the arc $x\ x_2\ x_3$ to be 29 inches; then $29'' \times 6'' \times \frac{3}{4}'' \times .26 = 33.93$ pounds, which is the weight of one side, and $33.93 \times 2 = 67.86$ pounds, which is the weight of both sides, $d_2 f_2$ and $e_2 p_2$.

Let us now assume that the counterbalance is divided into a number of slabs, as indicated by the dotted lines $d_3 f_3$, $d_4 f_4$, etc., each slab 1 inch thick, the divisions or cutting planes being parallel to the face $l\ m\ a\ y\ o\ n$ of the counterbalance. Let us now find the weight of one of these slabs. Each one of them is composed of two kinds of metal, namely, lead and cast-iron. Of course, lead predominates. The weight of lead is generally reckoned at 0.41 pound per cubic inch. Consequently the area bounded by the dotted lines $r\,s$, $t\,u$, and the arcs $s\,v\,t$, $r\,w\,u$, multiplied by .41, will give the number of pounds of lead in one slab. The area of this surface of lead is found by multiplying the length of the arc $x_4\,x_2\,x_5$ by width $v\,w$. The width $v\,w$ is, under the given conditions, equal to $4\frac{1}{2}$ inches; and assuming that by measurement we find the length of the arc $x_4\,x_2\,x_5$ equal to $27\frac{1}{2}$ inches, we have for the weight of lead in one slice, whose thickness is 1 inch, $27\frac{1}{2}'' \times 4\frac{1}{2}'' \times .41 = 50.7375$ pounds, say $50\frac{3}{4}$ pounds.

To this weight must be added the weight of the cast-iron included by the arcs $m\,a\,o$ and $s\,v\,t$; also that between the arcs $r\,w\,u$ and $l\,y\,n$, all 1 inch in depth. Let us assume that we have found by calculation the weight of this amount of cast-iron to be equal to $10\frac{1}{4}$ pounds, then the total weight of one slab will be equal to

$$50\tfrac{3}{4} + 10\tfrac{1}{4} = 61 \text{ pounds.}$$

Cut a templet to conform to the outline $l\,m\,a\,o\,n\,y$ of the counterbalance, and find its center of gravity $G$ by the method shown in Fig. 385; lay off this center of gravity on the drawing, and measure its distance from the center $j$ of the axle; this distance, we will say, is equal to $8\frac{1}{2}$ inches.

The moment of the force due to the weight applied to the crank-pin is equal to the product of the length of the crank into the weight applied to the pin; hence we have

$$300 \times 9 = 2700.$$

The moment of the force due to the weight of the counterbalance is also equal to 2,700; hence the total weight of the counterbalance must be equal to

$$\frac{2700}{8.5} = 317.64+ \text{ pounds.}$$

But we have already found that the weight of the two cast-iron sides $d_2\,f_2$ and $e_2\,p_2$ (Fig. 395) is equal to 67.86 pounds. Subtracting this weight from the total weight of the counterbalance, we have

$$317.64 - 67.86 = 249.78 \text{ pounds.}$$

This weight of 249.78 pounds must now be made up by the weight of the slabs into which the counterbalance has been divided. Therefore, we must now find the number of slabs required to make up the weight of 249.78 pounds. Since we have found that the weight of each slab is equal to 61 pounds, we have

$$\frac{249.78}{61} = 4.09, \text{ say 4 slabs.}$$

And lastly, since each slab is 1 inch thick, the thickness of the lead from $d$ to $e$ must be 4 inches, and the total thickness from $d_2$ to $e_2$ of the counterbalance must be equal to $4 + 1\frac{1}{2} = 5\frac{1}{2}$ inches. In this case we have left out the weight of the arms and rim, which must necessarily be cut out of the wheel to insert the counterbalance, but this weight is generally made up by filling the opening $g\,h\,i\,k$ with lead.

277. Figs. 396, 397 represent a 42-inch wheel center with lead counterbalance, designed in one of our prominent locomotive works. It is suitable for heavy freight engines with cylinders 20 inches diameter and up to 22 inches.

MODERN LOCOMOTIVE CONSTRUCTION. 253

Figs. 398, 399 represent a driving wheel with lead counterbalance. It is used on elevated railroads. We believe that in this wheel the arms and rim could have been made lighter, and still be strong enough to do excellent service.

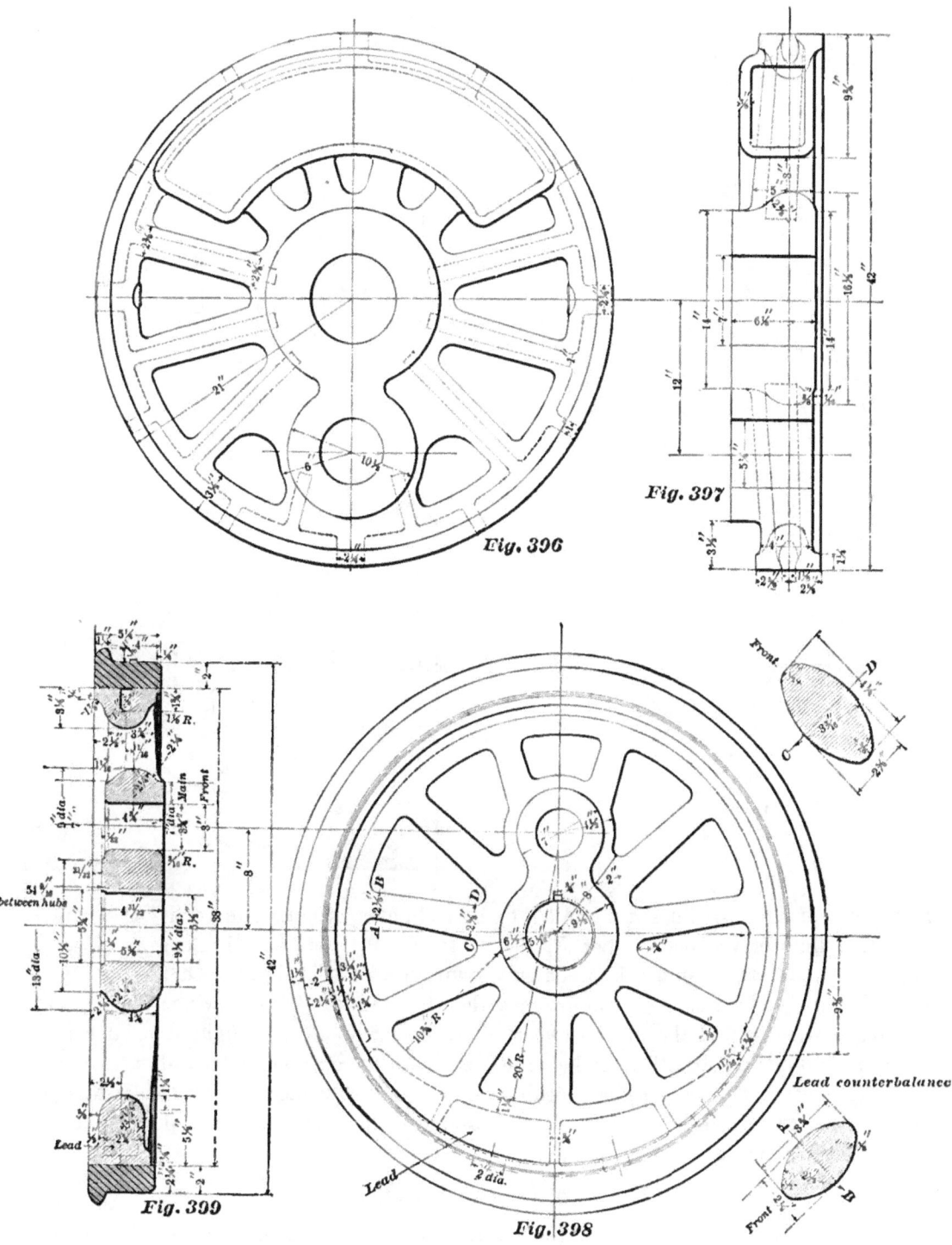

Fig. 396

Fig. 397

Fig. 399

Fig. 398

254    MODERN LOCOMOTIVE CONSTRUCTION.

278. In locomotive construction we have sometimes to find the areas of plane surfaces or figures similar to that shown in Fig. 400.

The area of such a figure may be found in the following manner:

Divide the line $a\,b$ into any number of equal parts, say five, and through the points of division $e, g, i, k$, draw lines perpendicular to $a\,b$ terminating in the curve $c\,h\,d$. The lines $c\,f, g\,h$, etc., are called ordinates, and for the sake of simplicity we

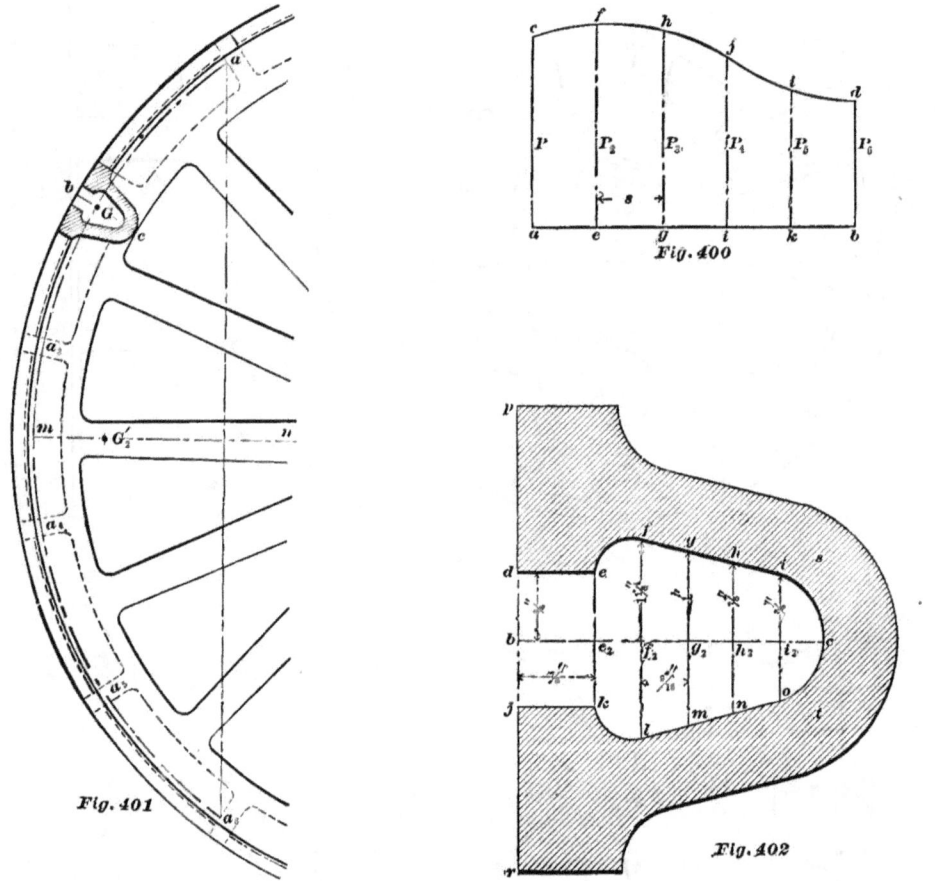

may also consider the lines $a\,c$ and $b\,d$ to be ordinates, although in reality they are bounding lines of the plane. Let $P, P_2, P_3, P_4, P_5, P_6$ represent the lengths of the ordinates, and $s$ the distance between any two successive ordinates—that is to say, $s = e\,g$ or $g\,i$. The area of this figure may then be found by the following:

RULE 51.—To find the area between a given curve and a straight line, such as $c\,h\,d$ and $a\,b$ in Fig. 400. To one-half the lengths of the extreme outer ordinates add the length of all the intermediate ordinates, and multiply the sum by the distance between any two successive ordinates; the product will be the area. Or, putting this rule in the shape of a formula, we have

$$(\tfrac{1}{2} P + P_2 + P_3 + P_4 + P_5 + \tfrac{1}{2} P_6) \times s = \text{area}.$$

EXAMPLE 83.—Suppose we find the length of $a\,c$ equal to $2\tfrac{7}{8}$ inches, $c\,f = 3, g\,h =$

$2\frac{15}{16}$, $i\,j = 2\frac{9}{16}$, $k\,l = 2\frac{1}{16}$, $b\,d = 2$, and the distance $s$ between any two successive ordinates equal to $1\frac{1}{4}$ inches; it is required to find the area.

$$\left(\frac{2\frac{7}{8}''}{2} + 3'' + 2\frac{15}{16}'' + 2\frac{9}{16}'' + 2\frac{1}{16}'' + \frac{2''}{2}\right) \times 1\frac{1}{4}'' = 16\frac{1}{4} \text{ square inches.}$$

The accuracy of the result depends on the number of ordinates; the greater the number, the greater the accuracy.

In the next article we will give practical applications of this rule.

279. In a number of locomotives the outer form of the rim of the driving wheel is uniform throughout. Such a wheel is shown in Fig. 358. There we notice that a portion of the rim, opposite to the crank, is cast solid, and the remaining portion of the rim is cast hollow. But, in many cases, the extra weight of metal gained by casting part of the rim solid is not sufficient for counterbalancing the whole weight applied to the crank-pin; consequently we often find the whole rim cast hollow, and of equal dimensions throughout, with a certain portion of the rim opposite the crank filled with lead, so as to obtain a greater weight in the same amount of space than can be obtained by casting a portion of the rim solid. Hence, it frequently happens that the weight of the lead in the rim, and its effect as a counterbalance, must be calculated.

Let Fig. 401 represent a part of a driving wheel whose rim is cast hollow, and of uniform cross-section throughout. The section around the center line $b\,c$ represents a cross-section of the rim; and Fig. 402 represents the same section on a larger scale. The portion of the rim from the rib $a$ to the rib $a_6$ is filled with lead. It is required to find the weight of the lead, and its effect as a counterbalance; that is to say, to determine the amount of weight applied to the crank-pin which the lead in the rim can counterbalance.

This problem includes two distinct problems, namely, to find the weight of the lead; second, to find the effect of the weight of the lead as a counterbalance.

For the sake of simplicity we shall leave the ribs $a_3$, $a_4$, $a_5$ which are cast in the rim out of consideration, and proceed as if the hollow part of the rim from the rib $a$ to the rib $a_6$ had been a clear space and then filled with lead.

### WEIGHT OF THE LEAD IN THE RIM.

In looking at this counterbalance, or body of lead, from a theoretical standpoint, we may consider this body or solid to be generated by a surface which is equal in extent to the cross-section of lead revolving about the center of the axle, and this surface we may call the generating surface. The contents (that is, the number of cubic inches) of this solid is obtained by multiplying the area of the generating surface in square inches by the length of the path (or arc, in this case) in inches described by the center of gravity of the generating surface; the product will be the number of cubic inches in the counterbalance. And lastly, the number of cubic inches multiplied by the weight of one cubic inch of metal will be the weight of the counterbalance. Consequently we have the following:

RULE 52.—Multiply the area in square inches of the cross-section of the lead by the length of the arc in inches, described by the center of gravity of this cross-section; the product will be the number of cubic inches in the counterbalance. This last product, multiplied by the weight of one cubic inch of lead, namely, .41 pound, will be the weight of the counterbalance.

From the foregoing we see that in determining the number of cubic inches in the counterbalance two distinct factors enter into our calculation, namely, the area of the cross-section of the lead, and the length of path which the center of gravity of this section will describe.

The outline of the cross-section of the lead is represented by the outline $d\ e\ h\ c\ n\ k\ j$ of the cavity in Fig. 402. The area of this cross-section can be found by Rule 51. Thus: Draw the line $b\ c$ perpendicular to $p\ r$. If the outline of the section is symmetrical, the line $b\ c$ must be drawn through the center of the section; if the outline of this section is not symmetrical, we first draw a line $s\ t$ (any length) parallel to line $p\ r$, and touching the curve $i\ c\ o$ in one point, as $c$, and then through this point, that is, the point of tangency, draw the line $b\ c$ perpendicular to $p\ r$, as before.

Let us assume that the outline of the section is symmetrical. Through the point $e$ draw a line $e\ e_2$ perpendicular to the line $b\ c$. Divide the distance from $e_2$ to $c$ into any number of equal parts, say five; through the points of division $f_2, g_2, h_2$, and $i_2$ draw lines perpendicular to $b\ c$, cutting the outline of the section in the points $f, g, h, i$. Suppose now that we find, by measurement, the line $e\ e_2$ to be equal to $\frac{3}{4}$ inch; $f f_2 = 1\frac{1}{8}$; $g\ g_2 = 1$; $h\ h_2 = \frac{7}{8}$; $i\ i_2 = \frac{3}{4}$; and $c$ of course $= 0$; also, the distance, such as $f_2\ g_2$, or $g_2\ h_2$, that is, the distance between any two successive ordinates or perpendiculars, equal to $\frac{9}{16}$ inch. The area of the surface $e_2\ c\ h\ f\ e$ will then, according to Rule 51, be equal to

$$\left( \frac{\frac{3''}{4}}{2} + 1\frac{1}{8}'' + 1'' + \frac{7}{8}'' + \frac{3}{4}'' + \frac{0}{2} \right) \times \frac{9}{16} = 2.32+ \text{ square inches.}$$

To this we must add the area of the rectangle $b\ d\ e\ e_2$; and since $b\ e_2$ is equal to $\frac{7}{8}$ inch, and $e\ e_2 = \frac{3}{4}$ inch, we have $.875 \times .75 = .65+$ square inch; hence $2.32 + .65 = 2.97$ square inches, which is the area of the section above the line $b\ c$; and $2.97 \times 2 = 5.9$ square inches, the total area of the cross-section of the lead.

If the outline of the section is not symmetrical, as we have assumed it to be, then we find area of the surface above the line $b\ c$, and that below the line $b\ c$, each one separately, in a manner precisely similar to the foregoing, and add the two together; the sum will be the total area of the surface.

Our next step will be to find the length of the path described by the center of gravity of the cross-section of the lead. Cut a templet to the outline $d\ e\ h\ c\ n\ k\ j$ of the cavity (Fig. 402), and find its center of gravity $G$ by the method shown in Fig. 378, and mark this point $G$ in its correct position from $b$ in the section shown in Fig. 401. From the center of the axle describe an arc passing through the center $G$, and terminating in the sides of the brackets $a$ and $a_6$. This arc will represent the path of the center of gravity $G$ of the cross-section, while this cross-section, or generating surface, is revolving about the center of the axle. Now suppose that, by measurement, we find the length of this arc from $a$ to $a_6$ to be 57 inches, then the total number of cubic inches in the lead will be equal to the product obtained by multiplying the area in square inches of the cross-section, previously found, by the length in inches of the arc $a\ a_4\ a_6$; hence we have $5.9'' \times 57'' = 336.3$ cubic inches. Multiplying the cubic inches by the weight of one cubic inch of lead, we have 336.3 × .41 = 137.883 pounds, which is the total weight of the lead in the rim.

### EFFECT OF THE LEAD COUNTERBALANCE IN THE RIM.

280. Our next step will be to determine how much of the weight applied to the crank-pin will be counterbalanced by the weight of the lead in the rim. To do this we must find the center of gravity $G_2$ (Fig. 401) of the whole amount of lead, and the correct distance between this center of gravity and the center of the axle. But here a little difficulty arises; we see that the thickness of the lead is not uniform, that is to say, the lines $k\ e$, $l f$, $m\ g$, etc., in the cross-section of the lead, as shown in Fig. 402, are not equal in length; therefore we cannot find the center of gravity of the lead by the method shown in Fig. 385, or by any method previously given; hence we adopt the following method:

In the first place we shall assume that the area of the cross-section of the lead is infinitely reduced, so that the whole counterbalance will be represented by the arc $a\ m\ a_6$ (Fig. 401), which is described from the center of the axle and passes through the center of gravity $G$ of the cross-section; and we shall also assume that the whole weight of the lead is concentrated along this arc, or, in other words, the weight of this arc $a\ m\ a_6$ is equal to the whole weight of the lead. Join the extremities $a$ and $a_6$ of this arc by a straight line, which will be the chord. We have now reduced the conditions of the problem to those of a very simple one, for we have now only to find the center of gravity of the arc $a\ m\ a_6$.

In J. Weisbach's "Theoretical Mechanics" we find that the center of gravity of an arc of a circle must lie in the radius drawn through the middle of the arc, because this radius is an axis of symmetry of the arc; consequently in our problem the center of gravity $G_2$ of the arc $a\ m\ a_6$ must lie in the line $n\ m$, which is drawn through the middle $m$ of the arc to the center of the axle. Again, we find that the distance from the center of gravity of the arc to the center from which the arc has been described is to the radius of the arc as the chord is to the arc. To indicate these proportions by symbols, let

Length of the arc be represented by................................................$b$
Length of the chord  "        "         "  ................................................$s$
Length of radius     "        "         "  ................................................$r$
Distance of center of gravity "         "  ................................................$y$

Then we have

$$y : r : : s : b.\ \ \text{Consequently,}$$

$$y = \frac{s\ r}{b}.$$

From the foregoing we can establish the following rule:

RULE 53.—To find the center of gravity of the lead in the rim, multiply the length in inches of the chord joining the extremities of an arc which is described from the center of the axle and passing through the center of gravity of the cross-section of the lead by its radius in inches, and divide this product by the length of the arc in inches;

the quotient will be the distance from the center of the axle to the center of gravity of the arc.

We have already seen that the length of the arc $a\,m\,a_6$ is 57 inches; now suppose we find by measurement that the chord $a\,a_6$ is 48½ inches, and the radius 29½ inches, then the distance of the center of gravity $G_2$ of the lead in Fig. 401 from the center of axle will be equal to

$$\frac{48.5'' \times 29.5''}{57''} = 25.1 \text{ inches.}$$

We have found that the weight of the lead is 137.883 pounds, consequently the moment of the force due to the weight will be equal to

$$137.883 \times 25.1 = 3460.86+.$$

If we now assume that the length of the crank is 12 inches, then our lead will counterbalance a weight applied to the crank-pin equal to

$$\frac{3460.86}{12} = 288.4 \text{ pounds.}$$

### WEIGHT OF CRANK-PIN HUB.

281. In Art. 254 it was shown that, in order to determine the amount of weight required to counterbalance the weight of the crank, we must first find the center of

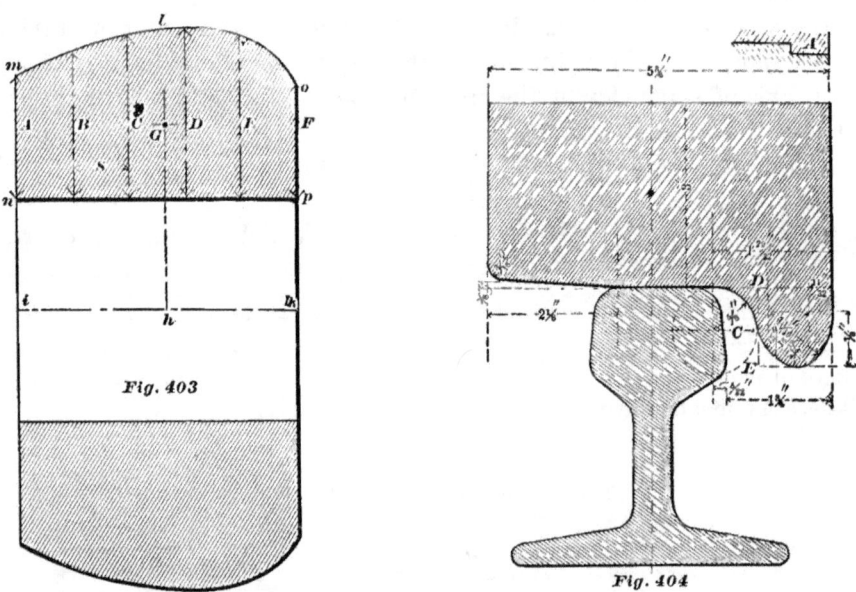

Fig. 403

Fig. 404

gravity of the crank. In Art. 270 it will also be seen that, on account of the difficulty of determining accurately the center of gravity of the crank, many draftsmen and engineers will often, instead of counterbalancing the weight of the crank referred to the crank-pin, content themselves by simply adding the weight of the crank-pin hub to the other weights applied to the crank-pin, and then counterbalancing the sum of these weights. Hence the question may arise: How can we find the weight of the crank-pin hub?

The weight of the crank-pin hub can be determined by the same method and rules which were employed for finding the weight of lead in the rim of a wheel, as explained in Art. 279. Thus, for instance: Let Fig. 403 represent the longitudinal section of the crank-pin hub whose weight we are to determine. We first find the area of the section of the metal $l\,m\,n\,o\,p$. To do this we follow Rule 51. Therefore, divide the distance $n\,p$ into any number of equal parts, and through the points of division draw lines perpendicular to the line $n\,p$, terminating in the curve $m\,l\,o$. Let $A$, $B$, $C$, etc., represent the length in inches of the perpendicular lines (the lengths being obtained by measurement). Then, according to Rule 51,

$$\left(\frac{A}{2} + B + C + D + E + \frac{F}{2}\right) \times s = \text{area in square inches.}$$

We must now find the center of gravity $G$ of the surface $l\,m\,n\,o\,p$. To do this, cut a templet to the outline of this surface, and find its center of gravity by the method shown in Fig. 377. Mark off this center of gravity $G$ on the section of the hub, and measure its distance $G\,h$ from the center line $i\,k$; twice the distance $G\,h$ will be equal to the diameter of the circle whose circumference will be the path of the point $G$ as the surface $l\,m\,n\,o\,p$ revolves around the center line $i\,k$. According to Rule 52, the number of cubic inches in the hub will be equal to the product obtained in multiplying the circumference in inches of the circle described by the center of gravity $G$, by the area in square inches of the surface $l\,m\,n\,o\,p$. This last product, multiplied by the weight of one cubic inch of cast-iron (.26), will be the weight of the crank-pin hub.

### DRIVING WHEEL TIRES.

282. At present, nearly all driving wheel tires are made of steel. The most common practice is to shrink the tires on the wheel centers, as explained in Art. 248. When tires are to be shrunk on, they are bored out to a uniform diameter throughout, so that their sections will appear like that shown in Fig. 404. Of course the inside diameter of the tire must be a certain amount less than the diameter of the wheel center; care must be taken not to allow too much for shrinkage, as this will draw the tire too tight, and will be liable to burst it when the engine is running; on the other hand, with an insufficient allowance for shrinkage, the tire will, in a short time, become loose; the shrinkage diameters adopted by the American Railway Master-Mechanics' Association are given in Art. 248.

283. When steel tires are properly shrunk on the wheel centers in this manner, they will remain tight and resist all the lateral thrust caused by the flanges bearing against the rails, until they are worn considerably. Then these tires need watching, as the constant rolling action is liable to loosen them. When this is the case, shimming pieces are often placed between the tires and wheel centers. Occasionally the excellent plan as shown at $A$ in Fig. 404 is adopted. Here it will be seen that a slight projection or flange is left on the periphery of the wheel center near its inner face, or flanged side of the wheel. The purpose of this design is that the projection shall receive the thrust caused by the flanges bearing against the rails, and prevent the

tire from slipping inward should it at any time become loose. Yet it seems that the general inclination is to avoid the extra expense incurred in putting the tires on the wheel centers in this manner, and consequently the most common practice is to bore out the tires straight.

284. Very seldom do we find tires which have not been shrunk on, but placed cold on the wheel centers; in fact, we know of only one road in the United States

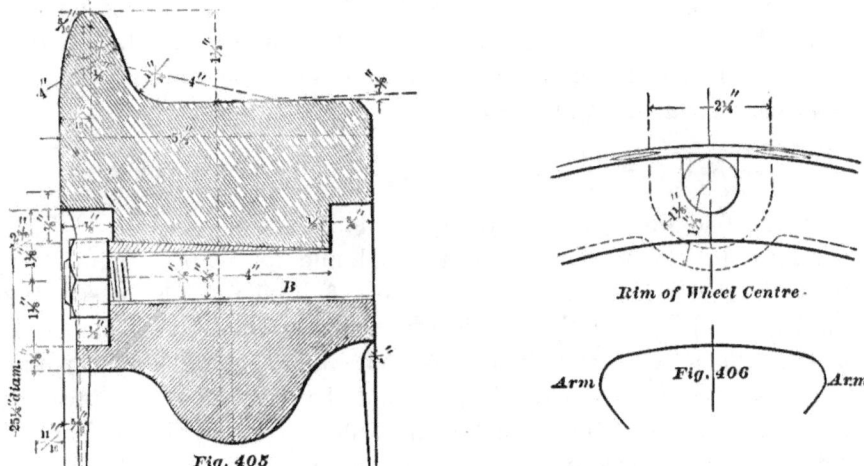

Fig. 405     Fig. 406

where this practice prevails. On this road the tires are bored out, tapered, and the periphery of the wheel center turned to suit, as shown in Fig. 405. The large diameter of the bore of the tire is on the flanged side, or, in other words, on the inside of the wheel. The tire is prevented from slipping outward by the hook-headed bolts $B$. The taper prevents the tire from slipping inwards, and resists the thrust caused by the flange bearing against the rails. Eight hook-headed bolts $B$ are generally used for a tire 63 inches inside diameter; and six bolts $B$ for a tire $35\frac{1}{4}$ inches inside diameter. The nuts on these bolts are not allowed to project beyond the inside of tire; consequently, recesses for the nuts are cast in the rim of the wheel center; another view of one of the recesses, and metal partially surrounding it, cast to the rim, is shown in Fig. 406.

The advantage claimed for this mode of putting tires on the wheel centers is that they can be removed when necessary with less labor and delay than will be required for removing tires which are shrunk on the wheel centers, and also, should the constant rolling action loosen the tires at any time, they can be quickly tightened. We decidedly prefer the tires shrunk on wheel's center, as we believe that, with these, safety is promoted and better results obtained.

285. In fitting up a pair of driving wheels, the wheel centers are first pressed on the axles with a pressure equal to that given in Art. 252. The keys are then driven, and the tires shrunk on. After this the wheels and axle are placed in a quartering machine and the holes bored for the crank-pins. It is very important to have the crank-pins exactly in line with the axle, and at equal angles in all the different driving wheels, and such results are obtained in a correctly designed quartering machine.

The crank-pins are then pressed into the wheel centers with a pressure of about six tons for every inch in diameter of the crank-pin fit, providing the holes are perfectly true and smooth. If the holes are not perfectly true, which may not only be due to bad workmanship, but may be, and sometimes is, the result of the bad practice of shrinking the tires on the wheel centers after the crank-pin holes have been bored, a pressure of nine tons per inch in diameter is necessary for pressing the crank-pins into the wheels. The last operation is to turn the tires to the correct gauge.

### CLEARANCE BETWEEN FLANGES AND RAILS.

286. The tires are placed on the wheel centers so as to allow a certain amount of clearance, $C$ (Fig. 404), between the flanges and the rails. The most common amount of clearance allowed at $C$ for each wheel is $\frac{3}{8}$ of an inch, making the total clearance between the rails and the flanges of a pair of driving wheels $\frac{3}{4}$ inch. On a few roads this clearance for each wheel is only $\frac{1}{4}$ inch, and, on the other hand, we occasionally find it increased to $\frac{1}{2}$ inch. We are in favor of $\frac{3}{8}$ inch clearance for each wheel. Should the distance between the rails of a curve be established, and any doubt exist as to the sufficiency of this amount of clearance in running over the curve, the proper amount of clearance can readily be obtained by making a plan of the curve, and also a plan of the wheels with the correct distances between the axles drawn upon the former; the distance between the flanges of a pair of driving wheels can then be regulated to allow a necessary amount of clearance, which will prevent the wheels from binding in running over the curve.

### PLAIN TIRES.

287. Fig. 407 represents a cross-section of a tire without a flange; tires of this kind are generally called "plain tires." These tires are generally wider than the flanged tires under the same engine.

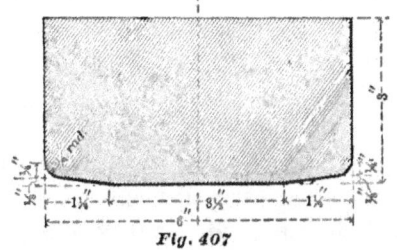

Fig. 407

The width of the plain tires must be made to suit the curves over which the engine has to run, and should be sufficiently wide not to leave the track at any time. To determine this width, a plan of the curve and wheel base must be made, and the width of the plain tire regulated so as to cover the rails at all times. As a consequence, the width of the plain tires varies, under the different classes of engines, from $5\frac{3}{4}$ to 7 inches.

### DISTRIBUTION OF FLANGED TIRES IN THE VARIOUS CLASSES OF LOCOMOTIVES.

288. In a large majority of eight-wheeled passenger engines, in which four of the whole number of wheels are driving wheels, as shown in Fig. 1, all the driving wheels have flanged tires. We have noticed only a very few of this class of engines in which one pair of drivers—the front ones—had plain tires, leaving only one pair of driving wheels—the rear ones—to guide the engine over a curve. This we believe to be dangerous practice. All wheels in this class of engines should have flanges.

In a great number of Mogul engines, in which six wheels of the whole number are driving wheels, as shown in Fig. 2, the front and rear driving wheels have flanged tires; the middle pair have plain tires. We believe this to be the best practice, for the following reasons: All locomotives have a tendency to sway in front from side to side; this is objectionable. Now, a Mogul engine has only a two-wheeled truck (generally called a pony truck) in front, and such a truck without the aid of the flanges on the first pair of drivers is not suitable to guide the engine steadily on a straight track, neither is it suitable to guide it safely over a curve. In short, more than two wheels with flanges (particularly when these wheels are truck wheels) are needed to guide the engine steadily in front.

In ten-wheeled engines, in which six wheels of the whole number are driving wheels, as shown in Fig. 3, the rear pair of drivers, and the pair next to it, have flanged tires. In these engines the four-wheeled truck in front is generally considered to be sufficient to guide the engine steadily on a straight track and safely over a curve without the aid of flanges on the front driving wheels.

In consolidation engines, in which eight wheels of the whole number are driving wheels, as shown in Fig. 4, the distribution of flanged tires somewhat differs on the various railroads. All these engines have in front a two-wheeled—that is, a pony—truck, and since, as we have stated before, a two-wheeled truck is generally considered insufficient to guide an engine steadily on a straight track or safely over a curve, we find that nearly every engine of this class has flanged tires on the front drivers. As to the other driving wheels under the same engines, we often find the rear pair, and the pair next to it, with flanged tires, leaving only one pair of driving wheels (the pair next to the front ones) with plain tires.

This arrangement seems to indicate that some designers consider two pairs of the whole number of wheels, including truck wheels, to be necessary for the purpose of guiding the rear end of the locomotive, and two pairs of wheels to guide the front end.

But this arrangement is by no means a universal one, as we frequently meet with consolidation engines in which only the rear and front pairs of driving wheels have flanged tires, leaving the two intermediate pairs of driving wheels with plain tires. This arrangement seems to indicate that if one pair of wheels with flanges is sufficient to guide, as is generally the case, the rear end of a Mogul engine, one pair of wheels with flanges will also be sufficient to guide the rear end of a consolidation engine, and that plain tires on the two intermediate driving wheels will allow the engine to curve easier. In a few instances we find the flanged tires distributed so as to bring the flanges on alternate driving wheels. In such cases the rear and third pair of driving wheels, counting from the rear end, will have flanged tires, the second pair from the rear and the front pair will have plain tires. Our favorite arrangement is to have flanges on the front and rear driving wheels; these, we believe, will guide the engine steadily, and allow it to curve easily.

Lastly, occasionally we meet with consolidation, Mogul, and ten-wheeled engines under which all the driving wheels have flanged tires.

## DEPTH OF FLANGES.

289. The depth $D\,E$ of the flanges of tires (Fig. 408) varies, according to the judgment of the designer, from 1 to $1\frac{1}{4}$ inches; and in a few instances the flanges are made $1\frac{1}{2}$ inches deep, as shown in Fig. 405. Many master-mechanics claim that flanges 1 inch deep are perfectly safe, and to prove their assertion point to engines with

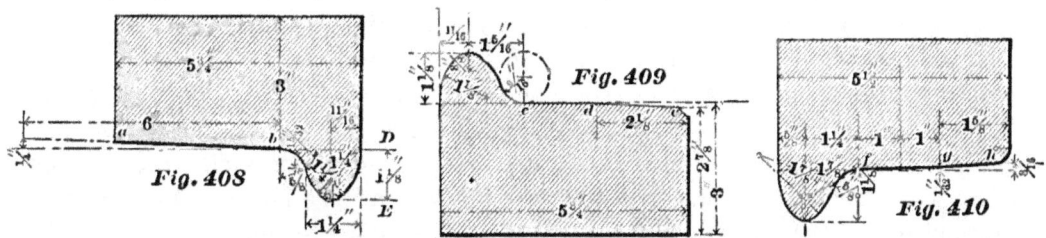

flanges 1 inch deep on the drivers which are and have been running daily without any trouble or accidents; yet others claim that flanges $1\frac{1}{4}$ inches deep are safer, and adopt this depth for all their driving wheel flanges. In a large majority of locomotives the driving wheel flanges are $1\frac{1}{8}$ inches deep—an arithmetical mean of 1 and $1\frac{1}{4}$.

## FORMS OF TREAD ON DRIVING WHEELS.

290. At present various forms of tread on driving wheels are used. Fig. 408 represents a section of a tire in which the tread $a\,b$ is a surface of uniform taper. This taper varies on the different roads from $\frac{1}{8}$ to $\frac{3}{4}$ of an inch in 12 inches. This form of tread is usually called the cone tread.

Fig. 409 represents a section of a tire in which the tread is composed of two surfaces; one surface is represented by the line $c\,d$, and is turned to a uniform diameter; the other surface is represented by line $d\,e$, and is turned to a uniform taper; in some cases this taper is as much as $\frac{1}{4}$ of an inch in $1\frac{1}{4}$ inches. This form of tread is often called the straight tread.

Fig. 410 represents a section of tire in which the tread is also composed of two surfaces, $f\,g$ and $g\,h$. The surface $f\,g$ is turned to a slight taper, as shown; and the surface $g\,h$ is turned to a greater taper, whose dimensions are also given. This form of tread is a modification of the cone tread, and its advantages will be presently explained.

## BEST FORM OF TREAD.

291. The question now arises: Which is the best form of tread for locomotive tires? We have already seen that all locomotives have a tendency to sway from side to side at the front end, and such a sinuous motion is objectionable. Tires with a cone tread, as shown in Fig. 408, will certainly reduce to some extent this objectionable sinuous motion. We may therefore claim for the cone tread, particularly in engines which have only a pony truck to guide the front end, and where some dependence must be placed on the front drivers to guide, in some measure, the engine steadily, that the cone tread will help to keep the engine in the center of the track,

and to some extent reduce the wear on the flanges. True, the taper of the tread near the base of the flange will soon wear off, and a channel or groove in the tire will be formed, as shown in Fig. 411. In this case the form of the ridge near the flange will, to some extent, answer the same purpose as that for which the cone tread was originally designed. Hence we may say that the cone tread is particularly desirable for engines in which the tires are new, or have not been worn. Indeed, this fact has often been proven by experience on roads, and more distinctly so on roads with sharp curves, where straight treads had to be abandoned and replaced by cone treads, so as to obtain more satisfactory results, cause the engine to run with greater safety over the curves, and reduce the wear of the flanges when new. On the other hand, the claim that a cone tread will cause the engine to run over a curve with less friction and less wear on the tires than with treads of other forms is a fallacy. For instance, the argument that the centrifugal force will cause the engine to run towards the outer rails of a curve, and thus cause the outer driving wheels to work on their large diameter and the inner driving wheels to work on their small diameter, thereby creating a rolling motion similar to that of a cone on a flat surface, cannot be sustained when sound principles are applied.

It is true that when a single cone is rolled over a flat surface it will run in a curve whose radius is dependent on the taper of the cone. But if we now take two equal cones and fix their axes rigidly and parallel to each other in a frame, so as to obtain conditions similar to those of parallel axles and wheels under an engine, and then roll the cones over a flat surface, the results thus obtained will greatly differ from the results noticed in rolling one of the cones separately. The two cones thus held together will roll in a curve which approaches a straight line; considerable sliding friction will also be created, so that the forces required for rolling both cones held together will be considerably greater than the sum of the two forces required for rolling each cone separately.

The claim that the centrifugal force will cause the engine to run towards the outer rails of the curved track is also very doubtful, because, to obtain such a result, the radius of the curve would have to be suitable for the speed of the engine, or the engine would have to be run at a speed suitable for the radius of the curve, and these are conditions which cannot be obtained in practice. Hence we conclude that the cone tread will not lessen the wear or friction on the tires in running over a curve, but it has this advantage, that it will generally prevent, to some extent, the sinuous motion of the locomotive, and that on this account it will somewhat lessen the wear of the flanges.

The tread shown in Fig. 410, and treads similar to it, have in late years greatly grown in favor; and we believe these to be the best to adopt, as they possess not only the advantage of the cone tread, but, furthermore, possess the advantage of wearing to a better form than the cone tread, because the increased taper of the tread near the edge of the tire will reduce the outer ridge of the groove or channel shown in Fig. 411, the groove being always an objectionable feature.

The straight tread shown in Fig. 409 possesses only the advantage of wearing to a form approaching that of Fig. 410, but it does not possess the advantage of steadily guiding the engine when the tires are new.

292. In the Proceedings Twentieth Annual Convention, 1887, of the American Railway Master-Mechanics' Association, we see it reported that the form of the tread, such as shown in Fig. 412, has been adopted as a standard, which is the same form of

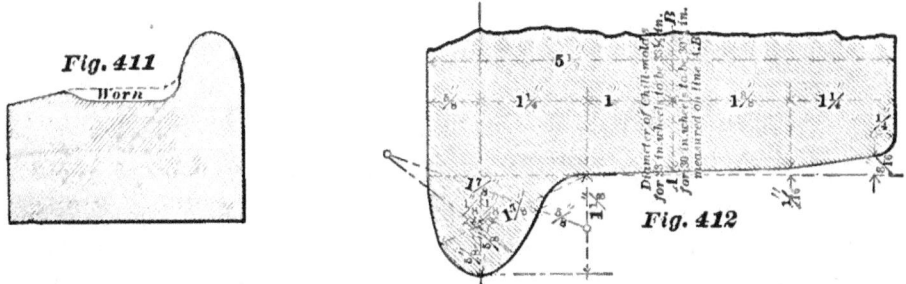

tread as that adopted by the Master Car Builders' Association, and has been illustrated in the report of their twenty-first annual convention, from which our illustration has been taken. Figs. 409, 410, and 411 have been taken from the report of the proceedings of the seventeenth annual convention of the American Railway Master-Mechanics Association.

### THE LIMIT OF WEAR OF TIRES.

293. A fixed limit to which the thickness of a tire can be reduced by wear without impairing the safety of running the engine cannot be established, as the weight on the drivers, the climate, and quality of the steel will have some influence on the limit of wear. But generally, experience seems to indicate that in warm climates tires made of good homogeneous steel may remain in use until their thickness has been reduced to $1\frac{1}{4}$ inches; for light engines, whose weight does not exceed 10,000 pounds on each driver, the tires may remain in use until their thickness has been reduced to $1\frac{1}{8}$ inches. In colder climates, although sometimes we there see engines running with tires reduced to $1\frac{1}{4}$ inches in thickness, we believe that safety will be promoted by removing the tires before this limit has been reached.

### THICKNESS AND WIDTH OF TIRE.

294. On many roads the thickness of the tire when new is 3 inches, measured at the base of the flange as indicated by the dimension line in Fig. 408. On some roads this thickness has been considerably increased, so that we now find many locomotives with tires 4 inches thick. The advantage claimed for thick tires is that they will, to some extent, reduce the expense of keeping the engine in working order, because, generally, tires, of whatever original thickness, are not allowed to wear below a thickness of $1\frac{1}{4}$ inches, and are then taken off the wheel center; consequently the interval between the renewals of tires 4 inches thick will be greater than the interval between the renewals of 3-inch tires, and thereby time and labor are saved when the former thickness has been adopted. Again, the amount of steel thrown away, so to speak, when the tire is condemned on account of its reduction, will, in comparison with the original weight of the tire, be less for tires 4 inches thick than for those whose original thickness was below 4 inches. On the other hand, with the use of heavy

tires a greater dead weight than desirable, that is to say, a weight not supported by the springs, is placed on the rails, and such a procedure must in time injure the rails It is therefore probable that in the future the thickness of tires will not exceed 4 inches.

The width of flanged tires generally varies from 5½ to 5¾ inches.

### DISTANCE BETWEEN THE BACKS OF FLANGES ON TIRES.

295. It is important that the distance between the backs of flanges on tires should be suitable for the gauge of the road on which the engine has to run. Increasing this distance will obviously decrease the thickness of the flanges, which is not desirable. Decreasing the distance between the backs of flanges beyond a certain limit will interfere with the guard rail on the different lines of railroads. For a gauge of 4 feet 8½ inches the distance between the backs of flanges is generally made 4 feet 5⅜ inches. On a few roads we find this distance decreased to 4 feet 5¼ inches; and on some other roads increased to 4 feet 5½ inches.

# CHAPTER VII.

## MAIN-RODS.—SIDE-RODS.—CRANK-PINS.

### MAIN-RODS AND SIDE-RODS.

296. Figs. 413, 414 represent a main-rod, and Figs. 415, 416 represent a side-rod. Both were designed for a four-wheeled connected engine, such as shown in Fig. 1, cylinders 17 × 24 inches.

The office of the main-rod is to transmit motion from the crosshead to the main drivers; it connects the crosshead pin and the main crank-pin, and therefore is sometimes called the connecting-rod. The term main-rod is mostly used in this country, and will be adopted in the following descriptions.

The office of the side-rod is to transmit motion from the main driving wheels to the other driving wheels; it forms a connection or coupling between the drivers, and therefore is sometimes called a coupling-rod; or again, because the side-rod on one side of the engine is always parallel to the side-rod on the opposite side, it is sometimes called the parallel-rod. But the term side-rod is by far the most popular one, and will be adopted in these articles.

Several different designs of main- and side-rods are in use, as will soon be shown; but the designs here represented, we believe, are the most common ones for the class of engine named. The end of the main-rod marked $F$, Fig. 413, is usually called the front end; and the opposite end, marked $R$, the rear end.

The design of the front end of a main-rod depends on the kind of crosshead to be employed. The design of the front end $F$ shown in Fig. 413 is only suitable for the class of crossheads shown in Figs. 234 and 237.

297. In both rods the number of bolts $e\,e\,e$ required, and their diameters, for holding firmly the straps $a\,a$ to the butt ends of the rods, depend on the magnitude of the forces which these rods have to transmit. In side-rods we generally find two bolts through each strap to be sufficient; but in main-rods sometimes more than two bolts through each strap will be required. The manner of determining the number of bolts in the main-rod and the diameters of bolts through all rods will be explained hereafter. These bolts are generally turned to a taper of $\frac{1}{8}$ inch in 12 inches; that is to say, the difference of the two diameters 12 inches apart is $\frac{1}{8}$ of an inch; sometimes this taper is only $\frac{1}{16}$ inch in 12 inches. These bolts must have an extremely good fit in, and be driven tight into both the straps and butt ends of the rods; the object of the taper is simply this, that when it becomes necessary to refit the brasses

268    MODERN LOCOMOTIVE CONSTRUCTION.

$b\ b\ b$, the bolts can be readily driven out without impairing or upsetting their ends. Another advantage of the taper is that, should these bolts at any time become somewhat loose, they can to some extent be quickly tightened by turning—a small amount—off the under side of the head. Each one of these bolts should have two

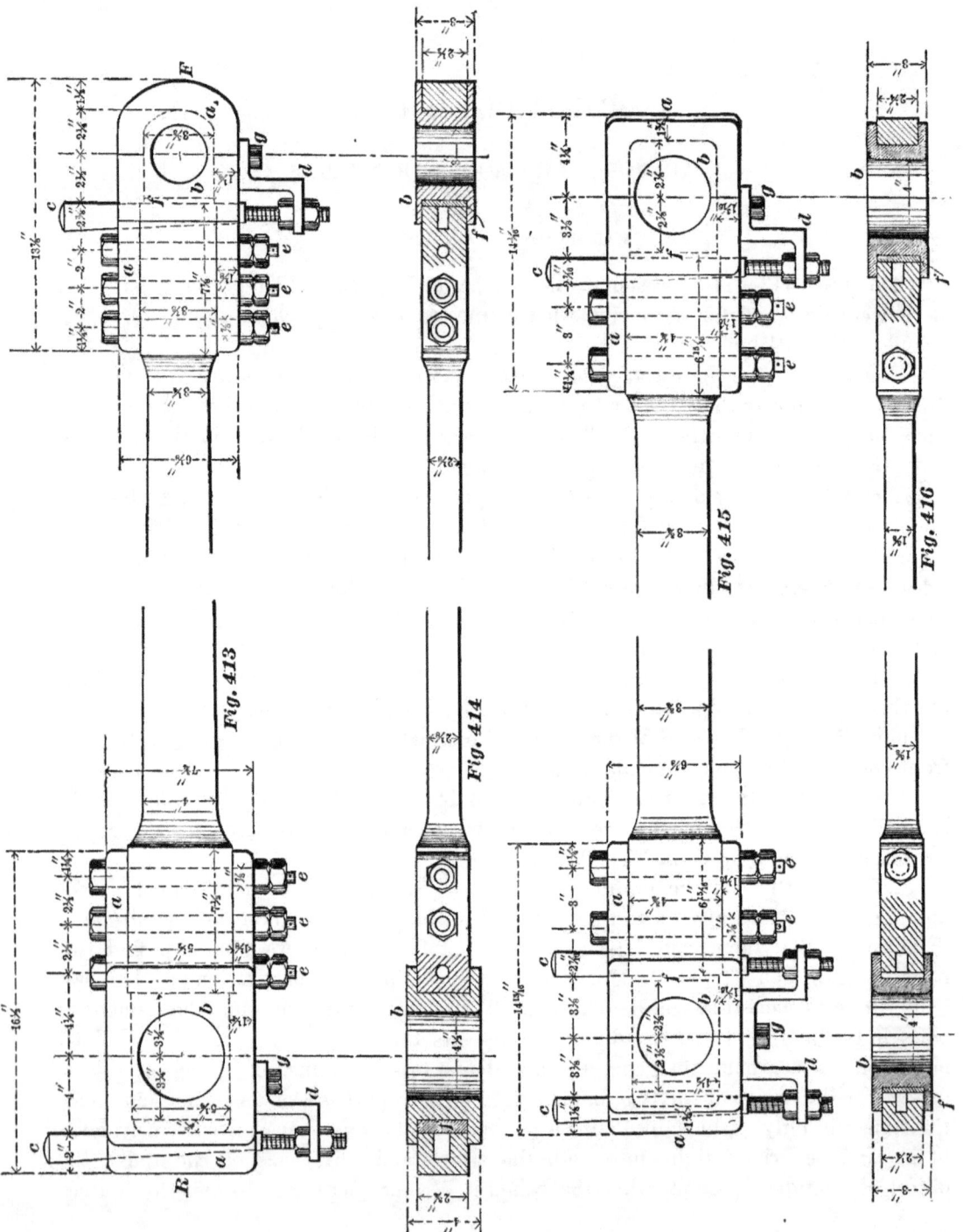

MODERN LOCOMOTIVE CONSTRUCTION. 269

nuts, and since these nuts are always placed at the under side of the strap, greater security should be provided by inserting split pins at the ends of the bolts.

298. The keys are nearly always made of steel. Main-rods have generally one key at each end; in the design shown in Fig. 413, the key is placed at the back of the crosshead pin, and the key in the opposite end of the rod is placed at the back of the main crank-pin. This is good practice, as, with this arrangement of keys, the brasses

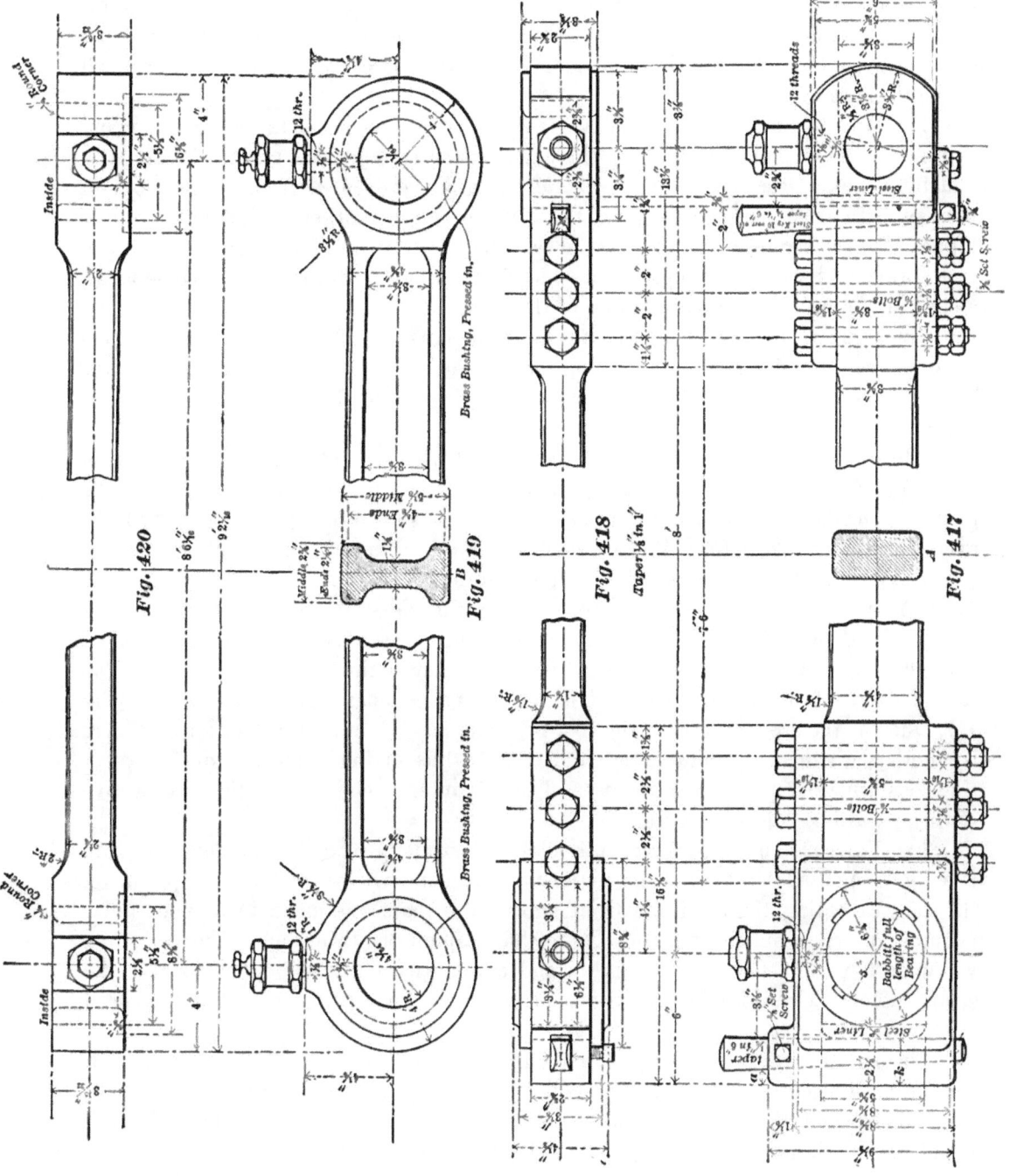

Fig. 420  Fig. 419  Fig. 418  Fig. 417

can be adjusted to some extent, without perceptibly altering the length of the main-rod. Yet this arrangement of keys is by no means a universal practice, as there are many main-rods with the key at the front of the crank-pin, and one at the back of the crosshead pin. With this arrangement the rod will be lengthened when the keys are driven further into the straps.

Side-rods, designed for four-wheeled connected passenger engines, generally have two keys through one end, and one key through the opposite end; and indeed, for this class of engines this arrangement of keys gives satisfactory results. But in other classes of engines we sometimes find side-rods with two keys at each end, as will presently be shown.

The taper of the keys in all rods varies from ⅝ to 1¼ inches in 12 inches. In many engines the small end of the key is threaded, passed through the guard $d\,d$, Fig. 415, and by means of the nuts on each side of the guard prevented from slipping out of position. In other engines we find the keys held in position by small set screws tapped into the straps or the rod, as the case may require, and for greater security, so as to prevent the key from flying out should the set screw at any time become loose, a split pin is inserted at the small end of the key.

Liners are inserted between the keys and the brasses. The object of these liners is to prevent the keys from indenting or cutting the soft surface of the brasses. These liners are generally made of steel, sometimes of wrought-iron. Their thickness varies from ¼ to ¾ inch.

299. Figs. 417, 418 represent a main-rod, and Figs. 419, 420 represent a side-rod for a four-wheeled connected engine, such as is shown in Fig. 1; cylinders 18 × 24 inches. The design of the main-rod is similar to that shown in Figs. 413, 414, with the exception that the keys (Fig. 417) are plain and are held in position by set screws.

The design of the side-rod, Figs. 419, 420, differs greatly from that shown in Fig. 415. As will be noticed, straps are not used for this side-rod. These rods are forged in one piece, the ends bored out, and brass bushings pressed in. The cross-section of the rod here represented also differs greatly from that of the ordinary side-rod. The cross-section of an ordinary side-rod is rectangular, similar to that shown at $A$, Fig 417, whereas the cross-section of the rod, Fig. 419, has the appearance of an I. There is another distinct type illustrated in Art. 301, thus giving three distinct types of side-rods which at present are in use. The advantages claimed by their respective advocates will be considered later.

300. Figs. 421 and 422 represent a main-rod strap with key. This form of strap is very often used; in fact, in the majority of locomotives we find the straps on all the rods, excepting those on the front end of the main-rod, made to a rectangular form, as shown in our illustration. As to the strap on the front end of the main-rod, we are often compelled to round off its end as shown in Fig. 417, so as to give the strap sufficient clearance in the crosshead while the rod oscillates on the crosshead pin.

The length $c\,d$ of the space, or that part of the opening of the strap marked $A$, should be sufficiently great to admit the brasses and the liner $l$ as shown. The length $d\,e$ of that part of the opening marked $B$ is determined by the number of bolts through the strap and the width of the key, as will be presently explained.

We occasionally meet with straps whose openings are of equal width throughout; that is to say, the distance between $t$ and $t_2$ is equal to that between $s$ and $s_2$. But we believe it is safe to say that, in a large majority of straps, the thickness of the metal at $f$ is greater than the thickness at $g$; thus making the width $s\ s_2$ less than the width of the opening at $t\ t_2$. The straps are planed so as to make the surface $t$ parallel to $t_2$; and $s$ parallel to $s_2$, leaving a projection in line with $d$. Since the portion of the strap marked $g$ is weakened by the bolt holes $i\ i$, we may be led to the conclusion that this strap is badly proportioned, and such a conclusion will be correct, if only the strength of the strap is considered. Indeed, if we are required to design a strap which shall be simply of equal strength throughout, we would make the thickness at $g$ greater than that at $f$, so as to allow for the loss of strength caused by the holes $i\ i$. But in designing straps for locomotive rods, other considerations must be

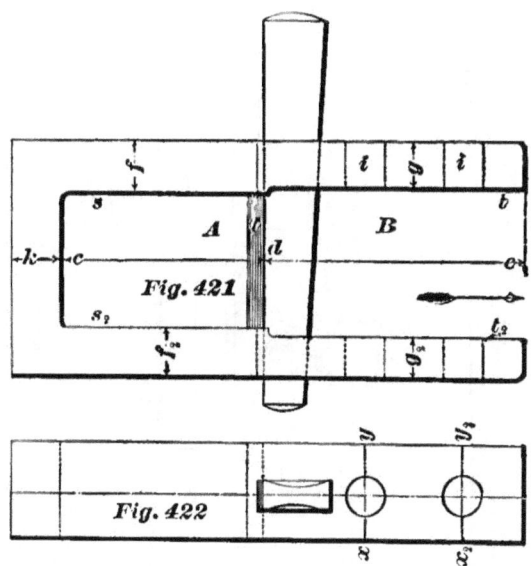

taken into account. One of the aims of a locomotive designer is to design an engine which can be kept on the road in good working order at a minimum cost, and also reduce as much as possible the time during which the engine is kept out of service for the necessary repairs; and these are the conditions kept in view, or which should be kept in view, when a strap for a locomotive rod is to be designed. Consequently, the thickness of the straps at $f$ is greater than at $g$ for the following reason: In practice it is found that the inner surfaces $s\ s_2$ will wear unevenly, and the brasses become loose long before the strap needs any other repairs. Now this extra thickness of metal at $f$ will allow the surfaces $s\ s_2$ to be trued up or re-planed without touching the inner surfaces $t\ t_2$. New brasses can then be fitted in the space $A$ and the rod restored to good working order in a comparatively short time, and at a minimum cost. On the other hand, if there had not been any extra thickness of metal at $f$, then as soon as the inner surfaces of the strap become worn, they will have to be re-planed from end to end, making the opening of the strap—that is, the width from $t$ to $t_2$—too wide for the end of the rod; and therefore, in this case, the strap will have to be heated and upset at $k$, so as to close the opening to fit the end of the rod. In doing so the holes $i\ i$ will be thrown out of line, and otherwise cause considerable expense and an extra expenditure of time (which always means delay in getting the engine into service) before the rod can be brought into working order.

The usual practice is to make the thickness of the strap at $f$ $\frac{1}{8}$ of an inch greater than at $g$; occasionally we find the difference between these thicknesses to be only $\frac{1}{16}$ of an inch. When there is no key through the end $k$ of the strap, the thickness at $k$ is generally $\frac{1}{4}$ of an inch greater than at $g$ for small engines; and from $\frac{3}{8}$ to $\frac{1}{2}$ inch greater at $k$ than at $g$ for large engines. When there is a key through the end $k$ of the strap, as shown in Fig. 417, the thickness of the metal at $k$ is determined by the width of the key. In small engines, say engines with cylinders 14 inches in diameter, the thickness at $k$ is generally such as to leave $\frac{1}{2}$ inch metal at $a$ (Fig. 417), that is, $\frac{1}{2}$

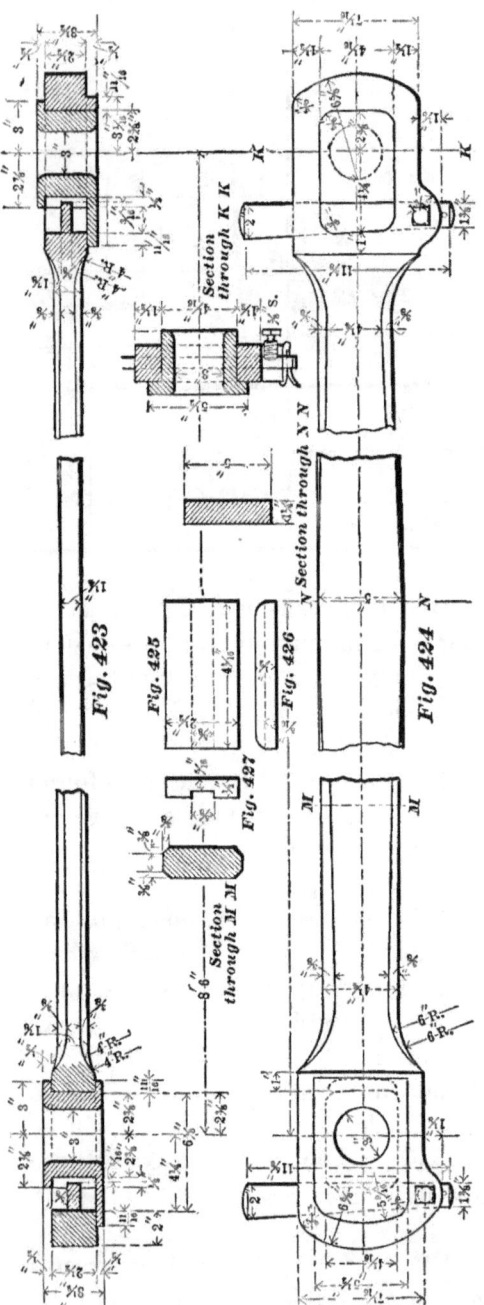

inch metal at the outside of the wide end of the key. As the diameters of the cylinders are increased, the amount of metal at $a$ is also increased at a rate which will give about 1 inch metal at $a$ for engines with cylinders 20 inches in diameter. These dimensions here given are about the average of those in common use.

The width of the strap depends upon the length of the crank-pin journal, or the length of the crosshead pin. By deducting from the lengths of these journals the thickness of the brass flanges, the width of the strap is at once determined. Hence in designing straps for locomotive main- or side-rods, about the only calculations which we have to make are those for finding the correct diameters and the number of bolts through the straps, and the correct thickness of the strap at $g$, Fig. 421.

301. Figs. 423, 424 represent another side-rod designed for a four-wheeled connected engine, such as is shown in Fig. 1; cylinders 17 × 24 inches. The whole design of this rod differs from the designs of the rods previously shown. Straps are not used, but the keys are retained, so that the brasses can be adjusted. The rod itself is made thick and narrow at the ends; and thin and wide at the center. Figs. 425, 426, 427 represent the liner used between the keys and the brasses. The advantages claimed for this design will be considered hereafter

### MAIN-ROD BOLTS.

302. A bolt may be subjected to a single or a double shearing stress. Thus: Let $A$ and $B$, Fig. 428, represent two plates which are connected by a bolt $C$. Now assume that a force is acting on the plate $A$ in the direction of arrow 2; and another force acting on the plate $B$ in the direction of the arrow 3. In this case the bolt is subjected to a single shearing stress,

because, if the forces are great enough, the bolt will be severed in only one place, and the area through which the bolt will be severed is equal to the cross-sectional area of the bolt.

In Fig. 429 the conditions are changed. Here we have a bolt connecting a rod and a strap. Assume now that a force is acting on $A$ in the direction of the arrow 2, and another force acting on the strap in the direction of the arrow 3. In this case the bolt is subjected to a double shearing stress, because, if the forces are great enough, the bolt will be severed in two places, and the area through which the bolt will be severed will be equal to twice the cross-sectional area of the bolt. From this we infer that, if the diameter of the bolt in Fig. 428 is equal to the diameter of the bolt in Fig. 429, the force required to shear the bolt in the latter figure will be equal to twice the force required to shear the bolt in the former figure. Or, conversely, when the bolts in both figures are subjected to the same shearing forces, the cross-

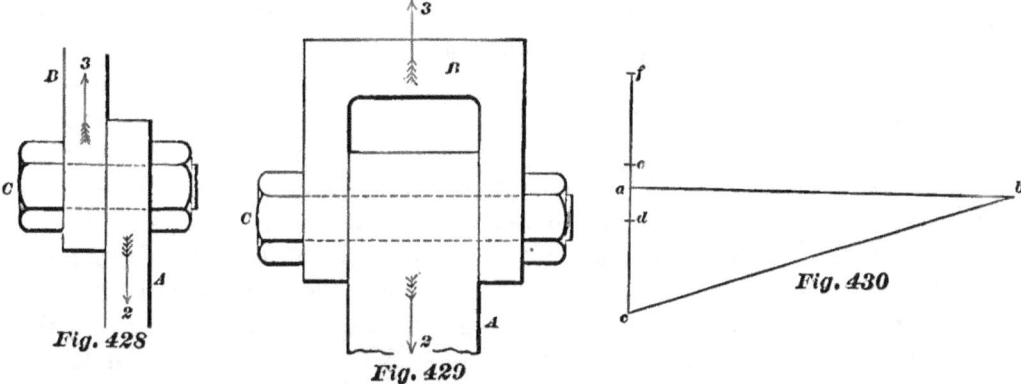

sectional area of the bolt in Fig. 428 must be equal to twice the cross-sectional area of the bolt in Fig. 429. From these considerations we learn that the area sheared is proportional to the shearing force to which the bolt is subjected.

303. In determining the diameters and the number of bolts through the main-rod straps, we may assume, without impairing the results of our calculations, that these bolts are simply subjected to a double shearing stress.

Here then the question arises: How great will be the shearing force to which the bolts through the main-rod straps are subjected? To this we answer: The shearing force to which the bolts are subjected will be equal to the maximum pressure on the main-rod. To find this maximum pressure we adopt the following graphical method:

Fig. 430. Draw the straight line $ab$, and let it represent the center line of motion of the piston. On this line lay off any point $a$, and let this point represent the center of the driving axle. Through the point $a$ draw the line $cf$ perpendicular to the line $ab$, and let the line $cf$ represent the vertical direction through which the axle box can move in the pedestal. On the line $cf$ lay off a point $d$; this point is to represent the center of the axle when the axle box touches the pedestal cap, consequently the distance between the points $a$ and $d$ must be equal to the distance between the center line of motion $ab$, and the lowest position that the center of the axle can occupy in the pedestal. Again, on the line $cf$ lay off a point $e$; this point is to represent the center of the axle when the axle box touches the upper end of the pedestal, consequently the distance between the points *a* and *e* must be equal to the distance between the center line of motion *a b* and the highest position that the center of the axle can occupy in the pedestal. If now we find that the distance *a d* is greater than the distance *a e*, then from the point *d* lay off on the line *c f* a point *e*; the distance between the points *d* and *c* must be equal to one-half the stroke, or, in other words, equal to the length of the crank. If, on the other hand, the distance *a e* is greater than the distance *a d*, then from the point *e* lay off on the line *c f* a point *f*; the distance between the points *c* and *f* must be equal to one-half the stroke. But generally in locomotives, the distance *a d* will be found to be greater than *a e*, hence we shall confine our attention to that which happens below the center line of motion *a b*. From the point *c* as a center, and with a radius equal to the length of the connecting-rod, describe an arc cutting the line *a b* in the point *b*; join the points *c* and *b* by a straight line, and thus completing the right-angled triangle *a c b*. Now the length of the side *a b* of this triangle will represent the total steam pressure on the piston; the length of the side *c b* will represent the maximum pressure on the main-rod, and according to what has been stated before, the length of the side *c b* will also represent the shearing force to which the bolts in the rod are subjected. Therefore, as soon as we know the pressure which the length of the side *a b* does represent, we will have no difficulty in determining the shearing force on the bolts; because, as we have seen, the line *a b* represents the total steam pressure, and this pressure is easily found by multiplying the area of the piston by the pressure per square inch; the pressure on the main-rod due to the steam pressure will be as much greater than the total pressure on the piston, as the length of the line *c b* is greater than the length of the line *a b*, and consequently this pressure can be found by a simple rule of proportion. In order to show plainly the manner of applying these principles, we will take the following example:

EXAMPLE 84.—It is required to find the shearing force to which the main-rod bolts are subjected in a locomotive whose cylinders are 16 inches diameter; stroke, 24 inches; maximum steam pressure in the cylinders is 120 pounds per square inch; length of the connecting-rod, 84 inches; the distance (*a d*, Fig. 430) below the center line of motion of the piston through which the center of axle can move is 3 inches.

In the first place, let us find the lengths of all the sides of a right-angled triangle, such as shown in Fig. 430, whose hypothenuse shall represent the pressure on the main-rod due to the steam pressure given in our example.

The lengths of two sides of this triangle are already known, for we know that the side, or hypothenuse, *c b* must be equal to the length of the connecting-rod, namely, 84 inches. The length of the side *a c* must be equal to the sum of the distance *a d*, which is 3 inches, and one-half the stroke, which is 12 inches; hence, the side *a c* will be $12 + 3 = 15$ inches. The length of the side *a b* we must find by the well-known rule given in geometry for finding any side of a right-angled triangle when two of its sides are known. In the case before us we must subtract the square of the side *a c* from the square of the side *c b*, and extract the square root of the remainder.

The square of the side *b c* is equal to $84 \times 84 = 7056$.

The square of the side $a\,c$ is equal to $15 \times 15 = 225$.

Subtracting the latter square from the former, we have $7056 - 225 = 6831$.

Extracting the square root of 6,831, we have

$$\sqrt{6831} = 82.64 \text{ inches,}$$

which is the length of the side $a\,b$.

The area of a piston 16 inches in diameter is equal to 201.06 square inches, and the total steam pressure on one piston will be equal to $201.06 \times 120 = 24127.20$ pounds.

Hence line $a\,b$, which we have found to be 82.64 inches long, represents 24,127.20 pounds. The line $c\,b$ we know to be 84 inches long, and since the pressure represented by the side $c\,b$ will be as much greater than 24,127.20 pounds as $c\,b$ is longer than $a\,b$, we have

$$\frac{84 \times 24127.20}{82.64} = 24524.25 \text{ pounds,}$$

which is the pressure represented by the line $c\,b$, and consequently is the pressure on the main-rod, or the shearing force to which the bolts in the main-rod are subjected.

304. Our next step will be to find the area necessary to resist this shearing force, and this area will be equal to twice the total cross-sectional area of all the bolts through one end of the rod. In order to find this area we must first establish the stress which should be allowed per square inch, and this can best be established by finding the stress allowed by builders. For the sake of simplicity, we shall consider that the bolts are subjected to a shearing stress only, and shall consider that the total stress is equal to the total pressure on the main-rod. Now, assuming, as we have done before, that the pressure in the cylinders on locomotives at present in service, whose safety valves are set to 130 pounds, will be 120 pounds per square inch, and then determining by calculation the stress (due to the pressure of 120 pounds) which has been allowed per square inch of cross-sectional area of the main-rod bolts, we find that it varies in different locomotives from 7,000 to 9,000 pounds, and in one case we found it to be as high as 12,000 pounds per square inch. Our experience leads us to believe that, when the best quality of iron is used, 8,000 pounds per square inch of the cross-sectional area of the main-rod bolts will give good results, and should be adopted. The best quality of wrought-iron of which these bolts are generally made possesses an ultimate shearing strength of about 56,000 pounds per square inch; if we now assume that these bolts are simply subjected to a shearing stress, and allow 8,000 pounds per square inch of section, we adopt 7 as a factor of safety. Hence, if the ultimate shearing strength of the iron is less than 56,000 pounds per square inch, say it is only 49,000 pounds, then the safe working stress to be allowed per square inch will be equal to

$$\frac{49000}{7} = 7000 \text{ pounds.}$$

From the foregoing remarks we conclude that twice the total cross-sectional area of the bolts—that is, the area which has to resist the shearing force—must be proportioned so that the stress per square inch will be 8,000 pounds, provided the best quality of iron is used.

After this, when the number and diameters of the bolts are to be established, we may be compelled to change this stress of 8,000 pounds per square inch, because the general practice in locomotive building is to avoid $\frac{1}{64}$ and $\frac{1}{32}$ of an inch in the diameters of the bolts, and therefore, in establishing the nearest number of bolts and adopting the nearest practical diameters to those for which the result of the calculations call, the stress may be somewhat greater or less than 8,000 pounds per square inch; indeed, we may have to be satisfied as long as the stress falls within the limits of 7,500 to 8,500 per square inch for the best quality of iron. For an inferior quality of iron the stress should be less.

Now, having established the stress to be allowed per square inch, we can easily find the total cross-sectional area of the main-rod bolts through one end of the rod by the following rule:

RULE 54.—Divide the total pressure on the main-rod, as found by the diagram, Fig. 430, by 8,000; the quotient will be twice the total cross-sectional area of the main-rod bolts through one of its ends.

EXAMPLE 85.—The total pressure on the main-rod given in Example 84 is 24,524.25 pounds; what will be twice the total cross-sectional area of the bolts?

$$\frac{24524.25}{8000} = 3.065 \text{ square inches.}$$

305. These bolts, as we have stated before, are tapered, hence when we speak of the diameters of the bolts we mean their small diameters. In a large number of locomotives the rear strap is wider than the front or crosshead strap. Careful observation seems to indicate that the diameter of any one of these bolts should be equal to about one-third the width of the rear strap; in some engines the diameters are a little greater, and in others a little less, than this proportion. We may therefore assume that it is good practice to make the diameter of the bolt (as near as possible consistent with the avoidance of $\frac{1}{64}$ or $\frac{1}{32}$ of an inch in the diameter) equal to one-third of the width of the rear strap. Hence we have the following rule:

RULE 55.—Divide the width of the rear strap in inches by 3; the quotient will be the diameter of the bolt.

EXAMPLE 86.—The width of the strap is $2\frac{3}{4}$ inches; find the diameter of the bolts.

$$\frac{2.75}{3} = .916,$$

which is nearly equal to $\frac{59}{64}$ inch. Avoiding $\frac{1}{64}$ or $\frac{1}{32}$ inch, we say the diameter of the bolts should be $\frac{15}{16}$ inch. Some builders will make these bolts $\frac{7}{8}$ inch diameter.

306. When we know the diameters of the bolts, and also the total cross-sectional area which has to resist the shearing force, the number is easily determined by the following rule:

RULE 56.—Divide the total cross-sectional area of the bolts, as found by Rule 54, by twice the cross-sectional area of one bolt; the quotient will be the number of bolts required.

Example 87.—The total cross-sectional area of the bolts subjected to shearing stress is 3.065 square inches, the diameter of each bolt is $\frac{15}{16}$ inch. How many bolts will be required? The cross-sectional area of a $\frac{15}{16}$-inch bolt is .69 square inch; hence

$$\frac{3.065}{2 \times .69} = 2.2, \text{ say 2 bolts.}$$

In this case the stress per inch, when the taper of the bolt is taken into account, which, for the sake of simplicity, has been left out of consideration, will not exceed 8,500 pounds.

Example 88.—The total pressure on one main-rod of a locomotive—cylinders 18 × 24—is 31,000 pounds; the width of the strap is $2\frac{3}{4}$ inches; find the diameter and number of bolts.

According to Rule 54, twice the total cross-sectional area of the bolts should be

$$\frac{31000}{8000} = 3.87 \text{ square inches.}$$

According to Rule 55, the diameter of each bolt should be

$$\frac{2.75}{3} = .916, \text{ say } \frac{15}{16} \text{ inch.}$$

The cross-sectional area of a bolt $\frac{15}{16}$ inch diameter is .69 square inch; hence, according to Rule 56, the number of bolts required will be

$$\frac{3.87}{2 \times .69} = 2.8, \text{ say 3 bolts.}$$

Some locomotive builders use three bolts $\frac{7}{8}$ inch in diameter for the same size of engine.

Example 89.—The total pressure on one main-rod of a locomotive—cylinders 20 × 24—is 38,000 pounds, strap 3 inches wide; find the diameter and number of bolts.

According to Rule 54, the total cross-sectional area of the bolts will be

$$\frac{38000}{8000} = 4.75.$$

According to Rule 55, the diameter of the bolts will be 1 inch. The cross-sectional area of a bolt 1 inch in diameter is .7854; hence, according to Rule 56, the number of bolts through each end of rod will be

$$\frac{4.75}{2 \times .7854} = 3.$$

There are engines of the same size running with only 2 bolts 1 inch in diameter through each end. We believe that 3 bolts, 1 inch diameter, for a maximum steam pressure of 120 pounds in a cylinder 20 inches diameter, will be safer and give better results.

Example 90.—What should be the diameter of the bolt shown in the rear end of the main-rod, Figs. 431, 432? The cylinder is 12 × 16 inches; maximum steam pressure in the cylinder, 120 pounds; the distance through which the axle box can move below the center line of motion of the piston is 2 inches.

Although the design of this rod is different from any we have previously shown, the foregoing rules are applicable. Here we will first have to find the total maximum pressure on the rod, as explained in Art. 303, and illustrated in diagram, Fig. 430. The area of a piston 12 inches in diameter is 113.1 square inches, hence the total pressure on the piston is equal to

$$113.1 \times 120 = 13572 \text{ pounds};$$

consequently the line $a\ b$ in our diagram, Fig. 430, represents 13,572 pounds. But the length of the line $a\ b$ is not yet known, and must be found according to the instructions given in Art. 303.

In order to suit the conditions given in the example, the length of the line $a\ c$ must be 10 inches—that is, the sum of half the stroke (8 inches) and the distance (2 inches) through which the axle box can move below the center line of motion of the piston. The length of the line $c\ b$ is equal to the length of the connecting-rod—that is, the distance between the centers of journals—and, as will be seen in Figs. 431, 432, this distance, or length of the connecting-rod, is 60 inches. Therefore the length of the line $a\ b$ will be equal to

$$\sqrt{60^2 - 10^2} = 59.16 \text{ inches.}$$

Consequently, according to Art. 303, the line $c\ b$ will represent

$$\frac{60 \times 13572}{59.16} = 13764.7 \text{ pounds,}$$

which is the maximum pressure on the main-rod.

Twice the total cross-sectional area of the bolt to resist shearing must be, according to Rule 54,

$$\frac{13764.7}{8000} = 1.72 \text{ square inches,}$$

and

$$\frac{1.72}{2} = .86 \text{ square inch,}$$

which will be the cross-sectional area of the bolt. The diameter of the bolt whose cross-sectional area is .86 square inch is nearly $1\frac{1}{16}$ inches, agreeing very closely with diameter of the bolt given in the illustration.

307. Figs. 431, 432 represent a main-rod, and Figs. 433, 434 a side-rod used on engines running on one of the elevated roads; the cylinders of these engines are 12 inches diameter and 16 inches stroke. The rods are very good ones, and well adapted for these engines. The design of the main-rod differs from the designs of rods previously given. Straps are not used; the rear end is an open one, which, after the bearings have been placed in position, is closed by the steel block $A$, firmly held in position by the bolt $B$. This bolt must be strong enough to resist the pull of the rod. The front end of the rod is designed to suit a class of crossheads with a single slide, such as is shown in Fig. 248.

The design of the side-rod also differs from the designs of side-rods previously given. Here the straps have been retained, but keys are not used.

MODERN LOCOMOTIVE CONSTRUCTION. 279

308. In the previous examples we have made the diameters of the main-rod bolts equal to one-third of the width of the rear strap as nearly as possible. The rear strap, as we have stated before, is generally made a little wider than the front one, so as to make the former stronger than the latter; the reason for this will be presently

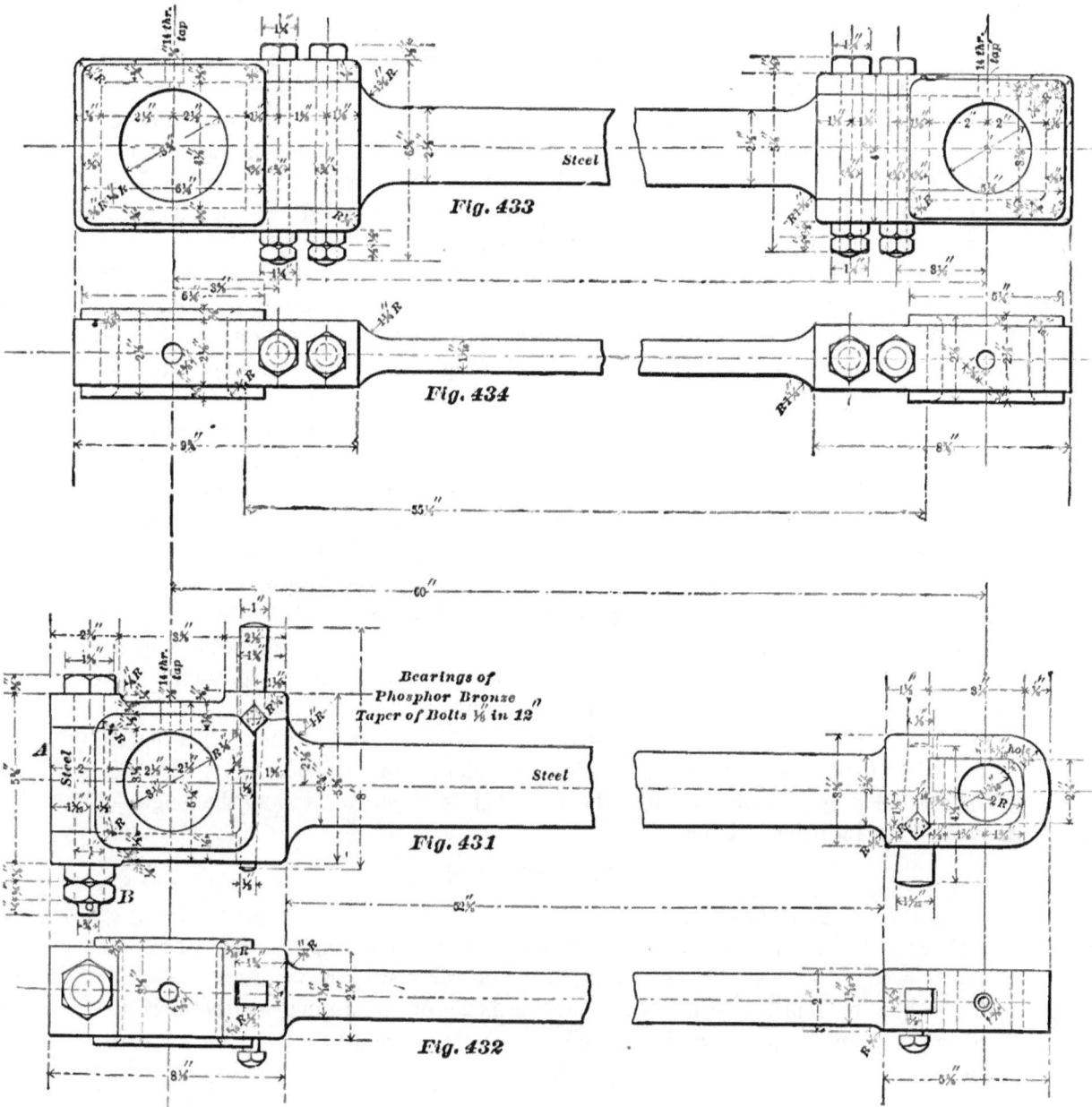

explained. But, although the width of the rear strap differs from the width of the front one, the diameters of the bolts are nearly always made the same for each end.

Again, in the previous examples, the diameters of the bolts and their number were made to suit a maximum steam pressure of 120 pounds per square inch of piston. The stress of 8,000 pounds per square inch of the cross-sectional area of the bolts was also established; and since this stress should not be changed, no matter how great or small the maximum steam pressure in the cylinders may be, it follows that the rules previously given for determining the diameters and number of bolts through the main-rod are also applicable when the maximum steam pressure in the cylinder is greater or less than 120 pounds per square inch. When the steam pressure is greater than 120 pounds per square inch, then we shall generally require three bolts through each end of the main-rod for locomotives having cylinders 17 inches in diameter and upwards. Since the greatest number of bolts used through each strap is three (at least we have not met with cases in which this number was exceeded), the problems for solution may present themselves in the following form.

EXAMPLE 91.—Three bolts are to be used through one end of a main-rod for a locomotive having cylinders 18 × 24 inches. The length of the main-rod is 90 inches; the maximum steam pressure in the cylinder is 160 pounds; the vertical distance below the center line of motion of the piston through which the center of axle can move is 3 inches. It is required to find the diameter of the bolts.

In Art. 303 we have stated that the shearing force to which the bolts through one end of the main-rod are subjected is represented by the length of the hypothenuse $c\,b$ of a right-angled triangle, Fig. 430, in which the length of the side $a\,b$ represents the total steam pressure on the piston; hence our first step, in the solution of our problem, will be to find the lengths of the sides of such a triangle. In Art. 303 we also have stated that the length of the hypothenuse must be equal to the length of the connecting-rod; hence, in this case the length of the hypothenuse must be 90 inches. The length of the side $a\,c$, that is, the shortest side, must be equal to the sum of the length of the crank, and the vertical distance below the center line of motion through which the center of the axle can move; hence, according to the conditions given in the example, the length of the side $a\,c$ must be equal to $12 + 3 = 15$ inches. The length of the side $a\,b$ must be found by calculation as explained in Art. 303, thus:

Remembering that the length of the hypothenuse is 90 inches, and the length of the side $a\,c$ is 15 inches, we have

$$\sqrt{90^2 - 15^2} = 88.74 \text{ inches},$$

which is the length of the side $a\,b$.

Now, having found the lengths of the sides of the right-angled triangle, we can easily determine the shearing force to which the bolts are subjected; thus:

The area of a piston 18 inches in diameter is 254.46 square inches; therefore the total pressure on the piston at 160 pounds per square inch will be

$$254.46 \times 160 = 40713.60 \text{ pounds}.$$

According to the remarks in Art. 303, the length of the side $a\,b$, namely, 88.74 inches, represents a pressure of 40713.60 pounds; that is to say, the length of the side $a\,b$ represents the total steam pressure on the piston. But we also know that the maximum pressure on the main-rod is represented by the length of the hypothenuse of the same triangle, and that the maximum pressure on the main-rod is as much greater as the length of the hypothenuse is greater than the length of the side $a\,b$. Hence we have

$$\frac{40713.60 \times 90}{88.74} = 41291.68 \text{ pounds,}$$

which is the maximum pressure on the main-rod; and this pressure also represents the total shearing force to which the three bolts are subjected.

Since the stress per square inch is to be 8,000 pounds, twice the total cross-sectional area of the bolts—that is, the whole area which has to resist the shearing force—is found by Rule 54, and is equal to

$$\frac{41291.68}{8000} = 5.16 \text{ square inches.}$$

But our example requires that three bolts shall resist the shearing force, and since the bolts are subjected to a double shearing stress, twice the total area of the bolts which has to resist the shearing force will be equal to six times the cross-sectional area of one bolt; hence we have

$$\frac{5.16}{6} = .86 \text{ square inch,}$$

which is the cross-sectional area of one bolt. The diameter of a circle whose area is .86 inch is nearly $1\frac{1}{16}$ inches; consequently the diameter of the bolts should be $1\frac{1}{16}$ inches.

309. Figs. 435, 436 represent a main-rod, and Figs. 437, 438 represent a side-rod for a Mogul engine, that is to say, a locomotive having six driving wheels and a pony, or two-wheeled truck.

In these engines the side-rods have to connect three pairs of driving wheels, and transmit motion to the front and rear pair. We have already seen that the design of the pedestal permits the driving axles to move up and down, so as to enable the driving wheels to adjust themselves to any unevenness of the track, consequently the centers of the axles will not always lie in a horizontal line. Under these conditions we cannot connect the three driving wheels on one side of the engine by a side-rod in which the crank-pin bearings are held rigidly in line. Consequently the side-rods in Mogul engines are made in two pieces, forming a front and rear side-rod for each side of the engine, as shown in Figs. 437, 438.

The front and rear side-rods are connected by the pin $S$, which is placed at the back of the main-pin $M$. As far as the working of the engine is concerned, the pin $S$ could be placed in front of the main-pin $M$; but for the sake of convenience it is always best to place it at the back of the main crank-pin, so that it will at no time be covered by the main-rod, which, in nearly all Mogul engines, is placed outside of the side-rods. In fact, it often happens that, with the main-rods placed outside of the side-rods, the available space between the side- and main-rods will not be sufficient for the nuts on the pin $S$, and consequently this pin must be placed at the back of the main-pin $M$ as shown. The pin $S$ should also be placed as near as possible to the main crank-pin, so as to reduce the stress to which the strap around the main-pin is subjected to a minimum.

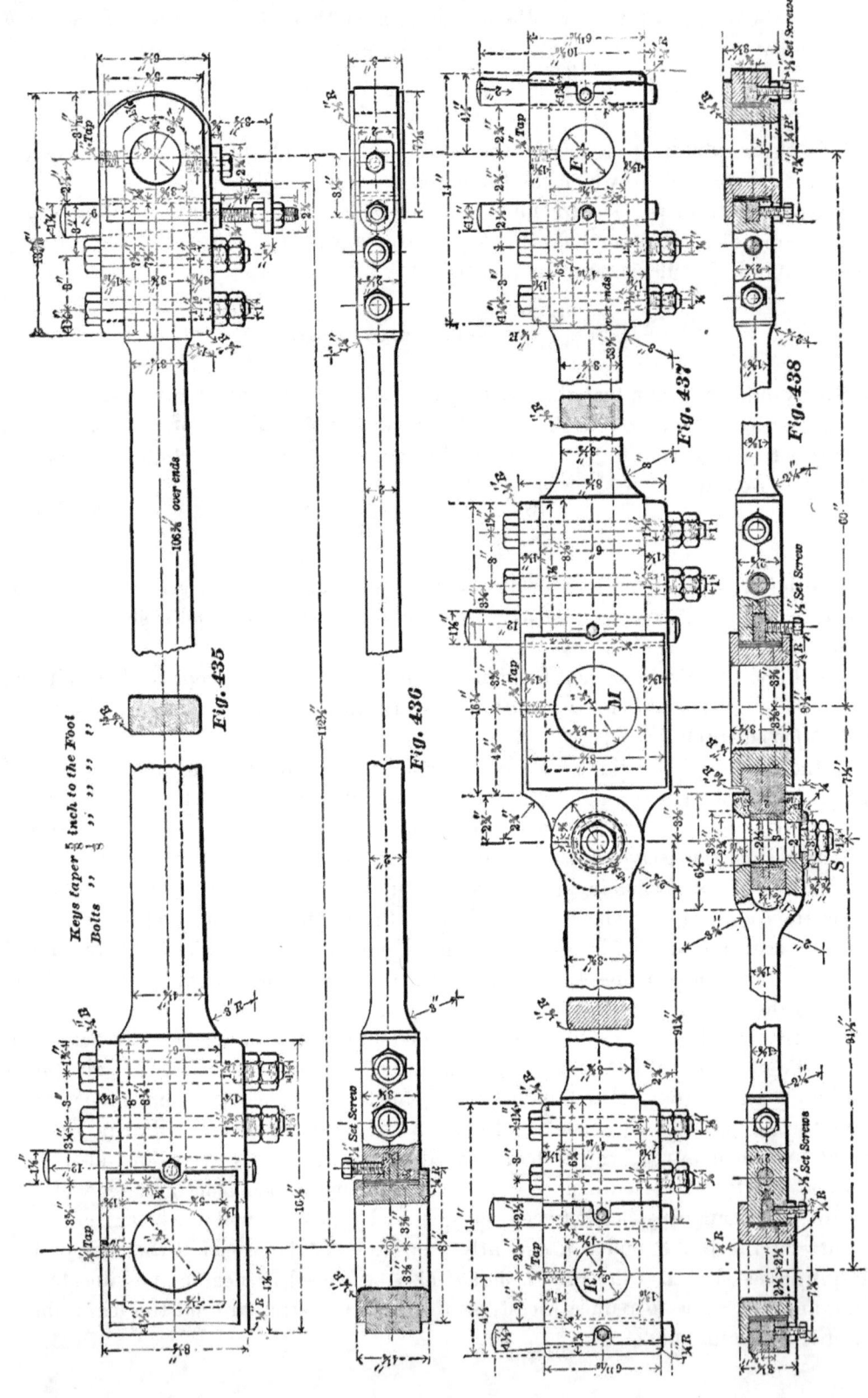

Fig. 435  Fig. 436  Fig. 437  Fig. 438

From the foregoing remarks we may conclude that in Mogul engines the front side-rods contain the bearings for the front crank-pin $F$ and for the main crank-pin $M$; the rear side-rod simply contains the bearing for the rear crank-pin $R$.

## MAIN-ROD STRAPS.

310. In Art. 300 we have stated that in designing the straps for locomotive main- and side-rods, about the only calculations which we will have to make are those for finding the correct diameters for the bolts, number required, and the thickness of the strap represented by $g$, in Fig. 421.

The rules for finding the number of bolts and their diameters have been given; hence it now only remains for us to establish rules for finding the thickness of the strap at $g$.

The weakest part of any locomotive main- or side-rod strap is in the plane $x\,y$ or $x_2\,y_2$ (Fig. 422), passed through the axis of the bolt. Consequently, when the width of the strap is given, the thickness at $g$ must be determined by calculation so as to give a sufficient cross-sectional area in the plane $x\,y$ to resist the forces acting on the strap. Of course, in the foregoing remarks we have assumed that the key has the best possible shape for the work it has to do (more of this hereafter), and that its thickness, as well as the diameter of the hole for the oil-cup, does not exceed the diameter of the bolts.

The stress\* in the main-rod straps is greater than that in the side-rod straps; we shall, therefore, in this article, consider the strength of the main-rod straps only.

Both the front and the rear straps are subjected to a tensile force—that is, a force tending to tear the straps. But the centrifugal force to which the rear end of the rod is subjected brings into play on both straps a force which acts in a direction perpendicular to the length of the rod, or, in short, a transverse force; this force acts with the greatest intensity at the back end of the rod, and becomes zero at the center of the crosshead pin. Yet there are portions of the front strap, which on account of their distances from the center of the crosshead pin, are more or less subjected to a transverse force. Also, noticing that the bolts through the straps must necessarily be placed at some distance from the center of the pins, the transverse forces on both straps will act with a leverage, and therefore will act with a greater effect, and cause a greater stress in the straps, than they would do if the bolts could be closer to the center of the pins. Consequently, these latter forces must not be neglected in our calculations.

But the transverse force acting on the rear strap is greater than the transverse force acting on the front one; and since the tensile forces are equal on both straps, it follows that the total stress in the rear strap is greater than the total stress in the front one.

Again, the stress per square inch of cross-sectional area should be the same in both straps; hence, it follows that, since the total stress is greater in the rear strap than that in the front one, the former should be made stronger than the latter, and this we often find to be the case in practice. But many master-mechanics prefer to

---

\* "Stress" may be defined as the resistance to the alteration of form, and in this sense the word "stress" is here used.

make these straps of equal strength, for the following reason: The crosshead pin will wear in time to an oval form, making it smaller in the direction of the axis of the cylinder. If now the brasses in the front end of the rod do not touch each other, as is often the case, and the rod begins to pound, the key may be driven accidentally or carelessly too tight, causing the brasses to bind on the large part of the crosshead pin, throwing on the front strap an extra stress, which may, unless the front strap is strong enough to resist this extra force, cause considerable damage.

There is another fact which must not be lost sight of in proportioning a strap, namely, the bolt holes in the strap will in time wear to an oval shape, and then they must be re-reamed, thereby weakening the strap; therefore it is necessary, in designing a strap, to make a slight allowance for re-reaming.

Now, in order to determine accurately the thickness $g$ of the strap, we should know the exact magnitudes of the forces to which they are subjected. But to find the exact magnitudes of these forces will be a difficult matter. Hence, taking all the given conditions into consideration, it will be an easier way, and probably the most practical one, to base our calculations on the proportions of straps used at present in locomotives running at high speeds, doing excellent service.

We have seen that the weakest part of the strap is in the plane $x\,y$; hence, our first step will be to determine the cross-sectional area of the strap in this plane.

Suppose, for the sake of simplicity, that the strap is subjected to a tensile force—that is to say, a force acting in the direction of the length of the rod, or in a direction indicated by the arrow in Fig. 421—tending to pull the strap apart. In this strap we have two bolts, which we may assume resist an equal amount of the pull, or, in other words, each bolt resists one-half of the pull. We therefore conclude that the metal of the strap in the plane $x_2\,y_2$ has to resist one-half of the tensile force or pull to which the strap is subjected. But the force, acting on the metal in the plane $x_2\,y_2$, is transmitted to the plane $x\,y$, and this plane must also resist the tensile force transmitted to it by its own bolt. Therefore the metal of the strap in the plane $x\,y$ must resist the whole tensile force to which the strap is subjected; and the area of this metal must be proportioned accordingly. If we had three bolts through the strap, as is often the case, the conditions would not be changed—that is to say, the weakest part of the strap, namely, its portion in the plane $x\,y$, must be made strong enough to resist the whole tensile force, and treated just the same as if no other portion of the strap had to resist any part of the force acting upon it.

If, then, the straps are subjected to a tensile force pure and simple, as we have supposed, we can easily find the cross-sectional area at $x\,y$ by allowing a stress of 10,000 pounds per square inch, as we have done, on the weakest part of a piston-rod, and consequently obtain the number of square inches in the cross-sectional area, by dividing the maximum pressure on the main-rod by 10,000; the quotient will be the required area through both wings $g\,g_2$ of the strap.

But we have seen that these straps are subjected to forces acting in a direction perpendicular to the length of the rod, and these forces must not be neglected. But since it is difficult to determine the exact magnitude of these forces, we make allowances for them by reducing the stress per square inch due to the tensile force acting on these straps—that is to say, we assume the straps to be subjected to a tensile force only, and reduce the stress of 10,000 pounds per square inch of cross-sectional area, so as to obtain a larger area.

Here, then, the question arises, How much stress per square inch shall we allow? For an answer to this question we must turn to the straps at present in use. In these straps we find that the stress per square inch of cross-sectional area in the plane $x\,y$ varies, for the rear straps, from 6,000 to 7,000 pounds per square inch; and when the front straps are made weaker than the rear ones, the stress per square inch for the former is in the neighborhood of 7,000 to 7,500 pounds per square inch. Our experience leads us to believe that a stress of 6,500 pounds per square inch of cross-sectional area for rear strap, and a stress of 7,000 pounds per square inch for the front one, both made of the best quality of hammered iron, is good practice. These figures will be adopted in the following calculations. Hence we have the following rule:

RULE 57.—To find the thickness at $g$ (Fig. 421) of the rear strap on the main-rod when the width of the same is given: Divide the maximum pressure on the main-rod by 6,500; the quotient will be the required number of square inches in the cross-sectional area at $x\,y$ (Fig. 422). From the width of the strap subtract the diameter of the bolt; the remainder will be the width of the metal at the weakest part of the strap. Divide the required cross-sectional area at $x\,y$ by the width of metal at the weakest part of the strap; one-half of this quotient will be the thickness of the strap at $g$.

For finding the thickness of the front main-rod strap we use the same rule, with the exception that, instead of dividing the maximum pressure on the main-rod by 6,500, we divide it by 7,000.

EXAMPLE 92.—In a locomotive with cylinders 18 × 24 inches, and a maximum steam pressure in the cylinders of 120 pounds per square inch, we find by the method given in Art. 303 that the maximum pressure on the rod is 31,000 pounds; the width of the front and rear straps is $2\frac{3}{4}$ inches; the diameter of each bolt through the straps is $\frac{15}{16}$ inch; it is required to find the thickness of the straps at $g$ (Fig. 421).

The total cross-sectional area at $x\,y$ of the rear strap will be

$$\frac{31000}{6500} = 4.76 \text{ square inches.}$$

The width of the metal at the weakest part of the strap—that is, at $x\,y$—will be equal to

$$2\tfrac{3}{4} - \tfrac{15}{16} = 1\tfrac{13}{16} = 1.8125 \text{ inches,}$$

and

$$\frac{4.76}{1.8125} = 2.62 \text{ inches,}$$

will be the sum of the thickness of both wings $g\,g_2$ of the strap. Therefore,

$$\frac{2.62}{2} = 1.31 \text{ inches,}$$

say $1\frac{5}{16}$ inches, is the thickness of the rear strap at $g$.

For the thickness of the front strap, we have

$$\frac{31000}{7000} = 4.42 \text{ square inches}$$

in the cross-sectional area at $x\,y$.

and
$$\frac{4.42}{1.8125} = 2.43,$$

$$\frac{2.43}{2} = 1.21 \text{ inches, say } 1\tfrac{3}{16} \text{ inches.}$$

NOTE.—Some master-mechanics make the thickness of the front strap equal to that of the rear one; therefore, in such cases, special calculations for the front strap will not be required.

311. Figs. 439, 440 represent two views of a main-rod for a consolidation engine—that is, an engine with four pairs of drivers, and a pony truck, as shown in Fig. 4.

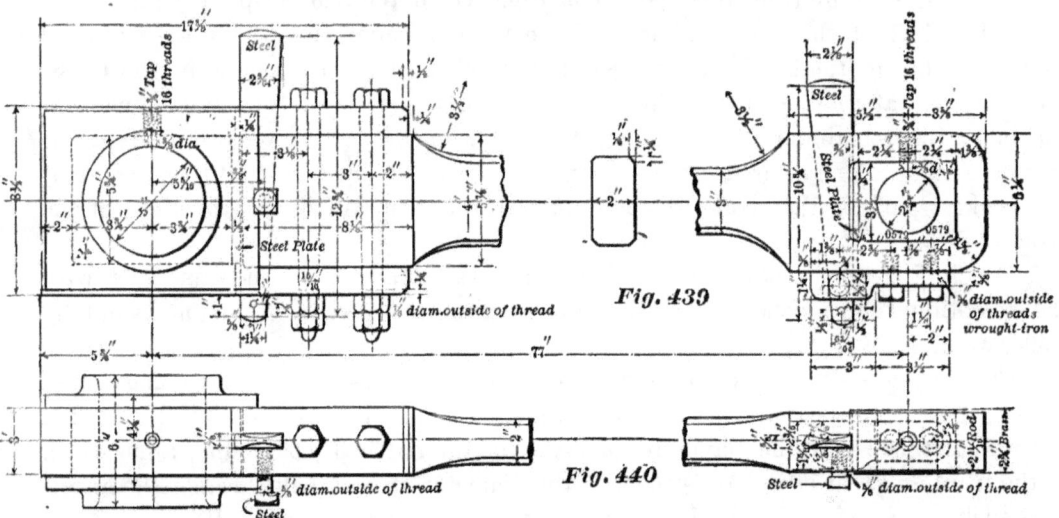

Fig. 439

Fig. 440

The engine for which these rods were designed has cylinders 20 inches diameter and 24 inches stroke, and crossheads like that shown in Figs. 244, 246, and 247.

For a high speed and a maximum steam pressure of 120 pounds in the cylinders, the rear strap on this rod is, in our opinion, too weak; for the above given maximum pressure and for high speeds, safer and better results will be obtained by making the thickness of the strap around the bolts at least $1\tfrac{7}{16}$ inches; and also three $1\tfrac{5}{16}$ inch bolts should be used in place of two.

### SIDE-ROD STRAPS FOR EIGHT-WHEELED PASSENGER ENGINES.

312. In comparing the side-rod straps belonging to different locomotives of one and the same class and size, but designed in different locomotive establishments or by different master-mechanics, we find quite a variation in the dimensions of corresponding parts of the different side-rod straps around similar crank-pins. This is, no doubt, due to the fact that it is impossible to determine exactly the magnitude of the forces to which the side-rods are subjected.

We have already seen that the main-rods are subjected to a tensile force, and also to a transverse force due to the centrifugal action at one of its ends. The side-rods are subjected to similar forces, but whose sum is of less magnitude than that of the forces acting on the main-rods. The magnitude of the tensile force acting on the main-rod is dependent on the whole pressure on the piston, whereas on side-rods the magnitude of the tensile force is dependent on the weight on the driving wheels, and partly also on the condition of the road-bed, and on the condition of the working parts under the engine; but the latter conditions will affect the tensile force acting on the side-rods to a greater degree than it will affect the tensile forces acting on the main-rods. If, for instance, the road-bed is not level, or the play between the axle box and the wedges has been increased by wear, or the engine is running over a sharp curve, the driving axles, as well as the side-rods, may at any time be thrown out of line with each other, thereby suddenly increasing the tensile force on the side-rods on one or the other side of the engine; and when, under these conditions, the engine is running at a high rate of speed, this extra tensile force will act on the side-rods only, because these rods will be affected by the stored-up energy in the engine to turn the wheels, whereas the main-rods cannot be subjected to a greater pressure than that due to the pressure on the piston. Now, with these emergencies to provide for, it should not be a matter of surprise to hear of straps breaking; but the frequency of such occurrences can be avoided by basing our calculation on the designs of such straps which experience has taught us to be correct.

In designing a side-rod strap we are guided by the same reasoning as that given in connection with the design of the main-rod straps, and therefore conclude that the weakest part of the side-rod strap is in the plane $x\,y$ (Fig. 422) passed through the axis of the bolt. Since the width of the side-rod strap depends upon the dimensions of the crank-pin, we shall consider that the width has been given, and all that remains for us to determine is the thickness $g$ (Fig. 421) of the wing of the strap.

In eight-wheeled passenger engines two driving wheels are connected on each side of the engine; consequently, each main-rod in this class of engines has to transmit motion to two driving wheels; and the side-rod has to transmit motion to only one driving wheel. The main driving wheels generally have to support a greater weight than the rear ones, as the former have to support a portion of the weight of the connecting-rods, a portion of the weight of the valve gear, and often have a heavier counterbalance than the latter; but for the purpose of finding the proportions of the side-rod straps, we may assume that each driving wheel, whether front or rear, supports an equal amount of weight. Again, the whole of the total steam pressure on the piston is not utilized for the purpose of giving motion to the driving wheels; yet for the sake of simplicity we may assume that such is the case. Now, in order to simplify matters still more, we may again assume, as we did in relation to the main-rod, that the side-rods are subjected to a tensile force only. Consequently, since the main-rod in eight-wheeled passenger engines has to transmit motion to two driving wheels, and since the side-rod is, so to speak, only a connecting link between these two drivers, and therefore has only to transmit motion to one of them, it follows that, under the foregoing assumptions, the tensile force to which the side-rods are subjected will be equal to one-half the pressure on the piston. Comparing the cross-sectional area in the plane $x\,y$ of the side-rod straps, at present working successfully, we find that the stress per square inch of the cross-sectional area in the plane $x\,y$, made by different makers, varies, in round figures, from 3,500 to 4,700 pounds. Our experience leads us to believe that, for eight-wheeled passenger engines, it is good practice to make an allowance for a stress of 4,200 pounds per square inch of the cross-sectional area through the weakest part of the strap (that is, in the plane $x\,y$), under the assumption that the side-rods are subjected to a tensile force only, and that the magnitude of this force is equal to one-half the steam pressure on the piston; this stress of 4,200 pounds per square inch of the weakest part of the strap will be adopted in the following calculations.

313. In Art. 310 it will be seen that for main-rod straps the stress allowed per square inch in the plane $x\,y$ is 6,500 pounds, but for the side-rod straps we have now established a stress of 4,200 pounds per square inch in a similar plane. This difference is due to the fact, as stated before, that side-rods are subjected to an additional tensile force when the engine is running over uneven road-beds, curves, etc. Therefore, in order to find the thickness at $g$ of the side-rod strap (see Fig. 421), we divide the total steam pressure on the piston by 2; the quotient will be the assumed tensile force acting on the strap; dividing this quotient by 4,200, we obtain the number of square inches in the smallest cross-sectional area of the strap—that is to say, in the plane $x\,y$. Dividing this cross-sectional area by the width of the strap minus the diameter of the bolt, we obtain the sum of the thickness at $g$ and $g_2$; one-half of this sum will be the required thickness at $g$. This manner of finding the required thickness can be made simpler, hence the following:

RULE 58.—Divide the total steam pressure on the piston by 16,800; divide this quotient by the width of the strap from which the diameter of the bolt has been subtracted; the last quotient will be the thickness at $g$ of one of the wings of the side-rod strap.

EXAMPLE 93.—Find the thickness at $g$ of the side-rod strap for an eight-wheeled passenger engine; cylinders, 17 inches diameter; maximum steam pressure on the piston, 120 pounds per square inch; width of strap, $2\frac{1}{4}$ inches; diameter of bolts through the straps, $\frac{7}{8}$ inch.

The total pressure on the piston is equal to the product of its area in square inches into the steam pressure per square inch; consequently the total pressure on the piston will be

$$226.98 \times 120 = 27237.60 \text{ pounds.}$$

Dividing this pressure by 16,800, we have

$$\frac{27237.60}{16800} = 1.621.$$

Dividing this quotient by the width of the strap minus the diameter of the bolt, we obtain

$$\frac{1.621}{2\frac{1}{4} - \frac{7}{8}} = 1.17+, \text{ say } 1\frac{1}{8} \text{ inches,}$$

for thickness of the side-rod strap at $g$, Fig. 421.

**314.** In Art. 309 we have given the reasons for the use of two side-rods on each side of a Mogul engine. For similar reasons we need three side-rods on each side of a consolidation engine, namely, the front, central, and rear side-rods.

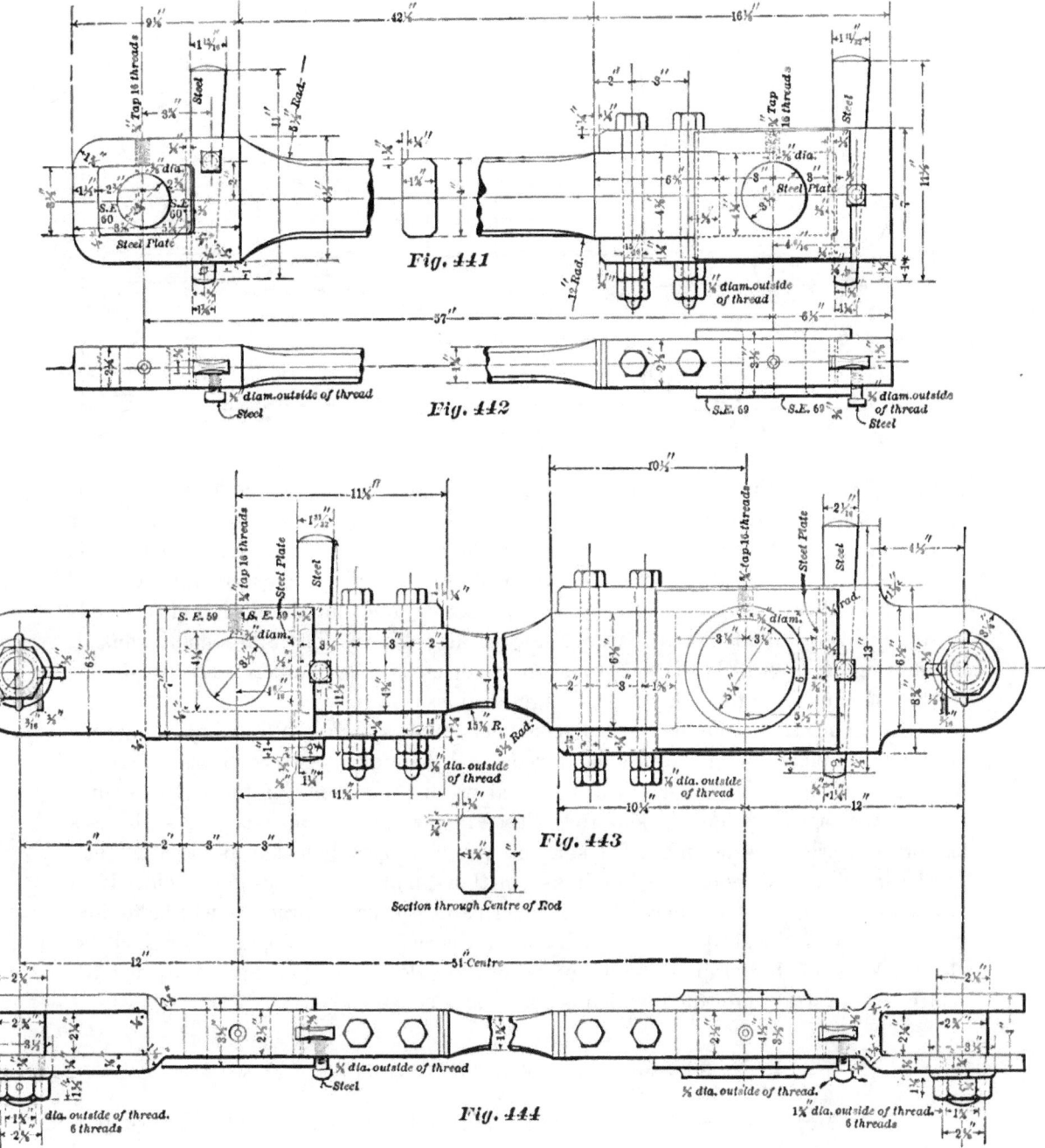

Fig. 441
Fig. 442
Fig. 443
Fig. 444

Figs. 441, 442 represent the front side-rod; Figs. 443, 444 represent the central side-rod; and Figs. 445, 446 represent the rear side-rod for a consolidation engine with cylinders 20 × 24 inches. It will be seen that the central side-rod connects two wheels; the straps on this rod have forked ends, to which the front and rear side-rods are connected. This manner of connecting side-rods differs from the connection of the side-rods shown in Figs. 437, 438, in which the rear side-rod has the forked end, and

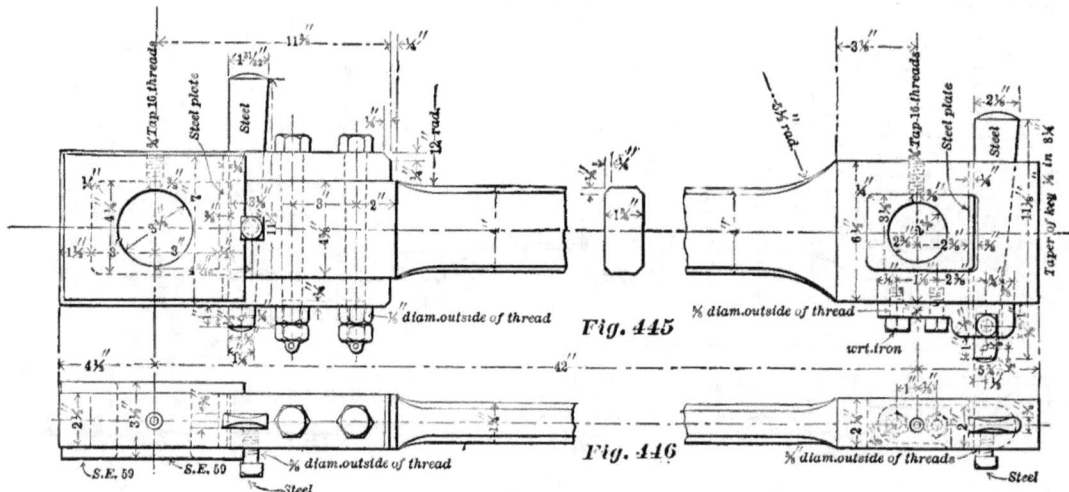

Fig. 445

Fig. 446

the strap around the main crank-pin is forged solid. Again, in the front and rear side-rods for the consolidation engine, provision has been made to take up the wear of the bearings in the ends of these rods which are connected to the central-rod. This makes a very good arrangement; but it must not be understood that this design of side-rods is always adopted in consolidation engines, and that the design of side-rods shown in Figs. 437, 438 is only suitable for Mogul engines. There are many consolidation engines in which the side-rods are connected in a manner precisely similar to that of connecting the side-rods in Mogul engines.

315. In nearly all eight-wheeled passenger engines, 4 feet 8½ inches gauge, the side-rods are placed outside of the main-rods, and therefore the brass bearings, straps, etc., at each end of the side-rod will be equal in size. In some of the narrow-gauge engines we sometimes find the side-rods plased inside of the main-rods. In such cases the brass bearing at one end of the side-rod will be larger than that at the other end of the same rod. Locomotive builders sometimes make the straps for such rods of equal thicknesses. We believe that in such cases the better practice will be to find the thickness of the strap at the small end of the rod by Rule 58, and then increase the thickness of the strap at the large end of the side-rod ten per cent., provided the widths of the straps are equal, which is generally the case.

### SIDE-ROD STRAPS FOR MOGUL ENGINES.

316. In Mogul engines the stress in the side-rods will—as in eight-wheeled passenger engines—depend on the weight on drivers, the condition of the road-bed, and the condition of the engine, as we have explained in connection with side-rods for passenger engines. But in Mogul engines we have two other elements—not found in passenger engines—which are detrimental to the strength of the side-rod strap, namely,

a larger number of driving wheels, and the knuckle joint—that is, the connection of the two side-rods as shown at $S$ in Fig. 438.

317. Fig. 447 represents the wheel base of a Mogul engine; the main- and side-rods are indicated simply by their center lines. In this class of engines the main pair of driving wheels $B$ is placed between the front pair $A$ and the rear pair $C$, but is not placed centrally between them. The rigid wheel base will often depend on the length of the boiler; and the distance between the wheels will in many cases depend on the general design of the boiler and the valve gear. Although these driving wheels are not placed at equal distances apart, the arrangement of the equalizing levers is such as to throw as nearly as possible the same amount of weight on each driver. For the purpose of

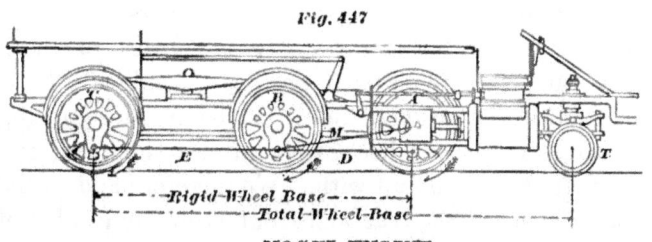

MOGUL ENGINE

designing the side-rod straps, we may assume that an equal amount of weight is placed on each driver. In order to simplify the rule for finding the thickness of the strap, we shall again assume, as we did in the case of passenger engines, that the whole steam pressure on the piston is utilized for the purpose of giving motion to the wheels. Now, since three drivers are connected on each side of the engine, and since the same amount of weight is assumed to be placed on each driver, it follows that one-third of the total steam pressure on one piston will, according to our assumption, be required to turn one driving wheel. When the driving wheels are turning in the direction as indicated by the arrows, and the crank-pins are below the centers of the axles, the front side-rod $D$ will be subjected, besides the transverse forces acting upon the rods, to a tensile force; and the rear side-rod $E$ will be subjected to a compressive force, each equal to one-third of the pressure on the piston, provided the engine is running over a straight and perfect level road. On the other hand, when the crank-pins are above the center of axle, the front side-rod will be subjected, besides the transverse forces acting upon the rods, to a compressive force and the rear side-rod to a tensile force, each again equal to one-third of the pressure on the piston. The exact magnitude of the transverse forces acting on the side-rods under the various conditions of the road-bed, etc., cannot be determined, but the total steam pressure on the piston is known; we therefore assume, as in the case of passenger engines, that the side-rods are simply subjected to a tensile force due to the pressure on the piston; design the straps accordingly, and make allowances for the other forces, as will be hereafter explained. If now we had no transverse forces acting on the straps to contend with, we would simply divide one-third of the maximum piston pressure by 10,000 pounds (which is about a fair allowance for stress per square inch when we have to provide against a simple tensile force), and thereby obtain the number of square inches in the cross-sectional area through the weakest part of the strap. But since we have to provide against the transverse forces, we must divide one-third of the maximum steam pressure on the piston by a number less than 10,000, and shall adopt, as before, 4,200. Hence, if we divide one-third of the maximum steam pressure on the piston by 4,200, we shall obtain the number of square inches in the cross-sectional area through the weakest part of the strap. Dividing this area by the width of the strap minus the diameter of the bolts through it, and again dividing the quotient thus obtained by 2, we obtain a thickness for the side-rod straps which we shall indicate by the letter $A$. But this thickness $A$ will not be sufficiently great, for the following reasons: In adopting the number 4,200, or, in other words, allowing one square inch for every 4,200 pounds of the pressure on the strap due to one-third of the maximum piston pressure, we provide for the transverse forces acting on the strap, and also for the extra tensile forces due to the condition of the road-bed and condition of the engine, such as will occur in passenger engines. This extra tensile force, due to the condition of the road-bed, etc., will be greater in Mogul engines, on account of the increased number of wheels, than in passenger engines; and besides this we have the knuckle joint to contend with. We therefore add to the thickness $A$ previously found, $\frac{3}{16}$ of an inch for the rear and front strap, and add $\frac{3}{8}$ of an inch for the central strap, for all Mogul locomotives having cylinders 13 inches diameter and upwards. For Mogul engines having cylinders whose diameters are less than 13 inches, add $\frac{1}{4}$ of an inch to the thickness $A$ for the front and rear straps, and $\frac{7}{16}$ of an inch to the thickness for the central strap. These rules can be stated in a simpler manner, as follows:

RULE 59.—To find the thickness $g$ (Fig. 421) for the side-rod straps around the front and rear crank pins in Mogul engines having cylinders 13 inches diameter and upwards: Divide the total maximum steam pressure on one piston by 25,200; divide the quotient thus obtained by the width of the strap from which the diameter of the bolts through it has been deducted, and add $\frac{3}{16}$ of an inch to the last quotient; the sum will be the required thickness.

For Mogul engines having cylinders less than 13 inches in diameter, divide the total maximum steam pressure on the piston by 25,200; divide the quotient thus obtained by the width of the strap from which the diameter of the bolts through it has been deducted, and add $\frac{1}{4}$ of an inch to the last quotient; the sum will be the required thickness $g$ for the side-rod strap around the front and rear crank-pin.

RULE 60.—To find the thickness $g$ for the side-rod strap around the main crank-pin in Mogul engines having cylinders 13 inches diameter and upwards: Divide the total maximum steam pressure on the piston by 25,200; divide the quotient thus obtained by the width of the strap from which the diameter of the bolts through it has been deducted, and add $\frac{3}{8}$ of an inch to the last quotient; the sum will be the required thickness.

For Mogul engines having cylinders less than 13 inches diameter, divide the total maximum steam pressure on the piston by 25,200; divide the quotient thus obtained by the width of the strap from which the diameter of the bolts through it has been deducted, and add $\frac{7}{16}$ of an inch to the last quotient; the sum will be the thickness $g$ for the central side-rod strap.

EXAMPLE 94.—Find the thickness $g$ (Fig. 421) for the side-rod straps for a Mogul engine whose cylinders are 18 inches diameter; maximum steam pressure on the piston, 120 pounds per square inch; width of front and rear straps, $2\frac{1}{4}$ inches; diameters of the bolts through these straps, $\frac{15}{16}$ inch; width of central strap, $2\frac{1}{2}$ inches; diameters of bolts through the same, $1\frac{1}{16}$ inches.

Let us first find the thickness for the front and rear straps. The total maximum steam pressure on the piston is found by multiplying the area of the piston in square inches by the steam pressure per square inch; hence we have

$$254.47 \times 120 = 30536.40 \text{ pounds.}$$

$$\frac{30536.40}{25200} = 1.211.$$

Subtracting the diameter of a side-rod bolt from the width of the strap, we obtain

$$2.25 - .9375 = 1.3125 \text{ inches,}$$

and

$$\frac{1.211}{1.3125} = .922, \text{ say } \tfrac{15}{16} \text{ of an inch,}$$

which is the thickness $A$, to which $\tfrac{3}{16}$ inch must be added. Hence $\tfrac{15}{16} + \tfrac{3}{16} = 1\tfrac{1}{8}$ inches, which is the thickness $g$ of the front and rear side-rod straps.

To find the thickness $g$ of the central side-rod strap, we divide, as before, the total maximum steam pressure on the piston by 25,200, and obtain 1.211. This quotient we divide by width of the central strap minus the diameter of the bolt. We have

$$\frac{1.211}{2.5 - 1.06} = .84, \text{ say } \tfrac{7}{8} \text{ of an inch,}$$

which is the thickness $A$. To this we must add $\tfrac{3}{8}$ of an inch; the sum $\tfrac{7}{8} + \tfrac{3}{8} = 1\tfrac{1}{4}$ inches, which is the thickness $g$ of the central side-rod strap.

EXAMPLE 95.—What should be the thickness of the side-rod straps for a Mogul engine whose cylinders are 11 inches diameter; rear and front straps, $1\tfrac{3}{4}$ inches wide; bolts, $\tfrac{3}{4}$ inch diameter; central side-rod strap, 2 inches wide; bolts, $\tfrac{3}{4}$ inch diameter; maximum steam pressure on the piston, 120 pounds per square inch?

Total maximum steam pressure on the piston will be equal to

$$95.03 \times 120 = 11403.60 \text{ pounds,}$$

and

$$\frac{11403.60}{25200} = .452.$$

To find the thickness $g$ for the front and rear strap, we have first .452 divided by the width of the straps minus the diameter of the bolts, equal to

$$\frac{.452}{1.75 - .75} = .452, \text{ say } \tfrac{1}{2} \text{ inch,}$$

which is the thickness $A$. To this we must, according to rule, add $\tfrac{1}{4}$ of an inch. We therefore obtain $\tfrac{1}{2} + \tfrac{1}{4} = \tfrac{3}{4}$ inch for the thickness $g$ for the front and rear side-rod straps.

For the thickness $g$ of the central side-rod straps we have

$$\frac{11403.60}{25200} = .452,$$

and

$$\frac{.452}{2 - .75} = .361, \text{ say } \tfrac{3}{8} \text{ inch,}$$

which is the thickness $A$. To this we must add $\frac{7}{16}$ inch. Therefore $\frac{3}{8} + \frac{7}{16} = \frac{13}{16}$ inch, which is the thickness $g$ for the central side-rod strap.

318. For all Mogul engines in which the maximum steam pressure on the piston is 120 pounds per square inch, we believe it is good practice not to make the thickness $g$ of any side-rod strap less than $\frac{3}{4}$ of an inch. If our calculations, according to the foregoing rules, call for a thickness less than $\frac{3}{4}$ inch, then the results indicate that the width of the strap is excessive, and it should be reduced.

### SIDE-ROD STRAPS FOR CONSOLIDATION ENGINES.

319. Fig. 448 represents the wheel base for a consolidation engine. Here we have four wheels connected on each side of the engine. The wheel marked $A$ is one of the first pair of drivers, $B$ one of the second pair, $C$ one of the third pair, and $D$ one of

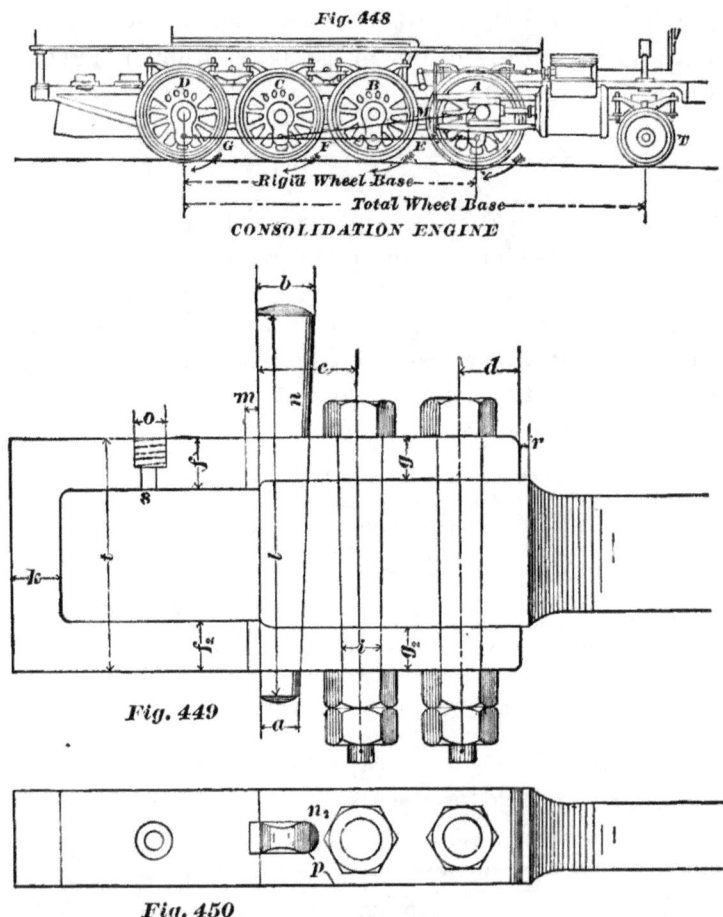

the rear or fourth pair of drivers. In some engines of this class the main-rods are connected to the second pair of drivers. The front side-rod $E$, the central side-rod $F$, and the rear side-rod $G$, and also the main-rod $M$, are represented by their center lines only.

In this class of engines the equalizing levers are arranged, as in the former class, to throw, as nearly as possible, an equal amount of weight on each driver; hence for the purpose of designing the side-rod straps we may again assume that all drivers have to bear an equal amount of weight; we may also assume, as in the former cases, that the whole steam pressure on the piston is utilized for rotating the wheels. Since four wheels are connected on each side of the engine, it will require, under the foregoing assumptions, one-fourth of the total steam pressure on the piston to turn each wheel.

When the wheels are connected, as shown in Fig. 448, the front side-rod $E$ will have to transmit motion to one wheel; that is, the wheel $A$; the central side-rod $F$ will have to transmit motion to the second wheel $B$, and by a little reflection it will be seen that the same side-rod $F$ has also to transmit motion, through the front rod $E$, to the front wheel $A$. We may therefore say that the work performed by the central side-rod $F$ is equal to twice that performed by the front rod $E$, and conclude that under our assumptions the tensile force acting on the side-rod $F$, due to the steam pressure on the piston, is equal to one-half of the total maximum pressure on the piston; and that the tensile force acting on the front side-rod $E$ is equal to one-fourth of the total maximum steam pressure on the piston. Such conclusion will be correct so long as the engine is in first-class condition, and running over a perfect and straight road. But when the engine is running over curves, and the road-bed is not perfect, and the wear has caused play between the axle boxes and the wedges, the ratio between the tensile forces acting on the central and front side-rod will not be exactly as two to one.

Again, since the action at one end of the central side-rod is equal to the reaction at the other end, we conclude that the straps on this rod should be of equal dimensions. Furthermore, practice has shown that the stress on the front and rear side-rods is somewhat less than that on the central rod. The thickness $g$ (Fig. 449) of the side-rod straps, obtained by the following rules, will agree with modern practice.

RULE 61.—To find the thickness at $g$ (Fig. 449) for the front and rear side-rod straps, for consolidation engines: Divide the total maximum steam pressure on the piston by 33,600; divide the quotient thus obtained by the width of the strap minus the diameter of the bolts through it; add $\frac{7}{16}$ of an inch to the last quotient; the sum will be the required thickness.

RULE 62.—For finding the thickness of the central side-rod straps, divide the total maximum steam pressure on the piston by 33,600; divide this quotient by the width of the strap, minus the diameter of the bolts through it, and add $\frac{5}{8}$ of an inch to the last quotient; the sum will be the required thickness at $g$ (Fig. 449).

EXAMPLE 96.—What should be the thickness of the side-rod straps for a consolidation engine having cylinders 20 inches diameter? Maximum steam pressure on the piston, 120 pounds. The width of the central side-rod straps, and also the width of the front and rear side-rod straps, is $2\frac{1}{2}$ inches; the diameter of the bolts through the central side-rod is $1\frac{1}{4}$ inches; the diameter of the bolts through the front and rear straps is 1 inch.

296   MODERN LOCOMOTIVE CONSTRUCTION.

The area of a piston 20 inches in diameter is 314.16 square inches. The total maximum steam pressure on the piston will be

$$314.16 \times 120 = 37699.20 \text{ pounds,}$$

and

$$\frac{37699.20}{33600} = 1.122.$$

The thickness at $g$ for the front and rear side-rod straps will be equal to

$$\frac{1.122}{2\tfrac{1}{2} - 1} + \tfrac{7}{16} = 1\tfrac{3}{16} \text{ inches, very nearly.}$$

The thickness for the central side-rod straps will be

$$\frac{1.122}{2\tfrac{1}{2} - 1\tfrac{1}{8}} + \tfrac{5}{8} = 1\tfrac{7}{16} \text{ inches, very nearly.}$$

320. After the thickness at $g$ (Fig. 449) for the side-rod straps has been obtained, we determine the thickness at $f$ and $k$ in a manner similar to that adopted for finding these thicknesses for the main-rod straps—namely, the thickness at $f$ is made $\tfrac{1}{8}$ of an inch greater than at $g$, and the thickness at $k$ is made $\tfrac{1}{4}$ of an inch thicker than at $g$ for small engines, and from $\tfrac{3}{8}$ to $\tfrac{1}{2}$ inch greater for large engines.

In some straps we find the hole $o$ for the oil-cup drilled through the whole thickness of the wing; in others, we find this hole drilled only part way through the wing, and then a smaller hole $s$ about $\tfrac{3}{8}$ of an inch in diameter drilled through the remaining part of the thickness, as shown in Fig. 449. The latter we believe to be the best practice, as this will not reduce the strength of the strap as much as when the large hole is drilled clear through.

### SIDE-ROD BOLTS.

321. In considering the strength of the bolts which fasten the straps to the main-rods, we have seen (Art. 303) that the principal force to which these bolts are subjected is a shearing force. In determining the number and diameter of these bolts we made their cross-sectional area proportional to this force, with certain allowances for the other forces to which they are subjected. It was further seen (Art. 308) that for the light main-rods two bolts through each strap are sufficient for the work they have to do; but that for the heavy class of main-rods three bolts through each strap must be used, so as to obtain the required cross-sectional area, and at the same time avoid the use of bolts of excessively large diameters; or, we may say, bolts whose diameters are out of proportion to other parts of the rod.

But now, in considering the strength of bolts required to hold the straps to side-rods, it may be stated, at once, that more than two bolts through each side-rod strap are not required, because two bolts will always give us a sufficient cross-sectional area without using bolts of excessively large diameters. Even in the heaviest locomotives which up to the present time have been built, it has been found that two bolts through the side-rod straps are sufficient to resist all the forces to which they are subjected, and yet the diameters of these bolts did not appear to be too large, or, in other words, the bolts did not require so much metal to be drilled out of the straps as to increase the thickness of the wings of the straps to an unreasonable extent. Of course, for practical reasons which are obvious, less than two bolts through each end of the side-rod cannot be used. Therefore we may say that the number of bolts through each side-rod strap (namely, two), for any locomotive, is established. In order to find the diameter of bolts for side-rod straps, we should know the exact magnitudes of the forces to which they are subjected; but to determine the magnitude of these forces accurately is impossible; in fact, the same remarks made in relation to forces to which the side-rod straps are subjected are also applicable to the forces which tend to break the bolts through the straps. We must therefore again allow experience to guide us in forming the following rules:

For all practical purposes we may proceed in our calculations for finding the diameters of the side-rod strap bolts as if these bolts were subjected to a simple shearing force only, due to the weight on the driving wheels.

Therefore, in the following calculations we shall simply find, first, the diameter of the bolts required to resist a shearing force, and then add to this diameter a certain amount to allow for the forces due to the unevenness of tracks, loose boxes, etc., which sum will also be sufficient for the stress due to the momentum of the rod.

322. Let us first consider the diameters of bolts required for side-rod straps in eight-wheeled passenger engines. We have already seen that, in this class of engines, there are two driving wheels on each side, and that the motion to the rear driving wheel is transmitted through the side-rod, which connects the two. Now let us assume, as we have done before, that the whole steam pressure on the piston is utilized in giving motion to the wheels. Under this assumption, the force acting in the direction of the length of the side-rod will be equal to one-half the total maximum steam pressure on the piston, and will represent an assumed shearing force, to which the bolts are subjected.

Now, having established, for the purpose of our calculations, a shearing force, we next determine an area proportional to this force, and this may be done in a manner similar to that adopted for finding cross-sectional area of the main-rod strap bolts, namely, divide the pressure on the side-rod, which in this case is assumed to be equal to one-half of the total maximum steam pressure on the piston, by 8,000; the quotient will give us an area proportional to our assumed shearing force; but since this area is greater than that required for the actual shearing force, we have also made, to a great extent, an allowance for the force due to the momentum. For the sake of brevity, hereafter we shall refer to this area as a simple shearing area, and the force to which it is proportioned the shearing force. Having found the required shearing area, the cross-sectional area of one bolt is readily found. Since in all side-rod straps two bolts are used, and since the shearing force tends to cut each bolt in two places, it follows that the shearing area must be equal to four times the cross-sectional area of one bolt; hence we divide the former area by 4; the quotient will be the cross-sectional area in inches of one bolt; the diameter corresponding to the last area will be the diameter of the bolt required to resist the shearing force. In order to allow for the forces due to uneven tracks, etc., we must add $\frac{1}{8}$ of an inch to the diameter thus found; the sum will be the required diameter of the side-rod bolts in eight-wheeled passenger engines. This rule can be stated in a simpler manner, as we shall presently show.

In Mogul and ten-wheeled engines we have three driving wheels connected on each side of the engines; we therefore divide one-third of the maximum steam pressure on the piston by 8,000; the quotient will be the shearing area in square inches; dividing this area by 4, we again obtain the cross-sectional area of one bolt, the diameter of which must also be increased by some given amount to resist the additional forces which come into play. This additional amount will be given in the rules which are to follow.

The diameters of the bolts through side-rod straps in consolidation engines are found in a manner similar to the foregoing. In these engines we have four wheels, connected on each side, consequently we divide one-fourth of the maximum steam pressure on the piston by 8,000, so as to obtain the shearing area of the bolts through the front and rear straps; dividing the latter by 4, we obtain the cross-sectional area of one bolt, whose corresponding diameter must again be increased by a certain amount, as will be given in the following rules:

RULE 63.—To find the diameter of a side-rod strap bolt for an eight-wheeled passenger engine: Divide the total maximum steam pressure on the piston by 64,000; the quotient will be the cross-sectional area of one bolt required to resist the shearing force.

To the corresponding diameter of this area add $\frac{1}{8}$ of an inch; the sum will be the required diameter of the bolts.

EXAMPLE 97.—The diameter of the cylinders of an eight-wheeled passenger engine (such as is shown in Fig. 1) is 18 inches; maximum steam pressure per square inch of piston, 120 pounds; find the diameter of the side-rod bolts.

The total maximum steam pressure on the piston is equal to its area multiplied by 120. The area of an 18-inch piston is equal to 254.47 square inches; and 254.47 × 120 = 30536.4 pounds.

$$\frac{30536.4}{64000} = 0.477 \text{ square inch.}$$

The nearest diameter of a bolt corresponding to a cross-sectional area of 0.477 square inch is $\frac{25}{32}$ inch; neglecting the $\frac{1}{32}$ of an inch and adding $\frac{1}{8}$ of an inch to the diameter found, we have $\frac{3}{4} + \frac{1}{8} = \frac{7}{8}$ inch, which is the required diameter of the side-rod strap bolts for eight-wheeled passenger engines.

RULE 64.—To find the diameters for the side-rod strap bolts in a Mogul engine: Divide the total maximum steam pressure on the piston by 96,000; the quotient will be the cross-sectional area in square inches of one bolt necessary to resist the shearing force. To the corresponding diameter, which we designate by the letter $A$, add $\frac{1}{4}$ of an inch; the sum will be the required diameter of the bolts through the straps around the front and rear crank-pin. Again, to the diameter $A$ add $\frac{3}{8}$ of an inch; the sum will be the required diameter of the bolts through the straps around the central or main crank-pin.

EXAMPLE 98.—Find the diameters for the side-rod bolts in a Mogul engine, having cylinders 19 inches in diameter; maximum steam pressure per square inch of piston,

120 pounds. The area of a 19-inch piston is 283.53 square inches; the total maximum pressure on the piston will be equal to 283.53 × 120 = 34,023.6 pounds.

$$\frac{34023.6}{96000} = 0.354 \text{ square inch.}$$

The nearest diameter corresponding to an area of 0.354 square inch is $\frac{11}{16}$ inch. Therefore $\frac{11}{16} + \frac{1}{4} = \frac{15}{16}$ inch, which is the diameter for the bolts through side-rod straps for the front and rear crank-pin. And $\frac{11}{16} + \frac{3}{8} = 1\frac{1}{16}$ inch, which is the diameter of the bolts through the side-rod strap for the central or main crank-pin.

RULE 65.—To find the diameters for the side-rod strap bolts in a consolidation engine: Divide the total maximum steam pressure on the piston by 128,000; the quotient will be the cross-sectional area in square inches of each bolt through the front and rear straps necessary to resist the shearing force. To the corresponding diameter, which we shall designate by the letter $B$, add $\frac{3}{8}$ of an inch; the sum will be the required diameter of the bolts through the straps for the front and rear crank-pins. Again, to the diameter $B$, add $\frac{1}{2}$ inch; the sum will be the diameter of the bolts through the straps for the second and third crank-pins.

EXAMPLE 99.—Find the diameters for the side-rod bolts in a consolidation engine having cylinders 20 inches in diameter; maximum steam pressure per square inch of piston, 120 pounds.

The area of a 20-inch piston is equal to 314.16 square inches; the total maximum steam pressure on the piston will be equal to 314.16 × 120 = 37699.2 pounds.

$$\frac{37699.2}{128000} = 0.294 \text{ square inch.}$$

The nearest diameter corresponding to an area of 0.294 square inch is $\frac{5}{8}$ inch. Therefore $\frac{5}{8} + \frac{3}{8} = 1$ inch, which is the diameter of the bolts through the straps around the front and rear crank-pins. And $\frac{5}{8} + \frac{1}{2} = 1\frac{1}{8}$ inches, which is the diameter of the bolts through the straps for the second and third crank-pins.

323. The bolts through the side-rod and also through the main-rod straps should be placed as close to the keys as possible, leaving only sufficient room to tighten the nuts. The distance $d$, Fig. 449 or Fig. 451, that is, the distance from end of the wing of the strap to the first bolt, is generally made equal to about one and a half times the diameter of the bolt. The distance from center to center of bolts varies from 2 to 3 inches, depending on the diameters of the bolts; for engines with cylinders 16 inches in diameter and upwards, this distance is generally 3 inches, and for engines having cylinders 10 or 11 inches, it is 2 inches, and in some cases even less than that. Good practice seems to indicate that these bolts should be as close to each other as a sufficient clearance for the wrench will allow.

The side-rod bolts are generally tapered, the taper varying from $\frac{1}{16}$ to $\frac{1}{8}$ of an inch in 12 inches. The diameters of the bolts found in the foregoing calculations are the small diameters.

324. The cross-section of the keys is usually rectangular. We believe the better practice will be to round off the side $n$, as shown in Figs. 449, 450, because it has been found that, when keys of rectangular cross-section are used, the strap is

liable to crack, as indicated at $p$ in Fig. 450, which shows that sharp corners at these points impair the strength of the strap.

The thickness of the key is generally made from $\frac{1}{8}$ to $\frac{1}{4}$ of an inch less than the diameters of the bolts. The width $a$ at the small end of the key (Figs. 449, 451) varies from one to one and a half times the diameter of the bolts; the latter is preferable for main-rods, the former for side-rods. The length $l$ of the key is usually made equal to one and a half times the total width of the strap.

The taper of these keys varies from $\frac{5}{8}$ to $1\frac{1}{4}$ inches in 12 inches; the former is the most common.

Although sometimes the keys are made of wrought-iron, the best practice is to make them of steel.

325. Figs. 451, 452 represent a main-rod whose front end is designed to connect to a crosshead working between two slides, similar to the one shown in Figs. 241, 243.

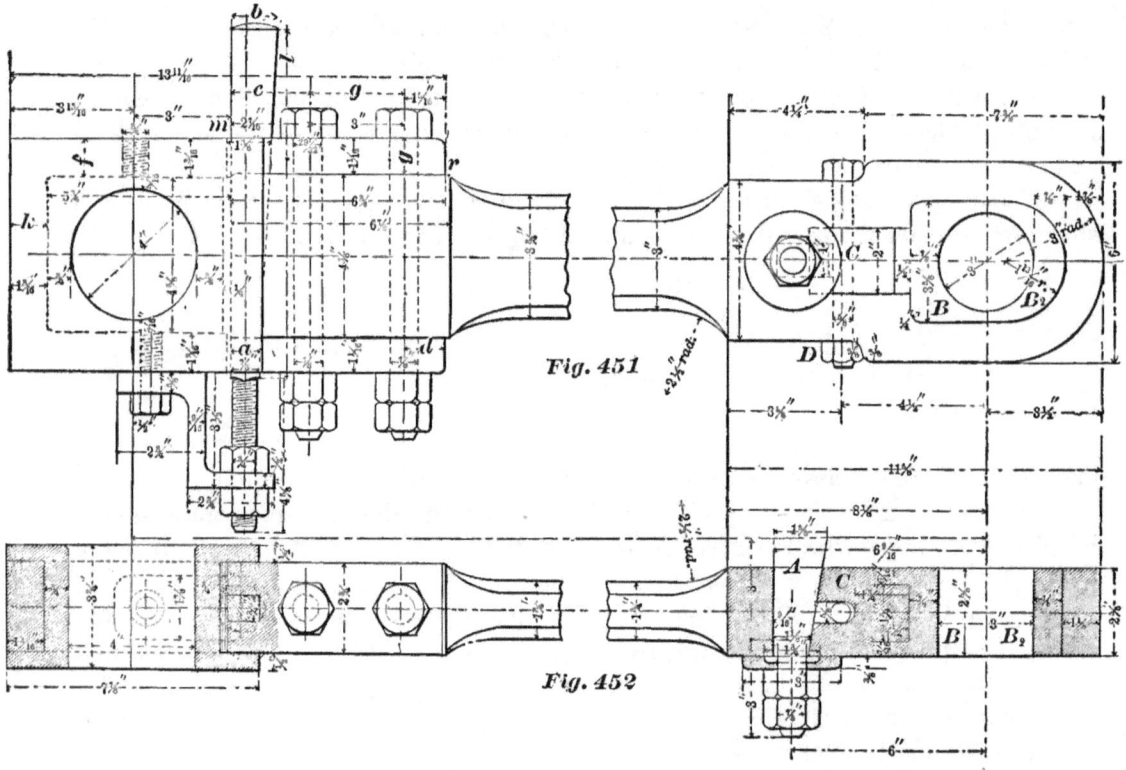

Fig. 451

Fig. 452

The key in the front end is inserted horizontally, because there is not sufficient room between the projecting ends of the crosshead to place the key vertically. The key is necessarily made short, so as to clear other parts of the machinery. It bears against a cast-iron block $C$, which, when the key is drawn in, forces the brasses $B$ $B_2$ against each other. The bolt $D$ simply prevents the cast-iron block from slipping out of position.

## FORMS OF RODS.

326. The favorite locomotive main-rod is the solid one of rectangular form—that is to say, a rod whose transverse section is similar to that shown in Fig. 453; they are made stiff enough so as not to buckle.

Main-rods are subjected alternately to a tensile and compressive force, due to the steam pressure on the piston; the intensity of these forces is increased by the obliquity of the rods, and also by positions of some of the mechanism which at times must work out of alignment when the engine is running over curves or uneven tracks. The compressive force has a tendency to buckle the rods in the direction of arrow 2 (Fig. 457); in order to prevent buckling in this direction, a definite thickness at $C$ and $D$ (Fig. 457) will be required; in all main-rods this thickness is uniform throughout. The main-rods are also subjected to a transverse force, due to the centripetal acceleration, and this force has a tendency to bend or break the rod in the direction of arrow 3 (Fig. 456);

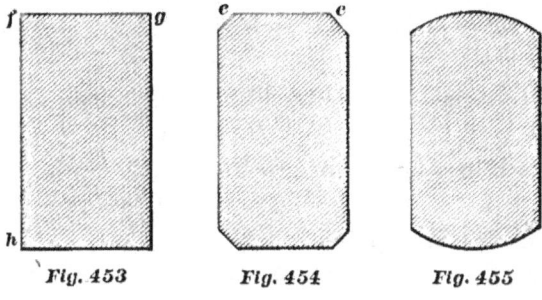

Fig. 453  Fig. 454  Fig. 455

to prevent any change of form in this direction, a definite depth at $A$ and $B$ will be required; this depth increases uniformly from $A$ to $B$.

The thickness and depth of main-rods, made by different builders and master-mechanics, for the same class and size of locomotives, vary somewhat, but the average of good practice seems to point to the following proportions:

In the smallest transverse section of a main-rod, that is, at $A$, the depth $fh$, Fig. 453, should be equal to $1\frac{3}{4}$ times the thickness $fg$; the depth at $B$, Fig. 456, should be 25 per cent. greater than that at $A$; and furthermore, the area of the transverse section at $A$ should be such as to contain 1 square inch for every 5,000 pounds

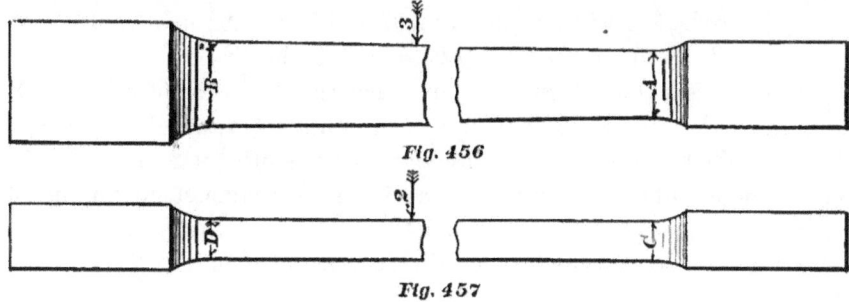

Fig. 456

Fig. 457

of the total maximum steam pressure on the piston. Hence, within the limits of ordinary locomotive practice, we may adopt the following rules, which are based upon the proportions just given.

RULE 66.—To find the area of the smallest transverse section of a main-rod, that is, the area of the cross-section at $A$, Fig. 456, divide the total maximum steam pressure on the piston by 5,000; the quotient will be the number of square inches in the area of the transverse section at $A$.

EXAMPLE 100.—The maximum steam pressure on the piston of a consolidation engine is 120 pounds per square inch, cylinders 20 inches diameter; what should be the number of square inches in transverse section through the smallest part of the main-rod?

The area of a 20-inch piston is 314.16 inches; the maximum steam pressure on the piston will be equal to

$$314.16 \times 120 = 37699.20 \text{ pounds,}$$

and the number of square inches required in the area of the smallest cross-section of the main-rod will be equal to

$$\frac{37699.20}{5000} = 7.53 \text{ square inches.}$$

RULE 67.—To find the thickness and depth of the main-rod at its smallest transverse section, that is, at $A$, Fig. 456, and also the depth of the rod at $B$, multiply the cross-sectional area of the smallest section of the rod, as found by Rule 66, by 4, and divide the product by 7; the square root of the quotient will be the required thickness $C$ or $D$ (Fig. 457) in inches.

To find the depth of the rod at $A$, multiply the thickness of the rod in inches by 1.75; the product will be the depth in inches at $A$. For the depth at $B$, increase the depth of $A$ by 25 per cent.

EXAMPLE 101.—What should be the thickness and depth of a main-rod for a consolidation engine having cylinders 20 inches diameter, steam pressure on piston 120 pounds per square inch?

Here we must first find the area in square inches of the smallest cross-section of the rod, that is, at $A$. In the last example we found this area to be 7.53 inches. Hence, the thickness of the rod will be equal to

$$\sqrt{\frac{7.53 \times 4}{7}} = 2.07 \text{ inches.}$$

The depth of the rod at $A$ will be equal to $2.07 \times 1.75 = 3.62$ inches.

The depth at $B$ will be equal to $3.62 \times 1.25 = 4.52$ inches.

Avoiding fractions less than $\frac{1}{16}$ inch, we find that the thickness of this rod should be $2\frac{1}{16}$ inches; the depth at $A$, $3\frac{5}{8}$ inches; and the depth at $B$, $4\frac{9}{16}$ inches.

EXAMPLE 102.—What should be the thickness and depth of a main-rod for an eight-wheeled passenger engine having cylinders 18 inches diameter, maximum steam pressure in cylinder 140 pounds per square inch?

The total maximum steam pressure on the piston is equal to $254.47 \times 140 = 35625.8$ pounds.

According to Rule 66, the area of the smallest cross-section should be equal to

$$\frac{35625.8}{5000} = 7.12+ \text{ square inches;}$$

and according to Rule 67, the thickness of the main-rod will be equal to

$$\sqrt{\frac{7.12 \times 4}{7}} = 2.02 \text{ inches.}$$

The depth of the rod at $A$ will be equal to

$$2.02 \times 1.75 = 3.53 \text{ inches.}$$

The depth of the rod at $B$ will be equal to $3.53 \times 1.25 = 4.41$ inches. Avoiding fractions less than $\frac{1}{16}$ inch, the thickness of the rod will be 2 inches; depth at $A$, $3\frac{1}{2}$ inches; and depth at $B$, $4\frac{7}{16}$ inches.

It will be noticed in these examples that in the small transverse section of the rod the side $fh$, Fig. 453, is $1\frac{3}{4}$ longer than the side $fg$. Should it be required to have a different ratio between these sides, say that $fh$ shall be $1\frac{5}{8}$ longer than $fg$, then multiply the area in square inches, as found by Rule 66, by 8, and divide the product by 13; the square root of the quotient will be the thickness; and the thickness thus found multiplied by $1\frac{5}{8}$, or 1.625, will give the depth of the rod at $A$.

The foregoing rules are applicable to locomotive main-rods only; and even in locomotive practice, these rules will give satisfactory results only so long as the length of the main-rod is not greater or much greater than 60 times the width of the rod found by these rules. Main-rods whose lengths are greater than 60 times the thickness, or connecting-rods for other engines in which this ratio and the maximum steam pressure on the piston differs greatly from ordinary locomotive practice, should be treated as upright columns or pillars, with rounded or pointed ends supporting a load; and the dimensions of these rods should be found by rules given in books treating on the strength of materials.

Sometimes we find locomotive main-rods with the edges chamfered, whose cross-sections will appear as shown in Fig. 454. This we believe to be bad practice, as it cuts the metal away in places where it is needed the most. Chamfered edges do not add to the beauty of a rod, but unnecessarily increase the expense of making them, and when done no advantage whatever is gained. The best practice is simply to take off the sharp corners to as small degree as possible, so as to prevent a person cutting his hands or otherwise hurting himself in oiling, cleaning, or inspecting a locomotive.

Sections of rods, as shown in Fig. 455, should also be avoided, because such forms only impair the strength of the rod without gaining any advantage.

327. Main-rods are often made of iron, sometimes of steel; when of the former, the best quality of hammered iron must be used. The rules for finding the dimensions of main-rods (given in Art. 326) are suitable for rods made of the best hammered iron. When made of steel they may be made slightly lighter. But since, in many cases, steel rods are adopted simply for the purpose of ensuring greater safety, and not so much for the purpose of reducing the weight, no difference in the dimensions between iron and steel rods is made.

For the sake of convenience in designing, we have given the following tables containing the dimensions for iron main-rods. These have been determined by the rules given in Art. 326. In the dimensions given we have avoided those containing less than one $\frac{1}{16}$ of an inch, and selected such as agreed nearest with the decimals found.

## TABLE 22.

THICKNESS AND DEPTH OF MAIN-RODS AT THE SMALL AND LARGE ENDS. RODS MADE OF BEST HAMMERED IRON. MAXIMUM STEAM PRESSURE PER SQUARE INCH OF PISTON, 120 POUNDS.

| Diameter of Cylinders. | Thickness. | Depth at Small End. | Depth at Large End. |
|---|---|---|---|
| 9″ | $1\frac{5}{16}″$ | $1\frac{5}{8}″$ | 2″ |
| 10″ | 1″ | $1\frac{13}{16}″$ | $2\frac{1}{4}″$ |
| 11″ | $1\frac{1}{8}″$ | 2″ | $2\frac{1}{2}″$ |
| 12″ | $1\frac{1}{4}″$ | $2\frac{3}{16}″$ | $2\frac{3}{4}″$ |
| 13″ | $1\frac{3}{8}″$ | $2\frac{3}{8}″$ | $2\frac{15}{16}″$ |
| 14″ | $1\frac{7}{16}″$ | $2\frac{1}{2}″$ | $3\frac{3}{16}″$ |
| 15″ | $1\frac{9}{16}″$ | $2\frac{3}{4}″$ | $3\frac{3}{8}″$ |
| 16″ | $1\frac{5}{8}″$ | $2\frac{7}{8}″$ | $3\frac{5}{8}″$ |
| 17″ | $1\frac{3}{4}″$ | $3\frac{1}{16}″$ | $3\frac{7}{8}″$ |
| 18″ | $1\frac{7}{8}″$ | $3\frac{1}{4}″$ | $4\frac{1}{16}″$ |
| 19″ | 2″ | $3\frac{7}{16}″$ | $4\frac{1}{4}″$ |
| 20″ | $2\frac{1}{16}″$ | $3\frac{5}{8}″$ | $4\frac{1}{2}″$ |
| 21″ | $2\frac{3}{16}″$ | $3\frac{13}{16}″$ | $4\frac{3}{4}″$ |
| 22″ | $2\frac{5}{16}″$ | 4″ | 5″ |

## TABLE 23.

THICKNESS AND DEPTH OF MAIN-RODS AT THE SMALL AND LARGE ENDS. RODS MADE OF BEST HAMMERED IRON. MAXIMUM STEAM PRESSURE PER SQUARE INCH OF PISTON, 130 POUNDS.

| Diameter of Cylinders. | Thickness. | Depth at Small End. | Depth at Large End. |
|---|---|---|---|
| 9″ | 1″ | $1\frac{11}{16}″$ | $2\frac{1}{8}″$ |
| 10″ | $1\frac{1}{16}″$ | $1\frac{7}{8}″$ | $2\frac{3}{8}″$ |
| 11″ | $1\frac{3}{16}″$ | $2\frac{1}{16}″$ | $2\frac{9}{16}″$ |
| 12″ | $1\frac{5}{16}″$ | $2\frac{1}{4}″$ | $2\frac{13}{16}″$ |
| 13″ | $1\frac{7}{16}″$ | $2\frac{1}{2}″$ | $3\frac{1}{16}″$ |
| 14″ | $1\frac{1}{2}″$ | $2\frac{5}{8}″$ | $3\frac{1}{4}″$ |
| 15″ | $1\frac{5}{8}″$ | $2\frac{13}{16}″$ | $3\frac{1}{2}″$ |
| 16″ | $1\frac{3}{4}″$ | 3″ | $3\frac{3}{4}″$ |
| 17″ | $1\frac{13}{16}″$ | $3\frac{3}{16}″$ | 4″ |
| 18″ | $1\frac{15}{16}″$ | $3\frac{3}{8}″$ | $4\frac{1}{4}″$ |
| 19″ | $2\frac{1}{16}″$ | $3\frac{9}{16}″$ | $4\frac{3}{8}″$ |
| 20″ | $2\frac{1}{4}″$ | $3\frac{3}{4}″$ | $4\frac{11}{16}″$ |
| 21″ | $2\frac{1}{4}″$ | $3\frac{15}{16}″$ | $4\frac{15}{16}″$ |
| 22″ | $2\frac{3}{8}″$ | $4\frac{1}{8}″$ | $5\frac{3}{16}″$ |

## TABLE 24.

THICKNESS AND DEPTH OF MAIN-RODS AT THE SMALL AND LARGE ENDS. RODS MADE OF BEST HAMMERED IRON. MAXIMUM STEAM PRESSURE PER SQUARE INCH OF PISTON, 140 POUNDS.

| Diameter of Cylinders. | Thickness. | Depth at Small End. | Depth at Large End. |
|---|---|---|---|
| 9″ | 1″ | $1\frac{3}{4}″$ | $2\frac{3}{16}″$ |
| 10″ | $1\frac{1}{8}″$ | $1\frac{15}{16}″$ | $2\frac{7}{16}″$ |
| 11″ | $1\frac{1}{4}″$ | $2\frac{1}{8}″$ | $2\frac{11}{16}″$ |
| 12″ | $1\frac{5}{16}″$ | $2\frac{3}{8}″$ | $2\frac{15}{16}″$ |
| 13″ | $1\frac{7}{16}″$ | $2\frac{9}{16}″$ | $3\frac{3}{16}″$ |
| 14″ | $1\frac{9}{16}″$ | $2\frac{3}{4}″$ | $3\frac{7}{16}″$ |
| 15″ | $1\frac{11}{16}″$ | $2\frac{15}{16}″$ | $3\frac{11}{16}″$ |
| 16″ | $1\frac{3}{4}″$ | $3\frac{1}{8}″$ | $3\frac{15}{16}″$ |
| 17″ | $1\frac{15}{16}″$ | $3\frac{5}{16}″$ | $4\frac{1}{8}″$ |
| 18″ | 2″ | $3\frac{1}{2}″$ | $4\frac{3}{8}″$ |
| 19″ | $2\frac{1}{8}″$ | $3\frac{11}{16}″$ | $4\frac{5}{8}″$ |
| 20″ | $2\frac{1}{4}″$ | $3\frac{15}{16}″$ | $4\frac{3}{4}″$ |
| 21″ | $2\frac{3}{8}″$ | $4\frac{1}{8}″$ | $5\frac{1}{4}″$ |
| 22″ | $2\frac{7}{16}″$ | $4\frac{5}{16}″$ | $5\frac{3}{8}″$ |

## TABLE 25.

THICKNESS AND DEPTH OF MAIN-RODS AT THE SMALL AND LARGE ENDS. RODS MADE OF BEST HAMMERED IRON. MAXIMUM STEAM PRESSURE PER SQUARE INCH OF PISTON, 150 POUNDS.

| Diameter of Cylinders. | Thickness. | Depth at Small End. | Depth at Large End. |
|---|---|---|---|
| 9″ | $1\frac{1}{16}″$ | $1\frac{13}{16}″$ | $2\frac{1}{4}″$ |
| 10″ | $1\frac{1}{8}″$ | $2″$ | $2\frac{1}{2}″$ |
| 11″ | $1\frac{1}{4}″$ | $2\frac{1}{4}″$ | $2\frac{3}{4}″$ |
| 12″ | $1\frac{3}{8}″$ | $2\frac{7}{16}″$ | $3″$ |
| 13″ | $1\frac{1}{2}″$ | $2\frac{5}{8}″$ | $3\frac{1}{4}″$ |
| 14″ | $1\frac{5}{8}″$ | $2\frac{13}{16}″$ | $3\frac{1}{2}″$ |
| 15″ | $1\frac{3}{4}″$ | $3″$ | $3\frac{3}{4}″$ |
| 16″ | $1\frac{7}{8}″$ | $3\frac{1}{4}″$ | $4″$ |
| 17″ | $1\frac{15}{16}″$ | $3\frac{7}{16}″$ | $4\frac{1}{4}″$ |
| 18″ | $2\frac{1}{16}″$ | $3\frac{5}{8}″$ | $4\frac{9}{16}″$ |
| 19″ | $2\frac{3}{16}″$ | $3\frac{7}{8}″$ | $4\frac{13}{16}″$ |
| 20″ | $2\frac{5}{16}″$ | $4\frac{1}{16}″$ | $5\frac{1}{16}″$ |
| 21″ | $2\frac{7}{16}″$ | $4\frac{1}{4}″$ | $5\frac{5}{16}″$ |
| 22″ | $2\frac{9}{16}″$ | $4\frac{7}{16}″$ | $5\frac{9}{16}″$ |

## TABLE 26.

THICKNESS AND DEPTH OF MAIN-RODS AT THE SMALL AND LARGE ENDS. RODS MADE OF BEST HAMMERED IRON. MAXIMUM STEAM PRESSURE PER SQUARE INCH OF PISTON, 160 POUNDS.

| Diameter of Cylinders. | Thickness. | Depth at Small End. | Depth at Large End. |
|---|---|---|---|
| 9″ | $1\frac{1}{8}″$ | $1\frac{7}{8}″$ | $2\frac{5}{16}″$ |
| 10″ | $1\frac{3}{16}″$ | $2\frac{1}{8}″$ | $2\frac{5}{8}″$ |
| 11″ | $1\frac{5}{16}″$ | $2\frac{5}{16}″$ | $2\frac{7}{8}″$ |
| 12″ | $1\frac{7}{16}″$ | $2\frac{1}{2}″$ | $3\frac{1}{8}″$ |
| 13″ | $1\frac{9}{16}″$ | $2\frac{11}{16}″$ | $3\frac{3}{8}″$ |
| 14″ | $1\frac{11}{16}″$ | $2\frac{13}{16}″$ | $3\frac{5}{8}″$ |
| 15″ | $1\frac{13}{16}″$ | $3\frac{1}{8}″$ | $3\frac{15}{16}″$ |
| 16″ | $1\frac{15}{16}″$ | $3\frac{5}{16}″$ | $4\frac{3}{16}″$ |
| 17″ | $2\frac{1}{16}″$ | $3\frac{9}{16}″$ | $4\frac{7}{16}″$ |
| 18″ | $2\frac{3}{16}″$ | $3\frac{3}{4}″$ | $4\frac{5}{8}″$ |
| 19″ | $2\frac{5}{16}″$ | $3\frac{15}{16}″$ | $4\frac{15}{16}″$ |
| 20″ | $2\frac{3}{8}″$ | $4\frac{3}{16}″$ | $5\frac{1}{4}″$ |
| 21″ | $2\frac{1}{2}″$ | $4\frac{3}{8}″$ | $5\frac{1}{2}″$ |
| 22″ | $2\frac{5}{8}″$ | $4\frac{5}{8}″$ | $5\frac{3}{4}″$ |

### SIDE-RODS.

328. When we consider all the conditions under which a side-rod must transmit motion from one wheel to another, it will be seen that to design such a rod is not as easy as to design a main-rod. We have seen that a main-rod should be stiff enough to do its work without buckling in any direction; and since we can estimate very closely the pressure to which it will be subjected, its strength to resist these pressures can be readily determined, as shown by the foregoing rules. Side-rods, however, labor under disadvantages to which the main-rods are not subjected. Wear will create play between the axle boxes and wedges, allowing the axles to run out of their proper adjustment, thereby throwing an extra stress on the side-rods; uneven tracks will throw the side-rods out of parallelism, which will again increase the stress on the rods; unequal wear of tires, which practically means a difference in the diameter of the

wheels, and consequently that one or the other wheel must slip a certain amount during each revolution; but this slip, due to the unequal diameters of the wheels, cannot take place through any other agency than the side-rod, and consequently the rod will again be subjected to an extra thrust or pull. But slip is not only due to the unequal wear of tires; it is also caused by the form of the tread of tires, and, as we have seen in previous articles, many tires have a cone tread; consequently, in curving, the wheels having such treads will run on one side of the engine on larger diameters than on the other side, and consequently slip must occur. Another feature which presents itself in connection with curving is that the play between the axle boxes and wedges will cause the axles to run out of parallelism, and all this tends to throw extra stress on the side-rods. Comparatively sudden stopping by the application of brakes, running over slippery places on the rails, or incautious use of sand often plays mischief with the side-rods.

Now, these conditions are the disadvantages under which a side-rod labors, and may at times throw on it extraordinary pressures which cannot be accurately determined, but can only be approximately estimated.

Side-rods should be made as light as possible, so as to reduce the stresses due to the action of the centrifugal force to a minimum, yet they must be strong enough to resist the tensile and compressive forces to which they are alternately subjected. When side-rods are subjected to a compressive force or thrust, they must not buckle in a vertical direction, that is, in the direction of arrow 2, Fig. 458; yet, under certain circumstances, it is desirable that they should, to a limited extent, slightly spring or buckle in a horizontal direction, that is, in the direction of arrow 3. The reason for desiring a slight spring of the side-rods in a horizontal direction is to obtain a certain

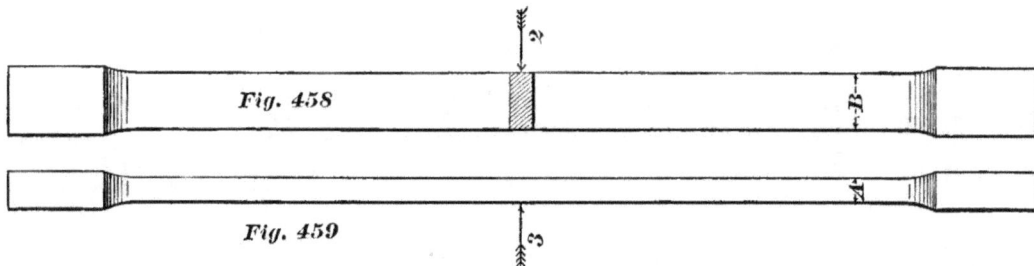

amount of flexibility, so as to avoid excessive jerks on the rod and crank-pin, and thereby lessen the danger of heating the crank-pin brasses, or breaking the crank-pins or side-rods. Here we notice a difference between the essential conditions demanded from a main-rod and a side-rod; the former must do its work without buckling in any direction, the latter should not buckle in a vertical direction, but should have a certain amount of flexibility by springing to a slight extent in a horizontal direction; and these requirements the designer should not lose sight of.

Now, a side-rod which shall meet all the demands made upon it must have a proper distribution of metal, and must also be of such a form as will reduce the cost of manufacture to a minimum. Consequently, various types of side-rods are now in use.

In the early stages of locomotive building, many side-rods with circular transverse sections were used, the diameter of the central section being larger than the diameters of the end sections. This type of rod was finally abandoned, because, although cheap to manufacture, it had the same rigidity vertically and laterally, which, as we have seen, is objectionable.

Probably the most popular type of side-rod at present in use is that shown in Figs. 458, 459. This rod has a uniform, rectangular tranverse section throughout. It has a certain amount of flexibility in the direction of arrow 3, and is, comparatively, not a costly rod to make. This rod is extensively used both for freight and passenger engines. On account of its cheapness, it is nearly always adopted for freight engines;

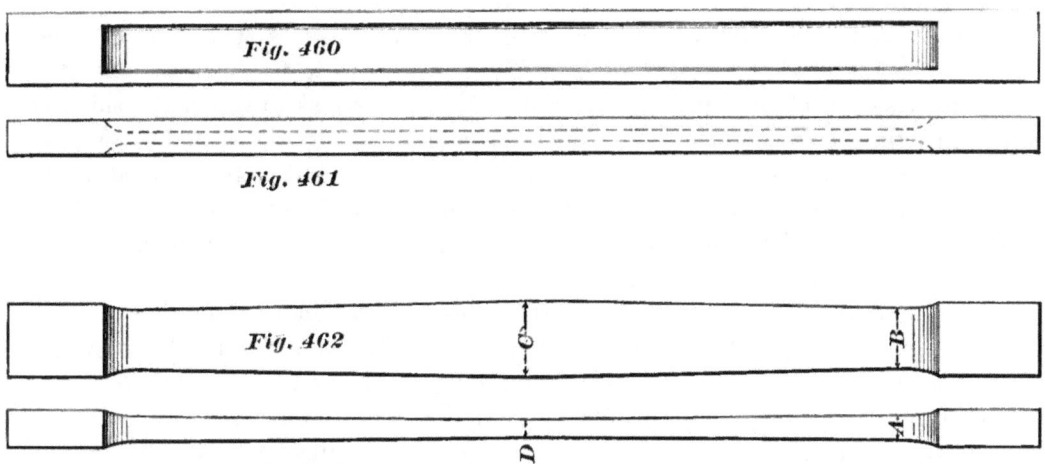

but for fast passenger service its metal is not considered to be correctly distributed, and, consequently, we now frequently meet with passenger engines for which a type of side-rod such as is shown in Figs. 460, 461 has been adopted. The transverse section of this rod is of the I form, as shown in Fig. 464, drawn to a larger scale than Figs. 460, 461. For some rods the section is made uniform throughout; in others, it is deeper at the center than at the ends. The advantage of this form of rod is that, with an amount of metal equal to that used for a rod with a solid rectangular section, its depth can be made greater than the depth of the latter, and consequently it is stronger to resist the action of the centrifugal force. On the other hand, the opinion prevails among a number of master-mechanics that this rod does not possess the required flexibility sideways, and we believe that, on this account, it is not generally adopted. A difference is also made by different designers in the distribution of metal throughout the transverse section; the proportions given in Fig. 464 we find sometimes adopted, whereas, for the same class and size of engines, we occasionally find the proportions of the cross-section to be like those shown in Fig. 419.

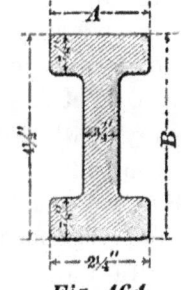

The type of side-rod shown in Figs. 462, 463 has been used on some railroads for a number of years, and is said to be one of the best type of rods in use. As will be seen, it is made deeper at the center than at the ends, but its thickness at the center is less than at the ends. In it are combined the best features of the rods shown in Figs. 458 and 460. On account of its increased depth at the center, it is stronger to resist the action of the centrifugal force than the rod shown in Fig. 458; and on account of its decreased thickness at the center, it has a greater flexibility than the one shown in Fig. 460. But it is an expensive rod to make, and therefore we believe it is not as often adopted as its merits deserve.

## PROPORTIONS OF SIDE-RODS.

329. In Art. 328 it was seen that there are many causes which at any time may increase the stress on a side-rod, and may increase it to such an extent as will cause fracture of or injury to the rod. The total stress to which the side-rods may at any time be subjected can only be determined by experience and close observation of the behavior of the side-rods in every-day service, and facts obtained in this way will enable us to establish rules for guidance in designing other side-rods for similar locomotives. The following rules are empirical, and will hold true only within the limits of ordinary locomotive practice.

In eight-wheeled passenger engines, the side-rods are longer than those used in consolidation engines; and since the length of the rods has an important bearing upon the size of the cross-section, that is to say, for longer rods we require a greater cross-section, it follows that the side-rods for consolidation engines have generally a smaller cross-section than that of the rods for passenger engines, diameter of cylinders and maximum steam pressure being the same in both cases. Again, in consolidation engines the front and rear side-rods have less work to do than the central side-rod, and therefore the cross-section of the latter rod is generally made greater than that of the front and rear rods.

In Mogul and ten-wheeled engines, the length of the rear side-rods is generally equal to the length of the side-rods in passenger engines of the same power; but the front side-rods in the former classes of engines are generally shorter, and therefore the cross-sectional area of the front rods is often made less than that of the rear side-rods. Yet this is not a universal practice, as in these classes of engines we meet with many in which all the side-rods are of equal cross-section. Similar remarks apply to consolidation engines; that is to say, in a number of engines of this class, there is no difference made in the cross-sectional area of the side-rods, whereas in others the cross-sectional areas for the front and rear side-rods are made less than that of the central rods.

Here, then, we see that practice differs, and therefore in establishing our rules we shall follow the average of good practice.

330. In comparing the side- and main-rods made by different builders, we find that the cross-sectional area of the side-rods is generally about ten per cent. less than the cross-section at the smallest part of the main-rod. Consequently, to find the cross-section of side-rods for passenger engines, we have the following rule:

RULE 68.—Divide the total maximum steam pressure on the piston by 5,500; the quotient will be the number of square inches in the cross-sectional area of the side-rod for eight-wheeled passenger engines.

EXAMPLE 103.—In a passenger engine having cylinders 18 inches in diameter, the maximum steam pressure on the piston is 140 pounds per square inch; what should be the cross-sectional area of the side-rod?

The maximum steam pressure on the piston is

$$254.47 \times 140 = 35625.8 \text{ pounds},$$

and $\dfrac{35625.8}{5500} = 6.47$ square inches in the cross-sectional area of the side-rod.

In practice a difference exists between the ratio of the thickness to depth of the side-rods, but observation indicates that two and a half times the thickness for the depth is a good proportion; and this we shall adopt for side-rods in passenger engines. Hence we have the following rule:

RULE 69.—To find the thickness and depth of side-rods for passenger engines: Multiply the cross-sectional area of the side-rod (as found by Rule 68) by 2, and divide the product by 5; the square root of this quotient will be the thickness. Multiply this thickness by $2\frac{1}{2}$; the product will be the depth of the side-rod.

EXAMPLE 104.—Find the thickness and depth for a side-rod for an eight-wheeled passenger engine with cylinder 17 inches diameter; maximum steam pressure on the piston, 150 pounds per square inch.

The maximum steam pressure on the piston is $226.98 \times 150 = 34{,}047$ pounds. According to Rule 68, the cross-sectional area of the side-rod should be

$$\frac{34047}{5500} = 6.19 \text{ square inches}.$$

According to Rule 69, the thickness of the side-rod should be

$$\sqrt{\frac{6.19 \times 2}{5}} = 1.57 \text{ inches} = 1\tfrac{9}{16} \text{ inches nearly}.$$

And the depth should be $1.57 \times 2.5 = 3.92$ inches $= 3\tfrac{15}{16}$ inches nearly. Hence the side-rod should be $1\tfrac{9}{16}$ inches thick, and $3\tfrac{15}{16}$ inches deep.

The foregoing rules will only hold true for side-rods made of the best quality of hammered iron, whose lengths for cylinders 9″, 10″, and 11″ in diameter do not exceed 6 feet 6 inches; for 12″, 13″, 14″ cylinders, 7 feet 6 inches; for 15″, 16″, 17″ cylinders, 8 feet 6 inches; and for cylinders 18 inches diameter and upwards, 9 feet. For shorter rods in this class of engines, the cross-sectional area could be somewhat reduced; but for the sake of uniformity of templates, etc., such close adjustment of the cross-sectional area to the length of the side-rod is not usually observed.

The appended tables have been arranged by the foregoing rules.

331. From what has been said in the beginning of the foregoing article, it will be seen that the dimensions of the side-rods given in the following tables can be used for the rear side-rods in Mogul, and also for the rear side-rods in ten-wheeled engines. And since the front side-rods in these classes of engines are shorter than the rear ones, we believe it to be good practice to reduce the cross-sectional area of the front rods. In nearly all Mogul and ten-wheeled engines, the thickness of the rear side-rods is equal to the thickness of the front ones; consequently, when we wish to reduce the cross-sectional

area of the front rods, we have only to reduce their depth, according to the following rule.

RULE 70.—To find the depth for the front side-rod: Multiply the depth of the rear side-rod (taken from the following tables) by .08; and subtract the product from the depth of the rear side-rod; the remainder will be the depth of the front rod.

EXAMPLE 105.—What should be the dimensions of the cross-section for a front side-rod in a Mogul engine, having cylinders 18 inches diameter, maximum steam pressure on the piston 140 pounds per square inch?

Looking in Table 29, we find that for a cylinder 18 inches diameter, the rear side-rod should be $1\frac{5}{8}$ inches thick, and 4 inches deep. Since the thickness of the rods is not changed, we know that the thickness of the front side-rod should be $1\frac{5}{8}$ inches. According to Rule 70, the depth of the front rod should be equal to 4 inches $- (4 \times .08) = 3.68$, say $3\frac{5}{8}$ inches.

## TABLE 27.

THICKNESS AND DEPTH OF SIDE-RODS OF UNIFORM RECTANGULAR CROSS-SECTION, MADE OF THE BEST HAMMERED IRON, FOR EIGHT-WHEELED PASSENGER ENGINES. MAXIMUM STEAM PRESSURE ON THE PISTON, 120 POUNDS PER SQUARE INCH.

| Diameter of Cylinders. | Thickness. | Depth. |
|---|---|---|
| 9″ | $\frac{3}{4}″$ | $1\frac{7}{8}″$ |
| 10″ | $\frac{13}{16}″$ | $2\frac{1}{16}″$ |
| 11″ | $\frac{15}{16}″$ | $2\frac{1}{4}″$ |
| 12″ | $1″$ | $2\frac{7}{16}″$ |
| 13″ | $1\frac{1}{16}″$ | $2\frac{11}{16}″$ |
| 14″ | $1\frac{3}{16}″$ | $2\frac{7}{8}″$ |
| 15″ | $1\frac{1}{4}″$ | $3\frac{1}{8}″$ |
| 16″ | $1\frac{5}{16}″$ | $3\frac{3}{8}″$ |
| 17″ | $1\frac{7}{16}″$ | $3\frac{1}{2}″$ |
| 18″ | $1\frac{1}{2}″$ | $3\frac{11}{16}″$ |
| 19″ | $1\frac{9}{16}″$ | $3\frac{15}{16}″$ |
| 20″ | $1\frac{5}{8}″$ | $4\frac{1}{8}″$ |
| 21″ | $1\frac{3}{4}″$ | $4\frac{5}{16}″$ |
| 22″ | $1\frac{13}{16}″$ | $4\frac{1}{2}″$ |

## TABLE 28.

THICKNESS AND DEPTH OF SIDE-RODS OF UNIFORM RECTANGULAR CROSS-SECTION, MADE OF THE BEST HAMMERED IRON, FOR EIGHT-WHEELED PASSENGER ENGINES. MAXIMUM STEAM PRESSURE ON THE PISTON, 130 POUNDS PER SQUARE INCH.

| Diameter of Cylinders. | Thickness. | Depth. |
|---|---|---|
| 9″ | $\frac{13}{16}″$ | $1\frac{15}{16}″$ |
| 10″ | $\frac{7}{8}″$ | $2\frac{1}{8}″$ |
| 11″ | $\frac{15}{16}″$ | $2\frac{3}{8}″$ |
| 12″ | $1″$ | $2\frac{9}{16}″$ |
| 13″ | $1\frac{1}{8}″$ | $2\frac{3}{4}″$ |
| 14″ | $1\frac{3}{16}″$ | $3″$ |
| 15″ | $1\frac{1}{4}″$ | $3\frac{3}{16}″$ |
| 16″ | $1\frac{3}{8}″$ | $3\frac{7}{16}″$ |
| 17″ | $1\frac{7}{16}″$ | $3\frac{5}{8}″$ |
| 18″ | $1\frac{9}{16}″$ | $3\frac{7}{8}″$ |
| 19″ | $1\frac{5}{8}″$ | $4\frac{1}{16}″$ |
| 20″ | $1\frac{3}{4}″$ | $4\frac{5}{16}″$ |
| 21″ | $1\frac{13}{16}″$ | $4\frac{1}{2}″$ |
| 22″ | $1\frac{7}{8}″$ | $4\frac{3}{4}″$ |

## TABLE 29.

THICKNESS AND DEPTH OF SIDE-RODS OF UNIFORM RECTANGULAR CROSS-SECTION, MADE OF THE BEST HAMMERED IRON, FOR EIGHT-WHEELED PASSENGER ENGINES. MAXIMUM STEAM PRESSURE ON THE PISTON, 140 POUNDS PER SQUARE INCH.

| Diameter of Cylinders. | Thickness. | Depth. |
|---|---|---|
| 9″ | $\frac{13}{16}$″ | 2″ |
| 10″ | $\frac{7}{8}$″ | $2\frac{3}{16}$″ |
| 11″ | $\frac{15}{16}$″ | $2\frac{7}{16}$″ |
| 12″ | $1\frac{1}{16}$″ | $2\frac{5}{8}$″ |
| 13″ | $1\frac{1}{8}$″ | $2\frac{7}{8}$″ |
| 14″ | $1\frac{1}{4}$″ | $3\frac{1}{16}$″ |
| 15″ | $1\frac{5}{16}$″ | $3\frac{5}{16}$″ |
| 16″ | $1\frac{7}{16}$″ | $3\frac{9}{16}$″ |
| 17″ | $1\frac{1}{2}$″ | $3\frac{3}{4}$″ |
| 18″ | $1\frac{5}{8}$″ | 4″ |
| 19″ | $1\frac{11}{16}$″ | $4\frac{1}{4}$″ |
| 20″ | $1\frac{3}{4}$″ | $4\frac{1}{2}$″ |
| 21″ | $1\frac{7}{8}$″ | $4\frac{11}{16}$″ |
| 22″ | 2″ | $4\frac{15}{16}$″ |

## TABLE 30.

THICKNESS AND DEPTH OF SIDE-RODS OF UNIFORM RECTANGULAR CROSS-SECTION, MADE OF THE BEST HAMMERED IRON, FOR EIGHT-WHEELED PASSENGER ENGINES. MAXIMUM STEAM PRESSURE ON THE PISTON, 150 POUNDS PER SQUARE INCH.

| Diameter of Cylinders. | Thickness. | Depth. |
|---|---|---|
| 9″ | $\frac{13}{16}$″ | $2\frac{1}{16}$″ |
| 10″ | $\frac{15}{16}$″ | $2\frac{5}{16}$″ |
| 11″ | 1″ | $2\frac{1}{2}$″ |
| 12″ | $1\frac{1}{8}$″ | $2\frac{3}{4}$″ |
| 13″ | $1\frac{1}{4}$″ | 3″ |
| 14″ | $1\frac{5}{16}$″ | $3\frac{1}{4}$″ |
| 15″ | $1\frac{3}{8}$″ | $3\frac{7}{16}$″ |
| 16″ | $1\frac{1}{2}$″ | $3\frac{11}{16}$″ |
| 17″ | $1\frac{9}{16}$″ | $3\frac{15}{16}$″ |
| 18″ | $1\frac{5}{8}$″ | $4\frac{1}{8}$″ |
| 19″ | $1\frac{3}{4}$″ | $4\frac{3}{8}$″ |
| 20″ | $1\frac{13}{16}$″ | $4\frac{5}{8}$″ |
| 21″ | $1\frac{15}{16}$″ | $4\frac{7}{8}$″ |
| 22″ | 2″ | $5\frac{1}{16}$″ |

## TABLE 31.

THICKNESS AND DEPTH OF SIDE-RODS OF UNIFORM RECTANGULAR CROSS-SECTION, MADE OF THE BEST HAMMERED IRON, FOR EIGHT-WHEELED PASSENGER ENGINES. MAXIMUM STEAM PRESSURE ON THE PISTON, 160 POUNDS PER SQUARE INCH.

| Diameter of Cylinders. | Thickness. | Depth. |
|---|---|---|
| 9″ | $\frac{7}{8}$″ | $2\frac{1}{8}$″ |
| 10″ | $\frac{15}{16}$″ | $2\frac{3}{8}$″ |
| 11″ | $1\frac{1}{16}$″ | $2\frac{5}{8}$″ |
| 12″ | $1\frac{1}{4}$″ | $2\frac{7}{8}$″ |
| 13″ | $1\frac{1}{4}$″ | $3\frac{1}{16}$″ |
| 14″ | $1\frac{5}{16}$″ | $3\frac{5}{16}$″ |
| 15″ | $1\frac{7}{16}$″ | $3\frac{9}{16}$″ |
| 16″ | $1\frac{1}{2}$″ | $3\frac{13}{16}$″ |
| 17″ | $1\frac{9}{16}$″ | $4\frac{1}{16}$″ |
| 18″ | $1\frac{1}{2}$″ | $4\frac{5}{16}$″ |
| 19″ | $1\frac{13}{16}$″ | $4\frac{1}{2}$″ |
| 20″ | $1\frac{15}{16}$″ | $4\frac{3}{4}$″ |
| 21″ | 2″ | 5″ |
| 22″ | $2\frac{1}{16}$″ | $5\frac{1}{4}$″ |

332. In finding the dimensions for the side-rods for consolidation engines, the best mode of procedure will be to find first the dimensions for the central one. We have already seen that these rods are shorter than those in passenger engines, and therefore the cross-sectional area of the central side-rods for consolidation engines is generally less than that of the side-rods for passenger engines. Observation indicates that the average of good practice is to give one square inch in the cross-sectional area for every 6,000 pounds of the maximum steam pressure on the piston; and that the depth of the central side-rod is about $2\frac{1}{2}$ times its thickness. Hence we have the following rules:

RULE 71.—To find the cross-sectional area of the central side-rods for consolidation engines: Divide the total maximum steam pressure on the piston by 6,000; the quotient will be the number of square inches in the cross-sectional area.

RULE 72.—To find the thickness and depth of the central side-rods for consolidation engines: Multiply the cross-sectional area (found by Rule 71) by 2, and divide the product by 5; the square root of this product will be the thickness. Multiply this thickness by $2\frac{1}{2}$; the product will be the depth.

EXAMPLE 106.—What should be the thickness and depth of a central side-rod for a consolidation engine having cylinders 20 inches diameter; maximum steam pressure on the piston, 140 pounds per square inch?

The maximum steam pressure on the piston is $314.16 \times 140 = 43982.4$ pounds.

According to Rule 71, the cross-sectional area should be

$$\frac{43982.4}{6000} = 7.33 \text{ square inches.}$$

And according to Rule 72, the thickness should be

$$\sqrt{\frac{7.33 \times 2}{5}} = 1.71 \text{ inches.}$$

The depth should be

$$1.71 \times 2.5 = 4.275 \text{ inches.}$$

Avoiding thirty-seconds of an inch, we find that the thickness should be $1\frac{3}{4}$ inches, and the depth, $4\frac{1}{4}$ inches.

The front and rear side-rods in consolidation engines have less work to do than the central ones, hence the cross-sectional area of the former can be less than that of the latter. In nearly all consolidation engines the thickness of all the side-rods remains the same; we have therefore only to find the depth of the front and rear rods, which can at once be obtained by deducting a certain amount from the depth of the central one; the remainder will be the required depth for the front and rear side-rods.

RULE 73.—To find the depth of the front and rear side-rods for consolidation engines: Multiply the depth of the central side-rod by .08, and subtract the product from the depth of the central one; the remainder will be the depth of the front and rear side-rods.

EXAMPLE 107.—What should be the thickness and depth of all the side-rods for a consolidation engine, having cylinders 22 inches diameter; maximum steam pressure on the piston, 140 pounds? We first find the dimensions of the central rod.

The total maximum steam pressure on the piston is

$$380.13 \times 140 = 53218.2 \text{ pounds.}$$

According to Rule 71, the cross-sectional area of this rod should be

$$\frac{53218.2}{6000} = 8.86 \text{ square inches.}$$

According to Rule 72, the thickness of all the side-rods should be

$$\sqrt{\frac{8.86 \times 2}{5}} = 1.88 \text{ inches.}$$

The depth of the central side-rod should be $1.88 \times 2.5 = 4.70$ inches. And the depth of the front and rear side-rods should be $4.70 - (4.70 \times .08) = 4.33$ inches.

Avoiding thirty-seconds of an inch, we find that the thickness of all the side-rods should be $1\frac{7}{8}$ inches; the depth of the central one should be $4\frac{11}{16}$ inches; and that of the front and rear rods, $4\frac{3}{8}$ inches.

The appended tables have been computed by the foregoing rules.

## TABLE 32.

THICKNESS AND DEPTH OF SIDE-RODS OF UNIFORM RECTANGULAR CROSS-SECTION, MADE OF THE BEST HAMMERED IRON, FOR CONSOLIDATION ENGINES. MAXIMUM STEAM PRESSURE ON THE PISTON, 120 POUNDS PER SQUARE INCH.

| Diameter of Cylinders. | Thickness of all the Side-rods. | Depth of Central Side-rod. | Depth of Front and Rear Side-rods. |
|---|---|---|---|
| 14″ | $1\frac{1}{16}''$ | $2\frac{5}{8}''$ | $2\frac{1}{2}''$ |
| 15″ | $1\frac{3}{16}''$ | $3''$ | $2\frac{3}{4}''$ |
| 16″ | $1\frac{1}{4}''$ | $3\frac{1}{8}''$ | $2\frac{7}{8}''$ |
| 17″ | $1\frac{5}{16}''$ | $3\frac{3}{8}''$ | $3\frac{1}{16}''$ |
| 18″ | $1\frac{7}{16}''$ | $3\frac{9}{16}''$ | $3\frac{1}{4}''$ |
| 19″ | $1\frac{1}{2}''$ | $3\frac{3}{4}''$ | $3\frac{7}{16}''$ |
| 20″ | $1\frac{9}{16}''$ | $3\frac{15}{16}''$ | $3\frac{5}{8}''$ |
| 21″ | $1\frac{11}{16}''$ | $4\frac{1}{4}''$ | $3\frac{13}{16}''$ |
| 22″ | $1\frac{3}{4}''$ | $4\frac{3}{8}''$ | $4''$ |

## TABLE 33.

THICKNESS AND DEPTH OF SIDE-RODS OF UNIFORM RECTANGULAR CROSS-SECTION, MADE OF THE BEST HAMMERED IRON, FOR CONSOLIDATION ENGINES. MAXIMUM STEAM PRESSURE ON THE PISTON, 130 POUNDS PER SQUARE INCH.

| Diameter of Cylinders. | Thickness of all the Side-rods. | Depth of Central Side-rod. | Depth of Front and Rear Side-rods. |
|---|---|---|---|
| 14″ | $1\frac{1}{8}''$ | $2\frac{7}{8}''$ | $2\frac{5}{8}''$ |
| 15″ | $1\frac{1}{4}''$ | $3\frac{1}{16}''$ | $2\frac{13}{16}''$ |
| 16″ | $1\frac{3}{8}''$ | $3\frac{3}{8}''$ | $3\frac{1}{16}''$ |
| 17″ | $1\frac{7}{16}''$ | $3\frac{1}{2}''$ | $3\frac{1}{4}''$ |
| 18″ | $1\frac{1}{2}''$ | $3\frac{5}{8}''$ | $3\frac{3}{8}''$ |
| 19″ | $1\frac{9}{16}''$ | $3\frac{7}{8}''$ | $3\frac{9}{16}''$ |
| 20″ | $1\frac{5}{8}''$ | $4\frac{1}{16}''$ | $3\frac{3}{4}''$ |
| 21″ | $1\frac{3}{4}''$ | $4\frac{3}{8}''$ | $4''$ |
| 22″ | $1\frac{13}{16}''$ | $4\frac{1}{2}''$ | $4\frac{1}{8}''$ |

## TABLE 34.

THICKNESS AND DEPTH OF SIDE-RODS OF UNIFORM RECTANGULAR CROSS-SECTION, MADE OF THE BEST HAMMERED IRON, FOR CONSOLIDATION ENGINES. MAXIMUM STEAM PRESSURE ON THE PISTON, 140 POUNDS PER SQUARE INCH.

| Diameter of Cylinders. | Thickness of all the Side-rods. | Depth of Central Side-rod. | Depth of Front and Rear Side-rods. |
|---|---|---|---|
| 14″ | $1\frac{3}{16}″$ | $3″$ | $2\frac{7}{8}″$ |
| 15″ | $1\frac{1}{4}″$ | $3\frac{3}{16}″$ | $2\frac{15}{16}″$ |
| 16″ | $1\frac{3}{8}″$ | $3\frac{7}{16}″$ | $3\frac{1}{8}″$ |
| 17″ | $1\frac{7}{16}″$ | $3\frac{5}{8}″$ | $3\frac{3}{8}″$ |
| 18″ | $1\frac{1}{2}″$ | $3\frac{7}{8}″$ | $3\frac{1}{2}″$ |
| 19″ | $1\frac{5}{8}″$ | $4\frac{1}{16}″$ | $3\frac{3}{4}″$ |
| 20″ | $1\frac{3}{4}″$ | $4\frac{1}{4}″$ | $3\frac{15}{16}″$ |
| 21″ | $1\frac{13}{16}″$ | $4\frac{1}{2}″$ | $4\frac{1}{8}″$ |
| 22″ | $1\frac{7}{8}″$ | $4\frac{11}{16}″$ | $4\frac{3}{8}″$ |

## TABLE 35.

THICKNESS AND DEPTH OF SIDE-RODS OF UNIFORM RECTANGULAR CROSS-SECTION, MADE OF THE BEST HAMMERED IRON, FOR CONSOLIDATION ENGINES. MAXIMUM STEAM PRESSURE ON THE PISTON, 150 POUNDS PER SQUARE INCH.

| Diameter of Cylinders. | Thickness of all the Side-rods. | Depth of Central Side-rod. | Depth of Front and Rear Side-rods. |
|---|---|---|---|
| 14″ | $1\frac{1}{4}″$ | $3\frac{1}{16}″$ | $2\frac{13}{16}″$ |
| 15″ | $1\frac{5}{16}″$ | $3\frac{5}{16}″$ | $3\frac{1}{16}″$ |
| 16″ | $1\frac{7}{16}″$ | $3\frac{1}{2}″$ | $3\frac{1}{4}″$ |
| 17″ | $1\frac{1}{2}″$ | $3\frac{3}{4}″$ | $3\frac{7}{16}″$ |
| 18″ | $1\frac{9}{16}″$ | $4″$ | $3\frac{5}{8}″$ |
| 19″ | $1\frac{11}{16}″$ | $4\frac{3}{16}″$ | $3\frac{7}{8}″$ |
| 20″ | $1\frac{3}{4}″$ | $4\frac{7}{16}″$ | $4\frac{1}{16}″$ |
| 21″ | $1\frac{7}{8}″$ | $4\frac{5}{8}″$ | $4\frac{1}{4}″$ |
| 22″ | $1\frac{15}{16}″$ | $4\frac{7}{8}″$ | $4\frac{7}{16}″$ |

## TABLE 36.

THICKNESS AND DEPTH OF SIDE-RODS OF UNIFORM RECTANGULAR CROSS-SECTION, MADE OF THE BEST HAMMERED IRON, FOR CONSOLIDATION ENGINES. MAXIMUM STEAM PRESSURE ON THE PISTON, 160 POUNDS PER SQUARE INCH.

| Diameter of Cylinders. | Thickness of all the Side-rods. | Depth of Central Side-rod. | Depth of Front and Rear Side-rods. |
|---|---|---|---|
| 14″ | $1\frac{1}{4}″$ | $3\frac{3}{16}″$ | $2\frac{15}{16}″$ |
| 15″ | $1\frac{3}{8}″$ | $3\frac{7}{16}″$ | $3\frac{1}{8}″$ |
| 16″ | $1\frac{7}{16}″$ | $3\frac{5}{8}″$ | $3\frac{3}{8}″$ |
| 17″ | $1\frac{9}{16}″$ | $3\frac{7}{8}″$ | $3\frac{9}{16}″$ |
| 18″ | $1\frac{5}{8}″$ | $4\frac{1}{8}″$ | $3\frac{3}{4}″$ |
| 19″ | $1\frac{3}{4}″$ | $4\frac{5}{16}″$ | $4″$ |
| 20″ | $1\frac{13}{16}″$ | $4\frac{9}{16}″$ | $4\frac{3}{16}″$ |
| 21″ | $1\frac{15}{16}″$ | $4\frac{13}{16}″$ | $4\frac{7}{16}″$ |
| 22″ | $2″$ | $5″$ | $4\frac{5}{8}″$ |

## ROD BRASSES.

**333.** All main- and side-rods for which straps are used are provided with brass boxes, generally called "brasses." These are made in pairs, one brass being an exact duplicate of the other.

All main-rod brasses for the crank-pin should be babbitted. We have known a few instances in which no Babbitt metal was used, but such, as far as we have seen, proved to be a failure. Even when these boxes were made of phosphor bronze, Babbitt metal was required to keep them cool.

Figs. 465, 466 represent the brasses in a main-rod for the crank-pin, and show the

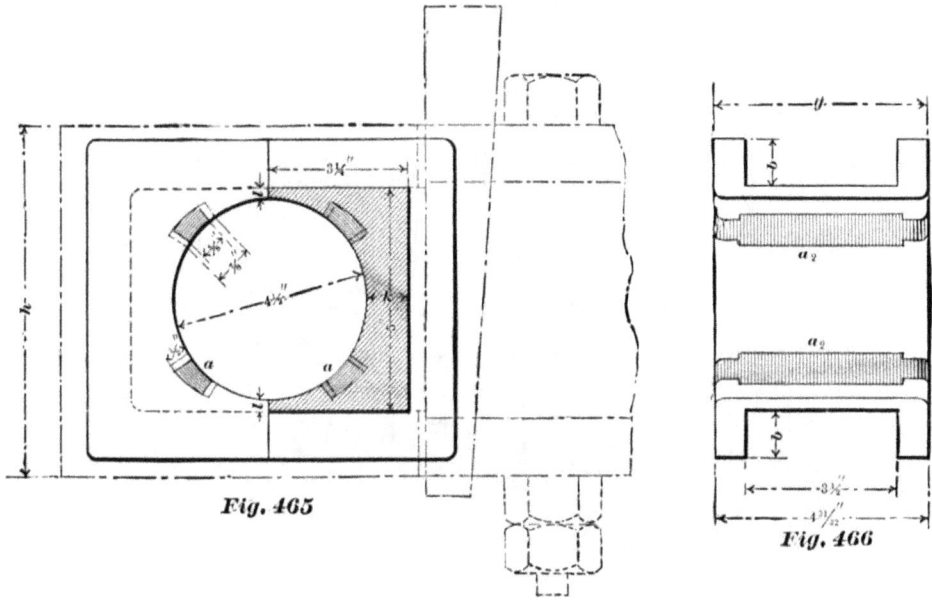

*Fig. 465*

*Fig. 466*

amount and the location of the Babbitt metal $a\ a\ a_2\ a_2$ in these brasses. Sometimes these strips of Babbitt metal are made of uniform width throughout, but we believe the best practice is to make the ends narrower than the central parts, as shown in Fig. 466, which will prevent the babbitt from slipping out of position.

In many cases these strips are placed at equal distances apart, as shown in Fig. 465, but we believe the best practice is to increase the distances between the strips and the joint of the brasses, so as to bring the center of the strips on lines drawn from the center of the hole to the corners of the brasses, or nearly so. With this arrangement the strips will be in those portions of the brasses which contain the greatest amount of metal, and will not be so detrimental to the strength of the brasses as in the positions shown.

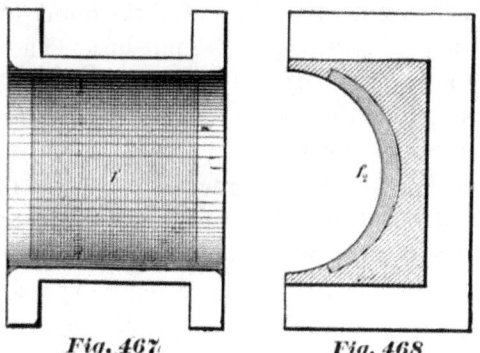

*Fig. 467*  *Fig. 468*

Side-rod brasses should also be babbitted, but there are many in use without it. When Babbitt metal is used, it is inserted either as shown in Figs. 465, 466, or as shown in Figs. 467, 468. The former method we believe to be the best one, because, with the Babbitt metal extending clear across the brasses, the crank-pin will wear more evenly than with the Babbitt metal inserted as shown in Figs. 467, 468. This latter method should never be adopted for the crank-pin brasses in main-rods.

334. In many locomotives the side-rod brasses are made similar in form to that shown in Figs. 467, 468, and in a few instances they are made similar to that shown in

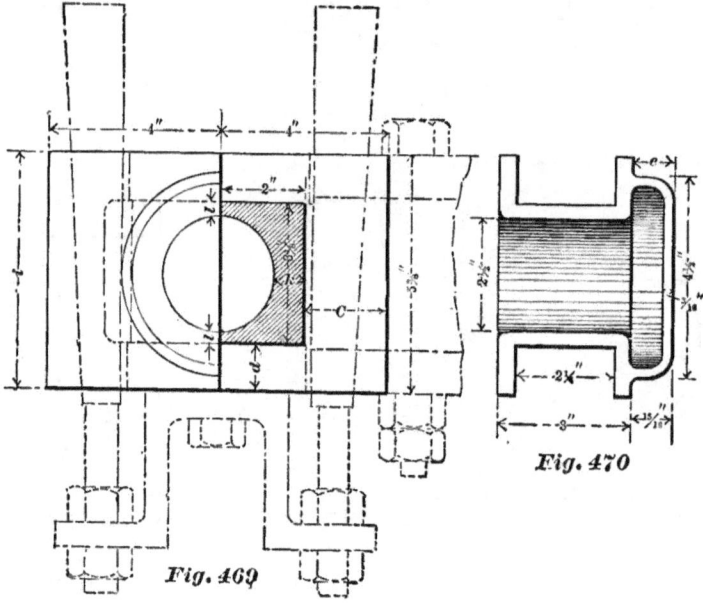

Figs. 469, 470. The difference between these two forms is, that one set is provided with caps $c$, as shown in Fig. 470, which are cast to the brasses; the other set is made up of plain brasses—that is to say, they have no caps.

These caps cover the end of the crank-pin; their purpose is to keep the crank-pin, as much as possible, free from dust. The caps answer the purpose for which they have been designed; but they are detrimental to the examination of the condition of the pin which they cover; and consequently they are not as frequently adopted as the ordinary plain brasses.

In Fig. 465 it will be noticed that the flanges of the brasses do not extend to the edges of the strap; there are many main-rods as well as side-rods which have brasses of this design. But there is an objection against the flanges stopping short of the edges of the strap. The brasses are exposed to considerable dust, and as soon as they become a little loose, the dust will work in between the flanges and strap, and wear ridges in the latter, so that, when it becomes necessary to replace the brasses, the straps must be re-planed before the new brasses can be used. Re-planing straps should be avoided as much as possible, as it reduces their strength; consequently we must prevent, as much as possible, unequal wear and the formation of ridges in the sides of the straps. This desired result is obtained, to some extent, by allowing the flanges of the brasses to cover the whole width $i$ (Fig. 469) of the strap, and also cover the solid end of the same. Since one brass is a duplicate of the other one, the depth of the flange at $C$ appears to be and is excessive; yet, on account of the practical advantages gained by making the flanges so deep, there are, probably, at present more brasses with deep flanges used than brasses with flanges stopping short of edges of the strap.

335. The thickness $l$ (Fig. 469) of the metal at the joint of the brasses, in main- and side-rods, is generally about $\frac{1}{4}$ of an inch.

The thickness $k$ of metal between the pin and the butt end of the rods, and also the thickness of the flanges, are given in the following table:

THICKNESS $k$ (FIG. 469) OF METAL IN MAIN- AND SIDE-ROD BRASSES.

| Diameter of Cylinders. | Thickness of Metal at $k$, Fig. 469. | Thickness of Flanges. |
|---|---|---|
| 9″ | $\frac{5}{8}$″ | $\frac{5}{8}$″ |
| 10″ | $\frac{5}{8}$″ | $\frac{5}{8}$″ |
| 11″ | $\frac{5}{8}$″ | $\frac{7}{16}$″ |
| 12″ | $\frac{3}{4}$″ | $\frac{7}{16}$″ |
| 13″ | $\frac{3}{4}$″ | $\frac{1}{2}$″ |
| 14″ | $\frac{7}{8}$″ | $\frac{1}{2}$″ |
| 15″ | $\frac{7}{8}$″ | $\frac{9}{16}$″ |
| 16″ | $\frac{7}{8}$″ | $\frac{9}{16}$″ |
| 17″ | 1″ | $\frac{5}{8}$″ |
| 18″ | 1″ | $\frac{5}{8}$″ |
| 19″ | 1″ | $\frac{11}{16}$″ |
| 20″ | 1″ | $\frac{11}{16}$″ |
| 21″ | $1\frac{1}{8}$″ | $\frac{3}{4}$″ |
| 22″ | $1\frac{1}{8}$″ | $\frac{3}{4}$″ |

The length of side-rods should be ascertained by actual measurement when the engine is hot. The brasses should have a somewhat loose fit on the crank-pins, so that, when the engine is in working order under steam, the side-rods can be moved on the crank-pin to just a perceptible extent.

The following proportions of the different metals for main- and side-rod brasses we believe will give good satisfaction:

Six pounds of copper, one pound of tin; to one hundred pounds of this mixture add one-half pound of zinc and one-half pound of lead.

## CRANK-PINS.

336. Crank-pins are made either of steel or of the best quality of hammered iron. In order to reduce the wear on iron crank-pins, they are frequently case-hardened. During the process of case-hardening, the crank-pin will, to some extent, alter its form, and therefore, after case-hardening, it must be trued up. In so doing, the case-hardened surface may be reduced to an uneven thickness, which in time may produce an uneven wear, and interfere with the cool and smooth running of the engine. On the other hand, steel crank-pins do not need to be case-hardened, they wear well without it, and therefore the chances of obtaining a wearing surface of different degrees of hardness are lessened, and the causes of heating and uneven wear are to some extent removed. Yet a wrought-iron pin has an advantage over a steel one; the latter, when

subjected to excessive pressure—which may happen even in the best designed engines—may break or snap off suddenly, and thereby cause considerable damage; on the other hand, a wrought-iron pin will bend to a greater extent before it breaks than a steel one, and consequently may give, in many instances, a timely warning of an excessive pressure, so that repairs or changes can be made before much damage has been done. But steel pins can resist a greater pressure than iron ones, and, since they do not need to be case-hardened, they are often preferred. Hence on some roads we find steel pins used exclusively, and on other roads iron pins are adopted. We prefer steel pins.

337. From the foregoing remarks we infer that in designing a crank-pin we must keep in view its strength, and also its liability of heating. To prevent heating, we must have a sufficient bearing surface, and, when a sufficient bearing surface has been provided, then the crank-pins, having such proportions as are adopted in modern locomotive practice, will also be strong enough for the work they have to do. Hence, in determining the dimensions of a crank-pin we shall be guided mostly by the pressure which the crank-pins have to resist. The pressure on the crank-pin is estimated by the pressure on its projected area; that is to say, by the pressure on a rectangular surface, whose length and breadth are equal to the length and diameter of the crank-pin journal.

In comparing the pressure per square inch of projected area of the crank-pins as made by different makers, we find a great difference; indeed, in some instances we find the pressure per square inch on the projected area to be about 1,000 pounds; in other cases the pressure is nearly 2,000 pounds per square inch. The low pressures on crank-pins we find to occur mostly in small engines, and the higher pressures mostly in large engines; which seems to indicate that the crank-pins in a number of small engines are somewhat large, and in a number of large engines the crank-pins are too small. The truth of these conclusions, we believe, is confirmed by experience and the results in practice.

In the rules which are to follow, we shall adopt 1,600 pounds per square inch of projected area of the crank-pin, and determine the size of all crank-pins according to this pressure.

### CRANK-PINS FOR EIGHT-WHEELED PASSENGER ENGINES.

338. In designing a main crank-pin, care must be taken not to make its journals too long, because an increase of length will weaken the pin; the diameters of the journals should not be larger than necessary, because enlarging the diameters will occasion a loss of work due to friction. Consequently, there should be a ratio between the diameter and the length of a locomotive crank-pin journal; and this ratio can best be established by the proportions of crank-pins now in actual and successful service.

In all locomotives which have more than one pair of drivers, the main crank-pins have two journals, as shown in Fig. 471. One of these journals is the main-rod journal; the other is the side-rod journal.

In wide-gauge (4 feet 8½ inches) eight-wheeled passenger engines, the main-rod is nearly always placed next to the wheels; in narrow-gauge eight-wheeled passenger engines we are frequently obliged to place the side-rod next to the wheel. If Fig. 471 represents a crank-pin designed for an eight-wheeled passenger engine (4 feet 8½ inches gauge), then the journal $B$ will represent the main-rod journal; and the journal $C$ will represent the side-rod journal. The portion $A$ of the pin which is pressed into the wheel is called the wheel fit.

Let Fig. 471 represent a main crank-pin for an eight-wheeled passenger engine: it is required to find the diameter $D$ and the length $L$ of the main-rod journal $B$; it is also required to find the diameter $d$ and the length $l$ of the side-rod journal $C$.

Let us commence by finding the dimensions of the main-rod journal $B$. Our first step will be to establish a ratio between its diameter $D$ and its length $L$. It is not often that we find in eight-wheeled passenger engines a crank-pin in which the length of the main journal exceeds its diameter; but there are a number of eight-wheeled passenger engines in which the length and diameter of the main-rod journal are equal to each other; and lastly, we believe it is safe to say that, in the majority of engines,

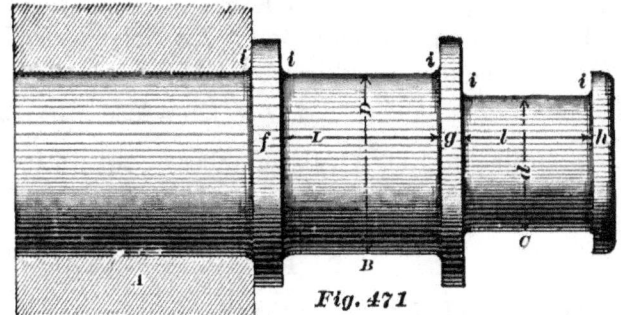

Fig. 471

the diameter of the main journal is greater than its length. In the latter cases the ratio between the diameters and lengths, as made by different builders, varies somewhat; but good practice seems to indicate that the diameter of the main-rod journal should be about 1⅛ times greater than its length. Occasionally crank-pins need to be trued up a little, for which a small allowance should be made. Hence, in determining the dimensions of the main-rod journal, we shall first find its diameter and length, whose ratio is as 1⅛ to 1, and then add, to allow for wear, about 1/16 to ⅛ inch to the diameter thus found. We say *about* 1/16 to ⅛ inch, because the diameter determined by calculation will in many cases contain a fraction of an inch, and when this fraction does not contain even ⅛ inch, we shall then add a little less, or in some cases a trifle more, than ⅛ inch, so as to make the fraction divisible by ⅛ inch; indeed, many locomotive builders do not adopt a diameter which cannot be divided by ¼ inch. If the diameter obtained by calculation contains even ⅛ inch, we simply add ⅛ inch for wear. When the length of the journal, as found by calculation, contains fractions which cannot be divided by ⅛ inch, we simply take the nearest fraction divisible by it to that found; hence, in some cases the lengths adopted may be a little less, and in others a little greater than that found by calculation.

For the sake of simplicity, we shall assume that the whole steam pressure on the piston is exerted to turn the wheels, allowing nothing for the friction of piston, etc.; we shall also neglect the pressure due to the obliquity of the main-rod.

Now, since the pressure per square inch of projected area of a steel crank-pin journal is to be 1,600 pounds, we can readily find, under the foregoing conditions, this area when the steam pressure on the piston is known, thus:

RULE 74.—For crank-pins made of steel, divide the total maximum steam pressure on the piston by 1,600; the quotient will be the number of square inches in the projected area of the main-rod journal for eight-wheeled passenger engines.

Now, since the diameter of the journal is to be $1\tfrac{1}{8}$ times its length, we have the following rule:

RULE 75.—Multiply the projected area (as found by Rule 74) by 8, and divide the product by 9; extract the square root of the quotient; the result will be the length of the journal. Multiply this length by 1.125, and add for wear so as to make the diameter divisible by $\tfrac{1}{8}$ inch; the sum will be the required diameter.

EXAMPLE 108.—Find the dimensions for the main-rod crank-pin journal for a passenger engine having cylinders 18 inches diameter; maximum steam pressure per square inch of piston, 130 pounds.

The area of an 18-inch piston is 254.47 square inches; hence, the maximum steam pressure on the piston will be

$$254.47 \times 130 = 33081.10 \text{ pounds.}$$

According to Rule 74, the number of square inches in the projected area of the main-rod journal will be

$$\frac{33081.10}{1600} = 20.67 \text{ square inches.}$$

According to Rule 75, we find the length to be

$$\sqrt{\frac{8 \times 20.67}{9}} = 4.28 \text{ inches.}$$

And the diameter we find to be

$$4.28 \times 1.125 = 4.815 \text{ inches;}$$

adding to this diameter .06 (which in this case is a little less than $\tfrac{1}{16}$ inch), we obtain $4\tfrac{7}{8}$ inches. Hence, the diameter of this journal should be $4\tfrac{7}{8}$ inches, and its length, $4\tfrac{1}{4}$ inches.

339. To determine the dimensions of the side-rod journal we proceed in manner similar to that adopted for finding the dimensions of the main journal. Our first step will be to compute the projected area. In good practice we find that in eight-wheeled passenger engines the projected area of the side-rod journal is equal to about 65 to 75 per cent. of that of the main-rod journal; we believe that about 67 per cent. is a good proportion. Hence, when we know the projected area of the main-rod journal, that of the side-rod journal may be found by making it equal to about 67 per cent. of the former. But this result can be obtained in a more direct way by the following rule, which will give results agreeing well with the average good practice.

RULE 76.—For steel crank-pins, divide the maximum pressure on the piston by 2,400; the quotient will be the number of square inches in the projected area of a side-rod journal for eight-wheeled passenger engines.

In many locomotives we find the length of the side-rod journal to be equal to its diameter; on the other hand, we find as many, if not a greater number of engines, in which the diameter of the side-rod journal is greater than its length. In the latter class, the ratio between the diameters and lengths, as made by different makers, varies somewhat, but good practice seems to indicate that this ratio should be equal to that of the main-rod journal, namely, the diamter should be $1\frac{1}{8}$ times greater than the length; and these porportions we shall adopt.

To the diameter thus found we shall also add $\frac{1}{16}$ to $\frac{1}{8}$ inch, so as to avoid fractions which cannot be divided by $\frac{1}{8}$ inch. As for the length of the side-rod journals, we shall simply adopt such as can be divided by $\frac{1}{8}$ inch, and which will be the nearest to the fraction found by calculation, and therefore may in some cases be a little less and in others greater than that obtained by the rule.

RULE 77.—To find the length and diameter of a steel side-rod journal for eight-wheeled passenger engine. Multiply the projected area of the side-rod journal (as found by Rule 76) by 8, and divide the product by 9; extract the square root of the quotient; the result will be the required length. Multiply the length by 1.125, add to the product from $\frac{1}{16}$ to $\frac{1}{8}$ inch, so as to obtain a numerical value divisible by $\frac{1}{8}$ inch; the sum will be the required diameter.

EXAMPLE 109.—Find the dimensions for the side-rod journal for a passenger engine having cylinders 18 inches diameter; maximum steam pressure per square inch of piston, 130 pounds.

We have already found, in Example 108, that the maximum steam pressure on the piston is 33081.10 pounds; hence, according to Rule 76, we have

$$\frac{33081.10}{2400} = 13.78 \text{ square inches,}$$

which is the projected area of the side-rod journal.

According to Rule 77, the length should be

$$\sqrt{\frac{8 \times 13.78}{9}} = 3.49 \text{ inches.}$$

For the diameter we have $3.49 \times 1.125 = 3.926$ inches; to this add .199 inch; the sum will be 4.125, which is the required diameter; hence, the side-rod journal should be $4\frac{1}{8}$ inches diameter, and $3\frac{1}{2}$ inches long.

In this manner the diameters and lengths of steel crank-pins given in the following tables have been obtained.

### TABLE 37.

DIMENSIONS OF STEEL CRANK-PIN JOURNALS FOR EIGHT-WHEELED PASSENGER ENGINES (FOUR WHEELS CONNECTED). MAXIMUM STEAM PRESSURE ON THE PISTON, 120 POUNDS PER SQUARE INCH. LETTERS AT THE HEAD OF COLUMNS REFER TO FIG. 471.

| Diameter of Cylinders. | Main-rod Journals. | | Side-rod Journals. | |
|---|---|---|---|---|
| | Diameter $D$ | Length $L$ | Diameter $d$ | Length $l$ |
| 9  | $2\frac{5}{8}$ | 2              | 2              | $1\frac{3}{4}$ |
| 10 | $2\frac{3}{4}$ | $2\frac{1}{4}$ | $2\frac{1}{4}$ | $1\frac{7}{8}$ |
| 11 | $2\frac{7}{8}$ | $2\frac{3}{8}$ | $2\frac{3}{8}$ | 2              |
| 12 | $3\frac{1}{8}$ | $2\frac{5}{8}$ | $2\frac{1}{2}$ | $2\frac{1}{8}$ |
| 13 | $3\frac{1}{4}$ | 3              | $2\frac{5}{8}$ | $2\frac{1}{4}$ |
| 14 | $3\frac{1}{2}$ | $3\frac{1}{8}$ | $3\frac{1}{8}$ | $2\frac{5}{8}$ |
| 15 | 4              | $3\frac{1}{4}$ | $3\frac{1}{4}$ | $2\frac{7}{8}$ |
| 16 | $4\frac{1}{4}$ | $3\frac{3}{8}$ | $3\frac{1}{4}$ | 3              |
| 17 | $4\frac{1}{2}$ | $3\frac{7}{8}$ | $3\frac{3}{8}$ | $3\frac{1}{8}$ |
| 18 | $4\frac{5}{8}$ | $4\frac{1}{8}$ | $3\frac{7}{8}$ | $3\frac{3}{8}$ |
| 19 | 5              | $4\frac{3}{8}$ | $4\frac{1}{8}$ | $3\frac{1}{2}$ |
| 20 | $5\frac{1}{4}$ | $4\frac{1}{2}$ | $4\frac{3}{8}$ | $3\frac{3}{4}$ |

## TABLE 38.

DIMENSIONS OF STEEL CRANK-PIN JOURNALS FOR EIGHT-WHEELED PASSENGER ENGINES) FOUR WHEELS CONNECTED). MAXIMUM STEAM PRESSURE ON THE PISTON, 130 POUNDS PER SQUARE INCH. LETTERS AT THE HEAD OF COLUMNS REFER TO FIG. 471.

| Diameter of Cylinders. | Main-rod Journals. | | Side-rod Journals. | |
|---|---|---|---|---|
| | Diameter $D$ | Length $L$ | Diameter $d$ | Length $l$ |
| 9  | $2\tfrac{1}{4}$ | $2\tfrac{1}{8}$ | $2\tfrac{1}{8}$ | $1\tfrac{3}{4}$ |
| 10 | $2\tfrac{5}{8}$ | $2\tfrac{3}{8}$ | $2\tfrac{1}{4}$ | $2$ |
| 11 | $3\tfrac{1}{8}$ | $2\tfrac{5}{8}$ | $2\tfrac{1}{2}$ | $2\tfrac{1}{4}$ |
| 12 | $3\tfrac{3}{8}$ | $2\tfrac{7}{8}$ | $2\tfrac{5}{8}$ | $2\tfrac{3}{8}$ |
| 13 | $3\tfrac{1}{2}$ | $3\tfrac{1}{8}$ | $2\tfrac{7}{8}$ | $2\tfrac{1}{2}$ |
| 14 | $3\tfrac{7}{8}$ | $3\tfrac{3}{8}$ | $3\tfrac{1}{8}$ | $2\tfrac{3}{4}$ |
| 15 | $4\tfrac{1}{4}$ | $3\tfrac{1}{2}$ | $3\tfrac{3}{8}$ | $3$ |
| 16 | $4\tfrac{3}{8}$ | $3\tfrac{3}{4}$ | $3\tfrac{5}{8}$ | $3\tfrac{1}{4}$ |
| 17 | $4\tfrac{5}{8}$ | $4$ | $3\tfrac{7}{8}$ | $3\tfrac{3}{8}$ |
| 18 | $4\tfrac{7}{8}$ | $4\tfrac{1}{4}$ | $4\tfrac{1}{8}$ | $3\tfrac{1}{2}$ |
| 19 | $5\tfrac{1}{4}$ | $4\tfrac{1}{2}$ | $4\tfrac{3}{8}$ | $3\tfrac{5}{8}$ |
| 20 | $5\tfrac{1}{2}$ | $4\tfrac{5}{8}$ | $4\tfrac{5}{8}$ | $3\tfrac{7}{8}$ |

## TABLE 39.

DIMENSIONS OF STEEL CRANK-PIN JOURNALS FOR EIGHT-WHEELED PASSENGER ENGINES (FOUR WHEELS CONNECTED). MAXIMUM STEAM PRESSURE ON THE PISTON, 140 POUNDS PER SQUARE INCH. LETTERS AT THE HEAD OF COLUMNS REFER TO FIG. 471.

| Diameter of Cylinders. | Main-rod Journals. | | Side-rod Journals. | |
|---|---|---|---|---|
| | Diameter $D$ | Length $L$ | Diameter $d$ | Length $l$ |
| 9  | $2\tfrac{3}{8}$ | $2\tfrac{1}{4}$ | $2\tfrac{1}{8}$ | $1\tfrac{7}{8}$ |
| 10 | $2\tfrac{7}{8}$ | $2\tfrac{1}{2}$ | $2\tfrac{3}{8}$ | $2$ |
| 11 | $3\tfrac{1}{8}$ | $2\tfrac{3}{4}$ | $2\tfrac{5}{8}$ | $2\tfrac{1}{4}$ |
| 12 | $3\tfrac{1}{2}$ | $3$ | $2\tfrac{7}{8}$ | $2\tfrac{1}{4}$ |
| 13 | $3\tfrac{3}{4}$ | $3\tfrac{1}{8}$ | $3\tfrac{1}{8}$ | $2\tfrac{5}{8}$ |
| 14 | $4$ | $3\tfrac{1}{4}$ | $3\tfrac{1}{4}$ | $2\tfrac{7}{8}$ |
| 15 | $4\tfrac{1}{4}$ | $3\tfrac{5}{8}$ | $3\tfrac{1}{2}$ | $3$ |
| 16 | $4\tfrac{3}{8}$ | $4$ | $3\tfrac{3}{4}$ | $3\tfrac{1}{4}$ |
| 17 | $4\tfrac{7}{8}$ | $4\tfrac{1}{4}$ | $4$ | $3\tfrac{1}{2}$ |
| 18 | $5\tfrac{1}{8}$ | $4\tfrac{1}{2}$ | $4\tfrac{1}{8}$ | $3\tfrac{5}{8}$ |
| 19 | $5\tfrac{3}{8}$ | $4\tfrac{5}{8}$ | $4\tfrac{3}{8}$ | $3\tfrac{7}{8}$ |
| 20 | $5\tfrac{5}{8}$ | $4\tfrac{7}{8}$ | $4\tfrac{5}{8}$ | $4$ |

## TABLE 40.

DIMENSIONS OF STEEL CRANK-PIN JOURNALS FOR EIGHT-WHEELED PASSENGER ENGINES (FOUR WHEELS CONNECTED). MAXIMUM STEAM PRESSURE ON THE PISTON, 150 POUNDS PER SQUARE INCH. LETTERS AT THE HEAD OF COLUMNS REFER TO FIG. 471.

| Diameter of Cylinders. | Main-rod Journals. | | Side-rod Journals. | |
|---|---|---|---|---|
| | Diameter $D$ | Length $L$ | Diameter $d$ | Length $l$ |
| 9  | $2\tfrac{3}{4}$ | $2\tfrac{3}{8}$ | $2\tfrac{1}{4}$ | $1\tfrac{7}{8}$ |
| 10 | $3$ | $2\tfrac{5}{8}$ | $2\tfrac{3}{8}$ | $2\tfrac{1}{8}$ |
| 11 | $3\tfrac{1}{4}$ | $2\tfrac{7}{8}$ | $2\tfrac{5}{8}$ | $2\tfrac{1}{4}$ |
| 12 | $3\tfrac{5}{8}$ | $3\tfrac{1}{8}$ | $3$ | $2\tfrac{1}{2}$ |
| 13 | $3\tfrac{7}{8}$ | $3\tfrac{3}{8}$ | $3\tfrac{1}{4}$ | $2\tfrac{3}{4}$ |
| 14 | $4\tfrac{1}{8}$ | $3\tfrac{5}{8}$ | $3\tfrac{3}{8}$ | $3$ |
| 15 | $4\tfrac{1}{4}$ | $3\tfrac{7}{8}$ | $3\tfrac{5}{8}$ | $3\tfrac{1}{4}$ |
| 16 | $4\tfrac{7}{8}$ | $4\tfrac{1}{4}$ | $3\tfrac{7}{8}$ | $3\tfrac{5}{8}$ |
| 17 | $5$ | $4\tfrac{5}{8}$ | $4\tfrac{1}{4}$ | $3\tfrac{1}{2}$ |
| 18 | $5\tfrac{1}{4}$ | $4\tfrac{5}{8}$ | $4\tfrac{5}{8}$ | $3\tfrac{3}{4}$ |
| 19 | $5\tfrac{5}{8}$ | $4\tfrac{7}{8}$ | $4\tfrac{5}{8}$ | $4$ |
| 20 | $5\tfrac{7}{8}$ | $5\tfrac{1}{8}$ | $4\tfrac{3}{4}$ | $4\tfrac{1}{8}$ |

## TABLE 41.

DIMENSIONS OF STEEL CRANK-PIN JOURNALS FOR EIGHT-WHEELED PASSENGER ENGINES (FOUR WHEELS CONNECTED). MAXIMUM STEAM PRESSURE ON THE PISTON, 160 POUNDS PER SQUARE INCH. LETTERS AT THE HEAD OF COLUMNS REFER TO FIG. 471.

| Diameter of Cylinders. | Main-rod Journals. | | Side-rod Journals. | |
|---|---|---|---|---|
| | Diameter $D$ | Length $L$ | Diameter $d$ | Length $l$ |
| 9  | $2\frac{3}{4}$ | $2\frac{5}{8}$ | $2\frac{1}{4}$ | 2 |
| 10 | $3\frac{1}{8}$ | $2\frac{5}{8}$ | $2\frac{1}{2}$ | $2\frac{1}{4}$ |
| 11 | $3\frac{3}{8}$ | $2\frac{7}{8}$ | $2\frac{3}{4}$ | $2\frac{5}{8}$ |
| 12 | $3\frac{5}{8}$ | $3\frac{1}{4}$ | 3 | $2\frac{5}{8}$ |
| 13 | 4 | $3\frac{1}{2}$ | $3\frac{1}{4}$ | $2\frac{7}{8}$ |
| 14 | $4\frac{1}{4}$ | $3\frac{3}{4}$ | $3\frac{1}{2}$ | 3 |
| 15 | $4\frac{5}{8}$ | 4 | $3\frac{3}{4}$ | $3\frac{1}{4}$ |
| 16 | $4\frac{7}{8}$ | $4\frac{1}{4}$ | 4 | $3\frac{1}{4}$ |
| 17 | $5\frac{1}{8}$ | $4\frac{1}{2}$ | $4\frac{1}{4}$ | $3\frac{3}{8}$ |
| 18 | $5\frac{1}{2}$ | $4\frac{3}{4}$ | $4\frac{1}{2}$ | $3\frac{7}{8}$ |
| 19 | $5\frac{3}{4}$ | 5 | $4\frac{3}{4}$ | $4\frac{1}{2}$ |
| 20 | $6\frac{1}{8}$ | $5\frac{1}{4}$ | 5 | $4\frac{5}{8}$ |

340. Fig. 472 represents a rear crank-pin for an eight-wheeled passenger engine; in fact, this figure and Fig. 471 represent a pair of crank-pins for an engine of this class.

Figs. 474, 475 represent another pair of crank-pins for the same class of engine; they were made of steel, and designed for an engine having cylinders 17 inches diameter. Fig. 474 represents the main, and Fig. 475, the rear crank-pin; their forms, as will be seen, differ somewhat from those of the pins previously referred to.

The general practice is to make the diameter of the outer collar (see Fig. 471) from 1 to $1\frac{1}{2}$ inches greater than the diameter $d$ of the journal $C$; the diameters of the middle collar and the collar next to the hub of the wheel are generally made $1\frac{1}{2}$ inches greater than the diameter $D$ of the journal $B$. The thickness $h$ of the outer collar is generally $\frac{1}{2}$ inch, sometimes $\frac{5}{8}$ inch. The thickness $g$ of the middle collar, and the thickness $f$ of the collar next to the hub of the wheel, will depend upon the distance between the line coinciding with the axis of the cylinder and the face of the hub of wheel. In many eight-wheeled passenger engines the thickness $g$ is $\frac{1}{2}$ inch, and the thickness $f$, $\frac{3}{4}$ inch.

Sometimes the hub of the wheel is made exceedingly deep, leaving no room for a collar next to the hub; in such cases the main crank-pin will appear as shown in Fig. 474. The diameter of the wheel fit of this crank-pin is made comparatively great, so as to obtain a shoulder against which the brasses of the main-rod can bear; this shoulder generally projects $\frac{1}{16}$ of an inch beyond the face of the hub.

The junctions $i\,i$ of the journal and the face of the collars (Fig. 471) should in every instance be curved surfaces turned to a radius of $\frac{1}{8}$ inch for small crank-pins, and increased up to a radius of $\frac{1}{4}$ inch for large pins.

For many rear crank-pins the shank $E$ is formed so as to leave a collar next to the hub of the wheel, as shown in Fig. 472. The diameter $n$ of this collar is made equal to that of the corresponding one on the main crank-pin, and its thickness $p$ is generally $\frac{5}{8}$ or $\frac{3}{4}$ inch. The diameter $m$ of the shank $E$ is generally made from $\frac{1}{4}$ to $\frac{1}{2}$ inch greater than the diameter $D$ of the main-rod journal.

324                    MODERN LOCOMOTIVE CONSTRUCTION.

Fig. 473 also represents a rear crank-pin for an eight-wheeled passenger engine. The shank $E$ of this pin has a uniform taper nearly throughout its whole length; the diameter $n$ is made—as the diameter $n$ of the collar of the shank in Fig. 472—equal to the diameter of the collar on the main crank-pin; that is, the collar next to the hub.

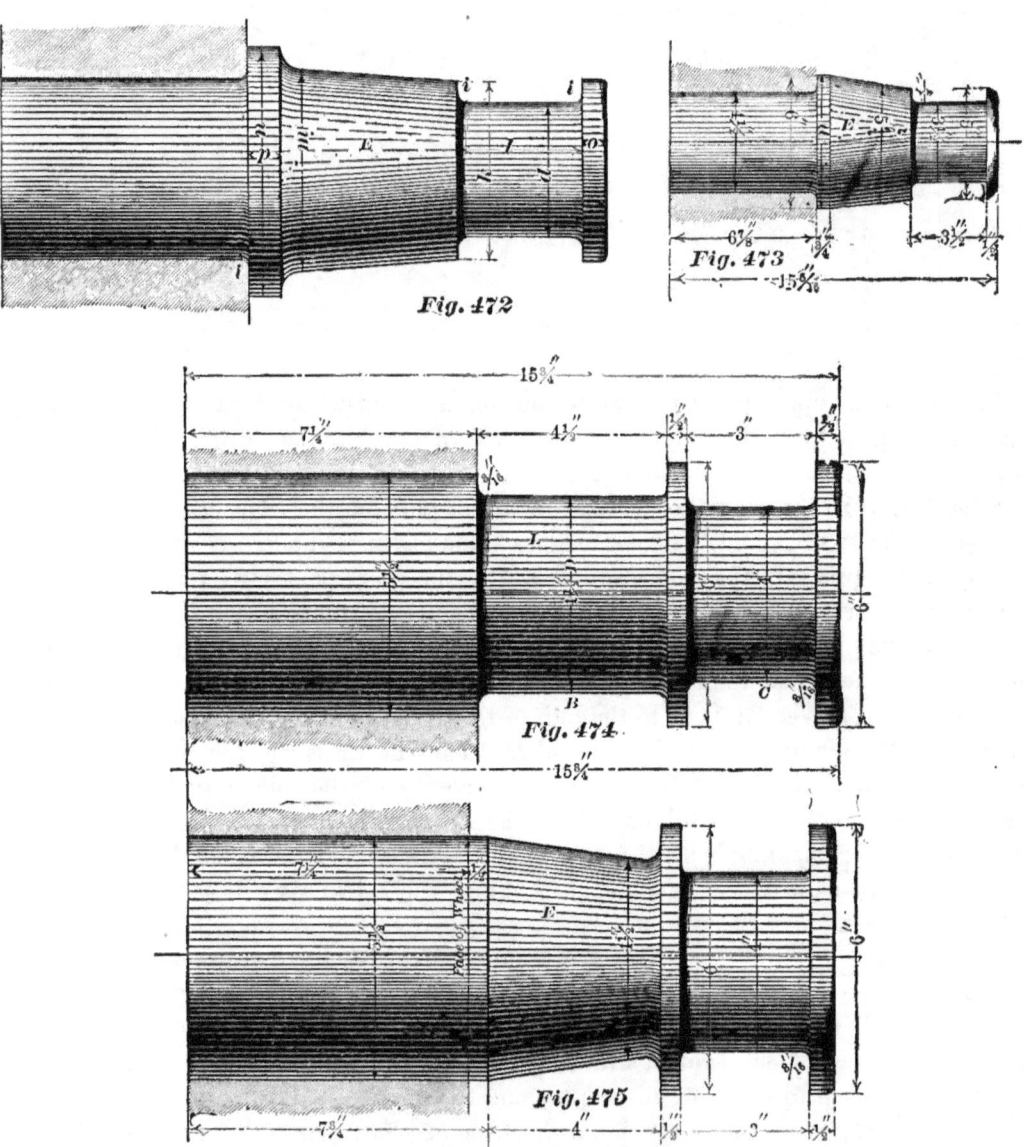

Fig. 472

Fig. 473

Fig. 474

Fig. 475

Making the form of the shank like that shown in Fig. 473 increases the weight of the pin unnecessarily; it does no good, and therefore this form of shank is not recommended. Indeed, in order to reduce the weight of the rear crank-pin, some locomotive builders make its shank $E$ like that shown in Fig. 479; this rear crank-pin has a collar on each side of the journal, and the diameter $r$, next to the inner collar, is generally made $\frac{1}{4}$ of an inch greater than the diameter $d$ of the journal.

Figs. 476, 477 also represent a pair of crank-pins for an eight-wheeled passenger engine having cylinders 17 inches diameter. It will be noticed that the shank $E$ of the rear crank-pin, Fig. 476, is different in form from those previously shown. Here the diameter $s$, in the center of the shank, is made less than the diameter $k$, or the diameter of the wheel fit. The object of this design of crank-pin is to reduce its rigidity, so that when the crank-pin is subjected to a sudden stress or shock, the slight flexibility which it may possess will lessen the effect of the shock, and

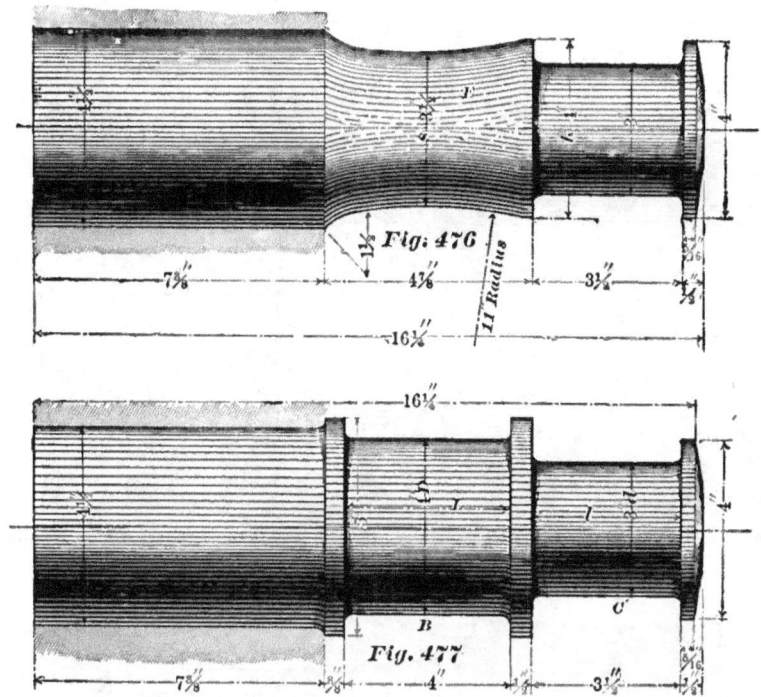

thus reduce the chances of breaking. Of course, the proportions of this crank-pin must be such that none of its fibers will be strained beyond the limits of elasticity. These crank-pins are used to quite an extent on one of our prominent roads, and give good satisfaction. On other roads this form of crank-pin is seldom found. The reason why this form is not generally adopted is probably on account of the difficulty of determining its correct proportions; in fact, these proportions are generally obtained by a tentative process rather than by computation.

Figs. 478, 479 represent a pair of crank-pins for an eight-wheeled passenger engine with cylinders 17 inches diameter; they are also often used for the same class of engines with cylinders 18 inches diameter.

These crank-pins are designed for engines which have solid-ended side-rods. One of these rods is shown in Fig. 419.

341. In eight-wheeled passenger engines the diameter of the wheel fit of the rear crank-pin is always made equal to that of the main crank-pin. This diameter should never be made less than the diameter $D$ of the journal next to the wheel; in fact, we believe it to be good practice to make the diameter of the wheel fit from $\frac{1}{8}$ to $\frac{1}{4}$ inch greater than the diameter $D$.

When the crank-pin has a collar next to the wheel, the junction of the wheel fit and the face of the collar should never be a sharp corner, but should be well rounded out.

The crank-pins are generally pressed into the wheels. When the crank-pin hole is perfectly true and smooth, the pin should be pressed in with a press-

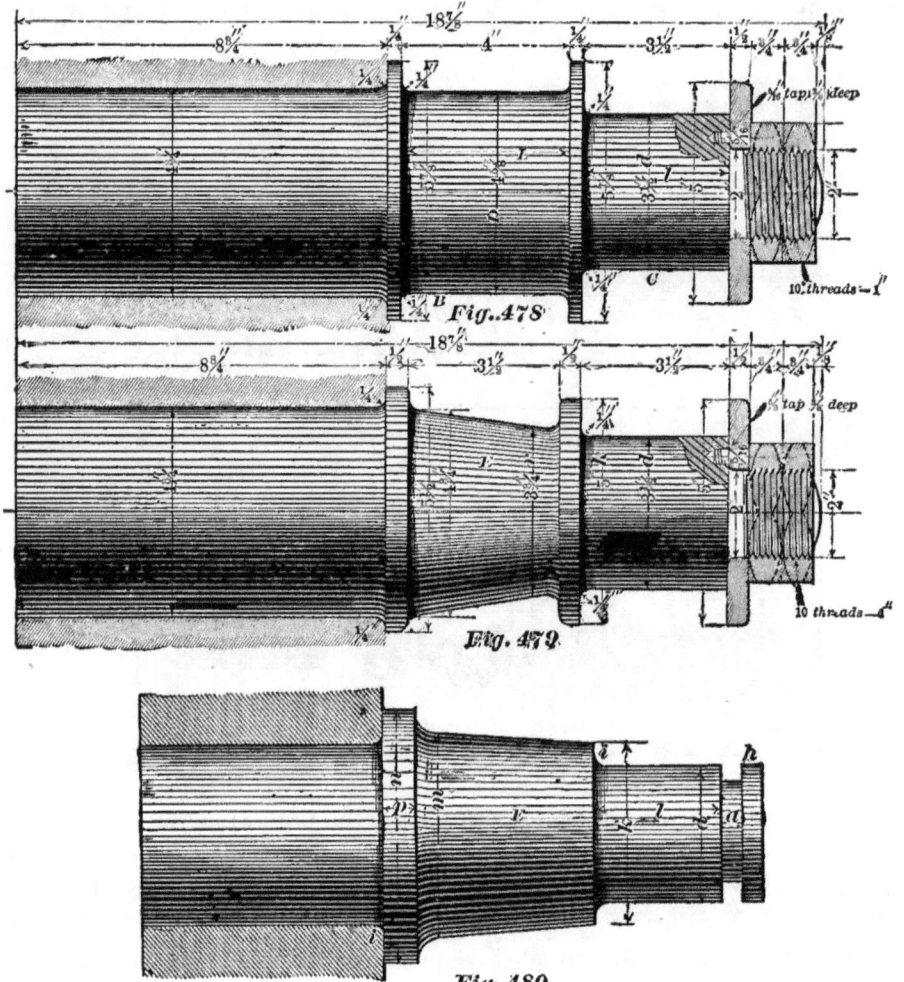

Fig. 478

Fig. 479

Fig. 480

ure equal to about six tons for every inch in diameter of the wheel fit. When the hole is not perfectly true, which may be the result of shrinking the tire on the wheel center after the hole for the crank-pin has been bored, or if the hole is not perfectly smooth, the pressure may have to be increased to nine tons for every inch in diameter of the wheel fit. From these remarks it appears that it is always best to shrink the tires on the wheel centers before the holes for the crank-pins are bored.

342. Fig. 480 represents another form of crank-pin used for solid-ended side-rods; it differs from that shown in Fig. 479 in the fact that it has no loose collar for holding the side-rod in position after the latter has been slipped on to the journal; instead of a loose collar a groove $a$ is turned into the journal near the end. The design of side-rod used for this pin is shown in Figs. 481 and 482. A solid brass bushing is forced into

the end of the side-rod; a brass plate B made in two pieces is made to fit into the groove a in the crank-pin journal; a brass cap C covers the end of the pin; four bolts D D extend through the whole width of this side-rod end and hold the cap C and the

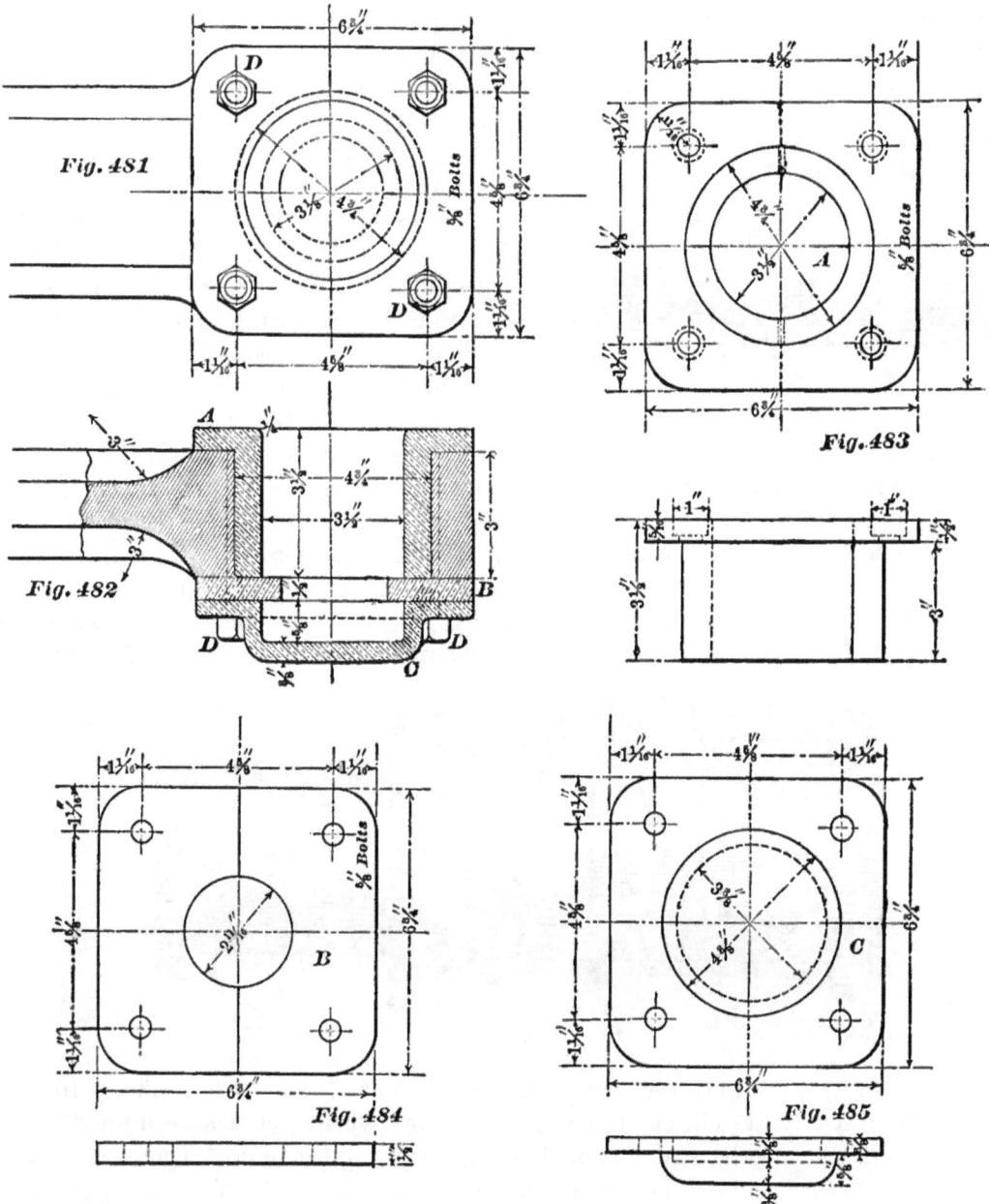

plate B firmly in position, and also prevent the brass bushing from turning around should it become loose through constant service. The bolt-heads are countersunk into the flange of the bushing, as shown in Fig. 483.

Fig. 483 represents in detail the brass bushing A; Fig. 484 represents the brass plate B; and Fig. 485 represents the brass cap C; these require no further explanation.

## MAIN CRANK-PINS FOR MOGUL, TEN-WHEELED, AND CONSOLIDATION ENGINES.

343. In ten-wheeled, Mogul, and consolidation engines, the arrangement of the side- and main-rods generally differs from the arrangement of the rods in passenger engines. In the latter class of engines we have seen that the main-rod takes hold of the inner journal of the main crank-pin; in the former classes of engines the main-rod generally takes hold of the outer journal of the main crank-pin, thus bringing the side-rods next to the wheels.

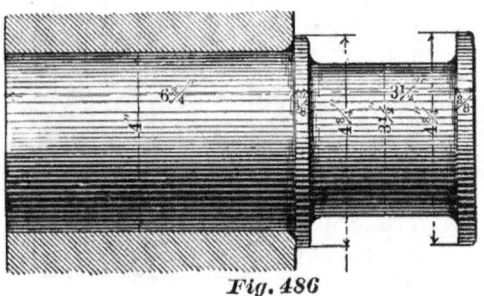
Fig. 486

Fig. 487 represents a main crank-pin for a consolidation engine having cylinders 20 inches diameter; and Fig. 486 represents one of the side-rod pins for the same engine. The main crank-pins for consolidation, Mogul, and ten-wheeled engines are generally similar in form; hence the rules by which the dimensions of the crank-pin journals for one of these classes of engines are determined can also be used for finding the dimensions of similar crank-pin journals for the other two classes of engines.

The following rules are for steel pins. In establishing these rules we shall again be guided by the dimensions of the crank-pins at present in use, and which give good satisfaction. Let us commence with the main-rod journal on the main crank-pin; this journal will be the outer one in Fig. 487; it is required to find the diameter $D$ and the

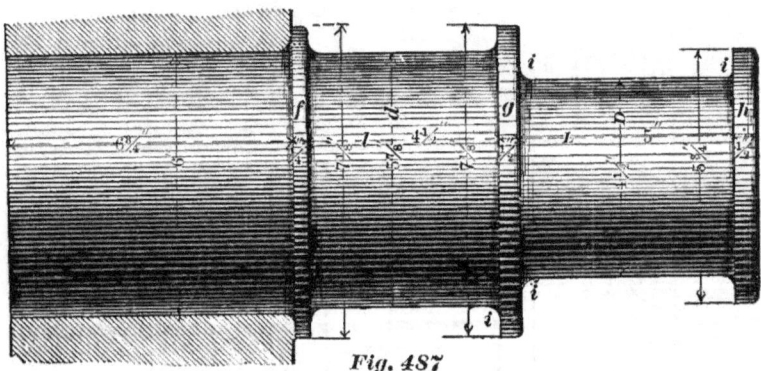
Fig. 487

length $L$. In Art. 337 it has been stated that, to prevent a locomotive crank-pin from heating, it must have a sufficient bearing surface, and when such has been provided, the crank-pin will also be strong enough for the work it has to do. These remarks again apply to the main-rod journal of the crank-pins, in which this journal is the outer one, as shown in Fig. 487; they also apply to the side-rod crank-pin, such as is shown in Fig. 486; but they do not apply to side-rod journal on the main crank-pins, as will presently be seen.

Since the pressure per square inch of the projected area of a steel crank-pin journal should not exceed 1,600 pounds, we readily find, by Rule 74, the projected area of the main-rod journal for consolidation, Mogul, and ten-wheeled engines. Thus:

EXAMPLE 110.—What should be the projected area of the main-rod journal on the main crank-pin for a Mogul engine having cylinders 18 inches diameter? Maximum steam pressure on the piston is 130 pounds per square inch.

Multiplying the area in square inches of the piston by the steam pressure per square inch, we have

$$254.47 \times 130 = 33081.10 \text{ pounds,}$$

which is the maximum steam pressure on the piston.

According to Rule 74, we have

$$\frac{33081.10}{1600} = 20.67 \text{ square inches,}$$

which is the projected area of the main-rod crank-pin journal.

Before we can find the diameter and the length of this journal we must establish a ratio between the diameter and the length. There are a few engines of the classes now under consideration in which the diameter of the main-rod crank-pin journal exceeds its length; and on the other hand we meet with a few engines in which the diameter is less than the length. But in a large majority of these engines the diameter of the main-rod crank-pin journal is equal to its length. We shall therefore adopt a rule by which we can find the diameter and the length which are equal to each other. To the diameter so found we shall add, for wear, about $\frac{1}{16}$ or $\frac{1}{8}$ inch, so as to obtain such diameters whose fractions, if they have any, are divisible by $\frac{1}{8}$ inch; as for the length, we shall adopt the nearest which contains fractions that can be divided by $\frac{1}{8}$ inch, and this may be either a little less or a little greater than the length found by the following rule:

RULE 78.—To find the diameter and length of the main-rod crank-pin journal: Extract the square root of the projected area, as found by Rule 74. If this square root does not contain any fractions, or if it does contain fractions which can be divided by $\frac{1}{8}$ inch, add to it $\frac{1}{8}$ of an inch for wear; the sum will be the diameter. If the square root contains fractions which cannot be divided by $\frac{1}{8}$ inch, add $\frac{1}{16}$ or a little more, so as to obtain diameters which are divisible by $\frac{1}{8}$ inch. The square root of the projected area will also be the length of the pin; if it is not divisible by $\frac{1}{8}$ inch, adopt the nearest length which is divisible by $\frac{1}{8}$ inch.

EXAMPLE 111.—Find the diameter and length of the main-rod crank-pin journal for a Mogul engine having cylinders 18 inches diameter, maximum steam pressure on piston 130 pounds per square inch.

In Example 110 we have found that the projected area of this journal is 20.67 square inches. The square root of 20.67 is 4.54 inches, which is a little more than $4\frac{1}{2}$ inches, hence the diameter is $4\frac{5}{8}$ inches; and the length is $4\frac{1}{2}$ inches.

344. The projected area of the side-rod journal of the main crank-pin, that is, the inner journal in Fig. 487, as made by different builders, varies somewhat; hence we find that in a number of engines the projected area of the side-rod journal is greater than that of the main-rod journal; and in a number of engines it is less; but in the majority of engines the projected areas of the two journals are equal, and these latter proportions we shall adopt. Hence the projected area of the side-rod journal of the main crank-pin is found by Rule 74.

True, if we had only to make provisions for the prevention of heating, a smaller area would suffice, but, since the outer journal of this pin is subjected to a greater pressure than is brought to bear on the side-rod journal, and since the pressure on the outer pin acts with a leverage, we require a large projected area so as to provide for the strength of the pin.

The ratio between the diameter and length of this side-rod journal, as made by different builders, also varies; but the most common practice is to make the diameter $1\frac{1}{4}$ times larger than the length; and these proportions we shall adopt. We have therefore the following rule:

RULE 79.—To find the length and diameter of the side-rod journal for the main crank-pin, when this journal is next to the wheels, divide the projected area, as found by Rule 74, by 5; multiply the quotient by 4, and extract the square root from the product; this square root will be the length of the side-rod journal. If this length is not divisible by $\frac{1}{8}$ inch, adopt the nearest one which can be divided by $\frac{1}{8}$ inch. For the diameter multiply the square root found as above by 1.25; if this product is divisible by $\frac{1}{8}$ inch, add to it $\frac{1}{8}$ inch for wear; the sum will be the required diameter; if this product is not divisible by $\frac{1}{8}$, add from $\frac{1}{16}$ to $\frac{1}{8}$ inch, so as to make it divisible by $\frac{1}{8}$ inch; the sum will be the required diameter.

EXAMPLE 112.—Find the length and diameter of the side-rod journal for the main crank-pin for a Mogul engine having cylinders 18 inches diameter; maximum steam pressure on the piston, 130 pounds per square inch. The projected area of this journal is, according to Rule 74, 20.67 square inches; in fact, this area we have found in Example 110.

According to Rule 79, we have

$$\frac{20.67 \times 4}{5} = 16.53.$$

The square root of 16.53 is

$$\sqrt{16.53} = 4.06 \text{ inches.}$$

Hence the length of this journal is 4 inches.

Again, for the diameter we have $4.06 \times 1.25 = 5.07$ inches, which is a little more than 5 inches; hence the diameter of this journal is $5\frac{1}{8}$ inches.

In a similar way we can determine the dimensions of the journals for any main crank-pin (made of steel) under different pressures for ten-wheeled, Mogul, and consolidation engines.

The dimensions of the main crank-pin journals given in the following tables have been computed by the foregoing rules.

## TABLE 42.

DIMENSIONS OF THE MAIN CRANK-PIN JOURNALS (STEEL) FOR MOGUL, TEN-WHEELED, AND CONSOLIDATION ENGINES. MAXIMUM STEAM PRESSURE ON THE PISTON, 120 POUNDS PER SQUARE INCH.

| Diameter of Cylinders. | Main-rod Journals. | | Side-rod Journals. | |
|---|---|---|---|---|
| | Diameter. | Length. | Diameter. | Length. |
| 9 | 2¼ inches. | 2⅛ inches. | 2½ inches. | 2 inches. |
| 10 | 2½ " | 2⅜ " | 2¾ " | 2⅛ " |
| 11 | 2¾ " | 2⅝ " | 3 " | 2⅜ " |
| 12 | 3 " | 2⅞ " | 3⅜ " | 2⅝ " |
| 13 | 3¼ " | 3⅛ " | 3⅝ " | 2¾ " |
| 14 | 3½ " | 3⅜ " | 3⅞ " | 3 " |
| 15 | 3¾ " | 3⅝ " | 4⅛ " | 3¼ " |
| 16 | 4 " | 3⅞ " | 4½ " | 3½ " |
| 17 | 4¼ " | 4⅛ " | 4¾ " | 3⅝ " |
| 18 | 4½ " | 4⅜ " | 5 " | 3⅞ " |
| 19 | 4¾ " | 4⅝ " | 5¼ " | 4⅛ " |
| 20 | 5 " | 4⅞ " | 5½ " | 4⅜ " |
| 21 | 5¼ " | 5⅛ " | 5¾ " | 4½ " |
| 22 | 5½ " | 5⅜ " | 6 " | 4¾ " |

## TABLE 43.

DIMENSIONS OF THE MAIN CRANK-PIN JOURNALS (STEEL) FOR MOGUL, TEN-WHEELED, AND CONSOLIDATION ENGINES. MAXIMUM STEAM PRESSURE ON THE PISTON, 130 POUNDS PER SQUARE INCH.

| Diameter of Cylinders. | Main-rod Journals. | | Side-rod Journals. | |
|---|---|---|---|---|
| | Diameter. | Length. | Diameter. | Length. |
| 9 | 2⅜ inches. | 2¼ inches. | 2⅝ inches. | 2 inches. |
| 10 | 2⅝ " | 2½ " | 2⅞ " | 2¼ " |
| 11 | 2⅞ " | 2¾ " | 3¼ " | 2½ " |
| 12 | 3⅛ " | 3 " | 3½ " | 2¾ " |
| 13 | 3⅜ " | 3¼ " | 3⅞ " | 3 " |
| 14 | 3⅝ " | 3½ " | 4 " | 3⅛ " |
| 15 | 3⅞ " | 3¾ " | 4¼ " | 3⅜ " |
| 16 | 4⅛ " | 4 " | 4⅝ " | 3⅝ " |
| 17 | 4⅜ " | 4¼ " | 4⅞ " | 3⅞ " |
| 18 | 4⅝ " | 4½ " | 5⅛ " | 4 " |
| 19 | 4⅞ " | 4¾ " | 5½ " | 4¼ " |
| 20 | 5⅛ " | 5 " | 5¾ " | 4½ " |
| 21 | 5⅜ " | 5¼ " | 6 " | 4¾ " |
| 22 | 5⅝ " | 5½ " | 6¼ " | 5 " |

## TABLE 44.

DIMENSIONS OF THE MAIN CRANK-PIN JOURNALS (STEEL) FOR MOGUL, TEN-WHEELED, AND CONSOLIDATION ENGINES. MAXIMUM STEAM PRESSURE ON THE PISTON, 140 POUNDS PER SQUARE INCH.

| Diameter of Cylinders. | Main-rod Journals. | | Side-rod Journals. | |
|---|---|---|---|---|
| | Diameter. | Length. | Diameter. | Length. |
| 9 | 2½ inches. | 2⅜ inches. | 2¾ inches. | 2⅛ inches. |
| 10 | 2¾ " | 2⅝ " | 3 " | 2⅜ " |
| 11 | 3 " | 2⅞ " | 3¼ " | 2½ " |
| 12 | 3¼ " | 3⅛ " | 3⅝ " | 2¾ " |
| 13 | 3½ " | 3⅜ " | 3⅞ " | 3 " |
| 14 | 3¾ " | 3⅝ " | 4⅛ " | 3¼ " |
| 15 | 4 " | 3⅞ " | 4½ " | 3½ " |
| 16 | 4¼ " | 4⅛ " | 4¾ " | 3¾ " |
| 17 | 4½ " | 4⅜ " | 5 " | 4 " |
| 18 | 4¾ " | 4⅝ " | 5⅜ " | 4¼ " |
| 19 | 5⅛ " | 5 " | 5⅝ " | 4½ " |
| 20 | 5⅜ " | 5¼ " | 5⅞ " | 4⅝ " |
| 21 | 5⅝ " | 5½ " | 6¼ " | 4⅞ " |
| 22 | 5⅞ " | 5¾ " | 6½ " | 5⅛ " |

## TABLE 45.

DIMENSIONS OF THE MAIN CRANK-PIN JOURNALS (STEEL) FOR MOGUL, TEN-WHEELED, AND CONSOLIDATION ENGINES. MAXIMUM STEAM PRESSURE ON THE PISTON, 150 POUNDS PER SQUARE INCH.

| Diameter of Cylinders. | Main-rod Journals. | | Side-rod Journals. | |
|---|---|---|---|---|
| | Diameter. | Length. | Diameter. | Length. |
| 9 | 2½ inches. | 2⅜ inches. | 2¾ inches. | 2⅛ inches. |
| 10 | 2¾ " | 2⅝ " | 3⅛ " | 2⅜ " |
| 11 | 3⅛ " | 3 " | 3⅜ " | 2⅝ " |
| 12 | 3⅜ " | 3¼ " | 3¾ " | 2⅞ " |
| 13 | 3⅝ " | 3½ " | 4 " | 3⅛ " |
| 14 | 3⅞ " | 3¾ " | 4¼ " | 3⅜ " |
| 15 | 4⅛ " | 4 " | 4⅝ " | 3⅝ " |
| 16 | 4½ " | 4⅜ " | 4⅞ " | 3⅞ " |
| 17 | 4¾ " | 4⅝ " | 5¼ " | 4⅛ " |
| 18 | 5 " | 4⅞ " | 5½ " | 4⅜ " |
| 19 | 5¼ " | 5⅛ " | 5⅞ " | 4⅝ " |
| 20 | 5½ " | 5⅜ " | 6⅛ " | 4⅞ " |
| 21 | 5¾ " | 5⅝ " | 6⅜ " | 5⅛ " |
| 22 | 6⅛ " | 6 " | 6⅝ " | 5⅜ " |

## TABLE 46.

DIMENSIONS OF THE MAIN CRANK-PIN JOURNALS (STEEL) FOR MOGUL, TEN-WHEELED, AND CONSOLIDATION ENGINES. MAXIMUM STEAM PRESSURE ON THE PISTON, 160 POUNDS PER SQUARE INCH.

| Diameter of Cylinders. | Main-rod Journals. | | Side-rod Journals. | |
|---|---|---|---|---|
| | Diameter. | Length. | Diameter. | Length. |
| 9 | 2⅝ inches. | 2½ inches. | 2⅞ inches. | 2¼ inches. |
| 10 | 2⅞ " | 2¾ " | 3¼ " | 2½ " |
| 11 | 3⅛ " | 3 " | 3½ " | 2¾ " |
| 12 | 3½ " | 3⅜ " | 3⅞ " | 3 " |
| 13 | 3¾ " | 3⅝ " | 4⅛ " | 3¼ " |
| 14 | 4 " | 3⅞ " | 4½ " | 3½ " |
| 15 | 4¼ " | 4⅛ " | 4¾ " | 3¾ " |
| 16 | 4½ " | 4⅜ " | 5⅛ " | 4 " |
| 17 | 4⅞ " | 4¾ " | 5½ " | 4¼ " |
| 18 | 5⅛ " | 5 " | 5¾ " | 4½ " |
| 19 | 5½ " | 5⅜ " | 6 " | 4¾ " |
| 20 | 5¾ " | 5⅝ " | 6⅜ " | 5 " |
| 21 | 6 " | 5⅞ " | 6⅝ " | 5¼ " |
| 22 | 6¼ " | 6⅛ " | 7 " | 5½ " |

There are very few Mogul engines built with cylinders 9 inches diameter, and we do not know of any consolidation engines with cylinders of such small diameter; it may therefore appear unnecessary to extend the tables to such small cylinders. But we have seen that, in narrow-gauge passenger engines, the side-rods are often placed next to the driving wheels; these engines generally have small cylinders, consequently these tables are useful for obtaining the dimensions of main crank-pins for this class, and other classes of engines whose side-rods are placed next to the driving wheels.

### SIDE-ROD PINS FOR TEN-WHEELED AND MOGUL ENGINES.

345. In comparing the side-rod pins for ten-wheeled and Mogul engines with the side-rod pins for eight-wheeled passenger engines whose cylinders are equal in size to those in the former classes of engines, and all subjected to the same steam pressure,

we find that the side-rod pins in ten-wheeled and Mogul engines are smaller than those in eight-wheeled passenger engines. The reason for this is that in passenger engines we have only two driving wheels on each side, and in ten-wheeled and Mogul engines we have three driving wheels on each side. With cylinders of equal size, and equal steam pressures, the thrust on the main-rod crank-pin journals in all the different classes of engines will be practically equal. Now assuming that the total weight on the driving wheels is equally distributed, the pressure on the side-rod pins in ten-wheeled and Mogul engines must be less than that on the side-rod pins in passenger engines, because in the latter class nearly all the pressure on the main pin is transmitted to two wheels, whereas, in the former class an equal amount of pressure is transmitted to three wheels. Hence, the rules previously given for determining the dimensions of the side-rod pin for eight-wheeled passenger engines are not suitable for finding the dimensions of the side-rod pins for ten-wheeled and Mogul engines.

The following rules will give results which agree closely with the average good practice:

RULE 80.—Divide the total steam pressure on the piston by 2,800; the quotient will be the number of square inches in the projected area of steel side-rod pins in the front and rear driving wheels under ten-wheeled and Mogul engines.

RULE 81.—To find the diameter and length of the front and rear side-rod pins in the above classes of engines, extract the square root of the projected area, as found by Rule 80. If this square root does not contain any fractions, or if it does contain fractions which can be divided by $\frac{1}{8}$ inch, add to it $\frac{1}{8}$ inch for wear; the sum will be the diameter of the pins. If the square root contains fractions which cannot be divided by $\frac{1}{8}$ inch, add about $\frac{1}{16}$ inch, or a little more, so as to obtain diameters which are divisible by $\frac{1}{8}$ inch. The square root of the projected area will also be the length of the pins; if it is not divisible by $\frac{1}{8}$ inch, adopt the nearest length which is divisible by $\frac{1}{8}$ inch.

EXAMPLE 113.—Find the diameter and length of the front and rear side-rod pins in a Mogul engine having cylinders 18 inches diameter; maximum steam pressure on the piston, 130 pounds per square inch.

The total steam pressure on the piston is equal to its area multiplied by the steam pressure per square inch; therefore,

$$254.47 \times 130 = 33081.10 \text{ pounds} = \text{total pressure on the piston.}$$

According to Rule 80, the projected area is equal to

$$\frac{33081.10}{2800} = 11.81 \text{ square inches.}$$

According to Rule 81, we must find the square root of 11.81, which is 3.43, or, we may say it is practically equal to $3\frac{7}{16}$ inches; hence, the diameter of this pin is $3\frac{1}{2}$ inches and its length $3\frac{3}{8}$ inches.

In a similar manner the dimensions of steel side-rod pins for ten-wheeled and Mogul engines in the following tables have been computed:

## TABLE 47.

DIMENSIONS OF STEEL SIDE-ROD PINS IN THE FRONT AND REAR WHEELS FOR TEN-WHEELED AND MOGUL ENGINES. MAXIMUM STEAM PRESSURE ON THE PISTON, 120 POUNDS PER SQUARE INCH.

| Diameter of Cylinders. | Diameter of Journals. | Length of Journals. |
|---|---|---|
| 9  | $1\frac{7}{8}$ inches. | $1\frac{5}{8}$ inches. |
| 10 | 2 " | $1\frac{7}{8}$ " |
| 11 | $2\frac{1}{8}$ " | 2 " |
| 12 | $2\frac{3}{8}$ " | $2\frac{1}{8}$ " |
| 13 | $2\frac{1}{2}$ " | $2\frac{3}{8}$ " |
| 14 | $2\frac{5}{8}$ " | $2\frac{1}{2}$ " |
| 15 | $2\frac{7}{8}$ " | $2\frac{3}{4}$ " |
| 16 | $3\frac{1}{8}$ " | 3 " |
| 17 | $3\frac{1}{4}$ " | $3\frac{1}{8}$ " |
| 18 | $3\frac{3}{8}$ " | $3\frac{3}{8}$ " |
| 19 | $3\frac{5}{8}$ " | $3\frac{1}{2}$ " |
| 20 | $3\frac{3}{4}$ " | $3\frac{5}{8}$ " |
| 21 | 4 " | $3\frac{7}{8}$ " |
| 22 | $4\frac{1}{8}$ " | 4 " |

## TABLE 48.

DIMENSIONS OF STEEL SIDE-ROD PINS IN THE FRONT AND REAR WHEELS FOR TEN-WHEELED AND MOGUL ENGINES. MAXIMUM STEAM PRESSURE ON THE PISTON, 130 POUNDS PER SQUARE INCH.

| Diameter of Cylinders. | Diameter of Journals. | Length of Journals. |
|---|---|---|
| 9  | $1\frac{7}{8}$ inches. | $1\frac{3}{4}$ inches |
| 10 | 2 " | $1\frac{7}{8}$ " |
| 11 | $2\frac{1}{4}$ " | $2\frac{1}{8}$ " |
| 12 | $2\frac{3}{8}$ " | $2\frac{1}{4}$ " |
| 13 | $2\frac{5}{8}$ " | $2\frac{1}{2}$ " |
| 14 | $2\frac{3}{4}$ " | $2\frac{5}{8}$ " |
| 15 | 3 " | $2\frac{7}{8}$ " |
| 16 | $3\frac{1}{8}$ " | 3 " |
| 17 | $3\frac{3}{8}$ " | $3\frac{1}{4}$ " |
| 18 | $3\frac{1}{2}$ " | $3\frac{3}{8}$ " |
| 19 | $3\frac{3}{4}$ " | $3\frac{5}{8}$ " |
| 20 | $3\frac{7}{8}$ " | $3\frac{3}{4}$ " |
| 21 | $4\frac{1}{8}$ " | 4 " |
| 22 | $4\frac{1}{4}$ " | $4\frac{1}{4}$ " |

## TABLE 49.

DIMENSIONS OF STEEL SIDE-ROD PINS IN THE FRONT AND REAR WHEELS FOR TEN-WHEELED AND MOGUL ENGINES. MAXIMUM STEAM PRESSURE ON THE PISTON, 140 POUNDS PER SQUARE INCH.

| Diameter of Cylinders. | Diameter of Journals. | Length of Journals. |
|---|---|---|
| 9  | $1\frac{7}{8}$ inches. | $1\frac{3}{4}$ inches. |
| 10 | $2\frac{1}{8}$ " | 2 " |
| 11 | $2\frac{1}{4}$ " | $2\frac{1}{8}$ " |
| 12 | $2\frac{1}{2}$ " | $2\frac{3}{8}$ " |
| 13 | $2\frac{5}{8}$ " | $2\frac{1}{2}$ " |
| 14 | $2\frac{7}{8}$ " | $2\frac{3}{4}$ " |
| 15 | $3\frac{1}{8}$ " | 3 " |
| 16 | $3\frac{1}{4}$ " | $3\frac{1}{8}$ " |
| 17 | $3\frac{1}{2}$ " | $3\frac{3}{8}$ " |
| 18 | $3\frac{5}{8}$ " | $3\frac{1}{2}$ " |
| 19 | $3\frac{7}{8}$ " | $3\frac{3}{4}$ " |
| 20 | 4 " | 4 " |
| 21 | $4\frac{1}{4}$ " | $4\frac{1}{8}$ " |
| 22 | $4\frac{3}{8}$ " | $4\frac{3}{8}$ " |

## TABLE 50.

DIMENSIONS OF STEEL SIDE-ROD PINS IN THE FRONT AND REAR WHEELS FOR TEN-WHEELED AND MOGUL ENGINES. MAXIMUM STEAM PRESSURE ON THE PISTON, 150 POUNDS PER SQUARE INCH.

| Diameter of Cylinders. | Diameter of Journals. | Length of Journals. |
|---|---|---|
| 9 | 2 inches. | 1⅞ inches. |
| 10 | 2⅛ " | 2 " |
| 11 | 2⅜ " | 2¼ " |
| 12 | 2⅝ " | 2½ " |
| 13 | 2¾ " | 2⅝ " |
| 14 | 3 " | 2⅞ " |
| 15 | 3⅛ " | 3 " |
| 16 | 3⅜ " | 3¼ " |
| 17 | 3⅝ " | 3½ " |
| 18 | 3¾ " | 3⅝ " |
| 19 | 4 " | 3⅞ " |
| 20 | 4¼ " | 4⅛ " |
| 21 | 4½ " | 4⅜ " |
| 22 | 4⅝ " | 4½ " |

## TABLE 51.

DIMENSIONS OF STEEL SIDE-ROD PINS IN THE FRONT AND REAR WHEELS FOR TEN-WHEELED AND MOGUL ENGINES. MAXIMUM STEAM PRESSURE ON THE PISTON, 160 POUNDS PER SQUARE INCH.

| Diameter of Cylinders. | Diameter of Journals. | Length of Journals. |
|---|---|---|
| 9 | 2⅛ inches. | 2 inches. |
| 10 | 2¼ " | 2⅛ " |
| 11 | 2½ " | 2⅜ " |
| 12 | 2⅝ " | 2½ " |
| 13 | 2⅞ " | 2¾ " |
| 14 | 3⅛ " | 3 " |
| 15 | 3¼ " | 3⅛ " |
| 16 | 3½ " | 3⅜ " |
| 17 | 3⅝ " | 3½ " |
| 18 | 3⅞ " | 3¾ " |
| 19 | 4⅛ " | 4 " |
| 20 | 4⅜ " | 4¼ " |
| 21 | 4½ " | 4⅜ " |
| 22 | 4¾ " | 4⅝ " |

### SIDE-ROD PINS FOR CONSOLIDATION ENGINES.

346. In the foregoing article we have seen that the side-rod pins for eight-wheeled passenger engines are larger than those for Mogul and ten-wheeled engines. If, now, we compare the relative pressures on the side-rod pins in Mogul and consolidation engines, we will find that for the latter class of engines we may make the side-rod pins still smaller; that is, say, they may be made smaller than those in Mogul engines. The reason for this will be seen by referring to Fig. 488, which shows the arrangements of the driving wheels on one side of a consolidation engine. The main-rod pin is marked *M*, and *A*, *B*, *D* are the side-rod pins. For the purpose of comparison, we may assume that in all locomotives the total weight on the drivers is equally distributed on the wheels; and we may also assume that the whole pressure on the main-rod crank-pin journal is required for turning the wheels (this, of course, is not exactly true). Under these conditions it will require one-fourth of the pressure on the main crank-pin

journal to turn each wheel. In Mogul engines we have only three driving wheels on each side of the engine; and with cylinders of the same size as those in a consolidation engine, and also equal steam pressures, the thrust on the main-rod crank-pin journal will practically be the same in both engines; and the pressure on the side-rod

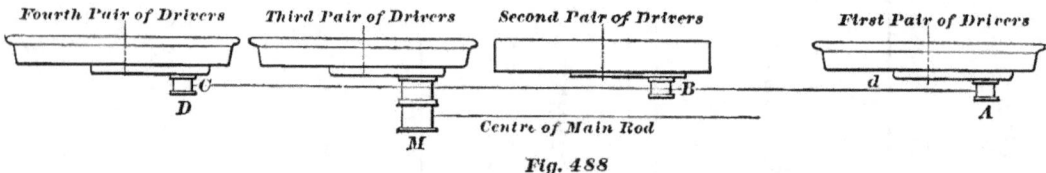

Fig. 488

pins for Mogul engines will be equal to one-third of that on main-rod journal instead of one-fourth, as in consolidation engines. Therefore, since the pressure on the side-rod pins in the latter class of engines is less than that in the former classes, it follows that the side-rod pins for consolidation engines may also be reduced in size. True, these pins are subjected to other pressures besides that due to pressure on the piston; but these may be provided for by choosing a proper divisor for the total steam pressure on the piston in determining the projected area, as we have done in the following rule:

RULE 82.—Divide the total maximum steam pressure on the piston by 3,200; the quotient will be the number of square inches in the projected area of any one of the steel side-rod pins $A$, $B$, $D$ (Fig. 488) for consolidation engines.

The length and diameter of these pins are equal, or nearly so, in the majority of engines of this class; hence the following rule:

RULE 83.—To find the length and diameter of steel side-rod pins for consolidation engines, extract the square root of the projected area as found by Rule 82; result will be the length of the pin; if this length contains a fraction not divisible by $\frac{1}{8}$ inch, then adopt the nearest length which can be divided by $\frac{1}{8}$ inch. For the diameter, add to the length found $\frac{1}{8}$ inch for wear; the sum will be the required diameter.

EXAMPLE 114.—Find the dimensions of the side-rod pins for a consolidation engine having cylinders 20 inches diameter; maximum steam pressure on the piston, 130 pounds per square inch.

The area of a piston 20 inches diameter is 314.16 square inches; hence the maximum steam pressure on the piston will be 314.16 × 130 = 40840.8 pounds. According to Rule 82, we have $\frac{40840.8}{3200}$ = 12.76 square inches, which is the projected area of the pin. The square root of 12.76 is 3.57. Hence, the length of the side-rod pin will be $3\frac{1}{2}$ inches, and its diameter will be $3\frac{5}{8}$ inches.

The dimensions given in the following tables have been computed by the foregoing rules.

There is a possibility, when a consolidation engine is running over an uneven track, causing the wheels to run out of alignment, that the side-rod pin $B$ will be subjected to a greater pressure than the side-rod pins $A$ and $D$. Consequently, we frequently find the side-rod pin $B$ made from $\frac{1}{4}$ to $\frac{3}{8}$ of an inch greater in diameter than that of the pins $A$ and $D$. This is good practice, but not a universal one, as in many engines all the side-rod pins are the same size. In computing the dimensions given in these tables, we have assumed that all the side-rod pins should be equal in size. If it is desirable to increase the size of the pin B, its diameter only should be increased; the length should remain as given; by so doing the center lines of the side-rods can be kept more readily in the same vertical plane, which is of importance.

### TABLE 52.

DIMENSIONS OF STEEL SIDE-ROD PINS FOR CONSOLIDATION ENGINES. MAXIMUM STEAM PRESSURE ON THE PISTON, 120 POUNDS PER SQUARE INCH.

| Diameter of Cylinders. | Diameter of Journals. | Length of Journals. |
|---|---|---|
| 14 | $2\frac{1}{2}$ inches. | $2\frac{5}{8}$ inches. |
| 15 | $2\frac{5}{8}$ " | $2\frac{1}{2}$ " |
| 16 | $2\frac{7}{8}$ " | $2\frac{5}{8}$ " |
| 17 | 3 " | $2\frac{7}{8}$ " |
| 18 | $3\frac{1}{8}$ " | 3 " |
| 19 | $3\frac{3}{8}$ " | $3\frac{1}{4}$ " |
| 20 | $3\frac{1}{2}$ " | $3\frac{1}{2}$ " |
| 21 | $3\frac{5}{8}$ " | $3\frac{5}{8}$ " |
| 22 | $3\frac{7}{8}$ " | $3\frac{3}{4}$ " |

### TABLE 53.

DIMENSIONS OF STEEL SIDE-ROD PINS FOR CONSOLIDATION ENGINES. MAXIMUM STEAM PRESSURE ON THE PISTON, 130 POUNDS PER SQUARE INCH.

| Diameter of Cylinders. | Diameter of Journals. | Length of Journals. |
|---|---|---|
| 14 | $2\frac{5}{8}$ inches. | $2\frac{1}{2}$ inches. |
| 15 | $2\frac{3}{4}$ " | $2\frac{5}{8}$ " |
| 16 | 3 " | $2\frac{7}{8}$ " |
| 17 | $3\frac{1}{4}$ " | 3 " |
| 18 | $3\frac{3}{8}$ " | $3\frac{1}{4}$ " |
| 19 | $3\frac{1}{2}$ " | $3\frac{3}{8}$ " |
| 20 | $3\frac{5}{8}$ " | $3\frac{1}{2}$ " |
| 21 | $3\frac{3}{4}$ " | $3\frac{5}{8}$ " |
| 22 | $4\frac{1}{4}$ " | 4 " |

### TABLE 54.

DIMENSIONS OF STEEL SIDE-ROD PINS FOR CONSOLIDATION ENGINES. MAXIMUM STEAM PRESSURE ON THE PISTON, 140 POUNDS PER SQUARE INCH.

| Diameter of Cylinders. | Diameter of Journals. | Length of Journals. |
|---|---|---|
| 14 | $2\frac{3}{8}$ inches. | $2\frac{1}{4}$ inches. |
| 15 | $2\frac{7}{8}$ " | $2\frac{3}{4}$ " |
| 16 | $3\frac{1}{8}$ " | 3 " |
| 17 | $3\frac{1}{4}$ " | $3\frac{1}{8}$ " |
| 18 | $3\frac{1}{2}$ " | $3\frac{3}{8}$ " |
| 19 | $3\frac{5}{8}$ " | $3\frac{1}{4}$ " |
| 20 | $3\frac{3}{4}$ " | $3\frac{5}{8}$ " |
| 21 | 4 " | $3\frac{7}{8}$ " |
| 22 | $4\frac{1}{4}$ " | $4\frac{1}{4}$ " |

## TABLE 55.

DIMENSIONS OF STEEL SIDE-ROD PINS FOR CONSOLIDATION ENGINES. MAXIMUM STEAM PRESSURE ON THE PISTON, 150 POUNDS PER SQUARE INCH.

| Diameter of Cylinders. | Diameter of Journals. | Length of Journals. |
|---|---|---|
| 14 | $2\frac{3}{4}$ inches. | $2\frac{5}{8}$ inches. |
| 15 | 3 " | $2\frac{7}{8}$ " |
| 16 | $3\frac{1}{8}$ " | 3 " |
| 17 | $3\frac{3}{8}$ " | $3\frac{1}{4}$ " |
| 18 | $3\frac{1}{2}$ " | $3\frac{1}{2}$ " |
| 19 | $3\frac{3}{4}$ " | $3\frac{5}{8}$ " |
| 20 | 4 " | $3\frac{7}{8}$ " |
| 21 | $4\frac{1}{8}$ " | 4 " |
| 22 | $4\frac{3}{8}$ " | $4\frac{1}{4}$ " |

## TABLE 56.

DIMENSIONS OF STEEL SIDE-ROD PINS FOR CONSOLIDATION ENGINES. MAXIMUM STEAM PRESSURE ON THE PISTON, 160 POUNDS PER SQUARE INCH.

| Diameter of Cylinders. | Diameter of Journals. | Length of Journals. |
|---|---|---|
| 14 | $2\frac{7}{8}$ inches. | $2\frac{3}{4}$ inches. |
| 15 | $3\frac{1}{8}$ " | 3 " |
| 16 | $3\frac{1}{4}$ " | $3\frac{1}{8}$ " |
| 17 | $3\frac{1}{2}$ " | $3\frac{3}{8}$ " |
| 18 | $3\frac{5}{8}$ " | $3\frac{1}{2}$ " |
| 19 | $3\frac{7}{8}$ " | $3\frac{3}{4}$ " |
| 20 | $4\frac{1}{8}$ " | 4 " |
| 21 | $4\frac{1}{4}$ " | $4\frac{1}{8}$ " |
| 22 | $4\frac{1}{2}$ " | $4\frac{3}{8}$ " |

### WHEEL FITS.

We have seen that in eight-wheeled passenger engines (two driving wheels on each side) the diameter of the wheel fit of the side-rod pin is equal to that of the main pin. In ten-wheeled, Mogul, and consolidation engines, the diameter of the wheel fit of the side-rod pins is less than that of the main pin; it is generally from $\frac{1}{4}$ to $\frac{1}{2}$ inch greater than the diameter of the journal. The wheel fit for the main pin should never be less than the diameter of the journal next to the wheels; in fact, it is better practice to increase it from $\frac{1}{8}$ to $\frac{1}{4}$ inch.

### KNUCKLE JOINTS.

347. The side-rods in all locomotives which have more than two driving wheels on each side have a knuckle joint; its form in many engines is similar to that shown in Figs. 489 and 490. In Mogul and ten-wheeled engines there is only one knuckle joint on each side of the engine; sometimes it is placed in the rear of the main pin, as shown

in Fig. 437 (Art. 309), and occasionally we find it placed in front of the main pin; there is an advantage in placing it in the rear (see Art. 309). In all consolidation engines one knuckle joint is placed in the rear of the main pin and another one in front of the side-rod pin $B$ (Fig. 488), or in general they are placed in the rear of and

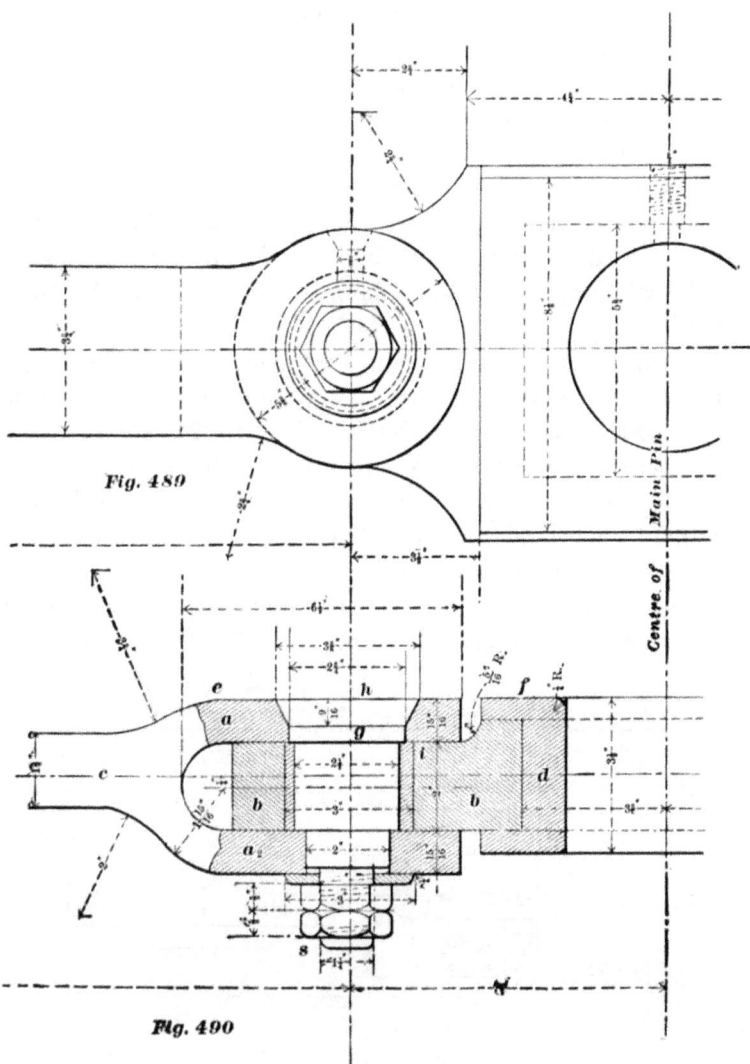

Fig. 489

Fig. 490

close to the pins in the third pair of drivers; and in the front of and close to the pins in the second pair of drivers. The solid ends $b\ b$ (Fig. 490) of the knuckle joints are generally forged to the central side-rod straps, and the forked ends are forged to the front and rear side-rods.

The center lines of the side-rods always lie in one vertical plane, represented by the line $C\ d$ in Fig. 488. This plane is also represented by the line $c\ d$ in Fig. 490. In this figure it will be noticed that the center line $b\ b$ of the knuckle joint does not coincide with the center line $c\ d$ of the side-rods; the reason for this is, that in a great number of engines the inner face $f$ of the flange of the main-rod brass is close to the outer face of the hub of wheel, consequently the inner face $e$ of the knuckle joint must not project beyond the face $f$, and therefore the center $b\ b$ of the forked end will often be out of line with center $c\ d$ of the rod.

348. The form of the pin through the knuckle joint is plainly shown in Fig. 490. A larger portion of its head $h$ is made conical, and the remainder, $g$, cylindrical; the diameter of this cylindrical portion is generally a little greater than the diameter of the body of the pin, so that the latter can be passed easily through the hole bored for the head. Another form of the knuckle-joint pin is shown in Fig. 491; here the holes in both wings $a\ a_2$ of the forked end are reamed out with one tapered reamer; this plan seems to be the most popular one.

The ratio between the length and the diameter of the pin, as made by different builders, varies somewhat, as will be seen by referring to Figs. 490 and 491; but we believe good results will be obtained by making the diameter 25 per cent. greater than the length of the pin.

Generally, the pins in the knuckle joints are made of wrought-iron, and are case hardened. Iron is to be preferred to steel, as iron pins, particularly when their form is like that shown in Fig. 491, are not as liable to break off in the shank as steel ones. In many engines these pins work in wrought-iron bushings case hardened; in a few instances they work in brass bearings, arranged as shown in Figs. 441, 445.

The knuckle-joint pins should be prevented from turning in their outer bearings; for this purpose dowel pins are inserted, as shown at $p$, Fig. 491.

So long as the side-rods remain in perfect alignment, the knuckle-joint pins do not rotate in their middle bearings; under other conditions the amount of rotation is

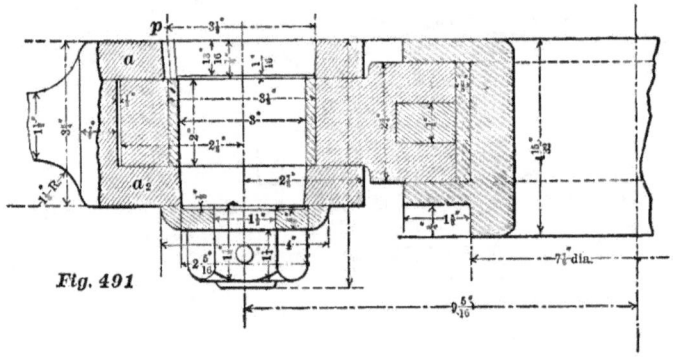

Fig. 491

very small. Hence their liability of heating is not so great as that of the crank-pins; consequently, the pressure per square inch of projected area of a knuckle-joint pin can be considerably greater than the pressure per square inch of projected area of a crank-pin. Careful observation seems to indicate that the projected area of a knuckle-joint pin may be at once determined from the pressure on the piston, and that for every 7,000 pounds of the maximum steam pressure on the piston one square inch of projected area should be allowed. Hence, for obtaining the length and diameter of a knuckle-joint pin, we have the following rules:

RULE 84.—Divide the total maximum steam pressure on the piston by 7,000; the quotient will be the number of square inches in the projected area of the pin.

RULE 85.—To find the length and diameter of the knuckle-joint pin, divide the projected area, as found by Rule 84, by 5, multiply the quotient by 4, and extract the square root of the product; the result will be the length of the pin. Multiply the length by 1.25; the product will be the diameter of the pin. Only fractions divisible by $\frac{1}{16}$ inch are adopted; hence, if the dimensions found by calculation contain fractions not divisible by $\frac{1}{16}$ inch, adopt the nearest one which can be so divided.

EXAMPLE 115.—It is required to find the dimensions of a knuckle-joint pin for a consolidation engine having cylinders 20 inches diameter; maximum steam pressure on the piston, 140 pounds per square inch.

The maximum pressure on the piston will be

$$314.16 \times 140 = 43982.4 \text{ pounds.}$$

According to Rule 84, we have

$$\frac{43982.4}{7000} = 6.283+ \text{ square inches in the projected area.}$$

According to Rule 85, we have

$$\frac{6.283}{5} \times 4 = 5.02+.$$

The square root of 5.02 is $\sqrt{5.02} = 2.24$ inches, which is the length of the pin. And the diameter will be

$$2.24 \times 1.25 = 2.80 \text{ inches.}$$

Adopting the nearest fractions which are divisible by $\frac{1}{16}$ inch, we have for the length $2\frac{1}{4}$ inches, and for the diameter, $2\frac{7}{8}$ inches. By the term "length," we mean only that portion of the pin which is covered by the bushing, or the brass bearing, in which it works. An increase in the steam pressure of 10 pounds per square inch of piston will only slightly increase the dimensions of the pins; hence, in the following tables we have given one set of dimensions, suitable for steam pressures varying from 120 to 140 pounds per square inch of piston, and another set for steam pressures varying from 140 to 160 pounds per square inch.

TABLE 57.

DIMENSIONS OF KNUCKLE-JOINT PINS FOR MOGUL, TEN-WHEELED, AND CONSOLIDATION ENGINES, SUITABLE FOR MAXIMUM STEAM PRESSURES ON PISTONS VARYING FROM 120 TO 140 POUNDS PER SQUARE INCH.

| Diameter of Cylinders. | Diameter of Pins. | Length of Pins. |
|---|---|---|
| 11 | $1\frac{1}{2}$ inches. | $1\frac{1}{4}$ inches. |
| 12 | $1\frac{5}{8}$ " | $1\frac{3}{8}$ " |
| 13 | $1\frac{3}{4}$ " | $1\frac{7}{16}$ " |
| 14 | 2 " | $1\frac{9}{16}$ " |
| 15 | $2\frac{1}{8}$ " | $1\frac{11}{16}$ " |
| 16 | $2\frac{1}{4}$ " | $1\frac{3}{4}$ " |
| 17 | $2\frac{3}{8}$ " | $1\frac{7}{8}$ " |
| 18 | $2\frac{1}{2}$ " | 2 " |
| 19 | $2\frac{5}{8}$ " | $2\frac{1}{8}$ " |
| 20 | $2\frac{7}{8}$ " | $2\frac{1}{4}$ " |
| 21 | 3 " | $2\frac{3}{8}$ " |
| 22 | $3\frac{1}{4}$ " | $2\frac{1}{2}$ " |

## TABLE 58.

DIMENSIONS OF KNUCKLE-JOINT PINS FOR MOGUL, TEN-WHEELED, AND CONSOLIDATION ENGINES, SUITABLE FOR MAXIMUM STEAM PRESSURES ON PISTONS VARYING FROM 140 TO 160 POUNDS PER SQUARE INCH.

| Diameter of Cylinders. | Diameter of Pins. | Length of Pins. |
|:---:|:---:|:---:|
| 11 | $1\frac{7}{8}$ inches. | $1\frac{5}{16}$ inches. |
| 12 | $1\frac{3}{4}$ " | $1\frac{7}{16}$ " |
| 13 | 2 " | $1\frac{9}{16}$ " |
| 14 | $2\frac{1}{8}$ " | $1\frac{11}{16}$ " |
| 15 | $2\frac{1}{4}$ " | $1\frac{13}{16}$ " |
| 16 | $2\frac{3}{8}$ " | $1\frac{15}{16}$ " |
| 17 | $2\frac{1}{2}$ " | 2 " |
| 18 | $2\frac{5}{8}$ " | $2\frac{1}{8}$ " |
| 19 | $2\frac{7}{8}$ " | $2\frac{1}{4}$ " |
| 20 | 3 " | $2\frac{3}{8}$ " |
| 21 | $3\frac{1}{8}$ " | $2\frac{1}{2}$ " |
| 22 | $3\frac{1}{4}$ " | $2\frac{5}{8}$ " |

# CHAPTER VIII.

THROTTLE PIPES.—THROTTLE VALVE GEAR.—SAFETY VALVES.—WHISTLE.—PUMPS.—CHECK VALVES.

### THROTTLE VALVES.

349. Throttle valves are occasionally placed in the smoke-box, close to the front flue sheet; when placed there, the throttle valve is simply a plain slide, arranged so as to open or close rectangular ports, which lead the steam into the steam pipes; but the general practice is to place the throttle valve inside of the dome; and for such cases a double poppet valve is used. The design of this valve, and that of the throttle pipe, is shown in Figs. 492 and 493. The throttle valve consists of two disks, $E\ E$, cast to three or four wings, $F\ F$. The upper portion of each one of these disks is generally bounded by a cylindrical surface, and the lower portion, by a conical surface; the conical portions of the disks fit into seats of corresponding form in the throttle pipe. The angle formed by an element of this conical surface and the axis of the valve is often equal to 45 degrees, but sometimes it is less, as shown in our illustrations. Necessity demands a greater diameter for the upper disk than for that of the lower one, so as to enable us to pass the lower valve through the upper opening. A difference in the diameters of these disks is in nowise objectionable; in fact, it is desirable and advantageous for the following reason: the throttle pipe is surrounded by the steam in the boiler, and when the valve is closed a greater pressure will be on the upper disk than on the lower one, because the former exposes a larger area to the steam pressure than the latter. Under these conditions the valve has a tendency to remain closed when steam is shut off, which is of great importance, as this reduces the liability of engines running away, thus sometimes avoiding serious accidents.

The throttle valve is placed in a vertical position, and as high in the dome as possible, leaving between it and the dome-cover sufficient room only for raising the valve so as to obtain around it the necessary amount of opening for the admission of steam. The vertical distance through which the valve must be raised rarely exceeds $1\frac{1}{4}$ inches; often it is less.

The valve is made to fit the valve-stem $G$ quite easy, so as to give the valve ample freedom to come in contact with its seat throughout. The stem $G$ connects to the bell crank $B$, and the latter connects to the valve-rod $H$, which passes through the end of the boiler and connects to the throttle lever. The valve-stem $G$ is always made of wrought-iron; the bell crank $B$ is sometimes made of cast-iron, frequently of wrought-iron. The valve-rod $H$ is usually a plain, round wrought-iron bar, with brass, cast- or wrought-iron ends $I$ screwed on to it.

The throttle pipe, sometimes called the stand pipe, is occasionally made in two pieces, P and C, as shown in Fig. 493; and in many engines it is made in one piece. When made in two pieces, the joint between the flanges M M should be a ground one. This design of throttle pipe (that is, one made in two pieces) is generally used for a dome, having a portion of its top riveted to the dome sheet, leaving a comparatively small opening for a man to enter the dome for the purpose of making the connections

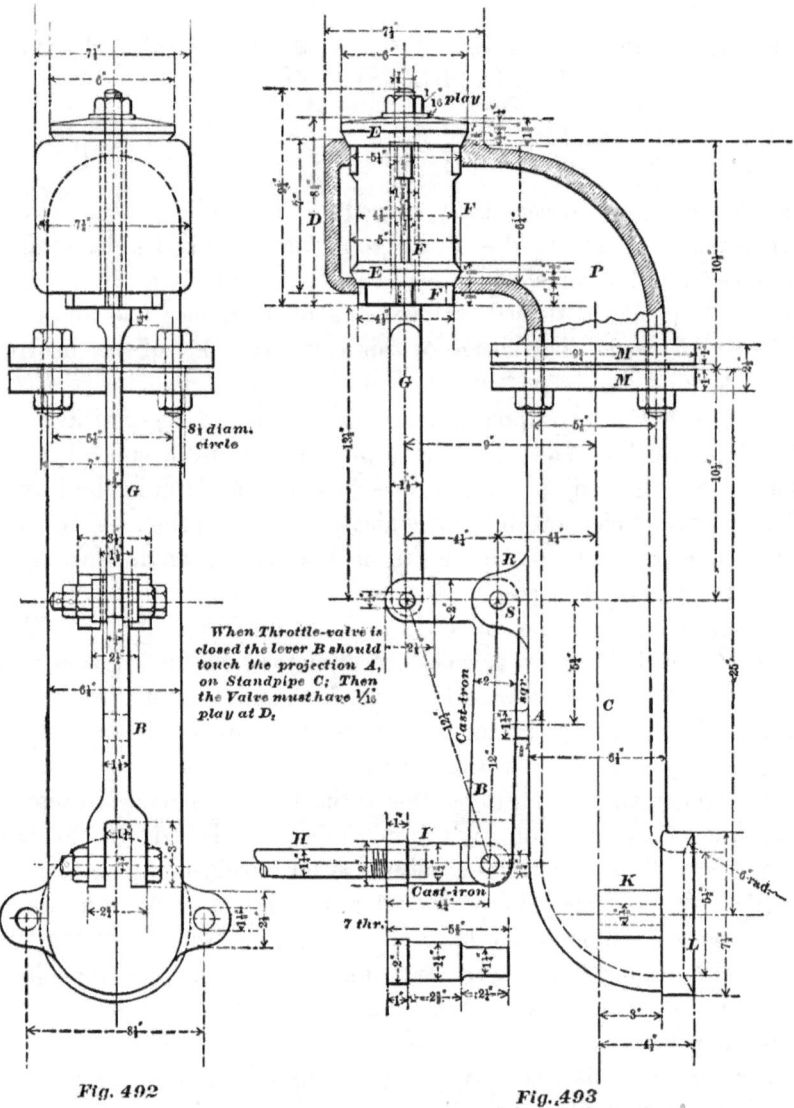

Fig. 492  Fig. 493

between the throttle and dry pipes, that between the bell crank and throttle rod, and others. In a dome with a small opening at top these connections cannot be conveniently made, and in some cases it is impossible to make them, with the throttle valve in position; hence the pipe is made in two pieces, so that everything can be properly and securely connected, before the upper portion P, containing the throttle valve, is placed in position. For domes whose whole top can be removed, throttle pipes made in one piece are suitable. Throttle pipes are always made of cast-iron, and therefore the throttle valves should also be made of the same metal, so as to obtain an equal rate of expansion in the valve and the pipe, thereby preventing leakage. It is on account of the difference in the rate of expansion of the different metals that brass valves in cast-iron pipes have proved to be a failure. Even cast-iron valves will expand lengthways a trifle more than the pipe, and this fact should not be overlooked in fitting the valve to its seat. In order to obtain a steam-tight joint, the valve is ground on its seats, until a perfect fit between both the upper and lower disks and their

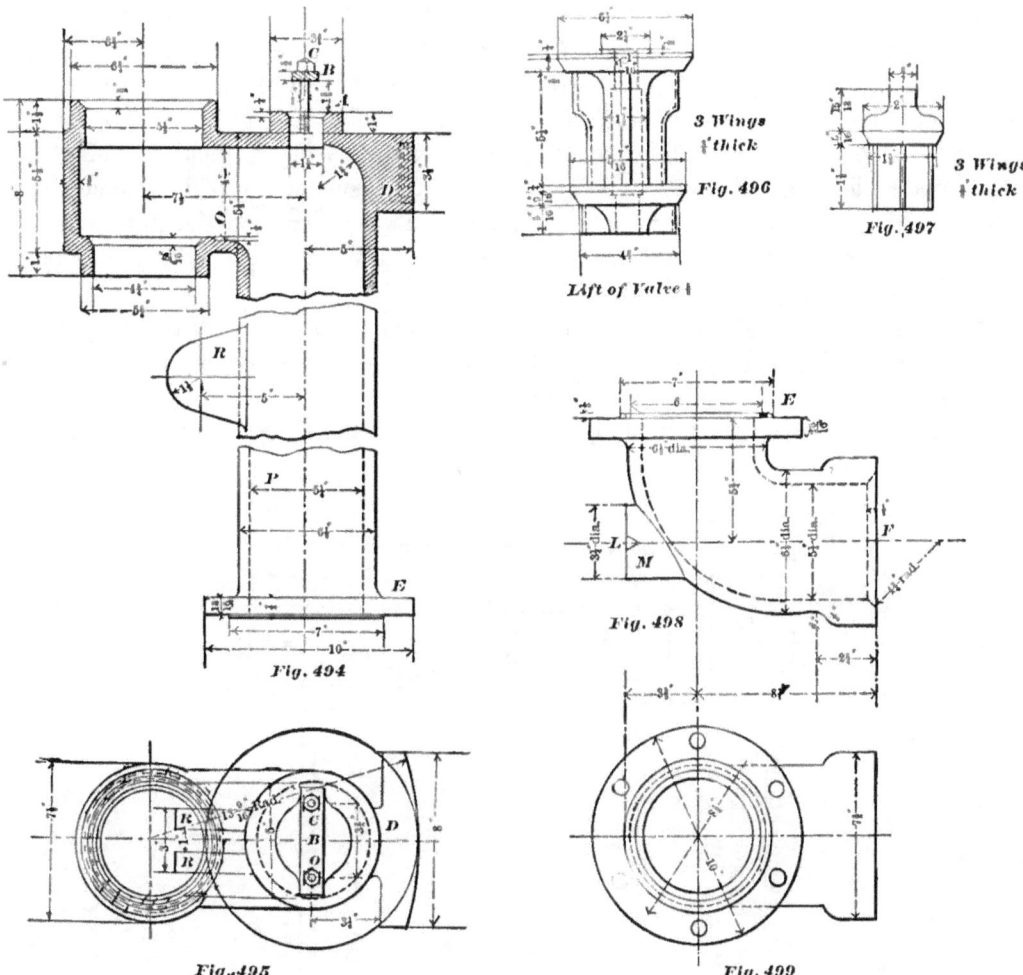

seats has been obtained; the emery should then be wiped off the upper disk and its seat, and a few extra turns given to the valves, so as to very slightly ease the fit between its lower disk and seat; fitting the valve in this manner will generally secure a steam-tight throttle when the engine is under steam.

350. Figs. 494, 495 represent another design of throttle pipe; Fig. 496 represents the valve. The principal difference between the throttle pipe shown in Fig. 493 and the one shown here is that the latter has at the top a seat $A$ for a small relief valve, which is shown in Fig. 497. The object of this relief valve is to prevent

the dry pipe $NN$ (Fig. 500) from bursting, which, without this valve, is liable to occur when the engine is suddenly reversed. Springs are not used for holding this valve on its seat; the steam pressure in the boiler is sufficient to do so. When the valve does lift, it is prevented from lifting too high by the small wrought-iron plate $B$, held in position by the two studs $CC$.

The elbow, Figs. 498, 499, is bolted to the throttle pipe; the joint $E$ is a ground joint.

The dry pipe $NN$ is made of wrought-iron; the thickness varies for different sizes of pipes from $\frac{5}{32}$ to $\frac{5}{16}$ inch; the former thickness is suitable for pipes 4 inches outside diameter. But dry pipes of the same diameter will not always have the same thickness, as master-mechanics will increase it to suit the steam pressure in the boiler; the thickness is also frequently increased for pipes longer than the average length of pipes. Dry pipes 7 inches outside diameter are the largest that we have seen used. We believe that for this size of pipe a thickness of $\frac{5}{16}$ inch is sufficient for the greatest length required in any locomotive. The smallest outside diameter of a dry pipe that we have seen used is 4 inches; the diameter for the next size is $4\frac{1}{2}$ inches; diameters larger than 5 inches increase by 1 inch. Dry pipes, like boiler tubes, are designated by their outside diameter.

351. A sleeve, generally made of brass, is attached to each end of the dry pipe. In some cases the dry pipe is slipped over the sleeves, but frequently the sleeves $I$ and $J$ are slipped over the dry pipe, as shown in Fig. 500.

When the diameter determined by the rule which we shall presently give agrees

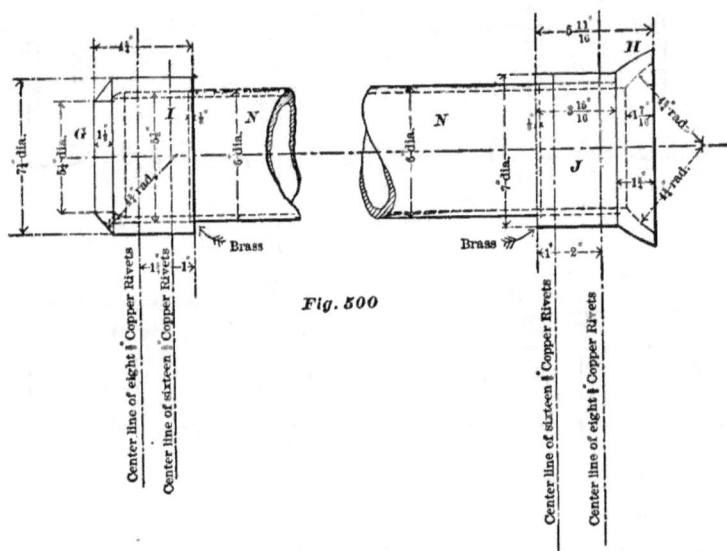

Fig. 500

with one of the standard diameters of pipes, the best practice is to put the dry pipe inside of the sleeves.

Some master-mechanics shrink the sleeves on to the pipe; others fasten them with rivets, generally $\frac{3}{8}$ inch diameter. Two rows of rivets, from $1\frac{1}{2}$ to 2 inches apart, are used. The pitch of rivets is generally from 2 to 3 inches. The rivets are arranged zigzag; in some instances twice as many rivets in one row as in the other are used, as shown in Fig. 500. Frequently, instead of using rivets, the holes through the sleeve and dry pipe are tapped, threaded plugs screwed in, and their ends slightly riveted over, to prevent them from turning and falling out. In our opinion, the best practice is to use iron rivets or plugs; copper rivets should be avoided, as the action of some kinds of water will produce corrosion between the iron and copper, and consequently cause leakage.

When the sleeves are placed on the outside of the pipe, and fastened with rivets or plugs, as mentioned, they are calked; or if the shape of the sleeve will allow it, the ends of the pipe are calked. Pipes placed on the outside of the sleeves always have their ends calked, but sleeves shrunk on the pipe are frequently not calked. Sometimes the ends of the pipe are threaded, and the sleeves screwed on; in such cases, calking will be a detriment.

352. The end $G$ of the sleeve $I$ (Fig. 500) is turned to a spherical form, and the elbow at $F$ (Fig. 498) is counterbored to a similar shape, so as to make a ball joint between

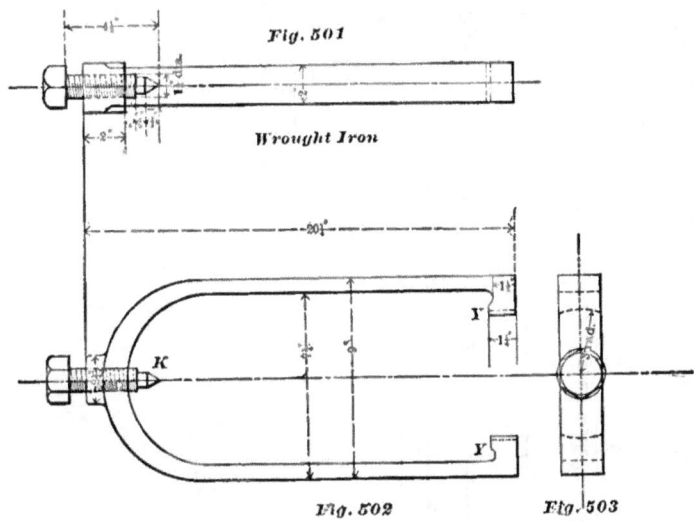

the two. For connecting the dry pipe to the elbow, the yoke shown in Figs. 501, 502, 503 is slipped over the sleeve $I$ and the elbow $F$; the lugs $Y Y$ are made to bear against the flat end of the sleeve, the point $K$ of the set screw is inserted in the countersunk cavity $L$ in the lug $M$ (Fig. 498), and the sleeve $I$ drawn tightly against spherical face $F$, and firmly held there. Although this mode of fastening the dry pipe to throttle pipe is often used, and gives good satisfaction, other designs for accomplishing the same thing are adopted; for instance, for a throttle pipe like that shown in Fig. 493, two hooked bolts instead of a yoke are used. But in all cases the joint between the throttle pipe and dry pipe is a ball joint, which affords ready means for adjusting the dry pipe to any inaccuracies which cannot be avoided in the construction of a boiler. The sleeve $J$ at the other end of the dry pipe (Fig. 500) is also made so as to form a ball joint, with a casting riveted to the front flue sheet; this casting or ring will be presently shown.

353. Figs. 504, 505 represent another throttle pipe, and Figs. 506, 507, 508 show some of its details. The design of this throttle pipe does not differ much from those previously shown. The principal differences are that the pipe is made in one piece, and that the sleeve $I$ is of a different form. The manner of fastening the

348                MODERN LOCOMOTIVE CONSTRUCTION.

dry pipe to the throttle pipe is plainly shown, and does not need any further explanation.

The favorite way of fastening the throttle pipe to the dome is plainly shown in

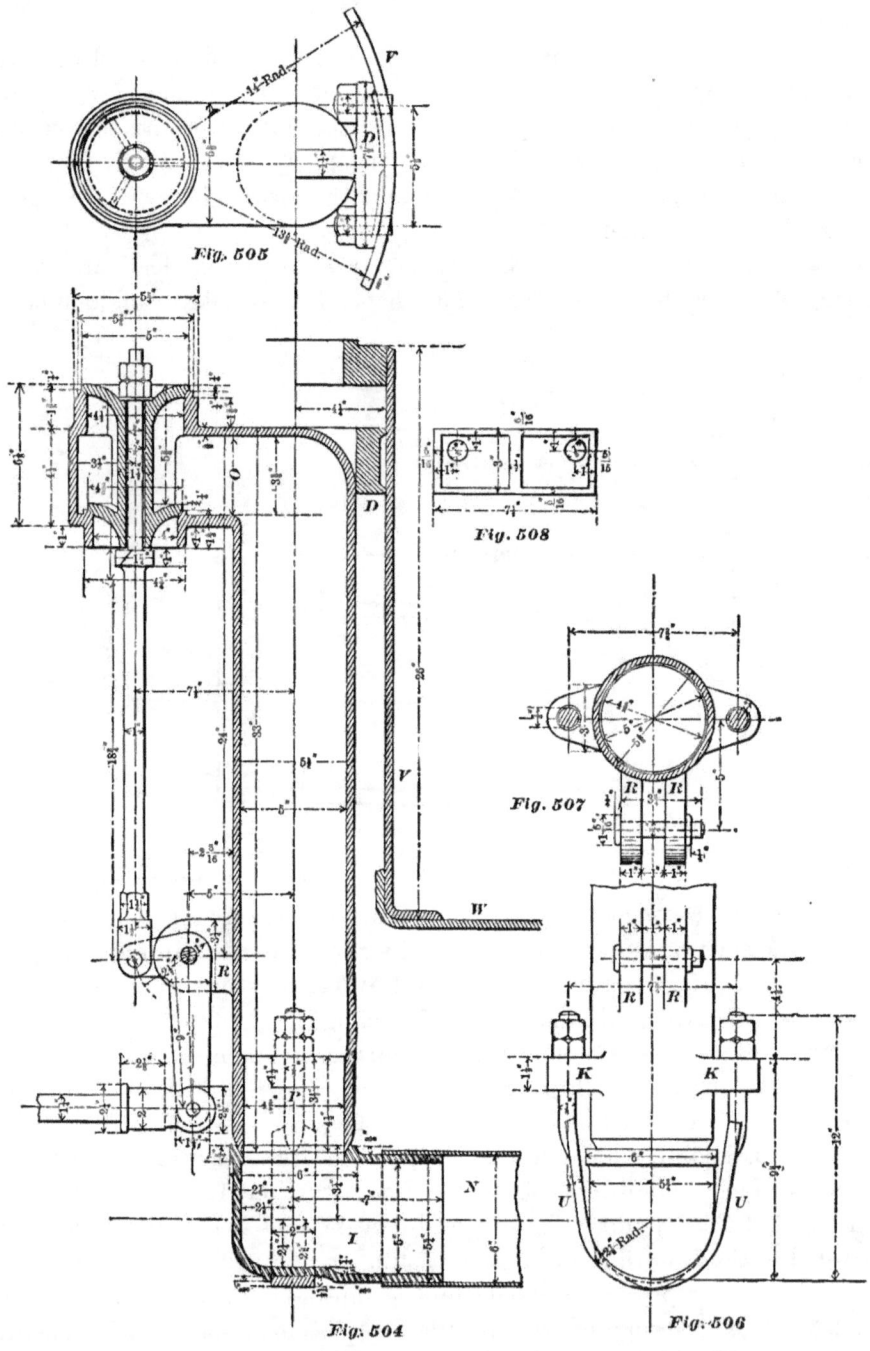

these figures. A bracket $D$ is cast to the throttle pipe, and fastened to the dome sheet $V$ by two studs. When possible, all dry pipes are allowed to rest on top of the crown bars. When this cannot be done, the dry pipe is suspended by a strap, usually made of $2 \times \frac{1}{2}$-inch iron, bolted to the boiler shell $W$.

The thickness of the throttle pipes is generally about $\frac{1}{2}$ to $\frac{5}{8}$ inch.

Fig. 504 represents a pipe exceptionally thin, the thickness being only $\frac{5}{16}$ of an inch; and for this reason the thickness at the lower end is increased, so as not to injure it in clamping the dry pipe to it.

The inner diameter of the throttle pipe is generally made proportionate to the diameter of the cylinder; the ratio between the two, as made by different builders, varies. Hence we sometimes find the inner diameter of the throttle pipe equal to one-quarter of the diameter of the cylinder, and frequently we find it to be equal to about one-third of the diameter of the cylinder. The latter we believe to be the best proportion, and should be adopted. When the inner diameter of the throttle pipe is not uniform throughout—for instance, if the throttle pipe is made similar to that shown in Fig. 504—the smaller diameter $P$ should be one-third of the diameter of the cylinder. The inner diameter of a throttle pipe should not be greater, in any case, than here given. If made much smaller, so that the cross-sectional area of the throttle pipe is less than one-tenth of the cross-sectional area of the cylinder, the initial steam pressure in the cylinder at high speeds will be reduced below the boiler pressure more than it would be otherwise, and the tractive power of the engine will be interfered with. On the other hand, practice seems to indicate that no advantage is gained by making the inner diameter of the throttle pipe greater than one-third of the diameter of the cylinder; in fact, throttle pipes and dry pipes too large in diameter are detriments to the engines, because an unnecessary quantity of steam held in these pipes must be worked off before the engine can be stopped, which is an objection in case of an emergency.

The cross-sectional area at $O$, Fig. 504, is generally rectangular in form; the length and breadth of this section should be so proportioned as to give an area equal to that through the cylindrical portion of the pipe.

354. The inner diameter of the dry pipe should be equal to that of the throttle pipe; but since in many cases the diameter of the pipe, determined by calculation, cannot be found among the standard diameters of dry pipes, the next larger size is adopted; and therefore we often find locomotives having dry pipes whose inner diameters are greater than those of the throttle pipes.

The outer diameter of the upper disk of the throttle valve is sometimes a little greater than the inner diameter of the throttle pipe; frequently it is less. A good rule is to make the outer diameter of the upper disk equal to one-third of the diameter of the cylinder. The outer diameter of the lower disk is made from $\frac{1}{8}$ to $\frac{1}{4}$ of an inch less than the diameter of the upper opening in the valve seat.

355. Fig. 510 represents a complete sectional view of the connections of the T-pipe and dry pipe $N$. The brass ring $B_2$ is riveted to the flue sheet $A$; another view of this ring is shown in Fig. 509. The six holes marked $s\ s$ in Fig. 509 are tapped for the studs marked $F\ F$ in Fig. 510; the remaining holes $r\ r$ are the rivet holes. The size of rivets and studs vary according to the size of engine; for small engines, say with cylinders 10 inches diameter, the rivets through the ring $B_2$ are generally $\frac{5}{8}$ inch diameter, and the studs $\frac{3}{4}$ inch diameter; for engines with cylinders

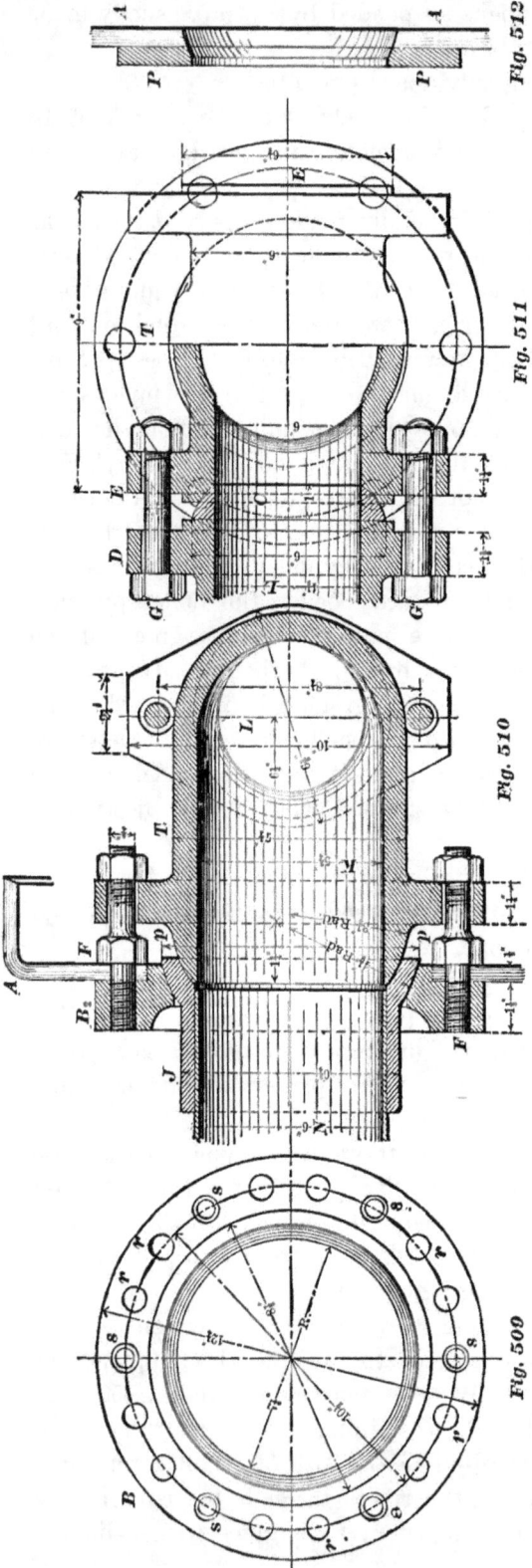

20 inches diameter, rivets ¾ inch diameter and studs 1 inch diameter are generally used. The flue sheet $A$ is bored out to receive the projection on the brass ring $B_2$. The spherical seat in this ring is made to fit the spherical surface on the sleeve $J$; this sleeve, we have seen in Art. 351, is riveted to the dry pipe $N$. The T-pipe has a spherical projection $p$, bearing against the surface of the counterbore in the sleeve $J$; some builders make this counterbore a conical surface; others make it a spherical surface as shown; but in all cases, the projection $p$ on the T-pipe is turned to a spherical form.

The diameter of the opening $R$ in the brass ring must be made sufficiently large to admit the sleeve on the other end of the dry pipe; this condition will determine to a great extent the size of the ball joint on the sleeve $J$. It will be seen that the studs $F\ F$ force the T-pipe against the sleeve $J$, and the latter is, in turn, pressed against the ring $B_2$, thus forming steam-tight joints between the whole.

Some builders do not use a brass ring $B_2$ for small locomotives, but use in place of it a wrought-iron plate $P\ P$, as shown in Fig. 512. In fact, some master-mechanics prefer the wrought-iron plate $P\ P$ for all sizes of engines, and consequently we frequently meet with large engines which have a plate of this kind in place of the brass ring. The plate is riveted to the flue sheet $A\ A$; the arrangement of rivets and studs for holding the T-pipe is similar to that in the brass ring as shown in Fig. 509. Both the flue sheet and the plate are then counterbored as shown, so as to form a bearing for the spherical part of the sleeve $J$.

356. The right-hand side of Fig. 511 represents an outside view of the T-pipe, and the left-hand side represents a section of the connection of the T-pipe and the steam pipe $D$. The steam pipes lead to the cylinders. A complete drawing of these pipes and their position in the smoke-box will be found in Fig. 24. In fact the illustrations here given simply show in detail and to a larger scale the connections of the dry pipe, T-pipe, and steam pipes.

The opening in the flanges $E\ E$ of the T-pipe are counterbored to a spherical form for the brass rings $C$, which are inserted between the T-pipe and steam pipes. Usually two bolts $G\ G$ are used for connecting each steam pipe to the T-pipe.

The inside diameter $K$ of the T-pipe must be equal to that of the throttle pipe. The area of the opening $L$ in the branches of the T-pipe should be equal to the inner cross-sectional area of the steam pipe. The rule for finding this area has been given in Art. 46.

357. Fig. 511A shows a throttle pipe arranged to take a device for furnishing dry steam to the cylinders. This is accomplished by separating the steam from the water

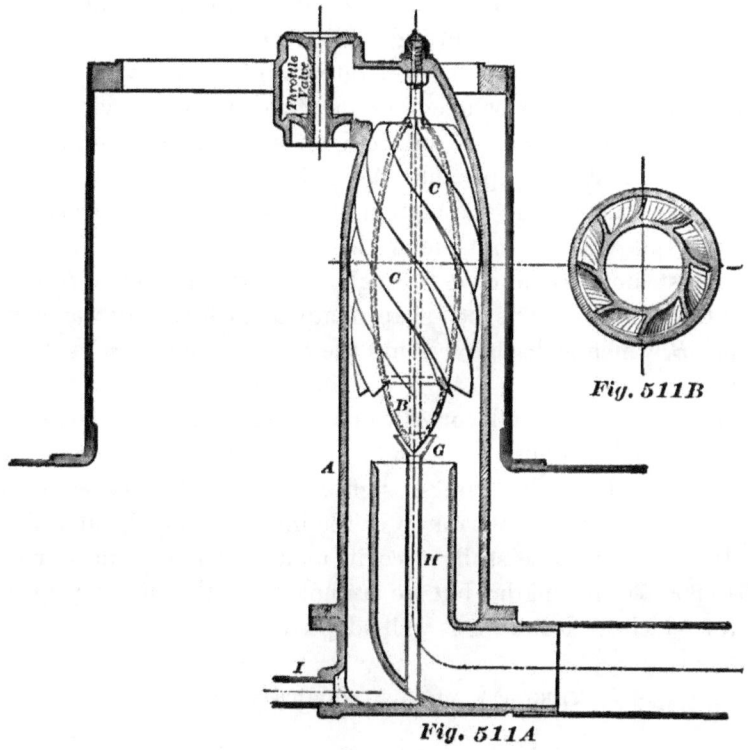

when the engine is running. The device is called a separator, and consists of a single casting with the necessary drain pipes for leading off the water after it has been separated from the steam. It will presently be seen that its construction is exceedingly simple; it is very durable, and requires very little or no attention.

The separator is cast in one piece. Its core $B$ is made hollow, and is gradually reduced from a comparatively large diameter at the center to a point at each end, so as to form a conoidal surface. A number of wings $C\ C$ are cast to this surface and extend spirally towards the ends of the core. This separator is set concentric with the throttle pipe, whose diameter is necessarily somewhat larger than that of an ordinary one. The separator does not rotate, but it is firmly attached to the pipe as shown.

In Fig. 511B it will be noticed that one side of each wing is formed tangential to the surface of the core, and the other side approaches a radial surface. The object of the whole construction is to divide the steam as it flows through the pipe into several smaller currents, and to give to each a compound whirling motion which is accomplished in the following manner. The core $B$ of the separator spreads the steam or, so to speak, expands it into an annular body, and the wings $C\ C$ divide it into several streams or currents, while their spiral forms impart to each current a whirling motion around the core; and the sides tangential to the surface of the core impart to each stream a whirling motion within itself. It will also be noticed that by expanding the steam into an annular body and cutting it up into several streams all the suspended particles of water will be affected by the whirling motion.

If, on the other hand, the solid stream as it enters the separator had not been expanded into an annular body, the whirling motion could not act on the particles of water in the center, and the action of the separator would thereby be impaired. The result of all this is that as the steam enters the throttle pipe a violent, compound whirling motion is imparted to all the particles of steam and water, all the heavier particles are thrown against the pipe, and the water thus separated from the steam flows into the annular chamber at the bottom of the throttle pipe, whence it is conducted through the tube $I$ to the outside of the boiler and may be fed back to it if desirable. The dry steam is conducted through the vertical branch $H$ into the dry pipe leading to the cylinders. The bell-shaped cup $G$ gathers any water which may flow along the core $B$, which is discharged into the tube $I$, which carries it off with the rest of the water.

In applying this separator to a locomotive nothing needs to be changed excepting the throttle pipe. There is nothing to get out of order, which is an important feature in mechanical devices which are placed out of sight and cannot be reached like a throttle pipe in a locomotive boiler. This separator is the invention of Mr. Joseph De Rycke of New York. It has been successfully used in many marine engines and on steam mains from 200 to 800 feet in length; but we are not aware that it has yet been applied to locomotives, for which we believe it is well adapted.

### THROTTLE VALVE CONNECTIONS.

358. There are various ways of attaching the throttle valve connections to the boiler. Sometimes we are compelled to run the throttle lever connections through the top of the boiler; but generally the throttle rod passes either through the back head of the boiler, or it passes through the sides of the dome. Figs. 513, 514, 515 represent a throttle valve lever and its attachment, suitable for engines in which the throttle rod $H$ is passed through the back head of the boiler.

The throttle lever is probably the simplest in design used on locomotives. The back head $P\ P$ of the boiler is bored out to receive the spherical portion of the stuffing-box $C$, the two forming a ball joint; this joint is a ground one, so as to make it perfectly steam tight. The stuffing-box is fastened to the boiler head by four studs, $L, M, K, K$; the studs $K, K$ are made long enough to take hold of the stuffing-box gland. The form of the nut on the stud $M$ is made suitable for receiving a pin, on which the two links $O, O$ vibrate. These links are connected to the throttle lever $A$, and act as a fulcrum. The throttle lever $A$ is connected to the throttle rod $H$ by means of the jaw $I$. In a few instances this jaw is screwed on to the rod $H$, but

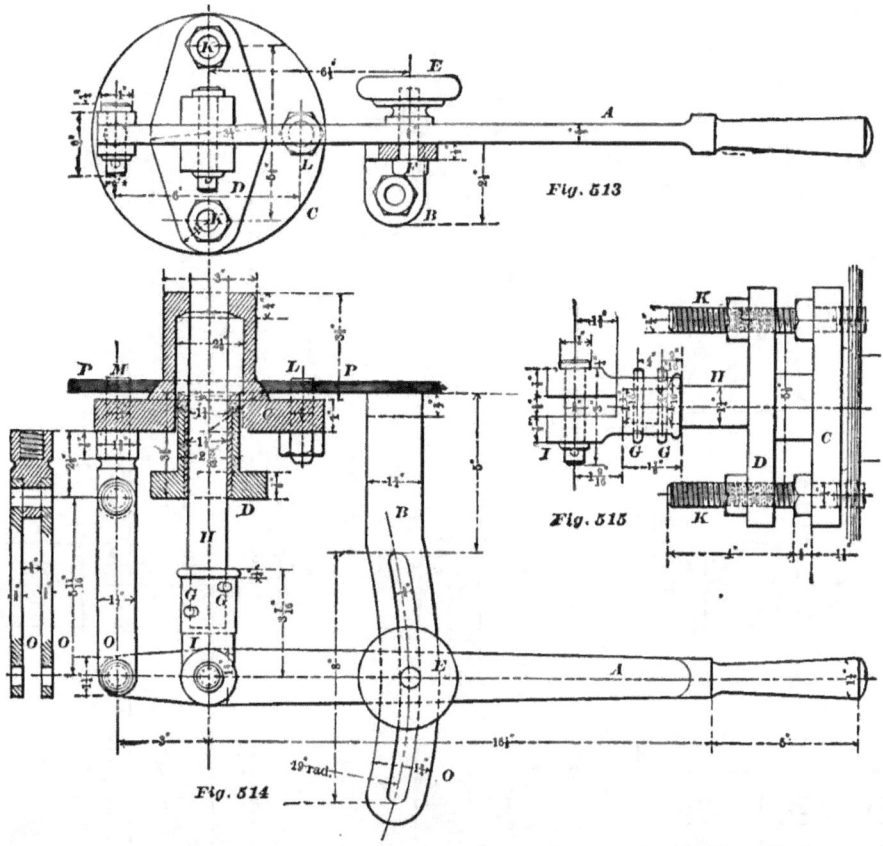

generally the jaw is bored out to a taper, accurately fitting the tapered end of the rod $H$, which is driven into the jaw, and held there by means of the tapered pins $G, G$; in some cases only one pin in place of two is used. The taper on the end of the rod $H$ is generally $\frac{1}{8}$ inch in 2 inches. The throttle lever rests on the quadrant $B$, which is fastened to the boiler head by means of one stud; in a few instances two studs are used for the same purpose. Through the quadrant $B$, a slot is cut for the clamping bolt $F$; the nut $E$ for this bolt is capped with wood. The throttle lever $A$ is clamped to the quadrant $B$ in any position which gives the throttle valve in the dome the desired degree of opening.

This design of lever is often adopted on account of its simplicity; but it is not a convenient one for the engineer to handle, because in order to open, close, or adjust the throttle valve with this kind of lever the engineer may have to use both hands, which is not only inconvenient, but in case of an emergency is objectionable.

**359.** Figs. 516, 517 represent a throttle lever and attachments designed to remove the objectionable feature inherent in the former one. The principal difference between the two designs lies in the design of the quadrant $B$.

In Fig. 516 it will be seen that on the convex edge of the quadrant $B$ notches are cut which engage with corresponding teeth on the end of the latch $S$; this latch is connected to the handle $R$ by the link $T$. It will readily be perceived that, with this arrangement, the engineer can

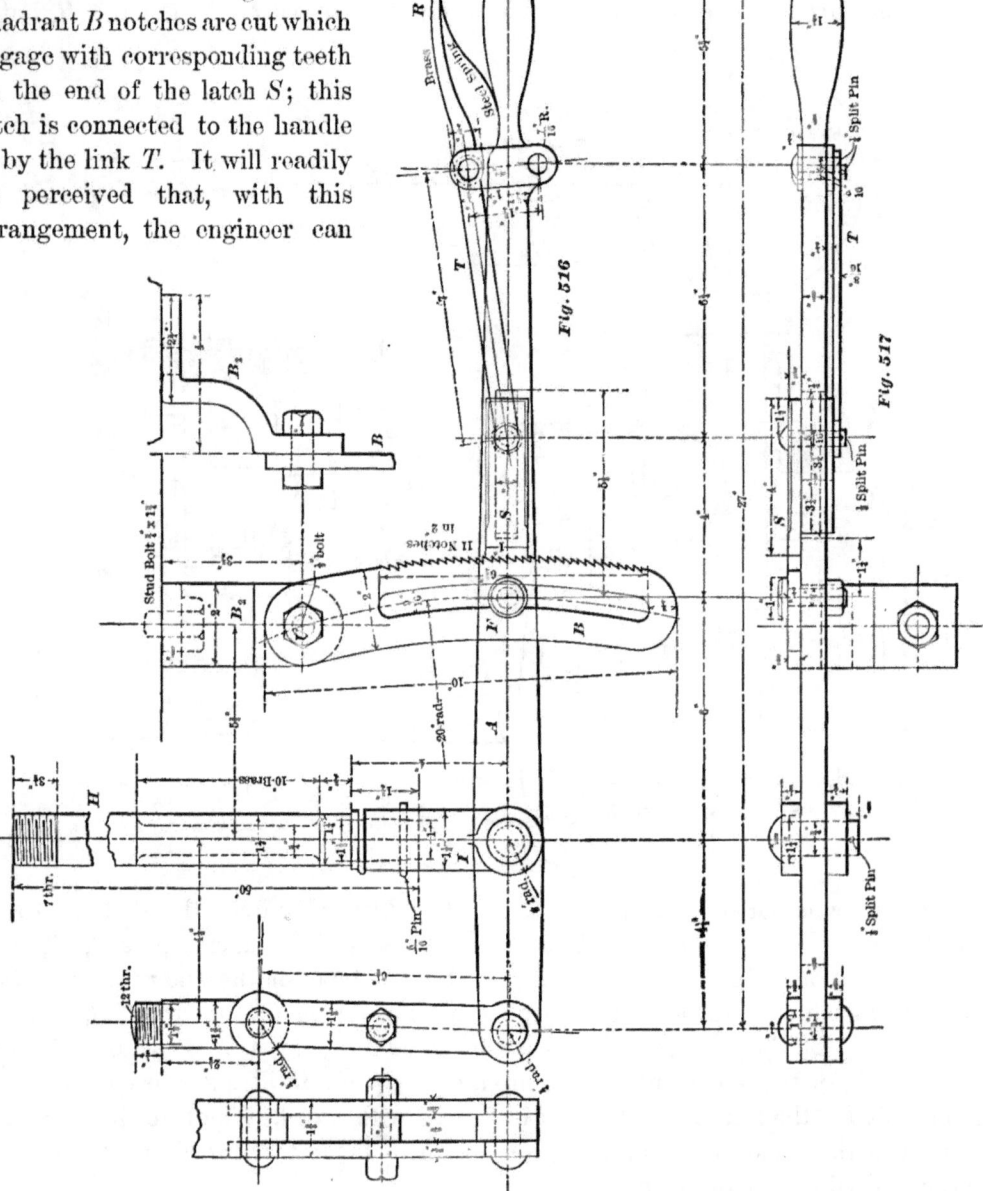

with one hand disengage the latch, move the lever into any position, and allow it to lock itself there.

The manner of fastening the quadrant $B$ (Fig. 516) to the boiler differs somewhat from that shown in Fig. 514. In the former figure it will be noticed that a bracket $B_2$

is fastened to the boiler, and the quadrant $B$ is attached to this bracket. In many engines the bolt $U$ does not hold the quadrant $B$ rigidly to the bracket, but allows it to vibrate a little, so as to adjust itself to any position of the lever $A$. Under these conditions, we need in the quadrant $B$ a slot cut equidistant from the notched edge of the arc. In this slot a bolt $F$ is accurately fitted, and prevents a disengagement of the quadrant $B$ and the latch $S$. These are usually placed above the lever; in such cases, the bolt $F$ will tend to prevent the lever from moving out of its appointed plane of action, and help to produce steadiness of motion.

360. The diameter of the throttle rod $H$ varies for the different sizes of engines; for small engines it is about $\frac{3}{4}$ inch, and for large engines about $1\frac{1}{4}$ inches.

To place the throttle rod $H$ in position, it must be passed through the stuffing-box; hence, collars on the rod are not admissible. When these rods are made of uniform diameter throughout, they must be turned throughout their whole length; to save time in turning, a large portion of the rod, extending to within a short distance from the ends, is forged about $\frac{1}{16}$ of an inch smaller in diameter than the required finished diameter at the ends, leaving at the throttle-lever end a portion to be finished, of a length only as may be required for the movement of the rod in the stuffing-box, and leaving at the throttle-pipe end a portion of such a length as may be required for the thread.

Sometimes that part of the rod which works in the stuffing-box is provided with a brass casing, as shown in Fig. 516. This brass casing is cast on the rod; its object is to prevent a collection of rust between the rod and stuffing-box. The portion of the rod covered by the brass casing is generally forged to an octagon form.

361. The stuffing-box is generally made of cast-iron, sometimes of brass. For large engines the stuffing-box gland is often made of cast-iron. Glands made of cast-iron have always a brass bushing. The bushing is sometimes driven into the gland with a hammer, and sometimes it is pressed in by a hydraulic press with a pressure of about 100 pounds.

For small engines, the gland is often made of brass. The principal proportions of the gland and stuffing-box are found by the rule given in Arts. 192, 193, 194, and 195.

362. The quadrants $B$, having a form similar to that shown in Fig. 514, are made of brass, and when they are made like that shown in Fig. 516 they should be made of the best hammered iron or steel, so as to prevent wear of the notches. The shape of the notches is similar to that of the teeth in an ordinary circular saw; the notches are cut so as to bring their radial sides towards the boiler. Notches of this kind will prevent the throttle valve from flying open, and allow it to be very easily closed.

363. Sometimes the throttle lever $A$ is placed in a horizontal position; in many engines it points upward, and occasionally it points downward.

The proper position of the throttle lever will depend on the position of the stuffing-box in the back head, and the position of the reverse lever.

The stuffing-box is placed as high in the back head as is possible and practical to do, and determines the position of that part of the throttle lever which is connected to the throttle rod. The handle of the throttle lever should be as close as possible to the handle of the reverse lever, the latter being placed in a convenient position for the engineer to reach; hence in this way the position of the end of the throttle lever is found, and the plane in which it is to move is established.

The distance between the extremity of the throttle-lever handle and that of the reverse lever should be about 2½ to 3 inches, so as to prevent the engineer from jamming his hand between the two; hence this condition will determine the length of that part of the throttle lever which extends from the center of the throttle rod to the extremity of the handle.

364. The objection raised to the throttle lever shown in Figs. 516, 517 is that the pitch of the teeth on the quadrant $B$ will limit the degree of opening of the throttle valve,

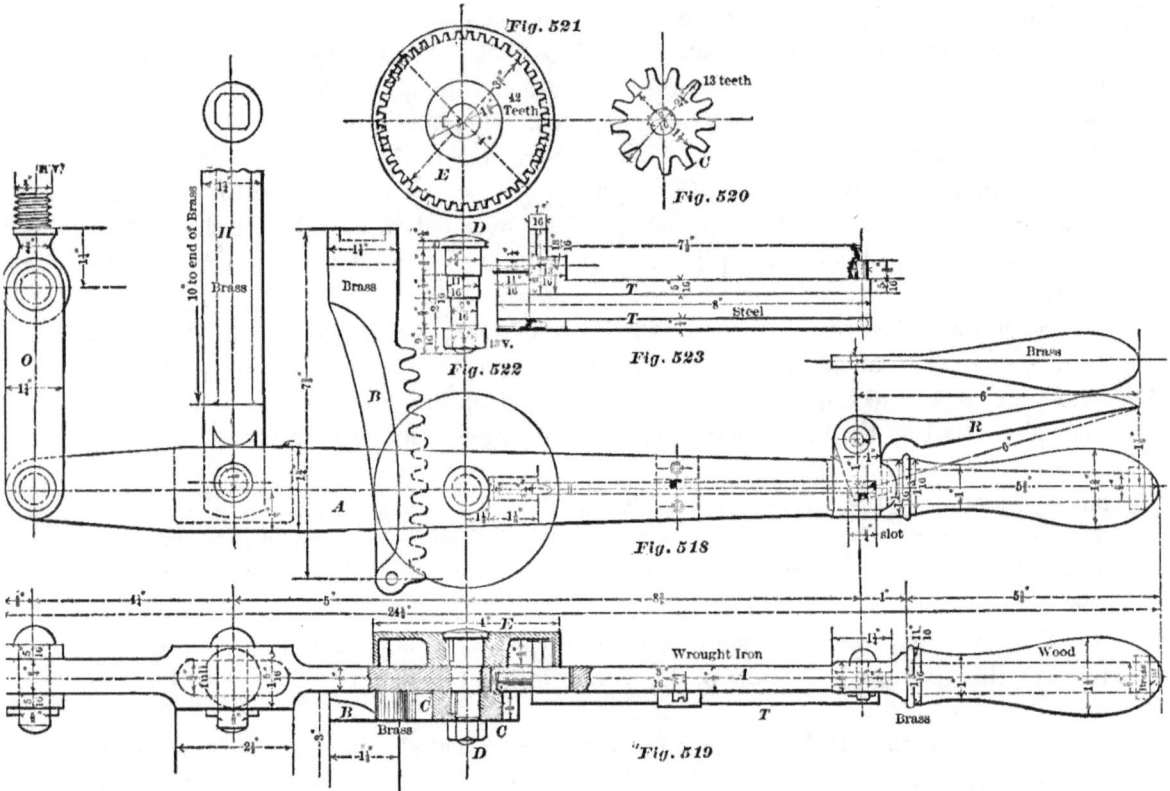

and in some cases will not be as close to the requirements of the engine as may be desirable. Again, on account of the fine pitch of the teeth in the quadrant $B$, strength, and consequently security, will be impaired; and also in some cases the wear of the teeth is objectionable.

Figs. 518, 519 represent a throttle-valve lever designed to overcome these objections. In this arrangement a curved rack $B$ instead of a quadrant is introduced; the rack is placed under the lever $A$. This rack engages with a small pinion $C$ keyed to the stud $D$; to the same stud is keyed another wheel $E$, larger in diameter than the pinion; the wheel $E$ is an internal-spur wheel, whose teeth engage with the link $T$, preventing the stud $D$ from turning, and thus locks the throttle lever in the desired position. The reason for placing the teeth inside of the wheel $E$ is simply to obtain a pleasing effect, exposing to view plain and polished surfaces, which can be kept clean. The link $T$ is connected to the handle $R$, the spring $S$ holds the link $T$ in contact with the teeth in the wheel $E$. In pressing the handle $R$ towards the throttle-lever handle, a disengagement of the link $T$ and the wheel $E$ takes place, enabling the engineer to move the throttle lever to and fro with ease.

In this arrangement the wear of the teeth in the rack will be less than the wear of the teeth in the quadrant shown in Fig. 516; also, because the pitch of the teeth in the rack and in the wheel $E$ is greater than the pitch of the teeth in the quadrant $B$ (Fig. 516), the strength of this arrangement, and security, is increased. A very close adjustment of the throttle valve to the requirements of the engine can also be obtained; indeed, this closeness of adjustment largely depends upon the difference between the diameters of the wheel $E$ and the pinion $C$. For instance, suppose that the pinion $C$ makes just one complete turn in lifting the throttle valve one inch, then the wheel $E$ must of course also make one complete turn during the same time; if now the wheel $E$ has 42 teeth, then it must be obvious that the throttle valve can be set to $\frac{1}{42}$ inch; and if a closer regulation is required without changing the pitch of the teeth in the wheel $E$, then we have only to increase its diameter so as to enable us to increase the number of teeth.

365. The method for finding the length and curvature of the pitch line for the rack $B$ is the same as that for finding the length and curvature of the quadrants $B$ in Figs. 514 and 516. In order to explain this method, we have shown in Fig. 524 a portion of the

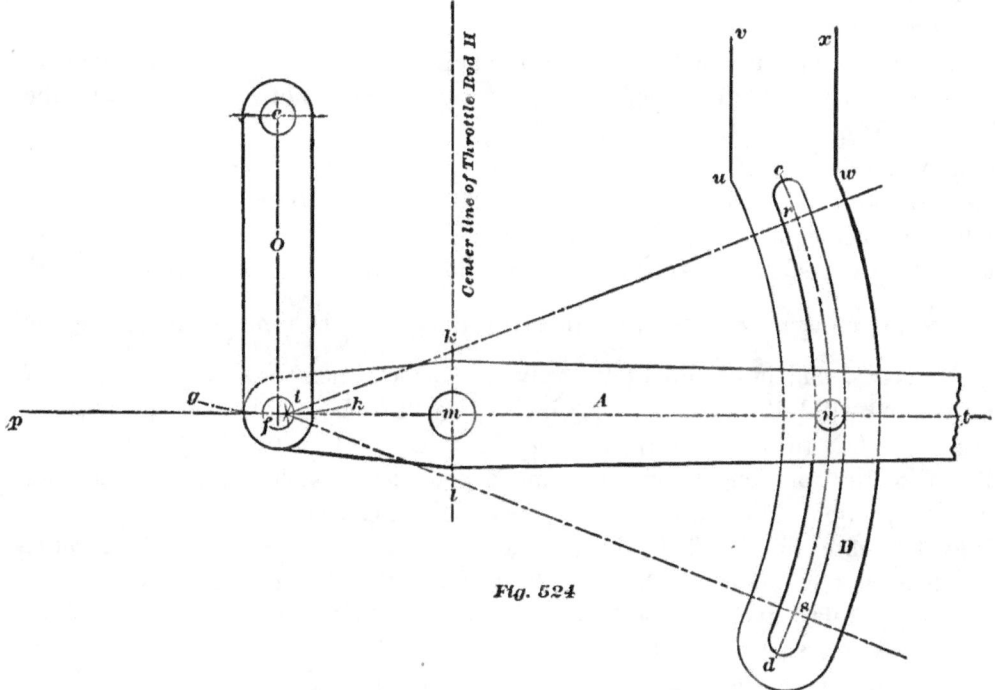

Fig. 524

throttle lever $A$, the links $O$, and a portion of the quadrant $B$. Before we can determine the length and curvature of the quadrant we must know the lift of the throttle valve; hence the following problems present themselves: first, to find the lift of the throttle valve; second, to find the length of the arc $c\,n\,d$; third, to find the radius of the same arc.

First, to find the lift of the throttle valve. To explain this, we shall refer to Fig. 504. In this figure we see that the smallest inner diameter ($4\frac{5}{8}$ inches) of the throttle pipe is at the bottom of the pipe; the area of a circle $4\frac{5}{8}$ inches diameter is 16.80 square inches; hence the throttle valve must have a lift which will allow such a quantity of steam to enter as can pass through an area of 16.80 square inches. Again, we see that the valve seats are of a conical form; but, for the sake of simplicity in finding the lift, the valve seats are assumed to be flat. Under these conditions the lift of the valve must be such that, when the circumferences of the inner edges of the valve seats are multiplied by the lift, the area thus obtained will be equal to the smallest inner cross-sectional area of the pipe, which in our case is 16.80 square inches.

In Fig. 504 we see that the diameter of the inner edge of the upper throttle-valve seat is $4\frac{1}{2}$ inches, hence its circumference will be $4.5 \times 3.1416 = 14.13+$ inches; the diameter of the inner edge of the lower valve seat is 4 inches, its circumference will be $4 \times 3.1416 = 12.56+$ inches; the sum of the two circumferences will be $14.13 + 12.56 = 26.69$ inches; hence in the case before us the lift will be $\frac{16.80}{26.69} = .62+$ inch. But this lift is suitable only for flat valve seats, and will not give us a sufficient opening for conical valves. In nearly all locomotives the inclination of the valve seat varies but little from an angle of 45 degrees from the axis, and therefore we will generally obtain good results by adding 50 per cent. to the lift just found; hence the lift for the valve shown in Fig. 504 should be $.62 + .31 = .93$ inch. From the foregoing we may establish the following rule:

RULE 86.—Divide the smallest cross-sectional area of the throttle pipe by the sum of the circumferences of the openings in the valve seats; add 50 per cent. to the quotient; the sum will be the lift of the valve.

If now the lengths of the arms of the bell crank to which the valve-stem and throttle rods are connected had been equal, the throttle rod $H$ would have to move through a distance of .93 inch. But in Fig. 504 we see that the arm of the bell crank to which the valve-stem connects is $2\frac{1}{2}$ inches long, and the other arm is 9 inches long, hence the movement of the throttle rod will be $\frac{9}{2\frac{1}{2}} = 3.6$ times greater than the lift of the valve; and if the lift of the valve is .93 inch, then the total movement of the throttle rod will be $3.6 \times .93 = 3.348$ inches, say $3\frac{3}{8}$ inches.

Second, to find the length of the arc $c\,d$, Fig. 524.

To make the solution of our problem as plain as possible, let us assume that Fig. 524 is a portion of the throttle work, as shown in Fig. 514.

Draw the center line $k\,l$ of the throttle rod $H$, and on it lay off two points, $k$ and $l$; the distance between these points must be equal to the travel or movement of the throttle rod; if this travel is to be $3\frac{3}{8}$ inches, as found by the foregoing calculations, then make the distance between $k$ and $l$ equal to $3\frac{3}{8}$ inches. When the throttle-valve is one-half open, or, in other words, when it stands in the center of its lift, the center line $p\,t$ of the throttle lever $A$ stands generally parallel to the back end of the boiler and the center line $e\,f$ of the link $O$ stands perpendicular to $p\,t$, as shown in Fig. 514. Under these conditions, draw through the center $m$ (Fig. 524) of the movement $k\,l$ a line $p\,t$ perpendicular to $k\,l$, and a line $e\,f$ perpendicular to $p\,t$, cutting the latter in the point $f$; the distance between the lines $k\,l$ and $e\,f$ must of course be equal to the given distance between the center line of the link $O$ and the center line of the throttle rod; in Fig. 514 we see that this distance is 3 inches. The point $f$ will be the center of the fulcrum pin through the end of the lever $A$, and the point $m$ will be the center of the pin through the lever $A$ and the throttle rod $H$. On the line $p\,t$ lay off a point $n$, and make the distance between $m$ and $n$ equal to the given distance between the center of the pin $m$ and the center of the clamping bolt; in Fig. 513 we see that this distance is $6\frac{1}{2}$ inches. Now, the center $e$ in the link $O$ will be stationary, the center $f$ will move along the arc $g\,h$ described from the center $e$, and the center $m$ will move along the straight line $k\,l$. Therefore from the point $k$ as a center, and with a radius equal to the distance between $f$ and $m$, describe a short arc cutting the arc $g\,h$ in the point $i$, join the points $i$ and $k$ by a straight line, and prolong it towards $r$. Again, from the point $l$ as a center, and with a radius equal to $f\,m$, describe a short arc cutting the arc $g\,h$; the point in which these two arcs intersect will very nearly coincide with the point $i$, previously found; for all practical purposes we may assume that these points coincide. Through the points $i$ and $l$ draw a straight line, and prolong it towards $s$. Make $k\,r$ equal to $m\,n$; also make $l\,s$ equal to $m\,n$.

When the throttle valve is closed, the center line of the throttle lever $A$ will coincide with the line $i\,r$, and the point $r$ will be the position of the center of the clamping bolt. When the throttle valve is full open, the center line of the throttle lever $A$ will coincide with the line $i\,s$, and the point $s$ will be the position of the center of the clamping bolt. The arc $r\,n\,s$ will represent the length of the path of the center of the clamping bolt. In practice it is customary to make the arc $r\,n\,s$ about 1 inch longer than length just found, consequently the length of the arc $c\,n\,d$ will be equal to the sum of the arc $r\,n\,s$, as found by construction, plus the diameter of the clamping bolt, plus 1 inch.

Third, to find the radius of the arc $c\,n\,d$. This arc will not coincide exactly with an arc of a circle, yet the difference is so slight that it may be neglected, and for all practical purposes we may assume that the arc $c\,n\,d$ is an arc of a circle. Now, the points $r\,n\,s$ are points in this arc, hence all that is necessary is to find a point $p$, from which an arc can be described which will pass through the three points $r\,n\,s$; the distance from $p$ to any one of these points will, of course, be the required radius.

Probably the quickest way to find the point $p$ is by trial; it can also be found in a geometrical way, by joining the points $r$ and $n$ by a straight line; also joining the points $n$ and $s$ by a straight line. Then bisect the lines $r\,n$ and $n\,s$ by perpendicular lines; the point in which these perpendiculars intersect will be the center $p$ from which the arc $r\,n\,s$ is to be described.

The lines $u\,v$ and $w\,x$ extend, and are perpendicular to the back head of the boiler; the distance between the center line of the throttle rod $H$ and the line $u\,v$ will depend on the position of rivets in the head of the boiler, and this distance should be so adjusted that the stud or studs which fasten the quadrant $B$ to the boiler will be clear of the rivet heads.

366. The following figures represent a throttle-lever arrangement for engines, in which the throttle rod passes through the side of the dome. Similar letters in the different views indicate the same details.

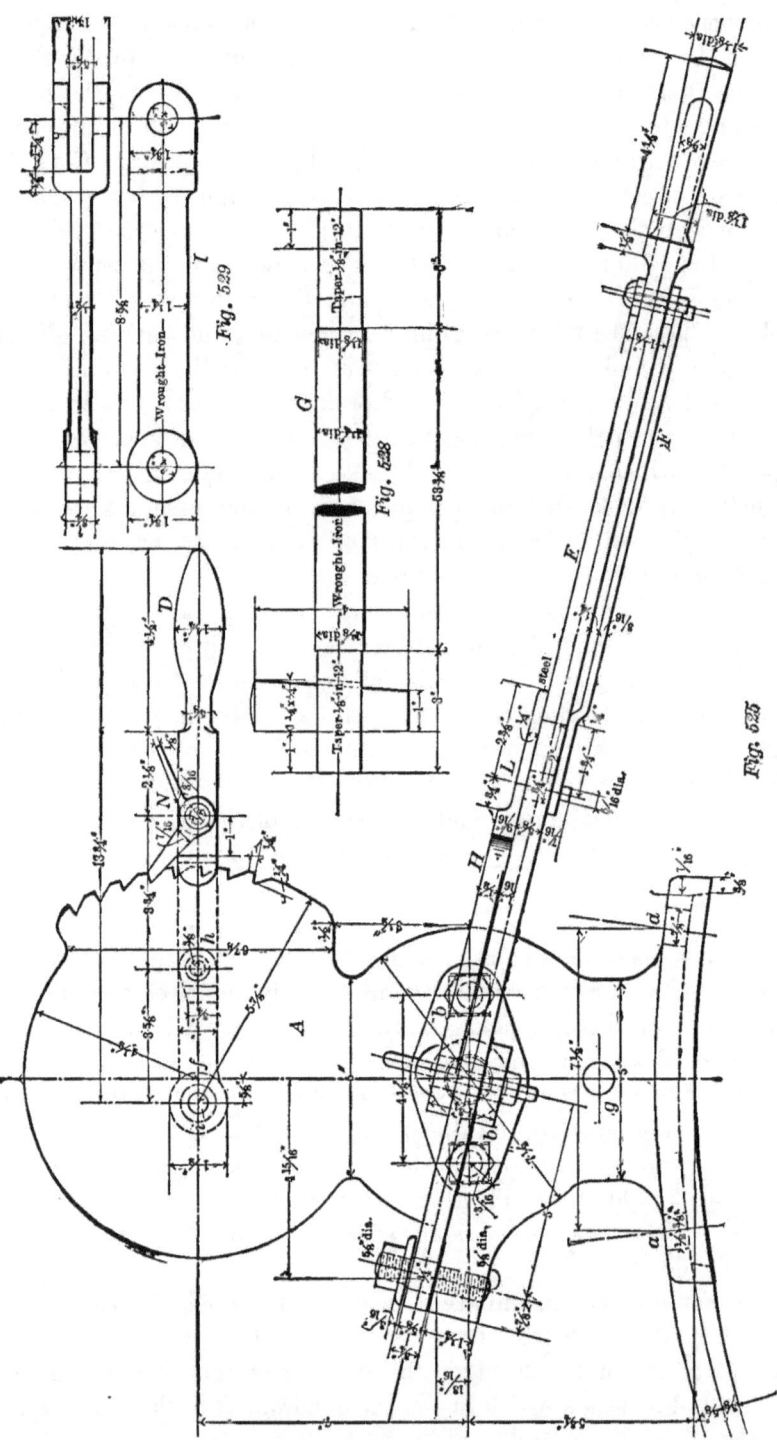

Fig. 525 represents this throttle-lever arrangement as seen from the back end of the boiler. Fig. 526 is a plan of the same; Fig. 527, a section of the steam-gauge stand, stuffing-box, gland, and steam-pipe connecting the steam-gauge stand to the dome; Fig. 528 shows the throttle rod, and Fig. 529 the link used for connecting the throttle lever to the steam-gauge stand.

The steam-gauge stand marked *A* is often made of cast-iron, sometimes of brass,

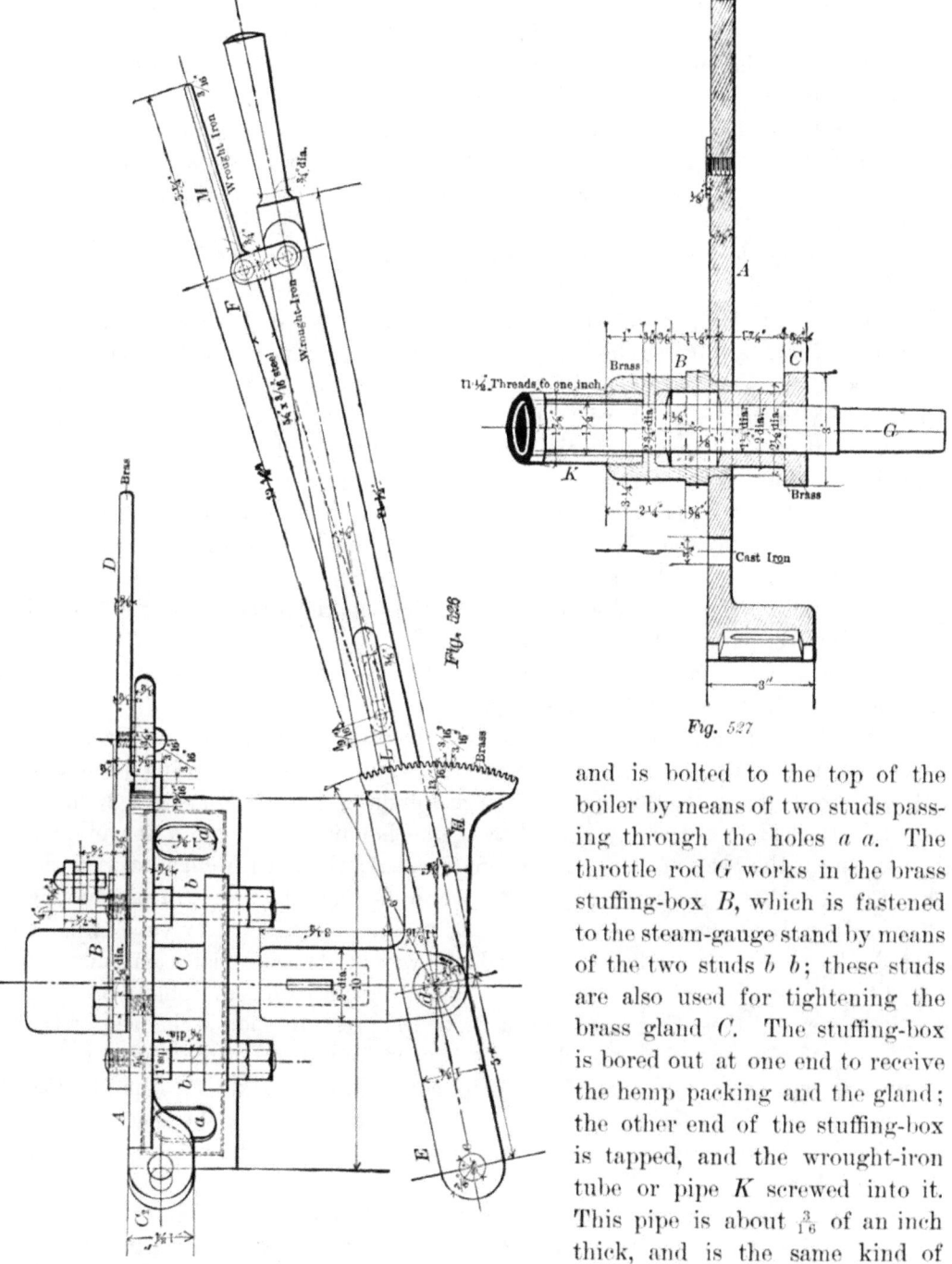

Fig. 527

and is bolted to the top of the boiler by means of two studs passing through the holes *a a*. The throttle rod *G* works in the brass stuffing-box *B*, which is fastened to the steam-gauge stand by means of the two studs *b b*; these studs are also used for tightening the brass gland *C*. The stuffing-box is bored out at one end to receive the hemp packing and the gland; the other end of the stuffing-box is tapped, and the wrought-iron tube or pipe *K* screwed into it. This pipe is about $\frac{3}{16}$ of an inch thick, and is the same kind of tubing as used for water grates, to which we shall refer later on. The other end of the pipe *K* is screwed into a small brass flange; the latter is riveted to the outside of the dome, and is completely covered by the dome casing. The pipe $K$ is not bored out; its inner diameter is somewhat larger than the diameter of throttle rod $G$, so as to give the latter ample freedom for its motion. The purpose of the pipe $K$ is to cover and protect the throttle rod, and in the meantime bring the stuffing-box $B$ and gland $C$—which are required in any case—within easy reach of the engineer.

In this design the jaw $H$ and the jaw at the opposite end of the throttle rod are keyed to the latter, as indicated in Fig. 528; this way of fastening the jaws to the throttle rod differs a little from the manner of fastening similar jaws on rods, as previously illustrated. The wrought-iron link $I$ forms a connection between the throttle lever $E$ and the lug $C_2$ cast to the steam-gauge stand $A$, and serves as a fulcrum for the former.

The manner of locking the lever $E$ differs greatly from any of the previous designs. The upper side of the jaw $H$ (Figs. 525, 526) is extended sideways and formed into a circular rack; the pitch of the teeth is very fine, so as to obtain a regulation of the lift of the throttle valve as close as possible to the requirements of the engine; yet with this arrangement it will be difficult, if not impracticable, to obtain as close a regulation as with the design shown in Fig. 518. A steel latch $L$, having three or four teeth cut in its end, engages with the rack. The lug forged to the bottom of the latch, and sliding in a slot cut through the lever, serves as a guide for the latch; the link $F$ connects the latch to the handle $M$, which, in being pressed towards the throttle-lever handle, disengages the latch from the rack, and leaves the lever free to move. In moving the lever to and fro, the latch $L$ will move faster than the pin $d$, and it is on account of the difference between the rates of these motions that when the latch $L$ engages with the circular rack the lever is locked.

The steam-gauge is fastened to the upper part of the stand $A$; the center $f$ of this part coincides with the center of the steam-gauge.

The handle $D$ $D$, Figs. 525, 526, is for the purpose of opening one of the safety valves, or regulating the pressure on the same; the pin $h$ connects a spring balance—not shown—to the lever $D$; this spring balance stands in a vertical position, with its upper end attached to the safety-valve lever; the handle $D$ swings on the pivot $i$, which is cast on the back of the steam-gauge stand $A$; the pawl $N$ engages with the teeth cut on the edge of the steam-gauge stand, and prevents the lever $D$ from moving upwards. In pulling the lever downwards, the pressure on the safety valve will be increased. The safety valves and spring balance will be described later on; all that we need to say here is that two safety valves are always used for a locomotive boiler, and it is only one of these that can be released, or the pressure upon it changed by the lever $D$; the other safety valve is or should be beyond the control of the engineer.

Fig. 530 represents a wrought-iron steam-gauge lamp bracket for the throttle valve gear shown in Fig. 525; its end $p$ is inserted in the hole $g$ in the lower part of the stand $A$, and fastened there; the steam-gauge lamp is screwed on to the end $l$ of the lamp bracket.

367. In this design of throttle-valve gear the pitch line of the teeth in the circular rack must be described from the center $d$, Fig. 526, and not from a center lying to the left of it—for instance, such as we were compelled to find by the construction shown in Fig. 524.

For obtaining the length of the circular arc—that is, the distance from $h$ to $i$, Fig. 531—we simply describe from the center $d$ the arc $h\,i$, which contains the outer extremities of the teeth, and then proceed as follows:

Let the point $d$, Fig. 531, represent the position of the center of the pin when the throttle valve is closed. Through the point $d$ draw the center line $m\,n$ of the valve-rod, and on this line mark off a point $d_2$; the distance between the points $d$ and $d_2$ must be equal to the distance through which the center $d$ of the pin will travel to open the throttle valve fully; this distance is found as explained in Art. 365, and is usually about two inches, or a little more; in some cases it may be as much as $2\tfrac{1}{2}$ inches.

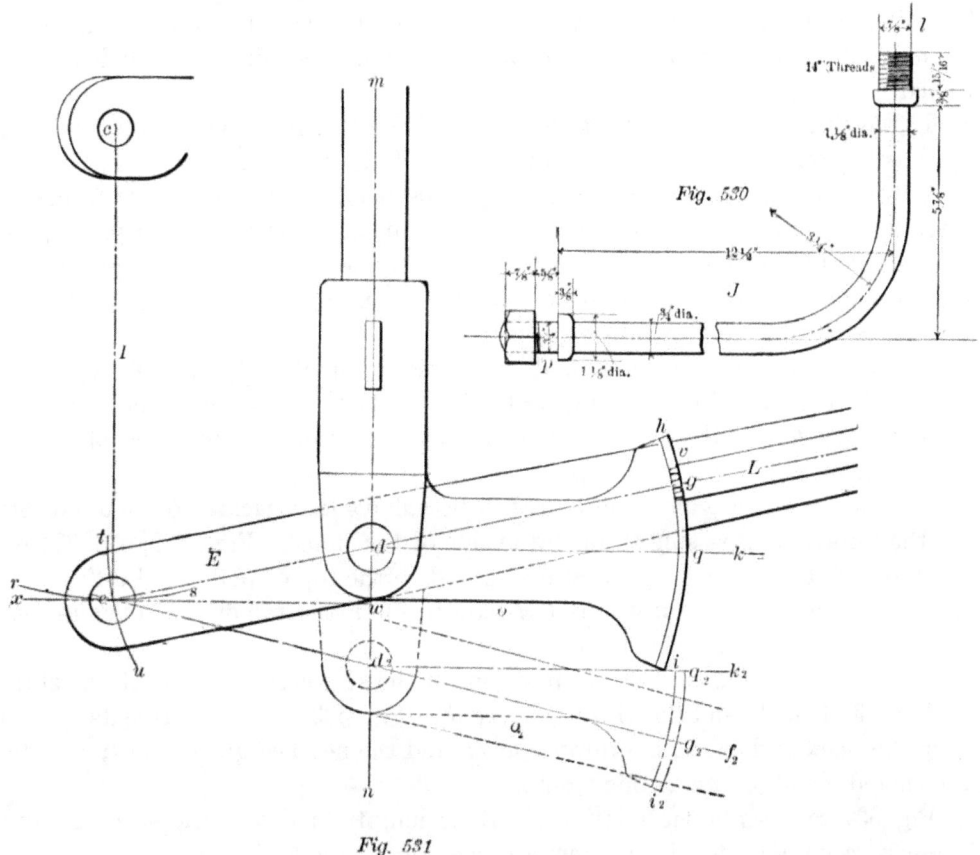

Fig. 531

Lay off a point $c$ to represent the center of the lug cast on the steam-gauge stand; the location of the point $c$ must, of course, correspond relatively to the position of the point $d$. From the point $c$ as a center, and with a radius equal to the distance between the centers of the holes in the link $I$ (Fig. 529), describe a short arc $r\,s$; also from the point $d$ as a center, and with a radius equal to the distance between the centers $d$ and $e$—that is, the given distance between the centers of the holes in the lever $E$—describe an arc $t\,u$ cutting $r\,s$ in the point $e$; the straight line joining the points $c$ and $e$ will be the center line of the link $I$. Through the points $e$ and $d$ draw a straight line, and prolong it towards $L$, cutting the arc $h\,i$ in the point $g$. Now the center line $e\,L$ indicates one of the extreme positions of the throttle lever $E$ (that is, when the throttle valve is closed), and theoretically the arc $h\,i$ need not extend beyond the edge $v$ of the latch $L$; but, in order to allow for wear and inaccuracies in fitting, the distance from $g$ to $h$ is usually such as to extend $\frac{1}{2}$ of an inch beyond $v$; hence the total distance from $g$ to $h$ measured on the arc $h\,i$ will be about $1\frac{3}{8}$ inches.

Through the point $d$ draw a line $d\,k$ perpendicular to $m\,n$, cutting the arc $h\,i$ in the point $q$, and thus obtain the distance $h\,q$—that is, the distance from the point $h$ to the line $d\,k$, measured on the arc $h\,i$.

If now a line $w\,x$, perpendicular to $m\,n$, be drawn through the point $w$—that is, the middle of the distance $d\,d_2$—and the line $w\,x$ passes through the point $e$, as shown, then the motion of the lever $E$ will be symmetrical on each side of the line $e\,w$; under these conditions we have only to make $i\,q$ equal $h\,q$, and thus obtain the whole length of the circular rack $h\,i$.

If the line $w\,x$ does not pass through the point $e$, then, the point $h$ having been found as before, the point $i_2$ will be found in the following manner:

Through the point $d_2$ draw the line $d_2\,k_2$, perpendicular to $m\,n$; also from $d_2$ as a center, and with a radius equal to $d\,e$, describe an arc to cut the arc $r\,s$; in practice the point of intersection thus found will generally be so near to the point $e$ that we may consider the former to coincide with the point $e$. Through the point $e$ and $d_2$ draw a straight line, and prolong it towards $f_2$.

From the point $d_2$ as a center, and with a radius equal to $d\,g$, describe the arc $q_2\,i_2$, cutting $e\,f_2$ in the point $g_2$, also cutting the horizontal line $d_2\,k_2$ in the point $q_2$. Make $g_2\,i_2$ equal to $g\,h$, add the arc $q_2\,i_2$ to the arc $h\,q$, and thus obtain the whole length of the circular rack.

368. In Art. 366 we have shown a throttle-valve gear attached to the top of boiler, with the throttle rod passing through the side of the dome. Figs. 532, 533, 534 represent another throttle-valve gear, also attached to the top of boiler, but differing from the former in having the throttle rod $H$ pass through the top of the boiler instead of passing through the side of the dome.

Fig. 532 represents the relative positions of the steam-gauge stand $A$, the stuffing-box $B$ with gland $C$, and the throttle lever $E$. Fig. 533 simply represents a plan of the stuffing-box and gland, the throttle lever, and the notched quadrant $D$; the steam-gauge stand is not shown in this figure.

Fig. 534 represents the relative positions longitudinally of the stuffing-box and steam-gauge stand; and Fig. 535 represents a plan of the latter.

The throttle rod $H$ stands in a vertical position. The ends of the throttle rod which pass through the lever $E$ and the crank $I$ are cut square.

In Fig. 532 the line $d$ is the center line of the boiler, and since the center line of the throttle pipe in the dome coincides with the line $d$, and since the center $f$ of the pin through the small crank $I$ should also coincide, or nearly so, with $d$, it follows that the stuffing-box must be placed on one side the center line $d$.

The joint between the stuffing-box and top of boiler is a ground ball joint; around it, the thickness of metal is increased by riveting a small plate $K$ to the inside of the boiler, thereby obtaining a sufficient depth of metal for the threads on the studs $a$, $a_2$, $a_2$, which fasten the stuffing-box to the boiler; the studs $a_2\,a_2$ are made long enough to take hold of the gland $C$.

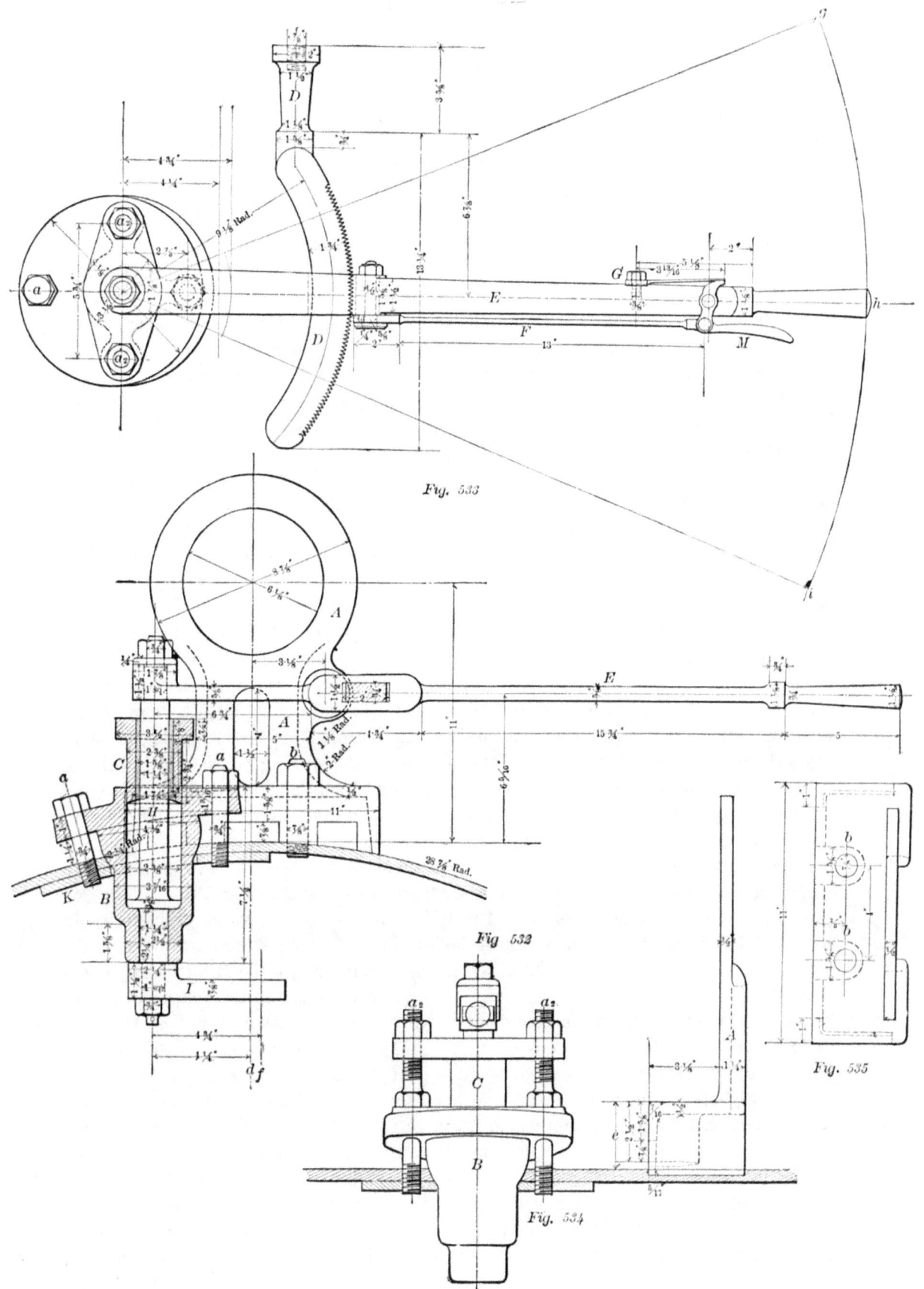

Fig. 533

Fig. 532

Fig. 534

Fig. 535

The steam-gauge stand $A$ is fastened to the top of boiler with two studs, $b$ $b$. The depth $e$ of the steam-gauge stand flange may seem to be excessive; this depth, as well as the distance from the top of the stuffing-box flange to the top of boiler, will be governed by the following conditions:

The designs of throttle-valve gears shown in Figs. 525 and 532 are generally required for boilers which extend nearly to the rear end of the cab; the portion of the boiler inside of cab must be lagged, as well as the outer portion, so as to prevent a loss of heat by radiation, and also to prevent the cab from becoming uncomfortably hot for the engineer. The distance between the outer face of lagging and the boiler usually varies from about $1\frac{1}{2}$ to 2 inches; now, in order to make a nice and easy finish of the lagging around the steam-gauge stand and stuffing-box, the upper faces of their flanges are made to extend about $\frac{1}{4}$ inch beyond the lagging, hence the excessive depth $e$ of the steam-gauge stand flange and the seemingly unnecessary height of the stuffing-box flange.

The quadrant $D$ is bolted to the steam-gauge stand; this quadrant must, of course, be described from the center of the throttle rod $H$. It will be noticed that in this design the quadrant $D$ is made to pass through the throttle lever $E$, instead of being placed below or above it, as shown in some of the other designs of throttle-valve gear. The manner of locking the throttle lever $E$ is so plainly shown in Fig. 533 that an explanation is unnecessary.

The arc $g$ $h$ $i$, Fig. 533, represents the path of the end of the throttle lever; the distance between its extremities $g$ and $i$ is usually about 12 inches, and should not exceed 18 inches. Now, to keep the movement of the end of the throttle lever within these limits, and in the meantime give the throttle valve the required lift, no more and no less, we must assign a suitable length to the crank $I$ in Fig. 532. But in many cases the boiler braces will determine the position of the stuffing-box $B$, which will also fix the length of the crank $I$; the length thus found may not be suitable for keeping the movement of the throttle lever within the given limits; under these conditions we must give such lengths to the arms of bell crank $B$, Fig. 493, as will produce the desired results. The given limit of the movement of the throttle lever will also, in many cases, determine the distance between the holes $e$ and $d$ in Fig. 531.

369. We have already seen that the design of the throttle-valve gear shown in Figs. 525, 526 is used on engines whose boilers extend nearly to the rear end of the cab. This class of engines, or the class of engines in which the throttle-rod passes through the side of dome, generally present first-class opportunities for making provisions for attaching the various kinds of valves and cocks without screwing each one directly into the boiler shell. Consequently, in many of the locomotives of these classes built in recent years, we find a throttle-valve gear like that shown in Figs. 536, 537, or others, very similar in design to the one here shown. In these illustrations we have only represented the most prominent features of this design of throttle-valve gear; for the sake of simplicity the throttle lever, with its attachments for locking it, is not shown; in fact, any one of the throttle levers previously illustrated, with only a slight modification in a few of them, can be used in this kind of gear. Its principal feature is the steam stand $B$, which is simply a rectangular box, generally made of brass. In Fig. 536 we see a longitudinal section of this box, and Fig. 540 shows a cross-

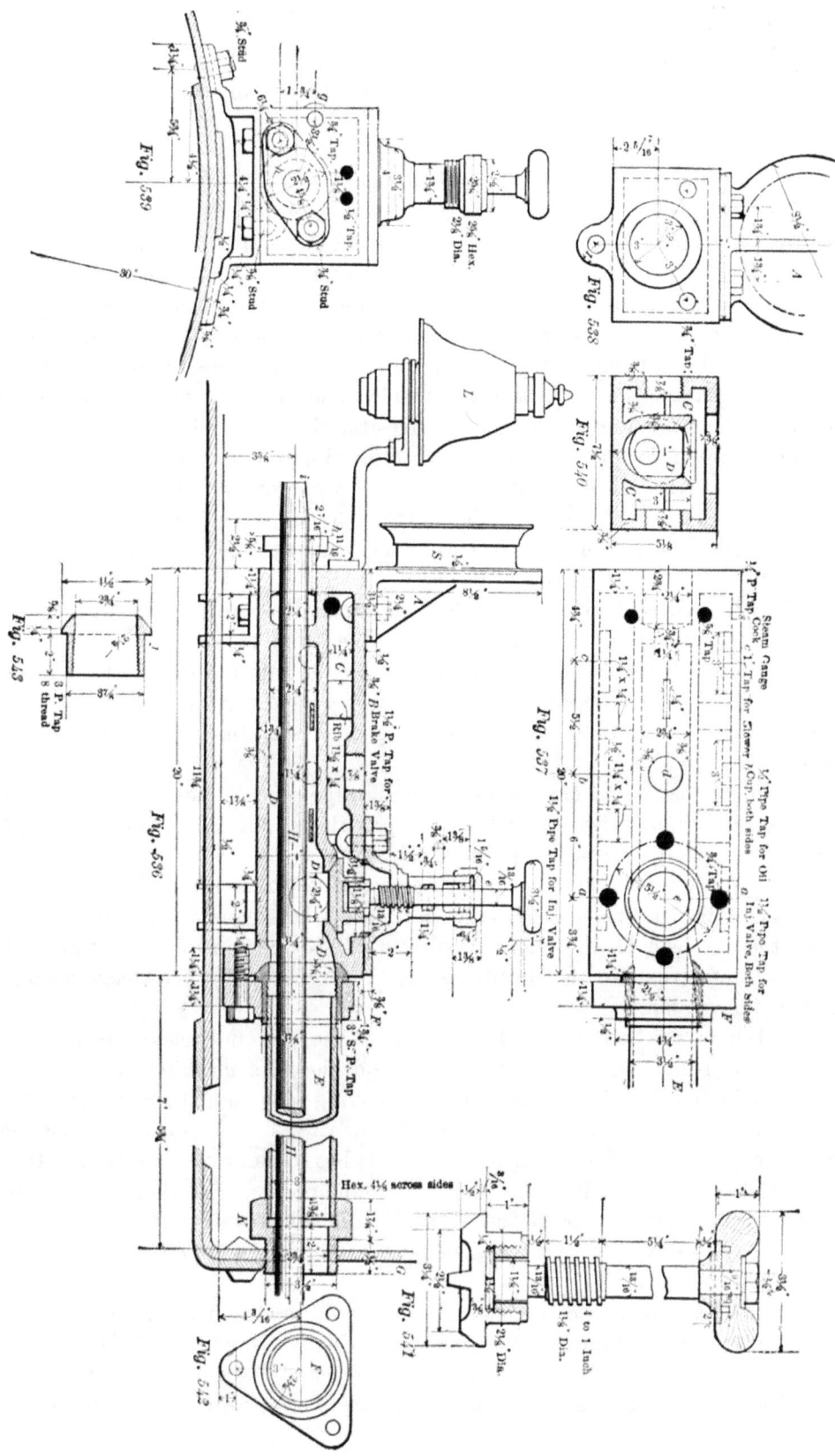

section of the same. These figures plainly indicate that the steam stand $B$ is divided into two compartments or chambers, $D$ and $C$; the chamber $C$ nearly surrounds the chamber $D$. Communication between these two chambers is either opened or closed by means of the valve $e$.

The throttle rod $H$ passes through the chamber $D$, and also through the heavy wrought-iron pipe $E$; the latter forms a connection between the steam stand $B$ and the dome $G$. The rear end of the steam stand is bored out so as to form a stuffing-box; $h$ is the stuffing-box gland. The end $i$ of the throttle rod $H$ is fastened to the throttle jaw (not shown here), and this throttle jaw connects to the throttle lever.

The steam-pipe $E$ is connected to the dome by means of a thimble $K$, which takes the place of a brass flange. A part of the outer portion of this thimble is hexagonal in form, the remaining outer portion is threaded and screwed into the dome sheet. A portion of this thimble is tapped and receives the threaded end of the pipe $E$. This is a favorite way, in locomotive practice, of connecting a pipe of the kind here shown to the boiler. On the other end of the pipe $E$ a wrought-iron sleeve $f$ is screwed. A separate view of this sleeve is shown in Fig. 543, and, as will be seen, it forms a ball joint with the steam stand; this sleeve is held against the stand by the flange $F$, of which a separate view is shown in Fig. 542.

Fig. 537 represents a plan of the steam stand $B$; here it is plainly seen that its sides have a number of tapped holes; into these the various valves and cocks are screwed, which otherwise would have to be screwed into the shell of the boiler. For instance, the holes $a\ a$ receive the injector valves; $b\ b$ receive the cylinder oil-cups; $c$ receives the blower valve; and $s$ the steam-gauge cock; the hole $d$ on top of the stand takes the brake valve.

Steam is conveyed from the dome through the pipe $E$, and enters the chamber $D$ in the steam stand; when the valve $e$ is open the steam enters the chamber $C$, and supplies all the valves attached to the steam stand.

Fig. 541 shows the spindle of the valve $e$ on a larger scale; Fig. 538 shows the front end of the steam stand $B$, and a portion of the steam-gauge stand $A$; Fig. 539 shows the rear end of the stand $B$, with stuffing-box gland $h$; the tapped hole $g$ receives the fulcrum for the throttle lever. In Fig. 536, $S$ is the steam-gauge, and $L$ the steam-gauge lamp.

We believe this arrangement to be one of the best and neatest in use. All the holes in the steam stand $B$ can, of course, be drilled in a machine, and all the valves, etc., fitted in it before it is taken into the erecting shop, and therefore less time and labor will be required for attaching the different valves, cocks, etc., to the engine than must be expended when each one of the valves has to be fitted directly into the boiler shell. But besides this advantage, the steam stand possesses another one, namely, with the valve $e$, the steam can be at once shut off from all the valves attached to the stand, consequently, if one of these valves gets out of order, it can be repaired with full steam pressure in the boiler.

The relative position of the steam stand $B$ will greatly depend upon the position of the reverse lever; it must be placed in a position which will bring the throttle-valve lever, as well as the reverse lever, within easy reach of the engineer; consequently we often find that this design of throttle-valve gear is placed quite a distance in front of the back head of the boiler, and differs from the position generally assigned to the throttle-valve gear in ordinary eight-wheeled passenger engines. In fact, in the latter class of engines the boiler seldom extends more than 12 to 15 inches into the cab; hence, the steam stand illustrated in Figs. 536, 537 is not suitable for this class of engines, because there is no room for it. The short extension of the boiler into the cab, and general design of passenger engines, necessitate the use of throttle-valve gears such as have been illustrated in Figs. 514, 517, 519. When one of the latter class of throttle-valve gears has to be used, the steam-gauge stand becomes an independent fixture, and, for the sake of convenience to the engineer, it is generally fastened to the curved part of the back head of the boiler.

### STEAM-GAUGE STAND.

370. Fig. 544 represents a steam-gauge stand for passenger engines and for that class of engines whose boiler projects but little into the cab. This stand is arranged for a steam-gauge and clock, the latter being placed above the former. In this figure we also see an outside view of the spring balance $S$ connected to the lever $C$. The rod $E$ extends upwards and is connected to the safety-valve lever. A portion of the lever $C$ is represented in section, so as to show the spiral spring underneath the pawl $D$. The spiral spring keeps the pawl engaged with the circular rack $e$, and prevents the lever $C$ from being pulled upwards by the tension of the spring balance. The lever $C$ swings on the pivot $f$, which is cast to the steam-gauge stand; hence, in pulling the lever $C$ downwards the tension of the spring will be increased, and therefore the force which presses the safety valve against the seat will also be increased. Pressing the pawl $D$ towards the lever $C$ disengages the pawl and rack, allowing the lever to move upwards, thus enabling the engineer to blow off steam when necessary.

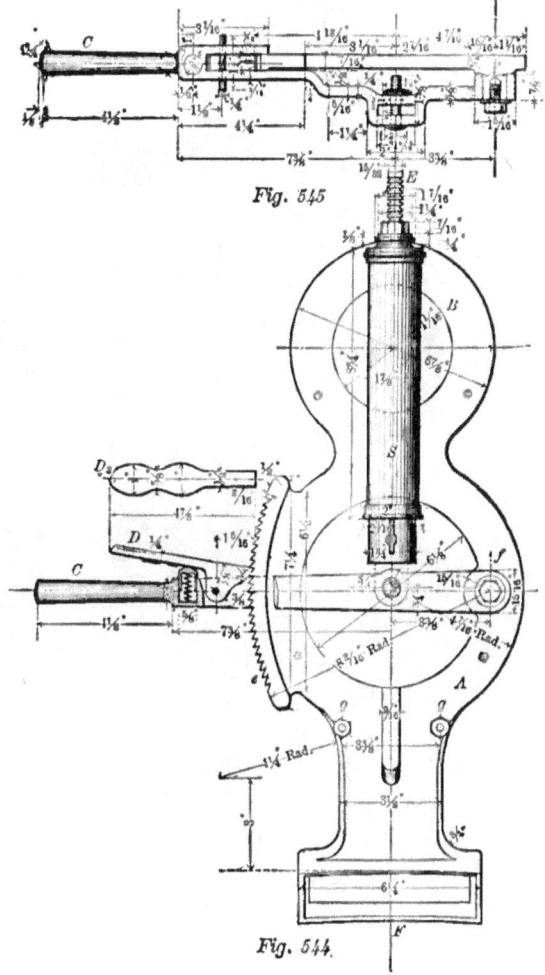

Fig. 545

Fig. 544.

Another view of the pawl is shown at $D_2$. The nuts $g\ g$ fasten the steam-gauge lamp to the stand. Fig. 545 represents a plan of the lever $C$, and a section of the steam-gauge stand.

Fig. 546 represents a side view of the same steam-gauge stand. This side view is drawn to a larger scale, so as to enable us to illustrate more distinctly a section of the

370  MODERN LOCOMOTIVE CONSTRUCTION.

spring balance. This spring balance consists of an outer and inner casing, a spring which connects the two, and nuts for regulating the tension of the spring. The

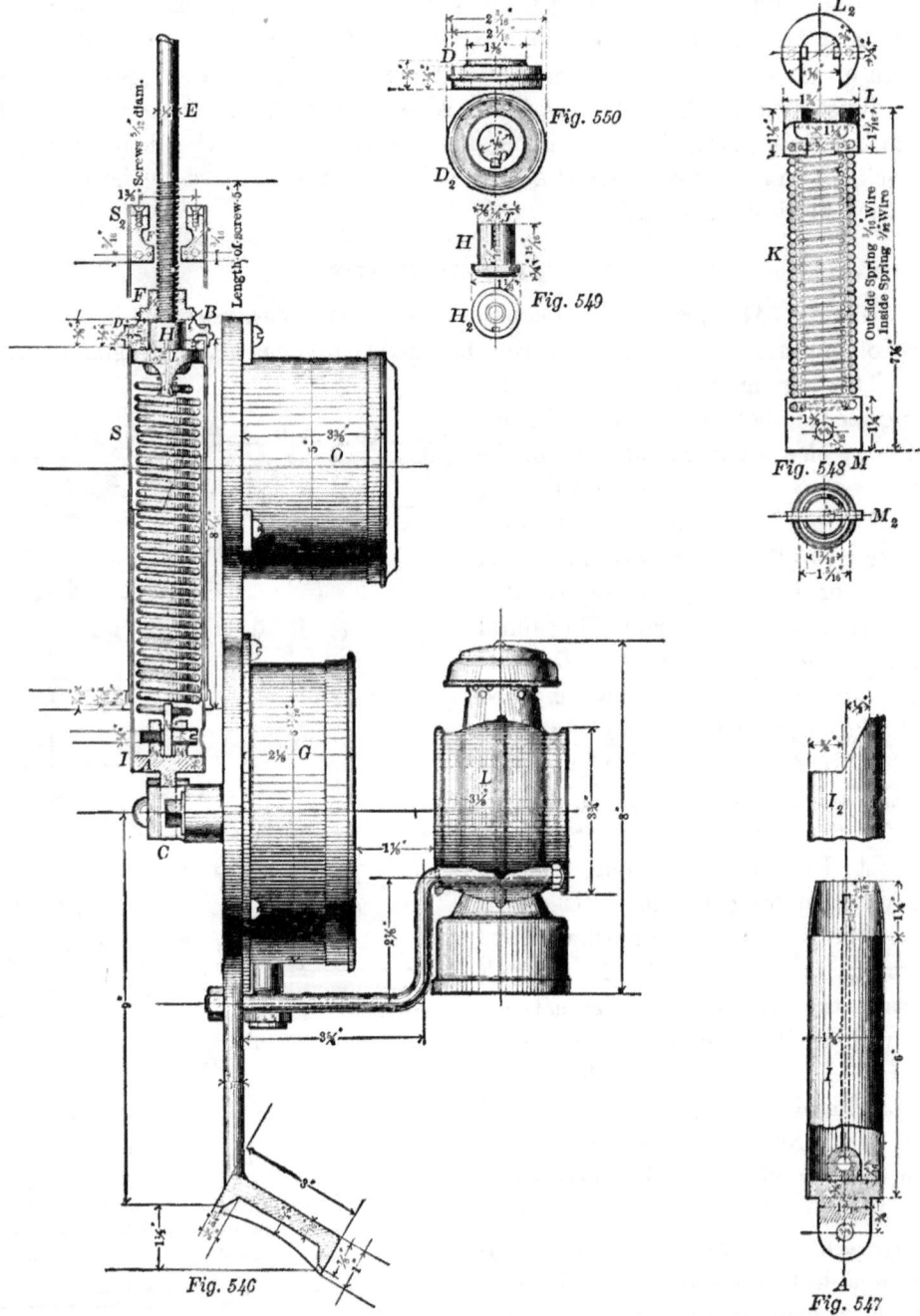

casings are made of brass tubes. The outer casing is open at the bottom, and a small brass head $B$ is brazed in its upper end; this head is bored out to receive the brass nut $H$, of which separate views are shown in Fig. 549. The inner casing is open at the top, and closed at the bottom by the brass head $A$ brazed to it. A separate view of the inner casing is shown in Fig. 547; a portion of the upper end of this casing is cut off for convenience in putting the spring balance together. Fig. 548 represents the spiral springs, one placed inside of the other, and fastened to the brass end-pieces $L$ and $M$; a plan of the end-piece $L$ is shown at $L_2$, and a plan of the lower end-piece $M$ is shown at $M_2$; in this figure the ends of the two springs are also seen. The piece $L$ is fastened to the head of the outer casing by means of two screws, as shown at $S_2$, Fig. 546, which is another section of the upper part of the outer casing; the end-piece $M$ is attached to the head at the bottom of the inner casing.

The upper end of the outer casing fits in the recess of the cap $D$, of which separate views are shown in Fig. 550. This cap is not fastened to the casing. The feather $p$, shown in Fig. 550, engages with the groove cut in the outer surface of the nut $H$; hence, in turning the cap, the nut must also turn, causing an increase or decrease in the tension of the spring. The nut $F$, Fig. 546, is simply a jam nut.

Examining the section in Fig. 546, it will be seen that the head of the nut $H$ bears against the under side of the upper end-piece $L$ of the springs; consequently the outer casing will not be subjected to any vertical stress due to the pressure on the safety valve; the two small screws connecting the head of the outer casing and the end-piece $L$ are simply for the purpose of preventing the piece $L$ from turning, thereby keeping the springs free from any torsional strain.

The tension of the springs can, of course, be regulated to a limited extent by means of the lever $C$, of which other views are shown in Figs. 544, 545. The nut $H$ and cap $D$ are for the purpose of closer adjustment of the tension.

In Fig. 546, $O$ represents the clock, $G$ the steam-gauge, and $L$ the lamp.

## SAFETY VALVE, DOME, AND CASING.

**371.** Fig. 551 represents a common safety valve, its attachments, and a portion of the dome top marked $D$. Occasionally the opening for the common safety valve in dome top is bushed with brass, but generally it is not bushed. The safety valve $A$ is made of brass; it consists of a hollow cone with four wings, $a\ a$, cast to it, which guide the valve in the opening. Frequently the valve seat is made flat, leaving only a bearing of $\frac{3}{16}$ inch all around, as shown in the illustration, but this is not the best form. The seat should have an inclination of 45 degrees to the center line of its axis, thereby obtaining an additional face-to-face metal impingement, which insures tightness under a high boiler pressure. This is an important matter, particularly for the higher pressures as are now used in locomotives, because with an increased metal impingement the valve will keep tight to a limit nearer to the blowing-off point than those with flat seats. An angle less than 45 degrees would be still better to insure against leakage, but with this comes the danger of the valve sticking to its seat. Hence, the seat beveled to an angle of 45 degrees we believe to be the best.

The surface of the seat should not be conical; it should be spherical, so that the valve will always be tight even when there is not the proper alignment of motion from the want of accuracy, of workmanship, or from wear. The radius of this surface is found in the following manner: Draw the valve seat as shown in Fig. 551A; bisect

372  MODERN LOCOMOTIVE CONSTRUCTION.

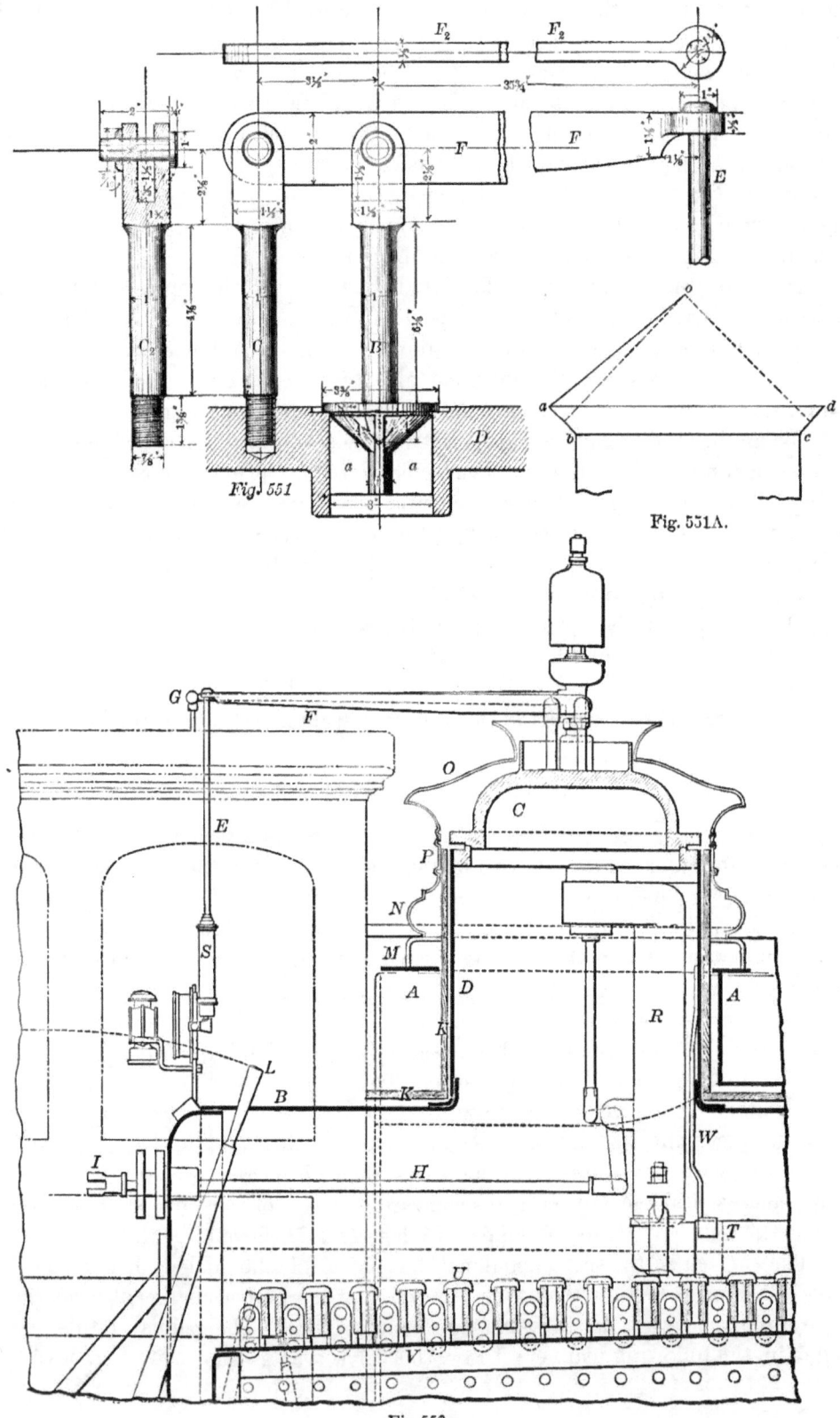

Fig. 551

Fig. 551A.

Fig. 552

$a\,b$ and $c\,d$ by perpendiculars, cutting each other in the point $o$; then $o\,a$ will be the required radius.

Two views of the safety-valve lever $F$ are shown in Fig. 551, $F_2$ being the plan. The rounded end of the wrought-iron valve spindle $B$ sets in the hollow part of the valve. The wrought-iron fulcrum $C$ is screwed into the dome top. Another view of this fulcrum is shown at $C_2$. The rod $E$ is a portion of the rod marked $E$ in Fig. 546.

The opening in the top of dome for this kind of safety valve is three inches in diameter for all locomotives, excepting very small ones, say with cylinders nine or ten inches in diameter; and even for these engines the safety-valve opening is sometimes three inches in diameter.

This form of safety valve is often adopted when the dome is close to the cab, as shown in Fig. 552; it is placed on the right-hand side of the engine, a pop being placed on the other side.

When the dome is placed on the center of the boiler, the common safety valve here shown is not suitable, because its lever will be too long, and therefore a pop valve is used in its place. Some master-mechanics use the latter valve exclusively on all engines. The advantage claimed for the common safety valve with the spring balance arranged as illustrated is that it can be adjusted very conveniently—without going outside of the cab—to blow off at any desired steam pressure. On the other hand, the pop valve has a greater venting capacity, and is therefore sometimes preferred. These valves will be described later.

372. Fig. 552 represents a section of a portion of the boiler $B$ and the dome $D$; it shows plainly the position of the steam-gauge stand in the cab, also the manner of connecting the spring balance $S$, by means of the rod $E$, to the safety-valve lever $F$. The whistle lever is marked $G$; details of the whistle and connections will be shown later. We also see the position of the throttle pipe in the dome, and the general arrangement of the throttle gear. The throttle lever, which is not shown, connects to the jaw $I$, and the manner of opening the throttle valve, by pulling out the throttle rod $H$, can readily be traced.

The steam-pipe $T$ is allowed to rest on the crown bars $U$, being secured in position by the clamp $W$, which is bolted to the side of the dome. We also see the relative position of the reverse lever $L$, which is shown in full gear forward. The reverse lever is, with very few exceptions, always placed on the right-hand side of the engine; it is shown here for the sake of completeness; had we strictly followed the rules of drawing we could not have shown the reverse lever, because that side of the engine is cut off.

The section here shown is that of a switching engine with a saddle tank $A\,A$, but the relative positions of steam-gauge stand, reverse lever, and throttle lever do not differ from those in ordinary eight-wheeled passenger engines. In the latter class of engine we have, of course, no tank on the top of boiler, and therefore the dome casing extends to the top of the lagging $K$. The casing here shown consists of a cast-iron ring $M$, which, in passenger engines, is fitted to the top of the lagging, and the sheet-iron or brass casing, which is made in three parts, namely, the lower ring $N$, the body $P$, and the upper ring $O$. The casing is not fastened to the dome, but is kept in place by the lagging around the dome, to which it is fitted pretty closely, and can readily be lifted off when repairs to the boiler become necessary.

In our illustration the boiler extends a little further into the cab than it generally does in passenger engines. In some of these engines the lagging around the boiler extends only up to the cab; in others it extends to the back head of the boiler.

## TENSION ON SAFETY-VALVE SPRINGS.

373. The tension on the springs in the spring balance $S$ (Fig. 546), the length of safety-valve lever, etc., are determined by well-known rules. Before we give these rules, let us first establish a formula from which they may be derived; such a course will give us a clearer conception of them.

In Fig. 553 the line $e\ e_2$ represents the center line of the rod marked $E$ in Figs. 546, 551. This rod is, of course, subjected to a tensile stress due to the steam pressure

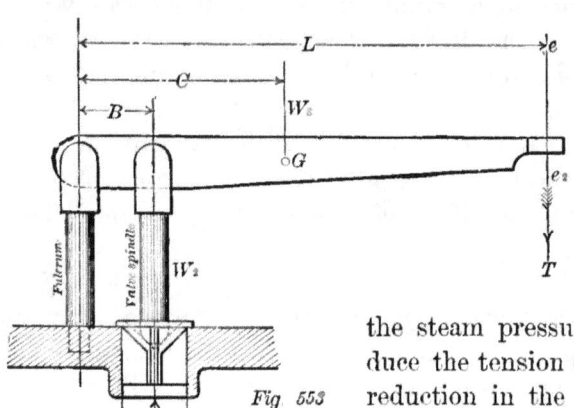

Fig 553

on the safety valve, and this stress is transmitted to the spring balance; hence we may say that the tension on the spring is equal to the stress on the rod whose center line is represented by the line $e\ e_2$ in Fig. 553. The weight of the safety-valve lever, weight of valve, and weight of valve spindle will, of course, help to resist the steam pressure on the valve, and will therefore reduce the tension on the springs, and in some cases this reduction in the tension will be considerable. For the sake of simplicity we shall, in the first place, give the rules in which the weights of the safety-valve lever, valve, and valve spindle are neglected.

Let $L$ represent the distance in inches from the center of the fulcrum to the center line $e\ e_2$; this distance is often called the length of the safety-valve lever.

$B$, the distance in inches from the center of the fulcrum to the center of the valve spindle.

$T$, the tension in pounds on the springs.

$A$, the area in square inches of the safety valve; this area must always be taken equal to the cross-sectional area of the safety-valve opening $D$.

$P$, the pressure of the steam in pounds per square inch of the safety-valve area.

$W_2$, the weight in pounds of the safety valve and its spindle.

$W_3$, the weight in pounds of the safety-valve lever.

$C$, the distance in inches from the center of fulcrum to the center of gravity $G$ of the lever.

In neglecting the weight of the safety-valve lever, valve, and spindle, the symbols $W_2$, $W_3$, and $C$ will not be used; we have given them here so as to make our table of symbols complete.

The total steam pressure in pounds on the safety valve is evidently equal to the product obtained by multiplying the steam pressure $P$ per square inch by the area $A$ of the valve; hence the total pressure on the valve is equal to $P \times A$. But this total steam pressure acts with a leverage $B$, and is resisted by the tension $T$ acting with a leverage $L$. Now in order to compare the intensity with which the pressure on the valve acts, with the intensity with which the tension acts, we must find the moment of each of these forces.

The moment of the total steam pressure acting on the valve is equal to $P \times A \times B$.
The moment of the tension is equal to $T \times L$.

When the steam pressure on the valve is just sufficient to raise the valve, we have then a condition of equilibrium, in which the moment of the total steam pressure is equal to the moment of the tension, and these conditions are represented by the formula

$$P \times A \times B = T \times L.$$

Putting this formula in words, we have: The product obtained by multiplying the steam pressure per square inch by the area in square inches, and by the distance from the center of the valve to the center of the fulcrum, is equal to the product obtained by multiplying the tension in pounds by distance from the line of action of the tension to the center of the fulcrum.

From this formula we derive the well-known rules which will enable us to solve any problem relating to the safety valve, and these rules hold true when a weight is substituted for the springs, as in safety valve for stationary boilers; all we need to remember is that the center of the weight will lie in the line $c\ c_2$. We must also bear in mind that, in the following rules, the weight of the safety-valve lever, valve, and spindle are neglected.

EXAMPLE 116.—The length $L$ (Fig. 553) is $38\frac{1}{2}$ inches; the distance $B$ from the center of the valve to the center of the fulcrum is $3\frac{1}{2}$ inches; the steam pressure $P$ per square inch is 120 pounds; the safety valve is 3 inches diameter. What will be the tension on the springs?

The area $A$ of a safety valve 3 inches diameter is 7.06 square inches. Here, then, we have given $P$, $A$, $B$, and $L$; it is required to find $T$.

We know that
$$P \times A \times B = T \times L;$$
hence, to find $T$, we have
$$\frac{P \times A \times B}{L} = T, \qquad (a)$$
which reads:

RULE 87.—The steam pressure in pounds per square inch, multiplied by the area in square inches of the safety valve, and this product again multiplied by the distance in inches from the center of the valve to the center of the fulcrum, and the last product divided by the length of the lever in inches, will give the tension in pounds of the springs.

Substituting the numerical values for the symbols in formula $(a)$, we have

$$\frac{120 \times 7.06 \times 3.5}{38.5} = 77 \text{ pounds}$$

for the tension of the springs.

EXAMPLE 117.—The tension $T$ is 77 pounds; the distance $B$ (Fig. 553) is $3\frac{1}{2}$ inches;

the area $A$ of the valve, 7.06 square inches; steam pressure $P$, 120 pounds per square inch. Find the length $L$ of the safety-valve lever.

Here we have

$$\frac{P \times A \times B}{T} = L, \qquad (b)$$

which reads:

RULE 88.—The steam pressure in pounds per square inch, multiplied by the area in square inches of the safety valve, and this product again multiplied by the distance from the center of the valve to the center of the fulcrum, and the last product divided by the tension in pounds, will give a quotient which is numerically equal to the length of the lever in inches.

Substituting the numerical values for the symbols in formula $(b)$, we have

$$\frac{120 \times 7.06 \times 3.5}{77} = 38.5 \text{ inches}$$

for the length of the safety-valve lever.

EXAMPLE 118.—The tension $T$ is 77 pounds; length $L$ of the safety-valve lever, $38\frac{1}{2}$ inches; area $A$ of the valve, 7.06 square inches; distance $B$ from the center of the valve to the center of the fulcrum, $3\frac{1}{2}$ inches. Find the steam pressure per square inch on the safety valve.

Here we have

$$\frac{T \times L}{A \times B} = P, \qquad (c)$$

which reads:

RULE 89.—The product obtained by multiplying the tension in pounds by the length of the lever in inches, divided by the product obtained by multiplying the area in square inches of the valve by the distance in inches from the center of the valve to the center of the fulcrum, will give a quotient which is numerically equal to the steam pressure per square inch.

Substituting the numerical values for the symbols in formula $(c)$, we have

$$\frac{77 \times 38.5}{7.06 \times 3.5} = 119.97 \text{ pounds}$$

steam pressure per square inch of the safety valve.

EXAMPLE 119.—The tension $T$ is 77 pounds; length of lever, $38\frac{1}{2}$ inches; steam pressure, 120 pounds; distance from the center of the valve to the center of fulcrum, $3\frac{1}{2}$ inches. Find the area of the valve.

Here we have

$$\frac{T \times L}{P \times B} = A, \qquad (d)$$

which reads:

RULE 90.—The product obtained by multiplying the tension in pounds by the length of the safety-valve lever in inches, divided by the product obtained by multiplying the steam pressure per square inch by the distance from the center of the valve to the center of the fulcrum in inches, will give a quotient which is numerically equal to the number of square inches in the area of the safety valve.

Substituting the numerical values for the symbols in formula $(d)$, we have

$$\frac{77 \times 38.5}{120 \times 3.5} = 7.05 \text{ square inches}$$

in the area of the valve.

EXAMPLE 120.—The tension $T$ is 77 pounds; length of lever $L$, $38\frac{1}{2}$ inches; steam pressure $P$, 120 pounds; area $A$, 7.06 square inches. Find the distance from the center of the valve to the center of the fulcrum.

Here we have
$$\frac{T \times L}{P \times A} = B, \qquad (e)$$
which reads:

RULE 91.—The product obtained by multiplying the tension in pounds by the length of the lever in inches, divided by the product obtained by multiplying the steam pressure per square inch by the area in square inches of the valve, will give a quotient which is numerically equal to the distance in inches from the center of the valve to the center of the fulcrum.

Substituting the numerical values for the symbols in formula ($e$), we have

$$\frac{77 \times 38.5}{120 \times 7.06} = 3.49 \text{ inches},$$

which is the distance from the center of the valve to the center of the fulcrum.

When the weight of the safety-valve, lever, etc., are taken into account, the formulas become a little more complicated; but if the foregoing formulas and rules are understood, there will not be any difficulty in forming a clear conception of the rules in the next article.

374. In the following rules relating to safety-valve problems, the weight of the valve, lever, and spindle is to be taken into account. These weights must be accurately ascertained, either by actual weighing or by computation.

The weight of the safety-valve lever will act on the valve with a leverage which is equal to the distance from the center of gravity of the lever to the fulcrum. In other words, we assume that the whole weight of the safety-valve lever is concentrated at its center of gravity $G$ (Fig. 553), and acts with a leverage $C$.

When the safety-valve lever is of uniform thickness and width throughout, and the shape of one end exactly like that of the opposite end, we may, for all practical purposes, assume the center of gravity to lie in the center of the lever, and, indeed, it will be there exactly, provided no holes are drilled through the lever, and the metal is homogeneous.

When the lever is not of uniform thickness throughout, then, in order to find the center of gravity, the lever should be balanced on a knife-edge, and when in equilibrium, the center of gravity will lie in a vertical line drawn across the lever from the knife-edge.

When the lever is of uniform thickness throughout, but not of uniform width, we may also find the center of gravity by balancing the lever on a knife-edge. This method may not always be convenient; in such cases we may adopt the following method, which will give us an approximate position of the center of gravity; but it should be distinctly understood that this method is only applicable to levers which have a uniform thickness. Nearly all safety-valve levers for locomotives are of uniform thickness, with the exception of the small hub around the center line $e\ e_2$, in Fig. 553. To allow for this hub, assume the lower edge of the lever to extend clear to its end and proceed as follows: Cut a template out of stiff paper, conforming to the width of the lever. Anywhere near one of the edges of this template punch a small hole, for instance at $A$ (Fig. 553a), and suspend the template from a pin passed through this hole, allowing the template to have plenty of freedom to vibrate; also, from the same pin suspend a plummet-line, and along it draw a pencil line $A B$ on the template. In a similar way suspend the template from another hole $C$, punched anywhere near the edge opposite the hole $A$; along the plummet-line draw on the template another pencil line $C D$, cutting $A B$ in the point $G$, which will be the position of the center of gravity.

Fig. 553a

The preliminary details having been arranged, we are in a position to establish a formula, from which all subsequent rules relating to the safety-valve can be deduced.

Since these rules will be interesting examples of the principle of moments, it may be advantageous to repeat the definition of the moment of a force given in Art. 256.

The moment of a force with respect to a point is the product obtained by multiplying the force by the perpendicular distance from the point to the direction of the force.

Now the point referred to in this definition is the center of the fulcrum-pin in Fig. 553. About this point there are four forces acting—namely, the steam pressure acting in the direction of the vertical line through the center of the valve; the total steam pressure is evidently equal to $P \times A$ (here the same symbols are used as given in Art. 373), hence, according to our definition, the moment of this pressure about the fulcrum is equal to $P \times A \times B$. Second, the tension acting in the direction of the vertical line $e\ e_2$, hence its moment about the fulcrum is equal to $T \times L$. Third, the weight $W_2$ of the valve and spindle acting in a direction of the vertical line through the center of the valve, hence its moment about the fulcrum is equal to $W_2 \times B$. And lastly, the weight $W_3$ of the lever, acting in a vertical line through the center of gravity $G$, hence its moment about the fulcrum is equal to $W_3 \times C$.

The moment $P \times A \times B$ acts upwards, all the other moments act downwards; and when the steam pressure is just sufficient to raise the valve, we have then a condition in which the upward moment is equal to the sum of the downward moments. Summing up the downward moments, we have:

Moment of the tension $T$ about the fulcrum $= T \times L$.
Moment of the weight $W_2$ about the fulcrum $= W_2 \times B$.
Moment of the weight $W_3$ about the fulcrum $= W_3 \times C$.
Sum of the downward moments $= (T \times L) + (W_2 \times B) + (W_3 \times C)$.

Since the sum of these moments must be equal to the upward moment, we have:

$$P \times A \times B = (T \times L) + (W_2 \times B) + (W_3 \times C). \qquad (f)$$

From this formula all rules relating to the safety valve can be deduced.

EXAMPLE 121.—Tension of the springs $T = 72.27$ pounds.

Length $L$ of lever = 38.5 inches.
Weight $W_3$ of lever = 11 pounds.
Distance $C$ of center of gravity of lever from the fulcrum = 15 inches.
Weight $W_2$ of valve and spindle = 5 pounds.
Distance $B$ from center of valve to fulcrum = 3.5 inches.
Area $A$ of the valve = 7.06 square inches.
Find the steam pressure $P$ per square inch.

Here we are to find $P$; hence from formula (*b*) we obtain

$$P = \frac{(T \times L) + (W_2 \times B) + (W_3 \times C)}{A \times B}, \qquad (g)$$

which reads:

RULE 92.—Add the moment of the tension, the moment of weight of the valve and spindle, and the moment of weight of the lever; divide this sum by the product obtained by multiplying the area of the valve by the distance from the fulcrum to the center of the valve; the quotient will be the steam pressure per square inch on the valve.

In this and the following rules, all the dimensions should be taken in inches, and the weights in pounds.

Substituting the numerical values for the symbols in formula (*g*), we have

$$P = \frac{(72.27 \times 38.5) + (5 \times 3.5) + (11 \times 15)}{7.06 \times 3.5} = 119.9+ \text{ pounds.}$$

EXAMPLE 122.—The steam pressure per square inch is 120 pounds; the weights and dimensions of the safety valve are as given in Example 121, with the exception of the area of the valve, which is to be found.

Here we have

$$A = \frac{(T \times L) + (W_2 \times B) + (W_3 \times C)}{P \times B}, \qquad (h)$$

which reads:

RULE 93.—Add the moment of the tension, the moment of the weight of valve and spindle, and the moment of the lever; divide this sum by the product obtained by multiplying the steam pressure per square inch by the distance from the fulcrum to the center of the valve; the quotient will be the area of the valve in square inches.

Substituting the numerical values for the symbols in formula (*h*), we obtain

$$A = \frac{(72.27 \times 38.5) + (5 \times 3.5) + (11 \times 15)}{120 \times 3.5} = 7.05 \text{ square inches.}$$

EXAMPLE 123.—The steam pressure is 120 pounds, the weights and dimensions of the safety valve are as given in Example 121, with the exception of the distance from the fulcrum to the valve, which is to be found.

Here we are to find $B$, hence

$$B = \frac{(T \times L) + (W_2 \times B) + (W_3 \times C)}{A \times P}, \qquad (i)$$

which reads:

RULE 94.—Add the moment of the tension, the moment of the weight of the valve and spindle, and the moment of the weight of the lever; divide this sum by the product obtained by multiplying the area of the valve by the steam pressure; the quotient will be the distance from the fulcrum to the center of the valve in inches.

Substituting the numerical values for the symbols in formula ($i$), we obtain

$$B = \frac{(72.27 \times 38.5) + (5 \times 3.5) + (11 \times 15)}{7.06 \times 120} = 3.49 \text{ inches.}$$

In order to find the tension we must change our original formula ($f$) to the following:

$$(P \times A \times B) - (W_2 \times B) - (W_3 \times C) = T \times L. \qquad (j)$$

From this we obtain

$$T = \frac{(P \times A \times B) - (W_2 \times B) - (W_3 \times C)}{L}, \qquad (k)$$

which reads:

RULE 95.—From the moment of the steam pressure subtract the moment of the weight of valve and spindle, also subtract the moment of the lever; divide the remainder by the length of the lever; the quotient will be the tension in pounds.

EXAMPLE 124.—The steam pressure is 120 pounds per square inch; all other dimensions are as given in Example 121, excepting the tension, which is to be found.

Substituting the numerical values for the symbols in formula ($k$), we have

$$T = \frac{(120 \times 7.06 \times 3.5) - (5 \times 3.5) - (11 \times 15)}{38.5} = 72.27 \text{ pounds.}$$

For finding the length $L$ of the safety-valve lever when all other dimensions and weights are given, we have the following formula:

$$L = \frac{(P \times A \times B) - (W_2 \times B) - (W_3 \times C)}{T}. \qquad (l)$$

In this formula we have taken into account $W_3$, which is the weight of the lever, and $C$, which is the distance from the fulcrum to the center of gravity of the lever, and, since these cannot be accurately determined unless the length $L$ of the lever is known, we are compelled to assume a value for $W_3 \times C$.

Probably under these circumstances it will be best to find the length $L$ of the lever by formula ($b$), Art. 373; the length $L$ thus found will be somewhat longer than that obtained by formula ($l$).

### DOME TOPS.

375. The safety valves are generally attached to a cast-iron dome top, the proportions of which are shown in Figs. 554, 555; the relative positions of the safety valves and the whistle are also given.

The safety valve, such as is shown in Fig. 553, is placed in the opening $A$, and the locked safety valve, or pop valve, is placed in the opening $B$. The whistle is screwed into the central hub $E$, and stands forward of the safety valves.

When the ordinary plain safety valve is used, we do not require the hubs $f, f$, shown in Fig. 555; yet these are generally cast to the dome top so that any other safety valve can readily be attached. The basin $C$ is simply for the purpose of collecting the water due to the condensation of steam as it flows through the safety valves and whistle.

Fig. 556 represents a plan of the dome ring, and the arrangements of the rivet holes $r\ r$, and the stud holes $s\ s$.

Fig. 556A represents, on a larger scale, the joint between the dome top and the ring; this joint is a ground one. $F$ represents a section of the dome-top flange, and $H$ a section of the ring. Here it will be seen that the holes $s$ for the studs $I$ are not drilled through the ring; this precaution is taken to prevent leakage around the studs.

Sometimes the rings are placed outside of the dome; in such cases bolts are used for fastening the dome top to the ring.

## WHISTLE.

376. Fig. 557 shows a section of the whistle, a section of a

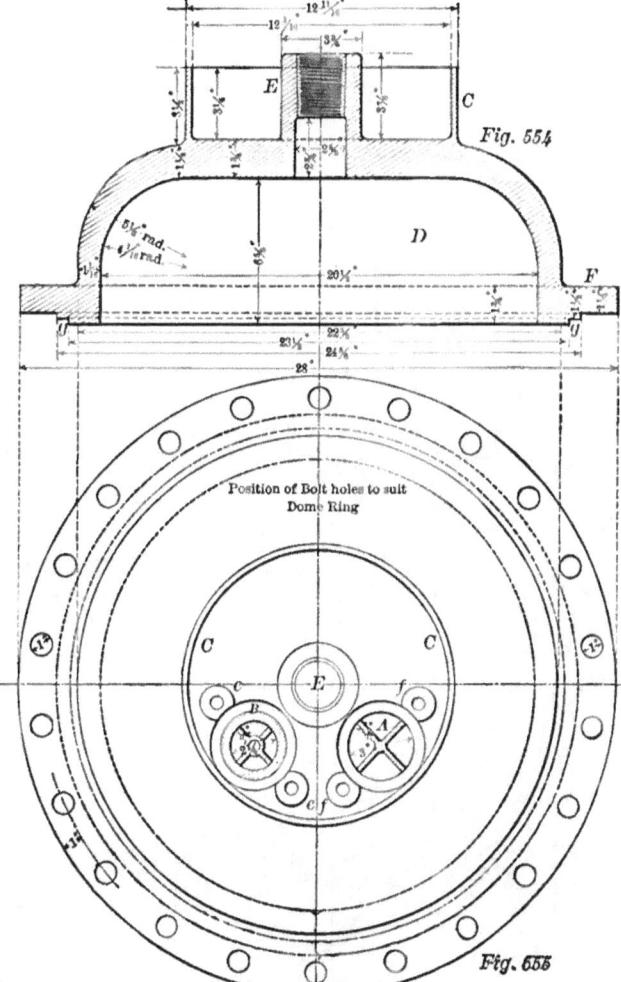

Fig. 554

Fig. 555

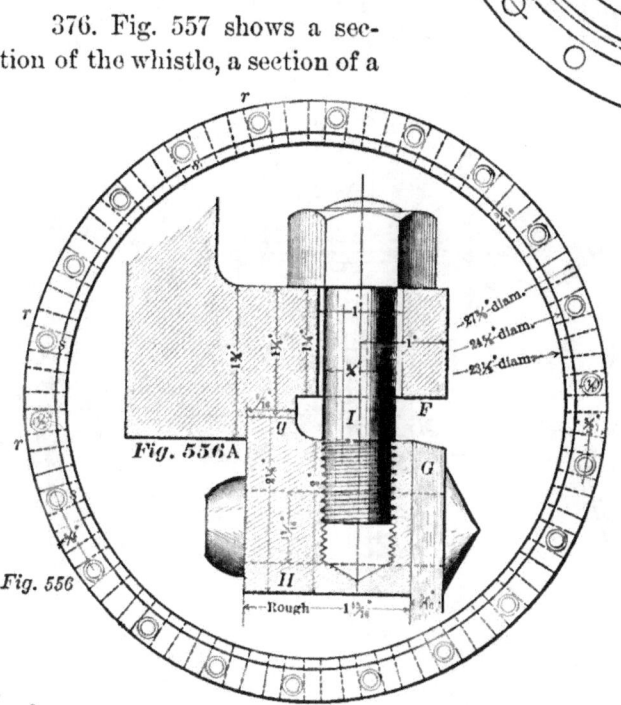

Fig. 556A

Fig. 556

common safety valve, and a section of a pop safety valve. Another section of the lower portion of the whistle is shown in Fig. 559. The whistle consists of the bell $O$, generally made of brass; the stem $P$, generally made of malleable iron—sometimes of wrought-iron; the brass bowl $N$ and the shank $M$ cast in one piece, the brass disk $W$, the brass valve $R$, and the wrought-iron lever $T$. The valve $R$ rests against the conical seat formed on the bottom of the shank. The valve is

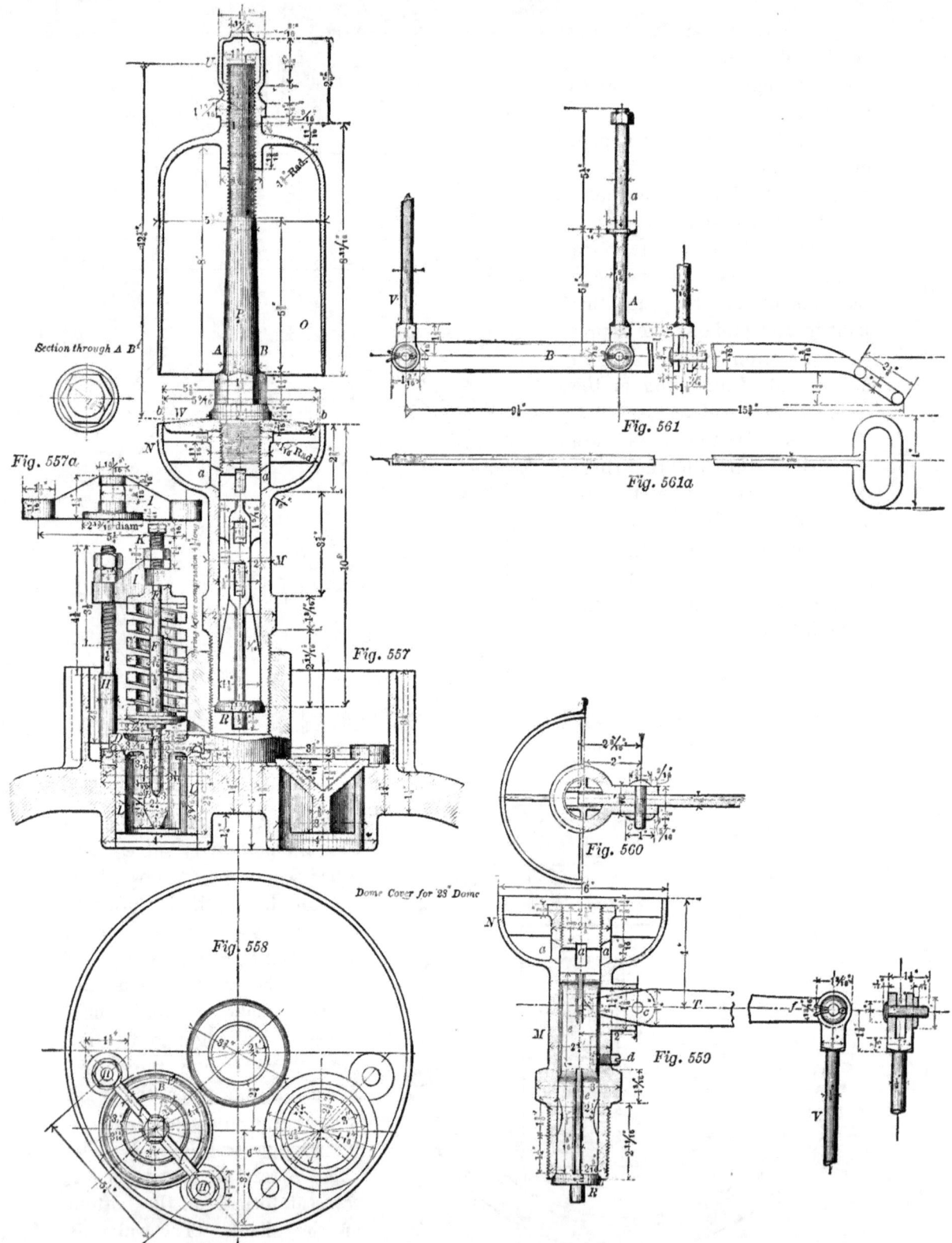

Fig. 557a
Fig. 557
Section through A B
Fig. 558 — Dome Cover for 28" Dome
Fig. 559
Fig. 560
Fig. 561
Fig. 561a

made with guides or wings $e\ e$ extending upwards in the shank for a considerable distance, so as to provide for a pocket for the screw $d$, which prevents the valve from turning, and from dropping into the boiler when the lever $T$ is at any time taken out; and also, for a pocket which receives the end of the lever $T$; the height at which the lever $T$ must be placed above the dome is generally determined by the height of the cab above which the lever $T$ must pass. The disk $W$ is held in position by the stem $P$, which is screwed into the hub cast in the center of bowl. An annular opening $b\ b$ is left between the disk $W$ and the inner surface of the bowl. The upper end of the bell $O$ is tapped, and can be set to any desired height on the stem $P$, and is secured in its position by the jam-nut $U$. The outer diameter of the bell must, of course, always be a little larger than the outer diameter of the annular opening $b\ b$. The lever $T$ works on the fulcrum $c$, and it must move the valve $R$ downwards when a communication with the steam space in the boiler is to be opened, enabling the steam to flow upwards in the shank, then pass through openings $a\ a$, and finally flow out through the annular opening $b\ b$, striking the lower end of the bell $O$, thereby producing either a deep or shrill sound, according to the size and proportions of the whistle.

Fig. 560 represents part of the plan of the bowl, and a section through the valve and fulcrum $c$. The size of whistle is designated by the outer diameter of the bell; the whistle here given is called a 6-inch whistle, and this size is the most common one, used on nearly all locomotives; sometimes a 4-inch whistle is adopted for small locomotives running on ordinary surface roads.

Fig. 561 represents another whistle lever, $B$, which is placed in the cab. The rod marked $V$ in Figs. 561 and 559 represents one and the same rod, which passes through the roof of the cab and connects the lever $B$ to the lever $T$ (Fig. 559). The lever $B$ works on the fulcrum $A$, whose shank $a$ passes through the roof of the cab and is fastened there. A plan of the lever $B$ is shown in Fig. 561$a$. This arrangement of whistle is often, but not exclusively used; indeed, sometimes the whistle is operated simply by a cord.

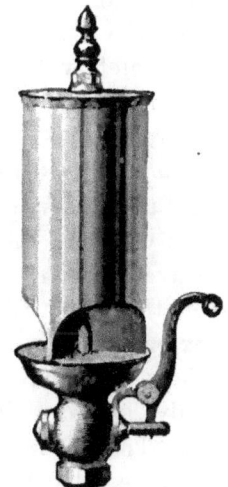

Fig. 562

## CHIME WHISTLE.

377. Fig. 562 represents a single bell chime whistle;* the peculiar features of this whistle are found in the construction of the bell, which is divided into three compartments. One of these compartments extends throughout the whole length of the bell; the second compartment is made somewhat shorter, and the third still shorter. The whistle valve need not differ in construction from that of any other whistle, and can be made to suit the taste and experience of the designer. This whistle produces three distinct tones, which harmonize and give an agreeable musical chord; and when they are used on passenger trains exclusively, serve to distinguish the latter from freight trains. These whistles have been adopted for passenger service on several railroads, and are favorably endorsed.

* Patented and made by the Crosby Steam Gauge and Valve Co., of Boston.

## POP SAFETY VALVES.

378. In Fig. 557 the section $A$ is that of a common safety valve, which has been illustrated in Fig. 551. $B$ is a section of a pop safety valve, first introduced on locomotives by George W. Richardson. The openings in the dome top for both safety valves are generally 3 inches diameter, but for the pop valve the opening is reduced by the brass bushing $L$, making the opening for the safety valve $2\frac{1}{4}$ inches diameter, which is the size of all locomotive pop safety valves. The brass bushing $L$ is pressed tightly into the dome top. On the top of this bushing a conical valve seat $C$ is formed, on which the valve $B$ rests. The valve is made with wings or guides extending nearly to the bottom of the bushing. In the center of the valve a hole of considerable depth is drilled, and on the bottom of this hole a spindle $F$ rests, which fits very loosely in the hole. The disk $G$, which is pressed on the spindle, supports the spring $S$; the upper end of this spring acts against a disk cast to the cross-bar $I$, usually made of brass. On account of showing the valve in section, one-half of the cross-bar is cut off, and the remaining half is shown foreshortened. A full view of the cross-bar is given in Fig. 557a. The upper end of the spindle $F$ is guided by the cross-bar. Two wrought-iron studs, $H$ $H$, are screwed into the dome top; one of these only is shown in Fig. 557. The nuts on these studs regulate the height at which the cross-bar is to be placed above the valve, and thereby regulating the resistance of the spring. The set-screw $K$ is for the purpose of preventing the valve from lifting too high.

When common safety valves are held down by springs arranged as shown in Fig. 552, a difficulty presents itself, namely, that the resistance of the spring increases with the lift, and therefore the lift will be insufficient, and will not be as great as that of a safety valve held down by an ordinary weight; even with the latter arrangement, the lift of the valve in many cases is less than desired. The pop valve is designed to overcome this difficulty, and therefore the diameter of the upper end of the valve $B$ is made considerably greater than the diameter of the opening, and a groove is turned in the lower face of this enlarged end of the valve; another groove $E$ is turned in the upper face of the bushing, both grooves being outside of the valve seat. Now, as the valve lifts these grooves fill with steam, causing it to act with considerable energy on the increased surfaces of the valve and seat, enabling it to overcome to some extent the increased resistance of the springs, and giving it a lift which will increase the venting capacity of the pop valve to more than double that of the ordinary safety valve loaded with a weight.

The general design of this valve and its seat is shown much plainer in Fig. 557b; but the valve here represented has an additional piece, namely, the adjustable screw ring $K$. The purpose of this ring is to regulate the difference between the blowing-off pressure and that at the time of the closing of the valve. If the boiler pressure is reduced too much before the valve closes, loosen the set-screws $L$ $L$, and turn the ring up a notch at a time; if it reduces the pressure too little, turn the ring down a notch at a time, until the desired pressure is reached, and then turn down the set-screws.

Sometimes solid nickel valve seats are used, and the spring is nickel-plated so as to prevent corrosion.

The valve shown in Fig. 557b represents one of Richardson's patent open locomo-

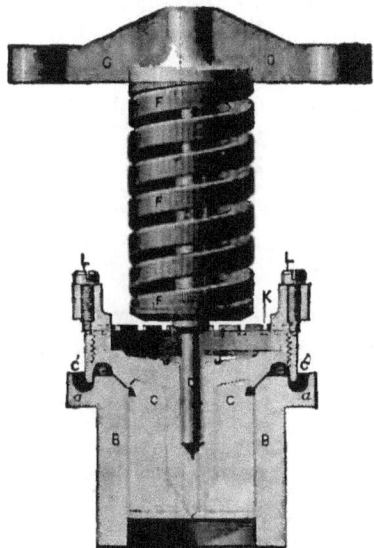

Fig. 557b.

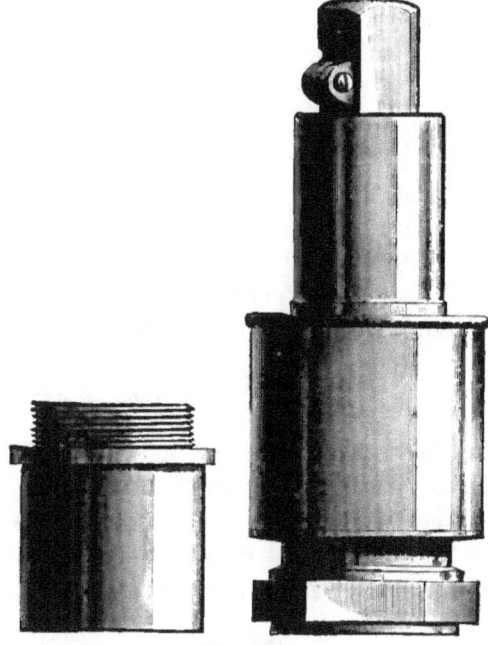

Fig. 557c.

tive pops; and Fig. 557c shows an encased one. The casing greatly reduces the noise of the escaping steam, and the lock-up device prevents tampering with the valve.

Fig. 563 represents a Crosby pop safety valve. In this design the valve $B$ rests upon two flat annular seats $V V$ and $W W$, which lie in the same plane, and form a part of the shell $A A$. This shell may be said to consist of two distinct parts; namely, the inner cylindrical chamber $C C$, and the outer cylinder $A A$; these two are connected by the hollow arms $D D$ radiating horizontally, and allowing the steam to pass between the arms and act against that portion of the lower surface of the valve $B$ which is exposed between the annular valve seats. The valve $B$ is made with wings or guides $X X$, which project into cylindrical chamber $C$. When the valve is raised against the resistance of the spring $S$, the steam flows over the inner annular valve seat $W$, passes into the cylindrical chamber $C$, and out through the passages $E E$ formed in the arms $D D$. The flange $G G$ is for the purpose of

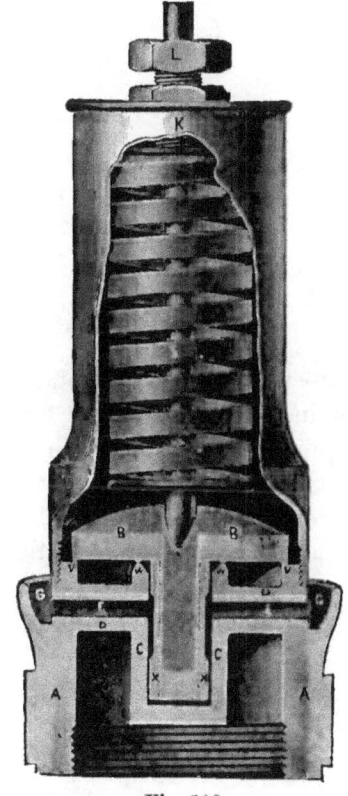

Fig. 563

turning the current of steam upwards. The tension of the spring $S$ is regulated by the screw bolt $L$. The casing around the spring serves for a frame against which the end of the spring acts, and also reduces the noise of the escaping steam. In this valve also, provisions have been made to overcome the increasing resistance of the spring when the valve is raised off its seat, for we have already seen that when the valve is closed the steam acts on that portion of the lower surface of the valve which is confined within the annular valve seats $V$ and $W$; and now, when the valve is raised off its seat, the whole lower surface of the valve is exposed to the action of the steam.

The pressure which the spring $S$ in this valve has to resist when the valve is closed will be equal to the area of the lower surface of the valve, which is confined within the outer edge of the annular valve seat $W$, and the inner edge of the annular valve seat $V$, multiplied by the steam pressure per square inch.

In the Richardson safety valve, the pressure which the spring has to resist when the valve is closed will be equal to the area of the safety-valve opening multiplied by the steam pressure per square inch.

### HELICAL SPRINGS.

379. Rules relating to the strength of helical springs—such as are used for safety valves—have been given by different authorities; some of these rules are not satisfactory, as they do not give results agreeing with practice. The best we have seen are given in "Manual of Rules, Tables and Data for Mechanical Engineers," by D. K. Clark, from which the following formulas have been taken:

$$E = \frac{d^3 \times w}{D^4 \times C}, \qquad (1)$$

in which:

$E$ = Compression or extension of one coil, in inches.
$d$ = Diameter from center to center of steel bar composing the spring in inches.
$D$ = Diameter, or side of square of the steel bar, of which the spring is made, in sixteenths of an inch.
$C$ = A constant, which from experiments made may be taken as 22 for round steel, and 30 for square steel.
$w$ = Load on spring, in pounds.

The deflection of one coil is to be multiplied by the number of free coils to obtain the total deflection for a given spring. The deflection obtained by this formula for springs made of $\frac{3}{8}$ square steel agrees very closely with practice. But for springs made of steel less than $\frac{3}{8}$ of an inch square we would suggest to increase the constant (30), as experiments seem to indicate that steel rolled to the smaller sizes does not deflect as much proportionally. For steel $\frac{1}{4}$ of an inch square a constant of 40 will give better results than a constant of 30.

To find the size of steel for a given diameter of spring and pressure, we have the following formulæ, also taken from D. K. Clark's work:

$$D = \sqrt[3]{\frac{w \times d}{3}} \text{ for round steel,} \qquad (2)$$

$$D = \sqrt[3]{\frac{w \times d}{4.29}} \text{ for square steel.} \qquad (3)$$

The letters given in these formulæ represent the same quantities as given for the first formula.

EXAMPLE 125.—How much must a helical spring be compressed to resist a steam pressure of 120 pounds per square inch? Safety-valve opening, $2\frac{1}{4}$ inches diameter; spring made of $\frac{3}{8}$-inch square steel; diameter of spring from center to center of coil, 2 inches; 6 free coils.

In applying formula (1) we have $d^3 = 2 \times 2 \times 2$. Total pressure on the valve is equal to its area multiplied by the steam pressure $= 3.97 \times 120 = 476.4$ pounds $= w$. Steel $\frac{3}{8}$ inch square $= \frac{6}{16}$, hence $D^4 = 6 \times 6 \times 6 \times 6$. And for the constant $C$ in this example we shall use 30. Hence we have

$$E = \frac{2 \times 2 \times 2 \times 476.4}{6 \times 6 \times 6 \times 6 \times 30} = \frac{3811.2}{38880} = .098.$$

Here, then, the compression for 1 coil is .098 of an inch; consequently for 6 free coils the compression will be $.098 \times 6 = .588$, or nearly $\frac{19}{32}$ of an inch.

EXAMPLE 126.—The total pressure which a helical spring has to resist is 476.4 pounds; diameter of coil from center to center of steel bar composing it is to be 2 inches; find the size of square steel required.

According to formula (3), we have

$$D = \sqrt[3]{\frac{476.4 \times 2}{4.29}} = \sqrt[3]{\frac{952.8}{4.29}} = \sqrt[3]{222} = 6.05 \text{ sixteenths inch,}$$

say $\frac{6}{16} = \frac{3}{8}$ of an inch square for the size of steel bar.

## DOME TOP MADE IN TWO PIECES.

380. In Figs. 554, 555 we have shown a dome top made in one piece, but frequently dome tops are made in two pieces. In the latter design, one piece is called the dome cover, and the other the dome ring.

Fig. 564 represents a section, and Fig. 565 a plan of the dome cover; Figs. 566 and 567 represent the section and plan of the dome ring. The dome ring is riveted to the dome sheet; the manner of fastening the dome cover to the ring and also their dimensions are plainly indicated in the illustrations.

## PUMPS.

381. In nearly all modern locomotives the water is supplied to the boiler by injectors; in a few engines the pump, which in former years was used exclusively, still holds its place, and even in these few cases we sometimes find only one pump which is placed on one side of the engine, and an injector on the opposite side. Pumps are often worked directly from the crosshead; these are called full-stroke pumps. Sometimes they are worked from an eccentric fastened to one of the driving axles, and others are worked from a small crank attached to the crank-pin. The stroke of the latter class of pumps is generally less than that of the piston, and therefore they are called short-stroke pumps.

Figs. 568, 569, and 570 represent a full-stroke pump designed for an eight-wheeled passenger engine. Fig. 568 represents a section; Fig. 569 a plan; Fig. 570 an end view of the pump, and Fig. 570*a* a section through the lower stuffing-box and gland. The pump consists of the barrel *B*, the lower air-chamber *A*, the upper air-chamber *C*, the valves *L L*, the valve seats *I I*, and the cages *K K*. The valves are cylindrical

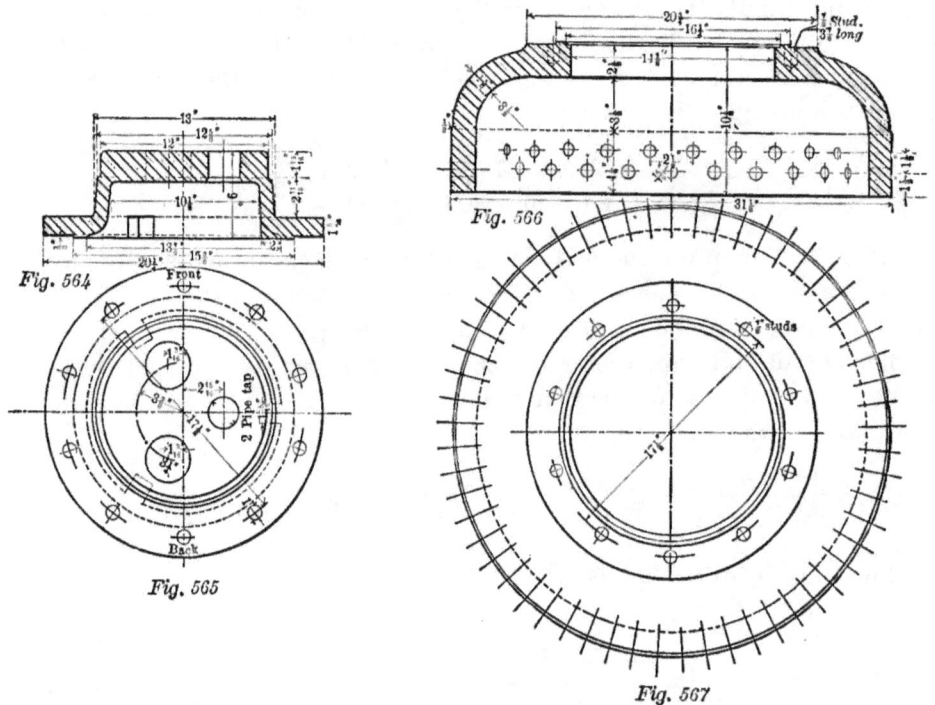

in form, and rest on the seats *I I*, the latter resembling ordinary disks. The upper valve seat rests on the face of the flange of the barrel, and the lower valve seat rests on the face of the flange on the air-chamber. The cages rest on the valve seats, the whole being clamped together and held in position by the bolts through the flanges of the air-chambers, and those of the barrel. The joints between the flanges, valve seats, and cages are ground joints. An enlarged section and plan of the cage and valve seat are shown in Figs. 571 and 572. The purpose of the cage is to guide the valve, and prevent it from lifting too high.

The barrel and air-chambers are often made of brass; sometimes of cast-iron; the valves, seats, and cages are always made of brass.

The stuffing-box on the lower air-chamber receives the end of the suction pipe, and a water-tight connection is made by means of the hemp packing in the stuffing-box *E*. The stuffing-box on the upper chamber receives the end of the delivery pipe, and here, also, a water-tight connection is obtained by means of the hemp packing in the stuffing-box *G*. The suction pipe extends to the rear end of the engine, where it is connected by a rubber hose to the tank. Since the suction pipe is comparatively a straight pipe, it is often made of iron; sometimes of brass. The delivery pipe extends to the check valve on the boiler, and because the delivery pipes have to be bent, they are made of copper.

MODERN LOCOMOTIVE CONSTRUCTION. 389

The manner of fastening the pump to the frame $F$ is plainly shown in Fig. 569.

Fig. 573 represents the plunger; it is made of a wrought-iron bar, with a tapered shank $a$ turned at one end. This shank fits in a lug either cast or bolted to the crosshead.

In a pump of the size here shown, the lift of the lower valve—sometimes called the suction valve—is one-quarter of an inch; and the lift of the upper valve—sometimes

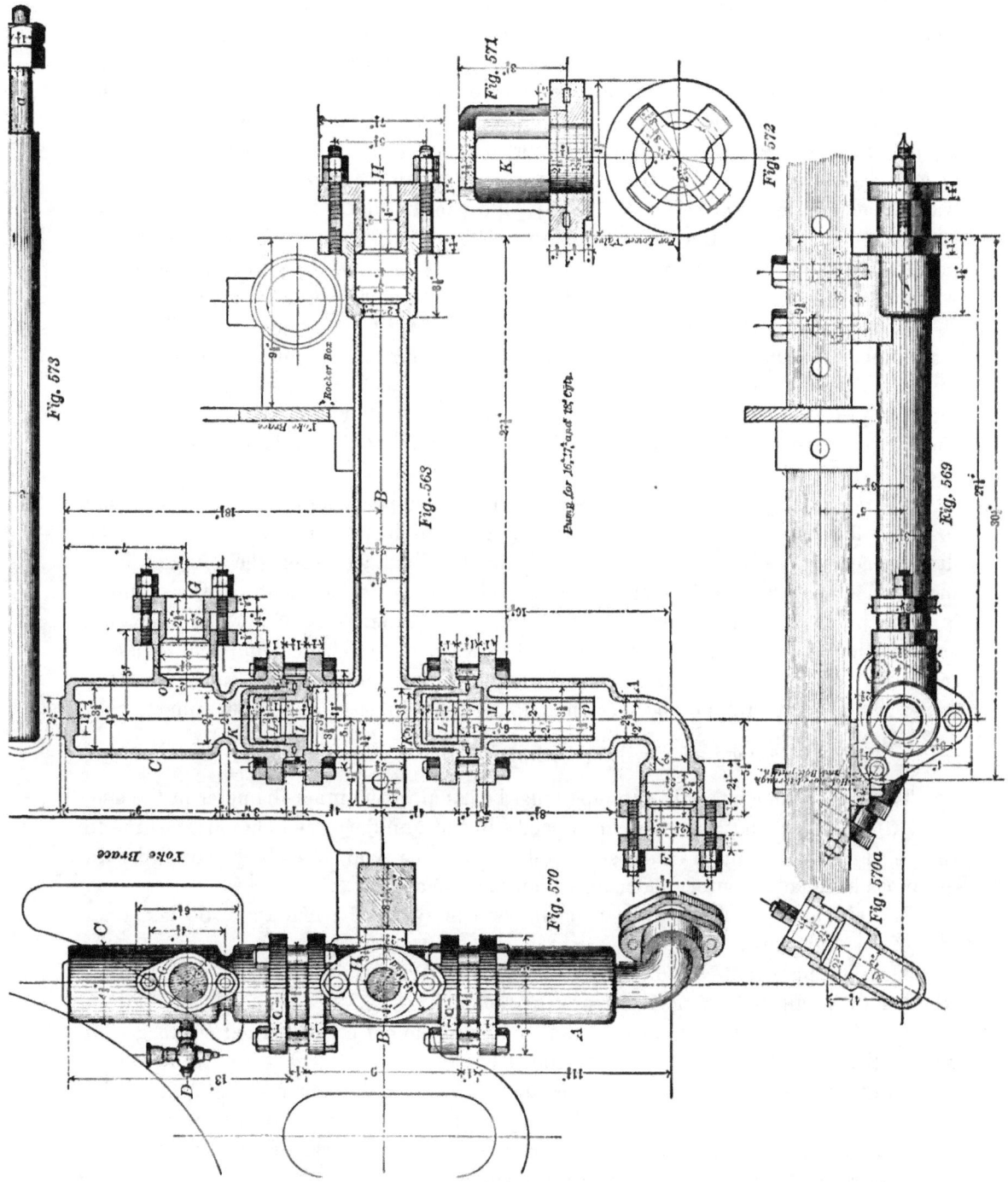

called the delivery valve—is $\frac{5}{16}$ of an inch. The successful working of the pumps depends to a considerable extent on the correct amount of lift, hence the necessity of exercising great care in determining the lift; too much lift will prevent a quick closing of the valve; it will also cause it to pound, thereby ruining the valve seat.

382. The air-chambers are for the purpose of relieving the pump and its pipes from sudden shocks, which are liable to occur by the rapid motion of the pump plunger. For instance, as soon as the water rises above the top of the opening $o$ in the upper air-chamber, the air in the latter will be compressed, and act as a cushion, thereby reducing the intensity of a shock. The lower air-chamber is arranged somewhat differently; a pipe $M$ extends from the top to within a short distance from the bottom of the chamber, so as to leave an annular air space. This pipe $M$ is called a dip pipe. As soon as the water reaches the lower end $p$ of the dip pipe, the air in the annular space is compressed, and has a similar effect as the air in the upper chamber. It must readily be perceived that when the lower air-chamber does not contain a dip pipe, the chamber will soon be rendered useless, because the air in it will be replaced by water.

In many locomotive pumps the water is discharged through the top of the upper air-chamber, instead of through its side, as shown in our illustrations. In cases of this kind the upper chamber must be arranged similar to the lower one; that is to say, it must be provided with a dip pipe extending from the top of the chamber to within a short distance from its lower end; otherwise the chamber will soon be filled with water, and rendered useless.

The air capacity above the water line in the upper chamber should be equal to the total displacement of the pump plunger; in fact, one and a half times the displacement will give better results. Thus, for instance: Let the plunger be 2 inches in diameter, and 24 inches stroke. The total displacement of the plunger is found by multiplying its cross-sectional area by the stroke. Now, the area of a cross-section 2 inches in diameter is 3.14 square inches, hence the total displacement will be $3.14 \times 24 = 75.36$ cubic inches. Consequently the air capacity of the upper chamber should not be less than 75.36 cubic inches, and 75.36 cubic inches $+ \frac{75.36}{2} = 113.04$ cubic inches will be better.

The inner diameter of the dip pipe must be equal to the inner diameter of the suction or feed pipe; and since the air capacity in the annular space should be equal to the air capacity of a plain chamber, it follows that many air-chambers provided with dip pipes have larger outer dimensions than plain chambers.

The air capacity of the lower air-chamber can always be made a little less than that of the upper one.

383. The small pet-cock $D$, shown in Fig. 570, is for the purpose of ascertaining whether the pump is feeding water into the boiler.

Fig. 574 represents different views and details of the pet-cock (marked $D$ in Fig. 570) and its fittings. The lower end of the rod $A$ fits in a square pocket cast into the pet-cock plug. In many engines this rod extends a little above the running board; the lever $B$, attached to the top of the rod $A$, is connected to the reach-rod $C$, which leads into the cab, enabling the engineer to open or close the cock, and thus determine whether the pump is feeding water into the boiler.

## CHECK VALVES.

384. Figs. 575, 576, 577 represent the check valve. Its purpose is to prevent the water in the boiler from flowing back into the pump, and also to prevent the water from flowing out of the boiler and doing serious damage in case of accidents to the pump or delivery pipe. The check valve consists of a brass or cast-iron case $A$, the valve $L$, the

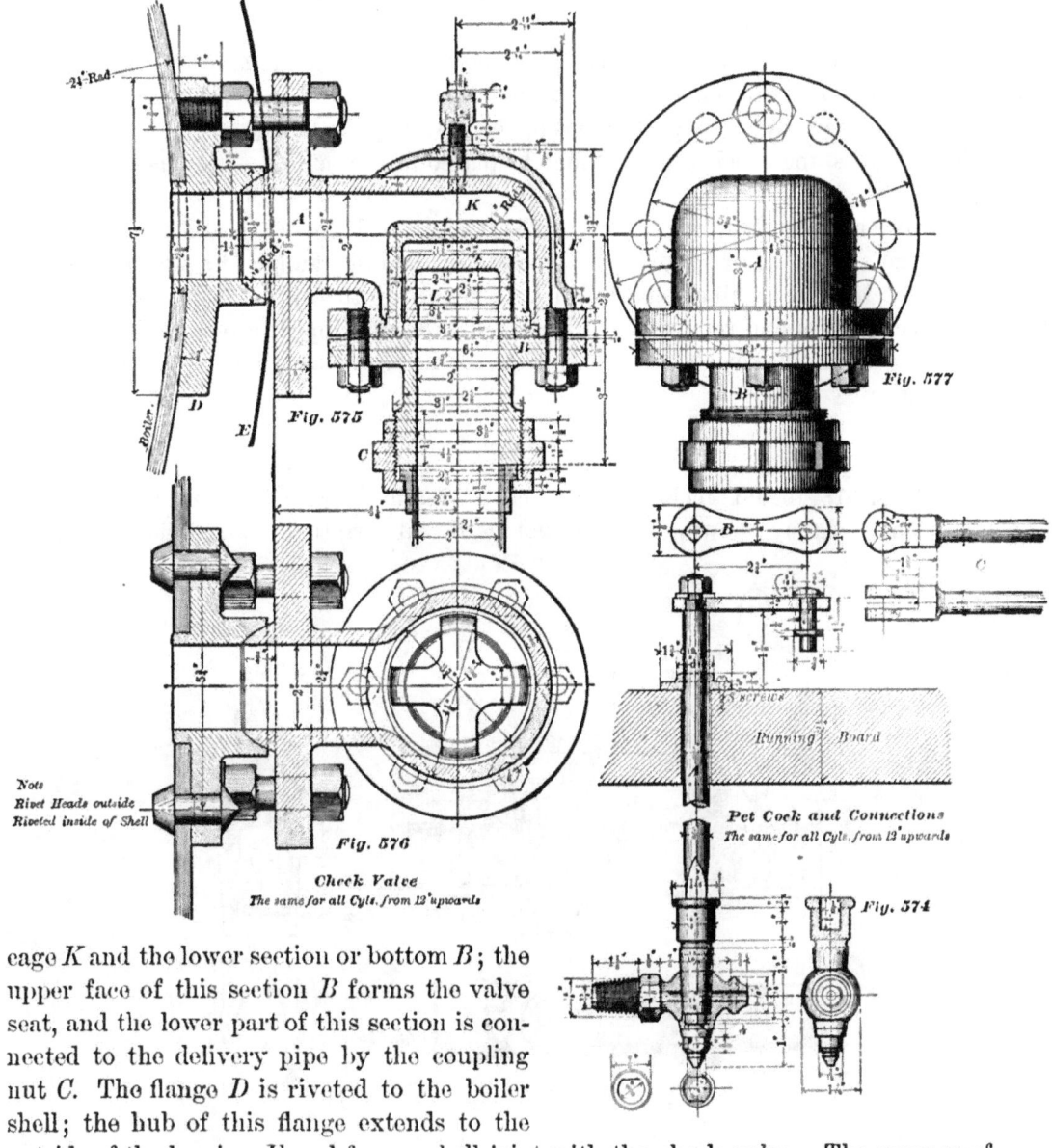

cage $K$ and the lower section or bottom $B$; the upper face of this section $B$ forms the valve seat, and the lower part of this section is connected to the delivery pipe by the coupling nut $C$. The flange $D$ is riveted to the boiler shell; the hub of this flange extends to the outside of the lagging $E$, and forms a ball joint with the check valve. The manner of fastening the check valve to the boiler is plainly shown. $F$ is simply a false cover; it is not shown in Fig. 577.

The check valve should be placed towards the front of the boiler; it is usually placed at a distance of 1½ to 2 feet from, and in the rear of, the front flue sheet, so as to feed the water into the coolest part of the boiler, and also prevent as much as possible the collections of any impurities, which may enter into the boiler with the water, around the hot sheets in the furnace. These impurities generally collect under the check-valve opening in the boiler in the form of mud, and pile up towards the front flue sheet. If the check valve is connected to the back end of the boiler, as has been done in a few instances, the impurities will collect in the water space around the fire-box, causing the sheets to be burnt.

It is also important that the valve L should stand in a vertical position, consequently the center of the check-valve opening in the boiler is generally placed in a horizontal plane passing through the axis of the barrel of the boiler.

For injectors, the check valves should be placed in the same position as those for pumps.

In many engines we find the check valve attached to the boiler in a manner different from that shown in our illustrations; instead of the brass flange D, a wrought-iron plate (reinforcing plate), about ½ inch thick, is riveted to the inside of the boiler, and both the boiler sheet and reinforcing plate are drilled and tapped to receive the shank of the check valve. Nearly all the check valves for injectors are attached to the boiler in this manner.

### FEED-COCKS.

385. Figs. 578 to 581 inclusive represent different views of the feed-cock; its construction is plainly shown, and does not need a description. The kind of feed-

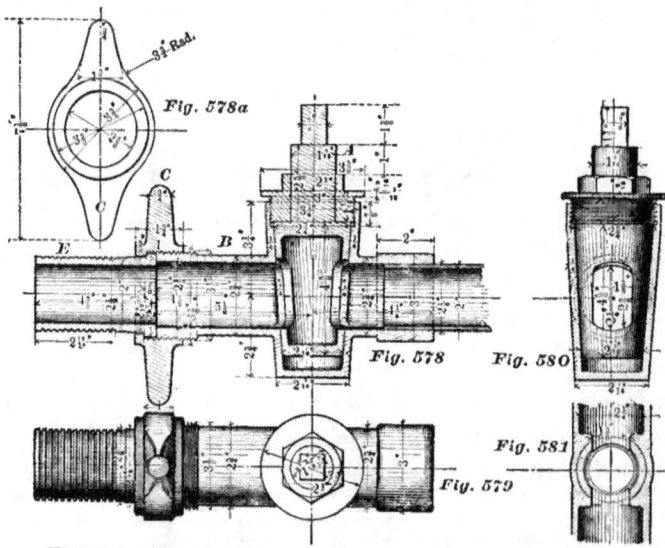

Feed Cock. The same for all Cyls. from 12" upwards.

cock here shown is preferable to one whose plug extends through the bottom of the casing, and adjusted by a nut at the bottom; feed-cocks of the latter class are liable to leak; or, when adjusted to prevent leaking, will often require too much power to open or close them.

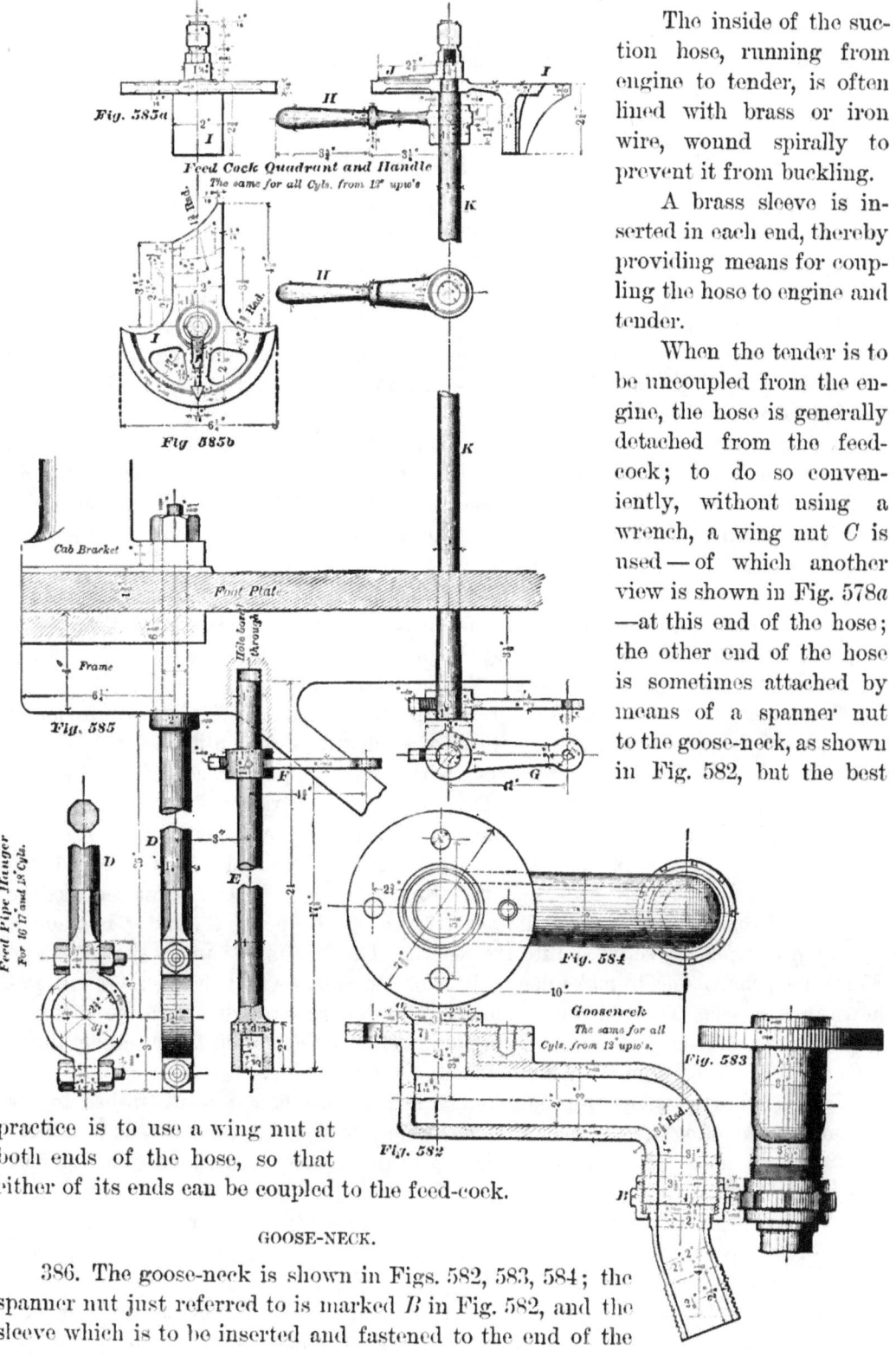

The inside of the suction hose, running from engine to tender, is often lined with brass or iron wire, wound spirally to prevent it from buckling.

A brass sleeve is inserted in each end, thereby providing means for coupling the hose to engine and tender.

When the tender is to be uncoupled from the engine, the hose is generally detached from the feed-cock; to do so conveniently, without using a wrench, a wing nut $C$ is used—of which another view is shown in Fig. 578$a$—at this end of the hose; the other end of the hose is sometimes attached by means of a spanner nut to the goose-neck, as shown in Fig. 582, but the best practice is to use a wing nut at both ends of the hose, so that either of its ends can be coupled to the feed-cock.

### GOOSE-NECK.

386. The goose-neck is shown in Figs. 582, 583, 584; the spanner nut just referred to is marked $B$ in Fig. 582, and the sleeve which is to be inserted and fastened to the end of the

hose is also shown in this figure. The goose-neck is made of cast-iron, and is bolted to the bottom of the tank. The conical counterbore $a$ forms the valve seat. The manner of operating this valve will be shown later.

### FEED-PIPE HANGERS AND CONNECTIONS.—POSITION OF PUMPS.

387. The feed-cock is held in position by clamping its branch $B$ in the feed-pipe hanger $D$, which is shown in Fig. 585. The shank of this hanger takes the place of a bolt for bolting the frame, foot plate, and cab bracket together.

The socket in the feed-cock rod $E$ fits the square end of the feed-cock plug $A$; the other end of the rod $E$ works in a bearing drilled into the frame. The crank or lever $F$ on the rod $E$ is connected to the crank $G$ on the quadrant rod $K$; the upper end of this rod works in a bearing drilled through the quadrant $I$, of which other views are shown in Figs. 585$a$ and 585$b$.

The quadrant $I$ is bolted to the back end of the boiler in such a position as to bring the handle $H$ within easy reach of the engineer, enabling him to open, close, and regulate the amount of opening in the feed-cock. The pointer $J$ fastened to the upper end of the quadrant rod indicates on the quadrant the amount of opening in the feed-cock.

In order to obtain a close regulation of feed-water, the opening in the feed-cock plug may be made square, with a diagonal of the square coinciding with the axis of the plug; with this arrangement a closer regulation can be obtained in that position of the feed-cock plug where close regulation is most desirable.

For the majority of injectors at present in use, the feed-cock is not required, and consequently the quadrant and rod are also abolished; but non-lifting injectors do require a feed-cock; for these, a feed-cock with a square opening, as described above, is recommended; the opening is generally $\frac{7}{8}$ of an inch square.

The feed-pipe hanger $D$ is, of course, retained in all engines, and for injectors this hanger takes hold of a brass sleeve; the rear end of this sleeve is threaded like the rear branch of the feed-cock, and the front end of the sleeve is formed like the front branch of the feed-cock, and brazed to the feed-pipe, if the latter is made of copper; iron pipes are screwed into the sleeve. The feed-pipe hanger shown in Fig. 585 is an expensive one to make, hence in many engines we find the hangers made as shown in Fig. 586. The rod $A$ is often made of square wrought-iron; the shank $b$, turned at the end, holds the cast-iron clamps $c$, $c$, which support the sleeve above referred to. The cast-iron clamps are usually $1\frac{3}{4}$ inches wide.

For cold climates a heater pipe about $\frac{3}{4}$ inch inside diameter is attached to the suction pipe, enabling the engineer to blow steam into the latter, to prevent freezing.

388. The pumps can be attached directly to the frames, as illustrated in Fig. 569, only in eight-wheeled passenger engines. In Mogul, ten-wheeled, and consolidation engines there is no room to place them in similar positions, therefore, in the latter classes of engines, we often find them attached to the guides. Figs. 587 and 588 show a pump designed for fastening it to the guide and guide-yoke; the only difference between this pump and the one previously shown is in the position of the air-chambers, and the position and design of the lugs. The type of guide for which this pump was

designed is shown in Fig. 241. The lug near the stuffing-box (Fig. 588) is bolted to the top of the guide, and the lug near the air-chamber is bolted to the guide-yoke.

The illustrations (Figs. 587, 588) show the air-chambers placed in the neighborhood of the center of the barrel; the object aimed at in this design is to concentrate the weight of the pump as much as possible near one of the points of support. As far as the distribution of weight is concerned, the design is correct; but in placing the air-chambers at or near the center of the barrel, the direction of the flow of water is interfered with, which is an objection. The proper place for the air-chambers, in the class of pumps here shown, is at the end of the barrel; and although they cannot always be placed there, it should be remembered that any change in the direction of the flow of water, such, for instance, as is caused by placing the air-chamber in the center of the barrel, has a tendency to reduce the efficiency of the pump, and this should be avoided as much as possible.

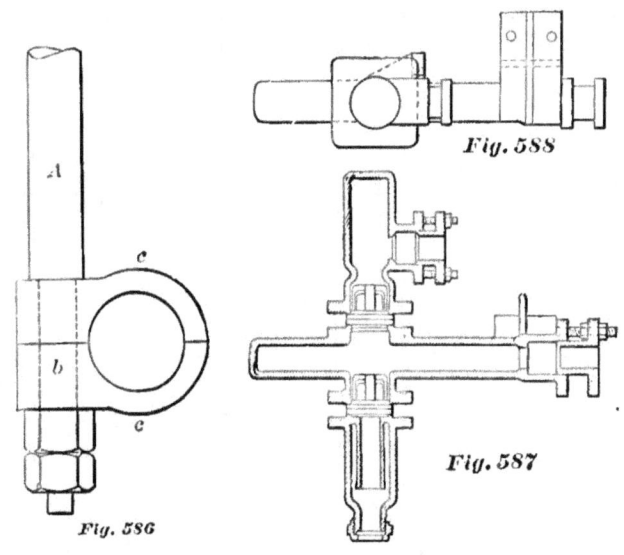

It may also be well to remark here that in all pumps the suction valve should be placed as near as possible to the plunger, leaving only a sufficient water-way between them. Necessary changes in the form and size of the water passages should be made gradually; sudden enlargements and contraction should always be avoided.

### SHORT-STROKE PUMPS.

389. We have previously referred to short-stroke pumps; sections and other views of this class of pumps are given in Figs. 589 to 592. These pumps are placed under the boiler, and are bolted to a cross-brace A extending from frame to frame. The plunger D is worked from an eccentric placed on one of the driving axles. Fig. 593 shows separate views of the pump-rod jaw C, to which the pump-rod B is connected. The valves and cages in this pump are of the same design as those in the full-stroke pumps previously illustrated. This pump is designed for a 12-inch cylinder.

Figs. 594 to 596 represent another short-stroke pump. The pump is fastened to the draw-bar, and is worked from a pin attached to one of the crank-pins; hence the pump is placed outside of the driving wheels. It will be noticed that the valves L and cages K are made somewhat different from those previously illustrated; this difference is not due to any particular necessity, but is simply a matter of choice.

## SIZE OF PUMPS.

390. To find the size of pump required, we should estimate the consumption of steam, and this may be approximately obtained by calculating the weight of steam in the cylinder from its pressure and volume at the time of its release. In locomotives, the average pressure of the steam at the time of its release does not vary much, and therefore we may make the pump capacity directly proportional to the cylinder

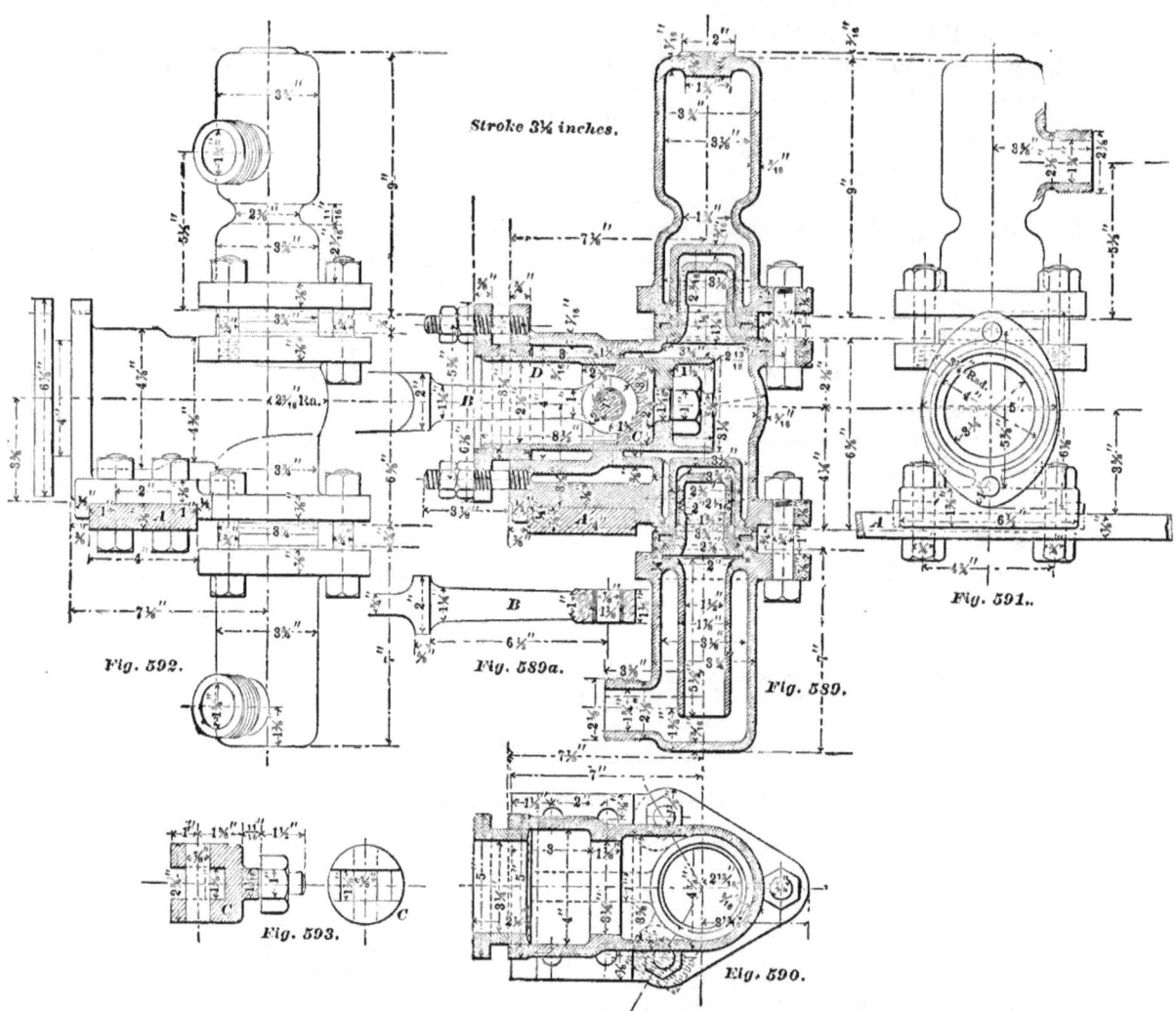

Fig. 592.  Fig. 589a.  Fig. 589.  Fig. 591.  Fig. 593.  Fig. 590.

capacity, without finding the amount of steam consumed. Since the stroke of a full-stroke pump is equal to that of the piston in the steam cylinder, we may further simplify the computation and make the cross-sectional area of the plunger directly proportional to the cross-sectional area of the cylinder. Practice indicates that for locomotives having two pumps, good results will be obtained by making the cross-sectional area of each plunger equal to $\frac{1}{72}$ of the cross-sectional area of one cylinder. This proportion is not strictly adhered to by the different builders; indeed, many

MODERN LOCOMOTIVE CONSTRUCTION. 397

builders use the same size of pump for two or three different sizes of cylinders; for instance, the pump illustrated in Fig. 568 is used for cylinders 16, 17, and 18 inches in diameter. But the proportion here given we believe to be a good one to adopt in designing a full-stroke locomotive pump. Hence the following:

RULE 96.—Divide the cross-sectional area of the cylinder by 72; the quotient will

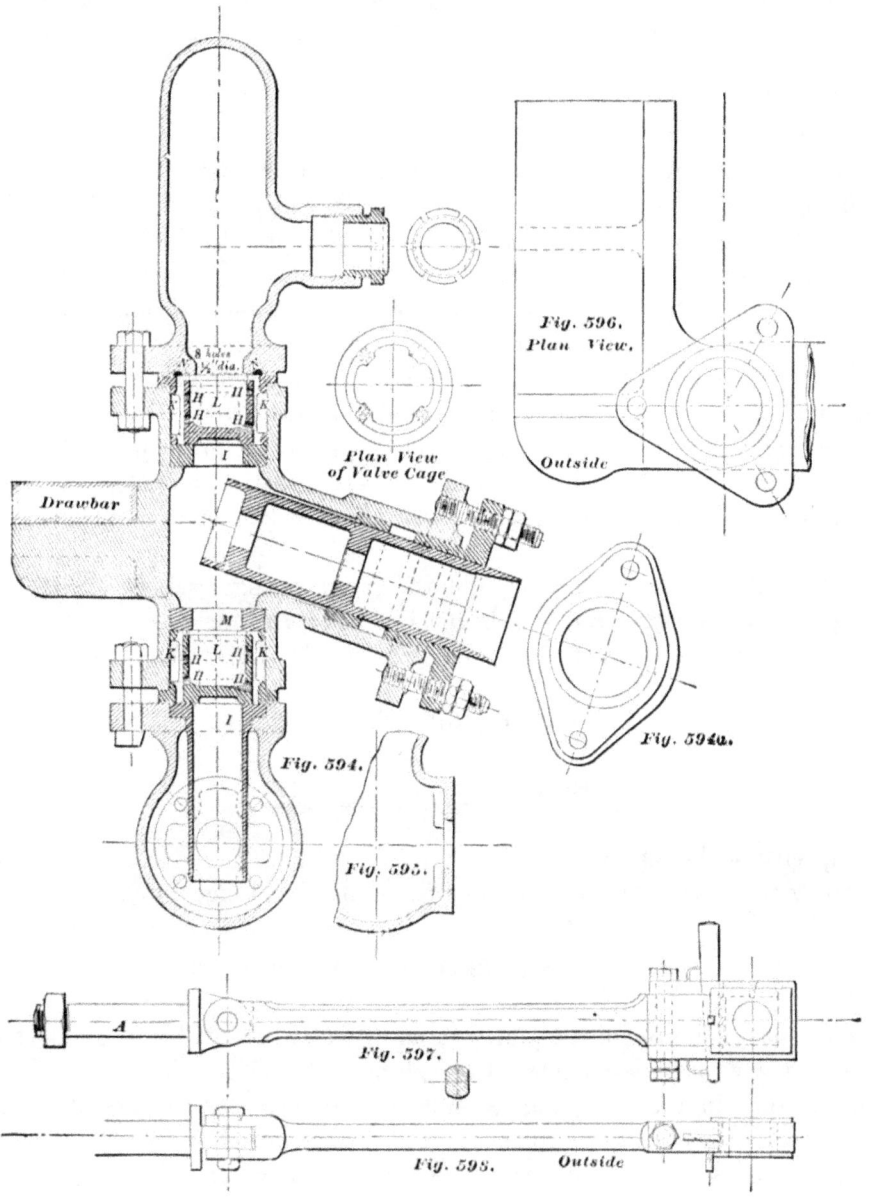

be the cross-sectional area of the pump plunger for locomotives in which two full-stroke pumps are to be used.

EXAMPLE 127.—What should be the diameter of the pump plunger for a full-stroke pump in a locomotive having cylinders 17 inches diameter?

The cross-sectional area of a cylinder 17 inches diameter is 226.98 square inches, and $\frac{226.98}{72} = 3.15$ square inches for the cross-sectional area of the plunger; the corresponding diameter is 2 inches (very nearly), hence the diameter of the plunger should be 2 inches.

Let us take another example. Find the diameter of the pump plungers for a full-stroke pump in a locomotive having cylinders 10 inches diameter. Here we have $\frac{78.54}{72} = 1.09$ square inches for the cross-sectional area of the pump plunger, and the corresponding diameter is $1\frac{3}{16}$, nearly.

In a similar manner we find that the diameter of the pump plungers for full-stroke pumps for cylinders 20 inches in diameter will be nearly $2\frac{3}{8}$ inches. These results agree very closely with the average locomotive practice.

The capacity of a full-stroke pump designed by the foregoing rule will be $\frac{1}{72}$ of the capacity of one steam cylinder; and short-stroke pumps should have the same capacity. We may therefore establish the following:

RULE 97.—Multiply the cross-sectional area of the cylinder in square inches by the length of stroke of piston in inches, and divide the product by 72; the quotient will be the capacity of the pump in cubic inches. Dividing this capacity by the length of stroke of plunger in inches, we obtain the cross-sectional area of the plunger in square inches; or, dividing the capacity of the pump by the cross-sectional area of the plunger, we obtain the stroke of plunger.

EXAMPLE 128.—Find the diameter of the pump plunger; its stroke is 7 inches; the diameter of the steam cylinder is 18 inches; stroke, 24 inches.

The cross-sectional area of the steam cylinder is 254.47 square inches; hence its capacity is

$$254.47 \times 24 = 6107.28 \text{ cubic inches,}$$

and

$$\frac{6107.28}{72} = 84.82 \text{ cubic inches}$$

for the capacity of the pump.

Dividing the capacity of the pump by the stroke of plunger, we have

$$\frac{84.82}{7} = 12.11 \text{ square inches}$$

for the cross-sectional area of the plunger; and its diameter will be $3\frac{15}{16}$ inches nearly; hence we may say that the diameter of the plunger should be 4 inches.

Suppose that in the foregoing example the diameter—4 inches—of the plunger had been given instead of the stroke, and that it is required to find the stroke of the plunger. Under these conditions we proceed in the following manner:

We first find the cross-sectional area of a plunger 4 inches diameter, which is 12.56 square inches; now, dividing the pump capacity by 12.56, we have $\frac{84.82}{12.56} = 6.75$ inches, which is the stroke of the pump plunger. These results agree closely with the size of the pump illustrated in Fig. 594, which is an exact copy of a working drawing;

the diameter of the plunger is 4 inches; stroke, 7 inches; this pump was designed for 18 × 24 inch cylinder.

EXAMPLE 129.—Find the diameter of a short-stroke pump plunger whose stroke is $3\frac{1}{2}$ inches, the locomotive having cylinders 12 inches in diameter, stroke, 20 inches.

The capacity of the steam cylinder is 113.10 × 20 = 2262 cubic inches. That of the pump should be

$$\frac{2262}{72} = 31.41 \text{ cubic inches;}$$

and the cross-sectional area of the plunger will be

$$\frac{31.41}{3.5} = 8.97 \text{ square inches;}$$

and its diameter will be $3\frac{3}{8}$ inches, nearly. Here, again, we have results agreeing closely with dimension in Fig. 589, which is also a copy of a working drawing.

Of course the fact of using only one pump and an injector for the same locomotive will not make any difference in the sizes of pumps found by the foregoing rules. When no injector is used, two pumps of the sizes here given will be required for each engine.

# CHAPTER IX.

### SPRING GEAR.

391. Fig 599 represents the spring gear for the driving wheels under an eight-wheeled passenger locomotive, with cylinders 17 inches diameter and 24 inches stroke. Of course in this class of engines we have only two driving axles; these are marked $F$, $F_2$. The spring saddles, their position on the driving-boxes, and the manner of placing the springs on the saddles, have been illustrated in Figs. 303, 304. In the illustrations before us we have only shown the center lines $S$, $S_2$ of the spring saddles. This design of spring gear is probably the most common one used for eight-wheeled engines 4 feet 8½ inches gauge; a few builders make changes in the minor details, but the design as a whole remains the same. $A$, $B$, and $C$ are the spring hangers; separate views of the hanger $A$ are shown in Fig. 603, of $B$, in Fig. 604, and of $C$, in Fig. 605. Figs. 601, 602 show separate views of the equalizing lever $E$, and Fig. 600 shows separate views of the lever fulcrum $D$; all of these are made of wrought-iron.

In this design the lever fulcrum is bolted to the frame with two bolts, but we believe it to be better practice to fasten it with four bolts whenever the design of engine will admit that number. The central slot in the equalizing lever is cut sufficiently long to allow the lever to vibrate around the gib or key through the lever fulcrum. The equalizing lever is connected to the springs by the link hangers $B$, $B_2$ passed through the slots in the springs, and in the ends of the equalizing lever; the outer ends of the springs are connected to the frame by the link hangers $A$ and $C$; the springs and equalizing lever form a system of levers free to turn about their respective fulcrums.

Fig. 606 represents the driving-wheel spring gear for a ten-wheeled engine. The only difference between this spring gear and the one shown in Fig. 599 is that the former has an additional spring and equalizing lever on each side of the engine.

These springs support the greatest portion of the weight of the engine; a smaller portion is supported by the trucks; the axles, wheels, driving-boxes, spring saddles, and springs, the side-rods, a part of the main-rods, part of the eccentric-rods and the eccentrics are directly supported by the track; and these weights subtracted from the weight on the driving wheels will give the load on the driving-wheel springs.

The purpose of the equalizing levers is to distribute the weight equally on the driving axles, also to reduce the effects of shocks caused by the rails, and to allow the

MODERN LOCOMOTIVE CONSTRUCTION. 401

wheels to adjust themselves readily to any unevenness in the track without throwing an undue strain on the frames and other parts of the locomotive. It will readily be

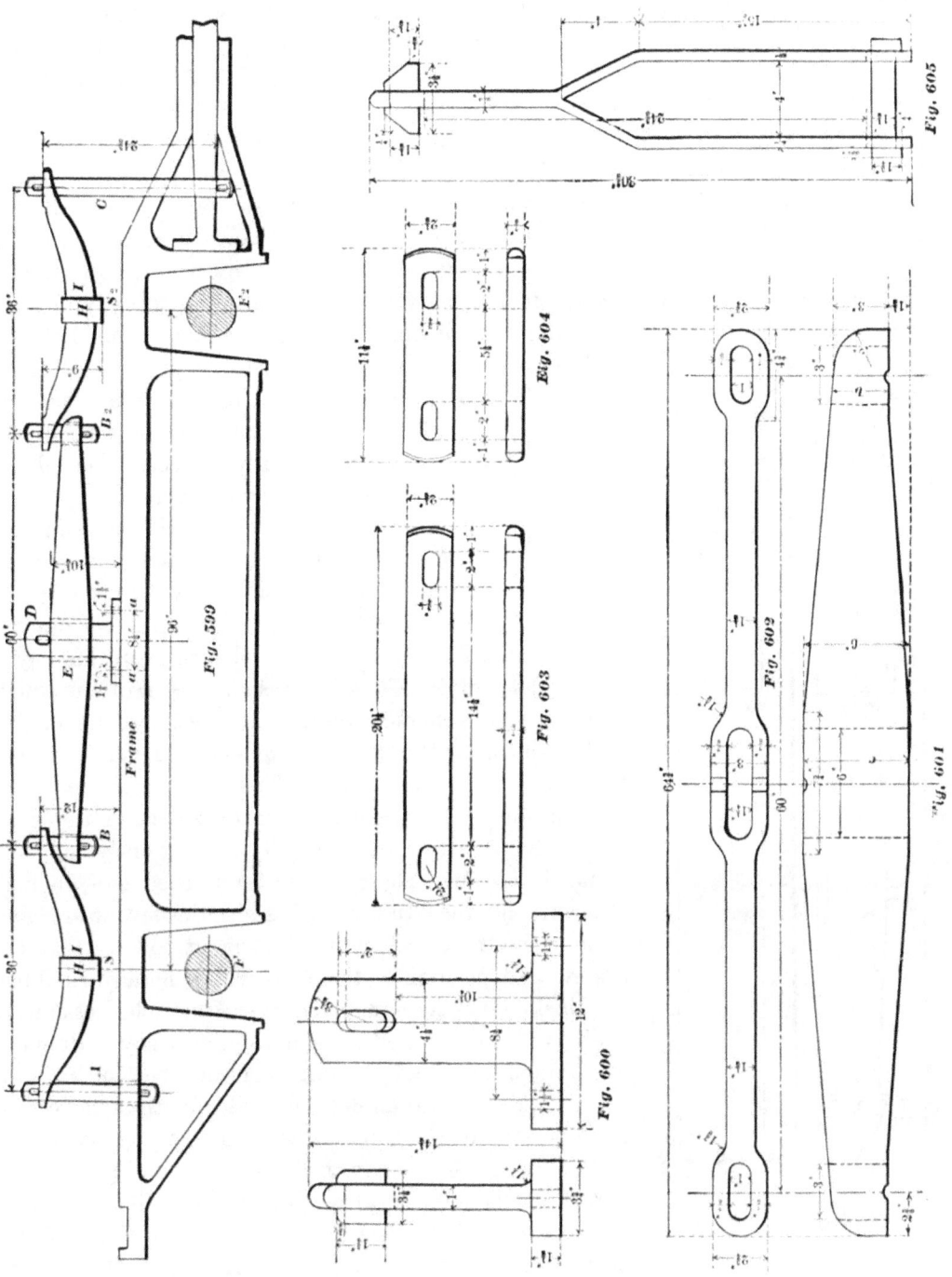

seen that when one wheel receives, through the unevenness of the road, a shock, it is immediately transferred to the spring; a part of this shock will be transferred through the outer spring hanger to the frame, and the other part will be transferred to the

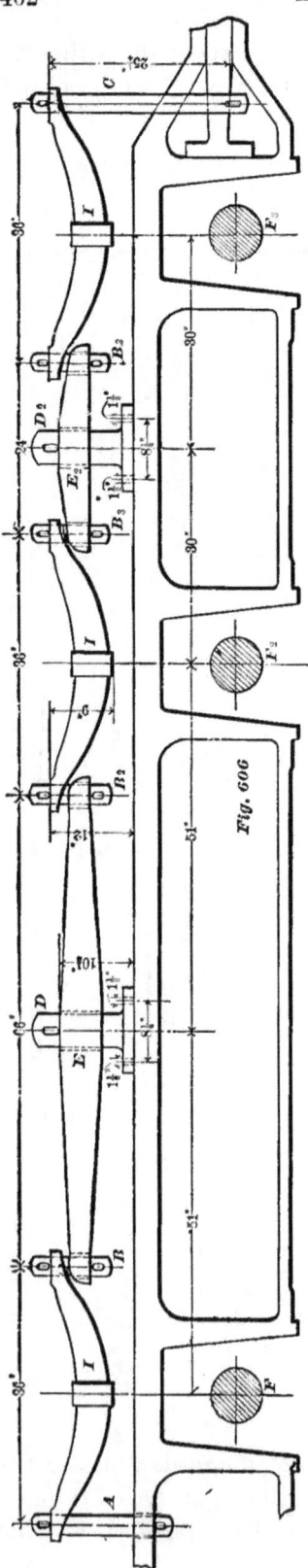

Fig. 606

equalizing lever, and from thence thrown on the next spring; or, again, if one spring becomes momentarily burdened by an oscillation of the engine, the equalizing lever will immediately transfer a part of this load to the next wheel, thereby distributing the effects of the shock among all the axles. If, on the other hand, an equalizing lever is not used, the whole effect of the shock must be resisted by one spring, and this spring must be made strong enough to enable it to do so; consequently the spring must be made heavier than it need to be with an equalizing lever; but making the spring heavier will also reduce its elasticity, which, in turn, will greatly increase the danger of breaking the axle, saddle, spring hangers, and spring; heavy springs will also make the riding on the engine very uncomfortable, and, in some cases, to such a degree as to be almost unbearable. From the foregoing remarks we can readily conceive the advantages gained by the use of equalizing levers.

In eight-wheeled passenger engines, and also in tenwheeled engines, all the driving-wheel springs are connected by equalizing levers. But we will presently see that for Mogul and consolidation engines it is not practicable to connect all the driving-wheel springs in this way.

In determining the thickness and depth of the equalizing lever we generally find that the design of the engine will establish the thickness. For instance, in many engines the pads which connect the boiler to the frame are placed at each side of the lever fulcrum $D$, and the nuts which fasten the pads to the boiler will be along one side of the equalizing lever. There should be at least $\frac{1}{8}$ of an inch clearance between these; and since the levers are generally made of a symmetrical form, it follows that the design and position of the pads will generally establish the thickness of the equalizing lever; this thickness rarely exceeds $1\frac{1}{2}$ inches; and for small engines, say with cylinders 9 inches in diameter, will sometimes be $\frac{7}{8}$ inch.

392. Before we can determine the depth of the equalizing lever we must know the load to which it is subjected. Take, for instance, the spring over the journal $F$ in Fig. 599. The load on this spring will be equal to the pressure on the journal $F$; one-half of this load will be transferred to the spring hanger $A$, the other half to the spring hanger $B$. In order to produce equilibrium, the force acting at the other end $B_2$ of the lever must be equal to that at $B$. The force at $B_2$ is equal to one-half of the

reaction of the spring over the journal $F_2$, and this reaction is equal to the pressure on this journal. This mode of reasoning shows that the pressure on the journals will be equalized; in other words, the pressure on the journal $F$ will be equal to that on the journal $F_2$. It further shows that the tension on each spring hanger is equal to one-half of the pressure on one journal, or one-quarter of the sum of the pressures on the two journals $F$ and $F_2$; and the tension on the fulcrum $D$ will be equal to one-half the sum of the pressures on the two journals. Consequently the equalizing lever $E$ must be considered as a beam loaded at the center, and freely supported at the ends, the length of the lever being equal to the distance between the centers of the spring hangers $B$ and $B_2$, and the load equal to one-half the sum of the pressures on the journals $F$ and $F_2$. Thus, for instance, if the pressure on each journal is 1,000 pounds, then the sum of the pressures will be 2,000 pounds; the tension on each spring hanger will be 500 pounds; the tension on the fulcrum $D$ will be 1,000 pounds, and consequently the load on the equalizing lever will also be 1,000 pounds.

393. Spring gears, such as are shown in Figs. 599 and 606, cannot be used in many narrow-gauge engines, because in these engines the width of the fire-box is generally made so great as to leave insufficient room for the springs between the fire-box and the driving wheels. Figs. 607, 608 show a portion of a general plan of an eight-wheeled passenger engine, 3 feet gauge; the spring gear is plainly shown, and besides this, the design and arrangement of other details are given, which we shall first describe very briefly, as we believe they will be interesting and instructive to the reader. The ash-pan $A$ here shown is made of sheet-iron. In order to obtain a sufficient grate surface, the width of the fire-box $B$ is such as to cause the reduction in the width of those portions of the frames $F$ which lie alongside the fire-box, the lower brace of the frame remaining the full width throughout. This class of frames we have called "slab frames"; they have been illustrated in Figs. 298 and 299. $C$ is the rear damper handle; $E$, the rigging for the front damper handle; $G$, the pads securing the frames to the boiler, and yet allowing the boiler freedom for expansion; $H$, the foot plate; $I$, the injector; $J$, the draw bar; $K$, the lever for shaking the grates; and $L$, the reversing lever.

For the spring gear two equalizing levers $M_1$ $M_2$ are placed on the top of each driving-box $O$; the equalizing levers $M_2$ on the front box are connected to the spring hanger $P_5$; this spring hanger is of the T form, its upper branches forming hubs for taking up the space between the two equalizing levers, the whole being connected by a pin about ¾ inch in diameter; the lower end of the hanger $P_5$ passes through slots cut in the braces of the frame, a spiral spring is placed between the bottom of the frame, and the gib which passes through the lower end of the hanger. The other ends of the same equalizing levers are connected to the spring hanger $P_4$. The form of this hanger is shown in Fig. 609. The jaws $a$ $a$ are connected to the levers, and the lower end takes hold of the spring. The other end of the spring is connected by means of the hanger $P_1$ to the equalizing lever $N$ below the frame; the form of the spring hangers $P_1$ and $P_3$ is shown in Fig. 610. The lever $N$ works on the pin $Q$ shown in Fig. 611; the holes drilled in the boiler pad $G$ and the plate $D$ form bearings for the pin $Q$. A pin or roller $b$ is inserted between the spring and spring seat $C$, as shown in Fig. 612. The equalizing levers on the rear box, and spring hangers for the same, are like those

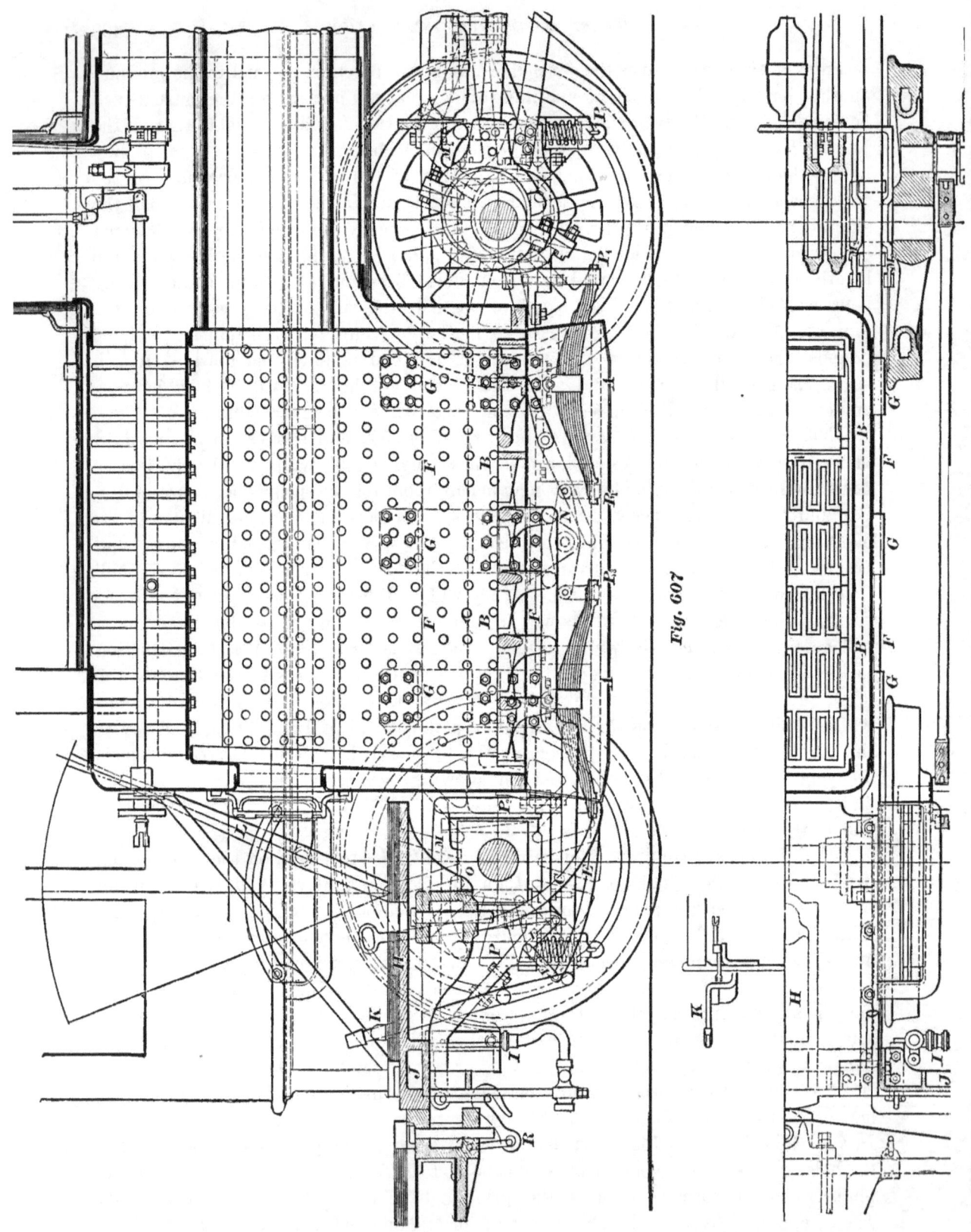

Fig. 607

we have just described. All the boiler pads extend to and are fastened to the lower brace of the frame, so as to strengthen the latter and enable it to carry the weight thrown upon it.

394. Now let us return to the spring gear shown in Fig. 599, and find by calculation the depth of the equalizing lever $E$.

EXAMPLE 130.—Find the depth of an equalizing lever for a 17 × 24 inch eight-

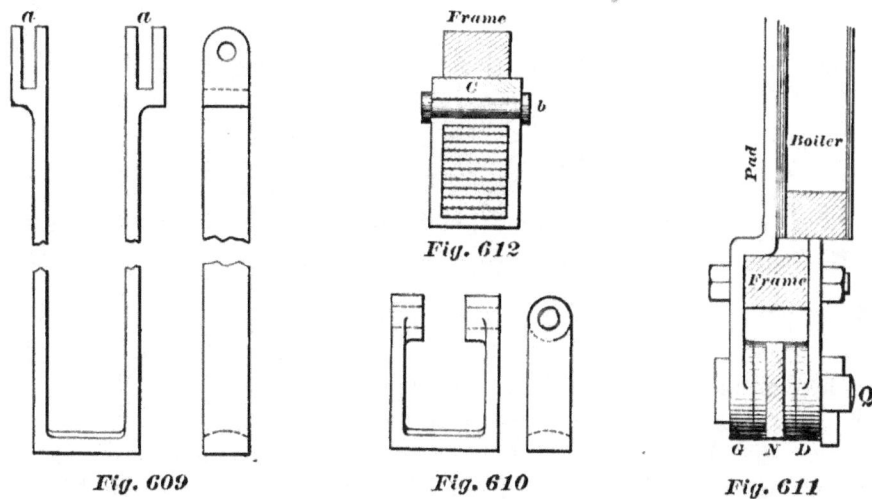

Fig. 609     Fig. 610     Fig. 611

Fig. 612

wheeled passenger locomotive; the thickness of the lever is to be $1\frac{1}{2}$ inches; the distance from the center of the spring hanger $B$ to the center $B_2$ is 60 inches.

In Table 5 (Art. 24) we find that the weight on the drivers for this class and size of engine is 52,020 pounds. From this weight we must subtract the weight supported directly by the track, such as driving wheels, axles, etc., as stated in Art. 391. Supposing the total weight to be subtracted (that of four driving wheels, two axles, four driving boxes, etc.) amounts to 12,000 pounds, we then have 52,020 − 12,000 = 40,020 pounds to be supported by four springs; hence each spring will have to support

$$\frac{40020}{4} = 10005 \text{ pounds.}$$

Since the load which the equalizing lever has to support is equal to one-half of the sum of the loads on two springs, we may say that the total load on the lever is 10,005 pounds; and since the length of the equalizing lever is measured from center to center of the spring hangers, we may consider the equalizing lever to be a simple beam 60 inches long, having a rectangular cross-section, and freely supported at the ends; its thickness is $1\frac{1}{2}$ inches and loaded at the center with a weight of 10,005 pounds. It is now required to find the depth of this beam. In books treating on the strength of material we find the following equation for a beam of this kind, loaded under the foregoing conditions: $\frac{1}{4} W l = \frac{1}{6} f b d^2$, in which $W$ represents the load in pounds; $l$, the length of the lever in inches; $f$, the stress in pounds per square inch on the outer fibers of the lever—that is, the fibers running lengthways of the lever; $b$, the breadth of the lever in inches; and $d$, the depth of the lever in inches at the center. Usually for $f$ a value of 12,000 pounds is assigned, so that our equation will read: $\frac{1}{4} \times W \times l = \frac{1}{6} \times 12000 \times b \times d^2$; this equation may be reduced to

$$W \times l = 8000 \times b \times d^2.$$

Hence, to find $d^2$ we have

$$\frac{W \times l}{8000 \times b} = d^2;$$

substituting the numerical values for the symbols, we obtain

$$\frac{10005 \times 60}{8000 \times 1\frac{1}{2}} = d^2 = 50.02,$$

which, as will be seen by the symbol $d^2$, is the square of the depth of the lever at the center. Consequently, to find the depth $d$ we extract the square root of 50.02, or

$$d = \sqrt{50.02} = 7.07 \text{ inches,}$$

which is the depth at the center of the equalizing lever.

From the foregoing we may establish the following:

RULE 98.—To find the depth at the center of an equalizing lever for an eight-wheeled passenger engine. Subtract from the weight in pounds on the driving wheels that portion of the weight which is directly supported by the rails; divide the remainder by 4; the quotient will be the load at the center of the equalizing lever. Multiply this load by the length of the lever in inches, and call the result product $A$. Multiply the breadth in inches by 8,000, and call the result product $B$. Divide the product $A$ by product $B$, and find the square root of the quotient; the result will be the depth at the center of the equalizing lever.

If there is a notch cut across the lever, so as to form a bearing for the gib in the fulcrum, as shown in Fig. 601, the depth found by the foregoing rule will be the distance from the bottom of the notch to the bottom of the lever.

If the lever has a uniform breadth, and tapers uniformly towards its ends, as shown in Fig. 601, the depths at the ends should be equal to one-half of that at the center. This proportion will give us an equalizing lever which is at no place weaker than at the center.

It would seem that the thickness of the metal at the sides of the slots cut through the lever should be equal to one-half of the thickness of the solid part of the lever; but practice seems to indicate that better results are obtained by increasing it about 15 per cent.

The lever shown in Figs. 601 and 602 was made for a 17 × 24 inch eight-wheeled engine. Comparing the depth given in these figures with the results of our calculation, we find that the latter call for a greater depth. The reason for this difference is twofold: first, the weight on the drivers under the engine, for which the lever in Figs. 601, 602 was designed, was less than the weight taken in our example; second, the lever must have been made of a better quality of wrought-iron than is usually adopted for this class of work.

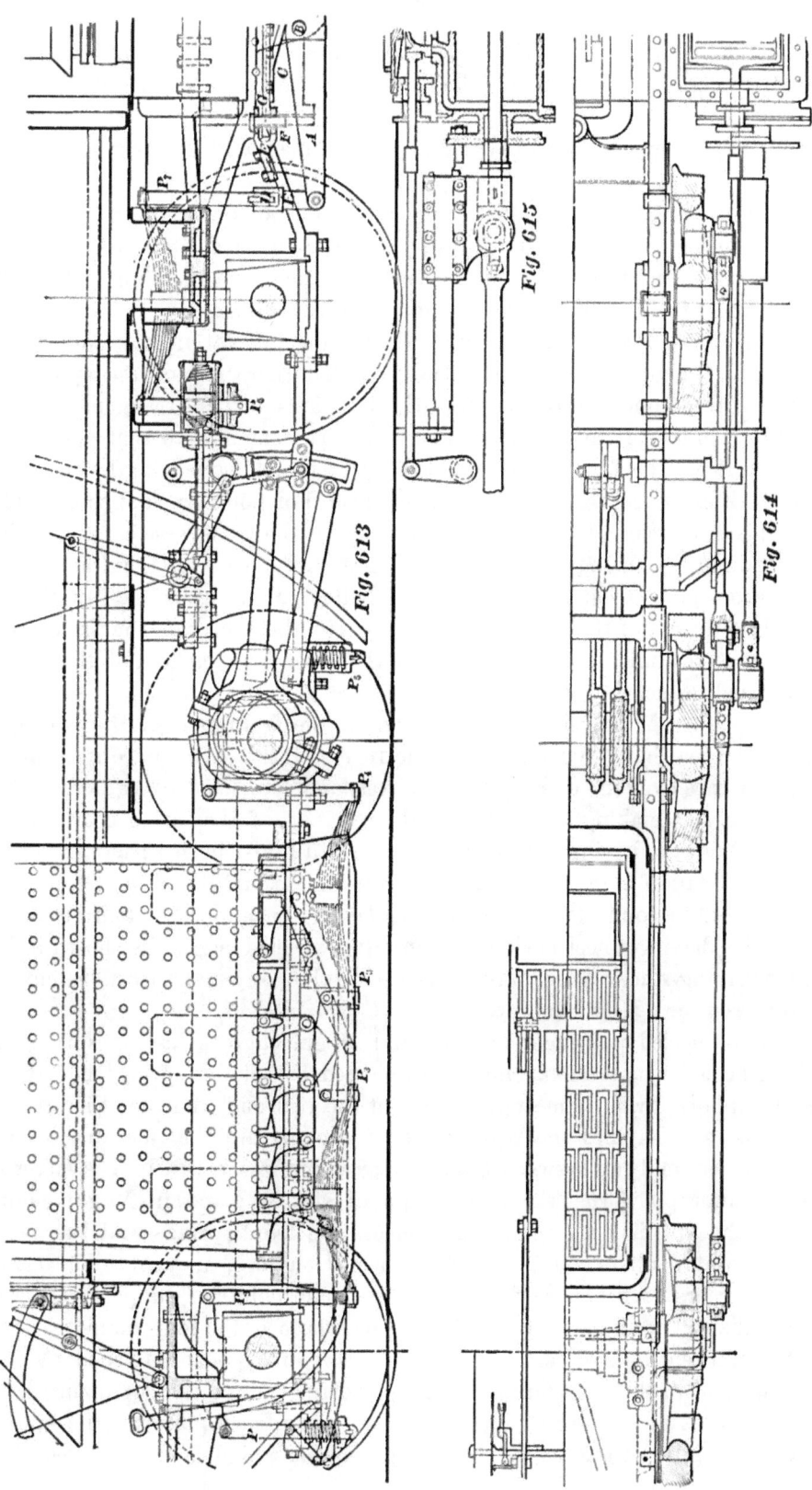

If for any reason the depth of the equalizing lever is limited, compelling us to find the thickness instead of the depth of the lever, we may use the following formula:

$\dfrac{W \times l}{8000 \times d^2} = b$, in which the symbols denote the same quantities as given on page 405.

The depth of the short equalizing lever in Fig. 606 is also found by Rule 98. In regard to the load which the short lever has to support at its center, we only need to say that it is equal to the load at the center of the long equalizing lever. This will be evident from the fact that they are connected by a spring.

395. Figs. 613, 614 show a portion of the sectional elevation and plan of a narrow-gauge Mogul locomotive. It will be noticed that there is not an equalizing lever between the front and central driving-wheel springs. This arrangement divides the spring gear into two distinct parts. The rear part is similar to that described in the foregoing article; the front part consists of a system of equalizing levers connecting the front driving-wheel springs to the two-wheeled or pony-truck springs. The front spring hangers $P_7$ (Fig. 613) connect the springs to the transverse equalizing lever $D$; the longitudinal equalizing lever $A$ is placed midway between the frames; it works on the fulcrum pin $B$ held in the casting $C$ bolted to the under-side of the cylinder saddle; the rear end of the lever $A$ is connected to the center of the transverse lever $D$ by means of the link $E$; the front end of the lever $A$ takes hold of the king bolt in the pony truck, which is not shown here.

In wide-gauge Mogul engines the design of the front part of the spring gear is similar to the one here shown; but at the rear end, the springs are generally placed above the frames over the driving-wheel boxes, and connected by equalizing levers as shown in Fig. 599, making the design of the rear part of the spring gear similar in all respects to that of a driving-wheel spring gear for a four-wheeled passenger engine.

In consolidation engines the springs over the second, third, and fourth driving axle are generally connected by equalizing levers, forming a system similar to the design of the driving-wheel spring gear in a ten-wheeled engine, as shown in Fig. 606. The front driving-wheel springs are connected to the pony truck by a system of levers like those used for a Mogul engine.

In eight-wheeled passenger engines, and Mogul engines having spring gears as here described, the mass of machinery supported by all the springs has three main points of support; two of these points are at the rear end, and the other at the front. In both classes of engines the rear points of support are the fulcrums of the main equalizing levers midway between the two rear driving wheels. In passenger engines the truck center pin forms the front point of support; and in Mogul engines the fulcrum of the equalizing lever which connects the front springs and the pony truck forms the front point of support. Ten-wheeled engines, and consolidation engines with spring gears as here described, have five main points of support; the fulcrums of the equalizing levers between the driving wheels form the four main rear points of support. In a ten-wheeled engine the front point of support is formed by the truck center pin; and in the consolidation engine the fulcrum of the equalizing lever connecting the front driving-wheel springs and the pony truck performs the same office.

396. The center of gravity of a passenger engine will always be between the three

points of support, as it should be, in order to make the engine ride steadily. The center of gravity of ten-wheeled, Mogul, and consolidation engines should always lie between the front point of support and the two points—one on each side of the engine—lying midway between those driving wheel springs which are connected by equalizing levers. There is danger of changing this condition; for instance, if in Mogul engines all the driving-wheel springs are connected by equalizing levers, the two rear points of support just referred to will be moved forward and the center of gravity will be at the back of these points, instead of lying between these and the front point of support; the consequence will be that the rear end of the engine will have a constant tendency to drag downwards, and interfere with the steady riding of the engine. The same remarks apply to consolidation engines. Here, then, we perceive the reason for not having equalizing levers between the front springs and the adjacent ones. There is another advantage gained with this arrangement. When the pony-truck wheels pass over any unevenness of the track, or obstacles, the truck springs will be relieved of some of the strain, a portion of it being thrown on the front driving-wheel springs.

### EQUALIZING-LEVER FULCRUM.

397. The design of the engine generally determines the height of the equalizing-lever fulcrum, which in the majority of cases will have to be made as short as possible, so that the bulge of the fire-box will not prevent the equalizing lever from being taken off without removing the fulcrum. This fact must not be overlooked when the distance from the top of frame to the center of the boiler is to be determined; it will sometimes compel us to place the boiler higher than we otherwise should. Since it is always the aim to keep the boiler as low as possible, it follows that there is no room to spare for the equalizing-lever fulcrum, and its length is cut down so as to leave sufficient room only for the vibration of the equalizing lever without striking the frame or top of bolts which secure the fulcrum to the frame.

398. The principal stress to which the fulcrum is subjected is a tensile stress; and since its weakest section is through $a\ b$, Fig. 615a, it follows that the area of this cross-section must be sufficiently large to resist the tensile stress. Careful observations indicate that the general practice is to allow

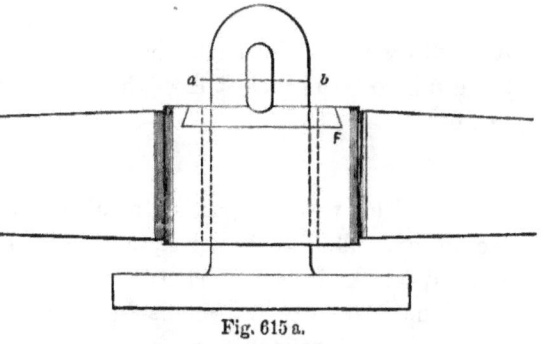

Fig. 615 a.

3,000 pounds per square inch of cross-section. The tensile stress on fulcrum is equal to the load on the equalizing lever, consequently, with this data, the area of the cross-section through $a\ b$ (Fig. 615a) of the fulcrum is easily computed by the following rule:

RULE 99.—Divide the load on the equalizing lever by 3,000; the quotient will be the number of square inches in the cross-section $a\ b$ of the fulcrum.

EXAMPLE 131.—In Art. 394 we have found that the load on the equalizing lever is 10,005 pounds. Find the cross-sectional area through the weakest part of the fulcrum.

Here we have

$$\frac{10005}{3000} = 3.33+ \text{ square inches, say } 3\tfrac{3}{8} \text{ square inches.}$$

The ratio of the thickness and width of the fulcrum is arbitrary, and in deciding upon these dimensions good judgment must be used; but usually, on account of the cramped space, the fulcrum will have to be made as thin as possible. If, now, the thickness of the fulcrum is to be 1 inch, which is about the average thickness, then

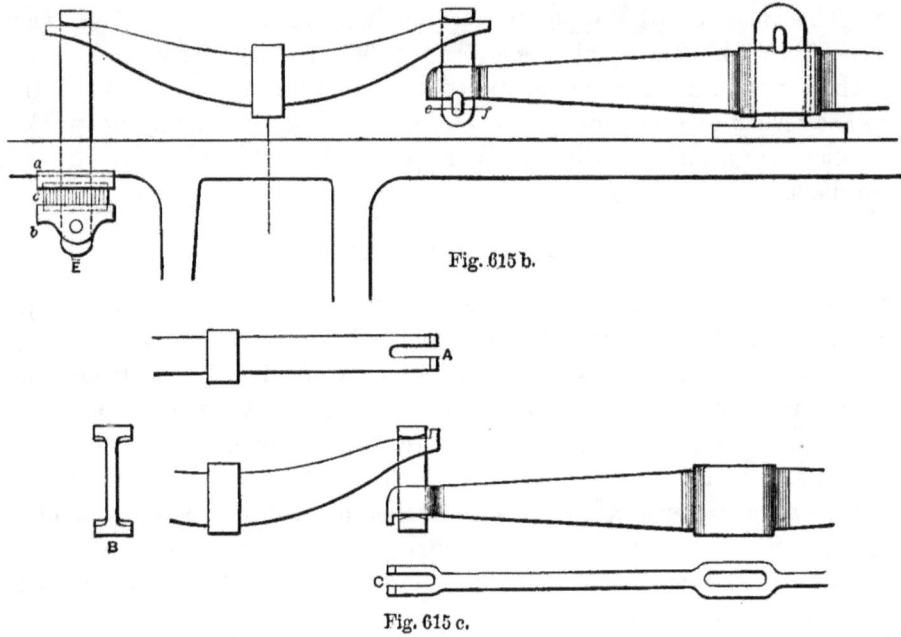

Fig. 615 b.

Fig. 615 c.

its width will have to be $3\tfrac{3}{8}$ inches plus the thickness of the gib; if the thickness of the gib is to be $1\tfrac{1}{8}$ inches, then the width of the fulcrum will have to be $3\tfrac{3}{8} + 1\tfrac{1}{8} = 4\tfrac{1}{2}$ inches.

### SPRING HANGERS.

399. The weakest part of a spring hanger, shown in Fig. 615b, is through the section $e\,f$. The stress per square inch of this area is also 3,000 pounds, the same as allowed for the fulcrum; hence the following rule:

RULE 100.—Divide one-half the load on the spring by 3,000; the quotient is the number of square inches in the cross-section through the weakest part of the spring hanger.

EXAMPLE 132.—The load which a spring has to sustain is 10,005 pounds. Find the area of the weakest part of the spring hanger.

Here we have

$$\frac{10005}{2} = 5002.5 \text{ pounds stress on the hanger;}$$

and

$$\frac{5002.5}{3000} = 1.667 \text{ square inches in the cross-sectional area.}$$

The ratio of its thickness and width is also arbitrary. If the thickness is established, we divide the cross-sectional area by the thickness; the quotient plus the thickness of the gib will be the width of the hanger. Hence, if the thickness of the hanger is ⅞ inch, and the thickness of the gib is ¾ inch, then the width of the hanger will be

$$\frac{1.667}{.875} + .75 = 2.65 \text{ inches, say } 2\tfrac{5}{8} \text{ inches.}$$

If gibs are not used as shown in Fig. 615c, and if the load on the spring and the thickness of the hanger remain the same as before, then the width of the hanger will be simply

$$\frac{1.667}{.875} = 1.9, \text{ say 2 inches.}$$

The foregoing results agree well with the ordinary practice, but it seems that the tendency is to make the spring hangers rather heavy, and the equalizing levers are often made too light.

400. In Figs. 603 and 604 are shown spring hangers made of flat bars; indeed, this is the simplest form of hangers. There are other forms used, as shown in Figs. 615b and 615c. It will be seen that the one shown in Fig. 615c has the form of an I, as shown at B. When this hanger is used, slots in the springs have to be cut through to the ends as shown at A; and the ends of the equalizing lever are forked as shown at C. The small projections forged to the ends of the spring and to the ends of the equalizing lever prevent the hanger from disengaging itself.

In Fig. 615b the spring hangers have a T-head forged to one of their ends; the opposite ends are plain, and secured by either pins or gibs. It will also be noticed that the pin through the bottom of the hanger E does not bear against the under-side of the frame. In this case two castings a and b are introduced between the pin and the frame, with a rubber block c, about 2 to 2½ inches thick, between these castings. Sometimes a helical spring is used in place of the rubber, as shown at P in Fig. 607. This arrangement is somewhat expensive, and is not always used when the main-springs are placed over the axle-box; but when the springs are placed as shown in Fig. 607, the helical spring on the hanger must be used.

Sometimes the spring hangers are secured at their ends by a pin D, of the form shown in Fig. 615d. This pin is cut from a hexagonal bar; the corners are turned off at the center so as to form a bearing for the hanger; the corners which remain at each end form, so to speak, shoulders which prevent the pin from moving out of position. Of course, for a pin of this kind, no slots in the hangers are needed; they have simply holes drilled through them large enough to admit the hexagonal part.

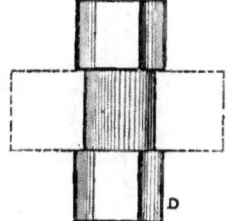

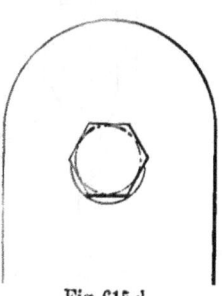

Fig. 615 d.

401. The gib through the equalizing fulcrum tends to cut into the top of the lever and thereby weaken it. Consequently we often find a steel plate driven into the upper side of the lever, as shown at F in Fig. 615a. Another

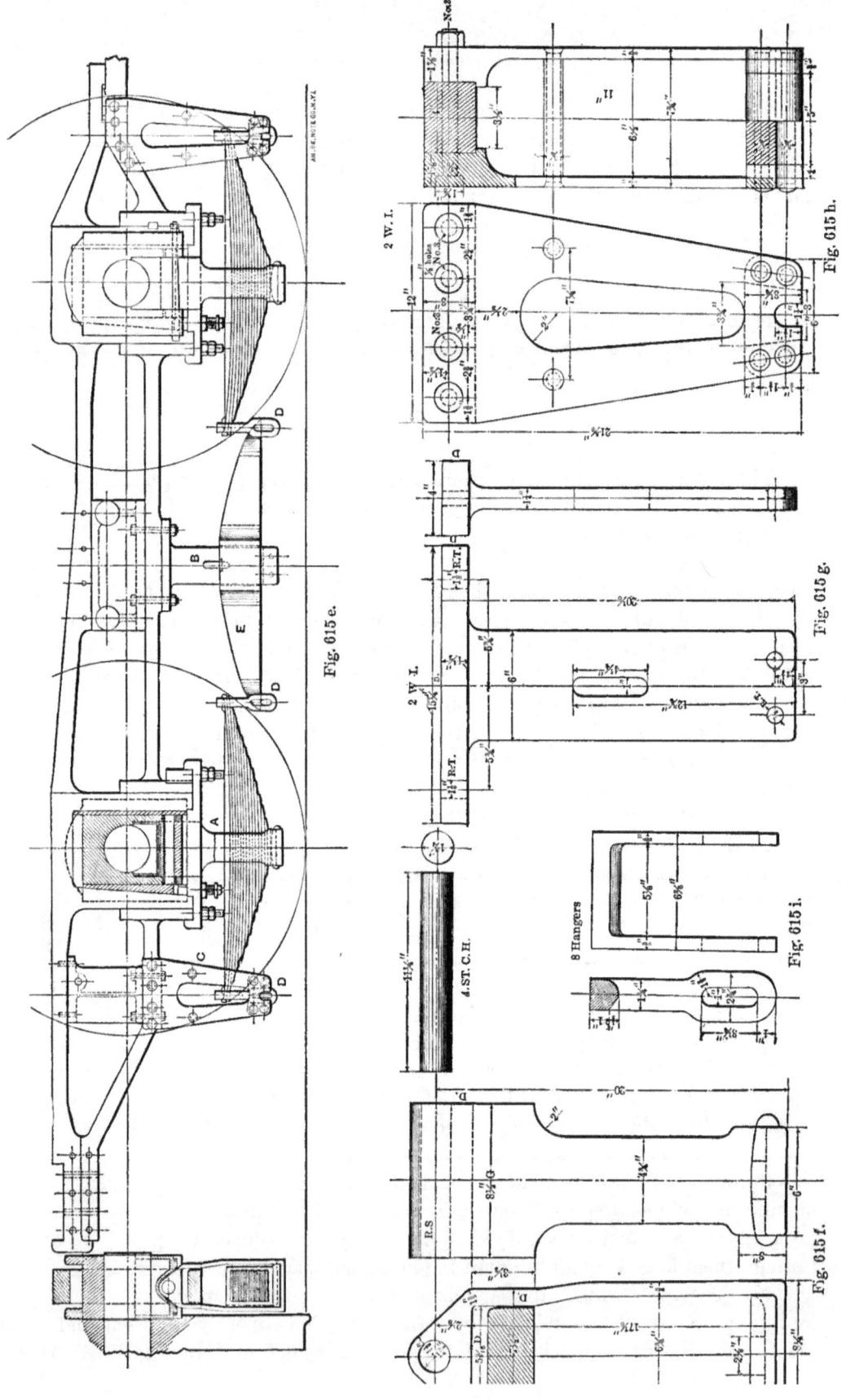

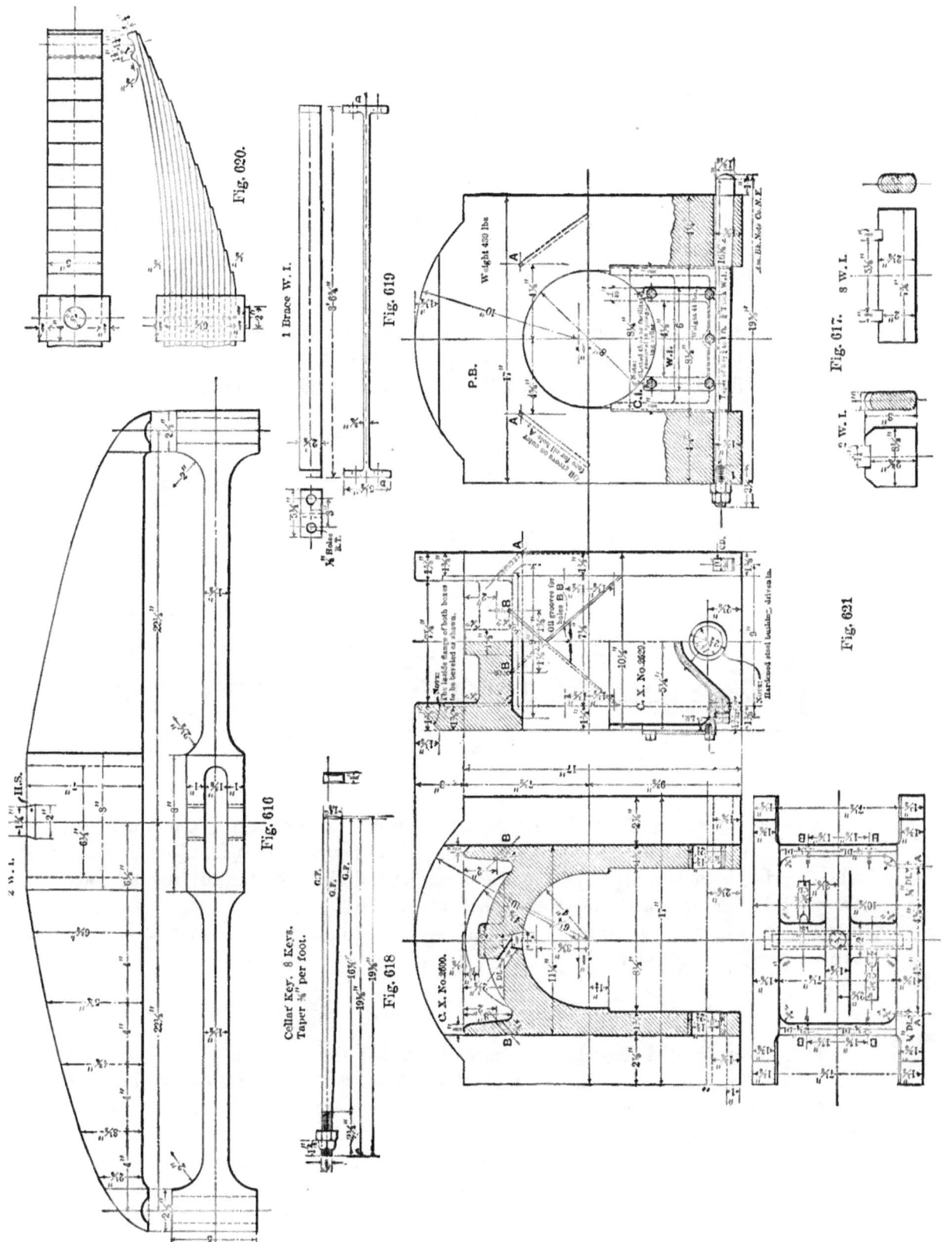

mode of preventing the evil effects of the wear under the gib is to place a loose steel plate between the top of equalizing lever and the gib.

### SPRING GEAR USED BY THE PENNSYLVANIA RAILROAD.

402. Fig. 615e shows a spring gear used by the Pennsylvania Railroad under their standard eight-wheeled passenger engine; cylinders, 18½ × 24 inches; weight of engine in working order, 106,500 pounds; weight on first pair of drivers, 36,500 pounds; weight on second pair of drivers, 36,850 pounds; weight on truck, 33,150 pounds; steam pressure, 160 pounds. The central stirrup *A* is shown on a larger scale in Fig. 615*f*; the spring-hanger stirrup *C*, in Fig. 615*h*; the equalizing fulcrum *B*, in Fig. 615*g*; spring hanger *D*, in Fig. 615*i*; and equalizing lever, in Fig. 616.

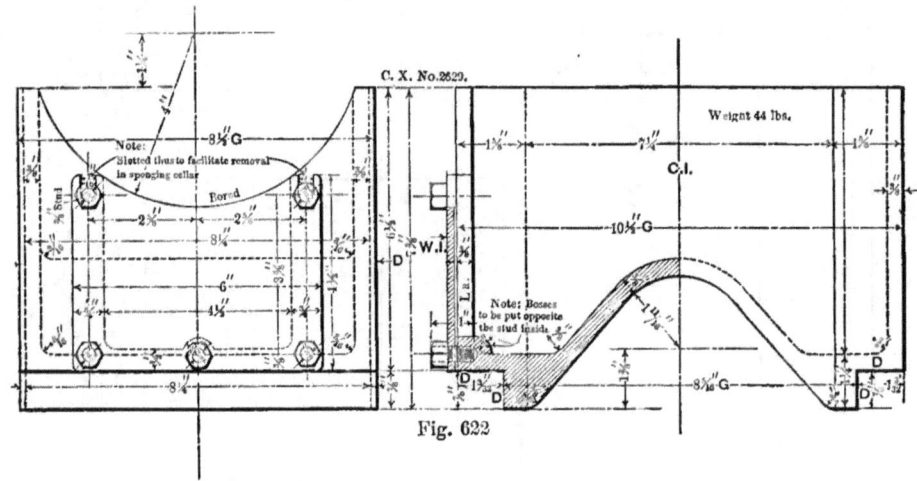

Fig. 622

The gibs are shown in Fig. 617; the transverse brace for connecting the equalizing lever fulcrum is shown in Fig. 619; and the cellar key, in Fig. 618. The driving-wheel spring is shown separately in Fig. 620; several views of the driving axle-box are given in Fig. 621; and the cellar is shown in Fig. 622.

The drawings show the general arrangement and details so plainly that further explanation is not necessary.

### DRIVING-WHEEL SPRINGS.

403. When the driving-wheel springs are loaded, their lengths vary from 30 to 48 inches; the usual length is 36 inches. The term "length of spring" is always understood to mean the distance *a*, Fig. 622*a*, from center to center of spring hangers. Sometimes the term "span" is used in place of length. The length of spring will depend much on the design of engine; no regular rule for determining it can be given, but good judgment guided by experience must be used.

404. Springs 36 inches long are generally 3½ inches wide; springs shorter than 36 inches are often made 3 inches wide; and the longer springs, 5 inches wide, as will be seen in Fig. 620.

405. The set of spring is the distance $b$, Fig. 622$a$, measured from the top, at the center, of the long plate or leaf to the bearings of the gibs. The set of the spring when loaded should be such that when the axle-box bears against the top of pedestal the leaves will be straight, as shown in Fig. 622$b$; and since the play between the axle-box and top of pedestal varies, in different classes of engines, from $2\frac{1}{4}$ to 3 inches, it follows that the set of springs under engines in working order will vary from $2\frac{1}{4}$ to 3 inches, according to size of engine.

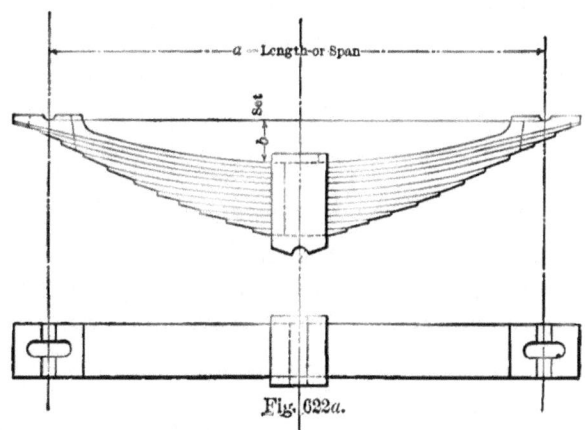

406. The usual thickness of the leaves is $\frac{3}{8}$ inch, sometimes it is $\frac{1}{2}$ inch; the former thickness is often adopted for springs 36 inches long; for springs much longer than this, the leaves are made $\frac{1}{2}$ inch thick; and for comparatively short springs the thickness is $\frac{5}{16}$ inch. The greater the thickness the greater will be the stress on the outer fibers of the plate; hence, for a durable spring the thickness of plates should be reduced as much as is consistent with good practice.

407. After the length, width of spring, and thickness of leaves have been decided upon, the number of leaves will have to be computed; this can be done by the following rule:

RULE 101.—Multiply the load in tons (2,000 pounds per ton) which the spring has to sustain by the length of spring in inches, and multiply this product by 11; call this product $A$. Multiply the width of the spring in inches by the square of the thickness in sixteenths of an inch of one leaf; call this product $B$. Divide product $A$ by the product $B$; the quotient will give the number of leaves required. Or, in symbols, we have

$$\frac{\text{Load in tons} \times \text{length of spring in inches} \times 11}{\text{Breadth in inches} \times (\text{thickness of one leaf in sixteenths})^2} = \text{number of leaves.}$$

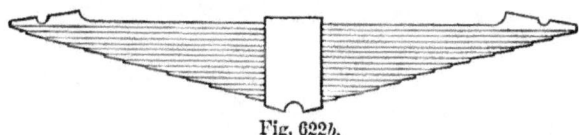

Fig. 622$b$.

The load on the spring is found in the same manner as the load was found on the equalizing lever, explained in Art. 394; in fact, the load on the spring is equal to the load on the equalizing lever.

EXAMPLE 133.—The load which a spring has to sustain is 5 tons; length of spring, 36 inches; width, $3\frac{1}{2}$ inches; thickness of leaves, $\frac{3}{8}$ inch. Find the number of leaves required to sustain the given load.

According to the foregoing rule, we have

$$\frac{5 \times 36 \times 11}{3.5 \times 6^2} = 15.7.$$

This answer calls for more than 15 leaves, and less than 16; to be on the safe side, it is advisable to adopt 16 leaves.

408. In ordering a spring it is necessary to know its deflection, so that the set without the load can be given. The following rule may be used for finding the deflection:

RULE 102.—Multiply the cube of the length in inches by 1.5; call this product $A$. Multiply the width of the plate in inches by the cube of its thickness in sixteenths, and multiply this product by the number of plates or leaves; call this product $B$. Divide product $A$ by product $B$; the quotient will be the deflection in sixteenths of an inch per ton of 2,000 pounds.

In symbols, we have

$$\frac{(\text{Length of spring in inches})^3 \times 1.5}{\text{Width of plate in inches} \times (\text{thickness in sixteenths})^3 \times \text{number of plates}} = \text{deflection in sixteenths per ton.}$$

EXAMPLE 134.—The length of spring is 36 inches; width, $3\frac{1}{2}$ inches; thickness of plates, $\frac{3}{8}$ inch; number of plates, 16; load to be sustained, 5 tons. Find the deflection of the springs.

Here we have

$$\frac{36^3 \times 1.5}{3.5 \times 6^3 \times 16} = 5.79 \text{ sixteenths of an inch deflection per ton.}$$

The load is 5 tons, hence the total deflection is $5.79 \times 5 = 28.9$ sixteenths, say $\frac{29}{16} = 1\frac{13}{16}$ inches deflection for a load of 5 tons. According to Art. 405, the spring should have a set, when loaded, equal to the play between top of axle-box and top of pedestal; if this is equal to $2\frac{1}{2}$ inches, then the total set before the spring is loaded should be $2\frac{1}{2} + 1\frac{13}{16} = 4\frac{5}{16}$ inches.

## CHAPTER X.

BOILERS.—GRATE SURFACE.—HEATING SURFACE.—RIVETED JOINTS.—EXTENSION FRONTS.

### BOILERS.

409. Figs. 623, 624, 625, 626 represent different views of a boiler for an eight-wheeled passenger engine with cylinders 18 inches diameter and 24 inches stroke. Figs. 633, 634, 635 represent a boiler and its details for a consolidation engine with cylinders 20 inches diameter and 24 inches stroke. Both boilers are designed for burning bituminous or soft coal.

In all boilers provision must be made for cleaning and washing, and for this purpose every boiler must be provided with hand holes at each corner of the fire-box; they are generally placed between the fire-box ring $a$, Fig. 623, and the first row stay bolts; another hand hole must be placed in the bottom of the front tube sheet, as shown at $b$, Fig. 626. Occasionally we find two or three hand holes placed in each side of the fire-box about 1 inch above the crown sheet. We have seen a brass plug placed in the fire-box flue sheet directly under the flues, but this practice should be condemned, because plugs in the fire-box are liable to burn out, causing considerable trouble and annoying delays.

410. The hand holes are made either oval or circular in form. The average size of oval holes is shown in Fig. 632. The forms of plates for these holes are shown in Figs. 641, 642, 643. They are made of cast-iron, with a wrought-iron bolt through their centers to clamp them to the sheet. The average sizes of circular holes and mud plugs used in place of oval ones are shown in Fig. 637. The mud plugs are usually made of brass; they have generally a square recess, sometimes a square projection, for screwing them into the holes. Plugs with recesses are to be preferred, because they take up less room. The taper of the plugs is about 1 inch in 12 inches; the thread is of a comparatively fine pitch, 12 or 14 threads per inch. Sometimes reinforcing plates are used, as shown in Fig. 637. They are riveted to the inside of the sheet, so as to obtain more perfect threads in the holes, but this is not a common practice, although it is a good one.

411. A mud drum is sometimes riveted to the bottom of the boiler near the front flue sheet, as shown in Fig. 644. The diameter of the drum is generally 15 inches; depth, from 10 to 12 inches. A wrought-iron ring is riveted to the outside, at the bottom end, to which a cast-iron head is bolted; the bolts should have large square heads, one of their sides bearing against the outside of the drum to prevent them from

418                    MODERN LOCOMOTIVE CONSTRUCTION.

turning in screwing up the nuts, otherwise the lagging around the drum may have to be removed (which is not desirable) when the drum head is to be taken off. A blow-off cock is screwed into the center of the head, and worked by means of a rod extend-

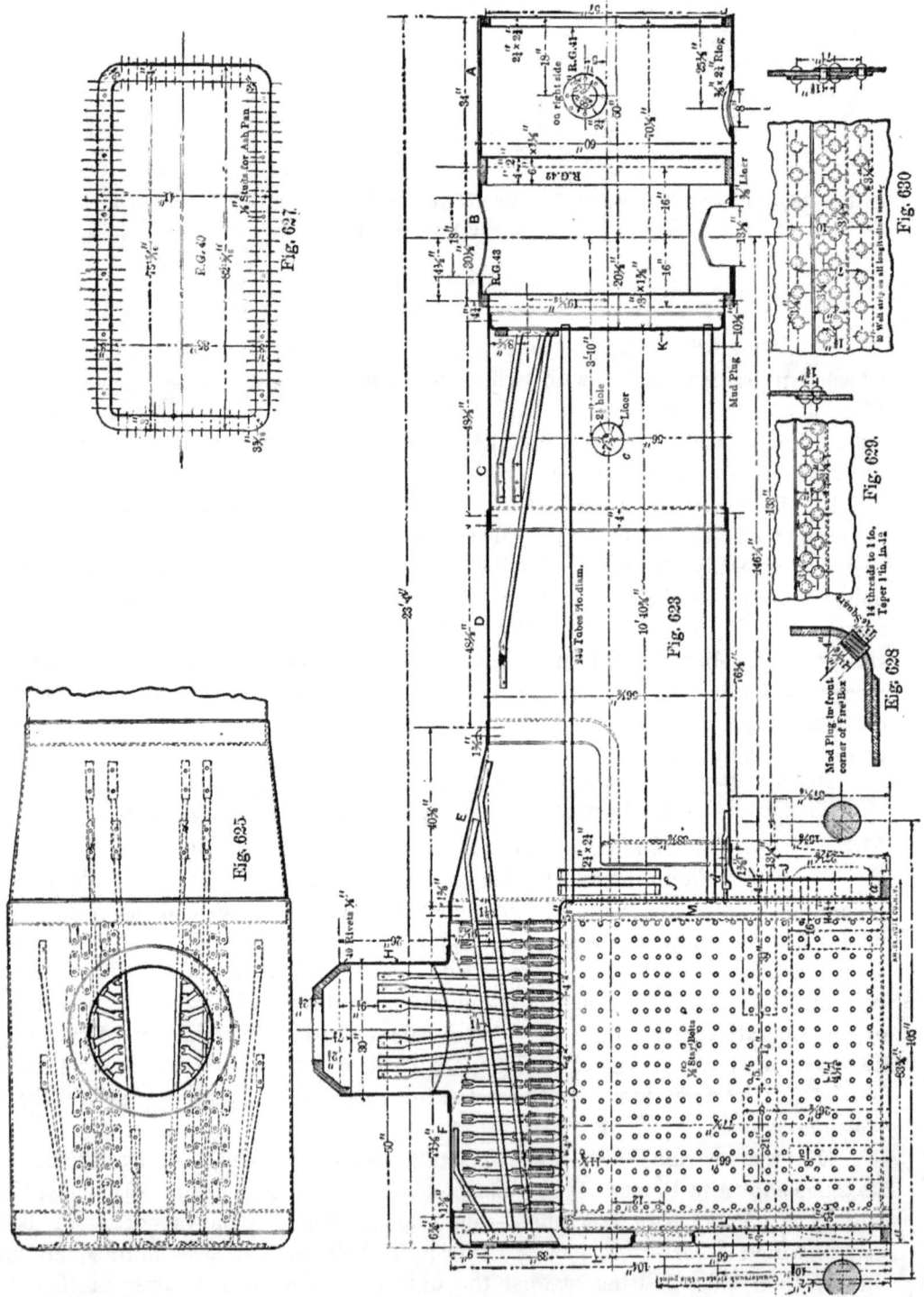

ing to the outside of the frames. The writer does not favor the use of mud drums, and believes that better results will be obtained by screwing the blow-off cock directly into the bottom of the boiler, in about the same position as that occupied by the mud drum. Although this is not a general practice, we believe it to be a good one, because the check valves are nearly always placed near the front end, as indicated at *c* in Fig. 623, and the mud and other impurities which are carried with the water

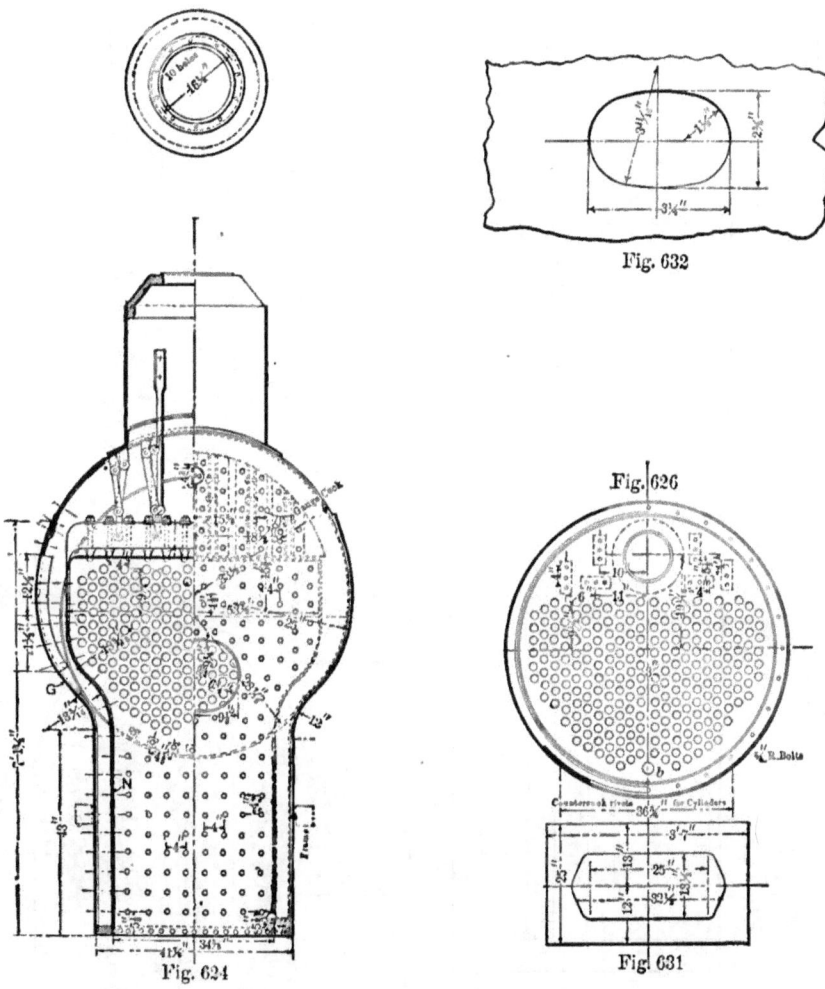

into the boiler will settle directly under the check-valve openings and often pile up in a wedge form, highest at the front flue sheet, forming nearly an angle of 45 degrees with the same; hence the utility of having a blow-off cock at the front end of the boiler must be readily perceived. Whether or not a blow-off cock is placed there, one is always attached to the fire-box as low as possible; it is screwed in the back head of the boiler whenever the driving axle will permit its use there; sometimes it is placed in the front of the fire-box, and occasionally in the sides; it is placed in the latter position, either because there is no room for it anywhere else, or because in some designs of engines it is more convenient to have it there.

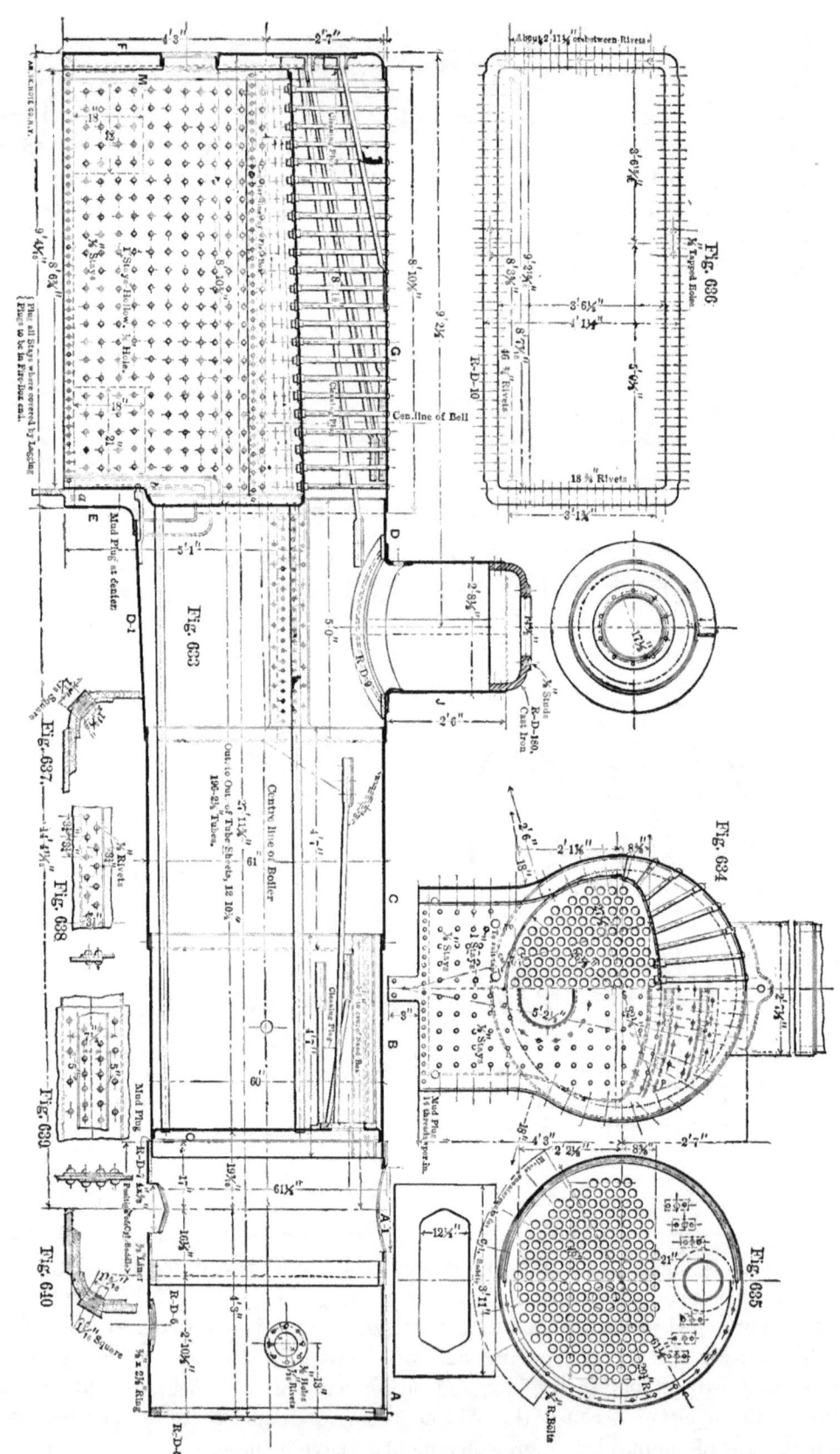

412. It may also be well to notice that the hand-hole plates or mud plugs in the bottom of the fire-box should be placed in such positions as to make access to them easy, and convenient for washing and cleaning the water space around the furnace.

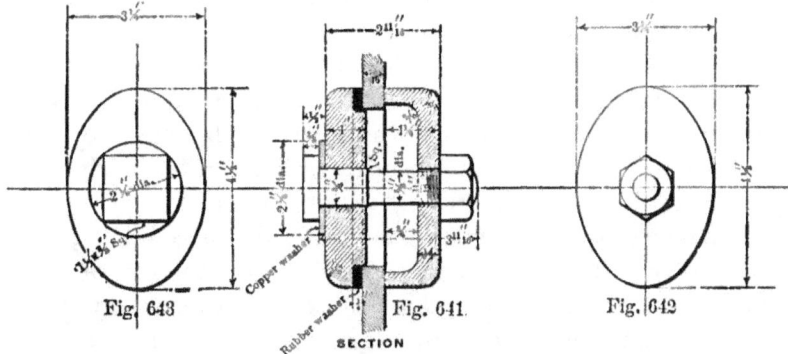

Fig. 643    Fig. 641    Fig. 642
SECTION

When the fire-boxes extend downwards between the driving axles, it is often difficult to place the hand-hole plates in desirable positions, particularly at the rear end, because the rear driving axle is generally closer to the fire-box than the front axle; the distance from the center of the rear axle to the fire-box varies from 6 to 7 inches, according to the size of engine, leaving in many cases a clearance of only $\frac{1}{2}$ inch between the flanges of the rear driving-boxes and fire-box, thereby compelling us to be satisfied with such positions of the hand holes as are not exactly desirable.

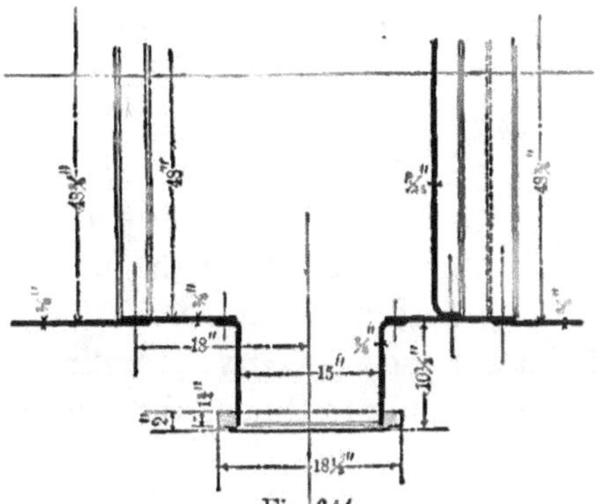

Fig. 644

### GRATE SURFACE.

413. Locomotive boilers may be divided into two classes, namely, bituminous or soft-coal burners, and anthracite or hard-coal burners. We shall consider the soft-coal burners first.

In a large number of eight-wheeled passenger, Mogul, and ten-wheeled engines, the fire-box is placed between the two rear axles, and in a few of the larger engines it is placed above the axles, extending over the rear one. The advantage of placing the fire between the axles is that a deep fire-box can be obtained so as to accommodate the depth of soft-coal fires; the depth of these fires varies from 15 to 24 inches, according to the quality of the coal used and the nature of the service. If the fire-box is not placed between the axles, then in order to obtain the required depth of fire the boiler must be raised. For fast running engines it is always advisable to keep the boiler as low as possible, and since eight-wheeled passenger engines are generally designed for high speeds, we do not often find the fire-box in this class of engines placed above the rear driving axle.

Since the available space in passenger engines, say with cylinders 18 inches diameter and upwards, is insufficient for a size of fire-box which can give the highest economy of fuel, it follows that great care must be taken not to give a greater amount of clearance between the fire-box and other mechanism than is absolutely necessary. The distance between the frames limits the width of the fire-box; hence in designing a large eight-wheeled passenger engine which is to have the fire-box between the axles, all that can be done is to exercise good judgment in determining the distance between the driving axles, which, as we have seen in Art. 205, is limited by the length of the side-rod, and then use the available space to the best advantage. In smaller engines, and also in locomotives which have the fire-box above the axles, the space for the fire-box is not restricted to such a small extent, and in such cases the question arises: What is the proper area for the grate surface?

414. It is impossible to give any hard-and-fast rule for computing the grate area suitable for the many various conditions of service and character of fuel. But it is reasonable to assume that the grate surface should be governed by the horse-power developed when the engine is exerting its maximum continuous effort. To compute the horse-power we must know the piston speed and the mean effective pressure on the piston. But the horse-power is also limited by the tractive force, therefore locomotive builders usually adopt a certain ratio of grate surface to the tractive force; but they do not agree on this ratio, and the consequence is that it varies considerably. We find that an allowance of 1 square foot of grate surface for every 600 pounds of tractive force agrees very closely with the average practice. Hence we can establish the following rule:

RULE 103.—Divide the tractive force, as found by Rule 3, by 600; the quotient will be the number of square feet of grate area for soft-coal burning engines.

EXAMPLE 135.—Find the number of square feet of grate surface for a soft-coal burning passenger engine with cylinders 15 × 24 inches; driving wheels, 55 inches diameter; mean effective pressure on the piston, 90 pounds per square inch.

According to Rule 3, the tractive force of this engine is

$$\frac{15^2 \times 90 \times 24}{55} = 8836 \text{ pounds.}$$

According to Rule 103, we have

$$\frac{8836}{600} = 14.72 \text{ square feet for the grate area.}$$

If, now, the furnace is to be 35 inches = 2.91 feet wide, then its length will have to be
$$\frac{14.72}{2.91} = 5 \text{ feet.}$$

EXAMPLE 136.—Find the number of square feet of grate area for a soft-coal burning passenger engine with 18 × 24 inch cylinders; drivers, 61 inches diameter; mean effective steam pressure on the piston, 90 pounds per square inch.

The tractive force of this engine is

$$\frac{18^2 \times 90 \times 24}{61} = 11472 \text{ pounds.}$$

And the grate surface will be

$$\frac{11472}{600} = 19.12 \text{ square feet.}$$

If, now, the width of the furnace is to be 2.91 feet, then its length will have to be

$$\frac{19.12}{2.91} = 6.57 \text{ feet.}$$

If there is no room for this length of furnace between the axles, then we must place the furnace above the axles, or be satisfied with less grate surface.

In general, if the grate surface determined by the foregoing rule is too large for a fire-box to be placed between the axles, then we must place it above them, or if this cannot be done, we must be either satisfied with a reduced steaming capacity of the boiler, or reduce the area of the exhaust nozzles, which will to some extent make up for the loss sustained by an insufficient grate area. Although this mode of procedure is a general one, it is by no means free from objections, because the reduction of the diameter of the exhaust nozzle not only increases the back pressure in the cylinders, but it also tends to lift the fuel, and draw some of it unconsumed through the flues, thereby creating a waste of fuel. Even with a grate area as large as is found by the given rule we shall need a blast of considerable force.

The grate area in the following tables have been computed by Rule 103; the mean effective steam pressure on the piston has been taken at 90 pounds per square inch for all the engines. It will be found that these grate areas agree very closely with the average practice.

### TABLE 59.

CALCULATED GRATE AREA FOR SOFT-COAL BURNING EIGHT-WHEELED PASSENGER ENGINES.

| Size of Cylinders. | Diameter of Driving Wheels. | Grate Area. |
|---|---|---|
| Column 1. | Column 2. | Column 3. |
| Inches. | Inches. | Square feet. |
| 10 × 20 | 45 | 6.6 |
| 11 × 22 | 45 | 8.8 |
| 12 × 22 | 48 | 9.9 |
| 13 × 22 | 49 | 11.3 |
| 14 × 24 | 55 | 12.8 |
| 15 × 24 | 55 | 14.7 |
| 16 × 24 | 58 | 15.8 |
| 17 × 24 | 60 | 17.3 |
| 18 × 24 | 61 | 19.1 |

### TABLE 60.

CALCULATED GRATE AREA FOR SOFT-COAL BURNING CONSOLIDATION ENGINES.

| Size of Cylinders. | Diameter of Driving Wheels. | Grate Area. |
|---|---|---|
| Column 1. | Column 2. | Column 3. |
| Inches. | Inches. | Square feet. |
| 14 × 16 | 36 | 13.0 |
| 15 × 18 | 36 | 16.8 |
| 20 × 24 | 48 | 30.0 |
| 22 × 24 | 50 | 34.8 |

Comparing the grate area of the engines with cylinders 14 and 15 inches diameter, given in Table 60, with the grate area of engines having cylinders 14 and 15 inches in diameter, as given in Table 59, we find that the length of stroke and the diameter of wheels affect the grate area to small extent only. Hence, a number of locomotive builders adopt the same grate area for a given size of cylinder for all classes of soft-coal burning engines.

415. Usually when the fire-box is placed above the axles, it is still kept between the frames, which, of course, limits its width but gives us more available space for length. Sometimes this practice is changed by placing the fire-box entirely above the top of frames; such a course will give us a greater width, but it will also raise the boiler higher than it would be by keeping the fire-box between the frames and placing it simply above the axles. To overcome the objection to raising the boiler too high, the fire-box has been made of a form as shown in Figs. 645 and 646, which are so plain that further explanation is unnecessary. This design was brought out by Mr. John Headden, during the time he held the position of superintendent of the Rogers Locomotive Works. Several of these locomotives have been built, and, as far as we know, have given good satisfaction; yet this design, although it embraces excellent points, is not free from objections—for instance, the top of the rear end of frames must be made somewhat crooked; and secondly, the springs cannot be placed above the frames, which, after all, seems to be the favorite arrangement.

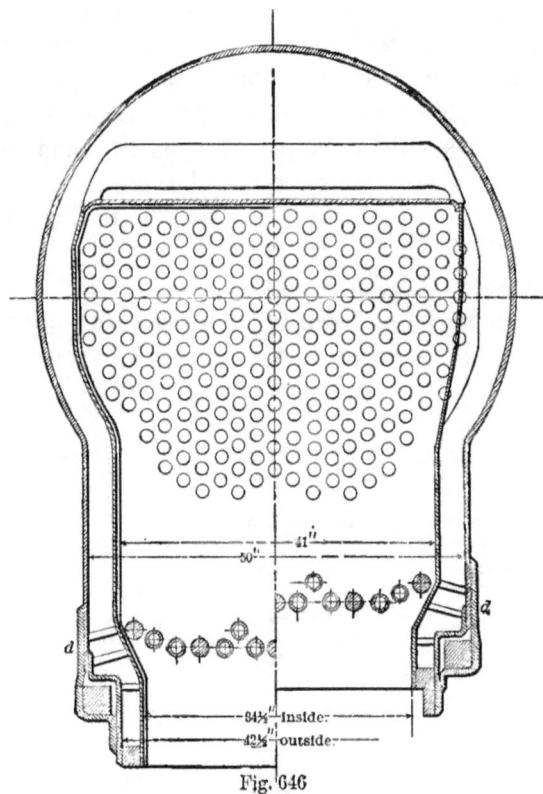

Fig. 646

## ANTHRACITE, OR HARD-COAL BURNING ENGINES.

416. In this class of engines we require a larger grate surface than in bituminous or soft-coal burning engines, because in the former shallower fires are carried, ranging from 6 to 15 inches deep, according to the quality of coal and the nature of the service of the engine, while in soft-coal burning engines the depth of fires varies from 15 to 24 inches. Since both kinds of coal contain about the same number of units of heat, in round numbers about 14,000, it follows that in order to evaporate the same amount of water with both kinds of coal, the grate surface for the hard coal must be greater than that for soft coal.

The reason for the difference in the depths of fires may be stated as follows: When bituminous coal is heated in the furnace it parts readily with the hydrocarbons in the form of gas, leaving the solid portion of coal as a spongy, porous mass (coke);

# MODERN LOCOMOTIVE CONSTRUCTION.

425

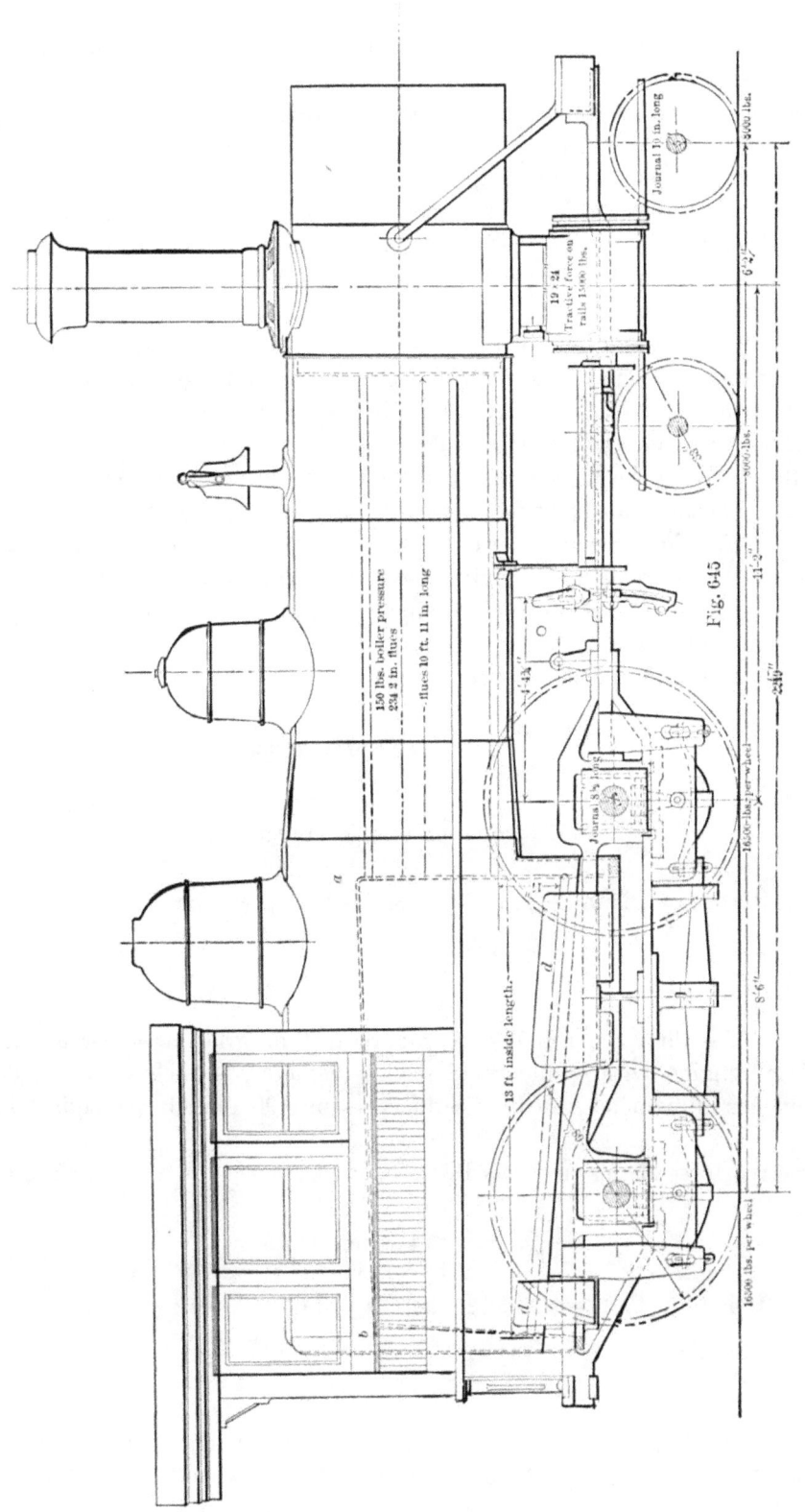

Fig. 645

the lumps break up into smaller pieces, allowing the air to come in contact with the interior of the solid coal.

The anthracite coal, on the contrary, does not break to pieces so readily, if at all, thereby permitting the air to come in contact with the exterior surface only. Hence, this coal requires a freer intermingling of air with it, and therefore a comparatively shallow fire must be carried. But for shallow fires the depth of furnace can be reduced, enabling us to place the fire-box above the axles without raising the boiler to an undesirable height. Hence in hard-coal burners the fire-boxes are generally placed above the axles.

417. The grate area adopted for this class of engines by the different builders also varies considerably. We find that the tractive force as found by Rule 3, divided by 500, will give us a grate area in square feet which agrees very closely with the average practice. Hence we have the following rule:

RULE 104.—Divide the tractive force as found by Rule 3, by 500; the quotient will be the grate surface in square feet for hard-coal burning engines.

EXAMPLE 137.—Find the number of square feet of grate surface for a hard-coal burning eight-wheeled passenger engine having cylinders 15 inches diameter, 24 inches stroke; driving wheels, 55 inches diameter; mean effective pressure, 90 pounds per square inch of piston.

According to Rule 3, the tractive force is

$$\frac{15^2 \times 90 \times 24}{55} = 8836 \text{ pounds,}$$

and

$$\frac{8836}{500} = 17.6 \text{ square feet of grate surface.}$$

If the width of grate is to be 2.91 feet, then its length will be

$$\frac{17.6}{2.91} = 6 \text{ feet.}$$

EXAMPLE 138.—Find the number of square feet of grate area for a hard-coal burning Mogul engine with cylinders 18 inches diameter, 24 inches stroke; driving wheels, 51 inches in diameter; mean effective pressure, 90 pounds per square inch of piston.

The tractive force of this engine is 13722.3 pounds, hence the grate surface will be

$$\frac{13722.3}{500} = 27.44 \text{ square feet.}$$

If the grate is to be 2.91 feet wide, its length will be

$$\frac{27.44}{2.91} = 9.4 \text{ feet.}$$

EXAMPLE 139.—Find the grate area for a hard-coal burning consolidation engine with cylinders 20 inches diameter, 24 inches stroke; driving wheels, 48 inches diameter; mean effective pressure, 90 pounds per square inch of piston.

The tractive force of this engine is 18,000 pounds, hence the grate surface will be

$$\frac{18000}{500} = 36 \text{ square feet.}$$

If the width of grate is to be 2.91 feet, then its length will be

$$\frac{36}{2.91} = 12.3 \text{ feet.}$$

The grate areas in the following tables have been computed by the foregoing rule.

### TABLE 61.

CALCULATED GRATE AREA FOR HARD-COAL BURNING EIGHT-WHEELED PASSENGER ENGINES.

| Size of Cylinders. | Diameter of Driving Wheels. | Grate Area. |
|---|---|---|
| Column 1. | Column 2. | Column 3. |
| Inches. | Inches. | Square feet. |
| 10 × 20 | 45 | 8.0 |
| 11 × 22 | 45 | 10.6 |
| 12 × 22 | 48 | 11.8 |
| 13 × 22 | 49 | 13.6 |
| 14 × 24 | 55 | 15.3 |
| 15 × 24 | 55 | 17.6 |
| 16 × 24 | 58 | 19.0 |
| 17 × 24 | 60 | 20.8 |
| 18 × 24 | 61 | 22.9 |

### TABLE 62.

CALCULATED GRATE AREA FOR HARD-COAL BURNING CONSOLIDATION ENGINES.

| Size of Cylinders. | Diameter of Driving Wheels. | Grate Area. |
|---|---|---|
| Column 1. | Column 2. | Column 3. |
| Inches. | Inches. | Square feet. |
| 14 × 16 | 36 | 15.6 |
| 15 × 18 | 36 | 20.2 |
| 20 × 24 | 48 | 36.0 |
| 22 × 24 | 50 | 41.8 |

The tendency is to make the grate area for the larger hard-coal burning engines a little less than given in the tables, so as not to get a length of furnace which is inconvenient for firing; but for the smaller engines the tendency is to make the grate area a little greater than given in the tables, as such furnaces will not be too long to fire. Furnaces over 12 feet in length are difficult to fire, and should be avoided.

### GREATEST WIDTH OF FIRE-BOX.

418. In all ordinary wide-gauge (4′ ″ 8½″) locomotives the outside width of the fire-box cannot exceed the distance from the inner to outer sides of the frames, because the clearance between the tires and the frames is usually from 1 to 1¼ inches, and

428                    MODERN LOCOMOTIVE CONSTRUCTION.

less clearance than this between the fire-box and the tires is impracticable; even with this clearance the rivets in the fire-box, in the neighborhood of the tires, will frequently have to be countersunk to prevent contact.

### DEPTH OF HARD AND SOFT COAL FURNACES.

419. The same practical considerations which determine the depth of a soft-coal burning furnace will also determine the depth of a hard-coal burning furnace. The depth of the furnace will depend, first, on the number of flues and the depth of the fires; second, it will depend on the clearance which must be given between the bulged part of the fire-box and the springs or the flanges of the wheels; third, it will depend on the manner of fastening the frames to the fire-box.

First. To find the depth of the furnace, we must lay in the tubes as shown in Fig. 624, and then lay in the flange of the tube sheet so that its inner surface will be about ¾ of an inch, or not more than 1 inch above the top of the upper row of tubes; in this way we establish the position of the crown sheet. We then add the required depth below the flues for the fuel, and this generally establishes the necessary depth of the furnace. If, now, the fire-box is to be placed on top of frames, we have simply to raise the boiler high enough for this depth of furnace.

Second. In hard-coal burning engines the boiler will generally set so high as to clear the springs and the flanges of the driving wheels, but to be certain, it is always best to lay in the frames as shown in Fig. 654, and also draw in the springs and wheels in the position they will occupy when the engine is in working order. There should be at least 4 inches clearance between the flanges $a$ of the wheels and the bulge $b$, so as to allow for the vertical movement of the wheels in the pedestals; there should also be about 4 inches clearance between the ends of the springs (not shown here) and the bulge, so as to allow the springs to be placed in position before they are strapped down. If there is less than 4 inches of clearance the boiler should be raised bodily and the fire-box made deeper, allowing the bottom to come within about 1 inch above the top of frames. It is also necessary to lay in the lifting-shaft and see that there is clearance between the link motion and the lagging around the barrel of the boiler. For soft-coal burning engines we proceed in precisely the same way, and then provide for the third condition, which, as we have seen, is, that the depth of the furnace will depend on the manner of fastening the fire-box to the frames. Of course, when the fire-box is placed above the frames, and we have met all the practical requirements just mentioned, the manner of fastening the fire-box to the frames will not affect the depth of the furnace. But when the fire-box is placed between the frames as is shown in Fig. 654, it is customary to allow its lower end $c$ to extend a short distance below the lower braces $d$ of the frames so as to bring the heads of the rivets through the ring of the fire-box below the under side of the lower braces, otherwise the heads of the rivets will in many cases have to be countersunk, which in good locomotive practice is avoided as much as possible. This arrangement allows the pads to be attached to the lower brace of the frame as well as to the upper one, thereby securing the frames rigidly in a lateral position, the fire-box acting as a brace between them. Sometimes the required depth of the ash-pan $f$ will not allow the fire-box to extend so far downwards; in such cases the bottom $c$ of the fire-box just reaches the top $g$ of the lower brace of the frame.

The provisions made for fastening the fire-box to the frames as just explained may give us, in some cases, a deeper furnace than is required for the depth of the fire;

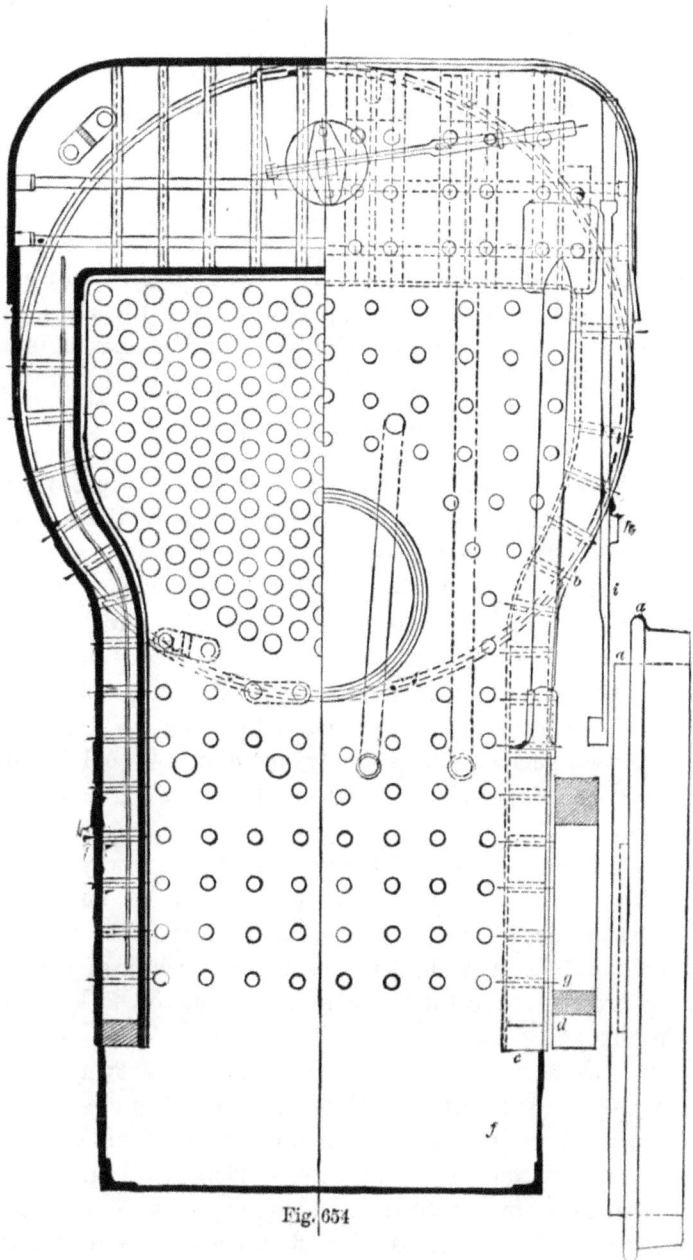

Fig. 654

it is for this reason that we have said that the depth of the furnace will depend on the manner of fastening the fire-box to the frames. This class of boilers is often used for passenger engines, and since the driving wheels of this class of engines are of a large diameter comparatively, there is sometimes trouble in finding room for the reach-rod $h$

(Fig. 654), which connects the reversing lever $i$ to the lifting-shaft; hence the cross-section of the reach-rod should also be drawn in the end view, and sufficient room allowed for it; to do so may sometimes compel us to raise the boiler a little. Now, having provided for all these practical requirements, we have not only established the depth of the furnace, but we have also established the height of the boiler above the frames; for we cannot place it lower without interfering with the action of other mechanism, and we cannot place it higher without reducing the stability of the engine; the boiler should always be kept as low as possible.

### FIRE-BOXES FOR WOOD-BURNING LOCOMOTIVES.

420. For wood-burning locomotives a very deep fire-box is required; consequently, in this class of engines, it is nearly always placed between the axles, thereby obtaining the same size of grate surface as is used for soft-coal burning engines with fire-boxes placed in a similar position.

### SLOPING CROWN SHEETS.

421. When a locomotive has to run down a hill, the water level in the boiler will of course remain horizontal, hence the depth of the water at the rear end of the engine above the center line of the boiler will be less than at the front end. If, now, the crown sheet has been placed horizontally, that is to say, parallel with the center line of the boiler, there is danger of the rear end of the crown sheet projecting above the water level, which may cause it to be burnt, and lead to serious or fatal accidents. In order to keep it well covered, it is customary to slope the crown sheet of a long furnace downwards towards the rear end, as is shown in Fig. 633.

For short furnaces, such as are generally found in soft-coal burning engines, it is not deemed necessary to slope the crown sheet unless the engine has to run over very steep grades.

But in hard-coal burners, in which the furnaces are always comparatively long, this precaution should be taken. It may be asked, What becomes of the front end of the crown sheet when the engine is running up-hill? To this we only need to reply, that the front end of the crown sheet is closer to the center of the boiler, and consequently it cannot project above the water as readily as the back end when the engine is running down-hill.

The amount of slope should be such as to bring the crown sheet parallel to the water level when the engine is running down the steepest grade.

422. When crown bars are used for the purpose of staying the crown sheet, the latter is generally made flat across the furnace, as shown in Fig. 624. Sometimes it is slightly curved crossways, concave to the fire, having about $1\frac{1}{2}$ inches rise in the center. The advantage of this is that the matter deposited from the water tends to flow off, and therefore prevents incrustation. For some kinds of water the crown bars cannot be used, as they tend to obstruct the movements of the matter deposited from the water, and therefore tend to promote incrustation, which of course is hurtful to the crown sheet. In such cases radial stay bolts are used, and in order to obtain as many perfect threads as possible in the crown sheet, the latter is curved crossways to a considerable

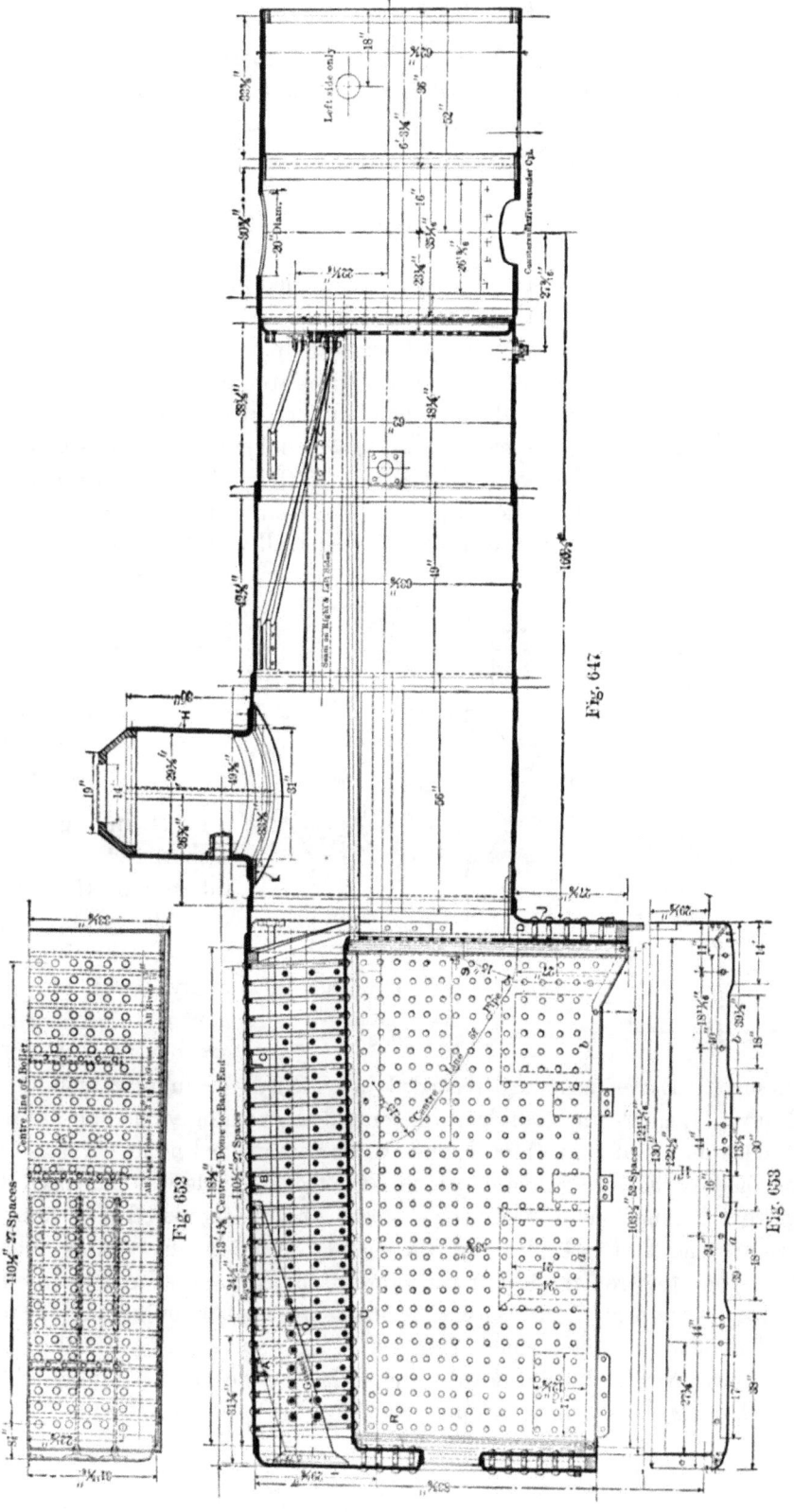

Fig. 647
Fig. 652
Fig. 653

extent, as is shown in Fig. 634. This form of crown sheet possesses the further advantage of being better adapted for receiving the radiant heat. But we prefer the crown bars whenever the quality of water will permit their use, as we believe that with crown bars a safer and stronger boiler can be made.

### BELPAIRE FIRE-BOX.

423. The desire to avoid radial stay bolts has led to the adoption, on some roads, of the Belpaire fire-box, shown in Figs. 647 and 648.

The difference between an ordinary and a Belpaire fire-box is that in the latter the furnace crown sheet and the outer crown sheet are made flat and placed parallel to each other. The advantage of the Belpaire fire-box is that it gives more steam space, and sometimes it is asserted that it increases the strength of the boiler; but in this assertion we have no faith, for the reason that the cylindrical form is the most natural one to which all vessels subjected to an internal steam pressure tend to conform, and therefore the latter must be the strongest.

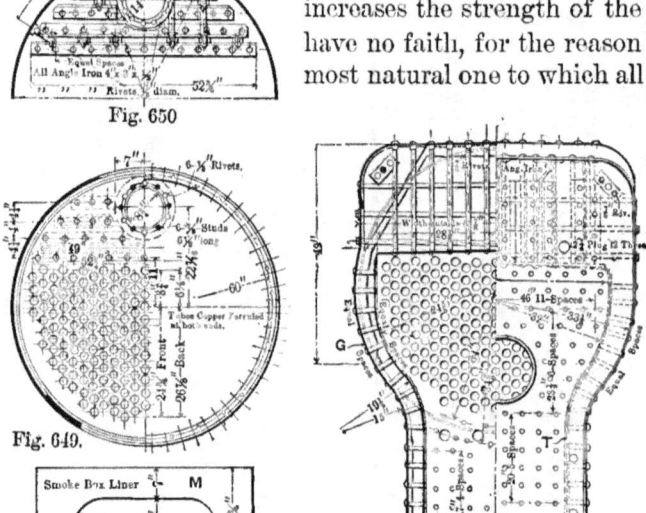

Fig. 650 Fig. 649. Fig. 651 Fig. 648

### INCLINATION OF THE FURNACE-DOOR SHEETS AND SIDE SHEETS.

424. In Fig. 655 it will be seen that the water space at the top of the furnace-door sheet is greater than at the bottom—the difference is generally about 1½ inches; the aim is to give the steam a greater freedom of parting from the sheet. Experiments are recorded in which a rectangular metallic box, submerged in water, and heated from within, generated steam only one-half as fast from its vertical sides as it did from the top, and the bottom yielded none. Again, by slightly inclining the box the rate of evaporation on the elevated side was increased, the steam parting from it much more easily; the steam on the depressed side hung so sluggishly as to lead to overheating of the metal. For similar reasons the width of the water space towards the top of the sides of the furnace is also increased; in fact, in some boilers we find the furnace side sheets to have a bulge only near the flue sheet, and none at rear end, where they are straight and placed parallel to each other, and sometimes even inclined towards each other at the top. Although this form of fire-box is by no means a universal one, we believe it to be a good one.

MODERN LOCOMOTIVE CONSTRUCTION.          433

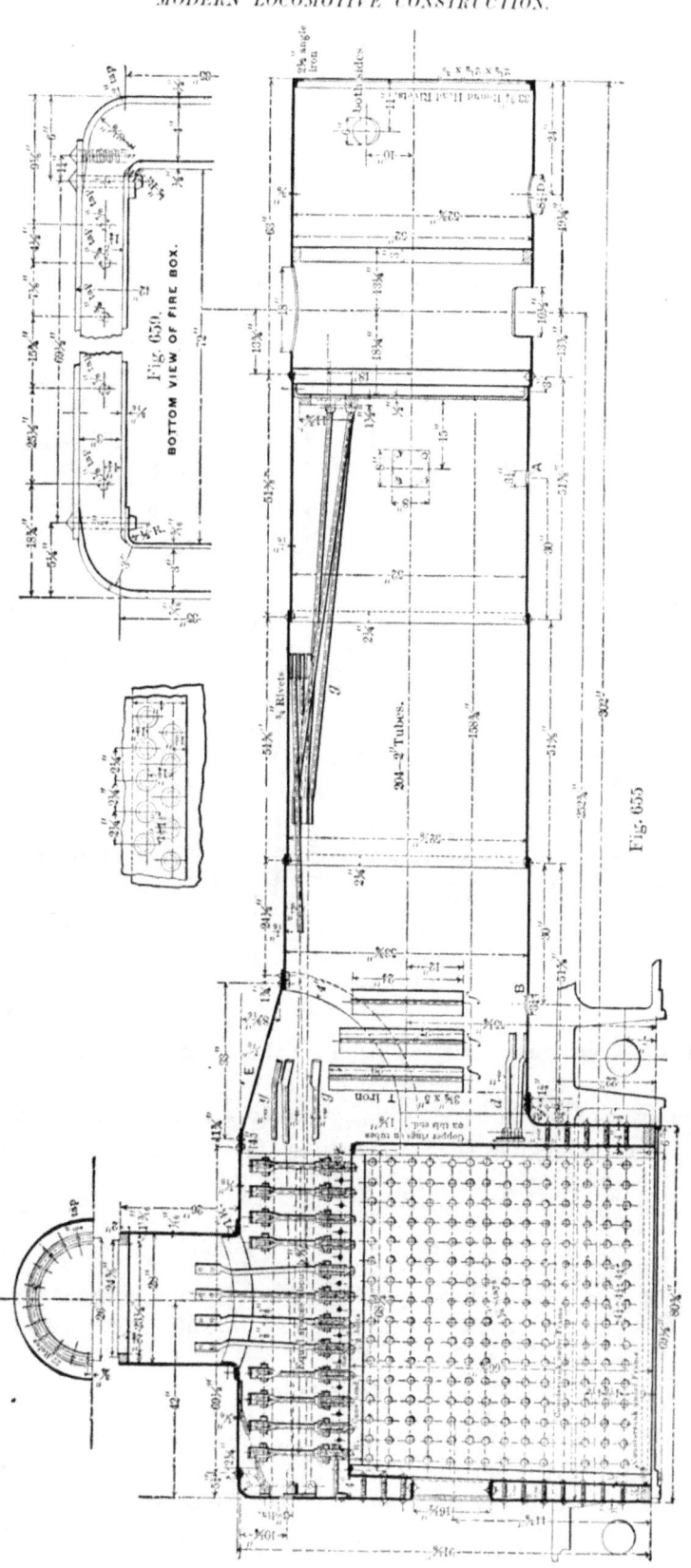

Fig. 659. BOTTOM VIEW OF FIRE BOX.

Fig. 655

## WIDTH OF WATER SPACE.

425. In engines having cylinders 16 inches in diameter and upwards, the water space at the bottom of the rear end of the fire-box is usually 3 or $3\frac{1}{2}$ inches wide; at the bottom of the sides it is also 3 to $3\frac{1}{2}$ inches; and at the bottom of the front end it is usually from $3\frac{1}{2}$ to 4 inches wide.

For smaller engines the water space is reduced; for an engine with cylinders 9 inches in diameter the water space at the rear end and sides is generally $2\frac{1}{2}$ inches wide; and at the bottom of the front end, 3 inches wide.

We have seen the water space at the bottom of the rear end and the sides 2 inches wide, but such a narrow water space should be avoided.

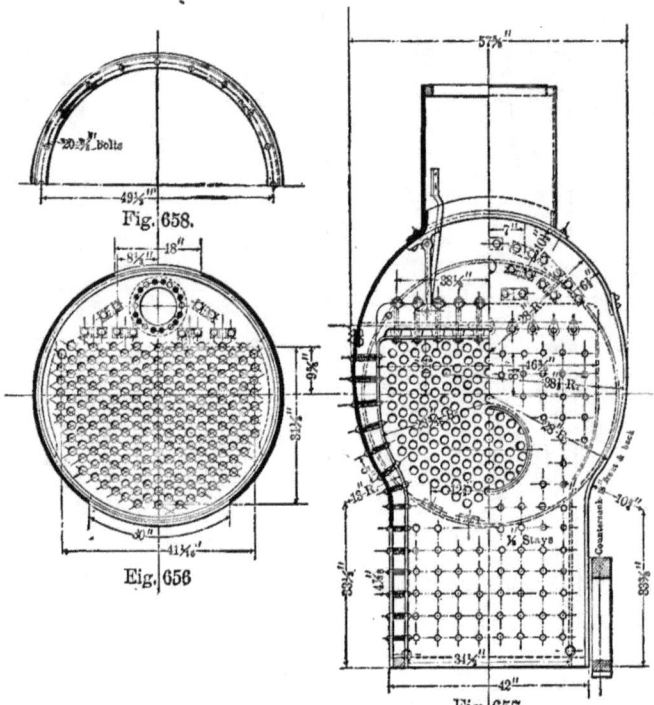

## TUBE SHEETS.

426. The furnace-tube sheet is sometimes made in two pieces, as shown in Fig. 633. With this arrangement there is no particular advantage to be gained, excepting the additional heating surface in the fire-box, which is more effective than that of the tubes. On the other hand, there is an objection to making the furnace-tube sheet in this way, as it has been found that the bend of the flange at $b$ is liable to wear and give trouble.

The upper part of this tube sheet is generally $\frac{1}{2}$ inch thick, and the lower part $\frac{3}{8}$ inch thick. In many engines the furnace-tube sheet is made in one piece, as shown in Fig. 655; these sheets are generally $\frac{1}{2}$ inch thick throughout.

## THICKNESS OF FURNACE SHEETS.

427. The thickness of the furnace-door and side sheets is generally $\frac{5}{16}$ inch, that of the crown sheet is generally $\frac{3}{8}$ inch; and these thicknesses are used for either iron or steel.

## FIRE-BOX RING.

428. The ring or frame at the bottom of the fire-box is made of bar-iron, and its thickness varies in different engines from 2 to $2\frac{1}{4}$ inches, according to the judgment and experience of the different builders; its width must, of course, conform to the water space.

The rivets are usually ¾ inch in diameter, pass through the rings, furnace and fire-box sheets, and are driven on the outside. At the corners where there is no room for passing rivets through all this metal, copper studs ¾ inch in diameter are screwed into the ring and riveted over on the outer fire-box sheets.

### RIVETS IN FURNACE SHEETS.

429. In the larger classes of engines all the rivets in the furnace sheets are usually ¾ of an inch in diameter, and are driven on the inside. It is good practice to

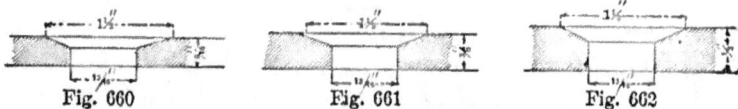

countersink the rivet holes in the furnace sheets, making the depth of the countersink equal to ⅛ of the thickness of the sheets, and 1½ inches diameter for ¾ rivets. Sections of these holes for the various thicknesses of sheets are shown in Figs. 660, 661, and 662. The rivets are driven with points slightly raised above the countersink. Deep rivet heads in the furnace are liable to burn off.

### FUSIBLE PLUGS.

430. Fusible plugs are sometimes used as a safeguard against the collapse of the furnace crown sheet from overheating through a shortness of water. Sections of the

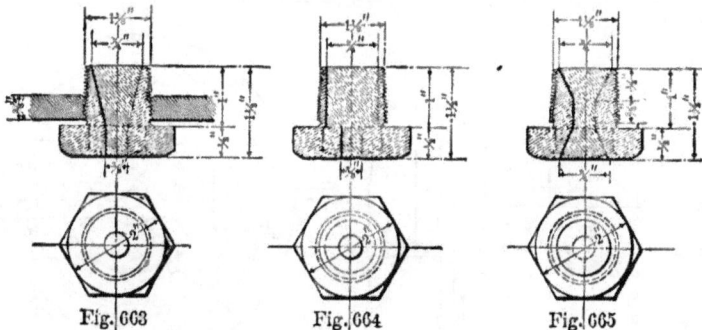

different forms of these plugs are shown in Figs. 663, 664, and 665. They consist of a brass shell containing an alloy of tin, lead, and bismuth.

The plug is screwed into the crown sheet at a distance of 18 to 24 inches from the tube sheet. The water above the crown sheet keeps the alloy at a comparatively low temperature, and prevents it from being melted. When the water in the boiler is so low as to uncover the plug, the alloy is supposed to fuse, allow the steam to escape, retard combustion, and in the meantime relieve the boiler of its pressure. Whether this action of the plug can always be relied upon is very questionable; we believe its efficiency is sometimes over-rated. A long exposure to the heat in the furnace may cause an alteration in the nature of the alloy and render it valueless. Again, incrustation on the plug may become strong enough to withstand the pressure of the steam and prevent its escape after the alloy has been melted. It is therefore good practice, when these plugs must be used, to renew them at short intervals, say every two or three months.

### FIRE-DOOR OPENINGS.

431. In the majority of locomotives the fire-door opening is formed by flanging the furnace-door sheet outwards, and the back head inwards, bringing the seam in the water space, as shown in Fig. 666. Sometimes the opening is formed by riveting a flange to the back head, and a strip connecting this flange to the flange of the furnace sheet, as shown in Fig. 667; but this way of forming the opening is not as good as the one previously mentioned. Occasionally we find the opening made as shown in Fig. 668; both sheets are flanged outwards and riveted on the outside of the back head, the same rivets taking hold of a bar about 1¾ or 2 inches wide by ½ inch thick. This bar

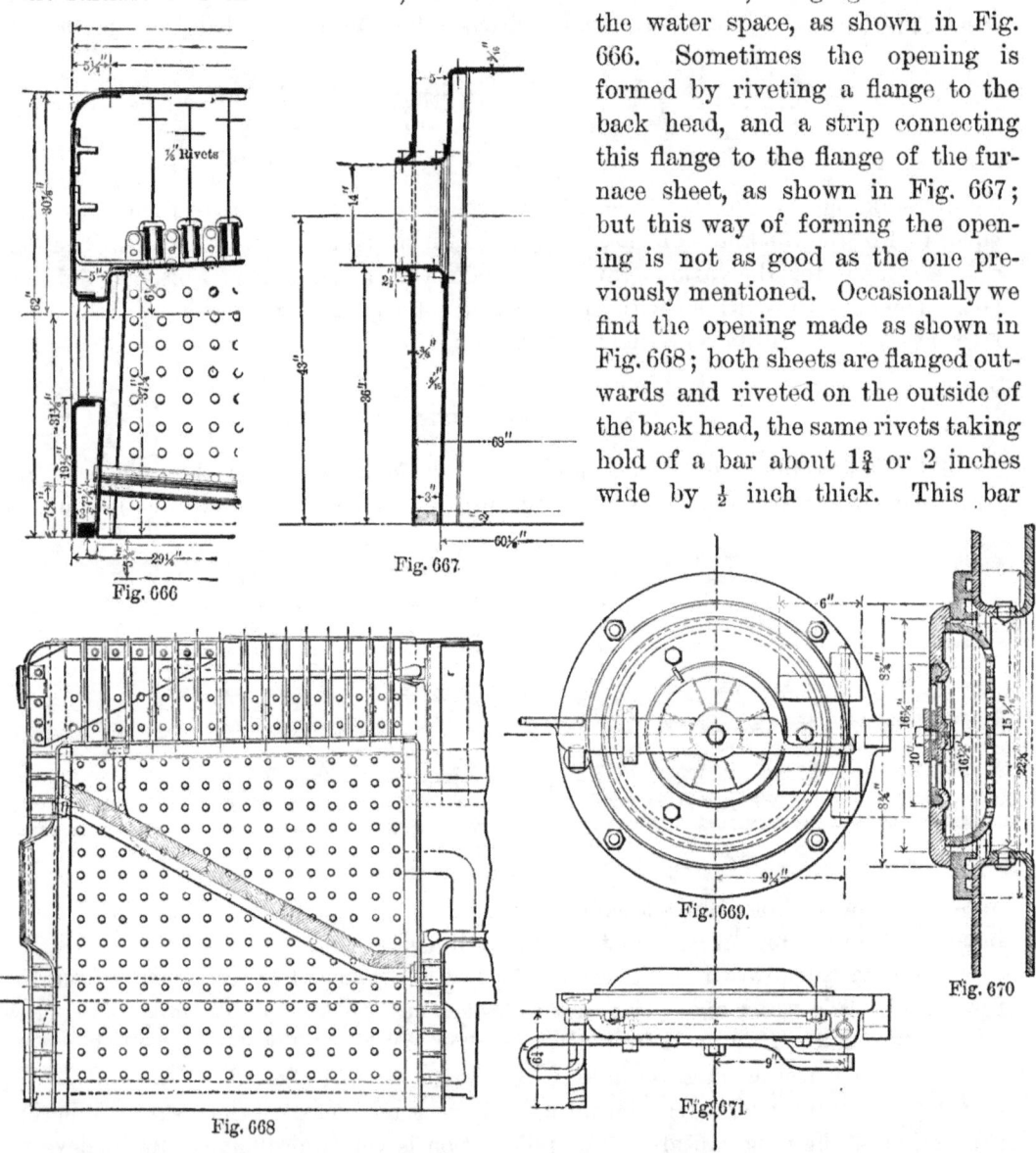

Fig. 666.
Fig. 667.
Fig. 668
Fig. 669.
Fig. 670
Fig. 671

extends around the opening; it forms a rest for the fire tools and prevents wear on the edge of the flange. It will be noticed that the opening is greater in the furnace than it is in the boiler head; the object of this is to give the fireman a greater range with the fire tools; we believe this to be a good door opening. In many locomotives the fire-door opening is oval in form; a good size is 14 × 17 inches in the clear; of course some builders adopt a different size, but do not vary much from the size here given. Sometimes the opening is made circular in form, about $16\frac{1}{2}$ inches in diameter, as shown in Figs. 669, 670, 671, which also show the construction of the cast-iron door with its frame bolted to the boiler head. The bottom of the opening should be about 6 inches above the top of the foot-plate.

### DENTS IN SIDE OF FIRE-BOX.

432. Figs. 647 to 653 represent a boiler for an engine which has two axles below the fire-box. The dents $a$ and $b$ in the side of the fire-box are for the purpose of clearing the spring saddles.

### TUBES.

433. The tubes are generally made of iron, sometimes of steel, seldom of copper. When made of iron they are manufactured from strips and lap welded; when made of steel they are generally "solid drawn." Steel tubes will probably be the favorite ones in the near future. They are thinner than iron tubes, and therefore the ends of the former, through a distance of about 6 inches, are made thicker than the body of the tubes; these ends are usually called "safe ends."

In the ordinary locomotive boiler the tubes are 2 inches external diameter; for small boilers they are sometimes $1\frac{1}{2}$ inches external diameter, but it is doubtful whether anything is gained by making them so small. The writer was once instructed to design a boiler with $\frac{3}{4}$-inch copper tubes; the boiler was made, but their heating surface, on account of the small diameter, was not effective; they were replaced by 2-inch iron tubes, and then the boiler steamed well.

When the length of the tubes exceeds 11 feet, it is advisable to increase the diameter, say to $2\frac{1}{4}$ or $2\frac{1}{2}$ inches. (See Art. 437.)

Formerly the thickness of iron flues 2 inches external diameter was No. 13 Birmingham wire-gauge, but of late the thickness has been increased to about No. 12 gauge, making the inside diameter equal to 1.78 inch. The thickness of $2\frac{1}{2}$-inch tubes is also about No. 12 Birmingham wire-gauge, making the inside diameter equal to 2.26 inches. The thickness of $1\frac{1}{2}$-inch tubes is No. 13 wire-gauge, and the inside diameter is 1.31 inch.

Although the primary object of the tubes is to carry off the gases and heat the water surrounding them, they also serve as stays for the tube sheets. Consequently many mechanics not only expand the tubes to make them steam-tight, but also bead them over to give them a better hold on the tube sheets so as to prevent the steam pressure from drawing them out of the holes.

Now, beading the tubes simply for the purpose of giving them a better hold is unnecessary, because experiments have shown that when a 2-inch tube is properly expanded it will resist a pull of 5,000 pounds, which is greater than the stress to which a locomotive tube will ever be subjected. Hence, we frequently find the tubes not beaded on the front flue sheet; they are simply expanded and allowed to project $\frac{1}{8}$ of an inch, but they are, or rather should be, always beaded on the furnace tube sheet, for the following reason:

438                MODERN LOCOMOTIVE CONSTRUCTION.

The ends of the tubes in the furnace are liable to be exposed to cold currents of air when the furnace door is opened, which in time will cause them to leak and give considerable trouble. To avoid this leakage as much as possible, copper ferrules are inserted between the tubes and the sides of the holes in the tube sheet; hence the tube should be beaded over to prevent the ferrule from dropping out, and at the same time protect the ferrule as well as the end of tube from wear caused by the impact of the unconsumed fuel which is drawn against them.

Copper ferrules are seldom placed on the front ends of the tubes, although the use of ferrules on these ends we believe to be good practice and advantageous when the tubes have to be taken out for making repairs, because with ferrules, the holes through the front tube sheet, through which the tubes must be drawn, are necessarily larger and will permit a slight incrustation on the tubes to be drawn through the holes, and therefore involve less labor and time than when the holes are smaller.

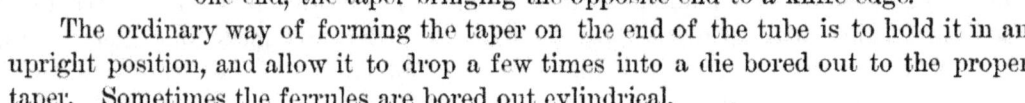
Fig. 672.

Without ferrules, the holes are drilled $\frac{1}{32}$ inch, and with ferrules $\frac{1}{16}$ inch larger in diameter than that of the tubes.

434. Fig. 672 shows the ends of a tube with a copper ferrule. The outside of the ferrule is turned straight, and the inside is bored out tapered. The length of the ferrule is about $\frac{1}{4}$ inch greater than the thickness of the sheet; and its greatest thickness is about $\frac{1}{8}$ inch at one end, the taper bringing the opposite end to a knife-edge.

The ordinary way of forming the taper on the end of the tube is to hold it in an upright position, and allow it to drop a few times into a die bored out to the proper taper. Sometimes the ferrules are bored out cylindrical.

## CROSS-SECTIONAL AREA OF TUBES.

435. A too great aggregate cross-sectional area of tubes produces a slow velocity of the gases, which will permit a deposit of soot, and cause a reduction in the rate of evaporation. On the other hand, too small an area checks the draft, and besides this, it leaves no allowance for a further obstruction to the draft caused by the lodgment of cinders in the lower tubes, which is liable to occur in locomotives. Here, then, the question arises: What should be this aggregate cross-sectional area, so as to obtain the best results?

In Mr. B. F. Isherwood's "Experimental Researches of Steam Engineering" we find that the best aggregate cross-sectional area of the tubes is $\frac{4}{31}$ of the grate surface; and it has this property, that it is the best for all types of boilers, for all rates of combustion, and for all ratios of heating to grate surface.

The aggregate area may be reduced without loss or much inconvenience to $\frac{1}{9}$ of the grate surface, but it cannot be increased beyond $\frac{1}{7}$ without serious sacrifice to the economic results. The horizontal fire-tube boiler is much more sensibly affected by this area than the vertical water-tube boiler, and requires a much nicer adjustment of it. It is also more affected by the difference in ratio of the heating to the grate surface, using the same rate of combustion.

The aggregate cross-sectional area of the tubes in American locomotives of the larger sizes is about $\frac{1}{8}$ of the area of the grate surface, and agrees with the conclusions of Mr. Isherwood; but in the smaller engines we sometimes find this area to be as large as ¼ of the grate surface. The reason for this will be presently seen. The following table gives the aggregate area of tubes as found in locomotives running on some of our best roads.

TABLE 63.

TABLE OF AGGREGATE TUBE AREA IN SOFT-COAL BURNING ENGINES.

| Diameter of Cylinder. | Stroke. | Number of Tubes. | Diameter of Tubes. | Grate Area. | Aggregate Tube Area. | Ratio of Grate to Tube Area. |
|---|---|---|---|---|---|---|
| Column 1. | Column 2. | Column 3. | Column 4. | Column 5. | Column 6. | Column 7. |
| Inches. | Inches. | | Inches. | Square feet. | Square feet. | |
| 9 | 16 | 100 | 1½ | 7.08 | 1.38 | 5.1 to 1 |
| 9 | 16 | 45 | 1¾ | 4.02 | 0.62 | 6.4 to 1 |
| 10 | 18 | 110 | 1¾ | 8.02 | 1.52 | 5.2 to 1 |
| 10 | 18 | 62 | 2 | 7.11 | 1.06 | 6.7 to 1 |
| 11 | 18 | 120 | 1¾ | 8.50 | 1.66 | 5.1 to 1 |
| 12 | 20 | 130 | 2 | 13.45 | 2.23 | 6.0 to 1 |
| 12 | 20 | 90 | 2 | 7.29 | 1.55 | 4.7 to 1 |
| 13 | 20 | 140 | 2 | 14.16 | 2.41 | 5.8 to 1 |
| 14 | 20 | 145 | 2 | 14.87 | 2.49 | 5.9 to 1 |
| 14 | 20 | 115 | 2 | 10.70 | 1.96 | 5.4 to 1 |
| 15 | 22 | 151 | 2 | 15.58 | 2.60 | 5.9 to 1 |
| 15 | 22 | 126 | 2 | 11.86 | 2.17 | 5.4 to 1 |
| 16 | 24 | 163 | 2 | 16.29 | 2.80 | 5.8 to 1 |
| 16 | 24 | 180 | 2 | 15.28 | 3.10 | 4.9 to 1 |
| 17 | 24 | 184 | 2 | 17.00 | 3.16 | 5.3 to 1 |
| 17 | 24 | 196 | 2 | 16.28 | 3.37 | 4.6 to 1 |
| 18 | 24 | 194 | 2 | 18.41 | 3.34 | 5.5 to 1 |
| 18 | 24 | 200 | 2 | 17.24 | 3.44 | 5.0 to 1 |
| 19 | 24 | 246 | 2 | 28.00 | 4.23 | 6.6 to 1 |
| 19 | 24 | 210 | 2 | 18.14 | 3.61 | 5.0 to 1 |
| 20 | 24 | 252 | 2 | 31.16 | 4.33 | 7.1 to 1 |

In examining the foregoing table our attention is drawn to the fact that the grate areas are not proportionate to the size of engines; indeed, the grate areas vary considerably for the same size of engine. This variation is partly accounted for by the fact that the proportions of boilers are not always determined by fixed rules, and much depends on the individual experience and fancy of the designer.

We have already seen that the aggregate tube area should be proportionate to the grate area; we shall therefore assume that the grate areas given in Tables 59 and 60 are correct, and that the ratios of these to the tube areas are governed by the following practical considerations.

If the diameter and length of a locomotive boiler had not been limited by the service for which the engines is intended, then probably the best proportion for the total cross-sectional area of the tubes would be $\frac{1}{7}$ of the grate surface, which will provide for the loss of area by the lodgment of cinders in the lower tubes, and leave about $\frac{1}{9}$ of unimpaired area. But often we shall have to be satisfied with an aggregate area less than $\frac{1}{7}$ of the grate surface. For instance, in large locomotives the diameter of the boiler is limited by the distance between the wheels, which in turn is limited by the gauge of the track; and if we make the grate surfaces equal to the given areas in Tables 59 and 60, then it will be difficult to obtain the desired number of tubes without encroaching on the steam space, and we will be compelled to use a smaller number, with a total cross-sectional area equal to about $\frac{1}{8}$ of the grate surface. If, on the other hand, we make the total area of tubes in small engines equal to ¼ of the grate surface, then we shall have an insufficient heating surface; because the wheel base in these small engines demands comparatively short tubes; therefore, in order to obtain a sufficient heating surface we must increase the number of tubes, and consequently increase their aggregate cross-sectional area, which in small engines is sometimes equal to ¼ of the grate surface.

Here, then, we see the reason for the variation of the ratio of tube to grate area in the different classes of engines as given in Table 64.

Indeed, it may be said that in American locomotives the aggregate cross-sectional area of the tubes varies from ¼ to ⅛ of the grate surface.

In the following table we have given the number of tubes as found by calculation, and these will serve as a guide in designing new locomotives.

The number of flues here given agree closely with the number used in locomotives in actual service, and can therefore be recommended.

In Column 3 we have given the grate area as calculated by Rule 103, reduced to square inches.

Column 4 gives the ratio of the grate surface to the aggregate tube area; it commences with a ratio of 4 and gradually increases to 8, for the reason stated above.

Column 5 gives the aggregate cross-sectional area of the tubes in square inches, and is, of course, obtained by dividing the grate area in Column 3 by the ratio given in Column 4.

Column 6 gives the number of tubes 2 inches outside diameter. The inner diameter of these tubes has been taken at 1.78 inches, and the cross-sectional area of one tube at 2.48 square inches; therefore the number of flues in Column 6 are obtained by dividing the numbers in Column 5 by 2.48.

### TABLE 64.

TABLE OF CALCULATED AGGREGATE TUBE AREA AND NUMBER OF TUBES.

| Diameter of Cylinder. | Stroke. | Grate Area. | Ratio of Grate Area to Aggregate Tube Area. | Aggregate Cross-sectional Area of Tubes. | Number of Tubes. |
|---|---|---|---|---|---|
| Column 1. | Column 2. | Column 3. | Column 4. | Column 5. | Column 6. |
| Inches. | Inches. | Square inches. | | Square Inches. | |
| 10 | 20 | 950.40 | 4 to 1 | 237.6 | 95 |
| 11 | 22 | 1267.20 | 4 to 1 | 316.8 | 127 |
| 12 | 22 | 1425.60 | 4.5 to 1 | 316.8 | 127 |
| 13 | 22 | 1627.20 | 5 to 1 | 325.4 | 131 |
| 14 | 24 | 1843.20 | 5 to 1 | 368.6 | 148 |
| 15 | 24 | 2116.80 | 5.5 to 1 | 384.8 | 155 |
| 16 | 24 | 2275.20 | 5.5 to 1 | 413.6 | 166 |
| 17 | 24 | 2491.20 | 6 to 1 | 415.2 | 167 |
| 18 | 24 | 2753.20 | 6.5 to 1 | 423.5 | 170 |
| 20 | 24 | 4320.00 | 7.5 to 1 | 576.0 | 232 |
| 22 | 24 | 5011.20 | 8 to 1 | 626.4 | 252 |

All tubes are 2 inches in diameter.

436. It may appear that the foregoing table is only suitable for soft-coal burning engines, because in Column 3 we have given the grate surface for this class of engines; and that for hard-coal burning engines there should be a greater number of tubes,

because in these engines the grate surface is larger than in soft-coal burners. This to some extent is true; but when we remember that for the smaller engines the total area of tubes given in the table is greater than it should be for the given grate area, and that in the larger engines we have not the room for a greater number of tubes than given, we conclude that the same number of tubes should be used in hard- and soft-coal burners.

### RATIO OF DIAMETER TO LENGTH OF TUBE.

437. The tubes for all the engines given in Table 64 are 2 inches external diameter, and indeed some builders seldom use larger tubes; but we believe it to be good practice not to allow the external diameter to be less than $\frac{1}{65}$ part of the length of the tubes. Thus, for instance: if the tube is 12 feet long, then its external diameter should be $\frac{12 \times 12}{65} = 2.2$, say $2\frac{1}{4}$ inches. Increasing the diameter will stiffen the tube and consequently prevent sagging to some extent; a comparatively large diameter will also allow the flame to extend further into the tube, and make this heating surface more effective. But it must be remembered that by increasing the diameter and keeping the aggregate cross-sectional area the same as for smaller tubes, the heating surface will be decreased. This can be best explained by taking an example.

438. In Table 64 we see that for an engine with cylinders 18 inches diameter we need 170 tubes 2 inches external diameter. The circumference of a 2-inch tube is $2 \times 3.14 = 6.28$ inches, and for 170 tubes the circumference is equal to $6.28 \times 170 = 1067.60$ inches, or 88.96 feet; hence for every foot of length of the tubes we have 88.96 square feet of heating surface; and the aggregate area of the tubes is (according to Table 64) 423.1 square inches. Now suppose we increase the external diameter of these tubes to $2\frac{1}{2}$ inches, but leaving the length as before.

The inner cross-sectional area of one of these tubes is 4.011 square inches; consequently, since the aggregate area of the tubes is not to be changed, we have $\frac{423.1}{4.011} = 105$ tubes $2\frac{1}{2}$ inches diameter instead of 170 tubes 2 inches diameter.

The outer circumference of a $2\frac{1}{2}$-inch tube is 7.85 inches, and the sum of the circumference of all the tubes is $7.85 \times 105 = 824.25$ inches, or 68.68 feet; hence for every foot of length of the tubes we have 68.58 square feet of heating surface. But the 2-inch tubes, with the same aggregate tube area, have 88.96 square feet, hence by increasing the tubes to $2\frac{1}{2}$ inches we lose $88.96 - 68.68 = 20.28$ square feet of heating surface for every foot of length of the tubes, which amounts to nearly 23 per cent. loss of the total tube heating surface.

Although in large boilers we may sacrifice this amount of heating surface for other advantages to be gained, we cannot afford to lose this amount in small boilers, because in these boilers we have had to make the aggregate area of tubes larger than desirable for the very purpose of gaining heating surface (see Art. 435), and therefore it would be decidedly bad practice to sacrifice some of this heating surface by making the diameter of the tubes greater than is absolutely necessary. Therefore in small boilers the diameter of the tubes should not be greater than 2 inches, neither should it be less than 2 inches, because such a reduction will tend to reduce the efficiency of the tube heating surface; yet in large boilers the diameter of the tubes may often be increased, with advantage, to 2¼ or 2½ inches.

### LENGTH OF TUBES.

439. The length of the tubes is limited by the positions of the tube sheets. The position of the furnace tube sheet is of course established as soon as the size of furnace has been determined.

The front tube sheet is placed as far forward as possible, allowing only the heads of the rivets through this tube sheet and shell to clear the cylinder saddle; and the distance between these tube sheets will, of course, establish the length of the tubes; since the position of the cylinder saddle depends upon the length of wheel base, it may be said that the wheel base determines the length of tubes, leaving us little or no choice in the matter.

### ARRANGEMENT OF TUBES.

440. The tubes should be arranged to allow the steam as it is formed to ascend in straight lines as nearly as is possible for it to do, therefore the favorite arrangement is like that shown in Fig. 672a.

The tubes are usually spaced off on a flue board, and from that transferred to the tube sheets. The best way to proceed in drawing the tubes on the flue board will be

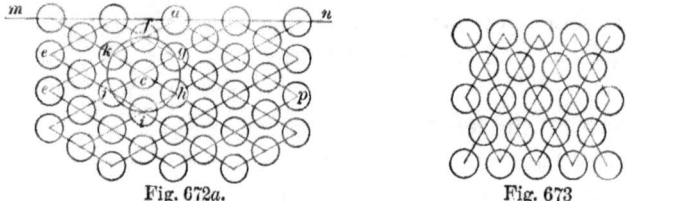

Fig. 672a.   Fig. 673.   Fig. 674.

to establish first the position of one tube in the upper row, say the tube $a$, Fig. 672a, and through its center draw the line $a\ e$ making an angle of 30 degrees with the horizontal line $m\ n$; also, through the center of the tube $a$ draw the line $a\ p$ making the same angle with $m\ n$. On the lines $a\ e$ and $a\ p$ lay off the centers of the tubes, and through these centers draw lines parallel to $a\ e$ and $a\ p$; the intersection of these lines will give the centers of other tubes; the centers above the lines $a\ e$ and $a\ p$ are found in a similar way. All these lines can be readily drawn to the correct angle with the aid of a **T** and set square, the latter containing the angles of 30, 60, and 90 degrees.

If the tubes have been correctly located, then a circle described from the center of any tube, say $c$, and with a radius equal to the distance between the centers of tubes, will pass through the centers of the six nearest tubes, as $f\ g\ h\ i\ j\ k$, shown in Fig. 672a. When the tubes are arranged as here shown, they are said to be in vertical rows. Tubes may also be arranged in vertical rows as shown in Fig. 674, but this arrangement takes up too much room, and therefore it is very seldom adopted in locomotive boilers.

Tubes placed as shown in Fig. 673 are said to be arranged in horizontal rows, but this arrangement obstructs the upward passage of the steam, and therefore is seldom adopted.

441. The space between the tubes depends sometimes on the number of tubes to be placed in the boiler; but the best practice is to make the diameter of the boiler to suit the number of tubes given in Table 64, and with such spaces between them as have been found to give good results. When tubes are widely spaced they are more easily cleaned from incrustation, and there is also less liability to prime. The clear space between two tubes should never be less than $\frac{1}{2}$ inch.

When there are more than 120 tubes in a boiler the clear space between the tubes should be increased $\frac{1}{16}$ of an inch for every fifteen additional tubes. From the foregoing we may establish the following rule:

RULE 105.—To find the clear space between the tubes, divide the number of tubes in the boiler by 15, and multiply the quotient by $\frac{1}{16}$ of an inch; the product will be the required clear space between the tubes. Add to this the diameter of the tube; the sum will be the distance between the centers. This rule will hold good only when there are more than 120 tubes in the boiler. For a smaller number of tubes the space should always be $\frac{1}{2}$ inch.

EXAMPLE 140.—What should be the distance from center to center of tubes in a boiler having 135 tubes 2 inches diameter? Here we have $\frac{135}{15} = 9$; and $9 \times \frac{1}{16} = \frac{9}{16}$ inch for the space between the tubes. Adding this to the diameter of the tube, we have: $\frac{9}{16} + 2 = 2\frac{9}{16}$ inches from center to center of tubes.

In a similar way we find that the space between the tubes in a boiler with 195 tubes should be $\frac{195}{15} = 13$; and $13 \times \frac{1}{16} = \frac{13}{16}$ inch. If the tubes are $2\frac{1}{2}$ inches outside diameter, then the distance from center to center should be $2\frac{1}{2} + \frac{13}{16} = 3\frac{5}{16}$ inches. We believe that the circulation will be improved by arranging the two central vertical rows of tubes, as shown in Fig. 626, and making the clear space between them from $\frac{1}{4}$ to $\frac{1}{2}$ inch greater than the space between the other tubes. Although this arrangement is sometimes adopted, it is not a general practice; they are usually arranged as shown in Fig. 656.

### STEAM SPACE.

442. The distance from top of the upper row of flues to the top of the boiler varies from $\frac{1}{4}$ to $\frac{1}{8}$ of the diameter of the boiler; we prefer $\frac{1}{8}$, because a liberal steam space tends to prevent priming; it must also be remembered that when the tubes are placed too high the water surface is contracted, which by itself is probably a greater cause for priming than simply a contracted steam space. In all cases the steam space should be large enough to allow a man to enter the boiler to make repairs when necessary.

### DIAMETER OF BOILER SHELL AND DESIGN OF BOILER.

443. Having established the number and size of tubes, also the height of steam space, we are in a position to determine the diameter of boiler, which has simply to

be made large enough to admit the required number of tubes with sufficient steam space above them, and with a clearance of not less than 2 inches between any tube and the boiler shell.

We have now sufficient data for determining the principal dimensions of a locomotive boiler; and from the foregoing remarks we conclude that the proper mode of procedure in designing a boiler is as follows:

First. Find the grate area as explained in Art. 414.

Second. Find the aggregate cross-sectional area of the tubes according to Art. 435.

Third. Divide the aggregate area of the tubes by the inner cross-sectional area of one tube; the quotient will be the required number of tubes.

Fourth. Locate the tubes—that is to say, make an end view of the tubes placed at the proper distance apart, and draw an end view of the boiler-shell which will admit the required number of tubes, leaving a steam space equal to $\frac{1}{8}$ of the diameter of the shell in height, and a 2-inch space between the side and bottom tubes and shell.

Fifth. Make an outline drawing of the boiler, an end view, and a longitudinal section, and see to it that there is ample clearance between the boiler and the mechanism attached to it, and make provision for fastening the boiler to the frames.

EXAMPLE 141.—Find the principal dimensions of a boiler for an eight-wheeled passenger engine having cylinders 16 inches diameter and 24 inches stroke; driving wheels, 58 inches diameter; mean effective steam pressure, 90 pounds per square inch; soft-coal burner; tubes, 2 inches outside diameter.

First. According to Rule 103, we divide the tractive force by 600; the quotient will be the grate surface in square feet. The tractive force of this engine is (according to Rule 3) 9,533 pounds; hence we have

$$\frac{9533}{600} = 15.8 \text{ square feet.}$$

Second. According to Table 64, the aggregate area of the tubes for this size of engine should be $\frac{1}{5.5}$ part of the grate area; we therefore have $\frac{15.8 \times 144}{5.5} = 414.4$ square inches for the aggregate area of the tubes.

Third. To find the number of tubes. Referring to Art. 435, we see that the inner cross-sectional area of a tube 2 inches outside diameter is 2.48 square inches; hence, dividing the aggregate area of the tubes by the cross-sectional area of one tube, we have $\frac{413.6}{2.48} = 166$, which is the required number of tubes. Referring to Art. 441, we see that the clear space between the tubes should be $\frac{166}{15} = 11$, and $11 \times \frac{1}{16} = \frac{11}{16}$ of an inch, and $2 + \frac{11}{16} = 2\frac{11}{16}$ inches from center to center of tubes.

Fourth. To find the diameter of boiler shell. Lay in about 200 tubes $2\frac{11}{16}$ inches from center to center, and then find by trial a circle which will take in 166 tubes, leaving a clear space of about $\frac{1}{8}$ of its diameter in height above the upper row of tubes, and not less than 2 inches clearance between the side and bottom tubes and shell; the diameter of this circle will be the inside diameter of shell. It may be remarked here that the grate surface, cross-sectional tube area, and number of tubes in this example could have been found at once without any calculation by referring to Table 64

Fifth. A longitudinal section and end view of the boiler should now be drawn, and all such mechanism as may come in contact with boiler should be located and examined in regard to clearance, and allowances made for fastening the boiler to the frames.

If the fire-box has to be placed between the driving axles, it may be that on account of insufficient room the grate area of 15.8 square feet, as previously found, will be somewhat too large, and will have to be reduced. We shall need about 6 inches from the center of the rear driving axle to rear end of fire-box, and about 13 to 14 inches from the center of the front axle to the front end of the fire-box; but the reduction of the grate, if any, will be comparatively small, so that no change will need to be made in the number of tubes.

### HEATING SURFACE.

444. The heating surface throughout the boiler is not equally effective; the relative value will depend on its position. A square foot of heating surface in the furnace will evaporate considerably more water than a square foot of tube surface; and a square foot of heating surface in the rear end of the tubes will be more effective than a square foot in the front end; the tops of the flues are more effective than the bottoms. The relative value of the different parts of a tube as a heating surface is generally represented as follows:

Let Fig. 675 represent the end of a tube. If now the efficiency of the upper part of the tube is considered to be equal to 1, the efficiency of the sides will be equal to $\frac{1}{2}$, and the value of the bottoms will be 0. Hence the average efficiency of the whole tube surface will be $\dfrac{0 + \frac{1}{2} + \frac{1}{2} + 1}{4} = \frac{1}{2}$. This shows that the whole surface of the tube is only half as effective as it would be if all the different parts had been as valuable as the top.

445. Experiments also indicate that the heating surface placed perpendicular to the current of heated gases, so as to receive the heat by direct impact, is more effective than a heating surface placed diagonally to the current; approximately, one square foot of the former is as effective as 4 square feet of the latter, and it will require 8 square feet of heating surface placed parallel to the current to transmit as much heat as 1 square foot placed perpendicular to the current.

446. In computing the heating surface of a locomotive boiler the difference of the efficiency is not taken into account, and the whole surface is treated as if there existed no difference.

All the surface above the top of grate bars, in contact with the water and transmitting heat to it, is considered to be heating surface.

Many builders endeavor to obtain 400 square feet of heating surface for every cubic foot of piston displacement during one stroke. If, for instance, the cylinders are 16 inches diameter and 24 inches stroke, the piston displacement in one cylinder will be 2.79 cubic feet, and consequently the total heating surface should be 2.79 × 400 =

1,116 square feet. But in many cases the wheel base and gauge of track will limit the heating surface, and we may have to be satisfied with 320 square feet per cubic foot of piston displacement.

Some master-mechanics take into account the diameter of the wheel and mean effective pressure per square inch of piston, and consequently proportion the heating surface to the tractive force, allowing from 1 square foot of heating surface for every 10, up to 12 pounds of tractive force. Thus, for instance, the tractive force of an eight-wheeled passenger engine with cylinders 16 × 24 inches, mean effective steam pressure 90 pounds per square inch, and driving wheels 58 inches diameter, will be 9,533 pounds. Now, allowing 1 square foot of heating surface for every 10 pounds of tractive force, we have $\frac{9533}{10} = 953$ square feet of heating surface, which is less than found before.

If we allow 1 square foot of heating surface for every 10 pounds of tractive force, and 1 square foot of grate surface for every 600 pounds of tractive force, then the ratio of heating to grate surface will be as 60 to 1, which agrees well with the average practice. The ratio of heating to grate surface varies from 45 to 1 to 70 to 1.

For hard-coal burning engines 1 square foot heating is also allowed for every 10 pounds of tractive force; and allowing 1 square foot of grate surface for every 500 pounds of tractive force, the ratio of heating to grate surface will be 50 to 1, and this again agrees well with the average practice.

The heating surface in the tubes is from 6 to 8 times greater than the heating surface in the fire-box; probably a fair average will be 8 to 1, so that when the total heating is 953 square feet, that in the tubes will be 847.2 square feet.

447. The foregoing proportion will aid us in estimating the length of the tubes. For example, let it be required to find the length of the tubes for an eight-wheeled passenger engine, with 16 × 24 inch cylinders; diameter of driving wheels, 58 inches; mean effective steam pressure, 90 pounds per square inch.

The tractive force of this engine is 9,533 pounds; its total heating surface will be $\frac{9533}{10} = 953$ square feet; and the heating surface in the tubes will be $953 - \frac{953}{9} = 847.2$ square feet. According to Table 64, we find that this engine should have 166 tubes 2 inches outside diameter. The circumference of a 2-inch tube is 6.28 inches, and for 166 tubes the sum of the circumferences will be 166 × 6.28 = 1042.48 inches, or 86.87 feet. Dividing the required tube heating surface of 847.2 square feet by 86.87 feet, we have $\frac{847.2}{86.87} = 9.7$ feet for the length of the tubes. Whether we can use tubes of this length will depend on the wheel base.

The value of the tube heating surface is often overrated, but still it has value, and designers should strive to obtain such a length for the tubes as to give a liberal heating surface.

### RIVETED JOINTS.

448. The common practice in American locomotive boiler construction is to use single-riveted lap joints for the circular seams, and double-riveted lap joints for the longitudinal seams; or a double-riveted lap joint for the circular seams, and double-

riveted lap joints with welt pieces for the longitudinal seams. Sometimes welt pieces are also put over the circular seams up to the water line, for the purpose of preventing furrowing. Sometimes the longitudinal seams are butt joints.

The single-riveted lap joint is represented in Fig. 676. It is the simplest kind of riveted joints. A double-riveted lap joint is represented in Fig. 677. The latter joint

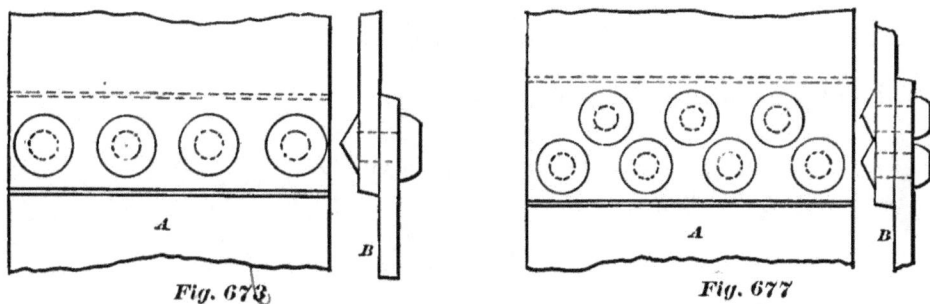

Fig. 676.   Fig. 677

is, of course, stronger than the former. The reason for using a stronger joint for the longitudinal seams is, that every inch of this seam has to resist twice the stress of every inch in the circular seam. To prove this we will take the following illustration:

Let Fig. 678 represent a cylinder 36 inches diameter, one inch long, and conceive the shell to be very thin, so that for the purpose of investigation we may leave the thickness out of consideration; also let the steam pressure in the cylinder be 100 pounds per square inch.

The stress tending to part the sheet on any longitudinal line, as $a\,b$, will be equal to one-half the product obtained by multiplying the diameter, $d\,a$, by the steam pressure per square inch; hence we have

$$\frac{36 \times 100}{2} = 1800 \text{ pounds,}$$

which is the stress on the line $a\,b$ or $d\,c$, and since these lines are one inch long, we may say that this is the stress per inch of the longitudinal seam. The total stress on any circular line will be equal to the area of the head in square inches multiplied by the steam pressure per square inch. The area of the head is 1017.88 square inches, hence the total pressure on the head will be $1017.88 \times 100 = 101{,}788$ pounds. But this pressure is resisted by the circumference of the cylinder, which is equal to

$$36 \times 3.1416 = 113.09+ \text{ inches.}$$

Here, then, we have 113.09 inches to resist 101,788 pounds, consequently each inch will have to resist

$$\frac{101788}{113.09} = 900 \text{ pounds,}$$

which is just one-half of the stress per inch on the longitudinal line $a\,b$.

This can be proved in another way. Let $p$ denote the steam pressure per square inch; $d$, the diameter in inches of a shell one inch long; $T_l$, the tension or stress per inch on the longitudinal seam; $T_c$, the tension per inch on the circular seam. Then for the longitudinal seam we have

$$T_l = \frac{d \times p}{2},$$

and for the circular seam we have

$$T_c = \frac{d^2 \times .7854}{d \times 3.1416} \times p.$$

This last equation can be written as follows:

$$T_c = \frac{d \times d \times .7854}{d \times 4 \times .7854} \times p.$$

By canceling we have

$$T_c = \frac{d \times p}{4}.$$

But

$$T_l = \frac{d \times p}{2},$$

which shows the tension or stress per inch of the circular seam is just one-half of that on one inch in the longitudinal seam. But from the foregoing it must not be understood that the double-riveted lap joints, when used in a boiler for the longitudinal seams, are twice as strong as the single-riveted lap joints used for the circular seams.

### EFFECTS OF TENSION ON RIVETED JOINTS.

449. When a riveted joint is subjected to tension, fracture may occur in several ways, depending on the defects of construction.

Let the shaded portion in Fig. 679 represent a strip of a boiler shell, with a single-riveted lap joint, and let the width $a$ be equal to the pitch of the rivets. It is evident that the strip is held together by the section of the metal whose width is equal to $b$; that is, the cross-sectional area of the metal between the rivets; it is also held together by the cross-sectional area of one rivet. Now, fracture may occur in the following ways:

First. By the metal breaking across in front of the rivet, as shown at $c$, Fig. 679, the action being similar to that of the fracture of a beam loaded at the center and fixed

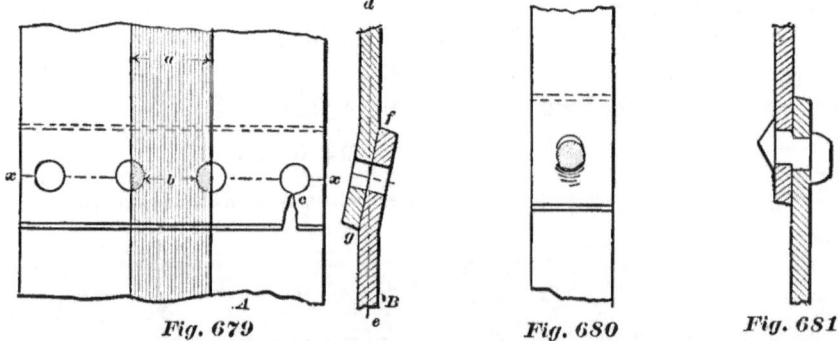

Fig. 679   Fig. 680   Fig. 681

at the ends. The cause of failure lies in the fact of punching or drilling the rivet holes too close to the edge of the plate. It is therefore of great importance to place the rivets at a proper distance from the edge of the plate.

Prof. W. C. Unwin, in his "Elements of Machine Design," gives the following distances from the center of rivets to the edges of iron and steel plates:

TABLE 65.

| Diameter of Rivets. | Iron Plates. Distance from Edge of Plate to Center Line of Rivets. | Steel Plates. Distance from Edge of Plate to Center Line of Rivets. |
|---|---|---|
| ½ inch. | 1.00 inch. | 0.86 inch. |
| ⅝ " | 1.14 " | 0.98 " |
| ¾ " | 1.29 " | 1.12 " |
| ⅞ " | 1.41 " | 1.22 " |
| 1 " | 1.55 " | 1.35 " |
| 1⅛ " | 1.67 " | 1.46 " |
| 1¼ " | 1.80 " | 1.57 " |

Mr. R. Wilson, in his "Treatise on Steam Boilers," says: "The lap (that is, from edge to edge of plates) for single riveting should be equal to 3 times the diameter of the rivet, and never more than 3.3 times the diameter."

The ordinary practical rule is to make the distance from center line of rivets to the edge of plate equal to 1½ times the diameter of the rivet. For thin plates, up to ½ inch thick, we would recommend to make this distance 1⅝ times the diameter of the rivet for iron and steel plates.

If the lap is too great, there will be difficulty, owing to the elasticity of the metal, in calking the joint so as to make it steam-tight.

Second. Fracture may occur by crushing the plate and rivet, as shown in Fig. 680, causing the joint to become leaky and insecure. But if the diameter of the rivet is of the proportion to thickness of plate as given in Table 66, trouble of this kind need not be anticipated.

Third. Fracture may occur by shearing the rivet, as shown in Fig. 681.

This is caused by placing the rivets too far apart, or using rivets too small in diameter. Here, then, the following question presents itself: What shall be the diameter of the rivets? This question leads us to consider the diameter of the smallest hole which can be punched through a plate of given thickness. In punching the hole, the area sheared by the punch is equal to $\pi dt$—in which $\pi$ denotes the ratio of the diameter to the circumference, and is always equal to 3.1416; $d$, the diameter of hole; and $t$, the thickness of plate, all in inches. Now let $c_s$ denote the resistance to shearing per square inch of metal, and let $R_s$ be the total resistance to shearing; then we have

$$R_s = \pi dt c_s.$$

The strength of the punch is equal to its cross-sectional area multiplied by the resistance to crushing per square inch. Let $c_c$ represent the resistance to crushing per square inch; and $R_c$ the whole resistance to crushing. Remembering that the cross-sectional area of the punch is equal to $\frac{\pi}{4}d^2$, we have

$$R_c = \frac{\pi}{4}d^2 c_c.$$

And when the total resistance to crushing is equal to the total resistance to shearing, we have
$$R_c = R_s,$$
or,
$$\frac{\pi}{4}d^2 c_c = \pi d t c_s;$$
clearing of fractions, we have
$$\pi d^2 c_c = 4\pi d t c_s.$$
Hence,
$$d = \frac{4 t c_s}{c_c}.$$

Therefore the diameter of the punch can never be less than $\frac{4tc_s}{c_c}$; if it is less, the punch will be crushed. If, for instance, the thickness $t$ of the plate is $\frac{1}{2}$ inch, and the resistance $c_s$ to shearing is 20 tons per square inch, and the resistance $c_c$ to crushing is 80 tons per square inch, then by substituting for the letters their values in the formula, we have
$$d = \frac{4 \times \frac{1}{2} \times 20}{80} = \frac{1}{2} \text{ inch}$$
for the smallest diameter of the punch which can be used for a plate $\frac{1}{2}$ inch thick; or, as will be seen in this particular case, the diameter of the punch is equal to the thickness of the plate.

In practice, of course, the diameter of the rivet holes is always larger than the thickness of the plate, so as to reduce the pressure per square inch on the punch.

In practice the diameter of the rivet is generally equal to $\frac{7}{8}$ of the thickness of the plate plus $\frac{3}{8}$ of an inch. Or, if $d$ denotes the diameter of the rivet in inches, and $t$ the thickness of the plate in inches, we may give in place of the foregoing rule the symbolic expression,
$$d = \tfrac{7}{8}t + \tfrac{3}{8} \text{ of an inch.}$$

The diameters of the rivets in Table 66 have been found by the foregoing rule. The first column gives the thickness of the plates, and the second, the diameters of the rivets in the nearest $\frac{1}{16}$ of an inch found by calculations.

TABLE 66.

| Thickness of Plate. | Diameter of Rivets. |
|---|---|
| $\frac{3}{16}$ inch. | $\frac{1}{2}$ inch. |
| $\frac{1}{4}$ " | $\frac{9}{16}$ " |
| $\frac{5}{16}$ " | $\frac{5}{8}$ " |
| $\frac{3}{8}$ " | $\frac{11}{16}$ " |
| $\frac{7}{16}$ " | $\frac{3}{4}$ " |
| $\frac{1}{2}$ " | $\frac{7}{8}$ " |
| $\frac{9}{16}$ " | $\frac{15}{16}$ " |
| $\frac{5}{8}$ " | 1 " |
| $\frac{11}{16}$ " | $1\frac{1}{16}$ " |
| $\frac{3}{4}$ " | $1\frac{1}{16}$ " |
| $\frac{13}{16}$ " | $1\frac{1}{8}$ " |
| $\frac{7}{8}$ " | |

Fourth. Fracture may occur along the center line $x\ x$ of rivets, Fig. 679. It is caused by placing the rivets too close to each other. This leads us to the consideration of the pitch of rivets—that is, the distance between their centers.

The tensile strength of iron plates in the direction of the grain varies from about 42,000 to 50,000 pounds per square inch. Now, for the purpose of calculating the pitch of rivets, we should know the exact tensile strength; sometimes it is stamped on the plates, but when this is omitted we should cut testing strips, and find the tensile strength by actual tests. In the absence of this knowledge we shall assume that the tensile strength is 45,000 pounds per square inch.

Referring to Fig. 679, let the shaded portion represent a strip of boiler shell; the width $a$ of this strip is equal to the pitch of the rivets.

Along the center line $x\ x$ of the rivets the width of the strip is necessarily reduced to the width $b$, and the amount of this reduction is equal to the diameter of the rivet. Now, if a square inch of metal can resist 45,000 pounds at $a$, it would appear that a square inch of metal will also resist 45,000 pounds at $b$. But this is not true; the reasons for this statement are as follows: First, referring to $B$, Fig. 679, we notice that the line $d\ e$, which represents the direction in which the pull or tension acts, does not pass through the center of the thickness of those portions of the plates which make up the riveted joint; hence the action of the tension on the joint is oblique, and therefore the plates at the joint cannot resist as great a pull as they can directly above or below the joint.

Second. Punching will reduce the tenacity of the plate along the line of rivet holes. The probable cause of the reduction of tenacity or injury is, that in punching the metal immediately surrounding the hole is squeezed laterally into the plate, giving this portion of the metal a permanent set, thereby reducing the strength of the plate. We believe that with a spiral punch the injury will not be as great as when the plates are punched with a common flat-ended punch. The recorded results of experiments made for determining the amount of reduction of strength caused by punching vary so much that it is impossible to state the correct amount. But experiments seem to indicate that, if the holes are punched somewhat too small, so that a ring of about .06 of an inch or more can be reamed out to bring the holes to the right size, the injury to the plate will practically amount to nothing; or, if the holes are punched to the right size, and the plates are annealed after punching, the original tenacity will be restored.

In the following calculations we shall assume that the plates are not annealed, and that the holes are punched to the right size with an ordinary flat-ended punch, all of which is a common practice. And we shall further assume that the oblique action of the pull on the joint, combined with the loss due to punching, reduces the original strength of 45,000 pounds per square inch to 40,000 pounds per square inch; the latter amount we shall hereafter, for the sake of brevity, call the apparent strength.

It is reasonable to assume that in new boilers properly made friction exists between the parts of the plates which make up the joints, and this friction adds strength to the joints. But the contraction and expansion will in time reduce this friction to nothing; we shall therefore neglect it in computing the strength of the joint. Now, if the apparent strength of the plate at the joint is 40,000 pounds per square inch, as we have assumed, it will be evident that, if we multiply 40,000 pounds by the area of the section at $b$—that is, multiply 40,000 pounds by the thickness of the plate, and by the width $b$, we obtain the total stress which our shaded strip in Fig.

679 can resist, provided the rivet is strong enough. Let $R_r$ represent the total resistance of the plate at $b$; and let the distance in inches between the sides of the rivets be denoted by $b$; $t$, the thickness in inches of the plate; and $c_r$, the apparent strength per square inch, which is equal to 40,000 pounds. We then have

$$R_r = b \times t \times c_r. \tag{1}$$

Since the width $a$ of the shaded strip in Fig. 679 is equal to the pitch of the rivets, it follows that only one whole rivet can hold the two parts of the strip together. Now it must be readily perceived that, in order to make one part of the joint as strong as the other, one rivet must be capable of resisting just as great a pull as the plate at its section $b$.

In a lap joint the rivets are subjected, to a small extent, to an oblique shearing stress, and it is perhaps for this reason, and on account of the bending action of the plates, that the rivets do not offer as great a resistance to shearing as they would do when shearing takes place in a plane perpendicular to the axis of the rivets. Again, rivets in punched holes seem to offer a greater resistance to shearing than those in drilled holes. The difference is probably due to the sharp edges of the drilled holes, which seem to shear the rivets with less pressure or load than the blunter edges of a punched hole. We shall assume that the shearing resistance of iron rivets in punched holes is 46,000 pounds per square inch. The total shearing resistance of the rivet will then be equal to its cross-sectional area multiplied by 46,000. Now, putting $R_s$ for the total shearing resistance of the rivet, $d$, the diameter of the rivet in inches, and $c_s$ for the shearing resistance per square inch = 46,000 pounds, we have

$$R_s = .7854 \times d^2 \times c_s. \tag{2}$$

But since the total shearing resistance of the rivet must be equal to the strength of the plate at its section $b$ (see Fig. 679), we have $R_s = R_r$; and according to Equation 1, $R_r = b \times t \times c_r$; in which $b$ is the distance between the sides of the rivets. Now, this distance $b$ is evidently equal to the pitch of the rivets minus the diameter of the rivet. Putting $p$ for the pitch and $d$ for the diameter, we have

$$R_r = (p - d) \times t \times c_r.$$

Since $R_s = R_r$, we have

$$.7854 \times d^2 \times c_s = (p - d) \times t \times c_r.$$

From the foregoing we get

$$\frac{.7854 \times d^2 \times c_s}{t \times c_r} + d = p.$$

But $.7854 \times d^2$ is equal to the cross-sectional area of the rivet; if we now put $a$ for this area, we have

$$\frac{a \times c_s}{t \times c_r} + d = p$$

Replacing $c_s$ and $c_r$ by their values as previously assumed, we have

$$\frac{a \times 46000}{t \times 40000} + d = p. \tag{105}$$

EXAMPLE 141a.—Find the pitch of rivets in a single-riveted lap joint for an iron plate $\tfrac{3}{4}$ of an inch thick.

In Table 66 we find that the diameter of the rivet for a $\tfrac{3}{4}$-inch plate should be $1\tfrac{1}{16}$ inches. The cross-sectional area of the rivet is .8866 square inch. Now, substituting for the symbols in Formula 105 their values, we have

$$\frac{.8866 \times 46000}{.75 \times 40000} + 1\tfrac{1}{16} = p = 2\tfrac{7}{16} \text{ inches.}$$

In this manner we have found the pitch of rivets in the nearest $\tfrac{1}{16}$ of an inch given in Column 3, Table 67. It will be noticed that this pitch does not increase regularly with the thickness of the plates; it is therefore not adopted in practice. The pitch given in Column 4 (same table) is recommended, as it agrees closer with the average practice.

In Table 67 it will be noticed that the pitch of rivets as recommended for thin plates is less than the calculated pitch. The reason for this reduction is to avoid the difficulty in calking. On the other hand, for thick plates the pitch of rivets as recommended is greater than the calculated pitch. The reason for this increase is twofold: First. In Formula 105 we have taken the nominal diameter of the rivet, not the real diameter—that is to say, the holes are always punched somewhat greater than the nominal diameter of the rivet; this, of course, decreases the amount of metal between the rivets; and since the rivet generally fills the holes, the real diameter of the rivet is larger than its nominal diameter, and for this increase no allowance was made in the formula, hence we see the propriety of increasing the calculated pitch. Second. The edges of the plates will corrode or wear faster than the rivets. This fact indicates that the calculated pitch should be increased, provided it does not interfere with calking, and since thick plates are not so liable to spring, a limited increase of the calculated pitch, as given in Column 4, can be made without endangering the tightness of the joint. Without this increase of pitch the life of the boiler is shortened. Of course, for thin plates an increase of the calculated pitch is prevented by the difficulty of calking.

### TABLE 67.

PITCH OF RIVETS FOR SINGLE-RIVETED LAP JOINTS FOR WROUGHT-IRON PLATES PUNCHED AND NOT ANNEALED.

| Thickness of Plates. | Diameter of Rivets. | Pitch as Calculated by Formula 105. | Pitch as Recommended. |
|---|---|---|---|
| Column 1. | Column 2. | Column 3. | Column 4. |
| $\tfrac{3}{16}$ inch. | $\tfrac{1}{2}$ inch. | $1\tfrac{11}{16}$ inches. | $1\tfrac{1}{2}$ inches. |
| $\tfrac{1}{4}$ " | $\tfrac{9}{16}$ " | $1\tfrac{5}{8}$ " | $1\tfrac{3}{4}$ " |
| $\tfrac{5}{16}$ " | $\tfrac{11}{16}$ " | $2\tfrac{1}{16}$ " | $2$ " |
| $\tfrac{3}{8}$ " | $\tfrac{3}{4}$ " | $2\tfrac{3}{8}$ " | $2\tfrac{1}{4}$ " |
| $\tfrac{7}{16}$ " | $\tfrac{13}{16}$ " | $2\tfrac{3}{16}$ " | $2\tfrac{1}{4}$ " |
| $\tfrac{1}{2}$ " | $\tfrac{13}{16}$ " | $2\tfrac{1}{4}$ " | $2\tfrac{3}{8}$ " |
| $\tfrac{9}{16}$ " | $\tfrac{7}{8}$ " | $2\tfrac{3}{8}$ " | $2\tfrac{1}{2}$ " |
| $\tfrac{5}{8}$ " | $\tfrac{15}{16}$ " | $2\tfrac{3}{16}$ " | $2\tfrac{1}{2}$ " |
| $\tfrac{11}{16}$ " | $1$ " | $2\tfrac{5}{8}$ " | $2\tfrac{5}{8}$ " |
| $\tfrac{3}{4}$ " | $1\tfrac{1}{16}$ " | $2\tfrac{7}{16}$ " | $2\tfrac{3}{4}$ " |
| $\tfrac{13}{16}$ " | $1\tfrac{1}{16}$ " | $2\tfrac{5}{16}$ " | $3$ " |
| $\tfrac{7}{8}$ " | $1\tfrac{1}{8}$ " | $2\tfrac{1}{4}$ " | $3$ " |

Many engineers assume the resistance of the plate between the rivet holes to be equal to the shearing resistance of the rivets. Under these conditions the formula for finding the pitch of rivets will be simpler than Formula 105. It is as follows:

$$\frac{a}{t} + d = p, \qquad (106)$$

in which $a$ denotes the cross-sectional area of the rivet in square inches; $t$, the thickness of the plate in inches; $d$, the diameter of the rivet in inches; and $p$, the pitch in inches.

The pitch found by this formula will be less than that given in Table 67. We have stated that the shearing resistance of the rivets in drilled holes is not as great as that of the rivets in punched holes, consequently when the holes are drilled it is advisable to reduce the pitch which is given in Table 67, and adopt the pitch given in the following table, which has been calculated by the formula,

$$\frac{a}{t} + d = p.$$

This pitch is also more suitable for steel plates and iron rivets, or in all cases where the tensile strength of the plate and the shearing strength of the rivets are equal or nearly so.

### TABLE 68.

PITCH OF RIVETS FOR SINGLE-RIVETED LAP JOINTS, CALCULATED BY FORMULA $\frac{a}{t} + d = p$; SUITABLE FOR WROUGHT-IRON PLATES WITH DRILLED HOLES, OR STEEL PLATES WITH IRON RIVETS.

| Thickness of Plates. | Diameter of Rivets. | Pitch of Rivets as Calculated by Formula. | Pitch of Rivets Recommended. |
|---|---|---|---|
| Column 1. | Column 2. | Column 3. | Column 4. |
| $\frac{3}{16}$ inch. | $\frac{1}{2}$ inch. | $1\frac{9}{16}$ inches. | $1\frac{1}{4}$ inches. |
| $\frac{1}{4}$ " | $\frac{9}{16}$ " | $1\frac{9}{16}$ " | $1\frac{3}{8}$ " |
| $\frac{5}{16}$ " | $\frac{5}{8}$ " | $1\frac{3}{4}$ " | $1\frac{5}{8}$ " |
| $\frac{3}{8}$ " | $\frac{3}{4}$ " | $1\frac{15}{16}$ " | $1\frac{7}{8}$ " |
| $\frac{7}{16}$ " | $\frac{13}{16}$ " | $2$ " | $2$ " |
| $\frac{1}{2}$ " | $\frac{13}{16}$ " | $1\frac{15}{16}$ " | $2\frac{1}{8}$ " |
| $\frac{9}{16}$ " | $\frac{7}{8}$ " | $2\frac{1}{16}$ " | $2\frac{3}{8}$ " |
| $\frac{5}{8}$ " | $\frac{15}{16}$ " | $2\frac{1}{8}$ " | $2\frac{1}{2}$ " |
| $\frac{11}{16}$ " | $1$ " | $2\frac{1}{4}$ " | $2\frac{5}{8}$ " |
| $\frac{3}{4}$ " | $1\frac{1}{16}$ " | $2\frac{1}{4}$ " | $2\frac{5}{8}$ " |
| $\frac{13}{16}$ " | $1\frac{1}{16}$ " | $2\frac{3}{16}$ " | $2\frac{5}{8}$ " |
| $\frac{7}{8}$ " | $1\frac{1}{8}$ " | $2\frac{1}{4}$ " | $2\frac{3}{4}$ " |

### DOUBLE-RIVETED LAP JOINTS.

**450.** We will now consider double-riveted lap joints. Let the shaded portion, Fig. 682, represent a strip whose width $b$ is equal to the pitch of a double-riveted lap joint. Here it is evident that two rivets hold the joint together. In all other respects the conditions are just the same as those for a single-riveted lap joint, and the remarks relating to it given in Art. 449 are also applicable to the double-riveted lap joint.

Since there are two rivets in the shaded strip (Fig. 682), the formula

$$\frac{a \times 46000}{t \times 40000} + d = p$$

as given for single-riveted joint, must be slightly changed so as to adapt it for a double-riveted joint. It is as follows:

$$\frac{2a \times 46000}{t \times 40000} + d = p, \qquad (107)$$

in which $a$ denotes the cross-sectional area in square inches of the rivet; $t$, the thickness of the plate in inches; $d$, the diameter of the rivet in inches; and $p$, the pitch in inches.

The pitch given in Column 3 in Table 69 has been calculated by the foregoing formula.

### TABLE 69.

PITCH OF RIVETS FOR A DOUBLE-RIVETED LAP JOINT, WROUGHT-IRON PLATES, PUNCHED AND NOT ANNEALED.

| Thickness of Plates. | Diameter of Rivets. | Pitch of Rivets as Calculated by Formula. | Pitch of Rivets Recommended. | Distance $C$ between the Rows of Rivets. |
|---|---|---|---|---|
| Column 1. | Column 2. | Column 3. | Column 4. | Column 5. |
| $\frac{3}{16}$ inch. | $\frac{1}{2}$ inch. | $2\frac{3}{4}$ inches. | 2 inches. | $1\frac{1}{4}$ inches. |
| $\frac{1}{4}$ " | $\frac{7}{16}$ " | $2\frac{3}{16}$ " | $2\frac{1}{4}$ " | $1\frac{3}{16}$ " |
| $\frac{5}{16}$ " | $\frac{11}{16}$ " | $3\frac{3}{8}$ " | $2\frac{1}{4}$ " | $1\frac{1}{4}$ " |
| $\frac{3}{8}$ " | $\frac{3}{4}$ " | $3\frac{1}{4}$ " | $2\frac{1}{2}$ " | $1\frac{5}{16}$ " |
| $\frac{7}{16}$ " | $\frac{13}{16}$ " | $3\frac{1}{4}$ " | $2\frac{3}{4}$ " | $1\frac{3}{8}$ " |
| $\frac{1}{2}$ " | $\frac{13}{16}$ " | $3\frac{3}{8}$ " | 3 " | $1\frac{1}{2}$ " |
| $\frac{9}{16}$ " | $\frac{7}{8}$ " | $3\frac{3}{8}$ " | $3\frac{1}{4}$ " | $1\frac{5}{8}$ " |
| $\frac{5}{8}$ " | $\frac{15}{16}$ " | $3\frac{3}{8}$ " | $3\frac{1}{2}$ " | $1\frac{3}{4}$ " |
| $1\frac{1}{16}$ " | 1 " | $3\frac{5}{8}$ " | $3\frac{5}{8}$ " | $1\frac{13}{16}$ " |
| $\frac{3}{4}$ " | $1\frac{1}{16}$ " | $3\frac{1}{4}$ " | $3\frac{3}{4}$ " | $1\frac{7}{8}$ " |
| $\frac{13}{16}$ " | $1\frac{1}{16}$ " | $3\frac{3}{16}$ " | $3\frac{7}{8}$ " | $1\frac{15}{16}$ " |
| $\frac{7}{8}$ " | $1\frac{1}{8}$ " | $3\frac{3}{4}$ " | 4 " | 2 " |

The pitch recommended in Column 4 is, of course, the distance $P$ from center to center of rivets measured on the center line of one row of rivets; the distance $C$ given in Column 5 is the perpendicular distance between the two rows of rivets (Fig. 682).

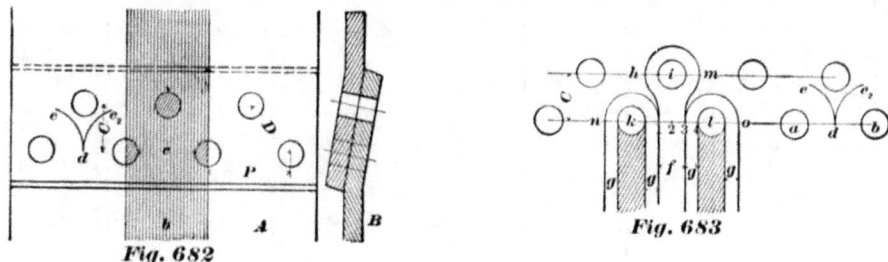

Fig. 682    Fig. 683

The distances $C$ have been adjusted to suit the conditions shown graphically in Fig. 683. In this figure we have divided the metal between the sides of any two rivets, $k$ and $l$, for instance, in four equal parts, and from the center of rivets $k$, $l$, and $i$

described circles whose diameters are equal to the diameter of one rivet plus two of the four equal parts laid off between the rivets. Now, lines drawn perpendicular to the line $k\,l$ through the points of division 1 and 3 will be tangent to the circles around the centers $k$ and $l$, and drawing lines perpendicular to $k\,l$ and tangent to the opposite sides $n$ and $o$ of these circles, and also drawing lines in the same direction and tangent to the circumference of the rivets, we may assume that these lines represent straps $g\,g$ pulling on the rivets $k$ and $l$; and we may further assume that an eye bar $f$ is pulling on the rivet $i$. In order to make the eye of the bar $f$ as strong as the straps $g\,g$, the outlines of the eye bar $f$ and the straps must not overlap each other; in fact, to be on the safe side a small space should be left between the circles $n$ 1 around $k$, $o$ 3 around $l$, and $h\,m$ around $i$. Hence the distances $C$ given in all the tables have been adjusted so that the rivets in the upper row will fall outside of the arcs $d\,e$ and $d\,e_2$ (Fig. 682), whose radii are equal to half the pitch drawn from centers of two adjacent rivets in the lower row.

If we assume that the apparent tenacity of the plates between the rivets is equal to the shearing resistance of the rivets, then Formula 107 will become

$$\frac{2a}{t} + d = p, \qquad (108)$$

in which $a$ represents the cross-sectional area of the rivet in inches; $t$, the thickness of the plate in inches; $d$, the diameter of the rivet in inches; and $p$, the pitch in inches as before.

From this formula the pitch given in Column 3, Table 70, has been calculated.

The pitch recommended in this table we believe to be more suitable for iron plates with drilled holes, or steel plates with iron rivets, than the pitch given in Table 69.

TABLE 70.

PITCH OF RIVETS FOR DOUBLE-RIVETED LAP JOINTS, CALCULATED BY FORMULA $\frac{2a}{t} + d = p$, SUITABLE FOR WROUGHT-IRON PLATES WITH DRILLED HOLES OR STEEL PLATES WITH IRON RIVETS.

| Thickness of Plates. | Diameter of Rivets. | Pitch of Rivets as Calculated by Formula. | Pitch of Rivets Recommended. | Distance $C$ between the Rows of Rivets. |
|---|---|---|---|---|
| Column 1. | Column 2. | Column 3. | Column 4. | Column 5. |
| $\frac{3}{16}$ inch. | $\frac{1}{2}$ inch. | $2\frac{5}{8}$ inches. | 2 inches. | $1\frac{1}{4}$ inches. |
| $\frac{1}{4}$ " | $\frac{9}{16}$ " | $2\frac{13}{16}$ " | $2\frac{1}{8}$ " | $1\frac{3}{16}$ " |
| $\frac{5}{16}$ " | $\frac{11}{16}$ " | $3\frac{1}{16}$ " | $2\frac{1}{4}$ " | $1\frac{5}{16}$ " |
| $\frac{3}{8}$ " | $\frac{3}{4}$ " | $3\frac{1}{8}$ " | $2\frac{1}{2}$ " | $1\frac{7}{16}$ " |
| $\frac{7}{16}$ " | $\frac{13}{16}$ " | $3\frac{3}{16}$ " | $2\frac{5}{8}$ " | $1\frac{1}{2}$ " |
| $\frac{1}{2}$ " | $\frac{7}{8}$ " | $3\frac{1}{4}$ " | $2\frac{3}{4}$ " | $1\frac{5}{8}$ " |
| $\frac{9}{16}$ " | $\frac{15}{16}$ " | 3 " | 3 " | $1\frac{3}{4}$ " |
| $\frac{5}{8}$ " | 1 " | $3\frac{3}{16}$ " | $3\frac{1}{8}$ " | $1\frac{13}{16}$ " |
| $\frac{11}{16}$ " | $1\frac{1}{16}$ " | $3\frac{1}{4}$ " | $3\frac{1}{4}$ " | $1\frac{7}{8}$ " |
| $\frac{3}{4}$ " | $1\frac{1}{8}$ " | $3\frac{7}{16}$ " | $3\frac{3}{8}$ " | $1\frac{15}{16}$ " |
| $\frac{13}{16}$ " | $1\frac{3}{16}$ " | $3\frac{9}{16}$ " | $3\frac{3}{8}$ " | $1\frac{15}{16}$ " |
| $\frac{7}{8}$ " | $1\frac{1}{4}$ " | $3\frac{5}{8}$ " | $3\frac{1}{2}$ " | 2 " |

It should not be understood that the pitch for single and double-riveted lap joints as given in the foregoing tables must be used in all cases. But when the tenacity of the plates and the shearing resistance of the rivets are not known, we believe that the pitch given in the tables is as good as can be adopted. On the other hand, when the tenacity of the plates and the shearing resistance of the rivets are known, the pitch should be determined by the given formulas, taking care to substitute the proper values for the symbols $c_r$ and $c_s$, and making such allowances for calking and wear of plates as in the judgment of the designer are necessary.

## STRENGTH OF RIVETED JOINTS COMPARED WITH THAT OF THE SOLID PLATE.

**451.** Let us now compare the strength of a single-riveted lap joint with the strength of a solid plate. Referring to Table 67, we find in Column 4 that the pitch recommended for a plate $\frac{3}{16}$ inch thick is $1\frac{1}{2}$ inches, and in Column 3 we notice that in order to make the plate between the rivets as strong as the rivets, the pitch should have been $1\frac{11}{16}$ inches; hence we conclude that, by adopting $1\frac{1}{2}$ inches for the pitch, the plate will be weaker than the rivets, and therefore, for comparing the strength of the lap joint with the strength of the solid plate, we only need to take into consideration the strength of the plate between the rivets.

In a plate of this thickness the diameter of the rivets is $\frac{1}{2}$ inch. Now, assuming that the rivet holes are punched $\frac{1}{16}$ of an inch larger in diameter, we have for the width of the metal between the rivets $1\frac{1}{2} - \frac{9}{16} = \frac{15}{16} = .937$ inch. Multiplying this width by the thickness $\frac{3}{16} = .187$ inch, we have $.937 \times .187 = .175+$ square inch for the area of the metal. According to Art. 449, the apparent strength of the metal at $b$ (see Fig. 679) is 40,000 pounds per square inch, hence the resistance to tearing of the metal between the rivets is $.175 \times 40000 = 7000$ pounds.

The width $a$ of the solid strip (Fig. 679) is equal to the pitch, $1\frac{1}{2}$ inches; the cross-sectional area of this strip is $1.5 \times .187 = .2805$ square inch. We have assumed that the tenacity of the plate above and below the joint is 45,000 pounds, hence the resistance to tearing of the solid part of the plate is $.2805 \times 45000 = 12622.5$ pounds. Therefore the strength of the single-riveted lap joint compared with the strength of the solid plate is

$$\frac{7000 \times 100}{12622.5} = 55 \text{ per cent.}$$

Now let us take a plate $\frac{7}{8}$ inch thick; for this thickness the pitch recommended in Column 4, Table 67, is 3 inches, but in Column 3 in the same table we find that the pitch should have been $2\frac{1}{2}$ inches, hence we conclude that by adopting a pitch of 3 inches, the metal between the rivets is stronger than the rivets; consequently, in comparing the strength of the joint with that of the solid plate, we only need to take the strength of the rivet into consideration.

Assuming, again, that the rivet holes have been punched $\frac{1}{16}$ of an inch larger in diameter than the rivets, the diameter of the rivet when properly driven becomes $1\frac{3}{16}$ instead of $1\frac{1}{8}$, as given in the table. The cross-sectional area of a rivet $1\frac{3}{16}$ inches diameter is 1.107 square inches, and for the shearing strength we have adopted 46,000 pounds per square inch, therefore the total shearing resistance of the rivet is $1.107 \times 46000 = 50922$ pounds. The width $a$ of the strip (Fig. 679) is equal to the pitch, 3 inches; multiplying this by the thickness $\frac{7}{8} = .875$ inch, we have $3 \times .875 = 2.625$ square inches for the cross-sectional area of the strip. The tenacity of the plate we have taken at 45,000 per square inch, consequently the resistance to tearing of the solid part of the strip will be

$$2.625 \times 45000 = 118125 \text{ pounds.}$$

And the strength of the joint compared with that of the solid plate will be

$$\frac{50922 \times 100}{118125} = 43 \text{ per cent.}$$

Calculating by the foregoing methods the strength of the metal between the rivets, and also the strength of the rivets for each thickness of plate, and comparing the weaker of the two with the strength of the solid plate, we obtain the percentages given in the following table, and these represent the efficiency of the joints in which the pitch is equal to that recommended in Table 67.

### TABLE 71.

EFFICIENCY OF SINGLE-RIVETED LAP JOINTS, IRON PLATES, PUNCHED HOLES, NOT ANNEALED.

| Thickness of Plates. | Diameter of Rivets. | Pitch of Rivets. | Efficiency of Joints. |
|---|---|---|---|
| Column 1. | Column 2. | Column 3. | Column 4. |
| $\frac{3}{16}$ inch. | $\frac{1}{2}$ inch. | $1\frac{1}{2}$ inches. | 55 per cent. |
| $\frac{1}{4}$ " | $\frac{9}{16}$ " | $1\frac{3}{4}$ " | 57 " |
| $\frac{5}{16}$ " | $\frac{11}{16}$ " | 2 " | 55 " |
| $\frac{3}{8}$ " | $\frac{3}{4}$ " | $2\frac{1}{8}$ " | 54 " |
| $\frac{7}{16}$ " | $\frac{13}{16}$ " | $2\frac{1}{4}$ " | 54 " |
| $\frac{1}{2}$ " | $\frac{7}{8}$ " | $2\frac{3}{8}$ " | 53 " |
| $\frac{9}{16}$ " | $\frac{15}{16}$ " | $2\frac{1}{2}$ " | 50 " |
| $\frac{5}{8}$ " | $\frac{15}{16}$ " | $2\frac{5}{8}$ " | 49 " |
| $\frac{11}{16}$ " | 1 " | $2\frac{3}{4}$ " | 47 " |
| $\frac{3}{4}$ " | $1\frac{1}{16}$ " | $2\frac{7}{8}$ " | 47 " |
| $\frac{13}{16}$ " | $1\frac{1}{16}$ " | 3 " | 41 " |
| $\frac{7}{8}$ " | $1\frac{1}{8}$ " | 3 " | 43 " |

When the tenacity of the plates, apparent strength of metal between the rivets, and the shearing strength of rivets differ from the values which we have assumed, then of course the efficiency of the joints will also differ from that given in the foregoing table, but with the proper selection of the material for the boiler the difference will not be very great.

Mr. Fairbairn gives 56 per cent. for the efficiency of a single-riveted joint. This agrees very closely with the efficiency of thin plates given in our table, but it seems that for thick plates 56 per cent. is too great.

In a way similar to the foregoing we find the efficiency of a double-riveted lap joint. The results are given in the following table; they have been calculated for the pitch given in Table 69.

## TABLE 72.

EFFICIENCY OF DOUBLE-RIVETED LAP JOINTS, IRON PLATES, PUNCHED HOLES, NOT ANNEALED.

| Thickness of Plates. | Diameter of Rivets. | Pitch of Rivets. | Efficiency of Joints. |
|---|---|---|---|
| Column 1. | Column 2. | Column 3. | Column 4. |
| $\tfrac{3}{16}$ inch. | $\tfrac{1}{2}$ inch. | 2 inches. | 63 per cent. |
| $\tfrac{1}{4}$ " | $\tfrac{9}{16}$ " | $2\tfrac{1}{8}$ " | 62 " |
| $\tfrac{5}{16}$ " | $\tfrac{5}{8}$ " | $2\tfrac{1}{4}$ " | 59 " |
| $\tfrac{3}{8}$ " | $\tfrac{11}{16}$ " | $2\tfrac{3}{8}$ " | 59 " |
| $\tfrac{7}{16}$ " | $\tfrac{3}{4}$ " | $2\tfrac{5}{8}$ " | 60 " |
| $\tfrac{1}{2}$ " | $\tfrac{13}{16}$ " | 3 " | 61 " |
| $\tfrac{9}{16}$ " | $\tfrac{7}{8}$ " | $3\tfrac{1}{8}$ " | 63 " |
| $\tfrac{5}{8}$ " | $\tfrac{15}{16}$ " | $3\tfrac{1}{4}$ " | 63 " |
| $\tfrac{11}{16}$ " | 1 " | $3\tfrac{3}{8}$ " | 62 " |
| $\tfrac{3}{4}$ " | $1\tfrac{1}{16}$ " | $3\tfrac{1}{2}$ " | 62 " |
| $\tfrac{13}{16}$ " | $1\tfrac{1}{8}$ " | $3\tfrac{3}{4}$ " | 63 " |
| $\tfrac{7}{8}$ " | $1\tfrac{1}{4}$ " | 4 " | 63 " |

This table shows us that for the assumed values of the tenacity of the plates, shearing strength of rivets, etc., the efficiency of double-riveted lap joints varies from 60 to 63 per cent. Mr. Fairbairn gives 70 per cent. for the efficiency of these joints.

In Art. 448, we have intimated that the double-riveted lap joint has less than twice the strength of the single joint. We are now in a position to state how much stronger one is than the other. Referring to Table 72, we may say that the average strength of the double-riveted joint is 62 per cent. of that of the solid plate; and referring to Table 71, we may say that the average strength of the single-riveted joint is 49 per cent. of that of the solid plate. Consequently the double-riveted joint is 1.26, say $1\tfrac{1}{4}$ times as strong as the single-riveted joint; and we will find the same difference by adopting Mr. Fairbairn's values.

### RIVETED JOINTS WITH WELT PIECES.

452. Fig. 684 shows an excellent longitudinal seam; it is stronger than ordinary double-riveted lap joints, and differs from the latter by having a welt piece added on the inside, extending along the whole length of the joint. The welt piece makes the joint stiffer, and therefore will somewhat increase the apparent strength of metal between the rivets, consequently the pitch of the rivets in this joint can and should be made a little less than that given in the table; by so doing, the difficulty of drawing the three thicknesses together will be reduced.

The inside welt piece not only adds strength to the joint, but it also serves another very useful purpose, namely, it prevents furrowing—that is,

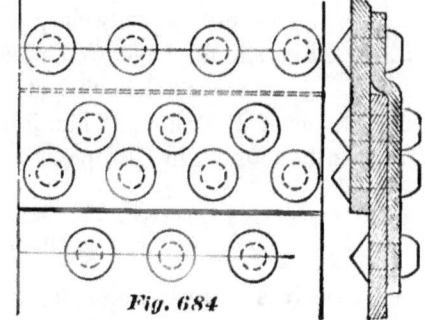

*Fig. 684*

the wearing or eating away of the metal on the inside of the boiler close to the edges of the joint, forming in some cases clear and distinct grooves. As to the cause of furrowing, engineers do not fully agree, but the weight of evidence seems to indicate that furrowing occurs to a greater extent with the use of bad water than with the use of good water. Again, furrowing occurs only along the seams below the water-line, and seldom, if ever, above it. This seems to indicate that there must be a chemical action of the water on the iron. The cause is also attributed to the form of the lap joint. Referring to Fig. 679, we notice that the line $fg$ of the lap is not in line with the center line $de$ of the thickness of the shell; consequently, when the boiler is subjected to a steam pressure, the tendency will be to draw the line $fg$ to coincide with the line $de$, causing a disturbance in the fibers of the iron near the edge of the plates, exposing a raw place to the chemical action of the water, and thereby promoting furrowing; hence it is sometimes said that furrowing is caused by a combined chemical and mechanical action. But whatever may be the cause, the fact remains that furrowing does occur below the water-line, and not above it. Locomotive boilers made of $\frac{5}{16}$ inch iron have been known to furrow nearly through the thickness of the iron in eighteen months. On the other hand, boilers with welt pieces have been known not to furrow during twenty-five years of hard service. This indicates an absolute necessity of placing all the longitudinal seams above the water-line whenever it is possible to do so, and that all transverse seams should have welt pieces extending to above the water-line. Indeed, this has become the practice on roads where the water is bad.

In the report of the proceedings of the American Railway Master-Mechanics' Association, an instance is recorded where furrowing was prevented by putting in an old boiler a sheet $\frac{3}{16}$ inch thick, extending about one-third around the circle of the barrel and throughout its whole length, and riveted lightly to the barrel.

This sheet or liner was first placed in the old boiler for the purpose of strengthening it; but when the boiler was examined after about two or three years' service, it was found that furrowing had not continued.

From the foregoing facts we learn that welt pieces not only increase the strength of boilers, but they also add to their life; and we may conclude that all longitudinal seams in any boiler should have welt pieces; below the water-line the welt pieces are needed for strength and to prevent furrowing, above the water-line they are needed for strength.

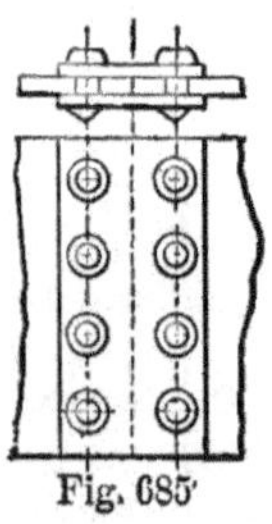

For similar reasons all single-riveted transverse or circular seams should have welt pieces all around; and double-riveted transverse seams should have welt pieces extending to above the water-line.

Fig. 685.

453. Fig. 685 shows a butt joint having a welt piece inside as well as outside of the shell. This joint is not so often used in this country, but it is frequently adopted in Europe, where it is the favorite one.

### THICKNESS OF BOILER SHELL.

454. It is scarcely necessary to say that the seam is the weakest part of the boiler, and the weakest part must be made strong enough to resist the pressure.

In Tables 71 and 72 we have given the strength of joints compared with that of the solid plate. This comparison will now enable us to compute the thickness of the shell for any diameter and steam pressure.

EXAMPLE 142.—It is required to find the thickness of the plate in a steel boiler 50 inches inside diameter, subjected to a steam pressure of 150 pounds per square inch. The ultimate tensile strength of the steel is assumed to be 65,000 pounds per square inch. Longitudinal seams are to be ordinary lap joints double-riveted with welt pieces, holes punched, plates not annealed after punching.

In example of this kind we need to take the strength of the longitudinal seams only into account; if these are strong enough, the circular seams will also be strong enough, because the stress per square inch on the longitudinal seams is twice as great as that on the circular seams, but the former are not twice as strong as the latter.

For the sake of simplicity let us employ for the relative strength of the seam to that of the solid plate the value given by Mr. Fairbairn, which for a double-riveted joint is 70 per cent. of the solid plate (Art. 451).

The ultimate strength of the solid plate as given in the example is 65,000 pounds per square inch; hence the strength of the seam is found by the following proportion:

$$100 : 70 :: 65000 : x.$$

Working out this proportion, we have

$$\frac{70 \times 65000}{100} = 45500 \text{ pounds per square inch}$$

of the plate in the seam. But this 45,000 pounds per square inch is the ultimate strength of the seam—that is to say, if the joint is subjected to this stress it will break. The general custom is to subject the joint to not more than $\frac{1}{5}$ of its ultimate strength, or, in other words, a factor of safety of 5 is adopted; hence the limit of the stress to which the joint should be subjected is $\frac{45500}{5} = 9100$ pounds per square inch, and this value (9100 pounds per square inch) can always be employed for double-riveted joints with welt pieces, in plates whose ultimate tensile strength is 65,000 pounds per square inch; we shall therefore call this value a constant. Now the total stress to which a strip one inch wide of the longitudinal joint will be subjected is numerically equal to the inner radius in inches of the boiler multiplied by the steam pressure per square inch. Let $P$ denote the steam pressure in pounds per square inch, and $R$ the inner radius in inches of the boiler; then the total stress to which a strip of the seam one inch wide will be subjected is equal to $P \times R$.

The stress which a strip one inch wide of the joint can resist with safety is numerically equal to the thickness of the plate multiplied by the constant previously found. Let $T$ be the thickness of the plate in inches; $C$, the constant; then the resistance which a 1-inch strip of the joint can offer with safety is equal to $T \times C$. Since a strip one inch wide has to resist a stress equal to $P \times R$, we have

$$T \times C = P \times R.$$

From this we obtain

$$T = \frac{P \times R}{C}.$$

Substituting for the symbols their values, we have

$$T = \frac{150 \times 25}{9100} = .412 \text{ inch, say } \tfrac{7}{16} \text{ of an inch,}$$

which is the thickness of the plate.

In working out this example, we have assumed that the strength of the joint is 70 per cent. of that of the solid plate; this value is somewhat too high for a double-joint without welt pieces—its strength is probably not over 60 per cent. of the solid plate (see Table 72). But if welt pieces are used, as they should be in all boilers, then the value of 70 per cent. for the joint is not too great and may be safely adopted.

In a similar way we may find the thickness of plates for boilers of any diameter, but it must be remembered that the value of the constant $C$ changes with the kind and quality of the material employed, and with the kind of joint adopted.

For the sake of convenience we give the following formulas for computing the thickness of plates for the ordinary class of boiler work, and for computing the pressure which ordinary boilers made of iron whose original ultimate tensile strength is 45,000 pounds per square inch, and those made of steel with a tenacity of 65,000 pounds per square inch will stand. These tenacities we believe to be about the average in ordinary boiler work. The factor of safety is 5, and for the relative strength of joints we have adopted Mr. Fairbairn's values.

For iron boilers with single-riveted longitudinal lap joints, welt pieces inside:

$$T = \frac{P \times R}{5040}. \qquad P = \frac{T \times 5040}{R}.$$

For steel boilers with single-riveted longitudinal lap joints, with welt pieces inside:

$$T = \frac{P \times R}{7280}. \qquad P = \frac{T \times 7280}{R}$$

For iron boilers with double-riveted longitudinal lap joints, with welt pieces inside:

$$T = \frac{P \times R}{6300}. \qquad P = \frac{T \times 6300}{R}.$$

For steel boilers with double-riveted longitudinal lap joints, with welt pieces inside:

$$T = \frac{P \times R}{9100}. \qquad P = \frac{T \times 9100}{R}.$$

In all these formulas $T$ denotes the thickness of the plate in inches; $P$, the steam pressure per square inch; and $R$, the inside radius in inches of the barrel.

### STEEL, IRON, AND COPPER FIRE-BOXES.

**455.** In Europe copper is used to a great extent for fire-boxes. In this country experience indicates that steel is decidedly the best material for this purpose, although some master-mechanics still use iron and believe that it gives as good results as steel. The failure of iron fire-boxes is generally caused by blistering; the failure of steel fire-boxes is generally caused by cracking. But with careful firing it has not been an unusual occurrence for a locomotive with a steel fire-box to make a mileage of 200,000 miles before the fire-box failed; in the reports of proceedings of the American Railway Master-Mechanics one instance is recorded where a mileage as high as 505,890 miles was obtained before the steel fire-box failed.

## STAY BOLTS.

**456.** Stay bolts for the fire-box are usually made of iron $\frac{7}{8}$ inch diameter, with 12 threads per inch; when the furnace side sheets are $\frac{1}{4}$ inch thick, the distance from center to center of stay bolts should not exceed 4 inches; for furnace sheets $\frac{5}{16}$ inch thick the distance from center to center of stay bolts can be increased, but should never exceed $4\frac{1}{2}$ inches.

For high steam pressure a good rule is to space the stay bolts so that the stress per square inch of the smallest cross-section of the bolt will not exceed 6,000 pounds per square inch. (See Art. 482.) The stay bolts are screwed into both sheets, and riveted over cold.

**457.** Sometimes one or two rows of hollow stay bolts are placed directly over the fuel; the purpose of these is to admit air to aid combustion. Sometimes three or four short pieces of 2-inch boiler tubes are inserted and expanded in each side of the fire-box in place of hollow stay bolts for the same purpose, but whether such devices will accomplish their purpose is very doubtful, as the air admitted is of too low a temperature to ignite the gases.

Occasionally we find holes drilled into the two upper rows of stay bolts in the sides of the fire-box; these holes are about $\frac{1}{8}$ of an inch in diameter, and extend in the direction of the axes of the bolts to a depth of about $\frac{3}{4}$ to 1 inch from the outside of the box; the purpose of these holes is to sound an alarm of danger in case any of them have been broken.

**458.** The crown sheet is often stayed in a similar manner—that is to say, it is stayed by radial stay bolts screwed into the outer and fire-box crown sheets, and riveted over cold; these stay bolts are shown in Fig. 634.

For stays of this kind the furnace crown sheet is of a necessity curved considerably, almost approaching a cylindrical form. The reason for this is to make the stay bolts enter both crown sheets as nearly as possible in a line normal to both sheets, so as to obtain as many full threads as can be had in either sheet. Another advantage gained by this curvature is that the impurities in the water as they are precipitated cannot find a ready lodgment on the crown sheet; the strong circulation washes the impurities off the sheet and keeps it comparatively clean. Hence this form of crown sheet and the manner of staying it are well adapted for muddy water, and have been favorably received. But these curved crown sheets have also a disadvantage, namely, they compel us to throw out too many tubes at the upper corners of the furnace, and in order to make up the right number of tubes more must be added in the center at the top of furnace. This arrangement compels us either to be satisfied with less than the desirable amount of steam room, or we must increase the diameter of the boiler, which is not always an easy thing to do.

**459.** To overcome the objectionable feature of this form of crown sheet and still have the stay bolts normal to the sheets, the Belpaire boiler, referred to in Art. 423, has sometimes been adopted. Besides the objections to the Belpaire boiler given in Art. 423, we may mention that the impurities of the water have a chance to settle on its furnace crown sheet; furthermore, the stay bolts through this sheet tend to entrap the impurities of the water, causing them to pile around the stay bolts in heaps of conical form, and covering a considerable portion of the crown sheet; all this increases the liability to overheating, which may lead to disastrous results, unless great care is taken to keep the crown sheet clean by frequent inspection and washing. It is our opinion that the Belpaire boiler is not the right kind to use on roads where pure water cannot be obtained.

460. In the Belpaire boilers the distances between the centers of stay bolts in the crown sheets vary from $4\frac{1}{2}$ to $4\frac{3}{4}$ inches, seldom exceeding the latter. In ordinary boilers with curved crown sheets, the distances between the stay bolts are measured on the furnace crown sheet, and also vary from $4\frac{1}{2}$ to $4\frac{3}{4}$ inches; the distances between the stay bolts measured on the outer crown sheet in this type of boilers are of course much greater, but this is of no consequence, as this outer crown sheet does not require as much bracing as that in the Belpaire box. Boilers whose furnace crown sheets are stayed by stay bolts usually have the dome placed on the barrel. When the dome is placed over the furnace, crown bars will have to be used.

## CROWN BARS.

461. Crown bars are generally made of two pieces of bar iron, as shown in section $B$, Fig. 686. These bars vary from 4 to $5\frac{1}{2}$ inches in depth, and from $\frac{5}{8}$ to $\frac{7}{8}$ inch in thick-

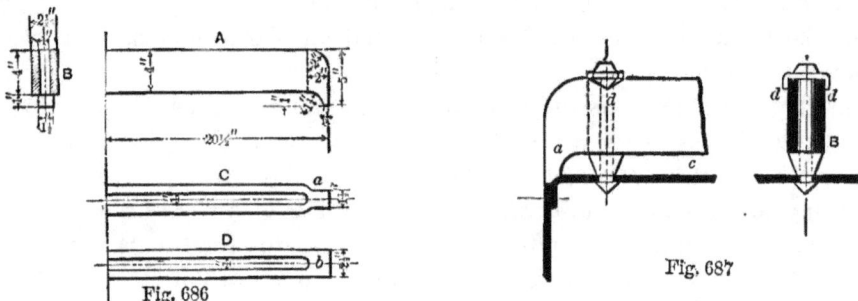

Fig. 686

Fig. 687

ness. The ends $a$ are sometimes bent and welded together, as shown at $C$, Fig. 686; and sometimes the ends are left straight and a piece $b$ set between them and the whole welded together, as shown at $D$, Fig. 686. The remaining portion of the bars are left a sufficient distance apart for the crown-bar bolts to pass through.

Sometimes the crown bars are placed lengthways of the furnace, but the usual practice is to place them across the crown sheet; by doing so they will be shorter, and consequently, with the same cross-section, will be stronger than if placed lengthways. The ends of the crown bars rest on the edges of the side sheets, and, to a small extent, on the corners of the crown sheet, as shown at $a$ in Fig. 687. The distance from center $b$ of the crown bar to center of the next one varies from $4\frac{1}{2}$ to 5 inches, seldom exceeding the latter; in fact, a distance of 5 inches between the centers is somewhat excessive; and yet this distance cannot be made much less than $4\frac{1}{2}$ inches, as there must be sufficient room left to put in the bolts which connect the crown-bar braces to the crown bar. The distance $c$ between the bottom of the crown bars and the top of crown sheet is sometimes 1 inch, but in the majority of boilers it is $1\frac{1}{2}$ inches; the latter distance we believe will be more satisfactory, because it allows a freer circulation and reduces the liability of the mud filling up the spaces.

## CROWN-BAR BOLTS.

462. The crown-bar bolts are generally ⅞ or 1 inch in diameter; they are placed from 4½ to 5 inches from center to center, but the former distance is preferable. In many boilers the crown-bar bolts have a button-head; the head is placed on the underside of the crown sheet; the nuts of these bolts bear against wrought-iron washers which are

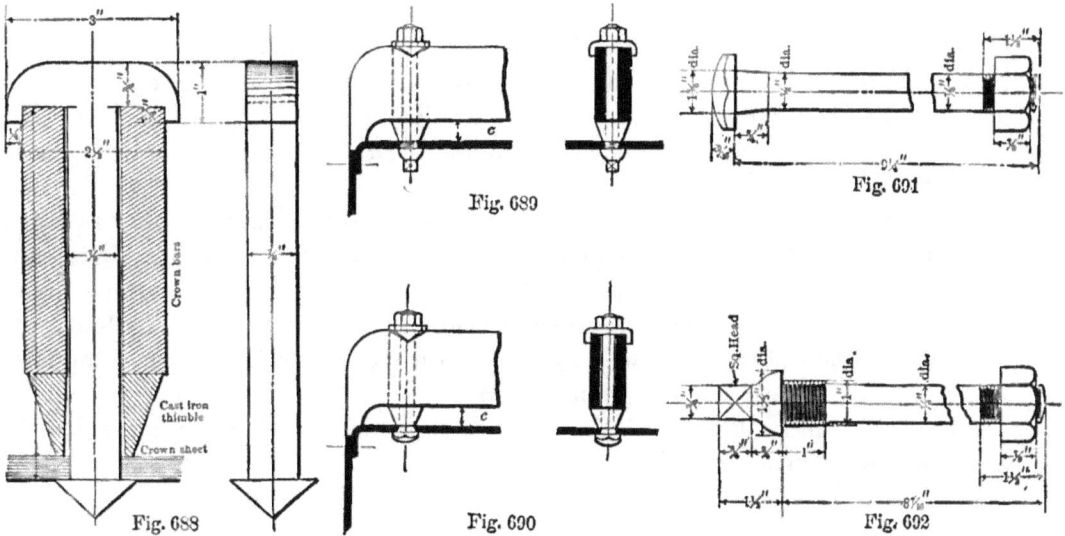

lipped over the top of crown bars. These washers are made in a very easy manner; they are simply square plates each having two corners turned over to form the lips, as shown at $d$ in Fig. 687.

Occasionally the crown-bar bolts have a T-head extending over the crown bars; the ends of these bolts are riveted over on the underside of the crown sheet, as shown in Fig. 688. Sometimes rivets are used in place of bolts, as shown in Fig. 687, and riveted over on the underside.

Occasionally the crown-bar bolts are of a form as shown in Fig. 689; these are screwed into the crown sheet, and a nut at the other end secures the bar to the sheet.

The crown-bar bolts shown in Fig. 690 we believe to be the best kind; they have a slight taper under the head, the crown sheet is reamed out to fit this taper, and the crown bars are secured in place by means of nuts bearing against the washers on the top. The advantage of this form is that, should leaks occur, the bolts can be readily taken out, and the tapered part extended by turning a small portion off the head and refitting the bolt in crown sheet.

Fig. 691 shows a bolt of this kind on a larger scale, and Fig. 692 shows the crown-bar bolt as used in Fig. 689.

463. The thimbles between the crown bars and crown sheet are sometimes made of wrought-iron ¼ or ⅜ inch thick. They are formed simply by bending the iron over a mandrel; the ends are not welded. Washers of this kind cover up too much of the crown sheet. To overcome this objection the washers are often made of cast-iron and tapered towards the crown sheet, as shown in Fig. 688, leaving at the bottom of the

washer about ⅛ of an inch metal around the bolt; the upper diameter is made sufficiently large to cover, or nearly so, the whole width of the crown bar. With these washers a greater surface of the crown sheet is in contact with the water, and overheating around the bolt is not so liable to occur.

CROWN-BAR BRACES.

464. For ordinary locomotives there should be at least four braces running from each crown bar to the outer crown sheet. The appearance of so many crown bars on the top of furnace may give an impression that the braces are superfluous, but such is not the case, as can be easily shown by computing the load which a crown bar can support.

For example: Say the crown bar is 54 inches long—this length we may assume to be the distance from inside to inside of the side sheets on which the ends of the crown bar rest; let the depth be 5 inches; and the thickness, ¾ inch; it is required to find the load which the crown bar can support without being reinforced by any braces.

For all practical purposes we may assume the crown bar to be a beam supported at the ends with a load uniformly distributed.

The load which any bar of a uniform rectangular cross-section can support is found by the following formula:

$$W = n\frac{Sbd^2}{6l},$$

in which $W$ denotes the load in pounds; $S$, the safe stress per square inch on the fibers most remote from the neutral surface; for wrought-iron this stress is usually taken at 12,000 pounds; $b$, the breadth; $d$, the depth; and $l$ the length, all in inches. The value of $n$ will depend on the manner in which the beam is supported and loaded; in this case the value of $n$ is 8. Hence the foregoing formula may be written as follows:

$$W = 8 \times \frac{12000 \times b \times d^2}{6 \times l}$$

This formula may again be reduced to

$$W = \frac{16000 \times b \times d^2}{l}.$$

Hence from the foregoing we have the following rule: Multiply 16,000 by the breadth, and by the square of the depth, all in inches, and divide the product by the length in inches; the quotient will be the load, uniformly distributed, which the crown bar can safely support.

We have seen that the crown bar is made of two pieces, each of which is ¾ inch in thickness; we may therefore say that the total thickness of the crown bar is 1½ inches. Now, substituting for the symbols in the last formula their values, we have

$$\frac{16000 \times 1.5 \times 5^2}{54} = 11{,}111 \text{ pounds (the fraction being neglected)},$$

and this is the load, uniformly distributed, which the crown bar can support.

Now let us compute the load which the crown bar has to support. Assume that these bars are placed 5 inches from center to center, and that the steam pressure is 150 pounds per square inch. The total steam pressure on a strip of the crown sheet 5 inches wide and 54 inches long will be

$$5 \times 54 \times 150 = 40500 \text{ pounds.}$$

Now, neglecting the load which the sheet itself can support, we may say that this is the load, uniformly distributed, which the crown bar must support under the given conditions.

But we have found by computation that the crown bar can support only 11,111 pounds, which leaves $40500 - 11,111 = 29389$ pounds which must be supported by the braces.

This result also enables us to compute the cross-sectional area of the braces. These should never be subjected to a greater tensile stress than 6,000 pounds per square inch of cross-section. Now, adopting 6,000 pounds for the stress per square inch, and dividing the total load which the braces have to support (29,389 pounds) by this stress per square inch, we obtain the aggregate number of square inches in the cross-sectional area of the braces, thus:

$$\frac{29389}{6000} = 4.89 \text{ square inches.}$$

We may assume that each end of the crown bar sustains one-half the load of one brace, and if there are to be four braces to each crown bar, and we wish to find the cross-sectional area of one brace, we proceed as if there are five braces to sustain a load of 29,389 pounds. Now, dividing the total cross-sectional area of the braces as previously found, namely, 4.89 square inches, by the number of braces, we have $\frac{4.89}{5} = 0.97$ square inch for each brace; the corresponding diameter is nearly $1\frac{1}{8}$ inches. In a similar way we find the diameters of the braces for any other steam pressure.

### TRANSVERSE BRACES.

465. The transverse braces $b$, which are placed above the furnace crown sheet, Fig. 693, for staying the outer sides of the fire-box, are secured to the side sheets in different ways. Sometimes they are screwed into the side sheets and then riveted over cold, as shown at $a$, Fig. 694. In cases of this kind one transverse brace $b$ is placed in each space between the crown bars (see Fig. 693). Then, again, we find the transverse braces fastened to crow-feet $c$ by means of pin bolts, Fig. 695. In cases of this kind a transverse brace is placed in every other space between the crown bars, as shown in Fig. 696, or in every space between the crown bars, as shown in Fig. 697. When these braces are placed in every other space the crow-feet $c$ stand horizontally, as shown in Fig. 696, and when placed in every space the crow-feet $c$ stand vertically, as shown in Fig. 697. The crow-feet are riveted to the side sheets; each crow-foot has two rivets. These rivets are laid off in straight lines generally parallel to the furnace crown sheet; the horizontal distance between the centers of

468                    MODERN LOCOMOTIVE CONSTRUCTION.

these rivets will of course depend on the distance between the centers of crown bars; if the latter are spaced 4½ inches apart, the horizontal distance between the centers of rivets will also be 4½ inches; furthermore, these rivets will generally fall in the ver-

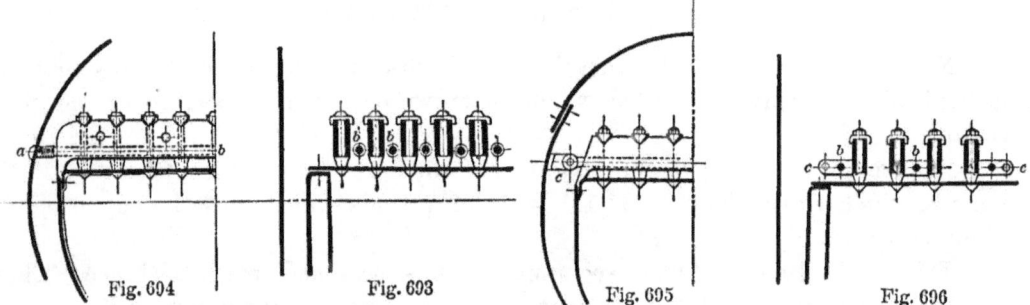

Fig. 694.   Fig. 693.   Fig. 695.   Fig. 696.

-tical lines drawn through the centers of stay bolts, or nearly so, giving the rivets the appearance of rows of stay bolts.

466. It may be well here to draw attention to the horizontal seams $d$ of the outer sides and crown sheets, Fig. 698. Considerable trouble will be experienced in the

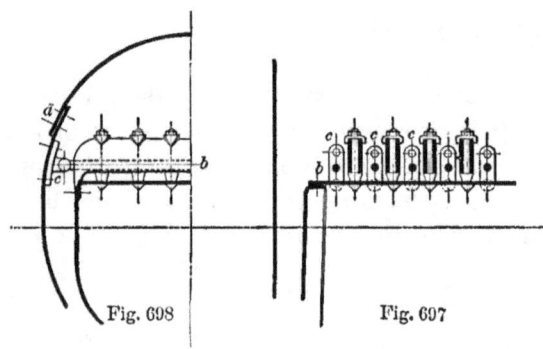

Fig. 698.   Fig. 697.

attempt to place one of these seams between two rows of stay bolts or between the upper row of stay bolts and crow-feet, on account of insufficient room. Consequently these seams are generally placed above the crow-feet. Sometimes the side sheets and outer crown are all made of one sheet, thus avoiding the side seams. This we believe to be the best practice, although there is one objection to it, namely, it makes the sheet very heavy for handling, and to flange the dome opening is somewhat troublesome, unless the boiler shop is specially fitted up for the purpose.

### BOILER BRACES.

467. Considerable space is left between the bottom of the tubes and the upper row of stay bolts in the furnace tube-sheet (see Fig. 624), and this portion of the tube sheet must be stayed. For this purpose braces $d$, Fig. 623, are run from the tube sheet to the bottom of the shell. These braces are sometimes attached to the crow-feet which are riveted to the tube sheet, and the other ends of the braces are riveted directly to the shell. Since this portion of the tube sheet is exposed to a great heat, it is advisable to place cast-iron thimbles of the same form as those under the crown bars between the tube sheet and the crow-feet, so as to allow as great a surface as possible of the former to come in contact with the water, thereby preventing overheating.

The tapered course $E$, Fig. 623, leaves another flat place in each of the sides of the shell which must be stayed. Sometimes they are stayed by braces running across the boiler; in such cases, of course, the tubes are spaced so as to leave room for these braces. But the general practice is to rivet stiffening pieces to the sides, as shown at $f$ in Fig. 623. These stiffening pieces are often made of bar iron about $2\frac{1}{4}$ inches square, and we believe that this is the best form. We recommend a distance of $3\frac{1}{2}$ inches from center to center of these pieces. Their length should be such as to extend a foot or so both ways on the cylindrical part of the shell. Sometimes the stiffening pieces $f$ are made of **T**-iron, as shown in Fig. 655, and then again we find them made of angle iron placed back to back.

The manner of staying the back head is plainly shown in Figs. 624, 634, and 657. Crow-feet are generally riveted to the back head, and braces $g$ (Fig. 655) extend from these to the shell of the boiler. Sometimes **T**-irons are used in place of crow-feet.

The front tube sheet is stayed in a manner similar to that of the back head. In all cases the rivets which secure the crow-feet or **T**-iron to the back head and front tube sheet should be spaced so as to bring them $4\frac{1}{2}$ inches apart from center to center, and arranged in rows like the stay bolts. The braces should be placed as nearly horizontal as possible, so as to reduce the stress in them. Again, the ends of these braces which are riveted to the shell should be kept a considerable distance apart, so as to distribute the stress over the shell as much as possible. For computing the stress in these braces see Art. 485.

The braces $g$ which we just described are usually called diagonal braces, to distinguish them from tie rods, which are sometimes used in place of the diagonal braces.

468. The tie rod is shown in Fig. 699. It extends from the back head to the front tube sheet, and it has a hexagonal head at one of its ends. The diameter of the portion near the head is larger than that of the body of the rod; this enlarged part is about 1 inch long, with a thread

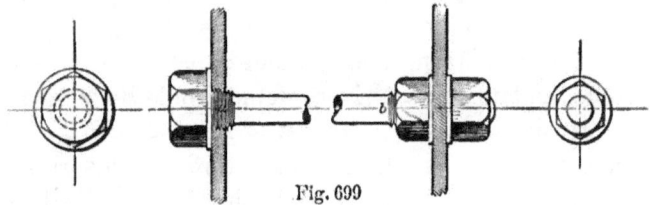

Fig. 699

cut on it, and is screwed into the back head. In order to secure a steam-tight joint a copper washer is placed between the head and the sheet.

The end $b$ of the rod is also made larger in diameter than that of the body of the rod, and has a thread cut on it, but it is not so large in diameter as the part near the head. If, for instance, the body of the rod is $\frac{7}{8}$ inch in diameter, the part near the head will be $1\frac{1}{4}$ inches diameter outside of the thread, and the end $b$ will be 1 inch diameter, also measured outside of the thread. The end $b$ of the rod is not screwed into the front tube sheet, but simply passed through it, and is secured to the tube sheet by means of two nuts, one inside and the other outside of the sheet; copper washers are placed between the sheet and the nuts. Great care must be taken in screwing up the inner nut, which should bear but slightly against the sheet, so as to avoid buckling the rod; the joint is made steam-tight by screwing up tightly the outer nut.

These tie rods are generally placed 5 or $5\frac{1}{2}$ inches from center to center. The diameter of the rods will depend on the steam pressure, and should be such that the stress per square inch will not exceed 6,000 pounds. To illustrate we will take the following example:

EXAMPLE 143.—What should be the diameter of the tie rods placed 5 inches from center to center, steam pressure 150 pounds per square inch?

The total surface which each tie rod has to support is 5 × 5 = 25 square inches; and since the steam pressure is 150 pounds per square inch, the total tension on the rod will be 25 × 150 = 3750 pounds. The stress is not to exceed 6,000 pounds per square inch, hence the cross-sectional area of the smallest part of the rod will be $\frac{3750}{6000}$ = .625 square inch; the corresponding diameter is nearly $1\frac{5}{16}$ inch.

469. Fig. 647 shows a boiler in which the back head is stayed by gusset plates instead of diagonal braces or tie rods. Sometimes the front head is stayed in a similar way. The usual way of fastening the gusset plates to the boiler sheets is to rivet their ends to two angle irons, and these are in turn riveted to the boiler sheets.

### DOMES.

470. A common way of fastening the dome to the shell is shown in Fig. 655. As will be seen, the outer crown is flanged up into the dome, and the dome is flanged to fit the outer crown.

The dome flange is riveted to the shell by a single row of rivets; their pitch is to be taken from the tables in Art. 449. The vertical flange of the shell is also riveted to the dome by a single row of rivets, but the pitch of these is double that of the rivets through dome flange and outer crown. It is often assumed that this manner of fastening the dome to the shell is sufficiently strong, but our experience has led us to believe that it is not strong enough, and is particularly weak for the high steam pressure adopted in late years. Every dome should have a wrought-iron stiffening-ring riveted to the inside of boiler, as shown in Fig. 633 or Fig. 647. The rivets through the dome flange and shell should also pass through this ring, and in addition to these rivets another row should pass through the ring and shell; the pitch of the rivets in this last row is usually double that of the rivets through the dome flange. Without this stiffening ring the boiler is liable to spread directly under the dome, thereby throwing an excessive stress on the dome flanges, and causing leaks. This action has been fully confirmed by experiments on the New York Elevated Railroad.

### SHORT SMOKE-BOXES.

471. A few years ago, short smoke-boxes, shown in Figs. 700 and 701, were almost universally used, and even at the present time they are often put on. The length of these boxes is such as to give but very little more than sufficient room for the steam pipes, exhaust nozzles, and draft or petticoat pipe.

The exhaust nozzle (not shown here) must necessarily be short. The petticoat pipe $a$, through which the exhaust steam passes, is made telescopic, so that it can be lengthened or shortened; the purpose of changing its length is to obtain an even draft on the fire. This pipe, after it has been correctly adjusted in position, is held by the braces $b$ which extend to the sides of the smoke-box, one on each side of the pipe. Boxes of this kind have smoke-stacks of the form as shown in Figs. 769, 770, of which a description is given further on. These boxes are of no use for holding sparks; they are not designed for such a duty, consequently the sparks are thrown out of the stack while the engine is running, thereby frequently doing much harm by set-

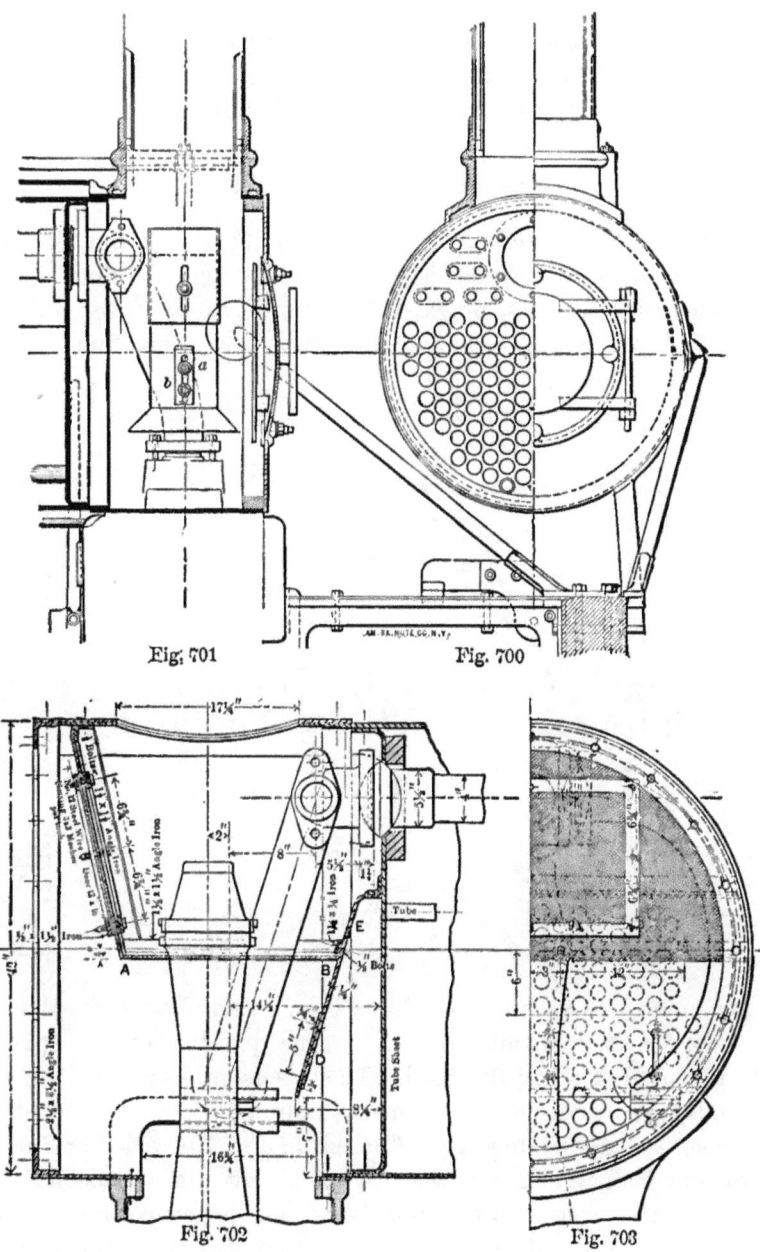

Fig. 701     Fig. 700

Fig. 702     Fig. 703

ting fire to objects along the road, and putting the railroad companies to a great expense in paying for the damages.

Figs. 702 and 703 represent another smoke-box, which may be properly classed with the short ones. It is used on the New York Elevated Railroad engines, and is designed for a straight stack similar to the one shown in Fig. 778 or Fig. 781. Stacks of this kind have, of course, no netting, consequently the netting is placed inside of the smoke-box. The exhaust nozzles extend above the horizontal netting $A\ B$, and this netting terminates at, and is fastened to, the diaphragm plate $D\ E$. The lower portion of this plate is adjustable, and answers the same purpose as the petticoat pipe, namely, to create an even draft on the fire. In this box there is some room provided for retaining the sparks, and for short runs it is well suited.

### EXTENSION FRONTS.—BRICK ARCHES.

472. Various spark arresters have been invented and designed, but when put into service proved themselves to be of little or of no practical value.

The extended smoke-boxes, or extension fronts, as they are sometimes called, shown in Figs. 704 and 705, were condemned after they were first brought out, but

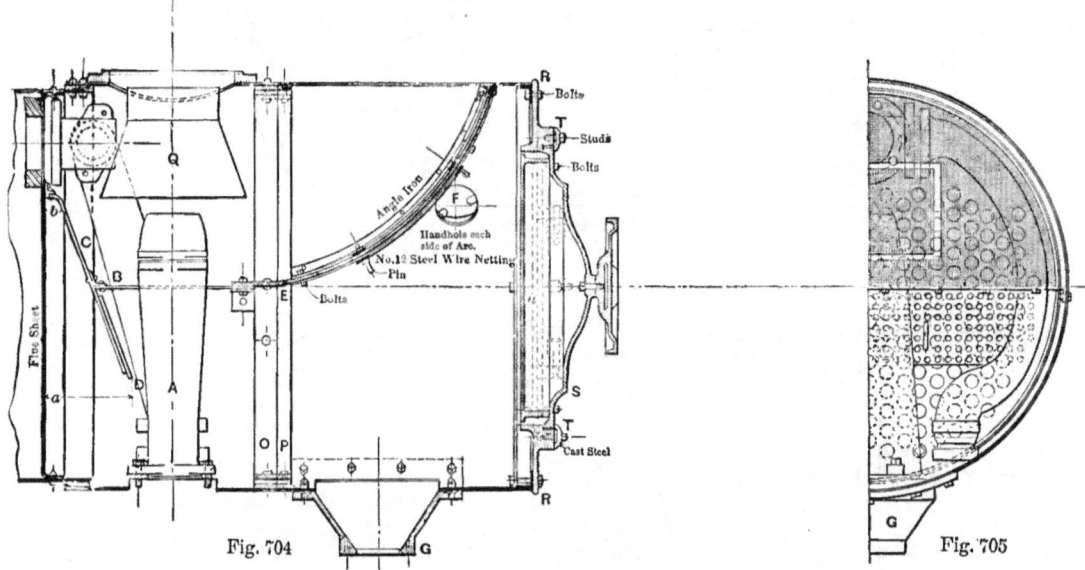

they were tried again, and in late years have been received with great favor, and we believe justly so, for they certainly retain a large quantity of the sparks, and to a great extent prevent fires along the road. The extension front has its enemies, but it has more friends, and is considered by many railroad men to be one of the greatest boiler improvements made in late years. Comparing Fig. 704 with Fig. 701, we find that the boxes are practically alike, with the exception that the extension front is about twice as long or a little more than the short box. The primary object of the extension front is to hold the sparks and carry them to a designated place where the box can be emptied and the sparks can do no harm, instead of scattering them along the road to start fires, the worst use that sparks can be put to. But besides this advantage which the extension front possesses, it is also claimed that it will save fuel. This may be explained as follows: We have already seen that with a short box the sparks are thrown out of the stack, and we may here add that many of the sparks and cinders are broken up in the stack by being thrown violently against the netting. Now to lift these sparks and cinders, and give them the velocity which they attain in the stack, break up some of them, and throw all out of the stack, requires an expenditure of energy, and this energy is supplied by the exhaust steam. Besides this, the exhaust steam has its legitimate work to do, namely, to create a forced draft. In the extension front some of the dust and finer cinders will also be thrown out of the stack, and indeed this cannot be avoided so long as an opening for the escape of the exhaust is required. But it is also a fact that the extension front becomes filled with cinders, and therefore not near so many cinders are thrown out of the stack, neither are these broken up as in the short box, consequently the exhaust steam in the extension front has less work to do than in the short box. Again, in the extension front the exhaust nozzle $A$ (Fig. 704) extends to above the netting $E$, and the exhaust steam passes out through a straight stack, and meets no obstruction; this greater freedom of escape also reduces the work of the exhaust steam. We may therefore say that nearly the whole force of the exhaust steam is expended in creating the required draft, and it has no extra work to perform. Now, since in the extension front the exhaust steam has less work to perform than in the short box, we can make the exhaust nozzles a little larger in diameter, and in fact they are usually made larger in an extension front than in a short box. But increasing the diameter of the exhaust nozzle will give less back pressure in the cylinder; it also gives a smoother draft, and is not so liable to draw unconsumed fine coal through the flues. Hence a lighter fire may be carried, and, in fact, lighter fires are generally carried, in locomotives with an extension front than in others; this also gives more time for the fuel to burn. All these things tend to and do save fuel, but there is such a thing as overestimating the advantages of an extension front.

In many engines a brick arch, as is shown in Fig. 668, is used in connection with the extension front, and since this arch prevents unconsumed fuel from being drawn through the flues, it must also promote the economy of fuel. The exact amount of fuel saved by the brick arch and that saved by the extension front cannot be stated, as reliable experiments to determine these amounts have not, to our knowledge, been made. But that the brick arch in connection with the extension front does save fuel is beyond a doubt.

473. The comparatively large capacity of the extension front affects to a slight extent the useful action of the exhaust, because the exhaust steam has to create a partial vacuum in a larger space than in a short box, and this increased capacity absorbs a part of the exhausting action of the blast before the tubes are appreciably affected; and it may be said that, within limits, the smaller we make the capacity of the smoke-box, the more will the exhausting action be felt by the tubes. Mr. D. K. Clark, in his treatise on Railway Machinery, gives for the most suitable capacity of the smoke-box 3 cubic feet for every square foot of grate. Now the capacity of the modern extension front is not much larger than this, and when partly filled with cinders is in some cases less. We may therefore conclude that although the increased capacity may affect the useful action of the exhaust, it does not affect it to any hurtful extent.

474. That the extension front has sometimes been a failure cannot be denied, but this was probably due to faulty design, bad workmanship, and lack of attention when the engine was running. In order to make an extension front work successfully

it must be fitted up perfectly air-tight, otherwise the smoldering cinders which it holds will take fire, which will warp the sheets and render the box useless. Care should also be taken not to allow the front to fill up too much; such a condition will cause the sparks to be thrown out of the stack. The diaphragm plate $C$ (Fig. 704) and netting $E$ must be properly arranged, also suitable exhaust nozzles adopted and ample provision made for emptying the box.

The diaphragm plate $C$ is generally made solid; sometimes its lower part $D$ is perforated, as shown in Fig. 705. This plate $C$ is fastened to the tube sheet by an angle iron placed directly over the top row of tubes.

The horizontal distance $a$ from the lower edge of the diaphragm to the tube sheet is greater than the distance $b$ between the plate and tube sheet at the top. The distance $a$ at the bottom will depend on the number of tubes; it should be such as to give a horizontal area for the passage of gases equal to the total cross-sectional area of the tubes. At the top a distance of $2\frac{1}{2}$ to 3 inches is usually sufficient. We have already seen that the lower part of the diaphragm plate is adjustable, or, in other words, it is made so that it can be raised or lowered, and the extent of the total adjustment is about 6 inches. The means provided for fastening the lower portion $D$ of the diaphram to the upper part consist generally of four $\frac{7}{8}$-inch bolts passed through the upper plate and sliding in suitable slots cut into the lower plate, as shown in Fig. 705. When the lower portion of the diaphragm plate is in its lowest position, the area in a vertical plane between its bottom edge and the shell of the smoke-box should not be less than the total cross-sectional area of the tubes.

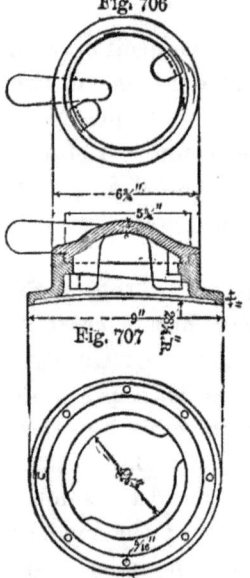

A horizontal plate $B$ (Fig. 704) is usually fastened to the upper part of the diaphragm plate; it extends a little beyond the exhaust nozzle towards the front of the box; the purpose of this is to prevent the sparks from flying into the smoke-stack. The netting is bolted to this plate and extends to the top of smoke-box as shown. The netting must be provided with a door so as to give ready access to the upper part of the steam pipes and exhaust nozzles.

A hole $F$ (Fig. 704) is cut in each side of the smoke-box to afford means for looking into it and examining its condition. These holes are closed by cast-iron caps which fit cast-iron flanges riveted to the shell. Of course care must be taken to make an air-tight joint between the caps and flanges. Different views of these caps and flanges are shown in Figs. 706, 707, and 708.

475. The cast-iron cinder-box $G$ for discharging the cinders, shown at the bottom of the smoke-box, Figs. 704 and 705, is usually riveted to the shell, and is generally closed by means of a cast-iron wedge fitted air-tight. Sometimes means are provided for blowing out the cinders by steam. One form of cinder-box is shown on a larger scale in Figs. 709, 710. The flange $G$ is riveted to the smoke-box. The opening in this flange is closed by the wedge $H$, which is driven home air-tight in the passage-way formed between the

flanges *G* and *I*. A wrought-iron pipe *J* is riveted to the flange *I* for the purpose of preventing the cinders and ashes from falling on the truck when the smoke-box is to be emptied. The flanges *G* and *I*, also the wedge *H*, are planed tapering, and the wedge *H* fits the planed surface of the passage-way very accurately, so as to make an air-tight fit. The cinder-box in Fig. 704 is shown in Figs. 711, 712, and 713, on a larger scale, with the attachments for opening and closing it. The construction of this box is similar to that shown in Fig. 710, with this difference, that the wedge *H*,

instead of being driven home, is pulled out of or forced in the passage-way by means of the screw *K*. The hand-wheel *L* on this screw is placed outside of the engine frame *M*. This makes a very convenient arrangement for opening and closing the cinder-box.

Cinder-boxes are sometimes made much deeper than those shown in any of the figures. The objection to deep cast-iron cinder-boxes is that, should the cinders in them become ignited through a small leakage of air, the box is liable to become red-hot, and in this condition crack or break off, thereby rendering the whole extension front useless.

476. The shell of the smoke-box is sometimes made in two courses; this is done for convenience of handling the plates. These courses butt against each other, and are connected by two heavy wrought-iron rings *O*, *P*, Fig. 704, one riveted to each course; the rings are then bolted together as shown. The length of the courses should be such as to enable the ring *O* in the inner course to take the bolts through the cylinder saddle and smoke-box. We prefer to make the smoke-box of one sheet, even if it is somewhat heavy to handle. In this case we also need a heavy wrought-iron ring *O*, as shown in Fig. 714, placed in a position to take the bolts through the cylinder saddle. The purpose of this ring is to stiffen the smoke-box and distribute the stress through a larger part of it.

## SMOKE-BOX FRONTS.

477. The manner of closing up the front end of the smoke-box is plainly shown in Fig. 704. An angle-iron ring is riveted to the outer end of the box, to which the cast-iron front is bolted. Frequently a wrought-iron ring $3 \times 1\frac{1}{2}$ inches in cross-section is used in place of the angle-iron ring. The front consists of a cast-iron ring

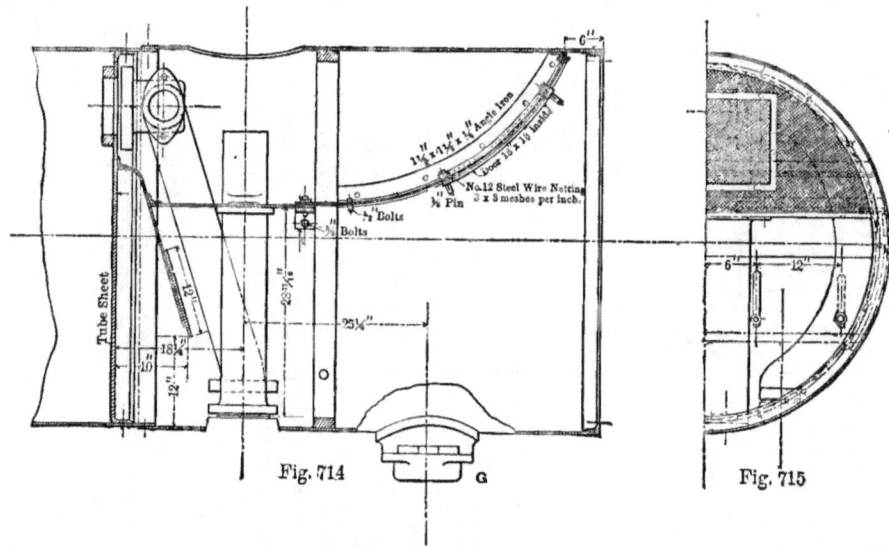

$R$ and a cast-iron door $S$ sufficiently large in diameter to permit the taking out of any one of the tubes. The door is hinged to the ring, and in closing it is made airtight by means of red-lead, and is then fastened by six or eight clamps $T$ attached to the outside of the ring $R$. Sometimes the clamps are placed inside; in many such cases there are only three or four clamps used, and arranged so as to unlock simultaneously by one handle placed outside. We believe the plan of placing the clamps outside, as shown in Fig. 704, is the best one, as by this method a tighter joint can be secured.

The cast-iron ring and door should be made sufficiently heavy and of such forms as are best adapted to prevent them from warping. The forms shown in Fig. 704 we believe to be good ones. The door is provided in many cases with a wrought-iron liner about $\frac{3}{16}$ inch thick, placed a short distance from the inside of the door. Sometimes the liner is made of cast-iron, as shown at $u$, Fig. 704. The object of this liner is to protect the door as much as possible from excessive heat.

478. In the extension front shown in Fig. 704, a petticoat pipe $Q$ is introduced, but this is not a general practice; in the majority of extension fronts a pipe of this kind is not used.

Long exhaust pipes are always adopted for extension fronts, bringing the top of the exhaust nozzles to within a short distance from the top of box.

In Art. 471 we have seen that in short smoke-boxes the exhaust nozzle is placed comparatively low, and the exhaust steam is led through the petticoat pipe into the stack. The following reason for the difference in the lengths of the exhaust nozzles in the two kinds of smoke-boxes may be given. In the short box shown in Fig. 701 diaphragm plates are not used, and therefore an adjustable petticoat pipe is needed to make the draft pull evenly all over the fire, and consequently the exhaust nozzles must be placed low, so that the object for which the petticoat pipe has been designed can be accomplished. On the other hand, in the extension front the pull of the draft on the fire is regulated by the lower portion of the diaphragm plate, and there is nothing to prevent the exhaust nozzle from being placed pretty close to the top of the box and thus leading the exhaust steam directly into the stack without giving it an opportunity to spread in the smoke-box.

### BRICK ARCHES.

479. In Fig. 668 the ordinary form of a brick arch for furnaces is represented. It is usually 4 inches thick, and is supported by four wrought-iron tubes. These tubes are generally 1⅞ inches outside diameter and about ¼ inch thick—in fact, they are made of the same kind of pipe as is used for water grates (see Art. 493). The two central supporting tubes, as shown in this particular case, extend from the tube sheet to the door sheet; the two outer ones extend to the crown sheet. The brick arch runs through the whole length of furnace and touches the sides, excepting at the two rear corners of the furnace, where openings about 12 inches square are left for the gases to pass through.

Sometimes the brick arch extends only through a part of the furnace, as shown in Fig. 716. The arch shown in this figure is a hollow one. Air is admitted into

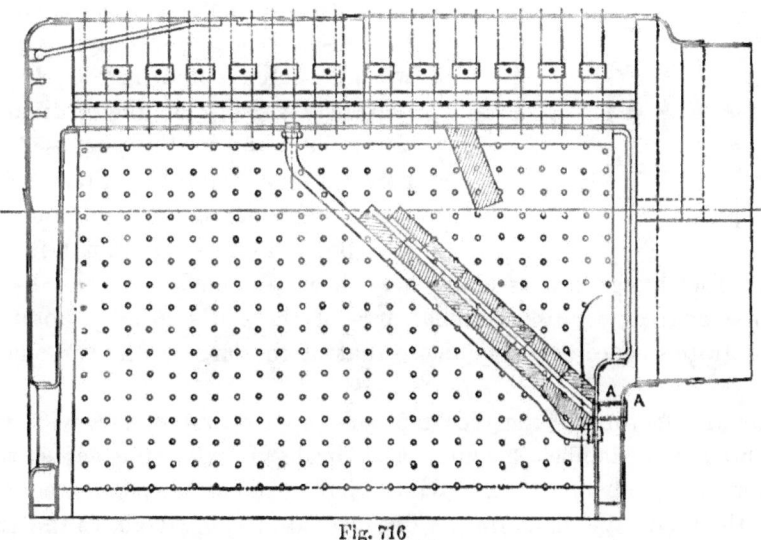

Fig. 716

the space between the bricks through openings $A$ in the front end of the fire-box; these openings are made by placing short pieces of 2-inch tube through the front water space, and expanding the ends of these tubes in the front leg and tube sheet. The object of the hollow brick arch is to raise the temperature of the air up to or over 400 degrees before it is allowed to mingle with the gases. This heated air is then permitted to escape through the openings at the other end of the arch, and mingle with the gases above the arch; the air, being thus raised to a high temperature, will ignite the gases more readily than at a lower temperature, and thus produce a more perfect combustion. Hollow brick arches require more care and give more trouble than solid ones, and therefore the former are not so often used. In a few cases the arch is supported by angle irons fastened to the side sheets of the furnace.

480. The tubes which support the brick arches are threaded at each end, 12 threads per inch; the ends are fitted in a nut shown in Fig. 717; the outside of the nut is tapered and threaded. In placing one of the supporting tubes in position, the nuts are first screwed on the ends of the tube, and then the nuts are screwed into the furnace sheets until a steam-tight joint is secured. These nuts are made either of wrought-iron or brass.

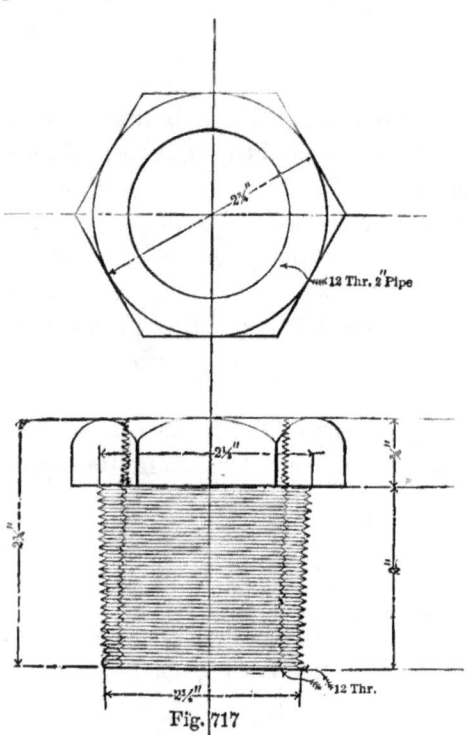

Fig. 717

## WOOTTEN BOILER.

481. The Wootten boiler, shown in Figs. 718 and 719, was designed by John E. Wootten, General Manager of the Philadelphia and Reading R. R., and patented by him July 1, 1877. This boiler, we believe, was originally designed for the purpose of burning finely broken-up coal, generally called "Buckwheat," which could not be burnt advantageously in any of the ordinary locomotive boilers, and for this purpose the Wootten boiler is well adapted. Afterwards the ordinary anthracite and bituminous coals were also burnt in this boiler, but it seems to us that with this fuel better results could have been obtained if it had been possible to increase the aggregate cross-sectional area of the tubes so as to obtain a ratio of tube area and grate surface nearer equal to that in the large ordinary boilers as given in Table 64.

The distinctive features of the Wootten boiler are a comparatively wide and shallow fire-box, a combustion chamber $A$, and a brick bridge $B$ extending across the fire-box end of the combustion chamber. The width of the fire-box may be extended as far as the width of the roadway will permit. The fire-box is placed above the frames and extends over the rear driving axle, consequently the fire-box, like those of other boilers with the furnace placed above the frames, must of necessity be made shallow, so as not to raise the boiler too high above the track. In a Wootten boiler in which finely broken-up coal is burnt a brick arch is of greater necessity than in other boilers; it serves to prevent the fine coal from being drawn into the tubes when the proper thickness of fire is carried. Quite a number of these boilers are now in use, and for burning fine coal a better boiler can probably not be found.

## STRESS ON STAY BOLTS.

**482.** Before we leave the subject of boiler construction, it may be advantageous to examine the stress on stay bolts and oblique braces. Fig. 720 shows a number of stay bolts placed in horizontal and vertical rows; the distance between centers is 4¼ inches,

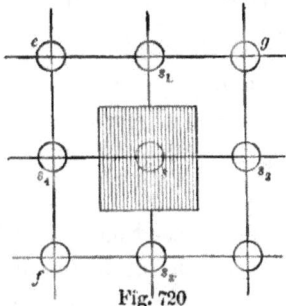
Fig. 720

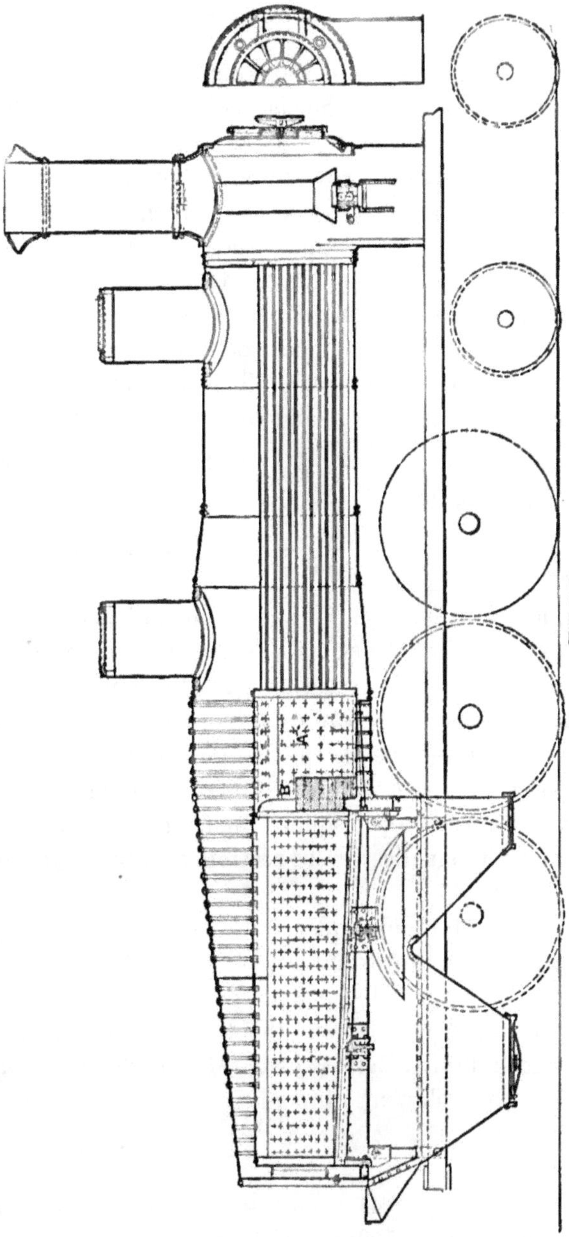

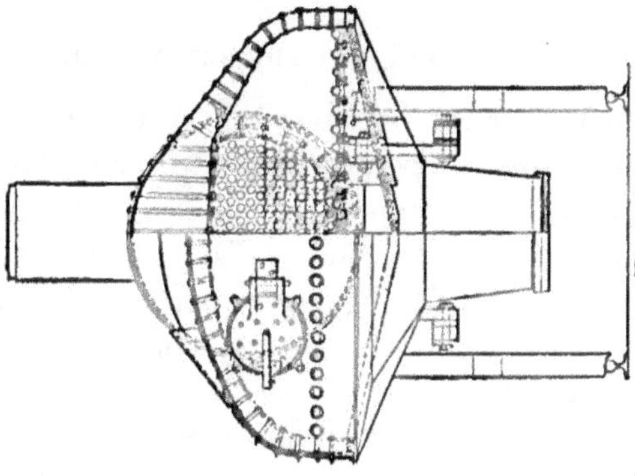

and they are supposed to sustain flat surfaces similar to those in a fire-box. It is now required to find the stress on each stay bolt, the steam pressure being 150 pounds per square inch. Each stay bolt has to support a portion of the surface, whose length and breadth is equal to the distance between the centers of the stay bolts; for instance, the bolt $s$ will have to support that portion of the surface which is shaded, and the sides of this surface pass through the center of the spaces between the bolt $s$ and those nearest to it, as $s_1$, $s_2$, $s_3$, and $s_4$; the sides of this surface must also be parallel to center lines $c\,g$ and $e\,f$ drawn through the horizontal and vertical rows, consequently the stay bolt $s$ has to support a square surface whose sides are 4¼ inches long. The area of this surface is $4.25 \times 4.25 = 18.0625$ square inches; and since the steam pressure is 150 pounds per square inch, the pressure on this surface, and therefore the stress on the stay bolt $s$, will be $18.0625 \times 150 = 2709.375$ pounds. This pressure has to be resisted by the smallest cross-section of the bolt, which is at the bottom of the thread. Now suppose that these stay bolts are ⅞ inch diameter, and at the bottom of the thread they are, say, ¾ inch diameter, then the area of the smallest cross-section will be equal to that of a circle ¾ inch diameter, which is equal to .44 square inch. Here, then, we see that on .44 square inch of metal the stress is 2709.375 pounds. In practice it is always necessary to know how much that will be equivalent to per square inch, so that a comparison can be made with the limit of the stress, which is always given per square inch. The equivalent stress per square inch is readily found by the rule of proportion, and the statement takes the following form:

$$.44 : 1 :: 2709.375 : \text{stress per square inch,}$$

from which we get

$$\frac{2709.375}{.44} = 6157.6 \text{ pounds per square inch.}$$

The limit of safe stress per square inch of stay bolts should not exceed 6,000 pounds, hence we see that the stress is somewhat too great, and therefore the diameter of the bolt should be made larger, or the stay bolts should be placed closer to each other. From the foregoing we can establish a rule for finding the stress on the stay bolt.

RULE 106.—Multiply the distance between two stay bolts on the horizontal row by the distance between two stay bolts on the vertical row, and multiply this product by the steam pressure per square inch. Divide this last product by the area in square inches of the smallest cross-section of the bolt; the quotient will be the stress per square inch.

483. The foregoing also indicates the method for finding the distances between the stay bolts. For example: What should be the distance between the stay bolts for a steam pressure of 150 pounds per square inch, the area of the smallest cross-section being .44 square inch, and the limit of the stress 6,000 pounds per square inch? Now, with a limit of stress of 6,000 pounds per square inch, that on .44 square inch is found by the following proportion:

$$1 : 0.44 :: 6000 : x,$$

from which we get $.44 \times 6000 = 2640$ pounds on an area of .44 square inch. The steam pressure is 150 pounds per square inch, consequently the area of the surface which the bolt can support is equal to $\frac{2640}{150} = 17.6$ square inches. If, now, the vertical distance between the stay bolts is equal to their horizontal distance, and if these rows are perpendicular to each other, then the form of the surface which each stay bolt has to support will be a square, and the sides of this surface will be equal to the square root of $17.6 = \sqrt{17.6} = 4.19$ inches, which is the distance between the stay bolts. From the foregoing we can establish the following rule for finding the distance between the centers of the stay bolts:

RULE 107.—Multiply the limit of the stress per square inch (6,000 pounds) by the area in square inches of the smallest cross-section of the bolt, and divide this product by the steam pressure per square inch; the quotient will be the area in square inches which the bolt can support. If, now, the horizontal distances between the stay bolts are equal to the vertical distances, then find the square root of the above quotient; the result will be the distance in inches between the centers of the stay bolts.

### THICKNESS OF STAYED SHEETS.

484. So far we have assumed that the sheets through which the stay bolts pass are sufficiently thick not to bulge between the stay bolts. If we have any doubt as to this thickness, we can find out what it should be by the following rule:

RULE 108.—When the horizontal distances between the stay bolts are equal to the vertical distances, as shown in Fig. 720, multiply the square of the distance between the stay bolts by the steam pressure per square inch, and divide the product by 8,000; multiply this quotient by $\frac{2}{9}$; the square root of this last product will be the thickness of the plate whose tenacity is 64,000 pounds per square inch. This rule is expressed by symbols, as follows:

$$t = \sqrt{\frac{2}{9} \times \frac{a^2 \times p}{f}},$$

in which $t$ denotes the thickness of plate in inches; $a$, the distance between the stay bolts; $p$, the steam pressure per square inch; and $f$ the working pressure, which will depend on the tenacity of the plate. If the tenacity is 64,000 pounds per square inch, which is about correct for steel sheets, and adopting a factor of safety of 8, then the value of $f$ will be 8,000, as given in the rule.

EXAMPLE 144.—What should be the thickness of a steel plate (tenacity of 64,000 pounds per square inch) subjected to a pressure of 150 pounds per square inch, stay bolts $4\frac{1}{4}$ inches from center to center?

Substituting for the symbols in the formula their values, we have

$$t = \sqrt{\frac{2}{9} \times \frac{4.25^2 \times 150}{8000}} = .27 \text{ inch.}$$

Since the sheets in the fire-box are never less than $\frac{1}{4}$ inch thick, and often are $\frac{5}{16}$ inch thick, we conclude that the stay bolts are spaced sufficiently close in this case to prevent the sheets from bulging.

### STRESS IN OBLIQUE BRACES.

485. Sometimes the flat surfaces, such as the boiler heads, are stayed by braces similar to that shown in Fig. 722; the end $g$ of this brace is riveted to the boiler shell, and the other end is connected to a crow-foot $h$. If, now, we wish to find the stress per square inch on the brace $B$, we must first find the pressure which the crow-foot $h$ has to resist. Let Fig. 721 represent the position of the crow-feet on the sheet. Now, assume that the horizontal distance between center of one crow-foot and that of the next one is 9 inches, and the vertical distance from the center of one row to the next one is $4\frac{1}{2}$ inches; each crow-foot will have to support a surface, as indicated by the shaded portion $a\ b\ c\ d$, 9 inches long and $4\frac{1}{2}$ inches wide. If, now, the pressure is 150 pounds

per square inch, then the total pressure which the crow-foot will have to resist is equal to 9 × 4.5 × 150 = 6075 pounds. This pressure or force acts in a direction perpendicular to the sheet $CD$. Therefore, through any point $e$ on the center line of the brace $B$ draw a line $ef$ perpendicular to $CD$, and make the length of this line to

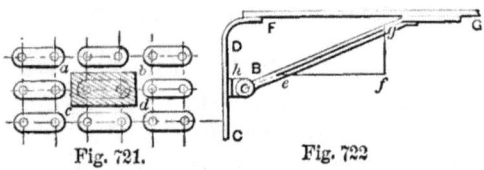

Fig. 721.   Fig. 722.

represent the pressure of 6,075 pounds. This can be done as follows: Let any unit of measurement represent a certain number of pounds—for instance, let 1 inch represent 1,000 pounds; under these conditions the line $cb$ must be 6.075 inches long.

Through the end $f$ draw a line $fg$ perpendicular to $FG$, meeting the center line of the brace in the point $g$, thereby completing the triangle $efg$. Now, the stress on the brace will be represented by the side $eg$ of the triangle; if this side measures 7 inches, then the stress on the brace will be 7 × 1000 = 7000 pounds, because we have adopted a scale of 1,000 pounds per inch. If the limit of the stress is 6,000 pounds per square inch, then the cross-sectional area of the brace will have to be $\frac{7000}{6000} = 1.166$ square inches, and the corresponding diameter will be $1\frac{1}{4}$ inches nearly; hence if the brace is made of round iron, it will have to be $1\frac{1}{4}$ inches diameter.

### BOILER FASTENINGS TO FRAMES.

486. Fig. 723 shows the ordinary way of fastening the frames to a fire-box which extends to a short distance below the frames. Four clamps or pads are attached to each side of the fire-box. They are made of wrought-iron plates $\frac{5}{8}$ to $\frac{3}{4}$ inch in

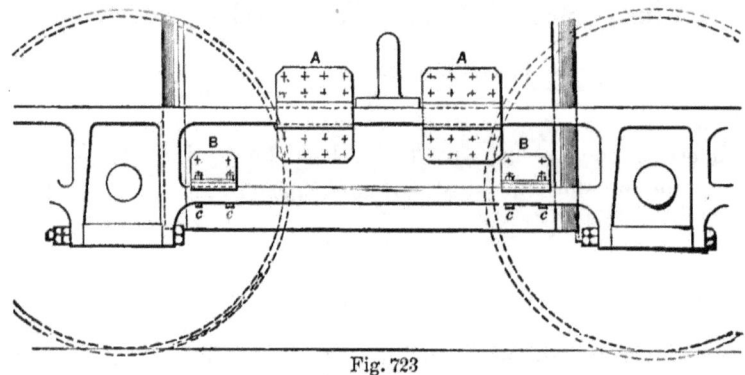

Fig. 723

thickness. The two upper pads $AA$ are planed to fit around the three sides of the frame, then heated and fitted to the boiler. Liners are placed between the inner sides of the frames and outer sides of the fire-box, after which the pads are bolted to the boiler by studs $\frac{7}{8}$ inch diameter. The two lower pads $BB$ are lipped over the outside of the lower frame brace and fastened to it by two bolts $cc$ through each pad. These bolts are driven into the frame brace, but work in slots cut in the pads; these slots are cut large enough to admit a thimble over each bolt. These thimbles rest on top of frame brace and project a little over the faces of the pads, so that the plates, which are bolted rigidly to the top of thimbles, will not touch the pads, and give the latter freedom to move in the direction of the frame brace as the boiler expands. The pads are of course fastened to the fire-box in a manner similar to that of the upper ones.

487. Fig. 724 shows the method of fastening the frames to a fire-box placed above the axles and extending to a short distance below the tops of frames. The pads B B are bent to an L form, and are fastened to the fire-box like those described above

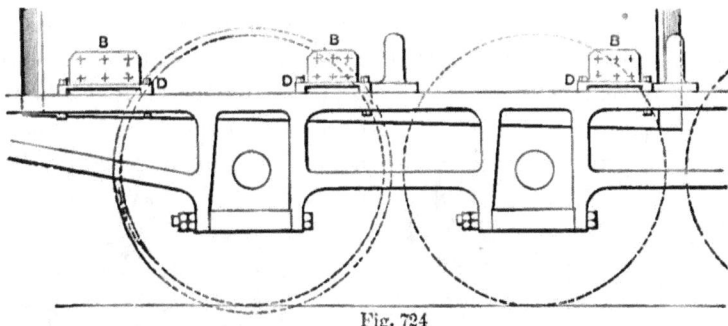

Fig. 724

They are prevented from moving laterally by the clamps D D, which embrace the lower parts of the pads and are bolted to the top of frame, giving the pads sufficient freedom to move longitudinally as the boiler expands.

488. Fig. 725 shows one method of fastening the frames to a fire-box placed above the frames, the width of the fire-box being equal to the distance from outside to outside of frames. In this case a stud is forged to each pad E E, and corresponding studs are attached to the side of the frame. The links C C passed over these studs

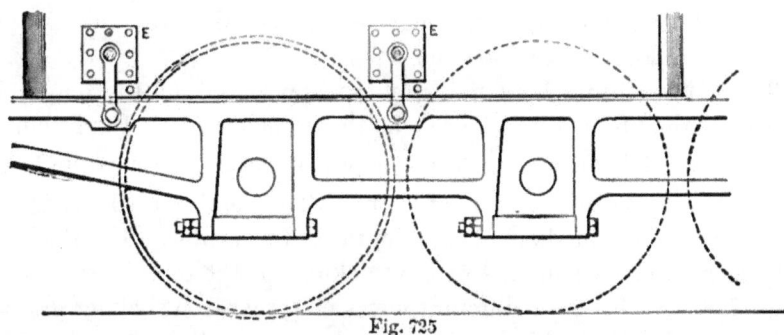

Fig. 725

support the rear end of the boiler. This manner of fastening the frames to fire-box is considered to be defective and insecure, and some master-mechanics believe it to be the cause of breaking the frames. A better way is to fasten the pads to the ends of the fire-box and allow them to rest on transverse braces bolted to the top of frames. The pads must be attached to these braces in such a manner as to allow the boiler freedom to expand.

489. In order to obtain a good hold for the studs through the pads, a plate about ⅜ inch thick, and about as wide and long as the pad, is placed on the inside of the fire-box shell for each pad. These plates are not riveted to the shell, they are held in position by the stay bolts which are screwed into them.

## GRATE-BARS.

490. Grate-bars may be divided into three classes; one class embraces those designed for burning wood; the second class embraces those for burning bituminous or soft coal; and in the third class we may place the grate-bars for burning anthracite or hard coal.

Figs. 726, 727, and 728 show different views of grate-bars $A$ designed for burning wood. They are generally made of cast-iron, cast in groups of two or three bars, and rest on wrought-iron bearers $B$ which are supported by the straps or hangers $C$; this type of hanger is only used in furnaces which do not have a fire-box ring; in furnaces which have a fire-box ring, the

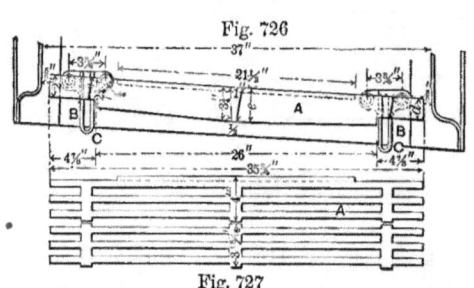

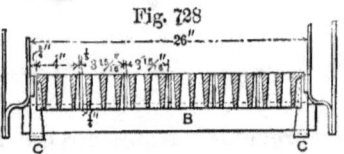

bearers are made of cast-iron, and bolted to the bottom of the ring. The grate-bars are generally $\frac{5}{8}$ inch thick at the top and tapered to about $\frac{1}{4}$ inch at the bottom; the space between the bars at the top is usually $\frac{5}{8}$ or $\frac{3}{4}$ inch wide.

Occasionally we find the grate-bars made of wrought-iron bolted together in groups of two, three, or four bars.

491. The depth $e$ at the center of the grate-bar should have a certain proportion to its length. The following is a good rule:

RULE 109.—For cast-iron bars, multiply the square root of the length in inches by the decimal .6; the product will be the depth in inches at $e$. Expressing this rule in symbols, we have $.6 \sqrt{\text{length in inches}} = $ depth at center. For wrought-iron bars, we have $.5 \sqrt{\text{length in inches}} = $ depth at center. The depth $d$ at the ends of the bars should never be less than one-half of the depth at the center. The thickness at the bottom of the bars should be about $\frac{1}{3}$ of the thickness at the top.

492. Figs. 728$A$ to 731 show different views of a cast-iron rocking grate designed for burning soft coal. Many kinds of soft coal tend to clink, and thereby prevent free combustion. Hence for burning soft coal it is necessary to adopt a grate to which a rocking motion can be imparted, thereby breaking up the clinkers and keeping the fire clean. There are many types of rocking grates in use; we have shown only two of the principal types.

The grate-bar, Figs. 728$A$ and 729 (usually called a finger grate), consists of a hollow center-piece $A$ with projections or fingers cast to each side of it, and arranged so as to make the fingers of one grate pass between those of the next grates, leaving a space of $\frac{1}{2}$ inch or $\frac{5}{8}$ inch wide between the fingers. These center-pieces $A$ and pivots $B$ are cast in one piece; the pivots rest in indentations cast in the side or bearing bars $C$, which are bolted to the bottom of the fire-box ring. A finger at one end of each grate-bar projects downwards and is formed to act as an arm, as shown at $D$;

MODERN LOCOMOTIVE CONSTRUCTION. 485

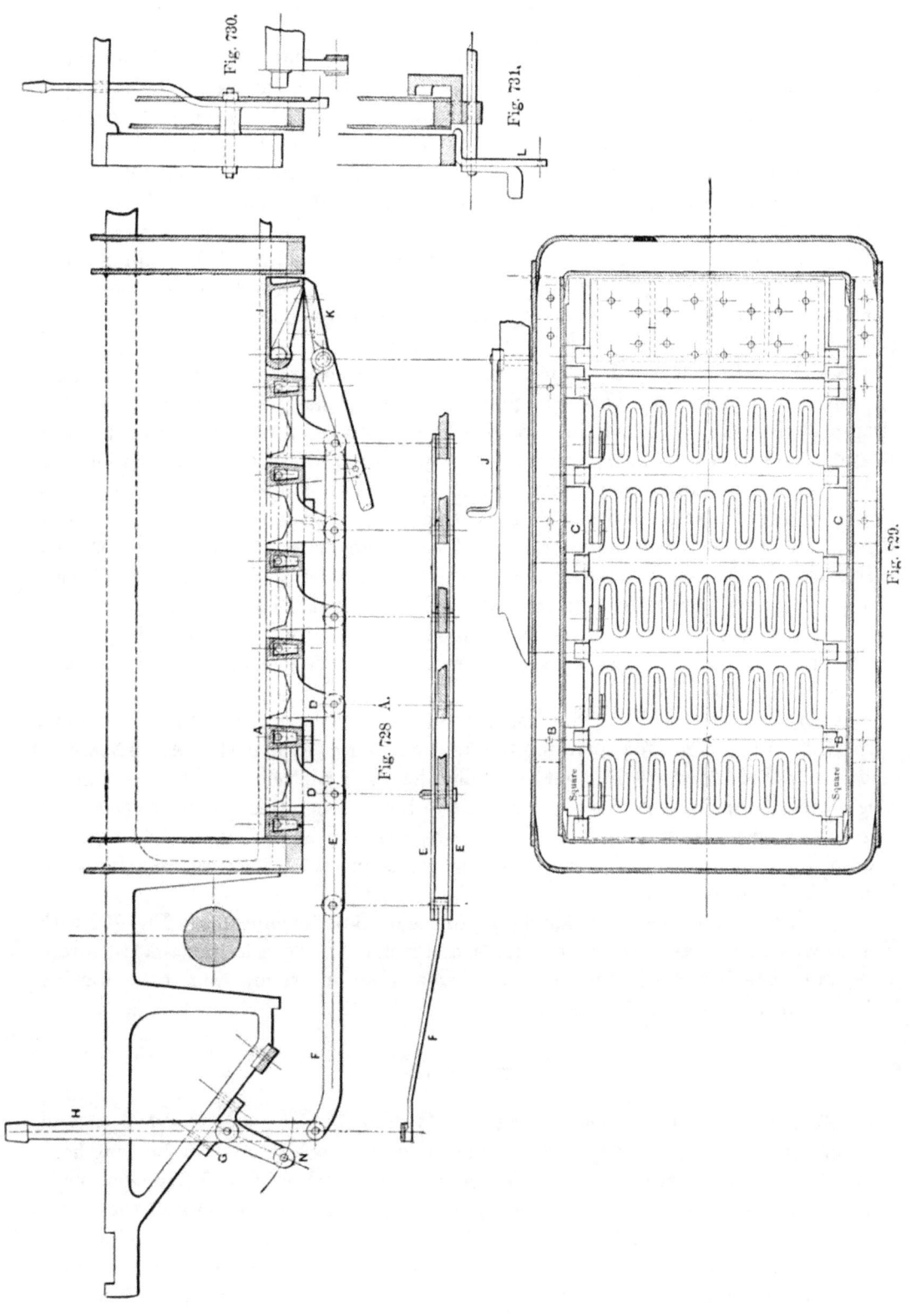

all these arms are attached to the wrought-iron bar $E$. The rear end of this bar is attached to the wrought-iron link $F$, and this in turn is connected to the bottom of the shaking lever $H$. This lever extends upwards through the foot-plate and projects about 6 to 9 inches above it, and works on the fulcrum fastened to the bracket $G$.

In order to obtain sufficient power for rocking the grates, the upper end of the shaking lever $H$ is made to fit in the socket of a handle (not shown) which is usually about 2 feet or 2 feet 6 inches long, and when not in use it is put out of the way. It will be seen that with this arrangement a rocking motion is imparted simultaneously to all the grate-bars. After the fire has been cleaned the grate-bars are prevented from turning by inserting a pin through the shaking lever and a wrought-iron bracket fastened for this purpose to the top of the foot-plate.

A drop-plate $I$ is placed at the front of the furnace for the purpose of dumping the fire. This drop-plate works on pivots similar to those on the grate-bars. The drop-plate is held up in position or allowed to drop by the wrought-iron arms $K$ forged to a shaft which extends across the furnace, and works in bearings fastened to the bottom of the furnace or engine frames. This shaft is operated by the wrought-iron lever $J$, which is generally held in position by a bracket $L$ (Fig. 731). The lever $J$ is placed outside of the engine frame on the fireman's side. With the type of lever here shown, the fireman has to step off the engine in order to dump the fire. Sometimes a long handle extending upwards through the running board is attached to the end of the lever $J$, so that the drop-plate can be raised or dropped without stepping off the engine. Drop-plates as here shown are used in soft-coal burning engines, and seldom in hard-coal burners.

It may be here stated that the cast-iron bracket $G$ also supports at its lower end a fulcrum for a bell crank for operating the front damper as explained in Art. 495.

Figs. 732 to 738 show different views and details of another type of rocking grate. The grates are operated in a manner similar to that of operating the grates shown in Figs. 728$A$ and 729, and need no further explanation, excepting to state that the drop-plate is operated by the handle $H_2$, which is placed next to the shaking-lever handle $H$ shown in Fig. 738.

The bar which connects the handle $H_2$ to the drop-plate coincides in Fig. 732 with the bar which connects the cast-iron grates, and it may therefore appear that the drop-plate and grate-bars are all connected to one bar; but an examination of the drawing will show that this is not the case.

## WATER GRATES.

493. Fig. 739 shows an elevation; Fig. 740, a half plan; and Fig. 741, an end view of a water grate. This type of grate is almost universally used for burning hard coal. It consists of wrought-iron tubes $A$ $A$, $1\frac{7}{8}$ or 2 inches outside diameter, made extra heavy, the thickness being about $\frac{1}{4}$ of an inch. It will be noticed that these tubes are placed in an inclined position, lower at the front than at the back end; the inclination is about $\frac{1}{2}$ inch to the foot; and one of the objects in placing these grates in this position is to obtain a continuous circulation of water through them, so as to prevent them from being burnt.

# MODERN LOCOMOTIVE CONSTRUCTION.

487

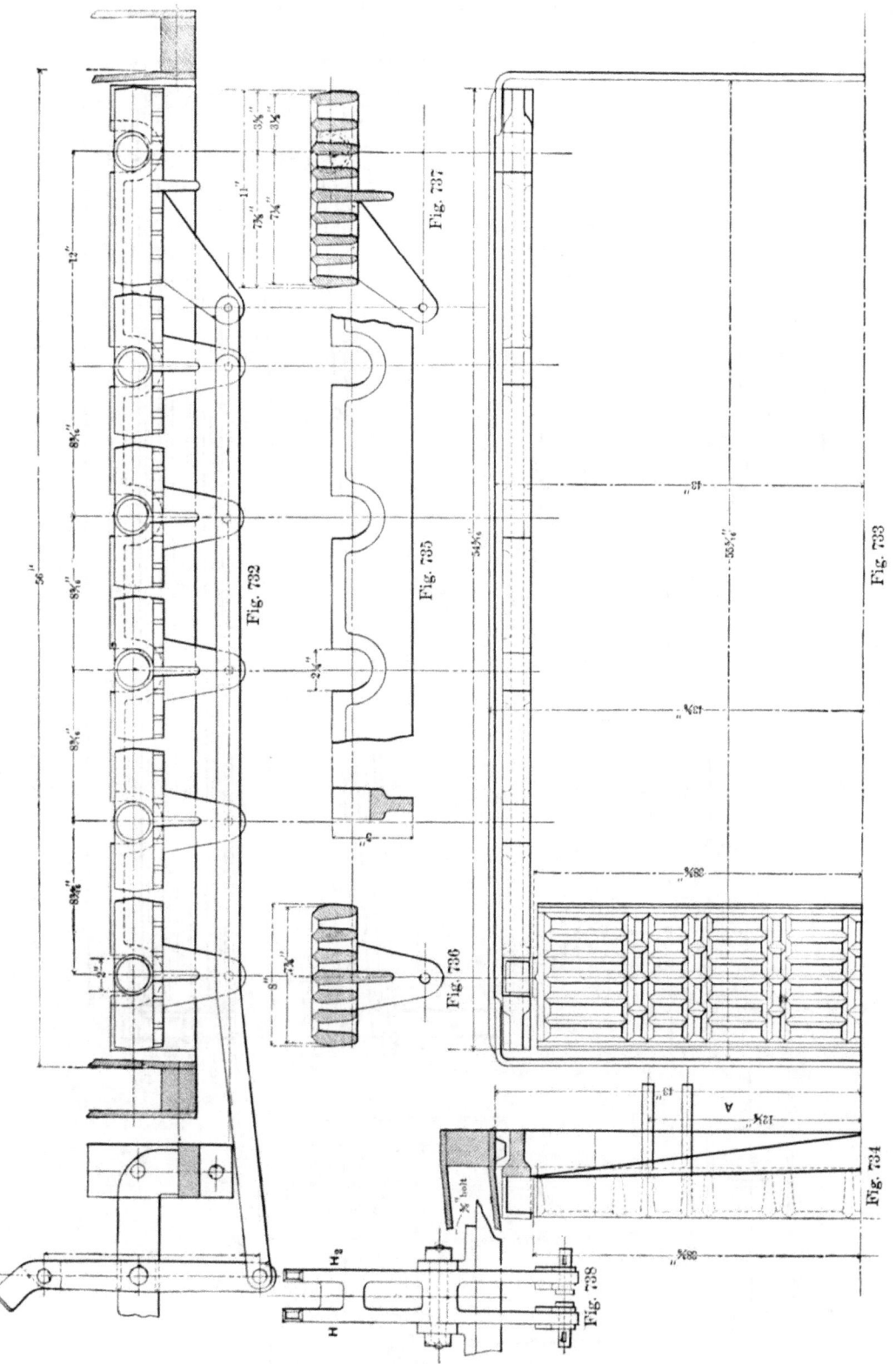

488　MODERN LOCOMOTIVE CONSTRUCTION.

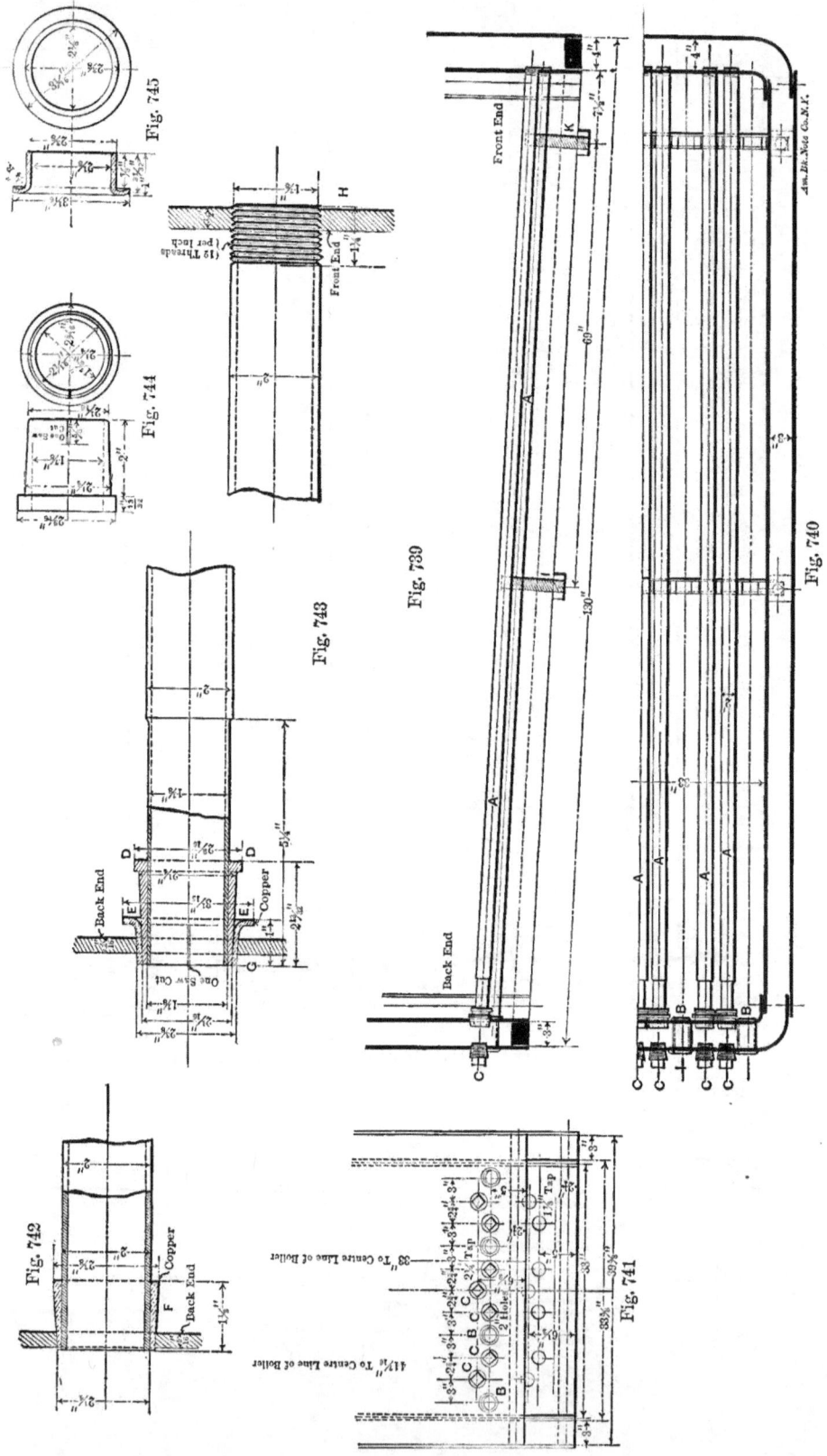

The front ends of these tubes are threaded, 12 threads per inch, and screwed into the tube sheet or front sheet of the furnace, as shown in Fig. 743. A small portion of the other ends of the tubes are turned, with wrought-iron ferrules $D$ fitted over them, and copper ferrules $E$ are placed on the outside of the wrought-iron ones, as shown in Fig. 743. These ends of the tubes are inserted into corresponding holes in the furnace-door sheet; the wrought-iron and copper ferrules are then driven in tightly, and the whole expanded on the water space side of the furnace-door sheet. Sometimes cast-iron ferrules in place of the wrought-iron ones are used; separate views of a cast-iron ferrule are shown in Fig. 744, and separate views of the copper ferrules are shown in Fig. 745.

In Fig. 744 it will be noticed that the end of the cast-iron ferrule is cut open a short distance on one side only; care must be taken that this cut does not extend beyond the copper ferrule when placed in position; the object of the cut is to make a tight joint when the ferrule is driven home, as it cannot be expanded. Wrought-iron ferrules are left solid.

In some cases nothing but a tapered copper ferrule is used, as shown in Fig. 742, which is expanded with the tube on the water space side of the sheet.

The brass plugs $C\ C$ (Figs. 739, 740, and 741) are for the purpose of closing up the holes in the back head; these holes are, of course, required for passing the tubes into the furnace; they also afford an opportunity for expanding the ends of the tubes.

In many engines the water tubes are arranged as indicated by the brass plugs $C\ C$ in Fig. 741—that is to say, some of the tubes are placed above the others; but this is by no means a universal practice, frequently we find all of them placed in one plane.

494. The ferrules $B\ B$, Figs. 740, 741, are usually made of ordinary 2-inch boiler tubes; they form the openings through which the dead bars are passed. These bars are made of solid wrought-iron about $1\frac{3}{8}$ inches diameter. They have usually an eye

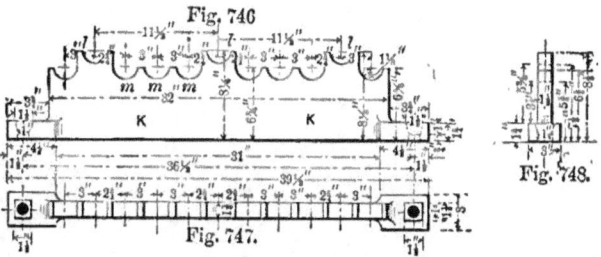

forged to one end, which projects beyond the back end of the fire-box and provides means for pulling the dead bars out. They extend to within 1 inch or less of the front sheet of the furnace, and are supported at the front end by the cast-iron bearer $K$ (Fig. 739); separate views of this bearer are given in Figs. 746, 747, and 748.

Another bearer $I$ similar in form to that of the bearer $K$ is used for supporting the center of the dead bars, and also the water tubes. Sometimes the front bearer $K$ supports only the ends of the dead bars; in such cases the indentations for the water grates shown in Fig. 746 are left off; but the central bearing $I$ always supports the tubes as well as the dead bars.

Some master-mechanics consider it dangerous practice to put the plugs $C\ C$ in the back head, because should one of these plugs blow out the engineer and fireman are liable to be seriously injured. We therefore meet with engines in which the water tubes have been passed into the furnace through openings in the front end, bringing the plugs $C\ C$ in the front sheet; hence, in this case, the bottom of the back head has no other large holes excepting those for the openings through which the dead bars are passed into the furnace. With this arrangement the water tubes are, so to speak, turned end for end, the threaded ends of the tubes are screwed into the furnace-door sheet, and the ferrules on the tubes are driven into the front sheet of the furnace. This manner of placing the water tubes in the fire-box is not free from objections, as it makes the cleaning of the tubes very unhandy and difficult.

# CHAPTER XI.

### ASH-PANS.—SMOKE-STACKS.—EXHAUST-PIPES.

#### ASH-PANS.

495. Fig. 749 shows an elevation; Fig. 750, part of a plan; and Fig. 751, part of an end view of the simplest kind of an ash-pan. This type is used for boilers whose fire-boxes extend downwards between the driving axles, consequently it is used for eight-wheeled passenger engines, Mogul, and ten-wheeled engines.

The function of an ash-pan is twofold, namely, to concentrate the current of air as it flows into the furnace, and afford means (but it does not always do so) for regulating a supply of air to the furnace.

The other function is the collecting and holding a quantity of ashes without choking the draft and burning the grate-bars. To meet these requirements the depth

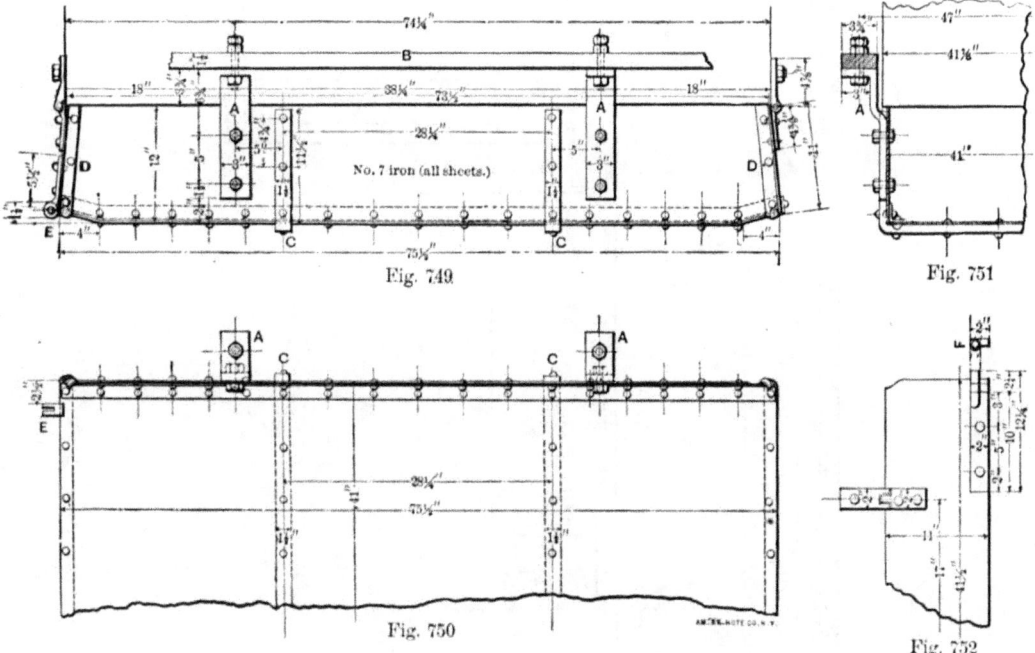

Fig. 749  Fig. 751

Fig. 750  Fig. 752

of this ash-pan is, in large engines, generally 12 inches, and in small engines, 10 inches, seldom less than 9 inches. The width of the ash-pan is generally equal, or nearly so, to the outside width of the fire-box. It is fastened by the hangers $A$ (two on each side) to the lower brace $B$ of the engine frame as shown in the illustrations.

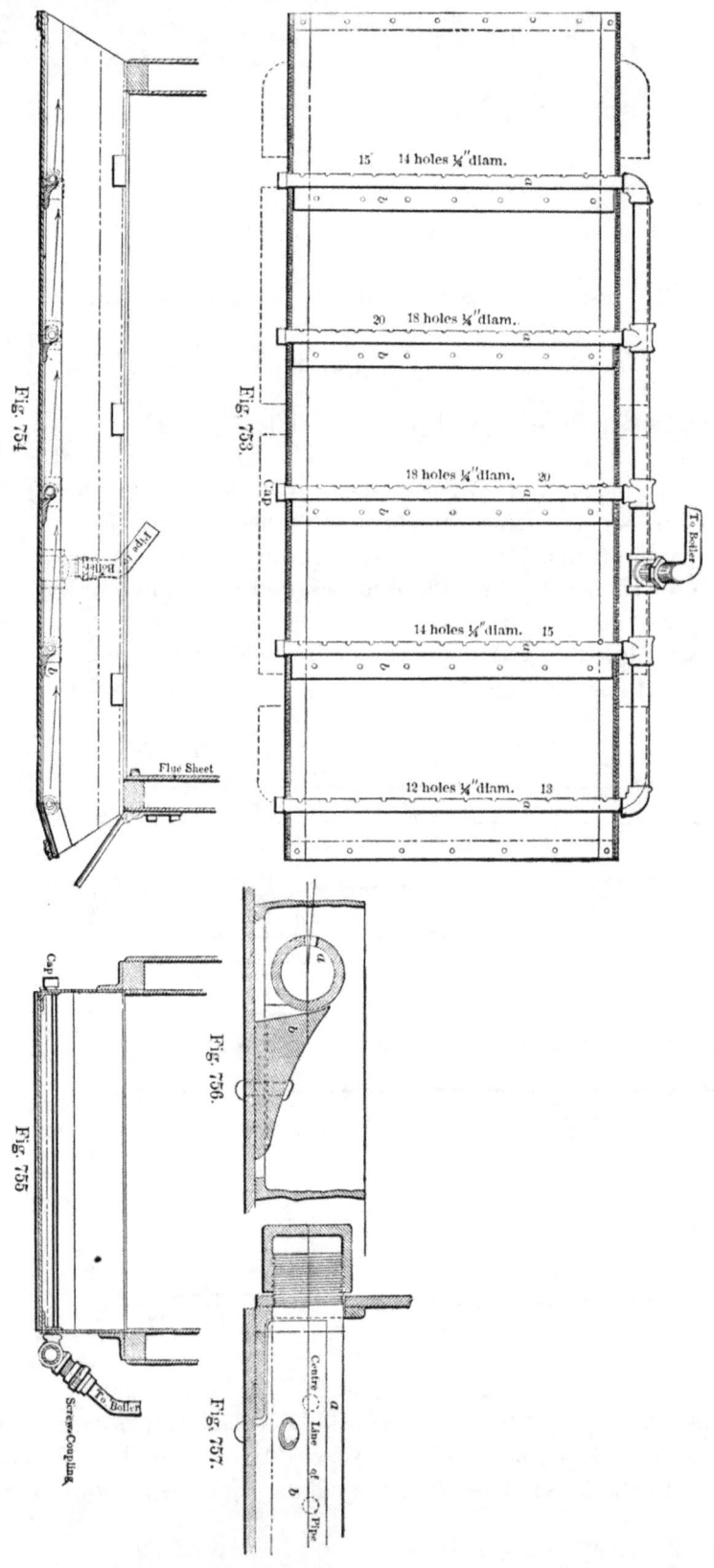

Sometimes the width of the ash-pan is equal to the width of the furnace; in cases of this kind, an angle iron is riveted to each side of the ash-pan, which is fastened to the bottom of the fire-box ring by studs with nuts, or studs with keys which wedge the angle iron to the bottom of the furnace ring.

The ash-pan shown in Figs. 749, 750 is made of wrought-iron. All the sheets are made of the same thickness, No. 7 or No. 8 Birmingham wire gauge. In order to stiffen the pan, two straps $C\ C$, $1\frac{1}{2} \times \frac{3}{4}$ inch, are riveted to the bottom and sides, and half-round bands are riveted to ends of the ash-pan. The ash-pan doors or dampers are hinged to the fire-box. The back damper is operated by a handle extending through the foot-plate. This handle is connected to the jaw $E$, which is riveted to the damper. The front damper is connected to a reach-rod, one end of which works on the pin $F$ (Fig. 752); the other end is connected to the bell crank suspended from the lower pin $N$ in the bracket $G$, Fig 728A; the bell-crank is in turn connected to a handle extending through the foot-plate alongside of the back damper handle. The whole arrangement is shown in Fig. 607, and it will there be seen that both dampers are operated from the foot-plate. No provision for dropping the ashes is made in this type of ash-pan; the ashes must be raked out.

496. A similar form of ash-pan is shown in Figs. 753, 754, 755. A number of pipes are placed cross-ways close to the bottom of this pan, for cleaning it out by

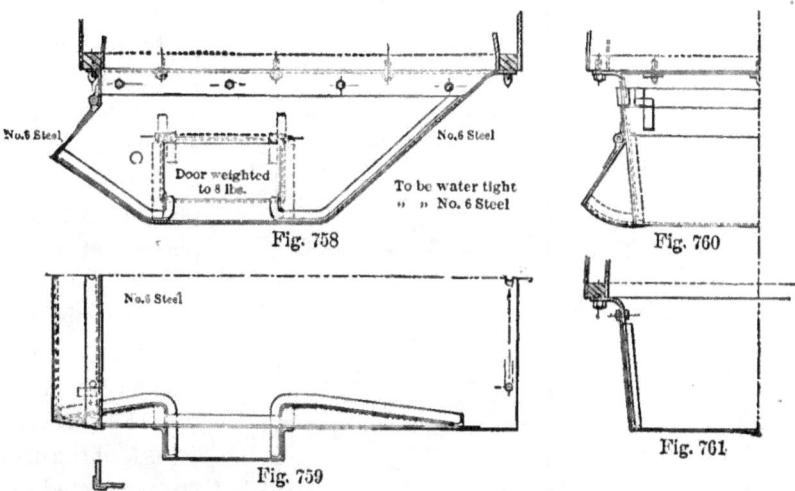

means of steam jets. The arrangement is shown so plainly that further explanation is unnecessary. This device is patented.

Figs. 758, 759, 760, and 761 show different views of an ash-pan with side doors for cleaning it.

497. Figs. 762, 763, and 764 show different views of a wrought-iron ash-pan for a consolidation engine. This pan is made in three sections, and their forms are such as to clear and protect the driving axles from ashes falling upon them. The ends of these sections often overlap each other about 3 or 4 inches, the lap being over the axles. Sometimes the ends butt against each other, and the joints are covered with plates which are fastened to the sections by set screws. It is not necessary to place the joints of the sections directly over the center of axles as here shown; indeed, these

494 MODERN LOCOMOTIVE CONSTRUCTION.

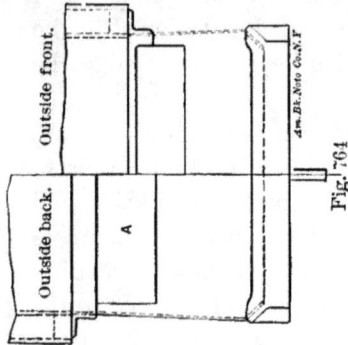

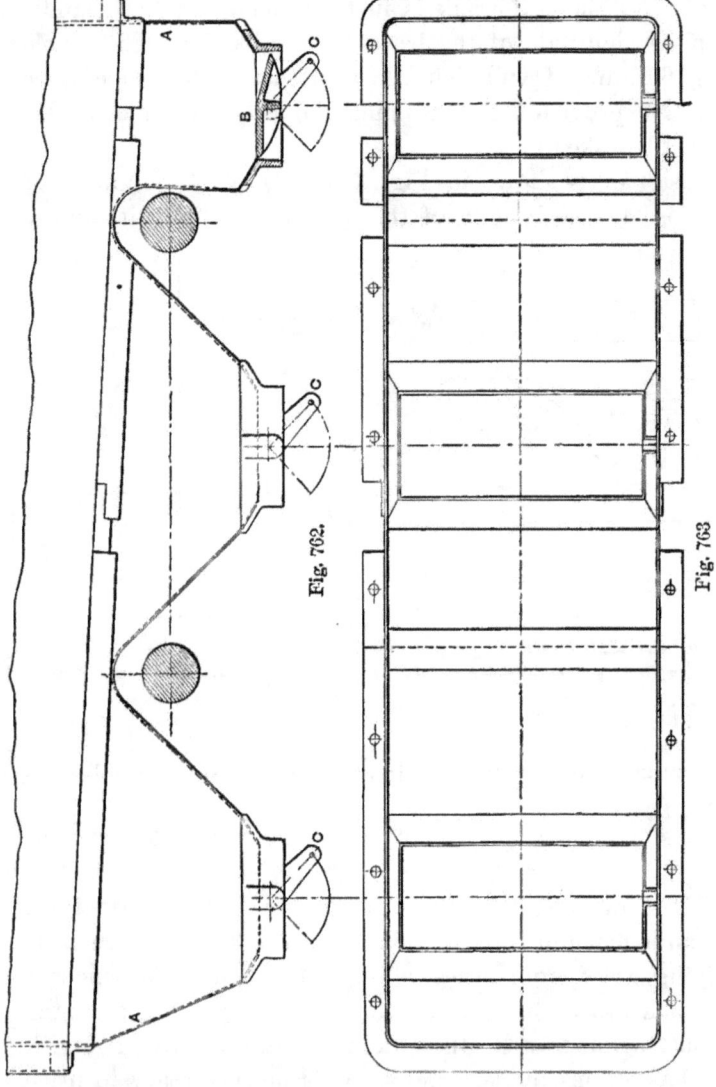

joints cannot always be placed there, because the length of the middle section must be adjusted so as to permit it to be placed under the engine with the driving axles in position, and therefore the middle section will frequently not reach from center to center of axles, and of course the end sections will have to be made longer so as to meet it.

Frequently, ash-pans of this class have no dampers for regulating the supply of air to the furnace. In the ash-pan here shown the air is admitted through the openings $A$, 31 × 8 inches, cut in the ends of the ash-pan near the top. If these openings are found to be too large for the average work which the engine has to do, they are partly covered by the movable plate fastened to each end of the ash-pan.

Each section of the ash-pan is provided with a drop-plate $B$; these plates work on pivots placed centrally on the ends of the plates.

The pivots rest in bearings in the cast-iron frame riveted to the bottom of each section. The arms $C$ of the drop-plates are connected to a reach-rod, and this rod is connected to suitable levers and handles, so that all drop-plates can be turned simultaneously from the foot-plate and allow the ashes to drop. Sometimes the drop-plates are made to slide instead of turning them on pivots.

498. Figs. 765, 766, and 767 show different views of a cast-iron ash-pan similar in form to the one which has just been described.

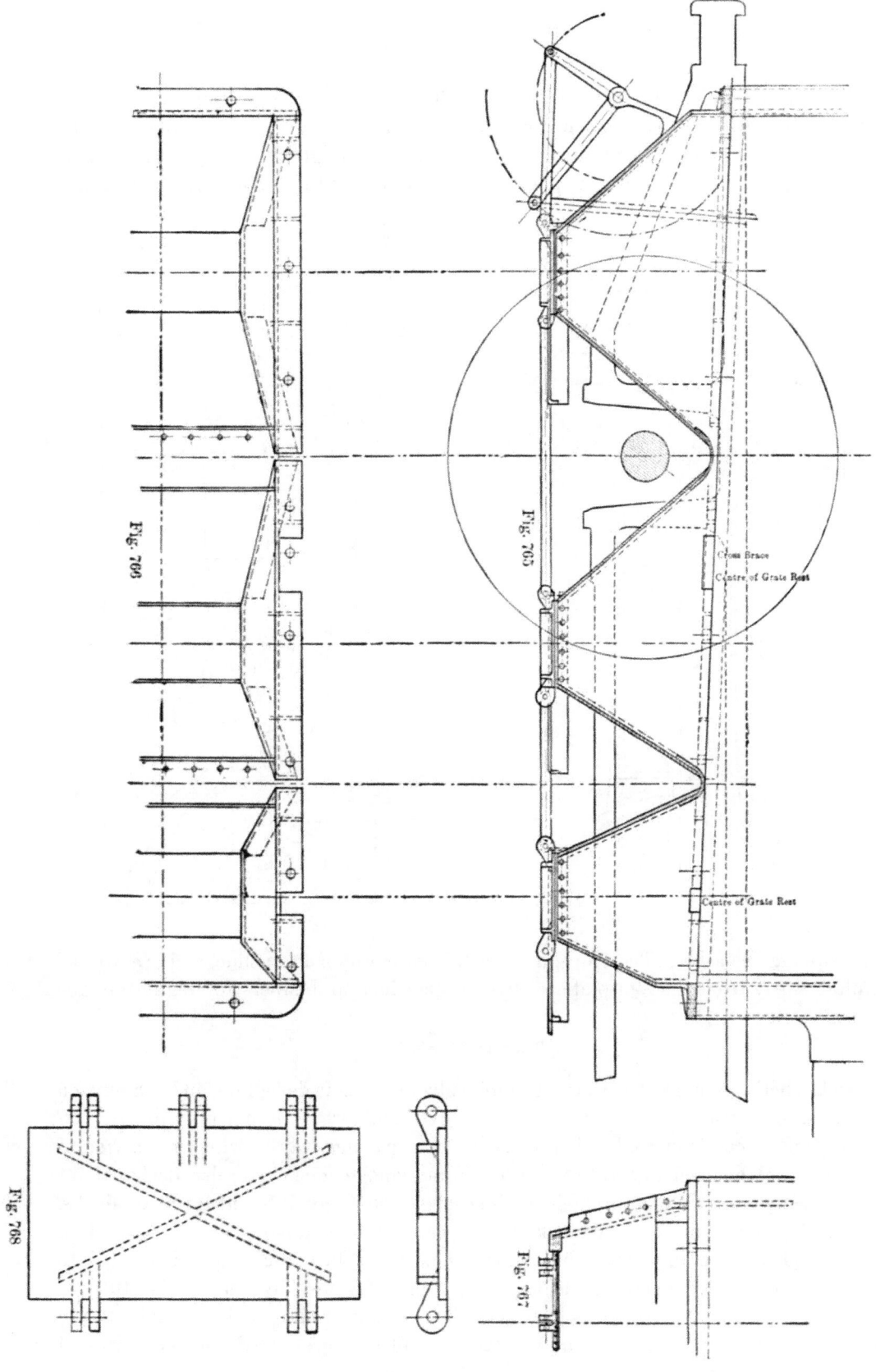

The thickness of the metal is ½ inch. The sides of each section have flanges cast to them; the flanges are turned outwards and are bolted to the end plates. This arrangement prevents the bolts from being burnt. Although this ash-pan passes over one axle only, it is nevertheless made in three sections for the convenience of handling

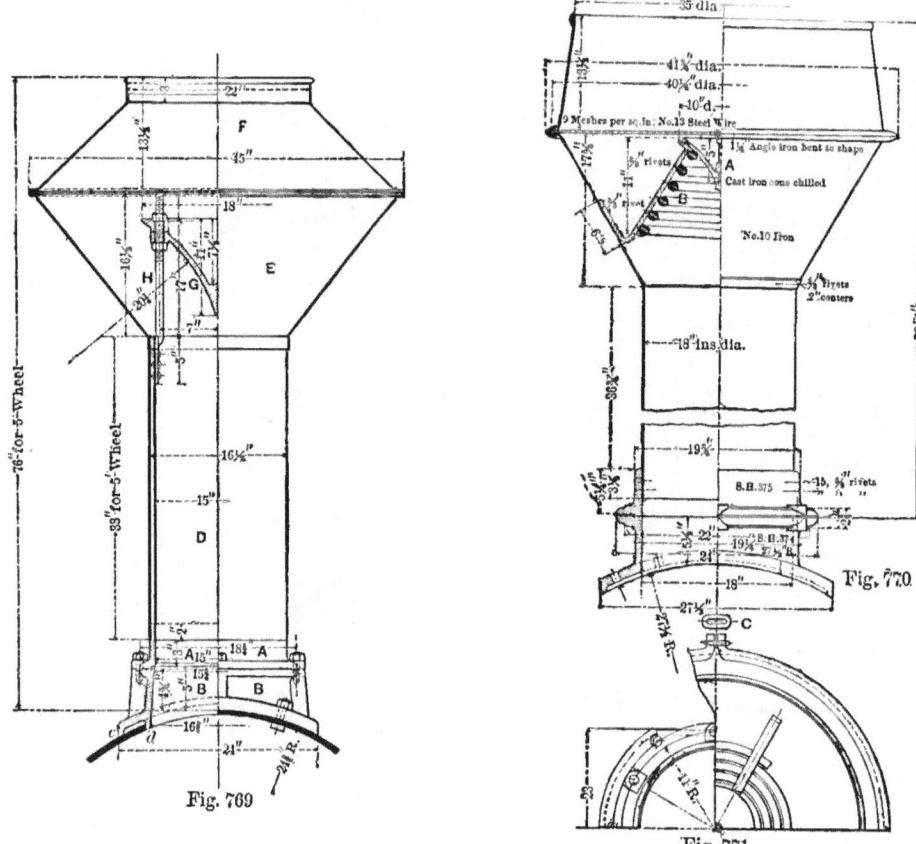

and dropping the ashes. The drop-plates in this case are made to slide, and are worked simultaneously from the foot-plate. This ash-pan has no dampers for regulating the supply of air.

### SMOKE-STACKS.

499. There are a great variety of smoke-stacks. Their design depends chiefly on the kind of fuel used. The duty of a locomotive smoke-stack is not only to carry off the products of combustion, but it also serves as a passage-way in which the action of the exhaust is enabled to create a draft. Some smoke-stacks are also designed for spark arresters, and this requirement is the cause of so many different forms of stacks.

Fig. 769 shows an ordinary stack, usually called the diamond stack. It is used on soft-coal burning engines with short smoke-boxes. A cast-iron ring $A$ is riveted to the bottom of the cylindrical shells, and this ring is fastened by four or six studs to the cast-iron saddle $BB$, which is in turn bolted by four or six ⅞ or 1 inch bolts to the top of smoke-box. The outer chipping strip $c$ is fitted closely to the smoke-box, and the inner strip $d$ is allowed to project into the box for the purpose of preventing the condensed steam from running along the outside of the box.

The cylindrical part $D$ of the stack often consists of two shells, leaving an annular space about $\frac{5}{8}$ inch wide between them. Sometimes four 1-inch holes are drilled through the outer shell just above the flange $A$, and another four holes are drilled through the outer shell near the top, for the purpose of creating a circulation of air through the annular space. This arrangement prevents the outer shell from becoming overheated and blistering the paint. The outer shell also serves another purpose: it does not permit direct contact between the outer air and the inner shell, thereby preventing to some extent condensation of the exhaust steam, and consequently tending to maintain the force of the draft. The thickness of the inner shell is about No. 8 Birmingham wire gauge, and the thickness of the outer shell when painted is about No. 10 B. W. G.; and when the outer shell is not painted it is made of Russia iron.

A wrought-iron ring is placed at the top between the two shells and riveted to them and also to the lower hood $E$. The netting is placed between the two hoods $E$ and $F$, and the whole bolted together.

A cast-iron cone or deflector $G$ is supported by three cone bolts $H$, which are riveted to the inner shell. The threaded parts of these bolts are of sufficient length to adjust to some extent the position of the cone $G$. The purpose of this cone is to arrest the sparks or unconsumed fuel and prevent injury, as much as possible, to the netting. In a few cases the whole stack has been made of cast-iron, but these have not given satisfaction, as they are too heavy to handle, and are liable to break off. The cylindrical part of the stack does not always consist of two shells, as will be seen in Fig. 770.

500. Figs. 770 and 771 show an elevation and part of the plan of another diamond stack. The principal difference between this stack and the one previously described is that the former has in addition to the cast-iron cone $A$ another spark arrester $B$, whose form is that of a cone-shaped spiral; it is made of round bar iron, and is supported by wrought-iron brackets. This spiral cone cannot be adjusted after it has been placed in position.

The lower and upper hoods with the netting between them are clamped together by an angle iron partly closed to shape. The ends of this angle iron are turned outwards and drawn together by a link or stirrup, as shown at $C$ in Fig. 771.

501. Fig. 772 shows another smoke-stack for a soft-coal burning engine with short smoke-box.

Fig. 773 shows the foregoing stack changed to suit a wood-burning engine with short smoke-box. The whole change consists in the form of the upper hood.

502. The common type of stack for wood-burning engines is shown in Fig. 774. The annular space $A$ between the two cylindrical shells is designed for a receptacle for sparks, and is therefore made much wider than the annular space shown in Fig. 769.

The outer shell is provided at the bottom with a hand-hole casting and cover (not shown here) for taking the cinders and ashes out of the annular space. The ordinary cone or deflector is also used. The upper hood is made of netting $C$, stiffened by the straps $d$. No cast-iron flange at the bottom of the cylindrical shells is used; the latter

498    MODERN LOCOMOTIVE CONSTRUCTION.

are bolted directly to the saddle $G$, the outer shell being generally bolted to the saddle by three bolts $e$, and the inner shell bolted to the same by three bolts $f$.

503. Fig. 775 shows the celebrated Radley & Hunter stack, which in former times was the favorite for wood-burning engines. It has no netting, but in place of it a

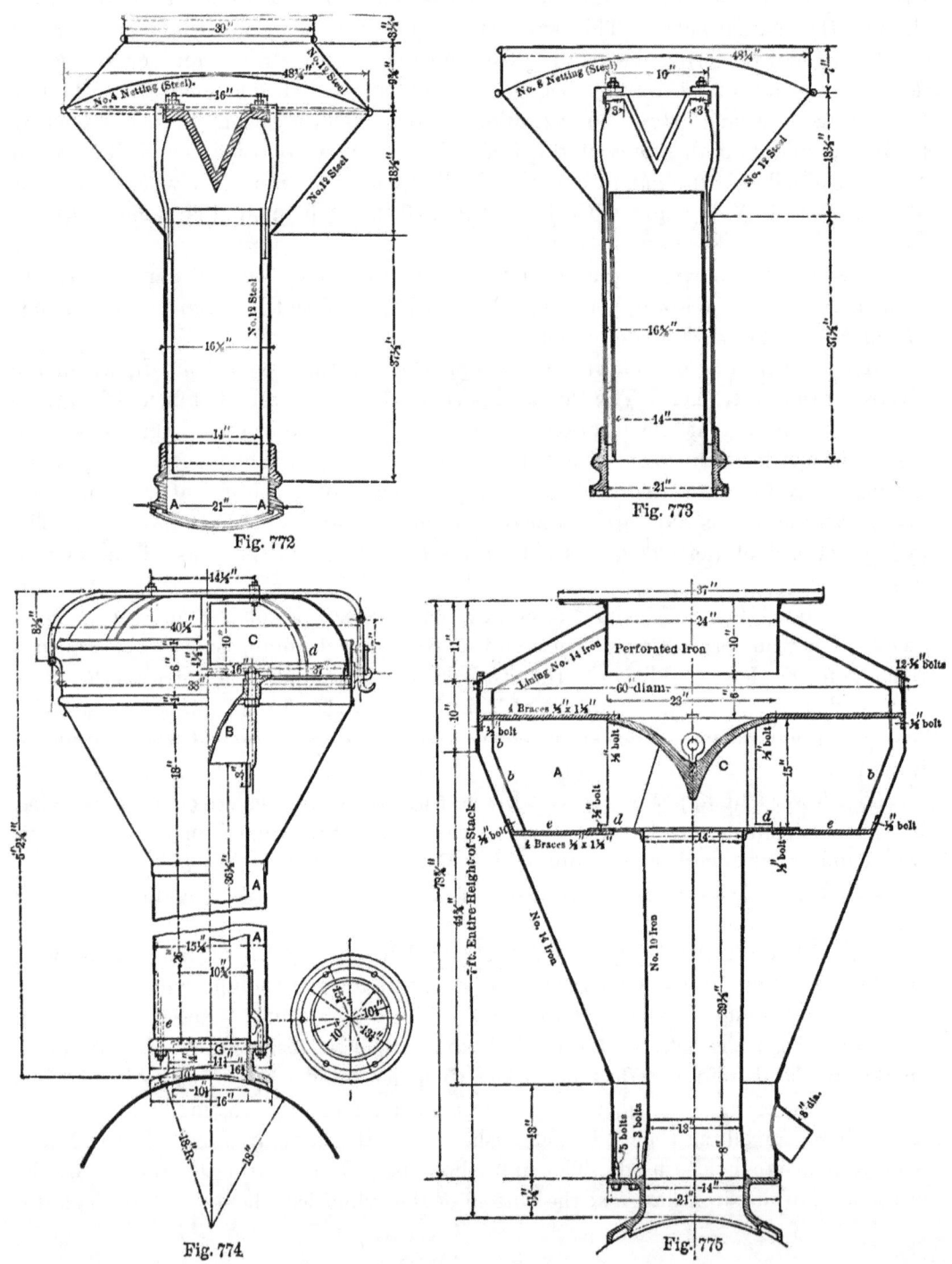

Fig. 772

Fig. 773

Fig. 774

Fig. 775

wrought-iron perforated liner $A$ is used; the holes are of a rectangular form, and are here only indicated in section at $b\ b$. The cast-iron cone $C$ has supports cast to it which rest on the wrought-iron plate $d\ d$ riveted to the inner shell, and steadied by the wrought-iron bracket $e\ e$.

504. Figs. 776 and 777 show an elevation and part plan of another wood-burning stack. Its main feature is the damper on the top of stack; this damper has connections leading to the cab, so that it can be opened or closed from there. This stack is chiefly used for plantation districts, and when running through or near these districts the damper $A$ is closed so as to avoid setting fire to the crops.

505. Fig. 778 shows a straight stack, and Figs. 779 and 780 show a section and plan of its saddle and flange. This stack is used either for soft or hard coal, but since it has no netting for arresting the sparks it is suitable only for extension fronts or such smoke-boxes as contain a netting. The cast-iron top consists of three pieces, namely, the ring $C$, the flare $B$, and the cap $A$. The ring $C$ rests on the top of the outer shell, the flare $B$ rests on this ring, and the cap $A$ is placed on the top of the flare; these are not riveted nor bolted together, but they are firmly held together by expanding the top of the inner shell over the flange on the cap $A$.

506. Fig. 781 shows a stack whose outer form is similar to that of the one we have just described, but the form of the inner shell of this stack differs from the foregoing. In Fig. 781 the diameter of the top of the inner shell is much larger than the diameter at a short distance above the base; we may therefore class it with the so-called tapered stacks.

Mr. William S. Hudson introduced stacks similar to that shown in Fig. 781 on engines built by the Rogers Locomotive Works, Paterson, N. J., some twenty-five years ago, hence the tapered stack shown in the next figure cannot be considered to be a modern improvement, as it is frequently said to be, although the tapered stack is now used to a greater extent than formerly.

507. Fig. 782 shows a tapered stack. The saddle is made of cast-iron; the stack is usually made of wrought-iron about $\frac{1}{4}$ inch in thickness. Sometimes the stack is made of cast-iron about $\frac{5}{16}$ inch thick. Its simplicity, and consequently its cheapness, recommends its adoption, and it has become of late the favorite stack for hard-coal burning engines; it is also frequently used for soft-coal burners. It has no netting, and it is therefore suitable only for extension fronts, although on one of our prominent roads it is used for short smoke-boxes which have no netting; but such practice is not to be recommended, as there is nothing to prevent red-hot cinders or unconsumed fuel from being thrown out of the stack.

Making the stack larger in diameter at the top than at the bottom makes it conform more to the path of the gases than that of a straight stack, consequently friction will be reduced; enlarging the upper end also reduces the velocity of the products of combustion in their ascent, consequently the height to which they are thrown into the air will also be reduced—all of which tends to lessen the work of the exhaust steam, and enables it to expend its force in its legitimate duty, that of creating a draft. The amount of taper will depend on the kind of exhaust nozzle used; generally the increase of diameter is about 1 inch or a little more per foot in height.

500     MODERN LOCOMOTIVE CONSTRUCTION.

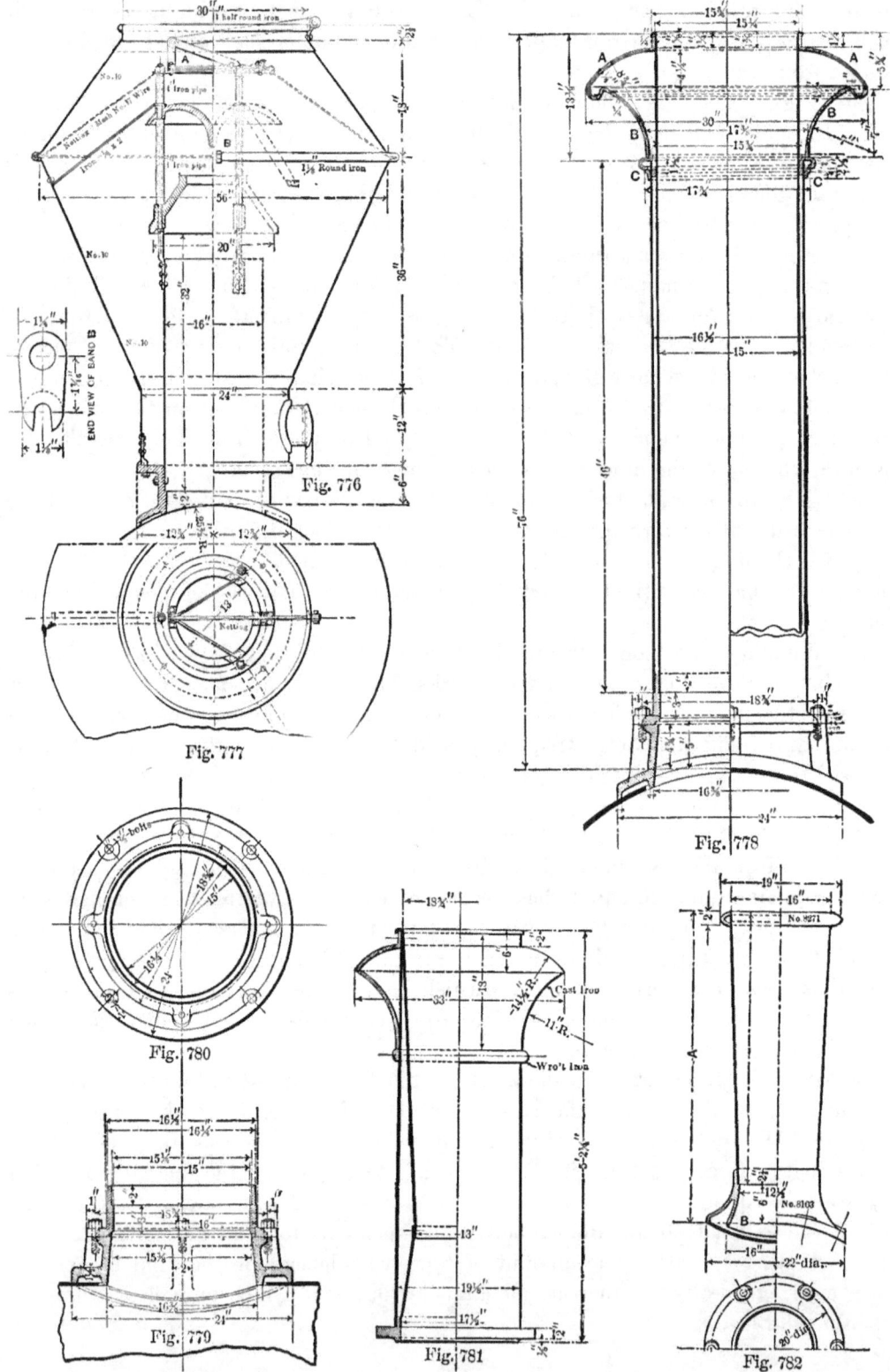

Fig. 776
Fig. 777
Fig. 778
Fig. 779
Fig. 780
Fig. 781
Fig. 782

If the diameter at the bottom of the stack is too great, soot is liable to collect on the inside near the bottom of the stack; on the other hand, if a correct taper has been given, the exhaust steam will keep the stack clean throughout its length.

508. Figs. 783 and 784 show a tapered stack with a variable exhaust damper applied. This damper is a recent invention of Mr. H. A. Luttgens, who for many years has been the chief draftsman at the Rogers Locomotive Works, Paterson, N. J. The damper is very simple in construction, and can be easily applied to any stack by removing the base or saddle and putting the damper in its place. It consists of a cast-iron register-plate $B$ resting upon a turned

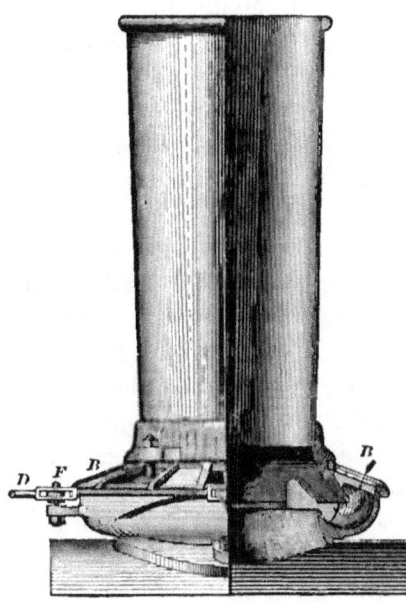

Fig. 783

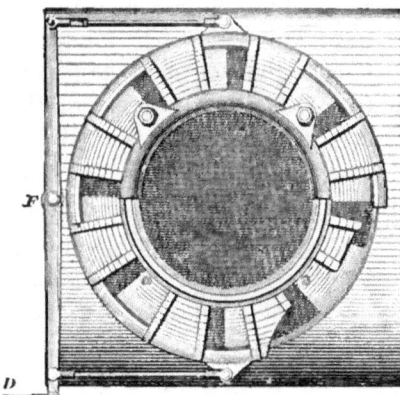

Fig. 784

surface covered with an improved Chinese paint; this paint is heat proof, and enters into the pores of the cast-iron, forming a hard and durable protection to the iron.

The register-plate is provided with a number of openings which correspond to the apertures in the base. It is connected by two links to the lever working on the fulcrum $F$, and this lever is worked by the rod $D$, which extends into the cab, and is so arranged that either the engineer or fireman can open or close the apertures in the base. In the plan of the stack these apertures show partly open, and in this position air is admitted into the bottom of the stack, as indicated by the arrows at $B$ in the elevation.

With this device the engineer is enabled to regulate the draft as required, by admitting more or less air, or shutting it off at will. The advantage of regulating the draft in this manner will readily be perceived; it does away with the necessity of opening the fire-door and admitting a current of cold air into the furnace, which often results in injury to the furnace sheets and tube joints. Evidence also seems to indicate that with this damper a considerable saving of fuel can be secured.

On the switching engines running on the Long Island Railroad, the dampers are closed at first upon a new fire, but during the remainder of the day each engine is run with an open damper; the result claimed for this is a noiseless and smokeless engine, without waste of steam at the safety-valve, and using from 3,000 to 4,000 pounds of inferior coal, where 3 tons would be about the usual allowance. These switching engines have 18 × 24 inch cylinders, and are on the move continuously. In other cases it is claimed that a saving of fuel from 15 to 30 per cent. has been secured; although we have no reason for doubting these statements, it seems hardly possible that so favorable results can be obtained in every case. Many of these dampers have been put in practical use and seem to establish an excellent reputation. Whatever merits may be attributed to them, it is evident that they correct some defects in the steaming of a locomotive. In the southern States there are quite a number of engines running with these dampers, and it is claimed that they have proved themselves valuable on account of their spark-arresting quality, and have prevented fires in the cotton districts. Undoubtedly, as the adoption of these dampers extends their advantages will be more appreciated.

509. In extension fronts where long exhaust nozzles reach nearly to the top of the smoke-box, some attention must be given to the inner shape of smoke-stack saddle, because the free access to the stack of the products of combustion will be somewhat affected by this shape. If the entrance of the saddle into the smoke-box is made square, as shown at $A$ $A$ in Fig. 772, the distance between the top of the exhaust nozzle and the top of the smoke-box should be equal to about the smallest inner diameter of the stack. When the entrance of the saddle into the smoke-box is of a bell form, as shown at $B$, Fig. 782, then the distance from the top of the exhaust nozzle and the top of smoke-box can be made a little less. In every case care must be taken not to impede the access of the gases to the stack, and the steam must be discharged through the gases and not above them.

510. Locomotive stacks cannot be made long enough to create a natural draft, consequently other means for obtaining the required draft must be provided. This is accomplished by the action of the exhaust steam, which may be described briefly as follows: As the exhaust steam passes through the stack it acts like a piston in a cylinder, taking with it a portion of the gases in the smoke-box. The blasts, which occur in quick succession, create a partial vacuum in the smoke-box and furnace, causing the external pressure of the atmosphere to force air through the openings in the grate and through the fuel, from whence the air and products of combustion are drawn through the tubes and finally ejected through the smoke-stack into the outer air. From the foregoing it will be seen that the stack alone, or the blast without the stack, cannot create the required draft, but the two must act in conjunction.

### DIAMETERS OF STACKS.

511. It may therefore be reasonably assumed that the stacks should have a definite size, but on this matter engineers do not seem to agree. Our experience seems to indicate, and is partly confirmed by practice, that the internal area of the smallest cross-section of the stack should be $\frac{1}{17}$ of the area of the grate surface.

The first column in the following table gives the sizes of cylinders; the second column gives the grate area in square inches for soft coal as found by Rule 103, and previously tabulated in Tables 59 and 60; the third column gives the smallest cross-sectional area of the stack equal to $\frac{1}{17}$ of the grate area; and the fourth column gives the corresponding diameter in the nearest $\frac{1}{4}$ inch.

## TABLE 73.

CALCULATED DIAMETERS OF STACKS.

| Size of Cylinders. | Grate Area. | Cross-sectional Area at the Smallest Part of the Stack. | Diameters of Stacks. |
|---|---|---|---|
| Column 1. | Column 2. | Column 3. | Column 4. |
| 10 × 20 inches. | 950.40 sq. in. | 55.90 sq. in. | 8½ inches. |
| 11 × 22 " | 1267.20 " | 74.54 " | 9¾ " |
| 12 × 22 " | 1425.60 " | 83.85 " | 10¼ " |
| 13 × 22 " | 1627.20 " | 95.71 " | 11 " |
| 14 × 24 " | 1843.20 " | 108.42 " | 11¾ " |
| 15 × 24 " | 2116.80 " | 124.51 " | 12⅝ " |
| 16 × 24 " | 2275.20 " | 133.83 " | 13 " |
| 17 × 24 " | 2491.20 " | 146.54 " | 13⅝ " |
| 18 × 24 " | 2750.40 " | 161.77 " | 14⅜ " |
| 20 × 24 " | 4320.00 " | 254.11 " | 18 " |
| 22 × 24 " | 5011.20 " | 294.77 " | 19⅜ " |

The foregoing diameters of stacks have been determined by the grate area of soft-coal burning engines. For hard-coal burning engines the grate area is larger, and therefore it would seem that the diameters of stacks should also be greater for this class of engines; but since in hard-coal burning engines lighter fires are carried, the diameters of stacks given in the foregoing table need not be changed.

The following table gives the diameters of stacks in actual service. A comparison shows that the calculated diameters agree very closely with the diameters of stacks in actual use.

## TABLE 74.

DIAMETERS OF STACKS IN ACTUAL SERVICE.

| Diameters of Cylinders. | Stroke. | Smallest Inside Diameters of Stacks. |
|---|---|---|
| Column 1. | Column 2. | Column 3. |
| 9 inches. | 16 inches. | 7½ inches to 8¾ inches. |
| 10 " | 18 " | 8½ " |
| 11 " | 18 " | 9¼ " |
| 12 " | 20 " | 9½ " to 10 " |
| 13 " | 20 " | 11 " |
| 14 " | 20 " | 11 " to 11¾ " |
| 15 " | 22 " | 12¾ " to 13 " and 14 inches. |
| 16 " | 24 " | 13½ " to 14 " " 14½ " |
| 17 " | 24 " | 14¼ " to 15 " " 15½ " |
| 18 " | 24 " | 14 " to 15 " " 16½ " |
| 19 " | 24 " | 16 " to 17 " |
| 20 " | 24 " | 17 " to 18 " |
| 21 " | 24 " | 18 " |
| 22 " | 24 " | 19 " |

512. It frequently occurs that the length of the stack is limited by the distance between the track and the bridges under which the engine has to pass, consequently the height of the engine measured from track to the top of smoke-stack is limited to 14 feet 9 inches, or 15 feet, seldom exceeding the latter. But in cases where the height of the stack is not limited by the bridges, the question arises: What shall be its length? Since the stack cannot be made high enough to create a natural

draft, we must assign to it a length suitable for the action of the exhaust steam. Mr. D. K. Clark, in his treatise on Railway Machinery, recommends a length equal to four diameters of the stack. This proportion we believe to be a good one, although some builders adopt a greater length when not limited by the conditions previously given. Hence, the length of a tapered stack, shown in Fig. 782, should be equal to four times its smallest inside diameter, and the length of the cylindrical part of the diamond stacks, shown in Fig. 769, should be equal to four times the inner diameter of the inner shell, and the height of the inner pipe in wood-burning stacks should also be equal to four times its inner diameter.

### EXHAUST PIPES AND NOZZLES.

513. Figs. 785, 786, 787 show different views of a double exhaust pipe, and Figs. 788, 789 show its nozzle.

This pipe is comparatively short; it is used in connection with stacks which have deflectors or cones, and netting for arresting the sparks and cinders; and it may be

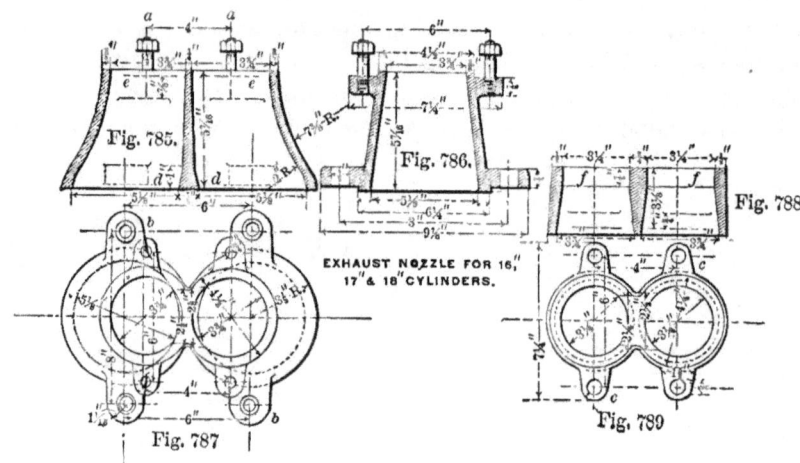

said that this pipe is generally used in short smoke-boxes with petticoat pipes, through which the exhaust steam passes after it leaves the nozzle.

The exhaust pipe is bolted to the cylinder saddle by studs passing through the lugs $b\ b$, and the nozzle is fastened to the top of the pipe by the studs $a\ a$, which pass through the lugs $c\ c$ of the nozzle. The object of making the nozzle separate from the pipe is to provide ready means for replacing it by a larger or smaller one, so that the force of the blast can be decreased or increased as occasion may require. Usually three nozzles of different sizes are sent with each engine.

The openings $d\ d$, Fig. 785, at the bottom of the pipe coincide, of course, with the openings in the cylinder saddle, and the openings $e\ e$ at the top of the pipe are placed as close to each other as it is practical to do.

The openings $f\ f$, Fig. 788, at the top of the nozzle are bored out cylindrically through a distance of about 1 inch, so as to prevent as much as possible the spreading of the exhaust steam. The axes of these openings $f\ f$ lie in a transverse plane perpendicular to the axis of the boiler, but the planes parallel to the axis of the boiler passed through these axes of the openings $ff$ slightly incline towards each other at the top, so as to direct the blast towards the bottom center of the cone in the stack. The passages through the exhaust pipe gradually decrease in size, and this is done for the purpose of increasing the velocity of the exhaust steam as it passes out of the nozzle, thereby giving the blast a sufficient force to create the required draft.

514. Figs. 790, 791, 792 show another short exhaust pipe; the form of the bottom of this pipe is similar to that of the one which has just been described, but the top of the pipe is designed for one orifice only, through which the steam from both

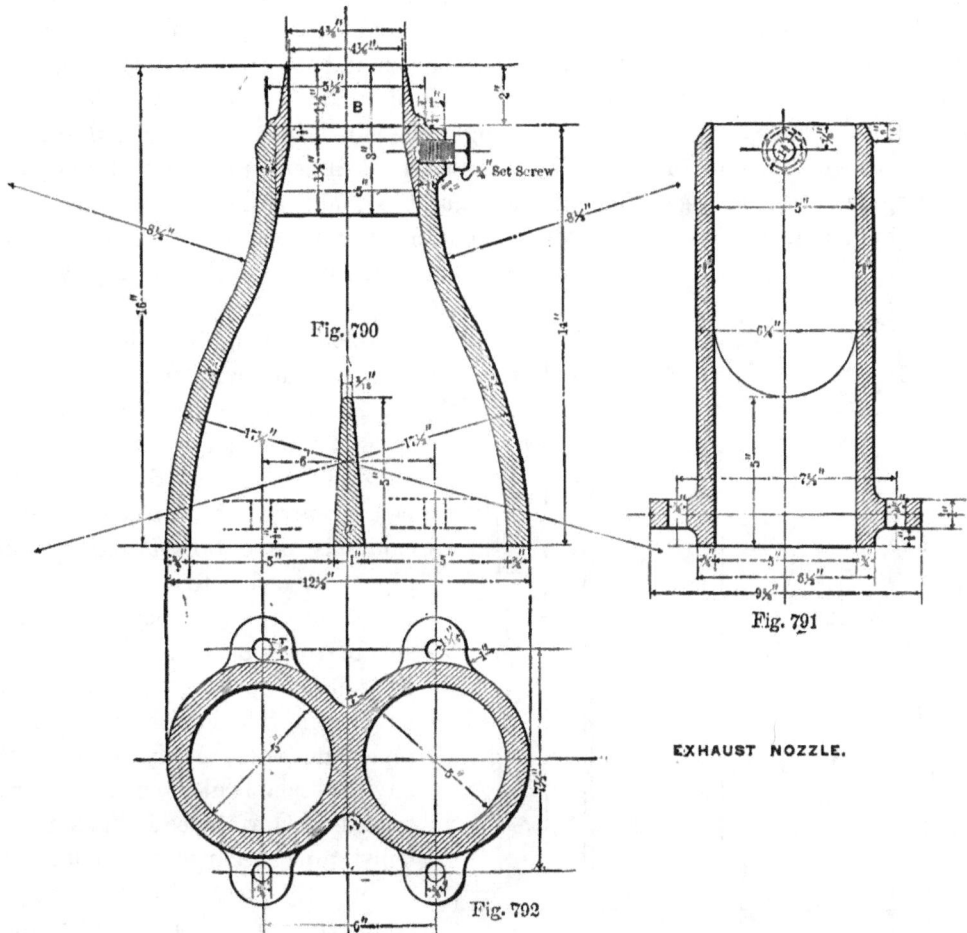

EXHAUST NOZZLE.

cylinders is discharged; this pipe is therefore called a single exhaust pipe. A thimble $B$ is inserted and fastened by a set screw in the top of the pipe; the object of using a thimble is to provide means for changing, in an easy manner, the size of the orifice by using a larger or smaller thimble. Usually three thimbles of different sizes are sent with each engine.

The upper part of the thimble is bored out cylindrically and must point direct to the center of the cone in the stack. It will be well to notice the outside form of the

506                MODERN LOCOMOTIVE CONSTRUCTION.

thimble; it is tapered, smaller at the top than at the bottom, and the upper edge of the pipe is chamfered off; this is done to facilitate the approach of the gases to the exhaust steam. For similar reasons the outside of the double nozzle in Figs. 788, 789 should have been tapered more than as is there shown.

The bridge which divides the pipe at the bottom into two passages prevents, or should prevent, a flow of exhaust steam from one cylinder into the other one, and consequently the bridge in these short pipes must be made as high as possible.

515. It is important that the passages through the double exhaust pipe and nozzle, as well as the passages through the single exhaust pipe and thimble, should be smooth, continuous, and with easy curvature; all sudden bends and corners should be avoided, and the cross-sections of each passage should be similar throughout. By attending to these particulars the back pressure in the cylinders will be reduced. Either the double exhaust pipe or the single one can be used in one and the same engine, but which one of these two is best to adopt is difficult to decide, and engineers do not agree on this subject. The advocates of the double exhaust pipe claim that by its use the exhaust from one cylinder cannot possibly interfere with the exhaust of the other one, and therefore the back pressure in either cylinder cannot be increased by the exhaust steam from one cylinder flowing back into the other, as they say is liable to occur with the single exhaust pipe. On the other hand, the advocates of the single exhaust pipe claim, and justly so, that the blast should be concentric with the stack, and this can only be obtained with a single pipe. In order to prove that, with the use of the single pipe, the exhaust steam from one cylinder cannot flow back into the other, indicator cards have been taken with each kind of pipe, and these cards do not show any appreciable difference in the back pressure. Our choice is the single exhaust pipe, because, we believe, if it is correctly designed it will give good results, and it is easier to make and to keep in repair.

516. With these short single exhaust pipes a petticoat pipe must also be used; but when a diaphragm plate is employed, as shown in Fig. 714, the petticoat pipe, in the majority of cases, is dispensed with, or in the few cases where it is used it is very short; consequently the exhaust pipe used in connection with a diaphragm plate is made much longer than that shown in Figs. 790, 791. Since diaphragm plates are employed in nearly all extension fronts, it may be said that the long single exhaust nozzle belongs to the extension fronts.

517. Figs. 793, 794, 795, 796 show different views of a single long exhaust pipe; its general construction does not differ from that shown in Figs. 790 and 791, and therefore the remarks relating to the latter apply equally well to the long pipe.

These pipes should be made as long as possible, leaving only a sufficient space between the top of the thimble and the bottom of the stack for the free access of the gases to the stack. In Art. 509 we have seen that when the stack has a square entrance to the smoke-box the distance from the top of the thimble to the bottom of the stack should be equal to the diameter of the stack; and when the stack has a bell-shaped entrance, the exhaust pipe can be made somewhat longer. These conditions enable us to determine the length of the exhaust pipe. The bridges in the long exhaust pipes are of course much higher than those in shorter ones, and therefore the danger of the exhaust from one cylinder flowing back into the other is much reduced, and single pipes can be used with confidence in extension fronts. Some master-mechanics make the cross-section of the body of the exhaust pipe comparatively small, so as to get rid of the exhaust steam as quickly as possible, thereby creating a strong blast with decisive intervals. Others prefer to make the body of the pipe comparatively large, and contracting it near the top, thereby obtaining a more constant and milder draft. Either plan can be advantageously employed; for shallow fires we should recommend to make the cross-section of the body of the exhaust pipe comparatively large, so as to obtain a mild and constant draft which will not tear up the fire. On the other hand, for a deep fire we should recommend to reduce the cross-sectional area of the body of the pipe, so as to obtain a blast sufficiently strong to draw the air through the increased depth of fire.

### AREA OF ORIFICES IN EXHAUST NOZZLES.

518. The area of the orifices in the exhaust nozzles or thimbles will depend on the quality and quantity of the coal to be burnt, size of cylinder, and the condition of the outer atmosphere. It is therefore impossible to give rules for computing the exact diameter of the orifices. All that can be done is to give a rule by which an approximate diameter can be found, which may then be used as a basis from which the exhaust pipe can be designed. The exact diameter of orifice can only be found by actual trials, and such sizes should be adopted as will give the greatest economy in fuel. We have seen that among the things which affect the size of exhaust nozzles are the quantity of coal to be burnt and the size of cylinders, and these two things affect its size more than anything else. The quantity of coal to be burnt will of course depend to a great extent on the grate area, and since this area is made proportional to the tractive force which takes in account the size of cylinders, we may at once determine the size of exhaust nozzle from the grate area.

Our experience leads us to believe that the area of each orifice in double exhaust nozzles should be $\frac{1}{400}$ part of the grate area. Adopting this proportion, we have:

RULE 110.—Divide the grate area in square inches (as found by Rule 103) by 400; the quotient will be the area in square inches of each orifice in a double exhaust nozzle for either soft- or hard-coal burners.

In this way we have found the areas of the orifices given in Column 3 in the following table, and in Column 4 the corresponding diameters are given.

### TABLE 75.

DIAMETERS OF ORIFICES IN DOUBLE EXHAUST NOZZLES FOR HARD AND SOFT COAL BURNERS AS COMPUTED BY RULE 110.

| Size of Cylinders. | Grate Area. | Area of each Orifice. | Diameter of each Orifice. |
|---|---|---|---|
| Column 1. | Column 2. | Column 3. | Column 4. |
| 10 × 20 inches. | 954.40 sq. in. | 2.38 sq. in. | 1¾ inches. |
| 11 × 22 " | 1267.20 " | 3.16 " | 2 " |
| 12 × 22 " | 1425.60 " | 3.56 " | 2⅛ " |
| 13 × 22 " | 1627.20 " | 4.06 " | 2¼ " |
| 14 × 24 " | 1843.20 " | 4.60 " | 2$\frac{7}{16}$ " |
| 15 × 24 " | 2116.80 " | 5.29 " | 2$\frac{9}{16}$ " |
| 16 × 24 " | 2275.20 " | 5.68 " | 2$\frac{11}{16}$ " |
| 17 × 24 " | 2491.20 " | 6.22 " | 2$\frac{13}{16}$ " |
| 18 × 24 " | 2750.40 " | 6.87 " | 2$\frac{15}{16}$ " |
| 20 × 24 " | 4320.00 " | 10.80 " | 3$\frac{7}{16}$ " |
| 22 × 24 " | 5011.20 " | 12.52 " | 4 " |

The grate areas given in this table are the same as those given in Tables 59 and 60.

The size of orifices in single exhaust nozzles or thimbles can be found by the following rule:

RULE 111.—Divide the grate area in square inches (as found by Rule 103) by 200; the quotient will be the area in square inches of the orifice in a single exhaust nozzle or thimble for either hard- or soft-coal burners.

The sizes in the following table have been found by this rule.

### TABLE 76.

DIAMETERS OF ORIFICES IN SINGLE EXHAUST NOZZLES OR THIMBLES FOR HARD AND SOFT COAL BURNERS AS COMPUTED BY RULE 111.

| Size of Cylinders. | Grate Area. | Area of Orifice. | Diameter of Orifice. |
|---|---|---|---|
| Column 1. | Column 2. | Column 3. | Column 4. |
| 10 × 20 inches. | 954.40 sq. in. | 4.72 sq. in. | 2¼ inches. |
| 11 × 22 " | 1267.20 " | 6.33 " | 2⅞ " |
| 12 × 22 " | 1425.60 " | 7.12 " | 3$\frac{1}{16}$ " |
| 13 × 22 " | 1627.20 " | 8.13 " | 3¼ " |
| 14 × 24 " | 1843.20 " | 9.21 " | 3$\frac{7}{16}$ " |
| 15 × 24 " | 2116.80 " | 10.58 " | 2$\frac{11}{16}$ " |
| 16 × 24 " | 2275.20 " | 11.37 " | 3$\frac{13}{16}$ " |
| 17 × 24 " | 2491.20 " | 12.45 " | 4 " |
| 18 × 24 " | 2750.40 " | 13.75 " | 4$\frac{3}{16}$ " |
| 20 × 24 " | 4320.00 " | 21.60 " | 5¼ " |
| 22 × 24 " | 5011.20 " | 25.05 " | 5$\frac{11}{16}$ " |

The grate areas given in this table are the same as those given in Tables 59 and 60.

The diameters of orifices as computed by the foregoing rules agree very closely with the diameters in actual use, as will be seen by a comparison with those given in the following table, which contains the sizes of orifices as found in locomotives in regular service.

In Columns 2 and 3 are given the sizes of three nozzles, comprising a set for each engine such as are generally furnished by locomotive builders. Whenever thimbles are used in place of nozzles, the diameter of the hole in top of the exhaust pipe is made $\frac{1}{2}$ inch greater than the diameter of largest orifice in a set for the smaller engines; and about $\frac{3}{4}$ of an inch greater for the larger engines.

## TABLE 77.

SIZES OF ORIFICES IN EXHAUST NOZZLE IN ACTUAL SERVICE FOR HARD AND SOFT COAL BURNERS.

| Size of Cylinders. | Double Nozzles. Diameter of Orifices in inches. | Single Nozzles. Diameter of Orifices in inches. |
|---|---|---|
| Column 1. | Column 2. | Column 3. |
| 9 × 16 inches. | $1\frac{1}{4}$, $1\frac{3}{8}$, $1\frac{1}{2}$. | |
| 12 × 20 " | $1\frac{5}{8}$, $1\frac{7}{8}$, $2\frac{1}{4}$. | |
| 13 × 20 " | $1\frac{3}{4}$, 2, $2\frac{1}{4}$. | |
| 14 × 24 " | $1\frac{7}{8}$, $2\frac{1}{4}$, $2\frac{3}{8}$. | $2\frac{7}{8}$, $3\frac{1}{4}$, $3\frac{5}{8}$. |
| 15 × 24 " | 2, $2\frac{1}{4}$, $2\frac{1}{2}$. | $3\frac{1}{4}$, $3\frac{3}{8}$, $3\frac{5}{8}$. |
| 16 × 24 " | $2\frac{1}{4}$, $2\frac{1}{2}$, $2\frac{3}{4}$. | $3\frac{3}{8}$, $3\frac{5}{8}$, $3\frac{7}{8}$. |
| 17 × 24 " | $2\frac{1}{2}$, $2\frac{3}{4}$, 3. | $3\frac{7}{8}$, 4, $4\frac{1}{4}$. |
| 18 × 24 " | $2\frac{3}{4}$, 3, $3\frac{1}{4}$. | 4, $4\frac{1}{4}$, $4\frac{1}{2}$. |
| 19 × 24 " | 3, $3\frac{1}{4}$, $3\frac{1}{2}$. | $4\frac{1}{2}$, $4\frac{3}{4}$, 5. |
| 20 × 24 " | $3\frac{1}{4}$, $3\frac{1}{2}$, $3\frac{3}{4}$. | $4\frac{3}{4}$, 5, $5\frac{1}{4}$. |

# CHAPTER XII.

### SAND-BOXES.—BELLS.—PILOTS.—ENGINE-BRACES.

#### SAND-BOXES.

519. The sand-boxes are usually placed on top of boilers; sometimes they are placed underneath the running boards. The capacity of a sand-box placed on top of

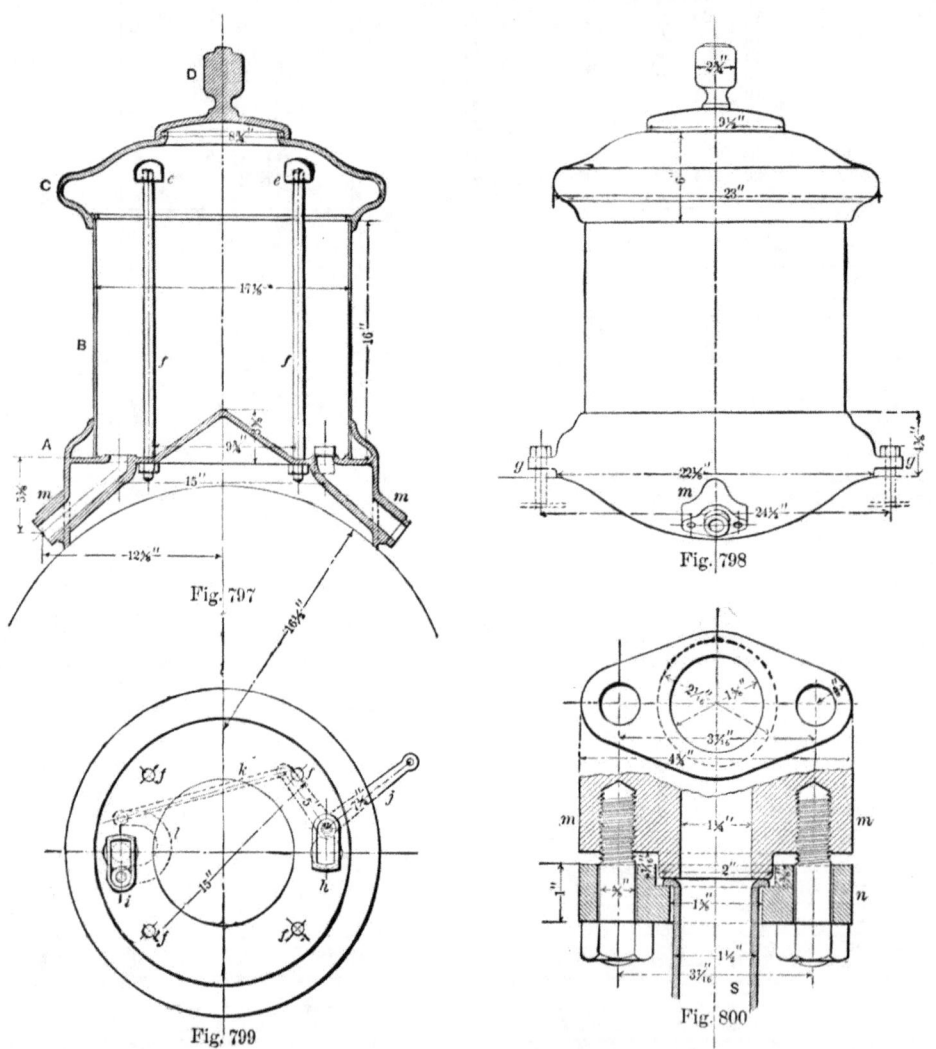

Fig. 797
Fig. 798
Fig. 799
Fig. 800

boiler is generally about 7 cubic feet, excepting those which are placed on small engines, which contain less.

The sand should be perfectly dry, so as to enable it to flow easily through the pipes which lead it to the rails. It should be used sparingly, not simply for the sake of economy, but mainly to avoid an increase of train resistance, which will occur when the wheels under the cars have to run on sanded rails; the purpose of putting sand on the rails is to assist the engine to overcome the train resistance; hence the latter should not be increased by an injudicious use of sand.

Fig. 797 shows a section, Fig. 798, an elevation, and Fig. 799, a plan, of a small sand-box of the ordinary form. It consists of a cast-iron base $A$, a wrought-iron body $B$, generally No. 12 B W. G., a cast-iron top $C$, and a cover $D$. The wrought-iron body $B$ is not riveted to the base or top; the body is simply set in these castings and the whole clamped together by the rods $f\,f$ which are tapped into the lugs $e\,e$ cast to the sand-box top, with the nuts on the lower ends of the rods bearing against the underside of the base. The sand is shut off or allowed to escape by the valves $h$ and $i$. The valve $h$ is worked directly by a bell crank, and the valve $i$ is worked by the bent lever $l$, whose free end is connected by a link $k$ to one of the arms of the bell crank. The free end of the arm $j$ of the bell crank is connected to a rod extending to the cab, within easy reach of the engineer; this rod, or sand-box reach-rod, as it is often called, is sometimes run through the hand rail. It will

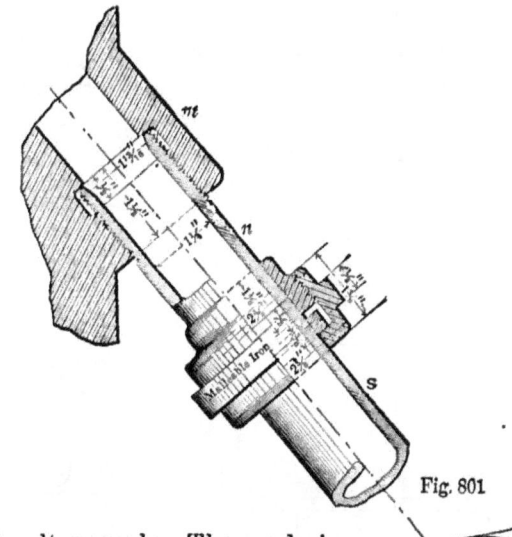

Fig. 801

be seen that both valves are worked simultaneously. The sand-pipes, which are usually made of wrought-iron, $1\frac{1}{2}$ inches outside diameter, are fastened to the lugs $m$; one way of fastening them is shown on a larger scale in Fig. 800. The end of the sand-pipe $S$ is turned over on a flange $n$, and this flange is secured to the lug $m$ by two studs  Fig. 801 shows another method of fastening the sand-pipe to the base. The lug $m$ is tapped, a nipple is screwed into it, and the sand-pipe is attached to the nipple by a nut, plainly shown in the illustration.

The sand-box (Fig. 798) is set on top of the lagging, and secured to the boiler by two studs tapped into the boiler shell and passing through the lugs $g\,g$, which are cast to the base.

Sometimes the sand-box rests directly on the boiler shell, and the lagging fitted around it. Some master-mechanics object to this method, as sparks are liable to fly between the base and lagging and set fire to the latter.

Figs. 802, 803 show a large sand-box. It consists of a cast-iron base $A$; a cast-iron lower ring $B$; a sheet-iron body $C$; an upper ring $D$; a top $E$; and a cover $F$. The whole, excepting the cover, is clamped together by the rods $f$.

Of course the sand-boxes must be water-tight, and since none of the joints are calked it is necessary to adopt such form of joints as will not permit the water to flow into the box. It is for this reason that the body C is made to overlap the upper edge of the lower ring, as shown at p, Fig. 802; and the upper ring overlaps the top of the body C, as shown at r; the joint s is not recommended, because, unless it is extremely well made, it will allow the water to flow into the box; the joint s in Fig. 804 is a better one.

The manner of operating the valves is plainly shown and needs no further explanation. The reach-rod, which extends to the cab, is attached to the free end of the lever j.

Figs. 804, 805 show a sand-box arranged for four sand-pipes, and consequently it has four valves; these are connected so that only two can be operated simultaneously

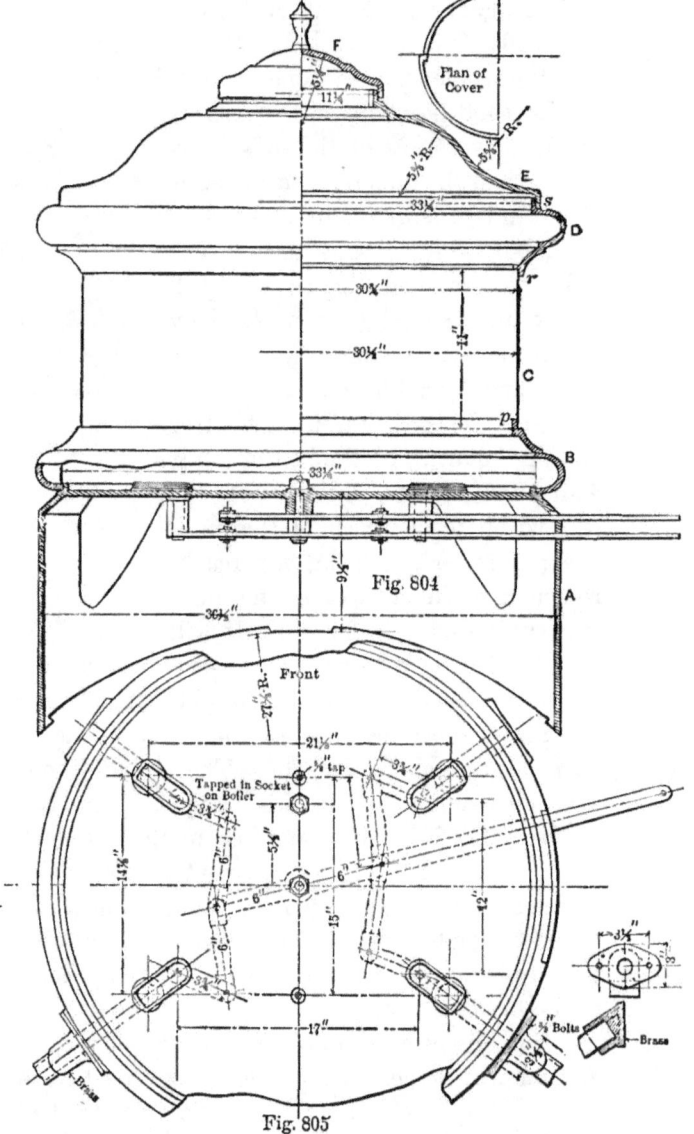

with one lever and reach-rod. Otherwise the construction of this box is the same as that shown in Fig. 802.

Figs. 806, 807 show a form of sand-box which in late years has been extensively adopted. It is copied from English design, and its advantages are, that it is simple in construction, and can be kept clean with less labor than other types. We do not favor the joint between the body and base, as this joint is liable to let water flow into the box. A better way is to allow the body to overlap the top of the base, and this can easily be done without interfering with the outer form of the box.

520. In eight-wheeled passenger engines, the sand-pipes are placed in front of the main drivers; in Mogul, ten-wheeled, and consolidation engines, they are sometimes placed in front of the front drivers; in others, in front of the main drivers, and occasionally on both sides of the main drivers. In switching engines it is desirable to have the sand-pipes on each side of a pair of drivers, and in such cases the sand-boxes with four sand-pipes are often used. The latter boxes are also frequently used on other engines.

BELLS.

521. Fig. 808 shows a locomotive bell $A$, with its cast-iron stand $B$ and cast-iron

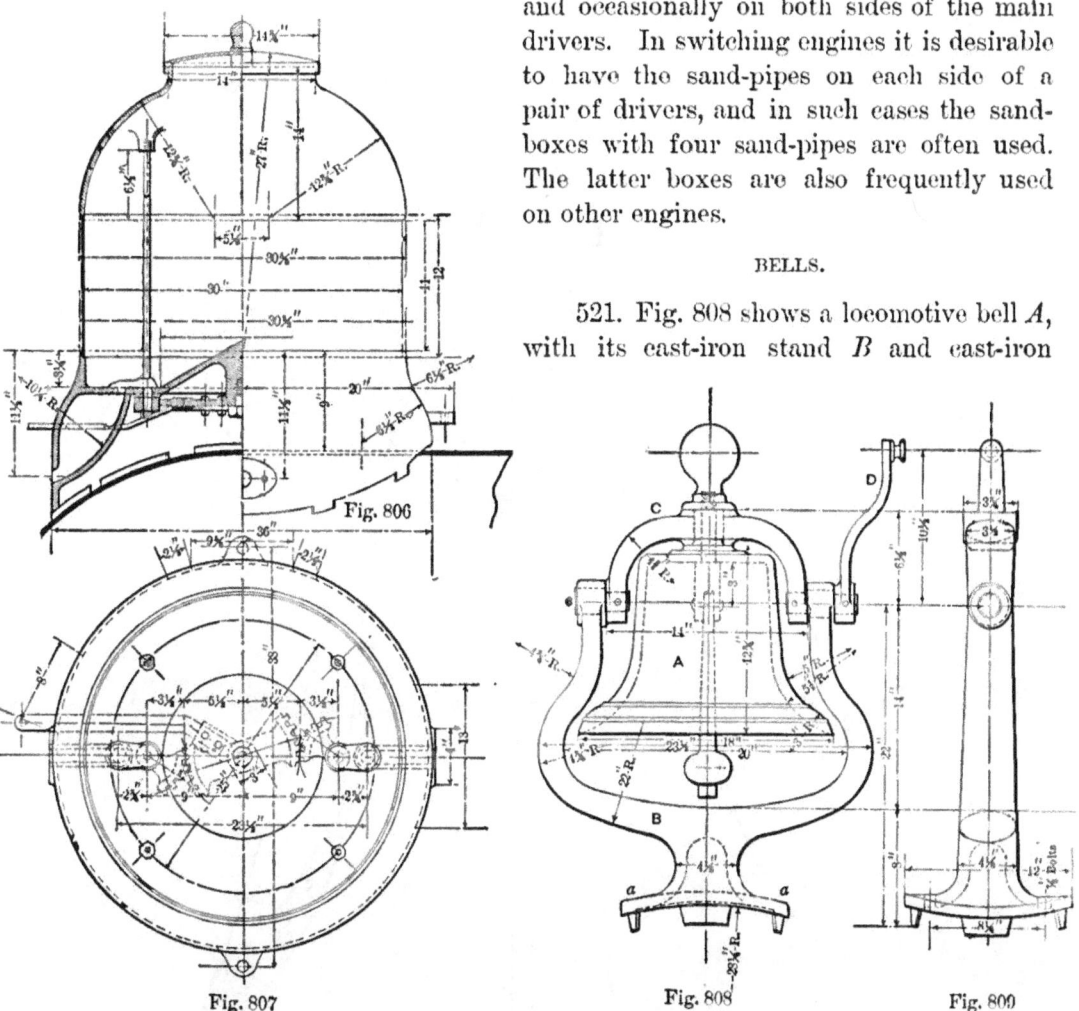

Fig. 806
Fig. 807
Fig. 808
Fig. 809

yoke $C$. Fig. 809 simply shows a side elevation of the stand and yoke. The stand is placed on top of boiler and fastened to the shell by two studs tapped into the shell. The position of the bell is generally such as will harmonize with and give a pleasing appearance to the whole.

The foot $a$ on the stand $B$ should be sufficiently deep to bring its upper surface about ¼ inch above the lagging, which should be fitted closely to the sides of the foot, so as to prevent sparks from setting fire to it.

The yoke turns on wrought-iron pivots $c$; these are driven into the yoke, and held in position by a dowel pin; the driven part of the pivot is made either straight or tapered, and the projecting part of the pivot is often made about ⅛ inch larger in diameter than the driven part. The bell is generally worked from the cab by a bell-rope attached to the handle *D*; sometimes, by an automatic bell-ringer driven by steam.

## CONSTRUCTION OF BELL.

522. The size of the bell is generally designated by the diameter of its mouth; if this is 12 or 18 inches in diameter, the bell is said to be a 12- or 18-inch bell. After

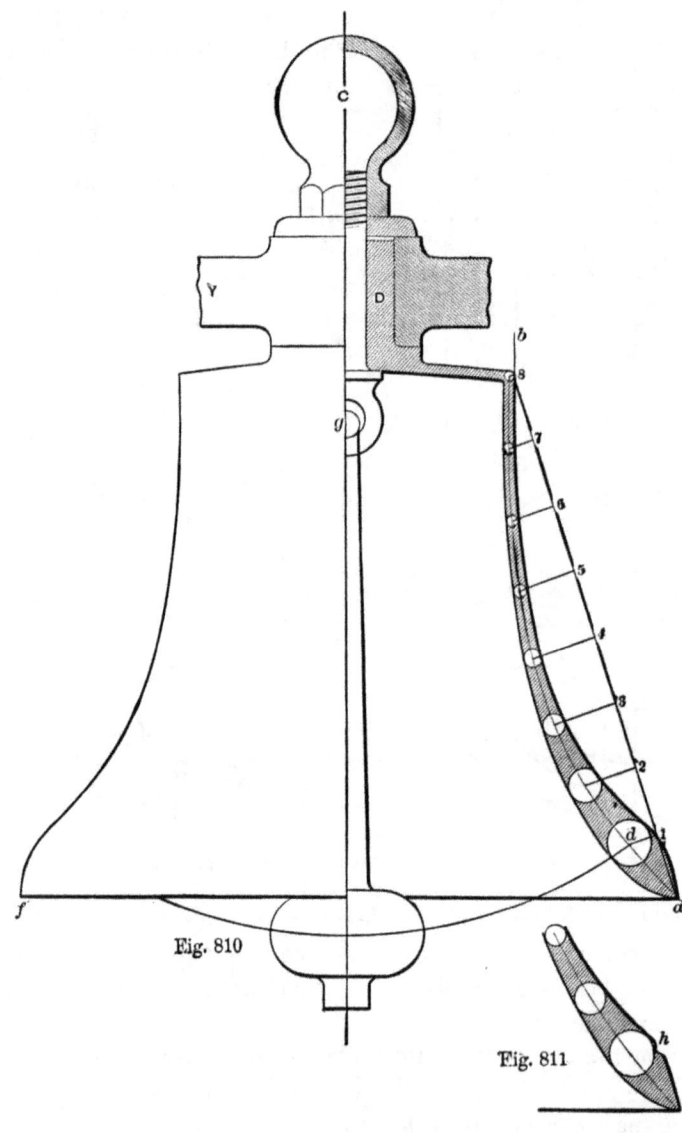

Fig. 810

Fig. 811

this diameter has been established, the other dimensions of the bell, excepting its shank, by which the bell is fastened to yoke, are derived from this diameter. For large locomotives 18- or 19-inch bells are generally used, and for the smaller engines

13-inch bells seem to be the favorite ones. For designing a bell of any size, the following method may be adopted and satisfactory results expected.

Draw the diameter $fa$, Fig. 810, of the mouth of the bell; also draw the center line $CC$ perpendicular to $fa$. Divide the diameter $fa$ into 10 equal parts; each part is called a stroke; this diameter, divided into strokes, forms a scale from which the other dimensions of the bell are laid off. Hence, for the sake of convenience, draw a line $fa$ equal in length to the diameter of the mouth of the bell on a separate piece of paper, which is to serve as a scale, divide $fa$ into 10 equal parts, and again divide one of the end divisions into 10 equal parts, and thus complete the scale. Since one of these parts (a stroke) is divided into 10 equal parts, we have constructed a decimal scale.

Parallel to the center line $CC$ draw a line $b$; the distance between $b$ and $CC$ must be equal to $2\frac{1}{2}$ strokes; in other words, the distance between these lines must be equal to one-half of $Ca$. The distance from $b$ to $CC$ represents one-half the diameter of the crown, consequently the diameter of the crown is equal to one-half the diameter $fa$ of the mouth of the bell. From the point $a$ as a center, and with a radius equal to 8 strokes, describe a short arc cutting the straight line $b$ in the point 8; join the points $a$ and 8 by a straight line; divide this line into 8 equal parts; each part will then be equal to a stroke. Mark the points of division 1, 2, 3, etc., as shown, and through these points draw lines perpendicular to $a\,8$. These lines are ordinates to the curve through center of the metal of the bell, and must be made equal to the length given in the following table; these lengths must, of course, be measured from the line $a\,8$, with the scale of strokes.

## TABLE 78.

Length of ordinate through point .................... 1 = 0.41 stroke.
" " " " " .................... 2 = 0.86 "
" " " " " .................... 3 = 1.02 "
" " " " " .................... 4 = 1.00 "
" " " " " .................... 5 = 0.87 "
" " " " " .................... 6 = 0.66 "
" " " " " .................... 7 = 0.39 "
" " " " " .................... 8 = 0.09 "

Through the ends of these ordinates draw a curve, which will be the curve through the center of the metal. From the points in which the ordinates meet this curve as centers describe circles of the following diameter:

## TABLE 79.

Diameter of circle on ordinate .................... 1 = 0.70 stroke.
" " " " " .................... 2 = 0.45 "
" " " " " .................... 3 = 0.33 "
" " " " " .................... 4 = 0.26 "
" " " " " .................... 5 = 0.22 "
" " " " " .................... 6 = 0.20 "
" " " " " .................... 7 = 0.19 "
" " " " " .................... 8 = 0.18 "

Tangent to these circles draw the outer and inner curves, which will determine the thickness of the metal. At the bottom of the bell describe an arc from a center on the line $fa$, so that the arc will be tangent to the outer curve and pass through the point $a$. Another arc with about the same radius must be described passing through the point $a$, and tangent to the inner curve.

The crown of the bell is sometimes slightly curved as shown, sometimes it is flat; in either case the lines which represent the outer and inner surfaces of the crown are drawn tangent to the circle on ordinate 8. After a bell has been drawn full size by the method here given, the drawing can be measured with an ordinary rule, and its dimensions in inches obtained.

For determining the diameter and length of the shank $D$, good judgment is required. For an 18-inch bell the shank is generally from $2\frac{1}{4}$ to $2\frac{3}{8}$ inches in diameter, and about $2\frac{1}{2}$ to $2\frac{3}{4}$ inches long. The bolt for fastening the bell to the yoke $Y$ is from $\frac{7}{8}$ to 1 inch in diameter. The length of the clapper should be such that an arc passing through the center $d$ of the circle on ordinate 1, and described from the center $g$, shall pass through the center of the ball on the clapper. The weight of the clapper should be from $\frac{1}{40}$ to $\frac{1}{50}$ the weight of the bell; the heavier weight is to be used for the smaller bells.

The proportions here given answer well for an ordinary locomotive bell. Should it be desirable to use a greater or smaller thickness of metal, make the ordinates through the points of division on the line $8\,a$ the same length as before; and the diameters of the circles on these ordinates are found by the following table:

TABLE 80.

```
Diameter of circle on ordinate .......................... 1 = 1    stroke.
   "       "    "   "    "    .......................... 2 = 0.653   "
   "       "    "   "    "    .......................... 3 = 0.474   "
   "       "    "   "    "    .......................... 4 = 0.380   "
   "       "    "   "    "    .......................... 5 = 0.327   "
   "       "    "   "    "    .......................... 6 = 0.291   "
   "       "    "   "    "    .......................... 7 = 0.279   "
   "       "    "   "    "    .......................... 8 = 0.267   "
```

If it is now desirable to make the thickness of metal on ordinate 1 equal to, say, $1\frac{1}{4}$ inches, describe a circle $1\frac{1}{4}$ inches diameter; the diameters of the circles on the other ordinates are found in the following manner: Multiply $1\frac{1}{4}$ inch by 0.653, which is the diameter given in Table 80 for the circle on ordinate 2; for the circle on ordinate 3 multiply $1\frac{1}{4}$ inches by 0.474, which is the diameter given in the table for ordinate 3, and so on in succession for all the other circles, and then proceed as before. In a similar way we find the diameters of the circles for any other thickness, either more or less than an inch on ordinate 1.

Increasing the thickness of the metal at the bottom of the bell will make the diameter of the crown a little larger than one-half the diameter of the mouth, but this difference will not affect the tone of the bell to any appreciable extent.

If it is desirable to have a fillet $h$ near the bottom of the bell, it should be drawn tangent to the circle on ordinate 1, as shown in Fig. 811. A good mixture for the metal is 4 of copper to 1 of tin; to every hundred pounds of this mixture add $\frac{1}{2}$ pound of zinc, and $\frac{1}{2}$ pound of lead.

## PILOTS.

523. Figs. 812, 813, 814 show a wooden pilot of ordinary design. The drawing is very complete, and therefore a few remarks only are necessary. The height of all pilots should be such as to leave 1 inch clearance between the top of rails and the bottom of the pilot when the engine frames rest on top of the driving boxes, consequently when the engines stand at their ordinary working height there will be from 3 to 5 inches clearance between the bottom of the pilots and the rails. A wrought-iron band about 3 inches wide and ½ inch thick is fastened to the sides of the lower side rails $l$ of the pilot, and this band extends partly over the sides of the rear rail $m$. The pilot is bolted to the bumper beam $C$; its front end is braced by two rods $D$, which run up to the casting $E$ fastened to the top of bumper beam. The bottom of the rear end of the pilot is

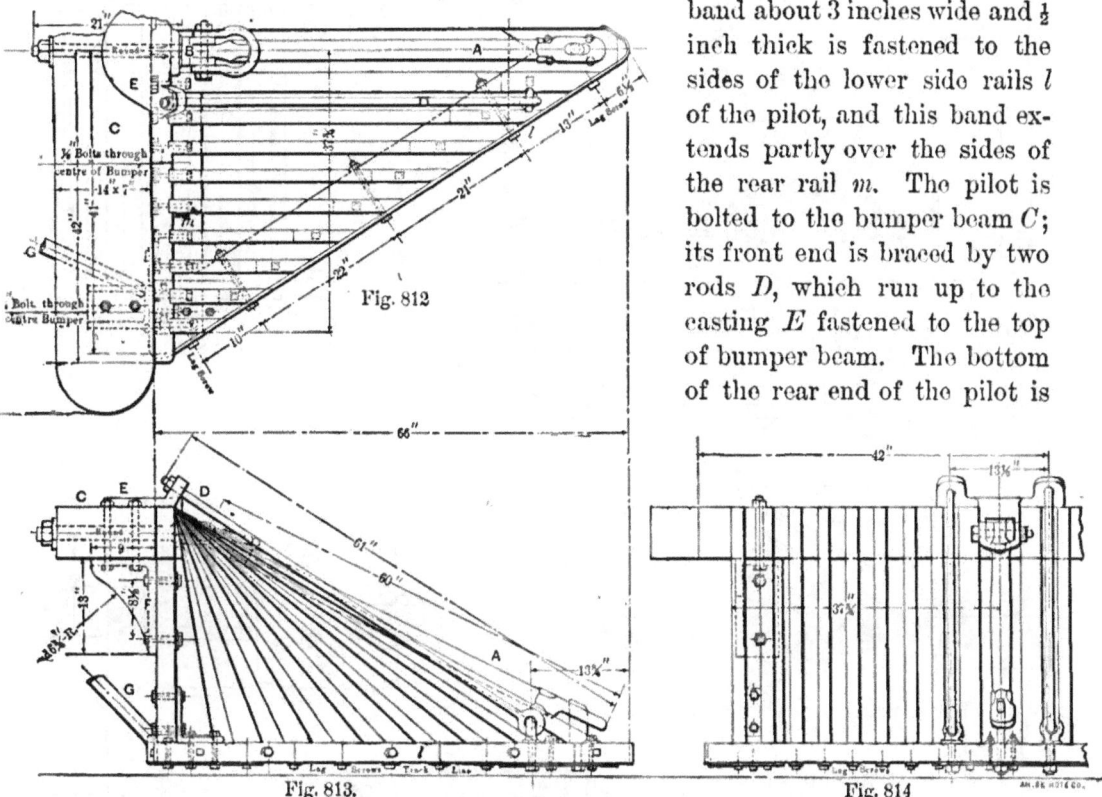

Fig. 812
Fig. 813.
Fig. 814.

braced by the braces $G$, which cross each other and are bolted to the engine frames, or sometimes to the cylinder saddle. For further security the cast-iron knees $F$ are used. The pulling bar $A$ is attached to the jaw $B$, whose shank passes through the bumper beam and is fastened to it.

Figs. 815, 816, 817 show another wooden pilot, of slightly different construction. Instead of bracing its front end by two braces, only one brace $D$ is used, and this brace is placed inside of the pilot and bolted to the bottom of the bumper beam. The pulling bar $A$ is attached to a cast-iron draw-head $B$. The draw-heads are made of various forms. The one here shown has its upper edge flaring forward; the object of this flare is to hold obstructions which may slide along the top of the pilot, and prevent them from smashing the front end of the smoke-box.

Figs. 818, 819 show a wrought-iron draw-head which is sometimes used in place of the cast-iron head. It is bolted to the front of the bumper beam; it not only serves as a draw-head, but also as a bumper bar. The brace A is, of course, bolted to the top of bumper beam.

Figs. 820, 821 show an iron pilot with two wooden bumper blocks B; these blocks

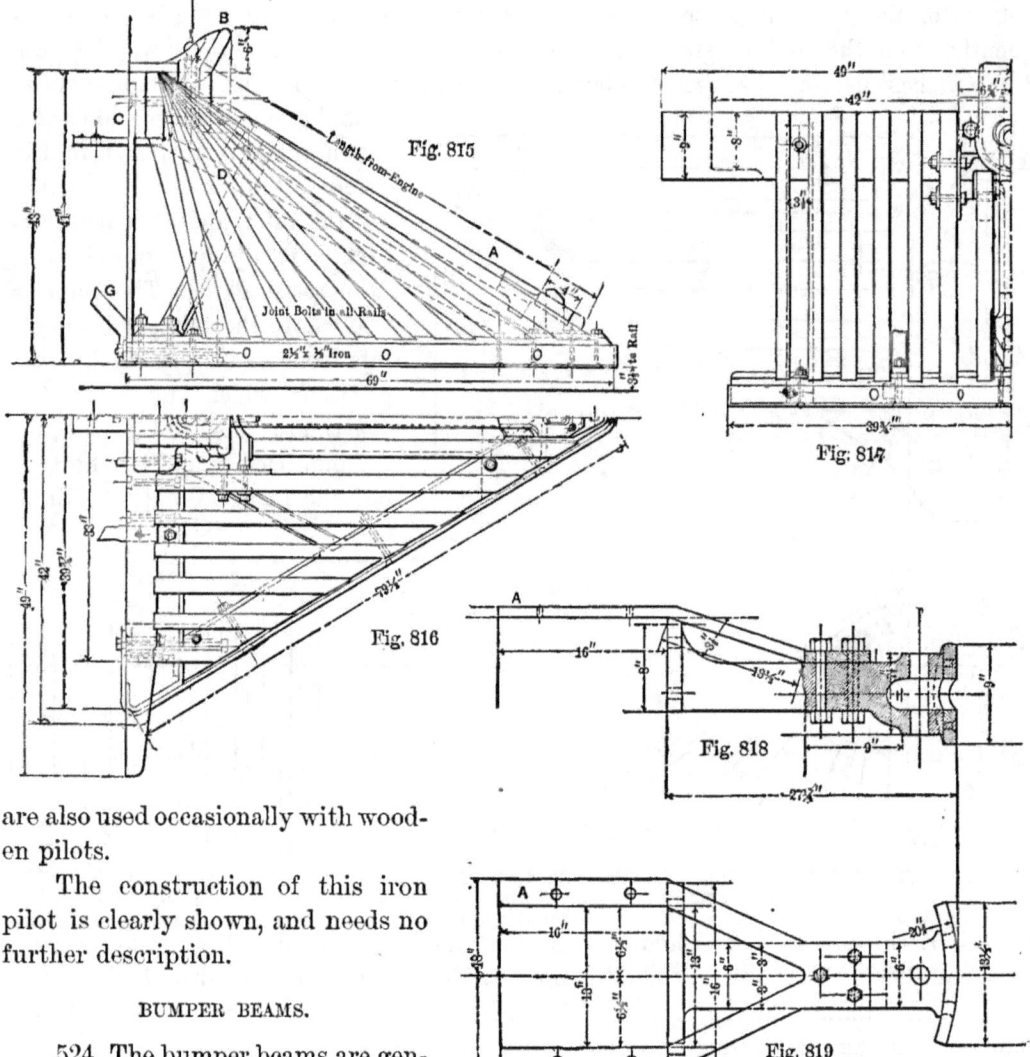

are also used occasionally with wooden pilots.

The construction of this iron pilot is clearly shown, and needs no further description.

### BUMPER BEAMS.

524. The bumper beams are generally made of oak. They are made long enough to project 1 inch beyond the cylinder flanges; the object of this is to prevent obstructions on the track from striking the cylinders.

Sometimes the cross-section of the bumper beam is rectangular, as shown in Fig. 813. The usual size of this cross section is 7 × 14 or 15 inches; frequently the cross-section is square or nearly so; 9 × 10 inches is often used for engines of medium size.

The bumper beams are fastened to the frames in various ways; the manner of fastening them often depends on the distance from the rail to the draw-head on the cars.

Fig. 822 shows the beam bolted to the end a of the frame by a horizontal bolt c

# MODERN LOCOMOTIVE CONSTRUCTION. 519

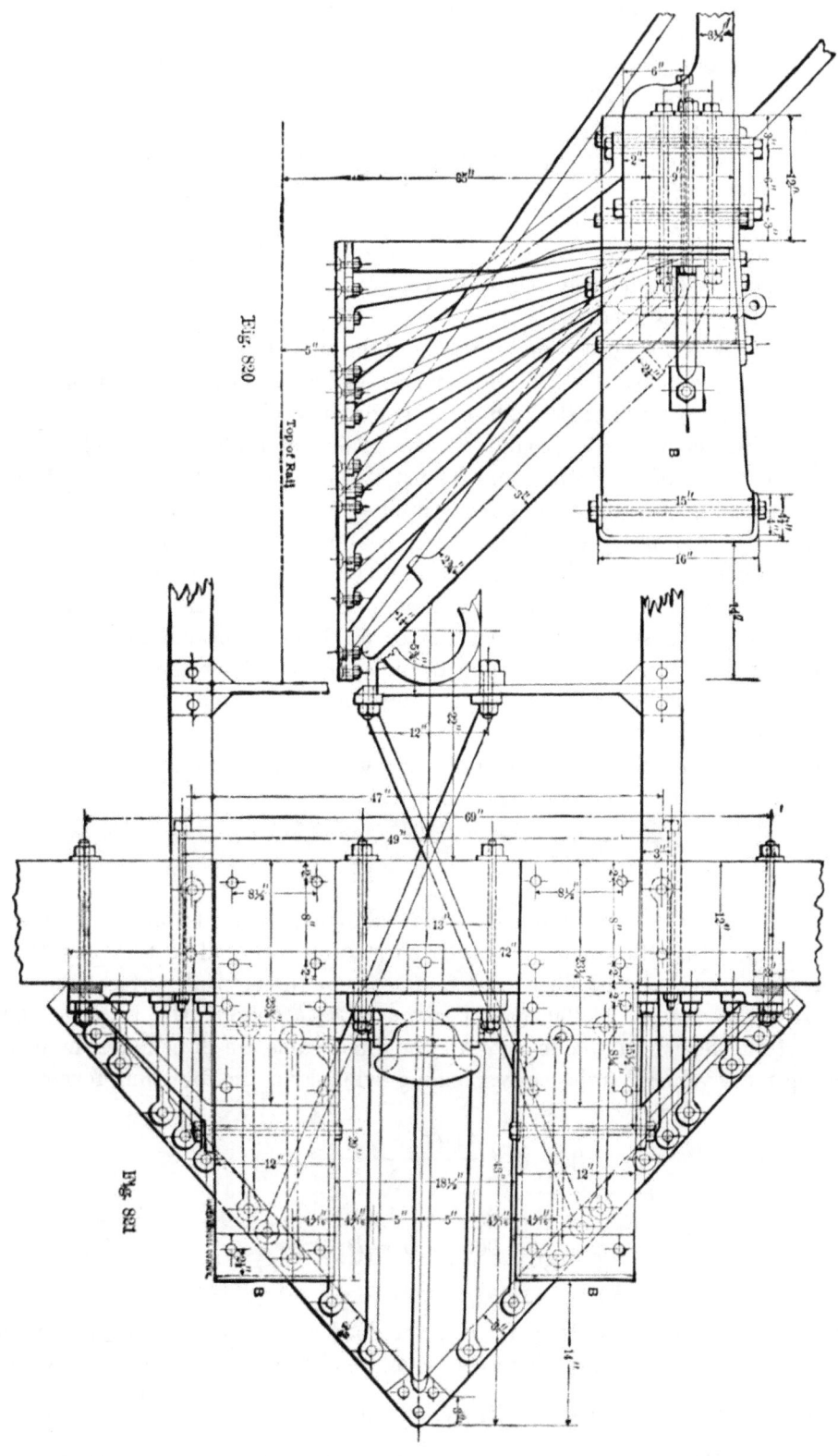

Fig. 820

Fig. 821

and two vertical bolts $b\ b$, which also pass through the foot of the bumper brace $A$; this foot is lipped over a projection on the frame, so as to reduce as much as possible the stress in the frame $F$.

Sometimes a casting shown in Figs. 300, 301 is used; a wrought-iron plate about 1 inch thick extending across the engine is bolted to the front faces of these castings and the beam bolted to the plate.

525. In ordinary service, the principal stresses in the beam are those due to the pull and push of the engine, the weight of the pilot, and the stress due to removing comparatively slight obstructions.

The simplest way to proceed in determining the size of cross-section is to assume that the beam has to resist the pull and push of the engine only, and adopt for this work a factor of safety sufficiently high to allow for the other stresses.

In calculating the strength of bumper beams, they should be considered as beams supported by the ends of the frames and loaded at the center. When a draw-head is used as shown in Fig. 816, the load is really applied at two points when the engine is pulling, and it is uniformly distributed over a short distance when the engine is pushing; therefore, if we consider the beam to be loaded at the center as stated, we shall obtain a somewhat larger beam than necessary, but the error will be on the side of safety; we shall therefore consider all bumper beams to be loaded at the center. The load is numerically equal to the adhesion of the driving wheels, and the direction in which the load acts is of course horizontal instead of vertical as in ordinary beams.

For computing the width or breadth of beam we use the formula

$$W = n\,\frac{Sbd^2}{6l},$$

in which $W$ denotes the load in pounds; the value of $n$ depends on the manner of loading and supporting the beam—in this case the value of $n$ will be 4; $S$ denotes the stress per square inch on the fiber most remote from the neutral surface, and for a breaking stress a value of 14,400 may be given to $S$; $b$ denotes the breadth; $d$, the depth; and $l$, the length of the beam. All the dimensions are to be taken in inches. Substituting these values for the corresponding symbols in the foregoing formula, we get,

$$W = 4 \times \frac{14400 \times b \times d^2}{6 \times l}.$$

This reduces to

$$W = \frac{9600 \times b \times d^2}{l}.$$

The above gives us the breaking load; for a safe load which a beam can support, and which is subjected to shocks like a bumper beam, we should adopt a factor of safety of 15. Therefore, instead of using a multiplier of 9600 we should use $\dfrac{9600}{15} = 640$. In order to allow for the minor stresses to which the bumper beam is subjected, we must make a further reduction, say to 480. Hence, for the safe load on the bumper beam we have the following formula:

$$W = \frac{480 \times b \times d^2}{l}; \qquad (a)$$

or,

$$W \times l = 480 \times b \times d^2. \qquad (b)$$

We are now in a position to apply the formula.

EXAMPLE 145.—Find the length of a side of a cross-section of a square bumper beam for an eight-wheeled passenger engine with cylinders 17 inches diameter and 18 inches stroke; the distance between the centers of frames is 47 inches.

In Table 5 we find that the adhesion of a 17 × 18 inch eight-wheeled passenger engine is 10,404 pounds. Now, substituting in the last formula for the symbols their values, we have,

$$10404 \times 47 = b \times d^2 \times 480.$$

Since in square sections $b$ is equal to $d$, we have,

$$10404 \times 47 = d^3 \times 480;$$

hence,

$$d^3 = \frac{10404 \times 47}{480} = 1018.72,$$

and

$$d = \sqrt[3]{1018.72} = 10.1 \text{ inches nearly.}$$

This size of beam will answer the purpose when a draw-head as shown in Fig. 815 is used, or in which no large hole is bored through the center or dangerous section. When a pulling jaw, as shown in Fig. 812, is employed, a large hole must be bored through the center of the beam, thereby greatly reducing its strength, which must not be neglected. To show how formula (b) can be applied in this case we will take the following example:

EXAMPLE 146.—The cross-section of a bumper beam for an eight-wheeled passenger engine with 17 × 18 inch cylinders is to be rectangular, as shown in Fig. 813; the breadth is 7 inches; diameter of hole through center, 2½ inches; distance between frames 47 inches. What must be the depth of the beam?

The hole through the center reduces the breadth from 7 inches to $7 - 2\frac{1}{2} = 4\frac{1}{2}$ inches, and this value must be taken for $b$ in the formula.

Now, substituting in formula (b) for the symbols their numerical values, we have,

$$10404 \times 47 = 4.5 \times d^2 \times 480;$$

hence,

$$d^2 = \frac{10404 \times 47}{4.5 \times 480} = \frac{488988}{2160} = 226.38,$$

and

$$d = \sqrt{226.38} = 15 \text{ inches.}$$

When the cross-section of a bumper beam is rectangular, it is always best to choose first the breadth $b$, which in many cases is arbitrary, and for choosing this dimension good judgment must be used. The depth may then be found by the foregoing formula, from which the following rule may be established for computing the depth of beams of rectangular cross-section.

RULE 112.—Multiply the adhesion in pounds on the drivers by the distance in inches between the centers of the engine frames; call this product $A$. Multiply the breadth in inches of the bumper beam by a constant of 480; call this product $B$. Divide product $A$ by the product $B$, and extract the square root from the quotient; the result will be the required depth in inches of the beam.

### FINISH OF FRONT END.

526. Figs. 822, 823 show the general finish of a front end of an engine with a short smoke-box. It consists of a bumper plate $E$ covering the beam and extending backwards up to the cylinder saddle. Its side edges are curved so as to allow sufficient room for taking off the cylinder heads and removing the pistons when necessary. Side plates riveted to the bumper plate extend along these edges and along the front of the bumper beam.

Sometimes the bumper sheet $E$ extends only from outside to outside of frames, leaving those portions of the beam which project beyond the frames exposed; or if it is desirable to protect these portions, they are covered by short plates, and the ends of the beam are covered with cast-iron caps.

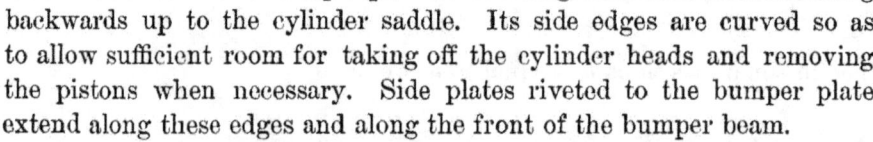

### BOILER SUPPORTS AND FRAME BRACES.

527. For short smoke-boxes the type of bumper brace $A$ as shown in Fig. 822 is always used. Its upper end is sometimes made rectangular, as shown, and bolted—sometimes riveted—to the smoke-box; the bolts should be turned and driven into reamed holes, two of the bolts passing through the smoke-box ring. Sometimes the upper end is made circular in form, with one bolt passing through the smoke-box ring.

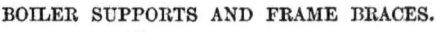

This type of brace is occasionally adopted for extension fronts, but in the majority of cases the type shown in Figs. 824, 825 is the favorite one. The foot $a$ of this brace is sometimes set on top of and bolted to the bumper beam, but usually it is placed close to the rear of it on the top of engine frame, and bolted to the latter. Its upper end $b$ is riveted to the extension front.

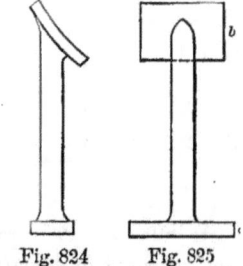

528. The next brace, extending from the engine frames to the boiler, is the guide-yoke. These braces may be divided into two principal classes: one class embraces those which do not extend from frame to frame and consequently a separate guide-yoke is required for each side of the engine; the second class embraces those which extend across both frames.

Figs. 826, 827 show a guide-yoke which does not extend across the engine; it has a foot $a$ forged to it, which is bolted to the frame; the holes $d\ d$ take the rocker-box bolts; this box also serves to hold the guide-yoke in position. The upper end is riveted to the boiler by the angle iron $b$. The holes $c\ c$ take the shanks of the guide blocks. The opening $e$ must be made long enough to clear the connecting-rod. This brace is often used on eight-wheeled passenger engines. Its thickness is $\frac{3}{4}$ or $\frac{7}{8}$ inch in large engines, and a thickness of $\frac{5}{8}$ inch is sufficient for smaller ones. Figs. 828, 829 show the second kind of guide-yoke; it is generally used on consolidation engines, and frequently on Mogul and ten-wheeled engines. Some-

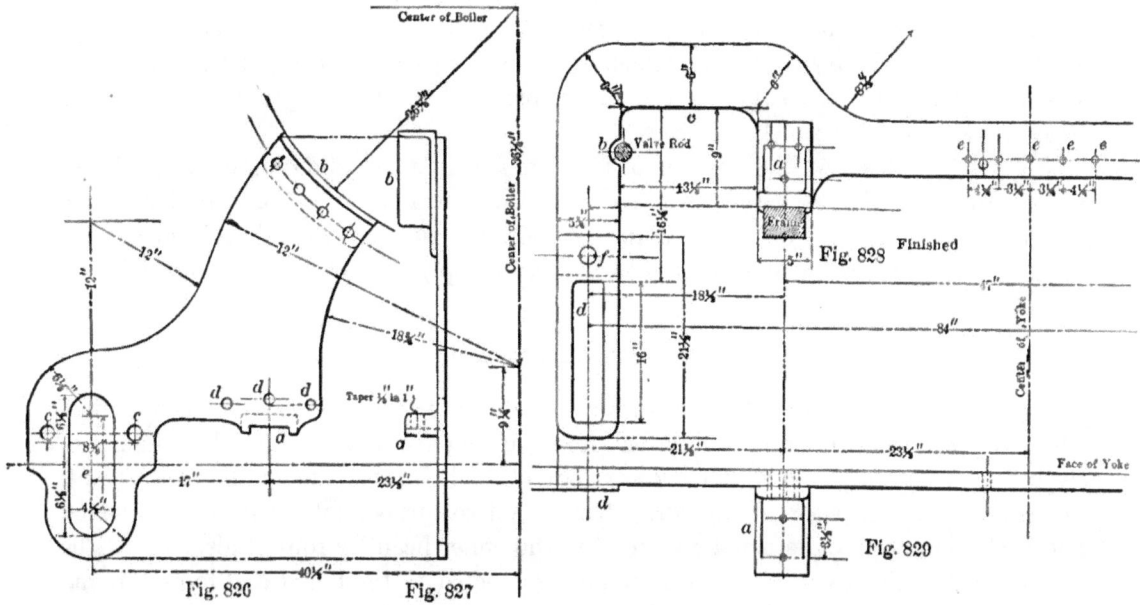

times the feet by which the guide-yoke is fastened to the frames are forged to it, but we believe that the best practice is to use cast-iron brackets $a$ bolted to it and to the frames, as shown in the figures.

The edge $c$ must be of sufficient height above the frames to clear the side-rods. At $b$ the brace is cut out to clear the valve-rod. The piece $d$ is simply a guard for the connecting-rod. The hole $f$ takes the shank of the guide block.

529. A wrought-iron plate, usually called the belly-brace, about $\frac{3}{8}$ or $\frac{1}{2}$ inch thick, is bolted to the center of the brace at $e\ e\ e$, Fig. 828, extending to the bottom of the boiler. This plate is either flanged, or has an angle iron riveted to it to fit the boiler. This flange or angle iron should not be fastened to the boiler, as it is in some cases. The object of the belly-brace is simply to prevent a lateral movement of the frames, which the curvature of the upper flange or angle iron will do without fastening it to the boiler.

530. Fig. 830 shows the position of the frame braces in an eight-wheeled passenger engine. The brace $A$ is bolted to the frame, and extends to the boiler, to which it is riveted. Separate views of this brace are shown in Figs. 831, 832. The brace $B$ (Fig. 830) extends from one frame to the other, and is bolted to them by studs.

Separate views of this brace are shown in Figs. 833, 834. A belly-brace, shown in Figs. 835, 836, is bolted to it. The holes $a$ (Fig. 835) take the rod for the lifting-shaft spring balance.

The brace $C$ (Fig. 830) is an ordinary lip-brace; it is shown separately in Fig. 837.

531. Fig. 838 shows the position of frame braces in a Mogul engine. These engines have a two-wheeled truck, and consequently the braces $A\ A$ in rear of the bumper beam are required for the truck center-pin guide. These braces are shown separately in Fig. 839. A cast-iron thimble $B$ is in some engines placed between the two frame splices $S$ and $T$, and the whole bolted together. The braces $C\ C$ simply extend from frame to frame, and have a belly-brace. They are shown separately in Fig. 840. $D\ D$ represent ordinary lip-braces, which are shown separately in Fig. 837. The brace $E$ takes the pin for and supports the radius bar of the truck; separate views of this brace are shown in Fig. 841.

532. Fig. 842 shows the position of frame braces in a consolidation engine. These braces are lettered in the same way as for a Mogul frame, Fig. 838. Similar letters indicate the same kind of brace in the two engines, so that what has been said in regard to the braces in Mogul engines will also apply to those in the consolidation engine.

### FOOT-PLATE BRACES.

533. A foot-plate brace $B$ is shown in Figs. 843, 844; two are used for each engine. They are generally made of round-bar iron, varying from 2 to $2\frac{1}{2}$ inches diameter according to size of engine. The lower foot of each brace rests on the top of foot-plate $A$, and is secured to it and draw-bar $C$ by two turned bolts driven into reamed holes. The upper foot is usually secured to the boiler head by four studs. It will be noticed that in this case the brace is rigidly connected to the boiler and foot-plate, no attention being given to the expansion of the boiler; the brace is supposed to spring enough for the expansion. The advantage claimed for this rigid connection is that it tends to prevent the frames from being permanently injured at $D$ when the rear end of the engine has to be hoisted for taking out the driving wheels, because when this has to be done the pedestal cap must of course be removed, thereby exposing the weak part $D$ of the frames to the danger of bending. In some cases the bolt holes in the lower foot of the brace are made oblong to allow for the expansion, but from what has been said it may be inferred, and correctly too, that this practice is liable to injure the frame at $D$, and therefore it is not often followed. It is also very doubtful whether the oblong holes will in every case answer their purpose, because in cases of this kind the braces are made of flat-iron 4 to 5 inches wide and from 1 to $1\frac{1}{4}$ inches thick, which makes a very stiff brace, and when the boiler expands it is liable to cant so as to wedge the foot between the bolt-heads and the foot-plate, thereby rendering the oblong holes useless for their intended purpose. We prefer the brace and the manner of fastening it as shown in Fig. 843.

In some engines there are no foot-plate braces used; in such cases special provisions are made for hoisting the rear end of engine.

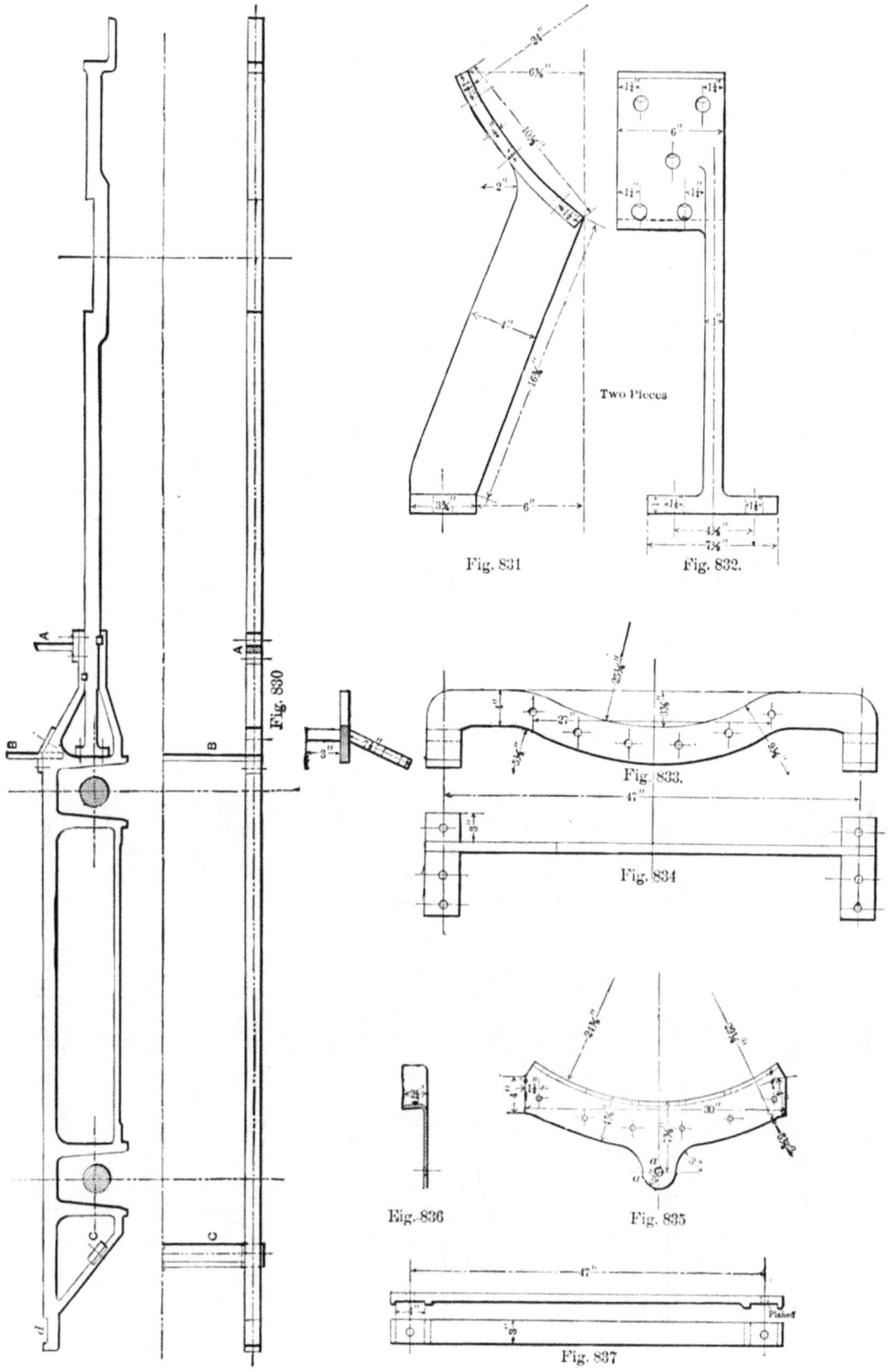

Fig. 830  Fig. 831  Fig. 832.  Fig. 833.  Fig. 834  Fig. 836  Fig. 835  Fig. 837

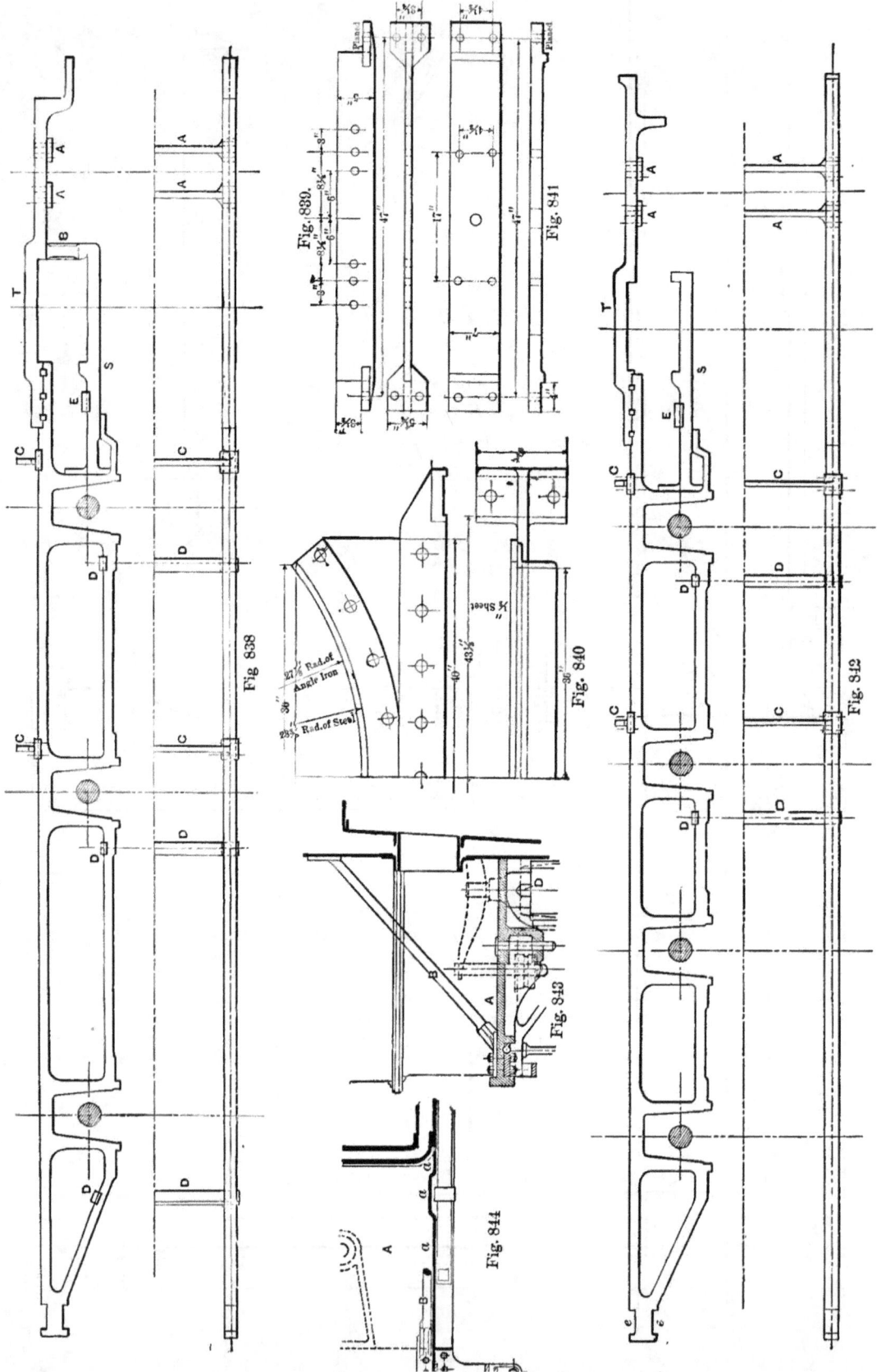

## FOOT-PLATES.

534. Figs. 845, 846, 847, 848 show different views of a cast-iron foot-plate $A$. It reaches from the rear end of the draw-bar $D$ to within ¾ inch of the boiler, and finishes flush with the outside of the frames, with the exception of the small portions $a\ a$ (Fig. 845), which are cut out to clear the spring saddles. A part $h$ of the rear end lips over the draw-bar $D$, and forms a rubbing plate. A rib $k$ butts against the front edge of the draw-bar $D$, and the ribs $m\ m$ bear against the inner sides of the frames. The ribs $l\ l$ extend from the rib $k$ to the pocket $n$, which

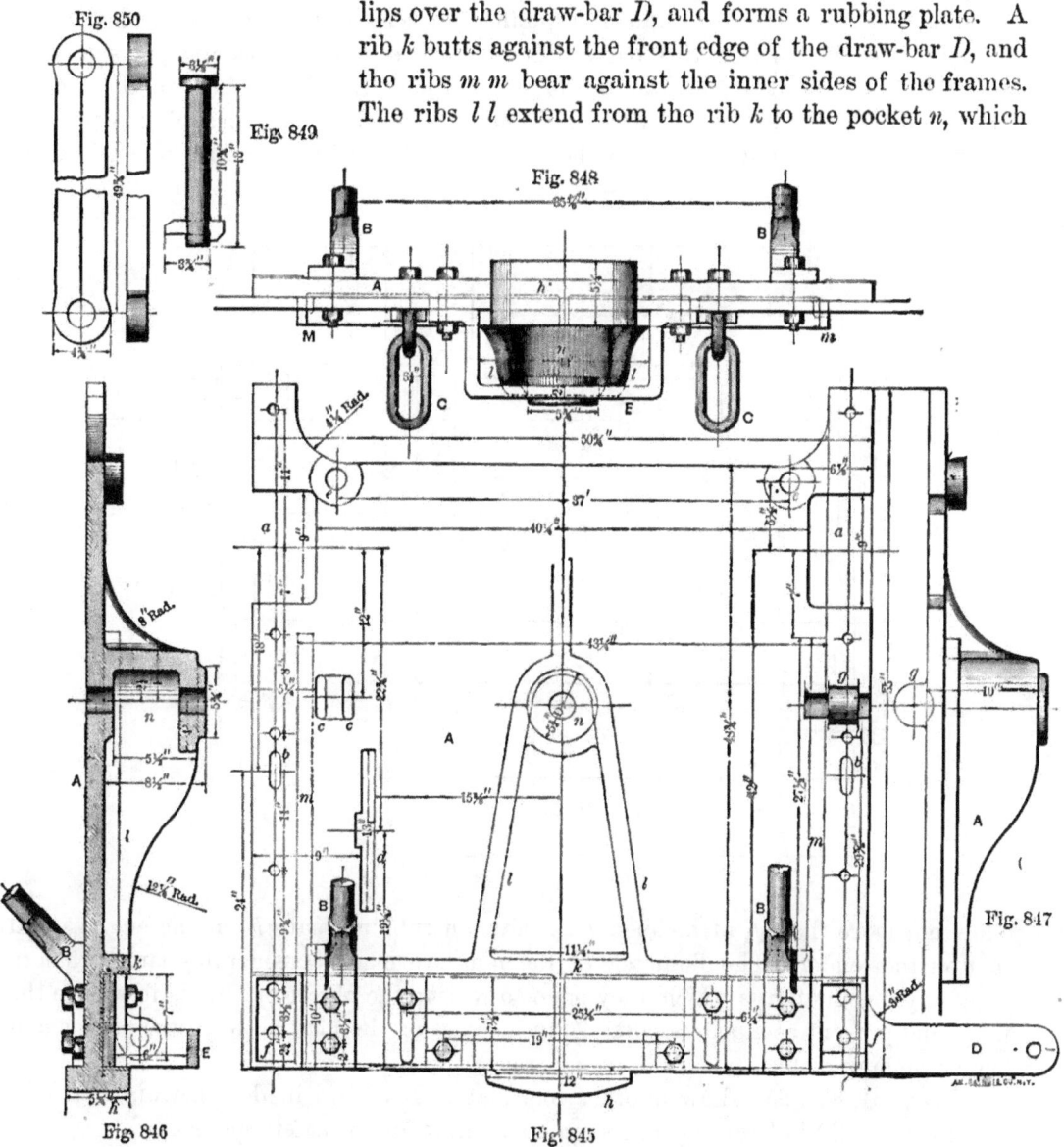

holds the pulling-bar pin shown separately in Fig. 849. The pocket $n$ should always be placed as far forward as possible, so as to relieve the frames of lateral stresses.

The spring hangers pass through the slots $b\ b$ cut through foot-plate and frames; the ash-pan damper handles pass through the slots $c\ c$, and the shaking lever works in the slot *d*. The holes *e e* are cast through the front end of the plate for the feed-cock rods, which are required only when pumps are used. The hub *g g* takes the end of the reverse lever. *B B* show the lower ends of the foot-plate braces; *C C*, the safety links which couple to the safety hooks attached to the tender; and *E* shows the pulling-bar support.

Fig. 850 shows the wrought-iron pulling-bar which connects the tender to the engine. The pin holes in this bar are bored; one of them takes the pin shown in Fig. 849, and the other one takes the pin through the draw-head on the tender. These pins should always be turned and made to fit the holes through the pulling-bar nicely. The distance between the centers of these holes should be such as to

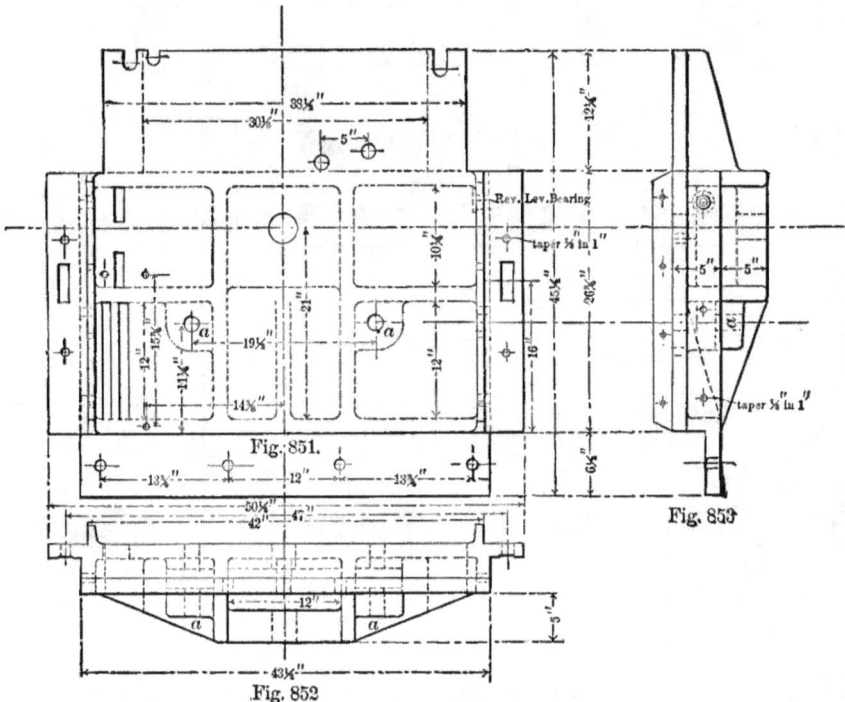

Fig. 851.
Fig. 852
Fig. 853

allow not more than $\frac{1}{16}$ of an inch play between rubbing-plate *h* on the engines and that on the tender. The diameters of the pins are made considerably larger than is necessary for the forces which they have to resist; the object of this is to reduce the wear, and prevent as much as possible an increase of the play between the engine and tender rubbing-plates.

Figs. 851, 852, 853 show another foot-plate. It differs in design from the foregoing principally in having pockets *a a a* cast in it for the safety chains.

Since weight at the rear end of an engine is in many cases not objectionable—in fact, it is often desirable—a liberal amount of metal is put in the foot-plates; they are much stronger than they need to be for the forces they have to resist.

A wooden floor is generally fastened to the top of the foot-plates.

## DRAW-BARS.

535. Fig. 854 shows two views of a draw-bar. It connects the ends of the two frames, and for this purpose it is notched at $a\ a$ and laid in the recess $d$ cut in the ends of frames (see Fig. 830); the ends of frames are finished flush with the rear edge of the bar. The ends $b\ b$ of the bar project beyond the outer sides of the frames and support the house brackets, of which separate views are shown in Figs. 858 to 861. This form

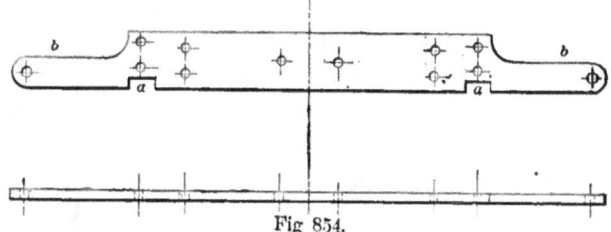

Fig. 854.

of draw-bar is generally used in eight-wheeled passenger engines, or engines which have a foot-plate. Sometimes the draw-bar is placed in a vertical position and bolted to the ends of the frames. The projecting ends of this draw-bar also support the house brackets, but in cases of this kind the foot of the house bracket is formed as shown in Figs. 864, 865.

In consolidation engines, or other classes of engines in which hard coal is burnt, the boiler extends to within a short distance of the ends of the frames, leaving no room for a cast-iron or other kind of foot-plate. In these engines a form of draw-bar as

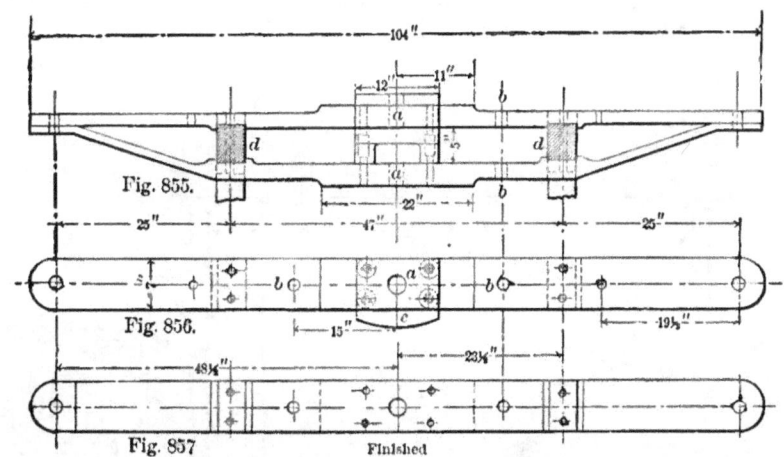

shown in Fig. 855 is used; Fig. 856 shows a plan of the upper bar, and Fig. 857 that of the lower one. These bars are fitted into recesses cut in the ends $d\ d$ of the frames; these recesses are shown at $e\ e$, Fig. 842. The holes $a\ a$, Figs. 855, 856, take the pulling-bar pin, and the holes $b\ b$ take the safety-chain pins. The chaffing block $c$ is bolted between the two bars.

## HOUSE BRACKETS.

536. Figs. 858, 859, 860, 861 show different views of a house bracket, which is used in connection with the draw-bar shown in Fig. 854. The house bracket is bolted to the draw-bar $d$ by the shank of the step column $e$ and the bolt $l$; it is also bolted to the engine frames $f$, the foot-plate $a$, and the draw-bar by the shank of the feed-pipe hanger

530   MODERN LOCOMOTIVE CONSTRUCTION.

$h$ and the bolt $m$. The flange $i$, which is cast to the bracket, holds the side-sheet which extends forward to the boiler, and whose width extends from the top of foot-plate to the underside of the running board $b$. A longitudinal section of this side-sheet is shown at $a\ a\ a$ in Fig. 844.

The wheel cover of the form shown in Fig. 862 is bolted to flange $k$. The house or cab $H$ is bolted to the running board $b$. The wrought-iron cab handle

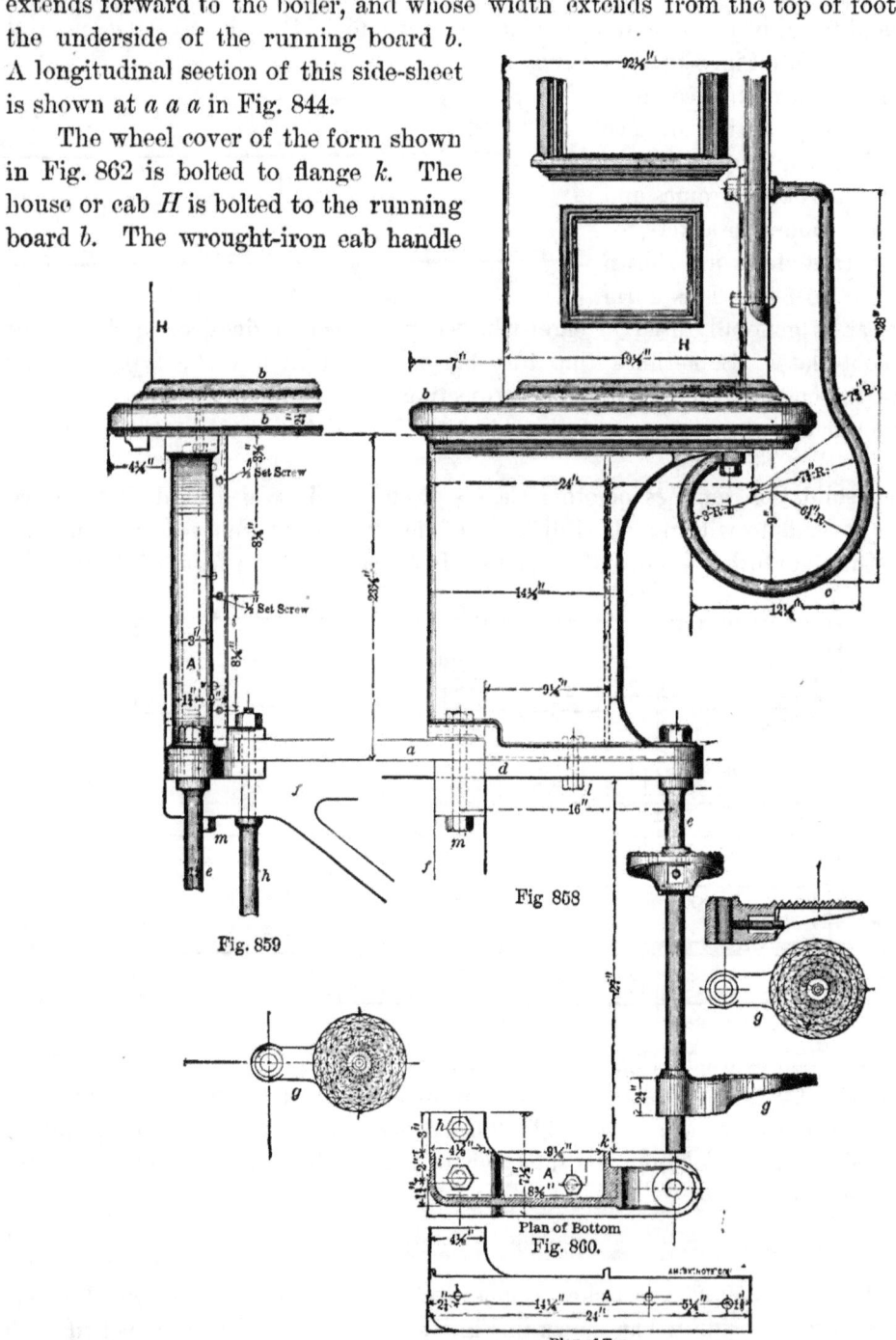

is marked $c$. Another form of wheel cover is shown in Fig. 863. It is usually bolted to the frame by two brackets, and sometimes it is also bolted to the running board.

MODERN LOCOMOTIVE CONSTRUCTION. 531

Some master-mechanics prefer the latter because it prevents the mud from being thrown on the working parts of the engine.

Figs. 864, 865, 866 show another house bracket; it is used in connection with drawbars placed vertically, as mentioned in Art. 535. The cab handle *c* is cast to the bracket.

### RUNNING BOARDS.

537. The running boards are fastened to the sides of the boiler. They are made of various lengths and forms; in a few cases they are three or four inches longer than

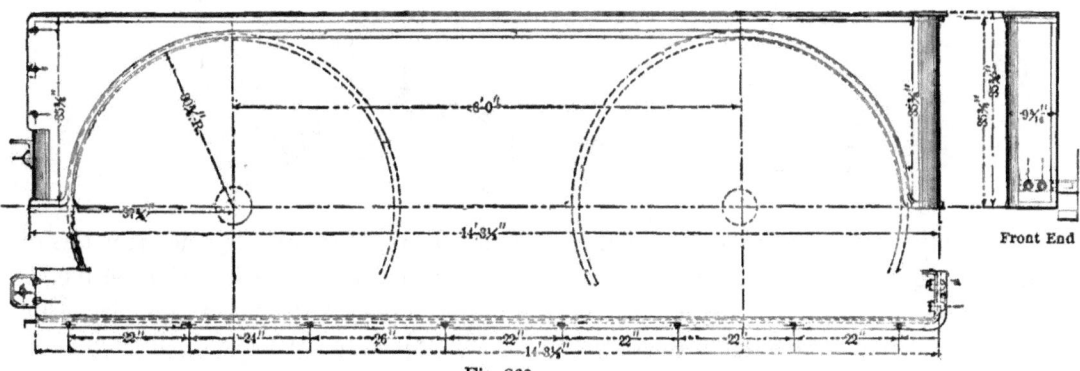

Fig. 862

the cab, but frequently they extend from the rear end of the cab to the smokebox. In ordinary passenger and freight engines, the rear end of the running board is supported by the house bracket, and along the side of the boiler it is supported by wrought-iron brackets placed from 28 to 36 inches from center to center; separate views of these brackets are shown in Fig. 872; these are generally riveted, sometimes bolted, to the boiler. Running boards are frequently made of wood usually 2 inches thick, with their outside edges faced with sheet-brass, or iron bands or angle iron; the latter, we believe, makes the best job.

Fig. 867 shows a wooden running board. Sometimes they are made of wrought-iron, steel, or cast-iron. Fig. 870 shows one made of steel finished off with an angle iron riveted to its outer edges.

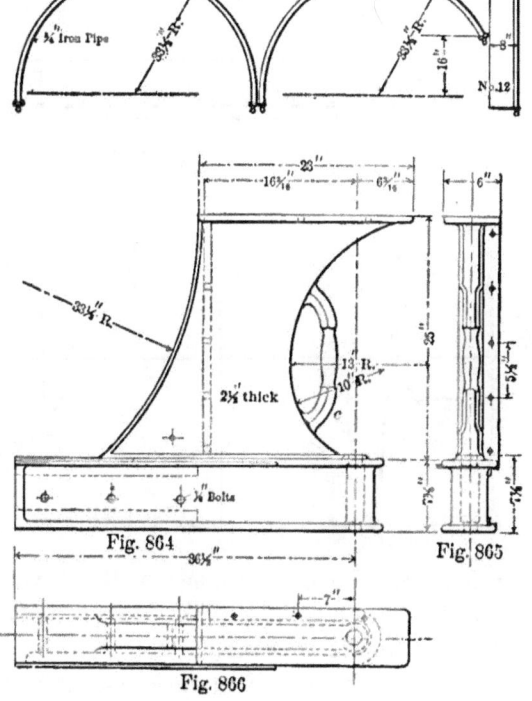

In regular passenger engines, such as is shown in Fig. 1, the engineer stands on the foot-plate; and in consolidation engines with the boiler extending to the draw-bar, or in other hard-coal burning engines which have no foot-plate, the engineer stands on the running board. For determining the distance at which the running board is to be placed above the foot-plate, good judgment must be used. In engines with foot-plates the running board is placed at a convenient height to serve as a seat

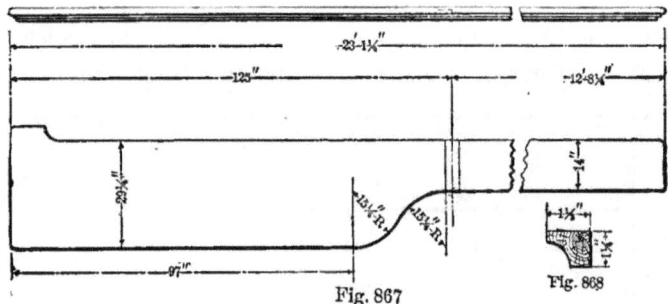

Fig. 867    Fig. 868

for the engineer and fireman. Sometimes this height is determined by the diameters of the driving wheels; if these are large, the running board is placed at about 4 inches above the flanges of the drivers, and in many passenger engines they are placed an inch or two above the reach-rod which connects the reversing lever to the lifting-shaft

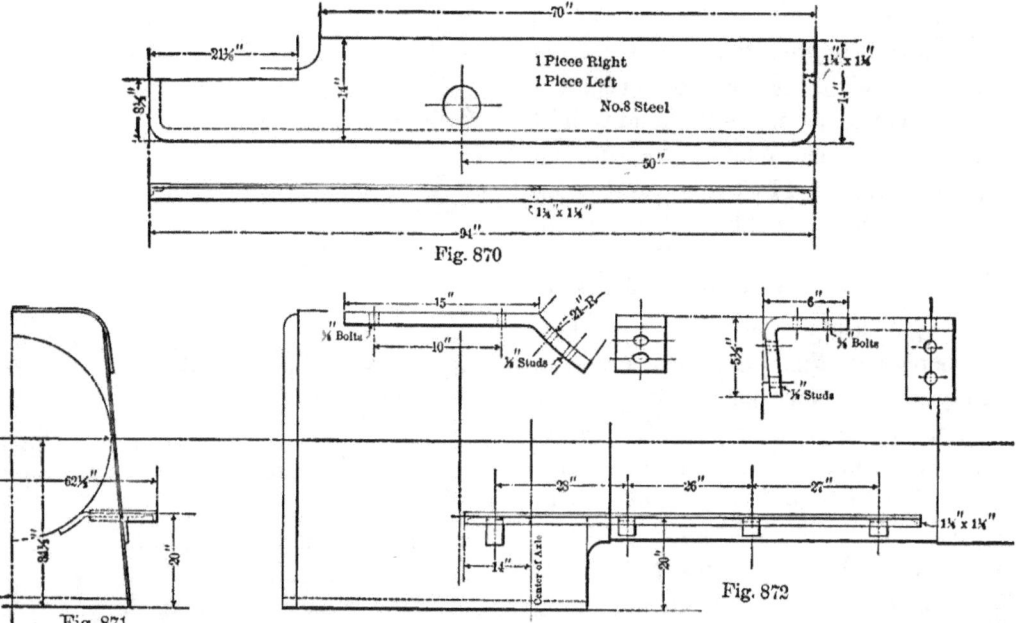

In hard-coal burning engines, or those which have no foot-plate, the running board is placed at a height which will enable the engineer to reach any of the cocks or valves placed on top of the boiler.

In some classes of engines, particularly switching engines, no house brackets are used, the cab being placed directly on the foot-plate. In such cases the position of the running board is a matter of choice and good judgment.

Figs. 871, 872 show the position of a running board for an engine with the cab placed on the foot-plate.

## CABS.

538. Figs. 873, 874 show different views of an ordinary cab. Its height often depends on the position of the running board. For engines in which the engineer stands on the foot-plate, the minimum clear height above the foot-plate should not be

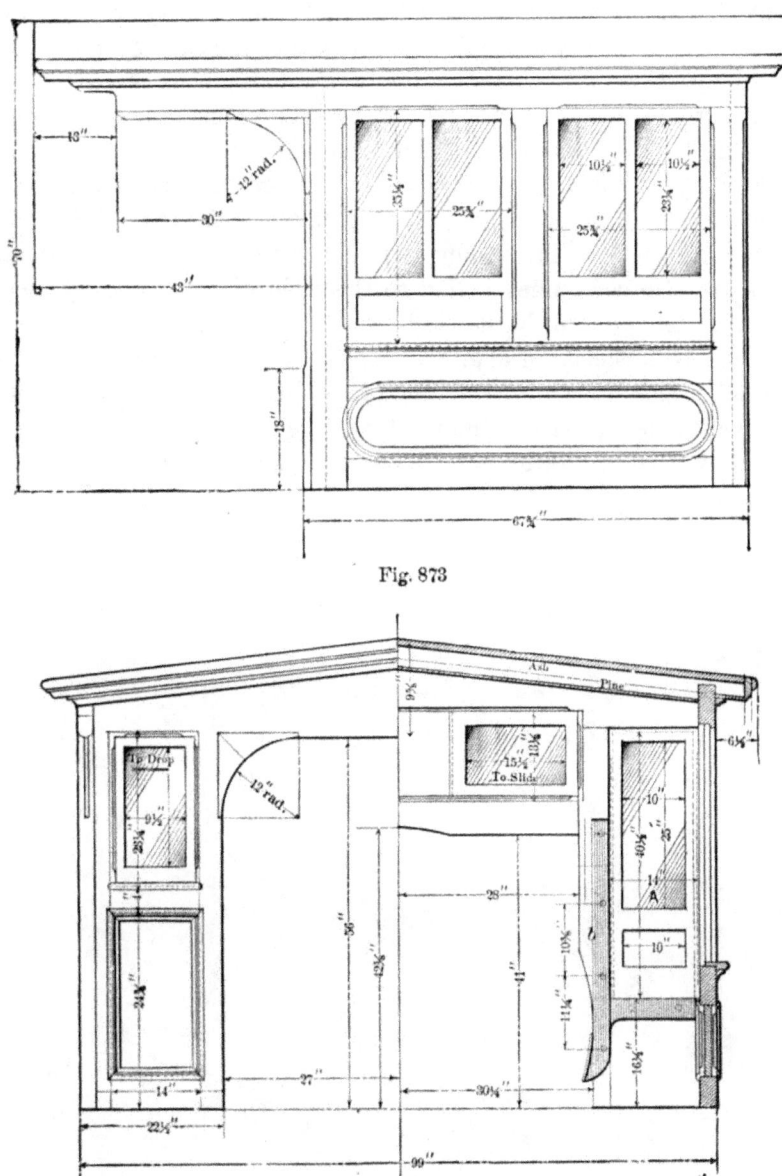

Fig. 873

Fig. 874

less than 6 feet; and for engines in which the engineer stands on the running board the minimum height should be 6 feet above the latter.

In engines with foot-plates the distance from the rear boiler head to the front end of the cab varies from 12 to 15 inches, so as to allow sufficient room for the valves and cocks which are attached to the boiler; and the cab is made wide enough to allow room in the front end for a door $A$ at each side of the boiler; these doors should be at least 14 inches wide.

In engines without foot-plates the width between the sides of the boiler and the inside of cab should not be less than 20 inches; 24 inches is better, if the width of the road will allow it. In nearly all engines the length of the cab depends on the length of arc described by the end of the reverse-lever handle; usually from 9 to 12 inches between the extreme positions of the reverse-lever handle and ends of the cab is allowed, making the cab from 5 feet 6 inches to 6 feet long.

A space of about 2 inches is usually left between the woodwork in the front end and the boiler shell, and this opening is closed by wrought-iron plates $b$ fitted closely to the boiler and bolted to the woodwork; they serve as braces for holding the cab. These plates are also sometimes bolted to the shell of the boiler by angle plates or brackets. In consolidation or hard-coal burning engines, doors are required in the rear end of the cab. In this class of engines the space between the rear end of the cab and the boiler head is closed by wrought-iron plates, leaving the furnace door exposed so that the boiler can be fired from the tender. The front windows in the sides of the cab are generally fixed in position, and the rear ones are made to slide for the convenience of looking out.

# CHAPTER XIII.

### ENGINE TRUCKS.

539. Figs. 875, 876, 877, 878 show different views of the ordinary four-wheeled truck. The axle-boxes $A$ work in cast-iron pedestals $B$, which are bolted to the wrought-iron frame $C$. Sometimes these pedestals are made of wrought-iron; the general form of these is shown in Fig. 879. The frame is supported by two springs $D\ D$ (one on each side), and these are attached by their hangers to the equalizing bars $E$, one on each side of the spring. The ends of these bars are turned downwards and rest in pockets cast in the upper end of the axle-box. We believe the better way is to make the ends of these bars perfectly plain and allow them to rest on a convex surface of the box, as shown in Fig. 881. A longitudinal brace $F$ (Fig. 876) on each side of the truck connects the bottoms of the pedestals. The center swing casting $I$ is supported by four hangers which swing on the pins $H$, and these are supported by the transverse bars $G\ G$ bolted to the top of frame. The lips $a\ a$ cast to the

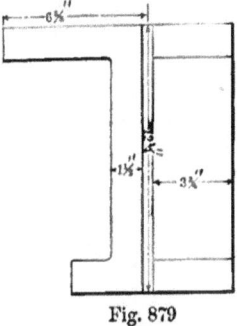

Fig. 879

center casting $I$ are for the purpose of holding up the front end of the engine in case a hanger has been broken. The annular groove $b$ on top of the casting receives the center pin which is bolted to the cylinder saddles. The outer diameter of this groove should not be much greater than 11 inches, because by increasing this diameter the leverage with which the friction between the pin and casting acts will also be increased, and may prevent the truck from turning as freely as it should do in running over a curve, and may cause it to run off the track.

The transverse bars $G$ are stiffened sideways by the longitudinal braces $K\ K$.

Two shackles $L$ for the safety chain are generally bolted to the front end of the frame, the other ends of the chains are attached to the bumper or to the engine frames.

Figs. 880, 881, 882, 883 show different views of another four-wheeled engine truck. The principal difference between the foregoing truck and this one is that in the latter the swing center casting $I$ is supported by a cast-iron center plate $M$ instead of wrought-iron transverse bars; otherwise the designs are similar, so that a further description of this truck is unnecessary.

Figs. 880, 881 show the wheel covers attached to the truck frame, and although this is good practice, it is by no means a universal one. In many cases the wheel

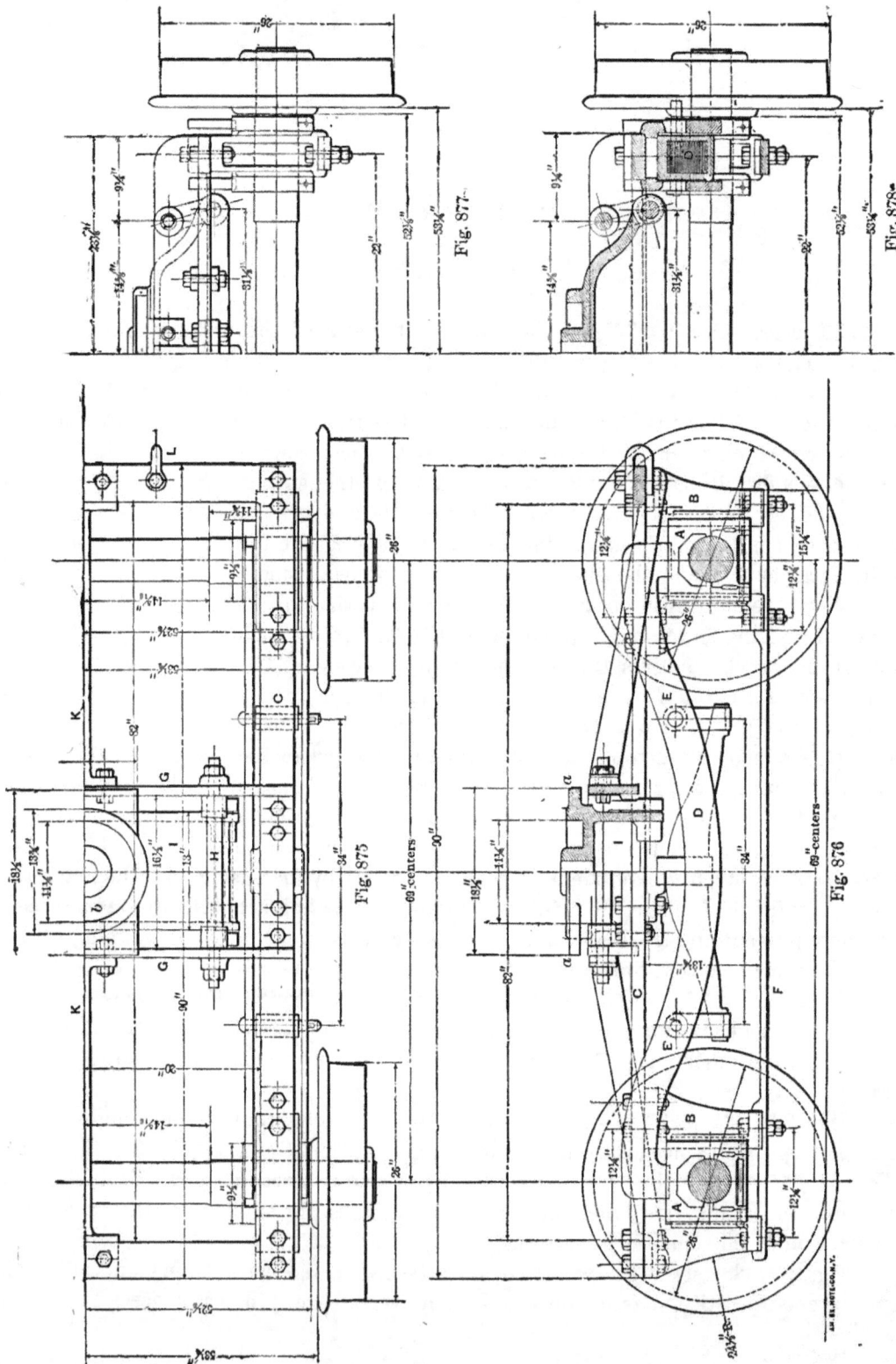

# MODERN LOCOMOTIVE CONSTRUCTION.

537

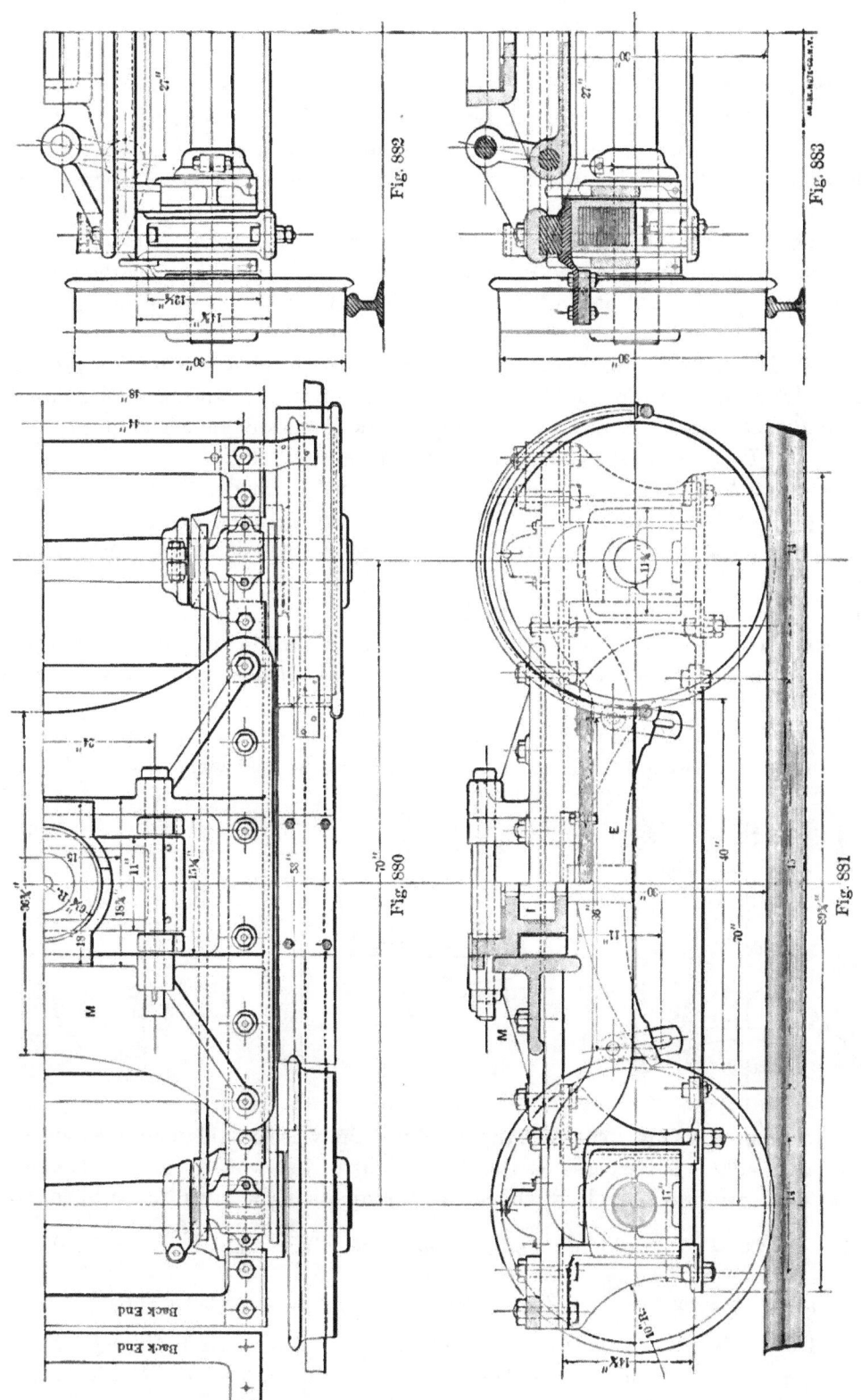

covers are fastened to the engine frames and are made much wider than shown in Fig. 880, so that they will always cover the wheels when running over a curve.

On some roads, swing center castings are not used; in such cases a center plate as shown in Figs. 884, 885 is often adopted; the annular groove $b$ takes the center pin as before.

Fig. 886A, 886B, and 886C show different views of another four-wheeled truck. This truck was designed by the Pennsylvania R. R., and is used under their Standard passenger engines illustrated in Fig. 998. The construction is so plainly shown that further explanation is not necessary.

540. The distance from center to center of axles must be such as to prevent the wheels from striking the cylinder heads when the engine is running over a curve. It is found that 68 to 70 inches between the centers of axles is sufficient for all ordinary curves and for a piston stroke not exceeding 24 inches.

The equalizing bars $E\ E$ (see Fig. 876) are generally made 1 inch thick, hence the usual problem is to find the depth of the bar. When bars are symmetrically formed and symmetrically loaded, we need to consider only one-half of the bar, as shown in Fig. 886.

To illustrate let us take the following:

EXAMPLE 147.—Find the depth of the equalizing bar $E$ (Fig. 876), 1 inch thick, for an eight-wheeled passenger engine with cylinders 18 inches diameter and 24 inches stroke.

Referring to Table 5, we find that the total weight on the truck is 28,680 pounds. This includes the weight of the truck; hence, to find the load which the equalizing bars

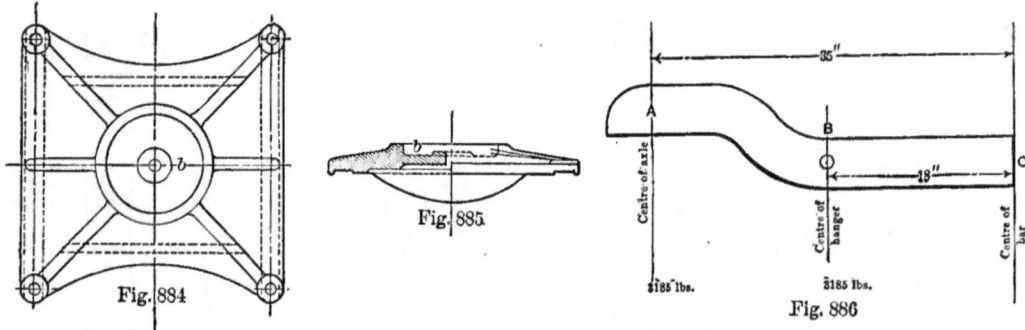

have to support, we must subtract the weight of the wheels, axles, and axle-boxes from the total weight. Let us assume that the weight of the wheels, etc., is 3,200 pounds; under these conditions the load which the four equalizing bars will have to support is $28680 - 3200 = 25480$ pounds; and the load on each bar will be $\dfrac{25480}{4} = 6370$ pounds. One-half of this load, $\dfrac{6370}{2} = 3185$ pounds, is supported by each spring-hanger pin (Fig. 886) at 18 inches from the center of the bar. The reaction of each axle-box is also equal to 3,185 pounds. All these conditions are represented in Fig. 886, which shows one-half of the bar. At $B$, 18 inches from the center $C$, equal to one-half the distance between the spring-hanger pins, we have a force of 3,185 pounds acting ver-

MODERN LOCOMOTIVE CONSTRUCTION. 539

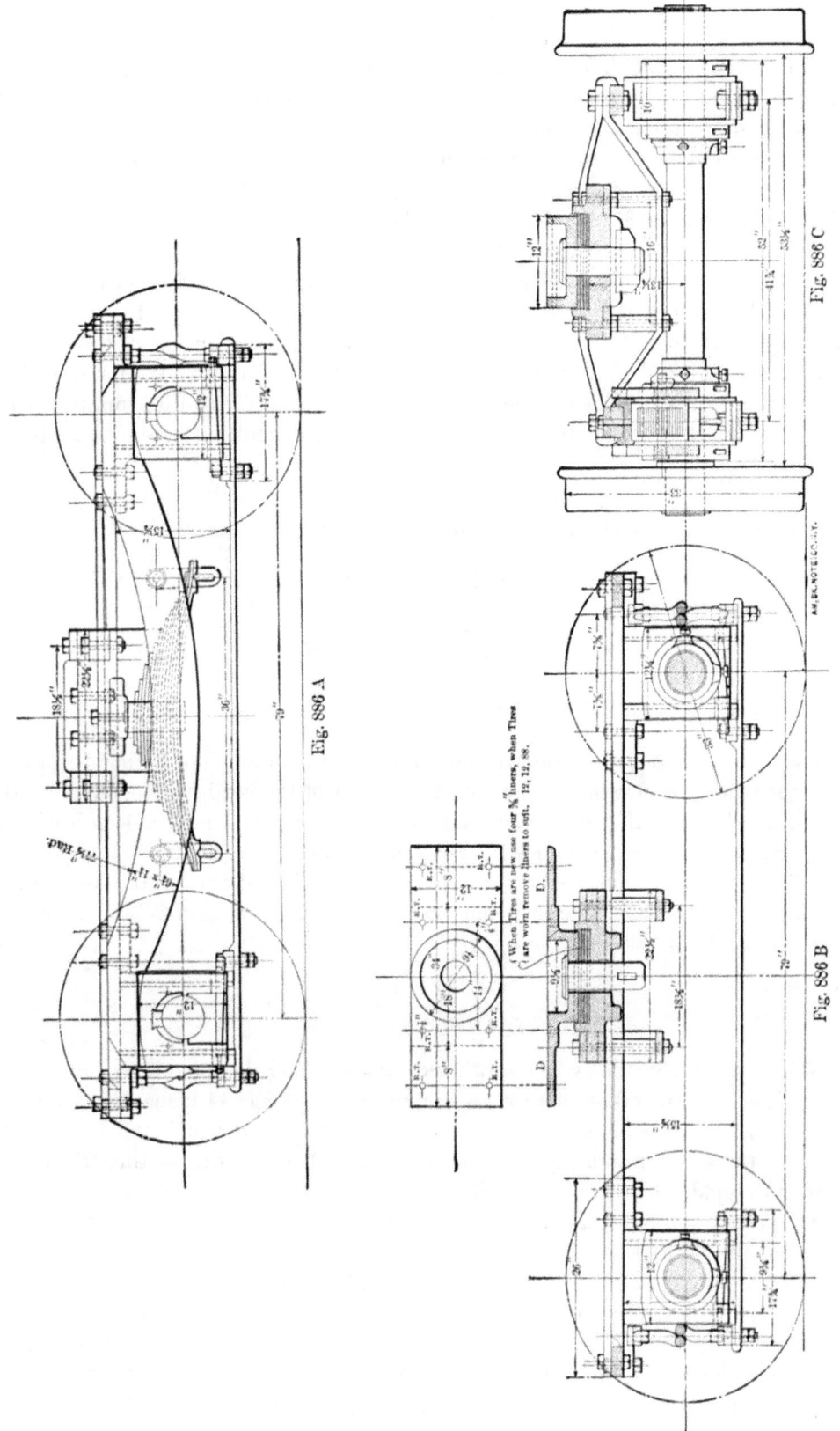

Fig. 886 A
Fig. 886 B
Fig. 886 C

tically downwards; at $A$, 35 inches from $C$, equal to one-half the distance between the centers of the axles, we have a force of 3,185 pounds acting vertically upwards. The force $B$ tends to turn the lever downwards about some point in $C$, and the force $A$ tends to turn the lever in the opposite direction. The effects of these forces in producing rotation are measured by their moments. According to Art. 256 the moment of the force $B$ is equal to $3185 \times 1.5 = 4777.5$ foot-pounds, and the moment of the force $A$ is equal to $3185 \times 2.91 = 9268.35$ foot-pounds. Subtracting the moments of $B$ from that of $A$, we have $9268.35 - 4777.5 = 4490.85$ foot-pounds, and this is bending moment to which the lever in Fig. 886 is subjected; let us designate it by $M$. The resisting moment is equal to $b \times d^2 \times S$, in which $b$ is the breadth in inches of the bar; $d$, its depth in inches; and $S$, a constant multiplier depending on the kind and quality of the material. For wrought-iron we may adopt 200. Now, for equilibrium the bending moment $M$ must be equal to resisting moment; this condition is represented by the following formula:

$$M = b \times d^2 \times S.$$

Now replacing the symbols by their values, we have

$$4490.85 = 1 \times d^2 \times 200,$$

from which we get

$$\frac{4490.85}{200} = 22.4542 = d^2,$$

and

$$d = \sqrt{22.4542} = 4.73 \text{ inches.}$$

Here we have made no allowance for the hole which must be drilled through the bar at the section $B$, nor have we taken the weight of the bar into account; but these will not affect the result much—indeed, if we make the bar $4\frac{7}{8}$ inches deep it will have sufficient strength to resist the load. For a more precise method of finding the resistance of materials, we must refer the reader to the "Text-Book of the Mechanics of Materials and of Beams, Columns, and Shafts," by Professor Mansfield Merriman, one of the best books treating on these subjects.

## TWO-WHEELED TRUCK.

541. Figs. 887, 888 show a two-wheeled truck, which is sometimes called a pony truck. This truck was designed for an engine with cylinders 14 inches diameter. The weight of the front end of the engine is sustained by the equalizing bar $A$, which works on the fulcrum pin $R$, and this in turn is held by the casting $T$ bolted to the cylinder saddle.

Frequently two holes about 5 inches from center to center are drilled for the pin $R$ through the lever $A$ and casting $T$; the pin is placed in either one of these holes, whereby the weight on the truck can to some extent be adjusted to suit the requirements of the engine. In some engines the fulcrum pin $R$ is not used; the upper face of the equalizing bar $A$ rests against a convex surface formed in the cylinder saddles or a pocket bolted to the saddles. But when a fulcrum pin $R$ is used we see no reason for placing it out of the center (vertically), as is often done, and as is shown in

Fig. 887; indeed, there is an objection to this, as it makes the bar weaker than when the pin is placed in the center.

The rear end of the equalizing bar $A$ is connected by a link $B$ (see Fig. 887) to a transverse equalizing bar $C$, which is connected to the driving-wheel spring hangers

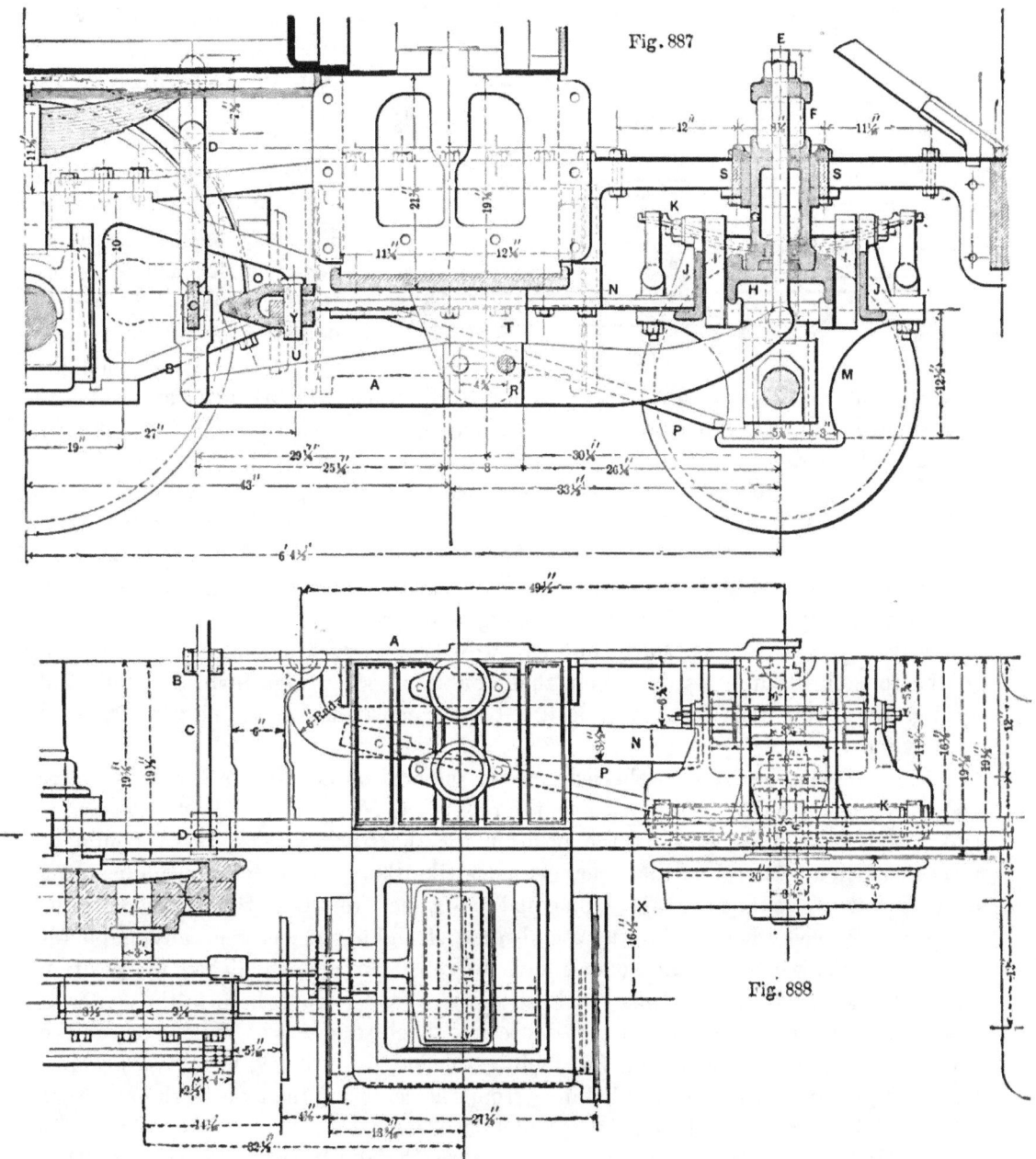

$DD$. The front end of the equalizing bar $A$ is connected to the king-bolt $E$, which transmits the pressure on to the cylindrical rubber spring $F$; sometimes a steel spiral spring, as shown at $F$ in Fig. 891, is used in place of the rubber. The spring rests on the center pin $G$ (Fig. 887), which is supported by the swing center casting $H$.

This center pin G slides up and down in the cast-iron guide which is bolted to the transverse engine braces S S.

The hangers I I connect the swing center casting to the cast-iron frame J, of which separate views are shown in Figs. 894, 895. This frame is supported by the

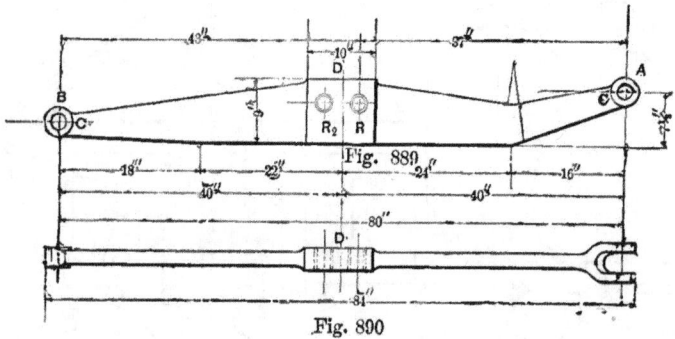

Fig. 889
Fig. 890

truck springs K K, which rest on the spring saddles, and these are in turn supported by the axle-boxes.

The cast-iron pedestals M are bolted to the frame J. The rear end of the radius bar N is supported by the transverse brace O, which is bolted to the engine frames; the brace O also holds the pin Y around which the radius bar swings; the front ends of the latter are bolted to the frame J, and an oblique brace P on each side of the truck connects the pedestals to the radius bar.

Figs. 891, 892, 893 show another two-wheeled truck designed for a consolidation engine with cylinders 20 inches diameter. The construction of this truck is similar to that of the one just described, with the exception that a wrought-iron frame J of rectangular form is used in place of a cast-iron one; the transverse braces L L bolted to this frame support the swing center casting as before.

Figs. 897, 898, 899, 900 show another two-wheeled truck of similar construction to the foregoing, with this exception, that double spiral springs instead of elliptical springs are used. This truck was designed for a consolidation engine with 20 × 24 inch cylinder.

542. The length of a two-wheeled truck is the horizontal distance from the center of the axle to the center of the pin Y in the radius bar N (see Fig. 887). To determine this distance we must first fix the position for the truck wheels; these should be placed sufficiently ahead so that they cannot strike the cylinder heads when running over a curve. A distance X (Fig. 888), equal to 6 inches from the cylinder heads to the side of the wheels when the engine stands on a straight track, is generally ample for any curve over which the engine may have to run. Having established the position of the truck wheels, we have also established the distance from these to the center of the rigid wheel base. We mention this because this distance is of importance in the following graphical construction for finding the length of truck, which, as we have seen, is equal to the horizontal distance from the center of the axle to the center of the pin Y, Fig. 887, around which the radius bar swings.

To find the length of the truck, draw, as in Fig. 901A, two lines O Y and O X perpendicular to each other, meeting in the point O; make O Y and O X equal to the distance from the center of the rigid wheel base to the center of the truck wheels. On the line O X lay off a point A; the distance from A to O must be equal to one-half of the rigid wheel base. Join the points A and Y by a straight line A Y, bisect this line by a perpendicular B C, cutting O Y in the point B; the distance O B will be

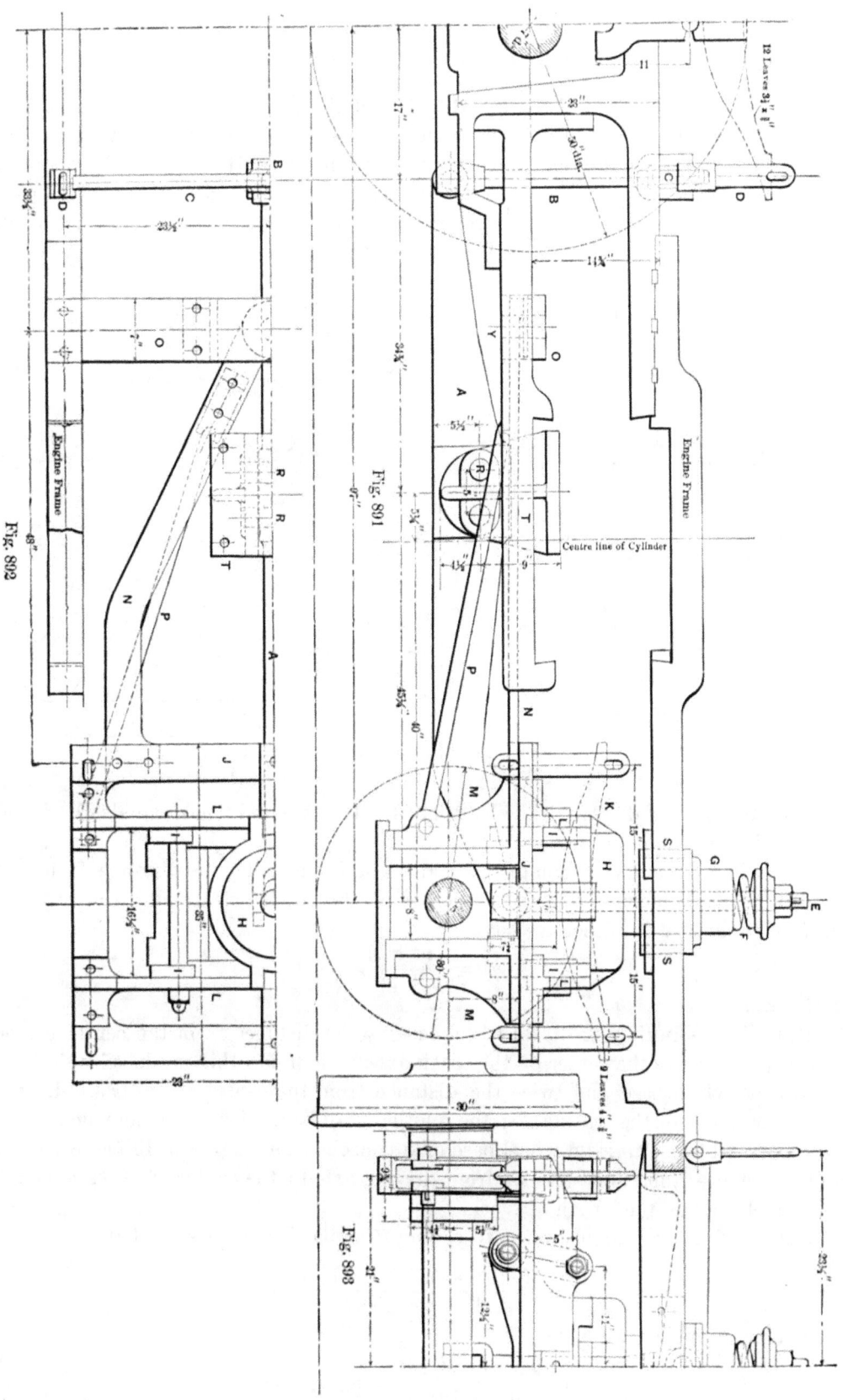

the length of the two-wheeled truck. It will be noticed that in this construction we have not taken the radius of the curve into account, and indeed we have a perfect right to omit it, because the radius of the curve will not affect the length of the truck; if it is correct for one radius, it will also be correct for any other radius. This construction holds good for all classes of engines having a two-wheeled truck; in all these engines the rigid wheel base is equal to the distance between the centers of

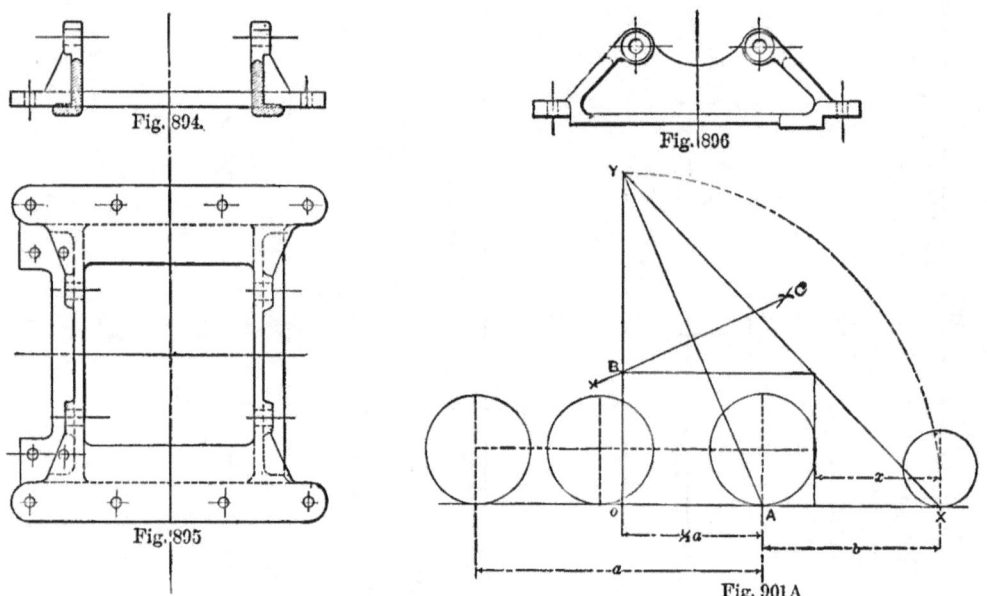

front and rear pair of drivers. The length of the two-wheeled truck can also be found by the following computation:

Let $a$ in Fig. 901A designate the rigid wheel base; $b$, the distance from the center of the front driving axle to the center of the truck axle; and $x$, the required length of engine truck. Then we have

$$x = \frac{b(a+b)}{a+2b},$$

which reads:

RULE 113.—Multiply the total wheel base by the distance from the center of the front driving axle to the center of the truck axle, and divide this product by the sum of the rigid wheel base and twice the distance from the center of the front driving axle to the center of the truck axle; the quotient will be the length of the truck.

EXAMPLE 148.—The rigid wheel base of a consolidation engine is 13 feet 8 inches, and the distance from the center of front driving axle to the center of truck axle is 7 feet 10 inches; find the length of truck.

Substituting for symbols in the foregoing formula their values, we have

$$x = \frac{7'\ 10'' \times (13'\ 8'' + 7'\ 10'')}{13'\ 8'' + 15'\ 8''},$$

or, reducing to inches, we have

$$x = \frac{94 \times (164 + 94)}{164 + 188} = 68.9 \text{ inches}$$

MODERN LOCOMOTIVE CONSTRUCTION. 545

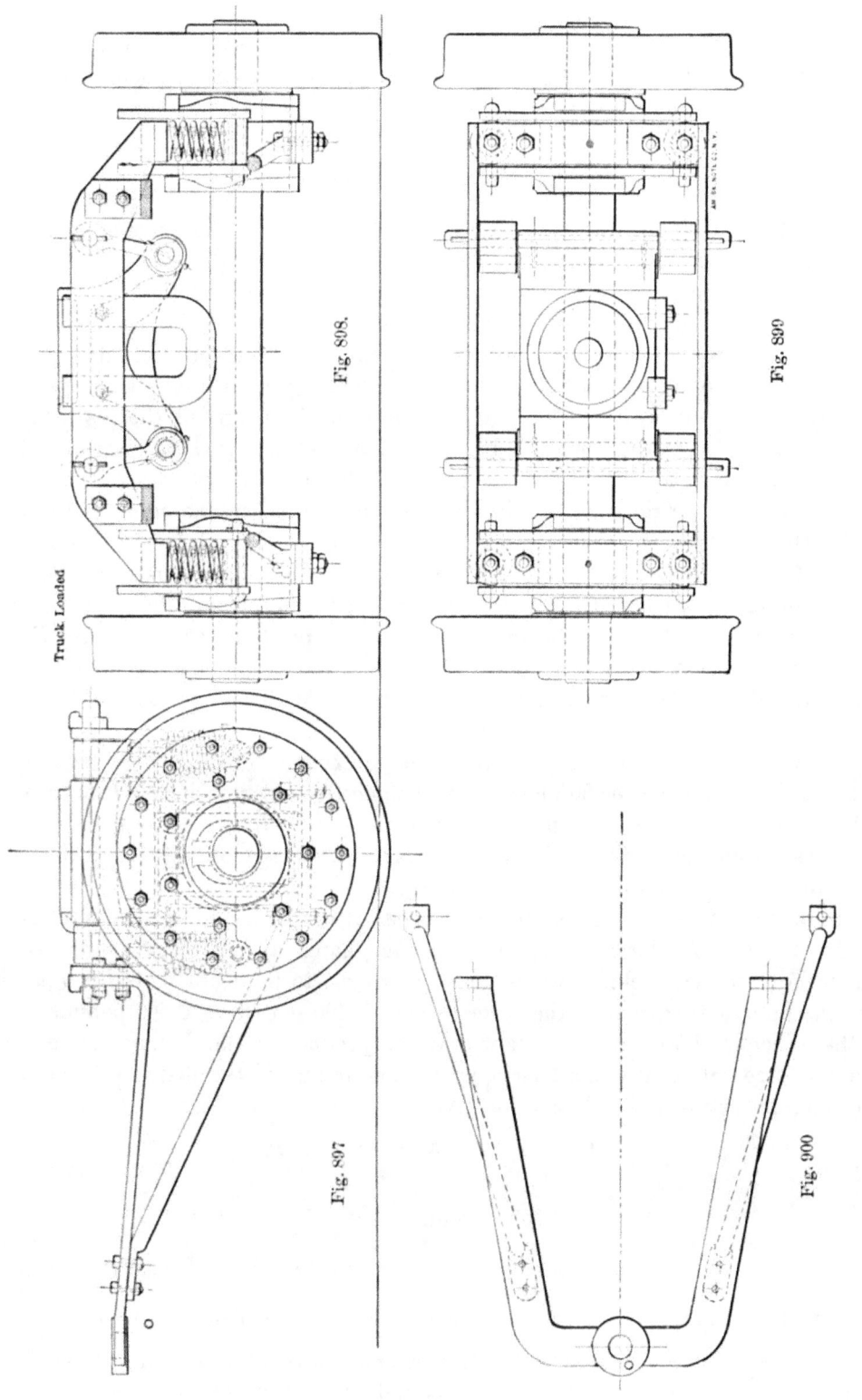

Fig. 898.
Truck Loaded
Fig. 899.
Fig. 897.
Fig. 900.

for the length of truck. This is the theoretical value. In practice it is customary to deduct 10 per cent. so as to insure against running off the track when the engine is running over a curve; this will give us a length of $68.9 - 6.89 = 62.01$, say 62 inches.

### ENGINE-TRUCK EQUALIZING LEVER.

**543.** The length of the equalizing lever $A$ (Fig. 887) is of course equal to the distance from the center of the truck axle to the front spring hangers $D$ of the front driving-wheel springs. We have already seen that the weight of the front end of the engine is carried by this equalizing lever; and it will readily be perceived that a portion of this weight is transmitted to the front hangers of the front driving-wheel springs, and the other portion is transmitted to the king-bolt through the truck center pin. If the fulcrum $R$ (Fig. 889) is in the center of the length of the lever, then the weight transmitted to the truck will be equal to that transmitted to the front driving-wheel spring hanger. But these springs act like a lever with its fulcrum at the center, hence the weight on the driving axle will in this case be equal to twice that transmitted to the spring hangers. But in many cases the fulcrum $R$ is not in the center of the length of the equalizing lever, and in practice we usually know only the weight on the truck. Hence the following practical problem often presents itself:

The weight on the truck being known, and the position of the fulcrum $R$ being established, it is required to find the weight transmitted to front driving-wheel springs, so that the size of the latter can be computed. To show how problems of this kind can be solved, we shall give an example.

EXAMPLE 149.—Let the length of the equalizing lever (Fig. 889) between the centers of holes $A$ and $B$ be 80 inches; the distance from center of hole $B$ to the center of fulcrum $R$ be 43 inches; then the distance from $A$ to $R$ will be 37 inches; let the whole weight on the truck wheels be 14,400 pounds. It is required to find the weight transmitted to the front driving-wheel springs.

In order to find the force acting on the end $A$ of the lever, we must subtract the weight of the truck wheels, axles, boxes, springs, hangers, and spring saddle from the total weight on the truck. Assume that the weight to be deducted is 1,900 pounds; then the force acting at $A$ of the lever will be $14400 - 1900 = 12500$ pounds. Now, by the principle of the lever we know that the product of the distance from $A$ to $R$ into the force acting at $A$ must be equal to the product of the distance from $B$ to $R$ into the force acting at $B$. Hence we have

$$12500 \times 37 = 43 \times \text{force at } B,$$

and

$$\frac{12500 \times 37}{43} = 10755.8 \text{ pounds for the force acting at } B.$$

But there are two driving-wheel springs to which this weight is transmitted, hence on the end of each spring we have a force acting vertically which is equal to $\frac{10755.8}{2} = 5377.9$ pounds, and at the center of each spring we have a force tending to straighten the spring equal to $5377.9 \times 2 = 10755.8$ pounds, and the spring must be made strong enough to resist this force or load.

544. At D (Fig. 890) the thickness of the equalizing lever is increased and the holes $R\ R_2$ are bushed with case-hardened wrought-iron thimbles so as to reduce the wear as much as possible.

To find the depth of the equalizing lever when its thickness has been established; or to find the thickness of the lever when its depth has been established, are problems which often present themselves to the designer; their solutions are readily found as follows:

Take, for example, the lever shown in Fig. 889. Its length from $A$ to $B$ is 80 inches; the force acting at its end $A$ is 12,500 pounds; the fulcrum pin is at $R$, 37 inches from $A$; find the thickness and depth of the lever. One of these dimensions is first arbitrarily chosen; suppose that we decide to make its thickness $2\frac{1}{4}$ inches, we have now to find simply its depth.

The dangerous section is on the vertical line through the center of $R$, and the bending moment for this section is numerically equal to the product of the distance $A\ R$ into the force acting at $A$; hence we have for the bending moment

$$\frac{37 \times 12500}{12} = 38541.66 \text{ foot-pounds.}$$

Let us designate this bending moment by $M$, and let the depth in inches be designated by $d$, and the breadth in inches by $b$. The resisting moment will then be equal to $d^2 \times b \times 200$. But the bending moment is equal to the resisting moment, and this condition expressed in symbols is

$$M = d^2 \times b \times 200.$$

Substituting for the symbols their values, we have

$$38541.66 = d^2 \times 2.25 \times 200;$$

hence

$$d^2 = \frac{38541.66}{450} = 85.64,$$

and

$$d = \sqrt{85.64} = 9.25 \text{ inches.}$$

If we had chosen arbitrarily the depth instead of the thickness of the lever, its thickness could have been found in a similar manner. For example, find the thickness of the equalizing lever shown in Fig. 889; it is 80 inches long, its depth at the center is $9\frac{1}{4}$ inches, it has a force of 12,500 pounds acting at $A$, 37 inches from the fulcrum $R$. The bending moment $M$ we have already found to be 38541.66 foot-pounds, and

$$M = d^2 \times b \times 200.$$

$$d^2 = 9.25 \times 9.25 = 85.5625.$$

Now, substituting for the symbols their values, we have

$$38541.66 = 85.5625 \times b \times 200;$$

hence

$$b = \frac{38541.66}{17112.5} = 2.25 \text{ inches.}$$

548  MODERN LOCOMOTIVE CONSTRUCTION.

The lever is of course weakened by drilling the holes for the fulcrum pin, but this is made up by the extra thickness allowed in the center of the lever for wear. The

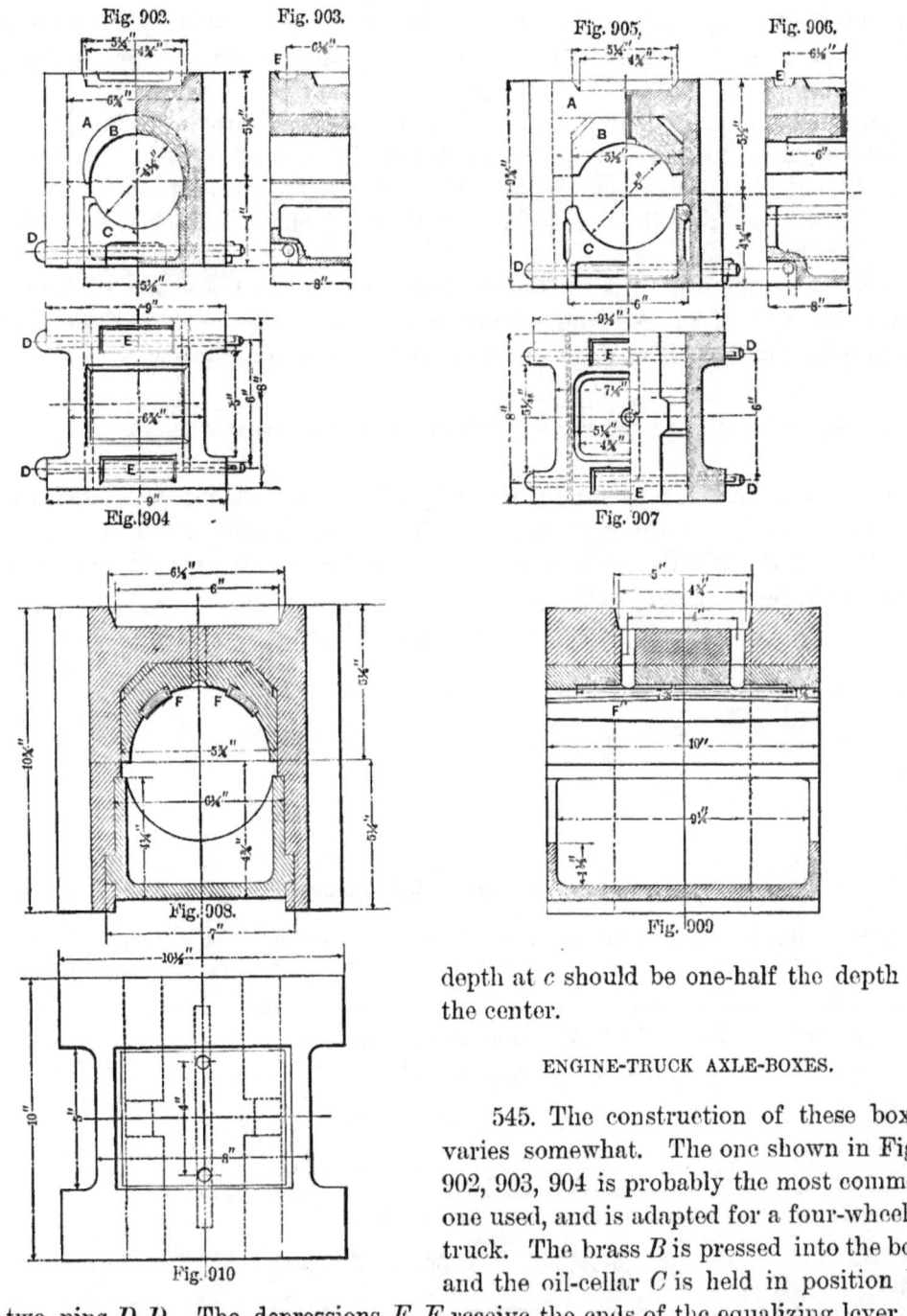

depth at $c$ should be one-half the depth at the center.

ENGINE-TRUCK AXLE-BOXES.

545. The construction of these boxes varies somewhat. The one shown in Figs. 902, 903, 904 is probably the most common one used, and is adapted for a four-wheeled truck. The brass $B$ is pressed into the box, and the oil-cellar $C$ is held in position by the two pins $D\ D$. The depressions $E\ E$ receive the ends of the equalizing lever.

Figs. 905, 906, 907 show another engine-truck box, which differs from the former by having the brass of polygonal form laid into the box. Since in both of these boxes the oil-cellars are held in place by the pins D D, they can be used in trucks which have no inside collars on the axles. These collars are considered by many master-mechanics to be of very little use; in fact, for ready access to the box, and easy inspection, they are in the way, and are therefore not used on many axles.

Figs. 908, 909, 910 show a box in which the oil-cellar is slid in end-ways and is prevented from slipping out by the hub of the wheel and the collar on the axle, which in this case must be used. The brass has two strips of Babbitt metal, F F, which project beyond its bearing. It is believed that with Babbitt metal projecting in this manner heating of the journal will be to a great extent prevented. The boxes in Figs. 902 and 905 are also used for two-wheeled trucks.

### ENGINE-TRUCK AXLE JOURNAL.

546. In Table 81 we give the sizes of engine-truck axle journals as we have found them in actual service, under engines built by different firms. It will be noticed that the sizes of these journals vary; they do not bear a certain ratio to the weight on the truck or size of engine. Yet this table will aid us in establishing a rule for finding the diameter and length of a journal.

### TABLE 81.

DIMENSIONS OF ENGINE-TRUCK JOURNALS, FOR EIGHT- AND TEN-WHEELED ENGINES, AS USED IN ACTUAL SERVICE.

| Size of Cylinders. | Diameter of Journals. | Length of Journals. |
|---|---|---|
| Column 1. | Column 2. | Column 3. |
| 11 × 15 inches. | 4 inches. | 6 inches. |
| 13 × 20 " | 4 " | 6 " |
| 14 × 20 " | 4 " | 6 " |
| 16 × 24 " | 4½ " | 8 " |
| 17 × 24 " | 4½ " | 8 " |
| 18 × 24 " | 5 " | 12 " |
| 19 × 24 " | 5 " | 8 " |
| 19 × 24 " | 4 " | 8¼ " |
| 19 × 26 " | 5¼ " | 13 " |
| 20 × 24 " | 5 " | 12 " |

The surface velocities of the truck journals are very high, varying from 6 to 10 feet per second. For such high velocities it is advisable not to allow the pressure on the journal to exceed 80 pounds per square inch of projected area. The pressure on the journal is, of course, found by subtracting from the weight on the truck (as given in Tables 5 to 8) the weight of wheels and axles, and dividing the remainder by the number of journals; the quotient will be the weight on the projected area of one journal, and dividing this by 80 will give us the number of square inches in the projected area. For many practical purposes we can get results sufficiently accurate by dividing the whole weight on the truck, including the weight of wheels and axles, by the number of journals, and then divide this quotient by 120; the last quotient will be the number of square inches in the projected area of one journal. For example: Referring to Table 5, we find that the weight on truck for an eight-wheeled passenger engine with cylinders 16 × 24 inches is 23,832 pounds; dividing this by 4, the number of journals in the truck, we have $\frac{23832}{4} = 5958$, which we may assume to be the pressure in pounds on the projected area of one journal; and dividing this quotient by 120, we have $\frac{5958}{120} = 49.65$ square inches in the projected area of one journal. After this area has been found it is an easy matter to find the diameter, provided we know the ratio of the diameter and length of journal. Referring to Table 81, it is seen that a fair average ratio is 1 to 2—that is, the length is twice the diameter. Adopting this as a standard, we have the following rule for finding the diameter:

RULE 114.—Divide the projected area of the journal in square inches by 2, and extract the square root of the quotient; the result will be the diameter in inches; the length will be equal to twice the diameter.

EXAMPLE 150.—Compute the diameter and length of the engine-truck journals for an eight-wheeled passenger engine with 16 × 24 inch cylinder.

We have already found that the projected area of each journal in this class and size of engine should be 49.65 square inches. Hence, according to rule, we have $\frac{49.65}{2} = 24.82$, and the square root of 24.82 is 5 very nearly; hence the diameter of the journal should be 5 inches and its length 10 inches.

In this way we have computed the dimensions of the journal in the following table. In Column 2 the weight on the truck is given, which has been taken from Table 5; the projected areas are given in Column 3; the diameter of the journals in the nearest quarter of an inch in Column 4; and the length in Column 5.

TABLE 82.

DIMENSIONS OF ENGINE-TRUCK JOURNALS FOR EIGHT-WHEELED PASSENGER ENGINES.

| Column 1. | | Column 2. | Column 3. | Column 4. | Column 5. |
|---|---|---|---|---|---|
| Cylinders. | | Weight on Truck in Pounds. | Projected Area of One Journal in Square Inches. | Diameter of Journal. | Length of Journal. |
| Diameter. | Stroke. | | | | |
| 10 inches. | 20 inches. | 10,000 | 20.83 | $3\frac{1}{4}$ inches. | $6\frac{1}{2}$ inches. |
| 11 " | 20 " | 13,310 | 27.72 | $3\frac{3}{4}$ " | $7\frac{1}{2}$ " |
| 12 " | 22 " | 14,850 | 30.93 | 4 " | 8 " |
| 13 " | 22 " | 17,070 | 35.56 | $4\frac{1}{4}$ " | $8\frac{1}{2}$ " |
| 14 " | 24 " | 19,242 | 40.08 | $4\frac{1}{2}$ " | 9 " |
| 15 " | 24 " | 22,090 | 46.02 | $4\frac{3}{4}$ " | $9\frac{1}{2}$ " |
| 16 " | 24 " | 23,832 | 49.65 | 5 " | 10 " |
| 17 " | 24 " | 26,010 | 54.18 | $5\frac{1}{4}$ " | $10\frac{1}{2}$ " |
| 18 " | 24 " | 28,680 | 59.75 | $5\frac{1}{2}$ " | 11 " |

Comparing these dimensions of journals with those in actual use, as given in Table 81, we notice that they agree fairly well up to 17 × 24 inches cylinders. For the 17 and 18 inches cylinders the computed diameters are somewhat too large and may be reduced $\frac{1}{4}$ of an inch. The diameters of journals found by the foregoing computations are always large enough, even if they are reduced a little, to resist all the forces which tend to break the axles; hence, computations for strength are not necessary.

The following table gives the dimensions of journals in two-wheeled trucks for consolidation engines. These have been computed in the same manner as was followed for finding those of a four-wheeled truck under an eight-wheeled passenger engine. Of course, for consolidation engines we divide the total weight on the journals by 2 instead of 4 for finding the weight on each journal.

TABLE 83.

DIMENSIONS OF ENGINE-TRUCK JOURNALS FOR CONSOLIDATION ENGINES.

| Column 1. | | Column 2. | Column 3. | Column 4. | Column 5. |
|---|---|---|---|---|---|
| Cylinders. | | Weight on Truck in Pounds. | Projected Area of One Journal in Square Inches. | Diameter of Journal. | Length of Journal. |
| Diameter. | Stroke. | | | | |
| 14 inches. | 16 inches. | 6,272 | 26.13 | $3\frac{3}{4}$ inches. | $7\frac{1}{4}$ inches. |
| 15 " | 18 " | 8,100 | 33.75 | 4 " | 8 " |
| 20 " | 24 " | 14,400 | 60.75 | $5\frac{1}{2}$ " | 11 " |
| 22 " | 24 " | 16,727 | 69.69 | $5\frac{3}{4}$ " | $11\frac{1}{2}$ " |

It may be advantageous to show how the rule for finding the diameter and length of journals has been found when their ratio is known, as it will enable us to establish rules for any other ratio of diameter to length. Let $a$ denote the number of square inches in the projected area of the journal, and $x$ the diameter in inches of the journal. If, now, the length is to be twice the diameter, we denote the length by $2x$.

Multiplying the diameter by the length, we obtain the projected area. This condition is expressed in symbols:
$$x \times 2x = a.$$

Performing the multiplication as indicated by the first member of the equation, we have
$$2x^2 = a,$$
from which we get
$$x^2 = \frac{a}{2},$$
and
$$x = \sqrt{\frac{a}{2}}.$$

This last expression reads: The diameter is equal to the square root of one-half the area, which is the same as given in Rule 114. If, now, the length of journal is $2\frac{1}{2}$ times the diameter, and using the same symbols as before, we have
$$x \times 2\frac{1}{2}x = a,$$
$$2\frac{1}{2}x^2 = a,$$
$$x^2 = \frac{a}{2\frac{1}{2}},$$
and
$$x = \sqrt{\frac{a}{2\frac{1}{2}}}.$$

From the foregoing we learn that the diameter of the journal is equal to the square root of the quotient which is obtained by dividing the projected area of the journal by the ratio of diameter to length.

# CHAPTER XIV.

### OIL-CUPS.—VALVES.—COCKS.—INJECTOR.

#### OIL-CUPS.

547. A great diversity of opinion exists in regard to the best form of oil-cups; in fact, since there is more or less trouble caused by the oil-cups breaking off at their shanks, they are sometimes considered to be a nuisance, and therefore on a few roads oil-cups of any kind are not used, the oil being fed through simple oil-holes. Of the various kinds adopted we shall show the construction of the principal ones.

Fig. 911 shows the simplest form of oil-cup. It is made of brass in one piece; its reservoir is filled with waste and oil. This cup is sometimes used for link hangers,

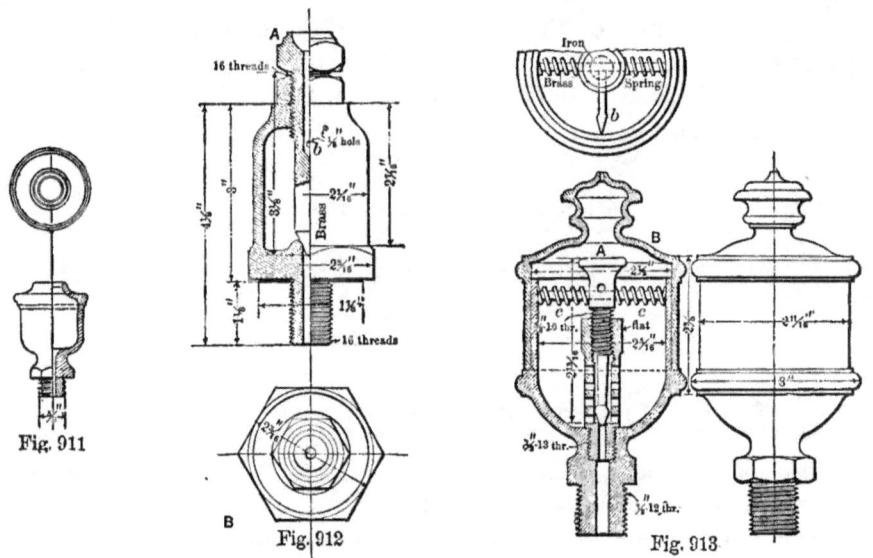

rocker-boxes, and other stationary bearings. Fig. 912 shows an oil-cup suitable for the guides. The flow of oil is regulated by the brass spindle $A$, whose conical end fits the seat in the bottom of the cup. For the purpose of filling the cup, the upper part of the spindle is made hollow, from which a hole $b$ leads into the reservoir of the cup.

Fig. 913 shows another form of guide oil-cup. In this cup the flow of oil is also regulated by an adjustable spindle $A$. A pointer $b$ is fastened to the upper end of this spindle for the purpose of indicating the extent of opening for the oil to flow through, and when set, the spindle is prevented from turning by the springs $c\ c$, which bear against the inside of the cup. After the supply of oil has been poured into it the whole is covered by the brass casing $B$. The aim in the design of these cups is, of course, to feed the oil gradually, and keep the slides constantly and regularly lubricated.

Fig. 914 shows the Rieker oil-cup. It is used on the rear ends of the main-rods and on the ends of the side-rods. The oil is thrown upwards to the top of the tube $a$ by the motion of the rods, and its flow is regulated by the needle on the end of spindle $A$.

Fig. 915 shows a cup after the pattern of the Nathan Manufacturing Co.'s patented oil-cup. A glass shell $B$ is placed inside of the brass casing $A$, and the whole is made oil-

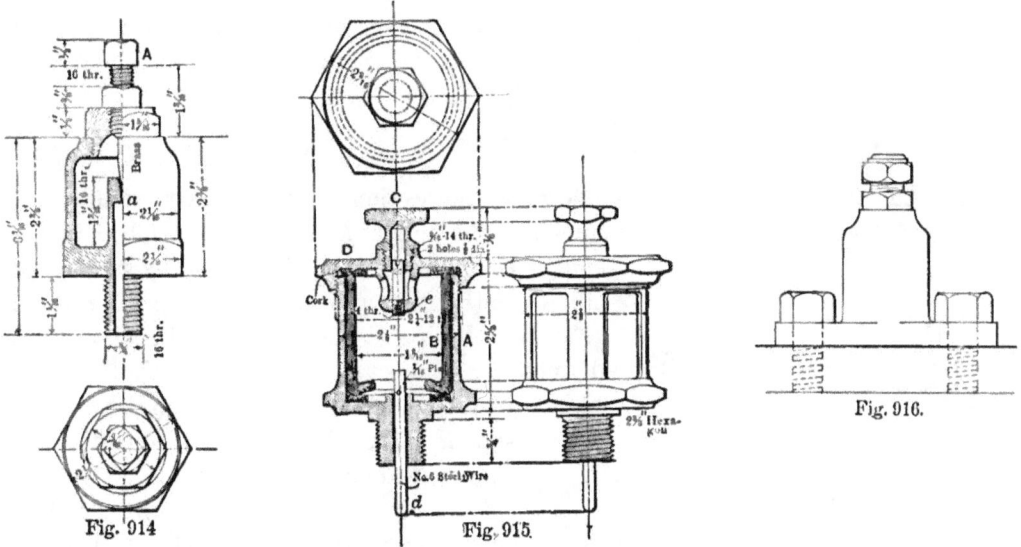

tight by cork packing placed at the top and bottom of the glass. When the cup is to be filled the nut $C$ must be taken off. A small air-hole should be drilled through the cover $D$ to admit air on top of the oil. When these cups are designed for the rear end

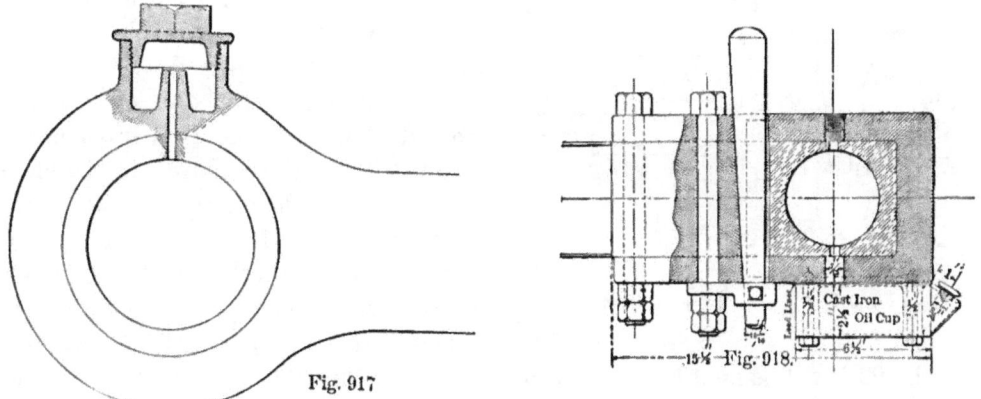

of the main-rods and for the side-rods, they have a steel spindle $d$, which works up and down, its movement being due to the motion of the rods, thereby feeding a certain amount of oil regularly onto the crank-pin journals. The lift of these spindles, and consequently the amount of oil to be fed, is regulated by the screw $e$. When the cup is at any time taken off the rods, the spindle $d$ is prevented from falling out of the cup by a small pin driven through its upper end. The advantage of these cups is that the oil in the reservoir is constantly exposed to view.

Since much trouble is experienced with the oil-cups breaking off at the shanks, some master-mechanics fasten the cups in the manner shown in Fig. 916. On some roads the rod oil-cups are forged to the rods or straps, as shown in Fig. 917.

An excellent way of keeping the crank pins and side-rod pins lubricated is by the use of an oil-cellar fastened to the bottom of the strap, as shown in Fig. 918. This cellar is filled with waste and oil, the waste extending through the oil-hole up to and touching the crank pin; the capillary force draws the oil up the waste and lubricates the pins.

## CYLINDER OIL-CUPS.

548. Figs. 919, 920 show an outside view and section of an ordinary cylinder oil-cup; one of these is used for each cylinder. The shank $D$ is usually attached to the side of the boiler inside of the cab by nipples or elbows, so that the cup stands in a vertical position. A copper oil-pipe $F$, usually $\frac{9}{16}$ or $\frac{11}{16}$ inch outside diameter, is connected to the shank $E$; the other end of this pipe is connected to the steam-chest plug shown in Fig. 923, and described further on. The conical end of the spindle $B$ (Fig. 920) acts as a valve by which the oil-hole $H$ in the stem $C$ can be opened or closed. The end of the stem $C$ has attached to it a valve $C_2$ for admitting steam into the oil-pipe $F$ for the purpose of blowing out any matter that may collect in it from time to time. Of course the valve $C_2$ is always closed when oil is to be fed into the cylinder. The oil is poured into the cup $A$, and when the end of the spindle $B$ is lifted off the seat on $H$ the oil can flow into the chamber $G$ and into the oil-pipe $F$; but it cannot flow into the steam-chest and cylinder until the throttle valve is closed, because so long as there is a steam pressure in the steam-chest the valve in the steam-chest

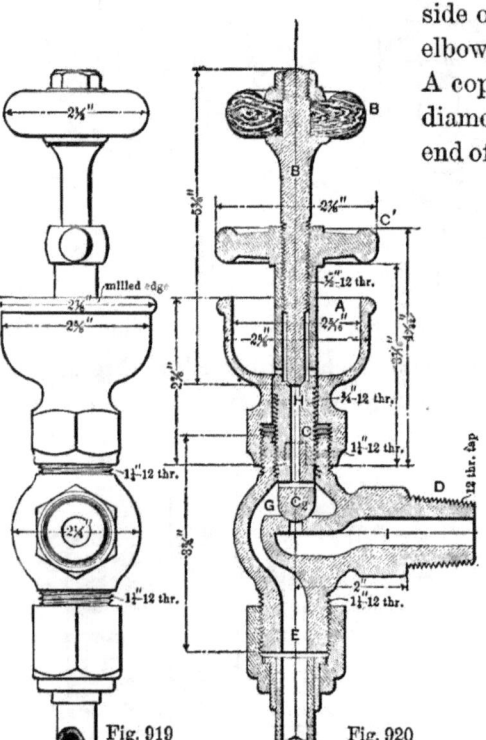
Fig. 919

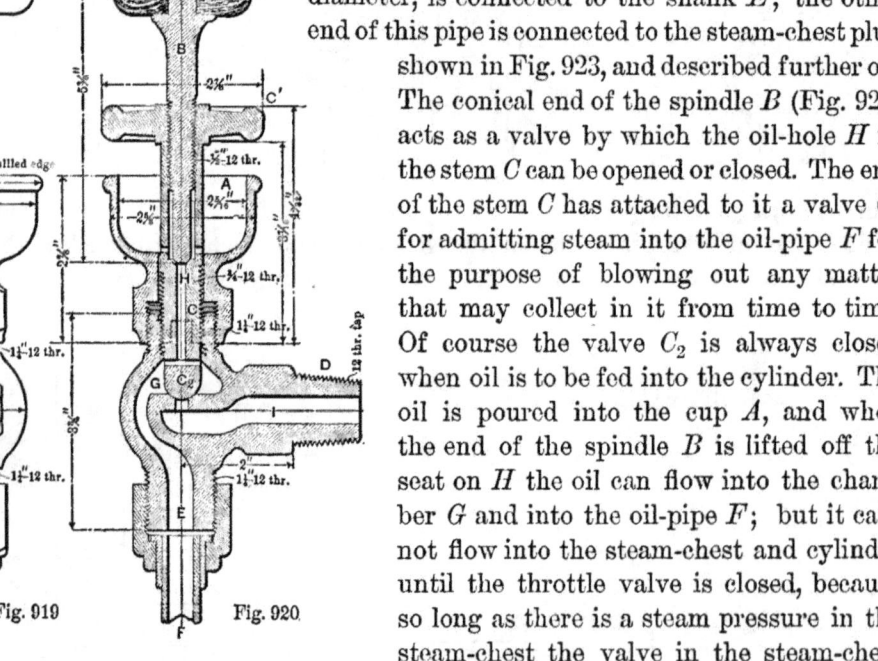
Fig. 920

plug (Fig. 923) will be kept closed; but as soon as the throttle valve is closed a partial vacuum will be formed in the steam-chest, and while the engine is still in motion the oil in the pipe $F$ will be sucked in the steam-chest and cylinder. Whenever the valve $C_2$ is to be opened care must be taken to first close the valve on the hole $H$, otherwise the engineer is liable to be scalded.

Figs. 921, 922 show another cylinder oil-cup somewhat different in design from the foregoing, but both work on the same principle. The shank $D$ is attached to the boiler, and the oil-pipe is connected to the shank E. The cup A is cast to the stem B, whose bottom end acts as a valve and closes or opens the hole leading into the chamber G. The cup A also forms a handle for turning the stem B. Oil is poured into the cup A, from whence it flows into the cup below, and when the valve B is opened the oil is drawn into the steam-chest as soon as the throttle valve is closed. A valve is fitted into the end of the stem C and admits steam into the oil-pipe for the purpose of cleaning it.

Fig. 923 shows a steam-chest plug; it is usually made of brass. Its shank C is screwed into the steam-chest cover, and the nut D holds down the steam-chest false cover. The oil-pipe is connected to the upper end of the plug by the nut A. This end contains a small valve B, which is free to move up or down. When the engine is working, the steam in the chest lifts the valve B, presses it against the end of the oil-pipe and prevents the steam from entering it. From the foregoing it will be seen that the cylinder can be lubricated only when the steam is shut off, as we have stated in the description of the cylinder oil-cups, and then nearly the whole quantity of oil in the cup will be drawn into the cylinder during a few revolutions of the wheels, making the feed irregular and not nearly as constant as is desirable. The small valve B in the plug not only relieves the oil-pipes of considerable internal pressure, but it also serves another useful purpose. If the small valve B is not used, the pipes will be continually full of steam, which is liable to condense and be forced out with the oil through the cups in case these are opened before

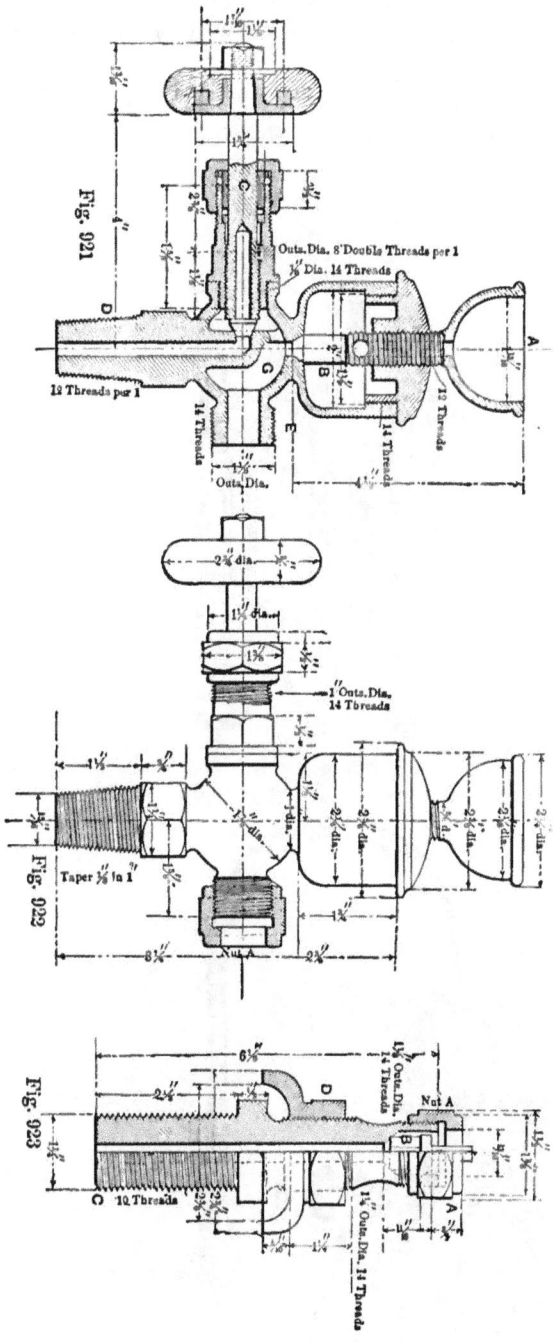

the pressure in the steam-chest has been reduced. The occurrence of this nuisance is prevented by the use of the small valve B.

## SIGHT-FEED LUBRICATORS.

549. During recent years sight-feed lubricators for the cylinders have to a great extent displaced the ordinary cylinder oil-cups previously described. Several kinds are manufactured.

Figs. 924, 925, 926, and 926A show one of these made and patented by the Nathan Manufacturing Company, of New York. With these lubricators the feed is regular and

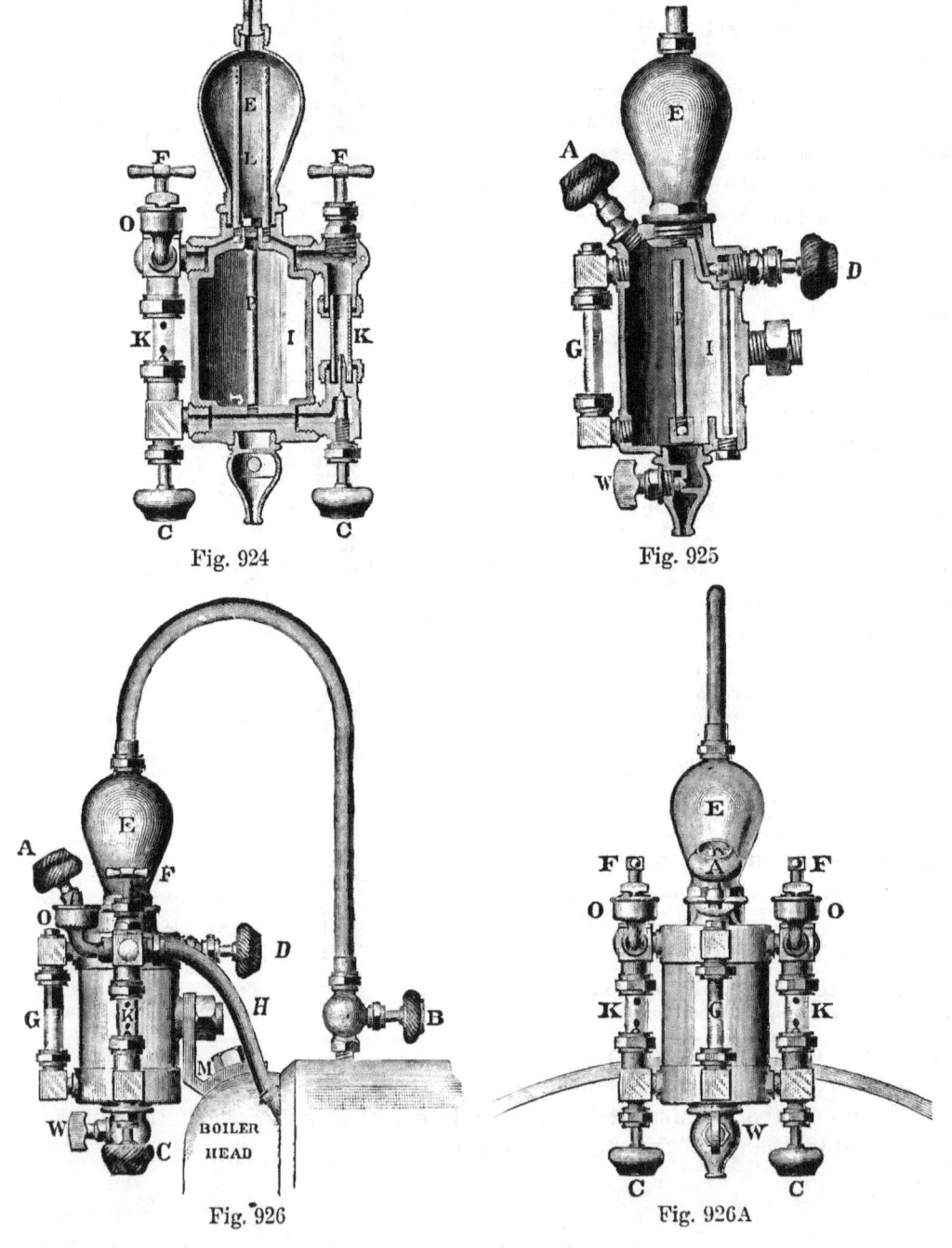

Fig. 924

Fig. 925

Fig. 926

Fig. 926A

continuous, whether steaming or with steam shut off, and when going up or down grade. The flow of oil is constantly in sight, showing at all times whether the lubricator is working satisfactorily or not. The lubricators are placed inside of the cab, and are usually attached to the rear end of the boiler, as shown in Fig. 926, within sight and easy reach of the engineer or the fireman. The principle upon which it works is that the water, which is heavier than the oil, displaces the oil in the cup, causing it to flow drop by drop through a body of water in the sight-feed glass, and then it enters the oil-pipes which lead to the steam-chest. Steam is taken from the top of boiler or from the dome, and is conducted into the condenser $E$, where it is condensed and furnishes the working water column. The water is led to the bottom of the reservoir $I$ by an inside pipe; its flow is regulated by the valve $D$, Fig. 925. The oil which floats on the water in the reservoir $I$ is carried upwards until it enters the top of the pipe $P$, from whence it flows downwards, then through the channel $J$, and finally enters into the bottom of the sight-feed glass $K$, through which it flows upwards drop by drop, and then enters the oil-pipe which leads the oil into the steam-chest and cylinders. The quantity of oil entering the sight-feed glass is regulated by the valves $C$, Fig. 924. Inside of the condenser $E$ there are two entirely separate steam conduits $L$, which allow the minimum quantity of steam to enter into oil-pipe $H$ (see Fig. 926); this steam becomes saturated with the oil and forms a steam lubricant. These lubricators are arranged to form two distinct oilers, one for each cylinder, thereby avoiding the possibility of feeding all the oil into one cylinder; each cylinder is lubricated independently of the other. Each side is also furnished with an independent hand or auxiliary oiler $O\ O$; these work on the same principle as the ordinary cylinder oil-cups shown in Fig. 921; they communicate directly with the outlet passages of the lubricator, and are used in case a sight-feed or gauge glass has been broken. Such an accident necessitates the shutting off of the sight lubricator. The glass tube $G$ shows the height of water in the reservoir $I$. The cock $W$ is simply a waste cock for draining the reservoir when necessary. $A$ is the filling plug, and $B$, Fig. 926, the steam valve. The safety valves $F\ F$ are always kept open, except when one of the glasses is broken. In such cases the valves $F$, $D$, and $B$ must be closed, so as to shut off the lubricator and allow the cylinders to be lubricated by the auxiliary oilers $O\ O$.

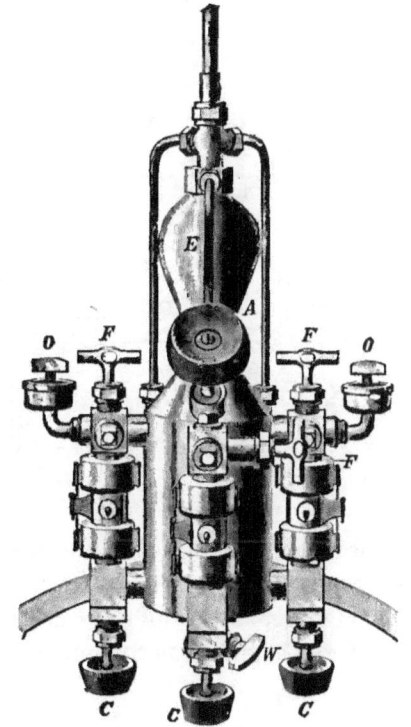

Fig. 926 B

The oil-pipe $H$, one on each side of the engine, is run along the boiler underneath the lagging, and is connected to the steam-chest plug. For sight lubricators the valve $B$ in the steam-chest plug (Fig. 923) must be removed so as to maintain the proper lubrication when the engine is running.

Fig. 926B shows a combined sight-feed lubricator for oiling the cylinders and air-brakes, and is a simple and effective device for the purpose. Its general appearance and construction does not differ much from that of the lubricator shown in Fig. 924, and works on the same principle. The same letters in all these lubricators indicate similar parts.

### BLOWER VALVES.

550. Fig. 927 shows the construction of an ordinary blower valve. Its shank $A$ is either screwed into the boiler shell or into the steam chamber shown in Fig. 929. The

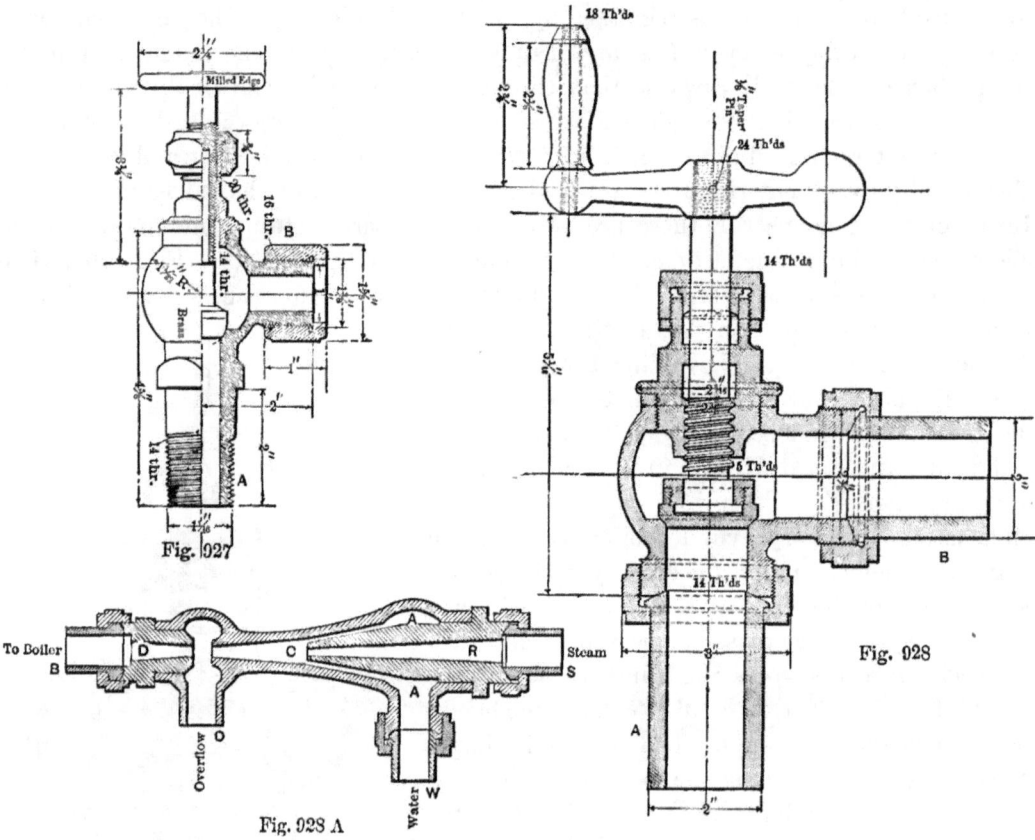

blower pipe is attached to the nipple $B$. This pipe is usually made of iron, sometimes of brass, ¾ inch inside diameter. It is placed along the side of the boiler underneath the lagging, and terminates in the smoke-box. Its duty is, of course, to create a draft when the engine is not running.

### INJECTOR.

551. Up to 1853, when the Giffard injector made its appearance, pumps were used exclusively for feeding locomotive boilers. In 1860 this injector was introduced by Messrs. Wm. Sellers & Co., of Philadelphia, Pa., who had also added many improvements to the original instrument. Its advantages were recognized, and it gained the confidence of practical men, gradually increasing in favor, and finally superseded the

pumps, so that now we rarely find a locomotive which is not equipped with injectors, generally one on each side of boiler, in place of pumps.

Practical tests and the results of many years of constant service under varying and trying conditions have placed the injectors, with their various modifications as now made by different manufacturers, beyond the experimental stage; and the old notions that the operation of an injector is incomprehensible, that its parts are liable to be impaired and involve nice adjustment to meet the practical requirements, have been removed by familiarity with the instrument. Its action is reliable, its construction is simple and compact, it can be easily examined, the cost of repairs is comparatively low, and the amount of feed water to be fed into the boiler can be regulated with it as well as with an ordinary pump. Its inherent advantages are that the feed water enters the boiler comparatively hot without the use of a feed-water heater, thereby reducing the liability of subjecting the boiler to an undue stress as might occur by feeding colder water into the boiler; it is an independent feeder, as with it a certain quantity of water can always be supplied to the boiler when the speed of the engine is irregular, or even when the engine is standing still; it requires no mechanism, such as eccentrics or cranks, or other attachments, for its operation; and it is easily applied to a locomotive without requiring any change in the mechanism of the engine.

The numerous kinds of injectors now made are the developments of the elementary form indicated in Fig. 928A, in which all the minor details have been omitted so as to show plainly the principles of its construction and action. It consists of a receiving tube $R$, a combining tube $C$, and a delivery tube $D$. These parts are common to all forms of injectors, with various modifications. The steam pipe from the boiler leading the steam to the injector is attached to the end $S$; the suction pipe supplying water to the instrument is attached to the nozzle $W$; and the delivery pipe leading to the boiler is attached to the end $B$. The action of the injector may be briefly described as follows: Steam from the boiler enters at $S$ and flows into the receiving tube $R$ with a great velocity, causing a partial vacuum in the chamber $A$; this causes the water to flow through the nozzle $W$ and around the receiving tube, from whence it is drawn into the combining tube $C$, where it combines with the steam, and then flows through the delivery tube into the delivery pipe and is led to the check valve, which is usually fastened to the side of the boiler, and forces its way into the boiler. If the supply of water is too great, a waste will occur at the overflow $O$; and if, on the other hand, the supply of steam is too great, air will be drawn through the same opening, which may cause a break in the feed.

At a casual glance it may appear to be impossible for an issuing jet of steam to force its way back into its own boiler, but this nevertheless does occur, and this action may be explained as follows:

We may assume that the steam pipe leading to the injector and the delivery pipe leading from the injector to the boiler form one continuous pipe. Here, then, we have a pipe into which steam enters at one end and water tends to enter at the other end, and both the steam and water are subjected to the same pressure. Under these conditions the velocity of the steam is much greater than that which the water would have if it could flow into the pipe. If, now, the steam during its flow is condensed, and the velocity of the water due to the condensation is not reduced to the velocity which the water at the opposite end of the pipe would have, then the water due to the condensation will have the greater momentum and will be enabled to overcome the force of water which tends to flow from the boiler, and the water due to condensation will force its way into the boiler. This is exactly what occurs when an injector is interposed; the steam enters the injector at a very high velocity, is condensed in the injector without losing much of its velocity, some of which is imparted to the water which rushes into the injector through the nozzle $W$; the resulting velocity is of course less than that of issuing jet of steam, but it is still greater, and consequently its momentum is also greater than the velocity of the water tending to flow out of the boiler would be. This enables the steam, with an additional amount of water, to overcome all resistances and force its way back into its own boiler.

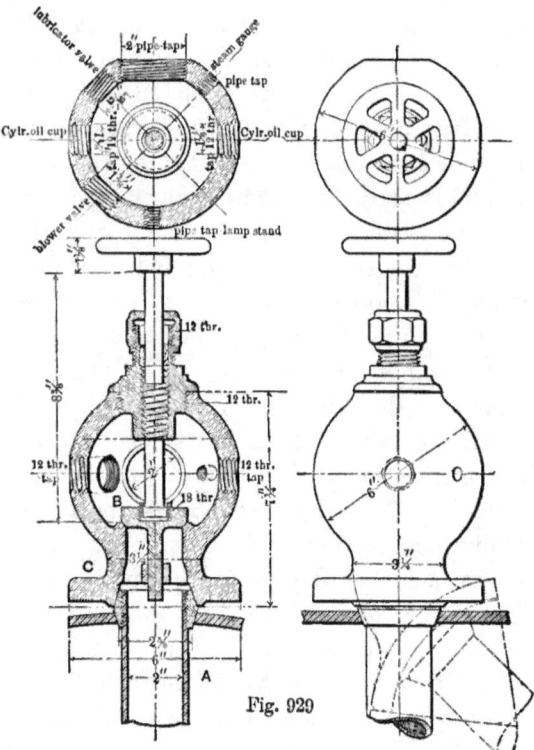

Fig. 929

There are many different forms of injectors manufactured, which need not be described here, as full information in regard to them, with illustrations, can be obtained in the many excellent catalogues distributed by the manufacturers.

With the higher steam pressures, say 150 pounds, the temperature of the feed water delivered by the injector may reach 120 degrees Fahrenheit, and for very low pressures it may reach 130 degrees.

When the injector is used as a boiler feeder it is a very efficient instrument, and it will require less of the fuel than a pump of the same capacity. The heat imparted to the feed water is not lost, as it is all returned to the boiler. But if an injector is used simply as a pump—that is to say, for raising water or similar purposes—the heat imparted to the delivery water is wasted, and on this account the efficiency of the injector is lower than that of a pump; or, in other words, it requires more steam to raise a given amount of water than will be required for running a pump doing the same amount of work.

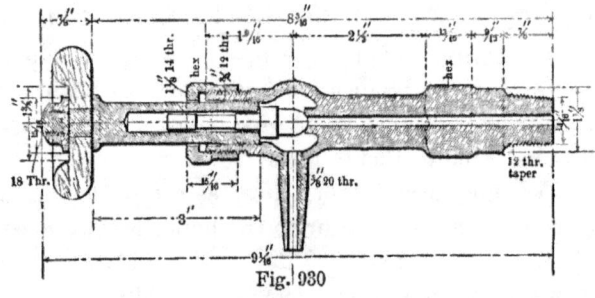

Fig. 930

Steam for working the injector should always be taken from the dome or the highest part of the boiler so as to obtain dry steam, as wet steam is liable to injure it.

A stop valve should always be placed between the steam space in the boiler and the injector. Fig. 928 shows the construction of such a valve. The nipple $B$ is either attached to the boiler or to the steam chamber, and the pipe leading to the injector is attached to the nipple $A$. The size of this valve depends on the size and kind of injector used. All pipes, whether steam, water supply, or delivery, must be of the same internal diameter as the hole in the corresponding branch of the injector, and all pipes should be as straight as practicable. When steam is taken from the dome a dry pipe is generally required to lead the steam to the stop valve.

For non-lifting injectors a small cock in the suction pipe is required for regulating the supply of water. This cock generally takes the place of the feed cock shown in Fig. 578, and is worked by a suitable mechanism from the foot-board.

552. We have already shown one form of steam chamber in Fig. 536. All the valves required in the cab are screwed into this chamber. Fig. 929 shows another form of a steam chamber; it is generally used on boilers which do not extend very far into the cab. The pipe $A$ is usually led into the dome so that dry steam will be supplied to all the valves attached to this chamber. The supply of steam can be shut

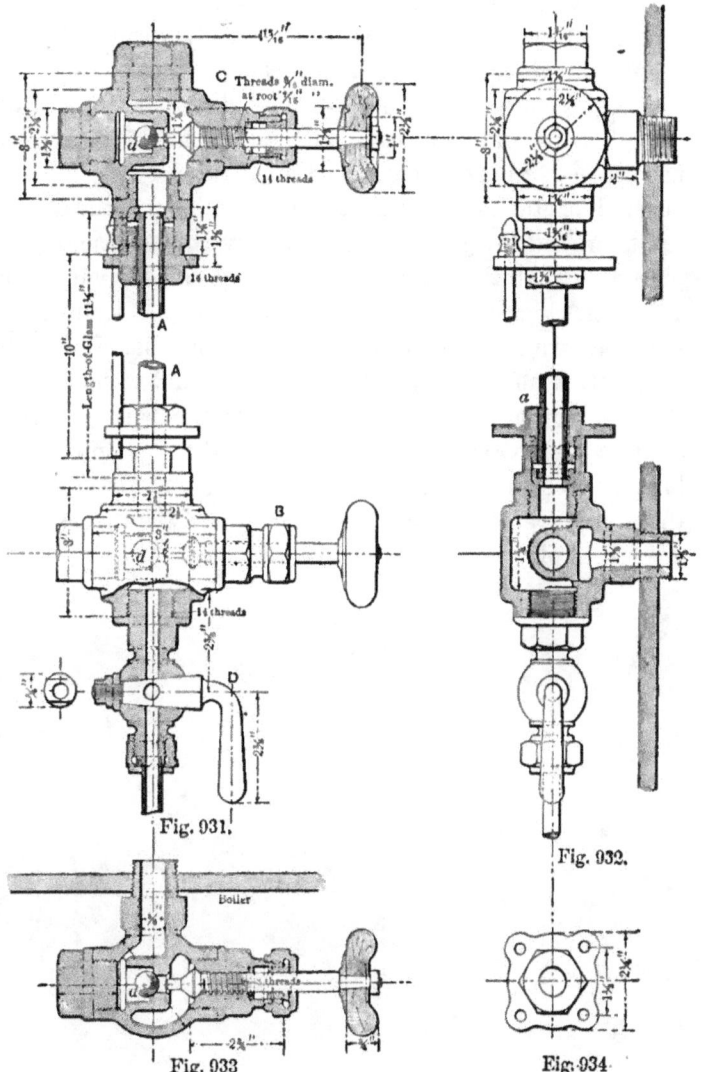

off by the valve $B$, for the purpose of repairing any one of the valves attached to the chamber when steam is in the boiler. The flange $C$ is bolted to the boiler by means of studs, and the joint between the shell and chamber is a ball joint, as shown. The dotted flange shows the form when the steam chamber has to be bolted on the side of the boiler.

553. Fig. 930 shows the construction of an ordinary gauge cock; it is made of brass, and usually three cocks are used for each boiler. They are frequently screwed into the rear head of the boiler, but sometimes into the side. The center of the lowest

gauge cock should be about 2 inches above the highest point of the crown sheet, and the upper cock should be placed a little above the intended water level. This will usually bring the gauge cocks from 3 to 4 inches apart. Consequently, when the upper gauge cock discharges water the indications are that there is too much water in the boiler; and it scarcely need be said that there is danger when the lower cock discharges steam.

In trying the gauge cocks the water is discharged into a drip pan, from whence it is led through a pipe to the road bed.

554. Figs. 931, 932, 933, 934 show different views of a water-gauge glass; the lower cock $B$ is in communication with the water in the boiler, and the upper cock $C$ communicates with the steam. The glass tube $A$ is usually from 11 to 15 inches long, its outer diameter is generally $\frac{5}{8}$ inch, and its thickness $\frac{1}{8}$ inch. Steam- and water-tight joints around the glass are secured by rubber packing. The lower cock $B$ should be placed so that the lower end of the glass at $a$ will indicate about 2 inches of water above the highest part of the crown sheet. The cock $D$ is used for blowing out the sediment which is liable to collect in the glass. The balls $d\ d$ are for the purpose of shutting off automatically the steam and water in case the glass has been broken. When everything is in working order the balls $d\ d$ roll away from their seats and allow a free passage for the steam and water into the glass. But should the glass break, the swift currents of the steam and water carry the balls against the seats, thereby preventing any further escape. When a new glass has been put in the balls are forced off the seats by the valve stems.

# CHAPTER XV.

## TENDERS.—TENDER TRUCKS.

### TENDERS.

555. Fig. 935 shows a side elevation of a tender; its frame is made of wood. All tender frames, whether made of wood or iron, are covered with planks, generally 2 inches thick; they form a floor on which the tank is placed. The usual method of fastening the tank to the frame is to rivet a wrought-iron bracket or knee $a\ a$ to each outer corner of the tank, and three or four brackets of the same kind are riveted to the sheets which form the coal space; a bolt through the frame and foot of each bracket holds the tank securely in place. Care should always be taken to secure the tank in such a way as will not cause it to be subjected to a longitudinal stress due to the pull of the engine. If the tank has to resist part of the pull of the engine, leakage is liable to occur.

When a wooden frame is used the front and back draw-heads are bolted to it by four bolts $b\ b$, which extend through the whole length of frame and must be made strong enough to transmit the whole pull of the engine to the cars behind it. The members of a wooden frame should never be subjected to a tensile stress; the only stress in a wooden tender frame should be that due to the weight of the tank, water and fuel, and the push of the engine.

556. The diameters of the longitudinal bolts $b\ b$ are easily found. The tension in these bolts cannot be greater than that due to the adhesion of the driving wheels. If, for instance, the weight on the drivers is 60,000 pounds, and if we assume the adhesion to be equal to $\frac{1}{4}$ of the weight on the drivers, then the tension in the four bolts will be $\frac{60000}{4} = 15000$ pounds, and the tension in one bolt will be $\frac{15000}{4} = 3750$ pounds. This tension or pull is frequently applied suddenly, and therefore the normal stress per square inch of cross-section of these bolts should not exceed 3,000 pounds, hence the smallest cross-sectional area of each bolt should be $\frac{3750}{3000} = 1.250$ square inches; the corresponding diameter is $1\frac{1}{4}$ inches; the smallest cross-section is at the bottom of the thread, hence this section should be $1\frac{1}{4}$ inches diameter, which will give us a little over $1\frac{3}{8}$ inches for the diameter outside of thread.

557. The iron trucks used under this tender (Fig. 935) are alike in every respect, excepting that the rear truck has two side bearings $r\ r$, on which the tender frame rests; the front truck has no side bearings, the front end of tender frame being supported by the center pin $s$, so that virtually the frame and tank with water and

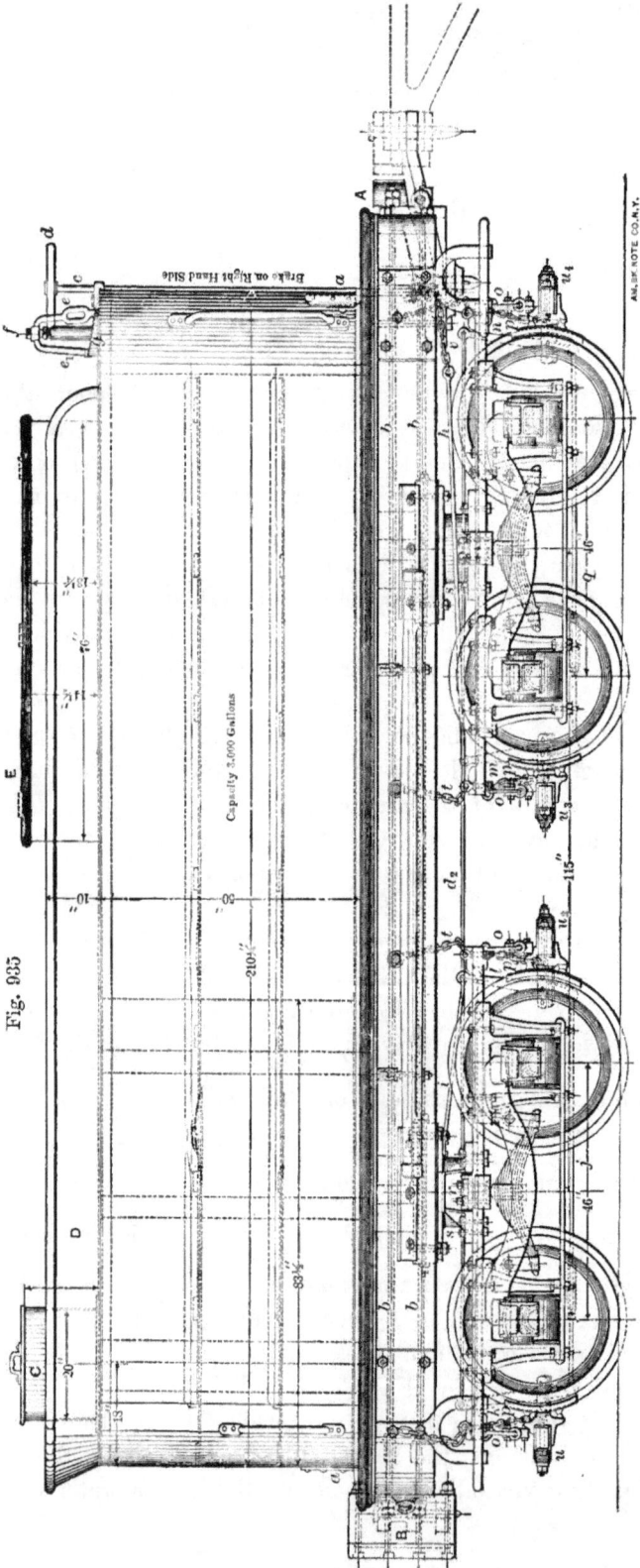

Fig. 935

fuel are supported by three points only. Although this is good practice, it is by no means a universal one, for under many tenders both trucks have side bearings and consequently support the frame and tank by four points. The objection to four points of support is that when the tender is running over any unevenness of the track some of the truck springs are liable to be compressed to a hurtful extent and the tender frame is liable to be twisted. With three supports the load will be more evenly distributed over all the springs under any conditions.

Trucks which have side bearings like the rear truck in Fig. 935 are called side-bearing trucks; and trucks whose center pin acts as a support, like the front truck in Fig. 935, are called center-bearing trucks.

558. Safety chains $t\ t$ are bolted to the truck frames and the sides of tender frame. The wooden brake beams $u\ u_2$, etc., are supported by their hangers $o\ o$; they also have safety chains $p\ p$ which can support the beams in case the hangers break.

559. The brakes in Fig. 935 are designed to be worked by hand. One end of the chain $v$ is attached to the bottom of the brake shaft $c$, the other end of the chain is connected to the rod $h$. In turning the shaft $c$ by the hand-wheel $d$ the chain $v$ is wound around

the bottom of the shaft, thereby pulling the rod $h$ towards the front of tender. This rod is connected to the rear-brake lever $m$ on the front truck; the rod $q$ connects the lower end of the lever $m$ and the lower end of its mate $n$; the fulcrums of these levers are supported by the wrought-iron jaws through the center of the brake beams. The upper end of the lever $n$ is connected to the rod $d_2$, which is in turn connected to the lever $k$ on the rear truck. The lower end of $k$ is connected to the lower end of the lever $l$ by the rod $j$, and the upper end of $l$ is held by the rod $i$, which is fastened to the tender frame. Now, it will readily be seen that a pull on the rod $h$ will put all the brakes in action; those on the front truck act before those on the rear truck.

The brake shaft $c$ is shown in detail in Fig. 936. Its upper end is held in position by a cast-iron bracket bolted to the tank; separate views of this bracket are shown in Fig. 937. The lower end of the shaft $c$ is supported by a step bearing, which is usually made of wrought-iron; it is bolted to the bottom of the tender frame, and the shaft is prevented from moving upwards by a key shown in Fig. 938. The hole $d$ takes the eye bolt shown in Fig. 939, to which the chain is attached.

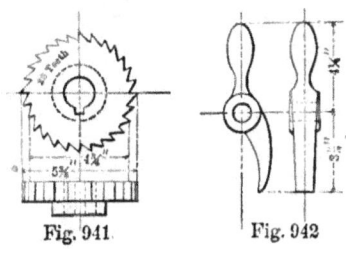

Fig. 941.   Fig. 942.

The casting shown in Fig. 940 is bolted to the top of tender floor. The brake shaft passes through the hole $a$. Just above this hole, the ratchet wheel which is shown in Fig. 941 is keyed to the brake shaft; this wheel en-

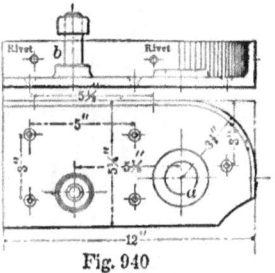

Fig. 940.

gages with the pawl shown in Fig. 942; it works on the pin $b$ (Fig. 940). The object of the pawl and ratchet wheel is, of course, to prevent the brake shaft from turning backwards, thereby holding the brakes in action. The pawl is worked by foot.

560. Figs. 943 to 946 show separate views of the wooden tender frame. Its construction is so plainly shown that further description is unnecessary.

561. The draw-head at the rear end of the tender frame has two pockets, as indicated in Figs. 944, 945, by which the tender can be coupled to cars of different heights. The number of pockets in the rear draw-head depends much on the service for which the engine is designed. In many engines this draw-head has only one pocket, and in switching engines three or even a greater number of pockets may be required.

The hole in this head for the coupling pin is a cored hole, and the pin is smooth forged; the pin has always a little play in the hole—in fact, more play than is admissible in the front draw-head.

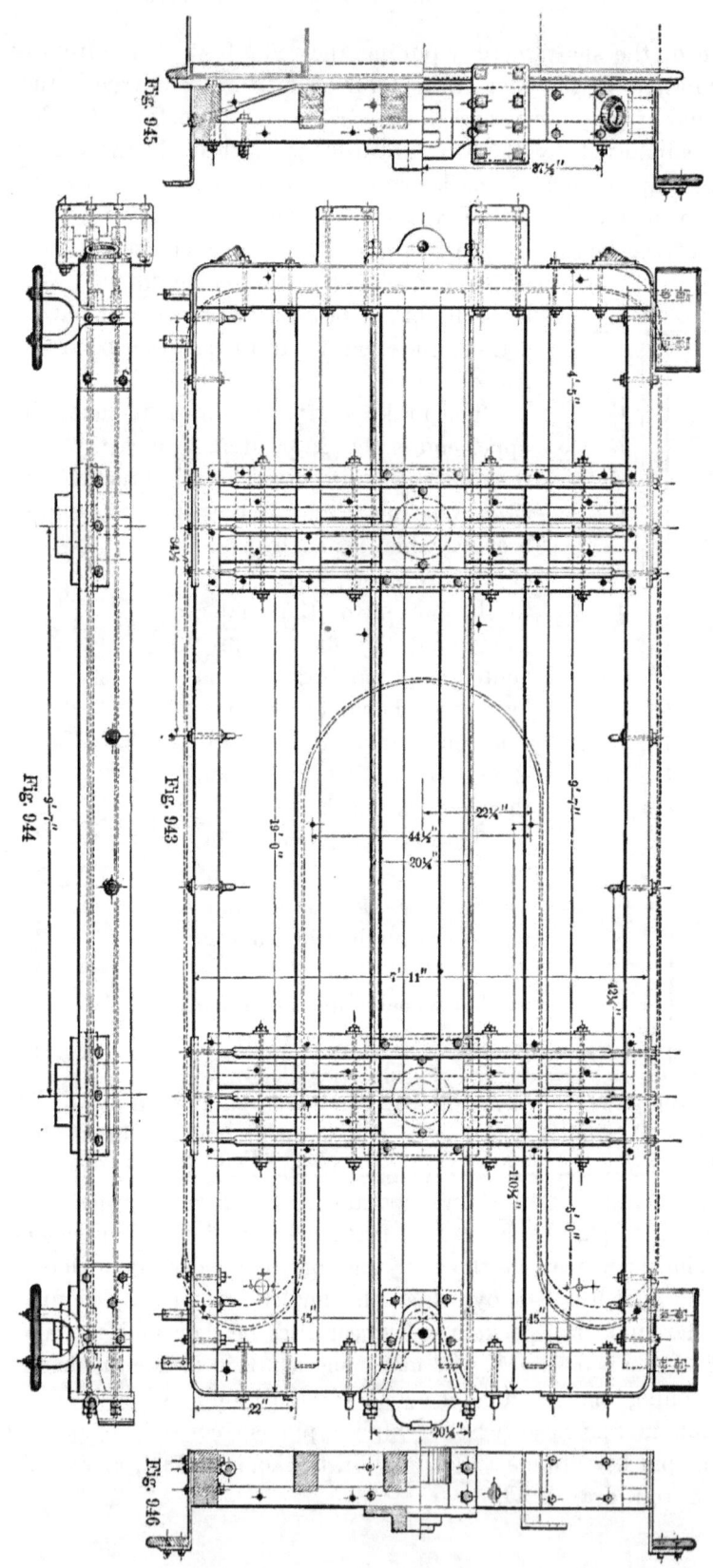

Figs. 947 to 950 show different views of the front draw-head. The designs of these heads differ in the various classes of engines. The one here shown was adopted for the tender illustrated in Fig. 935. The hole for the coupling pin is bored, and the pin is turned so as to reduce the play between engine and tender as much as possible.

## TANK.

**562.** Figs. 951 to 953 show separate views of the tank and the manner of bracing its sides and ends. Some of the braces are made to serve as swash plates, to prevent

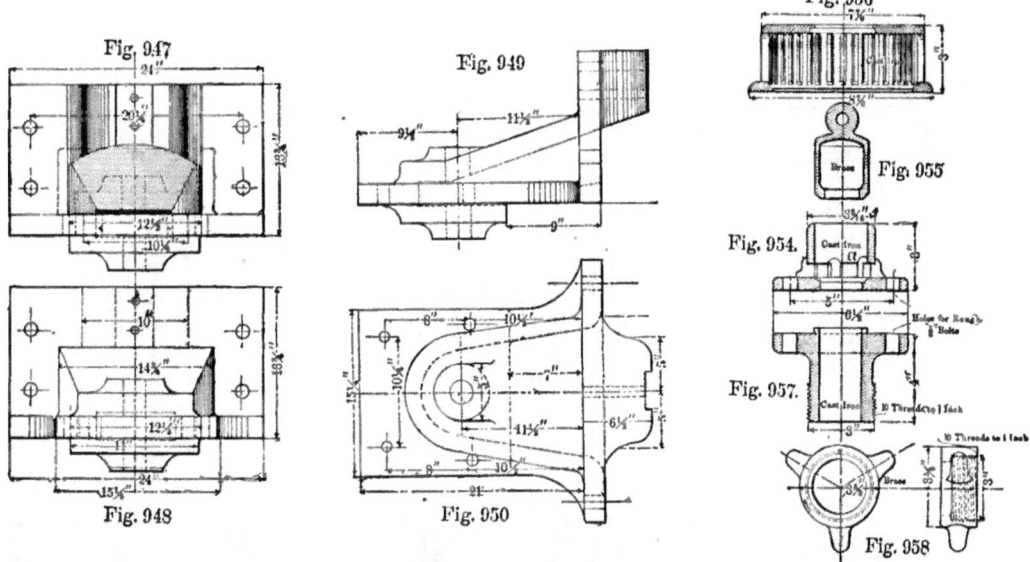

a violent motion of water when the engine is suddenly stopped or started. The tank is filled through the manhole $C$, whose cover is made of plate-iron, with a wooden block riveted to its under side as shown. The wings $D$ are riveted to the sides and rear end of tank, chiefly for the purpose of preventing fuel and water from dropping off the tank and destroying the outside appearance. The angle irons $w\ w$ riveted to the legs of the tank form a channel-way in which boards extending across the coal space are placed. The tank is generally made of iron, sometimes of steel. The outer sides are usually $\frac{3}{16}$ inch thick, plates around the fuel space $\frac{1}{4}$ inch thick, and the top and bottom sheets are also $\frac{1}{4}$ inch thick. The water capacities of tanks vary from 1,500 to 3,600 gallons, to suit the size of engine, and the fuel space will hold from 2 to 5 tons of coal.

The hole $y$ through the bottom sheet of tank (Fig. 951) is the outlet for the feed water; the hole $x$ in the top of tank allows the tank valve-rod to pass through the sheet; the centers of the holes $x$ and $y$ lie in the same vertical line.

**563.** Fig. 954 shows the tank valve seat; its hollow hub $a$ forms a guide for the valve $b$ shown in Fig. 955. This seat and valve is covered with a cast-iron strainer shown in Fig. 956; its purpose is to prevent any obstruction from entering the feed pipe which may render the pump or injector useless. The cast-iron nozzle shown in

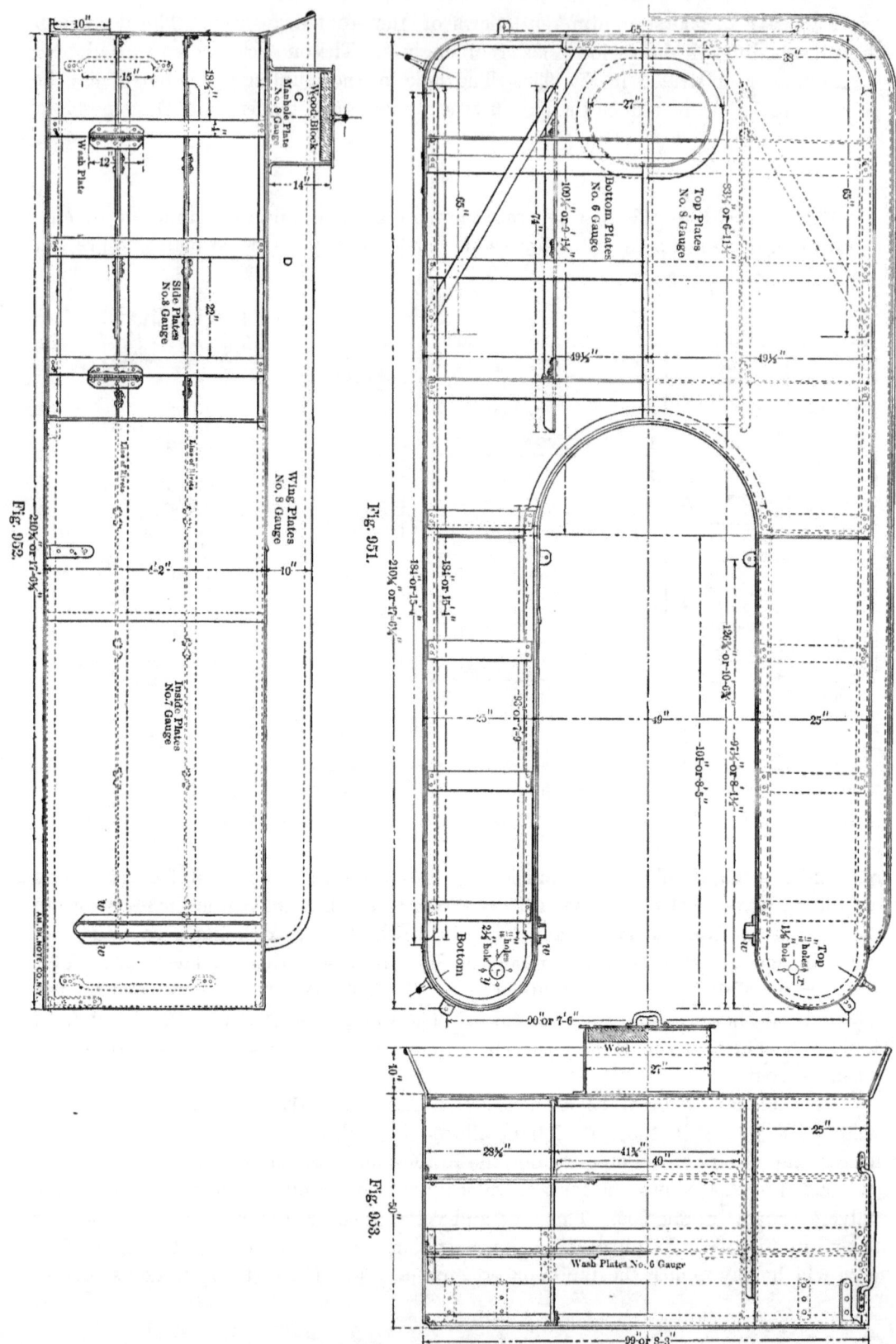

Fig. 957 is bolted to the under side of tank in line with the valve seat. By means of a horned nut (Fig. 958) a cast-iron or brass nipple is attached to the nozzle. The general appearance of the whole arrangement is shown in Fig. 959. A rubber hose is fastened to the nipple and leads the feed water to the feed pipe on the engine.

Fig. 960 shows the tank valve-rod; the jaw at its lower end is connected to the tank valve. This rod passes through the cast-iron stand $A$ shown in Fig. 961. This

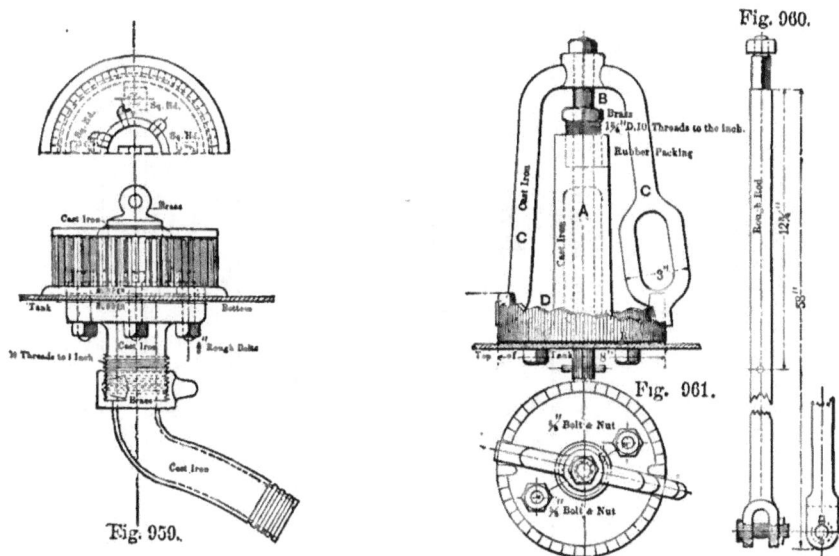

stand is bolted to the top of tank; its upper end is bored out larger than the body, and is threaded for the nut or gland $B$, which presses the packing against the valve-rod and makes a water-tight joint.

A cast-iron handle $C$ is fitted and fastened to the square end of the valve-rod. The bottom of this handle engages with the steps $D$, which gradually rise to a higher plane, so that by turning the handle in one direction the tank valve will be raised, and turning it in the opposite direction the tank valve will be lowered until finally it shuts off the feed water from the engine.

## IRON TENDER-FRAME.

564. Figs. 962 to 964 show a good construction of an iron tender-frame. It consists of four channel irons $A\ A$, 10 inches deep by $2\tfrac{5}{8}$ inches wide. These channel irons are placed longitudinally, and their ends are riveted by wrought-iron knee plates to the transverse end plates $B$ of wrought-iron, which are 1 inch thick. The ends of the channel irons are also held together by the plates $C\ C$, $\tfrac{1}{2}$ inch thick, riveted to the bottom flange of the channel irons, and further stiffness is secured by the braces $G\ G$. To the plates $C\ C$ the cast-iron draw-heads are bolted, which, as will be seen, differ in design from those shown on the frame in Fig. 943. The hole $D$ near the front end takes the coupling pin, and the holes $E\ E$ on each side of $D$ take the pins for the safety chain. Oak bumpers are bolted to the transverse plates $B\ B$ as shown. The

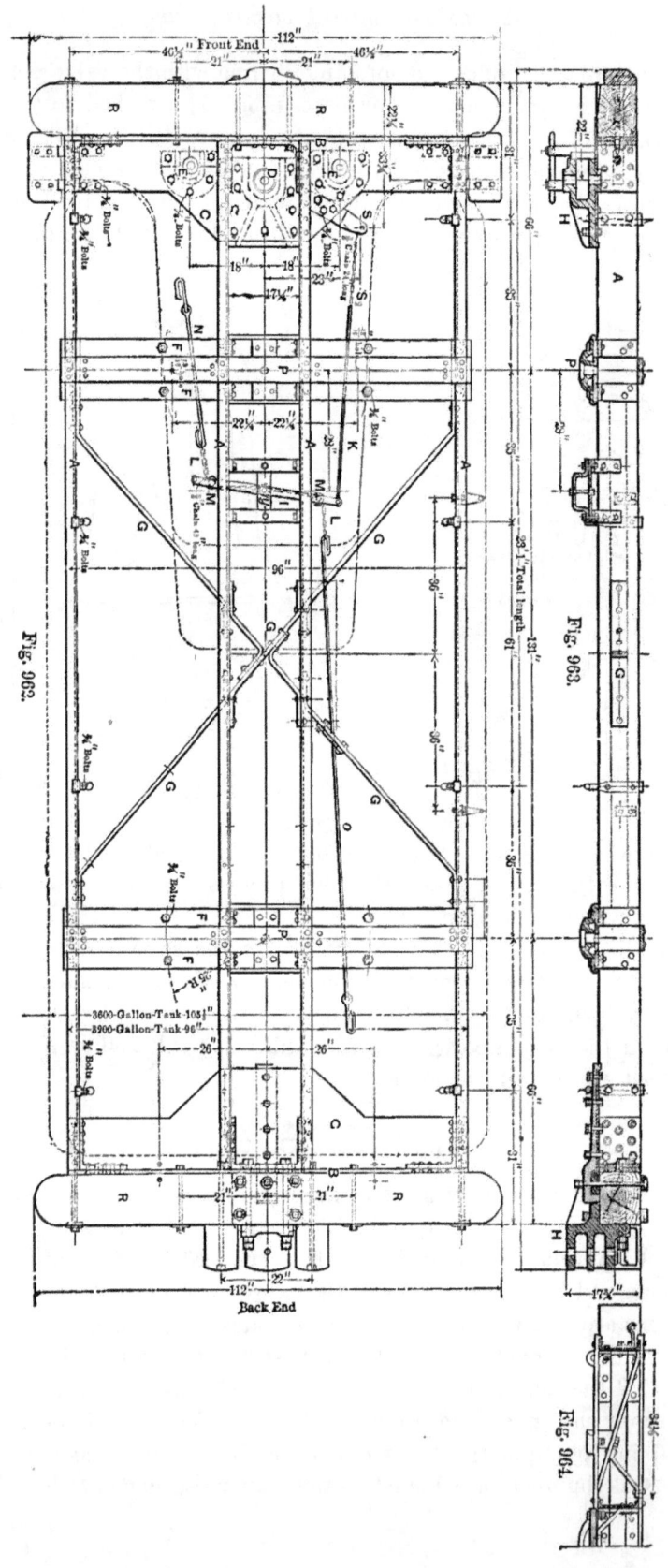

Fig. 962. Fig. 963. Fig. 964.

cast-iron sockets $P\ P$ for the truck center-pin are bolted to the transverse bars $F\ F$, which are riveted to the channel irons.

### BRAKE GEAR.

**565.** In the plan of this frame a very efficient brake gear is shown. The stand $S$ supports the upright brake shaft (not shown here) around which the chain $S_2$ is wound; this chain is connected to the rod $K$, which pulls on the lever $I$; this lever is fulcrumed at its center. A small chain wheel works on the fulcrum pin, and two wheels $M\ M$ of similar form work on the pivots fastened to the lever at a short distance from its ends. A chain $L\ L$ passes around these wheels as shown; one end of this chain is connected to the rod $N$, which works the brakes on the front truck, and the other end of the chain is fastened to a rod on the opposite end of lever which works the brakes on the rear truck. With this arrangement the brakes are put in action by hand, and the brake pressure on the front and rear truck is equalized by the chain $L\ L$. If it is desirable to put the brakes in action by air pressure, the end of the lever $I$ which engages with the rod $N$ is connected to the piston of the air cylinder without disturbing any of the other parts of the brake gear already described. With this arrangement the brakes can be put into action either by hand or by air pressure.

### TENDER TRUCKS.

**566.** There are quite a variety of tender trucks, but they all have one feature in common which differs from the engine truck, namely, all the axle journals are placed on

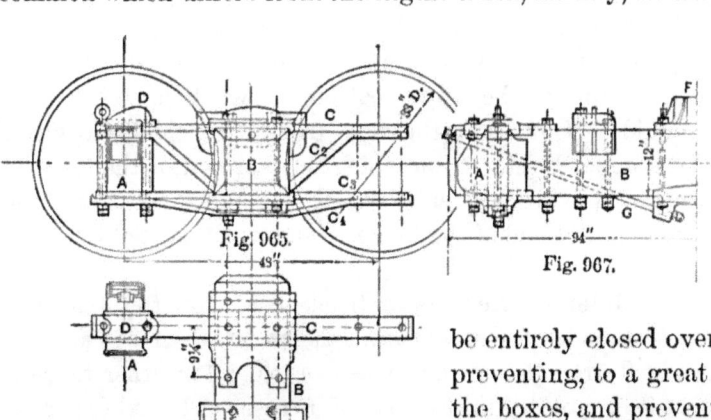

the outside of the wheels, which is not admissible on engine trucks, because their frames must be kept clear of the cylinders. In placing the journals outside of the wheels their bearings are more accessible, and the boxes can be entirely closed over the ends of axle, thereby preventing, to a great extent, dust from entering the boxes, and preventing oil from leaking out at the ends. Also in this position the journal bearings can be removed and replaced by new ones, and the boxes can be repacked with waste with much less difficulty than when the journals are on the inside of the wheels.

Figs. 965 to 967 show one of the simplest constructions of tender trucks. It consists of a wooden bolster $B$ (generally made of oak), which is supported by the wrought-iron bars $C$, $C_2$, $C_3$, and $C_4$. These bars are bolted direct to the axle-boxes $A\ A$. In this class of trucks the springs are simply laid on top of the truck frame.

For the rear truck here shown, which is a side-bearing truck, four springs are used; two of these springs (one on each side of truck) extend from the center of one axle to the center of the other one. The ends of these springs rest in the cast-iron pockets $D\ D$, which are bolted over each axle-box to the frame. Another pair of springs extend across the truck, one on each side of the center pin socket $F$; their ends rest in the

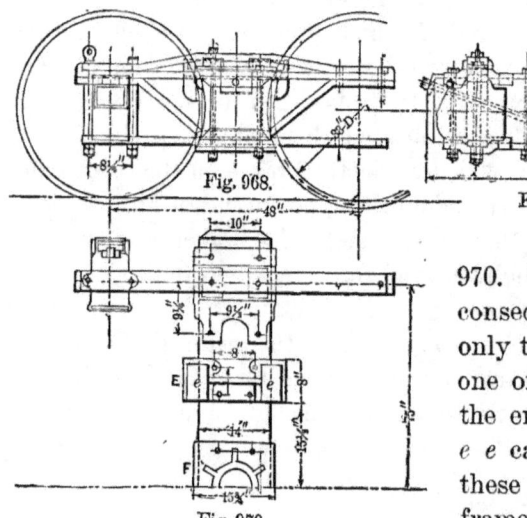

Fig. 968. Fig. 969. Fig. 970.

the pockets $e\ e$, which are cast in the bearings $E\ E$. The centers of these four springs support the rear end of the tender frame.

The front truck, which is similar in construction, is shown in Figs. 968 to 970. This truck is a center-bearing truck and consequently it has no outside springs. It has only two springs which extend across the truck, one on each side of the center-pin socket $F$; the ends of these springs rest in the pockets $e\ e$ cast in the bearings $E\ E$; the center of these springs support the front end of tender frame.

Figs. 971 to 974 show different views and sections of another type of tender truck. In this one the framing consists of the wrought-iron bars $C$, $C_2$, and $C_3$, which are bolted to the axle-boxes $A\ A$. The lower bolster $B_2$ is supported by the bars $C_2$ and $C_3$; on this bolster four springs $S\ S$ are laid, whose centers support the upper bolster $B$, which is free to move up and down between the guides $H\ H$. For the rear truck two side bearings $E$ are bolted to the top face of the upper bolster $B$, on which the rear end of the tender frame rests. These bearings make this truck a side-bearing one. For the front truck the bearings $E$ are not used; the front end of the tender frame is supported by the center-pin socket $F$.

Figs. 975 to 977 show different views of a truck used for the tender shown in Fig. 935. The frame $F$ is made of wrought-iron, the pedestals $A$ of cast-iron. In this case the brake beams $B$ are often made of ash or oak; for other tenders they are sometimes of wrought-iron built up in the form of a truss. The axle guards $C$ are simply wrought-iron straps and bent in the form of a U. Otherwise the construction of the truck is so plainly shown that a further description is unnecessary.

## TENDERS WITH WATER-SCOOPS.

567. The tanks for tenders heretofore shown are filled by means of a hose or pipe attached to the water tanks or hydrants in water stations. This often necessitates stops at comparatively short intervals, and consequently causes delays undesirable for express trains. In order to avoid such delays as much as possible some tenders are provided with water-scoops for taking water while the engine is running, the water

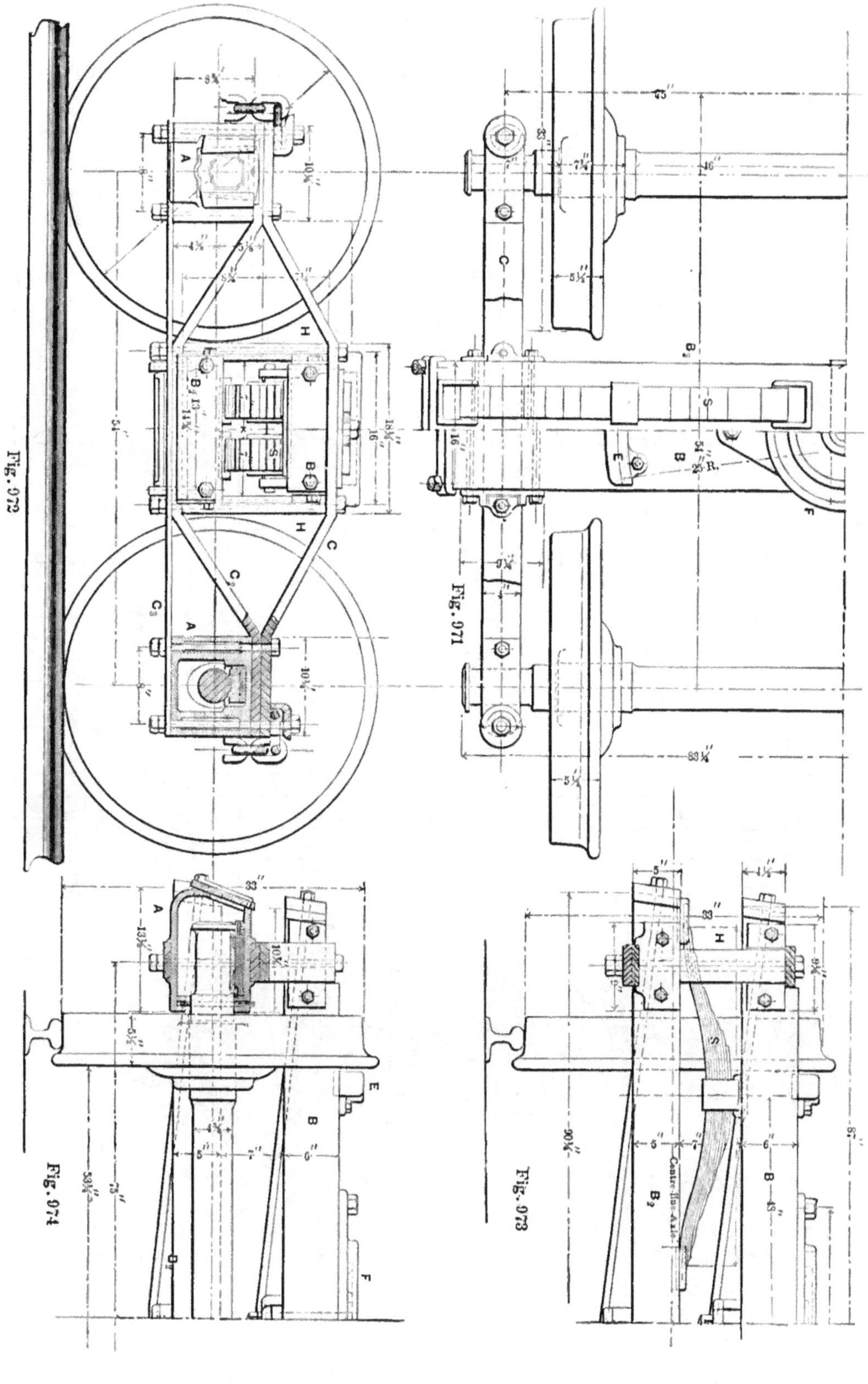

MODERN LOCOMOTIVE CONSTRUCTION.    573

Fig. 972

Fig. 971

Fig. 974

Fig. 973

being taken from a long narrow trough laid between the rails. The whole arrangement is shown in Figs. 978, 979, 980, and 980A.

The tank differs from the ordinary one by having a pipe *A*, **Fig. 978**, running through it leading the water up to the inside of the manhole, which is shown in dotted lines, from whence it is discharged into the tank. The smaller manhole, shown in full lines, simply indicates one as is used in the ordinary tank without the pipe *A*. The

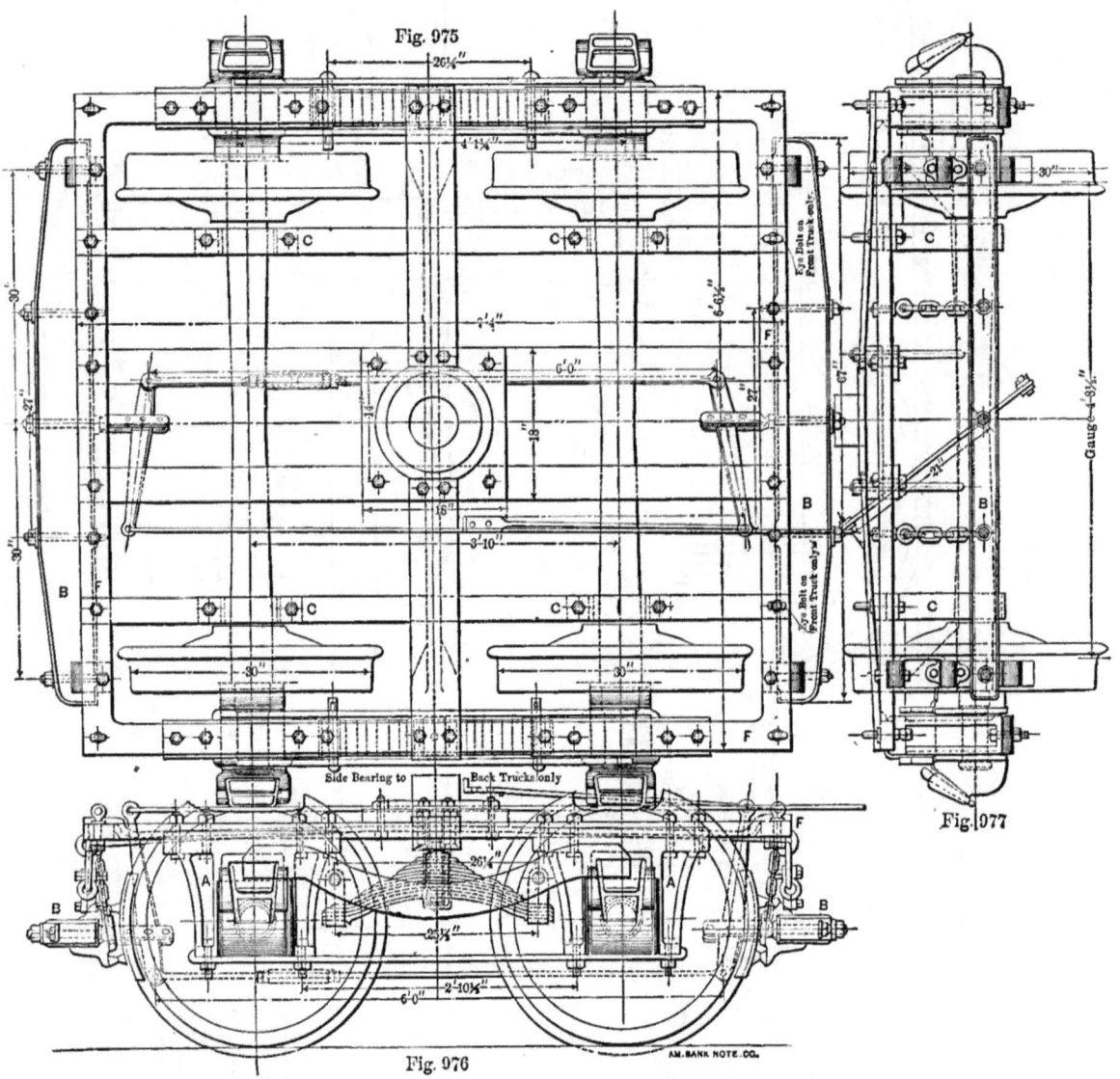

pipe *B* in Fig. 979 is a continuation of the pipe *A*, a water-tight joint being made between them. The scoop *C* is hinged to the pipe *B* so that the scoop can be raised or lowered by means of the system of levers shown plainly in Figs. 979, 980, and 980A; the raising and lowering being accomplished from the floor of the tender. The scoop is shown in its lowest position with its lower end dipping a few inches into the water in the trough. The bottom of the scoop acts like an inclined plane and takes advantage of the inertia of the water, which, being at rest in the trough and the engine running at a rate of 30 to 40 miles an hour, enables the scoop to lift the water through the pipe $A$, and is finally discharged into the tank. The height through which the water can be lifted will greatly depend on the speed of the train.

### TENDER-TRUCK AXLE-BOXES

568. Fig. 981 shows a longitudinal section of an ordinary tender-truck axle-box. Fig. 982 shows a horizontal section, Figs. 983 and 984 show respectively an outside end view and plan of the same box. It consists of a cast-iron casing $A$, a brass bearing $B$, and a cast-iron wedge $C$. This axle-box is suitable for a truck as shown in Fig. 972, and it is rigidly bolted to the frame by two turned bolts driven through the holes $D$, which are bored out at the ends only, and cored in the center somewhat larger than the diameter of the bolts. The brass $B$ rests on the journal $J$, and is held in position sideways by the projections $E E$ (Fig. 983) cast to the inner side of the casing $A$.

569. The wedge $C$ is placed in the box after the brass has been placed in position, and its purpose is simply to fill the space required for slipping the brass over the collar of the journal.

570. Many brasses have a convex back so as to give them only a small area of contact with the wedge, thereby giving freedom to the axle to adjust itself to any unevenness of the track. On account of this small area of contact the brass must be made comparatively thick so that its ends will not spring upwards and wear the journal more at its center than at its ends.

The brasses are bored, having frequently a radius from $\frac{1}{32}$ to $\frac{1}{16}$ inch greater than that of the journal. The edges $F F$ of the brass (Fig. 983) should be well rounded so as to prevent them from scraping the oil off the journal. The width of the bearing surface should

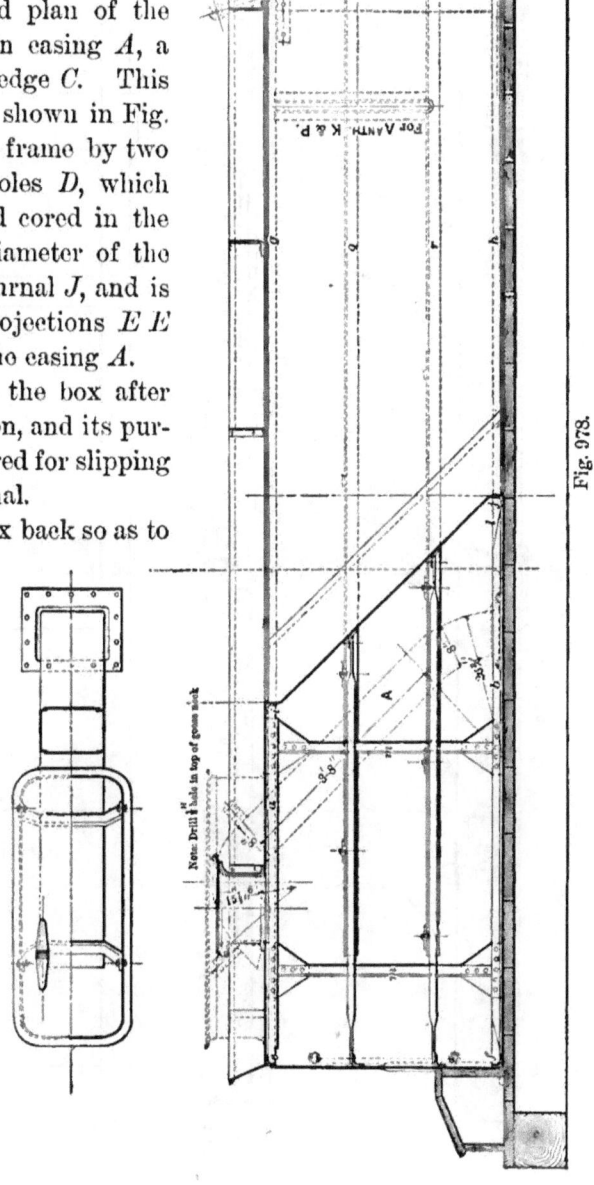

Fig. 978.

576 MODERN LOCOMOTIVE CONSTRUCTION.

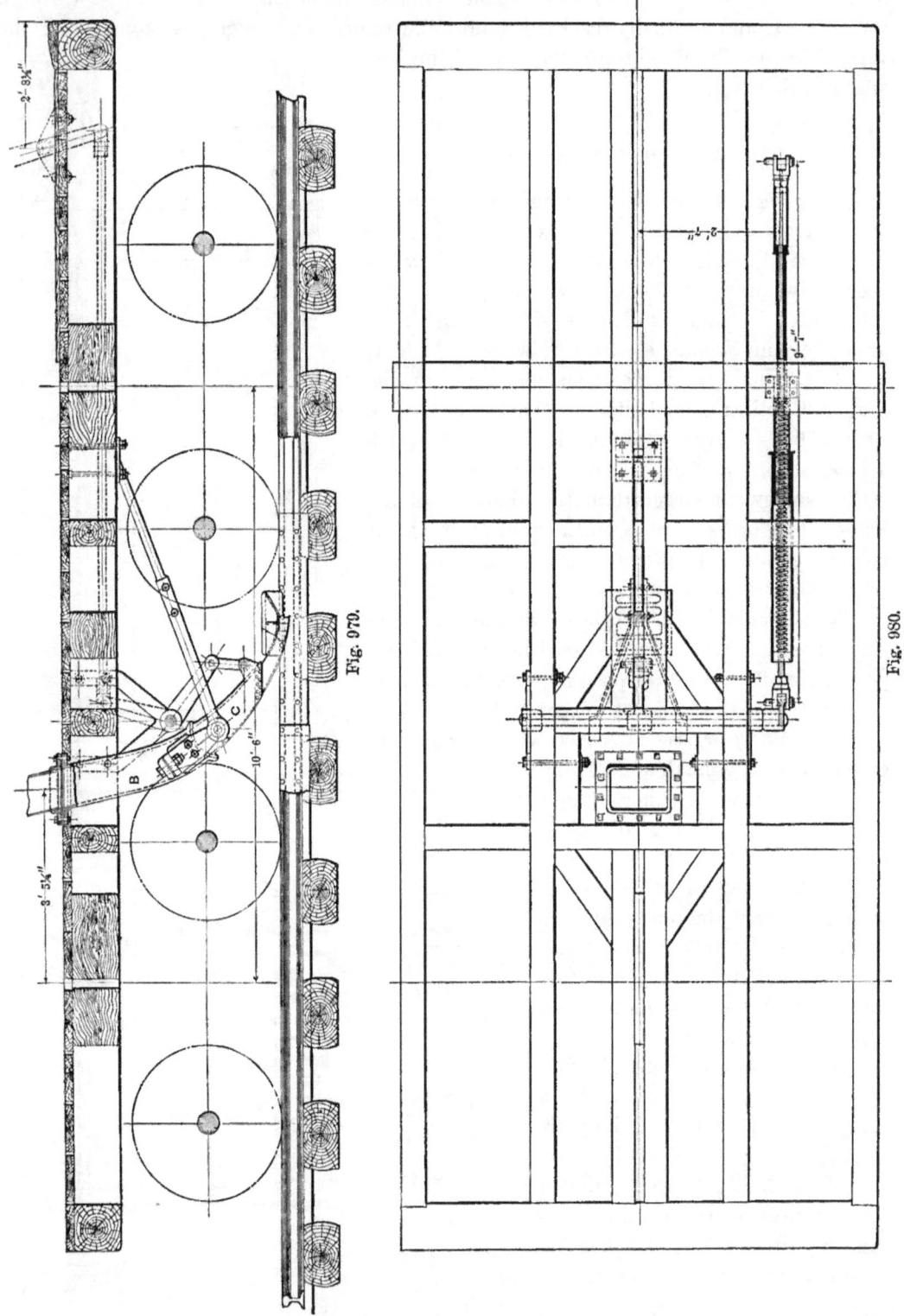

Fig. 979.

Fig. 980.

extend about one-third around the circumference of the journal, and the length of the brass is usually ¼ inch less than that of the journal.

571. Sometimes the bearing surface of the brass is composed of a lead lining, which, it is believed, prevents heating to a considerable extent, particularly when new brasses are used on worn journals. That lead lining has given good results cannot be denied, but reliable and definite values are lacking. This lining should not be more than $\frac{1}{16}$ inch thick; if it is more than this, the lead will be forced out at the edges so as to prevent a free flow of oil between the wearing surfaces, and otherwise give trouble.

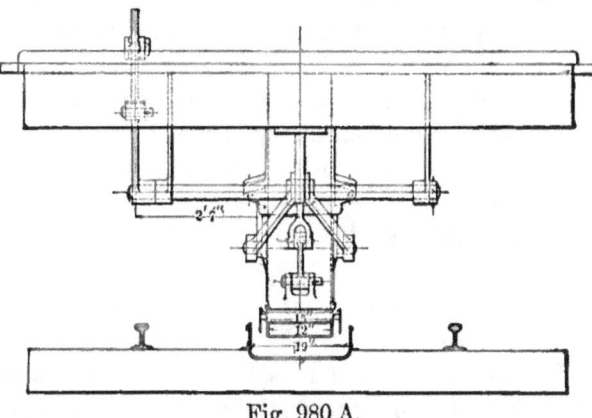

Fig. 980 A.

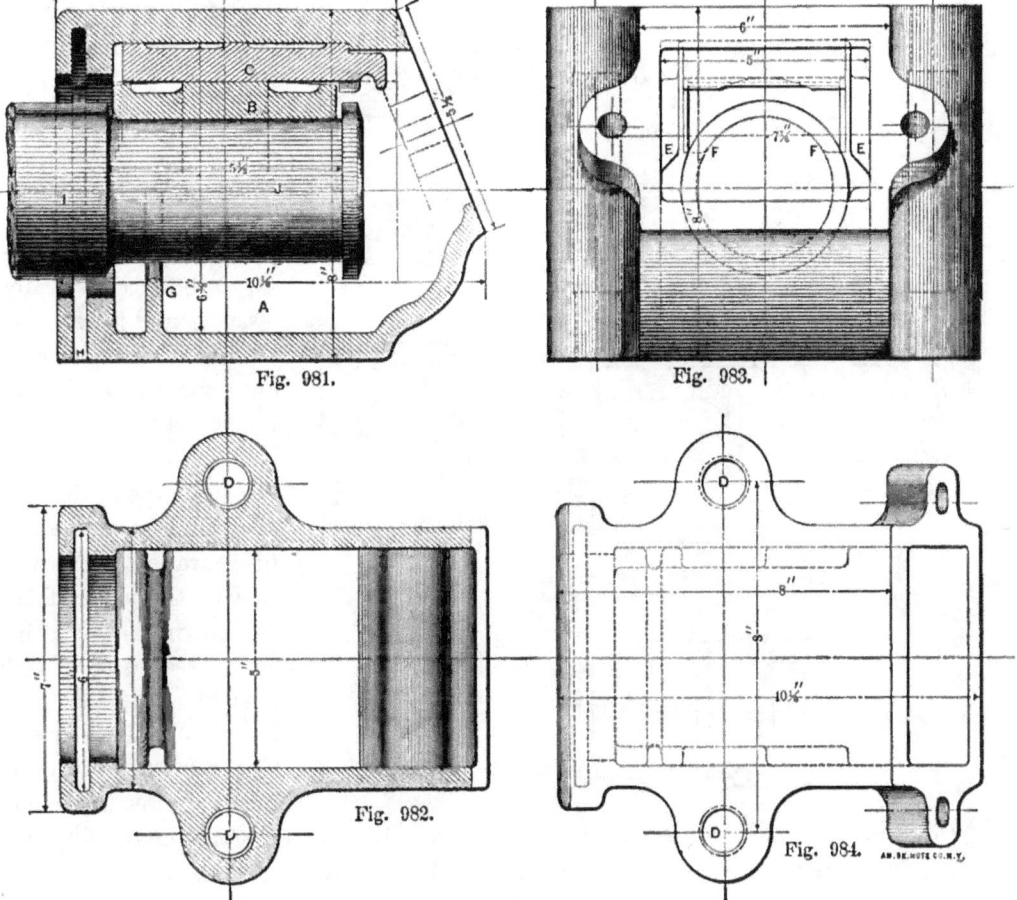

Fig. 981.   Fig. 983.

Fig. 982.   Fig. 984.

572. To prepare the brass for the lining it is first bored, then well heated over a coke fire, then cleaned with muriatic acid and tinned. After this it is placed at a

correct distance from a mandrel of suitable diameter, and warmed again to enable the lead, when poured between the mandrel and brass, to adhere to the tin. This process was patented by Mr. Hopkins, but the patent has now expired.

573. In designing the foregoing class of axle-box, care should be taken to have the centers of the holes $D$ in line with the center of the journal as shown.

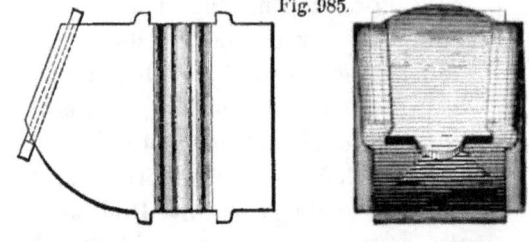

The bottom of the axle-box is filled with cotton or woolen waste saturated with oil, which bears against the bottom of the journal and keeps it lubricated.

The rib $G$ cast to the bottom of the box, Fig. 981, prevents the waste from being forced too far back. This rib is not used in all boxes; and when not used, the waste touches the end of the box. The opening $H$ takes the dust guard either made of wood or leather. The dust guard is made to fit the axle at $I$, and prevents the dust from getting in and the oil from leaking out.

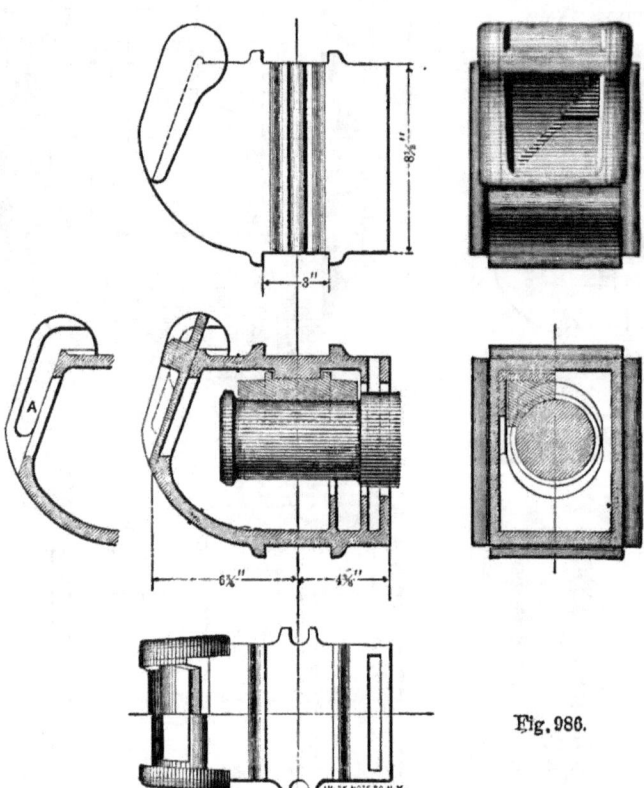

574. The front cover, which is not shown, is in this design of box fastened to it by two screw bolts. Trouble is sometimes occasioned by the loss of the screw bolts caused by carelessness and neglect to screw them in tight; consequently, on some roads the cover or lid is made in the form of a wedge, as shown in Fig. 985. On other roads the cover has a lug cast to each side which fit in tapered grooves $A$ $A$ cast to the sides of the box, as shown in Fig. 986. This cover wedges itself tightly in position when dropped into its place. The grooves are so arranged as to permit the box to be readily opened, but the cover cannot be conveniently removed wholly, and therefore the liability of losing it is much reduced, while the annoyance of dust flying into the box is to a great extent avoided.

575. The axle-box shown in Fig. 986 is similar in design to that shown in Fig. 981, but it has no wedge, and the dust guard enters at the top of the box instead of

entering at the bottom; the bolts which secure the box to the frame lie in grooves cast in the sides of the box instead of being driven into the holes. A very small amount of clearance is allowed for the bolts in the grooves. This is done not only for cheapness, but also to provide easy means for taking the bolts out when it becomes necessary to remove the box, thereby facilitating repairs.

576. Fig. 987 shows another box similar in design to that shown in Fig. 981, but with this difference: the sides of the box are arranged for a pedestal in which the box is free to move up or down. A box of this kind is suitable for a truck shown in Fig. 976. The pedestal must, of course, be placed central with the axle journal. It will also be noticed that the cover of this box is secured by one screw bolt only.

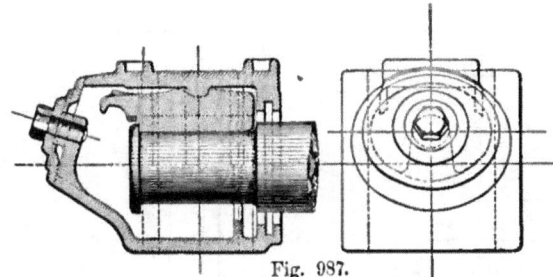

Fig. 987.

577. The design of box shown in Fig. 988 explains itself. It is made for an axle journal which has no end collar. The manner of holding its cover in position is somewhat peculiar; it is held by a spiral spring, and in order to open the box the cover must be sprung beyond the projections cast to the end of the box.

578. There are many other types of boxes used, their design depending chiefly on the form of brasses adopted, the manner of fastening the covers, and the type of truck

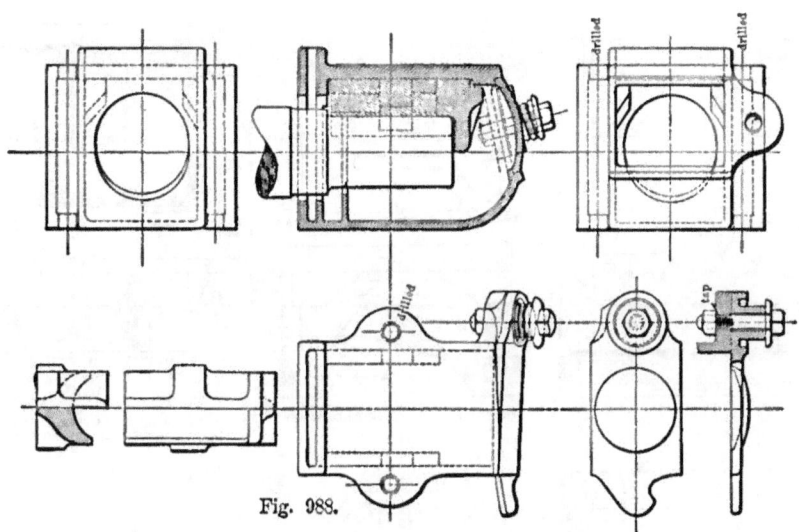

Fig. 988.

for which they are intended. But the features which enter into the design of the tender-truck boxes are shown in the foregoing illustrations.

Fig. 988A shows two views of a tender-truck axle-box, and Fig. 988B shows different views of its bearing and wedge. This box was adopted as a standard by the American Railway Master-Mechanics' Association.

## TENDER-TRUCK AXLES.

579. In designing a tender-truck axle the first problem which presents itself is to find the dimensions of the journals. These must not only be strong enough to hold the weight of the tender, fuel, and water, but they must also be so proportioned as not

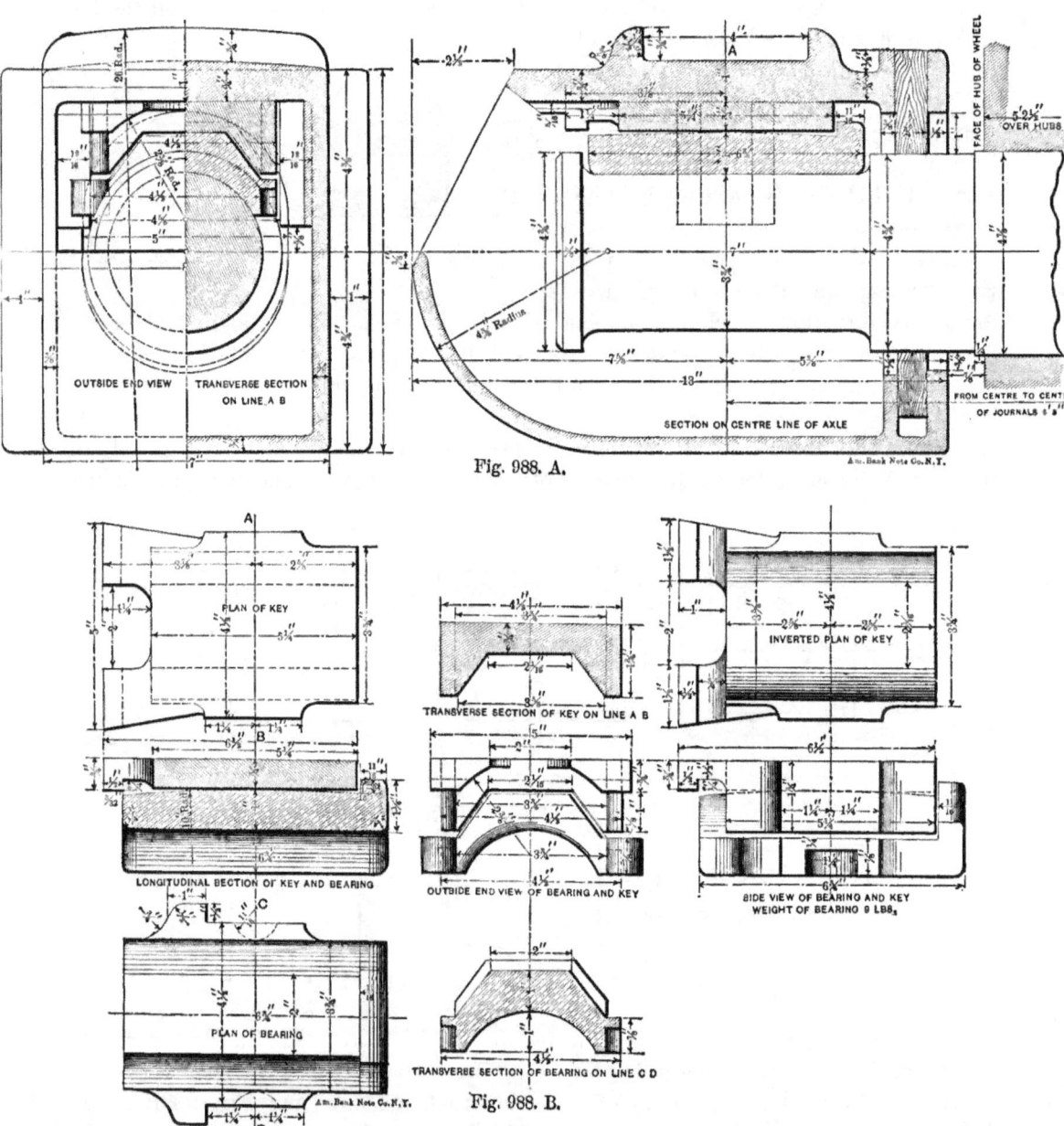

Fig. 988. A.

Fig. 988. B.

to heat; and generally, when they meet the requirements of the latter condition, they will also be strong enough to hold the weight placed upon them. To prevent heating, the pressure upon the journal must not exceed a certain limit.

Referring to Fig. 983, we notice that the brass touches only about one-third of the circumference of the journal; but for the sake of simplicity in making the computations it is usually assumed that the brass covers one-half of the circumference, so that pressure may be referred to the projected area of the journal, which, as we have seen, is equal to the product of the diameter into the length of the journal.

580. To obtain the weight on each journal we divide the total weight of tender, fuel, and water, minus the weight of wheels and axles, by the number of journals under the tender; the quotient will be the weight which each journal has to support. Dividing this weight by the projected area, we obtain the pressure per square inch of projected area. This pressure varies under different tenders from 170 to 350 pounds. We believe that the safest practice is not to allow it to exceed 225 pounds per square inch for a journal-surface speed of 5 feet per second.

581. On many roads the tender-truck journals are 3½ inches diameter and 7 inches long for tenders weighing, when empty, from 20,000 to 24,000 pounds, and with fuel

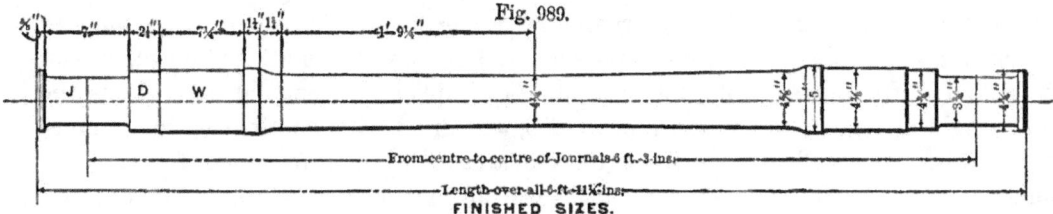

Master Car Builders' Standard Axle for 30,000 pound Cars. Master Mechanics' Standard Axle for Light Tenders.

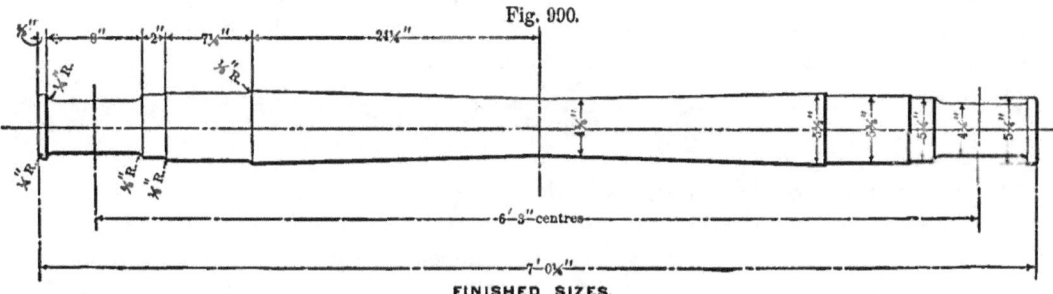

Master Car Builders' Standard Axle for 60,000 pound Cars. Master Mechanics' Standard Axle for Heavy Tenders.

and water weighing from 41,000 to 58,000 pounds. For tenders weighing, when empty, from 27,000 to 30,000 pounds, and with fuel and water weighing from 60,000 to 74,000 pounds, the journals are generally 4 inches diameter and 8 inches long. Other roads have adopted the Master Car Builders' standard for the tenders so as to avoid carrying extra sizes of axles for tenders in stock. These standards are illustrated in Figs. 989 and 990; they are recommended by the Master-Mechanics Association.

The axle shown in Fig. 989 has journals 3¾ inches in diameter and 7 inches long. It is suitable for tenders whose total weight varies from 40,000 to 58,000 pounds. The other axle shown in Fig. 990 has journals 4¼ inches diameter, 8 inches long. It is suitable for tenders weighing in complete working order from 60,000 pounds and upwards. These axles are made either of iron or steel.

582. It will be noticed that the pressure per square inch of projected area of the tender-truck axle is greater than that of the engine-truck axles. This is admissible, because the tender-truck wheels are usually larger in diameter than the engine-truck wheels. Again, in engine-trucks the journals are of necessity placed inside of the wheels, and therefore they have to be comparatively large in diameter and limited lengths so as to give the required strength to the axles; these conditions give a greater surface velocity to the engine-truck journals than that of the tender-truck journals, and consequently the pressure per square inch of projected area of the former journals cannot be as large as the pressure on the latter. The journals in tender-trucks are generally better protected from dust, and the load on them decreases as the fuel and water is used up, all of which tends to lessen the danger of heating.

583. To find the dimensions of journals for tenders weighing less than given in Art. 581, we subtract the weight of the wheels and axles from the total weight of the tender, water, and fuel, and divide the remainder by 225; the quotient will give the sum of the projected areas of the journals. Dividing the latter quotient by the number of journals, we obtain the projected area of each; if now the length is known, we can easily find the diameter. But for the sake of simplicity we may at once divide the total weight of tender, water, and fuel by 250, and divide this quotient by the number of journals, which will give us the projected area of each near enough for practical purposes, from which the diameter and length of journal can be easily found if we know the ratio between the two.

EXAMPLE 151.—The total weight of the tender, water, and fuel is 38,000 pounds; it has two four-wheeled trucks; the length of the journal is to be equal to twice its diameter; find the length and diameter of the journals.

Here we have
$$\frac{38000}{250} = 152 \text{ square inches}$$

for the projected area of eight journals, and

$$\frac{152}{8} = 19 \text{ square inches}$$

for the projected area of each journal.

The ratio between the length and diameter of journal is 2; hence the diameter can be found by the rule given in connection with engine-trucks, thus: $\sqrt{\frac{19}{2}} = 3.08$, say 3 inches for the diameter of the journal and $3 \times 2 = 6$ inches for its length.

584. Although journals are generally strong enough to support the weight placed upon them when they are correctly designed to prevent heating, the question may arise: What load can a journal support?

The worst condition to which a journal may be subjected is when the brass bears only on its outer end. In cases of this kind we may consider the journal to be a beam supported at one end and loaded at the other. For computing the load which a beam of this form can support with safety, we have the following formula:

$$L = \frac{S \times 3.1416 \times d^3}{32 \times l}, \qquad (a)$$

in which $L$ denotes the load in pounds; $S$, the stress per square inch on the fibers most remote from the neutral surface; for wrought-iron the value of $S$ is generally taken at 12,000 pounds, and for steel, 16,000 pounds; $d$ denotes the diameter in inches; and $l$, the length of the journal in inches. To show the application of this formula, we will take the following example:

EXAMPLE 152.—What load can a wrought-iron journal safely support, its diameter being $3\tfrac{3}{4}$ inches and its length 7 inches, under the assumption that the whole load is concentrated at the end of the journal?

Substituting in the formula for the symbols their values, we have,

$$L = \frac{12000 \times 3.1416 \times 3.75^3}{32 \times 7} = 8875 \text{ pounds.}$$

If this size of journal is used under a tender weighing 58,000 pounds, then the actual weight on each journal will not reach 7,250 pounds, which shows us that the journal is strong enough for the work it has to do.

If we consider the journal to be a beam supported at one end and uniformly loaded, then the load which it can support is computed by the following formula:

$$L = \frac{S \times 3.1416 \times d^3}{16 \times l}, \qquad (b)$$

in which the symbols denote the same quantities as before. Working out Example 152 by this formula, we find that this journal can support a load uniformly distributed of 17,750 pounds, which shows us that the journal is more than strong enough for a tender whose total weight is 58,000 pounds.

Formula ($a$) can be used for finding the load which can be supported by any beam of circular cross-section fixed at one end and loaded at the other.

Formula ($b$) can be used for finding the uniformly distributed load which can be supported by any beam of circular cross-section and fixed at one end.

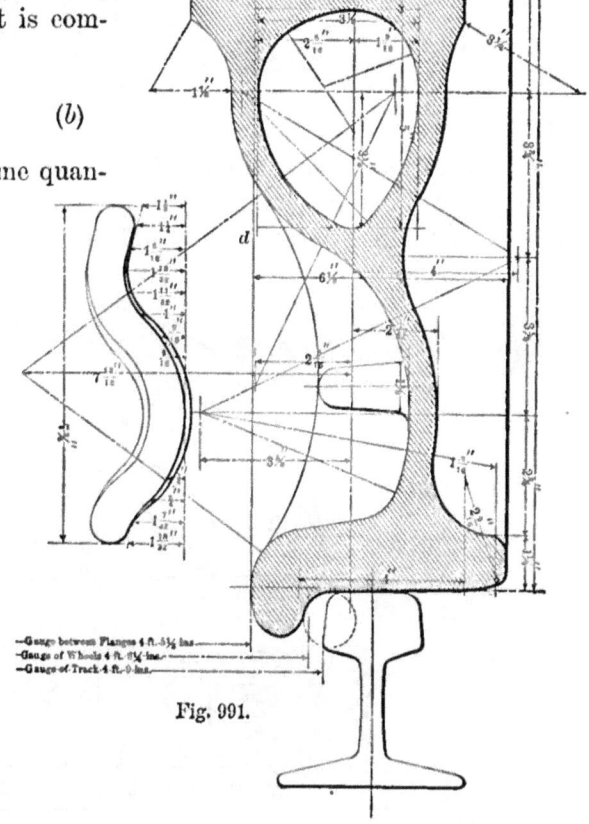

Fig. 991.

TRUCK WHEELS.

585. Of the many types of wheels now in use under cars and tenders, the cast-iron wheel with chilled treads is the most common one. A section of this wheel is shown

584                MODERN LOCOMOTIVE CONSTRUCTION.

in Fig. 991; its form should be such that no part of the wheel is unduly strained during cooling after it has been cast. The section in Fig. 991 is of a type used under cars and tenders on the Pennsylvania R. R.

586. For tender-trucks the face $a$ of the hub does not reach the outer face $c$ of the

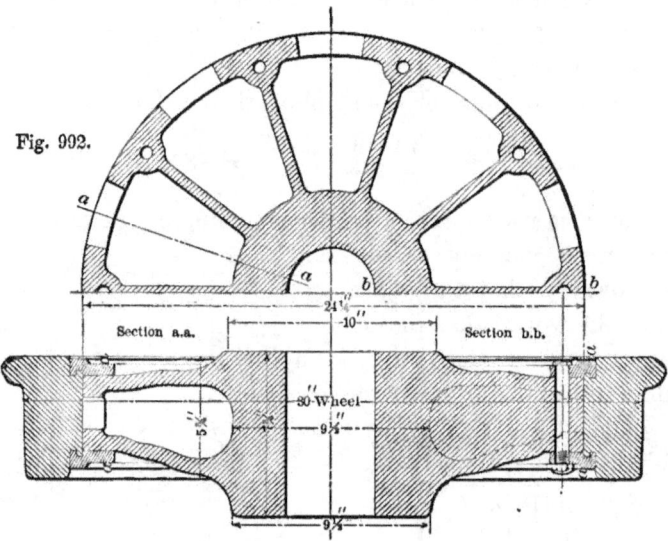

tread so as to allow sufficient space for the axle-box; and in order to obtain the necessary depth for the hub its inside face $b$ projects beyond the face of the flange $d$. In this respect the tender-truck wheel differs from the engine-truck wheel; in the latter

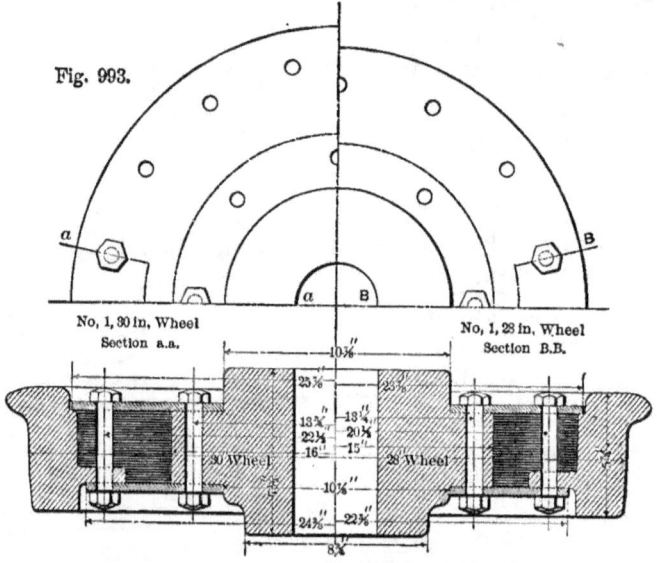

the hub is placed longitudinally, nearly central with the tread, so as to allow space for the axle-box, which in the engine-truck is placed on the inside of the wheel.

587. Fig. 992 shows a type of wheel manufactured by the Allan Paper Wheel Company, of Chicago, Ill. In this type the tire is shrunk on a cast-iron center and held by

two retaining rings. The form of these rings and that of the tire are such that, should the latter break across, the retaining rings will hold the broken tire in place.

Fig. 993 shows a paper wheel also manufactured by the Allan Paper Wheel Company. In this wheel the tire is joined to the hub by two wrought-iron plates.

588. Fig. 994 shows a steel wheel manufactured by the Boies Steel Wheel Company, of Scranton, Pa. Its construction is very simple. The wheel is composed of four principal parts: the steel tire, the two corrugated steel plates, and a cast-iron hub. The tire is shrunk on the corrugated plates, and the whole is firmly bolted together.

589. An excellent type of truck wheel is made at the Baldwin Locomotive Works, Philadelphia. The tire is placed on a wrought-iron center of the spoke type. The centers are made by an improved method patented by Samuel M. Vauclain, Superintendent of the Baldwin Locomotive Works. These wheels are very strong and have a fine finish, resembling a well-made cast-iron wheel having spokes of elliptical cross-section.

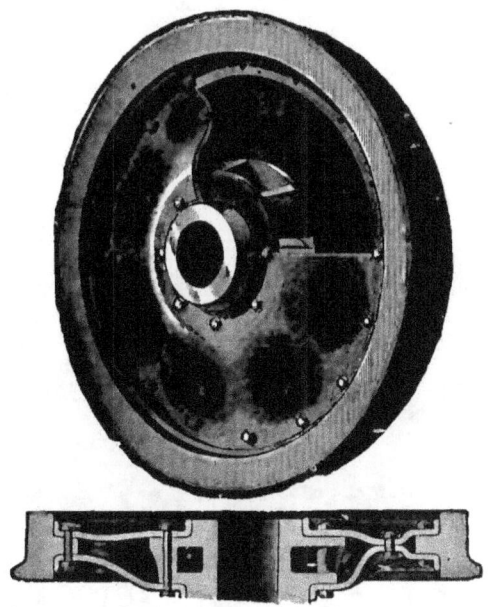

Fig. 994.

### GENERAL TYPES OF LOCOMOTIVES.

590. Fig. 995 shows a longitudinal section and a half plan of the machinery of an eight-wheeled passenger locomotive built by the Grant Locomotive Works, formerly at Paterson, N. J., now at Chicago, Ill. The right-hand side of Fig. 996 shows the rear end, and the left-hand side the front end, of the same engine with the smoke-box front and bumper removed. The left-hand side of Fig. 997 shows a transverse section taken in front of the guide-yoke, and the right-hand side shows a transverse section taken behind the sand-box. This engine has a short smoke-box, and is equipped with pumps, whose location, with the arrangement of suction and delivery pipes such as are generally adopted in this class of engine, is plainly shown.

591. Fig. 998 shows an elevation of another eight-wheeled passenger engine and a half plan of its machinery. This is the standard design adopted by the Pennsylvania R. R. In these illustrations is shown the manner of attaching the Westinghouse brake. The engine-truck is shown in Figs. 886A, 886B, and 886C. This engine is doing excellent service. Its principal dimensions are as follows:

SPECIFICATIONS FOR STANDARD P. R. R. LOCOMOTIVE WITH TENDER. CLASS "P"—68-INCH DRIVERS—160 POUNDS STEAM PRESSURE.

| | | | |
|---|---|---|---|
| Gauge | 4 ft. 9 in. | Tires | Steel. |
| Number of Pairs of Driving Wheels | 2. | Total Wheel Base | 22 ft. 8¼ in. |
| Diameter of Driving Wheels | 68 in. | Length of Rigid Wheel Base | 7 ft. 9 in. |
| Wheel Centers | Cast-iron. | Diameter of Driving-axle Bearing | 8 in. |

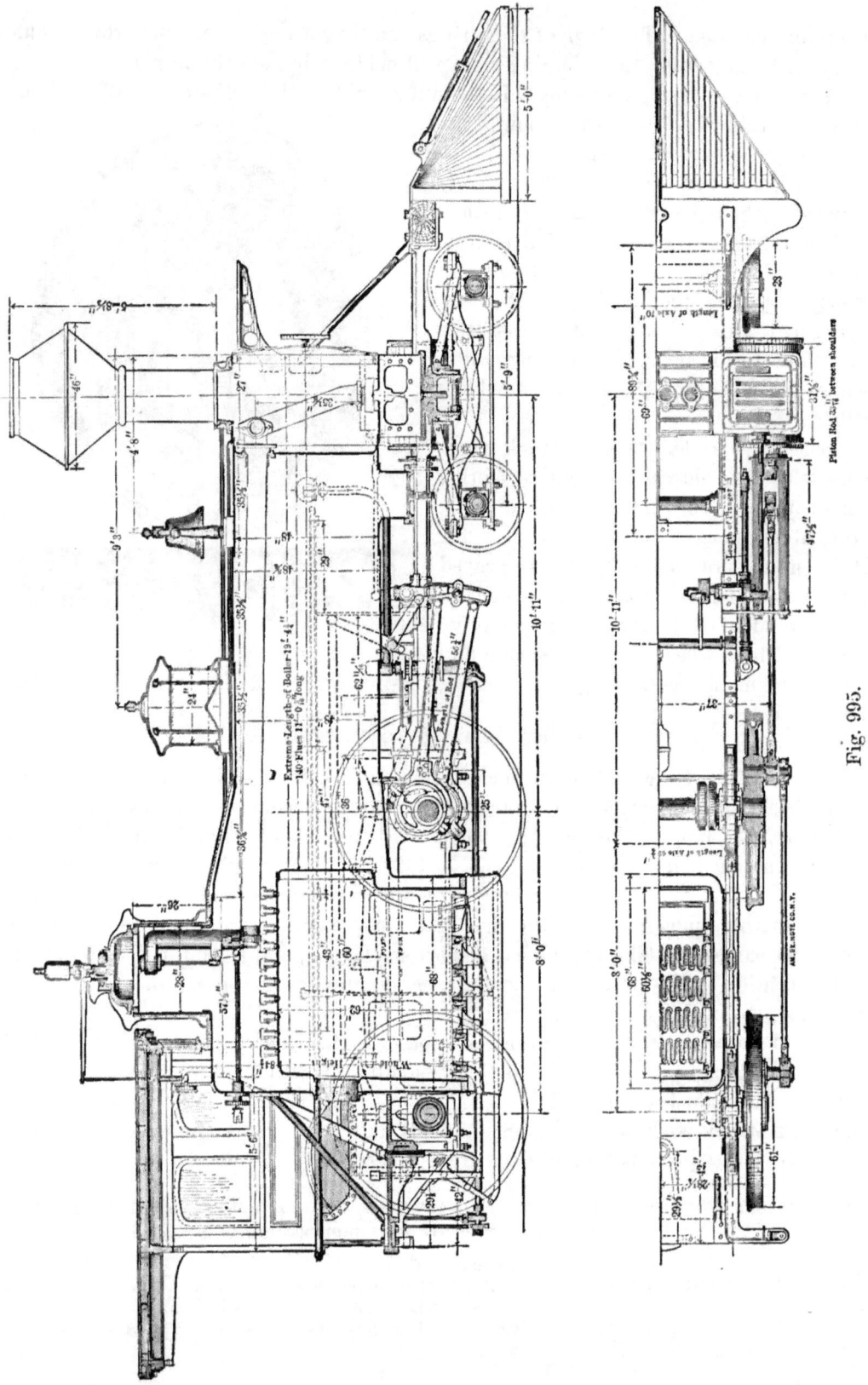

Fig. 995.

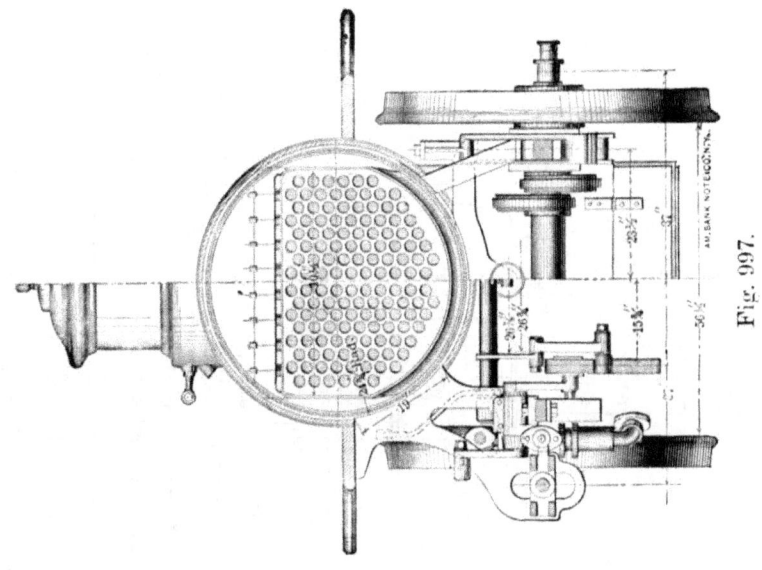

Fig. 997.

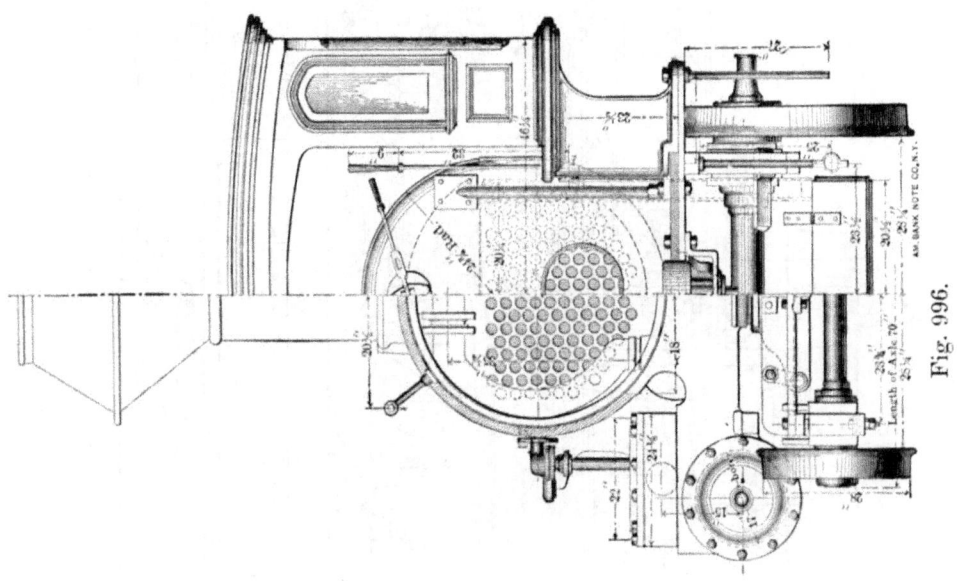

Fig. 996.

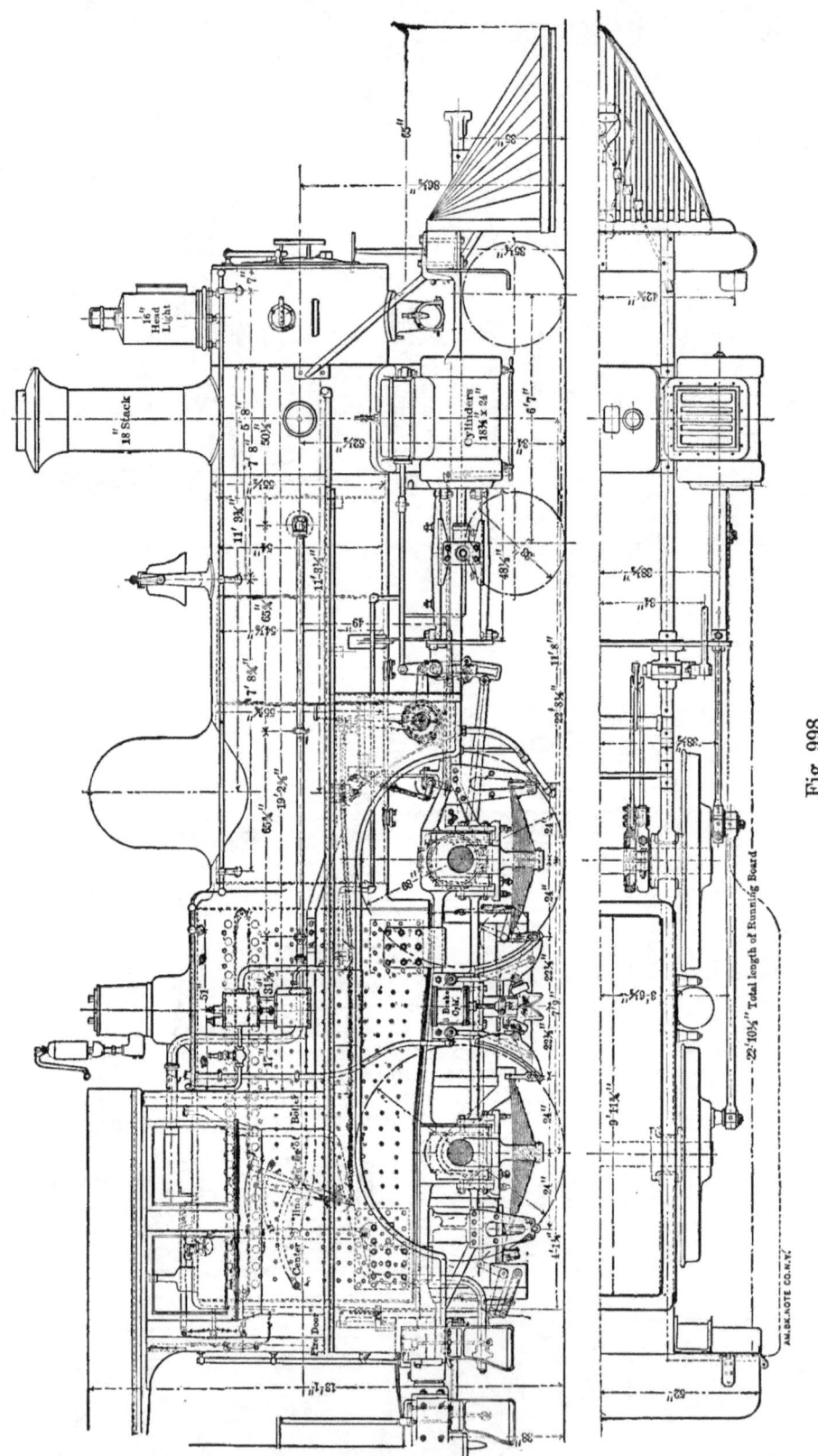

Fig. 998.

| | |
|---|---|
| Length of Driving-axle Bearing | 10¼ in. |
| Diameter of Main Crank-pin Bearing | 4⅝ in. |
| Length of Main Crank-pin bearing | 4¼ in. |
| Diameter of Parallel-rod Bearing } Front and Back | 3¾ in. |
| Length of Parallel-rod Bearing } | 3¼ in. |
| Number of Wheels in Front Truck | 4. |
| Diameter of Wheels in Front Truck | 33 in. |
| Material of Wheels in Front Truck, | Cast-iron Steel Tired. |
| Diameter of Truck-axle Bearing | 5¼ in. |
| Length of Truck-axle Bearing | 10 in. |
| Type of Truck | Rigid Center. |
| Cylinders and Steam-chests | Outside. |
| Spread of Cylinders | 77 in. |
| Diameter of Cylinders | 18¼ in. |
| Length of Stroke | 24 in. |
| Position of Valve Gear | Between Frames. |
| Type of Valve Gear | Shifting-link Motion. |
| Travel of Valve | 5 in. |
| Outside Lap of Valve | ⅞ in. |
| Inside Lap of Valve | None. |
| Lead of Valve | 1/16 in. |
| Throw of Eccentric | 5 in. |
| Length of Steam Ports | 17¼ in. |
| Width of Steam Ports | 1¼ in. |
| Width of Exhaust Port | 2¼ in. |
| Kind of Frames | Wrought-iron, Inside. |
| Distance between Centers of Frames | 44 in. |
| Boiler Material | Steel. |
| Thickness of Boiler Sheets, Dome | ⅜ in. |
| Thickness of Boiler Sheets, Barrel and Smoke-box | 7/16 in. |
| Thickness of Boiler Sheets, Outside Fire-box | 7/16 in. |
| Maximum Internal Diameter of Boiler } Belpaire | 56⅝ in. |
| Minimum Internal Diameter of Boiler } | 53¼ in. |
| Height to Center of Boiler, from Top of Rail | 86¼ in. |
| Number of Tubes | 210. |
| Inside Diameter of Tubes | 1¾ in. |
| Outside Diameter of Tubes | 2 in. |
| Tube Material | Wrought-iron. |
| Length of Tubes between Tube Sheets | 136 in. |
| External Heating Surface of Tubes | 1244 sq. ft. |
| Fire Area through Tubes | 3.5 sq. ft. |
| Length of Fire-box (Inside) | 9 ft. 11¼ in. |
| Width of Fire-box (Inside) | 3 ft. 4 in. |
| Height of Crown Sheet above Top of Grate (Center of Fire-box) | 3 ft. 8¼ in. |
| Inside Fire-box Material | Steel. |
| Thickness of Inside Fire-box Sheets, Sides | 7/16 in. |
| Thickness of Inside Fire-box, Crown | ⅜ in. |
| Thickness of Inside Fire-box, Back | ⅜ in. |
| Thickness of Tube Sheets, Front | ½ in. |
| Thickness of Tube Sheets, Back | ⅜ in. |
| Tube Sheet Material | Steel. |
| Heating Surface of Fire-box | 138 sq. ft. |
| Total Heating Surface | 1382 sq. ft. |
| Fire Grate Area | 33.25 sq. ft. |
| Diameter of Smoke-stack (Straight) | 18 in. |
| Height of Stack above Top of Rail | 15 ft. 0 in. |
| Width of Cab Roof | 9 ft. 6 in. |
| Height of Cab Roof from Rail | 12 ft. 10¼ in. |
| Width of Cab | 9 ft. |
| Size of Exhaust Nozzle | 2¾ x 3½ in. |
| Pressure of Steam per Square Inch | 160 lbs. |
| Nature of Fuel | Anthracite Coal. |
| Weight of Engine Empty | 96,100 lbs. |
| Weight on Drivers | 65,150 lbs. |
| Weight on Truck | 30,950 lbs. |
| Weight of Engine in Working Order | 106,500 lbs. |
| Weight on First Pair of Drivers | 36,500 lbs. |
| Weight on Second Pair of Drivers | 36,850 lbs. |
| Weight on Truck | 33,150 lbs. |
| Engine fitted with Driver Brake. | |
| Capacity of Tank | 3000 gal. |
| Capacity of Coal-box | 9900 lbs. |
| Number of Wheels under Tender | 8. |
| Diameter of Wheels under Tender | 33 in. |
| Material of Wheels under Tender, | Cast-iron Chilled Tread. |
| Diameter of Tender-truck Journals | 4 in. |
| Length of Tender-truck | 8 in. |
| Weight of Tender, Empty | 29,800 lbs. |
| Weight of Tender, Loaded | 65,500 lbs. |
| Tender fitted with Water-scoop. | |

It will be noticed that this engine has an extension smoke-box, and the driving-wheel springs are placed below the axle-boxes instead of above them, as shown in Fig. 995.

592. Fig. 999 shows an elevation, and Figs. 1000, 1001, and 1002 show end views and section of a ten-wheeled engine built by the Baldwin Locomotive Works, Philadelphia, Pa.

Fig. 1003 shows an elevation of a consolidation engine also built by the Baldwin Locomotive Works.

593. Fig. 1004 shows a powerful six-wheeled switching engine built by the Pennsylvania R. R. Its principal dimensions are as follows:

SPECIFICATIONS FOR STANDARD P. R. R. CLASS "M" SHIFTING ENGINE WITH TENDER.

| | |
|---|---|
| Gauge | 4 ft. 9 in. |
| Number of Pairs of Driving Wheels | 3. |
| Diameter of Driving Wheels | 50 in. |
| Wheel Centers | Cast-iron. |
| Tires | Steel. |
| Total Wheel Base | 10 ft. 8 in. |
| Length of Rigid Wheel Base | 10 ft. 8 in. |
| Diameter of Driving-axle Bearing | 7¼ in. |

590  MODERN LOCOMOTIVE CONSTRUCTION.

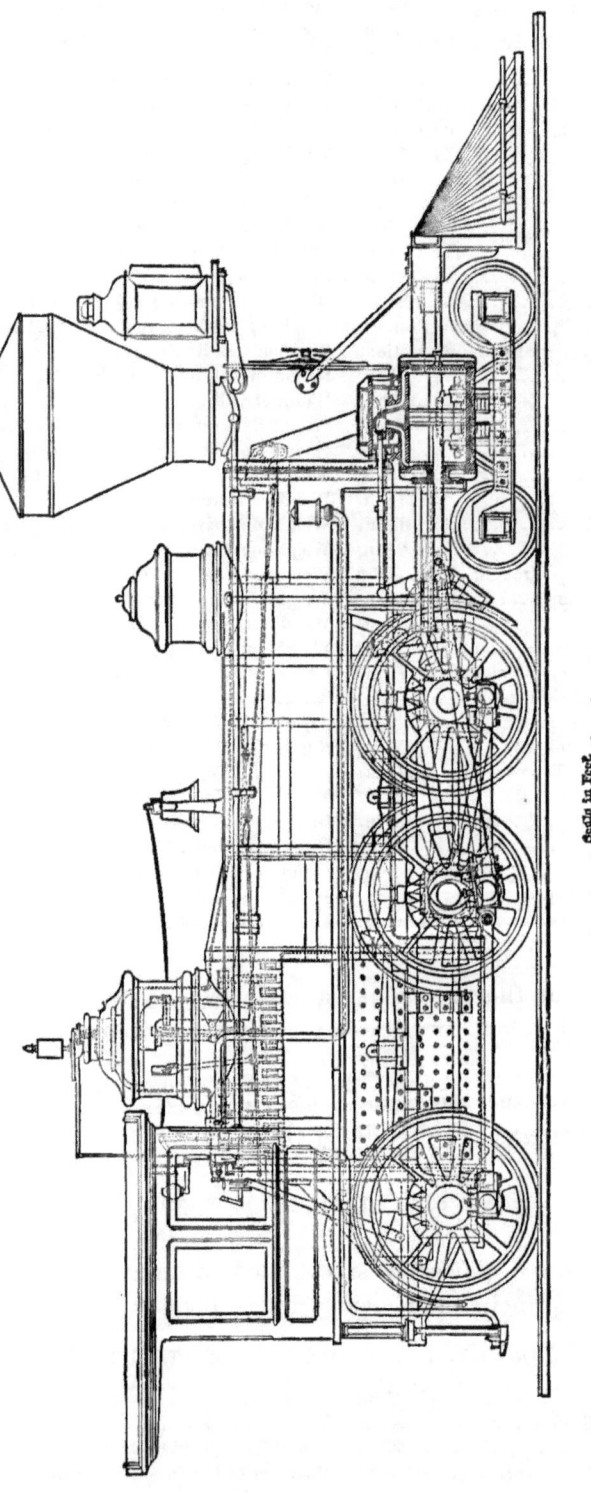

Fig. 999.

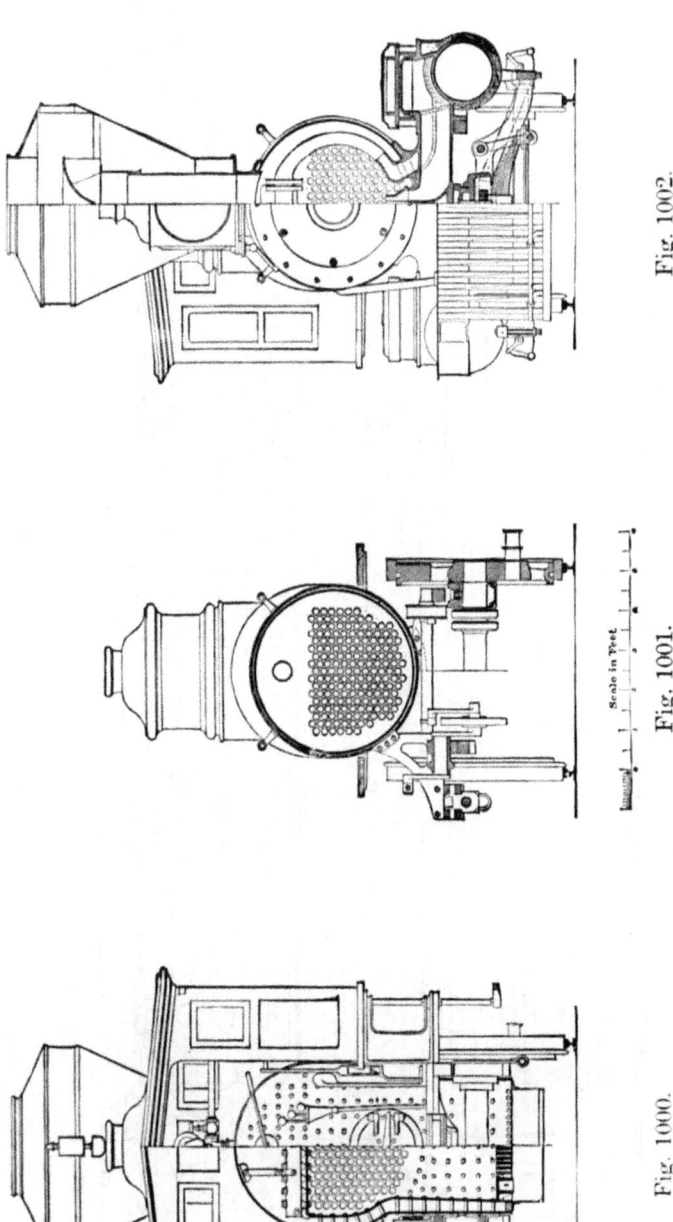

Fig. 1002.

Fig. 1001.

Fig. 1000.

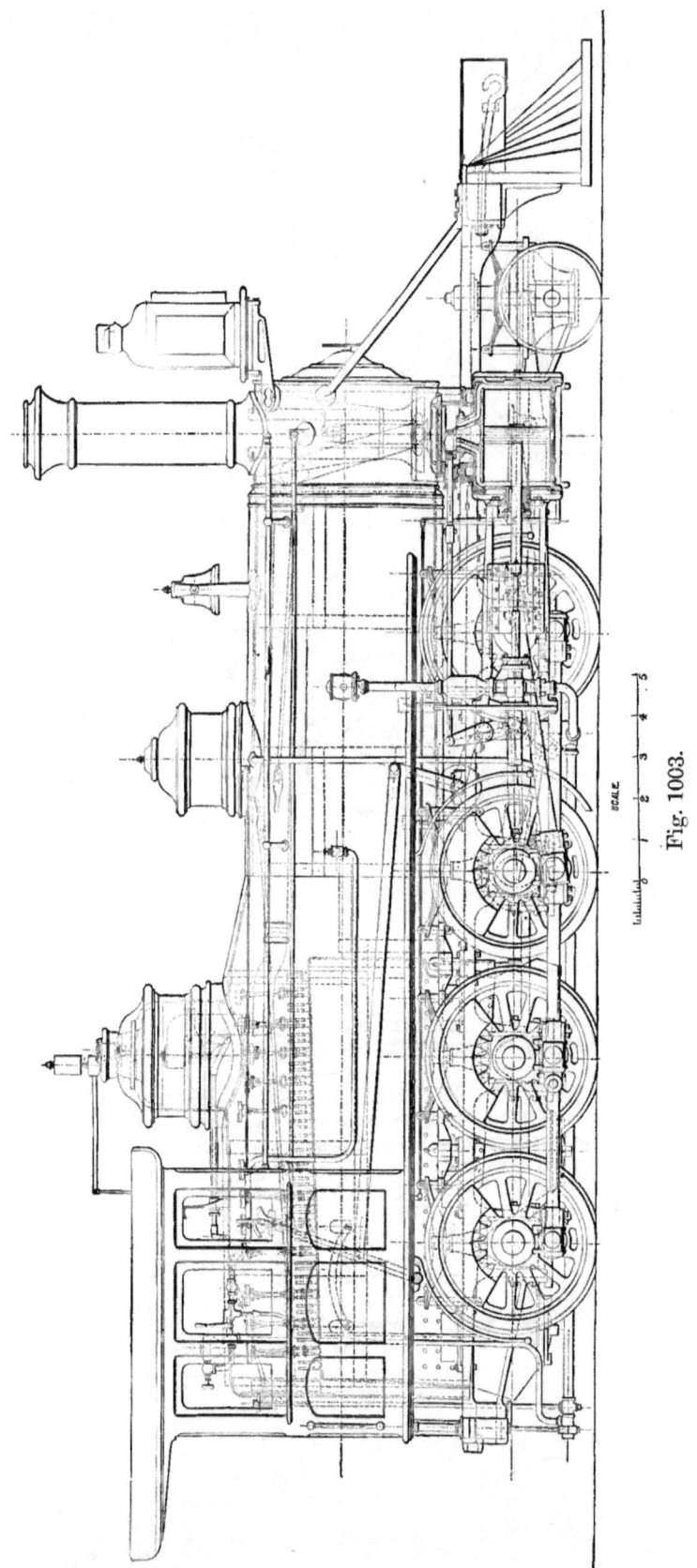

Fig. 1003.

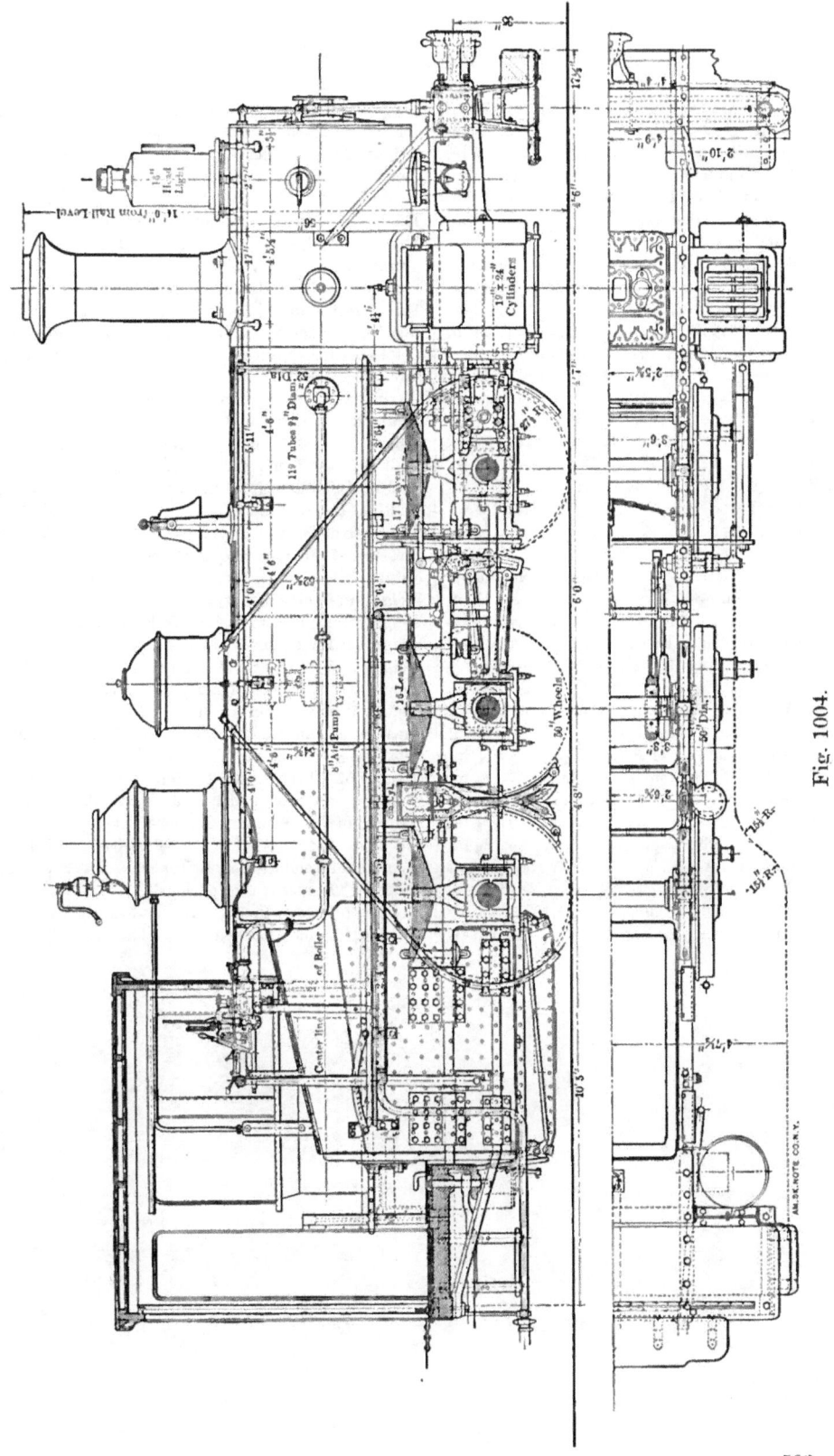

Fig. 1004.

| | |
|---|---|
| Length of Driving-axle Bearing | $7\frac{5}{8}$ in. |
| Diameter of Main Crank-pin Bearing | $4\frac{1}{2}$ in. |
| Length of Main Crank-pin Bearing | 5 in. |
| Diameter of Front and Third Parallel-rod Bearings | $3\frac{1}{2}$ in. |
| Length of Front and Third Parallel-rod Bearings | $3\frac{1}{4}$ in. |
| Diameter of Second Parallel-rod Bearing | $5\frac{3}{8}$ in. |
| Length of Second Parallel-rod Bearing | $4\frac{1}{2}$ in. |
| Cylinders and Steam-chests | Outside. |
| Spread of Cylinders | 84 in. |
| Diameter of Cylinders | 19 in. |
| Length of Stroke | 24 in. |
| Position of Valve Gear | Between Frames. |
| Type of Valve Gear | Shifting-link Motion. |
| Travel of Valve | 5 in. |
| Outside Lap of Valve | $\frac{3}{4}$ in. |
| Inside Lap of Valve | None. |
| Lead of Valve | $\frac{1}{8}$ in. |
| Throw of Eccentric | 5 in. |
| Length of Steam Ports | $15\frac{1}{2}$ in. |
| Width of Steam Ports | $1\frac{1}{4}$ in. |
| Width of Exhaust Port | $2\frac{1}{2}$ in. |
| Kind of Frames | Wrought-iron, Inside. |
| Distance between Centers of Frames | 47 in. |
| Boiler Material | Steel. |
| Thickness of Boiler Sheets, Dome | $\frac{5}{16}$ in. |
| Thickness of Boiler Sheets, Barrel, Outside Fire-box and Neck | $\frac{3}{8}$ in. |
| Smoke-box, Waist, and Sheet under Dome | $\frac{7}{16}$ in. |
| Maximum Internal Diameter of Boiler } Altoona | $53\frac{1}{4}$ in. |
| Minimum Internal Diameter of Boiler } Altoona | $51\frac{1}{4}$ in. |
| Height to Center of Boiler from Top of Rail | 76 in. |
| Number of Tubes | 119. |
| Inside Diameter of Tubes | $2\frac{1}{4}$ in. |
| Outside Diameter of Tubes | $2\frac{1}{2}$ in. |
| Tube Material | Wrought-iron. |
| Length of Tubes between Tube Sheets | $169\frac{15}{16}$ in. |
| External Heating Surface of Tubes | 1,102.97 sq. ft. |
| Fire Area through Tubes, less Ferrules | 3.29 sq. ft. |
| Length of Fire-box at Bottom (Inside) | $62\frac{5}{8}$ in. |
| Width of Fire-box at Bottom (Inside) | $34\frac{1}{4}$ in. |
| Height of Crown Sheet above Top of Grate (Center of Fire-box) | 53 in. |
| Inside Fire-box Material | Steel. |
| Thickness of Inside Fire-box Sheets, Sides | $\frac{1}{4}$ in. |
| Thickness of Inside Fire-box Sheets, Front, Back, and Crown | $\frac{5}{16}$ in. |
| Thickness of Tube Sheets | $\frac{1}{2}$ in. |
| Tube Sheet Material | Steel. |
| Heating Surface of Fire-box | 92.96 sq. ft. |
| Total Heating Surface | 1,195.93 sq. ft. |
| Fire-Grate Area | 15 sq. ft. |
| Maximum Diameter of Smoke-stack } Straight | 18 in. |
| Minimum Diameter of Smoke-stack } Straight | 18 in. |
| Height of Stack from Top of Rail | 14 ft. 0 in. |
| Width of Cab Roof | 9 ft. |
| Height of Cab Roof from Rail | 11 ft. $9\frac{3}{4}$ in. |
| Width of Cab | 8 ft. 6 in. |
| Size of Exhaust Nozzle | 3 x 4 in. |
| Pressure of Steam per Square Inch | 125 lbs. |
| Nature of Fuel | Bituminous Coal. |
| Weight of Engine, Empty | 77,000 lbs. |
| Weight of Engine in Working Order | 87,500 lbs. |
| Weight on First Pair of Drivers | 33,400 lbs. |
| Weight on Second Pair of Drivers | 29,500 lbs. |
| Weight on Third Pair of Drivers | 24,600 lbs. |
| Engine fitted with Driver Brake. | |
| Capacity of Tank | 2200 gal. |
| Capacity of Coal-box | 3200 lbs. |
| Number of Wheels under Tender | 8. |
| Diameter of Wheels under Tender | 33 in. |
| Material of Wheels under Tender-trucks, | Cast-iron Chilled Tread. |
| Diameter of Tender-truck Journals | $3\frac{1}{2}$ in. |
| Length of Tender-truck Journals | 7 in. |
| Weight of Tender, Empty | 21,300 lbs. |
| Weight of Tender, Loaded | 42,200 lbs. |

# CHAPTER XVI.

## USEFUL RULES, FORMULAS, AND DATA.

### DIAMETER OF CYLINDERS.

594. In Art. 23 we have given one method of computing the diameter of cylinders, when the stroke of piston, mean effective steam pressure, and weight on drivers are known. This method was mainly given for the purpose of showing the principles upon which Rule 3 for finding the tractive force was based. It is generally best to state rules of this kind in symbols; this will often enable us to very readily deduce from them other rules. Thus, for instance: Let $D$ denote the diameter of the driving wheels in inches; $d$, the diameter of the cylinder in inches; $s$, the stroke of piston in inches; $p$, the mean effective steam pressure per square inch of piston; and $T$ the tractive force in pounds; then Rule 3 will take the following form:

$$\frac{d^2 \times p \times s}{D} = T. \qquad (a)$$

This formula gives of course the tractive force, and this multiplied by 5 (see Art. 16) gives the weight on drivers.

From formula ($a$) we can easily deduce a simpler rule for finding the diameter of the cylinder than is given in Art. 23, the mean effective steam pressure on the piston, diameter of the driving wheels, stroke of piston, and tractive force being given.

Multiplying both sides of formula ($a$) by $D$, we get

$$d^2 \times p \times s = T \times D,$$

from which we obtain

$$d^2 = \frac{T \times D}{p \times s},$$

hence,

$$d = \sqrt{\frac{T \times D}{p \times s}}, \qquad (b)$$

which in ordinary language reads:

RULE 115.—Multiply the tractive force in pounds by the diameter of the driving wheel in inches; call this product $A$. Multiply the mean effective steam pressure per square inch of piston by the stroke in inches; call this product $B$. Divide product $A$ by product $B$, and find the square root of the quotient, which will be the diameter of the cylinder in inches.

EXAMPLE 153.—What should be the diameter of the cylinders for an eight-wheeled passenger engine—stroke of piston, 24 inches; mean effective steam pressure, 90 pounds per square inch of piston; diameter of driving wheels, 61 inches; weight on drivers, 57,360 pounds?

Taking, as before, $\frac{1}{5}$ of the weight on the drivers for the adhesion, and consequently for the tractive force, we have

$$\frac{57360}{5} = 11472 \text{ pounds.}$$

Now, substituting for the symbols in formula (b) their values, or working according to Rule 115, we have

$$d = \sqrt{\frac{11472 \times 61}{90 \times 24}} = \sqrt{329} = 18 \text{ inches}$$

for the diameter of the cylinders.

In the foregoing rule we have neglected the internal friction of the engine, which if taken into account would somewhat increase the diameter of the cylinders as found above. But since the tractive force depends on the adhesion, and since the latter is in many cases to some degree an uncertain quantity—for we have already stated that the adhesion varies from $\frac{1}{6}$ to $\frac{1}{4}$ of the weight on the driving wheels, depending on the condition of the rails—we may leave the internal friction of the engine out of consideration; of course care must be taken not to adopt too great a tractive force, for this would cause the engine to be over-cylindered.

The foregoing rule is frequently used by locomotive builders, and agrees very closely with the one recommended in the Report of the Proceedings of the Twentieth Annual Convention of the American Railway Master-Mechanics' Association.

### THE MEAN EFFECTIVE STEAM PRESSURE REQUIRED TO DO A GIVEN AMOUNT OF WORK.

595. From formula (a), Art. 594, we may deduce another one, namely, to find the mean effective pressure, thus:

$$p = \frac{T \times D}{d^2 \times s}, \qquad (c)$$

in which the symbols denote the same quantities as given in Art. 594.

In ordinary language this formula reads:

RULE 116.—Multiply the tractive force in pounds by the diameter of the driving wheels in inches, and divide this product by the square of the diameter of the cylinder in inches into the stroke in inches; the quotient will be the required mean effective pressure per square inch of piston.

EXAMPLE 154.—Find the required mean effective pressure per square inch of piston in an eight-wheeled passenger locomotive with cylinders 18 inches in diameter, 24 inches stroke; diameter of driving wheels, 61 inches; and weight on driving wheels, 57,360 pounds.

The tractive force will be

$$\frac{57360}{5} = 11472 \text{ pounds.}$$

According to formula (c) we have

$$p = \frac{11472 \times 61}{18^2 \times 24} = 90 \text{ pounds,}$$

that is to say, the required mean effective pressure per square inch of piston will be 90 pounds.

596. The foregoing rule enables us to compute the mean effective pressure required to do a given amount of work. But frequently the question arises: What will be the mean effective steam pressure when the boiler pressure and the point of cut-off are known?

To compute this with any degree of accuracy we must take the clearance into account. In commencing a new design of a locomotive it is often impossible to determine this clearance accurately, and therefore for preliminary calculations it is frequently neglected until the design is far enough advanced to make accurate computations. But in either case there are other rules of comparatively simple character, and definitions involved to which we shall first direct attention.

597. In all computations relating to the distribution and action of steam in the cylinder we must use the *absolute steam pressure*. The absolute steam pressure is equal to the sum of the pressure indicated by the steam gauge plus the atmospheric pressure; the latter is generally taken at 14.7 pounds per square inch; consequently, to find the absolute pressure add 14.7 pounds to the gauge pressure. If the steam gauge indicates 120 pounds, then the absolute pressure will be $120 + 14.7 = 134.7$ pounds.

### IDEAL INDICATOR-CARD.

598. In order to gain a clear conception of the following rules it will be advantageous to understand the meaning of the lines which form the outline of an ideal indicator-card such as is shown in Fig. 1005. The horizontal line $Z\,O$ is called the line of perfect vacuum, or the zero line; from this line all the absolute pressures, represented by lines drawn perpendicular to it, are laid off. The length of the line $Z\,O$ also represents the stroke of the piston.

The line $Z\,C$ represents the absolute initial steam pressure. By initial steam pressure is meant the pressure in the cylinder at or near the beginning of the stroke.

The line $C\,D$ represents the distance through which the piston travels before steam is cut off; hence the point $D$ represents the point of cut-off.

The curve $D\,F$ represents the expansion curve, and, as will be seen later on, this curve is usually assumed to be a rectangular hyperbola.

599. A card as shown in Fig. 1005 can only be obtained under the conditions that the exhaust opens exactly at the end of the forward stroke; closes exactly at the end of the return stroke; that the ports are fully opened and closed instantaneously, so as to avoid wire drawing of the steam; and that there is no compression. Of course such conditions never exist in any engine, and therefore a card of this kind cannot be obtained from an engine. But the card as here shown serves well for an introduction to the study of indicator-cards, and is an aid to the clear understanding of this subject.

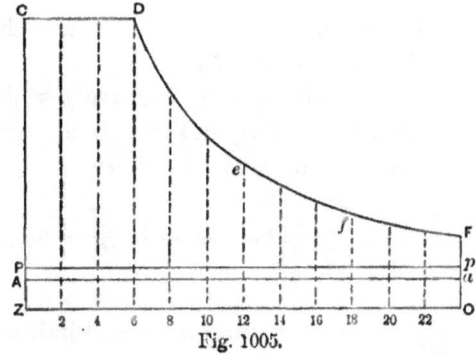

Fig. 1005.

600. We have already seen that the line $Z\,C$ represents the pressure at the beginning of the stroke; and in like manner any other line drawn perpendicular to $Z\,O$ and terminating in the line $C\,D$ or the curve $D\,F$ will represent the pressure at a corresponding point of the stroke. To illustrate: Let the zero line $Z\,O$ (Fig. 1005) represent a stroke of 24 inches; then the line $12\,e$ drawn through the center of $Z\,O$ will represent the pressure at half stroke; and in like manner the line $F\,O$ represents the terminal pressure, that is, the pressure at the end of the stroke. The length of these lines measured with a suitable scale will give the pressure in pounds at different points of the stroke; of course the same scale must be used for all the lines of pressure in a card.

601. For the sake of simplicity it is customary to assume that the expansion of steam follows the law of Mariotte, which is also frequently called Boyle's law. A curve $D\,F$ laid out according to this law will be a rectangular hyperbola.

Boyle's law states that the pressure of a perfect gas at a constant temperature varies inversely as the space it occupies.

From this we get,

$$\text{pressure} \times \text{volume} = \text{a constant quantity.}$$

Or, let $p$ denote the pressure in pounds; $v$, the volume; and $c$ a constant quantity; we have

$$p \times v = c. \qquad (a)$$

Now the volume of the cylinder or any part of it is equal to its area multiplied by its length, or the length of that part of the cylinder which is under consideration. Since the area of the cylinder is constant throughout its length, we need not pay any attention to the area when an indicator-card is under consideration, and therefore we may assume that the zero line $Z\,O$ denotes the whole volume of the cylinder, and any part of the line $Z\,O$ represents the volume of a corresponding part of the cylinder. Looking at the length of the line $Z\,O$ or any part of it in this light will greatly simplify matters, as will be seen in the following example.

EXAMPLE 155.—Let the stroke of the piston be 24 inches; absolute steam pressure, 150 pounds; cut-off at 6 inches of the stroke. Find the pressure at half stroke, and also the terminal pressure.

In this example we have $p = 150$ pounds; $v = 6$ inches; and $c = 150 \times 6 = 900$. This constant quantity will not change for any part of the stroke; hence formula ($a$) may, in this case, be written

$$p \times v = 900.$$

For half-stroke $v = 12$ inches; hence we have

$$p \times 12 = 900,$$

and therefore the pressure at half stroke will be

$$p = \frac{900}{12} = 75 \text{ pounds.}$$

For the terminal pressure, that is, the pressure at the end of the stroke, we have $v = 24$ inches, and therefore the terminal pressure will be

$$p = \frac{900}{24} = 37.5 \text{ pounds.}$$

In a similar way we find by formula (*a*) the pressure at any other part of the stroke; thus in the above example the pressure at 8 inches from the beginning of the stroke will be

$$p = \frac{900}{8} = 112.5 \text{ pounds};$$

and at 10 inches from the beginning of the stroke the pressure will be

$$p = \frac{900}{10} = 90 \text{ pounds};$$

and so on for any other part of the stroke.

602. If we now lay off these pressures on corresponding ordinates—that is, lines drawn from and perpendicular to $Z\,O$—and join their upper extremities, we obtain the rectangular hyperbola $D\,F$. Thus: To lay out the expansion curve to suit the conditions given in Example 155, we draw the line $Z\,O$ and make it to any convenient scale 24 inches long; divide this line into any number of equal parts, say 12, as shown in Fig. 1005; then the distance between any two successive points will represent 2 inches; we therefore mark the points of division (commencing from the beginning $Z$ of the stroke) 2, 4, 6, 8, etc.; through these points of division draw the lines, or ordinates, perpendicular to $Z\,O$. Now, steam being cut off at 6 inches, the ordinate $6\,D$ must be made to represent 150 pounds, which is the absolute initial pressure given in the example. To do so we adopt any scale of pressure; this scale may be the same one as used for laying off the length of $Z\,O$, or we may adopt a different scale; but whatever scale we do adopt to lay off one ordinate must be used for all the other ordinates in the card. Let us adopt 1 inch to represent 50 pounds, then $6\,D$ must be made 3 inches long to represent 150 pounds; we have already found that at 8 inches from the beginning of the stroke the pressure, according to formula (*a*), will be 112.5 pounds, and therefore the ordinate on point 8 must be $2\frac{1}{4}$ inches long; at 10 inches of the stroke the pressure will be 90 pounds, hence this ordinate must be $1\frac{8}{10}$ inches long. In a similar way we find the pressure for all the other points of the

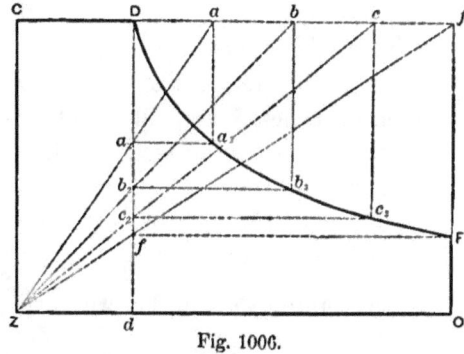

Fig. 1006.

stroke, and lay off these pressures on corresponding ordinates; the curve drawn through the upper extremities of these ordinates will be the rectangular hyperbola.

This curve can also be found by a graphical method, thus: Through the end of the stroke $O$ (Fig. 1006) draw $O\,f$ perpendicular to $Z\,O$, and prolong $C\,D$ to meet $O\,f$ in the point $f$, thus completing the rectangle $C\,Z\,O\,f$. Through the point of cut-off $D$ draw $D\,d$ perpendicular to $Z\,O$; through $Z$ and $f$ draw the diagonal $Z\,f$, cutting $D\,d$ in the point $f_2$; through the latter point draw $f_2\,F$ parallel to $Z\,O$, cutting $O\,f$ in $F$; this point will be one point in the curve, and $O\,F$ will be the terminal pressure. Take any point, as $a$, on the line $C\,f$, and draw the diagonal $Z\,a$, cutting $D\,d$ in the point $a_2$; through this point draw the line $a_2\,a_3$ parallel to $Z\,O$, and through $a$ draw $a\,a_3$ parallel to $Z\,C$, meeting $a_2\,a_3$ in the point $a_3$, which will be another point in the curve. By taking any number of points, such as $b$, $c$, on the line $C\,f$, at any distance apart (they need not be equal distances apart), we find in a manner similar to the above the points $b_3$, $c_3$ in the curve. A line drawn through all the points thus found will be the hyperbola.

### RATIO OF EXPANSION—CLEARANCE NEGLECTED.

603. The ratio of expansion is the number of times the volume of that part of the cylinder occupied by the steam up to the point of cut-off is contained in the whole volume of the cylinder. Hence, when the clearance is not taken into account, we have

$$\frac{\text{volume of cylinder}}{\text{volume to point of cut-off}} = \text{ratio of expansion,}$$

or,

$$\frac{\text{area of cylinder} \times \text{length of stroke}}{\text{area of cylinder} \times \text{distance to point of cut-off}} = \text{ratio of expansion.}$$

From which we get

$$\frac{\text{length of stroke}}{\text{distance to point of cut-off}} = \text{ratio of expansion.}$$

RULE 117.—Divide the length of stroke by the distance from the beginning of stroke to the point of cut-off; the quotient will be the ratio of expansion.

This rule expressed in symbols is as follows:

$$\frac{L}{l} = r,$$

in which $L$ denotes the length of the stroke; $l$, the distance from the beginning of the stroke to the point of cut-off; and $r$, the ratio of expansion. Of course when $L$ is taken in inches, $l$ must also be taken in inches; or if one is taken in feet, the other must also be taken in feet. Or if $L$ is regarded as 1 (unity), then $l$ must be taken as a fraction of 1.

EXAMPLE 156.—Stroke of piston is 24 inches; steam is cut off at 6 inches. Find the ratio of expansion.

According to Rule 117 we have $\frac{24}{6} = 4$, which is the ratio of expansion.

If we regard the stroke as 1 (unity), then in this example the cut-off must be regarded to take place at $\frac{6}{24} = \frac{1}{4}$ of the stroke; hence we have

$$1 \div \tfrac{1}{4} = 1 \times \tfrac{4}{1} = 4$$

for the ratio of expansion, which gives us the same result as before.

EXAMPLE 157.—Stroke of piston is 24 inches; steam is cut off at 16 inches. Find the ratio of expansion.

Here we have

$$\frac{24}{16} = 1.5 \text{ for the ratio of expansion.}$$

Or, since 16 inches is $\tfrac{2}{3}$ of the stroke, we have

$$1 \div \tfrac{2}{3} = 1 \times \tfrac{3}{2} = 1.5 \text{ for the ratio of expansion.}$$

## TERMINAL PRESSURE.

**604.** We have already seen that the terminal pressure can be found by the formula $p \times v = c$ (see Art. 601). To this we may now add the following:

RULE 118.—Divide the initial steam pressure by the ratio of expansion; the quotient will be the terminal pressure.

EXAMPLE 158.—The absolute initial steam pressure is 150 pounds; stroke of piston, 24 inches; steam is cut off at 6 inches. Find the terminal pressure.

According to Rule 117 the ratio of expansion is $\frac{24}{6} = 4$; and according to Rule 118 the terminal pressure is

$$\frac{150}{4} = 37.5 \text{ pounds.}$$

This rule holds good only for a card as shown in Fig. 1005, in which $CD$ is parallel to $ZO$, and the exhaust opens at the end of the stroke.

## MEAN PRESSURE.

**605.** We are now in a position to compute the mean pressure in the cylinder when the distribution of steam is as indicated in Fig. 1005, and in which clearance is not taken into account.

For this computation we need a table of hyperbolic logarithms as given below.

### TABLE 84.

#### HYPERBOLIC LOGARITHMS.

| Number. | Hyperbolic Log. | Number. | Hyperbolic Log. |
|---|---|---|---|
| 1.1 | .095 | 3.6 | 1.281 |
| 1.2 | .182 | 3.7 | 1.308 |
| 1.3 | .262 | 3.8 | 1.330 |
| 1.4 | .336 | 3.9 | 1.36 |
| 1.5 | .405 | 4 | 1.386 |
| 1.6 | .470 | 4.1 | 1.411 |
| 1.7 | .531 | 4.2 | 1.435 |
| 1.8 | .588 | 4.3 | 1.459 |
| 1.9 | .642 | 4.4 | 1.482 |
| 2 | .693 | 4.5 | 1.504 |
| 2.1 | .742 | 4.6 | 1.526 |
| 2.2 | .788 | 4.7 | 1.548 |
| 2.3 | .833 | 4.8 | 1.569 |
| 2.4 | .875 | 4.9 | 1.589 |
| 2.5 | .916 | 5 | 1.609 |
| 2.6 | .955 | 5.1 | 1.629 |
| 2.7 | .993 | 5.2 | 1.649 |
| 2.8 | 1.030 | 5.3 | 1.668 |
| 2.9 | 1.065 | 5.4 | 1.686 |
| 3 | 1.099 | 5.5 | 1.705 |
| 3.1 | 1.131 | 5.6 | 1.723 |
| 3.2 | 1.163 | 5.7 | 1.740 |
| 3.3 | 1.196 | 5.8 | 1.758 |
| 3.4 | 1.224 | 5.9 | 1.775 |
| 3.5 | 1.253 | 6 | 1.792 |

To find the hyperbolic logarithm of any other number not given in the table, multiply the common logarithm of the number by 2.302585 (many engineers simply use 2.3 for a multiplier); the product will be the hyperbolic logarithm of the number.

Tables of common logarithms are given in nearly all engineers' pocket-books; they may also be found in many school-books, and need not be given here.

For finding the mean pressure we have the following:

RULE 119.—Add 1 to the hyperbolic logarithm of the ratio of expansion; multiply this sum by the absolute initial steam pressure, and divide the product by the ratio of expansion; the quotient will be the absolute mean pressure per square inch.

Or in symbols, we have

$$\frac{1 + \text{hyperbolic logarithm } r}{r} \times p = p_m,$$

in which $r$ denotes the ratio of expansion; $p$, the absolute initial steam pressure, and $p_m$ the absolute mean pressure.

EXAMPLE 159.—The absolute initial pressure in the cylinder is 180 pounds; stroke of piston, 24 inches; steam is cut off at 6 inches of the stroke. Find the absolute mean pressure.

According to Rule 117 the ratio of expansion is

$$\frac{24}{6} = 4.$$

The hyperbolic logarithm of 4 (as found in the table) is 1.386; hence, according to Rule 119, we have

$$\frac{1 + 1.386}{4} \times 180 = 107.37 \text{ for the absolute mean pressure.}$$

606. So far we have not taken the back pressure into consideration; if we assume it to be uniform throughout the stroke, we can indicate it on the card, Fig. 1005, by drawing the line $P\,p$ parallel to $Z\,O$; the distance between these two lines must be laid off with the same scale as was used for laying off the initial pressure. If, for instance, we have used a scale of 1 inch to represent 50 pounds, and the absolute back pressure is 18 pounds, then the distance between the lines $Z\,O$ and $P\,p$ must be equal to $\frac{18}{50} = .36$ inch. If, now, we subtract the absolute back pressure from the absolute mean pressure, the remainder will be the mean *effective* pressure. Thus: In the previous example we have found the mean pressure to be 107.37 pounds; if, now, the back pressure is 18 pounds, the mean effective pressure will be $107.37 - 18 = 89.37$ pounds.

607. Since all the pressures are laid off from the zero line $Z\,O$, it is of the utmost importance to locate it correctly on a card taken by an indicator. To do so the atmospheric line $A\,a$ is traced by the pencil on the card before it is taken off the indicator-drum. When this line is to be traced the communications between the indicator and the engine cylinder are closed; the pencil will then stand in its neutral position, and will trace the atmospheric line while the indicator-drum revolves on its axis.

When the card is taken off, the zero line is drawn below the atmospheric line, and parallel to it at a distance which will represent the atmospheric pressure of 14.7 pounds. This must, of course, be laid off with the adopted scale of pressures; if, for instance, a scale of 1 inch to represent 50 pounds is to be used, the distance between the atmospheric and zero line must be .294 inch.

608. It should be distinctly understood that any scale may be used for laying off the pressures in the construction of an ideal card such as is shown in Fig. 1005, but whatever scale we may adopt must be used for laying off all the pressures on that particular card. Of course, when the pressures are to be measured on a card taken by an indicator, we must use a scale corresponding to the spring in the indicator, hence in cases of this kind there is no choice of scale.

609. Under the assumption that the expansion of steam follows Boyle's law, the mean pressure as found above will be correct when there is no clearance. But clearance we have in all engines, because the steam ports have volume, however short they may be; and besides, some play between the piston and cylinder heads is required to allow for inaccurate workmanship, and for taking up the wear of the rod brasses, and that between the driving boxes and wedges. It must also be remembered that in locomotives the cut-off is regulated by the link, and at short cut-offs there will be an early exhaust closure, which increases the compression; and in order to prevent the pressure due to compression becoming too great we require probably a greater clearance than in many stationary engines.

The clearance space being filled with steam at the moment of cut-off will have an important influence on the ratio of expansion, and therefore it must not be neglected in accurate computations. Consequently the amount of clearance must be determined accurately; but since it is often a difficult matter to compute it correctly, a practical method is frequently adopted by placing the piston at the end of the stroke and filling the clearance space with water whose quantity in cubic inches is accurately measured.

610. Our next step will be to indicate the clearance on the card, and compute its effect on the expansion. To make this plain we will take the following example:

EXAMPLE 160.—The cylinder is 16 inches in diameter; stroke of piston, 24 inches; cut-off at 6 inches; absolute initial steam pressure, 180 pounds; and the clearance space contains 385 cubic inches. Find the ratio of expansion and the mean pressure on the piston.

Our first step will be to find the ratio between the clearance and piston displacement.

The total volume of the piston displacement is found by multiplying the area of the piston by its stroke. The area of a 16-inch piston is 201 square inches, hence the piston displacement is

$$201 \times 24 = 4824 \text{ cubic inches.}$$

We must now find a part of the length of cylinder which will contain 385 cubic inches, the clearance space. This is done by dividing the 385 cubic inches by the area of the piston; we thus obtain

$$\frac{385}{201} = 1.91 \text{ inches,}$$

which means that a volume 16 inches diameter and 1.91 inches long contains as many cubic inches as the clearance.

When it is desirable to indicate this clearance on the card we proceed as follows: Let

$Z$ to $O$, which represents the stroke, Fig. 1007, be 4 inches long, then the distance corresponding to 1.91 inches will be $\frac{1.91 \times 4}{24} = .318$ inch, and this must be added to the card. Hence the distance from $Z$ to $B$, which represents the clearance, must be .318 inch. Through the point $B$ draw a line perpendicular to $Z O$, and complete the rectangle $B Z E C$.

If there had been no clearance, then according to Rule 117 the ratio of expansion would have been 4. But when clearance is taken into account the ratio of expansion is found as follows:

$$\text{Ratio of expansion} = \frac{\text{volume of cylinder} + \text{clearance}}{\text{volume to point of cut-off} + \text{clearance}},$$

or,

$$\text{Ratio of expansion} = \frac{\text{area of cylinder} \times (\text{length of stroke} + \text{clearance})}{\text{area of cylinder} \times (\text{length of stroke to point of cut-off} + \text{clearance})},$$

which reduces to

RULE 120.—Ratio of expansion $= \dfrac{\text{length of stroke} + \text{clearance}}{\text{length of stroke to point of cut-off} + \text{clearance}}$.

To express this rule in symbols, we have

$$r = \frac{L + c}{l + c},$$

in which $r$ denotes the ratio of expansion; $L$, the length of stroke in inches; $l$, the distance in inches from the beginning of stroke to point of cut-off; and $c$, the clearance.

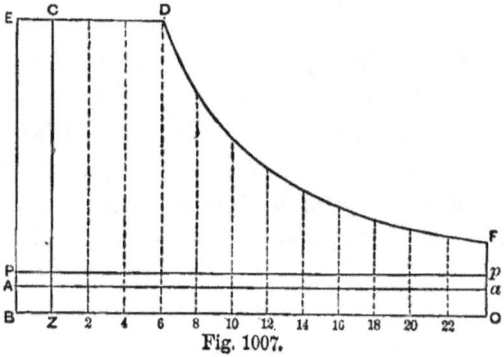
Fig. 1007.

Substituting for the symbols the values given in the example, we have

$$r = \frac{24 + 1.91}{6 + 1.91} = 3.2.$$

From this it will be seen that the effect of clearance is to make the effective cut-off comparatively later and decrease the ratio of expansion.

In the foregoing computation the values of $L$, $l$, and $c$ must always be expressed in the same unit; if one is taken in inches, the others must also be taken in inches; or if one is expressed in feet, the others must also be expressed in feet.

611. Sometimes the clearance is given in per cent. of the piston displacement. In cases of this kind, $L = 1$, and $l$ will be expressed by a fraction of the stroke at which steam is cut off. In Example 160 the clearance is eight per cent. of the piston displacement; and $l = .25$.

Hence the ratio of expansion is

$$r = \frac{1 + .08}{.25 + .08} = 3.2, \text{ as before.}$$

For finding the mean pressure on the piston we should use the true ratio of expansion as found above, and again employ Rule 119; but since this will give us the mean pressure from $B$ to $O$ (Fig. 1007) instead of from $Z$ to $O$, the length of the stroke, we must make a slight correction, as will presently be explained, otherwise the mean pressure will be too high.

We have found that with clearance the ratio of expansion is 3.2. Now the hyperbolic logarithm of 3.2 is 1.163; hence, according to Rule 119, the mean pressure from $B$ to $O$ (Fig. 1007) will be

$$\frac{1 + 1.163}{3.2} \times 180 = 121.66 \text{ pounds.}$$

The mean pressure from $Z$ to $O$ (Fig. 1007), that is, the length of the stroke, will be less than found above. To find this we must make a slight correction to the foregoing with the aid of the following rule:

RULE 121.—Multiply the mean pressure in pounds per square inch as found by Rule 119 by the stroke plus the clearance in inches; multiply the initial pressure by the clearance; subtract the last product from the first one; and divide the remainder by the stroke in inches; the quotient will be the mean pressure per square inch during the stroke.

Or, referring to Fig. 1007, we have in symbols,

$$P_m = \frac{(p_m \times \overline{BO}) - (p \times \overline{BZ})}{\overline{ZO}},$$

in which $P_m$ denotes the mean pressure during the stroke; $p_m$, the mean pressure as found by Rule 119; and $p$, the initial pressure.

Substituting for the symbols their values, and remembering that the clearance measured on the zero line is 1.91 inches, we have

$$P_m = \frac{(121.66 \times 25.91) - (180 \times 1.91)}{24} = 117 \text{ pounds.}$$

Hence the answer to example is: Ratio of expansion, 3.2; mean pressure, 117 pounds.

If, now, the back pressure is 18 pounds, the mean effective pressure will be

$$117 - 18 = 99 \text{ pounds.}$$

612. To sum up the whole matter, we have the following mode of procedure for finding the mean effective pressure when clearance is taken into account: Find the ratio of expansion as per Rule 120; find the mean pressure as per Rule 119; correct this mean pressure as per Rule 121, and subtract the back pressure; the result will be the mean effective pressure.

### HORSE-POWER.

613. In locomotive practice we have seldom to compute the horse-power; but should it be necessary to do so, we must find the mean effective pressure, taking into account the true ratio of expansion as above, and when this is known the horse-power is very easily found by the following:

RULE 122.—Multiply the mean effective pressure per square inch of piston by the area of the piston in square inches, by the length of the stroke in feet, and by the number of strokes per minute; divide this product by 33,000; the quotient will be the indicated horse-power for one cylinder.

This rule may be expressed in symbols, as follows:

$$I.\,H.\,P. = \frac{P \times L \times A \times N}{33000},$$

in which $P$ denotes the mean effective pressure per square inch; $L$, the length of stroke in feet; $A$, the area of the piston in square inches; and $N$, the number of strokes per minute.

In the foregoing formula we have arranged the symbols on the right-hand side to form the word *PLAN*, which we believe will be an aid to remember the rule. It should be remarked that the number of strokes per minute is equal to twice the number of revolutions of the wheels in the same time.

EXAMPLE 161.—Diameter of cylinder is 16 inches; stroke, 24 inches; cut-off at 6 inches; absolute initial pressure, 180 pounds; number of revolutions of wheels, 170 per minute; clearance, 8 per cent. Find the indicated horse-power.

In the solution of Example 160 we have found the mean effective pressure to be 99 pounds. The number of strokes per minute is $170 \times 2 = 340$, and the area of a 16-inch piston is 201 square inches.

According to Rule 122 we have

$$I.\,H.\,P. = \frac{99 \times 2 \times 201 \times 340}{33000} = 410.$$

This is for one cylinder; for two cylinders we have $410 \times 2 = 820$ $I.\,H.\,P.$

This result will be exact, provided the mean effective pressure $P$ has been correctly computed. This pressure, as found in the last example, is correct for a card as shown in Fig. 1007; but since the form of a card taken from an engine will always differ more or less from the one here shown, there will also be a difference in the mean effective pressure as computed above. But all preliminary computations are based upon a form of card as shown in Fig. 1007, and the results obtained will usually be sufficiently accurate for practical purposes; or, at all events, they will be a close approximation.

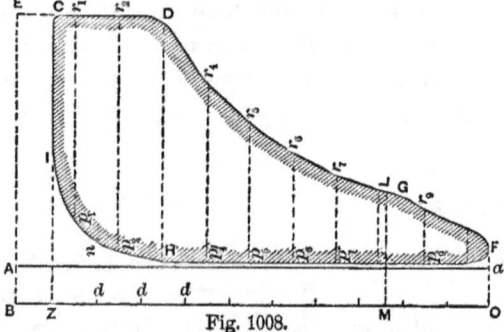

Fig. 1008.

CARDS TAKEN WITH AN INDICATOR.

614. When a valve gear has been correctly designed we may expect to get, with an indicator, a card similar in form to the one shown by the shaded portion in Fig. 1008, when steam is cut off at ¼ stroke. The distance between $B$ and $Z$ represents the clearance, which has been located on the card in precisely the same manner as that adopted for locating the clearance line in Fig. 1007.

It will be noticed that in this card the point of cut-off, exhaust opening and closure is not as decisively indicated as in the ideal cards previously shown, and this is due to the slowness with which the valve opens or closes the ports. Generally the expansion curve from $D$ to $G$ does not coincide exactly with the rectangular hyperbola; and from $G$ to $F$ a decided departure takes place.

615. In this diagram, as in the others, the line $A\,a$ is the atmospheric line. The line $Z\,O$, the zero or perfect vacuum line, and these are located as explained in Art. 607.

The names of the other lines are as follows:

    $I\,C$, admission line.   $G\,F$, exhaust line.
    $C\,D$, steam line.    $F\,H$, line of counter pressure.
    $D\,G$, expansion curve.   $H\,I$, compression line.

616. From a diagram of this kind, taken with an indicator, the mean effective pressure, and consequently the horse-power, when required, can be correctly computed. The mean effective pressure is usually obtained with the aid of the planimeter, which gives the area of the card (the shaded portion) in square inches; dividing this area by the length of the line $Z\,O$ (not $B\,O$) measured with an ordinary rule, we obtain the mean height of the card; and this multiplied by the scale of the spring used in the indicator will give us the mean effective pressure per square inch of piston.

The mean effective pressure can be obtained from this card in another way. Divide the length of the card $Z\,O$ into 10 equal parts, thereby obtaining the points of division $d\,d\,d$; through the center of each division draw lines perpendicular to $Z\,O$ or $A\,a$, and terminating in the upper lines $C\,D\,G\,F$. Measure the lines $p_1\,r_1$, $p_2\,r_2$, etc., from the lower boundary line $I\,H\,F$ to the upper one $C\,D\,G\,F$ with an ordinary rule. Add these lengths (all in inches), and divide the sum by the number of lines; the quotient will be the mean height of the card. Multiply this height by the scale of the spring used in the indicator; the product will be the mean effective pressure per square inch of piston.

### STEAM ACCOUNTED FOR BY THE INDICATOR.

617. By means of an indicator-card the weight of steam in the cylinder at every point of the stroke can be computed; but this will not include the water existing in the cylinder at the time, and which entered as steam; therefore, the steam accounted for by the indicator is not the full weight of steam that entered the cylinder, or the full weight of water required to supply the boiler. However, by adding a certain percentage to the weight of steam accounted for by indicator, we can generally determine very closely the amount of water taken out of the boiler. To make this plain let us take the following example:

EXAMPLE 162.—Compute the weight of steam accounted for by the indicator from a card as shown in Fig. 1008; cylinder, 16 inches diameter; stroke, 24 inches; clearance, 8 per cent.; number of revolutions per minute, 170; scale of spring, 80 pounds to the inch.

Our first step in the solution of this problem will be to select a point on the expansion curve, as near as possible to the end of the stroke, at which it is certain the exhaust has not commenced. The card shows that the exhaust commences at the point $G$, 19 inches from the beginning of the stroke, therefore let us select the point $L$, at 18 inches from the beginning of the stroke; through this point draw a line $L\ M$ perpendicular to the zero line, and terminating in the expansion curve at one end and in the zero line at the other end. Now measure this line with the scale of the spring; this will give us the pressure at 18 inches from the beginning of the stroke; let us assume that we found this pressure to be 60 pounds absolute.

The next step is to find the volume occupied by the steam up to this point; this is evidently equal to sum of the piston displacement up to this point plus the clearance space. In finding this volume of steam we must remember that at one end of the cylinder the volume is reduced by the space occupied by the piston-rod; consequently we must take the mean area of the cylinder, which is equal to the area corresponding to the diameter of the cylinder minus one-half of the piston-rod area. Let us assume that the latter is 3 square inches; now the area of a 16-inch cylinder being 201 square inches, we have for the mean area $201 - 3 = 198$ square inches. Consequently the volume occupied by the steam due to the piston displacement alone up to 18 inches of the stroke is $198 \times 18 = 3564$ cubic inches. To this we must now add the volume due to the clearance space, which is, as given in the example, 8 per cent. of the total piston displacement; and the latter is equal to the mean area of the cylinder multiplied by the whole length of stroke, hence the volume due to the clearance alone is equal to $198 \times 24 \times .08 = 380.16$ cubic inches. Now the total volume of steam occupied up to 18 inches of the stroke will be $3564 + 380.16 = 3944.16$ cubic inches, or

$$\frac{3944.16}{1728} = 2.282 \text{ cubic feet.}$$

The weight of a cubic foot of steam at a pressure of 60 pounds (absolute) is .1457 of a pound, hence the total weight of steam in the cylinder up to 18 inches of the stroke will be $2.282 \times .1457 = .3324$ of a pound.

From this we deduct the weight of steam saved—that is, the steam confined in the cylinder after the exhaust is closed. To find this we select a point on the line of counter-pressure at which it is certain that the exhaust is closed. Let us take the point $n$, 4 inches from the end of the stroke. The volume of steam confined up to this point will be

$$\frac{(198 \times 4) + 380.16}{1728} = .678 \text{ of a cubic foot.}$$

The absolute pressure at the point $n$ is found by measuring its distance from the zero line with the scale of the spring; let us assume that in this way we find the absolute pressure to be 23 pounds per square inch. The weight of a cubic foot of steam at this pressure is .0585 pounds, hence the weight of steam saved is $.678 \times .0585 = .0396$ of a pound.

Now the quantity of steam accounted for by the indicator is $.3324 - .0396 = .2928$ pound during each stroke. The wheels make 170 turns per minute, hence the number of strokes will be 340 per minute, or $340 \times 60 = 20400$ strokes per hour, and the steam used in one cylinder per hour as accounted for by the indicator will be

$$20400 \times .2928 = 5973.12 \text{ pounds.}$$

One gallon of water weighs 8.33 pounds, hence the quantity of water used per hour in one cylinder will be

$$\frac{5973.12}{8.33} = 717 \text{ gallons,}$$

and for two cylinders the amount of water per hour as accounted for by the indicator will be $717 \times 2 = 1434$ gallons.

The actual amount of water used will, of course, be considerably greater. For late cut-offs, say about ¾ of the stroke, we should add 20 per cent. for cylinder condensation. For early cut-offs, say at ¼ stroke, we should add 35 per cent. for cylinder condensation; hence, for a cut-off at ¼ stroke, the total amount of water used will be

$$1434 \times 1.35 = 1935.9 \text{ gallons.}$$

618. From the foregoing it must not be understood that a greater economy is obtained by late cut-offs; indeed, the contrary is true. But the above does show that with early cut-offs a greater cylinder condensation takes place, because a greater portion of the cylinder is exposed to a lower temperature at the end of each stroke, and therefore a greater portion of the cylinder wall is also cooled; and in order to bring this up to the temperature of the live steam, heat must be expended, and consequently a greater condensation will take place than when a lesser portion of the cylinder is exposed to a cooling condition as occurs in late cut-offs.

619. The mean effective pressure is a measure of the work done in the cylinder by the steam; hence the economy in the use of steam is increased by making the mean effective pressure for a given quantity of steam as high as possible and the pressure at the opening of the exhaust as low as possible, thereby obtaining a great amount of work out of a small quantity of steam. The weight of steam represents the weight of water that must be evaporated to produce it. If, now, the initial pressure is 150 pounds per square inch, and steam is cut off at ¼ stroke, the mean pressure will be, according to Rule 119,

$$\frac{1 + 1.386}{4} \times 150 = 89.4 \text{ pounds.}$$

If, on the other hand, steam follows the full stroke of the piston, the mean pressure will be 150 pounds; but in this case we use four times as much steam as is used in cutting off at ¼ stroke; here, then, is a gain with an early cut-off, but some of it is lost by the greater cylinder condensation. An excellent treatment of this subject will be found in "Indicator Practice and Steam-engine Economy," by Frank F. Hemenway; this book also contains all the necessary tables for making computations relating to the use of steam.

### GRADE.

620. By the term "grade" is meant the degree of inclination of the track from a horizontal line. In American practice the grade is designated by the rise of track per mile; for instance, if it is said that the grade is 150 feet, we understand that in a length of one mile of the track the rise is 150 feet.

To illustrate, let $AC$ in Fig. 1009 represent one mile of track; $AB$, a horizontal line; and $BC$, a line drawn vertically to $AB$; then $BC$ will represent the rise of the track per mile.

According to some text-books treating on "Mechanics," the term "grade" would mean the rise per mile of the horizontal line $AB$; but in ordinary railroad practice we generally understand it to mean the rise per mile of the length of the track $AC$; this latter definition we shall adopt in that which is to follow.

In "Mechanics" the triangle $ABC$ is called the section of an inclined plane; $AC$ is called the length of the plane; $AB$, its base; and $BC$, its height. The propositions

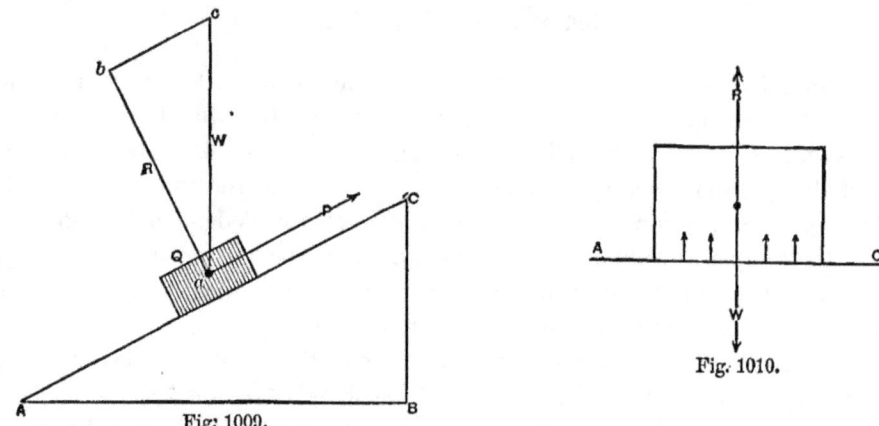

Fig. 1009.

Fig. 1010.

relating to a body moving on an inclined plane as given in "Mechanics" are also applicable to the solutions of problems of a train moving on a grade.

### NORMAL PRESSURE.

621. In the footnote on page 6 we have stated that the weight and pressure are equal only on a level or horizontal track, and not on a grade; we shall now find the difference between the weight and pressure of a body on an inclined plane.

Let $W$, Fig. 1010, be the weight of a body resting on a horizontal plane $AC$; each particle of this body gives rise to a reaction which is equal and opposite to its weight. We may therefore say that the total reaction of this body is equal to the sum of the small reactions, which may be replaced by their resultant $R$ passing through the center of gravity of the body. Consequently this resultant $R$ is equal to the weight of the body, but acts in an opposite direction. This shows us that the normal pressure on a horizontal track is equal to the weight of the train.

Let $Q$, Fig. 1009, represent a body resting on an inclined plane, and let its weight be denoted by $W$. Here, again, each particle of the body causes a reaction at right angles to the plane $AC$; these small reactions can be replaced by their sum, or, in other words, by their resultant $R$ acting through the center of gravity $a$ of the body perpendicular to $AC$, as indicated by the line $ab$, and this resultant is equal to the normal pressure of the body on the plane $AC$. To find the magnitude of this resultant we apply the principle of the parallelogram of forces, thus:

Through the center of gravity $a$ of the body draw a vertical line $ac$ of any definite length, to represent the weight $W$ of the body $Q$. Through $a$ draw a line $a\,b$ perpendicular to $A\,C$, and through $c$ draw a line $b\,c$ parallel to $A\,C$, meeting $a\,b$ in $b$. Now the line $a\,c$ represents the magnitude of the force or weight $W$, and the line $a\,b$ represents the force or magnitude of the resultant $R$. The parallelogram of forces teaches us that the resultant $R$ is as much smaller than the weight $W$ as the line $a\,b$ is shorter than the line $a\,c$. Hence we have

$$\overline{a\,c} : \overline{a\,b} :: W : R, \qquad (a)$$

which gives us

$$\frac{\overline{a\,b} \times W}{\overline{a\,c}} = R. \qquad (b)$$

Comparing the triangles $a\,b\,c$ and $A\,B\,C$, we find that they are similar; hence formula ($a$) may be stated as follows:

$$\text{Length of inclined plane} : \text{base of inclined plane} :: W : R, \qquad (c)$$

which gives us in place of formula ($b$)

$$\frac{\overline{A\,B} \times W}{\overline{A\,C}} = R, \qquad (d)$$

or,

$$\frac{\text{base of inclined plane} \times \text{weight of body}}{\text{length of inclined plane}} = \text{normal pressure } R.$$

Hence to find the normal pressure of a train on a grade, we have the following rule:

RULE 123.—Multiply the base $A\,B$ of the inclined plane by the weight of train, and divide this product by the length $A\,C$ of the inclined plane; the quotient will be the normal pressure.

EXAMPLE 163.—What will be the normal pressure of a train weighing 120 tons on a grade of 150 feet per mile? From the definition of grade given in Art. 620 we know that the length $A\,C$, in this case, is 5,280 feet (one mile), and the height $B\,C$ is 150 feet; the length of $A\,B$ must be found by computation, which need not be given here; it is sufficient for our purpose to say that in this case $A\,B$ will be 5279.4 feet.

Now, according to rule we have

$$\frac{5279.4 \times 120}{5280} = 119.98 \text{ tons normal pressure.}$$

This shows us that, although there is a difference between the normal pressure and the weight, it is so small that it may be neglected; and we may for all practical purposes assume that the normal pressure on all grades up to 350 feet per mile is equal to the weight of train.

### RESISTANCE DUE TO FRICTION.

622. In hauling a train up an inclined plane we have to overcome the resistance due to rolling and axle friction.

When the surfaces do not abrate or cut one another, it is sufficiently accurate to assume that the amount of friction varies directly as the normal pressure. Hence, multiplying the normal pressure by the coefficient of friction, we obtain the amount of friction. In Art. 621 we have shown how the normal pressure on an inclined plane is found; if we now denote the coefficient of friction by $F$, we have (see Fig. 1009)

$$\frac{\overline{AB} \times W}{\overline{AC}} \times F = \text{amount of friction.}$$

We have already seen that the difference between the normal pressure and the weight is so small that this difference can be neglected; hence in ordinary railroad practice we may say that

$$\text{Amount of friction} = W \times F.$$

In Art. 13 we have given a coefficient of friction of $7\frac{1}{2}$ pounds per ton, and in Art. 22 we have stated that this coefficient is not only sufficient to overcome the resistance of the cars due to friction, but it is also sufficient to overcome the frictional resistance of the engine. Many engineers prefer to compute the resistances of cars and engine separately. In doing so a coefficient of 7 pounds per ton is generally adopted to overcome the rolling and axle friction of the cars, the same is also adopted for the tender, and a coefficient of 8 pounds per ton is adopted to overcome the rolling and axle friction, and the friction of the machinery of the engine. These coefficients are only suitable when the train is in motion. For starting the train a coefficient of 8 pounds per ton should be used for overcoming the friction of the cars, and 10 pounds per ton for the engine.

### RESISTANCE DUE TO GRADE.

623. In hauling a train up a grade, work is performed. By the term "work" is meant the overcoming of resistances continually recurring along the path of motion. To do work, energy must be expended. By the term "energy" is meant the ability of an agent to do work. That which gives motion to the body is force, and the energy expended is equal to the product of this force into the distance through which it acts. From this we see that the amount of energy expended is expressed in foot-pounds, or foot-tons, etc. Since the energy expended is equal to the work done, the amount of work performed is also expressed in foot-pounds, or foot-tons, etc. When a body is moved up an inclined plane, energy must be expended to overcome gravity and friction. Let the force $P$, Fig. 1009, act in a direction parallel to the plane $AC$; then the energy expended on gravity and friction in moving the body from $A$ to $C$ is equal to the product of the force $P$ into the distance $AC$.

624. Let us determine the magnitude of the force $P$ required to overcome the action of gravity only, the corresponding energy expended, and work performed.

This force $P$ is found by the principle of the parallelogram of forces. Hence we construct the triangle $a\ b\ c$, in Fig. 1009, as we did for finding the reaction $R$ in Art. 621. Now $bc$ represents the magnitude of the force $P$, which is as much smaller than the weight $W$ of the body $Q$ as $bc$ is shorter than $ac$. But the triangles $a\ b\ c$ and $A\ B\ C$ are similar, hence we have

$$\overline{AC} : \overline{BC} :: W : P, \qquad (a)$$

from which we get

$$P = \frac{\overline{BC} \times W}{\overline{AC}}. \qquad (b)$$

But the force $P$ acts through the distance $AC$, hence the energy expended on gravity is found as follows:

$$\text{Energy expended} = \frac{\overline{BC} \times W}{\overline{AC}} \times \overline{AC} = \overline{BC} \times W. \quad (c)$$

But the work performed against gravity is equal to the energy expended. Hence we may say the work done on gravity is equal to the weight $W$ raised through the height $BC$, as formula (c) indicates.

625. In computing the hauling capacity of a locomotive on a given grade, we have to deal with the force $P$; formula (b), Art. 624, shows us that

$$P = \frac{\overline{BC} \times W}{\overline{AC}}.$$

In this formula, $BC$ is the rise of grade in feet per mile, and $AC$ is equal to 5,280 feet (1 mile). If we now make $W = 2000$ pounds (1 ton), then we have

$$P = \frac{\overline{BC} \times 2000}{5280},$$

in which $BC$ must be taken in feet. But

$$\frac{2000}{5280} = .3787,$$

hence the force $P$ in pounds is

$$P = \overline{BC} \times .3787. \quad (d)$$

From this we get the following:

RULE 124.—To find the force in pounds required to haul a train of one ton up a given grade, under the assumption that there is no friction: Multiply the rise in feet per mile by .3787; the product will be the force required.

RULE 125.—To find the force required to haul a train of any weight in tons up a grade, under the assumption that there is no friction: Multiply the constant .3787, as given in Rule 124, by the weight of train in tons, and by the rise of grade in feet; the product will be the required force in pounds. Of course, to move a body up an inclined plane friction cannot be neglected, hence the force $P$ must not only be sufficiently great to overcome the action of gravity, but it must be able to overcome that of friction also. The resistance due to friction has been given in Art. 622.

In order to show the application of the foregoing rules for finding the resistance of a train, including friction, running on a grade, we shall take the following example:

EXAMPLE 164.—What will be the force required to move a train of cars and tender up a grade of 150 feet, weight of train 100 tons?

According to Art. 622, we have
Resistance due to friction of one ton (2,000) = 7 pounds
According to Rule 124,
Resistance due to grade, 150 × .3787 = 56.8 pounds
Total resistance per ton = 63.8 pounds

The total resistance due to the weight of train of 100 tons will be

$$63.8 \times 100 = 6380 \text{ pounds}.$$

That is to say, the force $P$ (Fig. 1009) will have to be equal to 6,380 pounds to haul a train of the given weight up a grade of 150 feet, at a very low rate of speed.

### RESISTANCE DUE TO SPEED.

**626.** The resistance due to speed depends much on the state of the weather. In calm weather the resistance is less than in strong head-winds, but in what proportion the resistance increases is not accurately known; consequently, for computing the resistance due to speed several formulas have been proposed, which give results at variance with each other. The result obtained from any of these formulas should be considered to be an approximation only. The following will give probably as safe results as any that can be used in designing engines for given speeds:

$$\frac{S^2}{171} = \text{resistance per ton (2,000 pounds) of train,}$$

in which $S$ denotes the speed in miles per hour. This rule indicates that the resistance increases with the square of the speed, but recent observations seem to indicate that this is not exactly true, and the resistance is less; however, the error resulting from the use of this formula will be on the safe side. From this we get the following:

RULE 126.—For finding the resistance due to speed: Divide the square of the speed in miles per hour by the constant 171; the quotient will be the resistance due to speed per ton of load.

Multiplying this quotient by the weight of load in tons will give the resistance of the total weight due to the speed.

EXAMPLE 165.—What is the total resistance of the load (including cars and tender), the aggregate weight being 100 tons, running up a grade of 150 feet per mile at a rate of 30 miles per hour?

| | |
|---|---|
| Resistance due to axle and rolling friction | = 7.0 pounds per ton |
| Resistance due to grade = 150 × .3787 | = 56.8 pounds per ton |
| Resistance due to speed = $\frac{30^2}{171}$ | = 5.26 pounds per ton |
| Total resistance per ton | = 69.06 pounds |

Resistance for the whole weight of cars and tender = 69.06 × 100 = 6906 pounds.

### RESISTANCE DUE TO CURVES.

**627.** Curves are frequently designated by degrees, although the simplest way to designate a curve is by its radius, to which locomotive draftsmen must reduce it when given in degrees. A curve of one degree is usually assumed to have a radius of 5,730 feet; a two-degree curve, $\frac{5730}{2} = 2865$ feet; a three-degree curve, $\frac{5730}{3} = 1910$ feet; and so on. Hence, if the degree of the curve is given, its radius is approximately found by dividing 5,730 by the number of degrees. This rule is correct enough for ordinary curves over 500 feet radius.

The resistance due to curves is influenced by many circumstances. It depends on the length of train, whether the cars are empty or loaded, for an empty train will offer a greater resistance than a loaded one of the same weight; by the distance between the wheels under each car, diameter of wheels, shape of tread; by the width of track, its condition, the degree of elevation of the outer rails, and kind of coupling. With so many conditions entering into the solution of a problem, it is easy to be seen that we must depend on experimental data; but very extensive experiments, as far as we know, have not been made, and the results of the computation based on the insufficient data at hand must be considered only as approximations, as they are more or less liable to error. The following rule is frequently adopted by builders:

RULE 127.—Multiply the number of degrees of curvature by .5; the product will be the resistance in pounds per ton of train due to the curves on a road.

This rule indicates that $\frac{1}{2}$ pound per ton of train is allowed for each degree of curvature.

### HAULING CAPACITY OF LOCOMOTIVE ON A GRADE.

628. We are now in a position to compute approximately the hauling capacity of a locomotive up a given grade with a curved or straight track. In fact, this will now be a very simple matter; all that needs to be done is to fill out the following specification of items, and then proceed as shown in the example.

Resistance of cars and tender due to rolling and axle friction, in pounds = 7 pounds × weight of cars and tender in tons.

Resistance of cars and tender due to grade, in pounds = rise × .3787 × weight of cars and tender in tons.

Resistance of cars and tender due to speed, in pounds = $\dfrac{\text{(speed in miles per hour)}^2}{171}$ × weight of cars and tender in tons.

Resistance of cars and tender due to curves, in pounds = degrees of curve × .5 × weight of cars and tender in tons.

Resistance of engine due to rolling and axle friction and that of machinery, in pounds = 8 pounds × weight of engine in tons.

Resistance of engine due to grade, in pounds = rise × .3787 × weight of engine in tons.

Resistance of engine due to speed, in pounds = $\dfrac{\text{(speed in miles per hour)}^2}{171}$ × weight of engine in tons.

Resistance of engine due to curves, in pounds = degrees of curve × .5 × weight of engine in tons.

EXAMPLE 166.—What load can an eight-wheeled passenger engine with cylinders 18 × 24 inches haul up a grade of 150 feet per mile, the road having a curve of 716 feet radius on the grade? Total weight of engine, 48 tons; weight on drivers, 64,000 pounds; speed, 30 miles per hour.

Since the sum of the weight of cars, with load and weight of tender, is to be found, we will designate the sum of these weights by $W$.

The radius of the curve is given at 716 feet; hence, according to Art. 627, the curve is one of $\dfrac{5730}{716} = 8$ degrees.

| | |
|---|---|
| Resistance of cars and tender due to rolling and axle friction = 7 × $W$ | = 7.0 $W$ pounds. |
| Resistance of cars and tender due to grade = 150 × .3787 × $W$ | = 56.8 $W$ pounds. |
| Resistance of cars and tender due to speed = $\dfrac{30 \times 30}{171} \times W$ | = 5.2 $W$ pounds. |
| Resistance of cars and tender due to curves = 8 × .5 × $W$ | = 4.0 $W$ pounds. |
| Total resistance of unknown weights | = 73.0 $W$ pounds. |

| | | |
|---|---|---|
| Resistance of engine due to rolling and axle friction and that of machinery = 8 × 48 | = | 384 pounds. |
| Resistance of engine due to grade = 150 × .3787 × 48 | = | 2726.4 pounds. |
| Resistance of engine due to speed = $\dfrac{30 \times 30}{171} \times 48$ | = | 249.6 pounds. |
| Resistance of engine due to curves = 8 × .5 × 48 | = | 192 pounds. |
| Total resistance of known weights | = | 3552 pounds. |

The adhesion of driving wheels, and therefore the tractive force, is one-fifth of the weight on drivers; consequently we have $\dfrac{64000}{5} = 12800$ pounds to overcome a total resistance of 3552 pounds + 73 $W$ pounds.

Subtracting the resistance of known weights from the tractive force, we have 12800 − 3552 = 9248 pounds to overcome a resistance of 73 $W$ pounds; consequently the weight of cars, with load and weight of tender, will be

$$W = \frac{9248}{73} = 126.68 \text{ tons,}$$

that is, the given engine can haul under the conditions given in the example 126.68 tons, provided the boiler has a sufficient steaming capacity to do this amount of work.

Since the weight of train as found above is that which the engine can keep in uniform motion, it may seem that the engine cannot start this train, because the rolling and axle friction is greater at starting than when the train is in motion. But it must be remembered that in the foregoing computation we have made an allowance for a speed of 30 miles per hour; but at starting the speed is zero, and the allowance we have made for speed will generally be sufficient for overcoming the extra friction at starting. Hence we may say that this engine will also start the train on the given grade.

# CHAPTER XVII.

## COMPOUND LOCOMOTIVES.

629. A compound locomotive is one in which the expansion of steam is divided into separate stages. Although, strictly speaking, triple expansion engines or quadruple expansion engines are compounds, yet custom has sanctioned the application of the term "compound engine" to one in which the expansion of steam is divided into two stages only. The general American locomotive practice at present is to use one cylinder for each stage of expansion. The steam is admitted as near as possible to the boiler pressure into one cylinder, called the high-pressure cylinder, and is there expanded to a greater or lesser extent, and is then allowed to escape into a second cylinder called the low-pressure cylinder, where it is again expanded, and then discharged into the atmosphere in the usual way.

### CYLINDER CONDENSATION AND RE-EVAPORATION.

630. The amount of cylinder condensation and re-evaporation varies with the difference between the initial and final temperature in the cylinder. Assume that the absolute initial pressure in a simple engine is 165 pounds; at this pressure the steam has a temperature of 365.7 degrees Fahr.; if the final pressure is 33 pounds absolute, the temperature of the steam will then be 255.7 degrees, giving a difference of temperature of $365.7 - 255.7 = 110$ degrees, in the cylinder during every stroke. Of course it cannot be claimed that the range of temperature in the metal of the cylinder walls will be as great as the difference between the initial and final temperature of the steam; but that there is a difference in the temperature of the cylinder walls during each stroke is beyond a doubt, and we naturally infer from this that when the entering steam comes in contact with the surface of the metal whose temperature is below that of the steam, condensation takes place and reduces the work which otherwise the steam could perform.

631. As the steam is expanded its temperature falls below that of the cylinder walls, causing heat to be transferred from the latter to the former, and causing a re-evaporation; and when the exhaust takes place, much of the heat transferred from the cylinder walls to the steam is lost, causing a loss of work.

632. We have seen that in a compound engine the expansion is divided into two stages, each taking place in a separate cylinder. This reduces the variation of pressure and temperature in each cylinder, and therefore it is said that the cylinder condensation in a compound is less than in a non-compound, the total ratio of expansion being the same in both engines. But the advocates of simple engines, among whom

there are many engineers whose reputation gives weight to their opinion, point to the fact that in a compound engine the steam is exposed to a greater cylinder cooling surface, and therefore insist that the cylinder condensation is not reduced as much as is claimed by the advocates of the compound engines, and that the saving of fuel in the latter class, if any, cannot be due to a reduced cylinder condensation. This opinion cannot well be refuted, because it is extremely difficult to detect the cylinder condensation on the indicator-cards taken when the locomotives are running at a high speed and cutting off at an early part of the stroke.

633. In a compound engine, the steam due to re-evaporation that takes place in the high-pressure cylinder is not wholly lost, because it is admitted into the low-pressure cylinder and does work there. The re-evaporation in the low-pressure cylinder, however, causes a loss, because the steam due to it will be discharged into the atmosphere before it has a chance of doing a corresponding amount of work; but this loss will not be as great as in a simple engine.

634. There is certainly a gain in using steam at a high pressure and cutting off short so as to expand it to as low a terminal pressure as is practical. To do so a difficulty is encountered. The ratio of expansion is governed by the link motion, which is usually of the type shown in Fig. 29, and on account of its simplicity is retained in compounds. With this gear the distribution of steam in each cylinder is governed by one valve, and this may cause considerable difficulty in the attempt to keep the pressure due to compression at early cut-offs within desirable limits; and indeed this matter is not so easily disposed of in compounds as in simple engines. The clearance space affects the pressure due to compression. For smooth running it should be sufficient to arrest the motion of the reciprocating parts; this is a problem by itself, and need not be considered here. For economy of steam the pressure at the end of compression should be equal to the initial pressure; there is no advantage in compressing the steam to a higher degree. Now, if in a simple engine the absolute initial pressure is 160 pounds and the absolute back pressure is 18 pounds, we may compress the latter $\frac{160}{18} = 8.8$ times before the initial pressure is reached. If in a compound the initial pressure in the high-pressure cylinder is 160 pounds and the back pressure in the low-pressure cylinder is 18 pounds, we have the same range of compression, but this takes place in two cylinders; if, for instance, the receiver pressure is 65 pounds, then the range of compression in the H. P. cylinder will be from 65 to 160 pounds, and in order to reach the initial pressure the steam will have to be compressed about $\frac{160}{65} = 2.4$ times. In the L. P. cylinder the range of compression is from 18 to 65 pounds, and therefore the back pressure will have to be compressed about $\frac{65}{18} = 3.6$ times before the receiver pressure is reached. Now if the same kind of link motion and the same size of valves are used in both classes of engines, it will easily be perceived that there is danger of obtaining an excessive and hurtful pressure due to compression, unless the clearance space is larger in the compound than in the simple engine. From this it will be seen that a large percentage of clearance space may be of great advantage in compound engines. There is another way of avoiding an excessive compression, namely, giving the valve a large

inside clearance so as to secure a late exhaust closure; this is often resorted to, and in fact it is the noticeable difference between the slide valves of a compound and an ordinary locomotive. Hence, an increased percentage of clearance space, or inside clearance of the valves, or both, may be advantageously employed in compound locomotives.

635. The point at which the exhaust closure should take place so as to give any desired pressure at the end of compression can be found by the following formula:

$$d = 1 - \left(\frac{P}{p} - 1\right)c,$$

in which $d$ denotes the distance $H F$ (see Fig. 1008), or, in other words, the distance from the beginning $F$ of the return stroke to the point $H$ of the exhaust closure; $P$, the desired absolute pressure $B E$ at the end of compression, which may be equal to the initial pressure or less; $p$, the absolute back pressure; and $c$, the clearance $B Z$ in per cent. of the stroke.

In ordinary language the above formula reads:

RULE 128.—Divide the desired absolute pressure at the end of compression by the absolute back pressure; subtract 1 (one) from the quotient, and multiply the remainder by the clearance in per cent. of the stroke; subtract this product from 1 (one); the remainder will be the distance in per cent. from the beginning of the return stroke to the point at which the exhaust valve should close.

EXAMPLE 167.—The clearance space is 8 per cent., the pressure at the end of compression is to be 160 pounds absolute, and the absolute back pressure is 18 pounds: at what distance from the beginning of the return stroke should the exhaust valve close?

Substituting for the symbols in the above formula the values given in the example, we have

$$d = 1 - \left(\frac{160}{18} - 1\right) \times .08 = .37,$$

that is to say, the exhaust should close at .37th part of the stroke; if the latter is 24 inches, then the exhaust should close at 24 × .37 = 8.88 inches from the beginning of the return stroke.

636. With the same valves and valve gear in both classes of engines, we can always obtain a greater ratio of expansion in a compound than in a simple engine, because in cutting off at the same point in both classes the steam in the high-pressure cylinder will be expanded to the same extent as in the simple engine; but this is again expanded in the low-pressure cylinder, thereby obtaining an increased ratio of expansion, and therefore high-pressure steam can be used with better advantage in a compound than in an ordinary locomotive. Again, it must not be overlooked that the expansive working of steam is compulsory in a compound; even with the link motion set in full gear, there will be an expansion of steam in the compound greater than in a simple engine, and this contributes much to the success of the former.

637. In compounds the variation of steam pressure during a stroke is reduced, consequently the pressures on the crank-pins are more uniform, which reduces the tendency to slip the wheels, and gives greater durability to the parts.

638. The lack of reliable experiments leaves the amount of fuel that can be saved with a compound in dispute; indeed, the reports relating to this are very conflicting. Considerable of this dispute is probably due to the prejudice of the advocates of the simple engine on the one hand, and the enthusiasm of the advocates of the compound on the other hand, who are liable, though perfectly honest, to overestimate the economy of fuel. Reports seem to indicate that in a very few cases a good simple engine has given as good results as a compound; but in the majority of cases the compounds have given much better results. It is probably safe to say that the saving of fuel in favor of the compound will vary from 15 to 30 per cent.; the latter amount may be expected when the compound is doing the work for which she has been designed, and this saving will be decreased when the engine has more or less than this amount of work to do.

### TWO-CYLINDER COMPOUNDS.

639. The two-cylinder compounds may be divided into two distinct classes. First, the class which embraces those which always work as compounds except for a brief period at starting; they are so arranged that they change automatically from simple to compound working. Second, the class which embraces those which can be worked as simple or as compounds at the will of the engineer.

The outer appearance of either class does not differ much from that of the simple engine; indeed, it does not require many changes to convert a simple into a compound engine.

### LOCOMOTIVES WHICH ALWAYS WORK AS COMPOUNDS.

640. Fig. 1013 shows a partial end view of an engine which always works as a compound, excepting during the brief period at starting. The high-pressure cylinder is marked H. P., and the low-pressure cylinder L. P.; the latter is of course larger in diameter than the former. An ordinary steam pipe, not shown here, but similar in design to that shown in Fig. 24, is used to convey the steam from the boiler into the H. P. cylinder; after it has done work there it is discharged into the pipe $r$, which conveys the steam into the L. P. cylinder; this pipe $r$ is called the receiver; after the steam has done its work in the L. P. cylinder it is discharged into the atmosphere in the usual way. The steam in its passage to the L. P. cylinder has to pass through the intercepting valve placed in the saddle as shown, and of which different sections are given. This valve is the invention of Mr. Albert J. Pitkin, superintendent of the Schenectady Locomotive Works.

Fig. 1011 is a longitudinal elevation partly in section of the L. P. cylinder; the partial section is taken on the line 5 5 of Fig. 1013.

Fig. 1012 is a longitudinal sectional plan of the saddle castings of the H. P. and L. P. cylinders, and the regulator mechanism taken on the line 1 1 of Fig. 1013.

Fig. 1014 is a longitudinal sectional elevation of a portion of the regulator, taken on the line 2 2, Fig. 1012, and line 3 3, Fig. 1013.

Fig. 1015 is a transverse sectional elevation of the regulator, taken on the line 4 4, Fig. 1012.

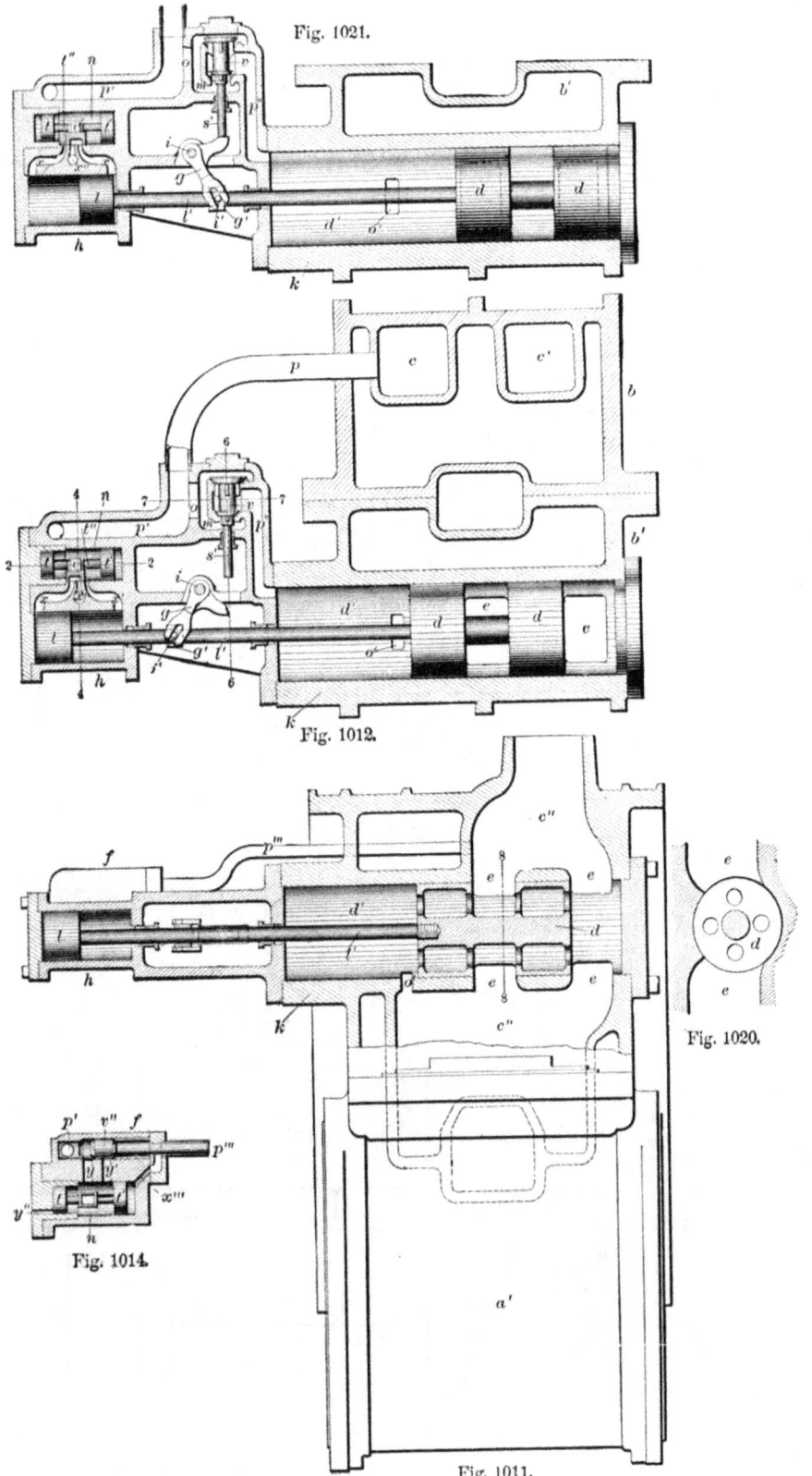

Fig. 1021.

Fig. 1012.

Fig. 1020.

Fig. 1014.

Fig. 1011.

621

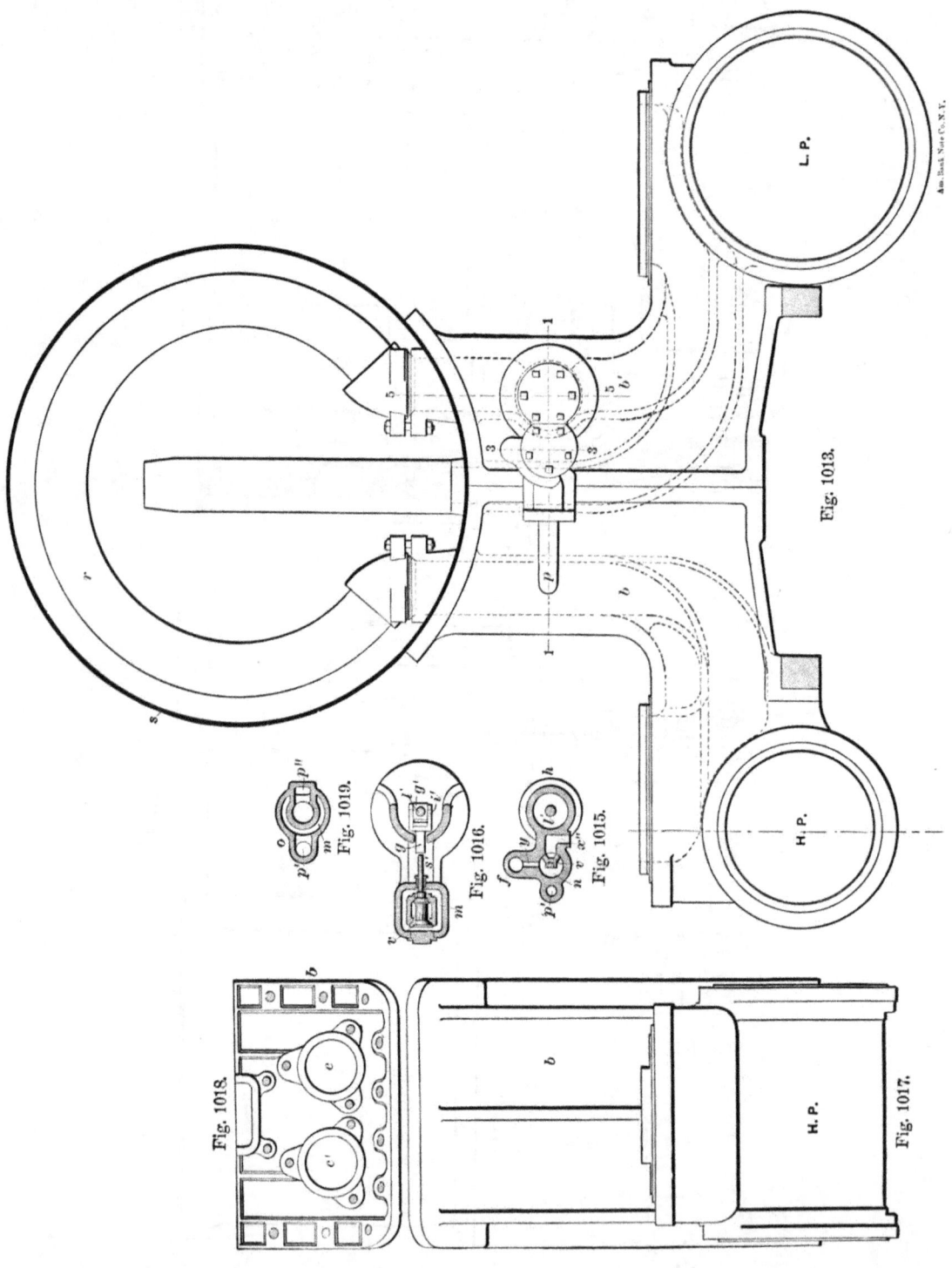

Fig. 1016 is a transverse sectional elevation of the regulator, taken on the line 6 6, Fig. 1012.

Fig. 1017 is a longitudinal elevation of the H. P. cylinder.

Fig. 1018 is a plan of the saddle connections of the H. P. cylinder.

Fig. 1019 is a longitudinal sectional elevation of a portion of the regulator on the line 7 7, Fig. 1012.

Fig. 1020 is a transverse sectional elevation of the intercepting valve and chamber on the line 8 8, Fig. 1011.

Fig. 1021 is a longitudinal sectional plan of the regulator and intercepting valve-chamber, taken on the line 1 1, Fig. 1013, showing the several parts in opposite positions to that in Fig. 1012.

The action of these valves is described as follows: Assuming the engine to be at rest, upon opening the throttle live steam from the boiler enters the H. P. cylinder steam-chest through the passage $c$, Figs. 1012 and 1018, while simultaneously this live steam passes through the pipe $p$ into the passage $p'$ of the regulator. From this passage it enters the auxiliary valve-chamber $f$ and forces the auxiliary valve $v''$ into the position shown in Fig. 1014. The live steam then flows through the port $y$, Fig. 1014, into the valve-chamber $n$, Fig. 1012. Owing to the difference in areas of the pistons $t$ and $t'$ the preponderance of the pressure will cause the pistons $t$ and $t'$ with the valve $v'$ to move to the opposite end of the chamber $n$ from that shown in Fig. 1012. This movement of the valve uncovers the port $x$ and allows the live steam to enter the cylinder $h$. This pressure upon the piston $l$ will cause it to move to the opposite end of the cylinder $h$ from that shown in Fig. 1012. This movement of the piston $l$ through the rod $l'$ causes the intercepting valve $d$ to close, thus cutting off all communication between the high- and low-pressure cylinders, as shown in Fig. 1021.

The angularity of the two arms of the lever $g$ in relation to the fixed position of the collar $g'$ upon the piston-rod $l'$ is such that, when the intercepting valve is being moved forward and closing, the shorter arm of the lever $g$ will strike the end of the spindle $s'$ at the time the intercepting valve $d$ has just closed line and line with its seat. The further movement of the intercepting valve, owing to its lap, will be sufficient to cause the valve $v$ to acquire its full opening. As soon as the valve $v$ is opened the live steam from the passage $p'$ flows through the opening $o$, the chamber $m$, the opening made by the valve $v$, the passage $p''$, through the intercepting valve chamber $d'$ and the opening $o'$ into the receiver, and thence on to the steam-chest of the low-pressure cylinder. This pressure being upon the under side of the intercepting valve, should any lost motion exist, raises it against the upper side of its chamber, and prevents any live steam from passing back through the receiver and acting as back pressure on the high-pressure cylinder. Stated concisely, the operation of starting is thus: Upon opening the throttle, live steam is admitted simultaneously to both the high- and low-pressure cylinders, and by means of this same live steam acting through a mechanism, separate and distinct from the intercepting valve itself, the intercepting valve is closed automatically and the engine starts with its full power as simple or non-compound engine. The engine now starting, the exhaust steam from the H. P. cylinder is accumulating in the receiver above the intercepting valve. This increasing pressure in the receiver is carried through the pipe $p'''$ into the auxiliary valve chamber $f$, Fig.

1014, thence through the ports $x'''$ into the valve chamber $n$, Fig. 1012, and exerts itself on the side of the piston $t'$, Fig. 1012, opposite to that acted upon by the live steam. As soon as the requisite pressure has accumulated in the receiver, and which is sufficient to overcome the live steam pressure on the unequal inner areas of the pistons $t$ and $t'$, these pistons with the slide valve $v'$ are caused to assume their original position, as shown in Fig. 1012, thus uncovering the port $x'$, allowing the live steam from the chamber $n$ to enter the corresponding end of the cylinder $h$. At the same time the slide valve $v'$ prevents the further entrance of the live steam to the cylinder $h$ through the port $x$, but does allow, by means of the cavity in the valve $v'$, the steam previously admitted through this port $x$ to escape through the exhaust port $x''$, Figs. 1012 and 1015, to the open air. The relief thus afforded allows the live steam entering the port $x'$ to force the piston $l$ back again to its former position, as shown in Fig. 1012, which at the same time opens the intercepting valve $d$, giving free communication between the high- and low-pressure cylinders. Since the backward movement of the intercepting valve $d$ and piston-rod $l$, Fig. 1012, carries back also the lever $g$, which allows the valve $v$ to close, thus cutting off the supply of live steam to the low-pressure cylinder, the engine continues to operate as a compound. Owing to the construction of the intercepting valve $d$, Figs. 1011, 1012, and 1020, which is clearly shown in the illustrations, any pressure in or around the pistons forming the valve has no influence whatever upon its movements. This pressure can neither start the valve in motion, nor retard its movement if it once be in motion. Therefore its movement is not derived from either live or exhaust steam acting upon it. The only use made of the exhaust steam from the receiver in any part of the mechanism, in ordinary operation, is to move the slide valve $v'$, Fig. 1012, as described. In the event of the intercepting valve being closed, as in the position shown in Fig. 1021, and the engine running with the throttle closed as in the case of a locomotive rolling down a grade, there would be no resisting pressure to cause an opening of the intercepting valve. Unless this valve should be opened, the constantly accumulating gases and vapor in the receiver above the intercepting valve would finally be sufficient, acting as back pressure on the H. P. piston, to become objectionable. To avoid the occurrence of such a condition, the auxiliary valve $v''$, Fig. 1014, is employed. This receiver pressure is carried to the auxiliary valve chamber $f$, Fig. 1014, by the pipe $p'''$ (Figs. 1011 and 1014), and acting upon the auxiliary valve $v''$ forces it to the opposite end of its chamber from that shown in Fig. 1014; and from the manner in which it seats itself, this receiver pressure cannot pass into the passage $p'$. The above-mentioned movement of the valve $v''$ uncovers the port $y'$, Fig. 1014, allowing the receiver pressure to enter the valve chamber $n$ between the two pistons $t$ and $t'$. At the same time this receiver pressure enters the end of the chamber $n$ through the port $x'''$. Since the pistons $t$ and $t'$ are of unequal area, the same pressure between the two pistons and on the opposite side of the larger piston, $t'$, would consequently force the pistons and the slide valve $v'$ to assume the position as shown in Fig. 1012, thus uncovering the port $x'$ allowing the receiver pressure to enter the cylinder $h$, and by its action force the piston $l$ backward as shown in Fig. 1012, thus opening the intercepting valve $d$.

The entire arrangement of the several parts of the mechanism is such that the intercepting valve is moved forward and backward automatically, and at proper intervals, to meet the requirements of any or all circumstances under which the engine may be operated.

In order that there may not be any undue slamming of the intercepting valve as it reaches the terminus of its stroke in either direction, the exhaust cavity of the valve $v'$, Figs. 1012 and 1015, is contracted in proper proportion to the volume of the exhaust escaping from the cylinder $h$, so as to form compression at the end of the stroke, thus allowing the intercepting valve to travel to and fro at a reduced speed consistent with its weight and length of travel.

The above is all the extra mechanism that is required for a compound engine of this class. In fact, to change a simple locomotive to a compound, all that is usually done is to take off one cylinder, replace it by one larger in diameter, with a slide valve and steam-chest necessarily a little larger than used in the simple system, and attach the intercepting valve with its auxiliaries.

### LOCOMOTIVES WHICH CAN BE WORKED AS COMPOUNDS OR NON-COMPOUNDS.

**641.** Figs. 1022, 1023, 1024 show the intercepting valve and its auxiliaries for a compound locomotive, which can be changed at will from a compound to a non-compound, started and run continuously with steam directly from the boiler in both cylinders, each doing half the work, and each exhausting into the stack and atmosphere directly. An outside view of this engine is shown in Fig. 1025. This type is built by the Rhode Island Locomotive Works, Providence, R. I. The intercepting valve and auxiliaries as shown in the following illustrations were invented by Mr. C. H. Batchellor, chief draftsman at the above works.

Fig. 1022 shows a front section of the intercepting valve at ports $d$ and $e$, also front view of a portion of the receiver with exhaust valve.

Fig. 1023 shows a longitudinal section of the same mechanism while running compound, and Fig. 1024 shows the same while running simple.

The same letters in the different views represent like parts. $A$, represents the intercepting valve casing; $B$, the reducing valve; $C$, the oil dash-pot; $D$, the pipe from the main steam pipe to the intercepting valve; $E$, the receiver; $F$, the exhaust valve; $a\ b\ c$, the intercepting valve pistons; $d$, a port from $D$ through $A$; $e$, a port from $A$ into the reducing valve $B$; $f$, a port from $A$ into the passage to L. P. steam-chest; $m$, a small pipe and passage connecting hand valve in cab to chamber $h$; $o$, port through exhaust-valve casing.

The operation of this device is as follows: The intercepting valve being in any position and the exhaust valve $F$ closed as in Fig. 1023, then on opening the throttle steam from the boiler will pass into the H. P. cylinder in the usual manner, and also through pipe $D$ into the intercepting valve $A$, causing the pistons $a\ b\ c$ to move into the position shown in Fig. 1024. In this position the receiver is closed to the L. P. cylinder by the piston $c$, and steam from $D$ passes through the ports $d$ and $e$ and reducing valve $B$ into the L. P. steam-chest, the pressure being reduced from the boiler pressure in the ratio of the cylinder areas. The pistons $a\ b\ c$ are so proportioned that they will automatically change to the compound position shown in Fig. 1023, when a predetermined pressure in the receiver $E$ has been reached by the exhaust from the

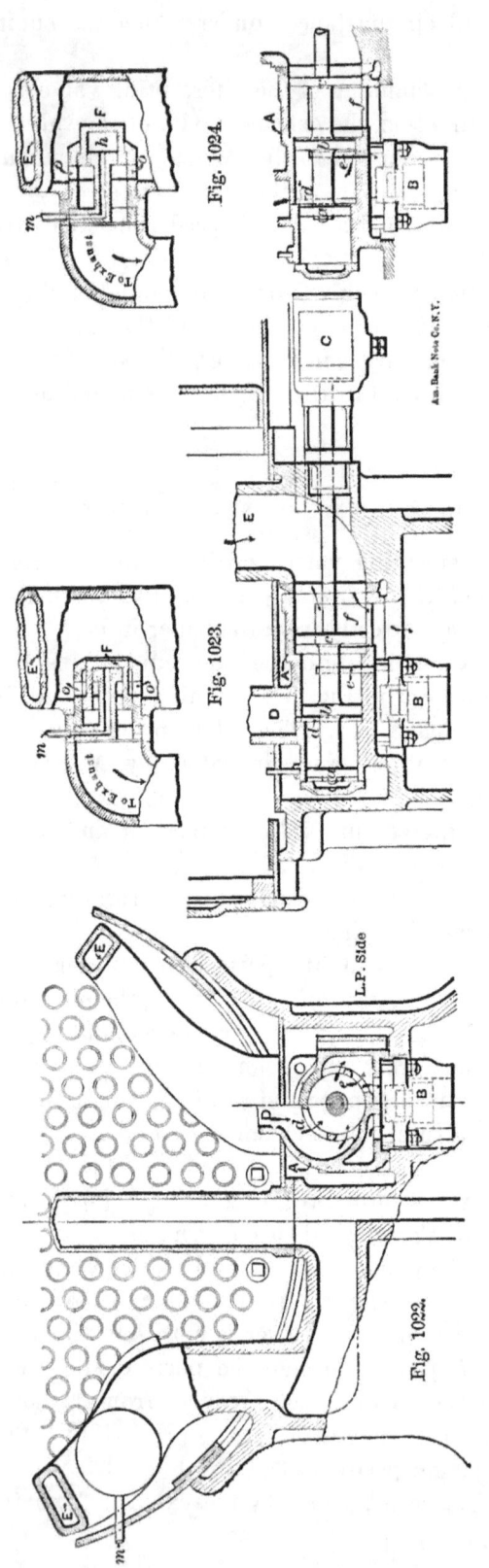

Fig. 1025.

H. P. cylinder. The engine thus starts with steam in both cylinders, and changes automatically to a compound at a desired receiver pressure.

The engine may be changed from a compound to a simple system at any time, at the will of the engineer, by opening the valve $F$ connecting the receiver to the exhaust pipe, allowing the exhaust from the H. P. cylinder to escape through the nozzle in the usual manner.

The exhaust valve $F$ is operated as follows: The small pipe $m$ leads from a hand valve in the cab connecting it to either steam or atmosphere. When desiring to run compound, $m$ is in connection with the atmosphere, the receiver steam keeping the valve $F$ in the position, as shown in Fig. 1023. To run simple $m$ is connected to the steam which will hold the valve $F$, as in Fig. 1024, the ports $o$ opening $E$ to the exhaust. The valve $F$ takes either position at any time at the will of the engineer.

It is obvious that in case of bad conditions of starting, the engine may be operated as a simple one by opening the exhaust valve before starting, and that upon its closure the pistons $a\ b\ c$ will automatically take the compound position.

### VALVE GEAR ADJUSTMENT IN TWO-CYLINDER COMPOUNDS.

642. In a two-cylinder compound locomotive the division of work is equalized by an adjustment of the valve gear so as to cut off at the proper time in each cylinder. For this purpose a later cut-off is frequently given in the low-pressure cylinder than in the high-pressure cylinder. Of course, for a correct adjustment of the valve gear indicator-cards will be required.

The difference in cut-offs in the two cylinders is frequently obtained by making the length of the high-pressure link-hanger about $\frac{1}{20}$ of the lift of the link less than that of the low-pressure link-hanger. This kind of adjustment is of course suitable only for engines which run mostly in forward gear; for others, which run as much in one direction as in the other, this adjustment is not suitable. In the latter cases the required cut-offs can be obtained by reducing the angular advance of the low-pressure eccentric, and also reducing to a corresponding degree the outside lap of the valve for the same cylinder.

### STEAM-PORT AREA FOR COMPOUND LOCOMOTIVE.

643. The steam-port area for the high-pressure cylinder is found by the same rule as given in Art. 43. This rule can be given in another form, so that the use of table given in Art. 43 is not necessary; thus:

RULE 129.—Multiply the speed of piston in feet per minute by the square of the diameter in inches, and divide the result by 7639; the quotient will be the area in square inches of the steam port in the H. P. cylinder. Expressing this rule by symbols, we have

$$\frac{\text{(Diameter of cylinder in inches)}^2 \times \text{speed of piston in feet}}{7639} = \text{area of steam ports}.$$

The ratio of width to length of steam port is the same as given in Art. 43.

For finding the steam-port area for the low-pressure cylinder, we have

RULE 130.—Multiply the piston speed in feet per minute by the square of the diameter of the cylinder in inches, and divide the product by 8800; the quotient will be the steam-port area for the low-pressure cylinder. Expressing this rule by symbols, we have

$$\frac{\text{(Diameter of cylinder in inches)}^2 \times \text{speed of piston in feet}}{8800} = \text{area of steam port}.$$

From this it will be seen that the steam-port area in the L. P. cylinder is not as great in proportion to the piston area as in the H. P. cylinder.

EXAMPLE 168.—What should be the dimensions of the steam ports in a compound locomotive with cylinders 17 and 24 inches diameter, piston speed 700 feet per minute?

For the area of steam ports in the H. P. cylinder, we have, according to rule,

$$\frac{17^2 \times 700}{7639} = 26.48 \text{ square inches.}$$

If we now decide to make the width of the steam port 1⅝ inches, then the length will be

$$\frac{26.48}{1.625} = 16.29, \text{ say } 16\tfrac{1}{4} \text{ inches.}$$

For the area of the steam ports in the L. P. cylinder, we have, according to rule,

$$\frac{24^2 \times 700}{8800} = 45.81 \text{ square inches.}$$

If we now decide to make the length of the steam port 22 inches, then we have for its width

$$\frac{45.81}{22} = 2.08, \text{ say } 2 \text{ inches.}$$

### DIAMETER OF CYLINDERS.

644. There exists a difference in opinion in regard to the proper diameters of cylinders in a two-cylinder compound, and consequently several rules for obtaining them have been recommended. We believe that the simplest way, and which will probably give as satisfactory results as any, is to find the diameter of the low-pressure cylinder by Rule 115, using 25 per cent. of the boiler pressure for the mean effective pressure $p$; then make the area of the H. P. cylinder one half that of the L. P. cylinder. According to this the volume of the L. P. cylinder is twice that of the H. P. cylinder, provided the stroke is the same in both cylinders. This ratio is not always adopted; frequently it is somewhat greater, making the volumes as 1 to 2.2, and occasionally we find this ratio somewhat less than 1 to 2.

EXAMPLE 169.—What should be the diameters of cylinders for a compound locomotive having a tractive force of 11,472 pounds; stroke of piston, 24 inches; diameter of driving wheels, 61 inches; boiler pressure, 170 pounds? For the mean effective pressure we take $170 \times .25 = 42.5$ pounds. The formula given in Art. 594 for finding the diameter of the cylinder is

$$d = \sqrt{\frac{T \times D}{p \times s}},$$

hence the diameter of the low-pressure cylinder will be

$$d = \sqrt{\frac{11472 \times 61}{42.5 \times 24}} = 26 \text{ inches (fraction omitted).}$$

The area of a 26-inch piston is 530.93 square inches. If we now decide to make the area of H. P. cylinder one half of that of L. P. cylinder, then we have $\dfrac{530.93}{2} = 265.46$ square inches for the area of H. P. cylinder, and the corresponding diameter will be $18\frac{3}{8}$ inches.

Referring to Table 5, page 17, we find that a non-compound eight-wheeled passenger engine with the same tractive force, same size of wheels, but with a mean effective pressure of 90 pounds per square inch, has cylinders 18 × 24 inches.

If in the foregoing example the weight on drivers had been given instead of the tractive force, we should have divided the weight on drivers by 5, which would have given us the tractive force, and then proceeded as before.

The foregoing method of finding the diameters of cylinders for a compound engine applies to those only in which the area of the L. P. cylinder is about twice that of the H. P. cylinder.

### VOLUME OF RECEIVER.

The volume of the receiver should not be less than that of the H. P. cylinder; in fact a receiver volume somewhat greater than this will give better results, as such will reduce the fluctuations of back pressure in the H. P. cylinder.

### FOUR-CYLINDER COMPOUND LOCOMOTIVES.

645. The four-cylinder compounds used to a great extent in the country are built by the Baldwin Locomotive Works of Philadelphia, and patented by Mr. Samuel M. Vauclain, superintendent of these works.

The general construction of boiler, frames, valve gear, driving and truck wheels, is the same as in an ordinary non-compound; the difference between these engines is entirely in the cylinders, pistons, cylinder cocks, crosshead, and valves, as shown in Figs. 1026, 1027; the latter shows the construction of the main valve, and Fig. 1028 shows the starting valve.

A piston valve, shown in section in Fig. 1027, is used for distributing the steam in the high- and low-pressure cylinders which are placed on each side of the engine; the flow of steam is clearly indicated by the arrows. The steam first enters the H. P. cylinder and propels the piston in it; on the return stroke it passes through the central chamber in the valve to the opposite end of the L. P. cylinder, where it expands and propels the large piston, and in the next stroke passes through a circular groove in the center of the valve, and is discharged through the exhaust port and exhaust pipe in the usual manner. The same operation takes place in both ends of the cylinders.

The centers of the high- and low-pressure cylinders are placed in one vertical plane, and the steam-chest is placed on the inside of the cylinders, as shown in Fig. 1026. Both piston-rods are connected to one crosshead, and the valve-rod connects to the upper rocker-arm in the usual manner.

The piston valve being balanced, it takes comparatively very little force to reverse the engine; and the pressure of the valve against its seat being reduced, it is not so liable to run dry as an ordinary slide valve working under the same high steam

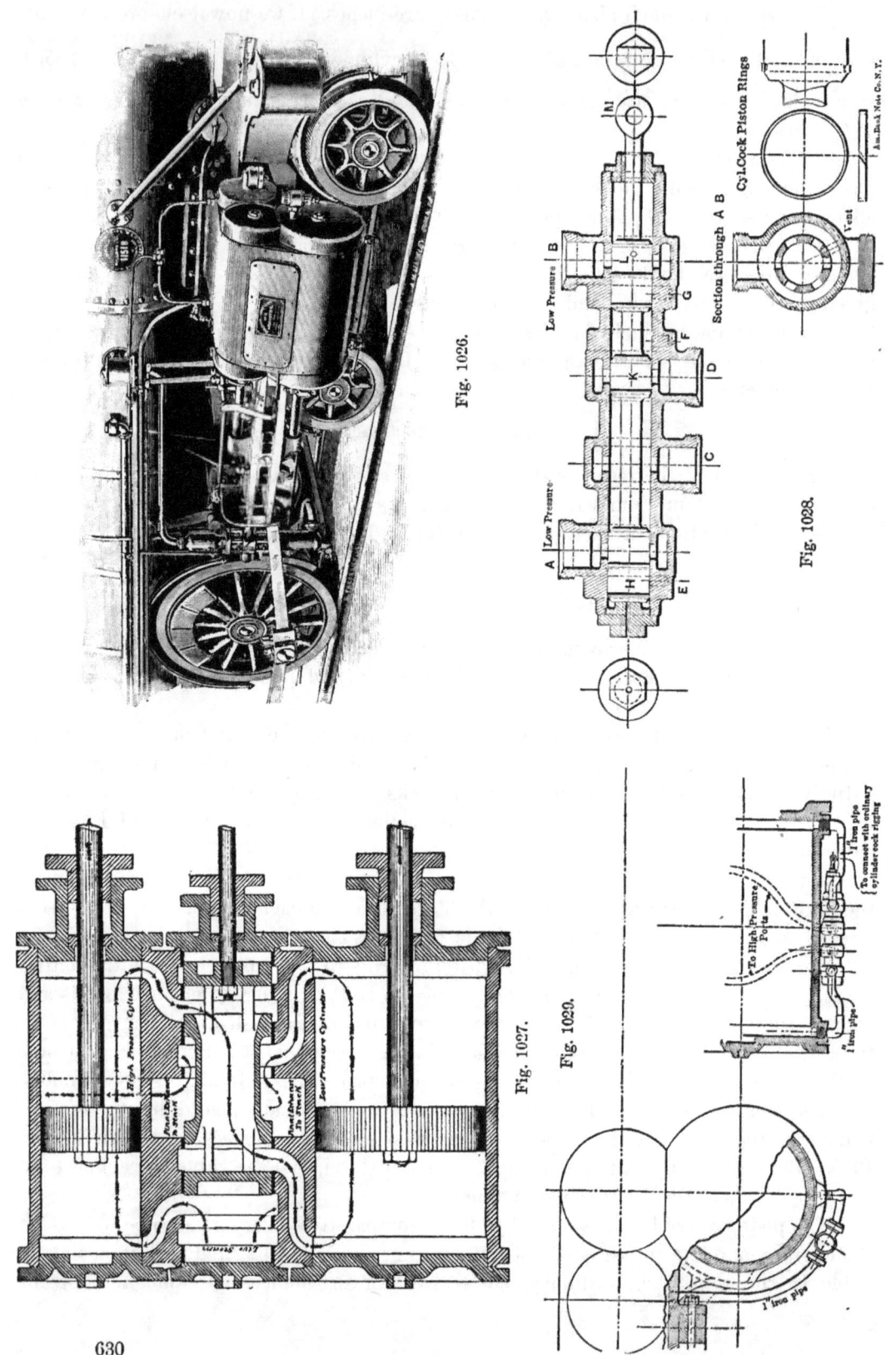

Fig. 1026.

Fig. 1027.

Fig. 1028.

Fig. 1029.

pressure, and therefore the piston valve is well adapted for compound engines in which high steam pressure is used.

646. Fig. 1028 shows a section of the starting valve. It is attached to the bottom of the L. P. cylinder, as shown in Fig. 1029, and is operated in the same way as ordinary cylinder cocks. It consists of a casing with a piston valve inside. The nozzles $A$ and $B$ are in communication with the L. P. cylinder, and the nozzles $C, D$ are connected by pipes to H. P. cylinder. The piston valves $H$ and $L$ fully cover the openings to the L. P. cylinder, while the piston $K$ covers the opening from one side of the H. P. cylinder; steam is therefore shut off from communication between the two cylinders and from the condensation vents $E$ and $G$.

In this position of the piston valves, the lever in the cab which operates them occupies the position as indicated at $P$, Fig. 1030. When this lever occupies the position of $P_2$ the valve is moved half stroke, still, however, covering the L. P. exits, but uncovering the port $D$, throwing the two ports $C$ and $D$ in communication, permitting steam from the inlet end of the H. P. cylinder to travel through the starting valve to the exhaust end of the H. P. cylinder, and consequently into the inlet of the L. P. cylinder, thus mixing live steam with the partially expanded steam. When the lever in the

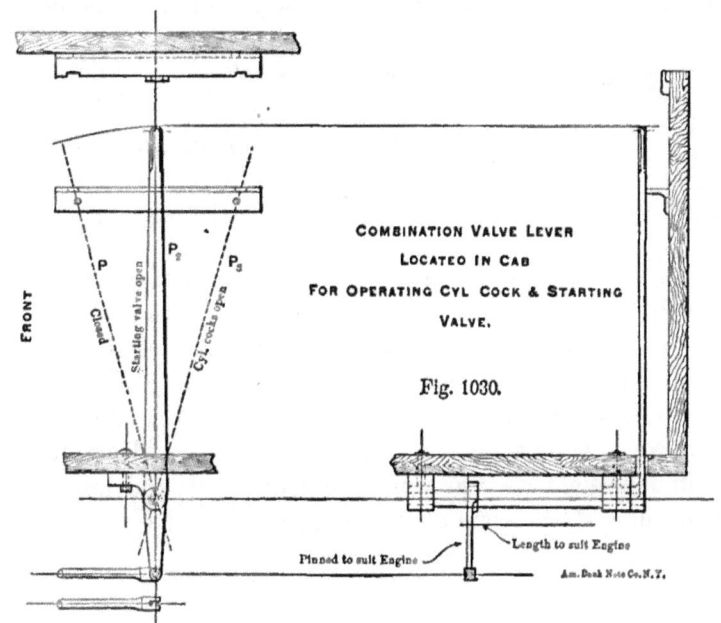

cab occupies the position of $P_3$ the piston valve has traveled to its extreme position and opened the vents $E$, $G$ of the low-pressure cylinder, while leaving the live steam inlet also open. The starting valve may be opened without opening the vents which act as cylinder cocks, but the latter cannot be opened without admitting live steam into the L. P. cylinder. Further, the rigging in the cab is so arranged that the starting valve may be kept open at will for any length of time, with the reverse lever in any position. This makes an extremely simple starting valve and enables the engineer to admit live steam into the L. P. cylinder at will.

### SIZE OF CYLINDERS IN FOUR-CYLINDER LOCOMOTIVES.

647. The formula used by the Baldwin Locomotive Works for finding the size of cylinders is as follows:

$$\text{Diameter of L. P. cylinder} = \sqrt{\frac{\text{weight on drivers in pounds} \times \text{diameter of drivers in inches}}{\text{boiler pressure in pounds per square inch} \times \text{stroke in inches} \times 2.7}}.$$

In ordinary language this reads:

RULE 131.—Multiply the weight on drivers in pounds by the diameter of the drivers in inches; call this product $A$. Multiply the boiler pressure in pounds per square inch by the stroke in inches and by the constant 2.7; call this product $B$. Divide product $A$ by product $B$, and extract the square root of the quotient. The result will be the diameter of the L. P. cylinder.

The area of the H. P. cylinder is made as nearly as possible one third of the area of the L. P. cylinder.

EXAMPLE 170.—What should be the diameters of the cylinders of a four-cylinder compound, the weight on drivers is 57,360 pounds; stroke of pistons, 24 inches; diameter of drivers, 61 inches; steam pressure, 180 pounds?

$$\text{Diameter of L. P. cylinder} = \sqrt{\frac{67360 \times 61}{180 \times 24 \times 2.7}} = 17.3, \text{ say } 17\tfrac{1}{4} \text{ inches.}$$

The area of this cylinder is 233.7055 square inches, consequently the area of the H. P. cylinder should be $\dfrac{233.7055}{3} = 77.9018$ square inches; the corresponding diameter is 10 inches very nearly. Hence the high-pressure cylinder should be 10 inches diameter and the low-pressure cylinder $17\tfrac{1}{4}$ inches diameter.

Up to this time about 200 engines of this class have been built. Besides these a great number of two-cylinder engines have also been built by various locomotive builders, and the average reports in regard to results as far as we can learn are very favorable, while a few are very contradictory. But the indications are that as compound locomotives are more generally used, and improvements made as experience may suggest, they will occupy a prominent place in railroad service.

THE END.

# INDEX.

## A

Absolute initial steam pressure, 597.
Absolute steam pressure, 597.
Action of eccentric, 80.
Action of exhaust steam, 502.
Action of spring equalizing levers, 400.
Adhesion, 7.
Adjustment of valve gear in two-cylinder compounds, 627.
Admission line, 607.
Admission of steam, to find the point of, 60.
Adoption of eccentric, reason for the, 38, 80.
Advance, linear, of valve, 45.
Advantage gained by dividing the steam passage into two branches, 22.
Advantage of cutting off early, 609.
Advantage of the present management of locomotives, 2.
Advantages claimed for Allen valve, 69.
Advantages of placing valve in central position, 44.
Advantages of single and double exhaust pipes, 506.
Air admitted through hollow brick arch, temperature of, 477.
Air chambers for pumps, 390.
Air chambers for pumps, capacity of, 390.
Air chambers for pumps, position of, 394.
Allen valve, 68.
Allowance for shrinkage in driving-wheel tires, 217.
Allowance for wear and re-planing of guides, 167.
American locomotives, shifting link for, 88.
Amount of axle and rolling friction, 5.
Amount of counterbalance, 228.
Amount of piston clearance, testing the, 125.
Amount of throw of eccentrics, 103.
Amount of weight that rails can bear, 8.
Angle of safety-valve bearing surface, 371.
Angle of surface in throttle valves, 343.
Angular advance affected by lap, 45.
Angular advance for shifting links, 91.
Angular advance for stationary links, to find, 91.
Angular advance of eccentric, 45.
Angular advance of eccentric for stationary link, 88, 91.
Angular advance of eccentrics; rocker-arms of equal lengths, 114.
Angular advance of eccentrics; rocker-arms of unequal lengths, 114.
Angular advance of eccentrics; rocker employed, center line of motion of valve gear not coinciding with that of piston, 116.
Angular advance of eccentric, to find, 98, 99.
Angular advance of eccentric when rocker is used, 111.
Angularity of the eccentric-rods, complicating influence of, 36.
Annealing, strength of plates restored by, 451.
Anthracite coal burning engines, 424.
Apparent strength of plates, 451.
Appearance of compounds, 620.
Appearance of locomotives, change in, 3.
Approximate rule for finding thrust against guides, 161.
Arc, center of gravity of an, 257.
Arc, definition of radius of link, 89.
Arc described by the end of reverse lever, length of, 109.
Arc for eccentric-rod pins, 100.
Arc, length of radius for link, 90.
Arc of link, definition of, 99.
Arc on throttle valve-rod jaw, length of, 363.
Arcs for reverse lever, 109.
Arcs for reverse lever, notches in, 109.
Arcs for reverse lever, to lay off notches on, 133.
Area, cross-sectional, of crown-bar braces, 466.
Area, cross-sectional, of engine-frame braces, 191.
Area, cross-sectional, of exhaust pipes, 507.
Area, cross-sectional, of rectangular part of throttle pipe, 349.
Area, cross-sectional, of slab-frame brace, 197.
Area of central side-rod for consolidation engines, cross-sectional, 312.
Area of crank-pins, projected, 318.
Area of crosshead-pin, projected, 174.
Area of equalizing lever fulcrum, cross-sectional, 409.
Area of front and rear side-rod pins for Mogul and ten-wheeled engines, projected, 333.
Area of grate surface, hard coal, 426.
Area of grate surface, soft coal, 422.
Area of irregular surfaces, 254.
Area of knuckle-joint pin in side-rods, projected, 340.
Area of orifices in exhaust nozzles, 507.
Area of pump plungers, full stroke, cross-sectional, 396.
Area of rim of wheel, cross-sectional, 256.
Area of safety valve, 376, 379.
Area of side-rod pins for consolidation engines, projected, 336.
Area of side-rods, cross-sectional, 308.
Area of sliding surface of crosshead gibs, 163.
Area of smallest transverse section of main-rod, 301.
Area of spring hangers, cross-sectional, 410.
Area of stacks, cross-sectional, 502.
Area of steam and exhaust ports, 26.
Area of steam passages, 31.
Area of steam pipes, 30.
Area of steam pipes, to compute, 30.
Area of steam pipes, to compute with aid of table, 31.
Area of steam ports in compounds, 627.
Area of steam port, to compute, 27.
Area of surface of counterbalance, 249.
Area of tubes, cross-sectional, 438.
Areas, table of proportional steam pipe, 31.
Areas, table of proportional steam port, 28.
Arm of a force, or lever arm, 225.
Arm of counterbalance, 242.
Arms of rockers, length of, 76.
Arms of rockers, thickness of, 77.
Arms of rockers, width of, 77.
Arms on lifting shaft, dimensions of, 107.
Arms on lifting shaft, location of, 107.
Arrangement of simple valve gear, 36.
Arrangement of steam ways and ports in cylinder and saddle, 20.
Arrangement of tubes, 442.
Asbestos paper for cylinder lagging, 24.
Ash-pan, cast-iron, 494.

Ash-pan dampers, 493, 494.
Ash-pans for consolidation engines, 494.
Ash-pans for eight-wheeled, Mogul, and ten-wheeled engines, 491.
Ash-pans with blowing-out arrangement, 493.
Ash-pans with side doors, 493.
Atmospheric line, 602, 607.
Attachments for safety valves, 371.
Axle and rolling friction, 5.
Axle and rolling friction, methods of finding, 6.
Axle-box brasses, 204.
Axle-box brasses, Babbitt metal in, 205.
Axle-box brasses for tender trucks, width of, 581.
Axle-box brasses, octagonal, objections to, 204.
Axle-box brasses, preparation of, for lead lining, 577.
Axle-box brasses, pressure for forcing into box, 205.
Axle-boxes, blocking up the, 126.
Axle-boxes, classification of, 203.
Axle-boxes, designing of driving, 206.
Axle-boxes for engine trucks, 548.
Axle-boxes for main axles, 203.
Axle-boxes for Mogul and consolidation engines, 212.
Axle-boxes for tender trucks, 575.
Axle-boxes for tender trucks, brasses for, 575.
Axle-boxes for tender trucks, lead lining for brasses, 577.
Axle-boxes for tender trucks, wedges for, 575.
Axle-boxes, play between wheels and, 203.
Axle-boxes, position of center lines on frames, 190.
Axle-boxes, proportions of, 205.
Axle-boxes, vertical clearance in engine pedestals, 189.
Axle-boxes, vertical movement of, 189.
Axle-boxes, width of driving, 208.
Axle-box for tender trucks, cotton or woolen waste in, 578.
Axle-box for tender trucks, cover for, 578.
Axle-box for tender trucks, design of, 578.
Axle-box for tender trucks, dust guard for, 578.
Axle-box for tender trucks, standard, 579.
Axle-box for tender trucks, types of, 579.
Axle-box for tender trucks with pedestals, 579.
Axle-box for tender trucks without collars on axle, 579.
Axle-box for tender trucks without wedge, 578.
Axle-box oil cellars, 204.
Axle-box, Pennsylvania R. R., main, 413.
Axle-box, pockets in, 204.
Axle, distance from fire-box to center of, 82.
Axle journal, diameter of driving, 209.
Axle journals for eight-wheeled, Mogul, ten-wheeled, and consolidation engines, 210.
Axle journals for engine trucks, 549.
Axle journals for tender trucks, 580.
Axle journals for tender trucks, diameter of, 581.
Axle journals for tender trucks, pressure on, 581.
Axle journals for tender trucks, to compute dimensions of, 582.
Axle journals for tender trucks, to compute load they can bear, 582.
Axle, key ways in, for eccentric, 81.
Axle, position of, for laying out the valve gear, 119.
Axles, distance between centers of engine truck, 538.
Axles, distance between, in consolidation engines, 188.
Axles, distance between, in eight-wheeled engines, 188.
Axles, distance between, in Mogul engines, 188.
Axles, distance between, in ten-wheeled engines, 188.
Axles, driving, 214.
Axles for tender and engine trucks, difference between pressure on, 582.
Axles for tender trucks, standard, 581.
Axles, greatest distance between centers of, 188.
Axles in soft-coal or wood-burning engines, space required between, 188.
Axles, under hard-coal burners, position of, 189.
Axle, to find position of eccentrics on, 132.

## B

Babbitted wings on crossheads, 151.
Babbitt metal for rod brasses, 315.

Babbitt metal in driving axle-box brasses, 205.
Back ends of engine frames suitable for foot-plates, 187.
Back pressure, 602.
Back pressure line, or line of counter-pressure, 607.
Backs of flanges of tires, distance between, 266.
Backward eccentric, 89.
Backward eccentric-rod, 89.
Backward stroke, 89.
Balanced slide valves, 66.
Balanced slide valves, hole in top of, 67.
Balanced slide valves, Richardson's, 67.
Balanced slide valves, springs for, 66.
Balance for safety-valve, spring, 362, 369.
Baldwin Locomotive Works, consolidation engine built by the, 589.
Baldwin Locomotive Works, ten-wheeled engine built by the, 589.
Ball joint between dry pipe and front flue sheet, 347.
Ball joint between dry pipe and T-pipe, 350.
Ball joint between throttle and dry pipes, 347.
Ball joint for steam pipes, 33.
Batchellor, C. H., intercepting valves for compounds, 625.
Bearers for water grate, 489.
Bearing surface of safety valves, angle of, 371.
Bell crank for throttle valve, 343.
Bells, construction of, 514.
Bells, stand and yoke, 513.
Belly brace, 523.
Belpaire boiler, form of crown sheet in, 463.
Belpaire boiler, stay bolts in, 464.
Blades in driving wheel springs, number of, 415.
Blades in driving-wheel springs, thickness of, 415.
Block link, clearance between ends of link and, 130.
Blocks, copper strips between guides and, 152.
Blocks for guides, 149.
Blower valves, 558.
Bodies, common center of gravity of any two, 240.
Boiler braces, 468.
Boiler, capacity of smoke-boxes on, 473.
Boiler, distance between centers of stay bolts, 480.
Boiler domes, 470.
Boiler, extension fronts, 472.
Boiler fastenings to frames, 482.
Boiler, gusset plates in, 470.
Boiler lagging, extension of, 374.
Boiler lagging, thickness of, 366.
Boiler, manner of staying back head of, 469.
Boiler, manner of staying front tube sheet, 469.
Boiler pads, 482.
Boiler pads, clearance between equalizing lever and, 402.
Boiler plates, formulas for computing the thickness of, 462.
Boiler plates, furrowing in, 459.
Boiler pressure, formulas for computing the, 462.
Boiler, reinforcing plates for pads on, 483.
Boiler rivets, stress in, 452.
Boilers, 417.
Boilers, anthracite coal burning, 421, 424.
Boilers, area of grate surface for hard coal, 426.
Boilers, area of grate surface for soft coal, 422.
Boilers, arrangement of tubes, 442.
Boilers, beading of tubes, 437.
Boilers, Belpaire fire-box, 432.
Boilers, bituminous coal burning, 421.
Boilers, blow-off cocks in, 418.
Boilers, butt joints in, 460.
Boilers, classification of, 421.
Boilers, copper ferrules on tubes, 438.
Boilers, cross-sectional area of tubes, 438.
Boilers, crown-bar bolts, 465.
Boilers, crown bars, 464.
Boilers, crown bars, strength of, 467.
Boilers, dents in side of fire-box, 437.
Boilers, depth of fires, 424.
Boilers, depth of hard and soft coal burning fire-boxes, 428.
Boilers, diameter and design of, 443.
Boilers, diameter of rivets, 450.

Boilers, diameter of tube affects heating surface, 441.
Boilers, distance of rivets from edge of plate, 448.
Boilers, fire-box by Mr. J. Headden, 424.
Boilers, fire-box ring, 434.
Boilers, fire-door opening, form of, 436.
Boilers, flue sheets, thickness of, 434.
Boilers, form of crown sheets in, 432, 463.
Boilers, furnace sheets, thickness of, 434.
Boilers, grate surface, 421.
Boilers, greatest width of fire-box, 427.
Boilers, hand holes in, 417.
Boilers, heating surface, 445.
Boiler shell, thickness of, 460.
Boiler, short smoke-boxes on, 470.
Boilers, inclination of furnace door and side sheets, 432.
Boilers, large diameter of tube will stiffen them, 441.
Boilers, length of tubes, 442.
Boilers, limit of size of fire-box, 422.
Boilers, mud drums on, 417.
Boilers, number of tubes, 440.
Boilers, position of blow-off cocks in, 418.
Boilers, position of fire-box relative to axles, 421.
Boilers, position of hand holes in, 421.
Boilers, radial stay bolts for crown sheet, 432, 463.
Boilers, rate of evaporation on inclined sheets, 432.
Boilers, ratio of diameter to length of tubes, 441.
Boilers, reinforcing plates for mud plugs in, 417.
Boilers, riveted joints, 446.
Boilers, rivets in furnace sheets, 435.
Boilers, single-riveted lap joints, 447.
Boilers, sloping crown sheet, 430.
Boilers, space between tubes, 443.
Boiler stay bolts, 463.
Boiler stay bolts, hollow, 463.
Boiler, steam chamber for receiving valves on, 561.
Boilers, steam space, 443.
Boilers, stress, longitudinal, 447.
Boilers, stress, transverse, 447.
Boilers, tie rod in, 469.
Boilers, transverse braces, 467.
Boiler, stress in oblique braces, 481.
Boiler, stress in stay bolts, 479.
Boilers, tubes, 437.
Boiler supports, 522.
Boilers, width of water space, 434.
Boilers, wood-burning fire-box, 430.
Boiler, Wootten, 478.
Bolts, allowable stress per square inch of section of rod, 275.
Bolts and wedges for engine frame, proportion of, 186.
Bolts, factor of safety for rod, 275.
Bolts for engine frames, 201.
Bolts for guides, 168.
Bolts for main- and side-rods, taper of, 267, 299.
Bolts for segments of counterbalance, 242.
Bolts for side-rods, eight-wheeled engines, cross-sectional area of, 297.
Bolts for side-rods, eight-wheeled engines, stress in, 297.
Bolts for side-rods for consolidation engines, diameter of, 298.
Bolts for side-rods for Mogul engines, diameter of, 298.
Bolts for side-rods for ten-wheeled engines, diameter of, 298.
Bolts for side-rods, limited number of, 296.
Bolts for side-rods, number and diameter of, 267.
Bolts for side-rods, strength of, 296.
Bolts in cylinder heads, 23.
Bolts in engine-frame pedestal caps, number of, 194.
Bolts in main-rod, number and diameter of, 267.
Bolts in side-rods and main-rods, position of, 299.
Bolts in skeleton links, difficulty with, 103.
Bolts, longitudinal, through tender frames, 563.
Bolts, objection to, in cylinder heads, 24.
Bolts, shearing stress in rod, 272.
Bolts, stress in cylinder head, 24.
Bolts through cylinder saddle and front splice, 199.
Bolts through frame and splice, diameter of, 198.
Bolts through frame and splice, stress in, 198.

Bolts through front straps of main-rod, diameter of, 279.
Bolts through rear strap of main-rod, diameter of, 276.
Bolts through rear strap of main-rod, number of, 276.
Bolts, to find the diameter of cylinder head, 23.
Boxes for sand, 510.
Box link, 99.
Boyle's law, 598.
Braces for crown bars, 466.
Braces for engine frames, equal depth throughout, 196.
Braces for engine frames, stress per square inch, 191.
Braces for engine truck, 535.
Braces for foot-plate, 524.
Braces, frame, in a consolidation engine, 524.
Braces, frame, in a Mogul engine, 524.
Braces, frame, in an eight-wheeled engine, 523.
Braces from frames to boilers, 522.
Bracket lamp, for steam gauge, 362.
Brackets for running boards, 531.
Brake, manner of attaching Westinghouse, 585.
Brakes, gear for tender trucks, 564, 571.
Brass casing on throttle valve-rod, 355.
Brass driving axle-boxes, 204.
Brasses, flanges on rod, 316.
Brasses for driving axle-boxes, 204.
Brasses for driving axle-boxes, octagonal, 204.
Brasses for driving-boxes, heating of, 206.
Brasses for main crank-pin, caps on, 316.
Brasses for rods, 315.
Brasses for solid-ended side-rods, 326.
Brasses for tender-truck axle-boxes, 575.
Brasses for tender trucks, lead lining for, 577.
Brasses in valve-rod end, 79.
Brasses, metal in rod, 317.
Brasses, pressure for forcing them into box, 205.
Brasses, thickness of metal in rod, 317.
Brass gibs for crossheads, 151.
Brass packing rings for pistons, 143.
Brass packing rings for pistons, width and depth of, 144.
Brass ring inside of stuffing-box, 179.
Breadth and length of crosshead gibs, 164.
Breadth of exhaust ports, 29.
Breadth of guides, 166.
Breadth of link, 105.
Breadth of steam and exhaust ports, 26.
Breadth of steam ports, 29.
Brick arch, 473, 477.
Bridges in cylinder, 22.
Bridges in cylinder, thickness of, 25.
Bridges, weight on driving wheels limited by, 8.
Buckling of side-rods, 306.
Built-up crosshead for four slides, 152.
Built-up engine frame, 195.
Built-up pistons, 138.
Bumper beams, 518.
Bumper beams, computation of breadth of, 520.
Bumper beams, stress in, 520.
Bumper brace for extension fronts, 522.
Bumper brace for short smoke-boxes, 522.
Bumper plate or sheet, 522.
Bushing for eccentric-rod pins, 103.
Bushing for eccentric-rod pins, loose, 103.
Bushing for eccentric-rod pins, pressure for, 103.
Bushing for eccentric-rod pins, thickness of, 103.
Bushing for glands, 178.
Bushing for link hanger, 106.
Bushing for reach-rod pin in lifting shaft, 106.
Bushing for reach-rod pin in reverse lever, 109.
Bushing for throttle valve-rod gland, 355.
Bushing for valve-rod end, 79.

## C

Cab brackets, 529.
Cabs, 533.
Capacity, hauling, of a locomotive on a grade, 615.
Capacity of air chambers for pumps, 390.
Capacity of pumps, 398.
Capacity of sand-boxes, 510.

# INDEX.

Capacity of smoke-boxes, 473.
Capacity of tanks for tenders, 567.
Cap for engine-frame pedestals, number of bolts in, 194.
Caps, cast-iron, on sides of extension fronts, 474.
Caps for engine-frame pedestals, thickness of, 194.
Caps for frame pedestals, 182.
Caps on main crank-pin brasses, 316.
Cards, ideal indicator, 597.
Cards, taken with an indicator, 606.
Case-hardening of crank-pins, 317.
Casing for dome, 373.
Casing on throttle lever-rod, brass, 355.
Casting for front end of frame splice, 200.
Cast-iron ash-pan, 494.
Cast-iron guides, 168.
Cast-iron links, 102.
Cast-iron, selection of, for cylinders, 23.
Cause of variable motion of crank-pin, 50.
Cellar, oil, for Pennsylvania R. R. driving axle-box, 414.
Center-bearing tender-trucks, 564.
Center line of motion of valve gear, 43.
Center lines, position of, on frames, 190.
Center of eccentric, 43.
Center of gravity of a body, 224.
Center of gravity of an arc, 257.
Center of gravity of any two bodies, 240.
Center of gravity of counterbalance, 229.
Center of gravity of crank, to avoid finding, 247.
Center of gravity of engines, position of, 408.
Center of gravity of lead in rim of wheel, 257.
Center of gravity of safety-valve levers, 377.
Center of saddle-pin, to find position of, 123.
Center of travel of valve, important position, 44.
Centers of axles, greatest distance between, 188.
Central side-rod for consolidation engines, 289.
Central side-rod for consolidation engines, cross-sectional area of, 312.
Chamber in steam-gauge stand for valves, cocks, etc., 366.
Chamber on top of boiler for receiving valves, etc., 561.
Change in appearance of locomotives, 3.
Change of lead with shifting link, 93.
Changing position of eccentric-rods, result of, 122.
Check valves, 391.
Chime whistle, 383.
Cinder-box, manner of opening the, 475.
Cinder-box on extension fronts, 474.
Circular arc on throttle valve-rod jaw, length of, 363.
Classification of boilers, 421.
Classification of driving axle-boxes, 203.
Classification of links, 99.
Classification of locomotives, 3.
Classification of pistons, 138.
Classifications of slide valves, 39.
Clearance between driving-boxes and wheels, 203.
Clearance between ends of link and link block, 130.
Clearance between equalizing lever and boiler pads, 402.
Clearance between wheels of pony truck and cylinder heads, 542.
Clearance, effect on expansion, 603.
Clearance of axle-boxes in pedestals, vertical, 189.
Clearance of slide valve, 59.
Clearance of slide valve, its purpose, 59.
Clearance, piston and engine, 23.
Clearance, piston, testing the amount of, 128.
Clearance, practical method of determining engine, 603.
Clearances between flanges of wheels and rails, 261.
Clearance, to indicate on card, 603.
Coal, units of heat in, 424.
Cocks, blow-off, in boilers, 418.
Cocks, feed, 392.
Common center of gravity of bodies, principles relating to, 239.
Common safety valves, 371.
Comparison between old and new locomotives, 2.
Comparison of strength of riveted joint with that of solid plate, 457.
Complete locomotive valve gear, 35.

Complicating influence of the angularity of the eccentric-rod, 36.
Compound engines, always working as compounds, 620.
Compound engines, appearance of, 620.
Compound engines, compression of steam in, 618.
Compound engines, cylinder condensation in, 617.
Compound engines, diameter of cylinders for two-cylinder, 628.
Compound engines, diameter of cylinders for four-cylinder, 631.
Compound engines, engine clearance in, 618.
Compound engines, expansive working of steam in, 619.
Compound engines, experiments with, 620.
Compound engines, four-cylinder, 629.
Compound engines, fuel saved in, 620.
Compound engines in railroad service, 632.
Compound engines, inside clearance of valves in, 618.
Compound engines, intercepting valves, A. J. Pitkin, 620.
Compound engines, intercepting valve, C. H. Batchellor, 625.
Compound engines, piston valve for four-cylinder, 629.
Compound engines, pressure on crank-pins in, 619.
Compound engines, ratio of expansion in, 619.
Compound engines, receiver in, 620.
Compound engines, re-evaporation in cylinders in, 618.
Compound engines, steam-port area in, 627.
Compound engines, two-cylinder, 620.
Compound engines, valve-gear adjustment in two-cylinder, 627.
Compound engines, variation of pressure in cylinders in, 617.
Compound engines, volume of receiver in, 629.
Compound engines, working as compounds or non-compounds, 625.
Compound locomotives, 617.
Compression line, 607.
Compression of helical springs, 386.
Compression, to find point of, 60.
Compressive force on main-rods, 301.
Computation of breadth and thickness of link, 105.
Computation of breadth of bumper beams, 520.
Computation of common center of gravity of three equal weights, 241.
Computation of common center of gravity of four equal weights, 241.
Computation of common center of gravity of five equal weights, 242.
Computation of depth of equalizing lever in four-wheeled engine trucks, 538.
Computation of diameter of cylinder, 12, 595.
Computation of diameter of rocker shaft, 75.
Computation of mean effective pressure with aid of ordinates, 607.
Computation of mean effective pressure with aid of planimeter, 607.
Computation of pressure at any point of stroke, 598.
Computation of required mean effective steam pressure, 596.
Computation of steam-pipe area, 30.
Computation of steam-pipe area with aid of table, 31.
Computation of steam-port area, 27.
Computation of strength of crown bars, 466.
Computation of terminal pressure, 599.
Computation of travel of valve, 40.
Computation of thickness of cylinder walls, 25.
Computation of thrust against guides, 159.
Computation of tractive force, 14, 16, 17, 595.
Computation of weight on driving wheels, 595.
Computation of weight on engine trucks, 15.
Computation of width of rocker-arms, 77.
Computations relating to the safety valve, 374.
Condition and use of sand, 511.
Conditions a slide valve must fulfill, 38.
Conditions under which side-rods work, 305.
Connecting-rod, practical example in finding thrust of, 158.
Connecting-rod, to find thrust of, 156.
Connection of eccentric-rods to link affects the lead, 129.

INDEX.                                                                637

Connection of eccentric-rods to links, 88, 95.
Connection of reach-rod for link motion, 106.
Connections for throttle valve, 352.
Connections for throttle valve with rod through side of dome, 360.
Connections of T- and dry-pipes, 349.
Consolidation engine built by the Baldwin Locomotive Works, 589.
Consolidation engine, computation of weight on trucks, 15.
Consolidation engine, driving-wheel spring-gear for, 408.
Consolidation engine, frame braces in a, 524.
Consolidation engine, frame for, 195.
Consolidation engine, main-rod for, 286.
Consolidation engines, diameter side-rod bolts, 298.
Consolidation engines, distance between centers of axles, 188.
Consolidation engines, driving axle-boxes for, 212.
Consolidation engines, front splice for, 200, 201.
Consolidation engines, knuckle joint in side-rods for, 339.
Consolidation engines, pedestals for, 212.
Consolidation engines, side-rods for, 312.
Consolidation engines, side-rod straps, 294.
Consolidation engines, size of driving axle-journals, 210.
Consolidation engines, thickness of side-rod straps, 295.
Consolidation locomotives, diameter of driving wheels of, 10.
Consolidation locomotives, table of weights and hauling capacity of, 19.
Constant lead with stationary link, 88, 89.
Construction of Allen valve, 68.
Construction of bells, 514.
Construction of extension fronts, 472.
Construction of lifting shaft, 106.
Construction of rectangular hyperbola, 599.
Construction of reverse lever, 108.
Construction of sand-boxes, 511.
Construction of slide valve, practical, 57.
Construction of smoke-box shell, 475.
Construction of throttle pipe, 344.
Copper ferrules on boiler tubes, 438.
Copper fire-boxes, 462.
Copper strips between guides and blocks, 152.
Correct motion of valve will depend on position of saddle-pin, lifting shaft, and length of arms, 118.
Cotton or woolen waste in tender-truck axle-boxes, 578.
Counterbalance, amount of, 228.
Counterbalance, area of surface of, 249.
Counterbalance, bolts for segments of, 242.
Counterbalance, center of gravity of, 229.
Counterbalance, common center of gravity of two segments, 236.
Counterbalance, common center of gravity of three segments, 238.
Counterbalance, common center of gravity of four segments, 238.
Counterbalance, common center of gravity of five segments, 239.
Counterbalance, cubic inches in two segments of a, 237.
Counterbalanced, weights to be, 243.
Counterbalance for an eight-wheeled engine, 243.
Counterbalance for lifting shaft, 107.
Counterbalance, form of segment of, 242.
Counterbalance for Mogul, ten-wheeled, and consolidation engines, 250.
Counterbalance, geometrical method of finding the center of gravity of, 230.
Counterbalance in driving wheels, 221.
Counterbalance in rim of wheel, effect of lead, 257.
Counterbalance in rim of wheel, lead, 255.
Counterbalance in two segments, to find weight of each, 236.
Counterbalance, lead, 250.
Counterbalance, lever arm of, 242.
Counterbalance, number of cubic inches in a, 235.
Counterbalance, number of segments in, 244.
Counterbalance, practical method of finding the center of gravity of, 231.

Counterbalance, practical method of finding the common center of gravity of a number of segments, 239.
Counterbalance, thickness of, 235.
Counterbalance, thickness of solid, 248.
Counterbalance, thickness of two segments in a, 237.
Counterbalance, to compute the weight of a simple, 225.
Counterbalance, to find weight of, to balance crank and an additional load on crank-pin, 233.
Counterbalance, use of two weights or segments in, 235.
Counterbalance, weight of lead in rim of wheel, 255.
Counterbalance, weight of solid, 249.
Counterbore, 23.
Counter-pressure line, 607.
Courses in extension fronts, number of, 475.
Cover for tender-truck axle-boxes, 578.
Crank-pin brasses for solid-ended side-rods, 326.
Crank-pin, eight-wheeled engine, dimensions of main-rod journal on, 319.
Crank-pin for eight-wheeled engine, main, 319.
Crank-pin hub, weight of, 258.
Crank-pin, length of journal of, 318.
Crank-pin, main, side-rod journal on, for eight-wheeled engines, 320.
Crank-pin, ratio of length and diameter, 318.
Crank-pin, relation of its motion to that of piston, 49.
Crank-pins, 317.
Crank-pins, collars on, 323.
Crank-pins for eight-wheeled engines, 318.
Crank-pins for eight-wheeled engines, diameter of wheel fit, 325.
Crank-pins for Mogul, ten-wheeled, and consolidation engines, 328.
Crank-pins for Mogul, ten-wheeled, and consolidation engines, wheel fit, 337.
Crank-pins for narrow-gauge engines, 332.
Crank-pins for side-rods for consolidation engines, 335.
Crank-pins for side-rods for Mogul and ten-wheeled engines, 332.
Crank-pins for solid-ended side-rods, 325, 326.
Crank-pins, heating of, 318.
Crank-pin, side-rod journal on main, for Mogul, ten-wheeled, and consolidation engines, 329.
Crank-pins, pressure for forcing into wheel, 326.
Crank-pins, pressure required to force into hub, 260, 318.
Crank-pins, projected area of, 318.
Crank-pins, shank of, 323.
Crank-pins, strength of, 318.
Crank-pin, to find position of, for full and half stroke, 120.
Crank, relative position to that of eccentric, 46.
Crank, to find dead centers of, 97.
Crank, to find center of gravity of, 234.
Crank, to find position of piston corresponding to that of, 51.
Crank, weight of, referred to the crank-pin, 228.
Crosby pop safety valves, 385.
Crosshead, built-up, 152.
Crosshead classified, 149.
Crosshead, clearance between guide blocks and, 166.
Crosshead gibs, 149, 151.
Crosshead gibs, area of sliding surface of, 163.
Crosshead gibs, length and breadth of, 164.
Crosshead gibs, thickness of, 165.
Crosshead gib, wear of upper, 162.
Crosshead, greatest pressure of, against guides, 163.
Crosshead guides, 149.
Crosshead hubs, diameter of, 165.
Crosshead hubs, stress in, 165.
Crosshead keys, 149.
Crosshead, manner of fastening to piston-rod, 145.
Crosshead-pin, 149.
Crosshead-pin, position of, 153.
Crosshead-pin, diameter of, 174.
Crosshead-pin, length of, 173.
Crosshead-pin, pressure on, 174.
Crosshead-pin, projected area of, 174.
Crosshead-pins, dowel-pins for, 176.
Crosshead-pins, form of, 176.
Crosshead-pins, heating of, 174.

Crosshead-pins, proportions of, 172.
Crosshead-pins, reamers for, 176.
Crosshead-pins, securing of, 176.
Crosshead-pins, taper of, 176.
Crosshead-pin, strength of, 174.
Crosshead, position of cylinders will determine the form of, 150.
Crosshead, pressure between guides and, 153, 163.
Crossheads, function of, 149.
Crossheads, proportions of, 163.
Crossheads with babbitted wings, 151.
Crossheads with glass disks in wings, 151.
Crossheads, width of, 165.
Crosshead wings, 149.
Crosshead with four slides, 149, 150.
Crosshead with four slides, loose pin, 152.
Crosshead with one guide, 155.
Crosshead without gibs, case-hardened guides, 151.
Crosshead with pin cast in one piece, objections to, 151.
Cross-sectional area of exhaust pipes, 507.
Cross-sectional area of frame braces, 192.
Cross-sectional area of frame brace, slab form, 197.
Cross-sectional area of full-stroke pump-plunger, 396.
Cross-sectional area of rectangular part of throttle pipe, 349.
Cross-sectional area of rim of wheel, 256.
Cross-sectional area of side-rods, 308.
Cross-sectional area of stacks, 502.
Cross-section of exhaust passage, 32.
Crown-bar bolts, 465.
Crown-bar braces, 466.
Crown-bar braces, cross-sectional area of, 467.
Crown bars, 464.
Crown bars, distance between crown sheet and, 464.
Crown bars, position of, 464.
Crown-bar thimbles, 465.
Crown-bar washers, 465.
Crown sheet, form of, 432, 463.
Crown sheet, form of, in Belpaire boilers, 463.
Crown sheet, radial stay bolts to, 463.
Crown sheet, sloping, 430.
Curvature of reversing links, difference in, 88.
Curvature of throttle lever quadrants, to determine, 357.
Curves on railroads, degree of, 614.
Curves on railroads, radius of, 614.
Curves, resistance due to, 614.
Cut-off affected by lead, 53.
Cut-off affected by length of eccentric-rods, 73.
Cut-off affected by travel of valve, 54.
Cut-off, equalized, 72.
Cut-off, equalized, affected by position of lifting shaft, 73.
Cut-off equalized by means of link, 72.
Cut-off, equalized, exhaust regular with, 73.
Cut-off, point of, 39.
Cut-offs, adjusted with links, 89.
Cut-offs, sharp, obtained with a long travel of valve, 40.
Cut-off, to find, length of connecting-rod given, 69.
Cut-off, to find point of, 52, 60.
Cutting off early, advantage of, 609.
Cylinder and cylinder heads, joints between, 23.
Cylinder bridges, 22.
Cylinder cocks, 22.
Cylinder condensation and re-evaporation, 617.
Cylinder condensation cannot be detected on indicator-cards, 618.
Cylinder flanges, thickness of, 24.
Cylinder-head bolts, objection to, 24.
Cylinder-head bolts, stress in, 24.
Cylinder-head bolts, to find diameter of, 23.
Cylinder heads, 21.
Cylinder heads, thickness of, 24.
Cylinder-head studs, 24.
Cylinder lagging, 24.
Cylinder lagging, asbestos paper for, 24.
Cylinder oil-cups, 554.
Cylinders, 21.
Cylinder saddles cast separate, 20.
Cylinders, arrangement of steam-ways and ports, 20.

Cylinders cast with half saddles, 20.
Cylinders, classification of, 20.
Cylinders, computation of diameter, 12, 595.
Cylinders, manner of fastening to frame, 20.
Cylinders, position of, American practice, 20.
Cylinders, selection of iron for, 23.
Cylinder, thickness of bridges, 25.
Cylinder walls, computation of thickness of, 25.
Cylinder walls, thickness of, 24.
Cylinder walls, thickness of, in ferry boats, 25.

## D

Data required for choice of type of locomotive, 5.
Data used for computing weight of locomotives, 15.
Dead bars in water grates, 489.
Dead centers of crank, to find, 97.
Dead centers, to locate, 126.
Degree of curves on railroads, 614.
Dents in side of fire-box, 437.
Depth of brass packing-rings for pistons, 144.
Depth of central side-rods for consolidation engines, 312.
Depth of engine-frame pedestals, 189.
Depth of equalizing lever for pony trucks, 546.
Depth of equalizing lever in four-wheeled engine trucks, 538.
Depth of equalizing levers for driving-wheel springs, 402, 405.
Depth of fires in locomotive boilers, 424.
Depth of flanges of tires, 263.
Depth of frame splices for Mogul and consolidation engines, 201.
Depth of front frame splice, 199.
Depth of grate bars for burning wood, 484.
Depth of lower engine frame brace, 193.
Depth of main-rods, 301, 303.
Depth of piston at center, 139.
Depth of piston spider, 139.
Depth of side-rods for eight-wheeled engines, 309.
Depth of side-rods for Mogul engines, 310.
Depth of single guides, 167.
Depth of upper frame brace, 193.
Depth of upper frame brace, slab form, 197.
Depths of hard and soft coal burning furnaces, 428.
Designing driving axle-boxes, 206.
Designing engine frames, 188.
Design of front end of main-rod, 267.
Design of reverse lever, 108.
Design of tender-truck axle-boxes, 578.
Diagram showing the events of the distribution of steam, 63.
Diameter and depth of mud drums, 417.
Diameter and design of boiler, 443.
Diameter of boiler tubes, 437.
Diameter of bolts for segments of counterbalance, 242.
Diameter of bolts in main-rod, 267.
Diameter of bolts in side-rods, 267.
Diameter of bolts through frame and splice, 198.
Diameter of crosshead-hubs, 165.
Diameter of crosshead-pins, 174.
Diameter of cylinder-head bolts, to find, 23.
Diameter of cylinders, computation of, 12, 595.
Diameter of cylinders for two-cylinder compounds, 628.
Diameter of cylinders for four-cylinder compounds, 631.
Diameter of driving-axle journal, 209.
Diameter of driving wheels, limit of, 9.
Diameter of driving wheels, to compute, 9.
Diameter of eccentric, 81.
Diameter of eccentric, to determine the, 82.
Diameter of exhaust nozzle orifice, 507.
Diameter of front and rear side-rod pin journals for Mogul and ten-wheeled engines, 333.
Diameter of full-stroke pump plungers, 398.
Diameter of guide bolts, 168.
Diameter of holes in tube sheet for copper ferrules, 438.
Diameter of link saddle-pin, 106.
Diameter of main driving-axle journal, 212.

Diameter of main-rod crank-pin journal for Mogul, ten-wheeled, and consolidation engines, 328.
Diameter of piston-rods, 145, 147.
Diameter of pop safety valves, 384.
Diameter of reverse-lever pin, 109.
Diameter of rivets in boilers, 450.
Diameter of rocker shaft, 74.
Diameter of short-stroke pump plungers, 398.
Diameter of side-rod bolts for consolidation engines, 298.
Diameter of side-rod bolts for eight-wheeled engines, 297.
Diameter of side-rod bolts for Mogul engines, 298.
Diameter of side-rod bolts for ten-wheeled engines, 298.
Diameter of side-rod pin journals for consolidation engines, 336.
Diameter of smallest hole that can be punched through boiler plates, 449.
Diameter of stacks, 502.
Diameter of studs for stuffing-boxes, 180.
Diameter of throttle pipes, 349.
Diameter of throttle valves, 349.
Diameter of tubes affects heating surface, 441.
Diameter of wedge bolts, 186.
Diameter of wheel centers, standard, 217.
Diameters of wheel fits of crank-pins, 325, 337.
Diamond stack with double shell, 496.
Diamond stack with single shell, 496.
Diaphragm plates in extension fronts, 474.
Diaphragm plates in extension fronts, position of, 474.
Difference between tender and engine truck axles, 582.
Difference in curvature of reversing links, 88.
Difference in lead is affected by the length of eccentric-rods, 94.
Difficulty with skeleton links, 103.
Dimensions of crosshead-pins, 173.
Dimensions of elliptical springs for lifting-shaft counterbalance, 108.
Dimensions of engine frame braces, 191.
Dimensions of engine frame pedestals, 186.
Dimensions of guides, 166.
Dimensions of lifting shaft and its arms, 107.
Dimensions of link-blocks, 101.
Dimensions of link hanger, 106.
Dimensions of main-rod crank-pin journal for eight-wheeled engines, 319.
Dimensions of pistons and rods, 146.
Dimensions of reach-rods for link motion, 108.
Dimensions of rockers, 78.
Dimensions of rod brasses, 317.
Dimensions of tender-truck axle journals, 581.
Dimensions of tender-truck axle journals, to compute, 582.
Dimensions of volute springs for lifting-shaft counterbalance, 108.
Dip pipe in an air chamber of pumps, 390.
Dished driving wheels, 220.
Distance between axles in consolidation engines, 188.
Distance between axles in eight-wheeled engines, 188.
Distance between axles in Mogul engines, 188.
Distance between axles in ten-wheeled engines, 188.
Distance between backs of flanges of tires, 266.
Distance between bolts in cylinder heads, 23.
Distance between bottom of crown bars and crown sheet, 464.
Distance between centers of axles, greatest, 188.
Distance between centers of boiler stay bolts, 463.
Distance between centers of engine-truck axles, 538.
Distance between crown bars, 464.
Distance between eccentric-rod pin arc and link arc, 104.
Distance between guides, four in a set, 153.
Distance between guides, two in a set, 155, 170.
Distance between pony-truck wheels and cylinder heads, 542.
Distance between throttle-lever handle and reverse lever, 356.
Distance from center of axle to fire-box, 82.
Distance from center of safety valve to fulcrum, 377, 380.
Distance of rivets from edge of plate, 448.

Distribution of flanged tires in various classes of locomotives, 261.
Distribution of steam by slide valve, 38.
Distribution of steam, events of, 60.
Dome casing, 373.
Domes on boilers, 470.
Dome top, joint between ring and, 381.
Dome top made in two pieces, 387.
Dome-top ring, 381.
Dome tops, 380.
Door sheet, inclination of furnace, 432.
Doors in front of smoke-boxes, 476.
Double exhaust pipes, 504.
Double exhaust pipes, advantages of, 506.
Double poppet throttle valve, 343.
Double-riveted lap joint, pitch of rivets in, 455.
Double-riveted lap joints, 454.
Dowel pins for crosshead-pins, 176.
Draft pipe in short smoke-boxes, 470.
Draw bars, 529.
Draw-heads for tender, 565.
Draw-head, wrought-iron, on bumper beam, 517.
Driving axle-box brasses, 204.
Driving axle-box brasses, pressure for forcing into box, 205.
Driving axle-boxes, 203.
Driving axle-boxes, classification of, 203.
Driving axle-boxes for Mogul and consolidation engines, 212.
Driving axle-boxes, play between wheels and, 203.
Driving axle-boxes, proportions of, 205.
Driving axle-box oil-cellars, 204.
Driving axle-box, Pennsylvania R. R., 413.
Driving axle-box, Pennsylvania R. R., cellar, 414.
Driving axle-box, pockets in, 204.
Driving axle-box, width of, 208.
Driving axle journal, length of, 208.
Driving axle journals for eight-wheeled, Mogul, ten-wheeled, and consolidation engines, 210.
Driving axles, 214.
Driving axle, wheel fits on, 214.
Driving-boxes, location of center lines on engine frames, 190.
Driving-boxes, vertical clearance in pedestals for, 189.
Driving-boxes, vertical movement of, 189.
Driving wheel, center of gravity of lead in rim of, 257.
Driving-wheel counterbalance, 221.
Driving-wheel covers, 530.
Driving wheel, cross-sectional area of rim of, 256.
Driving wheel, effect of lead counterbalance in the rim of, 257.
Driving-wheel keys, 220.
Driving wheels, 215.
Driving wheels, clearance between rails and flanges of, 261.
Driving wheels, diameter of, 9, 10.
Driving wheels, fitting up a pair of, 260.
Driving wheels, form of tread of, 263.
Driving wheels, pressure for forcing on axle, 220.
Driving-wheel spring gear for eight-wheeled engines, 400.
Driving-wheel spring gear for ten-wheeled engines, 400.
Driving-wheel springs, 414.
Driving-wheel springs, deflection of, 416.
Driving-wheel springs, length of, 414.
Driving-wheel springs, load on, 402.
Driving-wheel springs, number of blades in, 415.
Driving-wheel springs, set of, 415.
Driving-wheel springs, span of, 414.
Driving-wheel springs, thickness of blades of, 415.
Driving wheels, standard form of tread, 265.
Driving wheels, tables of diameters of, 10.
Driving wheels, taper of tread of, 263.
Driving wheels, to compute diameter of, 9.
Driving wheels, to compute weight on, 595.
Driving wheels, to find number of, 8.
Driving wheels, to find weight on, 8.
Driving wheels to suit a particular service, 9.

Driving wheels, weight of rail must be known to determine the number of, 8.
Driving wheels, weight on, limited by bridges, 8.
Driving wheels with solid spokes, 217.
Driving wheels with tires bolted to them, 260.
Driving-wheels, 215.
Driving-wheel tires, 259.
Drop plate in grates, 486.
Drop-plate shaft, 486.
Dry pipe and throttle pipe, ball joint between, 347.
Dry pipe and T-pipe, ball joint between, 350.
Dry-pipe and T-pipe connections, 349.
Dry pipe for throttle valve, 344, 346.
Dry-pipe ring on front flue sheet, ball joint between, 347.
Dry pipes, diameter of, 346, 349.
Dry pipes on crown bars, 348, 373.
Dry pipes, rivets through sleeve and, 346.
Dry pipes, suspension of, 349.
Dry-pipe yoke, 347.
Dunbar piston packing, 142.
Dust-guard in tender-truck axle-boxes, 578.
Duty of eccentrics, 80.
Duty of exhaust passage, 22.
Duty of slide valves, 35.
Duty of steam passage, 22.
Duty of steam-pipes, 30.
Duty of steam-ways, 22.

E

Early cut-offs, advantage of, 609.
Eccentric, action of, 80.
Eccentric, angular advance of, 45.
Eccentric, angular advance of, for shifting links, 88, 90.
Eccentric, angular advance of, for stationary links, 88, 90.
Eccentric, angular advance of, when rocker is used, 112.
Eccentric, backward, 89.
Eccentric, center of, 43.
Eccentric, diameter of, 81.
Eccentric, forward, 89.
Eccentricity of eccentric, 37, 82.
Eccentricity of eccentric, relation of throw to, 41.
Eccentricity of eccentric, to find, 83.
Eccentric, key-ways in, 81.
Eccentric, line from which it is set, 43.
Eccentric, position of, rocker-arms of equal lengths, 111.
Eccentric, position of (rocker not used), 41.
Eccentric, position of (valve with lead), 43.
Eccentric, relative position to that of crank, 46.
Eccentric-rod, backward, 89.
Eccentric-rod, complicating influence of, 36.
Eccentric-rod, definition of length of, 89.
Eccentric-rod, forward, 89.
Eccentric-rod pin arc, 100.
Eccentric-rod pin arc, distance between link arc and, 104.
Eccentric-rod pin bushing, 103.
Eccentric-rod pin bushing, loose, 103.
Eccentric-rod pin bushing, pressure required, 103.
Eccentric-rod pin bushing, thickness of, 103.
Eccentric-rod pins, distance between the, 103.
Eccentric-rod pins, size of, 103.
Eccentric-rod pins, wear of, 103.
Eccentric-rods, connection of, to links, 88.
Eccentric-rods, connection to link affects the lead, 129.
Eccentric-rods, correct way of connecting to links, 95.
Eccentric-rods, introduction of link will change lengths of, 118.
Eccentric-rods, length of, affects difference in lead, 94.
Eccentric-rods, length of, affects the cut-off, 73.
Eccentric-rods, long, tend to give a symmetrical motion to the valve, 37.
Eccentric-rods, manner of fastening, to eccentric, 81.
Eccentric-rods of infinite length give symmetrical motion, 37.
Eccentric-rods, result of changing position of, 122, 129.
Eccentric-rods, to connect to link, 129.
Eccentric-rods, to find correct lengths of, 122.
Eccentrics, amount of throw of, 104.
Eccentrics and straps, 79.

Eccentrics, duty of, 80.
Eccentrics made in one or two parts, 81.
Eccentrics not on main-axle, valve motion with, 136.
Eccentrics, position of, for full and half stroke, 123.
Eccentrics, position of, rocker-arms of unequal lengths, 114.
Eccentrics, position of, rocker employed, center line of motion of valve gear not coinciding with that of piston, 116.
Eccentrics, practical way of setting, 47.
Eccentrics, proportions of, 84.
Eccentrics, reason for adopting, 38, 80.
Eccentrics, set screws in, 81.
Eccentrics, space for, 82.
Eccentric-strap, form of, 81.
Eccentric-strap joints, 81.
Eccentric, throw of, 37, 82.
Eccentric, to determine diameter of, 82.
Eccentric, to find angular advance of, 97, 99.
Eccentric, to find angular advance of, for stationary links, 91.
Eccentric, to find position of, 43.
Eccentrics, to find position of, for full and half stroke, 121.
Eccentrics, to find position of, on axle, 132.
Eccentric will travel ahead of crank, when no rocker is used, 42.
Effect of lap on linear and angular advance, 45.
Effect of lead counterbalance in rim of wheel, 257.
Effect of tension on riveted joints, 448.
Efficiency of single-riveted lap joints, 458.
Eight-wheeled engine built by the Grant Locomotive Works, 585.
Eight-wheeled engine built by the Pennsylvania R. R., 585.
Eight-wheeled engine, counterbalance for an, 243.
Eight-wheeled engine, driving-wheel spring gear for, 400.
Eight-wheeled engine, frame braces in an, 523.
Eight-wheeled engines, crank-pins for, 318.
Eight-wheeled engines, cross-sectional area of side-rod bolts for, 297.
Eight-wheeled engines, cross-sectional area of side-rods, 308.
Eight-wheeled engines, diameter of side-rod bolts for, 297.
Eight-wheeled engines, distance between axles, 188.
Eight-wheeled engines, driving axle-boxes for, 210.
Eight-wheeled engines, driving axle-journals for, 210.
Eight-wheeled engines, main crank-pin for, 319.
Eight-wheeled engines, position of side-rods in, 290.
Eight-wheeled engine, spring gear for narrow-gauge, 403.
Eight-wheeled engines, side-rods for narrow-gauge, 290.
Eight-wheeled engines, stress in side-rod bolts for, 297.
Eight-wheeled engines, stress in side-rod straps, 288.
Eight-wheeled engines, thickness and depth of side-rods, 309.
Eight-wheeled engines, thickness of side-rod straps for, 286.
Eight-wheeled locomotives, computation of weight on trucks, 15.
Eight-wheeled locomotives, diameter of driving wheels, 10.
Eight-wheeled locomotives, table of weight and hauling capacity, 17.
Elevated Railroad, smoke-boxes on the New York, 471.
Elevated roads, main- and side-rods for engines on, 278.
Elliptical springs for lifting-shaft counterbalance, 107.
Elliptical springs for lifting-shaft counterbalance, dimensions of, 108.
Encased pop safety valves, 385.
Energy and work, 612.
Energy required to overcome the force of gravity, 612.
Engine clearance, 23.
Engine clearance and piston displacement, ratio of, 603.
Engine clearance, effect on expansion, 603.
Engine clearance in compounds, 618.
Engine clearance, practical method of determining, 603.
Engine clearance, to indicate on card, 603.

Engine draw-head, front, 517.
Engine, finish at front end of, 522.
Engine frame and splice, diameter of bolts through, 198.
Engine frame and splice forged in one piece, 201.
Engine-frame bolts, 201.
Engine-frame braces, dimensions of, 191.
Engine-frame braces, equal depth throughout, 196.
Engine-frame brace, slab form, cross-sectional area of, 197.
Engine-frame braces, stress per square inch, 191.
Engine frame, built-up, 195.
Engine frame for a consolidation locomotive, 195.
Engine frame, light, 196.
Engine frame, lower brace, depth of, 193.
Engine-frame pedestal legs, thickness of, 193.
Engine-frame pedestals, 182.
Engine-frame pedestals, depth of, 189.
Engine frame, position of center lines on, 190.
Engine frames, 182.
Engine frames, back ends suitable for foot-plates, 187.
Engine frames, designing, 188.
Engine frames for eight-wheeled passenger locomotives, 187.
Engine-frame splice, casting for front end of, 200.
Engine-frame splice for consolidation and Mogul locomotives, 200, 201.
Engine-frame splice, form of front end of, 200.
Engine-frame splice, depth of, 199.
Engine-frame splices, recess for cylinder saddle in, 199.
Engine frames, proportions of, 187.
Engine frames, slab, 196.
Engine frame, upper brace, depth of, 193.
Engine-frame wedges, thickness of, 186.
Engine frame, width of, 191.
Engine pedestal caps, number of bolts in, 194.
Engine pedestal caps, thickness of, 194.
Engine pedestals for Mogul, ten-wheeled, and consolidation engines, 212.
Engine pedestals, position of straight legs, 190.
Engine pedestals, taper of legs, 190.
Engine pedestals, width of opening of, 190.
Engines, hard-coal burning, 424.
Engines, soft-coal burning, 421.
Engines, space required between axles in soft-coal or wood-burning, 188.
Engine-truck axle-boxes, 548.
Engine-truck axle-journals, 549.
Engine-truck axle-journals, diameter and length of, 550.
Engine-truck axle-journals, pressure on, 549.
Engine-truck center-plates, 538.
Engine truck, distance between centers of axles in, 538.
Engine truck, equalizing lever for four-wheeled, 538.
Engine truck, four-wheeled, 535.
Engine truck, length of two-wheeled, 542.
Engine truck, Pennsylvania R. R., 538.
Engine-truck swing-center castings, 538.
Engine truck, two-wheeled, 540.
Engine truck, two-wheeled, cast-iron frame for, 542.
Engine truck, two-wheeled, clearance between wheels and cylinder heads, 542.
Engine truck, two-wheeled, computation of length of, 544.
Engine truck, two-wheeled, equalizing lever for, 546.
Engine truck, two-wheeled, graphical method of finding length of, 542.
Engine truck, two-wheeled, thickness and depth of equalizing lever, 547.
Engine-truck wheel covers, 535.
Equalized cut-off, 72.
Equalized cut-off affected by position of lifting shaft, 73.
Equalizing lever for driving-wheel springs, depth of, 402, 405.
Equalizing lever for driving-wheel springs, load on, 403.
Equalizing levers, clearance between boiler pads and, 402.
Equalizing levers for driving-wheel springs, 400.
Equalizing levers for driving-wheel springs, thickness of, 402, 408.
Equalizing levers, gibs and plates on top of, 411.

Equalizing levers, purpose of, 400.
Equalizing lever, thickness of metal outside of slots through, 406.
Equalizing the cut-off by means of a link, 72.
Erecting shop, practical example of setting the valve gear in a, 125.
Evaporation, rate of, on inclined sheets, 432.
Events of the distribution of steam, 60.
Events of the distribution of steam, diagram showing the, 63.
Exhaust closure, to find the point of, 619.
Exhaust line, 607.
Exhaust nozzles, area of orifice in, 507.
Exhaust nozzles, position of, in long and short smoke-boxes, 477.
Exhaust passage, 22.
Exhaust passage, cross-section of, 32.
Exhaust passage, duty of, 22.
Exhaust passage openings, size of, 32.
Exhaust passages, small space for, 33.
Exhaust passage, thickness of metal around, 25.
Exhaust pipes, advantages of single and double, 506.
Exhaust pipes and nozzles, 504.
Exhaust pipes, cross-sectional area of, 507.
Exhaust pipes, form of passages in, 506.
Exhaust pipes, long, 507.
Exhaust pipes, long and short, where used, 506.
Exhaust pipes, short double, 504.
Exhaust pipes, short single, 505.
Exhaust port, 22.
Exhaust ports, area of, 26.
Exhaust ports, length and breadth of, 26, 29.
Exhaust regular with equalized cut-offs, 73.
Exhaust steam, action of, 502.
Exhaust thimbles, 505.
Expansion curve, 597, 607.
Expansion of steam, lap required for, 49.
Expansion, ratio of, clearance neglected, 600.
Expansion, ratio of, with clearance, 604.
Expansive working of steam in a compound, 619.
Experiments with compound engines, 620.
Extension fronts, 472.
Extension fronts affect the exhaust, 473.
Extension fronts, blowing out by steam, 474.
Extension fronts, capacity of, 473.
Extension fronts, cast-iron caps on side of, 474.
Extension fronts, cinder-box on, 474.
Extension fronts, construction of, 473.
Extension fronts, diaphragm plates in, 474.
Extension fronts, length of, 475.
Extension fronts, long exhaust pipe in, 476.
Extension fronts, number of courses in, 475.
Extension fronts, position of diaphragm plates in, 474.
Extension fronts, rings in, 475.

## F

Factor of safety for rod bolts, 275.
Fastening domes to boilers, 470.
Fastenings for boiler to frames, 482.
Fastening water grates in furnace, 489.
Favorite form of main-rod, 301.
Feed-cock plug, opening in, 394.
Feed-cock quadrant, 394.
Feed-cock rod, 394.
Feed-cocks, 391.
Feed-pipe hangers and connections, 394.
Ferrule for reach-rod pin in lifting shaft, 106.
Ferrule for reach-rod pin in reverse lever, 109.
Ferrules, copper, on boiler tubes, 438.
Ferry-boats used in connection with railroads, 25.
Finger grate-bars, 484.
Finish of front end of engine, 522.
Fire-box, Belpaire, 432.
Fire-box, dents in sides of, 437.
Fire-box, depths of hard- and soft-coal burning, 428.
Fire-box designed by Mr. J. Headden, 424.
Fire-box, distance from center of axle to, 82.

Fire-box, door and side sheets, inclination of, 432.
Fire-boxes, steel, iron, and copper, 462.
Fire-box, greatest width of, 427.
Fire-box, limit of size, 422.
Fire-door opening, 436.
Fire-box, position of, for soft-coal or wood-burning engines, 188.
Fire-box relative to axles, position of, 421.
Fire-box ring, 434.
Fire-box, rivets in, 435.
Fire-box sheets, thickness of, 434.
Fire-box, wood-burning, 430.
Fitting up a pair of driving wheels, 260.
Flanged tires, distribution of, 261.
Flanged tires, thickness and width of, 265.
Flanges of tires, depth of, 263.
Flanges of tires, distance between backs of, 266.
Flanges of wheels, clearance between rails and, 261.
Flanges on driving axle-boxes, form of, 204.
Flanges on engine-frame wedges, thickness of, 186.
Flanges on rod brasses, 316.
Flanges, thickness of cylinder, 24.
Flexibility of side-rods, 306.
Follower bolts for pistons, 139.
Follower plate for pistons, 138, 139.
Foot-plate braces, 524.
Foot-plates, 527.
Foot-plates, back ends of engine frames suitable for, 187.
Force acting on the ends of equalizing lever for pony truck, 546.
Force a locomotive must exert to haul a train, 7.
Force, moment of a, 226.
Force of gravity, energy required to overcome, 612.
Force which a rocker must overcome, 75.
Form and size of steam and exhaust ports, 26.
Form of crosshead determined by position of cylinders, 150.
Form of crosshead-pins, 176.
Form of crown sheet, 432, 463.
Form of eccentric strap, 81.
Form of main-rod, 301.
Form of passages in exhaust pipes, 506.
Form of piston and valve-rod glands, 179.
Form of piston packing, 140.
Form of saddles for smoke-stacks, 502.
Form of safety-valve seat, 371.
Form of segment of counterbalance, 242.
Form of slide-valve, ordinary, 34.
Form of templet for segment, 246.
Form of tread of driving wheels, 263.
Form of tread of driving wheel, standard, 265.
Forms of driving-wheel spring hangers, various, 411.
Formula for computing load on crown bars, 466.
Formulas for computing boiler pressure, 462.
Formulas for computing thickness of boiler plates, 462.
Formulas, rules, and data, 595.
Forward eccentric, 89.
Forward eccentric-rod, 89.
Forward stroke, 89.
Four-cylinder compound engines, 629.
Four-cylinder compound engines, diameter of cylinders, 631.
Four-wheeled engine truck, 535.
Frame and splice, diameter of bolts through, 198.
Frame bolts, 201.
Frame brace, engine, depth of lower, 193.
Frame brace, engine, depth of upper, 193.
Frame brace, engine, equal depth throughout, 196.
Frame braces, belly brace, 523.
Frame braces, bumper brace, 522.
Frame braces, engine, dimensions of, 191.
Frame braces, engine, stress per square inch, 191.
Frame braces, guide yoke, 522.
Frame braces in a consolidation engine, 524.
Frame braces in a Mogul engine, 524.
Frame braces in an eight-wheeled engine, 523.
Frame brace, slab form, depth of, 197.
Frame, engine, built-up, 195.

Frame, engine, width of, 191.
Frame for a consolidation engine, 195.
Frame for two-wheeled engine truck, 542.
Frame pedestal caps, number of bolts in, 194.
Frame pedestal caps, thickness of, 194.
Frame pedestal, dimensions of, 186.
Frame pedestal legs, thickness of, 193.
Frame pedestals, 182.
Frame pedestals, wedges for, 184.
Frames, engine, light, 196.
Frames for engine, designing, 188.
Frames for engine, proportions of, 187.
Frames for tender, iron, 569.
Frames for tender, wooden, 565.
Frame splice and frame forged in one piece, 201.
Frame splice, casting for front end of, 200.
Frame splice, depth of, 199.
Frame splice for consolidation and Mogul engines, 200.
Frame splices for passenger locomotives, 187, 197.
Frame splice, recess for cylinder saddle in, 199.
Frames, position of center lines on engine, 190.
Frames, slab, 196.
Freight locomotive, management of, 2.
Friction in the joints of boiler plates, 451.
Friction of slide-valve, 64.
Friction, resistance due to, 611.
Front draw-head on engine, 517.
Front draw-heads on tenders, 567.
Front end of main-rod, design of, 267.
Front flue-sheet ring for dry pipe, 347.
Front side-rod for consolidation engines, 289.
Front side-rod for Mogul engines, 281.
Front side-rod pins' for Mogul and ten-wheeled engines, projected area of, 333.
Front side-rods for consolidation engines, 312.
Fronts on smoke-boxes, 476.
Front driving-wheel springs in Mogul and consolidation engines, load on, 546.
Front strap of main-rod, diameter of bolts through, 279.
Fuel saved in compounds, 620.
Fulcrum for driving-wheel spring equalizing lever, 400, 409.
Fulcrum for driving-wheel spring equalizing lever, area of, 409.
Fulcrum for driving-wheel spring equalizing lever, load on, 403.
Fulcrum for driving-wheel spring equalizing lever, ratio of thickness and width, 410.
Fulcrum for driving-wheel spring equalizing lever, stress in, 409.
Full gear of link motion, 89.
Full-stroke pump plungers, diameter of, 398.
Full-stroke pump plungers, cross-sectional area of, 396.
Full-stroke pumps, 387.
Function of crossheads, 149.
Function of frame pedestals, 182.
Furrowing in boiler plates, 459.
Fusible plugs, 435.

## G

Gauge cocks, 561.
Gear for throttle valves with rod through end of boiler, 352.
Gear for throttle valves with rod through side of dome, 359.
Gear for throttle valves with rod through top of boiler, 359, 364, 366.
Geometrical method of finding the center of gravity of counterbalance, 230.
Gib of crosshead, wear of upper, 162.
Gibs and plates on top of equalizing lever, 411.
Gibs for crossheads, 149, 151.
Gibs for crossheads, area of sliding surface of, 163.
Gibs for crossheads, length and breadth of, 164.
Gibs for crossheads, thickness of, 165.
Gland for throttle valve-rod, 355.
Glands and stuffing-boxes, proportions of, 176.
Glands and stuffing-boxes, studs for, 180.

Glands, bushing for, 178.
Glands for piston-rods, 21.
Glands for valve-rods and piston-rods, metal in, 178.
Glands, length of, 179.
Glass disks in wings of crossheads, 151.
Goose-neck, 393.
Grade, 609.
Grade, hauling capacity of a locomotive on a, 615.
Grade, resistance due to, 612.
Grate-bars, 484.
Grate-bars, finger, 484.
Grate-bars for burning wood, 484.
Grate-bars for burning wood, depth of, 484.
Grate-bars, rocking, for burning soft coal, 484.
Grate-bars, shaking lever for, 486.
Grate dead-bars, 489.
Grate, drop-plate in furnace, 486.
Grate surface, 421.
Grate surface, area of, soft-coal, 422.
Grates, water, 486.
Gravity, energy required to overcome the force of, 612.
Guide-blocks, 149.
Guide-blocks, clearance between crosshead and, 166.
Guide-bolts, 168.
Guides, allowance for wear and re-planing, 167.
Guides, cast-iron, 168.
Guides, computation of thrust against, 159.
Guides, copper slips between blocks and, 152.
Guides, depth of single, 167.
Guides, dimensions of, 166.
Guides for crossheads, 149.
Guides, four in a set, distance between, 153.
Guides, greatest pressure of crosshead against, 163.
Guides, length and breadth, 166.
Guides, practical examples of finding thrust against, 158.
Guides, pressure between crosshead and, 153, 163.
Guides, tapered, 167.
Guides, thrust against, 156.
Guides, to compute thickness of, 166.
Guides, two in a set, distance between, 155, 170.
Guide-yoke, 149, 522.
Gusset plates in boiler, 470.

## H

Half gear of link motion, 89.
Hand holes in boilers, 417.
Handle for opening safety-valves, 362, 369.
Handle for shaking lever, 486.
Hanger for link, 100.
Hanger for link, dimensions of, 106.
Hanger, link, 87.
Hangers for driving-wheel springs, 400, 410.
Hangers for driving-wheel springs, cross-sectional area of, 410.
Hangers for driving-wheel springs, ratio of thickness to width, 411.
Hangers for driving-wheel springs, stress per square inch, 410.
Hangers for driving-wheel springs, tension on, 403.
Hangers for driving-wheel springs, various forms of, 411.
Hangers for feed-pipe, 394.
Hard-coal burners, position of axles under, 189.
Hauling capacity of a locomotive on a grade, 615.
Hauling capacity of locomotives, table of, 17, 18, 19.
Heads for pistons, 138.
Heads, thickness of cylinder, 24.
Heater pipe, 394.
Heating of crank-pins, 318.
Heating of crosshead-pins, 174.
Heating of driving-box brasses, 206.
Heating surface affected by diameter of tube, 441.
Heating surface per cubic foot of piston-drop displacement, 445.
Heating surface proportioned to tractive power, 446.
Heating surface, ratio of fire-box to tube, 446.
Height of stacks, 503.
Height of valve-seats, 29.

Helical springs, compression of, 386.
Helical springs, size of steel for, 386.
Hole in top of balanced slide-valves, 67.
Holes in rocker-arms, taper of, 74.
Holes in tube sheet for copper ferrules on tubes, diameter of, 438.
Hole, the smallest that can be punched through boiler plates, 449.
Hollow brick arches, 477.
Hollow stay bolts in boilers, 463.
Horse-power, 605.
Hose, suction, 393.
House brackets, 529.
Houses, 533.
Hub on rocker-arms, 78.
Hubs for crossheads, diameter of, 165.
Hubs for crossheads, stress in, 165.
Hyperbola, rectangular, 598.
Hyperbola, rectangular, construction of, 599.
Hyperbolic logarithms, 601.

## I

I cross-section for side-rods, 307.
Important position, center of the travel of valve is an, 44.
Inclination of furnace door and side sheets, 432.
Inclination of water grates, 486.
Indicator-card, ideal, 597.
Indicator-card, scale for, 603.
Indicator-cards, measurement of pressures on, 598.
Indicator-cards taken with an indicator, 606.
Indicator, steam accounted for by the, 607.
Infinite lengths of eccentric-rods give symmetrical motion, 37.
Influence of engine clearance on expansion, 603.
Influence of rocker-arms and link on travel of valve, 37.
Influence of rocker on the motion of the valve, 36.
Initial steam pressure, 597.
Injectors, 558.
Injector stop-valve, 561.
Inside clearance, its purpose, 59.
Inside clearance of valves in compounds, 618.
Inside lap, 59.
Inside lead, 59.
Intercepting valve in compounds, A. J. Pitkin, 620.
Intercepting valve in compounds, C. H. Batchellor, 625.
Introduction of link will change the lengths of eccentric-rods, 118.
Introduction of link will not change position of eccentrics nor rockers, 118.
Iron fire-boxes, 462.
Iron pilot, 518.
Iron plates, tensile strength of, 451.
Iron tender-frame, 569.
Irregular surfaces, area of, 254.

## J

Jaw for throttle-valve rod, 353, 362.
Jaw for throttle-valve rod, length of circular arc on, 363.
Joint between dome-top and ring, 381.
Joint between throttle and dry pipes, ball, 347.
Joint in valve-rod, knuckle, 76, 79.
Joints between cylinder and cylinder heads, 23.
Joints for steam-pipes, ball, 33.
Joints in boiler plates, friction in, 451.
Joints in boilers, butt, 460.
Joints in eccentric-straps, 81.
Joints, pitch of rivets in double-riveted lap, 455.
Joints, pitch of rivets in single-riveted lap, 450, 453.
Journal, diameter of driving-axle, 209.
Journal, length of driving-axle, 208.
Journal of main crank-pin for Mogul, ten-wheeled, and consolidation engines, 328.
Journal of main driving-axle, diameter of, 212.
Journal of side-rod journals for consolidation engines, 336.
Journals for tender-truck axles, 580.
Journals for tender-truck axles, diameter of, 581.

Journals for tender-truck axles, pressure on, 581.
Journals of crank-pin, eight-wheeled engines, 318.
Journals of driving-axle, pressure per square inch of projected area, 206.
Journals of driving-axle, projected area of, 206.
Journals of front and rear side-rod pin for Mogul and ten-wheeled engines, 333.
Journals on engine-truck axles, 549.
Journals on engine-truck axles, diameter and length of, 550.
Journals on engine-truck axles, pressure on, 549.
Journals, to find diameter and length of, when the ratio between them is known, 551.

### K

Keys for crossheads, 149.
Keys for cylinder saddle and front splice, 199.
Keys for driving-wheels, 220.
Keys for main- and side-rods, form of, 299.
Keys for main- and side-rods, thickness, width, and taper of, 300.
Keys for piston-rods, taper of, 145.
Keys for pistons, strength of, 148.
Keys in valve-rod end, 79.
Keys, taper of main- and side-rods, 270.
Key, transverse, in front end of main-rod, 300.
Key-way in axle for eccentrics, 81.
Key-ways in eccentric, 81.
Knuckle-joint for side-rods, 338.
Knuckle-joint in valve-rod, 79.
Knuckle-joint of side-rods, pin through, 281.
Knuckle-joint pin for side-rods, pressure on, 340.

### L

Lagging, asbestos paper for cylinder, 24.
Lagging on boiler, extension of, 374.
Lagging on boiler, thickness of, 366.
Lamp bracket for steam-gauge, 362.
Lap and travel of valve, to find, 56.
Lap at each end of valve is equal, 72.
Lap, effect of, on linear and angular advance, 45.
Lap, inside, 59.
Lap joints, double-riveted, 454.
Lap joints, pitch of rivets in double-riveted, 455.
Lap joints, single-riveted, 447.
Lap joints, single-riveted, efficiency of, 458.
Lap of valve, to find, 55.
Lap, outside, 39.
Lap, problems relating to, of the slide-valve, 52.
Lap required for the expansion of steam, 49.
Latch for reverse lever, 109.
Latch for reverse lever, position of, 109.
Latch, May's reverse lever, 110.
Late cut-offs, disadvantage of, 609.
Laying out a valve gear, 118.
Lead affected by the connection of eccentric-rods to link, 129.
Lead affects point of cut-off, 53.
Lead, amount of, 95.
Lead, change of, with shifting link, 93.
Lead constant with stationary link, 88, 89.
Lead counterbalance, 250.
Lead counterbalance in rim of wheel, 255.
Lead counterbalance in rim of wheel, effect of, 257.
Lead in rim of wheel, center of gravity of, 257.
Lead in rim of wheel, weight of, 255.
Lead is equal at each end of valve, full stroke, 72, 102.
Lead, length of eccentric-rods effects difference in, 94.
Lead lining for tender-truck axle-box brasses, 577.
Lead lining, preparation of brass for, 577.
Lead of valve, 42.
Lead variable with shifting link, 88.
Leaves in driving-wheel springs, number of, 415.
Leaves in driving-wheel-springs, thickness of, 415.
Legs, straight, engine pedestal, position of, 190.
Legs, taper of engine pedestal, 190.
Length and breath of crosshead gibs, 164.

Length of arc described by top of reverse lever, 109.
Length of bumper beams, 518.
Length of circular arc on throttle-valve rod jaw, 363.
Length of crank-pin journal, 318.
Length of crosshead-pins, 173.
Length of driving-axle journal, 208.
Length of driving-wheel springs, 414.
Length of eccentric-rod, definition of, 89.
Length of eccentric-rods affects cut-off, 73.
Length of eccentric-rods affects difference in lead, 94.
Length of eccentric-rods, to find, 96, 129.
Length of eccentric-rods will be changed by the introduction of links, 118.
Length of engine pony-truck, computation of, 544.
Length of engine-pony truck, graphical method of finding, 542.
Length of equalizing lever for engine pony-truck, 546.
Length of exhaust ports, 29.
Length of front and rear side-rod pin journals for Mogul and ten-wheeled engines, 333.
Length of guides, 166.
Length of link, 104.
Length of main-rod crank-pin journal for eight-wheeled engines, 320.
Length of main-rod crank-pin journal for Mogul, ten-wheeled, and consolidation engines, 328.
Length of radius for stationary links, 90.
Length of radius of shifting link, 104.
Length of reverse lever, 109.
Length of rocker-arms, 76.
Length of rocker-shaft, 74.
Length of safety-valve lever, 374, 376, 380.
Length of side-rod pin journals for consolidation engines, 336.
Length of side-rods, how taken, 317.
Length of smoke-stacks, 503.
Length of steam-ports, 26.
Length of throttle-lever quadrants, to determine the, 357.
Length of tubes, 442.
Length of valve-seat, 30.
Lengths of eccentric-rods, to find correct, 122.
Lever arm of counterbalance, 242.
Lever arm, or arm of a force, 225.
Lever for opening safety-valve, 362, 369.
Lever for shaking grates, 486.
Lever for throttle valve, 352, 354, 356.
Lever for throttle valve, position of, 355.
Lever, reverse, 87, 108.
Levers for driving-wheel springs, depth of equalizing, 400, 402, 405.
Levers for driving-wheel springs, equalizing, 400.
Levers for driving-wheel springs, thickness of equalizing, 402, 408.
Levers for driving-wheel springs, thickness of metal outside of slots through, 406.
Levers for whistle, 383.
Lifting shaft, 87, 106.
Lifting-shaft arms, 87, 107.
Lifting-shaft arms, dimensions of, 107.
Lifting-shaft counterbalance springs, dimensions of, 108.
Lifting shaft, diameter of, 107.
Lifting shaft, location of, 107.
Lifting shaft, object of, 36.
Lifting-shaft pin, 100, 106.
Lifting shaft, position for full gear backward, 106.
Lifting shaft, position for full gear forward, 106.
Lifting shaft, position for midgear, 106.
Lifting shaft, to find position of, 124.
Lifting shaft will affect the cut-off, position of, 73
Lift of pump valves, 389.
Lift of throttle valve, 358.
Limited number of bolts in side-rods, 296.
Limit of diameter of driving wheels, 9.
Limit of size of fire-box, 422.
Limit of wear of tires, 265.
Linear advance affected by lap, 45.
Linear advance of valve, 45.
Line, atmospheric, 602, 607.

Line from which eccentric is set, 43.
Line of admission, 607.
Line of compression, 607.
Line of counter-pressure, 607.
Line of direction of a force, 226.
Line of exhaust, 607.
Line of perfect vacuum, 597, 607.
Line of perfect vacuum, location of, 602.
Liners for main- and side-rods, 270.
Lines, position of center, on engine frames, 190.
Link arc, definition of, 99.
Link arc, distance between eccentric rod-pin arc and, 104.
Link-block, 87, 101.
Link-block pin, 100.
Link-block pin, diameter of, 100.
Link-blocks, proportions of, 101.
Link-blocks, slip of, 102.
Link, box, 100.
Link, breadth of, 105.
Link, clearance between link-block and ends of, 130.
Link, definition of radius of, 89, 100.
Link hanger, 87, 100, 106.
Link-hanger bushing, 106.
Link hanger, dimensions of, 106.
Link, introduction of link will not change position of eccentrics or rockers, 118.
Link, length of, 99.
Link motion, 86.
Link motion, dimensions of reach-rod for, 108.
Link motion, reach-rod for, 87.
Link motion, reach-rod for, connection of, 106.
Link, open, 100.
Link, radius of, to find, 121.
Link saddle, 87, 100.
Link saddle-pin, 87, 100.
Link saddle-pin, diameter and length of, 106.
Links, cast-iron, 102.
Links, classification of, 99.
Links, connection of eccentric-rods to, 88.
Links, difference in curvature of, 88.
Links, difficulty with skeleton, 103.
Link, skeleton, 99.
Links, method of attaching, 87.
Link, solid, 99.
Links, point of cut-off adjusted with, 89.
Links, proportions of, 102.
Links, safety, between engine and tender, 528.
Links, shifting, 88.
Links, stationary, 88.
Links, steel, 102.
Link, Stephenson's, object of, 36.
Link, suspension of, 100.
Links, wrought-iron, 102.
Link, thickness of, 105.
Link, to connect eccentric-rods to, 129.
Link used as a means for equalizing the cut-off, 72.
Load on driving-wheel equalizing lever, 403.
Load on driving-wheel springs, 402.
Load on front springs in ten-wheeled, Mogul, and consolidation engines, 546.
Load supported by crown bars, 466.
Locate the dead centers, to, 126.
Location of reverse lever, 108, 373.
Location of rocker, 118.
Locomotive, consolidation, built by the Baldwin Locomotive Works, 589.
Locomotive, eight-wheeled, built by the Grant Locomotive Works, 585.
Locomotive, eight-wheeled, Pennsylvania R. R. standard, 585.
Locomotive frame, built-up, 195.
Locomotive frame for a consolidation engine, 195.
Locomotive frames, 182.
Locomotive frames, light, 196.
Locomotive, hauling capacity on a grade, 615.
Locomotive, ten-wheeled, built by the Baldwin Locomotive Works, 589.

Locomotive, practical example of setting the valve gear of a, 125.
Locomotive pumps, location of, 585.
Locomotives, advantage of present management of, 2.
Locomotives, change in appearance of, 3.
Locomotives, classification of, 3.
Locomotives, compound, 617.
Locomotives, comparison between old and new, 2.
Locomotives, compound, built by the Baldwin Locomotive Works, 629.
Locomotives, compound, built by the Rhode Island Locomotive Works, 625.
Locomotives, compound, built by the Schenectady Locomotive Works, 620.
Locomotives, consolidation, 3.
Locomotives, consolidation, distance between centers of axles, 188.
Locomotives, data required for choice type of, 5.
Locomotives, data used for computing weight of, 15.
Locomotives, diameter of driving wheels for consolidation, 10.
Locomotives, diameter of driving wheels for eight-wheeled, 10.
Locomotives, diameter of driving wheels for Mogul, 10.
Locomotives, diameter of driving wheels for ten-wheeled, 10.
Locomotives, eight-wheeled, 3.
Locomotives, eight-wheeled, distance between centers of axles, 188.
Locomotives, force that must be exerted to haul a train, 7.
Locomotive, six-wheeled shifting, built by the Pennsylvania R. R., 589.
Locomotives, large, limit of total wheel-base, 189.
Locomotives, management of, 2.
Locomotives, Mogul, 3.
Locomotives, Mogul, distance between centers of axles, 188.
Locomotives, parts made stronger of modern, 2.
Locomotives, points of support of, 408.
Locomotives, position of center of gravity, 408.
Locomotives, small, total wheel-base of, 189.
Locomotives, ten-wheeled, 3.
Locomotives, ten-wheeled, distance between centers of axles, 188.
Locomotives, types of, 585.
Locomotives, weight of, 15.
Locomotives, work done by, 12.
Logarithms, hyperbolic, 601.
Long eccentric-rods tend to give a symmetrical motion to the valve, 37.
Long exhaust pipes, 507.
Long exhaust pipes, where used, 506.
Longitudinal bolts through tender-frames, 563.
Longitudinal play of driving boxes, 203.
Longitudinal stress in boiler shell, 447.
Long smoke-boxes, 472.
Long smoke-boxes affect the exhaust, 473.
Long smoke-boxes, blowing out by steam, 474.
Long smoke-boxes, cast-iron caps on side of, 474.
Long smoke-boxes, cinder-box on, 474.
Long smoke-boxes, construction of, 473.
Long smoke-boxes, diaphragm plates, 474.
Long smoke-boxes, length of, 475.
Long smoke-boxes, netting in, 474.
Long smoke-boxes, petticoat pipe in, 476.
Long smoke-boxes, rings in, 475.
Long wedge for frame pedestals, 184.
Lower engine-frame brace, depth of, 193.

## M

Main crank-pin for a consolidation engine, 328.
Main crank-pin for eight-wheeled engines, 319.
Main driving-axle journals, diameter of, 212.
Main-rod, area of smallest transverse section of, 301.
Main-rod bolts, 272.
Main-rod brasses, 315.

Main-rod, design of front end of, 267.
Main-rod, favorite form of, 301.
Main-rod for crosshead with two slides, 300.
Main-rod journal on crank-pin, eight-wheeled engine, dimensions of, 319.
Main-rod, liners for, 270.
Main-rod, number and diameters of bolts in, 267.
Main-rods and side-rods, 267.
Main-rods, diameter of bolts through front strap of, 279.
Main-rods, diameter of bolts through rear strap of, 276.
Main-rods for a consolidation engine, 286.
Main-rods for engines on elevated roads, 278.
Main-rods, form of keys for, 299.
Main-rods for Mogul engines, 281.
Main-rods, material for, 303.
Main-rods, number of bolts through rear strap of, 276.
Main-rods, oil-holes in straps for, 296.
Main-rods, pressure per square inch of cross-section, 301.
Main-rods, ratio of depth and thickness of, 301.
Main-rods, sections of, to be avoided, 303.
Main-rods, tensile and compressive force on, 301.
Main-rods, thickness and depth of, 301, 303.
Main-rods, thickness, width, and taper of keys for, 270, 300.
Main-rod straps, stress per square inch of cross-sectional area of, 285.
Main-rod straps, thickness of, 283.
Main-rods with chamfered edges, 303.
Main-rod with transverse key in front end, 300.
Management of locomotives, 2.
Manner of fastening piston-rods, 145.
Mariotte's law, 598.
Material for piston-rods, 147.
Material for valve-rod and piston-rod glands, 178.
May's reverse-lever latch, 110.
Mean effective pressure computed with the aid of ordinates, 607.
Mean effective pressure computed with the aid of planimeter, 607.
Mean effective steam pressure, computation of required, 596.
Mean effective steam pressure for a given cut-off, 597, 602, 605.
Mean pressure, 601.
Mean pressure, computation of, 602.
Measurement of pressure on cards, 598.
Metal in rod brasses, 317.
Method, correct, of connecting eccentric-rods to links, 95.
Method for determining engine clearance, practical, 603.
Method of attaching links, 87.
Method of equalizing cut-off, 73.
Method of finding the amount of rolling and axle friction, 6.
Method of finding the tractive power or force, 11.
Method of setting a simple valve-gear, practical, 96.
Mid-gear of link motion, 89.
Mogul engine, counterbalance for a, 250.
Mogul engine, driving-wheel spring-gear for a narrow-gauge, 408.
Mogul engine, frame braces in a, 524.
Mogul engine frame splices, 200, 201.
Mogul engines, computation of weight on trucks, 15.
Mogul engines, crank-pins for, 328.
Mogul engines, diameter of driving wheels of, 10.
Mogul engines, diameter of side-rod bolts for, 298.
Mogul engines, distance between centers of axles, 188.
Mogul engines, driving axle-boxes for, 212.
Mogul engines, knuckle-joint in side-rods for, 338.
Mogul engines, least thickness of side-rod straps for, 294.
Mogul engines, pedestals for, 212.
Mogul engines, side-rod pins for, 332.
Mogul engines, side-rods for, 281, 309.
Mogul engines, size of driving-axle journals, 210.
Mogul engines, stress in side-rod straps for, 291.
Mogul engines, thickness of straps for side-rods for, 292.
Mogul engine, table of weights and hauling capacity of, 18.
Moment of a force, 226, 378.

Moment of steam pressure on safety-valves, 375.
Moment of tension on safety-valve springs, 375, 378.
Motion of valve influenced by the rocker, 36.
Motion of valve will depend on position of saddle-pin, lifting shaft, length of its arms, 119.
Movement of axle-boxes, 189.
Mud drums, 417.
Mud plugs in boilers, 417.

## N

Names of lines on ideal indicator-cards, 597.
Narrow-gauge eight-wheeled engines, side-rods for, 290.
Narrow-gauge engines, crank-pins for, 332.
Netting in extension fronts, 474.
New York Elevated Railroad, smoke-boxes on, 471.
Normal pressure on rails, 610.
Notches in reverse-lever quadrants, 109.
Notches in reverse-lever quadrant, to lay off, 133.
Nozzles for exhaust pipes, 504.
Number of bolts in a segment of counterbalance, 242.
Number of bolts in engine-frame pedestal caps, 194.
Number of bolts in guides, 168.
Number of bolts in main-rods, 267.
Number of bolts in side-rods, 267.
Number of bolts in side-rods, limited, 297.
Number of bolts through frame and splice, 198.
Number of courses in smoke-box shell, 475.
Number of driving wheels, to find, 8.
Number of driving wheels, weight of rails must be known to determine, 8.
Number of leaves in driving-wheel springs, 415.
Number of safety-valves, 362.
Number of segments in counterbalance, 244.
Number of studs in stuffing-boxes, 180.
Number of tubes, 440.
Nuts on tubes for supporting brick arches, 478.

## O

Objections to bolts in cylinder heads, 24.
Objections to crosshead with pin cast in one piece, 151.
Objections to octagonal driving-box brasses, 204.
Object of lifting shaft, 36.
Object of rocker, 36.
Object of Stephenson's link, 36.
Oblique braces, stress in, 481.
Offset in rocker, 117.
Offset in rocker, to find, 119.
Oil-cellars for driving axle-boxes, 204.
Oil-cellars for driving axle-box, Pennsylvania R. R., 414.
Oil-cups, 552.
Oil-cups for cylinders, 554.
Oil-grooves in driving-box brasses, 205.
Oil-holes in main- and side-rod straps, 296.
Opening for fire door, 436.
Opening, width of engine pedestal, 190.
Open links, 99.
Orifices in exhaust nozzles, area of, 507.
Outside lap, 39.

## P

Pads on boilers, 482.
Pads, reinforcing plates inside of boiler for, 483.
Parts to be counterbalanced, 243.
Passages, form of exhaust-pipe, 506.
Passenger locomotive, management of, 2.
Passenger trains, remarks relating to, 2.
Pedestal caps, 182.
Pedestal jaw, 182.
Pedestal legs, engine, thickness of, 193.
Pedestals, depth of engine-frame, 189.
Pedestals, engine, vertical clearance for axle-boxes, 189.
Pedestals for engine frames, dimensions of, 186.
Pedestals for engine frames, function of, 182.
Pedestals for Mogul, ten-wheeled, and consolidation engines, 212.
Pedestals, taper of legs in engine, 190.

Pedestals, width of opening of engine, 190.
Pennsylvania R. R. engine truck, 538.
Pennsylvania R. R., six-wheeled shifting engine built by the, 589.
Pennsylvania R. R. Standard eight-wheeled engine, 585.
Perfect vacuum line, 597, 607.
Perfect vacuum line, location of, 602.
Petticoat pipe in extension fronts, 476.
Petticoat pipe in short smoke-boxes, 470.
Pilots, iron, 518.
Pilots, wooden, 517.
Pin for crosshead, 149.
Pin for lifting shaft, 100.
Pin for link-block, 100.
Pin for link-block, diameter of, 100.
Pin for link-saddle, 87, 100.
Pin for reach-rod, 106.
Pin for reverse-lever, diameter of, 109.
Pin in knuckle-joint of side-rods, 281, 340.
Pins for crossheads, diameter of, 174.
Pins for crossheads, length of, 173.
Pins for crossheads, securing of, 176.
Pins for eccentric-rods, distance between, 103.
Pins for eccentric-rods, size of, 103.
Pins for lifting shaft, 106.
Pins for rockers, 74.
Pins, link-saddle, diameter and length of, 106.
Pipe connecting throttle-valve stuffing-box to dome, 361.
Pipe for heating feed-water, 394.
Pipes, exhaust, 504.
Pipes, sand, 511.
Piston, cause of its variable motion, 50.
Piston clearance, 23.
Piston clearance, testing amount of, 128.
Piston displacement and engine clearance, ratio of, 603.
Piston follower-bolts, 139.
Piston heads, 138.
Piston, how to obtain a symmetrical motion, 50.
Piston illustrated, 146.
Piston keys, 139.
Piston keys, strength of, 148.
Piston packing, 138.
Piston packing, brass, 143.
Piston packing, Dunbar, 142.
Piston packing, form of, 140.
Piston packing rings, position of, 143.
Piston packing, width of, 139.
Piston, relation of its motion to that of crank-pin, 49.
Piston-rod gland, 21.
Piston-rod gland, form of, 179.
Piston-rod keys, taper of, 145.
Piston-rods, 21.
Piston-rods, diameter of, 145, 147.
Piston-rods, glands for, 178.
Piston-rods, manner of fastening to piston, 145.
Piston-rods, material for, 147.
Piston-rods, stress in, 144.
Piston-rods, taper at ends, 145.
Piston-rods, weakest part of, 148.
Pistons, 21, 138.
Pistons, classified, 138.
Pistons, depth at the center, 139.
Pistons, follower-plate for, 138, 139.
Piston, solid, 140.
Piston speed, to determine, 33.
Piston spider, 138.
Piston spider, depth of, 139.
Pistons with one face spherical, 139.
Piston, to find its position corresponding to that of crank, 51.
Piston T-rings, 140, 143.
Piston valve for four-cylinder compounds, 629.
Pitch of rivets in double-riveted lap joints, 455.
Pitch of rivets in single-riveted lap joints, 453.
Pitkin, A. J., intercepting valves for compounds, 620.
Plain throttle-valve lever, 352.
Plain tires, 261.
Plate for bumpers, 522.

Plates and gibs on top of equalizing lever, 411.
Plates, apparent strength of, 451.
Plates for mud plugs in boilers, reinforcing, 417.
Plates, friction in the joints of boiler, 451.
Plates in boilers, formulas for computing the thickness of, 462.
Plates in extension fronts, diaphragm, 474.
Plates, smallest hole that can be punched through, 449.
Plates, strength of, restored by annealing, 451.
Plates, strength of, restored by reaming the holes, 451.
Plates, stress in the joints of boiler, 451.
Plates, tensile strength of iron, 451, 462.
Plates, tensile strength of steel, 462.
Play between driving boxes and hub of wheel, 203.
Plugs, fusible, 435.
Pockets in driving boxes, 204.
Point of admission, to find, 60.
Point of compression, to find, 60.
Point of cut-off, 39.
Point of cut-off adjusted with links, 89.
Point of cut-off affected by lead, 53.
Point of cut-off affected by length of eccentric-rods, 73.
Point of cut-off affected by travel of valve, 54.
Point of cut-off, to find, 52, 60.
Point of cut-off, to find, length of connecting-rod given, 69.
Point of exhaust closure, to find, 619.
Point of release, to find, 60.
Point of suppression, to find, 60.
Points of support of engines, 408.
Pony truck, 540.
Pony truck, cast-iron frame for, 542.
Pony truck, clearance between wheels and cylinder heads, 542.
Pony truck, equalizing lever for, 546.
Pony truck, graphical method of finding length of, 542.
Pony truck, length of, 542.
Pony truck, thickness and depth of equalizing lever for, 547.
Pop safety-valve, 373, 380, 384.
Pop safety-valves, Crosby, 385.
Pop safety-valves, diameter of, 384.
Pop safety-valves, encased, 385.
Pop safety-valves, George W. Richardson's, 384.
Position of axle for laying out the valve gear, 119.
Position of blow-off cocks, 418.
Position of bolts in side-rods and main-rods, 299.
Position of center lines on engine frame, 190.
Position of center of gravity of counterbalance, 229.
Position of center of gravity of engines, 408.
Position of check-valves, 391.
Position of crank-pin for full and half stroke, to find, 120.
Position of crosshead-pin, 153.
Position of crown bars, 464.
Position of cylinders, American practice, 20.
Position of diaphragm plates in smoke-boxes, 474.
Position of eccentric, line from which it is set, 43.
Position of eccentric; rocker arms of equal lengths, 111.
Position of eccentric; rocker-arms of unequal lengths, 114.
Position of eccentric (rocker not used), 41.
Position of eccentric; rockers employed; center line of motion of valve-gear not coinciding with that of piston, 116.
Position of eccentric-rods, result of changing, 122.
Position of eccentrics for full and half stroke, 123.
Position of eccentrics on axle, to find, 132.
Position of eccentric, to find, 44.
Position of eccentric (valve having lead), 43.
Position of exhaust nozzles in long and short smoke-boxes, 477.
Position of fire-box for soft-coal burning engines, 188.
Position of fire-box relative to axles, 421.
Position of lifting shaft affects cut-off, 73.
Position of lifting shaft, to find, 124.
Position of notches in reverse-lever quadrant, 110.
Position of pump air-chambers, 394.
Position of reverse lever, 108, 373.

Position of reverse-lever latch, 109.
Position of reverse lever, to find, for full gear forward and backward, 130.
Position of rocker, 118.
Position of running boards, 532.
Position of saddle-pin, to find, 123.
Position of safety-valves, 380.
Position of sand pipes, 513.
Position of side-rods in eight-wheeled engines, 290.
Position of steam-gauge stand, 373.
Position of straight legs in engine pedestals, 190.
Position of throttle lever, 355.
Position of throttle-valve rod stuffing-box, 355.
Position of valve, central, an important one, 44.
Position of wheels under hard-coal burners, 189.
Position of whistle, 380.
Position, relative, of crank to eccentric, 46.
Positions of eccentrics for full and half stroke, to find, 121.
Power, horse, 605.
Power required to work a plain slide-valve, 63.
Practical construction of slide-valve, 57.
Practical example of finding thrust of connecting-rod, 158.
Practical example of setting the valve gear of a locomotive, 125.
Practical method of finding the center of gravity of counterbalance, 231.
Practical method of finding the common center of gravity of a number of segments in counterbalance, 239.
Practical method of setting a simple valve gear, 96.
Practical way of determining engine clearance, 603.
Practical way of setting eccentrics, 47.
Preference of studs in cylinder heads, 24.
Preparation of truck brasses for lead lining, 577.
Pressure, back, 602.
Pressure between crossheads and guides, 153, 163.
Pressure, computation of, at any point of the stroke, 598.
Pressure, computation of required mean effective, 596.
Pressure, computation of terminal, 599, 601.
Pressure for a given cut-off, mean effective, 597, 602, 605.
Pressure for eccentric-rod pin bushing, 103.
Pressure for forcing brasses and axle-boxes, 205.
Pressure for forcing bushing into throttle-valve gland, 355.
Pressure for forcing crank-pins into hub, 260, 326.
Pressure for forcing driving wheels on axle, 220.
Pressure, mean, 601.
Pressure, mean, computation of, 602.
Pressure, mean effective, computed with the aid of ordinates, 607.
Pressure, mean effective, computed with the aid of planimeter, 607.
Pressure, measurement, on cards, 598.
Pressure on crank-pins, 318.
Pressure on crank-pins in compound locomotives, 619.
Pressure on crosshead-pin, 174.
Pressure on knuckle-joint pin in side-rods, 340.
Pressure on rails, normal, 610.
Pressure on slide-valve, 64, 65.
Pressure on springs of pop safety-valves, 386.
Pressure on tender and engine-truck axles, difference between, 582.
Pressure per square inch of cross-section of main-rods, 301.
Pressure per square inch of projected area of driving-axle journals, 206.
Pressure per square inch of projected area on engine-truck axle journals, 549.
Pressure per square inch on journals for given velocities, 210.
Pressure, terminal, 598.
Pressure, variation of, in cylinders, is reduced in compound engines, 617.
Pressure which boilers will stand, formulas for, 462.
Primitive slide-valve, 48.
Principles relating to the common center of gravity of bodies, 239.

Principles to be remembered in laying out a valve gear, 99.
Problems relating to lap of slide-valve, 52.
Problems relating to slide-valves reduced to simplest forms, 35.
Projected area of crank-pins, 318.
Projected area of crosshead-pins, 174.
Projected area of driving-axle journals, 206.
Projected area of front and rear side-rod pins in Mogul and ten-wheeled engines, 333.
Projections on the inside of tires, 259.
Proportions of crosshead-pins, 172.
Proportions of crossheads, 163.
Proportions of driving boxes, 205.
Proportions of eccentrics, 84.
Proportions of engine frames, 187.
Proportions of link-blocks, 101.
Proportions of links, 102.
Proportions of main- and side-rod keys, 299.
Proportions of main- and side-rod straps, 270.
Proportions of side-rods, 308.
Proportions of wedges and bolts for engine-frame pedestals, 186.
Provisions for shutting off steam in all boiler valves, cocks, etc., 366.
Pulling-bar between engine and tender, 528.
Pulling-bar pin, 527.
Pulling-bar support, 528.
Pump, 387.
Pump air-chambers, 390.
Pump, lift of valves, 389.
Pump pet-cock, 390.
Pump plunger, 389.
Pump plunger, cross-sectional area of full-stroke, 396.
Pump plunger, cross-sectional area of short-stroke, 398.
Pumps, capacity of, 398.
Pumps, capacity of air-chambers for, 390.
Pumps, dip-pipe in air-chamber of, 390.
Pump, size of, 396.
Pumps, position of, 394.
Pumps, short-stroke, 387, 395.
Pump, to find stroke of, 398.
Punching reduces tenacity of plates, 451.
Punch, spiral, injury to plates, 451.
Purpose of giving lap to the valve, 49.
Purpose of inside clearance, 59.
Purpose of inside lap, 59.

**Q**

Quadrant for feed-cock, 394.
Quadrants for reverse lever, position of notches in, 110.
Quadrants for reverse levers, 109.
Quadrants for throttle lever, to determine the length and curvature of, 357.
Quadrants for throttle-valve lever, 353, 354, 355, 356.
Quadrants, to lay off notches on reverse-lever, 133.

**R**

Radial stay-bolts for crown sheet, 432, 463.
Radius, length of, for stationary links, 90.
Radius of a curve on railroads, 614.
Radius of link, definition of, 89, 100.
Radius of link, length of, 104.
Radius of link, to find, 121.
Radius of throttle-lever quadrant, 357.
Railroad service, compound engine in, 632.
Rails can bear, amount of weight that, 8.
Rails, clearance between flanges of wheels and, 261.
Rails, weight of, must be known to determine number of driving wheels, 8.
Rankine, Prof. W. J. M., table of pressures for given velocities of axle journals, 210.
Rate of evaporation on inclined sheets, 432.
Ratio between diameter and length of journal given, to find diameter and length, 551.
Ratio of cross-sectional area of tubes to grate surface, 438.

Ratio of depth and thickness of main-rods, 301.
Ratio of depth and thickness of side-rods, 309.
Ratio of diameter and length of knuckle-joint pin, 340.
Ratio of diameter to length of tubes, 441.
Ratio of engine clearance and piston displacement, 603.
Ratio of expansion, clearance neglected, 600.
Ratio of expansion in compounds, 619.
Ratio of expansion, with clearance, 604.
Ratio of fire-box to tube-heating surface, 446.
Ratio of length and diameter of main crank-pin for eight-wheeled engines, 318.
Ratio of length and diameter of main crank-pin journals for Mogul, ten-wheeled, and consolidation engines, 329.
Ratio of length and diameter of side-rod journals on main crank-pin for Mogul, ten-wheeled, and consolidation engines, 330.
Ratio of thickness to width of equalizing-lever fulcrum, 410.
Ratio of thickness to width of spring hangers, 411.
Reach-rod for link motion, 87.
Reach-rod for link motion, connection of, 106.
Reach-rod for link motion, dimensions of, 108.
Reach-rod pin, 106.
Reamers for crosshead-pins, 176.
Reaming rivet-holes restores strength of plate, 451.
Rear draw-heads for tenders, 565.
Rear side-rod pins for Mogul and ten-wheeled engines, projected area of, 333.
Rear side-rods for consolidation engines, 289, 312.
Rear side-rods for Mogul engines, 281.
Rear straps of main-rods, diameter of bolts through, 276.
Receiver in compounds, 620.
Receiver in compounds, volume of, 629.
Recess in front splice for cylinder saddle, 199.
Reciprocating parts counterbalanced, 243.
Rectangular hyperbola, 598.
Rectangular hyperbola, construction of, 599.
Re-evaporation in compounds is not wholly lost, 618.
Re-evaporation in cylinders, 617.
Regulation of feed-water, 394.
Reinforcing plates for mud plugs, 417.
Reinforcing plates inside of boiler for pads, 483.
Relation between motion of crank-pin and that of piston, 49.
Relative position of eccentric to that of crank, 46.
Release, to find point of, 60.
Relief-valve on throttle pipes, 345.
Remarks relating to passenger trains, 2.
Remarks relating to valve motions, 136.
Re-planing and wear of guides, allowance for, 168.
Resistance due to curves, 614.
Resistance due to friction, 611.
Resistance due to grade, 612.
Resistance due to speed, 614.
Resistance train, 5.
Result of changing position of eccentric-rods, 122.
Reverse lever, 87.
Reverse lever, construction of, 108.
Reverse-lever latch, 109.
Reverse-lever latch, May's, 110.
Reverse lever, length of, 109.
Reverse lever, length of arc described by top of, 109.
Reverse lever, location of, 108, 373.
Reverse-lever pin, diameter of, 109.
Reverse-lever quadrants, 109.
Reverse-lever quadrants, notches in, 109.
Reverse-lever quadrant, to lay off notches on, 133.
Reverse lever, thickness of, 109.
Reverse lever, to find position of, for full gear forward and backward, 130.
Reverse shaft, 87.
Reverse-shaft arms, 87.
Reverse-shaft arms, dimensions of, 107.
Reverse shaft, construction of, 106.
Reverse-shaft counterbalance, 107.
Reverse shaft, diameter of, 107.
Reverse shaft, location of, 107.

Reverse-shaft pin, 100, 106.
Reverse shaft, position for full gear backward, 106.
Reverse shaft, position for full gear forward, 106.
Reverse shaft, position for midgear, 106.
Reverse shaft, to find position of, 124.
Revolving parts counterbalanced, 243.
Rhode Island Locomotive Works, compound locomotives built by the, 625.
Richardson's balanced slide-valves, 67.
Richardson's, George W., pop safety-valves, 384.
Rigid wheel base, 5.
Rim of wheel, area of cross-section of, 256.
Rim of wheel, center of gravity of lead in, 257.
Rim of wheel, effect of lead counterbalance in, 257.
Rim of wheel, lead counterbalance in, 255.
Ring for dome-top, 381.
Ring for fire-box, 434.
Ring in smoke-boxes, 475.
Ring on front flue-sheet for dry pipe, 347.
Rings in stuffing-boxes, 179.
Riveted joints, 446.
Riveted joints, comparison of the strength of solid plate with that of, 457.
Riveted joints, effects of tension on, 448.
Riveted joints, efficiency of single, 458.
Riveted joints, friction in, 451.
Riveted joints, stress in, 451.
Riveted joints with welt pieces, 459.
Riveted lap-joints, double, 454.
Riveted lap-joints, single, 447.
Rivets and studs in dry and T-pipe connections, 349.
Rivets, diameter of, 450.
Rivets from edge of plate, distance of, 448.
Rivets in fire-box, 435.
Rivets, pitch of, in double-riveted lap-joints, 455.
Rivets, pitch of, in single-riveted lap-joints, 450.
Rivets, stress in boiler, 452.
Rivets through dry pipe and sleeves, 346.
Rocker-arms, computation of thickness of, 77.
Rocker-arms, computation of width of, 77.
Rocker-arms, hub on, 78.
Rocker-arms, length of, 76.
Rocker-arms, taper of holes in, 74.
Rocker, location of, 118.
Rocker, object of, 36.
Rocker, off-set in, 117, 119.
Rocker-pins, 74.
Rockers, 74.
Rockers, dimensions of, 78.
Rocker-shaft, computation of diameter of, 75.
Rocker-shaft, diameter of, 74.
Rocker-shaft, length of, 74.
Rockers, stress in, 74.
Rocker, the force it must overcome, 75.
Rocking grate-bars for burning soft coal, 484.
Rod brasses, 315.
Rod brasses, babbitted, 315.
Rod brasses, flanges on, 316.
Rod brasses, metal in, 317.
Rod for feed-cock, 394.
Rods for piston, manner of fastening, 145.
Rods for pistons, stress in, 144.
Roller between spring-saddle and spring, 203.
Roller valves, 65.
Rolling and axle friction, 5.

### RULES.

Rule 1. To compute the force an engine must exert to haul a train, 7.
" 2. To compute number of driving wheels, 8.
" 3. To compute the tractive force, 17.
" 4. To compute thickness of cylinder walls, 25.
" 5. To compute steam-port area, 27.
" 6. To compute steam-port area with aid of table, 28.
" 7. To compute steam-pipe area, 30.
" 8. To compute steam-pipe area with aid of table, 31.
" 9. To compute piston speed, 33.

Rule 10. To compute travel of valve without lap, 40.
" 11. To compute travel of valve without lap, 40.
" 12. To compute travel of valve with lap, 41.
" 13. To compute travel of valve with lap, 41.
" 14. To compute diameter of rocker-shaft, 76.
" 15. To compute width of rocker-arms, 77.
" 16. To compute thickness of rocker-arms, 77.
" 17. To find center line of motion of valve gear, 112.
" 18. To compute diameter of piston-rods, 147.
" 19. To compute thrust of connecting-rod, 160.
" 20. To compute thrust of a locomotive connecting-rod, 161.
" 21. To compute approximately thrust against guides, 161.
" 22. To compute thrust against guide for any position of connecting-rod, 162.
" 23. To compute area of sliding surface of crosshead gibs, 163.
" 24. To compute approximately area of sliding surface of crosshead gibs, 164.
" 25. To compute length and breadth of crosshead gibs, 164.
" 26. To compute diameter of crosshead hubs, 165.
" 27. To compute thickness of guides, 166.
" 28. To compute depth of single guides, 168.
" 29. To compute diameter and length of crosshead-pin, 174.
" 30. To compute diameter and length of crosshead-pin, 175.
" 31. To compute thickness of walls for stuffing-box, 176.
" 32. To compute thickness of flange of stuffing-box, 177.
" 33. To compute thickness of packing in stuffing-box, 178.
" 33a. To compute cross-sectional area of upper engine frame-braces, 192.
" 34. To compute thickness of flange on gland, 179.
" 34a. To compute depth of upper engine frame-brace, 193.
" 35. To compute diameter of studs for stuffing-boxes, 180.
" 35a. To compute depth of lower engine frame-brace, 194.
" 36. To compute depth of lower engine frame-brace, 194.
" 37. To compute depth of frame-brace, slab form, 197.
" 38. To compute diameter of bolts through frame and splice, 198.
" 39. To compute number of bolts through frame and splice, 198.
" 40. To compute depth of front frame-splice, 199.
" 41. To compute diameter of driving-axle journal, 209.
" 42. To compute weight of a simple counterbalance, 225.
" 43. To compute weight of crank referred to crank-pin, 229.
" 44. To compute weight of counterbalance, 235.
" 45. To compute number of cubic inches in counterbalance, 235.
" 46. To compute thickness of counterbalance, 235.
" 47. To find common center of gravity of three segments in counterbalance, 238.
" 48. To find common center of gravity of four segments in counterbalance, 238.
" 49. To find common center of gravity of five segments in counterbalance, 239.
" 50. To find common center of gravity of any two bodies, 240.
" 51. To compute area of irregular surfaces, 254.
" 52. To compute weight of lead in rim of wheels, 255.
" 53. To compute center of gravity of lead in rim of wheel, 257.
" 54. To compute cross-sectional area of main-rod bolts, 276.

Rule 55. To compute diameter of bolts through rear strap of main-rod, 276.
" 56. To compute number of bolts through rear strap of main-rod, 276.
" 57. To compute thickness of main-rod straps, 285.
" 58. To compute thickness of side-rod straps, 288.
" 59. To compute thickness of side-rod straps, Mogul engines, 292.
" 60. To compute thickness of side-rod strap, main-pin, Mogul engines, 292.
" 61. To compute thickness of front and rear side-rod straps, consolidation engine, 295.
" 62. To compute thickness of central side-rod straps, consolidation engine, 295.
" 63. To compute diameter of side-rod bolts for eight-wheeled engines, 298.
" 64. To compute diameter of ride-rod bolts for Mogul engines, 298.
" 65. To compute diameter of side-rod bolts for consolidation engines, 299.
" 66. To compute area of smallest transverse section of main-rod, 301.
" 67. To compute thickness and depth of main-rod, 302.
" 68. To compute cross-sectional area of side-rods for eight-wheeled engines, 308.
" 69. To compute thickness and depth of side-rods for eight-wheeled engines, 309.
" 70. To compute depth for front side-rod, Mogul engine, 310.
" 71. To compute cross-sectional area of central side-rod, consolidation engine, 312.
" 72. To compute thickness and depth of central side-rod, consolidation engine, 312.
" 73. To compute thickness and depth of rear and front side-rods for consolidation engines, 312.
" 74. To compute projected area of main-rod crank-pin journal for eight-wheeled engines, 320.
" 75. To compute diameter and length of main-rod crank-pin journal for eight-wheeled engines, 320.
" 76. To compute projected area of main crank-pin side-rod journal for eight-wheeled engines, 320.
" 77. To compute diameter and length of main crank-pin side-rod journal for eight-wheeled engines, 321.
" 78. To compute diameter and length of main crank-pin journal for Mogul, ten-wheeled, and consolidation engines, 329.
" 79. To compute diameter and length of side-rod journals on main crank-pin for Mogul, ten-wheeled, and consolidation engines, 330.
" 80. To compute projected area of front and rear side-rod pins in Mogul and ten-wheeled engines, 333.
" 81. To compute diameter and length of front and rear side-rod pins in Mogul and ten-wheeled engines, 333.
" 82. To compute projected area of side-rod pins for consolidation engines, 336.
" 83. To compute diameter and length of side-rod pins for consolidation engines, 336.
" 84. To compute projected area of knuckle-joint pin in side-rods, 340.
" 85. To compute diameter and length of knuckle-joint pin in side-rods, 341.
" 86. To compute lift of throttle-valve, 358.
" 87. To compute tension on safety-valve springs, 375.
" 88. To compute length of safety-valve lever, 376.
" 89. To compute steam pressure on safety-valve, 376.
" 90. To compute area of safety-valve, 376.
" 91. To compute distance from center of safety-valve to fulcrum, 377.
" 92. To compute steam pressure on safety-valve, weight of lever considered, 379.
" 93. To compute area of safety-valve, weight of lever considered, 379.

Rule 94. To compute distance from fulcrum to center of valve, weight of lever considered, 379.
" 95. To compute tension on safety-valve spring, weight of lever considered, 380.
" 96. To compute cross-sectional area of full-stroke pump plungers, 397.
" 97. To compute cross-sectional area of short-stroke pump plungers, 398.
" 98. To compute depth of equalizing lever for driving-wheel springs, 406.
" 99. To compute cross-sectional area of equalizing-lever fulcrum, 409.
" 100. To compute cross-sectional area of spring hangers, 410.
" 101. To compute number of leaves in elliptical springs, 415.
" 102. To compute deflection of elliptical springs, 416.
" 103. To compute area of grate surface, soft-coal, 422.
" 104. To compute area of grate surface, hard-coal, 426.
" 105. To compute space between boiler tubes, 443.
" 106. To compute stress in stay-bolts, 480.
" 107. To compute distance between centers of stay-bolts, 480.
" 108. To compute thickness of stayed sheets, 481.
" 109. To compute depth of grate-bars for burning wood, 484.
" 110. To compute area of orifices in double-exhaust nozzles, 507.
" 111. To compute area of orifices in single-exhaust nozzles, 508.
" 112. To compute depth of bumper beam, 522.
" 113. To compute length of engine pony-truck, 544.
" 114. To compute diameter and length of engine-truck axle-journals, 550.
" 115. To compute diameter of cylinders for simple engines, 595.
" 116. To compute required mean effective pressure, 596.
" 117. To compute ratio of expansion, clearance neglected, 600.
" 118. To compute terminal pressure, 601.
" 119. To compute mean pressure, without clearance, 602.
" 120. To compute ratio of expansion, with clearance, 604.
" 121. To compute mean pressure, with clearance, 605.
" 122. To compute horse-power, 605.
" 123. To compute normal pressure, 611.
" 124. To compute force required to haul a train on a grade, 613.
" 125. To compute force required to haul a train on a grade, 613.
" 126. To compute resistance due to speed, 614.
" 127. To compute resistance due to curves, 615.
" 128. To compute point of exhaust closure, 619.
" 129. To compute steam-port area in high-pressure cylinders in compound engines, 627.
" 130. To compute steam-port area in low-pressure cylinders in compounds, 627.
" 131. To compute diameter of cylinders for four-cylinder compounds, 632.

Rules, formulas, and data, 595.
Running-board brackets, 531.
Running board, position of, 532.

## S

Saddle for link, 87, 100.
Saddle-pin, 87, 100.
Saddle-pin for link, length of, 106.
Saddle pin, to find position of, 123.
Saddles for cylinders, 20.
Saddle, thickness of metal in sides of, 25.
Safety chains for tender trucks, 564.

Safety links between engine and tender, 528.
Safety valve, area of, 376, 379.
Safety-valve attachments, 371.
Safety-valve bearing surface, angle of, 371.
Safety valve, Crosby, 385.
Safety valve, distance from fulcrum to center of, 377, 380.
Safety valve, handle for opening, 362.
Safety-valve lever, 373.
Safety-valve lever, length of, 374, 376, 380.
Safety-valve levers, center of gravity of, 377.
Safety-valve opening in top of dome, diameter of, 373.
Safety valve, pop, 373, 380, 384.
Safety valves, common, 371.
Safety valves, computations relating to, 374.
Safety valves, diameter of pop, 384.
Safety valves, encased pop, 385.
Safety valves, number of, 362.
Safety valves, position of, 380.
Safety valves, pressure on springs of pop, 386.
Safety-valve spring balance, 362, 369, 370.
Safety-valve springs, tension on, 374, 375, 380.
Safety valves, steam pressure on, 376, 379.
Sand-boxes, 510.
Sand-boxes, construction of, 511.
Sand, condition and use of, 511.
Sand-pipes, 511.
Sand-pipes, position of, 513.
Schenectady Locomotive Works, compound engines built by the, 620.
Scoops, tenders with water, 572.
Segment, form of templet for, 246.
Segments in counterbalance, number of, 244.
Segments in counterbalance, use of two, 235.
Segments of a counterbalance, to find the common center of gravity of two, 236.
Segments of counterbalance, bolts for, 242.
Segments of counterbalance, common center of gravity of five, 239.
Segments of counterbalance, common center of gravity of four, 238.
Segments of counterbalance, common center of gravity of three, 238.
Segments of counterbalance, form of, 242.
Segments, two in a counterbalance, thickness of, 237.
Segments, two in a counterbalance, to find weight of each, 236.
Selection of iron for cylinders, 23.
Separator in throttle pipes, 351.
Set-screws in eccentric, 81.
Setting a simple valve gear, practical method of, 96.
Setting of eccentrics, practical way, 47.
Setting the valve gear of a locomotive, practical example, 125.
Shaft for drop-plate in furnace, 486.
Shaft, lifting, object of, 36.
Shaking lever for grate bars, 486.
Shaking-lever handle, 486.
Sheets for bumpers, 522.
Sheets, thickness of stayed, 481.
Shifting engine, six-wheeled, built by the Pennsylvania R. R., 589.
Shifting link, change of lead with, 93.
Shifting link for American locomotives, 88.
Shifting links, 88.
Shifting links, angular advance of eccentric for, 88.
Shifting links, curvature of, 88.
Shifting links, lead variable with, 88.
Shimming pieces under tires, 259.
Shoe for frame pedestals, 184.
Short double-exhaust pipes, 504.
Short exhaust pipes, where used, 506.
Short single-exhaust pipes, 505.
Short-stroke pump plungers, cross-sectional area of, 398.
Short-stroke pumps, 387, 395.
Short wedge for frame pedestals, 185.
Shrinkage allowance for driving-wheel tires, 217.
Shrinking tires on wheels, 215.

Side-bearing tender trucks, 564.
Side-rod bolts for consolidation engines, diameter of, 298.
Side-rod bolts for eight-wheeled engines, cross-sectional area of, 297.
Side-rod bolts for eight-wheeled engines, diameter of, 297.
Side-rod bolts for eight-wheeled engines, stress in, 297.
Side-rod bolts for Mogul engines, diameter of, 298.
Side-rod bolts for ten-wheeled engines, diameter of, 298.
Side-rod bolts, strength of, 296.
Side-rod brasses, 315.
Side-rod I section, solid ends, 270.
Side-rod pin for a consolidation engine, 328, 335.
Side-rod pins for eight-wheeled engines, 320.
Side-rod pins for Mogul and ten-wheeled engines, 332.
Side-rod pins, wheel fit, 337.
Side-rods and main-rods, 267.
Side-rods, buckling of, 306.
Side-rods, conditions under which they work, 305.
Side-rods, cross-sectional area of, 308.
Side-rods for consolidation engines, 289, 312.
Side-rods for eight-wheeled engines, position of, 290.
Side-rods for eight-wheeled engines, thickness and depth of, 309.
Side-rods for engines on elevated roads, 278.
Side-rods, form of keys for, 299, 300.
Side-rods for Mogul and ten-wheeled engines, 309.
Side-rods for Mogul engines, 281.
Side-rods for narrow-gauge eight-wheeled engines, 290.
Side-rods, four-wheeled connected, keys for, 270.
Side-rods, knuckle joint for, 338.
Side-rods, length of, how taken, 317.
Side-rods, liners for, 270.
Side-rods, number and diameter of bolts in, 267.
Side-rods, pin through knuckle joint of, 281.
Side-rods, proportions of, 308.
Side-rods, ratio of thickness and depth of, 309.
Side-rods, types of, 307.
Side rods with an I cross-section, 307.
Side-rod with solid end, 327.
Side sheets, inclination of furnace, 432.
Sight-feed lubricators, 556.
Simple valve gear, 36.
Single-exhaust pipes, advantages of, 506.
Single-riveted lap joints, 447.
Size of cylinders, 11.
Size of eccentric-rod pins, 103.
Size of pumps, 396.
Skeleton link, 99.
Skeleton links, difficulty with, 103.
Slab frame brace, cross-sectional area of, 197.
Slab frame brace, depth of, 197.
Slab frame braces, least thickness of, 197.
Slab frames, 196.
Sleeve on dry pipes, 346.
Slide throttle valve, 343.
Slide-valve, Allen, 68.
Slide-valve, Allen, advantages claimed for, 69.
Slide-valve, clearance of, 59.
Slide-valve, conditions it must fulfill, 38.
Slide-valve, friction of, 64.
Slide-valve, inside lap of, 59.
Slide-valve, inside lead of, 59.
Slide-valve, power required to work a, 63.
Slide-valve, practical construction of, 57.
Slide-valve, pressure on, 64, 65.
Slide-valve, primitive, 48.
Slide-valve, problems relating to lap of, 52.
Slide-valve, purpose of giving lap to, 49.
Slide-valves, 34.
Slide-valves, balanced, 66.
Slide-valves, balanced, Richardson's, 67.
Slide-valves, classification of, 39.
Slide-valves, duty of, 35.
Slide-valves, hole in top of balanced, 67.
Slide-valves, problems relating to, reduced to simplest form, 35.
Slide-valves, roller, 65.

Slide-valves, thickness of metal in, 34, 59.
Slide-valve, to find lap and travel of, 55, 56.
Slide-valve, travel of, 37, 82.
Slide-valve, travel of, affects point of cut-off, 54.
Sliding surface of crosshead gibs, area of, 163.
Slip of link-blocks, 102.
Sloping crown sheet, 430.
Smoke-box doors, 476.
Smoke-boxes, braces from frames to, 522.
Smoke-boxes, capacity of, 473.
Smoke-boxes, long, blowing out by steam, 474.
Smoke-boxes, long, cast-iron caps on side of, 474.
Smoke-boxes, long, cinder-box on, 474.
Smoke-boxes, long, construction of, 473.
Smoke-boxes, long, diaphragm plates in, 474.
Smoke-boxes, long, or extension fronts, 472.
Smoke-boxes, long, position of diaphragm plates in, 474.
Smoke-boxes, New York Elevated Railroad, 471.
Smoke-boxes, short, 470.
Smoke-boxes, short, petticoat pipe in, 470.
Smoke-box fronts, 476.
Smoke-box rings, 475.
Smoke-box shell, construction of, 475.
Smoke-box shell, length of, 475.
Smoke-box shell, number of courses in, 475.
Soft-coal burning engines, position of fire-box for, 188.
Soft-coal burning engines, space required between axles in, 188.
Solid link, 99.
Solid pistons, 140.
Space between tubes, 443.
Space for eccentrics, 82.
Space for steam and exhaust passages is limited, 33.
Specification for Pennsylvania R. R., eight-wheeled engine, 585.
Specification for Pennsylvania R. R., shifting engine, 589.
Speed of piston, to determine, 33.
Speed, resistance due to, 614.
Spider for pistons, 138.
Spider for pistons, depth of, 139.
Spiral punch, injury to plates, 451.
Splice and frame, diameter of bolts through, 198.
Splice and frame forged in one piece, 201.
Splice, casting for front end of frame, 200.
Splice, depth of front frame, 199.
Splice for consolidation and Mogul engine frames, 200, 201.
Splice for frames, form of front end of, 200.
Splices for frames, passenger engines, 187, 197.
Splices for frames, recess for cylinder saddle in, 199.
Spring balance for safety valve, 362, 369, 370.
Spring equalizing lever, load on driving wheel, 403.
Spring equalizing levers, purpose of, 400.
Spring gear, depth of equalizing lever for, 402, 405.
Spring gear, equalizing lever for driving wheel, 400.
Spring gear for driving wheels, eight-wheeled engine, 400.
Spring gear for driving wheels, ten-wheeled engines, 400.
Spring gear for narrow-gauge eight-wheeled engine, 403.
Spring gear, fulcrum for driving wheel, 400, 409.
Spring gear, load on fulcrum for driving wheel, 403.
Spring gear, Pennsylvania R. R., 414.
Spring gears for consolidation engines, driving wheel, 408.
Spring gears for Mogul engines, driving wheel, 408.
Spring gear, stress in equalizing fulcrum, 409.
Spring gear, thickness of equalizing lever for, 402, 408.
Spring hangers for driving-wheel springs, 400, 410.
Spring hangers, ratio of thickness to width, 411.
Spring hangers, stress per square inch, 410.
Spring hangers, various forms of, 411.
Spring hanger, tension on driving wheel, 403.
Springing of the valve-rod, 76.
Spring saddles for driving-wheel springs, 202, 400.
Springs for balanced slide-valves, 66.
Springs for driving wheels, 414.
Springs for driving wheels, deflection of, 416.
Springs for driving wheels, length of, 414.
Springs for driving wheels, number of blades in, 415.

Springs for driving wheels, set of, 415.
Springs for driving wheels, thickness of blades of, 415.
Springs for lifting-shaft counterbalance, 107.
Springs for lifting-shaft counterbalance, dimensions of, 108.
Springs, front, in ten-wheeled, Mogul, and consolidation engines, load on, 546.
Springs, helical, compression of, 386.
Springs, helical, size of steel for, 386.
Springs, load on driving wheel, 402.
Stack, diamond, with double shell, 496.
Stack, diamond, with single shell, 497.
Stack, H. A. Luttgens, 501.
Stack, Radley & Hunter, 498.
Stacks, diameter of, 502.
Stacks, form of saddles for, 502.
Stacks, length of, 503.
Stack, straight, 499.
Stack, tapered, 499.
Stack, wood-burning, 497.
Standard diameters of wheel centers, 217.
Standard tender-truck axle-boxes, 579.
Standard tender-truck axles, 581.
Stand for bells, 513.
Stand pipe for throttle valve, 344.
Stand to receive boiler cocks, valves, etc., 366.
Starting valve for four-cylinder locomotives, S. M. Vauclain, 631.
Stationary links, 88.
Stationary links, angular advance of eccentric for, 88, 90.
Stationary links, curvature of, 88.
Stationary links, lead constant with, 88, 89.
Stationary links, length of radius for, 90.
Stationary links, to find angular advance for, 91.
Stay bolts, distance between centers of, 480, 481.
Stay bolts for crown sheets, radial, 432.
Stay bolts in Belpaire boilers, 464.
Stay bolts in boilers, 463.
Stay bolts in boilers, hollow, 463.
Stay bolts, radial, to crown sheet, 463.
Staying back head of boiler, 469.
Staying front tube sheet, 469.
Steam accounted for by the indicator, 607.
Steam, back pressure, 602.
Steam chamber for receiving valves on boiler, 561.
Steam-chest seats, 21.
Steam-chests, vacuum valves in, 67.
Steam, compression of, in compounds, 618.
Steam, diagram showing events of distribution of, 63.
Steam, events of distribution of, 60.
Steam, expansive working of, in compounds, 619.
Steam-gauge lamp bracket, 362.
Steam-gauge stand, 362, 369.
Steam-gauge stand and chamber arranged to receive valves, cocks, etc., 366.
Steam-gauge stand, position of, 373.
Steam, lap required for expansion of, 49.
Steam line, 607.
Steam passage, 21.
Steam passage divided into two branches, advantage gained, 22.
Steam passage, duty of, 22.
Steam passage openings, size of, 32.
Steam passages, small space for, 33.
Steam passage, thickness of metal around, 25.
Steam-pipe area, 31.
Steam-pipe areas, table of proportional, 31.
Steam pipes, 30.
Steam pipes, ball joint for, 33.
Steam pipes, thickness of, 33.
Steam pipes, to compute area of, 30.
Steam pipes, to compute area of, with aid of table, 31.
Steam-port area in compounds, 627.
Steam-port areas, table of, 28.
Steam-port area, to compute, 27.
Steam ports, 22.
Steam ports, area of, 26.
Steam ports, length and breadth of, 26.

Steam pressure, absolute, 597.
Steam pressure, computation at any point of stroke, 598.
Steam pressure, computation of mean effective, with aid of ordinates, 607.
Steam pressure, computation of mean effective, with aid of planimeter, 607.
Steam pressure, computation of required mean effective, 596.
Steam pressure, computation of terminal, 599, 601.
Steam pressure for a given cut-off, mean effective, 597, 602, 605.
Steam pressure, initial, 597.
Steam pressure, mean, 601.
Steam pressure, mean, computation of, 602.
Steam pressure, terminal, 598.
Steam pressure which boilers will stand, formulas for, 462.
Steam space in boiler, 443.
Steam, temperature falls with the expansion of, 617.
Steam, to find point of admission, 60.
Steam, to find point of compression of, 60.
Steam, to find point of cutting off, 60.
Steam, to find point of release, 60.
Steam ways, duty of, 22.
Steel crank-pins, 317.
Steel fire-boxes, 462.
Steel links, 102.
Stephenson's link motion, 86.
Stephenson's link, object of, 36.
Straight legs in engine pedestal, position of, 190.
Straps for eccentric, form of, 81.
Straps for eccentrics, 79.
Straps for eccentrics, joints in, 81.
Straps for main- and side-rods, proportions of, 270.
Straps for main-rods, diameter of bolts through front, 279.
Straps for main-rods, diameter of bolts through rear, 276.
Straps for main-rods, number of bolts through rear, 276.
Straps for side-rods, consolidation engines, 294.
Straps for side-rods, eight-wheeled passenger engine, thickness of, 286.
Straps for side-rods for consolidation engines, thickness of, 295.
Straps for side-rods for Mogul engines, 290.
Straps for side-rods for Mogul engines, thickness of, 292.
Straps, least thickness of side-rod, 294.
Straps, oil-holes in main- and side-rod, 296.
Straps, thickness of main-rod, 283.
Strength of crank-pins, 318.
Strength of crosshead-pins, 174.
Strength of crown bars, computation of, 466.
Strength of iron plates, tensile, 451, 462.
Strength of piston keys, 148.
Strength of plates, apparent, 451.
Strength of plates restored by annealing, 451.
Strength of plates restored by reaming the holes, 451.
Strength of riveted joints compared with that of solid plate, 457.
Strength of steel plates, tensile, 462.
Stress in boiler rivets, 452.
Stress in boiler shell, longitudinally, 447.
Stress in boiler shell, transverse, 447.
Stress in bolts through frame and splice, 198.
Stress in bumper beams, 520.
Stress in crosshead hubs, 165.
Stress in cylinder-head bolts, 23.
Stress in oblique braces, 481.
Stress in piston-rods, 144.
Stress in riveted joints, 451.
Stress in rockers, 74.
Stress in rod-bolts, shearing, 272.
Stress in side-rod straps, eight-wheeled engines, 288.
Stress in side-rod straps for Mogul engines, 291.
Stress on stay bolts, 479.
Stress per square inch in engine frame braces, 191.
Stress per square inch of cross-sectional area of main-rod straps, 285.

Stress per square inch of section of rod-bolts, allowable, 275.
Stroke, backward, 89.
Stroke, forward, 89.
Stroke of pump, to find, 398.
Studs and rivets in dry and T-pipe connections, 349.
Studs for glands and stuffing-boxes, 180.
Studs for throttle-valve stuffing-box, 353.
Studs in cylinder head, 24.
Stuffing-box, brass ring in, 179.
Stuffing-boxes and glands, proportions of, 176.
Stuffing-box for throttle-valve rod, 352, 355.
Stuffing-box for throttle-valve rod, position of, 355.
Stuffing-box gland for throttle-valve rod, 355.
Suction hose, 393.
Support for pulling-bar, 528.
Supports for boilers, 522.
Supports of engines, points of, 408.
Surface of counterbalance, area of, 249.
Surfaces, area of irregular, 254.
Suspension of link, 100.
Symmetrical motion, eccentric-rods of infinite length give, 37.
Symmetrical motion of piston, how to obtain, 50.

## T

### TABLES.

Table 1. Diameter of driving wheels, eight-wheeled locomotive, 10.
" 2. Diameter of driving wheels, Mogul locomotive, 10.
" 3. Diameter of driving wheels, ten-wheeled locomotive, 10.
" 4. Diameter of driving wheels, consolidation locomotive, 10.
" 5. Weight and hauling capacity of eight-wheeled locomotives, 17.
" 6. Weight and hauling capacity of Mogul locomotives, 18.
" 7. Weight and hauling capacity of ten-wheeled locomotives, 18.
" 8. Weight and hauling capacity of consolidation locomotives, 19.
" 9. Proportional steam-port area, 28.
" 10. Proportional steam-pipe areas, 31.
" 11. Size of steam and exhaust openings, 32.
" 12. Proportional dimensions of eccentrics, 85.
" 13. Breadth and thickness of link, 105.
" 14. Diameter of piston-rods, 148.
" 15. Average dimensions of crosshead-pins, 173.
" 16. Computed dimensions of crosshead-pins, 175.
" 17. Dimensions of driving-axle journals for Mogul engines, 211.
" 18. Dimensions of driving-axle journals for ten-wheeled engines, 211.
" 19. Dimensions of driving-axle journals for consolidation engines, 212.
" 20. Dimensions of driving-axle journals in actual service, 212.
" 21. Standard sizes of wheel centers, 217.
" 22. Thickness and depth of main-rods, pressure 120 pounds, 304.
" 23. Thickness and depth of main-rods, pressure 130 pounds, 304.
" 24. Thickness and depth of main-rods, pressure 140 pounds, 304.
" 25. Thickness and depth of main-rods, pressure 150 pounds, 305.
" 26. Thickness and depth of main-rods, pressure 160 pounds, 305.
" 27. Thickness and depth of side-rods for eight-wheeled engines, pressure 120 pounds, 310.
" 28. Thickness and depth of side-rods for eight-wheeled engines, pressure 130 pounds, 310.
" 29. Thickness and depth of side-rods for eight-wheeled engines, pressure 140 pounds, 311.
Table 30. Thickness and depth of side-rods for eight-wheeled engines, pressure 150 pounds, 311.
" 31. Thickness and depth of side-rods for eight-wheeled engines, pressure 160 pounds, 311.
" 32. Thickness and depth of side-rods for consolidation engines, pressure 120 pounds, 313.
" 33. Thickness and depth of side-rods for consolidation engines, pressure 130 pounds, 313.
" 34. Thickness and depth of side-rods for consolidation engines, pressure 140 pounds, 314.
" 35. Thickness and depth of side-rods for consolidation engines, pressure 150 pounds, 314.
" 36. Thickness and depth of side-rods for consolidation engines, pressure 160 pounds, 314.
" 37. Dimensions of crank-pin journals for eight-wheeled engines, pressure 120 pounds, 321.
" 38. Dimensions of crank-pin journals for eight-wheeled engines, pressure 130 pounds, 322.
" 39. Dimensions of crank-pin journals for eight-wheeled engines, pressure 140 pounds, 322.
" 40. Dimensions of crank-pin journals for eight-wheeled engines, pressure 150 pounds, 322.
" 41. Dimensions of crank-pin journals for eight-wheeled engines, pressure 160 pounds, 323.
" 42. Dimensions of main crank-pin journals for Mogul, ten-wheeled, and consolidation engines, pressure 120 pounds, 331.
" 43. Dimensions of main crank-pin journals for Mogul, ten-wheeled, and consolidation engines, pressure 130 pounds, 331.
" 44. Dimensions of main crank-pin journals for Mogul, ten-wheeled, and consolidation engines, pressure 140 pounds, 331.
" 45. Dimensions of main crank-pin journals for Mogul, ten-wheeled, and consolidation engines, pressure 150 pounds, 332.
" 46. Dimensions of main crank-pin journals for Mogul, ten-wheeled, and consolidation engines, pressure 160 pounds, 332.
" 47. Dimensions of front and rear side-rod pins for Mogul and ten-wheeled engines, pressure 120 pounds, 334.
" 48. Dimensions of front and rear side-rod pins for Mogul and ten-wheeled engines, pressure 130 pounds, 334.
" 49. Dimensions of front and rear side-rod pins for Mogul and ten-wheeled engines, pressure 140 pounds, 334.
" 50. Dimensions of front and rear side-rod pins for Mogul and ten-wheeled engines, pressure 150 pounds, 335.
" 51. Dimensions of front and rear side-rod pins for Mogul and ten-wheeled engines, pressure 160 pounds, 335.
" 52. Dimensions of side-rod pins for consolidation engines, pressure 120 pounds, 337.
" 53. Dimensions of side-rod pins for consolidation engines, pressure 130 pounds, 337.
" 54. Dimensions of side-rod pins for consolidation engines, pressure 140 pounds, 338.
" 55. Dimensions of side-rod pins for consolidation engines, pressure 150 pounds, 338.
" 56. Dimensions of side-rod pins for consolidation engines, pressure 160 pounds, 338.
" 57. Dimensions of knuckle-joint pins for side-rods, pressure 120 to 140 pounds, 341.
" 58. Dimensions of knuckle-joint pins for side-rods, pressure 140 to 160 pounds, 342.
" 59. Grate area for soft-coal burning eight-wheeled engines, 423.
" 60. Grate area for soft-coal burning consolidation engines, 423.
" 61. Grate area for hard-coal burning eight-wheeled engines, 427.
" 62. Grate area for hard-coal burning consolidation engines, 427.
" 63. Aggregate tube area as found in practice, 439.
" 64. Aggregate tube area and number of tubes, 440.

Table 65. Distance of rivets from edge of boiler plate, 449.
" 66. Diameter of rivets in boilers, 450.
" 67. Pitch of rivets for single-riveted lap joints, 453.
" 68. Pitch of rivets for single-riveted lap joints, 454.
" 69. Pitch of rivets for double-riveted lap joints, 455.
" 70. Pitch of rivets for double-riveted lap joints, 456.
" 71. Efficiency of single-riveted lap joints, 458.
" 72. Efficiency of single-riveted lap joints, 459.
" 73. Calculated diameters of stacks, 503.
" 74. Diameters of stacks in actual practice, 503.
" 75. Diameters of orifices in double exhaust nozzles, 508.
" 76. Diameters of orifices in single exhaust nozzles, 508.
" 77. Sizes of orifices in exhaust nozzles in actual service, 509.
" 78. Length of ordinates for the construction of bells, 515.
" 79. Diameter of circle on ordinates for the construction of bells, 515.
" 80. Diameter of circle on ordinates for the construction of bells, 516.
" 81. Dimensions of engine-truck journals in actual service, 549.
" 82. Dimensions of engine-truck journals computed, 550.
" 83. Dimensions of engine-truck journals for consolidation engines, 551.
" 84. Hyperbolic logarithms, 601.

Tanks, capacity of, 567.
Tanks for tenders, 567.
Tank sheets, thickness of, 567.
Tank valve, valve seat, and attachments, 567.
Taper at ends of piston-rod, 145.
Tapered guides, 167.
Tapered smoke-stacks, 499.
Taper of bolts in main- and side-rods, 267.
Taper of bolts in side-rods, 299.
Taper of crosshead-pins, 176.
Taper of engine-frame bolts, 201.
Taper of holes in rocker-arms, 74.
Taper of keys for main- and side-rods, 270, 300.
Taper of legs in engine pedestals, 190.
Taper of link-block pins, 100.
Taper of mud plugs in boilers, 417.
Taper of piston-rod keys, 145.
Taper of tread of driving wheels, 263.
Taper on end of throttle-valve rod, 353.
Temperature falls with the expansion of steam, 617.
Temperature of air admitted through hollow brick arch, 477.
Templet for segments, form of, 246.
Tenacity of plates reduced by punching, 451.
Tender- and engine-truck axles, difference between pressure on, 582.
Tender draw-heads, 565.
Tender-frame, iron, 569.
Tender-frames, longitudinal bolts through, 563.
Tender-frames, wooden, 565.
Tenders, 563.
Tenders, points of support under tank, 563.
Tenders, weight of, 581.
Tenders with water-scoops, 572.
Tender-truck axle-box brasses, 575.
Tender-truck axle-box brasses, width of, 581.
Tender-truck axle-box brasses with lead lining, 577.
Tender-truck axle-boxes, 575.
Tender-truck axle-boxes, cotton or woolen waste in, 578.
Tender-truck axle-boxes, covers, 578.
Tender-truck axle-boxes, design of, 578.
Tender-truck axle-boxes, dust guard for, 578.
Tender-truck axle-boxes for axles without collars, 579.
Tender-truck axle-boxes for pedestals, 579.
Tender-truck axle-boxes, standard, 579.

Tender-truck axle-boxes, types of, 579.
Tender-truck axle-boxes, without wedges, 578.
Tender-truck axle-box wedges, 575.
Tender-truck axle-journals, 580.
Tender-truck axle-journals, diameter of, 581.
Tender-truck axle-journals, pressure on, 581.
Tender-truck axle-journals, to compute dimensions of, 582.
Tender-truck axle-journals, to compute load they can bear, 582.
Tender-truck axles, standard, 581.
Tender-truck brake gear, 564, 571.
Tender-trucks, 571.
Tender-trucks, center-bearing, 564.
Tender-trucks, safety chains, 564.
Tender-trucks, side-bearing, 564.
Tensile force on main-rods, 301.
Tensile strength of iron plates, 451, 462.
Tensile strength of steel plates, 462.
Tension on driving-wheel spring fulcrum, 403.
Tension on driving-wheel spring hangers, 403.
Tension on safety-valve springs, 374, 375, 380.
Ten-wheeled engine, counterbalance for, 250.
Ten-wheeled engine, driving-axle boxes for, 212.
Ten-wheeled engine, driving-wheel spring gear for, 400.
Ten-wheeled engine, pedestals for, 212.
Ten-wheeled engines, crank-pins for, 328.
Ten-wheeled engines, distance between centers of axles, 188.
Ten-wheeled engine, size of driving-axle journal, 210.
Ten-wheeled engines, knuckle-joint for side-rods, 338.
Ten-wheeled engines, side-rod pins for, 332.
Ten-wheeled engines, side-rods for, 309.
Ten-wheeled locomotive, computation of weight on trucks, 15.
Ten-wheeled locomotives, diameter of driving wheels of, 10.
Ten-wheeled locomotives, table of weights and hauling capacity of, 18.
Terminal pressure, 598.
Terminal pressure, computation of, 599, 601.
Testing the amount of piston clearance, 128.
Thickness and width of tires, 265.
Thickness of blades in driving-wheel springs, 415.
Thickness of boiler lagging, 366.
Thickness of boiler plates, formulas for computing, 462.
Thickness of boiler shell, 460.
Thickness of brick arches, 477.
Thickness of bridges in cylinder, 25.
Thickness of bushing for eccentric-rod pins, 103.
Thickness of central side-rod, consolidation engine, 312.
Thickness of counterbalance, 235.
Thickness of crosshead gibs, 165.
Thickness of cylinder flanges, 24.
Thickness of cylinder heads, 24.
Thickness of cylinder walls, 24.
Thickness of cylinder walls, computation of, 25.
Thickness of cylinder walls in ferry-boats, 25.
Thickness of driving-wheel equalizing levers, 402, 408.
Thickness of dry pipe for throttle-valve, 346.
Thickness of engine-frame pedestal caps, 194.
Thickness of engine-frame pedestal legs, 193.
Thickness of equalizing lever in four-wheeled engine trucks, 538.
Thickness of flanges on wedges for engine frames, 186.
Thickness of flue sheets, 434.
Thickness of furnace sheets, 434.
Thickness of guides, 166.
Thickness of keys for main- and side-rods, 300.
Thickness of lead counterbalance, 251.
Thickness of liners for main- and side-rods, 270.
Thickness of link, 105.
Thickness of main-rods, 301, 303.
Thickness of main-rod straps, 283.
Thickness of metal around exhaust passage, 25.
Thickness of metal around steam passage, 25.
Thickness of metal in rod brasses, 317.
Thickness of metal in sides of saddle, 25.

Thickness of metal in slide-valve, 59.
Thickness of metal outside of slots through equalizing lever, 406.
Thickness of pipe connecting throttle-valve stuffing-box to dome, 361.
Thickness of plates in wrought-iron ash-pans, 493.
Thickness of reach-rod pin bushing, 106.
Thickness of reverse-lever, 109.
Thickness of rocker-arms, 77.
Thickness of segments of counterbalance, 243.
Thickness of side-rods for eight-wheeled engines, 309.
Thickness of side-rods for Mogul engines, 310.
Thickness of side-rod straps, consolidation engine, 295.
Thickness of side-rod straps, eight-wheeled passenger engines, 286.
Thickness of side-rod straps, least, 294.
Thickness of side-rod straps, Mogul engines, 292.
Thickness of slab frame braces, least, 197.
Thickness of slide-valves, 34.
Thickness of stayed sheets, 481.
Thickness of steam-pipes, 33.
Thickness of two segments in a counterbalance, 237.
Thickness of wedges for engine frames, 186.
Thimbles for crown bars, 465.
Thimbles for exhaust pipes, 505.
Thimbles for frame pedestals, 182.
Throttle-lever handle and reverse lever, distance between, 356.
Throttle lever, position of, 355.
Throttle-lever quadrants, to determine curvature and length of, 357.
Throttle pipe and dry pipe, ball-joint between, 347.
Throttle pipe, construction of, 344.
Throttle pipes, cross-sectional area of rectangular part, 349.
Throttle pipes, diameter of, 349.
Throttle pipes, thickness of, 349.
Throttle pipe with relief-valve, 345.
Throttle pipe with separator, 351.
Throttle-valve bell-crank, 343.
Throttle-valve connections, 352.
Throttle valve, diameter of, 349.
Throttle-valve gear on top of boiler, 359, 364, 366.
Throttle-valve gear with rod through end of boiler, 353.
Throttle-valve gear with rod through side of dome, 359.
Throttle-valve lever, 352, 354, 356.
Throttle valve, lift of, 358.
Throttle-valve quadrant, 353, 354, 355.
Throttle-valve rod, 343, 353.
Throttle-valve rod, diameter of, 355.
Throttle-valve rod gland, 355.
Throttle-valve rod jaw, 353, 362.
Throttle-valve rod jaw, length of circular arc on, 363.
Throttle-valve rod stuffing-box, 352, 355.
Throttle-valve rod through back head of boiler, 352.
Throttle-valve rod with brass casing, 355.
Throttle valves and pipes, 343, 347.
Throttle-valve stem, 343.
Throttle valve, to obtain a steam-tight joint, 345.
Throw of eccentric, 37, 82.
Throw of eccentrics, amount of, 104.
Thrust against guides, computation of, 159.
Thrust against guides for any position of connecting-rod, 162.
Thrust of connecting-rod, practical example in finding, 158.
Thrust of connecting-rod, to find, 156.
Tie rods in boilers, 469.
Tire for driving wheels, 215.
Tires bolted to rim of wheels, 260.
Tires, depth of flanges of, 263.
Tires, distance between backs of flanges of, 266.
Tires, distribution of flanged, 261.
Tires for driving wheels, 259.
Tires for driving wheels, shrinkage allowance, 217.
Tires, limit of wear of, 265.
Tires, manner of fastening on wheels, 215.
Tires, plain, 261.

Tires, shimming pieces under, 259.
Tires with a projection on the inside, 259.
Tops for domes, 380.
Tops for domes made in two pieces, 387.
Total wheel base, 5.
Total wheel base, limit of, large engines, 189.
Total wheel base of small engines, 189.
T-pipe and dry-pipe connections, 349.
T-pipe and dry pipe, ball-joint between, 350.
Tractive force, to compute, 595.
Tractive power depends on diameter of cylinders, stroke, diameter of drivers, mean effective pressure, 11.
Tractive power, method of finding, 11.
Tractive power or force, 11.
Tractive power, to compute, 14, 16, 17.
Train resistance, 5.
Transverse braces in boilers, 467.
Transverse force on main-rods, 301.
Transverse key in front end of main-rod, 300.
Transverse stress in boiler shell, 447.
Travel and lap of valve, to find, 56.
Travel of valve, 37, 82.
Travel of valve affects point of cut-off, 54.
Travel of valve, center of, important position, 44.
Travel of valve influenced by rocker-arms and link, 37.
Travel of valve, to compute, 40.
Travel of valve with lap, 41.
Tread of driving wheels, form of, 263.
Tread of driving wheels, standard form of, 265.
Triangle of forces for finding thrust of connecting-rod, 158.
T-ring for pistons, 140, 143.
Trucks, computation of weight on engine, 15.
Truck wheels, Allen Paper Wheel Co., 584.
Truck wheels, Boies Steel Wheel Co., 585.
Truck wheels, cast-iron, Pennsylvania R. R., 583.
Truck wheels, difference between engine and tender, 584.
Truck wheels, S. M. Vauclain's patent, 585.
Tubes, arrangement of, 442.
Tubes, cross-sectional area of, 438.
Tubes for supporting brick arches, 477.
Tubes, heating surface affected by diameter of, 441.
Tube sheet, manner of staying front, 469.
Tubes, length of, 442.
Tubes, number of, 440.
Tubes, ratio of diameter to length of, 441.
Tubes, space between, 443.
Tubes, thickness, length, and diameter of boiler, 437.
Two-cylinder compounds, adjustment of valve gear in, 627.
Two-cylinder compounds, diameter of cylinders for, 628.
Two-cylinder compound engines, 620.
Two-wheeled engine truck, 540.
Two-wheeled engine truck, clearance between wheels and cylinder heads, 542.
Two-wheeled engine truck, equalizing lever for, 546.
Two-wheeled engine truck, length of, 542.
Two-wheeled engine truck, thickness and depth of equalizing lever, 547.
Two-wheeled truck, computation of length of, 544.
Two-wheeled truck, frame for, 542.
Two-wheeled truck, graphical method of finding length of, 542.
Type of locomotive, data required for choice of, 5.
Types of locomotives, 3, 585.
Types of side-rods, 306.

## U

Units of heat in coal, 424.
Upper engine frame brace, depth of, 193.
Useful rules, formulas, and data, 595.
Use of sand, 511.

## V

Vacuum line, or zero line, 597, 607.
Vacuum line, or zero line, location of, 602.
Vacuum valves in steam chests, 67.

Valve, center of its travel is an important position, 44.
Valve, check, 391.
Valve connections, throttle, 352.
Valve, diameter of throttle, 349.
Valve gear, adjustment in two-cylinder compounds, 627.
Valve gear, center line of motion of, 43.
Valve gear, complete locomotive, 35.
Valve gear, laying out, 118.
Valve gear, position of axle for laying out, 119.
Valve gear, practical example of setting, 125.
Valve gear, practical method of setting a simple, 96.
Valve gear, principles to be remembered in laying out a, 99.
Valve gear, simple, 36.
Valve gears with rockers, 111.
Valve gear, to find the center line of motion of, 112.
Valve, its motion will depend on position of saddle-pin, lifting-shaft, and lengths of arms, 119.
Valve, lead, 42.
Valve, linear advance of, 45.
Valve motion, influence of rocker on, 36.
Valve motions, infinite lengths of eccentric-rods give symmetrical, 37.
Valve motion with eccentrics not on the main axle, 136.
Valve, piston, for four-cylinder compounds, 629.
Valve, purpose of giving lap to slide, 49.
Valve, relief, on throttle pipes, 345.
Valve-rod end, bushing for, 79.
Valve-rod end with brasses and keys, 79.
Valve-rod gland, form of, 179.
Valve-rod, glands for, 178.
Valve-rod joint, 76.
Valve-rod, knuckle joint in, 79.
Valve-rod, springing of, 76.
Valves, balanced slide, 66.
Valves, balanced slide, springs for, 66.
Valve seat, 21.
Valve seat, height of, 29.
Valve seat, length of, 30.
Valves for pumps, lift of, 389.
Valves, inside clearance of, in compounds, 618.
Valves, intercepting, in compounds, A. J. Pitkin, 620.
Valves, intercepting, in compounds, C. H. Batcheller, 625.
Valve, slide, Allen, 68.
Valve, slide, clearance of, 59.
Valve, slide, conditions it must fulfill, 38.
Valve, slide, friction of, 64.
Valve, slide, inside lap of, 59.
Valve, slide, inside lead, 59.
Valve, slide, power required to work a, 63.
Valve, slide, practical construction of, 57.
Valve, slide, pressure on, 64, 65.
Valve, slide, primitive form of, 48.
Valve, slide, problems relating to lap of, 52.
Valve, slide, thickness of metal, 59.
Valve, slide, to find lap and travel of, 56.
Valve, slide, to find lap of, 55.
Valve, slide, travel of, affects point of cut-off, 54.
Valves, roller slide, 65.
Valves, slide, 34.
Valves, slide, classification of, 39.
Valves, slide, duty of, 35.
Valves, slide, thickness of metal, 34.
Valve, throttle, 343.
Valve travel, 37, 82.
Valve travel influenced by rocker-arms and link, 37.
Valve, travel of, with lap, 40.
Valve, travel, to compute, 40.
Valve with lead, position of eccentric, 43.
Variable motion of piston, cause of, 50.
Variation of pressure in cylinders in compound engines, 617.
Vauclain, S. M., four-cylinder compounds, 629.
Vauclain, S. M., starting valve for four-cylinder compounds, 631.
Vertical clearance in engine pedestals for driving boxes, 189.
Vertical movement of driving boxes, 189.
Volume of receiver in compounds, 629.
Volute springs for lifting-shaft counterbalance, 107.
Volute springs for lifting-shaft counterbalance, dimensions of, 108.

## W

Walls, thickness of cylinder, 24.
Washers for crown bars, 465.
Water-grate bearers, 489.
Water grates, 486.
Water grates, inclination of, 486.
Water grates, manner of fastening in furnace, 489.
Water-gauge glass, 562.
Water-scoops for tenders, 572.
Water space, width of, 434.
Weakest part of piston-rods, 148.
Wear and re-planing of guides, allowance for, 167, 168.
Wear of cast-iron crossheads and case-hardened guides, 151.
Wear of eccentric-rod pins, 103.
Wear of tires, limit of, 265.
Wear of upper crosshead gib, 162.
Wedges and bolts for engine-frame pedestals, proportions of, 186.
Wedges for engine-frame pedestals, 184.
Wedges for tender-truck axle-boxes, 575.
Weight of counterbalance to balance crank and an additional load on crank-pin, 233.
Weight of crank-pin hub, 258.
Weight of crank referred to crank-pin, 228.
Weight of foot-board, 528.
Weight of lead in hollow rims of wheel for counterbalance, 255.
Weight of locomotives, data used for computing, 8, 15.
Weight of locomotives, table of, 17, 18, 19.
Weight of rails must be known to determine the number of driving wheels, 8.
Weight of tenders, 581.
Weight on drivers, to compute, 8, 14, 595.
Weight on driving wheels limited by bridges, 8.
Weight on engine trucks, computation of, 15.
Weights to be counterbalanced, 243.
Weights, to find common center of gravity of any two, 240.
Welt pieces on riveted joints, 459.
Westinghouse brake, manner of attaching, 585.
Wheel base of small engines, total, 189.
Wheel base, rigid, 5.
Wheel base, total, 5.
Wheel base, total, limit of, in large engines, 189.
Wheel, center of gravity of lead in rim of, 257.
Wheel centers, standard diameter of, 217.
Wheel covers for driving wheels, 530.
Wheel covers for engine trucks, 535.
Wheel, cross-sectional area of rim of, 256.
Wheel, effect of lead counterbalance in rim of, 257.
Wheel fit of crank-pins for ten-wheeled, Mogul, and consolidation engines, 337.
Wheel fit of crank-pins in eight-wheeled engines, 325.
Wheel fits on driving-axles, 214.
Wheels, clearance between rails and flanges of, 261.
Wheels, difference between engine and tender truck, 584.
Wheels, dished driving, 220.
Wheels, driving, 215.
Wheels, driving, pressure for forcing on axle, 220.
Wheels for trucks, Allen Paper Wheel Co., 584.
Wheels for trucks, Boies Steel Wheel Co., 585.
Wheels for trucks, cast-iron, Pennsylvania R. R., 583.
Wheels for trucks, S. M. Vanclain's patent, 585.
Wheels, tires for driving, 259.
Wheels under hard-coal burners, position of, 189.
Wheels with tires bolted to them, 260.
Whistle, 381.
Whistle, chime, 383.
Whistle levers, 383.
Whistle, position of, 380.
Width and thickness of flanged tires, 265.
Width of brass packing rings for pistons, 144.

Width of crossheads, 165.
Width of driving-axle box, 208.
Width of engine frames, 191.
Width of engine pedestal openings, 190.
Width of exhaust ports, 29.
Width of fire-box, greatest, 427.
Width of flanges on driving-axle boxes, 204.
Width of keys for main- and side-rods, 300.
Width of piston packing, 139.
Width of plain tires, 261.
Width of rocker-arm, 77.
Width of steam ports, 29, 30.
Width of tender-truck axle-box brasses, 581.
Wings on crosshead, 149.
Wings with glass disks on crossheads, 151.
Wood-burning engines, position of fire-box in, 188.
Wood-burning fire-boxes, 430.
Wood-burning stack, 497.

Wooden floor on top of foot-plates, 528.
Wooden pilots, 517.
Wooden tender frames, 565.
Woolen or cotton waste in tender-truck axle-boxes, 578.
Wootten boiler, 478.
Work and energy, 612.
Work done by a locomotive, 12.
Wrought-iron crank-pins, 317.
Wrought-iron draw-head on bumper beam, 517.

## Y

Yoke for dry pipe, 347.
Yokes for bells, 513.

## Z

Zero line, or line of perfect vacuum, 597, 607.
Zero line, or line of perfect vacuum, location of, 602.

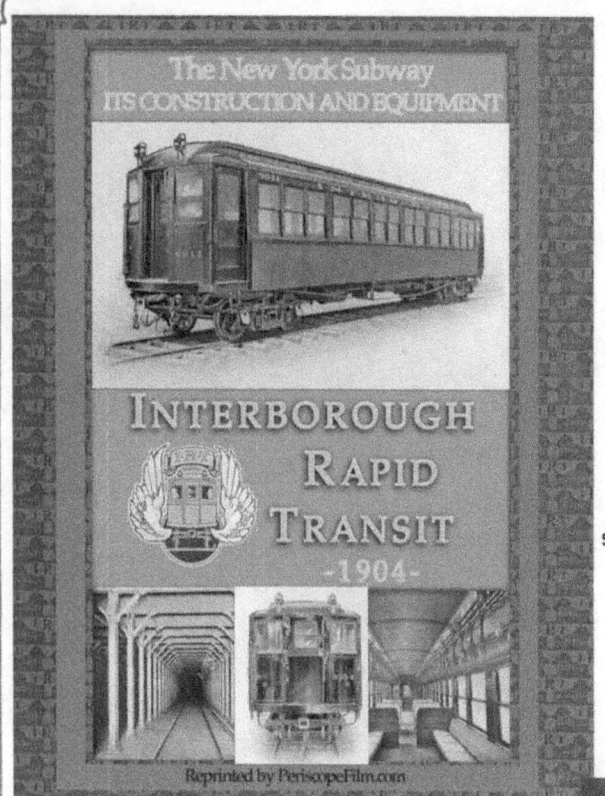

On October 27, 1904, the Interborough Rapid Transit Company opened the first subway in New York City. Running between City Hall and 145th Street at Broadway, the line was greeted with enthusiasm and, in some circles, trepidation. Created under the supervision of Chief Engineer S.L.F. Deyo, the arrival of the IRT foreshadowed the end of the "elevated" transit era on the island of Manhattan. The subway proved such a success that the IRT Co. soon achieved a monopoly on New York public transit. In 1940 the IRT and its rival the BMT were taken over by the City of New York. Today, the IRT subway lines still exist, primarily in Manhattan where they are operated as the "A Division" of the subway. Reprinted here is a special book created by the IRT, recounting the design and construction of the fledgling subway system. Originally created in 1904, it presents the IRT story with a flourish, and with numerous fascinating illustrations and rare photographs.

Originally written in the late 1900's and then periodically revised, A History of the Baldwin Locomotive Works chronicles the origins and growth of one of America's greatest industrial-era corporations. Founded in the early 1830's by Philadelphia jeweler Matthais Baldwin, the company built a huge number of steam locomotives before ceasing production in 1949. These included the 4-4-0 American type, 2-8-2 Mikado and 2-8-0 Consolidation. Hit hard by the loss of the steam engine market, Baldwin soldiered on for a brief while, producing electric and diesel engines. General Electric's dominance of the market proved too much, and Baldwin finally closed its doors in 1956. By that time over 70,500 Baldwin locomotives had been produced. This high quality reprint of the official company history dates from 1920. The book has been slightly reformatted, but care has been taken to preserve the integrity of the text.

## NOW AVAILABLE AT
## WWW.PERISCOPEFILM.COM

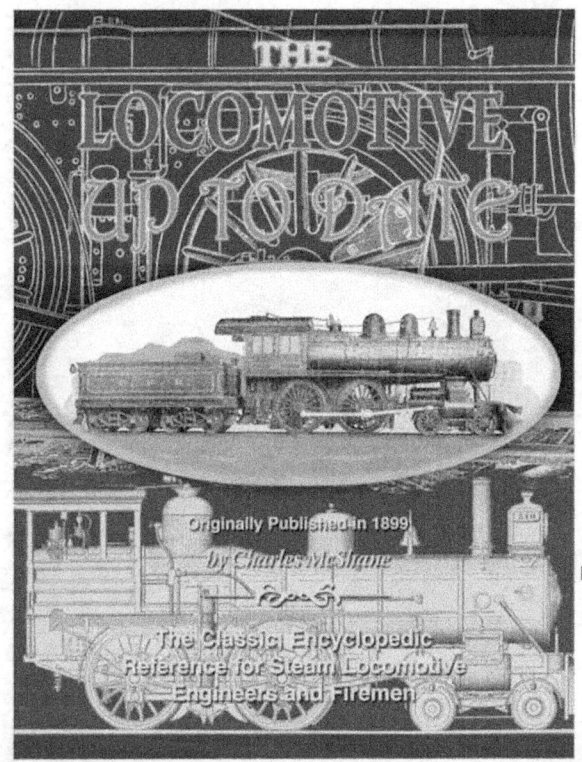

When it was originally published in 1899, **The Locomotive Up to Date** was hailed as "...the most definitive work ever published concerning the mechanism that has transformed the American nation: the steam locomotive." Filled with over 700 pages of text, diagrams and photos, this remains one of the most important railroading books ever written. From steam valves to sanders, trucks to side rods, it's a treasure trove of information, explaining in easy-to-understand language how the most sophisticated machines of the 19th Century were operated and maintained. This new edition is an exact duplicate of the original. Reformatted as an easy-to-read 8.5x11 volume, it's delightful for railroad enthusiasts of all ages.

Originally printed in 1898 and then periodically revised, **The Motorman...and His Duties** served as the definitive training text for a generation of streetcar operators. A must-have for the trolley or train enthusiast, it is also an important source of information for museum staff and docents. Lavishly illustrated with numerous photos and black and white line drawings, this affordable reprint contains all of the original text. Includes chapters on trolley car types and equipment, troubleshooting, brakes, controllers, electricity and principles, electric traction, multi-car control and has a convenient glossary in the back. If you've ever operated a trolley car, or just had an electric train set, this is a terrific book for your shelf!

## ALSO NOW AVAILABLE FROM PERISCOPEFILM.COM!

# THE CLASSIC 1911 TROLLEY CAR BUILDER'S REFERENCE BOOK

# ELECTRIC RAILWAY DICTIONARY

By Rodney Hitt
*Associate Editor, Electric Railway Journal*

REPRINTED BY PERISCOPEFILM.COM

THE CLASSIC 1915 TROLLEY CAR
AND INTERURBAN RAILWAY BOOK

# ELECTRIC RAILWAY ENGINEERING

By Francis H. Doane, A.M.B.

REPRINTED BY PERISCOPEFILM.COM

©2010 Periscope Film LLC
All Rights Reserved
ISBN #978-1-935700-20-3
www.PeriscopeFilm.com

www.ingramcontent.com/pod-product-compliance
Lightning Source LLC
Chambersburg PA
CBHW081752300426
44116CB00014B/2096